Child and Adolescent Psychological Disorders

Oxford Textbooks in
Clinical Psychology

EDITORIAL BOARD

Larry E. Beutler
Bruce Bongar
Gerald P. Koocher
John C. Norcross
Diane J. Willis

SERIES EDITOR

James N. Butcher

Child and Adolescent Psychological Disorders

A Comprehensive Textbook

Edited by

SANDRA D. NETHERTON
DEBORAH HOLMES
C. EUGENE WALKER

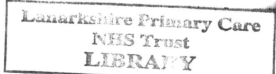
New York   Oxford
OXFORD UNIVERSITY PRESS
1999

Oxford University Press

Oxford   New York
Athens   Auckland   Bangkok   Bogotá   Buenos Aires   Calcutta
Cape Town   Chennai   Dar es Salaam   Delhi   Florence   Hong Kong   Istanbul
Karachi   Kuala Lumpur   Madrid   Melbourne   Mexico City   Mumbai
Nairobi   Paris   São Paulo   Singapore   Taipei   Tokyo   Toronto   Warsaw
and associated companies in
Berlin   Ibadan

Library of Congress Cataloging-in-Publication Data
Child and adolescent psychological disorders : a comprehensive
    textbook / edited by Sandra D. Netherton, Deborah Holmes, and C.
    Eugene Walker.
        p.   cm. — (Oxford textbooks in clinical psychology)
    Includes bibliographical references and index.
    ISBN 0-19-509961-3
        1. Child psychopathology.   2. Adolescent psychopathology.
3. Pediatrics—Psychological aspects.   4. Behavior disorders in
children.   5. Conduct disorders in adolescence.   I. Netherton,
Sandra D., 1960–   .   II. Holmes, Deborah Lott.   III. Walker, C.
Eugene.   IV. Series.
RJ499.C598   1999
618.92'89—DC21   98-7279
                                                CIP

9 8 7 6 5 4 3 2 1

Printed in the United States of America
on acid-free paper

Contents

Preface

The *Diagnostic and Statistical Manual of Mental Disorders*, Fourth Edition (DSM-IV), (American Psychiatric Association. 1994) and the *International Classification of Diseases*, Tenth Edition (ICD-10) (World Health Organization, 1992) are the primary diagnostic references for mental health professionals in psychiatry, psychology, social work, nursing, and other disciplines. DSM-IV provides brief descriptions of mental disorders in terms of their primary and associated features, age at onset, typical course, level of impairment, predisposing factors, complications, prevalence, sex ratio, and familial pattern. Diagnostic criteria are provided for each mental disorder, as well as descriptive guides for differential diagnosis. Although DSM-IV and ICD-10 are two of the primary training and reference tools for mental health professionals, their scope and utility are limited—they are diagnostic manuals and contain little information regarding assessment and treatment.

This textbook was developed to serve as a companion volume to DSM-IV and ICD-10. The text is intended to provide current information on in-depth assessment and treatment of child and adolescent mental disorders, which are the next steps after the diagnosis is established. The text was limited to child and adolescent disorders to make thorough coverage possible within a book of reasonable length. The diagnostic categories covered include diagnoses covered in the "disorders usually first diagnosed in infancy, childhood, and adolescence" section of DSM-IV, as well as selected other mental disorders that are often diagnosed prior to adulthood. Problems of infancy are given less coverage than those of childhood and adolescence due to the paucity of information and more limited psychological interventions available for this age group. Our goal has been to produce a text that is consistent with the educational and professional needs of the mental health professions.

Authors were selected based on their expertise in specific disorders and a record of publishing significant work in a given area. The contributors were encouraged to take an interdisciplinary approach and were provided with a chapter outline that could serve as a guide for the structure and content of their chapter. Chapter authors were asked to include, when possible, a brief review of the following diagnostic information: (1) historical development; (2) a critique; (3) epidemiology; and (4) relevant theoretical models. The bulk of the chapter content was to focus on specific assessment and treatment issues. Authors were encouraged, when possible, to base their recommendations on the empirically data-based literature. Many chapters are supplemented with identification of several references considered "essential reading" in the area.

Acknowledgments

The current text has resulted from the work, commitment, and support of numerous individuals. It is not the result of the efforts of any one person, but a collaborative effort that was sustained over time by the devotion, commitment, and efforts of many.

First, we would like to acknowledge the support and assistance of our editors, who have been helpful with their guidance and support. These include Gioia Stevens, Layla Voll, and Terri O'Prey. We would also like to acknowledge the input and assistance of our colleagues and students, who have provided suggestions and ideas on this project from inception to completion.

We wish to pay special tribute to our secretary, Elaine Lorton. Ms. Lorton was a consistent, steady force driving this project to completion. Her organizational skills, patience, and perseverance are, in many ways, the lifeforce that maintained this effort.

Finally, we would like to acknowledge the support of our families. As with many of the projects I have completed, my children were a sustaining force (C.E.W). I would like to acknowledge the love and support of my child throughout this process and his undying patience with the numerous hours that "Mommy had to work" (D.H.). As with all achievements in my life, I owe my love and gratitude to my parents. Without them, this would not have been possible (S.N.).

S.N.
D.H.
C.E.W.

Contributors

THOMAS S. ALTEPETER, PH.D., is a clinical psychologist in private practice in Oshkosh, Wisconsin, with particular expertise in the assessment and treatment of child behavior disorders, Attention-Deficit/Hyperactive Disorder, and mood disorders.

ARTHUR D. ANASTOPOULOS, PH.D., is Associate Professor, Department of Psychology, University of North Carolina, Greensboro. He has written extensively on Attention-Deficit/Hyperactivity Disorder, clinical child psychology, parent training, and cognitive therapy.

FRED J. BIASINI, PH.D., is Assistant Professor, Department of Psychology and Civitan International Research Center, University of Alabama at Birmingham. Special areas of interest and expertise include mental retardation and the impact of environmental and biological risk factors on child development.

KATHRYN M. BIGELOW is a doctoral candidate in the Department of Human Development and Family Life, University of Kansas, Lawrence. Her research focuses on developmental disabilities and child abuse and neglect.

CHARLES M. BORDUIN, PH.D., is Professor, Department of Psychology, University of Missouri-Columbia. Special areas of interest and expertise include service delivery in clinical child psychology, multisystemic treatment of child and adolescent behavior problems, socialization in the context of the family, and family therapy process and outcome.

SUSAN J. BRADLEY, M.D., is a consultant psychiatrist at the Child and Adolescent Gender Identity Clinic, Child and Family Studies Centre, Clarke Institute of Psychiatry, Toronto, with particular expertise on gender identity disorders, affect regulation, and anxiety disorders.

NORMAN W. BRAY, PH.D., is Professor, Department of Psychology, University of Alabama at Birmingham. Special areas of interest and expertise include neural network models of strategy development, children's problem-solving strategies, and mental retardation.

JOHN V. CAMPO, M.D., is Assistant Professor of Psychiatry and Pediatrics, Department of Psychiatry, Western Psychiatric Institute and Clinic, Pittsburgh. His research focuses on medically unexplained symptoms in children and adolescents and psychophysiologic disorders.

CHARLES R. CARLSON, PH.D., is Associate Professor, Department of Psychology, University of Kentucky at Lexington. He specializes in self-regulation skills training.

ROSARIO CASTILLO is a doctoral candidate in the Department of Psychology, University of Houston, working on child neuropsychology, cognitive functions in medical populations, and multicultural assessment.

MICHAEL D. CHAFETZ, PH.D., is a clinical psychologist with Psychological Resources PC, Kenner Regional Medical Center, Kenner, Louisiana, with a particular emphasis on neuropsychology, medical disabilities, and sex offender treatment.

EDWARD R. CHRISTOPHERSEN, PH.D., is Professor of Pediatrics, Developmental Medicine/Pediatric Psychology, Children's Mercy Hospital, Kansas City, Missouri. Special areas of interest and expertise include behavioral pediatrics and clinical child psychology.

MATTHEW J. CORDOVA, M.S., is a doctoral candidate in the Department of Psychology, University of Kentucky at Lexington.

SHANNON S. CROFT, M.D., is Child and Adolescent Fellow, Department of Psychiatry and Behavioral Sciences, Emory University School of Medicine.

ROBERT A. DAHMES, M.D. is a clinician at New Orleans Psychotherapy Associates, with special areas of interest and expertise in mood disorders, anxiety disorders, sexual abuse disorders, paraphilias, and ADHD.

RONALD M. DOCTOR, PH.D., is Professor, Department of Psychology, California State University, Northridge. His research focuses on anxiety disorders, trauma, PTSD, critical incidents, and child abuse.

STEPHEN J. DOLLINGER, PH.D., is Professor of Psychology and Director of Clinical Training, Department of Psychology, Southern Illinois University at Carbondale.

JEAN C. ELBERT, PH.D., is Associate Professor, Department of Pediatrics, University of Oklahoma Health Sciences Center, with a particular emphasis on children's learning and attentional disorders.

BRANDI J. FREEMAN, M.A. (Clinical Psychology), is a substance abuse specialist in the Substance Abuse Treatment Program, Division of Adolescent Medicine, Children's Hospital, Los Angeles. She works with special youth populations, including those living with HIV and substance abusers.

GARY GEFFKEN, PH.D., is Associate Professor of Clinical Psychology, Department of Psychiatry, University of Florida Health Science Center, Gainesville.

LISA A. GRUPE is a graduate research assistant at the Department of Psychology and Civitan International Research Center, University of Alabama at Birmingham, working on children's problem-solving strategies and mental retardation.

CARRIE A. HATCHER is a clinical psychology doctoral student in the Department of Psychology, University of Michigan. Her research focuses on religion, spirituality, and psychology.

NAAMITH HEIBLUM, M.S. (Clinical Psychology), is a doctoral candidate in clinical psychology at the University of Missouri-Columbia working on sexual and physical abuse of juvenile offenders, family and mental dysfunction, and delinquency treatment.

DEBORAH HOLMES is in private practice of psychology in Oklahoma City. She is a consultant to the Job Corps in Guthrie, Oklahoma, and an adjunct professor at the University of Oklahoma.

E. WAYNE HOLDEN, PH.D., is Director of Pediatric Psychology, Department of Pediatrics, University of Maryland School of Medicine, Baltimore. Special areas of interest and expertise include adjustment to chronic childhood illness and the effects of poverty on children.

LISA F. HUFFMAN is a graduate research assistant at the Department of Psychology and Civitan International Research Center, University of Alabama at Birmingham. Her research focuses on children's problem-solving strategies and mental retardation.

HEATHER C. HUSZTI, PH.D., is Associate Professor, Department of Pediatrics, University of Oklahoma Health Sciences Center.

CRAIG L. JOHNSON is Director of the Eating Disorders Program at Laureate Psychiatric Clinic and Hospital, Tulsa, Oklahoma; Professor of Clinical Psychology at the University of Tulsa, Oklahoma; and Senior Clinical Adviser for the National Eating Disorders Organization. He is also the author of *The Etiology and Treatment of Bulimia Nervosa: A Biopsychosocial Perspective* and *Psychodynamic Treatment of Anorexia Nervosa and Bulimia.*

NADINE J. KASLOW, PH.D., is Associate Professor, Department of Psychiatry and Behavioral Sciences, Emory University School of Medicine. Special areas of interest and expertise include depression and suicide in children and adults, family therapy, family violence, and family systems medicine.

CHRISTOPHER A. KEARNEY, PH.D., is Associate Professor, Department of Psychology, University of Nevada, Las Vegas. His work focuses on internalizing disorders and school refusal behavior in childhood.

MARIA LYNN KESSLER, PH.D., is in the Department of Psychology at The Citadel, The Military College of South Carolina. She has written extensively on child abuse and neglect, parenting, performance management, and applied behavior analysis.

JOHN N. KORGER, M.D., is a child and adolescent psychiatrist with Psychiatric Consultants in Oshkosh, Wisconsin, with particular expertise in child and adolescent behavior, ADHD, and mood and anxiety disorders.

KEVIN R. KRULL, PHD., is Assistant Professor, Department of Psychology, University of Houston. Special areas of interest and expertise include child neuropsychology, disorders of attention, neurotoxicity, and electrophysiology.

THOMAS R. LINSCHEID, PH.D., is Associate Professor of Pediatrics and Psychology, Ohio State University, Children's Hospital, Columbus, Ohio.

JOHN R. LUTZKER, PH.D., is Ross Professor and Chair, Department of Psychology, University of Judaism, Los Angeles. Special areas of interest and expertise include child abuse and neglect and developmental disabilities.

MICHAEL C. LUXEM, PH.D., is a fellow in the Department of Pediatrics, Children's Mercy Hospital, Kansas City, Missiouri, with a particular interest in the common behavior problems of young children.

RICHARD G. MACKENZIE, M.D., is Director, Division of Adolescent Medicine, Children's Hospital, Los Angeles.

LEE H. MATTHEWS, PH.D., is Chief Psychologist, DePaul-Tulane Behavioral Health Center and Research Neuropsychologist, Veteran Affairs, Medical Center, New Orleans.

LINDA MONACO is a graduate student in the Department of Clinical and Health Psychology, University of Florida, Gainesville.

LAURA BENNETT MURPHY, PH.D., is Assistant Professor, Department of Psychology, Otterbein College, Westerville, Ohio.

CHAD C. NELSON, PH.D., is a Pediatric Psychologist, Division of Pediatric Psychology/Neuropsychology, Mount Washington Pediatric

Hospital, Baltimore, Maryland. Special areas of interest and expertise include adjustment to illness, preparation for hospitalization and medical procedures, pediatric pain management, and pediatric HIV.

SANDRA D. NETHERTON, PH.D., is Clinical Assistant Professor, Department of Psychiatry and Behavioral Sciences, University of Oklahoma Health Sciences Center. Her research focuses on pediatric psychology, pain management, chronic illness, and death and bereavement.

STACEY STEINBERG NYE, PH.D. (Clinical Psychology), is a clinical psychologist at the Eating Disorders Program, St. Mary's Hill Hospital, Milwaukee, Wisconsin.

ROBERTA OLSON, PH.D., is Associate Professor, Departments of Counseling and Psychology, Oklahoma City University. Special areas of interest and expertise include mind-body relationships and psychotherapy outcome research.

STACY OVERSTREET, PH.D., is Assistant Professor, Department of Psychology, Tulane University, with particular interest in exposure to violence and trauma in childhood and the impact of diabetes in cognitive functioning.

LOREN PANKRATZ, PH.D., is a consultation psychologist in independent practice in Portland, Oregon, and also Clinical Professor in the Department of Psychiatry at Oregon Health Sciences University.

MARI RADZIK, PH.D., is Registered Psychologist, Risk Reduction Clinical Supervisor, Substance Abuse and Treatment Program, Division of Adolescent Medicine, Children's Hospital, Los Angeles. She focuses on individual and group psychotherapy with youth living with HIV and other chronic illnesses; gay, lesbian, and transgendered youth; eating disordered youth; and substance-using youth.

MANUEL D. REICH, D.O., is Assistant Professor of Psychiatry and Medical Director, Center for Pediatric Psychiatry and Medicine,

University of Pittsburgh Medical Center, Western Psychiatric Institute and Clinic. He frequently consults with allied mental health professionals and primary care physicians, with special areas of interest and expertise in children with chronic illness and psychoanalytic psychotherapy.

LYNN C. RICHMAN, PH.D., is Professor and Director of Pediatric Psychology, University of Iowa, with a particular interest in learning disorders, language disorders, and the neuropsychology of genetic disorders.

JAMES R. RODRIGUE, PH.D., is Associate professor, Department of Clinical and Health Psychology, University of Florida Health Science Center, Gainesville. His research focuses on child health psychology, health promotion, and family therapy.

CINDY M. SCHAEFFER, M.A. (Clinical Psychology), is a doctoral candidate in clinical psychology at the University of Missouri-Columbia working on sibling relations of delinquent adolescents, violent adolescent offenders, and community psychology.

CYNTHIA CUPIT SWENSON, PH.D., is Assistant Professor, Department of Psychiatry, Medical University of South Carolina. Special areas of interest and expertise include child trauma and family violence.

STEVEN D. THURBER, PH.D., is a licensed psychologist and Adjunct Professor, Department of Psychology, Boise State University, Idaho. His work focuses on pediatric and child clinical psychology and developmental psychopathology.

DAROLD A. TREFFERT, M.D., is a private practitioner with Associated Psychiatric Consultants, South Carolina, with particular expertise in autism. He is also the author of *Extraordinary People: An Exploration of the Savant Syndrome* (Harper & Row, 1989).

DIANE WADIAK, M.D., is a graduate student in the Department of Psychology, University of

Wyoming working on family factors in child-hood behavior disorders.

C. EUGENE WALKER, PH.D., is Professor Emeritus, Department of Psychiatry and Behavioral Sciences, University of Oklahoma Health Sciences Center. He has written extensively on pediatric psychology, behavioral treatment, and psychopathology.

HEATHER WALLACH, M.A. (Psychology), is a graduate student, Department of Psychology, Southern Illinois University at Carbondale.

SULA WOLFF, F.R.C.PSYCH., was formerly at the Department of Psychiatry, University of Edinburgh, Edinburgh, Scotland. Special areas of interest and expertise include personality disorder and its development.

KEVIN M. WOOD, PH.D., is a pediatric psychologist, Pediatric Psychology Division, University of Iowa, specializing in learning, attention, and memory and language disorders.

KENNETH J. ZUCKER, PH.D., is the Head of the Child and Adolescent Gender Identity Clinic, Child and Family Studies Centre, Clarke Institute of Psychiatry, Toronto. His research focuses on gender identity disorders, developmental psychopatholgy, and attachement and psychopathology.

Child and Adolescent Psychological Disorders

1

Brief History of DSM-IV and ICD-10

Sandra D. Netherton
C. Eugene Walker

INTRODUCTION

The current text is intended to focus on the assessment and treatment of mental disorders that affect infants, children, and adolescents. The disorders included were compiled on the basis of a review of the most recent version of the *Diagnostic and Statistical Manual of Mental Disorders*, Fourth Edition (DSM-IV; American Psychiatric Association, 1994). In anticipation of the release of this text in other parts of the world, relevant diagnostic information from the *International Classification of Diseases*, Tenth Edition (ICD-10; World Health Organization, 1992) has also been included.

Several DSM-IV diagnostic groups are included in addition to those found within the section entitled "Disorders Usually First Diagnosed in Infancy, Childhood, or Adolescence." Diagnostic groups selected from other sections of DSM-IV were chosen as representative of those disorders most pertinent to child and adolescent populations. Although there may be child or adolescent mental disorders that are omitted from this text, every attempt was made to develop a comprehensive text that is

thorough, yet manageable. The chapter authors of this edited volume are known to be knowledgeable and well versed in the assessment and treatment of the particular diagnoses about which they have written, and most have been prolific contributors to the scientific literature.

The development of this text was prompted by the publication of DSM-IV by the American Psychiatric Association (APA, 1994). The update of this basic reference provides a wealth of information for mental health professionals and is already being used extensively. Given the value and utility of the diagnostic manual to the provide valid diagnosis, a need was seen for a companion volume that would pick up where DSM-IV left off, describing current assessment and treatment approaches for diagnostic groups.

The diagnosis, assessment, and treatment of mental health disorders have an extensive and rich history. ICD and DSM have both undergone numerous revisions and provided the impetus for several theoretical, conceptual, pragmatic, and political challenges. Although the current chapter is not intended to provide a complete review of the history of the development of ICD-10 and DSM-IV, it may be valuable to provide an historical framework for these systems through which the reader can assimilate and integrate the diagnostic, assessment, and treatment information contained in this volume.

BRIEF HISTORY OF THE DIAGNOSIS OF MENTAL DISORDERS AND DSM-IV

The history of the classification of mental disorders most likely began with the origin of human beings. Based on recorded history, however, the description and classification of mental disorders began in ancient times (3000 to 2000 B.C.) with the Egyptian and Sumarian references to *senile dementia*, *melancholia*, and *hysteria*. Hippocrates (460–377 B.C.) and his followers expanded on this system with the addition of *phrenitis*, *mania*, *epilepsy*, and *Scythian disease* (akin to transvestism). His system of classification included these diagnostic categories under the medical domain and was based on empirical observation (Mack, Forman, Brown, & Frances, 1994). In contrast to the observationally derived system described by Hippocrates, Plato's approach to the categorization of mental disorders was couched in rational and logical thought. These two distinctive methods for the categorization of mental disorders have alternated and shared in popularity which they continue to do in current theoretical debates.

Substantial advances in the classification of mental disorders occurred also in conjunction with the Renaissance and the Enlightenment. Of considerable importance was the notion proposed by Syndeham (1624–1663) that different individuals with the same disease would have a similar presentation of symptoms. Thus, the classification of mental disorders could be approached best through the systematic observation and description of symptom patterns.

Jean Columbier and Francois Doublet published the *Instruction* in psychiatry in 1785 on the basis of information compiled from a group of physicians who were involved in the treatment of the mentally ill in France. The categories described in their volume, *manie* (mania), *mélancolie* (melancholy), *phrénensie* (frenzy), and *stupidité* (stupidity), are strikingly similar those described by Hippocrates more than 2000 years before this publication but represented one of the first diagnostic systems to be sanctioned by a group of professionals (an approach still being used in the development of DSM and ICD). The descriptive approach was also endorsed by Pinel (1798) and Esquirol (1838).

During the nineteenth century, the quest for an etiological explanation and classification system for mental disorders materialized again when Bayle (1822) attempted to group mental disorders according to the course of the disease and the accompanying brain lesions. His perspective was strongly supported by the work of Greisinger, who believed that all mental disorders had an underlying physical cause that originated in the brain. Bayle's quest was later realized by Morel, who eventually was able to successfully classify mental disorders according to the course of the disturbance (Menninger, 1963).

Emil Kraepelin made one of the most substantive contributions to the development of a nosology of mental disorders. His optimistic view was that with increased understanding and information, a classification system could be developed on the basis of etiology, symptomatology, and course and that these systems would ultimately converge in agreement (Kraepelin, 1896).

As noted in the introduction to DSM-IV, the inclusion of the "idiocy/insanity" category in the 1840 U.S. Census may be the first official recognition of the classification of mental disorders in the United States. By 1880, the mental disorders category of the U.S. Census was expanded to include seven additional diagnoses.

Dissatisfaction with the available classification systems prompted the cooperative efforts of the American Medico-Psychological Association and the National Committee for Mental Hygiene to publish a list of 22 disorders to be used in mental institutions throughout the United States (1918) (Kendell, 1975). This attempt was followed by the 1935 publication of the "Standard Classification" by the American Medical Association. After World War II and in view of the increased need to address the less severe mental disorders of veterans, the U.S. Army and the U.S. Navy developed a more comprehensive diagnostic system.

The first edition of the *Diagnostic and Statistical Manual of Mental Disorders* (DSM) was published by the American Psychiatric Association in 1952 (APA, 1952). This manual drew extensively from the systems utilized by the armed forces and was published in close concert with ICD-6. Provisions were made for future editions of DSM to be reviewed periodically, and a system was included for transferring DSM diagnoses to ICD codes.

Although DSM was only moderately well received, its success warranted the publication of another version. DSM-II was adopted in 1968 (APA, 1968). DSM-I and DSM-II experienced only limited success, in large part due to their reliance on theoretical descriptions and vague diagnostic criteria. These limitations, however, proved to serve as a strong impetus for the refinement of the APA's diagnostic system. It was the goal of the APA task force, formed in 1974, to modify the system so that it would provide more objective, clinically useful, and reliable diagnostic information that would be more palatable to clinicians and educators of various theoretical orientations (Zammit, 1995).

DSM-III (APA, 1980), proved to be a radical departure from the previously released versions. The dramatic alteration in the content of DSM-III has been largely attributed to the "Feighner criteria" derived from the work completed at Washington University in St. Louis (Feighner, Robins, Guze, Woodruff, Winokur, & Munoz, 1972) and on the Research Diagnostic Criteria (RDC; Spitzer, Endicott, & Robins, 1978). DSM-III was the first edition to use the multiaxial system. This version of DSM was very successful and became one of the most widely used diagnostic systems in the United States.

While DSM-III was a significant departure from the previously published editions, DSM-III-R included only minor changes to DSM-III (hence, the designation "Revised"). The publication of DSM-III-R was prompted primarily by the scientific data that had been accumulated by researchers using DSM-III and its

criteria. The need for this revision emphasized the importance of basing subsequent versions on available data, the empirical literature, and field trials (Frances, Widiger, & Pincus, 1989).

In anticipation of the publication of ICD-10 (WHO, 1992), APA appointed a task force to revise DSM-III-R in 1988. The responsibility of this task force was to develop a revised diagnostic system based on available empirical data that would be consistent with the new ICD. DSM-IV (APA, 1994) continues to be based on a descriptive approach to diagnosis but is expected to provide more reliable, empirically valid diagnoses.

BRIEF HISTORY OF THE INTERNATIONAL CLASSIFICATION OF DISEASES

The *International Classification of Diseases* is the standard recognized by the World Health Organization and used throughout the world. While its origin predates DSM by almost 100 years, the current versions of ICD are heavily influenced by the *Diagnostic and Statistical Manual* of the American Psychiatric Association, and the two systems, while not identical, are very compatible.

As Israel points out (1978), the roots of the *International Classification of Diseases* can be traced back two or three hundred years to John Graunt's analysis of the Bills of Mortality in London and can be traced through the eighteenth-century works of "Nosologica Methodica" of Francois de Lacroix as well as to Linnaeus' "Genera Morborum" and to the synopsis "Nosologiae Methodicae" of William Cullen. The original intent of these systems, as well as of ICD, which grew out of them, was not to standardize medical diagnosis and treatment but rather to statistically record and classify causes of death.

The modern history of ICD began at the meeting of the first International Statistical Conference, held in Brussels in 1853. The participants at this meeting were sufficiently impressed with the importance of gathering health statistics, particularly causes of death, that they assigned to William Farr, a medical statistician from England, and Marc d'Espine, of Geneva, the task of developing a nomenclature of causes of death that would be applicable in all countries.

The Second International Statistical Conference was held in Paris in 1855. At this meeting, Farr and d'Espine submitted their proposed lists of causes of death. The lists approached the problem in different manners. Farr's list organized causes of death into five main groups including epidemic diseases, constitutional or general diseases, local diseases arranged according to anatomical site, developmental diseases, and diseases resulting from violence. D'Espine's list was somewhat different in that it was organized according to the basic nature of the disease, for example, gouty, herpetic, hematic, and so forth (Israel, 1978). The conference combined these approaches and developed a list of 138 rubrics. This list was further revised in 1864, 1874, 1880, and 1886.

At a meeting of the International Statistical Institute (ISI) (this organization replaced the International Statistical Conference) in 1891, in Vienna, a committee was appointed, with Jacques Bertillon of Paris as chair, to review and prepare a new system of classification for causes of death. Bertillon made his report at the ISI meeting in Chicago in 1893. His report was well received and was adopted by a number of countries. In 1898 the American Public Health Association endorsed the Bertillon classification and suggested that this classification be revised every 10 years to keep up with new scientific evidence. In 1899 the ISI accepted the suggestion of the American Public Health Association and passed a resolution encouraging all countries to adopt the system. The first International Conference for the Revision of the Bertillon, or International Classification of Causes of Death, was convened in Paris, in 1890, at the invitation of the Government of France. Since that time, the system has been revised approximately every 10 years. Over the years, ICD has been endorsed by the Health Organization of the League of Nations and by the World Health Organization (WHO).

The sixth revision of ICD, which was published in 1946, was a major revision that expanded the system for the purpose of coding morbidity, as well as mortality, data. This revision was also the first to contain a separate section (section 5) devoted to "mental, psychoneurotic and personality disorders" (Kramer, 1994). It also proved adaptable enough to eventually be employed as a standard for diagnosing illnesses and for use by hospitals in classifying illnesses and health statistics.

Currently, there are several publications of interest to professionals in the mental health field, including *ICD-10 Classification of Mental and Behavioral Disorders: Clinical Descriptions and Diagnostic Guidelines* (WHO, 1992) and *ICD-10 Classification of Mental and Behavioral Disorders: Diagnostic Criteria for Research* (WHO, 1993), as well as ICD-10.

Although these publications are currently available in the United States, ICD-10 has not been completely adopted by U.S. officials. Adoption of ICD-10 is mandated by a treaty between WHO and the U.S. Department of Health and Human Services but is not expected to occur prior to the year 2000. Reasons for the delay include the difficulty of altering the computerized billing systems in the United States to the alphanumeric coding of ICD-10 (ICD-9 relies solely on numeric codes) and the fact that the comprehensive index of ICD-10 diagnostic codes has not been published. Therefore, the current version of DSM-IV uses ICD-9-CM codes, except in Appendix H, which contains ICD-10 codes.

The current edition of ICD is the tenth revision. It has been adopted, for all practical purposes, throughout the world. As noted earlier, ICD differs somewhat from DSM, but the two are completely compatible, and one can be translated into the other. The major difference between the two is a slight refinement and extension of certain categories in DSM over the more basic categories of ICD.

The format for these two diagnostic systems is also somewhat different. *ICD-10 Clinical Descriptions and Diagnostic Guidelines* provides descriptions of the diagnostic categories; however, the criteria described in these narratives are less stringent and do not detail explicit inclusion and exclusion criteria as well as DSM-IV does.

SUMMARY

The developmental histories of DSM-IV and ICD-10 have similar roots, and the classification systems have a long tradition of being interdependent. In their current versions, these diagnostic systems are generally compatible and have improved upon the degree of correspondence that existed between DSM-III/DSM-III-R and ICD-9-CM. In most cases, mental health professionals will find similar diagnoses described in each, although the diagnoses may be found within different classes of disorders and may be described in a different manner.

The publication of DSM-IV is yet another refinement in the most widely used diagnostic system for mental health professionals. These advances in the diagnostic procedures are a crucial step toward the continued development and growth of the disciplines involved in the provision of mental health services. The systematic use and study of these procedures, as well as assessment and treatment strategies, will promote further progress within the mental health fields. It is hoped that this text, in a similar manner, will contribute to the understanding and treatment of mental disorders in children and adolescents, as well as to the general quality and effectiveness of mental health services.

REFERENCES

American Psychiatric Association. (1952). *Diagnostic and statistical manual of mental disorders* (1st ed.). Washington, DC: Author.

American Psychiatric Association. (1968). *Diagnostic and statistical manual of mental disorders* (2nd ed.). Washington, DC: Author.

American Psychiatric Association. (1980). *Diagnostic and statistical manual of mental disorders* (3rd ed.). Washington, DC: Author.

American Psychiatric Association. (1987). *Diagnostic and statistical manual of mental disorders* (3rd ed., rev.). Washington, DC: Author.

American Psychiatric Association. (1994). *Diagnostic and statistical manual of mental disorders* (4th ed.). Washington, DC: Author.

Esquirol, J. E. D. (1838). *Des maladies mentales considerées sous les rapports medical, hygiénique et medico-légal.* Paris: Balliere.

Feighner, J. B., Robins, E., Guze, S., Woodruff, R. A., Winokur, G., & Munoz, R. (1972). Diagnostic criteria for use in psychiatric research. *Archives of General Psychiatry, 26,* 57–63.

Frances, A. J., Widiger, T. A., & Pincus, H. A. (1989). The development of DSM-IV. *Archives of General Psychiatry, 46,* 373–375.

Israel, R. A. (1978). The International Classification of Diseases: Two hundred years of development. *Public Health Reports, 93*(2), 150–152.

Kendell, R. E. (1975). *The role of diagnosis in psychiatry.* Oxford: Blackwell Scientific.

Kraepelin, E. (1896). *Psychiatrie* (6th ed.). Leipzig: Arno Press.

Kramer, M. E. (1994). The history of the International Classification of Diseases. In J. E. Mezzich, M. R. Jorge, & I. M. Salloum (Eds.), *Psychiatric epidemiology: Assessment concepts and methods* (pp. 81–99). Baltimore: Johns Hopkins University Press.

Mack, A. H., Forman, L., Brown, R., & Frances, A. (1994). A brief history of psychiatric classification: From the Ancients to DSM-IV. *Psychiatric Clinics of North America, 17*(3), 515–523.

Menninger, K. (1963). *The vital balance.* New York: Viking.

Pinel, P. (1798). *Nosographie philosophique ou la méthode de l'analyse appliquée à la médecine.* Paris: Maradon.

Spitzer, R. L., Endicott, J., & Robins, E. (1978). Research diagnostic criteria: Rationale and reliability. *Archives of General Psychiatry, 35,* 773–782.

Thangavelu, R., & Martin, R. L. (1995). ICD-10 and DSM-IV: Depiction of the diagnostic elephant. *Psychiatric Annals, 25,* 20–28.

World Health Organization. (1992). *International classification of diseases classification of mental and behavioral disorders: Clinical descriptions and diagnostic guidelines* (10th rev.). Geneva: Author.

World Health Organization. (1993). *International classification of diseases classification of mental and behavioral disorders: Diagnostic criteria for research* (10th rev.). Geneva: Author.

Zammit, G. K. (1995). The diagnosis of mental disorders using the DSM-IV. In G. K. Zammit & J. W. Hull (Eds.), *Guidebook for clinical psychology interns* (pp. 105–120). New York: Plenum Press.

2
Mental Retardation:
A Symptom and a Syndrome

Fred J. Biasini
Lisa Grupe
Lisa Huffman
Norman W. Bray

INTRODUCTION

Mental retardation is an idea, a condition, a syndrome, a symptom, and a source of pain and bewilderment to many families. Its history dates back to the beginning of man's time on earth. The idea of mental retardation can be found as far back in history as the therapeutic papyri of Thebes (Luxor), Egypt, around 1500 B.C. Although somewhat vague due to difficulties in translation, these documents clearly refer to disabilities of the mind and body due to brain damage (Scheerenberger, 1983). Mental retardation is also a condition or syndrome defined by a collection of symptoms, traits, and/or characteristics. It has been defined and renamed many times throughout history. For example, feeblemindedness and mental deficiency were used as labels during the late nineteenth century and in the early part of the twentieth. Consistent across all definitions are difficulties in learning, in social skills, and in everyday functioning, as well as age of onset (during childhood). Mental retardation has also been used as a defining characteristic or symptom of other disorders, such as Down syndrome and Prader-Willi syndrome. Finally, mental retardation is a challenge and a potential source of stress to the family of an individual with this disorder. From identification through treatment or education, families struggle with questions about cause and prognosis, as well as guilt, a sense of loss, and disillusionment about the future.

The objective of this chapter is to provide the reader with an overview of mental retardation, a developmental disability with a long and sometimes controversial history. Following a brief historical overview, the current diagnostic criteria, epidemiological information and the status of dual diagnosis are presented. Comprehensive assessment and common interventions are also reviewed in some detail.

Historical Perspective

The treatment of individuals with developmental disabilities has been dependent on the customs and beliefs of the era and the culture or locale. In ancient Greece and Rome, infanticide was a common practice. In Sparta, for example, neonates were examined by a state council of inspectors. If the council members suspected that the child was defective, the infant was thrown from a cliff to its death. By the second century A.D., individuals with disabilities, including children, who lived in the Roman Empire were frequently sold to be used for entertainment or amusement. The dawning of Christianity led to a decline in these barbaric practices and a movement toward care for the less fortunate; in fact, all of the early religious leaders—Jesus, Buddha, Mohammed, and Confucius—advocated humane treatment for the mentally retarded, developmentally disabled, or infirmed (Scheerenberger, 1983).

During the Middle Ages (476–1500 A.D.), the status and care of individuals with mental retardation varied greatly. Although more human practices evolved (i.e., decreases in infanticide and the establishment of foundling homes), many children were sold into slavery, abandoned, or left out in the cold. Toward the end of this era, in 1690, John Locke published his famous work *An Essay Concerning Human Understanding*. Locke believed that an individual was born without innate ideas, that the mind is a tabula rasa, a blank slate. This belief would profoundly influence the care and training provided to individuals with mental retardation. Locke also was the first to distinguish between mental retardation and mental illness: "Herein seems to lie the difference between idiots and madmen, that madmen put wrong ideas together and reason from them, but idiots make very few or no propositions and reason scarce at all" (Doll, 1962, p. 23).

A cornerstone event in the evolution of the care and treatment of the mentally retarded was the work of the physician Jean-Marc-Gaspard Itard (Scheerenberger, 1983), who was hired in 1800 by the Director of the National Institutes for Deaf-Mutes in France to work with a young boy named Victor. Victor had apparently lived his whole life in the woods of south-central France. After being captured and escaping several times, he had fled to the mountains of Aveyron. At about age 12, he was captured once again and sent to an orphanage, found to be deaf and mute, and moved to the Institute for Deaf-Mutes.

Building on the work of Locke and Condillac, who emphasized the importance of learning through the senses, Itard developed a broad educational program for Victor to develop his senses, intellect, and emotions. After 5 years of training, Victor continued to have significant difficulties in language and social interaction, though he acquired more skills and knowledge than many of Itard's contemporaries believed possible. Itard's educational approach became widely accepted and used in the education of the deaf. Near the end of his life, Itard had the opportunity to educate a group of children who were mentally retarded. He did not personally direct the education of these children but supervised the work of Edouard Seguin (Scheerenberger, 1983). Seguin developed a comprehensive approach to the education of children with mental retardation, known as the Physiological Method (Scheerenberger, 1983). Assuming a direct relationship between the senses and cognition, his approach began with sensory training, including vision, hearing, taste, smell, and eye-hand coordination. The curriculum extended from developing basic self-care skills to vocational education, with an emphasis on perception, coordination, imitation, positive reinforcement, memory, and generalization. In 1850 Seguin moved to the United States and became a driving force in the education of individuals with mental retardation. In 1876 he founded what would become the American Association on Mental Retardation. Many of Seguin's techniques have been modified and are still in use today.

Over the next 50 years, two key developments occurred in the United States: residential training schools were established in most states (19 state operated and 9 privately operated) by 1892, and the newly developed test of intelligence developed by Binet was translated in 1908 by Henry Goddard, Director of Research at the training school in Vineland, New Jersey. Goddard published an American version of the test in 1910. In 1935 Edgar Doll developed the Vineland Social Maturity Scale to assess the daily living skills and adaptive behavior of individuals suspected of having mental retardation. Psychologists and educators now believed that it was possible to determine who had mental retardation and to provide them with appropriate training in the residential training schools.

During the early part of the twentieth century, residential training schools proliferated, and individuals with mental retardation were enrolled. This practice was influenced by the availability of tests (primarily IQ) to diagnose mental retardation and by the belief that, with proper training, individuals with mental retardation could be "cured." When training schools were unable to "cure" mental retardation, they became overcrowded, and many of the students were moved back into society, where the focus of education began to change to special education classes in the community. The training schools, which were initially more educational in nature, became custodial living centers. Residential treatment became more a matter of warehousing individuals. Facilities became overcrowded and were frequently understaffed and underfunded. The living conditions were described as reprehensible and inhuman. Treatment was typically unavailable and appropriate equipment frequently nonexistent (Scheerenberger, 1983).

As a result of the disillusionment with residential treatment, advocacy groups, such as the National Association of Retarded Citizens and the President's Commission on Mental Retardation, were established from the 1950s through the 1970s. The Wyatt v. Stickney federal court action, in the 1970s, was a landmark class-action suit in Alabama that established the right to treatment of individuals living in residential facilities. Purely custodial care was no longer acceptable. Concurrent with this case, the U.S. Congress passed, in 1975, the Education for the Handicapped Act, now titled the Individuals with Disabilities Education Act. This Act guaranteed the appropriate education of all children with mental retardation and developmental disabilities, from school age through 21 years of age. This law was amended in 1986 to guarantee educational services to children with disabilities between the ages of 3 and 21 and provided incentives for states to develop infant and toddler service delivery systems. Today, most states guarantee

intervention services to children with disabilities between birth and 21 years of age.

Definition/Diagnosis/Classification

According to Scheerenberger (1983), the elements of the definition of mental retardation were well accepted in the United States by 1900. These included onset in childhood, existence of significant intellectual or cognitive limitations, and an inability to adapt to the demands of everyday life. An early classification scheme proposed by the American Association on Mental Deficiency (Retardation) in 1910 referred to individuals with mental retardation as feeble-minded, meaning that their development was halted at an early age or was in some way inadequate, making it difficult for them to keep pace with their peers and to manage their daily lives independently (Committee on Classification, 1910). Three levels of impairment were identified: *idiot*, individuals whose development is arrested at the level of a 2-year-old; *imbecile*, individuals whose development is equivalent to that of a child of between 2 and 7 years old at maturity; and *moron*, individuals whose mental development is equivalent to that of a 7- to 12-year-old at maturity.

Over the next 30 years, the definitions of mental retardation focused on one of three aspects of development: the inability to learn to perform common acts; deficits or delays in social development/competence; or low IQ (Yepsen, 1941). An example of a definition based on social competence was that proposed by Edgar Doll, who suggested that mental retardation referred to "social incompetence, due to mental subnormality, which has been developmentally arrested, which obtains at maturity, is of constitutional origin, and which is essentially incurable" (Doll, 1936, p. 38). Fred Kuhlman, who was highly influential in the early development of intelligence tests in the United States, believed mental retardation was "a mental condition resulting from a subnormal rate of development of some or all mental functions" (Kuhlman, 1941, p. 213).

As a result of the conflicting views and definitions of mental retardation, the growing number of labels used to refer to individuals with mental retardation, and a change in emphasis from a genetic or constitutional focus to a desire for a function-based definition, the American Association on Mental Deficiency (Retardation) proposed and adopted a three-part definition in 1959: "Mental retardation refers to subaverage general intellectual functioning which originates in the developmental period and is associated with impairment in adaptive behavior" (Heber, 1961, p. 3). Although this definition included the three components of low IQ (<85), impaired adaptive behavior, and origination before age 16, only IQ and age of onset were measurable with the existing psychometric techniques. Assessments of deficits in adaptive behavior were generally based on subjective interpretations by individual evaluators, even though the Vineland Social Maturity Scale was available (Scheerenberger, 1983).

In addition to the revised definition, a five-level classification scheme was introduced to replace the earlier three-level system, which had acquired a very negative connotation. The generic terms of borderline (IQ 67–83), mild (IQ 50–66), moderate (IQ 33–49), severe (IQ 16–32), and profound (IQ <16) were adopted.

Due to concern about the over- or misidentification of mental retardation, particularly in minority populations, the definition was revised in 1973 (Grossman, 1973), at which time the borderline classification was eliminated from the interpretation of significant subaverage general intellectual functioning. The upper IQ boundary changed from <85 to ≤70. This change significantly reduced the number of individuals who were identified as mentally retarded, impacting the eligibility criteria for special school services and governmental supports. Many children who might have benefited from special assistance were now ineligible for such help. A 1977 revision (Grossman, 1977) modified the upper IQ limit to 70–75 to account for measurement error. IQ performance resulting in scores of 71 through 75 were consistent with mental retardation only when significant deficits in adaptive behavior were also present.

The most recent change in the definition of mental retardation was adopted in 1992 by the American Association on Mental Retardation (AAMR): "Mental retardation refers to substantial limitations in present functioning. It is characterized by significantly subaverage intellectual functioning, existing concurrently with related limitations in two or more of the following applicable adaptive skill areas: communication, self-care, home living, social skills, community use, self-direction, health and safety, functional academics, leisure, and work. Mental retardation manifests before age 18" (AAMR, 1992, p. 5). On the surface, this latest definition does not appear very different from its recent predecessors. However, the focus on the functional status of the individual with mental retardation is much more delineated and critical in this definition. There is also a focus on the impact of environmental influences on adaptive skills development that was absent in previous definitions. Finally, this revision eliminates the severity-level classification scheme in favor of one that addresses the type and intensity of support needed: intermittent, limited, extensive, or pervasive. Practically, a child under age 18 must have an IQ ≤75 and deficits in at least two of the adaptive behavior domains indicated in the definition to obtain a diagnosis of mental retardation.

Educational Classifications

While the medical and psychosocial communities were developing an acceptable definition and classification system, the educational community adopted its own system of classification. Its three-level system separated school-age children with mental retardation into three groups on the basis of predicted ability to learn (Kirk, Karnes, & Kirk, 1955). Children who were *educable* could learn simple academic skills but could not progress above fourth-grade level. Children who were believed to be *trainable* could learn to care for their daily needs but could acquire very few academic skills. Children who appeared to be *untrainable* or totally dependent were considered in need of long-term care, possibly in a residential setting. Some form of this scheme is still in use today in many school systems across the country.

DSM-IV

The fourth edition of the *Diagnostic and Statistical Manual of Mental Disorders*, published by the American Psychiatric Association in 1994 (DSM-IV), attempts to blend the 1977 and the 1992 definitions put forth by the AAMR. It adopts the 1992 definition but retains the severity-level classification scheme from the 1977 definition. The upper IQ limit is 70, and an individual must have delays in at least two of the ten areas outlined in the 1992 definition to be classified as mentally retarded. In general, the overview of mental retardation in DSM-IV is thorough and easy to follow. However, it should be noted that comprehensive cognitive and adaptive skill assessment is necessary to make the diagnosis; it should not be made on the basis of an office visit or developmental screening.

ICD-10

ICD-10 is the tenth revision of the *International Classification of Diseases* (World Health Organization, 1993). It is currently in use in some countries around the world but will not be adopted for use in the United States until after the year 2000. ICD-10 differs from ICD-9 in at least two key ways. First, it includes more diagnoses and is, consequently, much larger. The second major difference is the coding scheme. The diagnostic codes have been changed from numeric codes to codes that begin with an alphabet letter and are followed by two or more numbers (e.g., mild mental retardation has changed from 317 to F70).

ICD-10 characterizes mental retardation as a condition resulting from a failure of the mind to develop completely. Unlike DSM-IV and the Classification Manual of the AAMR, ICD-10 suggests that cognitive, language, motor, social, and other adaptive behavior skills should all

be used to determine the level of intellectual impairment. ICD-10 also supports the idea of dual diagnosis, suggesting that mental retardation may be accompanied by physical or other mental disorders.

Four levels of mental retardation are specified in ICD-10: F70 mild (IQ 50–69), F71 moderate (IQ 35–49), F72 severe (IQ 20–34), and F73 profound (IQ below 20). IQ should not be used as the only determining factor. Clinical findings and adaptive behavior should also be used to determine level of intellectual functioning. Two additional classifications are possible: F78, other mental retardation, and F79, unspecified mental retardation. Other mental retardation (F78) should be used when associated physical or sensory impairments make it difficult to establish the degree of impairment. Unspecified mental retardation (F79) should be used when there is evidence of mental retardation but not enough information to establish a level of functioning (e.g., a toddler with significant delays in development who is too young to be assessed with an IQ measure).

Epidemiology

Over the past 50 years the prevalence and incidence of mental retardation have been affected by changes in the definition of mental retardation, improvements in medical care and technology, changing societal attitudes regarding the acceptance and treatment of an individual with mental retardation, and the expansion of educational services to children with disabilities from birth through age 21. The theoretical approach to determining the prevalence of mental retardation uses the normal bell curve to estimate the number of individuals whose IQ falls below the established criterion score. For example, 2.3% of the population of the United States has an IQ score below 70, and 5.5% has an IQ score below 75. However, this estimate does not account for adaptive behavior skills. On the basis of empirical sampling, Baroff (1991) suggests that only 0.9% of the population can be assumed to have mental retardation. Following a review of the most recent epidemiological studies, McLaren and Bryson (1987) report that the prevalence of mental retardation is approximately 1.25%, on the basis of total population screening. When school-age children are the source of prevalence statistics, individual states report rates from 0.3% to 2.5%, depending on the criteria used to determine eligibility for special educational services, the labels assigned during the eligibility process (e.g., developmental delay, learning disability, autism, and/or mental retardation), and the environmental and economic conditions within the state (U.S. Department of Education, 1994). It is estimated that approximately 89% of these children have mild mental retardation, 7% have moderate mental retardation, and 4% have severe to profound mental retardation. In addition, McLaren and Bryson (1987) report that the prevalence of mental retardation appears to increase with age up to about the age of 20, with significantly more males than females identified.

Etiology

There are several hundred disorders associated with mental retardation. Many of these disorders play a causal role in mental retardation. However, most of the causal relationships must be inferred (McLaren & Bryson, 1987). The American Association on Mental Retardation subdivides the disorders that may be associated with mental retardation into three general areas: prenatal causes, perinatal causes, and postnatal causes. For a complete listing of these disorders, the reader is referred to *Mental retardation: Definition, classification, and systems of support* (AAMR, 1992). It should be noted that some causes can be determined much more reliably than others. For example, chromosomal abnormalities such as Down syndrome can be assumed to be causal with more certainty than can be ascribed to some postnatal infections. It should also be noted that mental retardation is both a symptom of other disorders and a unique syndrome or disorder.

Causes Associated with Level of Mental Retardation

The most common factor associated with severe mental retardation (including the moderate, severe, and profound levels of mental retardation) has been chromosomal abnormality, particularly Down syndrome (McLaren & Bryson, 1987). In approximately 20% to 30% of the individuals identified with severe mental retardation, the cause has been attributed to prenatal factors, such as chromosomal abnormality. Perinatal factors such as perinatal hypoxia account for about 11%, and postnatal factors such as brain trauma account for 3% to 12% of severe mental retardation. In 30% to 40% of cases, the cause is reported to be unknown.

The etiology of mild mental retardation is much less delineated. Between 45% and 63% of the cases are attributed to unknown etiology. Fewer cases of prenatal and perinatal causes are reported, with the largest number attributed to multiple factors (prenatal) and hypoxia (perinatal). Very few postnatal causes have been linked to mild mental retardation (McLaren & Bryson, 1987).

Associated Disorders

A variety of disorders are associated with mental retardation. These include epilepsy, cerebral palsy, vision and hearing impairments, speech/language problems, and behavior problems (McLaren & Bryson, 1987). The number of associated disorders appears to increase with the level of severity of mental retardation (Baird & Sadovnick, 1985).

Psychopathology

Studies on the prevalence of mental health disorders among individuals with mental retardation suggest that between 10% and 40% meet the criteria for a dual diagnosis of mental retardation and a mental health disorder (Reiss, 1990). The range in prevalence rates appears to be due to varying types of population sampling. When case file surveys are conducted, the prevalence rates are consistently around 10%. The use of psychopathology rating scales in institutional or clinic samples produces the much higher 40% prevalence rate (Reiss, 1990). The actual prevalence may lie somewhere in between these two estimates. The discrepancy may be the result of the tendency of mental health professionals to consider behavior disorders in individuals with mental retardation as a symptom of their delayed development. Nevertheless, individuals with mental retardation appear to display the full range of psychopathology evidenced in the general population (Jacobson, 1990; Reiss, 1990). Individuals with mild cognitive limitations are more likely to be given a dual diagnosis than are children with more significant disabilities (Borthwick-Duffy & Eyman, 1990).

ASSESSMENT

Assessment of a child suspected of having a developmental disability, such as mental retardation, may establish whether a diagnosis of mental retardation or some other developmental disability is warranted, establish eligibility for special educational services, and/or aid in determining the educational or psychological services needed by the child and family. At a minimum, the assessment process should include an evaluation of the child's cognitive and adaptive or everyday functioning, including behavioral concerns, where appropriate, and an evaluation of the family, home, and/or classroom to establish goals, resources, and priorities.

Globally defined, child assessment is the systematic use of direct as well as indirect procedures to document the characteristics and resources of an individual child (Simeonsson & Bailey, 1992). The process may comprise various procedures and instruments that result in the confirmation of a diagnosis, documentation of developmental status, and the prescription of intervention/treatment (Simeonsson & Bailey, 1992). A variety of assessment instruments have been criticized for insensitivity to cultural differences and accused of resulting in misdiagnosis or mislabeling. However, assessments have many valid uses. They allow for the measurement of change and the evaluation of program effectiveness, and they provide a standard for evaluating how well all children have learned the basic cognitive and academic skills necessary for survival in our culture. Given that the use of existing standardized instruments to obtain developmental information as part of the assessment process may bring about certain challenges, there does not appear to be a reasonable alternative (Sattler, 1992). Thus, it becomes necessary to understand assessment and its purpose so that the tools that are available can be used correctly and the results interpreted in a valid way.

The four components of assessment (Sattler, 1992)—norm-referenced tests, interviews, observations, and informal assessment—complement one another and form a firm foundation for making decisions about children. The use of more than one assessment procedure provides a wealth of information about the child, permitting the evaluation of the biological, cognitive, social, and interpersonal variables that affect the child's current behavior. In the diagnostic assessment of children, it is important also to obtain information from parents and other significant individuals in the child's environment. For school-age children, teachers are an important additional source of information. Certainly, major discrepancies among the findings obtained from the various assessment procedures must be resolved before any diagnostic decisions or recommendations are made. For example, if the intelligence test results indicate that the child is currently functioning in the mentally retarded range, while the interview findings and adaptive behavior results suggest functioning in the average range, it becomes necessary to reconcile these disparate findings before making a diagnosis.

Developmental Delay or Mental Retardation

In diagnosing infants or preschoolers, it is important to distinguish between mental retardation and developmental delay. A diagnosis of mental retardation is appropriate only when cognitive ability and adaptive behavior are significantly below average functioning. In the absence of clear-cut evidence of mental retardation, it is more appropriate to use a diagnosis of developmental delay. This acknowledges a cognitive or behavioral deficit but leaves room for it to be transitory or of ambiguous origin (Sattler, 1992). In practice, children under the age of two should not be given a diagnosis of mental retardation unless the deficits are relatively severe and/or the child has a condition that is highly correlated with mental retardation (e.g., Down syndrome).

Cognitive/Developmental Assessment Tools

In assessing children's functioning, practitioners can use a number of instruments. These include:

• *Bayley Scales of Infant Development, Second Edition* (Bayley, 1993): The Bayley Scales is an individually administered instrument for assessing the development of infants and very young children. It is appropriate for children from 2 months to 3.5 years. It comprises three scales, the mental scale, the motor scale, and the behavior rating scale. The mental scale assesses the following areas: recognition memory, object permanence, shape discrimination, sustained attention, purposeful manipulation of objects, imitation (vocal/verbal and gestural), verbal comprehension, vocalization, early language skills, short-term memory, problem solving, numbers, counting, and expressive vocabulary. The motor scale addresses the areas of gross and fine motor abilities in a relatively traditional manner. The behavior rating scale is used to rate the child's behavioral and emotional status during the assessment. Performance on the mental and motor scales is interpreted through the use of standard scores ($M = 100$; $SD = 15$). The behavior rating scale is interpreted by the use of percentile ranks.

The Bayley Scales were standardized using a stratified sample of 1,700 infants and toddlers across 17 age groupings closely approximating the U.S. Census data from 1988. The manual includes validity studies and case examples. The Bayley Scales is one of the most popular infant assessment tools. It can also be used to obtain the developmental status of children older than 3.5 years who have very significant delays in development and cannot be evaluated using more age-appropriate cognitive measures (e.g., a 6-year-old with a developmental level of 2 years).

• *Mullen Scales of Early Learning* (MSEL) (Mullen, 1995): The MSEL is a relatively new assessment tool. It was developed by Eileen Mullen and standardized in phases between June 1981 and April 1989 on a sample of 1,849 subjects. According to the author, it can be used to assess learning styles and developmental status and to determine whether special services are indicated. It provides developmental information related to language, visual-perceptual skills, and motor skills (gross motor only for ages birth to 33 months) for infants, toddlers, and preschool children up to 68 months of age. Overall performance is summarized in the form of an early learning composite, a standard score with a mean of 100 and a standard deviation of 15. The MSEL is individually administered and, according to the authors, requires 25 to 40 minutes to complete. In general, this scale appears promising; however, there are only a few published studies that have utilized the MSEL.

• *The Differential Ability Scales* (DAS) (Elliott, 1990): The DAS consists of a battery of individually administered cognitive and achievement tests subdivided into three age brackets: lower preschool (2.5 years to 3 years, 5 months), upper preschool (3.5 years to 5 years, 11 months), and school age (6 years to 17 years, 11 months). The cognitive battery focuses on reasoning and conceptual abilities and provides a composite standard score, the *general conceptual ability* (GCA) score. Verbal and nonverbal cluster standard scores and individual subtest standard scores are also available. The DAS has several advantages over other similar measures. It has a built-in mechanism for assessing significantly delayed children who are over the age of 3.5 years. It can also provide information comparable to other similar instruments in about half the time. Finally, it is very well standardized and correlates highly with other cognitive measures (i.e., the Wechsler Scales).

• *Wechsler Preschool and Primary Scale of Intelligence-Revised* (WPPSI-R) (Wechsler, 1989): The WPPSI-R can be utilized for children ranging in age from 3 years to 7 years, 3 months. Though separate and distinct from the WISC-III (discussed later), it is similar in form and content. The WPPSI-R is considered a downward extension of the WISC-III. These two tests overlap between the ages of 6 and 7 years, 3 months. The WPPSI-R has a mean of 100 and standard deviation of 15, with scaled scores for each subtest having a mean of 10 and a standard deviation of 3. It contains 12 subtests organized into two major areas; the verbal scale includes Information, Similarities, Arithmetic, Vocabulary, Comprehension, and Sentences (optional) subtests, while the performance scale includes Picture Completion, Geometric Design, Block Design, Mazes, Object Assembly, and Animal Pegs (optional) subtests. The WPPSI contains nine subtests similar to those included in the WISC-III (Information, Vocabulary, Arithmetic, Similarities, Comprehension, Picture Completion, Mazes, Block Design, and Object Assembly) and three unique subtests (Sentences, Animal Pegs, and Geometric Design). Three separate IQ scores can be obtained: verbal scale IQ, performance scale IQ, and full-scale IQ. The WPPSI-R was standardized on 1,700 children divided equally by gender and stratified to match the 1986 U.S. census data. This instrument cannot be used with severely disabled children (IQs below 40) and, with younger children, may need to be administered over two sessions due to the length of time required to complete the assessment.

• *Wechsler Intelligence Scale for Children-III* (WISC-III) (Wechsler, 1991): The WISC-III can be utilized for children ranging in age from 6 years through 16 years of age. It is the middle-childhood to middle-adolescence version of the Wechsler Scale series. It contains 13 subtests

organized into two major areas; the verbal scale includes Information, Similarities, Arithmetic, Vocabulary, Comprehension, and Digit Span (optional) subtests; the performance scale includes Picture Completion, Picture Arrangement, Block Design, Object Assembly, Coding, and the optional subtests of Mazes and Symbol Search. Three separate IQ scores can be obtained: verbal scale IQ, performance scale IQ, and full-scale IQ. Each of these separate IQs are standard scores with a mean of 100 and a standard deviation of 15, with scaled scores for each subtest having a mean of 10 and a standard deviation of 3. The WISC-III was standardized on a sample of 2,200 American children selected as representative of the population on the basis of 1988 U.S. census data.

• *Wechsler Adult Intelligence Scale, III* (WAIS-III) (Wechsler, 1981): The WAIS-III covers an age range of 16 years, 0 months, to 89 years. The revised version contains about 80% of the original WAIS and was modified mainly due to cultural considerations. There are 14 subtests: the verbal scale (Information, Similarities, Arithmetic, Vocabulary, Comprehension, Letter-number Sequencing, and Digit Span) and the performance scale (Picture Completion, Picture Arrangement, Block Design, Object Assembly, Matrix Reasoning, Symbol Search, and Digit Symbol). The WAIS-III was standardized in the 1990s on a sample of 2,450 white and nonwhite Americans divided equally by sex. The WAIS-III has a mean of 100 and a standard deviation of 15, with the scaled scores for each subtest having a mean of 10 and a standard deviation of 3.

• *Stanford-Binet, Fourth Edition* (SB: FE) (Thorndike, Hagen, & Sattler, 1986): The SB: FE is appropriate for use on individuals ranging in age from 2 years to 23. It comprises 15 subtests, though only 6 (Vocabulary, Comprehension, Pattern Analysis, Quantitative, Bead Memory, and Memory for Sentences) are used in all age groups. The other 9 subtests (Picture Absurdities, Paper Folding and Cutting, Copying, Repeating Digits, Similarities, Form-Board Items, Memory for Objects, Number Series, and Equation Building) are administered on the basis of age. Unlike previous editions, the SB: FE uses a point scale similar to that of the Wechsler Scales, is more culturally sensitive, and includes some new items in the areas of memory for objects, number series, and equation building.

Once administered, the SB: FE yields three types of scores: age scores (or scaled scores), area scores (general intelligence, crystallized intelligence and short-term memory, specific factors, and specific factors plus short-term memory), and a composite score (similar to the full-scale IQ of the Wechsler). The SB: FE composite score has a mean of 100 and a standard deviation of 16 (unlike the Wechsler's standard deviation of 15).

Overlap between the WISC-III and the Stanford-Binet, Fourth Edition: The WISC-III is appropriate between the ages of 6 and 16, while the Stanford-Binet: Fourth Edition is appropriate between the ages of 2 and 23. While the child is between six and 16, either test is appropriate. Correlations range from .66 to .83 between the WISC-R Full Scale IQ and the Fourth Edition composite. Results from Thorndike, Hagen, and Sattler (1986b) show that, while the two tests yield approximately equal scores, they are not interchangeable. This is partly due to the fact that they operate on different standard deviations (Sattler, 1992).

Overlap between the WAIS-R and the Stanford-Binet, Fourth Edition: Results for individuals with and without mental retardation are similar in that the WAIS-R yields higher scores than the Stanford-Binet Fourth Edition.

Special Note: Assessment Tools for Individuals with Mental Retardation. The Stanford-Binet, Fourth Edition and the Wechsler Scales are useful instruments in assessing *mild* mental retardation; however, neither is designed to test individuals with severe or profound mental retardation. In addition, due to the high floor on the Wechsler Scales, the publisher recommends that a child obtain raw score credit in at least three subtests of the verbal scale and the performance scale before the practitioner assumes that the tests provide useful information. Raw score for six subtests, three verbal and three performance, are recommended for a valid full-scale IQ.

• *McCarthy Scales of Children's Abilities* (McCarthy, 1972): The McCarthy Scales can be used with children between the ages of 2.5 years and 8.5 years. It contains six scales: verbal scale, perceptual-performance scale, quantitative scale, memory scale, motor scale, and general cognitive scale. In addition to yielding a general cognitive index (GCI), the McCarthy Scales provide several ability profiles (verbal, nonverbal reasoning, number aptitude, short-term memory, and coordination). The overall GCI has a mean of 100 and a standard deviation of 16 and is an estimate of the child's ability to apply accumulated knowledge to the tasks in the scales. The ability profiles, in particular, make the McCarthy Scales useful for assessing young children with learning problems. The GCI is not interchangeable with the IQ score rendered by the Wechsler Scales; therefore, caution is advised in making placement decisions based on the GCI, especially in the case of children with mental retardation (Sattler, 1992).

Adaptive Behavior Assessment Tools

Adaptive behavior is an important and necessary part of the definition and diagnosis of mental retardation. It is the ability to perform daily activities required for personal and social sufficiency (Sattler, 1992). Assessment of adaptive behavior focuses on how well individuals can function and maintain themselves independently and how well they meet the personal and social demands imposed on them by their cultures. There are more than 200 adaptive behavior measures and scales. The most commonly used scale is the Vineland Adaptive Behavior Scales (Sparrow, Balla, & Cicchetti, 1984).

• *Vineland Adaptive Behavior Scales* (VABS) (Sparrow, Balla, & Cicchetti, 1984): The VABS is a revision of the Vineland Social Maturity Scale (Doll, 1953) and assesses the social competence of individuals with and without disabilities from birth to age 19. It is an indirect assessment in that the respondent is not the individual in question but someone familiar with the individual's behavior. The VABS measures four domains: communication, daily living skills, socialization, and motor skills. An adaptive behavior composite is a combination of the scores from the four domains. A maladaptive behavior domain is also available with two of the three forms of administration. Each of the domains and the composite has a mean of 100 and a standard deviation of 15. Three types of administration are available: the survey form (297 items), the expanded form (577 items, 297 of which are from the survey form), and the classroom edition (244 items for children age 3 to 13). The survey and the expanded forms were standardized on a representative sample selected to match the 1980 U.S. census data and include 3,000 individuals ranging in age from newborn to 18 years, 11 months. There are norms for individuals with mental retardation, children with behavior disorders, and individuals with physical handicaps. The classroom edition was standardized on a representative sample that matched the 1980 U.S. census data and that included 3,000 students, ages 3 years to 12 years, 11 months. Caution is advised when using this scale with children under the age of two because children with more significant delays frequently attain standard scores that appear to be in the low-average range of ability. In this case, more weight should be placed on the age equivalents that can be derived.

• *The American Association on Mental Retardation (AMMR) Adaptive Behavior Scale (ABS):* The ABS has two forms that address survival skills and maladaptive behaviors in individuals living in residential and community settings (ABS-RC:2; Nihira, Leland, & Lambert, 1993) or school-age children (ABS-S:2; Lamber, Nahira, & Leland, 1993). It is limited in scope and should be used with caution. A new scoring method has recently been devised that can generate scores consistent with the 10 adaptive behavior areas suggested in the 1992 definition of mental retardation (Bryant, Taylor, & Pedrotty-Rivera, 1996). The results of this assessment can be readily translated into objectives for intervention.

Achievement Tests

Intelligence tests are broader than achievement tests and sample a wider range of experiences, but both measure aptitude, learning, and achievement to some degree (Sattler, 1992). Achievement tests (such as tests in reading and mathematics) are heavily dependent on formal learning, are more culturally bound, and tend to sample more specific skills than do intelligence tests. Intelligence tests measure one's ability to apply information in new and different ways, whereas achievement tests measure mastery of factual information (Sattler, 1992). Intelligence tests are better predictors of scholastic achievement and therefore contribute more to the decision-making processes in schools and clinics, and they are a better predictor of educability and trainability than are other achievement tests because they sample the reasoning capacities developed outside school that should also be applied in school.

To determine if learning potential is being fully realized, results from an IQ test and standardized tests of academic achievement can be compared. If there is a significant difference between IQ and achievement, the child may benefit from special assistance in the academic area identified.

Achievement Assessment Tools

Among the achievement assessment tools that can be used with children with mild learning disorders are these:

• *Woodcock - Johnson Psycho - Educational Battery, Revised* (Woodcock & Johnson, 1990): The Woodcock-Johnson comprises 35 tests assessing cognitive ability (vocabulary, memory, concept formation, spacial relations, and quantitative concepts) and achievement (reading, spelling, math, capitalization, punctuation, and knowledge of science, humanities, and social studies). Though the test batteries can be used with individuals from age 2 through adulthood, not all tests are administered at every age. The cognitive ability battery and the achievement battery each have a recommended standard battery and supplemental batteries. The achievement battery can be used with preschool children (4- or 5-year-olds) through adults. They each provide scores that can be converted into standard scores with a mean of 100 and a standard deviation of 15. By comparing the tests of cognitive ability and the tests of achievement, the Woodcock-Johnson allows for the assessment of an aptitude/achievment discrepancy. The discrepancy reflects any disparity between cognitive and achievement capabilities. The Woodcock-Johnson was standardized on a representative sample of 6,359 individuals ranging in age from 2 to 95, from communities throughout the United States.

• *The Wide-Range Achievement Test, Revised (WRAT-R)* (Jastak & Wilkinson, 1984): The WRAT-R is a brief achievement test and contains three subtests: reading, spelling, and arithmetic. The WRAT-R is divided into two levels: Level One (ages 5 years, 0 months, to 11 years, 11 months), and Level Two (ages 12 years, 0 months, to 74 years, 11 months). The WRAT-R has a mean of 100 and a standard deviation of 15. It also provides *T* scores, scaled scores, grade-equivalent scores, and percentile ranks. It was standardized on a sample of 5,600 individuals in 28 age groups (ranging in age from 5 to 74 years).

A variety of other achievement tests are available for assessing academic performance. These include, but are not limited to, the Kaufman Test of Educational Achievement (Kaufman & Kaufman, 1985) and the Wechsler Individual Achievement Test (1992).

Other Assessment Tools

Other assessment tools include:

• *Peabody Picture Vocabulary Test, Revised (PPVT-R)* (Dunn & Dunn, 1981): The PPVT-R is appropriate for individuals between the ages of 2.5 and adulthood and measures receptive knowledge of vocabulary. It is a multiple-choice test requiring only a pointing response and no reading ability, thus making it useful for hearing individuals with a wide range of abilities,

particularly children with language-based disabilities. The revised edition is more sensitive to gender-based stereotypes and cultural issues; in fact, only 37% of the original items have been retained. The PPVT-R has two forms, L and M, with 175 plates in each form in ascending order of difficulty. Each plate consists of four clearly drawn pictures, one of which is the correct response to the word given by the experimenter. Standard scores have a mean of 100 and a standard deviation of 15. The PPVT-R was standardized on a national sample of 4,200 children (2.5–18 years of age) and 828 adults (19–40 years of age) divided equally by sex and based on 1970 U.S. census data. The PPVT-R was designed to assess breadth of receptive vocabulary and is not intended for use as a screening tool for measuring level of intellectual functioning. PPVT-R scores are not interchangeable with IQ scores obtained via the Stanford-Binet, Fourth Edition, or the Wechsler Tests.

• *Columbia Mental Maturity Scale*: The Columbia Mental Maturity Scale (Burgemeister, Blum, & Lorge, 1972) is a test of general reasoning ability that can be used with children who have significant physical limitations. It is appropriate for children between the ages of 3.5 years and 9 years, 11 months. The Columbia has a mean of 100 and a standard deviation of 16 and can be interpreted using age equivalents. When used in conjunction with the Peabody Picture Vocabulary Test, Revised, it can provide reasonably accurate cognitive-status information comparable to that derived from the more common intelligence tests.

• *Leiter International Performance Scale*: The Leiter International Performance Scale (Leiter, 1948) is a nonverbal assessment of intelligence. Although the norms are dated, it provides useful information about the cognitive status of children with hearing impairments or severe language disabilities. It can be used with subjects ages 2 through adult. It is currently under revision and will likely be a useful tool in the future (Roid & Miller, 1997).

For a description of a wide range of other specialty tests, the reader is referred to the *Assessment of Children* by Jerome Sattler (1992).

Dual Diagnosis

Appropriate assessment of psychopathology in people with dual diagnosis is important because: (a) it can suggest the form of treatment; (b) it may ensure access to and funding for special services; and (c) it can be used to evaluate subsequent interventions (Sturmey, 1995). Brain damage, epilepsy, and language disorders are risk factors for psychiatric disorders and are often associated with mental retardation (Rutter, Tizard, Graham, & Whitmore, 1976; Sturmey, 1995). Social isolation, stigmatization, and poor social skills put individuals with mental retardation at further risk for affective disorders (Reiss & Benson, 1985). The relationship between emotional disorders and mental retardation has been noted by many researchers (Bregman, 1991; Menolascino, 1977; Reiss, 1990). Rates of emotional disorders are more prevalent in children with mental retardation than in children without mental retardation (Bregman, 1988; Lewis & MacLean, 1982; Matson, 1982, Russell, 1985). As noted previously, epidemiological studies of psychiatric disorders in individuals with mental retardation show that this population experiences higher rates of psychopathology (Corbett, 1985; Gostason, 1985). Though children with mental retardation are diagnosed with psychiatric disorders more often than children without mental retardation, they are usually diagnosed with the *same types of disorders*. However, uncommon psychiatric disorders may be found in children with severe and profound levels of mental retardation (Batshaw & Perret, 1992).

An additional problem is the application of DSM-IV criteria to individuals with mental retardation. Though DSM has proven useful in diagnosing individuals with mild or moderate mental retardation (especially when the criteria are modified in some way, leading to problems in clearly operationalized definitions), many psychologists and psychiatrists rely more on biological markers, observable signs, and patterns of family psychopathology to diagnose individuals with severe and profound mental retardation, thus implying that DSM may not be as useful with this population (Sturmey, 1995). The mismatch between behaviors scripted in DSM-IV and psychopathology presented in individuals with mental retardation can lead to underdiagnosing of these individuals (Sturmey, 1995). Because DSM is so widely used by psychiatrists, psychologists, and health insurance companies, and because of the way it is coordinated with the International Classification of Diseases (ICD), it will continue to be the main diagnostic source. Practitioners should take care not to modify DSM criteria for their own use and instead should use the criteria as they are prescribed and document cases where the criteria are inadequate to make a comprehensive diagnosis (Sturmey, 1995).

Most psychologists in the mental health field have little exposure to individuals with mental retardation and are sometimes uncomfortable treating these individuals; in fact, many professionals seem unaware that this group can experience mental health problems (Reiss & Szyszko, 1983). Mental health and mental retardation systems have been separated in this country for many years, making it difficult administratively to serve people with both mental retardation and mental health disorders (Matson & Sevin, 1994). Recently, there has been a heightened awareness of the need to pursue behavioral-psychiatric assessment, diagnosis, and treatment of people with mental retardation and mental health problems (Bregman, 1991; Eaton & Menolascino, 1982; Reiss, 1990).

A variety of behavioral assessment tools are available and provide key information for practitioners in this area. A few of the commonly used measures or checklists include the Child Behavior Checklist (Achenbach & Edelbrock, 1986), the Conners Parent (or Teacher) Rating Scale (Conners, 1990), the Revised Behavior Problem Checklist (Quay & Peterson, 1987), and the Social Skills Rating System (Gresham & Elliott, 1990). These measures are only as reliable as the parent, guardian, or teacher completing them. However, they can provide useful information about the nature of the behavioral problems or competencies of the child. All of the scales mentioned focus primarily on behavioral difficulties, with the exception of the Social Skills Rating System, which includes items that address prosocial behaviors.

Interdisciplinary Approach

Because children with mental retardation often have other problems, it is necessary to involve a team of practitioners from different areas (e.g., child psychiatrist, social worker, child psychologist, special education teacher, speech and language specialist, and community agencies) in the comprehensive diagnosis. This type of interdisciplinary team approach is relatively new but is considered to be imperative for comprehensive assessment, treatment, and management of children with mental retardation (Lubetsky, Mueller, Madden, Walker, & Len, 1995). A natural extension of the interdisciplinary approach is the involvement of the family in the decision-making process. In fact, recent government and educational initiatives such as Public Law 99-457 and Public Law 102-119 *require* the involvement of parents and professionals in early intervention services (Lubetsky et al., 1995). A family-centered interdisciplinary approach begins with an assessment of the child (including school history, obtained from parents and school records), family (family marital and parenting history), and community resources. Medical, developmental, and psychiatric histories are obtained. A behavioral analysis and psychoeducational, speech, and language testing are completed. Medical and neurological assessments are performed. The team presents its findings to the parents, who are actively involved in evaluating and implementing treatment recommendations (Lubetsky et al., 1995).

INTERVENTION

Psychoeducational Intervention

As a result of federal legislation developed with the aid and encouragement of a number of advocacy groups (i.e., the Individuals with Disabilities Education Act; Public Law 94-142, Public Law 99-457, and Public Law 102-119), children and adolescents with mental retardation or related developmental disorders are entitled to free and appropriate intervention. Appropriate intervention should be based on the needs of the child as determined by a team of professionals, address the priorities and concerns of the family, and be provided in the least restrictive most inclusive setting (i.e., where the child has every opportunity to benefit from interacting with nondisabled peers and from the community resources available to all other children).

Infant/Toddler Services

Services to infants and toddlers can be home based, center based, or some combination of the two. The nature of the services should be determined on the basis of the results of the child assessment and the family's priorities for the child. These should be used to develop an Individual Family Service Plan for the child with the involvement of all parties participating in the intervention and coordinated by a Services Coordinator (case manager) who is available and acceptable to the family. The services may include assistive technology, intervention for sensory impairments, family counseling, parent training, health services, language services, nursing intervention, nutrition counseling, occupational therapy, physical therapy, case management, and transportation to services.

Preschool and School Services

Services to preschool children, ages 3 through 5, and school-aged children, 6 through 21, can be home based, but are more frequently center based. As in the case of infants and toddlers, a team evaluation and parent input are used to develop an intervention plan. This plan, the Individualized Education Plan (IEP), details the objectives for improving the child's skills and may include family or parent-focused activities. Services may include special education provided by a certified teacher and focused on the needs of the child, child counseling, occupational therapy, physical therapy, language therapy, recreational activities, school health services, transportation services, and parent training or counseling. These services should be provided in the most inclusive, least restrictive setting (e.g., a regular preschool program, Head Start Center, child's home).

Social/Interpersonal Intervention

Social and interpersonal interventions can be both preventive and therapeutic. As noted, children with mental retardation are at an increased risk for behavioral disorders. Therefore, a variety of group social and recreational activities should be included in the child's educational program. These activities should involve nondisabled peers and may include participation at birthday parties, attendance at recreational activities such as ball games and movies, participation in youth sports activities, and visits to community sites such as zoos. The goal of these activities should be to teach appropriate social skills relevant to group participation and building self-esteem.

Parents also may benefit from prevention activities. Respite care provided by trained individuals can afford parents the opportunity to address their own needs (e.g., personal time, medical appointments, socializing with peers). Parents can be much more effective when their own needs have been met. Social or parent support groups can also be an outlet for parents to discuss their feelings with individuals who have similar experiences. These groups may be syndrome specific (e.g., Parent Advocates for Down Syndrome) or more generic in nature.

Therapeutic interventions with the children and families may include family therapy, individual child behavior therapy, parent training, and group therapy for mildly mentally disabled children and adolescents that focuses on developing appropriate social skills. Child behavioral interventions can be used to teach self-care, vocational, leisure, interpersonal, and survival skills (e.g., finding a public restroom). Disruptive behaviors such as tantrumming, self-injury, noncompliance, and aggression toward others can also be addressed through behavioral techniques. The most frequent form of behavioral intervention for problematic behavior involves differential reinforcement of incompatible and/or other behaviors (Batshaw & Perret, 1992).

Psychopharmacological Intervention

Treatment specifying the use of medication should be considered only when a particular psychiatric condition known to benefit from a particular drug coexists with the mental retardation or developmental disability. This may take the form of a severe depression, obsessive-compulsive disorder, attention deficit hyperactivity disorder, or a variety of other psychiatric disorders. There are few well-controlled studies of drug treatments with children who have mental retardation. It should be noted that the use of medication as a form of chemical restraint should be avoided. In addition, when drug treatment is used, it should only be one component of an overall treatment approach (Batshaw & Perret, 1992).

FINAL COMMENTS

An invaluable resource in evaluating and treating children with mental retardation is the child's family. Consequently, including the families of children with or at risk for disabilities in every phase of intervention, from identification to planning to implementation through monitoring, should be considered. Including families in decisions about the treatment or management of their children's problems presents new challenges. Nevertheless, trying to understand and include families in the decision-making process can ultimately be rewarding and beneficial for all involved.

Level of Family Involvement

How and when should families be included in decision making? There is no standard formula for answering this question. Families, like individuals, vary tremendously. Nevertheless, there are some issues that must be considered when involving families in team decisions about their children with disabilities. First, the team must be receptive to including families in the decision-making process. This involves some effort on the part of the nonfamily team members to encourage family participation. In addition, the team must decide what child and family concerns are related to enhancing the development of the child. These should be the focus of generating family-oriented service delivery alternatives.

Second, the team must consider the level of knowledge and understanding of the family related to the disability of the child and/or the service and treatment options. If families are to participate in the decision-making process, they must have the knowledge necessary to select appropriate alternatives. It is unfair to assume that families will not understand or cannot make appropriate decisions about the care of their child. They are the consumers and need to be given the chance to make an informed choice.

Finally, once the family has an adequate understanding of the condition and service and treatment alternatives, they may need to be nurtured through the team decision-making process. Most families have never participated as members of a team of professionals and may initially be reticent or nonparticipatory in discussions unless they are specifically invited to speak. Certainly, as a primary care provider, the parent or family member has more at stake than the other team members. Over time, the cautious or reticent family member may become an active and vital team member.

Encouraging Parent Participation

Health and education professionals who participate as team members must actively pursue parent-professional partnerships in the decision-making process. The logical first step is to acknowledge the value of the parent-professional relationship. Parents should be viewed as equal partners who can make important and necessary contributions in the planning and decision-making process. If professionals are reluctant to or refuse to acknowledge parents as partners in the process, they run the risk of alienating them, resulting in a lack of interest or participation in necessary services. Once the nonfamily team members accept the parents or other relevant family members as equal partners in the planning process, strategies to encourage continued active participation should be developed and implemented.

REFERENCES

Achenbach, T. M., & Edelbrock, C. S. (1986). *Child Behavior Checklist*. Burlington, VT: Author.

*American Association on Mental Retardation. (1992). *Mental retardation: Definition, classification, and systems of supports*. Washington, DC: American Association on Mental Retardation.

Baird, P. A., & Sadovnick, A. D. (1985). Mental retardation in over half-a-million conservative livebirths: An epidemiological study. *American Journal of Mental Deficiency, 89*, 323–330.

Baroff, G. S. (1991). *Developmental disabilities: Psychological aspects*. Austin, TX: ProEd.

*Batshaw, M. L., & Perret, Y. M. (1992). *Children with disabilities*. Baltimore: Paul H. Brookes.

Bayley, N. (1993). *Bayley Scales of Infant Development: Second edition*. San Antonio, TX: The Psychological Corporation.

Borthwick-Duffy, S. A., & Eyman, R. K. (1990). Who are the dually diagnosed? *American Journal on Mental Retardation, 94*, 586–595.

Bregman, J. D. (1988). Treatment approaches for the mentally retarded. In R. Michels, A. M. Cooper, S. B. Guze et al. (Eds.), *Psychiatry* (pp. 1–11). Philadelphia: J. B. Lippencott.

Bregman, J. D. (1991). Current developments in the understanding of mental retardation. Part II: Psychopathology. *Journal of the American Academy of Child and Adolescent Psychiatry, 30*, 861–872.

Bryant, B. R., Taylor, R. L., & Pedrotty-Rivera, D. (1996). *AAA Assessment of Adaptive Areas*. Austin, TX: ProEd.

Burgemeister, B. B., Blum, L. H., & Lorge, I. (1972). *Columbia Mental Maturity Scale*. San Antonio, TX: Psychological Corporation.

Committee on Classifcation of Feeble-minded. (1910). *Journal of Psycho-Asthenics, 15*, 61–67.

Conners, C. K. (1990). *Manual for Conners' Rating Scales*. Toronto: Multi-Health Systems.

Corbett, J. A. (1985). Mental retardation: Psychiatric aspects. In M. Rutter & L. Hersov (Eds.), *Child and adolescent psychiatry: Modern approaches* (2nd ed., pp. 661–678). Oxford: Blackwell Scientific Publications.

Doll, E. A. (1936). Current thoughts on mental deficiency. *Journal of Psycho-Asthenics, 41,* 33–49.

Doll, E. A. (1953). *The measurement of social competence. A manual for the Vineland Social Maturity Scale*. Washington, DC: Educational Testing Bureau.

Doll, E. A. (1962). Trends and problems in the education of the mentally retarded, 1800–1940. *American Journal of Mental Deficiency, 72,* 175–183.

Dunn, L. M., & Dunn, L. M. (1981). *Peabody Picture Vocabulary Test—Revised*. Circle Pines, MN: American Guidance Service.

Eaton, L. A., & Menolascino, F. J. (1982). Psychiatric disorders in the mentally retarded: Types, problems, and challenges. *American Journal of Psychiatry, 139,* 1297–1303.

Elliot, C. D. (1990). *Differential ability scales*. San Antonio, TX: Psychological Corporation.

Gostason, R. (1985). Psychiatric illness among the mentally retarded: A Swedish population study. *Acta Psychiatrica Scandinavia, 70,* 1–117.

Gresham, F. M., & Elliot, S. N. (1990). *Social Skill Rating System*. Circle Pines, MN: American Guidance Service.

Grossman, H. J. (Ed.). (1973). *Manual on terminology in mental retardation (1973 rev.)*. Washington, DC: American Association on Mental Deficiency.

Grossman, H. J. (Ed.). (1977). *Manual on terminology in mental retardation (1977 rev.)*. Washington, DC: American Association on Mental Deficiency.

Heber, R. A. (1961). A manual on terminology and classification in mental retardation (2nd ed.). *Monograph supplement to the American Journal of Mental Deficiency*.

Jacobson, J. W. (1990). Do some mental disorders occur less frequently among persons with mental retardation? *American Journal of Mental Retardation, 94,* 596–602.

Jastak, S., & Wilkinson, G. S. (1984). *WRAT-R: Wide Range Achievement Test administration manual*. Los Angeles: Western Psychological Services.

Kaufman, A. S., & Kaufman, N. L. (1985). *Kaufman test of educational achievement*. Circle Pines, MN: American Guidance Service.

Kirk, S. A., Karnes, M. B., & Kirk, W. D. (1955). *You and your retarded child*. New York: Macmillan.

Kuhlman, F. (1941). Definition of mental deficiency. *American Journal of Mental Deficiency, 46,* 206–213.

Lambert, N., Nihara, K., & Leland, H. (1993). *AAMR Adaptive Behavior Scale—School* (2nd ed.). Austin, TX: ProEd.

Leiter, R. G. (1948). *Leiter International Performance Scale*. Wood Dale, IL: Stoelting Co.

Lewis, M. H., & MacLean, W. E. (1982). Issues in treating emotional disorders. In J. L. Matson & R. P. Barrett (Eds.), *Progress in behavior modification* (Vol. 1). San Diego: Academic Press.

Lubetsky, M. J., Mueller, L., Madden, K., Walker, R., & Len, D. (1995). Family-centered/interdisciplinary team approach to working with families of children who have mental retardation. *Mental Retardation, 33,* 251–256.

Matson, J. L. (1982). Depression in the mentally retarded: A review. *Education and Training in the Mentally Retarded, 17,* 159–163.

Matson, J. L., & Sevin, J. A. (1994). Theories of dual diagnosis in mental retardation. *Journal of Consulting and Clinical Psychology, 62,* 6–16.

McCarthy, D. A. (1972). *McCarthy Scales of Children's Abilities*. San Antonio: Psychological Corporation.

McLaren, J., & Bryson, S. E. (1987). Review of recent epidemiological studies in mental retardation: Prevalence, associated disorders, and etiology. *American Journal of Mental Retardation, 92,* 243–254.

Menolascino, F. J. (1977). *Challenges in mental retardation progressive ideology and services*. New York: Hyman Services Press.

Mullen, E. M. (1995). *Mullen scales of early learning: AGS edition*. Circle Pines, MN: American Guidance Service.

Nihira, K., Leland, H., & Lambert, N. (1993). *AAMD Adaptive Behavior Scale—Residential and Community* (2nd ed.). Austin, TX: ProEd.

Quay, H. C., & Peterson, D. R. (1987). *Manual for the Revised Behavior Problem Checklist*. Coral Gables, FL: Author, University of Miami.

Reiss, S. (1990). Prevalence of dual diagnosis in community-based programs in the Chicago metropolitan area. *American Journal on Mental Retardation, 94,* 578–584.

Reiss, S. A., & Benson, B. A. (1985). Psychosocial correlates of depression in mentally retarded adults: Minimal social support and stigmatization. *American Journal on Mental Deficiency, 89,* 331–337.

Reiss, S., & Szyszko, J. (1983). Diagnostic overshadowing and professional experience with mentally retarded persons. *American Journal of Mental Deficiency, 87,* 396–402.

Roid, G., & Miller, L. (1997). *Leiter International Performance Scale—Revised.* Wood Dale, IL: Stoelting Co.

Rubin, H. H., Goldman, J. J., & Rosenfeld, J. G. (1985). A comparison of WISC-R and WAIS-R IQs in a mentally retarded residential population. *Psychology in the Schools, 22,* 392- 397.

Russell, A. T. (1985). The mentally retarded, emotionally disturbed child and adolescent. In M. Sigman (Ed.), *Children with emotional disorder and developmental disabilities: Assessment and treatment* (pp. 111–136). New York: Grune & Stratton.

Rutter, M., Tizard, J., Yule, W., Graham, Y., & Whitmore, K. (1976). Isle of Wright studies: 1964–1974. *Psychological Medicine, 7,* 313–332.

*Sattler, J. M. (1992). *Assessment of children* (3rd ed.) San Diego: Author.

*Scheerenberger, R. C. (1983). *A history of mental retardation.* Baltimore: Paul H. Brookes.

Simeonsson, R. J., & Bailey, D. B. (1992). Essential elements of the assessment process. In L. Rowitz (Ed.), *Mental retardation in the year 2000* (pp. 25–41). New York: Springer-Verlag.

Sparrow, S. S., Balla, D. A., & Cicchetti, D. V. (1984). *Vineland Adaptive Behavior Scale, expanded form manual.* Circle Press, MN: American Guidance Services.

Sturmey, P. (1995). DSM-III-R and persons with dual diagnoses: Conceptual issues and strategies for future research. *Journal of Intellectual Disability Research, 39,* 357–364.

Thorndike, R. L., Hagen, E. P., & Sattler, J. M. (1986a). *Guide for administering and scoring the Stanford-Binet Intelligence Scale: Fourth edition.* Chicago: Riverside Publishing Co.

Thorndike, R. L., Hagen, E. P., & Sattler, J. M. (1986b). *Technical manual, Stanford-Binet Intelligence Scale: Fourth edition.* Chicago: Riverside Publishing Co.

U.S. Department of Education. (1994). *The sixteenth annual report to Congress on the implementation of the individuals with disabilities education act.* Washington, DC: U.S. Government Printing Office.

Wechsler, D. (1989) *Wechsler Preschool Primary Scale of Intelligence—Revised.* San Antonio: Psychological Corporation.

Wechsler, D. (1991). *Wechsler Intelligence Scale for Children—Third edition.* San Antonio: Psychological Corporation.

Wechsler, D. (1997). *Wechsler Adult Intelligence Scale—III.* San Antonio: Psychological Corporation.

Wechsler, D. (1992). *Wechsler Individual Achievement Test.* San Antonio, TX: Psychological Corporation.

Woodcock, R. W., & Johnson, M. B. (1990). *Woodcock-Johnson Psycho-Educational Battery—Revised.* Allen, TX: DLM Teaching Resources.

World Health Organization. (1993). *International classification of diseases* (10th Rev.). Geneva: Author.

Yepsen, L. (1941). Defining mental deficiency. *American Journal of Mental Deficiency, 46,* 200–205.

*Indicates references that the authors recommend for additional reading.

3
Learning and Motor Skills Disorders

Jean C. Elbert

INTRODUCTION
Historical Perspective

Otherwise intelligent individuals who fail to master basic skills in reading, written expression, or mathematics or who have impaired motor coordination have long been recognized in both medical and educational literature. The historical precursors of these developmental disorders described in DSM-IV were clinical reports of the sequelae of acquired brain insults in adults. Subsequent attention to difficulties experienced by children included Orton's (1937) descriptions of developmental reading problems and the observations of behavioral symptoms observed in brain injured adults, which were subsequently extended to children. Such symptoms as perceptual disturbance, distractibility, disinhibition, and perseveration in children were identified as the "Strauss Syndrome" (Strauss & Werner, 1942). By the 1960s, the existing knowledge base regarding children's learning disorders, as well as the central position espousing a neurological basis, was largely contained in several monographs relating to "minimal brain dysfunction in children" (e.g., Chalfant & Scheffelin, 1969).

Although educational classification is not synonymous with DSM-IV diagnoses, a brief review of the learning disabilities field is important, since both research and educational practice have emerged out of a field with both medical and educational underpinnings. The term "learning disabilities" (LD) originated with federal legislation designating "specific learning disabilities" as a handicapping condition in children, which, in turn, mandated public schools to provide special education services for eligible students (PL 94-142: Education of the Handicapped Act; U.S. Office of Education, 1977). It is important to underscore that these early practices, which influenced public policy in the identification and management of learning disorders, were not based on empirical research but rather, were fueled by advocacy efforts of parent and professional groups lobbying for improved educational opportunities for children with a variety of learning difficulties. Several aspects of diagnostic classification are important in a discussion of learning disorders. Many (medical) diagnoses in the *Diagnostic and Statistical Manual of Mental Disorders* of the American Psychiatric Association (Fourth Edition, 1994) (DSM-IV) and the World Health Organization's *International Classification of Diseases* (Tenth Edition, 1992) (ICD-10) are *categorical* in nature, that is, identification is made on the basis of discrete and dichotomous criteria (e.g., symptoms present or not present). In contrast, learning disorders represent a *dimensional* classification, reflecting skills or traits (e.g., reading scores) that are continuous in nature. Thus, while use of a common label such as learning disabilities may imply specificity and homogeneity, it must be stressed from the outset that individuals identified as having a learning disability constitute a highly heterogeneous group. Moreover, the problems inherent in specifying diagnostic criteria have resulted in lack of consensual agreement on definition, an issue that has plagued the field from its inception. The definition outlined in the Education for All Handicapped Children Act of 1975 (PL 94-142) and the subsequent Individuals with Disabilities Education Act (IDEA) Amendments of 1991 (PL 102-119) is the following:

> Specific learning disability means a disorder in one or more of the basic psychological processes involved in understanding or using language, spoken or written, in which the disorder may manifest itself in an imperfect ability to listen, think, speak, read, write, spell, or to do mathematical calculations. The term includes such conditions as perceptual handicaps, brain injury, minimal brain dysfunction, dyslexia, and developmental aphasia. The term does not include children who have learning problems which are primarily the result of visual, hearing, or motor handicaps, or mental retardation, or emotional disturbance, or of environmental, cultural, or economic disadvantage. (U.S. Office of Education, 1977, p. 65083)

Although there exist successive revisions of this definition, core elements to definitions of learning disabilities are the concepts of *discrepancy* (e.g., between expected and actual performance) and *exclusion* (e.g., of individuals for whom peripheral sensory impairment, generalized cognitive delay, primary psychiatric disorder, or sociocultural deprivation can be determined to be the primary cause of delayed

skill development). The definition presumed that there were distinct and qualitative differences between generally low-achieving children and those who achieve poorly in spite of unimpaired basic sensory, motor, and cognitive abilities. Finally, although the DSM-IV categories discussed in this chapter were originally subsumed under the global term "minimal brain dysfunction" popular in the 1960s, with the evolving definitions of "learning disabilities," disorders of motor functioning have tended to be separated from the academic skills disorders (U.S. Office of Education, 1977).

Criticisms of the original LD definition (e.g., Kavale & Forness, 1985) led to several subsequent attempts to refine the definition: the National Joint Committee on Learning Disabilities (Hammill, Leigh, McNutt, & Larsen, 1981), the Association for Children and Adults with Learning Disabilities (ACLD, 1985, subsequently renamed Learning Disabilities Association, LDA), and the Interagency Committee on Learning Disabilities, a multidisciplinary group mandated by the Health Research Extension Act of 1985 (PL 99-158; ICLD, 1987).

This latter refinement of the definition addressed etiology (presumed central nervous system dysfunction), added "problems in self-regulatory behavior, social perception, and social interaction" as a possible manifestation of a learning disability, and amended the exclusionary clause with the recognition of simultaneously occurring (i.e., comorbid) disorders, particularly ADHD. However, over the past 25 years, professionals have not agreed on a precise and unambiguous definition of LD. In view of the degree of heterogeneity involved, it is accepted that no global definition can be consistently operationalized or empirically validated. Instead, more discrete definitions of specific areas of deficit are needed, and the current DSM-IV categories represent examples.

The "discrepancy" issue has a long history of debate among those making public school–based identification of learning disorders. Following initial federal legislation, school-based learning disabilities classification has been defined as the presence of a severe discrepancy between ability and one or more of the seven designated areas of achievement[1] (Reynolds, 1990). In DSM-IV, the criteria for the reading, mathematics, and written expression disorders are specified only as "substantially below that expected, given the person's chronological age, measured intelligence, and age-appropriate education." Several methods have been used for computing this discrepancy, including deviation from grade level, expectancy formulas, simple standard score differences, and standard regression analyses, each of which has been criticized for statistical inadequacies or for ignoring the evidence for a bidirectional influence between intelligence and achievement (Siegel, 1989). An approach to the quantification of IQ-achievement discrepancies, which takes into consideration the psychometric regression effects of imperfect IQ-achievement test correlation, has been considered by some to be the best of current methods for determining a discrepancy (Heath & Kush, 1991). However, it is important to reiterate that current criteria for determining eligibility for public school LD services do not reflect scientific understanding but instead provide only a global rendering appropriate for program development.

The implementation of federal guidelines has largely been left up to individual states and their respective school systems. In actual educational practice, school-based criteria for identification of a learning disability have varied considerably, and it is not uncommon for a child to meet local identification criteria in one independent school district but not another, both within and across states. The determination of a severe IQ-achievement discrepancy varies widely, depending upon (1) whether a regression formula is used to account for the imperfect association between IQ and achievement, (2) the psychometric properties of the respective measures of intelligence and achievement used, (3) the level of severity (mild, moderate, severe) or the minimal level of discrepancy designated for "severe discrepancy" (e.g., ≥ 1,

1.5, 2 SD), and (4) whether accommodation is made for the individual whose underlying learning disorder may be reflected in lowered performance on global measures of full-scale IQ, thus reducing the discrepancy.

Finally, there has recently been considerable controversy and discussion as to the appropriateness of using the IQ-achievement discrepancy as the standard for determining learning disability in general, and reading disability in particular (e.g., Fletcher et al., 1994; Stanovich & Siegel, 1994). Long-held assumptions of fundamental differences between LD children with and without IQ-achievement discrepancies have clearly not been validated for those with reading disorders, since groups do not differ as a function of information processing, neurophysiological markers, genetic variables, or response to instruction (Lyon, 1996). Moreover, acculumating research evidence has pointed to a core deficit in processing phonological information, which is *not related to* IQ, thus suggesting that the discrepancy criterion becomes meaningless in the diagnosis of reading disability.

Brief Review of Theoretical Models

Among a variety of theoretical orientations of learning disabilities, perhaps the most prominent are: (1) a medical/biological model (emphasizing central nervous system dysfunction), (2) an educational/behavioral model (deemphasizing etiology and classification while focusing on the development of observable academic skills and targeted instruction), and (3) an interactionist viewpoint, holding that learning difficulties represent a broad continuum of causal factors, including factors primarily within the environment (e.g., poor or inconsistent instruction) and important psychosocial factors (e.g., motivation), as well as factors primarily within the child (e.g., evidence of "soft" neurological signs, clear history of genetic predisposition). Fundamental differences in the approach to assessment and intervention have arisen from these differing orientations

---

1. Areas of underachievement constituting a learning disability: (1) Listening Comprehension, (2) Oral Expression, (3) Basic Reading, (4) Reading Comprehension, (5) Written Expression, (6) Math Calculation, (7) Math Reasoning.

and are discussed more thoroughly in the following sections.

With the growing awareness that children with learning disabilities represent a very heterogeneous group, there has been considerable scientific interest in studying specific subtypes of learning disability. Such an effort is critical for a scientific validation of learning disorders, from those espousing a biological point of view (including rigorous description of the symptoms/characteristics, understanding of the biological underpinnings, predictions of risk, and well-designed intervention outcome studies), as well as from those with an educational/behavioral frame of reference, who might begin to validate LD subtypes based upon their response to intervention. Efforts at subtyping evolved from clinical-inferential models (such as grouping by patterns and levels of achievement) and neurocognitive classification models (based on differences in underlying psychological processes of attention, perception, memory, and language). Subsequently, subtyping efforts moved toward attempts at empirical classification using factor-analytic techniques. (See review of subtyping studies by Hooper & Willis, 1989.)

Beginning in the 1980s, the National Institutes of Health (NICHD branch) developed research initiatives to address the issues of definition, characteristics, measurement, classification, and etiology of learning disabilities, with more recent attention to investigating methods of intervention. From these efforts, a considerable body of research, involving theoretical models, taxonomic methodologies, and the identification of biological, psychological, and educational characteristics of children with learning disabilities, has evolved (see summary in Lyon, Gray, Kavanaugh, & Krasnegor, 1993). However, there is currently a considerable lag between research and practice. Such federally sponsored research has not appreciably influenced rigorous evaluation of existing educational practices with learning-disabled students (Martin, 1993) or of teacher preparation (Lyon, Vaasen, & Toomey, 1989). However, fueled by the movement for school reform in general education, some states have begun to alter instruc-

tional policy to reflect research findings (e.g., California State Board of Education, 1996). Continuing NICHD goals involve determining the most effective and empirically validated intervention for particular types of learning-disabled children in particular settings (Lyon, 1995a).

Epidemiology

Because of the failure to obtain consensus regarding definition and classification, estimates of the prevalence of learning disabilities have varied widely. Gaddes and Edgall (1994) estimate that the average elementary school population may include about 15% of children who are underachieving academically. Of these, approximately half (7.5%) are believed to demonstrate CNS dysfunction, including 2.5% with hard neurological signs, 5% with soft neurological signs, and an unspecified fraction with specific learning disability with no positive neurological signs. Predictably, when learning disabilities became a recognized condition requiring special education, prevalence of school-based LD tripled between 1976 and 1982. Following implementation of PL 94-142, in 1977, the percentage of children classified as LD had increased from 1.8% to 4.66% of the public school enrollment of children between the ages of 6 and 17 (U.S. Department of Education, 1991). Currently, more than 50% of all children receiving special education services are classified as learning disabled (with a corresponding underrepresentation of children in other categories of special education such as mentally retarded, speech/language impaired, and seriously emotionally distrubed/behavior disordered). While such an increase may reflect the vagueness in definition, some have suggested that this increased prevalence reflects sociocultural changes over the past 20 to 40 years, which have in turn increased both the risk for CNS disruption and the degree of psychosocial stress (Hallahan, 1992).

With regard to epidemiology of the specific learning disorders, recent studies have suggested that difficulty in acquiring basic reading skills occurs in 20% of the school-age population, with deficits in phonological processing in 80–90% of these children (Shaywitz, Escobar, Shaywitz, Fletcher, & Makuch, 1992). Whereas previous estimates implicated males over females at rates of 3–5:1, more current data from both epidemiologic studies and family studies have not found a significant gender difference (DeFries, 1989). The considerably higher incidence of males in school-based samples is now believed to reflect comorbidity; that is, males more frequently come to clinical attention because of their increased tendency to have co-occurring ADHD and/or disruptive behavior disorders.

Although mathematics disorders have received less attention and are generally believed to be less prevalent than reading disorders, their actual incidence is largely unknown, with estimates ranging from 6% to 8% of the population (Semrud-Clikeman & Hynd, 1992). An apparently higher incidence is suggested when those with both reading and math disorders are considered.

Even less attention has been devoted to the prevalence of disorders of written expression. While some have suggested that isolated disorders of writing (e.g., dysgraphia without dyslexia) occur rarely, the prevalence estimates for developmental language disorders in general (8–15%) suggest a higher frequency of written-language disorders. In addition, it is apparent that there are wide differences in emphasis on instruction of written language, in both regular and special education programs. Hooper and colleagues (1994) suggested that estimates of decreasing literacy, as assessed by written-language competency, likely reflect reduced emphasis in instruction, thus masking the prevalence of true disorders of written expression.

Finally, the incidence of developmental coordination disorder would be expected to vary as a function of whether it is assessed independently or in conjunction with other specific academic skills deficits. Gaddes and Edgall (1994) estimate that 5% of the school population of children have "soft" neurological signs (including motor clumsiness, perceptual deficits, and poor hand-eye coordination). Schoemaker and Kalverboer (1990) have estimated that "clumsy children" with no identifiable CNS damage or dysfunction make up 5% to 10% of elementary-school classes, and most studies report a higher incidence in males by 2–4:1.

Diagnostic Description and Critique of DSM-IV

The recognition of these childhood learning and motor skills disorders in DSM-IV is welcome, yet it should be emphasized that their publication comes at a time when debate on the definition of LD is continuing. Currently, they represent unitary constructs, a problem leading to overinclusiveness and lack of operational specificity. While for any classification model there are arguments for "splitting vs. lumping," it should be emphasized that there is evidence for differing neuropsychological profiles that accompany combinations of reading, spelling, math, and motor coordination disorders (e.g., Rourke and Finlayson, 1978) and for differentiation of subclasses (e.g., word decoding vs. reading comprehension difficulty). While research has yet to confirm etiologically distinct and empirically validated subtypes, the relative lack of specificity of the DSM-IV categories may serve to decrease their clinical usefulness. Currently, clinicians must exercise considerable judgment in determining the degree to which the poor achievement is of sufficient severity to meet diagnostic criteria and in distinguishing specific learning disorders from "underachievement."

For clinicians, it is also important to emphasize the increasing evidence for comorbidity of disorders. For example, while DSM-IV distinguishes between communication disorders and learning disorders, there are obvious degrees of overlap and/or co-occurrence, the primary one being the linkages among the current DSM-IV disorders involving speech or language (e.g., phonological disorder, expressive disorder, mixed expressive-receptive language disorder, reading disorder, and disorder of written expression). Such relationships between oral and written language have long been clinically recognized and validated by increasing research evidence for the continuum of language functions. Results of longitudinal studies linking impaired oral language abilities in preschoolers and their later reading and written language disorders (Catts, 1993; Scarborough, 1990) have led some to speculate that oral and written language disorders likely represent the same underlying deficit. Other combinations of skill deficits have been documented in specific neurological syndromes, for example, the Gerstmann Syndrome, which includes clustering of such symptoms as right-left disorientation, finger agnosia, writing, and math difficulties (Kinsbourne & Warrington, 1963).

Parallel to the DSM-IV nosology is the *International Classification of Diseases* World Health Organization, (1992). In this classification system, a distinction is made between developmental and acquired learning disorders, as ICD-10 includes parallel diagnoses under the general categories "mental and behavioral disorders" and "specific developmental disorders of scholastic skills" (p. 373).

In ICD-10, the category "specific reading disorder" (F81.0) includes the terms "backward reading," "developmental dyslexia," and "specific reading retardation" and excludes "reading difficulties secondary to emotional disorders" (F93).

In contrast to DSM-IV, ICD-10 contains a separate diagnostic category for "specific spelling disorder" (F81.1) (also labeled "specific spelling retardation [without reading disorder]," which excludes agraphia [R48.80] and spelling difficulties associated with a reading disorder [F81.0] or due to inadequate teaching [Z55.8]).

The category "specific disorder of arithmetic skills" (F81.2) is variously labeled "developmental acalculia," "arithmetical disorder," and "Gerstmann's syndrome" and excludes "acalculia" (R48.8), "arithmetic difficulties associated with a reading or spelling disorder" (F81.3), or difficulties "due to inadequate teaching" (Z55.8). Clearly, this diagnostic category is narrower and more exclusive than the comparable DSM-IV disorder.

Unlike DSM-IV, ICD-10 does not have a separate diagnostic category for disorder of written expression but lists developmental expressive writing disorder as "other developmental disorders of scholastic skills" (F81.8). Also included is the category "mixed disorder of scholastic skills" (F81.3), which includes mixed reading or spelling and math disorders, as well as a more general learning disability category, "developmental disorder of scholastic skills, unspecified" (F81.9).

The ICD-10 diagnosis that corresponds to DSM-IV's developmental coordination disorder is "specific developmental disorder of motor function" (also labeled clumsy child syndrome, coordination disorder, and dyspraxia). This definition clearly emphasizes features from the neurological examination and excludes the categories "abnormalities of gait and mobility" (R26), "lack of coordination" (R27), and "disorder secondary to mental retardation" (F70–F79).

Although DSM-IV provides a diagnostic label that can include comorbid disorders ("Learning Disorder Not Otherwise Specified" [315.9]), there is no formal diagnostic category in either DSM-IV or ICD-10 for a type of learning disability that has received growing attention and validation, both in clinical practice and in subtyping research: nonverbal learning disabilities, or "social-emotional learning disability" (Denckla, 1983). Children who exhibit impaired social skills, poor perception and interpretation of gesture and facial expression, and an inability to grasp the significance of situations have long been recognized by clinicians. Research evidence for a distinct nonverbal learning disability has been accumulating (e.g., Rourke, 1995), and a dysfunctional right hemisphere has increasingly been implicated (Voeller, 1990).

From the standpoint of etiology, although DSM-IV does not address the issue of CNS etiology in learning disorders, their occurrence in the context of "age-appropriate education" clearly presumes problems intrinsic to the child. However, for any individual child or adolescent, it is apparent that a variety of factors impact academic achievement. Factors both within the individual (e.g., impaired perception, memory, and/or conceptualization; social-emotional and motivational factors) and factors external to the individual (e.g., teacher competencies, emphasis and strategies of instruction) must clearly be considered in the diagnostic process. Although criteria are not specified, ICD-10 distinguishes between disorder and underachievement, with a diagnosis of "underachievement in school" (Z55.3), and notes the external factors with a diagnosis of "other problems related to education and literacy: inadequate teaching" (Z55.8).

Finally, it is important to again underscore that both DSM-IV and ICD-10 classification systems represent *medical* classifications that parallel, but are not interchangeable with, the seven *educational* categories of specific learning disability. Thus, providing a DSM-IV or ICD-10 diagnosis does not automatically lead to public school educational services, unless the child also meets eligibility criteria for learning disabilities placement in a particular state or local school district. In this regard, while motor handicaps were excluded from the original PL 94-142 definition of specific learning disability (U.S. Department of Health, Education, and Welfare, 1977), it is clear that disorders of math, spelling, and written expression are frequently accompanied by poor handwriting, the latter often involving impairment in perceptual-motor skills, fine motor planning, and/or sensorimotor integration. Thus, a clinician diagnosing this disorder may need to demonstrate the particular relevance of the motor handicap to reduced academic achievement.

As a preface to diagnostic assessment and treatment implications, the following sections provide summaries of important features of the individual disorders.

Reading Disorder (315.00)

Of the academic skills disorders in DSM-IV, reading disorder has clearly received the greatest attention, with regard to etiology, developmental course, variation in expression, and educational outcome. Although this DSM-IV diagnostic category includes disorders of both reading accuracy and of reading comprehension, it is clear from developmental, neuropsychological, and genetic studies that individuals who fail to master basic single-word-recognition skills (decoding) are a subgroup distinct from those who master such skills but fail to comprehend. For example, it is apparent that decoding and comprehension are dissociated in some individuals with mental retardation, autism, pervasive developmental disorder, and/or developmental language disorder, who may master word calling at a very early age but without comprehension (e.g., hyperlexia).

The term "reading disorder" typically refers to impaired word identification skills and is often used synonymously with "developmental dyslexia," "specific reading disability," or "specific reading retardation." The traditional model distinguishes dyslexia in individuals of normal general intelligence from the garden-variety poor readers whose delayed reading achievement relative to age is consistent with more generalized cognitive delays. However, as mentioned previously, the IQ-achievement discrepancy has not been supported for reading disorders. Second, some would hold that "developmental dyslexia" is not a synonym for the discrepancy-based reading disability described in either DSM-IV or the educational classification. Distinctions have also been made between dyslexia-pure and dyslexia-plus (the latter referring to dyslexia complicated by subclinical aspects of attention-deficit/hyperactivity disorder) and between pure reading disorders and those that occur in the context of persistent, concurrent language disorder (Denckla, 1993).

There is now a large body of converging evidence suggesting that a specific deficit in the ability to process phonological information may be causal in reading disorder (Wagner & Torgesen, 1987). Representative research currently demonstrates that (1) word recognition deficits also negatively affect comprehension in disabled readers, and (2) word recognition, phonological coding, and related segmental language skills are uniquely deficient in most disabled readers. Difficulty in segmenting and blending sounds, together with impaired ability to associate sounds (phonemes) with their component letters (graphemes), thus appears to be a primary factor in the failure to develop reading skills.

Single-word reading and spelling, but *not* reading comprehension, are genetically influenced (Pennington, 1991); moreover, the phonological deficit that underlies reading and spelling disorders has been shown to occur across the developmental age spectrum and is believed to be the core deficit in an inherited form of dyslexia (Pennington, Van Orden, Smith, Green, & Haith, 1990).

In addition to the word decoding/comprehension distinction, much of the learning disabilities subtyping research has focused on an attempt to delineate distinct neuropsychological subtypes of reading disability, with presumably different etiologies. Such clinically derived subtypes as dysphonetic, dyseidetic, and mixed dyslexia (Boder, 1973) and language disorder, articulatory and graphomotor dyscoordination, and visuospatial perceptual disorder (Mattis, French, & Rapin, 1975) have been heuristically useful. However, such efforts to isolate separate and genetically distinct subtypes of reading disability have to date been unsuccessful. Finally, recent controlled studies are accumulating evidence that the method of initial reading instruction clearly affects outcome and, by extension, the incidence of reading disability. In at-risk children, explicit instruction in alphabetic coding is more effective in developing reading skills than are approaches that rely exclusively on an implicit method (Foorman, 1995).

Disorder of Written Expression (315.2)

In contrast to the unitary nature of the DSM-IV diagnosis, writing is a complex, multidimensional process, and adequate written expression presumes competence in handwriting, written spelling, written syntax and sentence structure, the mechanics of capitalization and punctuation, logical, sequential organization, and formulation of ideas, to name some of the components. A wide variety of components is integrated in competent written language expression, including oral language, vocabulary knowledge and retrieval, fine-motor skills, orthographic coding, orthographic-motor integration, working memory, reading, verbal reasoning, and organization (e.g., Berninger, 1993).

Although both clinical experience and neuropsychological research confirm the relative independence of reading and written language skills in adults with acquired deficits (e.g., evidence for dysgraphia with and without dyslexia), these relationships are less well studied in children. Most studies suggest that poor spelling is one of the most frequent characteristics of reading-disabled children (Frith, 1980). The same phonological processing deficit that underlies reading is also believed to affect spelling. However, unlike reading, which can proceed with partial cues, spelling requires full cues; the letters must be in correct sequential order, and phonological strategies are not effective with irregular words.

Subtyping studies of writing and written language disorders have determined various subtypes based on patterns of neuropsychological performance: (1) fine-motor and linguistic deficits, (2) visual-spatial deficits, (3) attention and memory deficits, and (4) sequencing deficits (e.g., Sandler et al., 1992). With respect to this third subtype, some attention has been devoted to the writing disorders in LD children with co-occurring attention-deficit/hyperactivityl disorder (ADHD). Given the demands for focused attention, planning, and organization, together with the effortful processing involved in handwriting, it is not unexpected that disorders of written language are relatively common in children with both impaired attention and learning disabilities (Elbert, 1993).

Mathematics Disorder (315.1)

With regard to the question of specific disability versus generalized underachievement, it has been shown that underachievement in general, and underachievement in math in particular, is clearly related to such environmental factors as low socioeconomic status and impoverished home environment, with additional evidence for ethnic, gender, and cultural differences in math achievement (Stigler & Baranes, 1988–1989). In addition, there are widely differing approaches to educational instruction in math, with wide criticism of current math curriculum and teaching strategies, leading to arguments that many children labeled as learning or math disabled are in fact "curriculum disabled" (Hendrickson, 1983) and that their poor math achievement may reflect ineffective instruction, which compounds the difficulties of children with genuine learning disabilities. Finally, an additional factor that complicates the identification of children with specific math disorder is that there is wide variability in the development of mathematical skills in normally achieving children (e.g., O'Hare, Brown, & Aitken, 1991).

Geary's (1993) comprehensive review of cognitive and neurological components in math suggests that math-disordered children demonstrate two apparently distinct functional deficits. A "procedural" deficit, characterized by impaired computational skills, appears to follow a developmental-delay model, with a pattern of performance similar to that found in younger children. In contrast, a "memory-retrieval" deficit appears to reflect a more generalized problem in memory representation and retrieval, a difficulty more consistent with a developmental-difference model, since it persists throughout elementary school for many learning-disabled children. Neuropsychological studies of both children and adults suggest three primary math-related deficits: (1) *alexia and agraphia for numbers* (difficulties in reading and writing of numbers, a deficit reportedly rare in children and typically associated with left-hemisphere lesions); (2) *spatial acalculia* (characterized by difficulty in spatially representing numbers and thought to be associated with right-hemisphere dysfunction); and (3) *anarithmetria* (impaired retrieval of basic arithmetic facts from long-term memory and typically found to co-occur with verbal deficits). From available studies, the following math disability subtypes have

been suggested: (1) a semantic memory subtype (characterized by poor and inaccurate math-fact retrieval and frequently co-occurring in individuals with reading disorders), (2) a procedural subtype (characterized by use of immature procedures, errors in execution, and potential developmental delay in the understanding of concepts underlying procedures), (3) a visuospatial subtype (characterized by difficulty in spatially representing or interpreting numerical information, misaligning and rotating numbers, and making place-value errors), and (4) an attention subtype, characterized by an attentional-sequence disorder, including difficulties in allocating attention and following sequential steps in the execution of mathematical operations (Geary, 1993). However, it is not known whether the attentional type is specific to mathematics learning or reflects a more generalized learning disability in individuals with comorbid disorders.

Developmental Coordination Disorder (315.4)

Disabilities of a type and degree that qualitatively or quantitatively fall short of the threshold for diagnosing cerebral palsy have been reported for more than 50 years, and historically, neurological "soft signs" included some degree of impairment in motor function in what was once labeled "minimal brain dysfunction" (Nichols & Chen, 1981). Since several professional disciplines are involved in diagnosing these children (e.g., pediatric neurology, neuropsychology, physical and occupational therapy), it is not surprising that terminology has varied, with lack of operational definitions of such terms as "motor impairment," "developmental dyspraxia," "developmental dysgraphia," and "perceptual-motor difficulty." Among the wide-ranging difficulties of these children, impairments of the following types have been included: balance and posture, gross-motor coordination (running, jumping, skipping), fine-motor difficulty (buttoning, fastening, manipulating utensils), impaired visual-spatial/perceptual-motor integration and traditional hand-eye coordination (aiming, throwing, interception, catching), and specific graphomotor impairment (drawing, copying, handwriting).

Although it is widely held that children with impaired coordination do not represent a homogeneous group, the DSM-IV diagnosis is a unitary construct and presumes that gross neuromotor function is normal, implying more subtle motor deficiencies, or "soft" neurological signs. Since the initial description of these children, there has been little progress in characterizing a "pure" developmental coordination disorder. As neurologists, Denckla and Roeltgen (1992) distinguish disorders of motor function from developmental dyspraxia and developmental dysgraphia. "Developmental dyspraxia" is generally used to describe impairment in the planning and execution of skilled movements. Parallel to the traditional neurology definition of adult apraxia, Denckla and Roeltgen (1992) restrict the term "dyspraxia" to a disorder in the ability to use gesture, either meaningful or nonmeaningful; moreover, their definition presumes normal sensorimotor or perceptual-motor abilities. Alternatively, those in the occupational therapy field tend to use the term more broadly to define children who are unable to effectively plan and execute new motor actions or to generalize learned motor actions to new situations (e.g., Goodgold-Edwards & Cermak, 1990). They include children described as having "sensorimotor integration" difficulty and sharing some of the following difficulties: (1) learning rules about classes of motor actions, (2) using appropriate perceptual cues, (3) organizing and integrating sensory information, (4) solving problems and adapting behavior to new situations, (5) analyzing task requirements, (6) anticipating and preparing.

A most frequent use of the diagnosis "developmental coordination disorder" relates to children with handwriting problems. Use of the term "developmental dysgraphia" typically distinguishes between linguistic dysgraphia (associated with incorrect word or letter choice) and motor dysgraphias, which are associated with poor letter formation and production (Denckla & Roeltgen, 1992).

Despite lack of agreement about the existence of "pure" motor disorders, considerable clinical and research experience has documented the co-occurrence of motor problems with other learning disorders (e.g., Denckla's [1972] "motor dyscontrol" subtype; Mattis and colleagues' [1975] "articulatory and graphomotor dyscoordination" subtype; Sandler and colleagues' [1992] "writing disorder with fine-motor and linguistic deficits" subtype). Similarly, motor incoordination is frequently found in hyperactive children.

ASSESSMENT

Methods for the assessment of reading, written expression, math, and motor coordination clearly vary according to level of analysis (screening vs. comprehensive assessment), psychometric properties of instruments (formal standardized vs. informal criterion-referenced measures), and professional discipline. Diagnostic assessment is typically performed in order to determine a child's performance relative to normative standards, for the purpose of determining eligibility for learning disabilities services in public schools (simple classification) and/or for profiling individual strengths and weaknesses in order to determine specific needs for intervention. Typically such assessments are performed in the context of the aptitude-achievement discrepancy model discussed earlier, in which performance on a standardized measure of intelligence is compared against performance on measures of oral language, reading, written expression, and math. Despite criticisms of the standard diagnostic approach (e.g., Elliott & Fuchs, 1997), widespread demand for such assessment has led to the development of a number of broad-based achievement batteries, whose subtests include measures for a broad range of academic skills (see Table 3.1).

These well-standardized, norm-referenced, and comprehensive achievement test batteries

TABLE 3.1. General Academic Achievement Batteries

Measure/Reference	Age/Grade	Contents
Kaufman Test of Educational Achievement (KTEA) (Kaufman & Kaufman, 1993)	A: 6–17	Brief Form: Mathematics; Reading; Spelling; Comprehensive Form: Reading/Decoding; Reading Comprehension; Spelling; Mathematics Computation; Mathematics Applications
Peabody Individual Achievement Test-Revised (PIAT-R) (Markwardt, 1989)	A: 5–18	Information; Reading Recognition; Spelling; Reading Comprehension; Written Expression
Weschler Individual Achievement Test (WIAT) (Wechsler, 1993)	A: 5–19	Listening Comprehension; Oral Expression; Reading Recognition; Reading Comprehension; Spelling; Written Expression; Math
Wide-Range Achievement Test-3 (WRAT-3) (Wilkinson, 1993)	A: 5–adult	Reading; Spelling; Arithmetic
Woodcock-Johnson Psycho-Educational Battery-Revised (WJPEBR) (Woodcock & Johnson, 1989)	A: 5–adult	Letter/Word Identification; Word Attack; Passage Comprehension; Dictation; Proofing; Writing Fluency; Writing Samples; Math Calculation; Applied Problems; Quantitative Concepts

have the advantage of relatively brief administration time and good psychometric properties, and they are currently widely used in general psychoeducational evaluations of learning disabilities. However, the strength of these batteries in broad-based achievement screening is a corresponding weakness when a more detailed evaluation is needed. The addition of more specialized, curriculum-based and/or criterion-referenced assessment is often useful in providing the opportunity for error analyses and dynamic assessment. Tables 3.2–3.5 contain representative measures for more in-depth, comprehensive assessment.

Although assessment procedures specific to the DSM-IV categories of learning disorders are discussed separately in the following sections, it is important to point out that clinical evaluations typically include a broad and hypothesis-testing approach to the assessment of impaired learning, with additional assessment of attention, perception, memory, language, and reasoning abilities that relate to the academic skills disorders. While an extensive discussion of various theoretical frames of reference for assessment of learning disorders is beyond the scope of this chapter, the reader is referred to approaches to assessment arising out of the learning disabilities/special education field (e.g., Lyon, 1994) and child neuropsychology field (e.g., Hynd & Obrzut, 1981; Hynd & Willis, 1988), and to general references on child assessment (e.g., Reynolds & Kamphaus, 1990; Sattler, 1992). In view of the co-occurrence of learning disorders, a reasonable approach to comprehensive assessment involves an initial broad screening assessment of the wide range of academic skills, followed by more specialized assessment of the specific areas of difficulty.

In contrast to the more traditional psychometric assessment, which simply documents the discrepancy between aptitude or IQ measures and achievement (a model criticized because it emphasizes the end *product*, rather than the *process* of learning), alternative and more dynamic approaches to assessment include evaluation of specific cognitive problem-solving strategies, such as assessing not just what but how a child learns. Such approaches involve informal assessment of such metacognitive and executive functions as accessing, organizing, and coordinating mental activities, flexibility in thinking skills and shifting problem-solving strategies, and self-monitoring and motivation, the goal of which is to design highly specific and practical recommendations (see a review of such approaches in Meltzer, 1993). Other alternatives such as curriculum-based measurement would emphasize the assessment of skill mastery within a specific instructional curriculum (e.g., Elliot & Fuchs, 1997).

Assessment of Reading Skills

A comprehensive diagnostic evaluation of suspected reading disorder optimally involves assessment of the following skill levels: single words (oral reading accuracy, silent word comprehension), nonwords (oral reading accuracy), and context (oral reading accuracy and comprehension, silent reading comprehension). A variety of both norm-referenced and criterion-referenced measures specialized for reading are available for use in a more comprehensive reading assessment (see Table 3.2).

Since most impaired reading involves difficulties at the single-word (decoding) level,

reading assessment of sight word recognition/word decoding is important. The broad-based batteries do not lend themselves to a detailed analysis of the point of breakdown in impaired word recognition, such as rate and automaticity of "sight word" recognition, pattern of errors, relative accuracy in decoding phonetically regular versus nonregular words, decoding strategies for unknown words. Including a measure of nonsense word decoding in the assessment provides further information regarding impaired sound-symbol correspondence, since word familiarity cues are removed and an accurate response requires use of phonetic analysis. The Woodcock Reading Mastery Test-R (Woodcock, 1987) provides a broad-based reading evaluation, with a sufficient number of single-word items to allow informal error analysis. Informal analyses are often accomplished with criterion-referenced measures of reading subskills (e.g., knowledge of sound-symbol association for single consonants, consonant blends and digraphs, vowels and vowel combinations; knowledge and generalization of phonetic rules; knowledge of common prefixes and suffixes). Such reading inventories as the Decoding Skills Test (Richardson & Dibenedetto, 1985) and the Durrell Analysis of Reading Difficulty (Durrell & Catterson, 1980) include various aspects of subskill assessment.

Given the converging evidence that reading disability or dyslexia involves impaired phono-

TABLE 3.2. Specialized Assessment of Reading

Measure/Reference	Age/Grade	Contents
Decoding Skills Test (Richardson & Dibenedetto, 1985)	G: 1–5	Basic Reading, Phonics, Oral Reading
Durrell Analysis of Reading Difficulty (Durrell & Catterson, 1980)	G: 1–6	Oral Reading; Silent Reading; Listening Comprehension; Word Recognition/Analysis; Listening Vocabulary; Word Elements; Visual Memory; Auditory Analysis
Gates-MacGinitie Reading Tests (MacGinitie & MacGinitie, 1989)	G: K–12	Silent Reading; Vocabulary and Comprehension
Gray Oral Reading Tests-3 (GORT-3) (Wiederholt & Bryant, 1992)	A: 7–17	Oral Reading Accuracy/Comprehension
Woodcock Reading Mastery Tests-Revised (WRMT-R) (Woodcock, 1987)	A: 5–adult	Word Identification; Word Attack; Word Comprehension; Passage Comprehension

logical processing, formal assessment of these skills is increasingly viewed as being important in a child with suspected reading disorder. Examples of such measures include the Lindamood Auditory Conceptualization Test (Lindamood & Lindamood, 1979) and the Test of Phonological Awareness (Torgeson & Bryant, 1994).

Several issues should be considered in the assessment of reading comprehension: (1) length of the passage (sentence, paragraph, chapter), (2) the relative demands on comprehension, memory, and organization, (3) level of linguistic and syntactic complexity, (4) vocabulary level and semantic complexity (fiction, news, or technical material), (5) type of response required. Most standardized measures of child reading comprehension involve sentences of increasing length and complexity (e.g., Peabody Individual Achievement Test-R [Markwardt, 1989]) or, at most, brief paragraphs (e.g., Woodcock Reading Mastery Test-R [Woodcock, 1987]). This may not adequately assess the difficulties with comprehension experienced by middle school or high school students whose academic failure reflects difficulty with comprehension of literal, figurative, or multiple word meanings; impaired higher-level organization and abstract thinking skills necessary in making generalizations, drawing inferences, and forming conclusions; and/or poor verbal memory.

Assessment of Spelling and Written Language Skills

Since word identification, sound-symbol association, and spelling are all closely related skills, spelling is typically assessed in conjunction with reading and written language. Several issues need to be considered in assessing spelling: (1) oral versus written spelling, (2) recognition (multiple choice) versus recall, and (3) spelling of words in isolation versus spelling in context. The Kaufman Test of Educational Achievement (Kaufman & Kaufman, 1993), the Wechsler Individual Achievement Test (WIAT, 1992), and the Wide-Range Achievement Test-3 (Wilkinson, 1993) all include measures of written spelling of orally dictated words (see Table 3.1). An alternative measure of spelling from the Peabody Individual Achievement Test-R (Markwart, 1989) uses multiple-choice responses, thus involving recognition rather than recall. Additional normed and criterion-referenced measures of spelling are listed in Table 3.3, including a comparison

TABLE 3.3. Specialized Assessment of Spelling and Written Language

Measure/Reference	Age/Grade	Contents
Oral & Written Language Scales: Written Expression (Carrow-Woolfolk, 1995)	A: 5–21	Conventions; Syntactical Forms; Communication
Test of Early Written Language-2 (Hresko, Herron, & Peak, 1988)	A: 4–10	Spelling, Capitalization, Punctuation, Sentence Construction, Story Format, Thematic Maturity
Test of Written Expression (McGhee, Bryant, Larsen, & Rivera, 1995)	A: 6–15	Items (Capitalization, Punctuation, Spelling, Ideation, Semantics, Syntax); Essay (Ideation, Vocabulary, Grammar, Capitalization, Punctuation, Spelling)
Test of Written Language-3 (TOWL-3) (Hammill & Larsen, 1996)	A: 7–18	Spontaneous (Thematic Maturity, Contextual Vocabulary, Syntactic Maturity, Contextual Spelling, Contextual Style); Contrived (Vocabulary, Style & Spelling, Logical Sentences, Sentence Combining)
Test of Written Spelling-3 (TWS-3) (Larsen & Hammill, 1994)	A: 6–18	Predictable and Unpredictable Words

TABLE 3.4. Specialized Assessment of Math

Measure/Reference	Age/Grade	Contents
Key Math-Revised: Diagnostic Inventory of Essential Mathematics (Key Math-R) (Connolly, 1988)	G: 1–8	Basic Concepts; Operations; Applications
Sequential Assessment of Mathematics Inventories (SAMI) (Reisman & Hutchison, 1985)	G: K–8	Mathematical Language; Ordinality; Number & Notation; Measurement; Math Applications; Ordinality; Computation; Geometric Concepts; Word Problems
Stanford Diagnostic Mathematics Test (Beatty, Gardner, Madden, & Karlsen, 1985)	G: 1–12	Number System and Numerals; Computation; Applications
Test of Mathematical Abilities (TOMA-2) (Brown, Cronin & McEntire, 1994)	A: 8–18	Vocabulary; Computation; General Information; Story Problems
Test of Early Mathematical Abilities (TEMA-2) (Ginsburg & Baroody, 1990)	A: 3–8	Concepts; Counting; Calculation; Reading and Writing Numbers; Number Facts; Calculation Algorithms; Base-Ten Concepts

of phonetically regular and nonregular words (Test of Written Spelling-3 [Larsen & Hammill, 1994]) and spelling of words in sentences and paragraphs (Test of Written Language-3 [Hammill & Larsen, 1996]). Beyond establishing the level of difficulty, informal error analysis is necessary to determine the phonetic and orthographic patterns involved in poor spelling and to learn whether such errors occur in words spelled to dictation or only in the context of written language.

Because of the complex nature of written language expression, assessment of the writing skills named in DSM-IV is similarly more complex than the unitary construct implied in the diagnoses. Among the aspects of written expression that may be impaired are written syntax and morphology, sentence construction, mechanics (e.g., punctuation, capitalization), spelling in context, organization and formulation of ideas, and handwriting. On the basis of the performance of adults with acquired writing disorders, the neuropsychology literature suggests that assessment of writing/written language should include copying, writing to dictation, and spontaneous writing (Luria, 1980). Berninger (1994) has suggested that the following additional writing skills be included in assessment: handwriting quality (legibility)

and fluency and compositional quality and fluency. Several of the achievement batteries (Table 3.1) include a measure of written expression (e.g., Wechsler Individual Achievement Test [WIAT, 1992]); Woodcock-Johnson Psycho-Educational Battery-R [Woodcock & Johnson, 1989]), and other specialized measures have been developed that contain elements of written expression, for example, sentence dictation, sentence writing, and story composition (e.g., Test Of Written Language-3 [Hammill & Larsen, 1996]). However, given the complexity of the written-language process, currently available measures of spontaneous written expression have weaknesses in the scoring, which typically involves a relatively high degree of subjectivity on the part of the examiner.

Assessment of Mathematics Skills

At a minimum, assessment of mathematics skills should include evaluation of competence in computation, as well as math reasoning and problem solving. Most of the broad-based achievement batteries (Table 3.1) include such measures. While such widely used measures as the Wide-Range Achievement Test-3 (Wilkinson, 1993) might be useful in determining simple aptitude-achievement discrepancy, the relatively small number of items does not permit a detailed error analysis. More specialized diagnostic math tests are listed in Table 3.4.

In addition to determining broad areas of difficulty, informal error analysis and/or criterion-referenced assessment may be needed in order to design a specific intervention. Asking children to verbalize the steps in math problem solving (e.g., "think-aloud" procedures) is helpful in order to better delineate the pattern of difficulty and whether it reflects the deficits of a more generalized learning disability (e.g., the child with visual-spatial or graphomotor difficulty who can compute adequately but who cannot recall the right-to-left sequence of steps or keep numbers aligned) or difficulty with a specific level of analysis (e.g., problems with regrouping in subtraction, stemming from poor rule application). Similarly, problems with written math reasoning may reflect problems not specific to math but related to language (e.g., poor reading comprehension) or generalized difficulty with logical thinking and/or employing efficient problem-solving strategies. Attention and short-term memory, symbolic language integration, mental flexibility, nonverbal abstract reasoning and concept formation, and spatial memory have been linked to mathematics achievement (Batchelor, Gray, & Dean, 1990), suggesting that evaluation of impaired math skills may need to include more comprehensive psychoeducational and/or neuropsychological assessment.

Assessment of Coordination and Motor Skills

Since the threshold between less severe disorders of motor function and control and cerebral palsy is not clearly defined, children who present with obvious motor impairment should obtain a neurological exam to rule out other neuromotor or neuromuscular disorders. (Details of such assessment are beyond the scope of this chapter, and the reader is referred to Denckla, 1985; Deuel, 1992). Formal evaluation of the motor system generally includes assessment of muscles (bulk, strength, tone, and coordination) and reflexes (deep tendon and cutaneous). The clinical neurodevelopmental examination includes checking for: (1) the presence of subtle, minor, or "soft" versions of traditional neurological abnormalities and (2) the failure to meet developmental milestones for motor actions (Denckla & Roeltgen, 1992). The subtle neurologic signs looked for include involuntary (choreiform) movements, posturing, various asymmetries, pathological reflexes, subtle weaknesses, movement delays, and ataxia. Speed, rhythmicity, smoothness, duration, and freedom from overflow movements are evaluated. Assessment of motor function frequently occurs in infants and young children who are delayed in developing motor milestones. In order to rule out the presence of mental retardation (i.e., generalized, as opposed to specific, developmental delay), such an evaluation necessarily involves a more comprehensive assessment of cognitive and language skills. In view of the complex feedback relationship among attention, perceptual, and motor functions, the child with complex neuromotor problems may require a comprehensive neuropsychological assessment (see Hynd & Obrzut, 1981; Hynd & Willis, 1988). The broad-based neuropsychological assessment batteries include assessment of motor function (for example, measures of finger tapping and grip strength from the Reitan-Indiana Neuropsychological Test Battery for Children and the Halstead Neuropsychological Test Battery for Children [Selz, 1981] and the Luria-Nebraska Neuropsychological Battery for Children [Golden, 1981]). In addition to neurology and psychology, the occupational and physical therapy disciplines also specialize in the clinical evaluation of delayed or impaired motor skills.

Examples of both broad-band and narrowband tests of motor skills are listed in Table 3.5. The general psychological or psychoeducational assessment of children presenting with learning problems typically includes standardized measures of visual-motor integration, with such design-copying measures as the Bender Gestalt Test (Koppitz, 1963) and the Develop-

TABLE 3.5. Specialized Assessment of Motor Skills

Measure/Reference	Age/Grade	Contents
Bender Visual-Motor Gestalt Test (Koppitz, 1963)	A: 5–adult	Visual-Motor Integration
Bruininks-Oseretsky Test of Motor Proficiency (Bruininks, 1978)	A: 4–14	Running Speed/Agility; Balance; Bilateral Coordination; Strength; Upper-Limb Coordination; Response Speed; Visual-Motor Control; Upper-Limb Speed/Dexterity
Beery-Buktenica Developmental Test of Visual-Motor Integration (VMI) (Beery, 1997)	A: 3–18	Visual-Motor Integration; Motor Coordination
Peabody Developmental Motor Scales (Folio & Fewell, 1983)	A: infant–7	Gross-Motor and Fine-Motor Skills
Sensory Integration and Praxis Tests (Ayers, 1989)	A: 4–9	Praxis: (Verbal, Constructional, Postural, Oral, Sequencing); Bilateral Motor Coordination; Standing & Walking Balance; Motor Accuracy; Postrotary Nystagmus
Wide-Range Assessment of Visual-Motor Abilities (Adams & Sheslow, 1995)	A: 3–17	Visual-Spatial (Matching); Visual-Motor (Drawing); Motor (Pegboard)

mental Test of Visual-Motor Integration (Beery, 1997) as the most widely used screening measures. The Wide-Range Assessment of Visual Motor Abilities (Adams & Sheslow, 1995) provides an additional pegboard task to assess motor speed and dexterity. A normed broad-band test of motor skills is the Bruininks-Oseretsky Test of Motor Proficiency (Bruininks, 1978). (For more extensive reviews, see Cratty, 1994, and Sugden & Wright, 1998.)

Finally, assessment of dyspraxia (impaired gesture) and motor dysgraphia (impaired handwriting) also involve specialized assessment (Deuel, 1992; Denckla & Roeltgen, 1992). The Sensory Integration and Praxis Tests (Ayers, 1989) include a concentration of tasks to assess gesture.

Although several scales have been developed to rate handwriting samples (e.g., Phelps, Stempel, & Speck, 1985), there are currently no widely used standardized measures. Informal assessment typically includes such tasks as copying symbols and sentences, transcribing sentences, and comparing copied with self-generated writing. In addition, a variety of specific neuropsychological tests have been used to assess fine-motor function associated with poor handwriting, for example, measures of laterality (handedness), hand grip strength, hand fatigue, finger tapping, successive finger movements, and rapid hand taps (Beringer & Rutberg, 1992; O'Hare & Brown, 1989).

TREATMENT

Learning Disorders

Since children with learning disorders represent such a heterogeneous group, treatment methods vary widely. Traditional interventions for children with learning and coordination disorders include: (1) general educational management of learning-disabled children eligible for special education services in the public schools; (2) specific methods of instruction; (3) cognitive-behavioral techniques to teach efficient problem-solving strategies and to improve attitudinal/motivational problems, and (4) mental health approaches with children who have co-occurring social-emotional disorders. Finally, nontraditional and controversial therapies for these children abound and are reviewed by Silver (1995).

General Special Education Services

Since the initial legislation mandating special education services as part of a free and appropriate education for all students (PL 94-142), approximately half (51.3%) of all students with handicapping conditions are classified as learning disabled (U.S. Department of Education, 1993). Although a student might meet DSM-IV diagnostic criteria and/or school-based classification criteria for diagnosis of reading, mathematics, or written expression disorder, a school team must determine whether the student requires special education, that is, a specially designed curriculum not available to other students, using specialized methods and pacing of instruction, different texts or methods of input, and different standards for evaluating performance. If the student is not judged to require such an alternative educational program, he or she is not judged to be learning disabled from an educational perspective (Zigmond, 1995). For students who meet the school eligibility criteria, the school team must prepare an Individual Education Plan (IEP) outlining the strategies for improving academic performance and the method for assessing progress. The school system is then required to provide an array of educational placement options, including "pull-out" programs, such as a separate facility (residential facility or separate day school), a separate classroom, or a resource room (lab), and "mainstream" educational services, in which a student's needs are met by means of curriculum modification in the regular classroom. The law further mandates that the student's placement be consistent with the "least restrictive alternative." In the 1991–92 school year the majority (53.7%) of students classified as learning disabled were served through a resource room, and 22.5% were receiving regular classroom services, while only a small fraction of students (1.4%) were placed in separate facilities (U.S. Department of Education, 1993).

Current educational practice in special education has been criticized for the following reasons: (1) LD students may respond sufficiently to remedial instruction, such that they no longer qualify for special services, yet they may still be unable to cope with the mainstream curriculum, (2) LD students with mild learning disorders are precluded from receiving the educational support that might prevent the development of more severe problems, and (3) changes in psychometric test performance across repeated assessments result in some LD students being classified variously as educably mentally handicapped (e.g., mild MR) and learning disabled. The increasing number of children identified as LD in recent years has led both federal and state educational agencies to question the validity of both the LD definition and methods of assessment and identification. In the context of general educational reform, the "Regular Education Initiative" (Wang, Walbert, & Reynolds, 1992) is a movement away from the widespread practice of educating LD students in "pull-out" labs or resource programs and toward "full inclusion" of LD students in the mainstream classroom. Such a concept is distinguished from "mainstreaming" in that inclusion is intended to provide the regular classroom teacher with training, appropriate accommodations, auxiliary aids, and support from special educators. Research studies evaluating the efficacy of "pull-out" programs for the large population of children have shown mixed results (e.g., Carlberg & Kavale, 1980), and debate about the efficacy of current educational practices is likely to continue. Indeed, some have argued strongly that the inclusion movement will effectively eliminate individualized programming for children with learning disorders (e.g., Mather & Roberts, 1994).

Specific Educational Interventions

Since a detailed discussion of educational and remedial intervention is beyond the scope of this chapter, this section reviews some of the major trends in educational intervention for those with DSM-IV learning disorders. First, it is important to underscore that educational techniques abound that have gained popularity, yet that have not been reliably evaluated over large numbers of students. Second, the growing body of research in empirically validated interventions has not resulted in the parallel modification of educational practice and teacher training (Lyon et al., 1989). Future efforts may involve a redefining of learning disabilities in view of an individual's failure to respond to validated treatment protocols (Berninger, 1994).

READING DISORDER. Reading has attracted voluminous attention with regard to methods for basic acquisition, as well as remedial approaches for those who fail to master basic reading skills. In view of the different characteristics of those with single-word-decoding and reading comprehension disorders, instructional needs differ. First, a longstanding and continuing debate in regular education has been the approach to initial reading instruction. In general, debate has centered around the relative emphasis on a word decoding approach (in which the relationships between letters and sounds in words are made explicit, phonetic analysis and sound blending is taught, and vocabulary is controlled) and an approach in which emphasis is on meaning and the use of context to predict unknown words (Foorman, 1995). In the 1990s a major trend in general educational instruction is an application of the "whole language" approach, which is not one reading method per se but a coherent philosophy of language, curriculum, learning, and teaching (see reviews by Goodman, 1989; Symons, Woloshyn, & Pressley, 1994). The majority of children appear to acquire competence in reading irrespective of method of instruction, and 75% may intuitively master the alphabetic code without explicit instruction (Lieberman, Shankweiler, & Lieberman, 1989). However, those with a reading disability are within the 20% of children who fail to acquire adequate basic reading skills. Converging evidence of a phonological deficit in reading disability clearly suggests that these reading-disabled students require direct instruction in the phonological structure of the language (Foorman, 1995; Lyon, 1995b).

Educational instruction has focused on two areas: prevention of reading failure in at-risk preschool children and systematic remedial training for children who fail to respond to traditional instruction. Mounting evidence suggests that reading failure is predictable and that preschool training in phonemic awareness and segmentation generalize to improve the ability to learn word-decoding skills (e.g., Berninger, Thalberg, DeBruyn, & Smith, 1987). Moreover, the importance of early intervention with at-risk children is clearly underscored by the finding that initiating intervention after a child has failed for 2 to 3 years has limited success (Fletcher & Foorman, 1994). Clark (1988) provides an extensive review of specific methods of remedial instruction in word-decoding skills, including a discussion of the relative merits of explicit and incidental approaches to teaching phonics. Among the explicit approaches are various comprehensive programs for teaching reading, spelling, and writing that are based on a multisensory approach to utilizing combinations of visual, auditory, kinesthetic, and tactile information. In view of the complexity of evaluating reading methods, there is currently no definitive research that rigorously compares various phonics methods to guide the diagnostician in making recommendations for one method over another. However, aside from simple level of performance, the particular pattern of an individual's strengths and weaknesses should aid in determining educational intervention strategies, which should focus on an integration of decoding and comprehension and which should avoid the teaching of isolated skills. Making recommendations for specific educational programs clearly presumes that the mental health diagnostician has personal expertise in this area or consults with an educational or learning disabilities specialist.

Key components of effective instruction in comprehension include prereading activities, modeling, guided practice and feedback, and metacognitive instruction, with the use of semantic feature analysis, story grammar, story mapping, and mental imagery as useful teaching aids. A variety of reading comprehension interventions include: (1) cognitive interventions (e.g., teaching specific problem-solving skills, schema, or rules in approaching text, providing aids such as outlines, strategies for retaining and recalling factual information); (2) cognitive-behavioral interventions (e.g., self-monitoring, questioning, and evaluation techniques); (3) vocabulary interventions; (4) pre- and mid-reading interventions; (5) direct instruction (e.g. teacher cuing, signaling and reinforcement of attention, programmed materials, continuous evaluation and correction); and (6) computer-assisted interventions (e.g., mnemonic instruction, organizational approaches). (See reviews by Maria, 1990; Talbott, Lloyd, & Tankersley, 1994.)

DISORDER OF WRITTEN EXPRESSION. Attention to educational interventions for written-language disorders continues to lag behind reading methods. As a complex skill incorporating a variety of integrated cognitive processes, written language incorporates instruction in grammar, spelling, and mechanics (punctuation and capitalization), as well as the written formulation of ideas.

A number of multisensory methods of remedial instruction for dyslexic children include a comprehensive approach to the coordinated instruction of both reading and spelling (for reviews of spelling instruction see Clark, 1988; Fulk & Stormont-Spurgin, 1995; Gordon, Vaughn, & Schumm, 1993). A variety of spelling instructional techniques include direct instruction, study strategies, multisensory/modality training, and computer-assisted instruction. Suggested educational practices include: (1) use of error imitation and modeling, (2) reducing and spacing the introduction of new spelling words to three words, (3) writing, tracing letter tiles, and computer keyboard practice, as opposed to repetitive copying exercises, (4) structured peer tutoring, and (5) the use of various self-study techniques, including cognitive, self-questioning approaches.

As with any instruction, methods in written language instruction must be adjusted to accommodate developmental levels. Models

of writing instruction have included rule-and-skill instruction, facilitation of the substance and process of writing, and self-instructional strategy training. Methods of intervention for disorders of written expression have arisen out of several theoretical orientations, beginning with Johnson and Myklebust's (1967) hierarchy of language, Berninger's (1993) comprehensive, developmental neuropsychological model of writing, and Bos and Van Reusen's (1991) cognitive/metacognitive approaches to written composition. In the hierarchical model of language learning, a clinician is careful to determine whether the written language disorder parallels similar oral speech or language problems involving phonology, morphology, syntax, and formulation of ideas (Johnson, 1993). Thus, remediation of written language focuses on the linkages to parallel oral language problems and would work on both simultaneously. Finally, approaches surveyed by Bos and Van Reusen (1991) emphasize the importance of monitoring and regulation of such cognitive processes as planning, drafting, revision, editing—e.g., higher-order cognitive and metacognitive processes.

MATHEMATICS DISORDER. In a review of research on mathematics for learning-disabled students, three types of interventions have been described and are briefly described: (1) behavioral, (2) cognitive, and (3) alternative delivery systems (Mastropieri, Scruggs, & Shiah, 1991). Similar to work with reading-disabled students, various multisensory math procedures have been explored (Scott, 1993; Thornton & Toohey, 1985), incorporating visual, auditory, and kinesthetic strategies. Verbal problem-solving strategies have been found to be useful in assisting math disabled students in: (1) identifying the questions, (2) determining the correct operation, (3) recognizing and eliminating extraneous information, (4) deciding on number of steps, and (5) checking work. Montague and Bos (1986) found generalization of their cognitive strategy (read the problem aloud, paraphrase, visualize, state the problem, hypothesize, estimate, calculate, self-check) to problems of greater difficulty. Such alternative instructional techniques as cooperative learning have been found to be effective for both normally achieving and learning disabled students, particularly those of middle or high school age. Finally, while computer-assisted instruction and interactive video will undoubtedly increase in remedial math curricula, with some evidence of improvement in on-task behavior, there currently are insufficient data investigating or comparing particular programs to judge which ones may be effective.

In sum, although there has been considerable investigation of mathematics learning from the developmental and cognitive information-processing perspective (e.g., Resnick & Ford, 1981) and detailed study of the dyscalculia subtypes from the neuropsychological perspective (e.g., Novick & Arnold, 1988), well-controlled studies of various methods of instruction targeted to these specific types of learning disabilities have not emerged.

DEVELOPMENTAL COORDINATION DISORDER. With the exception of impaired handwriting, primary interventions with motor skills disorders are typically not undertaken by educators but generally involve the professional specialties of physical and/or occupational therapy. The current trends in federally mandated service delivery to children with developmental disorders, now extending to birth (PL 99-157), is to rely on community-based, rather than clinic-based, services. Such services to children may be delivered within the home or school setting, with more severe neurologically based motor disorders (e.g., cerebral palsy) being treated in multidisciplinary and rehabilitation centers. Approaches to intervention (for motor planning, dyspraxia, visual-motor integration, and dysgraphia) typically involve three approaches: circumventions, or "by-pass" methods; direct remedial interventions; and a combination of these approaches. Examples of circumventions are making adaptations in the requirements for activities that call for motor planning and coordination (for example, adaptive physical education; untimed tests; modifications in the requirements for handwriting; keyboard and word processing instruction; pro-

vision of appropriate tools, such as left-handed scissors; adaptive writing instruments; and special pencil grips). A survey of the allocation of time and types of fine-motor tasks expected of children in second, fourth, and sixth grade classrooms indicated that up to 60% of the school day may be allocated to fine-motor activities (McHale & Cermak, 1992). The majority (85%) of these activities involved paper-and-pencil tasks (e.g., copying from the board, doing repetitive writing, writing from dictation, taking notes, completing work sheets). Thus, the diagnostician may need to closely examine the demands for motor activities for the child with developmental coordination disorder and recommend modifications as appropriate.

Historically, direct intervention methods have included (1) "perceptual training," (2) multisensory approaches, which utilize intact perceptual and cognitive abilities (e.g., language and executive functioning) to assist in guiding and directing motor output, (3) such traditional physical therapy methods as muscle strengthening, and (4) interventions derived from a specific theoretical model of "Intersensory Integration." Denckla and Roeltgen (1992) note that false explanations of developmental sequences have frequently prompted interventions involving "perceptual training" for children with perceptual-motor disorders, with evidence that such training does not generalize to motor learning when the true difficulty is a motor output problem. Conversely, selective "motor training" is ineffective when visual-spatial disability accounts for much of the clumsiness noted in children with motor disorders. (For a review of such interventions, see Schoemaker & Kalverboer, 1990.)

Treatment approaches for developmental coordination disorder that have emerged in the rehabilitation therapies are based largely on clinical experience and assumptions about motor development. Two basic approaches have been used, a perceptual-motor approach (PM) and sensory integrative therapy (SI); however, studies of effectiveness have been equivocal. The objective of SI treatment is to enhance the brains's capacity to perceive and organize sensory information to produce a more normal, adaptive response and therefore to provide the foundation for mastering academic tasks. While initial studies of SI treatment appeared promising, more methodologically rigorous studies suggest that this approach may have some value for motor problems, but there is insufficient support of its effectiveness in treating academic problems (Polatajko, Kaplan, & Wilson, 1992).

Cognitive-Behavioral, Motivational, and Strategy Instruction

In addition to the information-processing deficits that underlie some learning disorders, it is now well known that considerable academic failure may also result from inefficient problem-solving strategies, poor self-regulatory skills, and passive learning in these children. In the past 10 years a major trend in intervention is the effort to teach a repertoire of specifically targeted strategies to promote efficient information processing. Some of these were discussed with regard to intervention in the specific subject areas of reading comprehension (e.g., Pressley, Johnson, Symons, McGoldrick, & Kurita, 1989), math problem-solving (e.g., Pressley, 1986), and written expression (e.g., Graham & Harris, 1993). Cognitive interventions have typically included the teaching of multiple-step procedures for both computation and word problems; others have included goal setting, verbalization and feedback regarding effort, use of manipulatives, mnemonic strategies, and various self-instructional strategies.

In addition to educationally targeted strategy instruction, similar efforts are often necessary for modifying motivation and achievement-related beliefs. Learning-disabled children are frequently unaware of the distinct processes involved in learning/remembering (metacognitive variables), are less knowledgeable about the world in general, and lack the ability to evaluate strategy effectiveness and to employ an alternative, more adaptive approach. Not specific to learning disabled children, such traits are also characteristic of

children with externalizing disorders, for example, those children co-morbid for LD and ADHD. Many of these children have lowered self-esteem, are characterized by "learned helplessness," tend to underestimate their intelligence, and tend to attribute their success to luck or external factors (i.e., external locus of control). A number of cognitive-behavioral treatments have been developed for enhancing children's motivation, including attribution retraining (e.g., Borowkowski, Weyhing, & Turner, 1986) and intensive short-term approaches to improving motivation (e.g., Rawson, 1992). While such techniques may be quite useful for enhancing motivation, it should be emphasized that motivational treatments are not substitutes for competent instruction in basic skill mastery and thus should be integrated with good skill instructional programs.

Other Psychosocial Approaches

Given the negative effects of lowered academic performance on self-esteem, together with evidence for an increased risk of internalizing disorders and other psychosocial problems, traditional mental health services are sometimes indicated. High levels of frustration, with associated performance anxiety and depression, are not uncommon in LD children, particularly the bright students who are painfully aware of their academic weaknesses. Moreover, intelligent students with severe reading or written language disorders may be dismissed as not trying by uninformed teachers who sense their high intellect and conclude that the problem is primarily motivational. Such situations clearly call for the diagnostician to inform school personnel about primary versus secondary emotional problems, while simultaneously providing therapeutic support to the student.

Second, learning disabled students are at higher risk for experiencing social rejection (Vaughn, McIntosh, & Spencer-Rowe, 1991), particularly those with nonverbal learning disabilities, who are frequently characterized by social misperception, reduced social competence, and concomitant socioemotional difficulties. Children with developmental coordination disorders may be particularly emotionally vulnerable. Denckla and Roeltgen (1992) have noted that the child deficient in self-care risks a combination of parental overprotection and exasperation; similarly, the clumsy child who is poor at games and sports is often excluded from socially relevant peer activities or experiences active teasing or rejection, often resulting in social withdrawal. Finally, while beyond the scope of this chapter, there is a considerable literature regarding the social functioning of individuals with learning disabilities (e.g., La Greca & Vaughn, 1992a; 1992b; Swanson & Malone, 1992), as well as methods for training appropriate reciprocal communication and social interaction skills.

COMMENTS

With the current impetus of the National Institutes of Health (NICHD branch), there has been considerable progress in improving our understanding of the learning disorders listed in DSM-IV, particularly reading disorder. At the same time, consensus is developing that assessment of learning disorders must move away from traditional psychometric assessment aimed at simple categorizing and labeling to a careful documentation of strengths and weaknesses aimed at targeting specific intervention strategies. The more recent cognitive-behavioral efforts toward assessment and teaching of learning strategies has greatly expanded our understanding of learning and response to instruction. As has been mentioned in this chapter, the extension of these research efforts to the development of valid prescriptions for effective interventions for particular types of children, with particular patterns of strengths and weaknesses, and in particular setting, is currently lacking. However, such an ambitious goal has been outlined by the NICHD (Lyon, 1995a), with large-scale studies under way to rigorously evaluate the effectiveness of a variety of individualized interventions

for well-defined groups of learning-disabled children.

REFERENCES

ACLD (1985). CLD offers new definition. *Special Education Today*, 2, 19.

Adams, W., & Sheslow, D. (1995). *Wide-Range Assessment of Visual-Motor Abilities*. Wilmington, DE: Wide Range.

American Psychiatric Association. (1994). *Diagnostic and statistical manual of mental disorders* (4th ed.). Washington, DC: Author.

Ayers, A. J. (1989). *Sensory Integration and Praxis Tests*. Los Angeles, CA: Western Psychological Services.

Batchelor, E. S., Gray, J. W., & Dean, R. S. (1990). Empirical testing of a cognitive model to account for neuropsychological functioning underlying arithmetic problem solving. *Journal of Learning Disabilities*, 23, 38–42.

Beatty, L. S., Gardner, E. G., Madden, R., & Karlsen, B. (1985). *Stanford Diagnostic Mathematics Test* (3rd ed.). San Antonio, TX: Psychological Corpora tion.

Beery, K. E. (1997). *The Beery-Buktenica Developmental Test of Visual-Motor Integration* (4th ed). Parsippany, NJ: Modern Curriculum Press.

Berninger, V. W. (1993). *Reading and writing acquisition. A developmental neuropsychological perspective*. DuBuque, IA: Brown & Benchmark.

Berninger, V. W. (1994). Future directions for research on writing disabilities: Integrating endogenous and exogenous variables. In G. R. Lyon (Ed.), *Frames of reference for the assessment of learning disabilities* (pp. 419–439). Baltimore, MD: Paul H. Brooks.

Berninger, V. W., & Rutberg, J. (1992). Relationship of finger function to beginning writing: Applications to diagnosis of writing abilities. *Developmental Medicine and Child Neurology*, 34, 198–215.

Berninger, V., Thalberg, S., DeBruyn, I., & Smith, R. (1987). Preventing reading disabilities by assessing and remediating phonemic skills. *School Psychology Review*, 16 (4), 554–565.

Boder, E. (1973). Developmental dyslexia: A diagnostic approach based on three atypical reading-spelling patterns. *Developmental Medicine and Child Neurology*, 15, 663–687.

Borowkowski, J. G., Weyhing, R. S., & Turner, L. A. (1986). Attributional training and the teaching of strategies. *Exceptional Children, 53,* 130–137.

Bos, C. S., & Van Reusen, A. K. (1991). Academic interventions with learning-disabled students: A cognitive/metacognitive approach. In J. E. Obrzut & G. W. Hynd (Eds.), *Neuropsychological foundations of learning disabilities* (pp. 659–683). San Diego, CA: Academic Press.

Brown, V. L., Cronin, M. E., & McEntire, E. (1994). *Test of Mathematical Abilities* (2nd ed.). Austin, TX: ProEd.

Bruininks, R. H. (1978). *Bruininks-Oseretsky Test of Motor Proficiency.* Circle Pines, MN: American Guidance Service.

California State Board of Education. (1996). *Teaching reading: A balanced, comprehensive approach to teaching reading in pre-kindergarten through grade three.* Sacramento, CA: California Department of Education.

Carlberg, C., & Kavale, K. (1980). The efficacy of special versus regular class placement for exceptional children: A meta-analysis. *Journal of Special Education, 14,* 295–309.

Carrow-Woolfolk, E. (1995). *Oral and Written Language Scales: Written Expression.* Circle Pines, MN: American Guidance Service.

Catts, H. W. (1993). The relationship between speech-language impairments and reading disabilities. *Journal of Speech and Hearing Research, 36* (5), 948–958.

Chalfant, J. C., & Scheffelin, M. A. (1969). *Central processing dysfunctions in Children: A review of research.* (NINDS Monograph, No. 9). Bethesda, MD: U.S. Department of Health, Education, and Welfare.

Clark, D. B. (1988). *Dyslexia: Theory & practice of remedial instruction.* Parkton, MD: York Press.

Connolly, A. J. (1988). *Key Math–Revised: A diagnostic inventory of essential mathematics.* Circle Pines, MN: American Guidance Service.

Cratty, B. J. (1994). *Clumsy-child syndromes: Descriptions, evaluation and remediation.* Chur, Switzerland: Harwood Academic Publishers.

DeFries, J. C. (1989). Gender ratios in children with reading disability and their affected relatives: A commentary. *Journal of Learning Disabilities, 22* (9), 544–545.

Denckla, M. B. (1972). Clinical syndromes in learning disabilities: The case for "splitting" vs. "lumping." *Journal of Learning Disabilities, 5,* 401–406.

Denckla, M. B. (1983). The neuropsychology of social-emotional learning disability. *Archives of Neurology, 40,* 461–462.

Denckla, M. B. (1985). Revised neurological examination of subtle signs. *Psychopharmacology Bulletin, 21,* 733–800, 1111–1124.

Denckla, M. B. (1993). A neurologist's overview of developmental dyslexia. *Annals of the New York Academy of Sciences, 682,* 23–26.

Denckla, M. B., & Roeltgen, D. P. (1992). Disorders of motor function and control. In I. Rapin & S. J. Segalowitz (Eds.), *Handbook of neuropsychology* (pp. 445–476). Amsterdam: Elsevier.

Deuel, R. K. (1992). Motor skill disorder. In S. R. Hooper, G. W. Hynd, & R. E. Mattison (Eds.), *Developmental disorders: Diagnostic criteria and clinical assessment* (pp. 239–281). Hillsdale, NJ: Lawrence Erlbaum.

Durrell, D. D., & Catterson, J. H. (1980). *Durrell Analysis of Reading Difficulty* (3rd ed.). San Antonio, TX: Psychological Corporation.

Elbert, J. C. (1993). Occurrence and pattern of impaired reading and written language in children with attention deficit disorders. *Annals of Dyslexia, 43,* 26–43.

Elliott, S. N., & Fuchs, L. S. (1997). The utility of curriculum-based measurement and performance assessment as alternatives to traditional intelligence and achievement tests. *School Psychology Review, 26* (2), 224–233.

Fletcher, J. M., & Foorman, B. (1994). Issues in definition and measurement of learning disabilities: The need for early intervention. In G. R. Lyon (Ed.), *Frames of reference for the assessment of learning disabilities: New views on measurement issues.* Baltimore, MD: Paul H. Brooks.

Fletcher, J. M., Francis, D. J., Rourke, B. P., Shaywitz, S. E., & Shaywitz, B. A. (1992). The validity of discrepancy-based definitions of reading disabilities. *Journal of Learning Disabilities, 25,* 55–61.

Fletcher, J. M., Shaywitz, S. E., Shankweiler, D., Katz, L., Liberman, I. Y., Steubing, K. K., Francis, D. J., Fowler, A. F., & Shaywitz, B. A. (1994). Cognitive profiles of reading disability: comparisons of discrepancy and low-achievement definitions. *Journal of Educational Psychology, 86,* 6–23.

Folio, M. R., & Fewell, R. (1983). *Peabody Developmental Motor Scales and Activity Cards.* Chicago: Riverside.

Foorman, B. R. (1995). Research on "the great debate": Code-oriented versus whole-language approaches to reading instruction. *School Psychology Review, 24* (3), 376–392.

Frith, U. (1980). *Cognitive processes in spelling.* London: Academic Press.

Fulk, B. M., & Stormont-Spurgin, M. (1995). Spelling interventions for students with disabilities: A review. *Journal of Special Education, 28* (4), 488–513.

Gaddes, W. H., & Edgall, D. (1994). *Learning disabilities and brain function: A neuropsychological approach* (3rd ed.). New York: Springer-Verlag.

Geary, D. C. (1993). Mathematical disabilities: Cognitive, neuropsychological, and genetic components. *Psychological Bulletin, 114* (2), 345–362.

Ginsburg, H. P. & Baroody, A. J. (1990). *Test of Early Mathematics Ability* (2nd ed.). Austin, TX: ProEd.

Golden, C. J. (1981). The Luria-Nebraska Children's Battery: Theory and formulation. In G. W. Hynd & J. E. Obrzut (Eds.), *Neuropsychological assessment and the school-age child: Issues and procedures* (pp. 277–302). New York: Grune & Stratton.

Goodgold-Edwards, S. A., & Cermak, S. A. (1990). Integrating motor control and motor learning concepts with neuropsychological perspectives on apraxia and developmental dyspraxia. *American Journal of Occupational Therapy, 44* (5), 431–439.

Goodman, K. S. (1989). Whole language is whole: A response to Heymsfield. *Educational Leadership, 46* (6), 69–70.

Gordon, J., Vaughn, S., & Schumm, J. S. (1993). Spelling interventions: A review of literature and implications for instruction for students with learning disabilities. *Learning Disabilities Research & Practice, 8* (3), 175–181.

Graham, S., & Harris, K. R. (1993). Teaching writing strategies to students with learning disabilities: Issues and recommendations. In L. J. Meltzer (Ed.), *Strategy assessment and instruction for students with learning disabilities: from theory to practice* (pp. 271–292). Austin, TX: ProEd.

Hallahan, D. P. (1992). Some thoughts on why the prevalence of learning disabilities has increased. *Journal of Learning Disabilities, 25* (8), 523–528.

Hammill, D. D., & Larsen, S. C. (1996). *Test of Written Language—3* (3rd ed.). Austin, TX: ProEd.

Hammill, D. D., Leigh, J. E., McNutt, G., & Larsen, S. C. (1981). A new definition of learning disabilities. *Learning Disability Quarterly, 4*, 336–342.

Heath, C. P., & Kush, J. C. (1991). Use of discrepancy formulas in the assessment of learning disabilities. In J. E. Obrzut & G. W. Hynd (Eds.), *Neuropsychological foundations of learning disabilities* (pp. 287–307). San Diego, CA: Academic Press.

Hendrickson, A. D. (1983), Prevention or cure: Another look at mathematics learning problems. In D. Carnine, D. Elkind, A. D. Hendrickson, D. Meichenbaum, R. L. Sieben, & F. Smith (Eds.), *Interdisciplinary voices in learning disabilities and remedial education* (pp. 93–107). Austin, TX: ProEd.

Hooper, S. R., Montgomery, J., Swartz, C., Reed, M. S., Sandler, A. D., Levine, M. D., Watson, T. E., & Wasileski, T. (1994). Measurement of written language expression. In G. R. Lyon, (Ed.), *Frames of reference for the assessment of learning disabilities* (pp. 375–417). Baltimore, MD: Paul H. Brooks.

Hooper, S. R., & Willis, W. G. (1989). *Learning disability subtyping: Neuropsychological foundations, conceptual models, and issues in clinical differentiation.* New York: Springer-Verlag.

Hresko, W. P., Herron, S. R., & Peak, P. K. (1998). *Test of Early Written Language-3* (3rd Edition.). Austin, TX: ProEd.

Hynd, G. W., & Obrzut, J. E. (Eds.). (1981). *Neuropsychological assessment and the school-age child: Issues and procedures.* New York: Grune & Stratton.

Hynd, G. W., & Willis, W. G. (1988). *Pediatric neuropsychology.* Orlando, FL: Grune & Stratton.

Interagency Committee on Learning Disabilities. (1987). *Learning disabilities: A report to the U.S. Congress.* Washington, DC: Author.

Johnson, D. J. (1993). Relationship between oral and written language. *School Psychology Review, 22* (4), 595–609.

Johnson, D. J., & Myklebust, H. R. (1967). *Learning disabilities: Educational principles and practices.* New York: Grune & Stratton.

Kaufman, A. S., & Kaufman, N. L. (1993). *Kaufman Test of Educational Achievement.* Circle Pines, MN: American Guidance Service.

Kavale, K. A., & Forness, S. R. (1985). *The science of learning disabilities.* San Diego, CA: College-Hill.

Kinsbourne, M., & Warrington, E. T. (1963). The developmental Gerstmann syndrome. *Archives of Neurology, 8*, 490–501.

Koppitz, E. M. (1963). *The Bender Gestalt Test for young children.* New York: Grune & Stratton.

La Greca, A. M., & Vaughn, S. (1992a). Social functioning of individuals with learning disabilities: Annotated bibliography. *School Psychology Review, 21* (3), 423–426.

La Greca, A. M., & Vaughn, S. (1992b). Social functioning of individuals with learning disabilities. *School Psychology Review, 21* (3), 340–347.

Larsen, S. C., & Hammill, D. D. (1994). *Test of Written Spelling* (3rd ed.). Austin, TX: ProEd.

Lieberman, I. Y., Shankweiler, D., & Lieberman, A. M. (1989). The alphabetic principle and learning to read. In D. Shankweiler & I. Y. Lieberman (Eds.), *Phonology and reading disability: Solving the reading puzzle* (pp. 1–33). Ann Arbor: University of Michigan Press.

Lindamood, C. H., & Lindamood, P. C. (1979). *Lindamood Auditory Conceptualization Test—Revised.* Hingham, MA: Teaching Resources.

Luria, A. R. (1980). *Higher cortical functions in man.* New York: Basic Books.

Lyon, G. R. (Ed.). (1994). *Frames of reference for the assessment of learning disabilities: New views on measurement issues.* Baltimore, MD: Paul H. Brooks.

Lyon, G. R. (1995a). Symposium discussion. Orton Dyslexia Society 46th Annual Conference, Houston, TX.

Lyon, G. R. (1995b). Teaching reading to children with learning disabilities using whole-language programs not advisable. *LDA Newsbriefs, 31* (2), 9. Pittsburgh, PA: Learning Disabilities Association.

Lyon, G. R. (1996). Learning disabilities. In E. J. Mash, & R. A. Barkley (Eds.), *Child psychopathology* (pp. 390–435). New York: Guilford Press.

Lyon, G. R., Gray, D. B., Kavanaugh, J. F., & Krasnegor, N. A. (Eds.). (1993). *Better understanding learning disabilities: New views from research and their implications for definition, classification, education, and public policy.* Baltimore, MD: Paul H. Brooks.

Lyon, G. R., Vaasen, M., & Toomey, F. (1989). Teachers' perceptions of their undergraduate and graduate preparation. *Teacher Education and Special Education, 12*, 164–169.

MacGinitie, W. H., & MacGinitie, R. K. (1989). *Gates-MacGinitie Reading Tests.* Chicago: Riverside Publishing Co.

Maria, K. (1990). *Reading comprehension instruction: Issues & strategies.* Parkton, MD: York Press.

Markwardt, F. C. (1989). *Peabody Individual Achievement Test—Revised.* Circle Pines, MN: American Guidance Service.

Martin, E. W. (1993) Learning disabilities and public policy: Myths and outcomes. In Lyon, G. R., Gray, D. B., Kavanaugh, J. K., & Krasnagor, N. A. (Eds.), *Better understanding learning disabilities: New views from research and their implications*

for education and public policies (pp. 325–342). Baltimore, MD: Paul H. Brooks.

Mastropieri, M. A., Scruggs, T. E., & Shiah, S. (1991). Mathematics instruction for learning disabled students: A review of research. *Learning Disabilities Research & Practice, 6*, 89–98.

Mather, N., Roberts, R. (1994). Learning disabilities: A field in danger of extinction? *Learning Disabilities Research & Practice, 9* (1), 49–58.

Mattis, S., French, J. H., & Rapin, I. (1975). Dyslexia in children and young adults: Three independent neuropsychological syndromes. *Developmental Medicine and Child Neurology, 17*, 150–163.

McHale, K., & Cermak, S. A. (1992). Fine-motor activities in elementary school: Preliminary findings and provisional implications for children with fine-motor problems. *American Journal of Occupational Therapy, 46* (10), 898–903.

McGhee, R., Bryant, B. R., Larsen, S. C., & Rivera, D. M. (1995). *Test of Written Expression.* Austin, TX: ProEd.

Meltzer, L. J. (Ed.). (1993). *Strategy assessment and instruction for students with learning disabilities: From theory to practice.* Austin, TX: ProEd.

Montague, M., & Bos, C. S. (1986). The effect of cognitive strategy training on verbal math problem-solving performance of learning-disabled adolescents. *Journal of Learning Disabilities, 19*, 26–33.

Nichols, P., & Chen, T. (1981). *Minimal brain dysfunction: A prospective study.* Hillsdale, NJ: Lawrence Erlbaum.

Novick, B. Z., & Arnold, M. M. (1988). *Fundamentals of clinical child neuropsychology.* Philadelphia: Grune & Stratton.

O'Hare, A. E., & Brown, J. K. (1989). Childhood dysgraphia. Part 2: A study of hand function. *Child: Care, Health, and Development, 15*, 151–166.

O'Hare, A. E., Brown, J. K., & Aitken, K. (1991). Dyscalculia in children. *Developmental Medicine and Child Neurology, 33*, 356–361.

Orton, S. (1937). *Reading, writing and speech problems in children.* New York: Norton.

Pennington, B. F. (1991). The genetics of dyslexia. *Journal of Child Psychology and Psychiatry, 31*, 193–201.

Pennington, B. F., Van Orden, G. C., Smith, S. D., Green, P. A., & Haith, M. (1990). Phonological processing skills and deficits in adult dyslexics. *Child Development, 61*, 1753–1778.

Phelps, J., Stempel, L., & Speck, G. (1985). The

children's handwriting scale: A new diagnostic tool. *Journal of Educational Research, 79,* 46–50.

Polatajko, H. J., Kaplan, B. J., & Wilson, B. N. (1992). Sensory integration treatment for children with learning disabilities: Its status 20 years later. *Occupational Therapy Journal of Research, 12* (6), 323–341.

Pressley, M. (1986). The relevance of the good strategy user model to the teaching of mathematics. *Educational Psychologist, 21,* 139–161.

Pressley, M., Johnson, C. J., Symons, S., McGoldrick, J. A., & Kurita, J. A. (1989). Strategies that improve children's memory and comprehension of text. *Elementary School Journal, 90,* 3–32.

Rawson, H. E. (1992). Effects of intensive short-term remediation on academic intrinsic motivation of "at-risk" children. *Journal of Instructional Psychology, 19* (4), 274–285.

Resnick, L., & Ford, W. W. (1981). *Psychology for mathematics instruction.* Hillsdale, NJ: Lawrence Erlbaum.

Reisman, F. K., & Hutchinson, T. A. (1985). *Sequential Assessment of Mathematics Inventories.* San Antonio, TX: Psychological Corporation.

Reynolds, C. R. (1990). Conceptual and technical problems in learning disability diagnosis. In C. R. Reynolds & R. W. Kamphaus (Eds.), *Handbook of psychological and educational assessment of children* (pp.571–592). New York: Guilford Press.

Reynolds, C. R., & Kamphaus, R. W. (1990). *Handbook of psychological and educational assessment of children: Intelligence and achievement.* New York: Guilford Press.

Richardson, E., & Dibenedetto, B. (1985). *Decoding Skills Test.* Parkton, MD: York Press.

Rourke, B. P. (Ed.). (1995). *Syndrome of nonverbal learning disabilities: Neurodevelopmental manifestations.* New York: Guilford Press.

Rourke, B. P., & Finlayson, M. A. J. (1978). Neuropsychological significance of variations in patterns of academic performance: Verbal and visual-spatial abilities. *Journal of Abnormal Child Psychology, 6,* 121–133.

Sandler, A. D., Watson, T. E., Footo, M., Levine, D., Coleman, W. L., & Hooper, S. R. (1992). Neurodevelopmental study of writing disorders in middle childhood. *Journal of Developmental and Behavioral Pediatrics, 13* (1), 17–23.

Sattler, J. M. (1992). *Assessment of children* (3rd ed., rev.). San Diego, CA: Author.

Scarborough, H. (1990). Very early language deficits in dyslexic children. *Child Development, 61,* 1728–1743.

Schoemaker, M. M., & Kalverboer, A. F. (1990). Treatment of clumsy children. In A. F. Kalverboer (Ed.), *Developmental biopsychology* (pp. 241–255). Ann Arbor: University of Michigan Press.

Scott, K. S. (1993). Multisensory mathematics for children with mild disabilities. *Exceptionality, 4* (2), 97–111.

Seltz, M. (1981). Halstead-Reitan Neuropsychological Test Batteries for Children. In G. W. Hynd & J. E. Obrzut (Eds.), *Neuropsychological assessment and the school-age child: Issues and procedures* (pp. 195–235). New York: Grune & Stratton.

Semrud-Clikeman, M., & Hynd, G. (1992). Developmental arithmetic disorder. In S. R. Hooper, G. W. Hynd, & R. E. Mattison (Eds.), *Developmental disorders: Diagnostic criteria and clinical assessment* (pp. 97–125). Hillsdale, NJ: Lawrence Erlbaum.

Shaywitz, S. E., Escobar, M. D., Shaywitz, B. A., Fletcher, J. M., & Makuch, R. (1992). Evidence that dyslexia may represent the lower tail of a normal distribution of reading ability. *New England Journal of Medicine, 326,* 145–150.

Siegel, L. S. (1989). IQ is irrelevant to the definition of learning disabilities. *Journal of Learning Disabilities, 22,* 469–486.

Silver, L. B. (1995). Controversial therapies. *Journal of Child Neurology, 10* (Suppl. 1), S96–S100.

Stanovich, K. E. (1991). Discrepancy definitions of reading disability: Has intelligence led us astray? *Reading Research Quarterly, 26,* 7–29.

Stanovich, K. E., & Siegel, L. S. (1994). Phenotypic performance profile of children with reading disabilities: A regression-based test of the phonological-core variable-difference model. *Journal of Educational Psychology, 86* (1), 24–53.

Stigler, J. W., & Baranes, R. (1988–1989). Culture and mathematics learning. *Review of Research in Education, 15,* 253–307.

Stott, D. H., Moyes, F. A., & Henderson, S. E. (1984). *Test of Motor Impairment,* Henderson revision. San Antonio, TX: Psychological Corporation.

Strauss, A. A., & Werner, H. (1942). *Disorders of conceptual thinking in the brain-injured child.* Vol. 1. New York: Grune & Stratton.

Sugden, D. A., & Wright, H. C. (1998). *Motor coordination disorders in children.* Thousand Oaks, CA: Sage.

Swanson, H. L., & Malone, S. (1992). Social skills and learning disabilities: A meta-analysis of the literature. *School Psychology Review, 21* (3), 427–443.

Symons, S., Woloshyn, V., & Pressley, M. (Eds.).

(1994). The scientific evaluation of the whole-language approach to literacy development [Special issue]. *Educational Psychologist, 29* (4).

Talbott, E., Lloyd, J. W., & Tankersley, M. (1994). Effects of reading comprehension interventions for students with learning disabilities. *Learning Disability Quarterly, 17* (3), 223–232.

Thornton, C. A., & Toohey, M. A. (1985). Basic math facts: Guidelines for teaching and learning. *Learning Disabilities Focus, 1,* 44–57.

Torgesen, J. K., & Bryant, B. R. (1994). *Test of Phonological Awareness.* Austin, TX: ProEd.

U.S. Department of Education. (1991). *Thirteenth annual report to Congress on the implementation of the Individuals with Disabilities Education Act.* Washington, DC: Author.

U.S. Department of Education. (1993). *Fifteenth Annual Report to Congress on the Implementation of the Individuals with Disabilities Education Act.* Washington, DC: Author.

U.S. Department of Health, Education, and Welfare, Office of Education. (1977, December). Part III. Additional procedures for evaluating specific learning disabilities. *Federal Register, 42* (250), 65083.

Vaughn, S., McIntosh, R., & Spencer-Rowe, J. C. (1991). Peer rejection is a stubborn thing: Increasing peer acceptance of rejected students with learning disabilities. *Learning Disabilities Research & Practice, 6* (2), 83–88.

Voeller, K. K. S. (1990). Right-hemisphere-deficit syndrome in children: A neurological perspective. *International Pediatrics, 5* (2), 163–170.

Wagner, R. K., & Torgesen, J. K. (1987). The nature of phonological processing and its causal role in the acquisition of reading skills. *Psychological Bulletin, 101,* 192–212.

Wang, M. C., Walberg, H. J., & Reynolds, M. C. (1992). A scenario for better—not separate—special education. *Educational Leadership, 44* (1), 26–31.

Wechsler, D. (1992). *Wechsler Individual Achievement Test.* San Antonio, TX: Psychological Corporation.

Wiederholt, J. L., & Bryant, B. R. (1992). *Gray Oral Reading Tests—Revised.* Austin, TX: ProEd.

Wilkinson, G. S. (1993) *The Wide-Range Achievement Test* (3rd ed.). Wilmington, DE: Wide-Range.

Woodcock, R. W. (1987). *Woodcock Reading Mastery Tests—Revised.* Circle Pines, MN: American Guidance Service.

Woodcock, R. W., & Johnson, M. B. (1989). *Woodcock-Johnson Psycho-Educational Battery—Revised.* Chicago: Riverside.

World Health Organization. (1992). *International statistical classification of diseases and related health problems.* Vol. 1. Mental and behavioral disorders (9th rev., Clinical modification). Geneva: Author.

Zigmond, N. (1995). Models for delivery of special-education services to students with learning disabilities in public schools. *Journal of Child Neurology, 10* (Suppl. 1), S86–S92.

4

Psychological Assessment and Treatment of Communication Disorders: Childhood Language Subtypes

Lynn C. Richman
Kevin M. Wood

INTRODUCTION

Historical Perspective

Identification and study of communication disorders has a long history dating to the late-ninetheenth-century studies of adult aphasia (Berndt, Caramazza, & Zurif, 1983). These early studies were usually based on autopsy findings of individuals with language disorders. Broca associated damage to the left hemisphere with speech deficits, and Wernicke later suggested that damage to different areas of the left hemisphere caused different types of language deficits. These language disorders became known as aphasia, which refers to language problems not related to peripheral problems, such as cleft palate or hearing loss. Early models continued to be developed, which associated specific types of aphasia with different brain regions. For more information on these models and aphasia terminology see Critchley (1967). These were the beginning steps in subtyping communication disorders. However, controversy arose regarding these attempts to associate specific language functions with isolated brain regions. One of the issues that remains controversial is the attempt to generalize from localization of brain damage associated with a specific language disorder to an assumption that specific speech and language functions are subserved by specific brain regions. For a more complete review of brain localization, especially laterality, see Corballis (1983). Neurological and aphasiological research continues to identify more precise brain-language relationships. An example is the distinction of phonological short-term memory associated with the left cerebral frontal region (Broca's area) and semantic language function associated with the temporal regions of the left hemisphere (Wernicke's area) through blood flow studies (Frackowiak, 1994). The adult brain damage and cerebral function studies provide a model for etiology of specific types of language disorders. However, childhood language disorders are often related to developmental differences rather than to traumatic brain injury (Geschwind & Galaburda, 1987). This chapter focuses on psychological aspects of the developmental language disorders of childhood.

A shift occurred from the adult, aphasia–brain damage model of language disorders to developmental models of childhood language disorders, which were referred to as developmental dysphasia. This transition in thinking was similar to the shift from adult brain damage models of alexia to childhood reading disorders without obvious brain damage, referred to as developmental dyslexia. For more complete reviews of these developmental disorders, see Benton (1975, 1978). During the 1960s and 70s, studies regarding etiology and treatment of language disorders in children began to merge with research on developmental learning disorders. Treatments were often focused on the assumed underlying cognitive disturbance, such as perceptual processing, linguistic processing, cognitive processing, and the relationship among these processes. For an extensive review of these diagnostic methods and treatment modalities for language-learning disorders, see Wiig and Semel (1976) and Irwin and Marge (1972).

Communication disorders is an extensive category that includes the primary speech and language disorders as well as other forms of communication deficits, such as those secondary to elective mutism, autism, cleft palate, and schizophrenia. The scope of this chapter includes speech and language disorders with an emphasis on the psychological (cognitive, behavioral, emotional) aspects of children and adolescents with various types of developmental language disorders. Language is defined as the symbolic system used for communication purposes with speech being one mode of communication. Language disorder is used to refer to the delay or deviance in development of speech and language.

Current approaches to diagnostic research in language disorders have focused on attempts to develop classification schemes for separate categories of language disorder subtypes. It is thought that delineating homogeneous subtypes of language disorders will allow valid classification of children with similar language disorders. This should lead to clinical treatment strategies designed for each subtype and outcome evaluation. Although early classification of childhood language disorders was based primarily on clinical-inferential groupings of symptoms according to adult aphasia models (Ludlow, 1980), more recent studies have applied more quantitative statistical models (Wilson & Risucci, 1986). The classification issues in language disorders are quite similar to the subtyping issues in the neuropsychology of learning disabled children (Fletcher, 1985). One of the most significant difficulties in comparing the different learning or language disorders subtyping studies is that researchers and clinicians use different tests and different methodological procedures.

Diagnostic Description of Language Disorders, including DSM-IV & ICD-10

Several recent research classification studies of child language disorders provide subgroups with some overlap in the dimensions of language functioning (Aram & Nation, 1975; Korkman & Hakkinen-Rihu, 1994; Rapin & Allen, 1983; Wilson & Risucci, 1986). These classification systems will be reviewed, along with the communication disorders classification of the *Diagnostic and Statistical Manual of Mental Disorders* (Fourth Edition) (DSM-IV) (American Psychiatric Association, 1994) and the *International Classification of Diseases and Related Health Problems* (Tenth Edition) (ICD-10) (World Health Organization, 1992). The classification subtypes of speech/language disorders from the research studies and DSM-IV are provided in Table 4.1.

The classifications identified in Table 4.1 are not equivalent, even though some subtypes use similar terminology. However, as pointed out by Wilson and Risucci (1986), their classification system, along with those of Aram and Nation (1975) and Rapin and Allen (1983), includes subtypes representative of the more general categories of expressive, receptive, and mixed expressive-receptive disorders. The most recent classification system listed (Korkman & Hakkinen-Rihu, 1994) also includes the equivalent of a receptive-expressive or global group, as well as subtypes of expressive and receptive (comprehension) disorder. Practitioners should view subtype classification as the prominent dimension of a child's disordered language,

TABLE 4.1. Classification Subtypes of Language Disorders

Aram & Nation (1975)	Korkman & Hakkinen-Rihu (1994)	Rapin & Allen (1983)	Wilson & Risucci (1986)	DSM IV (1994)
Generalized low performance	Global subtype: receptive & naming problem	Verbal auditory agnosia Semantic pragmatic	Global disorder	Mixed receptive expressive
Formulation-repetition Syntactic and speech programming disorder	Specific verbal dyspraxia subtype: phonological production & articulation problem no receptive problems	Phonologic-syntactic Verbal dyspraxia Phonological production problem	Expressive	Phonological disorder Expressive language disorder
Comprehension deficit	Specific comprehension subtype: problem in comprehension of complex verbal instructions, less impaired in auditory perceptual domain	Semantic-pragmatic disorder	Receptive-auditory semantic comprehension disorder	Mixed receptive-expressive
Nonspecific formulation Repetition disorder	Specific disnomia subtype: problem with name retrieval	Lexical syntactic	Auditory memory & retrieval	Phonological disorder Expressive language disorder

rather than consider subtypes as mutually exclusive categories representing groups of children with clear cut syndromes. As pointed out by Korkman & Hakkinen-Rihu (1994), children with language disorders often show symptoms across these dimensions, and individual children may show any combination of these language disorder dimensions.

The DSM-IV (APA, 1994) classification "communication disorders" includes three diagnostic categories identified in Table 4.1. Two other DMS-IV disorders are not included within most current research classifications or in clinical research on neuropsychological and psychiatric aspects of language disorders. One of these is stuttering, which is a disorder in speech fluency and timing. A similar stuttering category is included in ICD-10 (WHO, 1992). Approximately 60% to 80% of children who stutter recover before 16 years of age. This disorder is not discussed further in this chapter since it often spontaneously disappears and, when it is treated, treatment is usually by a speech specialist. When psychological problems do arise

secondary to stuttering, these should be treated according to the emotional manifestation (e.g., anxiety), rather than by any unique procedures. The other disorders in DSM-IV (1994) and ICD-10 (1992) not covered in this chapter are "communication disorder-not otherwise specified" (DMS-IV) and "developmental disorder of speech and language unspecified" (ICD-10). These diagnoses include communication disorders that do not meet criteria for any of the other communication disorders. The remaining three DSM-IV communication disorder diagnoses—"expressive language disorder," "mixed receptive–expressive language disorder," and "phonological disorder" (DSM-IV, 1994)—do have some relationship to established subtypes of language disorders identified in the literature.

Expressive Language Disorder

The DSM-IV diagnostic criteria for "expressive language disorder" overlaps with several previously identified "developmental language disorder" subtypes, as does the ICD-10 category "expressive language disorder." This disorder is characterized by impoverished speech and vocabulary, word finding problems, and simplified sentences. Associated features include the other types of language disorders, learning disorders, motor-coordination problems, and sometimes attention deficits. This chapter focuses primarily on the developmental type, which is reported to occur in approximately 5% of the population. As can be seen in Table 4.1, the diagnostic category "expressive language disorder" overlaps with several research-based language disorder subtypes, including the expressive type of Wilson and Risucci (1986), the specific verbal subtype of Korkman and Hakkinen-Rihu (1994), and the nonspecific formulation repetition disorder of Aram and Nation (1975), and it may also include symptoms of the disnomia and auditory memory subtypes.

Mixed Receptive-Expressive Disorder

The "mixed receptive-expressive disorder" of DSM-IV (1994) replaces the "global language disorder" of DSM-III-R. This diagnostic disorder includes the symptoms of the previously discussed expressive language disorder, along with impairment in receptive language development. Symptoms of receptive difficulty include difficulty comprehending words and sentences. The "receptive language disorder" category of ICD-10 is similar in most characteristics. One difference is that the ICD-10 preserves the pure receptive language disorder, while the DSM-IV combines the receptive and expressive types. This appears to be due to the fact that a pure receptive language disorder is rarely seen without some accompanying expressive problems. Generally, it is accepted that development of expressive language in children necessarily depends on the acquisition of receptive skills. However, Rapin and Allen (1983) indicate that some children with receptive language deficits develop well-formed, fluent expressive language, even though their expression may not always be relevant to the conversation due to their receptive deficit. They classify this language subtype as a semantic-pragmatic disorder. Wilson and Risucci (1986) identified a group of children with receptive deficits but without expressive deficits, although they subsequently collapsed several subgroups, including this one, into a more generic receptive-comprehension subtype. Korkman and Hakkinen-Rihu (1994) also identified a group of children with receptive deficits who demonstrated no fluency or naming deficits; this group was subsequently merged into a larger group labeled specific comprehension subtype. Given these findings, the clinician should be aware that there does appear to be a group of children with receptive language disorder who may, at least superficially, show normal expressive language, although they usually experience significant problems in the practical use of language. Rapin and Allen have described this group of children as showing "cocktail party" conversation, and these authors suggest that many of these children become hyperverbal and hyperlexic.

The most severe cases of receptive-expressive language disorder have been identified in the literature as having "global," "generalized," "comprehension," or "associative" language disorder. Children with this disorder may at times appear to be deaf or inattentive; they may have difficulty following verbal directions and show deficits in memory and sequencing verbal information. This disorder has a poor prognosis due to the generalized problems in language. This disorder almost invariably results in a significant learning disorder.

In summary, the mixed receptive-expressive language disorder is sometimes mild and may include children with associative language problems resulting in receptive language difficulty despite relatively normal expression due to intact rote memory and fluency. However, more often, this is a more severe disorder, with generalized language impairment requiring extensive language therapy, specialized learning assistance, and treatment of associated behavioral problems.

Phonological Disorder

The DSM-IV diagnosis of "phonological disorder" includes the previous DSM-III-R diagnosis of "developmental articulation disorder," along with other phonological problems. The primary symptoms of this disorder are developmental delays in use of speech sounds such as articulation errors and sound substitutions and omissions. This disorder has some features of Korkman and Hakkinen-Rihu's specific verbal dyspraxia disorder, Rapin and Allen's phonological production problem subtype, and Aram and Nation's formulation-repetition deficit subtype. This group of children often does not show other language or comprehension deficits, although children with global language disorders often show symptoms of the phonological disorder as well. Children with phonological disorder may also have symptoms that overlap with symptoms of children showing expressive language disorder. Many authors subsume phonological deficits within their expressive language disorder subtypes. The course of this disorder is variable, and some forms are thought to have a familial pattern. One interesting variant of the phonological disorder occurs when the speech production problem is accompanied by fine-motor incoordination in drawing or handwriting. This combination of symptoms has been associated with learning disorders and has been labeled "articulatory-graphomotor coordination disorder" (Mattis, French, & Rapin, 1975). The ICD-10 classification "specific speech articulation disorder" incorporates the DSM-IV classification "phonological disorder." However, this ICD-10 classification is broader and includes articulation disorders, which is subsumed under the "phonological disorder" classification of DSM-IV, and also dyslalia, which refers to any defective speech. The ICD-10 classification "other developmental disorders of speech and language" includes lisping or the misarticulation of sibilants, whereas lisping is included in the "phonological disorder" category of DSM-IV.

Other Diagnostic Considerations: Disnomia and Auditory Memory Deficits

One important type of language disorder not specifically addressed in the DSM-IV includes a disorder with deficits in word retrieval, object naming, and auditory memory, often referred to as Disnomia. Disnomia often occurs along with global language disorder and would then fall into the DSM-IV "receptive-expressive language disorder" diagnosis. However, as Korkman and Hakkinen-Rihu (1994) point out, specific disnomia may occur without more pervasive comprehension problems. This disorder is identified in Korkman and Hakkinen-Rihu's specific disnomia subtype, Wilson and Risucci's auditory memory and retrieval subtype, Aram and Nation's nonspecific formulation-repetition deficit type, and possibly Rapin and Allen's lexical-syntactic deficit syndrome. This group of children may show only mild symptoms during preschool years, but they may show unexplained dyslexia later (Korkman and Hakkinen-Rihu, 1994). Since the symptoms of disnomia (e.g., word retrieval, object naming, and auditory memory) often result in verbal expression problems, such as word omissions, decreased verbal flexibility, and diminished vocabulary, the DSM-IV diagnosis of "expressive language disorder" seems appropriate for these symptoms.

Some of the disagreement regarding the number and dimensions of language disorder subtypes is likely due to different clinical samples that vary on severity, age and socioeconomic status. Other reasons for inconsistent findings include the variety of language tests and the use of different theoretical models, (linguistic, psycholinguistic, neuropsychological), as well as varying methods of subtype derivation (clinical-inferential, diagnostic classification, and multifactoral-statistical). Wilson and Risucci (1986) provide a model for integrating various techniques and validating identified subtypes. They identified commonalties of subtypes derived from both clinical and statistical procedures with the same children. They also validated their groups according

to variables not used in the original classification and across ages. One unique difference of the Wilson and Risucci classification
is the recognition of an auditory memory
and retrieval deficit group not identified as
such by other classification systems. However,
Korkman and Hakkinen-Rihu (1994) identify a
problem with name retrieval in the disnomic
grouping, and Aram and Nation identify a
repetition deficit. For children with auditory
memory deficits that result in reduced verbal output, the DSM-IV diagnosis "expressive language disorder" appears to be the
best choice.

Epidemiology, Etiology, and Related Conditions

The reported prevalence of language disorders
(including all subtypes of speech and language
disorders) is quite variable, depending on definitions, selected symptoms, and populations
studied. Cantwell and Baker (1991) provide an
extensive listing of prevalence reports, which
provide estimates of occurrence from approximately 1% to 33% for speech and language
disorders, with an upward range of 17% for language disorders only. These authors point out
many reasons, including those stated earlier, for
the variance in these estimates. The frequency
of children with speech and language disorders
severe enough to warrant remedial intervention
is estimated to be between 5% and 10% in
preschool children (Aram & Hall, 1989). It is
estimated that approximately 50% to 80% of
these children continue to show language difficulties into adolescence and early adulthood
(Aram & Hall, 1989; Hall & Tomblin, 1978).
Generally, isolated phonological disorders have
the most favorable prognosis, with more general
language disorder (receptive-expressive type)
having the poorest outcome. Aram and Hall
(1989) report that academic difficulty is the
most frequently reported associated problem
(50–75%) for children with language disorders.
Other problems frequently associated with language disorders are social competence difficulty

(>50%) and behavior problems (70%) identified in a 10-year follow-up study with the Child
Behavior Checklist (Aram, Ekelman, & Nation,
1984).

The etiology of language disorders is varied. Developmental language disorders are
often considered to be genetic, with models of transmission similar to developmental
learning disorders (Ludlow & Cooper, 1983).
Language disorders may also be associated
with conditions such as brain injury, cleft
palate, cerebral palsy, stroke, and CNS infections. The diagnosis and treatment of these
language disorders associated with other conditions should utilize the same procedures
as those used with developmental language
disorders. The models for neurological and
biological aspects of developmental language
disorders are similar to those for developmental
dyslexia, which are reviewed extensively elsewhere (Galaburda, 1993; Pennington, 1991).
There is increasing evidence that some language disorders are related to atypical cerebral
organization (Segalowitz, 1983), which appears
to be related to familial genetic circumstances
for both dyslexia and developmental language
disorders (Pennington, 1991). For a review
of atypical cerebral lateralization of language
functions in developmental and organic cases,
see Geschwind and Galaburda (1987). Given
the current state of knowledge and research
in this area, neurological and genetic studies are not indicated for an individual clinical case of language disorder, unless there
are other genetic or neurological indications
such as associated dysmorphology or question
of seizural states. There are indications that
language disorders occur more frequently in
lower socioeconomic groups (Ludlow, 1980).
Early educational and language intervention
programs such as Head Start have attempted
to modify this situation, with variable success.
There are likely environmental conditions, such
as impoverished language interaction, that may
delay activation of critical brain maturation
and affect language emergence (Locke, 1992).
Although there are psychiatric conditions that
may show secondary language disorders (e.g.,
schizophrenia, autism), this chapter focuses on

neuropsychological models of primary childhood language disorders, as well as the secondary learning, behavioral, and emotional disorders.

The basis for learning disorders in many children with language disorders is somewhat evident, since reading and many academic functions are highly verbal (Segalowitz, 1983; Vellutino, 1979); however, the relationship between language disorders and behavioral or emotional disorders is somewhat less self-evident. There appear to be multiple paths to the development of behavior or emotional disorders in children with language disorders. Children with speech and language disorders have been shown to be at increased risk for behavioral and emotional problems (Cantwell & Baker, 1991; Piacentini, 1987). Cantwell and Baker (1991) found that approximately half of 600 children with speech and language disorders showed an Axis I clinical psychiatric disorder. Several other studies also identified more than 50% of children with language disorders as having behavioral disturbance (Stevenson & Richman, 1978) or psychopathology (Beitchman, Peterson, & Clegg, 1988). Furthermore, children with psychiatric disturbance have been shown to have a high incidence of speech and language disorders (Cantwell & Baker, 1991). The more severe psychiatric disorders of childhood (autism, pervasive developmental disorder, childhood schizophrenia, and psychosis) show the greatest frequency of language disorders, according to Cantwell & Baker (1991). Some less severe psychiatric disorders associated with language disorders are attention-deficit/hyperactivity disorder (ADHD) and conduct disorder.

Externalizing behavior disorders (e.g., ADHD, conduct disorders) have been shown to be associated with language disorders (Barkley, 1990; Beitchman, Peterson, & Clegg, 1985; Campbell, 1990; Cantwell & Baker, 1991; Landau & Milich, 1988). One model that may explain the relationship between externalizing behavior disorders and language disorders may be the hypothesis of a verbal mediation deficit underlying a deficiency in the self-control and maintenance of attention and behavior. This model, which has components put forth by Luria and Meichenbaum, suggests that there may be a fundamental requirement of a minimum level of verbal associative reasoning necessary to produce verbally mediated guidance in self-control mechanisms. A verbal mediation deficit has been associated with ADHD and conduct disorder (Barkley, 1990; Camp, 1997; Campbell, 1990; Hogan & Quay, 1984; Richman & Lindgren, 1981). Furthermore, different levels of associative language skills in language disordered children have been shown to be related to different externalizing and internalizing behavioral characteristics (Richman & Lindgren, 1981).

Review of Theoretical Models

At the current time, research efforts are attempting to refine the classifications of developmental language disorders and to derive models of neurocognitive specialization for specific language functions. The previously identified classification models (Aram & Nation, 1975; DSM-IV, 1994; ICD-10, 1992; Korkman & Hakkinen-Rihu, 1994; Rapin & Allen, 1988; Wilson & Risucci, 1986) all distinguish or clump various language disorder symptoms into categories such as expressive; repetitive or memory; or receptive, including comprehension or association and phonological, or into a category referred to as global, mixed or general. These subtyping models have been variously developed through a priori classification rules, clinical judgment, and statistical subtyping techniques. Furthermore, these subtype classifications are based on results of many different tests, with few classifications being subjected to external validation. For review of some of these important problems in classification and examples of empirical research classification, see Korkman and Hakkinen-Rihu (1994) and van Santen, Black, Wilson, and Risucci (1994).

The neural underpinnings of speech and language are just beginning to be better understood within a developmental model. For example, it is becoming increasingly clear that infants show early listening preferences to expressive voices (Fernald, 1991) and that the well-known left-hemisphere specialization for speech and language functions may also be supplemented by right-hemisphere involvement for social aspects of communication (Van Lancker et al., 1988). Some of these functional language systems have been demonstrated at very early ages, even at birth (Segalowitz, 1983) suggesting a basic biological substrate for language functions, which may subsequently be affected by trauma, maldevelopment, and/or environmental factors. Neural basis for the development of language is becoming increasingly complex, as the models must take into account complex brain functions, developmental variations, and learning paradigms. For a review of theorizing regarding current trends in neurobiological research on language, see Locke (1992).

Extensive research is still needed in order to validate neural theories, clarify objective classification procedures for subgrouping children with language disorders, determine the best instruments for assessment, and evaluate outcome of treatment recommendations. Nevertheless, the clinician must evaluate and treat children with language disorders on the basis of current knowledge and the clinical studies available. This chapter provides an assessment and treatment classification scheme based on classification models previously presented (Aram & Nation, 1975; DSM-IV, 1994; ICD-10, 1992; Korkman & Hakkinen-Rihu, 1994; Rabin & Allen, 1983; Wilson & Risucci, 1986). An outline of the classification model used in this chapter is presented first. This outline is based on a generic generalization from the classification systems reviewed earlier, as well as previous clinical research and experience (Richman, 1978, 1979, 1980, 1983; Richman & Eliason, 1992; Richman & Kitchell, 1981; Richman & Lindgren, 1980).

Outline for Language Disorder Classifications:

1. Expressive Language Disorder
   This is a disorder in producing vocal language, sometimes accompanied by articulation or phonological errors. Symptoms of this deficit include difficulty in naming objects or pictures (Denkla & Rudel, 1976; Wiig & Becker-Caplan, 1984), and in word fluency (Korkman and Hakkinen-Rihu, 1994). It may be difficult at times to distinguish this dimension from memory deficits, since difficulty in retrieval of words may occur in both (Wilson & Risucci, 1986).

2. Memory-Verbal Language Disorder
   This disorder may include difficulty in memory for isolated information (numbers, words), meaningful information (sentences, stories), or verbally mediated memory even when stimulus and response are nonverbal (Blank, 1968; Lindgren & Richman, 1980; Wood & Richman, 1988). This deficit may be evident in serial-order memory deficit rather than memory-span deficit per se (Bakker, 1972; Corkin, 1974; Wood, Richman, & Eliason, 1989).

3. Receptive Language Disorder
   This disorder may occur in somewhat isolated form in two subdimensions, Associative Language Deficit and Phonological Deficit. This disorder may also include deficits in all aspects of language, resulting in a global or general language deficit.

   a. Associative Language Disorder
      This is a disorder in verbal concept formation and language associations. It is a problem in categorization of objects, word associations and analogies, and semantic comprehension (Aram & Nation, 1975; Lindgren, Richman, & Eliason, 1986; Richman & Lindgren, 1980; Vellutino, 1979; Wilson & Risucci, 1986; Wood & Richman, 1988). Although this disorder may often be associated with a pervasive global language disorder, it does occur at times with adequate memory and superficially adequate expressive skills; it is then referred to as hyperverbal or hyperlexic syndromes

(Rapin & Allen, 1983; Richman & Kitchell, 1981).

b. Phonological Language Disorder
This disorder interferes with the ability to discriminate among sounds, synthesize phonetic units into words, or produce blends (Bradley & Bryant, 1985; Shankweiler & Liberman, 1976; Tallal & Piercy, 1973). Although the most common form of this disorder is articulation disorder, a more severe form is a disability in phonetic processing and awareness, which may or may not be accompanied by articulation deficit.

4. General Language Disorder
This global or pervasive language disorder may include all or any combination of the disorders listed in items 1–3. Almost all authors identify some form of this disorder which always has some components of both receptive and expressive language deficiency.

ASSESSMENT

The outline for language classifications is repeated throughout this chapter for consistency in the presentation of assessment (tests and clinical interpretation) and treatment. The reader may find it helpful to read a specific language disorder subtype in the sections on tests and on clinical interpretation of tests in the assessment section and then turn to the same language disorder subtype in the treatment section for consistency of assessment and treatment for each subtype. Also, the language disorder classifications presented here are not mutually exclusive, and there is considerable overlap in certain symptoms. Thus, the tests administered may reveal different characteristics for different language disorder subtypes, and the same test may be used for different purposes, depending on the language characteristic being considered. Due to this, the assessment procedures are outlined according to dimensions of language disorders, since these

dimensions may be useful in identifying patterns of several different language classification categories.

Assessment of children with language disorders is quite challenging because of the difficulty in accurately assessing levels of intellectual, cognitive, and achievement functions. This problem is partly related to the use of verbal and nonverbal assessment, which may produce different estimates of a child's ability. There is also difficulty interpreting behavioral and emotional content due to language symptoms that may interfere with self-report and affect judgments of parents and teachers. There are further difficulties in assessment decisions since it is sometimes difficult to judge whether language symptoms are indicative of neurological disorder (e.g., receptive language deficit vs. altered state of consciousness) or physiological arousal defect (e.g., auditory memory deficit vs. focused-attention deficit). It is extremely important to use tests that vary components of language (expressive, receptive, associative, memory), while also varying stimulus presentation (visual vs. verbal) and response mode (verbal vs. pointing).

Another problem in assessment of children with language disorders is test score interpretation. Although it is readily apparent that a child with an expressive language disorder may perform poorly on tasks requiring extensive verbal responding, it is sometimes less apparent that a child with a language disorder might also perform poorly on a visual-perceptual task due to that language disorder. Some children with memory deficits or associative language disorders may not remember or comprehend verbal instructions even on nonverbal tasks, including nonverbal intelligence-test items. Therefore, it is important to note this possibility and to use some nonverbal tasks that do not require verbal instructions. Examples of such tasks are intellectual tests designed for hearing-impaired children (Hiskey, 1966; Leiter, 1969).

Although verbal and nonverbal intellectual assessment with standard intelligence tests is usually part of any assessment battery, considerable caution should be used in interpreting verbal IQ scores for children with language disorders. Children with even mild forms of language disorder, such as mild expressive or memory deficit, often show significant subtest variability, with low scores on Information, Digit Span, or Vocabulary. Often the first sign of a language disorder is a low Verbal and a high Performance WISC profile (Richman, 1978, 1983; Richman & Lindgren, 1980). Specific symptoms and hypotheses related to this profile for language-disordered children are presented elsewhere (Richman, 1980, 1983; Richman & Eliason, 1992). The verbal IQ should often be considered invalid as an index of verbal reasoning skills for children with language disorders. The subtest profile of intelligence tests may be suggestive of certain language disorder subtypes (Richman & Lindgren, 1980), however, further neuropsychological assessment is needed in order to confirm such hypotheses. Although some authors recommend use of both verbal and nonverbal IQ scores for children with language disorders (Myklebust, 1971), it is recommended that the Full scale IQ not be used if there is a significant discrepancy between the two (Eisenson, 1972). Many authors recommend using only the nonverbal IQ for children with language disorders. However, it has been shown that even if nonverbal IQ were used as an index of intelligence, approximately 50% of children in special classes for the language impaired would be eliminated due to low IQ (Ludlow, 1980).

As recommended by Korkman and Hakkinen-Rihu (1994), it is probably best to consider previous attempts at subtyping groups of children with language disorders not so much as pure diagnostic groups but rather as dimensions of language characteristics or deficits that should be assessed. The dimensions of language deficits that have been identified on the basis of many attempts at subtyping language disorders include expressive (fluency, word finding), memory (store, retrieval), and receptive (associative, phonological awareness) elements. These dimensions are selected for assessment on the basis of previous research findings and are defined in the following sections.

Tests

There are few comprehensive neuropsychological assessment batteries designed specifically for children with language disorders. Some early tests that have subtests useful for language assessment include the Illinois Test of Psycholinguistic Abilities (McCarthy & Kirk, 1961), Neurosensory Center Comprehensive Examination for Aphasia (Crockett, 1974; Spreen & Benton, 1969), the Reynell Development Language Scale (Reynell, 1969), the Hiskey Nebraska Test of Learning Aptitude (Hiskey, 1966), Detroit Tests of Learning Aptitude (Hammill, 1985), and N EuroPSYological Investigation for Children (Korkman and Hakkinen-Rihu, 1994). Since there is no widely agreed-upon comprehensive battery, it is often recommended that clinicians avoid one general battery and utilize a variety of tests of language, including subtests from various batteries. An advantage of using a variety of tests rather than one comprehensive battery is that this allows the examiner to test hypotheses based on a child's symptoms and responses (Wilson & Risucci, 1986).

Tests should be categorized into neuropsychological dimensions, and several tests of the same dimension should be given. It is also important to use several tests of the same neuropsychological dimension that vary stimulus presentation (vocal-visual) and response requirements (vocal-pointing) in order to determine if the results are affected by input or output modes or by cross-modal transfer. There are numerous tests of each language dimension, and the choice of the specific test may not be critical as long as each dimension is adequately measured (Wilson & Risucci, 1986).

Some of the tests that have been shown to be useful in clinical and research reports are listed here.

1. Expressive Language
   Word Fluency (Neurosensory Center Examination for Aphasia—NCCEA; Spreen & Benton, 1969)—requires saying as many words as possible in one minute

that begin with a specific letter of the alphabet.

Boston Naming Test (Kaplan, Good-glass, & Weintraub, 1978)—requires naming of common pictures.

Visual Naming (NCCEA)—requires naming of a pictured object and naming specific parts.

2. Memory-Verbal

Digit Span (WISC-R)—memory for serial numbers.

Sentence Repetition (NCCEA)—memory for increasingly longer and more complex sentences.

Rey Auditory Verbal Learning Test (Lezak, 1983)—memory for 15 words over five trials.

Color Span Test (Richman & Lindgren, 1984)—memory for colors on four trials (visual presentation-pointing response; visual presentation-verbal response, verbal presentation-pointing response; verbal presentation-verbal response).

3. Receptive Language

a. Associative Language

Token Test (Multilingual Aphasia Examination MAE; Benton & Hamsher, 1978)—requires movement of colored shapes (circles, squares, large, small) according to verbal instructions.

Peabody Picture Vocabulary Test—requires pointing to one of four pictures based on word presented.

Association—Verbal

Similarities (WISC-R)—requires telling how the objects or ideas are alike.

Auditory Association (Illinois Test of Psycholinguistic Ability [ITPA]; McCarthy & Kirk, 1961)—requires the last word of a spoken incomplete analogy.

Associative—Visual

Picture Association (Hiskey-Nebraska Test of Learning Aptitude; Hiskey, 1966).

Picture Analogies (Hiskey-Nebraska Test of Learning Aptitude; Hiskey, 1966)—requires pointing to one of four pictures associated with two stimulus pictures.

Associative Picture Test (Richman, 1988)—requires pointing to one of three pictures associated with two stimulus pictures.

b. Receptive—Phonological

Sound Blending (ITPA)—requires the blending of individual phonemes presented separately into a word.

Auditory Discrimination (ITPA)—requires identifying whether two sounds are the same or different.

Clinical Interpretation of Language Test Results

Expressive Language Disorder

Children may show no language deficits on any tests other than Word Fluency, although some also show deficits on naming tests (Boston Naming, Visual Naming). Since there are few tests of purely expressive language functions, the clinician should look for other clinical signs of this disorder. Children with this disorder may show mild hesitancies in responding, which might suggest a word-finding problem. Some children with expressive problems are mute or say "I don't know" quickly during test questions. Other children may also have telegraphic speech, which is characterized by omissions of articles, prepositions, and connectives while maintaining the overall meaning. Children with word-finding or naming-problems may also show circumlocutions in speech, which is a roundabout way of speaking due to inability to produce a specific word. Often these children also have low scores on vocabulary tests. If children perform poorly on memory or associative language tests when a verbal response is required but perform better on these tests when only a pointing response is required, this may be due to an expressive language deficit, rather than a memory or associative language deficit per se.

Memory-Verbal Language Disorder

The most typical problem for memory-impaired children is a short-term automatic memory deficit for isolated information. The pattern of memory test results may alert the examiner to this type of difficulty. These children may have difficulty on Digit Span, although some children with good associative language skills are capable of using number associations (e.g., relative serial placements or groupings) and may not appear to have a memory deficit if this is the only memory test given. These children often perform better on memory for sentences, since they may use semantic associations. It is less likely that they will perform adequately on tests of memory for isolated words or colors, since these may have fewer associative relationships. These children usually perform below average on tests of verbal learning (e.g., Rey AVLT). The Color Span Test was developed in order to evaluate memory for isolated information in language-disordered children by varying stimulus and response possibilities (Richman & Lindgren, 1984). This test presents common colors visually or verbally and requires either a pointing or verbal response.

Children with auditory memory deficits often show expressive as well as memory deficits. These children are especially at risk for academic difficulties in early grades. Forgetting letters, numbers, words, math facts, and spelling are common symptoms. It is sometimes difficult to ascertain if a child has an auditory memory problem or an attention-deficit disorder, since children with either problem seem not to listen. If children appear to be inattentive only on memory tests, this may signify the avoidance of performance due to frustration with a memory deficit. Children with isolated memory deficits usually show more variability on memory tests, since they use their associative language strengths on memory for sentences and on later trials in verbal learning tests. Children with attention-deficit disorders are more likely to show variable attention throughout all other tests, unlike the child with a memory-verbal language disorder.

Receptive-Associative Language Disorder

Children with associative language deficits show deficits on all associative language tests whether the test is presented visually or verbally and whether the child responds by pointing or verbally. Some children with associative language disorder have intact short-term automatic memory skills and constitute an unusual symptomatic pattern. These children perform poorly on all associative language tests, but they may perform well on naming and memory tests. They may even learn to read words automatically without understanding what they read, a condition referred to as hyperlexia. Some of these children are also hyperverbal, although their expressive language may be pragmatically dysfunctional. A few children with these symptoms also show autistic features; in some cases, they show signs of thought disorder or schizophrenia.

Children who perform poorly on verbally presented and verbal-response associative language tests but perform better on tests that assess associative language functions through pictures and pointing responses probably do not have a primary associative language deficit. Children who perform poorly on Similarities and Auditory Association but achieve higher scores on Picture Association, for example, may have difficulty in verbal labeling or retrieval and, hence, may have expressive language disorder or memory-verbal language disorder, rather than associative language disorder.

Many children with associative language deficits perform poorly on almost all other language tests as well. These children usually also show low scores on all verbal IQ subtests. Thus, many of these children are more appropriately considered within the classifications of global, receptive-expressive, or general language disorder. Since this is a more severe disorder with poor prognosis, the examiner should be careful to spot any symptoms or test patterns that contradict this diagnosis.

Children with associative language deficits often show significant externalizing behavior disorders with oppositional, conduct, and attention disorders. These behavioral symptoms should alert the examiner to the fact that these children may have verbal mediation deficits that impair their ability to exert self-control or to self-monitor behavior.

Receptive-Phonological Disorder

Children with phonemic awareness deficits range from those with mild articulation errors and no other deficits to those with a severe fundamental deficit in the cognitive awareness of speech-sound association or meaning. At the milder levels, these children perform well on almost all language-neuropsychological tests. However, some of these children show deficits in almost all aspects of language due to their severe deficit, which interferes with language development and learning. One important clinical feature of even milder forms of this disorder is the potential for later reading disability or dyslexia. The phonetic coding problem in speech perception or production may present difficulty for the child in learning the early letter-sound associations, phonemic blends, segmentation, and synthesis important to the reading process.

Children with articulation or other vocal production difficulties (e.g., dyspraxia, dysarthria) should be assessed for other possible associated motor-coordination deficits. There is a group of children identified in the literature with motor speech and graphomotor problems in drawing and handwriting, referred to as having articulatory-graphomotor coordination disorder (Mattis, French, & Rapin, 1975). These children are often not appropriately diagnosed, since it is assumed they have only a developmental speech disorder. However, some of these children subsequently show later handwriting and reading disorders. The alert clinician should screen children with

phonological disorder for fine motor coordination difficulties to determine if early remedial educational interventions should occur.

General Language Disorder

The general, global, or mixed receptive-expressive disorder includes deficits in most or all language functions. The primary evaluation issue for this type of language disorder is to demonstrate adequate ability in nonverbal skills to differentiate this disorder from Mental Retardation and Pervasive Developmental Disorder. It is important to be aware that some of these children perform poorly even on the Performance Scale of the WISC-III due to their receptive disorder, which interferes with understanding directions, and/or their comprehensive disorder, which may interfere with self-guiding of even nonverbal responses. Use of tests designed for severe communication problems or hearing impairment such as the Hiskey-Nebraska or Leiter may be helpful in demonstrating adequate nonverbal intellectual skills.

Children with severe general language disorder often have significant behavioral and emotional deficits. Due to their significant difficulty in learning and understanding how to interact with others, they may have extreme social isolation or social interaction deficits. It is important for the clinician to have these children demonstrate their ability to perform nonverbally and to determine if nonverbal behavioral instructions and conditioning are beneficial in guiding or altering their behavior.

Educational Assessment of Children with Language Disorders

Although there are not specific educational tests designed for children with language disorder, there are specific educational test patterns that may assist the clinician. Children with expressive language disorders may show reading and comprehension deficits on oral reading tests. Their expressive deficit may interfere with fluent reading and slow down reading rate. Their focus on the expressive component in oral reading may distract their attention from meaning, resulting in an apparent reading comprehension deficit. Silent-reading tests are sometimes useful in assessing reading comprehension for these children. Children with memory-verbal language disorders often do not remember sight words, especially in isolation. They often perform better during reading of passages, since they are then able to use the context to aid memory. Reading comprehension tests usually rely on rote memory. Therefore, it is better to assess reading comprehension for children with memory deficits by having them answer inferential rather than isolated factual questions. Children with receptive-associative language disorder, who have good rote memory skills, may appear to read adequately in early grades due to adequate word recognition. However, it is important to determine if they know the meaning of words they read and to assess story comprehension, which is often weak. Children with phonological disorder may not be able to blend sounds. It should be determined whether they can synthesize individual sounds into words and whether they can break words down into their phonetic components. Children with general language disorder often do not show any meaningful reading patterns.

Math skills are often impaired for children with memory-verbal language disorder since these children have difficulty memorizing math facts. It is important to determine whether these children can figure out the process of how to calculate a math problem rather than test isolated memory for math facts, which is often impaired for them. On the other hand, children with good memory and poor association, like those with receptive-associative language disorder, may appear to have adequate math skills on tests of math memory. However, these children should also be assessed by having them translate word problems into math calculations, since ability in this area is often deficient. Math ability may be an isolated strength for children with general language disorder. It is important to note that assessment of math skills for this group of children should be primarily nonverbal, such as with the Arithmetic subtest of the WRAT-3.

Spelling and written language skills are usually impaired for most subtypes of language-disordered children. It is important to differentiate those children who can tell a story yet may not be able to write a story from those who can do neither adequately. It is also useful to analyze spelling errors to determine phonetic versus orthographic tendencies.

Behavioral/Emotional Assessment of Children with Language Disorders

The high incidence of psychological and psychiatric problems in children with language disorders is well established (Aram & Hall, 1989; Beitchman, 1985; Cantwell & Baker, 1991). In most cases, it is assumed that the language disorder and the psychological disorder have a common etiology, such as neurodevelopmental delay (Beitchman, 1985) or cognitive processing deficit (Cantwell & Baker, 1991). It has also been found that socioeconomic status and marital status were not related to the association of language disorders and psychiatry disorders in children (Beitchman, Peterson, & Clegg, 1988). However, the results of this study suggest that mothers' educational status may have a relationship to the child's clinical status, although whether this is a social or genetic effect is not clear.

Given the current research findings, there does not appear to be a reason to deviate from standard behavioral or emotional measures in assessment of a child with a language disorder, unless there are specific language requirements of the test itself (verbal or written self-report, reading comprehension) that might interfere. Younger children may have problems with the association or expression needed for projective tests. Young children with language disorders might be assessed via nonverbal personality self-report, such as preferred picture sorting on the Missouri Children's Picture Series (Sines et al., 1971). For adolescents, the MMPI-A may need to be administered via tape recording to avoid language-based reading problems.

Some behavioral ratings and diagnostic tests that have been used successfully with children and adolescents with language impairment include Child Behavior Checklist, Connor's Teacher Rating Scales (Aram, Ekelman, & Nation, 1984; Beitchman, Peterson, & Clegg, 1988), Rutter Parent and Teacher rating scale (Cantwell & Baker, 1985), Piers Harris Self-Concept Scale (Kapp, 1979), MMPI (Richman, 1983), and the Behavior Problem Checklist (Richman & Lindgren, 1981). Specific types of behavioral or emotional disorders have not been consistently identified in children with language disorders. Baker and Cantwell (1991) found externalizing behaviors (conduct, attention, oppositional) as well as internalizing behaviors (anxiety, phobia, depression). Beitchman et al. (1988) found multiple psychological disorders (avoidance, adjustment, attention) in language-disordered groups.

The clinician should be cautious in assuming that behavioral or emotional disorders are necessarily directly related to language disorders in children. Although studies show a high frequency of psychological problems in children with language disorders and a high occurrence of language disorders in children with psychiatric disturbance, causal factors have not been well established. It should always be remembered that many children with language disorders do not show psychological problems. An interesting aspect of clinical recognition of coexisting symptoms is cited by Prizant et al. (1990) and Gualtieri et al. (1983), who observe that speech and language pathologists may be more aware of psychiatric disorders in their clients than psychologists or psychiatrists are aware of language disorders in their clients.

TREATMENT

Medication Considerations

Although language disorders have been associated with other disorders that may require medication (e.g., ADHD or depression), factors independent of the child's language disorder subtype play an important part in determining whether medication is warranted. These factors include intellectual abilities, behavior and personality variables, and the environmental influence of home and school. It is the interaction of these factors with those unique aspects of the child's language disorder that may determine whether medication is warranted and what type of medication might be most appropriate.

Expressive Language Disorder

Children with primary expressive language disorder usually possess adequate associative language and memory functions. Therefore, they may have the capacity to effectively utilize verbal mediation as a means of controlling their own behavior and emotional reactions. Although these children may often exhibit halting speech, word-finding difficulties, and telegraphic speech patterns that influence the communication of their ideas, mild to moderate deficits of this nature usually do not generate emotional and behavioral reactions sufficient to warrant medication management. However, specific psychological predispositions or temperament (e.g., low frustration tolerance, oversensitivity, low self-esteem) may place a child with expressive deficits at risk for more severe problems that benefit from counseling and, in extreme cases, may warrant adjunct medication. Children with only expressive language disorders are rarely overactive and are more likely to show internalizing behavioral characteristics than externalizing characteristics. Thus, if a child with an expressive language disorder shows signs of inattention, this may be related more to excessive withdrawal and possible depressive characteristics, suggesting consideration of antidepressants rather than psychostimulants.

Memory-Verbal Language Disorder

Children with a primary memory language disorder usually possess adequate associative language skills, which may assist their capacity to verbally mediate their behavioral and emotional responses to perceived negative events. However, memory weaknesses may significantly hinder school learning, indirectly affect self-esteem/self-confidence, or influence how others perceive the child (e.g., inattentive, lazy, unmotivated). Therefore, children with this disorder are at a considerably high risk for adjustment difficulties, particularly when memory deficits are present with other predisposing psychological factors.

Since these children are often described as frequently off task and distractible and as having difficulty following directions, they may be viewed by teachers (or parents) as children with possible ADHD. Although they do not typically exhibit significantly high levels of impulsivity or hyperactivity, their significant inattention may require a careful diagnostic review in order to determine if a diagnosis of Attention-Deficit/Hyperactivity Disorder (predominantly inattention type) is applicable. Many children with memory language disorder have a coexisting attention-deficit disorder, and medication management with psychostimulants should be considered as a treatment option. Generally, children with verbal memory deficits and attention problems may benefit from low-dosage psychostimulants, such as methylphenidate (e.g., 0.3 mg/kg), but higher dosages are rarely needed.

Receptive Language Disorder

Since children with primary receptive language disorder exhibit deficiencies in verbal associative functions and/or basic phonological processing skills necessary for comprehending their verbal environment, they are at risk for significant behavioral and emotional problems. These problems often arise from their primary communication and comprehension deficits, although psychological problems may be secondary to chronic school failure, social rejection, and low self-esteem/self-confidence. The presence of comorbid factors such as behavior disorders and learning disabilities may further compound the child's sense of failure and hopelessness and limit the likelihood of positive outcomes using traditional psychotherapeutic approaches.

These children quite frequently exhibit significantly high levels of inattention, impulsivity, and hyperactivity and often, as a consequence, receive a diagnosis of Attention-Deficit/Hyperactivity Disorder (usually combined type). Therefore, medication management with psychostimulants may be necessary to address excessive hyperactivity and impulsivity arising from externalized anger and frustration. Also, severe emotional disturbances such as thought disorders or depression are sometimes seen in these children because of internalized emotions or negative perceptions. Those children without anxiety, depression, or other psychological disturbance who have high levels of impulsivity and hyperactivity are most likely to require up to moderate dosages (e.g., 0.5 mg/kg) of psychostimulants. Those children with more interalizing behaviors should receive comprehensive assessment of emotional status prior to consideration of medication management, since antidepressants, antianxiety drugs, or other psychiatric medication management may be indicated.

General Language Disorder

Children with more global language deficits may exhibit a pattern of severe behavioral and emotional disturbance similar to that seen in children with primary receptive language deficits. Deficiencies in verbal logic processing, associative functions, and verbal abstractions may contribute to the delayed development of rule-governed behavior and self-control frequently associated with significant attention deficits and hyperactivity. These children also tend to exhibit significant levels of impulsivity or frequent conduct problems due to limitations in the verbal mediation skills used to consider consequences of behavior. Thus, they are more likely to receive diagnoses of Attention-Deficit/Hyperactivity Disorder (combined type), oppositional defiant disorder, or conduct disorder, and psychostimulant medication may be warranted. However, these children often show dramatic improvement in activity level and behavior when nonverbal behavioral and educational interventions are instituted. Therefore, one should be cautious in recommending medication for these behaviors prior to consideration of alternative nonverbal behavior modifications, such as visual aids and pantomime.

Although it is recognized that emotional and/or behavioral disturbances are largely mediated by personality variables and environmental factors, it may be argued that the pervasive effects of global language deficits lower a threshold that permits these disorders to surface more easily. Medication management such as psychostimulants should occur only with other psychological intervention (e.g., behavioral modification, language therapy). These combined efforts may provide the emotional stability and behavioral guidance needed to survive in a society that places a high premium on effective communication and social interaction skills.

Home and School Considerations

In addition to providing an atmosphere of trust, acceptance, and patience in receiving impaired communication from the child, parents and educators can provide the child with a climate in which language skills may be taught, practiced, and generalized. The following section lists general suggestions and considerations for home and educational settings.

Expressive Language Disorder

Children with expressive difficulties often exhibit weak oral reading fluency, despite good reading comprehension skills. Teachers should assess whether this apparent weakness is due to limited knowledge of phonetic word-attack strategies or primarily a symptom of the language disorder.

Suggestions for children who exhibit isolated expressive deficits include the following:

a. Reading rate and fluency may be enhanced by practicing oral reading on easy passages.

b. Spelling weakness is often present secondary to the reading problem. Therefore, reducing the number of spelling words and allowing additional time on spelling tests may be beneficial.

c. Children with word-finding difficulties may benefit from instruction in mnemonic strategies (e.g., acronyms or cueing key words) that encourages use of their associative strengths to compensate for their individual weakness.

d. Although flash cards and other visual aids are not appropriate for some language-disorder groups, they may be helpful for children with expressive deficits. The use of the visual mode may assist formation of mental associations and, thus, enhance recall.

e. Teachers can model appropriate behavior for classmates of expressively delayed children. Allowing ample time for the child to respond in class discussions or during more directed questioning provides reinforcement for the child to respond. This also demonstrates appropriate social interaction to classmates. Parents should also demonstrate patient acceptance of their child's expressive attempts.

Memory Disorder

Memory-disordered children usually experience more significant learning problems than children with only expressive delays, and teachers play an even greater role in helping these children. Educational weaknesses are frequently exhibited in subject areas that require rapid recall, sequencing, and verbal labeling. Thus, sight vocabulary and spelling skills are often impaired, as are rapid recall of basic math facts (e.g., multiplication tables) and phonetic rules of reading. Since these children usually possess adequate associative language skills, they are often viewed by parents and teachers as bright, although underachieving. This perceived underachievement is often attributed to laziness, inattention, and/or lack of motivation. Without appropriate intervention, secondary behavioral and emotional difficulties are likely to surface, including limited motivation, low self-esteem, and increased frustration. As a consequence, these difficulties often compound existing academic problems.

Educational suggestions for children with primary memory deficits include the following:

a. Utilizing the child's language strength in associative reasoning should be a general guideline for educators. Using rhyming and visual imagery are two methods of aiding memory for isolated, less meaningful information.

b. Direct instruction in use of memory strategies such as "clumping" (i.e., grouping items on the basis of relatively similar features), cumulative verbal rehearsal, and acronyms may be helpful for specific memory demands across academic subject areas.

c. Parents and teachers should provide direct instruction in specific organization skills to help overcome memory deficits. Parents might assist the child in establishing a habit of organizing clothing and school materials (e.g., books, completed homework) during the evening before a school day. Parents might also initially assist the child in organizing his personal space (e.g., bedroom, playroom). Ideally, the assistance should include strategies for maintaining this organization. Teachers could use a similar approach when assisting students in organizing their desks and lockers.

d. Teachers and parents should frequently repeat, paraphrase, or shorten lengthy oral directions in order to enhance recall and understanding. The child's memory may be facilitated by using physical prompts (e.g., tap on shoulder) or verbal cues (e.g., stating child's name), which increase attending behavior.

e. Children with memory weaknesses should be encouraged to use checklists, assignment notebooks, assignment folders, and other advanced organizers to help them recall what is expected and to help them complete their daily classwork and homework.

f. Younger children who initially lack the ability to memorize basic math facts may benefit from access to a number line and, perhaps later, to a multiplication table sheet in order to help them keep pace with classmates when performing computational exercises. For older children with significant memory deficits, access to a calculator may be necessary.

g. Reading instruction should emphasize word-attack (decoding) skills that use phonetic and linguistic strategies, rather than strategies that encourage rote memory, such as the whole-word method. Decoding skills should be practiced through oral reading in a story context, which allows greater use of associative reasoning strengths to enhance memory. Reading comprehension (memory) may be enhanced by teaching the use of advanced organizers and focusing on the main ideas of stories.

h. Instructional techniques that emphasize primarily rote recall of isolated information should be avoided. Activities such as rapid tests of basic math facts and use of flash cards only provide more opportunity for memory-delayed children to fail.

Receptive Language Disorder

As noted earlier, children with receptive language deficits often possess a relative strength in rote memory functions but lack adequate associative reasoning skills. These deficits limit their ability to form verbal abstractions and to process verbal information in an efficient, logical manner. Since much early elementary education is devoted to memorizing isolated information, these children may initially appear successful, and deficits in associative functions may go undetected. When academic demands begin to place greater emphasis on higher-order verbal conceptualizations, usually about third grade, these weaknesses become apparent.

A deficit in phonemic segmentation sometimes represents an isolated receptive processing weakness. Children with this isolated subtype show difficulty decoding words because of deficits in blending sounds and sequencing syllables. These children do not always show associative reasoning deficits but often display reading comprehension difficulty secondary to inefficient decoding. In contrast, a rare subgroup of receptively delayed children demonstrates a highly developed word-calling ability but deficient comprehension, due to limitations in associative reasoning skills (Richman & Kitchell, 1981). Children who exhibit this hyperlexic characteristic are quite variable in their educational and behavioral functioning and are, therefore, difficult to diagnose and treat (Eliason & Richman, 1988; Richman & Lindgren, 1980, 1981).

Suggested educational procedures for children with receptive language deficits include the following:

a. Children with an isolated phonemic segmentation weakness may benefit from reading instruction that focuses on the fundamental aspects of phonemic awareness and synthesis. These children need to identify the individual phonemes of words through methods such as tapping rhythmically to the sounds of words. Phoneme discrimination may need to be taught through the use of headphones and the repetition of same and different sounds. Sound blending may also be improved by both seeing and listening to words simultaneously. Sometimes a child's phonemic awareness deficit is so severe that reading can be taught only by whole-word approaches.

b. Since older children with primary associative weaknesses very often display reading comprehension deficits, remedial instruction should focus directly on techniques of summarization that rely on both word and meaning cues; techniques of inferential comprehension (understanding beyond what is literally stated in text); and comprehension monitoring skills designed to check ongoing understanding.

c. Children with associative language deficits usually show extensive learning problems in many subject areas. Early diagnosis and remediation of their basic deficit through language therapy is very important. More extensive information on language therapy approaches can be found in Wiig and Semel (1976, 1980) and Eisenson (1972).

d. Hyperlexic children should be discouraged from reading in a "parrotlike" fashion, and they should be discouraged from memorizing dictionaries and encyclopedias, as they often do. They should read short passages to a monitor and then retell these in their own words to enhance comprehension. They also may benefit from language therapy (see [c]).

General Language Disorder

Children who possess deficient verbal associative reasoning and limitations in memory functions are likely to exhibit minimal verbal mediation skills. Their inability to develop cognitive strategies that would permit them to reflectively analyze and integrate verbal and behavioral information places them at considerable emotional, behavioral, and academic risk.

Educational considerations for these language-disordered children include the following:

a. Early and accurate diagnosis of these global language deficits can qualify these children for early in-home or center-based language therapy services. State and federal mandates oblige local educational agencies to provide such services at little or no cost to parents.

b. Initially, language therapy should incorporate both verbal and nonverbal (visual aids) approaches relating to time sequencing, relational concepts, and causality. Specific procedures can be found in texts by Eisenson (1972) and Wiig and Semel (1976, 1980).

c. The pervasive effects of global language deficits almost always include severe academic underachievement necessitating a level of supplemental assistance that may range from minimal "resource room" time to intensive, self-contained classroom instruction.

Explicit Therapy Considerations

Expressive Language Disorder

Since many children with expressive language problems show frustration related to verbal interaction, issues related to self-esteem, heightened anxiety, and social acceptance are likely to be the focus of therapy efforts. The child's cognitive strengths in associative reasoning and memory areas make use of conventional "talk therapies" permissible. Psychological predispositions, as well as the presence of comorbid learning, attention, or behavioral difficulties, may affect the severity of emotional and behavioral problems. The severity will dictate whether these problems can be effectively addressed within a school setting or require more intensive mental health assistance. Therapists should be alert to the important and difficult distinction between expressive language deficiency and emotional blocking or defensive reticence. Use of pictures and diagrams in aiding the child's expression is often a useful technique.

a. Programs designed to assist social skill development and positive peer interactions (Perske & Perske, 1988) are appropriate for those children who exhibit milder adjustment difficulties. Typically, these programs utilize a group counseling format and are applicable to either school or mental health settings. However, more involved adjustment difficulties may also require the individual therapy from a school counselor or mental health therapist.

b. For significant difficulties generated by negative beliefs or self-perceptions, rational-emotive or cognitive-behavioral therapeutic approaches are suggested. Procedures outlined by Ellis (1979), Meichenbaum and Jaremko (1983), Rathjen et al. (1978), and Vernon (1989) emphasize the active role cognitive processes play in determining stress and anxiety responses and in directing efforts to control thoughts in a more positive and productive manner. Aspects of these approaches typically include educating the child in how emotional responses are generated, identifying patterns of cognitive distortion, testing cognitions, rehearsing behavior, role-playing, coaching, providing performance feedback, and observing appropriate and inappropriate models. Some programs also encourage children to actively assist their peers in dealing with similar difficulties, using their newly acquired problem-solving skills.

Memory Disorder

Children with a primary memory disorder usually possess the capacity to understand verbal abstractions and higher-level conceptualizations. Thus, they may be receptive to "talk therapies." However, unlike individuals with primary expressive deficits, children with memory deficiency are likely to exhibit related learning, organizational, and attentional deficiencies. As a consequence, they may demonstrate more diverse emotional and behavioral problems requiring the services of mental health professionals.

a. Children with memory problems often do not have insight into their deficit, and they frequently give up or become defensive when tasks or interactions become difficult. Therefore, it is important for the therapist to assist the child to understand the deficit. The child must also learn to recognize when a memory problem negatively affects performance and interaction with others. A common problem is denial of the memory problem and projection of blame on others.

b. Memory-deficient children may respond to rational-emotive (Vernon, 1989) or cognitive-behavioral therapies (Camp et al., 1977; Meichenbaum et al., 1971), particularly if components of impulse-control and social-skill training are incorporated within the program. By utilizing their associative reasoning strengths, therapy can enhance the probability of their acquiring improved mediational skills used in reflective thought (e.g., thinking before acting).

c. Because organizational difficulties are prevalent among memory-delayed children, it is essential that treatment efforts be well structured and include sequentially ordered steps on which previously acquired skills are used to reinforce hierarchical understanding.

Receptive Language Disorder

Since children with receptive language deficits exhibit weakness in understanding spoken words, traditional "talk therapies" are not appropriate and may even be detrimental. Therapeutic efforts should attempt to utilize these children's cognitive strengths in memory and nonverbal skill areas by providing highly structured and repetitive therapy "exercises" within the context of relatively controlled settings (e.g., group therapy, the classroom). Guided behavioral instruction in social skills training, as well as in techniques of problem solving and impulse-control, would be suitable to their needs and competencies.

a. The "Think Aloud" program (Camp et al., 1977) provides considerable structure and detailed activities within a step-by-step format.

b. Cognitive-behavioral approaches might also prove beneficial, although the therapist needs to be cognizant of the child's limitations in verbal abstract conceptualization.

c. Given the increased likelihood of attention and impulsivity problems with receptively delayed children, therapeutic suggestions detailed by Barkley (1990) may provide mental health workers with the guidance necessary to assist parents and educators in their cooperative efforts.

d. Systematic applications of behavior modification techniques (Gambrill, 1977) may be warranted with more behaviorally involved children. A comprehensive program of this nature (i.e., involving home and school) often requires much professional time to develop, coordinate, and monitor, as well as considerable commitment on the part of teachers and parents.

General Language Disorder

The often severe and multiple symptoms of behavioral dysfunction exhibited by this group frequently warrant multidisciplinary efforts of psychologists, physicians, social workers, and educational specialists if meaningful behavioral improvements are to be realistically expected. The mental health professional may best serve not only as a source of guidance for the child and his parents but also as a coordinator (i.e., case manager) in directing and communicating with other involved professionals.

a. The pervasive effects of general language dysfunction necessitates a supportive interpersonal approach to treatment. Behavior modification techniques may be suitable for direct skill training and in dealing with specific problematic behaviors. However, it is essential that the critical factors (i.e., antecedent conditions) inherent in the child's primary environments (home and school) be identified and effectively changed if meaningful improvement is to be accomplished. Selective and timely application of other (structured) skill training (e.g., organizational and functional social skills) will also be needed and may be borrowed from more specific training programs.

COMMENTS

There is much work yet to be accomplished in developing more objective methods for diagnosis within the area of communication disorders. The research on subtypes of speech and language disorders and on the overlap between neuropsychological subtyping of learning disorders and language disorders has yielded some useful criteria for assessment. Unfortunately, most children with communication disorders are never evaluated, let alone treated, by psychologists or other mental health workers. If they are, they are usually treated for a behavioral or emotional disorder in isolation, without an awareness of the possible underlying language disorder. It is important that mental health clinicians become more aware of the relationships of language strengths and weakness and behavioral and emotional characteristics. Treatment approaches (e.g., behavior therapy, cognitive behavior modification, social-learning skills therapy, and psychodynamic therapy) may need to be considered depending on the language strengths and weaknesses of the client. Furthermore, since most children with language disorders experience associated learning disorders, treatment should also include educational interventions.

Considerable research into the developmental, genetic, and brain basis for language disorders is needed. However, the clinician, who must treat children with language, learning, and behavioral and emotional disorders, can learn from the current research. Assessment should acknowledge that there are subtypes of language-disordered children with unique strengths and weaknesses that need to be utilized in understanding the child and in developing treatment approaches. Behavioral modification approaches may not generalize for a child with a general language disorder unless nonverbal cues are associated with behavioral paradigms. Talk therapy for a child with associative language disorder is less likely to be effective than more memory-based strategies such as "stop, look, and listen" approaches unique to cognitive behavioral modification treatment. Children with good associative language functions, such as those with memory-verbal language disorder or expressive language disorder, may benefit from social-learning or psychodynamic approaches to emotional problems. In all cases, appropriate diagnosis of the language and learning disorder and consideration of possible related behavioral or emotional disorders should lead to more holistic treatment approaches.

Clinicians who treat behavioral and emotional disorders of children with language disorders should always entertain the possibility that language-based cognitive deficits can affect behavior. These relationships may be subtle and may relate to how language development produces verbal mediation skills, which in turn govern the self-regulation of behavior (Luria, 1966; Vygotsky, 1962). Also, deficiencies in verbal mediation (e.g., labeling, memory, associations) are related to deficits in verbal self-guidance needed to control attention, impulsivity, activity level, and aggression. Guidance can be provided to these children to improve their use of verbal mediation in self-control of behavior by avoiding strategies that may be ineffective. These children should be taught to use either verbal mediation strategies or their nonverbal strengths, depending on the type of language disorder. These treatment strategies should be taught, practiced in mock situations, and periodically strengthened by therapeutic or social reinforcement by clinicians, parents, and teachers. This approach of the primary mental health clinician adds to the possible medical, educational, and language therapies for children with language disorders and associated behavioral and emotional and learning disorders.

REFERENCES

American Psychiatric Association. (1994). *Diagnostic and statistical manual of mental disorders* (4th ed.). Washington, DC: American Psychiatric Association.

Aram, D. M., Ekelman, B. L., & Nation, J. E. (1984). Preschoolers with language disorders ten years later. *Journal of Speech and Hearing Research, 27,* 232–244.

Aram, D. M., & Hall, N. E. (1989). Longitudinal follow-up of children with preschool communication disorders: Treatment implications. *School Psychology Review, 18,* 487–501.

Aram, D. M., & Nation, J. E. (1975) Patterns of language behavior in children with developmental language disorders. *Journal of Speech and Hearing Research, 18,* 229–241.

Bakker, D. J. (1972). *Temporal order in disturbed reading.* Rotterdam: Rotterdam University Press.

Barkley, R. A. (1990). *Attention deficit disorder: A handbook for diagnosis and treatment.* New York: Guilford Press.

Beitchman, J. H. (1985). Speech and language impairment and psychiatric risk: Toward a model of neurodevelopmental immaturity. *Psychiatric Clinics of North American, 8,* 721–735.

Beitchman, J. H., Peterson, M., & Clegg, M. (1988). Speech and language impairment and psychiatric disorder. *Child Psychiatry and Human Development, 18,* 191–207.

Benton, A. L. (1975). Developmental dyslexia: Neurological aspects. In W. J. Friedlander (Ed.), *Advances in Neurology,* Vol. 7. New York: Raven Press.

Benton, A. L. (1978). The cognitive functions of children with developmental dysphasia. In M. A. Wyke (Ed.), *Developmental dysphasia.* New York: Academic Press.

Benton, A. L., & Hamsher, K. (1978). *Multilingual Aphasia Examination.* Iowa City: Department of Neurology, University of Iowa.

Berndt, R. S., Carmazza, A., & Zurif, E. (1983). Language functions: Syntax and semantics. In S. Segalowitz (Ed.), *Language functions and brain organization.* New York: Academic Press.

Blank, M. (1968). Cognitive processes in auditory discrimination in normal and retarded readers. *Child Development, 39,* 1091–1101.

Bradley, L., & Bryant, P. (1985). *Rhyme and reason in reading and spelling.* Ann Arbor, MI: University of Michigan Press.

Camp, B. W. (1977). Verbal mediation in young aggressive boys. *Journal of Educational Psychology*, 69, 129–135.

Camp, B. W., Blon, G. E., Hebert, F., & van Doorminck, W. J. (1977). "Think Aloud": A program for developing self-control in young aggressive boys. *Journal of Abnormal Psychology*, 5, 157–169.

Campbell, S. B. (1990). *Behavior problems in preschoolers: Clinical and developmental issues*. New York: Guilford Press.

*Cantwell, D. P., & Baker, L. (1991). *Psychiatric and developmental disorders in children with communication disorder*. Washington, DC: American Psychiatric Press.

Corballis, M. C. (1983). *Human laterality*. New York: Academic Press.

Corkin, S. (1974). Serial-ordering deficits in inferior readers. *Neuropsychologia*, 12, 347–354.

Critchley, M. (1967). Aphasiology nomenclature and definitions. *Cortex*, 3, 3–25.

Crockett, D. J. (1974). Component analysis of within correlations of language skills tests in normal children. *Journal of Special Education*, 8, 361–375.

Denkla, M., & Rudel, R. (1976). Rapid automatized naming (RAN): Dyslexia differentiated from other learning disabilities. *Neuropsychologia*, 14, 471–479.

Eisenson, J. (1972). *Aphasia in children*. New York: Harper & Row.

Eliason, M. J., & Richman, L. C. (1988). Behavior and attention in LD children. *LD Quarterly*, 11, 360–369.

Ellis, A. (1979). *Reason and emotion in psychotherapy*. Secaucus, NJ: Citadel Press.

Fernald, A. (1991). Prosody and focus in speech to infants and adults. *Developmental Psychology*, 27, 209–221.

Fletcher, J. M. (1985). External validation of learning disability typologies. In B. Rourke (Ed.), *Essentials of subtype analysis* (pp. 187–212). New York: Guilford Press.

Frackowiak, R. S. (1994). Functional mapping of verbal memory and language. *Trends in Neurosciences*, 17, 109–115.

Galaburda, A. M. (1993). *Dyslexia and development*. Cambridge, MA: Harvard University Press.

Gambrill, E. D. (1977). *Behavior modification: Handbook of assessment, intervention, and evaluation*. San Francisco: Jossey-Bass.

Geschwind, N., & Galaburda, A. M. (1987). *Cerebral lateralization: Biological mechanisms, associations and pathology*. Cambridge, MA: MIT Press.

Gualtieri, C. T., Loriath, U., Van Bourgondien, M., & Saleeby, N. (1983). Language disorders in children referred for psychiatric services. *Journal of the American Academy of Child Psychiatry*, 22, 165–171.

Hall, P. K., & Tomblin, J. B. (1978). A follow-up study of children with articulation and language disorders. *Journal of Speech and Hearing Research*, 43, 227–241.

Hammill, D. (1985). *Detroit Tests of Learning Aptitude*. Austin, TX: ProEd.

Hiskey, M. A. (1966). *Hiskey-Nebraska Test of Learning Aptitude*. Lincoln, NE: Union College Press.

Hogan, A. E., & Quay, H. C. (1984). Cognition in child and adolescent behavior disorder. In B. B. Lahey & A. E. Kazdin (Eds.), *Advances in Clinical Child Psychology* (Vol. 7, pp. 1–34). New York: Plenum.

Irwin, J. V., & Marge, M. (1972). *Principals of childhood language disabilities*. New York: Appleton-Century Crofts.

Kaplan, E. F., Goodglass, H., & Weintraub, S. (1978). *The Boston Naming Test*. Boston: E. Kaplan & H. Goodglass.

Kapp, K. (1979). Self-concept of the cleft lip and/or palate child. *Cleft Palate Journal*, 16, 171–176.

*Korkman, M., & Hakkinen-Rihu, P. (1994). A new classification of developmental language disorders. *Brain & Language*, 47, 96–116.

Landau, S., & Milich, R. (1988). Social communication patterns of attention-deficit-disordered boys. *Journal of Abnormal Child Psychology*, 16, 69–81.

Leiter, R. G. (1969). *Leiter International Performance Scale*. Chicago: Stoelting Co.

Lezak, M. (1983). *Neuropsychological assessment* (2nd ed.). New York: Oxford University Press.

Lindgren, S. D., Richman, L. C., & Eliason, M. J. (1986). Memory processes in reading disability subtypes. *Developmental Neuropsychology*, 2, 173–181.

Locke, J. L. (1992). Neural specializations for language: A developmental perspective. *Neurosciences*, 4, 425–431.

Ludlow, C. L. (1980). Children's language disorders: Recent research advances. *Annals of Neurology*, 7, 497–507.

*Ludlow, C. L., & Cooper, J. A. (1983). *Genetic aspects of speech and language disorders*. New York: Academic Press.

Luria, A. R. (1961). *The role of speech in the regulation of normal and abnormal behaviors*. New York: Liveright.

Mattis, S., French, J. H., & Rapin, I. (1975). Dyslexia in children and adults: Three independent neuropsychological syndromes. *Developmental Medicine and Child Neurology, 17,* 150–163.

McCarthy, J. J., & Kirk, S. A. (1961). *Illinois Test of Psycholinguistic Ability.* Urbana: University of Illinois Press.

Meichenbaum, D., & Goodman, J. (1971). Training impulsive children to talk to themselves. A means of developing self-control. *Journal of Abnormal Psychology, 77,* 115–126.

Meichenbaum, D., & Jaremko, M. E. (1983). *Stress reduction and prevention.* New York: Plenum Press.

Myklebust, H. R. (1971). *Progress in learning disabilities,* Vol. II. New York: Grune & Stratton.

*Pennington, B. F. (1991). *Diagnosing learning disorders.* New York: Guilford Press.

Perske, R., & Perske, M. (1988). *Circle of friends.* Nashville, TN: Abingdon Press.

*Piacentini, J. C. (1987). Language dysfunction and childhood behavior disorders. In B. Lahey & A. Kazdin (Eds.), *Advances in clinical child psychology* (Vol. 10, pp. 259–287). New York: Plenum Press.

*Prizant, B. M., Audet, L. R., Brurke, G. M., Hummel, L. J., Maher, S. R., & Theodore, G. (1990). Communication disorders and emotional/behavioral disorders in children and adolescents. *Journal of Speech and Hearing Disorders, 55,* 179–192.

Rapin, I., & Allen, D. A. (1983). Developmental language disorders: Nosologic considerations. In U. Kirk (Ed.), *Neuropsychology of language, reading and spelling.* New York: Academic Press.

Rathjen, D. P., Rathjen, E. D., & Hiniker, A. (1978). A cognitive analysis of social performance: Implications for assessment and treatment. In J. P. Foreyt & D. P. Rathjen (Eds.), *Cognitive behavior therapy.* New York: Plenum Press.

Reynell, J. (1969). *Reynell Developmental Language Scales.* Windsor, England: NFER Publishing.

Richman, L. C. (1978). Language mediation hypothesis: Implications of verbal/performance discrepancy and reading disability. *Perceptual and Motor Skills, 47,* 391–398.

Richman, L. C. (1979). Language variables related to reading ability of children with verbal deficits. *Psychology in the Schools, 16,* 299–305.

Richman, L. C. (1980). Cognitive patterns and learning disabilities in cleft palate children with verbal deficits. *Journal of Speech and Hearing Research, 23,* 447–456.

Richman, L. C. (1983). Language-learning disability issues, research and future directions. In M. Wolraich & D. Routh (Eds.), *Advances in developmental and behavioral pediatrics* (Vol. 4, pp. 87–107). Greenwich, CT: JAI Press.

Richman, L. C. (1982). Self-reported social, speech, and facial concerns and personality adjustment of adolescents with cleft lip and palate. *Cleft Palate Journal, 20,* 108–112.

Richman, L. C., & Eliason, M. (1992). Disorders of communication, developmental language disorders and cleft palate. In C. E. Walker & M. C. Roberts (Eds.), *Handbook of child clinical psychology-revised.* New York: Wiley.

Richman, L. C., & Kitchell, M. (1981). Hyperlexia as a variant of developmental language disorder. *Brain and Language, 12,* 203–212.

Richman, L., & Lindgren, S. (1980). Patterns of intellectual ability in children with verbal deficits. *Journal of Abnormal Child Psychology, 8,* 65–84.

Richman, L., & Lindgren, S. (1981). Verbal mediation deficits: Relation to behavior and achievement in children. *Journal of Abnormal Child Psychology, 90,* 99–104.

Richman, L., & Lindgren, S. (1984). *The Color Span Test.* L. Richman & S. Lindgren, University of Iowa, Iowa City, IA.

Richman, N., Stevenson, J. E., & Grahm, P. J. (1975). Prevalence of behavior problems in 3-year-old children: An epidemiological study in a London borough. *Journal of Child Psychology and Psychiatry, 16,* 277–287.

Rourke, B. P. (1985). *Neuropsychology of LD essentials of subtype analysis.* New York: Guilford Press.

*Segalowitz, S. (1983). *Language functions and brain organization.* New York: Academic Press.

Shankweiler, D., & Liberman, I. Y. (1976). Exploring the relations between reading and speech. In R. M. Knights & D. J. Bakker (Eds.), *The neuropsychology of learning disorders.* Baltimore: University Park Press.

Sines, J. O., Pauker, J. D., & Sines, L. K. (1971). *The Missouri Children's Picture Series test manual.* J. O. Sines, University of Iowa, Iowa City, IA.

Spreen, D., & Benton, A. (1969). *Neurosensory Center Comprehensive Examination of Aphasia.* Victoria: University of Victoria.

Stevenson, J. E., & Richman, N. (1978). Behavior, language and development in three-year-old children. *Journal of Autism and Child Schizophrenia, 8,* 299–313.

Sweeney, J. E., & Rourke, B. P. (1985). Spelling disability subtypes. In B. P. Rourke (Ed.), *Neu-*

ropsychology of learning disabilities: Essentials of subtype analysis. New York: Guilford Press.

Tallal, P., & Piercy, M. (1973). Developmental aphasia: Impaired rate of nonverbal processing as a function of sensory modality. *Neuropsychologia, 11,* 389–398.

Van Lancker, D. R., Cummings, J. L., Kreiman, J., & Dobkin, B. H. (1988). Phonagnosia: A dissociation between familiar and unfamiliar voices. *Cortex, 24,* 195–209.

van Santen, J. P. H., Black, L. M., Wilson, B. C., & Risucci, P. A. (1994). Modeling clinical judgment: A reanalysis of data from Wilson and Risucci's 1986 paper. *Brain & Language, 46,* 469–481.

Vellutino, F. R. (1979). *Dyslexia: Theory and research.* Cambridge, MA: MIT Press.

Vernon, A. (1989). *Thinking, feeling, behaving: An emotional curriculum for adolescents.* Champaign, IL: Research Press.

Vygotsky, L. (1962). *Thought and language.* Cambridge, MA: MIT Press.

Wiig, E., & Becker-Caplan, L. (1984). Linguistic retrieval strategies and word-finding difficulties among children with language disabilities. *Topics in Language Disorders, 4,* 1–81.

Wiig, E., & Semel, E. (1976). *Language disabilities in children and adolescents.* Columbus, OH: Merrill.

Wiig, E., & Semel, E. (1980). *Language assessment and intervention for the learning disabled.* Columbus, OH: Merrill.

Wilson, B. C., & Risucci, P. A. (1986). A model for clinical-quantitative classification. Generation I: Application to language-disordered preschool children. *Brain & Language, 27,* 281–309.

Wood, K. M., & Richman, L. C. (1988). Developmental trends within memory-deficient reading-disability subtypes. *Developmental Neuropsychology, 4,* 261–274.

Wood, K. M., Richman, L. C., & Eliason, M. J. (1989). Immediate memory functions in reading disability subtypes. *Brain and Language, 36,* 181–192.

World Health Organization. (1992). International statistical classification of diseases and related health problems (10th rev.). Geneva: Author.

*Indicates references that the authors recommend for additional reading.

5
Pervasive Developmental Disorders

Darold A. Treffert

The term "pervasive developmental disorders" (PDD) is used in both the *Diagnostic and Statistical Manual of Mental Disorders* (Fourth Edition) (DSM-IV) of the American Psychiatric Association and the World Health Organization's *International Classification of Diseases* (Tenth Edition) (ICD-10) to refer to a group of disorders, usually beginning in childhood, characterized by severe and pervasive impairment in communication, language, and social and interactive skills. They are often associated with stereotyped behavior, interests, and activities. This group of developmental conditions includes autistic disorder, Rett's disorder, childhood disintegrative disorder, Asperger's disorder, and pervasive developmental disorder not otherwise specified. These disorders are often associated with some degree of mental retardation, although there can be marked unevenness in performance on the various subscales of standard psychological tests. In several of these disorders, particularly autistic disorder and Asperger's disorder, that unevenness on testing may include areas of isolated but sometimes spectacular skills, linked with striking long-term memory ability within areas of prodigious skills.

Autistic disorder is the best known entity in the PDD group. While early infantile autism was first described by Kanner (1943), it was not until 1980 that infantile autism appeared as a separate diagnosis in DSM-III. During that intervening nearly 40-year time span, infantile autism, in its classic form, was considered a form of schizophrenia with onset in childhood. Therefore, no separate category existed, and it was classified as schizophrenia, childhood type. As early as 1964, however, Rimland (1964), in his book *Infantile Autism*, concluded that early infantile autism was not a form of childhood schizophrenia, and many other investigators shared that same view. Yet it was not until 1980 that infantile autism was listed as an entity separate from schizophrenia in DSM-III under a new group of disorders called pervasive developmental disorders, acknowledging therein a biological basis for these disorders and classifying them as developmental disabilities rather than a form of schizophrenia. Pervasive developmental disability has not been an especially well-accepted term among many clinicians, parents, and support-advocacy organizations for a number of reasons. Bernard Rimland, who has the largest database of autistic persons (more than

20,000 persons), along with others, feels the term autistic spectrum disorder would be more accurate for these entities, although not all would agree that Asperger's disorder, for example, is a form of autism. Failure to differentiate autism as an illness from autism as a symptom accounts for some of that confusion, since many persons with a number of mental and developmental disorders, including mental retardation, have autistic symptoms without having the illness of autism. In that sense, the term "early infantile autism" has lost much of its specificity and is used more casually and broadly to refer to "autistic" behaviors seen in a variety of conditions.

For those and other reasons, it is likely that PDD as a group of disorders may be merely a transient classification until biological markers for subtypes can be found. The beginning of wisdom is to call things by their right names. As more knowledge emerges about the specific and differential etiology of the disorders subsumed under PDD, they will be separately and more definitively classified. At the present time, however, both DSM-IV and ICD-10 list "pervasive developmental disorders" separate from other conditions, and that creates good uniformity between those two important systems of classification.

AUTISTIC DISORDER

History

Dr. Leo Kanner (1943), a child psychiatrist at Johns Hopkins Hospital, first published his description of a rare but unique behavior disorder in children that he later named early infantile autism (Kanner, 1944) In that article he described 20 patients whose behavior differed uniquely and markedly from that of normal children, yet who, when viewed as a group, were strikingly uniform in their psychopathology. All had been brought to the clinic assumed to be mentally retarded and deaf. Yet on careful testing it was apparent none were deaf, and "cognitive potentialities were only masked by the basic affective disorder; in fact, a few of the children

had started out by amazing their parents with phenomenal feats of rote repetition."

In that seminal article, Kanner goes on to describe the hallmarks of early infantile autism that, in my view, have not been better reported since that original description: the extreme autistic aloneness; mutism or language that fails to convey meaning to others; sometimes surprising, phenomenal rote memory; echolalia; literalness; reference to self in the third person; anxious, obsessive desire for sameness; good relation to objects, but not to people; fascination with spinning objects and rhythm; tendency to stare through but not at people; good cognitive potentialities expressed as sometimes astounding vocabulary and precise recollection of complex material yet not testable because of inaccessibility due to all the other affective and behavioral defects; and handsome faces that give the impression of overall serious-mindedness, anxiousness in the presence of others, but with a placid smile and an expression of beatitude, often accompanied by happy though monotonous humming and singing.

In that original group, there were 16 boys and 4 girls—a 4:1 male:female ratio that has been quite consistently found at that approximate level in all the studies since that time. Kanner noted an interesting common denominator in the backgrounds of all these children: all came from highly intelligent parents. That may have been a manifestation of Kanner's referral practice, although a broad-based statewide study in Wisconsin of all children carrying such a diagnosis did show a consistently higher educational level among parents of children with early infantile autism (Treffert, 1970). Kanner also suggested that higher social class might be associated with the disorder, but later studies have shown that this is not necessarily so.

Autistic disorder has come to be the most familiar of the PDD group to most professionals. That familiarity rose exponentially among the public as well when Dustin Hoffman portrayed with remarkable fidelity a high-functioning autistic person with savant abilities in the 1988 movie *Rain Man*. That movie gave both autism and savant syndrome high visibility, reflected in wide public interest now in those conditions. Savant syndrome is addressed separately later in this chapter.

Prevalence

Epidemiologic studies in the United States and elsewhere have found the incidence of autistic disorder to be about 4.5 cases per 10,000 children. Approximately half that number would qualify for the more narrowly defined early infantile autism group described by Kanner. The term "autistic" is generally more loosely applied, however, to a number of heterogeneous conditions in which autistic symptoms and behaviors are superimposed on mental retardation or other types of brain damage. If one includes these cases in autistic disorder, the incidence rises to as high as between 16 to 69 cases per 10,000 children, depending on various diagnostic criteria. Sex incidence is approximately 4:1, males to females. Some studies have suggested that a higher than expected number of autistic children are firstborn or lateborn. Siblings of autistic children have 50 times the risk of the normal population of developing the disorder. Monozygotic twins have an 80–90% concordance for autism, compared to 15–20% for dizygotic twins.

Diagnostic Description

Kanner's careful and detailed description of early infantile autism can hardly be improved upon 40 years later. DSM-IV, however, encompasses a wider spectrum of disorders than just early infantile autism. It uses the term "autistic disorder" for this particular condition as one of the pervasive developmental disorders and enumerates the following requisite criteria if this diagnosis is to be used:

1. Onset before age three of delays or abnormal functioning in at least one of three areas:
   a. social interaction
   b. language for social communication
   c. symbolic or imaginative play

2. Qualitative impairment in *social interaction* as manifested by at least *two* of the following:
   a. marked impairment in nonverbal behaviors such as eye-to-eye gaze, facial expression, body postures or gestures
   b. failure in developmentally appropriate peer relationships
   c. lack of spontaneity in sharing enjoyment, interests, or achievements with other people
   d. lack of social or emotional reciprocity

3. Qualitative impairment in *communication* as manifested by at least *one* of the following:
   a. delay in or lack of spoken language
   b. marked impairment in ability to initiate or sustain conversation with others if adequate speech does exist
   c. stereotyped, repetitive, or idiosyncratic language
   d. lack of developmentally appropriate varied, spontaneous, make-believe or imitative play

4. Restricted, repetitive, and stereotyped patterns of *behavior, interests, and activities* as manifested by at least *one* of the following:
   a. profound preoccupation with stereotyped and restricted patterns of interest that is abnormal in intensity or focus
   b. inflexible adherence to specific, nonfunctional routines or rituals
   c. stereotyped and repetitive motor mannerisms, such as hand flapping or complex whole-body movements
   d. persistent preoccupation with parts of objects

ICD-10, like DSM-IV, defines a number of separate disorders under the general heading "Pervasive Developmental Disorders." One of those is *childhood autism*, which is defined as impaired or abnormal development *before* 3 years of age that shows a *full* triad of impairments in (a) reciprocal social interaction; (b) communication; and (c) restricted, stereotyped, repetitive behavior. It also specifies and defines a condition called *atypical autism*, with onset of impaired or abnormal development *after* 3 years of age and with impairments in only *one* or *two* areas of the triad.

Etiology

There is no single cause for autistic disorder because it is not a single entity. Like schizophrenia or mental retardation, it is a *group* of disorders, with differing causes, that share some final common pathways of symptom expression, behaviorally and cognitively, over a full spectrum of severity. What can be said, though, is that the etiologic psychogenic and psychosocial theories that were espoused by a number of early researchers, including Kanner himself, have been replaced by a search for biological or organic causes, be they genetic, neuroanatomical secondary to developmental abnormality or injury, neurochemical, or immunological. The regrettable term "refrigerator mother," which implied that cold unemotional parenting caused autism by producing a reciprocal psychological aloofness in the child, has properly been discredited and discarded, and various paths of organic inquiry are vigorously being pursued.

The family and twin studies, noted briefly earlier, with their high concordance rate of monozygotic twins, their low concordance rate for dizygotic twins, and their incidence rate for siblings 50 times that for the general population, indicate that *genetic factors* play heavily in the transmission of some forms of autistic disorder. The fragile-X syndrome (which refers to a fragile site on the X chromosome when observed in a folate-deficient medium) has been found in a subgroup of persons diagnosed as autistic. That subgroup ranges from zero to as high as 20%, with a pooled prevalence of 8% (Campbell & Shay, 1995). There is dispute as to whether the fragile-X marker is associated with mental retardation rather than autism, since fragile-X syndrome occurs frequently in other forms of mental retardation without autism, but the fragile-X/autism link continues to be explored etiologically.

There have been a number of CNS *structural abnormalities* found in autistic persons, particularly since very-high-definition imaging studies such as MRI have been available. No single structural abnormality pervades the entire spectrum of autistic disorders, but findings of abnormalities continue to accumulate. Some studies have focused on the mesial temporal lobe, including the amygdala and hippocampus, as the site of organic pathology. These data come from imaging studies where there is demonstrated enlargement of the lateral ventricle or from autopsy data where microscopic cellular changes exist in these areas. The most consistently reported imaging abnormality involves changes in the cerebellum, beginning with Courchesne's work in 1987 and confirmed by his MRI study that compared 50 autistic subjects to 53 nondisabled controls (Courchesne, 1994). There also have been decreased numbers of cerebellar Purkinje cells on microscopic examination from autopsy specimens. A large-scale Japanese study (Hashimoto, 1995) on 102 autistic subjects found abnormally small cerebellum and brainstem size compared to those of a control group. Parietal lobe changes have also been reported (Chorchesne, 1993). Some MRI studies have suggested that autistic children have megalencephaly, or unusually large brains (Bailey et al., 1993). A study of 22 autistic subjects and 20 controls (Piven, 1995) found autistic persons to have significantly larger total brain, total tissue, and total lateral ventricle volumes than the controls. Such brain enlargement, found in 40% of subjects, may be a marker for one subgroup of autistic disorder. Other researchers (Pomeroy, 1990), using dichotic listening tests and the EEG, have postulated that left-hemisphere structural abnormality, from genetic, prenatal, or perinatal injury or injury from circulating testosterone in utero, results in a shift from standard left-hemisphere dominance to right-hemisphere dominance—so-called anomalous dominance. This asymmetry/reversal observation was supported by Dawson (1986) and coworkers, who found that on evoked potential responses most autistic persons processed speech on the right side, in contrast to normals, who processed speech on the left.

Neurochemical explanations continue to be explored as well. Numerous studies have shown high levels of *serotonin* in as many as a third of autistic persons as measured by whole blood or platelets. That is a nonspecific finding, however, to the extent that a large number of mentally retarded persons without autism also have elevated serotonin levels, as do some nonautistic relatives of autistic persons. Excess *dopamine* has also been suggested as contributing to some of the hyperactivity and stereotypies seen in autism because of the higher levels of dopamine found in CNS fluids or excretory products of autistic persons. *Vitamin B6* is a coenzyme in the serotonin and dopamine pathways, and an anomoly in the metabolism of this vitamin has been proposed as a possible etiologic agent in a least some subgroups of autism. A theory that autism is related to excess endogenous *opioids* has also been proposed, based on the similarities between autistic persons and opiate addicts in either intoxicated or withdrawal states and between autistic children and children exposed to opiates prenatally. One study showed higher CNS levels of endorphins in some autistic children (Pomeroy, 1990).

Finding of decreased immune system response in some autistic persons, and some immunological links between mothers and some autistic children, have raised the possibility of an *immune system* etiology. The greatly increased incidence of autism in children with congenital rubella has been often noted and has led to speculation about a *viral* cause of the disorder, although it may be that the associated blindness and auditory loss are the more significant variables, since other reports link congenital blindness and deafness also to increased incidence of autism. There have been reports (Iverson, 1990) of autism associated with other viral disorders, such as herpes simplex encephalitis and cytomegalovirus infection (CMV).

The causes of autistic disorder are multiple. Illustrating the importance of differential diagnosis in determining treatment approaches is the finding that 70% of patients with Landau-Kleffner Syndrome (LKS) have autistic-like symptoms and are often diagnosed as having autistic disorder (Rimland, 1991). LKS is also called acquired epileptic aphasia. It usually occurs between the ages of three and seven in formerly normal children who first lose the ability to understand others and then the ability to speak, coupled with many behavioral symptoms often seen in autistic disorders, including suspected deafness. EEGs are rather distinctively abnormal, with or without actual seizures. Surgical or steroid treatments can produce remarkable results in many LKS patients, unlike autistic disorder patients (Stefanatos et al., 1995). Tuberous sclerosis (Hunt & Shepard, 1993) and Tourette's disorder (Sverd, 1991) also must be considered in a differential diagnosis because of recent studies that link autism and those disorders.

The search for biological causes of autism proceeds. Until there is greater uniformity in the diagnosis of autistic disorder and its subtypes, however, there will be a continued lack of differentiation between organic findings as a marker of the disorder and organic findings as the cause of the disorder. New techniques are providing promising new paths to that critical distinction.

Assessment

The first step in the treatment of any medical, psychiatric, or psychological condition is to make an accurate diagnosis. That is certainly true with autistic disorder, with its various subgroups and their different etiologies. The first step in accurate diagnosis is to obtain a comprehensive *history*, with particular attention to developmental milestones, especially speech, since presence of meaningful speech before age five is often correlated with better prognosis. Parents often verify the presence of many of the typical autistic disorder symptoms enumerated earlier both on the DSM-IV chart and in Kanner's original description of the disorder, including, for example, lack of clinging to the parent when picked up as an infant, practice of staring "through" persons rather than at them, peculiar language, fascination with spinning objects, and suspected deafness.

Clinical observation shows typically a child who is handsome and attractive, detached from the people in the room, including the examiner, whom he or she largely ignores in favor of objects in the room, which are rather systematically, and often very actively, explored. There is little or no eye contact. Greetings or requests from the examiner are ignored as if the child were deaf. In some children, however, there seems to be hyperacusis (extreme, sometimes anguished sensitivity to certain sounds) and extreme sensitivity to some stimuli and activities surrounding the child, who seemingly blocks out others entirely. Language is absent, idiosyncratic, echolalic, or monotonous and repetitive. There may be toe-walking, spinning, or hand flapping, or the child may lick or hit him- or herself or objects. At times the child may withdraw even more, focusing instead on some familiar object or newly discovered item for long periods of time. There may be rituals that involve rocking, touching, smelling, or tasting. Activity level can be frenetic at times, then give way to a calm that excludes everyone present. The child usually does not seek or give affection; affect remains generally flattened and blank.

Because of the various biologic etiologies, as well as other conditions that can mimic autistic disorder, *physical examination*, including neurological exam, is vital to a complete differential diagnosis. The extent of *laboratory studies* is dictated in part by the presence of abnormal physical and neurological findings, if any. At a minimum, though, they should include an EEG, a CAT scan of the head, cytogenetic study for chromosomal abnormalities, including Fragile-X screen, and an auditory evaluation. There should be routine blood and urine screening studies, including blood lead level and tests for inborn errors of metabolism, such as phenylalanine, with more extensive laboratory work dictated by any additional abnormal history, physical, or neurologic findings. If any of the history, physical and neurological examination, imaging, EEG, or screening blood and urine studies provides clues to other disorders, those findings need to be followed up with other appropriate, more tailored, detailed testing.

Psychological testing is a challenge, given all the behavioral symptoms of the autistic child, as noted earlier. There should be some attempt, using scales that are not entirely language dependent, to assess intellectual ability. Those tests routinely used in assessing other developmental disabilities, such as the Vinland Social Maturity Scale, and other neurodevelopmental instruments should be used to the extent they can be. A specific speech and language appraisal is essential. The American Psychiatric Association publication *Treatments of Psychiatric Disorders* (Campbell & Schopler, 1989) provides a concise listing of the more popular psychological tests and summarizes the advantages and disadvantages of those tests, as well.

In addition to the more general psychological test instruments, a number of questionnaires and standard interview instruments have been developed specifically to aid in the assessment of autistic disorder and to differentiate autism from other developmental disorders. An article by Parks (1983) provides the most information on the applicability, validity, consistency, and reliability of five of the most commonly used such instruments: Behavior Rating Instrument for Autistic and Atypical Children (BRIAAC); Behaviour Observation Scale for Autism (BOS); Childhood Autism Rating Scale (CARS); Autism Behavior Checklist (ABC); and the Diagnostic Checklist Form E-2 from the Autistic Research Institute, San Diego, California. In the book *Children with Autism: Diagnosis and Intervention to Meet Their Needs*, Trevarthen (1996) and his coauthors describe those diagnostic instruments and others, including the Behavioural Summarized Evaluation (BSE); Autism Diagnostic Interview (ADI); Autism Diagnostic Observation Schedule (ADOS); Checklist for Autism in Toddlers (CHAT); and Pre-Linguistic Autism Diagnostic Observation Schedule (PL-ADOS).

Rimland developed the first diagnostic questionnaire in 1964. The original E-1 form consisted of 76 questions filled out by the parents regarding the child's prenatal and birth history, age at onset of symptoms, and behavioral symptoms and speech patterns. The E-2 scale was expanded in 1971 to 109 items, including 79 questions on the child's sex, age, birth order, birth weight, pregnancy and delivery data, health history in the first 3 months, developmental milestones, responsiveness to affection, posturing, suspected deafness, obsessiveness, fascination with spinning objects, and use of the first person in speech. This section also seeks information about the educational and psychiatric history of the parents and blood relatives. Then a section of 30 questions requires responses of very true, true, or false with regard to certain behaviors of the child before and after age two, such as whether certain sounds seem painful to the child, or whether the child avoids people or repeats phrases, sentences, or conversations, put his or her body in bizarre postures, or dislikes being held or touched. Those answers are then computer scored, and the autistic person is ranked on a scale according to how closely he or she approaches so-called "classic" infantile autism, with "not autistic" at the other end of the spectrum. The result is sent to the person or agency that submitted the form. This questionnaire has been given to more than 20,000 autistic or autistic-like persons and has yielded the largest database in the world on this condition.

There is a third part to the E-2 Diagnostic Checklist that is also useful. It asks parents to rate responses to treatment, in six increments ranging from "definitely helpful" to "much worse," for 74 different therapies and approaches, including 33 specific medications, 18 allergy or nutritional items, and 12 miscellaneous therapies, including behavior modification, sensory integration, and speech therapy. Other items can be inserted by the parent and commented upon. Systematic analysis of this part of the E-2 questionnaire has been helpful in assessing the effectiveness of the broad range of medication, dietary, and behavioral approaches currently being used for treatment in this large population.

For the clinician seeking a test rating scale that can be used as a direct-observation instrument, for use in an office, school, or home setting, rather than a parent-produced questionnaire, the Childhood Autism Rating Scale (CARS) is useful. The presence or absence of autism is assessed and the degree of severity classified. This scale can be a valuable adjunct in diagnostic efforts when combined with careful history, physical examination, and laboratory studies.

Treatment

Obviously, the treatment plan is dictated by what the evaluation produces. In some instances it becomes apparent that the diagnosis is *not* autistic disorder, but something else, such as Landau-Kleffner Syndrome, and other appropriate evaluations and referrals are made. Most of the time, though, one is left with a person with the diagnosis of autistic disorder, and treatment strategy is dictated by presenting symptoms, since there is no single definitive treatment for this disorder, with its varied etiologies. Intervention techniques, though, generally consist of several approaches applied together in a coordinated, comprehensive manner in a well-orchestrated, multidisciplinary treatment plan.

Educational Approaches

Individualized, carefully structured education plans, involving special education teachers, speech and language specialists, therapists, and family, are the backbone of successful intervention strategies with autistic children. The location of these efforts has been shifting from special education classrooms for mentally retarded persons to special classrooms for emotionally disturbed persons to regular classrooms in what has been called mainstreaming but more recently termed "full inclusion." There is debate, often heated, in the United States and in Europe over the benefits and drawbacks of full inclusion. The most successful strategy appears to be the availability of a full spectrum of different choices tailored to the needs of the individual autistic child, rather than full inclusion or full exclusion. More critical than *where* the specialized education takes place is *who* the teachers and supporting staff are and whether they have specialized training in working with autistic students as differentiated from other disability groups. The TEACCH program at the University of North Carolina is one setting that provides such a continuum (Schopler et al., 1984).

Behavioral Therapies

A study from the Princeton Child Development Institute (Fenske et al., 1985) reported that a carefully structured technique, called Intensive Early Behavioral Intervention, was very effective in 60% of autistic children enrolled before age five. A controlled study of this technique by Ivar Lovaas (1987) at UCLA gave it additional impetus when Lovaas reported good results, with 9 of 19 autistic children improving enough to be mainstreamed, compared to none in the control group of 40. This intensive early-behavior modification program, sometimes referred to simply as the Lovaas technique, relies on positive reinforcements as designed and supervised by trained therapists and teachers who carry out the protocols for as much as 40 hours per week, with parents continuing to carry out the program at home. An increasing number of therapists trained in the Lovaas technique are now available around the country. A two-year evaluation of a Lovaas-type program in Australia in 1994, reported by Birnbrauer and Leach, in which only 20 hours per week of therapy instead of the traditional 40 hours was offered still showed substantial gains in language, socialization, and adaptive behaviors for the children in the treatment group compared to a control group.

Behavior modification is probably the most extensively studied treatment technique, since it lends itself so readily to assessing specific behaviors and measuring quantitative change in those behaviors over time using consistent, specific, and uniform interventions. All these programs depend on providing a consistent, supportive environment in which external rewards are used in a consistent, uniform manner to positively reinforce desireable behaviors, educational goals, and social interaction, meanwhile extinguishing problem behaviors. Behavior modification techniques such as shaping, prompts, rewards, and time

out are common to all these programs. Studies support strongly the notion that the earlier such interventions occur, the better. Early childhood intervention programs are not only the most widely applied treatment intervention in the treatment of autistic disorder, but the most carefully studied and assessed to date.

Aversive reinforcement techniques, once popular, are much less commonly used now, although some programs continue to use them in very limited circumstances. A 1989 NIH Consensus Conference Report on Treatment of Destructive Behaviors in Persons with Developmental Disabilities found that aversives were necessary in some very limited instances to control highly harmful, especially self-injurious behaviors that are resistant to other approaches. Very careful controls on their use were recommended.

Psychotherapy

Psychodynamic psychotherapy or play therapy has little role in the treatment of autistic disorder in a curative sense, given the biologic basis for the condition. In many cases, language barriers and behavioral problems make such an intervention impossible, anyway. However, empathic, supportive, growth-reinforcing one-on-one individual or play therapy, depending on the age of the patient, or group interactions can be useful with the autistic child or adult, much as they are with any other developmentally disabled person as part of multidisciplinary, coordinated treatment effort.

Pharmacotherapy

Since autistic disorder is a group of conditions, rather than a single condition, no one psychopharmacologic intervention would be expected to be useful in *all* cases. Nevertheless, a variety of pharmacotherapies have been used with varying success in certain subgroups of patients who share certain common behavioral symptoms irrespective of their differential etiologies.

The *antipsychotic* drugs have been used in some autistic disorder patients since they became available more than 40 years ago with the discovery of chlorpromazine (Thorazine). At that time, autistic disorder was considered by many to be a form of childhood schizophrenia, and those medications that were effective in treating adult schizophrenia were tried on autistic patients, generally without much success. The high-potency antipsychotic drug haloperidol (Haldol) has been the most carefully studied of this class of medications in autistic disorder, and some controlled studies have found it to be useful with target symptoms of anger, irritability, and acting out compared to a placebo (Campbell & Shay, 1995). Antipsychotic medications generally do not reduce hallucinations, when they are present in autistic disorder, nearly as well as they reduce them in adult schizophrenia. Side effects of these medications include sedation, dry mouth, and extrapyramidal symptoms such as muscle spasm and tremor. Those extrapyramidal symptoms are reversible and can be easily controlled with other medication, such as Cogentin, administered along with the antipsychotic. Tardive dyskinesia is a long-term complication of this class of drugs in children and adults, however, and the risk-to-benefit ratio must carefully evaluated before using them. Tardive dyskinesia, like the short-term extrapyramidal symptoms, is a muscle movement disorder, but it is a long-term, irreversible condition that occurs as a serious, late complication in some persons who have been on antipsychotic drugs, even after use of those drugs is discontinued. The most common symptoms include involuntary movements of the mouth, tongue, and lips but also can include involuntary spasms or jerking of limb and trunk muscles.

Respiridone, a newer antipsychotic with apparently a lower risk of tardive dyskinesia and with fewer other side effects common to other antipsychotics, was used in one study (Purdon et al., 1994) of adult PPD patients and found to have useful effects. However, this was a noncontrolled study, and some patients remained on medications other than respiridone during the respiridone trial.

Fenfluramine, marketed as an appetite suppressant, gained some brief popularity as a treatment for autistic disorder in the 1980s.

Since some autistic persons appeared to have hyperserotenemia, as noted earlier, it was felt that perhaps fenfluramine, with its serotonin-depleting activity, might be useful. Some initial studies did show promise for that hoped-for outcome, but later controlled studies failed to show any such consistent useful effect.

Antidepressant medications, such as desimpramine and, more recently, clomipramine, have been used, since it was hoped that their effect on serotonin in autistic persons, just as in depressed persons, might be beneficial. Desimpramine is used in children for a variety of other disorders, ranging from bed-wetting to hyperactivity (ADHD). Recent reports of sudden death among some children on desimpramine, perhaps dose related, have caused a new look at that medication in children, particularly in the presence of any cardiac disease. Clomipramine was of more recent interest since, while it is basically an antidepressant drug, it also has a unique usefulness in treating obsessive-compulsive disorder (OCD) in adults. Since obsessive-compulsive, stereotypical, ritualistic behavior is so much a part of many autistic behavior patterns, it was hoped this drug might have special benefit on at least that part of the symptom profile. Several early studies have reported useful results in reducing some behavioral symptoms in autistic persons. One double-blind study (Gordon et al., 1993) found clomipramine in 12 autistic subjects to be more effective than desipramine or placebo on stereotypies, anger, and social interactive, self-injurious, and ritualistic behaviors. However, later studies found clomipramine to be no more effective than placebo in autistic children, none of whom improved on clomipramine, and significant side effects appeared. Trazadone, an antidepressant different from both clomipramine and desimpramine, has been reported to be useful in reducing self-injurious and aggressive behavior. Fluoxetine (Prozac), one of the newer SSRI antidepressants, has also been used with autistic children and adults with some useful effect on aggressive and obsessive-compulsive symptoms and self-injurious behaviors, although side effects were significantly distressing in some subjects (Cook et al., 1992). Fluvoxamine

(Luvox) is the most recent of the SSRI-type antidepressants/anti-OCD agents. A placebo-controlled, double-blind study of fluvoxamine in 30 adults with autistic disorder showed significantly improved language (decrease in echolalia), increases in social contacts, and greater responsiveness to others and decreases in repetitive behavior and aggressive and impulsive behaviors in 8 of 15 patients who received the drug and in none of the patients who received placebo (McDougal, 1995). A similar study in children is now under way.

Naltrexone blocks the effects of opioids in the body. Since some researchers have postulated, as noted earlier, that high levels of these compounds in some autistic persons account for some of the typical symptoms of autism, which resemble, in part, either intoxication or withdrawal from narcotic drugs, Naltrexone has been used as a treatment intervention by some clinicians. While some early findings suggested some success in modifying the autistic picture overall, a double-blind, placebo-controlled study in 41 autistic children ages three to eight (Campbell, 1993) reported the only significant finding to be that there was a decrease in hyperactivity, with a suggestion that Naltrexone might have been useful in decreasing self-injurious behaviors.

Clonadine is a medication used in treatment of hypertension because of its effects on the adrenergic system. It has been tried in autism, since some researchers have postulated that dysregulation and hyperarousal of the adrenergic system might account for some of symptoms in autism, particularly hyperactivity. One controlled study found clonodine to be superior to placebo in reducing some of the withdrawal, hyperactivity, anger, and sterotypies in autistic persons ages 5 to 33. A second double-blind study on hyperactive and impulsive male children ages 5 to 13 found mild decreases in hyperactivity and irritability ratings by teachers and parents, but clinicians' ratings showed no such overall effect of Clonodine on autistics (Campbell & Shay, 1995).

Rimland (1987) summarizes 12 studies, carried out in the United States and in Europe, to evaluate the usefulness of vitamin B6 and magnesium in the treatment of autism, an intervention begun in the 1960s. Those 12 studies showed positive results, according to Rimland, in producing "better eye contact, less self-stimulatory behaviors, more interest in the world around them, fewer tantrums, more speech and in general the children became more normal, although they were not completely cured." By 1994, according to Rimland, there were 18 studies on the use of high doses of vitamin B6 with magnesium; all showed some beneficial effects, and none showed adverse effects because of the safety of those products compared to more risky psychophamacologicals.

Other medications, reflecting various theoretical constructs, or empirical trials have been reported on as treatments for autistic disorder, including propranolol (a beta blocker), bromocripine (an anti-Parkinson agent involving dopamine systems), and buspirone (Buspar), which is particularly for self-injurious behaviors.

Facilitated Communication

While debates about the use of aversives and full inclusion have been heated at times, none has approached the controversy and contentiousness that surround the differing views about facilitated communication (FC), extending even into international arena. FC began as a program in Australia in which a nondisabled teacher, parent, or volunteer (facilitator) would give physical assistance such as touching the arm of an autistic or other developmentally disabled person, while the patient used his or her fingers, on the assisted hand, to type letters, words, and sentences on an electronic keyboard or other similar device. The program was expanded by Douglas Biklen of Syracuse University in the United States. Biklen claimed in his studies that autistic persons, some of whom were entirely nonverbal, could carry on sophisticated conversations using these keyboards, including writing poetry and complex essays. Questions immediately arose in Australia and in the United States about the extent to which the facilitator was unknowingly (iatrogenically) influencing the typed responses so that the person "talking" was really the facilitator, not the autistic person. Rimland (1994) has summarized 44 studies involving nearly 400 subjects done to date on FC, and he points out that in none of those studies "has a single subject been able to confirm Biklen's claim that many (he says vast majority) can communicate their own thoughts in sentences." Some subjects were able to label simple objects part of the time and could copy single words part of the time, and Rimland concludes FC might better be described, when it does work, as facilitated object naming or facilitated word copying. A 1993 PBS *Frontline* documentary titled "Prisoners of Silence" was particularly critical of FC and generated even more national debate. In an update on FC, Rimland (1994) lists five professional organizations, including the American Speech-Language-Hearing Association, the American Academy of Child and Adolescent Psychiatry (ASHA), the American Academy of Pediatrics, the American Association on Mental Retardation, and the American Psychological Association, that have adopted positions "opposing the acceptance of F/C as a valid mode of enhancing expression in the handicapped." That update contains the exact language from the 1994 ASHA statement (generally reflected in all the others), which states, in part, that there is "no conclusive evidence that facilitated massages can be reliably attributed to people with disabilities. Rather, most messages originate with the facilitator."

Course and Prognosis

Since autistic disorder is not a solitary illness, there is no uniform outcome. Also, the rapid changes in treatment and interventions, particularly in the 1990s, have changed the landscape so drastically, and usefully, in terms of where the autistic person is treated (from institution to community, from special education to mainstreaming), when treatment begins (intensive *early* intervention), with what techniques (new behavioral and biological methods), and by

whom (therapists, teachers, and parents) that the more grim prognoses of the past need to be revised, and one cannot rely on old outcome studies to view these new, more hopeful approaches.

More autistic persons reside at home now than in institutions, which sometimes in the past represented the only placement alternative. For those who cannot be at home, or who have no home, a whole spectrum of alternative facilities in the community is increasingly available, including foster homes, group homes, residential facilities, and supported living arrangements (apartments) specifically tailored to the unique needs of the autistic population. Recently, residential/work programs for autistic adults in rural areas, as alternatives to urban programs, have developed in the United States and in Europe. Thus, more and more autistic persons are being "mainstreamed," not just into the classroom but into the neighborhood, the workplace, and the community at large, sometimes in specially tailored programs. More such programs are needed nationwide.

But autistic disorder is a *spectrum* of disability ranging from mild to severe. Treatment programs and facilities must reflect that same spectrum. Some autistic persons are so disabled, so self-injurious, or so aggressive that they do need, at least at some times, even at this point of our knowledge about the disorder, to be in an in-patient setting. It is not an indictment of parent or program if some autistic disorder patients still do require in-patient or respite services periodically or, in severe cases, on a continuing basis. Just as occurred with other populations, deinstitutionalization of the autistic can be carried too far or managed inappropriately with this population, and abuses and neglect can occur in community facilities, as well as in in-patient settings. Both need to be adequately monitored.

By far the majority of autistic disorder patients do not require continuing institutional care. Some can live independently in the community, and that number may be as great as 10% in high-functioning autistic adults. There are only a few long-term follow-up studies at this time. One Canadian study (Szatmari et al., 1989) followed 16 high-functioning autistic persons (IQ above 65) from childhood to the late teens or adulthood. Five lived independently, one was married, and three dated regularly. Fourteen of the 16 required minimal or no supervision in handling finances and everyday needs. Eight had graduated from high school, and seven had university degrees. A longitudinal study (McEachin et al., 1993) of 15 high-functioning autistic children from infancy through childhood or preadolescence showed a varying but improving course; at the outset, all 15 met the diagnostic criteria for autism, whereas none met those criteria at the end of the study, even though some significant academic and social problems did persist as "subtle traces of their disorder."

With increased public awareness and better information about the disorder; with the help of organizations that actively support parents and caretakers, such as the Autism Society of America, which also provides up-to-date information to interested professional persons; with an increasing number of specially tailored community treatment programs and assisted living facilities; and with research that identifies, one by one, the subgroups that constitute autistic disorder and then discovers treatments appropriate to and effective in those specific subgroups, outcomes will improve even further. Interventions over the past 20 years have changed so drastically, overall for the better, that outcome studies, if they are to be meaningful, need to be done anew so that they accurately reflect outcome for those persons diagnosed with autistic disorder in the 1990s. Times, and outcomes, have changed.

Up-to-date information about autistic disorder itself, and about facilities, programs, support groups, and local resources for treatment of autism, can be obtained from the Autism Society of America, 1234 Massachusetts Avenue, N.W., Washington, D.C. 20005. For professionals, parents, and other interested persons, an excellent continuing source of broad-based, comprehensive information about current research in etiology, treatment, and program development as monitored on an ongoing basis is *Autism Research Review International*, a quarterly publication of the Autism Research Institute, 4182 Adams Avenue, San Diego, California 92116. It is dedicated to the review of biomedical and educational research in the field of autism and related disorders and uses an international and multidisciplinary network as information sources. *The Journal of Autism and Developmental Disorders* is another excellent resource for current information about research on and treatment of this disorder. An especially valuable resource for parents is the book *Children with Autism: A Parent's Guide* by Michael Powers (1989). In addition to detailed, understandable information about autistic disorder itself, the book contains information on helping families adjust to the diagnosis and on finding appropriate professionals to provide treatment and education and treatment programs. It also contains a discussion of legal rights and parent advocacy; a list of additional suggested readings; a resource guide to relevant national organizations; and an extremely useful, detailed list of regional research and treatment centers, as well as a state-by-state list of public and private agencies that provide assistance to people with special needs and to their families.

SAVANT SYNDROME IN AUTISTIC DISORDER

Approximately 10% of persons with autistic disorder have special abilities as part of what is called savant syndrome. Savant syndrome is a rare but spectacular condition in which persons with various developmental disabilities, including autistic disorder, have astonishing islands of ability or brilliance that stand in stark, markedly incongruous contrast to the overall handicap (Treffert, 1988, 1989). In some, savant skills are remarkable simply in contrast to the handicap (talented savants). In a much rarer form of the condition, the ability or brilliance is not only spectacular in contrast to the handicap, but would be spectacular even if viewed in a normal person (prodigious savant). There are fewer than 100 reported cases of the prodigious form in the world literature. Savant syndrome was first named *idiot savant* by Dr. J. Langdon Down (better known for having named Down's Syndrome) in 1887. The word "idiot" at that time was an accepted classification level of mental retardation (IQ below 25) and the word "savant" meant knowledgeable person derived from the french word *savoir*, meaning "to know." The term idiot savant has been largely discarded, appropriately, because of its colloquial, pejorative connotation and has been replaced by savant syndrome (Treffert, 1989). Actually, *idiot savant* was a misnomer because almost all of the reported cases have occurred in persons with IQs of 40 or above. The condition can be congenital or acquired in an otherwise normal individual following CNS injury or disease. It occurs in males more frequently than in females in an approximate 6:1 ratio.

Savant skills occur within a narrow but constant range of human mental functions, generally in six areas: calendar calculating, lightening calculating and mathematical ability, art (drawing or sculpting), music (usually piano with perfect pitch), mechanical abilities, and spatial skills. In rare instances unusual language abilities have been reported. Other skills much less frequently reported include map memorizing, visual measurement, extrasensory perception, unusual sensory discrimination (such as enhanced sense of touch and smell), and perfect appreciation (passing time without knowledge of a clock face). The most common savant skill is musical ability. A regularly recurring triad of musical genius, blindness, and autism is particularly striking in the world literature on this topic. Premature birth history is commonly reported in persons with savant syndrome.

In some cases of savant syndrome, a single special skill exists; in other cases several skills coexist. The skills tend to be right hemisphere in type—nonsymbolic, artistic, concrete, directly perceived—in contrast to left hemisphere type, which tend to be more sequential, logical, and symbolic (including language specialization).

Whatever the special skills, they are *always* linked with phenomenal memory. That memory, however, is of special type—very narrow but exceedingly deep—within its narrow

confines. Such memory is a type of "unconscious reckoning"—habit or procedural memory—which relies on more primitive circuitry (cortico-limbic) than higher level (cortico-striatal) cognitive or associative memory used more commonly and regularly in normal persons.

Approximately 10% of persons with autistic disorder have some savant abilities; that percentage is much greater than in other developmental disabilities, where in an institutionalized population that figure may be as low as 1:2000. Since other developmental disabilities are much more common than autism, however, the actual percentage of persons with savant syndrome turns out to be approximately half autistic disorder and half other developmental disabilities.

Theories to explain savant syndrome include eidetic imagery, inherited skills, concrete thinking and inability to think abstractly, compensation and reinforcement, and left brain injury with right brain compensation. Newer findings on cerebral lateralization, and some imaging and other studies that show left hemisphere damage in savants, suggest that the most plausible explanation for savant syndrome is left brain damage from prenatal, perinatal, or postnatal CNS damage with migratory right brain compensation *coupled with* corresponding damage to higher level cognitive (cortico-striatal) memory circuitry with compensatory takeover of lower level habit (cortical-limbic) memory. This accounts for the linking of predominately right brain skills with habit memory so characteristic of savant syndrome (Treffert, 1989). In talented savants, concreteness and impaired ability to think abstractly are locked in a very narrow band but, nevertheless, with constant practice and repetition can produce sufficient coding so that access to some noncognitive structure or unconscious algorithms can be automatically attained. In prodigious savants, some genetic factors may be operative as well, because practice alone cannot account for the access to vast rules of music, art, or mathematics, which seem innate in these persons. Once established, intense concentration, practice, compensatory drives, and reinforcement by family, teachers, and others play a major role in developing and polishing the savant skills and memory linked so characteristically and dramatically by this unique brain dysfunction.

One of the prenatal CNS injury mechanisms, which has implications not only for savant syndrome but for other disorders in which male sex is overrepresented, is the neurotoxic effect of circulating testosterone on the left hemisphere in the male fetus based on observations and reported by Geschwind and Galaburda (1987). Since the left brain completes its development later than the right brain, it is at risk for CNS damage from the circulating testosterone in male fetuses (which can be neurotoxic) for a longer period of time. Left brain CNS damage, with right brain compensation, may account for the high male:female ratio not only in savant syndrome, but in autism, stuttering, hyperactivity, and learning disabilities as well.

After the movie *Rain Man* depicted an autistic savant, that term became almost a household word. It is important to remember, however, that not all autistic persons are savants, and not all savants are autistic. What one sees in *Rain Man* are savant skills (lightening calculating, memorization, etc.) grafted *on to* autism (narrowed affect, obsessive sameness, rituals, etc.). It also is important to point out that the savant in the movie is a high functioning person with autistic disorder, but that autistic disorder consists of an entire spectrum of disabilities ranging from profoundly disturbed to high functioning—not all autistic savants function at such a high level.

For many years it was feared that helping the savant achieve a higher level of functioning with treatment—"eliminating the defect"—would result in a loss of special skills, that is, there would be a trade-off of right brain special skills for left brain language acquisition. That has not turned out to be the case. Quite to the contrary, "training the talent" is a valuable approach toward increasing socialization, language, and independence. Thus the special skills of the savant, rather then being seen as odd, frivolous, trivial, or distracting, become a useful treatment tool as a conduit toward normalization in these special persons. Some schools have begun to include persons with savant syndrome into classes for the gifted and talented as a method of enhancing further this conduit toward normalization.

WILLIAMS SYNDROME AND AUTISTIC DISORDER

In 1961 Williams described a genetic disorder in children with consistent findings of distinctive, characteristic facial features (often described as "elfin-like" or "pixie-like"); a heart defect (aortic stenosis); elevated calcium levels associated with "colic-like" symptoms as infants; autistic-like behaviors such as inflexibility, ritualism, obsessiveness, and hyperacusis; and developmental delays coupled with attention deficits and cognitive disability, usually with IQ less than 70. What is unique to Williams syndrome, however, in contrast to other forms of developmental disability, is a rich, expansive, grammatically complex vocabulary with striking conversation and richly expressive storytelling skills. Equally as striking, in contrast to the usual behavioral handicaps of autism, is the extremely outgoing, friendly, polite, expressive social skills that Williams syndrome persons show. They are typically unafraid of strangers and show a greater interest in contact with adults than with peers. Many are reported to have savant-like musical skills. This combination of a distinctive "elfin-like" appearance with what has been called a "cocktail party" personality (including expansive and expressive speech and musical ability) in persons with otherwise impaired cognition and many autistic features provides a most intriguing and unique mix of ability and disability. The unusual circumstance of impaired general cognition, but *spared* and even precocious language abilities, challenges theories about the ordinary linkage of language and cognition and raises new possibilities in thinking about language acquisition and brain function in autism, PDD, and other developmental disabilities (Wang & Bellugi, 1993).

Adding to the research interest in this condition is the fact that a specific genetic defect on chromosome 7 has been identified as the etiologic mechanism in the disorder. The genetic defect makes elastin production deficient, and it is thought that the elastin gene deletion accounts for the cardiovascular as well as neurodevelopmental brain abnormalities in persons with Williams syndrome. Gillberg and Rasmussen (1994) reported four cases of people with Williams syndrome who have classic concurrent autistic disorder (rather than simply autistic-like behavior). Their article explores the research significance of the concurrence of the two disorders and provides an excellent overview of the condition. The confluence of autistic disorder, mental retardation, and savant abilities seen in Williams syndrome (with the enhanced language so *atypical* of mental retardation and increased sociability and over-friendliness so *atypical* of autism, along with an overrepresentation of savant musical skills), provide a most intriguing mix from clinical, theoretical, and research points of view. If a diagnosis of Williams syndrome is suspected, the patient should be referred to a geneticist for specific laboratory tests to confirm the diagnosis. The national association for Williams syndrome provides information and support services to families of persons with Williams syndrome.

RETT'S DISORDER

Rett's disorder is a neurologic disorder in which progressive encephalopathy and deterioration occur usually (but not exclusively) in female infants beginning as early as 5 months of age after seemingly normal physical, motor, and intellectual development. Between the ages of 5 months and 48 months there is loss of previously acquired social, motor, and language skills with the appearance of unusual, but characteristic for this disorder, stereotyped hand-wringing or hand-washing type movements. There is deceleration of head growth, which previously had been normal. Autistic-like symptoms of social withdrawal, hyperactivity, and self-stimulation behaviors occur. Severely impaired expressive and receptive language defects are seen along with severe mental and psychomotor retardation. Seizures can occur in as many as two thirds of patients. EEG abnormalities are frequently seen. Abnormal gait and trunk movements are common, as are various skeletal abnormalities (including spasticity, scoliosis, and foot drop). The problems with poor social relatedness are often reported to improve somewhat with age.

Rett first described this disorder in 1966 in 22 girls. In 17 of 22 patients ammonia levels were elevated but that finding has not been consistent in later studies by Rett and others. Wider recognition of the disorder occurred when Hagberg and coworkers (1983) described 35 cases. Recent studies in Japan, the United States, and elsewhere have reported Rett's disorder symptoms in some males (Coleman, 1990; Philippart, 1990). An excellent overview of clinical features, differential diagnosis, assessment, laboratory studies, imaging data, and treatment is provided by Sekul and Percy in a 1992 review article.

The disorder appeared in DSM for the first time in the fourth edition. ICD-10 criteria for the disorder are the same as in DSM-IV and include the following:

1. apparently normal prenatal and perinatal development, including normal psychomotor development through the first 5 months and normal head circumference at birth
2. after a period of normal development, deceleration of head growth between the 5th and 48th month; loss of previously acquired purposeful hand skills with substitution somewhere between the 5th and 30th month of stereotyped hand movements such as hand-wringing or hand washing; loss of social engagement, although social interaction skills may develop later; poorly coordinated gait or trunk movements; and severely

impaired expressive and receptive language development coupled with severe psychomotor retardation.

Prevalence of Rett's disorder is estimated to be about 1:15000 births, with the vast majority of cases being reported in females—but not exclusively so as noted in the several studies reporting Rett's disorder in males.

The etiology of Rett's disorder is unknown, although genetic factors are heavily implicated. Biochemical abnormalities, including reduced B-Endorphins in spinal fluid of female Rett's disorder patients, have been reported, as have defects in the structure or enzyme systems of mitochondria in muscle tissue in girls with Rett's disorder (Ruch, 1989). Trauner and Haas (1987) have reported on characteristic EEG abnormalities in such patients.

Rett and Olsson (1985) and Budden (1986) differentiate Rett's disorder from autistic disorder as follows. In Rett's disorder the stereotypic hand movements are particularly characteristic and uniform and there is overall severe mental retardation, gait disturbance, often scoliosis, and microcephaly, as a part of the disorder. Rett patients also show a willingness to make eye contact, develop appropriate speech before the onset of deterioration, have severe problems with chewing and swallowing food, and have frequent seizure occurrence.

There is no specific treatment for Rett's disorder. Some reports have indicated that bromocriptine was effective in reducing some symptoms, including the stereotypic hand-washing activities. Other medications are sometimes useful in decreasing the hand stereotypies, which can become very severe and immobilizing.

Rett's disorder is a relatively new reported condition. Through June, 1995, 2237 cases were reported worldwide (1817 of those in the United States) to the Rett's Foundation, which exists as a case registry and information resource for parents and professionals. (The Rett's Foundation is located at 9121 Piscataway, Suite 2B, Clinton, Maryland 20735. 1-800-818-RETT.)

CHILDHOOD DISINTEGRATIVE DISORDER

This condition appeared as a separate entity for the first time in DSM-IV. It was originally described by Heller in 1908 and named "dementia infantilis." Heller described six children who showed severe regression in multiple areas of behavior and development after 3 to 4 years of normal development.

Symptoms of child disintegrative disorder as described in DSM-IV include the following:

1. Normal development of the child to at least age 2 as manifested by age-appropriate verbal and nonverbal communication, social relationships, play, and adaptive behavior.
2. Significant loss of those previously acquired skills before age 10 in at least two of five areas:
   a. expressive or receptive language
   b. social skills or adaptive behavior
   c. bowel or bladder control
   d. play
   e. motor skills
3. Abnormal functioning in at least two of the following areas:
   a. qualitative impairment in social interaction such as failure to develop peer relationships, lack of social or emotional reciprocity, or impairment in nonverbal behaviors
   b. qualitative impairment in communication such as delay or lack of spoken language, inability to initiate or sustain conversation, stereotyped and repetitive use of language, or lack of varied make-believe play
   c. restricted, repetitive, and stereotyped patterns of behavior, interests, mannerisms, and motor activities.

Childhood disintegrative disorder is an extremely rare condition, with approximately 77 cases reported in the world literature since Heller's 1908 report. The disorder is more common in males. In most cases, the onset of the disorder occurs at age three or four.

The essential feature, which distinguishes this disorder from autistic disorder, is marked regression after 2 years of apparently normal development. Mental retardation usually is a part of the disorder. Increased EEG abnormalities and seizures, as in Rett's disorder, are reported. Etiology is uncertain but generally appears to be a neurological development or degenerative process. There are reports of some accompanying neurological disorders such as Schilder's disease (adrenoleukodystrophy) or metachromic leukodystrophy in some cases, but often no specific neurological disease or process can be easily or readily identified.

Course of the disorder is variable. Onset can be gradual or abrupt. In some instances progressive deterioration occurs, but in other cases there is a period of regression followed by a static, plateaued course. There is no specific treatment for the disorder.

ICD-10 classifies this disorder as "Other Childhood Disintegrative Disorder," separating it thus from childhood autism, atypical autism, Rett's syndrome, Asperger's syndrome, and other pervasive developmental disorders, all of which would be included in a differential diagnosis, as would the neurological disorders specified above.

ASPERGER'S DISORDER

History

In 1944 an Austrian psychiatrist, Hans Asperger, described a condition in which persons with rather severe psychiatric impairments showed some exceptional skill or talent disproportionate to overall intellectual ability. Usually the skill involved an extraordinary capacity for memorization. He named the condition "autistic psychopathy." His description of what he called Asperger's disorder is nearly identical to Kanner's (1943) simultaneous description of infantile autism in the United States. The striking similarity between those two accounts did not become apparent, however, until about 1981 when Asperger's paper was translated into English for the first time. Until then, the term

Asperger's disorder was less familiar than infantile autism. Debate continues as to whether there are essential and distinctive differences between these two conditions or whether they are simply variants, primarily on a spectrum of severity, of the same disorder.

Clinical Description

In 1981 Wing reviewed Asperger's original cases and added 34 cases of her own. From those two groups of cases came the following picture of such patients: (1) Males outnumber females approximately 6:1. (2) Unlike in autistic disorder, onset of speech usually is not delayed, but, like autism, speech is repetitive, with monotone intonation and absence of use of first-person pronouns. (3) Nonverbal communication is flat, with little facial expression; the patient often seems to "stare through" persons in lieu of making direct eye contact. (4) Social interactions are severely restricted, naive, and peculiar. (5) Repetitive activities are preferred and are engaged in at length; there is resistance to change and intense attachment to particular possessions. (6) Motor coordination is particularly poor—patients are clumsy and posture and gait are peculiar. (7) There is excellent, often prodigious, memory with intense preoccupation and mastery of one or two subjects of interest, such as bus schedules, sports statistics, or history trivia, sometimes to the exclusion of learning in all other areas. (8) Language overall is rather limited except in the area of special ability, where conversation can be expansive, pedantic, and seemingly scholarly but shows little grasp of the meaning of words put forth so liberally. Even those dissertations tend to be carried out by rote.

The majority of symptoms of Asperger's disorder are the same as those of early infantile autism. Uta Frith (1991) edited a book that explores the links between autism and Asperger's syndrome. Several distinctive features of Asperger's are generally described: (1) clumsiness and poor motor coordination, not regularly seen in autism; (2) a higher level of social functioning than seen in autistic persons but still with bizarre, peculiar, and naive social interactions; (3) the use of facile, expansive language in several favorite subject areas but with no grasp of the meaning of the words used, in contrast to the mutism or globally impaired speech so often characteristic of autism; and (4) an average or above average measured IQ. Asperger believed his patients to be of high intelligence but provided no IQ scores to confirm that impression. Approximately 80% of Wing's cases were of average or above average intelligence.

Asperger's disorder was given official, separate recognition for the first time in DSM-IV and ICD-10. DSM-IV criteria include the following features:

1. Qualitative social interaction impairment as shown in at least *two* of the following ways:
   a. marked impairment in the use of nonverbal behaviors such as eye-to-eye gaze, facial expression, gestures, and body postures
   b. failure to develop peer relationships appropriate to developmental level
   c. lack of spontaneous seeking to share enjoyment, interests, or achievements with other people
   d. lack of social or emotional reciprocity
2. Restricted repetitive and stereotyped behavior, interests, and activities as shown by at least *one* of the following:
   a. encompassing preoccupation with one or more stereotyped, restricted patterns of interest that is abnormal in focus or intensity
   b. inflexible adherence to specific, nonfunctional routines or rituals
   c. stereotyped, repetitive motor mannerisms
   d. persistent preoccupation with parts of objects
3. Symptoms such as the above that cause clinically significant impairment in social, occupational, or other areas of functioning
4. No clinically significant general delay in language acquisition and use
5. No clinically significant delay in cognitive development or in the development of age-appropriate self-help skills, adaptive behavior (except social skills), and curiosity about the environment in childhood.

Prevalence and Etiology

A Swedish study (Gilberg & Gilberg, 1989) suggested that Asperger's disorder may occur in as many as 26 of every 10,000 nonretarded children and indicated that Asperger's was rarely found in conjunction with retardation. There appears to be an increased incidence of Asperger's disorder among relatives of those who have the disorder, suggesting a genetic component to the condition; a case of Asperger's in triplets fortifies the evidence for some genetic factors (Burgoine & Wing, 1983). While clumsiness is sometimes noted as a differentiating feature between Asperger's disorder and autism, some studies have shown no support for that observation. Several other clinicians, including Asperger himself, commented on face blindness (prosopagnosia) as being present in some Asperger's cases, perhaps denoting a subgroup of the disorder.

Several neuropsychologists have examined the NP profiles in persons with Asperger's disorder and contrasted them with NP profiles in persons with autistic disorder. Those cognitive profiles were found to be quite different from each other, suggesting two distinct disorders that share some clinical similarities but have different CNS dysfunctions. From those differing NP findings, it has been speculated that in Asperger's patients there may be a defect in *right* hemisphere function and relative superiority of *left* hemisphere verbal skills (in contrast to the opposite picture in autistic persons). However, Bonnet's (1987) study of six generations of a family with several cases of Asperger's disorder found evidence of *left* brain dysfunction in those with Asperger's disorder. Research reports have associated Asperger's disorders with acrocyanosis, Marfan's syndrome, and Tourette disorder. While generally no imaging findings specific to Asperger's disorder have been reported, one study (Berthier, 1994) did show abnormalities in the corpus callosum in 10 of 19 patients.

Assessment

Some neuropsychological test profiles have been reported to be consistently characteristic of Asperger's disorder. Stevens and Moffitt (1988) reviewed findings to date in their report of an Asperger's patient with exceptional mathematical ability who fit the generally reported NP profiles: Speech capabilities are superior to visuo-spatial abilities with good performance on tasks of abstraction; verbal IQs exceed performance scales by as high as 30 points; verbally based scores are particularly higher than visuo-spatial scores; abstract reasoning scores and tests of executive function tend to be within normal limits.

Treatment and Prognosis

Although there are no treatment approaches specific to Asperger's disorder, the same general multidisciplinary educational, social, and vocational approaches apply here as in the other pervasive developmental disorders. Since Asperger's disorder patients generally are rather high-functioning persons in the disability spectrum, behavioral symptoms are less intrusive and thus medication is less essential in attempting to modify the symptoms. Similarly, educational and vocational programs are geared toward that higher functioning and housing needs are more likely to include independent living arrangements.

Debate continues as to whether Asperger's disorder is separate from autistic disorder (which both Wing and Asperger believed to be the case) or whether it is a variant of autistic disorder with most persons operating at the high end of the spectrum in terms of overall function. Both DSM-IV and ICD-10 treat Asperger's disorder as an entity separate from autistic disorder. In a 1996 review of this question, Trevarthen and his coauthors, after examining the most recent data on this topic, concluded that autistic disorder and Asperger's disorder are better viewed as differing in level of impairment on a continuing spectrum of severity rather than being viewed as two separate conditions, a concept embodied in the term "autistic spectrum disorder" mentioned in the introduction to this chapter.

In general, since Asperger's disorder patients do function at a higher level overall than autistic disorder patients, as a group they are less disabled and more able to live and work more normally in the community than many autistic persons. In that sense the prognosis is generally more favorable in Asperger's disorder than in other pervasive developmental disorders.

PERVASIVE DEVELOPMENTAL DISORDER NOT OTHERWISE SPECIFIED

Both DSM-IV and ICD-10 contain the somewhat catch-all category of pervasive developmental disorder, NOS. In DSM-IV this category includes "atypical autism," which is defined as a condition where the criteria for autistic disorder as set forth in DSM-IV are not met because of late age of onset of symptoms or because those symptoms are subthreshold quantitatively. This PDD/NOS category is also applied, using DSM-IV terminology, when there is pervasive impairment in the development of reciprocal social interaction or verbal or nonverbal communication, or when stereotyped behavior, interests, and activities are present, but the criteria are not met for one of the other pervasive development disorders classified and described in DSM-IV.

It should be pointed out that ICD-10 has a separate classification for "atypical autism," rather than merely inclusion in the PDD/NOS category. Within ICD-10 atypical autism is defined as having onset after 3 years of age and having only two components of the full triad (impairment in reciprocal social interaction and communication along with restricted, stereotyped, repetitive behaviors) of components necessary for the diagnosis of childhood autism. Therefore, a clinician classifying a child as "atypical" for autistic disorder using DSM-IV terminology would apply the diagnosis of PDD/NOS. Using ICD-10 terminology, the clinician would apply the atypical autism diagnosis.

In day-to-day practice, autistic *behavior* (as opposed to autistic *disorder*) is often seen in a number of pervasive developmental disorders, other developmental disorders, or other psychiatric disorders such as schizophrenia or schizotypal personality disorders, for example. Occasionally a case of "classic" infantile autism is seen, but more often cases do not precisely fit any of the PDD categories. If the classification of pervasive development disorder itself is somewhat diffuse, as was pointed out in the introduction to this chapter, PDD/NOS is even more diffuse and its imprecision lends frustration to clinicians and families alike.

Regrettably, until PDD is spearated into the more distinct categories of disturbance—and etiology—that appear to exist, this somewhat nebulous, catch-all classification will have to do, for it is all the present state of knowledge will allow. However, with accelerating interest and activity in research into etiology of these various disorders, and with increasingly better technology and equipment to carry out necessary studies, PDD eventually can be separated into the several disorders it encompasses, and those that are only different quantitatively, rather than qualitatively, can be appropriately viewed as spectrum disorders.

This etiologic search, and the logical classification change that would result from it, is more than an academic exercise because, from more specific etiologies, individually targeted and hence more effective therapies will emerge. In the meantime, however, clinicians and families alike need to focus efforts on putting together broad-based, multidisciplinary treatment plans that specifically tailor programs to each person's uniqueness and *a*bilities as well as *dis*abilities, irrespective of which particular classification tag is applied.

REFERENCES

American Psychiatric Association. (1994). *Diagnostic and statistical manual of mental disorders* (4th ed.). Washington, DC: Author.

Asperger, H. (1944). Die "autistischen psychopathen" in kindersalter. *Arch Psychiatrie Nerven Krankh*, 117, 76.

Bailey, A., Luthert, P., Bolton, P., LeCouteur, A., Rutter, M., & Harding, B. (1993). Autism and megalencephaly. *Lancet*, 341.

Berthier, M. (1994). Corticocallosal abnormalities in Asperger's Syndrome. *American Journal of Roentgenology*, 162, 236–237.

Birnbrauer, J. & Leach, D. (1993): The Murdoch early intervention program after two years. *Behavior Change*, 10, 63–74.

Bonnet, K. (1987, September). A neurological locus for Asperger Syndrome and its genetics. Abstract of presentation to the Birth Defects Symposium.

Budden, S. (1986). Rett syndrome: Studies of 13 affected girls. *American Journal of Medical Genetics*, 24, 99–109.

Burgoine, E., & Wing, L. (1983). Identical triplets with Asperger's syndrome. *British Journal of Psychiatry*, 143, 261–265.

Campbell, M., et al. (1993). Naltrexone in autistic children: Behavioral symptoms and attentional learning. *Journal of the American Academy of Child and Adolescent Psychiatry*, 32, 1283–1291.

Campbell, M., & Schopler, E. (1989) Section 2: Pervasive developmental disorders. In American Psychiatric Association, *Treatments of psychiatric disorders: A task force report* (pp. 000) Washington, DC: American Psychiatric Press.

Campbell, M., & Shay, J. (1995). Pervasive developmental disorders. In H. Kaplan & B. Sadock (Eds.), *Comprehensive Textbook of Psychiatry VI* (pp. 000). Baltimore: Williams and Wilkins.

Coleman, M. (1990). Is classical Rett syndrome ever present in males? *Brain Development*, 12, 31–32.

Cook, E. et al. (1992). Fluoxetine treatment of children and adults with autistic disorder and mental retardation. *Journal of the American Academy of Child and Adolescent Psychiatry*, 31, 739–745.

Courchesne, E. (1993). Parietal lobe abnormalities dectected with MR in patients with infantile autism. *American Journal of Roentgenology, 160*, 387–393.

Courchesne, E. (1994). Abnormality of cerebellar vermian lobules VI and VII in patients with infantile autism. *American Journal of Roentgenology, 162*, 123–130.

Dawson, G., Phillips, S., Galpert, L., & Finley, C. (1986). Specialization and the language abilities of autistic children. *Child Development*, 57, 1440–1453.

Down, J. (1887). *On some of the mental affections of childhood and youth.* London: Churchill.

Fenske, C., Zalenski, S., Krantz, P., & McClannahan, L. (1985). Age at intervention and treatment outcome for autistic children in a comprehensive intervention program. *Annals and Intervention in Developmental Disabilities*, 5, 49–58.

Frith, U. (1991). *Autism and Asperger Syndrome.* Cambridge: Cambridge University Press.

Geschwind, N., & Galaburda, A. (1987). Cerebral lateralization: Biological mechanisms, associations and pathology. Cambridge, MA: MIT Press.

Gilberg, I., & Gilberg, C. (1989). Asperger's Syndrome—some epidemiologic considerations: A research note. *Journal of Child Psychology and Psychiatry*, 30, 631–638.

Gillberg, C., & Rasmussen, P. (1994). Brief report: Four case histories and a literature review of Williams Syndrome and Autistic Behavior, *Journal of Autism and Developmental Disorders*, 24, 381–392.

Gordon, C., State, R., Nelson, J., Hamberger, S., & Rapaport, J. (1993). A double-blind comparison of clomimpramine, desimipramine and placebo in treatment of autistic disorder. *Archives of General Psychiatry*, 50, 441–447.

Hagberg, B., Aicardi, J., Dias, K., & Ramos, O. (1983). A progressive syndrome of autism, dementia, ataxia and loss of purposeful hand use in girls. *Annals of Neurology*, 14, 471–479.

Hashimoto, T. et al. (1995). Development of the brainstem and cerebellum in autistic patients. *Journal of Autism and Developmental Disorders*, 25, 1–18.

Hunt, A., & Shepard, C. (1993). A prevalence study of autism in tuberous sclerosis. *Journal of Autism and Developmental Disorders*, 23, 323–339.

Iverson, S. (1990). Autism as one of several disabilities in two children with congenital cytomegalovirus infection. *Neuropediatrics*, 21, 102–103.

Kanner, L. (1943). Autistic disturbances of affective contact. *Nervous Child*, 2, 217–250.

Kanner, L. (1944). Early infantile autism. *Jouranl of Pediatrics*, 25, 200–217.

Lovaas, O. (1987). Behavioral treatment and normal education and intellectual functioning in young autistic children. *Journal of Consulting and Clinical Psychology*, 55, 3–9.

McDougal, C. (1995, August). Fluvoxamine improves adult autism's core effects. *Clinical Psychiatry News.*

McDougal, C., Price, C., & Goodman, W. (1990). Fluvoxamine treatment of co-incident autistic disorder and obsessive-compulsive disorder: A case report. *Journal of Autism and Developmental Disorders*, 20, 532–543.

McEachin, J., Smith, T., & Lovaas, I. (1993). Long-term outcome for children who received early intensive behavioral treatment. *American Journal on Mental Retardation*, 97, 359–391.

Parks, S. (1983). The assessment of autistic children: A selective review of available instruments. *Journal of Autism and Developmental Disorders*, 13, 255–267.

Philippart, M. (1990). The Rett Syndrome in males. *Brain Development*, 12, 33–36.

Piven, J. (1995). An MRI study of brain size in autism. *American Journal of Psychiatry*, 152, 1145–1149.

Pomeroy, J. (1990). Infantile autism and childhood psychosis. In B. Garfinkel, G. Carlson, & E. Weller (Eds.), *Psychiatric disorders in children and adolescents.* Philadelphia: W. B. Saunders.

Powers, M. (1989). Children with autism: A parent's guide. Rockville, MD: Woodbine House.

Purdon, S., Wilson, L., Labelle, A., & Jones, B. (1994). Risperidone in the treatment of PDD. *Canadian Journal of Psychiatry*, 39, 400–405.

Rett, A. (1966). Uber ein cerebral-atropisches Syndrom bei Hyperammonamie. Vienna: Bruder Hollinek.

Rett, A., & Olsson, B. (1985). Behavioral observations concerning differential diagnosis between Rett syndrome and autism. *Brain and Development*, 7.

Rimland, B. (1964). *Infantile autism.* New York: Appleton-Century Crofts.

Rimland, B. (1987), Vitamin B6 (and Magnesium) in the treatment of autism. *Autism Research Review International*, 1(4), 3.

Rimland, B. (1991). New surgical treatment offers hope for children with rare disorder often diagnosed as autism. *Autism Research Review International*, 5(1).

Rimland, B. (1994). Facilitated communication update. *Autism Research Review International*, 8(4), 6.

Ritvo, E., et al. (1986). Lower purkinje cell counts in

the cerebella of four autistic subjects. *American Journal of Psychiatry, 143,* 862–866.

Ruch, A., et al. (1989). Mitochondrial alterations in Rett syndrome. *Pediatric Neurology, 5,* 320–323.

Schopler, E., Mesibov, G., Shigley, R., & Bashford, A. (1984). Helping autistic children through their parents: The TEACCH model. In E. Schopler & G. Mesibov (Eds.), *The effects of autism on the family* (pp. 65–81). New York: Plenum Press.

Sekul, E., & Percy, A. (1992). Rett syndrome: Clinical features, genetic considerations, and the search for a biological marker. In *Current Neurology.* Mosby-Year Book, Inc.

Stefanatos, G., Grover, W., & Geller, E. (1995). Case study: Corticosteroid treatment of language regression in PPD. *Journal of the American Academy of Child and Adolescent Psychiatry.*

Stevens, D., & Moffitt, T. (1988). Neuropsychological profile of an Asperger's Syndrome case with exceptional mathematical skills. *Clinical Neuropsychologist, 2,* 228–238.

Sverd, J. (1991). Tourette's syndrome and autistic disorder: A significant relationship. *American Journal of Medical Genetics, 39,* 173–179.

Szatmari, G. et al. (1989). A follow-up study of high-functioning autistic children. *Journal of Autism and Developmental Disorders, 19,* 213–225.

Trauner, D., & Haas, R. (1987). Electroencephalographic abnormalities in Rett syndrome. *Pediatric Neurology, 3,* 331–334.

Treffert, D. (1970). The epidemiology of infantile autism. *Archives of General Psychiatry, 22,* 431–438.

Treffert, D. (1988). The idiot savant: A review of the syndrome. *American Journal of Psychiatry, 145,* 563–572.

Treffert, D. (1989). *Extraordinary people: Understanding savant syndrome.* New York: Ballantine.

Trevarthen, C., Aitken, K., Papoudi, D., & Robarts, J. (1996). *Children with autism: Diagnosis and interventions to meet their needs.* London: Jessica Kingsley Publishers.

Wang, P., & Bellugi, U. (1993). Williams Syndrome, Down Syndrome and cognitive neuroscience. *American Journal of Diseases of Children, 147,* 1246–1251.

Williams, J., Barratt-Boyes, B., & Lowe, J. (1961). Supravalvular aortic stenosis. *Circulation, 24,* 1311–1318.

Wing, L. (1981). Asperger's Syndrome: A clinical account. *Psychological Medicine, 11,* 115.

World Health Organization. (1992). *International statistical classification of diseases and related health problems* (ICD-10). Geneva: Author.

6

Attention-Deficit/Hyperactivity Disorder

Arthur D. Anastopoulos

INTRODUCTION

Attention-deficit/hyperactivity disorder (AD-HD) is the current terminology used by the American Psychiatric Association (1994) to describe children, adolescents, and adults who display chronic, pervasive, and developmentally inappropriate patterns of inattention, impulsivity, and/or hyperactivity. Although ADHD has long been recognized by child and adolescent health care professionals, it is only in recent times that the public has become keenly aware of its existence. Among the many factors that have undoubtedly contributed to this enhanced public awareness is the increased attention that ADHD has received from the media. Over the past 5 years in particular there has been a steady stream of local, regional, and national reports on ADHD, surfacing in newspaper and magazine articles and as a topic of discussion on various television and radio programs.

For the most part, this type of media exposure has been beneficial, because it has served to increase not only the public's awareness of ADHD but also their understanding and acceptance of this disorder. Not surprisingly, this change has had an impact on clinical practice. In their work with referred children and adolescents, for example, many educators and health care professionals now routinely encounter parents who are extremely well versed on the topic of ADHD. Because many of these better-informed parents wish to understand ADHD at a level that goes beyond what they can glean from the media, new demands have been placed on practitioners to respond to ADHD-related questions in a far more specific and in-depth manner than was previously necessary.

In order to meet this challenge, practitioners must work vigorously at maintaining a base of ADHD knowledge that is up to date and comprehensive. It is with this objective in mind that this chapter was written. As a way of clarifying the confusion that often exists over the different labels that have been applied to what we now term ADHD, this chapter begins with a brief historical review of the disorder. This is followed by a detailed description and critique of the two major classification schemes that educators and child health care professionals use in diagnosing this condition. As part of this discussion, relevant epidemiological and etiological issues are addressed. Against this background, current approaches to the assessment and treatment of ADHD in children and adolescents are then discussed.

Historical Perspective

For reasons that are not entirely clear, some individuals mockingly refer to ADHD as "the latest fad in psychiatry" or "the disorder of the 90s." Little justification exists for making such claims. A more accurate characterization would be to say that ADHD is the most recent in a long line of diagnostic labels that have been used to describe children and adolescents who display some combination of inattention, impulsivity, and/or hyperactivity. Although confusing to some, this periodic relabeling has not been without purpose. On the contrary, each diagnostic term has reflected shifts in the way that this disorder has been conceptualized at different points in time.

Two major trends characterize the history of this disorder. The first of these pertains to the issue of diagnostic uniformity. From Still's (1902) earliest account until the late 1960s, there was very little agreement within the field as to what to call this condition. Reflecting this lack of consensus, many different labels, including "minimal brain dysfunction" (Clements & Peters, 1962) and "hyperactive child syndrome" (Chess, 1960), were employed. As it became increasingly apparent that the simultaneous use of multiple labels would seriously limit scientific progress, many clinicians and researchers began to acknowledge the need for having a common diagnostic terminology. The publication of the second edition of the *Diagnostic and Statistical Manual of Mental Disorders* (DSM-II) by the American Psychiatric Association (APA, 1968) afforded the first real opportunity for this to occur through its presentation of "hyperkinetic reaction of childhood." Although other names continued to be used for this condition thereafter (Wender, 1973), momentum began to build in the direction of greater diagnostic uniformity. By the time that DSM-III (APA, 1980) arrived, most clinicians and researchers were committed to using a common

set of labels and guidelines and therefore readily adopted its criteria for "attention-deficit disorder with hyperactivity" (ADDH) and its various subtypes. Despite the fact that additional changes in the diagnostic guidelines for this disorder have been made since that time, this commitment to diagnostic uniformity has persisted to the present. As a result, most professionals now use the same diagnostic language in their descriptions of this disorder.

The other major historical trend pertains to the manner in which this disorder has been labeled. With the exception of Still's (1902) account, most of the early descriptions of this condition, such as "postencephalitic behavior disorder" (Hohman, 1922), reflected its presumed etiology. During the mid-1930s, a competing trend began to emerge in the form of various symptom-based descriptions, which included such terms as "restlessness syndrome" (Levin, 1938). Although both trends remained in evidence for the next 3 decades (Chess, 1960; Clements & Peters, 1962), they eventually began taking very different directions, with etiologically based descriptions declining in importance and symptom-based descriptions gaining in acceptance. When "hyperkinetic reaction of childhood" appeared in DSM-II, it marked the beginning of a new era in which only symptom-based descriptions were used as labels for this disorder. Such a tradition remained in place for DSM-III and DSM-III-R and continues to be an integral part of the current diagnostic guidelines.

DIAGNOSTIC DESCRIPTION OF ADHD

Primary Symptoms

Clinical descriptions of children with ADHD frequently include complaints of "not listening to instructions," "not finishing assigned work," "daydreaming," "becoming bored easily," and so forth. Common to all of these referral concerns is a diminished capacity for vigilance, that is, difficulties sustaining attention to task (Douglas, 1983). Such problems can occur in free-play settings (Routh & Schroeder, 1976) but most often surface in situations demanding sustained attention to dull, boring, repetitive tasks (Milich, Loney, & Landau, 1982). Clinic-referred children with ADHD may exhibit impulsivity as well. For example, they may interrupt others who might be busy or display tremendous difficulty waiting for their turn in game situations. They may also begin tasks before directions are completed, take unnecessary risks, talk out of turn, or make indiscreet remarks without regard for social consequences. When hyperactivity is present, this may be displayed not only motorically but verbally. Descriptions of physical restlessness might include statements such as "always on the go," "unable to sit still," and so forth. As for the verbal component, more often than not these complaints center around the child's "talking excessively" or being a "chatterbox or motor mouth." Whether mild or severe, what makes all of these behaviors manifestations of hyperactivity is their excessive, task-irrelevant, and developmentally inappropriate nature.

Although this point is not yet widely accepted, difficulties with rule-governed behavior and excessive performance variability may also represent primary deficits (Barkley, 1990; Kendall & Braswell, 1985). Several studies have demonstrated that children with ADHD display significant problems adhering to rules or complying with requests (Rapport et al., 1986). In line with these findings are the clinical reports of parents and teachers, who commonly voice concerns about the inability of children with ADHD to "follow through on instructions." Such difficulties may arise in a variety of contexts but most often occur in situations when adults are not present—that is, when there are increased demands for behavioral self-regulation.

Children with ADHD may also display tremendous inconsistency in their task performance, in terms of both their productivity and their accuracy (Douglas, 1972). Such variability may be evident with respect to their in-class performance or test scores, or it may involve fluctuations in their completion of homework or routine home chores. While it can be argued that all children display a certain amount of variability in these areas, it is clear from clinical experience and research findings that children with ADHD exhibit this to a much greater degree. Thus, instead of reflecting "laziness" as some might contend, the inconsistent performance of children with ADHD may represent yet another manifestation of this disorder. To the extent that it does, this allows for a characterization of ADHD as a disorder of variability, rather than inability.

Future descriptions of ADHD may indeed include deficiencies in rule-governed behavior and performance variability as defining features. In the meantime, however, most professionals in the field today regard inattention, impulsivity, and hyperactivity as the primary symptoms of ADHD. Although these symptoms traditionally have been viewed as distinct and separate components of the disorder, the validity of this assumption has recently been called into question. At a theoretical level, Barkley (1995) has proposed that all three primary symptoms, as well as many of its associated features, may stem from an underlying deficit in behavioral inhibition processes. From a strictly empirical point of view, recently reported factor-analytic results have further suggested that, while inattention symptoms do indeed tend to cluster apart from symptoms of impulsivity and hyperactivity, these latter two symptoms nonetheless routinely cluster together (DuPaul, 1991).

Diagnostic Criteria

Within North America today, the currently accepted criteria for making an ADHD diagnosis appear in the fourth edition of the *Diagnostic and Statistical Manual of Mental Disorders* (DSM-IV; APA, 1994). At the heart of this decision making process are two nine-item symptom listings—one pertaining to inattention symptoms, the other to hyperactivity-impulsivity concerns. Parents and/or teachers must report the presence of at least six of nine problem behaviors from either list to warrant consideration of an ADHD diagnosis. Such behaviors must have an onset prior to 7 years of age, a duration of at least 6 months, and a frequency above and beyond that expected of children of the same mental age. Furthermore, they must be evident in two or more settings, have a clear impact on psychosocial functioning, and not be due to other types of mental health or learning disorders that might better explain their presence.

As is evident from these criteria, the manner in which ADHD presents itself clinically can vary from child to child. For some children with ADHD, symptoms of inattention may be of relatively greater concern than impulsivity or hyperactivity problems. For others, impulsivity and hyperactivity difficulties may be more prominent. Reflecting these possible differences in clinical presentation, the new DSM-IV criteria not only allow for, but require, ADHD subtyping. For example, when more than six symptoms are present from both lists and all other criteria are met, a diagnosis of ADHD, Combined Type, is in order. If six or more inattention symptoms are present but fewer than six hyperactive-impulsive symptoms are evident, and all other criteria are met, the proper diagnosis would be "ADHD, predominantly inattentive type." Those familiar with prior diagnostic classification schemes will quickly recognize these DSM-IV categories as similar but not exact counterparts to what previously was known as "attention-deficit hyperactivity disorder" and "undifferentiated attention-deficit disorder" in DSM-III-R (APA, 1987) and "attention-deficit disorder with or without hyperactivity" in DSM-III (APA, 1980). Appearing for the first time in DSM-IV, however, is the subtyping condition known as "ADHD, predominantly hyperactive-impulsive type," which is the appropriate diagnosis to make whenever six or more hyperactive-impulsive symptoms arise, fewer than six inattention concerns are evident, and all other criteria are met. Along with these major subtyping categories, DSM-IV also makes available two additional classifications that have primary bearing on adolescents and adults. For example, a diagnosis of "ADHD, in partial remission," may be given to individuals who have clinical problems resulting from ADHD symptoms that currently do not meet criteria for any of the subtypes but nonetheless were part of a documented ADHD diagnosis at an earlier time. In similar cases where an earlier history of ADHD cannot be established with any degree of certainty, a diagnosis of "ADHD, not otherwise specified," would instead be made.

Although educators and child health care professionals in Europe and in many other parts of the world would certainly agree that symptoms of inattention and/or hyperactivity constitute a diagnostic condition, they would not refer to it as ADHD, nor would they follow DSM-IV guidelines in deciding whether or not a diagnosis was present. If any diagnosis was to be made at all, it would be "hyperkinetic disorder," the criteria for which appear in the tenth edition of the *International Classification of Diseases* (ICD-10; World Health Organization, 1993). Somewhat akin to DSM-IV, ICD-10 uses separate symptom listings, encompassing a total of 18 symptoms. Unlike DSM-IV, however, ICD-10 utilizes a nine-item inattention list, a five-item hyperactivity list, and a four-item list of impulsivity symptoms, each of which also differs in the symptom cut-points that they employ. For example, at least six inattention symptoms, three hyperactivity symptoms, and one impulsivity symptom must be present before one can consider a diagnosis of hyperkinetic disorder. ICD-10 further requires that these symptoms: (1) have an early childhood onset no later than 7 years of age, (2) have a duration of at least 6 months, (3) be developmentally deviant, and (4) not be due to pervasive developmental disorder or certain other psychiatric conditions (e.g., mood disorder).

What should be readily apparent from the preceding discussion is that the DSM-IV and the ICD-10 diagnostic guidelines are similar in a number of ways. That this is the case is by no means a chance occurrence, as systematic efforts were made during the development of DSM-IV to create a classification system that would allow for direct comparison with equivalent ICD-10 disorders. Thus, there is a fair amount of overlap in the content of the symptom lists across the two systems. Their criteria for onset and duration, as well as a portion of their exclusionary criteria, are essentially identical as well. Both systems also require clear evidence of cross-situational pervasiveness.

Amid these many similarities, however, important differences exist. Perhaps the most significant of these is that the symptom clusters and cut-points for DSM-IV were derived empirically from clinical field trials, whereas those in ICD-10 were determined primarily on the basis of committee consensus. Although both systems require evidence of cross-situational pervasiveness, ICD-10 is far more explicit and stringent about this. ICD-10 also differs from DSM-IV in that it does not allow for any diagnostic subtyping. Moreover, the co-occurring presence of a depressive episode or an anxiety disorder automatically precludes making an ICD-10 diagnosis of hyperkinetic disorder. By way of contrast, such conditions may preclude an ADHD diagnosis, but DSM-IV allows for the possibility of identifying them as comorbid disorders, along with ADHD.

Without question, the DSM-IV guidelines for ADHD and the ICD-10 criteria for hyperkinetic disorder represent major improvements over the earlier versions of these classification schemes. Nonetheless, much room for improvement remains in the quest for achieving higher levels of diagnostic reliability and validity, as well as clinical utility. One potentially critical area requiring further refinement in both systems is the extent to which impulsivity symptoms are addressed. Relatively few appear either in the ICD-10 impulsivity listing or among the nine hyperactive-impulsive items in DSM-IV. To the extent that symptoms of impulsivity are indeed the feature that most differentiates what we term ADHD or hyperkinetic disorder from other childhood psychiatric disorders, the necessity for including more of these items in subsequent revisions of DSM-IV and ICD-10 becomes even more apparent. Another problem area that will need to be addressed in subsequent revisions of both systems is the developmental appropriateness of the symptom descriptions. As it now stands, virtually all of the items employ wording that is far more appropriate for use with children

than with adolescents or adults. The practical implication of this shortcoming is that it potentially reduces the range of symptoms under consideration for adolescents and adults, thereby making their diagnostic cut-points more stringent. A related problem is the one-size-fits-all cut-point approach in both systems. Evidence now exists to suggest that symptoms of inattention, impulsivity, and hyperactivity can vary as a function of age and gender, and possibly race as well. By imposing the same cut-points for all individuals, there is an increased risk for overidentifying certain subgroups in the general population while underidentifying others. Future revisions of the DSM and ICD systems would be well advised to attend to this matter.

EPIDEMIOLOGY

Prevalence

Depending on the criteria employed, estimates of the incidence of ADHD may vary a great deal, ranging from as low as 2% up to as much as 25–30%. Using the diagnostic criteria put forth by DSM-IV, approximately 3–5% of the general child population meet criteria for some type of ADHD diagnosis (American Psychiatric Association, 1994). Although its actual incidence may fluctuate somewhat within the general population, ADHD is by no means specific to any particular subgroup. For example, it may be found among the rich and the poor, as well as among those with either very little or very high levels of education. It also cuts fairly evenly across diverse ethnic, racial, and religious lines. As is the case for other externalizing problems, however, ADHD does occur much more often in boys than in girls. The ratio within clinic samples, for example, has been reported to be as high as 6:1, whereas in community samples it occurs on the order of 3:1 (Barkley, 1990). This may represent a real difference as a function of gender but, as noted earlier, many other factors may contribute to this difference as well.

Developmental Course

Some children begin to show evidence of ADHD in early infancy (Hartsough & Lambert, 1985). Most, however, first display clear signs of developmentally deviant behavior between 3 and 4 years of age (Ross & Ross, 1982). For a smaller number of children, ADHD symptoms may not surface until 5 or 6 years of age, coinciding with school entrance.

During middle childhood, ADHD symptoms often become more chronic and pervasive, even though they may appear somewhat improved at times. It is during this same period that secondary complications, such as academic underachievement or oppositional-defiant behavior, frequently arise. Contrary to popular opinion, most children do not outgrow their ADHD problems upon reaching adolescence. As many as 70% continue to exhibit developmentally inappropriate levels of inattention and, to a lesser extent, symptoms of hyperactivity-impulsivity during their teen years (Weiss & Hechtman, 1986). Although the pattern of secondary complications accompanying ADHD in adolescence is highly similar to that found in younger ADHD populations (Barkley et al., 1991), certain differences do exist. Upon reaching adolescence, for example, additional problems may arise as the youngster tries to meet occupational responsibilities. Moreover, teens with ADHD are at increased risk for becoming involved in automobile accidents and for engaging in traffic violations (Barkley, Guevremont, Anastopoulos, DuPaul, & Shelton, 1993). Although adolescent and adult outcome data are scant, what research is available suggests that, while many children with ADHD continue to display these symptoms well into adolescence and adulthood, the vast majority learn to compensate for these problems and therefore make a satisfactory adult adjustment (Weiss & Hechtman, 1986; Wender, 1995). For those who do not, it is often the case that their comorbid problems, such as depression or alcoholism (Farrington, Loeber, & van Kammen, 1987), are of relatively greater clinical concern than their ADHD symptoms.

THEORETICAL MODELS

Biological Conceptualizations

Within the field today there is a consensus that neurochemical imbalances play a central role in the etiology of ADHD. More specifically, there may be abnormalities in one or more of the monoaminergic systems, involving either dopamine or norepinephrine mechanisms (Zametkin & Rapoport, 1986). The locus of this dysfunction purportedly lies within the prefrontal-limbic areas of the brain (Lou, Henriksen, Bruhn, Borner, & Nielsen, 1989). For a majority of children with ADHD, such neurological circumstances presumably arise from inborn biologic factors, including genetic transmission and pregnancy and birth complications (Biederman et al., 1987; Deutsch, 1987; Edelbrock, 1995; Streissguth et al., 1984). For relatively smaller numbers of children carrying this diagnosis, it can be acquired after birth, via head injury, neurological illness, elevated lead levels, and other biological complications (Ross & Ross, 1982). Despite their widespread public appeal, there is relatively little support for the assertions of Feingold (1975) and others that the ingestion of sugar or various other food substances directly causes ADHD (Wolraich et al., 1994).

Psychological Conceptualizations

Over the years, numerous psychological theories have been put forth to explain the manner in which ADHD affects psychosocial functioning. Many of the early accounts, which did not have the benefit of the etiological findings described earlier, focused almost exclusively on psychological processes that were believed to be at the core of ADHD difficulties. Among these were theories implicating core deficiencies in the regulation of behavior in response to situational demands (Routh, 1978), in self-directed instruction (Kendall & Braswell, 1985), in the self-regulation of arousal to environmental demands (Douglas, 1983), and in rule-governed behavior (Barkley, 1981). Although differing somewhat in their theoretical emphasis, each of these views shared the belief that poor executive functioning was a central problem.

Building on what we now know about the biology of ADHD, more recent theories have taken on a very distinctive neuropsychological flavor. Quay (1989), for example, has proposed that ADHD stems from an impairment in a neurologically based behavioral inhibition system. In an extensive elaboration of this same theme, Barkley (1995) has also contended that a deficit in behavioral inhibition is central to understanding the cognitive, behavioral, and social deficits observed within ADHD populations. Although less comprehensive in their scope, the theoretical views of many other investigators in the field are very much consistent with the notion that deficits in behavioral inhibition are at the core of many ADHD problems (Schachar, Tannock, & Logan, 1993; Sergeant, 1995; van der Meere, 1993).

Psychosocial Conceptualizations

Although a few environmental theories have been proposed to explain ADHD (Block, 1977; Willis & Lovaas, 1977), these have not received much support in the research literature. Thus, there seems to be little justification for claiming that poor parenting or chaotic home environments are in any way causally related to ADHD. When ADHD is found among children who come from such family circumstances, one might reasonably speculate that the parents of such children may themselves be individuals with childhood and adult histories of ADHD. If so, this would help to explain why their homes might be so chaotic and, at the same time, provide support for a genetic explanation for the child's ADHD condition. Under this same scenario, the resulting chaos in the home might then be viewed as a factor exacerbating, rather than causing, the child's preexisting, inborn ADHD condition.

ASSESSMENT STRATEGIES

Despite the existence of relatively clear diagnostic guidelines, establishing an ADHD diagnosis remains a difficult matter. One factor contributing to this situation is the availability of an enormous number and variety of clinical assessment procedures on the market. Because detailed information about the reliability and validity of such measures is not always readily available, clinicians frequently have little to go on in trying to determine how best to obtain a representative sample of a child's or adolescent's real-life behavior. The special nature of the ADHD population also presents many other assessment obstacles.

An especially important consideration is the degree to which ADHD symptoms vary as a function of situational demands. Contrary to the belief of many, ADHD is not an all-or-none phenomenon, either always present or never. Instead, it is a condition whose primary symptoms show significant fluctuations in response to different situational demands (Zentall, 1985). One of the most important factors determining this variation is the degree to which children with ADHD are interested in what they are doing. ADHD symptoms are much more likely to occur in situations that are highly repetitive, boring, or familiar than in those that are novel or stimulating (Barkley, 1977). Another determinant of situational variation is the amount of imposed structure. In free-play or low-demand settings, where children with ADHD have the freedom to do as they please, their behavior is relatively indistinguishable from that of normal children (Luk, 1985). Significant ADHD problems may arise, however, when others place demands on them or set rules for their behavior. Presumably due to increased demands for behavioral self-regulation, group settings are far more problematic for children with ADHD than are one-to-one situations. There is also an increased likelihood for ADHD symptoms to arise in situations where feedback is dispensed infrequently and/or on a delayed basis (Douglas, 1983).

Being aware of the situational variability of ADHD symptoms is central to understanding the frequently irregular clinical presentation of this disorder. Recognizing that this occurs, clinicians must, therefore, try to obtain information from individuals who observe identified children across different settings. At the very least, this should include input from parents and teachers. When appropriate, other significant caretakers, such as day care providers and babysitters, should provide similar input.

Another critical factor affecting the evaluation process is the increased likelihood that children and adolescents with ADHD will display comorbid conditions. For example, noncompliance, argumentativeness, temper outbursts, lying, stealing, and other manifestations of oppositional defiant disorder and conduct disorder may occur in up to 60% of the clinic-referred ADHD population (Barkley, Anastopoulos, Guevremont, & Fletcher, 1991; Loney & Milich, 1982). Virtually all children with ADHD experience some type of school difficulty. An especially common problem is that their levels of academic productivity and achievement are significantly lower than their estimated potential (Barkley, 1990). Depending on the definition used, as many as 20% to 30% may also exhibit dyslexia or other types of specific learning disabilities (Barkley, DuPaul, & McMurray, 1990). As a result of such complications, a relatively high percentage typically receives some form of special education assistance (Barkley, 1990). Significant peer socialization problems may occur as well (Pelham & Bender, 1982). At times, such difficulties involve deficiencies in establishing friendships (Grenell, Glass, & Katz, 1987). More often than not, however, maintaining satisfactory peer relations is of even greater clinical concern. Due to their inability to control their behavior in social situations, children and adolescents with ADHD frequently alienate their peers, who in turn respond with social rejection or avoidance (Cunningham & Siegel, 1987). Possibly as a result of such behavioral, academic, and/or social problems, children and adolescents with ADHD very often exhibit low self-esteem, low frustration tolerance, symptoms of depression and anxiety, and other emotional complications (Margalit & Arieli, 1984).

Taken together, what these findings clearly indicate is that the risk for comorbidity is quite high within the ADHD population. Thus, it is critical for clinicians to incorporate assessment methods that address not only primary ADHD symptoms but also other aspects of the identified child's or adolescent's psychosocial functioning. Although few would dispute the need for expanding the scope of an ADHD evaluation in this manner, little consensus exists with respect to which assessment instruments best serve this purpose. Because different procedures can indeed lead to very different conclusions about the presence or absence of various comorbid conditions, clinicians are well advised to become thoroughly familiar with the numerous conceptual and methodological issues that affect this very important decision-making process (Abikoff, Courtney, Pelham, & Koplewicz, 1993; Biederman et al., 1996; Frick et al., 1991; Hinshaw & Anderson, 1996; Pliszka, 1992).

Of additional importance is the need for gathering assessment data pertaining to parental, marital, and family functioning. Research has shown, for example, that parents of children with ADHD very often become overly directive and negative in their parenting style (Cunningham & Barkley, 1979). In addition to viewing themselves as less skilled and less knowledgeable in their parenting roles (Mash & Johnston, 1990), they may also experience considerable stress in their parenting roles, especially when comorbid oppositional-defiant features are present (Anastopoulos, Guevremont, Shelton, & DuPaul, 1992). Teens with ADHD are at increased risk for experiencing significant conflict with their parents, especially when oppositional-defiant disorder features are present (Barkley, Anastopoulos, Guevremont, & Fletcher, 1992). Depression and marital discord may arise as well (Lahey et al., 1988). Whether these parent and family complications result directly from the child's or adolescent's ADHD is not entirely clear at present. Clinical experience suggests that they probably do, at least in part, given the increased caretaking demands that children and adolescents with ADHD impose on their parents. These include more frequent displays of noncompliance, related to difficulties in following through on parental instructions (Cunningham & Barkley, 1979). In addition, parents of these children often find themselves involved in resolving various school, peer, and sibling difficulties, which occur throughout childhood

(Barkley, 1990) and into adolescence as well (Barkley et al., 1991).

Although gathering this type of parental and family information may not shed much light on whether or not an ADHD diagnosis is present, it nevertheless provides a context for understanding how problem behaviors may be maintained. Moreover, such information often serves as a basis for determining how likely it is that parents and other caretakers will implement recommended treatment strategies on behalf of their child or adolescent.

Implicit in the preceding discussion is the understanding that clinical evaluations of ADHD must be comprehensive and multidimensional in nature, so as to capture the situational variability of the disorder, its comorbid features, and its impact on home, school, and social functioning (Barkley, 1990). This multimethod assessment approach may include, for example, not only the traditional methods of parent and child interviews but also standardized child behavior rating scales, parent self-report measures, direct behavioral observations of ADHD symptoms in natural or analogue settings, and clinic-based psychological tests.

Interviews

Given their flexibility, unstructured and semistructured interviews with parents and children can yield a wealth of information pertaining to a child's psychosocial functioning. They do not, however, allow for accurate normative comparisons, which complicates the process of documenting developmental deviance. An alternative to these traditional approaches is the structured interview. In addition to avoiding the problems of unstructured and semistructured interviews, structured interviews allow for standardized administration across children, which facilitates data collection and research. Among the many procedures of this sort that have been employed in ADHD research are the Diagnostic Interview Schedule for Children (DISC; Costello, Edelbrock, Kalas, Kessler, & Klaric, 1982) and the Diagnostic Interview for Children and Adolescents (DICA; Herjanic,

Brown, & Wheatt, 1975), both of which are currently undergoing revision to be compatible with DSM-IV. While offering many advantages, structured interviews nevertheless possess certain limitations (Edelbrock & Costello, 1984), which makes them cumbersome to employ in typical clinical situations.

Behavior Rating Scales

Standardized behavior checklists and rating scales are often an indispensable part of the assessment of children and adolescents with ADHD. Their convenience, their applicability to multiple informants, their ability to gather information collapsed across long time intervals, and their provision of normative references have led to their widespread application in clinical practice. Although a large number and variety of such questionnaires are now available, most have not yet been adequately validated against the new DSM-IV criteria for ADHD. Among those having documented diagnostic utility with the DSM-III-R version of ADHD are the Child Behavior Checklist (CBCL; Achenbach, 1991), the Behavior Assessment System for Children (Reynolds & Kamphaus, 1992), the Revised Conners Parent and Teacher Rating Scales (Goyette, Conners, & Ulrich, 1978), the ADHD Rating Scale (DuPaul, 1991), the ADDES (McCarney, 1989), and the ADD-H Comprehensive Teacher Rating Scale (ACTeRS; Ullmann, Sleator, & Sprague, 1984). As might be expected, differences exist in the exact scope, format, and content of these instruments, but common to all is their emphasis on Likert-type ratings of individual ADHD symptoms, which, added together, yield a dimensional, developmentally sensitive assessment of this disorder. Illustrative of this process, appearing on the parent version of the CBCL, is the item "impulsive or acts without thinking," which parents endorse as being either a 0 ("not true"), 1 ("somewhat or sometimes true"), or 2 ("very true or often true"). The score for this item is then added to the ratings of all of the other items (e.g., "can't concentrate," "can't sit still, restless, or hyperactive") that make up the CBCL Attention Problems subscale to yield a quantitative assessment of overall ADHD tendencies. This total is then interpreted in the context of age- and/or gender-adjusted norms in order to document the degree to which primary ADHD symptoms deviate from developmental expectations. More specifically, Attention Problem subscale scores falling above the 98th percentile are considered to be within the clinically significant range, whereas those above the 93rd percentile are viewed to be of borderline significance.

In view of the relatively high incidence of parenting stress, marital discord, and psychopathology that exists among parents of children with ADHD, clinicians often must also incorporate parent self-report measures into the assessment process. This may include, but certainly is not limited to, such measures as the Symptom Checklist 90-Revised (SCL 90-R; Derogatis, 1986), the Parenting Stress Index (Abidin, 1983), the Beck Depression Scale (Beck, Rush, Shaw, & Emery, 1979), and the Locke-Wallace Marital Adjustment Scale (Locke & Wallace, 1959).

Clinic-Based Measures

Laboratory measures of sustained attention and impulsivity are commonly included in ADHD evaluations. Perhaps the most widely used instrument for assessing these particular ADHD features is the Continuous Performance Test (CPT). Numerous versions of the CPT exist, including the Conners (Conners, 1994), the Test of Variables of Attention (Greenberg, 1991), and the Gordon Diagnostic System (GDS; Gordon, 1983). Such procedures typically require the child or adolescent to watch a computer screen for anywhere from 9 to 22 minutes, during which time visual/auditory stimuli (e.g., letters, numbers) are presented in varying intervals. When designated target stimuli appear, the child or adolescent must respond either by pressing a button, space bar, or mouse (e.g., GDS) or by inhibiting or withholding such a response (e.g., Conners). One possible reason

for the widespread popularity and usage of CPTs is the degree to which they have been successful in differentiating groups of children with ADHD from normal controls. Despite such success at a group level, however, many of these measures produce unacceptably high false negative rates when applied to individual children or adolescents (DuPaul et al., 1992; Matier-Sharma et al., 1995). Although the exact reasons for this discrepancy are unclear, one possible explanation stems from a consideration of the fact that these procedures are typically administered in clinic settings under relatively novel, one-to-one, high-feedback conditions, which greatly reduces the likelihood of eliciting ADHD symptomatology.

Direct Observational Procedures

Also available are various observational assessment procedures, which more directly assess the behavior problems of children with ADHD, as well as their interactions with others. Among these are systems for observing behavior in classroom settings (Abikoff, Gittelman-Klein, & Klein, 1977; Jacob, O'Leary, & Rosenblad, 1978), systems for examining child behavior in clinic analogue situations (Roberts, 1987), and systems for assessing the clinic-based interactions between ADHD children and others (Mash & Barkley, 1986). Many of these coding systems target behaviors that reflect specific ADHD concerns, such as off-task behavior or fidgeting, or related concerns, such as noncompliance. With highly detailed definitions of such behaviors in mind (e.g., child fails to comply with parental request within 10 seconds), observers typically watch for their occurrence or nonoccurrence during designated intervals (e.g., every 30 seconds) over periods of time ranging from just a few minutes up to 20 or 30 minutes. Due to the fact that they attempt to capture behavior under conditions more representative of real-life circumstances, such procedures often times are more reliable and valid than clinic-based assessment devices.

Other Procedures

Information about intellectual functioning, level of academic achievement, and learning disabilities status needs to be incorporated into the assessment of children and adolescents suspected of having ADHD. Due to the fact that school personnel and other professionals very often address such concerns prior to the ADHD referral, such information usually can be obtained through review of school and medical records. If for some reason this is not available at the time of the ADHD workup, additional testing of this sort must then be conducted. A large number and variety of test instruments are available for this purpose, including the third edition of the Wechsler Intelligence Scale for Children (Wechsler, 1991) and the Wechsler Individual Achievement Test (Wechsler, 1992).

Practical Considerations

As noted earlier, the clinical evaluation of children and adolescents suspected of having ADHD generally requires a comprehensive multimethod assessment approach. As part of the evaluation process, clinicians must focus diagnostic attention not only on those behavioral difficulties suggestive of ADHD but also on various other aspects of the child's or adolescent's psychosocial functioning that are at increased risk for being problematic. Moreover, they must incorporate assessment procedures that yield information about parental, marital, and family functioning, so as to understand more fully the psychosocial context in which the child or adolescent functions.

The intuitive appeal of this rationale notwithstanding, many parents find the assessment approach incompatible with what they thought might be done to determine the presence or absence of ADHD. "After all," they might reason, "if you're trying to find out whether my child has ADHD, why are you spending so much time interviewing me and having me fill out questionnaires? Why aren't you spending more time testing my child?" Left unanswered, such matters can cause a parent to feel threatened or to question the competence of the evaluating clinician. This, in turn, can interfere with their acceptance of any diagnostic feedback, as well as their willingness to implement treatment recommendations.

In anticipation of such problems, clinicians must explain the rationale for their assessment approach. In particular, they need to mention that direct testing involves relatively novel and interesting psychological test materials that are administered under closely supervised, high-feedback, one-to-one conditions. Such circumstances decrease the likelihood that ADHD symptoms will surface. For this reason, therefore, a relatively more accurate sampling of a child's or adolescent's behavior stems from parent and teacher input, which is based on observations occurring in situational contexts (e.g., large-group setting) that are more likely to elicit ADHD symptomatology. This type of explanation very often serves to alleviate any parental concerns or doubts that might interfere with their receptivity to diagnostic and treatment feedback.

Although we have not discussed this point, it is also important to keep in mind that clinical use of the assessment procedures we have described does not have to be limited to the diagnostic phase of the assessment process. In many cases, these same procedures can serve as outcome measures in assessing the efficacy of various treatment approaches (e.g., stimulant medication trials), many of which are discussed in the next section.

TREATMENT APPROACHES

Many of the same factors that complicate the assessment process can affect treatment outcome as well. Foremost among these are the cross-situational pervasiveness of primary ADHD symptoms and the relatively high incidence of co-occurring or comorbid conditions. Such circumstances make it highly unlikely that any singular treatment approach can satisfactorily meet all of the clinical management needs of children and adolescents with ADHD. For this reason, clinicians must often employ multiple treatment strategies in combination, each of which addresses a different aspect of the child's or adolescent's psychosocial difficulties.

Among those treatments that have received adequate, or at the very least preliminary, empirical support are pharmacotherapy, parent training in contingency management methods/ parent counseling, classroom applications of contingency management techniques, and cognitive-behavioral training. Despite such support, these interventions should not be viewed as curative of ADHD. Instead, their value lies in their temporary reduction of ADHD symptom levels and in their reduction of related behavioral or emotional difficulties. When these treatments are removed, ADHD symptoms very often return to pretreatment levels of deviance. Thus, their effectiveness in improving prognosis presumably rests on their being maintained over long periods of time.

Pharmacotherapy

For many years, clinicians and researchers have employed medications in their management of children with ADHD. The rationale for doing so rests on the assumption that neurochemical imbalances are involved in the etiology of this disorder. Although the exact neurochemical mechanisms underlying their therapeutic action remain unclear, research has shown that at least two classes of medication—namely, stimulants and antidepressants—can be helpful in reducing ADHD symptomatology. Numerous studies have consistently demonstrated that stimulant medications are highly effective in the management of ADHD symptoms in a large percentage of the children and adolescents who take them (Taylor, 1986). According to some estimates, as many as 80–90% respond favorably, with a majority of these displaying behavior that is relatively normalized (Rapport, Denney, DuPaul, & Gardner, 1994). In addition to bringing about improvements in primary ADHD symptomatology, these medications very often can lead to increased child compliance and decreased aggressive behavior (Hinshaw, Henker, & Whalen, 1984). Although

certain side effects can arise from their use (e.g., decreased appetite, insomnia), these tend to be mild in nature, and most children tolerate them without great difficulty (Barkley, 1990), even over extended periods of time (Zeiner, 1995). For reasons such as these, many child health care professionals have incorporated stimulant regimens into their clinical practices.

The most commonly prescribed stimulants are methylphenidate (Ritalin), d-amphetamine (Dexedrine), and pemoline (Cylert). Of these, Ritalin is most often the medication of choice. Unlike many other types of medication, Ritalin acts rapidly, producing effects on behavior within 30 to 45 minutes after oral ingestion and peaking in its therapeutic impact within 2 to 4 hours. Its utility in managing behavior, however, typically dissipates within 3 to 7 hours, even though minuscule amounts of the medication may remain in the blood for up to 24 hours (Cantwell & Carlson, 1978). Available in standard 5-, 10-, and 15-milligram tablets, it is typically prescribed in twice-daily doses, but recent research has suggested that adding a third dose to the daily regimen can be tolerated fairly well by most children (Kent et al., 1995). Sustained-release 20-milligram capsules are available as well, which can be used either as a substitute for, or in combination with, standard dosage tablets. Many children take such medication exclusively on school days, but it can also be used on weekends and during school vacations, especially in cases where ADHD symptoms seriously interfere with home functioning. Although at one time "drug-free holidays" were the no-exceptions rule, the practice of extending the use of stimulant therapy into weekends and throughout the calendar year, if clinically indicated, is now considered acceptable by most experts in the field today.

Despite their overall utility, stimulants may not be appropriate for some children with ADHD, who nevertheless require a medication component in their overall clinical management. As a way of meeting the needs of such children, child health care professionals have recently turned to the use of tricyclic antidepressants, such as imipramine. Most often, these medications are employed in situations where certain side effects (e.g., motor tics), known to be exacerbated by stimulants, are present or where significant mood disturbances accompany ADHD symptomatology (Plizska, 1987). As a rule, antidepressants are given twice daily, usually in the morning and evening. Because they are longer-acting than stimulants, it takes more time to evaluate the therapeutic value of any given dose (Rapoport & Mikkelsen, 1978). Despite this limitation, recent research has suggested that low doses of these medications can produce increased vigilance and decreased impulsivity, as well as reductions in disruptive and aggressive behavior. Mood elevation may also occur, especially in children with significant pretreatment levels of depression or anxiety (Plizska, 1987). Such treatment effects, however, can diminish over time. Thus, antidepressants frequently are not the medication of choice for long-term management of ADHD.

Parent Training

As we have discussed earlier, ADHD is a condition characterized by deficiencies in regulating behavior in response to situational demands (Barkley, 1990). Such "demands" include not only the stimulus properties of the settings in which children function, but also the consequences for their behavior. To the extent that these situational parameters can be modified, one might reasonably anticipate corresponding changes in ADHD symptomatology. Assuming this to be valid, it provides ample justification for utilizing various behavior therapy techniques in the clinical management of children with ADHD.

Despite the plethora of research on parent training in behavior modification, very few studies have examined the efficacy of this approach with children specifically identified as having ADHD. What few studies exist can be interpreted with cautious optimism as supporting the use of behavioral parent training with such children (Anastopoulos, Shelton, DuPaul, & Guevremont, 1993; Pelham et al., 1988; Pisterman et al., 1989). Most of these interventions utilized weekly therapy sessions in either group or individual formats that were short-term in nature, spanning 6 to 10 weeks in length. By and large, most of these programs served to train parents in the use of specialized contingency management techniques, such as positive reinforcement, response cost, and/or time-out strategies. Some, however, combined contingency management training with didactic counseling, aimed at increasing parental knowledge and understanding of ADHD (Anastopoulos et al., 1993). In addition to producing changes in child behavior, parent training interventions have also led to improvements in various aspects of parental and family functioning, including decreased parenting stress and increased parenting self-esteem (Anastopoulos et al., 1993; Pisterman et al., 1989).

Classroom Contingency Management

In comparison with the parent training literature, relatively more research has addressed the use of behavior management methods for children with ADHD in the classroom. Such studies suggest that the contingent use of positive reinforcement alone can produce immediate, short-term improvements in classroom behavior, productivity, and accuracy (Pfiffner & Barkley, 1998). For most children with ADHD, secondary or tangible reinforcers seem to be more effective in improving behavior and academic performance than is teacher attention or other types social reinforcement (Pfiffner, Rosen, & O'Leary, 1985). The combination of positive reinforcement with various punishment strategies, such as response cost, typically leads to even greater improvements in behavior than either alone (Pfiffner & O'Leary, 1987). Despite the promising nature of such findings, many of these reported treatment gains subside when treatment is withdrawn (Barkley, Copeland, & Sivage, 1980). Of additional concern is the fact that these improvements in behavior and performance seldom generalize to settings where treatment is not in effect.

Cognitive-Behavioral Therapy

Over the past 20 years, clinicians and researchers have employed a large number and variety of cognitive-behavioral interventions with children who manifest ADHD symptomatology. Included among these are various self-monitoring, self-reinforcement, and self-instructional techniques. In a typical self-monitoring program, for example, a child works at his or her desk until a visual (e.g., teacher gesture) or auditory (e.g., tone from a tape recorder) cue arises, signaling the child to answer the question, "Am I paying attention to my work . . . Yes or No?" Such signals occur at predetermined intervals, providing the child with important feedback that purportedly serves to improve academic performance. Much of the appeal for this type of self-monitoring system, as well as other cognitive-behavioral programming, stems from their apparent focus on some of the primary deficits of ADHD, including inattention, impulsivity, poor organizational skills, and difficulties with rules and instructions. Also contributing to their popularity is their presumed potential for enhancing treatment generalization, above and beyond that achieved through more traditional contingency management programs.

Research on self-monitoring has shown that it can improve on-task behavior and academic productivity in some children with ADHD (Shapiro & Cole, 1995). The combination of self-monitoring and self-reinforcement can also lead to improvements in on-task behavior and academic accuracy, as well as in peer relations (Hinshaw, Henker, & Whalen, 1984). As for self-instructional training, the picture is less clear, with many recent studies (Abikoff & Gittelman, 1985) failing to replicate earlier reported successes (Bornstein & Quevillon, 1976; Meichenbaum & Goodman, 1971).

Readily apparent in these recent studies are several potential limitations. For example, in order to achieve desired treatment effects in the classroom, children with ADHD must be reinforced for utilizing self-instructional strategies. Hence, contrary to initial expectations, this form of treatment apparently does not free children from control by the social environment. Instead, what it seems to accomplish is to shift such external control to a slightly less direct form. Another limitation is that treatment effects seldom generalize to settings where self-instructional training is not in effect or to academic tasks that are not specifically part of the training process (Barkley et al., 1980). In this regard, self-instructional training apparently does not, as had been hoped, circumvent the problem of the situation-specificity of treatment effects, which has plagued the use of contingency management methods for many years.

Combined Interventions

What should be evident from the preceding discussion is that singular treatment approaches—whether they be pharmacological, behavioral, or cognitive-behavioral—are not, by themselves, sufficient to meet all of the clinical management needs of children with ADHD. In response to this situation, many child health care professionals have recently begun to employ multiple ADHD treatments in combination.

Despite the intuitive appeal of this clinical practice, there presently exists little empirical justification for utilizing such combinations. Although limited in number, studies generally have shown that, regardless of which combination is used, the therapeutic impact of the combined treatment package typically does not exceed that of either treatment alone. This certainly seems to be the case when stimulant medication therapy is combined with classroom contingency management (Gadow, 1985). Similar findings have emerged from studies examining the use of stimulant regimens in combination with cognitive-behavioral interventions (Hinshaw et al., 1984).

From a somewhat different perspective, there have been attempts to evaluate, retrospectively, the long-term effects of individualized multimodality intervention on ADHD outcome (Satterfield et al., 1980). Such multimodal interventions included medication, parent training, individual counseling, special education, family therapy, and/or other treatments as needed by the individual. The obtained results suggest that an individualized program of combined treatments, when continued over a period of several years, can produce improvements in the social adjustment of children with ADHD, in their rates of antisocial behavior, and in their academic achievement. Similar prospective multimodal intervention research is currently in progress under the sponsorship of the Child and Adolescent Branch of the National Institutes of Mental Health. Thus, in the not too distant future, additional light will be shed on this matter.

Adjunctive Procedures

Discussed in the preceding sections were numerous treatment strategies that directly target the needs of children with ADHD. What was not covered was the manner in which various comorbid features are typically addressed. When certain types of comorbid features, such as aggression, are present, very often they too diminish in frequency and severity when targeted ADHD symptoms come under the control of various interventions. This does not always occur, however. Moreover, there are numerous occasions when secondary emotional or behavioral features arise independent of the primary ADHD diagnosis and therefore are unresponsive to ADHD interventions. In situations such as these, it becomes necessary to consider the use of adjunctive intervention strategies. For example, it may become necessary to implement individual therapy for a child or adolescent to help the youngster adjust to parental divorce.

Due to the increased incidence of various psychosocial difficulties among the parents of such children, clinicians must sometimes recommend that they too receive therapy services, such as individual or marital counseling. In addition to providing therapeutic benefits for the parents themselves, these adjunctive procedures can produce indirect benefits for their children. For example, when parental distress is reduced, parents very often become better able to implement recommended treatment strategies, such as parent training, on behalf of their child.

On the assumption that increased knowledge of ADHD facilitates understanding and acceptance of this disorder, clinicians may also wish to provide ADHD counseling to interested children or adolescents and their parents. This, of course, can be accomplished in the context of face-to-face therapy discussions. In conjunction with such counseling efforts, clinicians can direct anyone who wishes to learn more about ADHD to the vast array of commercially available pamphlets, self-help books, audiotapes, and videotapes on the topic. Many such resources can be purchased through the ADD Warehouse, based in Plantation, Florida. Another way in which clinicians can be extremely useful to their clients is by directing them to any of the various ADHD support groups that now exist, such as CHADD. Such groups, which typically meet on a monthly basis, not only serve as additional sources of ADHD information but also provide ongoing opportunities for much needed emotional support and sharing.

Although intuitively appealing and sound on the basis of clinical experience, the use of such adjunctive procedures within an ADHD population has yet to be addressed empirically. This, therefore, appears to be a rather fruitful area for future clinical research.

SUMMARY AND CONCLUSIONS

Within the field there is a consensus that ADHD is a chronic and pervasive condition characterized by developmentally inappropriate levels of inattention, impulsivity, and/or hyperactivity. Most children and adolescents with ADHD presumably acquire this problem through inborn biological mechanisms. One of the more intriguing, and yet confusing, aspects of ADHD is that its primary features are subject to situational variation. Although it can occur alone, ADHD very often is accompanied by other types of educational, behavioral, emotional, social, and family complications.

Clinical evaluations of children and adolescents suspected of having ADHD must be multidimensional in nature so as to capture the disorder's situational variability and its secondary features. Moreover, some attempt must also be made to assess the extent to which parental and family functioning may be disrupted by its presence. For many of the same reasons, the clinical management of children and adolescents with ADHD must be multidimensional in nature. Among the many treatments that are available for dealing with this disorder, stimulant medication therapy is perhaps the one used most often and most effectively. Although not yet empirically validated, combining stimulant medication therapy with other types of treatments, such as parent training or classroom modifications, is regarded as acceptable and desirable clinical practice.

What should be readily apparent from the preceding discussion is that much progress has been made in our conceptual understanding of ADHD and in the way that we clinically manage it. Nonetheless, there remains much to learn.

In the conceptual domain, for example, further advances in neuroradiological imaging techniques should lead to a much clearer picture of the neurobiology of ADHD. This, in turn, should facilitate the development and refinement of current and future neuropsychological conceptualizations. Similar medical breakthroughs might also make it possible to assess the genetic hypothesis at the chromosomal and gene level.

Progress in this domain, however, is not entirely contingent on advances in medical technology. Another critical ingredient is the precision of our diagnostic tools. To the extent that we continue to compare findings from studies that use the same diagnostic label for samples that differ in many clinically important ways, scientific progress will be impeded. As was noted earlier, our current classification systems represent major improvements over earlier systems, but they are not without limitations. With these limitations in mind, future research must therefore seek to clarify, in far more detail than is currently available, how ADHD manifests itself across the life span, especially during adolescence and adulthood. In the context of such research, attention must also be directed to the moderating influence of gender, race, and various other variables, as well as to the manner in which various comorbid conditions unfold.

Future ADHD research must also take into consideration various fiscal realities. For example, getting to a clinic to have a child or adolescent evaluated or treated for ADHD may not be feasible for many families with limited financial resources. Even if they have the means to transport themselves to such a facility, they very likely may not have the necessary health insurance coverage or out-of-pocket monies to pay for the overall cost of a comprehensive multimethod evaluation or multimodal treatment program. To the extent that highly specialized multimethod assessments and multimodal treatments can be streamlined to reduce their cost and/or can be delivered in community settings, higher percentages of economically disadvantaged children and adolescents may then have access to such services.

This push for service delivery streamlining is, of course, not limited to the economically disadvantaged segment of the population. It also pertains to those who receive health care coverage from managed health care organizations. As such companies place increasing demands on practitioners to deliver assessment and treatment services in cost-effective ways, it becomes even more important for researchers to document that various methods of ADHD assessment and treatment are indeed in line with this cost-saving philosophy, while at the same time remaining clinically efficacious.

REFERENCES

Abidin, R. R. (1983). *The Parenting Stress Index.* Charlottesville, VA: Pediatric Psychology Press.

*Abikoff, H., Courtney, M., Pelham, W. E., & Koplewicz, H. S. (1993). Teachers' ratings of disruptive behaviors: The influence of halo effects. *Journal of Abnormal Child Psychology, 21,* 519–533.

Abikoff, H., & Gittelman, R. (1985). Does behavior therapy normalize the classroom behavior of hyperactive children? *Archives of General Psychiatry*, *41*, 449–454.

Abikoff, H., Gittelman-Klein, R., & Klein, D. (1977). Validation of a classroom observation code for hyperactive children. *Journal of Consulting and Clinical Psychology, 45*, 772–783.

*Achenbach, T. M. (1991). *Manual for the Child Behavior Checklist/4–18 and 1991 Profile.* Burlington: University of Vermont, Department of Psychiatry.

American Psychiatric Association. (1968). *Diagnostic and statistical manual of mental disorders* (2nd ed.). Washington, DC: Author.

American Psychiatric Association. (1980). *Diagnostic and statistical manual of mental disorders* (3rd ed.). Washington, DC: Author.

American Psychiatric Association. (1987). *Diagnostic and statistical manual of mental disorders* (3rd ed., rev.). Washington, DC: Author.

*American Psychiatric Association. (1994). *Diagnostic and statistical manual of mental disorders* (4th ed.). Washington, DC: Author.

Anastopoulos, A. D., Guevremont, D. C., Shelton, T. L., & DuPaul, G. J. (1992). Parenting stress among families of children with Attention Deficit Hyperactivity Disorder. *Journal of Abnormal Child Psychology, 20*, 503–520.

*Anastopoulos, A. D., Shelton, T., DuPaul, G. J., & Guevremont, D. C. (1993). Parent training for Attention Deficit Hyperactivity Disorder: Its impact on parent functioning. *Journal of Abnormal Child Psychology, 21*, 581–596.

Barkley, R. A. (1977). A review of stimulant drug research with hyperactive children. *Journal of Child Psychology and Psychiatry, 18*, 137–165.

Barkley, R. A. (1981). *Hyperactive children: A handbook for diagnosis and treatment.* New York: Guilford Press.

*Barkley, R. A. (1990). *Attention Deficit Hyperactivity Disorder: A handbook for diagnosis and treatment.* New York: Guilford Press.

*Barkley, R. A. (1995). Behavioral inhibition and executive functions: Constructing a unified theory of ADHD. Unpublished manuscript. University of Massachusetts Medical Center.

Barkley, R. A., Anastopoulos, A. D., Guevremont, D. C., & Fletcher, K. E. (1991). Adolescents with ADHD: Patterns of behavioral adjustment, academic functioning, and treatment utilization. *Journal of the American Academy of Child and Adolescent Psychiatry, 30*, 752–761.

Barkley, R. A., Anastopoulos, A. D., Guevremont, D. C., & Fletcher, K. E. (1992). Adolescents with Attention Deficit Hyperactivity Disorder:

Mother-adolescent interactions, family beliefs and conflicts, and maternal psychopathology. *Journal of Abnormal Child Psychology, 20*, 263–288.

Barkley, R. A., Copeland, A. P., & Sivage, C. (1980). A self-control classroom for hyperactive children. *Journal of Autism and Developmental Disorders, 10*, 75–89.

Barkley, R. A., DuPaul, G. J., & McMurray, M. (1990). A comprehensive evaluation of Attention Deficit Disorder with and without Hyperactivity defined by research criteria. *Journal of Consulting and Clinical Psychology, 58*, 775–789.

Barkley, R. A., Guevremont, D. C., Anastopoulos, A. D., DuPaul, G. J., & Shelton, T. L. (1993). Driving-related risks and outcomes of Attention Deficit Hyperactivity Disorder in adolescents and young adults: A 3- to 5-year follow-up survey. *Pediatrics, 92*, 212–218.

*Beck, A. T., Rush, A. J., Shaw, B. F., & Emery, G. (1979). *Cognitive therapy for depression.* New York: Guilford Press.

*Biederman, J., Faraone, S., Mick, E., Wozniak, J., Chen, L., Ouellette, C., Marrs, A., Moore, P., Garcia, J., Mennin, D., & Lelon, E. (1996). Attention-Deficit Hyperactivity Disorder and Juvenile Mania: An overlooked comorbidity? *Journal of the American Academy of Child and Adolescent Psychiatry, 35*, 997–1008.

Biederman, J., Munir, K., Knee, D., Armentano, M., Autor, S., Waternaux, C., & Tsuang, M. (1987). High rate of affective disorders in probands with attention deficit disorders and in their relatives: A controlled family study. *American Journal of Psychiatry, 144*, 330–333.

Block, G. H. (1977). Hyperactivity: A cultural perspective. *Journal of Learning Disabilities, 110*, 236–240.

Bornstein, P. H., & Quevillon, R. P. (1976). The effects of a self-instructional package on overactive preschool boys. *Journal of Applied Behavior Analysis, 9*, 179–188.

Cantwell, D., & Carlson, G. (1978). Stimulants. In J. Werry (Ed.), *Pediatric psychopharmacology* (pp. 171–207). New York: Brunner/Mazel.

Chess, S. (1960). Diagnosis and treatment of the hyperactive child. *New York State Journal of Medicine, 60*, 2379–2385.

Clements, S. D., & Peters, J. E. (1962). Minimal brain dysfunctions in the school-age child. *Archives of General Psychiatry, 6*, 185–197.

Conners, C. K. (1994). *The continuous performance test (CPT): Use as a diagnostic tool and measure of treatment outcome.* Paper presented at the annual meeting of the American Psychological Association, Los Angeles, CA.

Costello, A., Edelbrock, C., Kalas, R., Kessler, M., & Klaric, S. (1982). *The NIMH Diagnostic Interview Schedule for Children (DISC)*. Pittsburgh: Author.

Cunningham, C. E., & Barkley, R. A. (1979). The interactions of hyperactive and normal children with their mothers during free play and structured task. *Child Development, 50*, 217–224.

Cunningham, C. E., & Siegel, L. S. (1987). Peer interactions of normal and attention-deficit disordered boys during free-play, cooperative-task, and simulated classroom situations. *Journal of Abnormal Child Psychology, 15*, 247–268.

Derogatis, L. (1986). *Manual for the Symptom Checklist 90 Revised (SCL-90R)*. Baltimore, MD: Author.

Deutsch, K. (1987). *Genetic factors in Attention Deficit Disorders*. Paper presented at the symposium on Disorders of Brain, Development, and Cognition, Boston, MA.

Douglas, V. I. (1972). Stop, look, and listen: The problem of sustained attention and impulse control in hyperactive and normal children. *Canadian Journal of Behavioural Science, 4*, 259–282.

Douglas, V. I. (1983). Attention and cognitive problems. In M. Rutter (Ed.), *Developmental neuropsychiatry*. New York: Guilford Press.

*DuPaul, G. J. (1991). Parent and teacher ratings of ADHD symptoms: Psychometric properties in a community based sample. *Journal of Clinical Child Psychology, 20*, 245–253.

DuPaul, G. J, Anastopoulos, A. D., Shelton, T. L., Guevremont, D. C., & Metevia, L. (1992). Multimethod assessment of ADHD: The diagnostic utility of clinic based tests. *Journal of Clinical Child Psychology, 21*, 394–402.

Edelbrock, C. E. (1995). A twin study of competence and problem behaviors of childhood and early adolescence. *Journal of Child Psychology and Psychiatry, 36*, 775–785.

Edelbrock, C., & Costello, A. (1984). Structured psychiatric interviews for children and adolescents. In G. Goldstein & M. Hersen (Eds.), *Handbook of psychological assessment* (pp. 276–290). New York: Pergamon.

Farrington, D. P., Loeber, R., & van Kammen, W. B. (1987). *Long-term criminal outcomes of hyperactivity-impulsivity, attention deficit and conduct problems in childhood*. Paper presented at the Society for Life History Research meeting in St. Louis, MO.

Feingold, B. (1975). *Why your child is hyperactive*. New York: Random House.

Frick, P. J., Kamphaus, R. W., Lahey, B. B., Loeber, R., Christ, M. A. G., Hart, E. L., & Tannenbaum, L. E. (1991). Academic underachievement and the disruptive behavior disorders. *Journal of Consulting and Clinical Psychology, 59*, 289–294.

Gadow, K. D. (1985). Relative efficacy of pharmacological, behavioral, and combination treatments for enhancing academic performance. *Clinical Psychology Review, 5*, 513–533.

Gordon, M. (1983). *The Gordon Diagnostic System*. Boulder, CO: Clinical Diagnostic Systems.

Goyette, C. H., Conners, C. K., & Ulrich, R. F. (1978). Normative data on Revised Conners Parent and Teacher Rating Scales. *Journal of Abnormal Child Psychology*, 221–236.

Greenberg, L. M. (1991). Developmental normative data on the Test of Variables of Attention (T.O.V.A.). Unpublished manuscript.

Grenell, M. M., Glass, C. R., & Katz, K. S. (1987). Hyperactive children and peer interaction: Knowledge and performance of social skills. *Journal of Abnormal Child Psychology*, 1–13.

Hartsough, C. S., & Lambert, N. M. (1985). Medical factors in hyperactive and normal children: Prenatal, developmental, and health history findings. *American Journal of Orthopsychiatry, 55*, 190–201.

Herjanic, B., Brown, F., & Wheat, T. (1975). Are children reliable reporters? *Journal of Abnormal Child Psychology, 3*, 41-48.

*Hinshaw, S. P., & Anderson, C. A. (1996). Conduct and oppositional defiant disorders. In E. J. Mash & R. A. Barkley (Eds.), *Child psychopathology*. New York: Guilford Press.

Hinshaw, S. P., Henker, B., & Whalen, C. K. (1984). Self-control in hyperactive boys in anger-inducing situations: Effects of cognitive-behavioral training and of methylphenidate. *Journal of Abnormal Child Psychology, 12*, 55–77.

Hohman, L. B. (1922). Post-encephalitic behavior disorders in children. *Johns Hopkins Hospital Bulletin, 33*, 372–375.

Jacob, R. G., O'Leary, K. D., & Rosenblad, C. (1978). Formal and informal classroom settings: Effects on hyperactivity. *Journal of Abnormal Child Psychology, 6*, 47–59.

*Kendall, P. C., & Braswell, L. (1985). *Cognitive-behavioral therapy for impulsive children*. New York: Guilford Press.

Kent, J. D., Blader, J. C., Koplewicz, H. S., Abikoff, H., & Foley, C. A. (1995). Effects of late-afternoon methylphenidate administration on behavior and sleep in attention-deficit hyperactivity disorder. *Pediatrics, 96*, 320–325.

Lahey, B. B., Piacentini, J., McBurnett, K., Stone, P., Hatdagen, S., & Hynd, G. (1988). Psychopathology in the parents of children with conduct disorder and hyperactivity. *Journal of the American Academy of Child Psychiatry, 27*, 163–170.

Levin, P. M. (1938). Restlessness in children. *Archives of Neurology and Psychiatry, 39*, 764–770.

Locke, H. J., & Wallace, K. M. (1959). Short marital adjustment and prediction tests: Their reliability and validity. *Journal of Marriage and Family Living, 21*, 251–255.

Loney, J., & Milich, R. (1982). Hyperactivity, inattention, and aggression in clinical practice. In D. Routh & M. Wolraich (Eds.), *Advances in developmental and behavioral pediatrics* (vol. 3, pp. 113–147). Greenwich, CT: JAI Press.

Lou, H. C., Henriksen, L., Bruhn, P., Borner, H., & Nielsen, J. B. (1989). Striatal dysfunction in attention deficit and hyperkinetic disorder. *Archives of Neurology, 46*, 48–52.

Luk, S. (1985). Direct observations studies of hyperactive behaviors. *Journal of the American Academy of Child Psychiatry, 24*, 338–344.

Margalit, M., & Arieli, N. (1984). Emotional and behavioral aspects of hyperactivity. *Journal of Learning Disabilities, 17*, 374–376.

Mash, E. J., & Barkley, R. A. (1986). Assessment of family interaction with the Response-Class Matrix. In R. Prinz (Ed.), *Advances in behavioral assessment of children and families* (vol. 2, pp. 29–67). Greenwich, CT: JAI Press.

*Mash, E. J., & Johnston, C. (1990). Determinants of parenting stress: Illustrations from families of hyperactive children and families of physically abused children. *Journal of Clinical Child Psychology, 19*, 313–328.

*Matier-Sharma, K., Perachio, N., Newcorn, J. H., Sharma, V., & Halperin, J. M. (1995). Differential diagnosis of ADHD: Are objective measures of attention, impulsivity, and activity level helpful? *Child Neuropsychology, 1*, 118–127.

McCarney, S. B. (1989). *Attention Deficit Disorders Evaluation Scale (ADDES)*. Columbia, MO: Hawthorne Press.

Meichenbaum, D., & Goodman, J. (1971). Training impulsive children to talk to themselves: A means of developing self-control. *Journal of Abnormal Psychology, 77*, 115–126.

Milich, R., Loney, J., & Landau, S. (1982). The independent dimensions of hyperactivity and aggression: A validation with playroom observation data. *Journal of Abnormal Psychology, 91*, 183–198.

Pelham, W. E., & Bender, M. E. (1982). Peer relationships in hyperactive children: Description and treatment. In K. D. Gadow & I. Bialer (Eds.), *Advances in learning and behavioral disabilities* (vol. 1, pp. 365–436). Greenwich, CT: JAI.

*Pelham, W. W., Schnedler, R. W., Bender, M. E., Nilsson, D. E., Miller, J., Budrow, M. S., Ronnel, M., Paluchowski, C., & Marks, D. A. (1988). The combination of behavior therapy and methylphenidate in the treatment of Attention Deficit Disorders: A therapy outcome study. In L. Bloomingdale (Ed.), *Attention deficit disorders* (Vol. 3). New York: Spectrum.

Pfiffner, L. J., & Barkley, R. A. (1998). Treatment of ADHD in school settings. In R. A. Barkley (Ed.), *Attention-Deficit Hyperactivity Disorder: A handbook for diagnosis and treatment* (pp. 458–490). New York: Guilford Press.

Pfiffner, L. J., & O'Leary, S. G. (1987). The efficacy of all-positive management as a function of the prior use of negative consequences. *Journal of Applied Behavior Analysis, 20*, 265–271.

Pfiffner, L. J., Rosen, L. A., & O'Leary, S. G. (1985). The efficacy of an all-positive approach to classroom management. *Journal of Applied Behavior Analysis, 18*, 257–261.

Pisterman, S., McGrath, P., Firestone, P., & Goodman, J. T. (1989). Outcome of parent-mediated treatment of preschoolers with attention deficit disorder with hyperactivity. *Journal of Consulting and Clinical Psychology, 57*, 636–643.

Pliszka, S. R. (1987). Tricyclic antidepressants in the treatment of children with attention deficit disorder. *Journal of the American Academy of Child and Adolescent Psychiatry, 26*, 127–132.

Pliszka, S. R. (1992). Comorbidity of attention-deficit hyperactivity disorder and overanxious disorder. *Journal of the American Academy of Child and Adolescent Psychiatry, 31*, 197–203.

*Quay, H. C. (1989). The behavioral reward and inhibition systems in childhood behavior disorder. In L. M. Bloomingdale (Ed.), *Attention deficit disorder III: New research in treatment, psychopharmacology, and attention* (pp. 176–186). New York: Pergamon.

Rapoport, J., & Mikkelsen, E. (1978). Antidepressants. In J. Werry (Ed.), *Pediatric psychopharmacology* (pp. 208–233). New York: Brunner/Mazel.

*Rapport, M. D., Denney, C., DuPaul, G. J., & Gardner, M. J. (1994). Attention deficit disorder and methylphenidate normalization rates, clinical effectiveness, and response prediction in

76 children. *Journal of the American Academy of Child and Adolescent Psychiatry, 33,* 882–893.

*Rapport, M. D., Tucker, S. B., DuPaul, G. J., Merlo, M., & Stoner, G. (1986). Hyperactivity and frustration: The influence of control over and size of rewards in delaying gratification. *Journal of Abnormal Child Psychology, 14,* 181–204.

*Reynolds, C. R., & Kamphaus, R. W. (1992). *BASC: Behavior Assessment System for Children Manual.* Circle Pines, MN: American Guidance Service.

Roberts, M. A. (1987). How is playroom behavior observation used in the diagnosis of attention deficit disorder? In J. Loney (Ed.), *The young hyperactive child: Answers to questions about diagnosis, prognosis, and treatment* (pp. 65–74). New York: Haworth Press.

Ross, D. M., & Ross, S. A. (1982). *Hyperactivity: Current issues, research, and theory* (2nd ed.). New York: Wiley.

Routh, D. K. (1978). Hyperactivity. In P. Magrab (Ed.), *Psychological management of pediatric problems* (pp. 3–48). Baltimore: University Park Press.

Routh, D. K., & Schroeder, C. S. (1976). Standardized playroom measures as indices of hyperactivity. *Journal of Abnormal Child Psychology, 4,* 199–207.

Satterfield, J. H., Satterfield, B. T., & Cantwell, D. P. (1980). Three-year multimodality treatment study of 100 hyperactive boys. *Journal of Pediatrics, 98,* 650–655.

Schachar, R. J., Tannock, R., & Logan, G. (1993). Inhibitory control, impulsiveness, and attention deficit hyperactivity disorder. *Clinical Psychology Review, 13,* 721–739.

Sergeant, J. A. (1995). Hyperkinetic disorder revisited. In J. A. Sergeant (Ed.), *Eunethydis: European approaches to hyperkinetic disorder* (pp. 7–17). Amsterdam: Author.

*Shapiro, E. S., & Cole, C. L. (1994). *Behavior change in the classroom: Self-management interventions.* New York: Guilford Press.

Still, G. F. (1902). Some abnormal psychical conditions in children. *Lancet, I,* 1008–1012, 1077–1082, 1163–1168.

Streissguth, A. P., Martin, D. C., Barr, H. M., Sandman, B. M., Kirchner, G. L., & Darby, B. L. (1984). Intrauterine alcohol and nicotine exposure: Attention and reaction time in 4-year-old children. *Developmental Psychology, 20,* 533–541.

Taylor, E. (1986). *The overactive child.* Philadelphia: Lippincott.

Ullmann, R., Sleator, E., & Sprague, R. (1984). A new rating scale for diagnosis and monitoring of ADD children. *Psychopharmacology Bulletin, 20,* 160–164.

Van der Meere, J. (1993). *CPT and recent sustained attention data of adhd children.* Paper presented at the Society for Research in Child and Adolescent Psychopathology, Santa Fe, NM.

Wechsler, D. (1991). *Wechsler Intelligence Scale for Children* (3rd ed.). San Antonio, TX: Psychological Corporation.

Wechsler, D. (1992). *Wechsler Individual Achievement Test.* San Antonio, TX: Psychological Corporation.

*Weiss, G., & Hechtman, L. (1986). *Hyperactive children grown up.* New York: Guilford Press.

Wender, P. H. (1973). Minimal brain dysfunction in children. *Pediatric Clinics of North America, 20,* 187–202.

*Wender, P. H. (1995). *Attention-Deficit Hyperactivity Disorder in adults.* New York: Oxford University Press.

Willis, T. J., & Lovaas, I. (1977). A behavioral approach to treating hyperactive children: The parent's role. In J. B. Millichap (Ed.), *Learning disabilities and related disorders* (pp. 119–140). Chicago: Yearbook Medical Publications.

*Wolraich, M. L., Lindgren, S. D., Stumbo, P. J., Stegink, L. D., Appelbaum, M. I., & Kiritsy, M. C. (1994). Effects of diets high in sucrose or aspartame on the behavior and cognitive performance of children. *New England Journal of Medicine, 330,* 301–307.

*World Health Organization. (1993). *ICD-10 classification of mental and behavioral disorders: Diagnostic criteria for research.* Geneva: Author.

Zametkin, A. J., & Rapoport, J. L. (1986). The pathophysiology of Attention Deficit Disorder with Hyperactivity: A review. In B. Lahey & A. Kazdin (Eds.), *Advances in clinical child psychology* (vol. 9, pp. 177–216). New York: Plenum Press.

Zeiner, P. (1995). Body growth and cardiovascular function after extended treatment (1.75 years) with methylphenidate in boys with attention deficit hyperactivity disorder. *Journal of Child and Adolescent Psychopharmacology, 5,* 129–138.

*Zentall, S. S. (1985). A context for hyperactivity. In K. D. Gadow & I. Bialer (Eds.), *Advances in learning and behavioral disabilities* (vol. 4, pp. 273–343). Greenwich, CT: JAI Press.

*Indicates references that the author recommends for further reading.

7

Disruptive Behavior: Oppositional Defiant Disorder and Conduct Disorder

Thomas S. Altepeter
John N. Korger

INTRODUCTION

Children who exhibit overactive, noncompliant, oppositional, and aggressive behaviors are among the most commonly referred for professional help. Complaints about these children include annoying or aversive interpersonal behaviors (e.g., recurrent yelling, temper tantrums, impulsivity, excessive motor activity, lying, stealing), noncompliance with authority figures, defiance of social norms, and physically aggressive behaviors (e.g., hitting, fighting). Problems with older children and adolescents may also include truancy, curfew violations, theft, assault, rape, or alcohol or drug abuse. Typically, these problems do not occur in isolation but are exhibited over a period of months or years. Children who exhibit these behaviors tend to be diagnosed with one or more of the disruptive behavior disorders, including oppositional defiant disorder (ODD), conduct disorder (CD), and attention-deficit/hyperactive disorder (ADHD). The focus of this chapter is on the assessment and treatment of ODD and CD (ADHD is addressed in chapter 6 of this text).

Historical Perspective

There has been debate through the years about whether children with these types of problems exhibit variations of the same disorder or separate disorders and about how to define the various disorders. Issues of dispute have included the use of inclusionary and exclusionary criteria, whether subtyping (and which subtypes) contributes clarity, and the degree and significance of overlap between these disorders and similar disorders, such as ADHD. At the same time, the primary difficulties of the ODD or CD child/adolescent are generally agreed on. Primary features of ODD include a pattern of negativistic, defiant, noncompliant, and uncooperative behaviors. Primary features of CD include a pattern of behavior in which the basic rights of others and/or major age-appropriate norms or rules are violated. The primary feature that distinguishes ODD from CD is the emphasis in CD on the recurrent violation of the rights of others and/or societal norms and rules (APA, 1994). Secondary features common in children with ODD or CD include the following. First, these children are often inattentive, impulsive, and overactive, and 75% or more of the children with ODD/CD may have a co-existing ADHD (Stewart, Cummings, Singer, and deBois, 1981). Second, these children often exhibit deficits in social skills, including difficulties developing and maintaining peer relationships. In comparison to peers, these children are often more aggressive, less empathic, and more deficient in social-problem-solving skills, and they tend to misperceive the social environment, often incorrectly attributing hostile intentions to others (Lochman & Dodge, 1994). Third, they have an earlier first use of mood altering substances, and are more likely to abuse tobacco, alcohol, and/or other mood altering chemicals (Robins & McEvoy, 1990). Fourth, they are often sexually precocious and are more likely to engage in superficial sexual encounters. Additional difficulties may include low frustration tolerance; low self-esteem; mild to moderate depression; and mood lability.

The evolution of the *Diagnostic and Statistical Manual of Mental Disorders* (DSM) of the American Psychiatric Association has reflected the evolution in the theoretical conceptualizations of these disorders. DSM-I did not include disorders of childhood/adolescence. DSM-II included two diagnostic categories, "group delinquent reaction of childhood" (emphasizing identification with a delinquent peer group) and "unsocialized aggressive reaction of childhood" (emphasizing hostile disobedience, verbal and physical aggressiveness, and stealing). The presentation in DSM-III was broadened to include five categories: four subtypes of CD and a new category, oppositional disorder (OD). The CD subtypes were conceptualized along two bipolar dimensions, aggressive-nonaggressive and undersocialized-socialized. The nonaggressive types involved behaviors that lack confrontation with a victim (e.g., truancy, lying, stealing). The aggressive types involved behaviors that may include a violent confrontation with a victim (e.g., vandalism, breaking and entering, rape). The socialized-unsocialized dimension was concerned with whether the child formed an ongoing attachment with others (socialized) or not (unsocialized). The category of OD consisted of disobedient, negative, and provocative opposition,

devoid of more serious violations of rules and/or rights of others. The criteria were subsequently revised (DSM-III-R; APA, 1987). While the essential features of CD remained the same in the revision, the bipolar subtypes were replaced with three subtypes: group type, solitary aggressive type, and undifferentiated type. In the group type, problems occur primarily in the context of peer group activities. In the solitary aggressive type, physically aggressive acts may occur independent of peer group activities and may be directed at adults or peers. Finally, the undifferentiated type is a residual group that includes a mixture of problems that cannot be classified as either the solitary aggressive or group types.

Description/critique of DSM-IV

In the process of developing DSM-IV (APA, 1994), alternative ways of conceptualizing the relationship between ODD and CD were considered (APA, 1991). The first option was to retain the DSM-III-R distinction between ODD (characterized by negative, defiant behavior) and CD (characterized by antisocial behaviors). The second option was to collapse ODD/CD into one disorder containing several levels, with the distinction between the levels reflecting developmental trends and severity (e.g., Russo et al., 1994). In the end, DSM-IV maintained the distinction between ODD and CD, although reference is made to the overlap in comments such as ODD "includes some of the features contained in Conduct Disorder" (APA, 1994, p. 89), and "features of Oppositional Defiant Disorder are usually present in Conduct Disorder" (APA, 1994, p. 93). Once again, field trials were used to establish the validity of criteria and cutting scores (Frick et al., 1994). When criteria for both are met, CD takes precedence, and ODD is not diagnosed. Additional changes in the formulation of CD include: (1) expansion of criteria to include behaviors more characteristic of females; (2) arrangement of items into thematically related groups; and (3) use of new subtypes based on age of onset (i.e., early vs. late onset) to reflect the poorer prognosis associated with early onset. The criteria for ODD were modified slightly, deleting one item and adding an impairment criterion.

The DSM-IV criteria for ODD (APA, 1994, p. 91) include a pattern of oppositional, negative, and hostile behavior that lasts six months or longer and that causes "significant impairment in social, academic, or occupational functioning." During this time period, four or more behaviors must be present, including losing one's temper; arguing with adults; deliberately annoying others; blaming others for one's misdeeds; being angry and resentful; and being spiteful or vindictive. The DSM-IV criteria for CD (APA, 1994, p. 85) include a chronic pattern of behavior in which the "rights of others or major age-appropriate societal norms or rules are violated," causing "significant impairment in social, academic, or occupational functioning." During this period, three or more of 15 behavioral criteria must be evident. The criteria are clustered into four related groups, including: (1) aggression to people and animals (e.g., bullying or intimidation; acts of physical cruelty to people or animals); (2) destruction of property (e.g., fire-setting with the intent to cause damage; deliberately destroying others' property); (3) deceitfulness or theft (e.g., breaking into someone's house, building, or car; lying to obtain goods or favors or to avoid obligations); and (4) serious violations of rules (e.g., staying out at night past parental limits; running away from home overnight at least twice; repetitive truancy from school). Two subtypes are delineated, childhood-onset type (onset of at least one criterion prior to age 10 years), and adolescent-onset type (absence of any characteristic criteria prior to age 10 years). (The reader is referred to DSM-IV [APA, 1994] for a more detailed presentation of the diagnostic criteria.)

Comparison of DSM-IV with ICD-10

The descriptions in DSM-IV are both similar to and different from the conceptualizations of these disorders in the new *International Classification of Diseases* (ICD-10) (WHO, 1992, 1993). First, the overlap between ODD and CD is addressed in a similar manner in both DSM-IV and ICD-10. In both, ODD is seen as a milder disorder, but within the same spectrum as CD; however, this distinction is implemented in a slightly different manner. In DSM-IV, CD is an exclusionary criteria for ODD (i.e., if criteria for both are met, CD is diagnosed, and ODD is not), whereas in ICD-10 ODD is considered a mild subtype of CD, absent behaviors that violate the law and the basic rights of others (e.g., theft, cruelty, assault). Second, in ICD-10, overlap between ADHD (identified in ICD-10 as "hyperkinetic disorder") and CD is addressed by making ADHD an exclusionary criterion for CD. When the criteria for both are met, ADHD takes precedence, and CD is *not* diagnosed; the diagnosis is a subtype of ADHD, "hyperkinetic conduct disorder." Third, subtypes for CD in ICD-10 differ from those in DSM-IV. ICD-10 retains the distinction between "unsocialized" and "socialized" subtypes. Further, the subtype distinction of age of onset in DSM-IV is not made in ICD-10, although it is implied in the CD subtype of ODD, which "is characteristically seen in children below the age of 9 or 10" (WHO, 1992, p. 270). Finally, ICD-10 includes a CD subtype in which problems are limited to the family context. In this subtype, no significant conduct disturbances are evident outside the family context, and social relationships are within the normal range.

Developmental Course

While not all children who develop ODD or CD follow a common developmental course, there are some trends that do occur (Caspi, Elder, & Herbener, 1990). As early as infancy, many of these children exhibit a constellation of behavioral and temperamental characteristics, including irritability, overreactivity, nonadaptability, high activity level, and low tolerance of stimulation (Sanson et al., 1993). Often the child has one or more features that the parent(s) experience(s) as aversive. Patterson (1982) suggests that in early childhood the parental use of negative reinforcement begins to strengthen the frequency and intensity of aversive child behaviors. During the toddler phase (18–36 months) these children may exhibit a variety of difficult behaviors, including short attention span, impulsivity, restlessness and overactivity, and frequent temper tantrums. These children may be perceived by caretakers as noncompliant, negative, and oppositional, with rebellious motives often attributed to the child. During the preschool period (ages 3–6 years) these children can become increasingly noncompliant and exhibit more difficulties with frustration tolerance, greater displays of aggression, and increasing difficulties with peer relationships. Parents may resort to physical discipline to control the child's behavior, temporarily inhibiting the child's negative behavior but reinforcing the parent's use of physical punishment and increasing the probability that physical discipline will be used in the future. Thus, a gradually escalating level of reciprocal aggression may occur in the parent-child relationship. In addition, corporal punishment may provide ongoing modeling of aggressive behavior for the child, increasing the probability of future aggressive behavior by the child.

During the elementary school period (ages 6–11 years), behavior problems may continue in the home, school, and neighborhood settings. Parents may be confronted with school personnel who complain about the child's behavior. This may contribute to increased parental stress and increased parent-child tension. Difficulties with impulsivity, motor restlessness, and academic performance may be identified by the school. Peer and social problems generally continue. Due to their aggressiveness and behavior problems, these children are often rejected by non-ODD/CD peers. While some may have initial success in making friends, they may have difficulty maintaining friendships over time. Finally, minor delinquent behaviors, such as cheating, lying, and stealing, may emerge. During the middle-school years (ages 12 to 14), academic difficulties continue, and the child often loses interest in school. A pattern of truancy may emerge. Similarly, peer social relationships generally continue to be poor, with continued aggressions. If ongoing peer relationships are maintained, they are often in the context of groups of other ODD/CD children. Identification with an oppositional and delinquent peer group may solidify, and there may be increased lying, stealing, truancy, running away, initial alcohol and/or drug abuse, and initial sexual experiences. There may also be increased aggressive acting out, particularly in the form of brief explosive episodes in reaction to mounting stress and frustration. Problems with low self-esteem and depression may emerge.

During adolescence (ages 13–18 years), behavior and conduct problems generally escalate. Truancy from school may continue, and many adolescents with ODD or CD drop out or are expelled before they can graduate from high school. There may be an increased loyalty to the delinquent peer group and greater isolation from other peers. There may be many behaviors that violate societal rules or norms, including stealing, truancy, running away, alcohol and/or drug abuse, and sexual promiscuity (Robins & McEvoy, 1990). There may also be violent interpersonal behaviors, such as fighting, assault, and rape. Problems with low self-esteem and depression may continue, perhaps with suicidal ideation or attempts. Many of these adolescents are confronted by juvenile authorities for status offenses. Those who appear to have the greatest risk for juvenile convictions are those with an early history of aggressive behavior and those with comorbid CD/ADHD (Farrington, Loeber, & Van Kammen, 1990). Many will continue to exhibit difficulties well in adulthood. Common difficulties in adulthood may include substance abuse, poor marital and occupational adjustment, antisocial personality disorders, and criminal behavior (Caspi, Elder, & Herbener, 1990; Kazdin, 1985, 1987; Quinton, Rutter & Gulliver, 1990). Notably, various lines of research indicate that those who exhibit more aggressive behavior problems in childhood, and in more than one setting, are at greater risk to develop later antisocial behaviors and alcohol or drug abuse (Loeber, 1982, 1988,

Loeber et al., 1995; Offord & Bennett, 1994; Satterfield et al., 1995).

Epidemiology

Oppositional defiant disorder (ODD) occurs in 5–25% of school-age children (APA, 1994; Husain & Cantwell, 1991), twice as often in prepubertal males as in females, but relatively evenly in postpubertal males and females. Conduct disorder (CD) occurs in 5–20% of school-age children, and two to three times more frequently in males than in females (APA, 1994; Husain & Cantwell, 1991; Kazdin, 1987). For both ODD and CD, onset may occur at any time throughout childhood. ODD may develop as early as 3 and is usually evident by 8 years of age. ODD during early childhood may precede CD in later childhood or adolescence. Early onset and greater severity, particularly of aggressive behaviors, are associated with poorer prognosis in adolescence and adulthood. While these children represent a minority in the general population, they represent one of the groups most frequently referred to mental health professionals (APA, 1994; Husain & Cantwell, 1991), accounting for 35–50% of all clinic referrals (Herbert, 1978; Robins, 1981).

Comorbidity

Several other childhood disorders are highly associated with ODD/CD, and careful diagnosis is required to rule out other disorders and/or to identify and treat comorbidity. There is substantial overlap between the disruptive behavior disorders (CD, ODD, and ADHD), so, when the diagnosis involves one, the other two must be ruled out. The rate of ADHD among children with ODD/CD has been reported to be as high as 75% (Abikoff, Klein, Klass, & Ganeles, 1987; Safer & Allen, 1976). Mood disorders are also relatively common. In childhood, depressive disorders may be associated with oppositional and aggressive behavior. In adolescence, dysthymia or major depressive disorder

often coexists with ODD/CD. Although child-onset bipolar disorder is less common, recent evidence suggests some comorbidity between child-onset mania and ODD/CD (Kovacs & Pollock, 1995; Wozniak et al., 1995). Anxiety disorders, including separation anxiety, often present with oppositional behaviors and may be coexisting with ODD. Tourette's Syndrome is highly correlated with ADHD, but less so with ODD or CD. Neurologic abnormalities may present with unprovoked aggressive outbursts. Alcohol and other drug abuse is quite common in adolescents with ODD/CD and often impedes the efficacy of other forms of treatment unless also treated. Adjustment disorders and posttraumatic stress disorders may present with significant behavioral components, including oppositional, aggressive, and other acting-out behaviors. Recent evidence suggests that victims of physical and sexual abuse may experience high rates of ODD and aggressive acting-out behaviors (McLeer et al., 1994; Merry & Andrews, 1994; Pelcovitz et al., 1994). Specific developmental disorders (e.g., reading, arithmetic, expressive language disorders) are relatively common. The reader is referred to DSM-IV and several comprehensive reviews (Husain & Cantwell, 1991; Ollendick & Hersen, 1989; Walker & Roberts, 1992; Weiner, 1991) for detailed discussions of these disorders. In the majority of cases, the child meets the criteria for two or more disorders (e.g., CD, ADHD, and learning disability, or CD, major depressive disorder, and substance abuse). Obviously, in such cases, all appropriate diagnoses should be given and treatment planned accordingly.

Factors That Influence the Development of ODD/CD

ODD or CD may develop along multiple pathways. Genetic, temperamental, family interaction, and environmental stress variables have all been implicated in the development of ODD/CD. Concerning genetic factors, a higher incidence of psychiatric disorders have been noted among parents and other biological relatives of children with ODD or CD, including ODD, CD, ADHD, depression, alcoholism, substance abuse, antisocial personality, and criminal behavior (Frick et al., 1992; Kazdin, 1987; Loeber et al., 1995; Reich et al., 1993; Robins, 1981). In addition, several studies indicate a higher concordance among identical than fraternal twins, and a higher incidence of antisocial behavior in the biological fathers compared to adoptive fathers (Cadoret, 1978; Cloninger, Reich, & Guze, 1978; Jary & Stewart, 1985). These data suggest some genetic predisposition for ODD or CD, although specific mechanisms of transmission have not been identified.

There is considerable evidence for individual differences in "temperament." One proposed temperamental type is the "difficult child," who exhibits irritable, negative, nonadaptive behaviors starting in early infancy. Children who are temperamentally difficult in infancy tend to exhibit lower frustration tolerance and higher levels of aggressive behavior in later childhood (Chess & Thomas, 1990; Kolvin et al., 1982; Olweus, 1980; Sanson et al., 1993; Turecki & Tonner, 1985). However, the relationship between temperament and subsequent aggressive behavior is not clear. Other variables, such as modeling of aggressive behavior, maternal depression, and parental reinforcement of child aggression, may contribute more to aggressive behavior than temperament.

Family variables and patterns of interaction have been associated with the emergence of ODD/CD in children. In particular, deficiencies in fundamental parenting skills have been implicated in numerous studies. Problems have included inadequate monitoring of the child's behavior, insufficient involvement in the child's life, inadequate provision of positive reinforcement, insufficient problem-solving skills, interaction characterized by negative reinforcement and coercion, and an overreliance on harsh, aversive methods of physical discipline for behavioral management. Patterson (1982) provided a comprehensive analysis of family interaction patterns that may contribute to the development of conduct problems in chil-

dren, noting that negative reinforcement contributes to the escalation of reciprocal coercive interaction patterns in the family. Ultimately, negative reinforcement increase the probability of aversive and aggressive behaviors on the part of the child and parent (Patterson, 1982, 1986; Patterson & Stouthamer-Loeber, 1984).

In addition, ODD/CD children have relatively high rates of familial environmental stress and adversity (Schachar & Tannock, 1995). (This may be in part related to higher rates of psychopathology in parents and extended family members.) The home environments of these children are likely to contain low rates of cohesion and limited shared family activities, as well as higher rates of conflict, chronic parental marital discord, and parental adjustment notable for divorce, alcohol and drug abuse, under- or unemployment, and arrests or other legal problems. Severity and chronicity in these family adversity variables have been associated with higher rates of chronic aggression and delinquency in offspring (Haapasalo & Tremblay, 1994). Finally, these children appear to experience higher rates of physical and sexual abuse (McLeer et al., 1994).

ASSESSMENT

It is well recognized that there is considerable cross-situational variation in child behavior. Factors that influence the manner in which a child behaves include the relative degree of structure in a given environment, the novelty of the environment, contingencies operative within the environment, presence of caregiver(s), nature of the task, and prior learning history in similar situations. Children with disruptive behavior disorders exhibit an equally varied range of behavior and may exhibit behavioral and emotional problems to a greater or lesser extent across most settings, including the home, school, and community settings. Therefore, the evaluation (and subsequent treatment) of these children is by necessity comprehensive in scope. A thorough review of the assessment of disruptive behavior disorders is beyond the scope of this chapter.

Fortunately, several resources are available that address the salient issues involved in the assessment process, and the interested reader is referred to these for more detail (Breen & Altepeter, 1990; La Greca, 1990; Walker & Roberts, 1992; Weiner, 1991). What follows is a cursory review of pertinent aspects of the assessment of disruptive behavior disorders.

There is a need for standardization in the assessment of children with disruptive behavior disorders (Breen & Altepeter, 1990). The assessment process should strive to accurately understand the child's behavioral and emotional functioning across time and multiple settings, as well as the contexts in which the child normally functions. In addition, conclusions of such an assessment should have direct relevance for treatment, and should provide a baseline against which subsequent intervention can be evaluated. When possible, the assessment process should include the following major components. First, there is need for thorough medical, developmental, and social histories, including corroborative records when available. An accurate history enables one to situate the presenting concerns in the appropriate contexts and to begin to elucidate areas for potential intervention. Concerning the medical history, it is important to identify pre- or coexisting conditions that may contribute to the problems in question. Of particular note are possible histories of maternal alcohol or drug abuse during the pregnancy, birth trauma, prior head injury, prior seizures, or chronic infections (e.g., chronic sinus or ear infections). Exploring the developmental history and social background facilitates a broader understanding of the context and may provide direction about areas of intervention. For example, examining circumstances involved in reported "power struggles" during early developmental transitions (e.g., toilet training) may suggest a parent who lacks knowledge of normal child development or appropriate child management skills, is overly coercive, and so on. In families with histories of multiple disruptions and changes, there may be a history of disrupted and broken attachments between the child and primary caretakers. Finally, examining the child's social behaviors in other contexts (e.g., daycare, school) may help clarify the pervasiveness of the difficulties and whether interventions to improve social skill functioning are indicated.

Second, a comprehensive clinical interview with the custodial parent(s) and/or the child is essential. Exploring the history of behavioral difficulties and symptoms facilitates the diagnostic process, identification of possible precipitants, and evaluation of possible comorbidity. For example, a persistent course, dating back into the preschool years, of behavioral overactivity, impulsivity, and inattention (often misinterpreted by parents as intentional noncompliance) may raise the question of possible coexisting ADHD. On the other hand, a course that consists of a relatively sudden onset of problems, with no preceding history of difficulties, may raise questions of a possible depressive episode, separation anxiety, or a posttrauma reaction. One of several objective structured interviews, such as the Diagnostic Interview for Children and Adolescents (DICA; Herjanic & Reich, 1982) or the Diagnostic Interview Schedule for Children (DISC; Costello et al., 1987), may be helpful in reviewing the history and current presentation of symptoms.

Third, when possible, objective parent- and teacher-completed child behavior rating scales should be obtained. Currently there is a plethora of such questionnaires, varying widely in terms of psychometric acceptability. It is recommended that only those that have acceptable reliability and validity and an adequate normative base (including norms based on age and gender) be utilized. Depending on the specific circumstances, it is usually best that custodial parents and one or more teachers complete several questionnaires, including one broad-band questionnaire, such as the Child Behavior Checklist (CBCL; Achenbach, 1991a, 1991b) or the Revised Behavior Problem Checklist (Quay & Peterson, 1987), and one or more narrow-band questionnaire, such as the Conners Revised Parent and Revised Teacher Rating Scales (Conners, 1989), the New York Teacher Rating Scale (Miller et al., 1995), the ADD-H Comprehensive Teacher's Rating Scale (Ullmann, Sleator, & Sprague,

1988), or the Eyberg Child Behavior Rating Inventory (Burns & Patterson, 1991; Eyberg, 1980; Eyberg and Robinson, 1983). Such questionnaires have limitations, including the fact that they are typically high in face validity; therefore, they can be easily skewed to over- or underreport problems by informants inclined to do so. Ideally, one would look for consistency in score patterns across informants. For example, in situations where a child has an ODD or CD with no comorbidity, one would anticipate elevations on scales or factors that tap acting-out conduct problems (e.g., CBCL Aggressive, Delinquent scales; Conners's Conduct Problem factor). On the other hand, in situations where a child has ODD or CD with comorbid ADHD, one would anticipate these same elevations, along with elevations on scales that tap ADHD (e.g., CBCL Hyperactive scale; Conners's Hyperactive-Impulsive and Hyperactivity Index factors). Inconsistencies between informants raise questions that need to be explored and understood. For example, elevated scores produced by a parent but not a teacher may suggest that the child is having problems only at home; or that the child is not having problems anywhere but that the parent is overreporting for some reason; or that the child is having problems in multiple settings but that the teacher is underreporting for some reason.

Fourth, in preadolescents and adolescents, self-report questionnaires often provide information that is particularly helpful in assessing comorbidity. Commonly used measures include the Youth-Self Report (Achenbach, 1991c), the MMPI-A (Butcher et al., 1992), the Child Depression Inventory (Kovacs, 1992), and the Reynolds Adolescent Depression Scale (Reynolds, 1987).

Fifth, objective measures of attention span, impulse control, intellectual functioning, and academic skills may be indicated in some situations. When comorbid ADHD is suspected, an objective measure of attention span such as the Conners Continuous Performance Test (CPT; Conners, 1994) or the Gordon Diagnostic System (GDS; Gordon, 1982) may be indicated. The CPT and the GDS are objective instruments that assess vigilance, sustained attention, and impulse control and that have age-based normative data to facilitate interpretation. When comorbid cognitive disabilities or learning disabilities are suspected, standardized batteries of cognitive and academic skill functioning may be indicated.

Finally, although presenting complaints typically focus on the child, custodial parents may harbor some psychopathology (e.g., antisocial behavior, alcohol abuse, depression) that might help to maintain the child's problems and impede treatment efforts if not also addressed. In these situations, parent self-report measures (e.g., BDI [Beck, 1993]; MMPI-2 [Butcher et al., 1989]; SCL-90-R [Derogatis, 1983]) may be useful preliminary adjuncts, with more thorough evaluation and/or referral to an appropriate treatment source to follow as needed.

TREATMENT

As noted earlier, children with ODD/CD typically exhibit a wide variety of behavioral, social, and emotional problems across multiple settings, often in the context of heightened environmental conflicts and stressors. Although treatment is most often initiated in response to a specific set of complaints or concerns, it is helpful to keep in mind the broader array of problems that may exist and the possible future course for this child. In view of these broader perspectives, the goals of treatment should include ameliorating as much as possible the primary presenting concerns, identifying and ameliorating existing associated problems, and attempting to alter the long-term course toward a more favorable outcome, that is, primary prevention effort (Offord & Bennett, 1994; Yoshikawa, 1994). The treatment of these children commonly requires a comprehensive approach, involving multiple treatment targets and multiple treatment modalities (Barkley et al., 1992; Breen & Altepeter, 1990; Husain & Cantwell, 1991). Thus, it is recommended that a longitudinal, multimodal approach be adopted when working with ODD/CD children. Once presenting concerns are addressed, efforts should also be directed toward improving the quality of family interactions, parenting skills, and social skills of the child, with the goal of improving the long-term prognosis for the child. This may involve a variety of therapies, including pharmacotherapy, cognitive-behavioral therapy, social-skills training, communication training, marital or family therapy, and alcohol or other drug abuse treatment. With these comments as an overview, we now turn to a brief review of interventions that have been shown to have some efficacy in the treatment of children with ODD or CD.

Pharmacotherapy

A relatively high percentage of children with ODD or CD derive benefit from one or more psychotropic medications. This is in part associated with treatment of comorbid disorders, such as ADHD or depressive disorders and in part associated with efforts to treat aggressive behavior. Several reviews are available (e.g., Alessi et al., 1994; Campbell & Cueva, 1995; Campbell, Gonzalez & Silva, 1992; Campbell & Spencer, 1988; Eichelman, 1987), and the interested reader is referred to these.

Psychostimulants, including Ritalin (methylphenidate), Dexedrine (dextroamphetamine), and Cylert (pemoline), are commonly used with ODD/CD children, in part due to comorbidity with ADHD. These medicines have been found to reduce oppositional behavior, impulsivity and aggressive behavior, stealing, and destruction of property (Campbell, Green, & Deutsch, 1985; Campbell & Spencer, 1988; Dulcan, 1990; Hinshaw, 1991; Hinshaw, Heller, & McHale, 1992; Kline, 1991; Pelham et al., 1995). Therapeutic benefits tend to be greatest when there is a comorbid ADHD, although evidence suggests that stimulants may provide benefit in some children with ODD/CD without ADHD (Brown et al., 1991; Rapoport, 1983). Kline (1991), for example, found Ritalin to be more effective than Lithium in reducing aggression. Of these medications, Ritalin is the most commonly used and is typically administered in the range of 0.3–1.0 mg/kg/dose, three

doses per day. Dexedrine is generally administered in the range of 0.15–0.5 mg/kg/dose, three doses per day. Cylert is commonly administered in the range of .5–3.0 mg/kg, once daily in the morning. Possible adverse side effects of these medicines include appetite suppression, weight loss (or failure to maintain adequate weight gain), insomnia, behavioral or emotional rebound (i.e., increased irritability, excitability, or impulsivity after the dose wears off), and tics. Side effects for these medicines tend to be dose related. Cylert may have advantages over the other two, in preadolescents and adolescents, including once-per-day dosing (thus improving compliance), reduced potential for abuse, and lower street value.

Lithium has been used to treat acute mania, bipolar disorder, and aggressive behavior (Alessi et al., 1994; Sheard, 1978). Lithium has also been found to be effective in reducing aggressive behavior in neurologically normal delinquent children and adolescents with mood lability, irritability, restlessness, hostility, and explosiveness (Campbell et al., 1984, 1990, 1995; Platt et al., 1984). Lithium is commonly started at 150–300 mg/day and gradually titrated upward until serum concentrations reach 0.5–1.5 mEq/L. While exact dosing is individualized depending on serum levels and clinical response, most children and adolescents reach a stable full dose in the range of 600–1500 mg per day. Full therapeutic benefit may not be evident until 7–10 days after optimal serum level is reached. Potential adverse effects include weight gain, acne, nausea, headache, sleepiness, polyuria, and diarrhea. Adequate salt and fluid intake are required to help prevent toxicity.

Tegretol (carbamazepine) has been commonly used in Europe but not in the United States to treat ADHD. It is commonly used in the United States to treat ODD or CD with aggressive behavior (with or without EEG abnormalities). The most responsive symptoms include impulsivity, emotional instability, and aggression (Barratt, 1993; Kafantaris et al., 1992; Pliszka, 1991a; Trimble, 1990). Tegretol is commonly administered in the maintenance range of 5–20 mg/kg/day, divided into two or three doses per day. Typically a child is started at 50–100 mg at night, with daily dosing increased 50–100 mg every 7 days until a stable full dose is achieved. Therapeutic benefit may be evident in several days, but full therapeutic benefit may not be evident for 3–4 weeks. Potential side effects include drowsiness, lightheadedness, blurred vision, hyponatremia, skin rashes, liver toxicity, and leukopenia.

Clonidine has been used since the 1970s as an antihypertensive agent and since the 1980s to treat Tourette's disorder. More recently it has also been used to reduce excessive overactivity, low frustration tolerance, oppositionality, and aggressive behavior in children who have comorbid ADHD/ODD or ADHD/CD (Hunt, 1987; Hunt, Capper, & O'Connell, 1990; Kemph et al. 1993). Hunt et al. (1990, p. 89) concluded that "the most clonidine-responsive ADHD children . . . have a co-morbid oppositional or conduct disorder." Clonidine can be used in combination with a psychostimulant. Clonidine is commonly administered in the range of 0.15–0.4 mg/day in three or four divided doses per day (or comparable-dose transdermal patch). A child is typically started at 0.05 mg at night, with daily dosing increased 0.05 mg every 3–4 days until a stable full dose is achieved. Full therapeutic benefit may not be evident for 8–10 weeks. The most frequent adverse effect is initial sedation and fatigue, which may last for 2–4 weeks. There are several serious possible side effects, including transient but potentially serious rebound hypertension if the medication is suddenly withdrawn. This needs to be explained thoroughly to parents and appropriate plans made to ensure that the family does not let the prescription run out or fail or refuse to give the medication. When the medication is discontinued, it should be tapered gradually to reduce the risk of rebound hypertension. Tenex (guanfacine) is an antihypertensive agent similar to Clonidine in reducing overactivity, low frustration tolerance, oppositionality, and aggressive behavior. However, Tenex can be administered with less frequent dosing, and in some children it is less sedating and carries less risk of rebound hypertension than Clonidine.

Tenex is commonly administered in the range of 0.5–1.5 mg/day in two or three divided doses. Monitoring and side effects are otherwise comparable to those with Clonidine.

In situations where there is a comorbid anxiety, depression, or ADHD (and stimulants are contraindicated or have proven ineffective), an antidepressant medication may be indicated. Several agents have been used, including tricyclics (TCAs) (e.g., Imipramine, Desipramine) (Pliszka, 1987, 1991b; Riddle et al., 1988) or Wellbutrin (bupropion) (Barrickman et al., 1995). The most appropriate choice for each child depends on a number of factors, including symptom presentation, presence or absence of suicide risk, biomedical test data (e.g., EKG abnormality may exclude use of a TCA; EEG abnormality may exclude use of Wellbutrin), and prior positive response of a family member to one of the medications. TCAs are commonly administered in the range of 1–3 mg/kg/day, divided into three doses per day. Common side effects include dry mouth, nausea, constipation, dizziness (especially in adolescents), increased heart rate (especially if the child is using marijuana), blurred vision, fatigue, and excessive sweating. Due to their potentially lethal cardiovascular side effects, patients taking TCAs require careful monitoring, including a baseline EKG and pulse and blood pressure checks (Schroeder et al., 1989). Wellbutrin is typically administered in the range of 150–450 mg per day, divided into two or three doses per day. Potential side effects include initial restlessness or nausea, drowsiness, or fatigue. There is also an increased risk of seizure in individuals who have a history of seizures or abnormal EEG findings. Recent evidence (e.g., Gammon & Brown, 1993) suggests that SSRI antidepressants may also have a role to play in treating ODD or CD children with comorbid ADHD. These tend to have the effect of improving mood, reducing mood swings and irritability, and reducing oppositionality and aggressive behavior.

Finally, recent evidence suggests that one of the antianxiety agents, Buspar (buspirone), may help decrease aggressive and assaultive behavior in ODD/CD children, but without improvement in the ADHD features (Quiason et al., 1991; Sussman, 1994). Buspar is commonly started at 2.5–5 mg twice per day and titrated upward to 5–10 mg three times per day. Buspar has been found to have a relatively low side-effect profile, with reported side effects including dizziness, lightheadedness, headache, nausea, and insomnia.

Psychosocial Interventions

Cognitive Behavior Therapy

Cognitive behavior therapy (CBT) consists of strategies that emphasize the learning process, the influence of environmental contingencies, and the role of cognitive mediation in both the development and the remediation of various disorders. Aggressive children tend to misperceive social cues, to attribute hostile intent to others, to be hypervigilant in scanning the environment for hostile cues, and to have deficits in social problem-solving processes, such as generating alternative solutions, means-end thinking, and anticipating consequences (Kendall, 1993; Lochman & Dodge, 1994). The goal is to train the child in various cognitively mediated strategies, such as self-control and response-delay strategies, problem-solving skills, self-instructional training, and anticipation of consequences. It is assumed that the development and strengthening of these skills will lead to an increase in self-control and a corresponding decrease in impulsive and disruptive behaviors. A thorough review of the technical aspects of CBT with children who have disruptive behavior disorders is beyond the scope of this chapter. Fortunately, several resources are available that address the salient issues and processes, and the interested reader is referred to these for more detail (Braswell & Kendall, 1988; Camp & Bash, 1985; Kendall, 1993; Kendall & Braswell, 1985). What follows is a cursory review of pertinent aspects of the this form of treatment with ODD/CD children and adolescents.

Several comprehensive treatment manuals are available for use with disruptive children (e.g., Camp & Bash, 1985; Kendall & Braswell,

1985). The approach outlined by Kendall and Braswell (1985), for example, was designed for children who exhibit cognitive impulsivity, behavioral impulsivity, hyperactivity, and aggression. The program includes training in cognitive and behavioral self-control, utilizing strategies of problem solving, self-instructional training, behavioral contingencies, modeling, affective education, and role playing. The program is organized into four sequential instructional units and is designed to be implemented in 12 sessions. Throughout the program, modeling, self- and social rewards, and response-cost procedures are employed to shape child behavior. In addition, homework assignments are utilized to enhance generalization. The first unit focuses on orienting the child to the therapeutic program and fostering the acquisition of self-instructional procedures. The child is presented with nonthreatening problem-solving tasks. While working on these, self-statements are utilized to help the child "stop and think," examine the task demands, consider response alternatives, and evaluate response consequences. In the second unit, the nature of the task shifts from simple problem-solving tasks to grade-appropriate mathematical equations and abstract puzzles. The goals are to further shape the previously acquired skills and to begin to generalize these to other problem-solving situations where the child's impulsivity may lead to incorrect responding and, perhaps, behavior problems. In the third unit, the nature of the task shifts from equations and puzzles to social and interpersonal situations, including common childhood games that may be problematic or conflictual. These sessions are intended to further generalize the self-instructional skills to social situations, help the child learn to inhibit impulsive responding, and develop greater adherence to rules. Some of these situations involve exploration of emotional responses, and the child generalizes self-instructional methods to inhibit impulsive emotional responding. The final unit involves further generalization of self-instructional skills to social situations through role playing.

Numerous studies have demonstrated that cognitive-behavioral interventions, including problem-solving skills training, produce positive changes in aggressive and conduct-disordered children, with positive changes maintained up to three years (Baer & Nietzel, 1991; Braswell & Kendall, 1988; Kazdin, 1987; Lochman, 1990, 1992). While statistically significant changes have been noted, at times they have been of limited clinical significance. Given the inconsistencies in outcome studies, it may be useful to review conditions that might facilitate better outcomes in the clinical situation. Several child variables have been identified that might mediate outcome. First, younger children, those with lower general intelligence, and those who are cognitively less mature all seem to benefit less from CBT than do children with more mature cognitive abilities. In terms of specific levels of cognitive functioning, it appears that the child must exhibit some functional use of logic characteristic of concrete operations, which typically emerge at about 7–8 years. Second, there is evidence that more aggressive children derive less benefit from CBT interventions than do less aggressive children. However, these findings are preliminary, and it is uncertain whether interventions could be modified to produce better outcomes with more aggressive children. Third, there is no evidence that gender, race, or SES mediate outcome. In addition, several therapeutic process variables may also mediate treatment outcome. First, modeling by the therapist has been shown to be a potent means of conveying targeted skills and coping methods. In addition, outcome is enhanced to a greater degree when the therapist vocalizes his or her thoughts while modeling the targeted skills. Second, treatment that includes role playing, or performance-based learning experiences, has generally produced better outcome. Third, utilizing contingency management procedures as a formal part of the treatment package to shape and maintain appropriate skills appears to contribute to better outcome. Methods that have been utilized successfully include social reinforcement delivered by the therapist and self-reinforcing self-statements contingent upon emitting the correct behavior or skill; token programs (e.g., tokens intermittently redeemed from a menu of rewards) for emitting the correct response or targeted behavior; and mild punishments, in the form of response-cost (e.g., loss of token) contingencies. Finally, the intervention program must be of sufficient duration to ensure that the skills and behaviors become firmly established in the child's repertoire and, if possible, that contingencies are arranged in the natural setting to facilitate generalization and guard against extinction. Booster sessions held 12 to 18 months after treatment completion may help maintain gains.

Parent Management Training

Parent management training (PMT) refers to a set of procedures based on respondent and operant learning principles, designed to alter the reciprocal interactions between parents and children. The goals of these procedures include increasing appropriate proactive, competent parent child-management behaviors and decreasing general child noncompliance and oppositional and aggressive behaviors in children. The literature examining PMT is extensive, and several comprehensive reviews are available (Altepeter & Walker, 1992; Dangel & Polster, 1984; O'Dell, 1985). Several programs have been designed specifically for use with parents of disruptive, behavior-disordered children (e.g., Barkley, 1987; Forehand & McMahon, 1981; Webster-Stratton, 1987, 1994). Our goal here is to review the typical components of PMT and then to discuss several approaches that have demonstrated utility with disruptive behavior disordered children.

PMT involves teaching parents to consistently utilize techniques, based on operant and respondent learning principles, to more effectively manage their child(ren)'s behavior. The underlying assumption is that parenting deficits, including ineffective child management methods, play a role in the development and maintenance of child noncompliance and behavior problems. Parent trainers (therapists) typically employ a variety of interventions through the course of a PMT, including didactic instruction, modeling, behavioral rehearsal, shaping, reinforcement, and homework assignments. Evidence suggests that use of positive reinforcements or reward systems for parents who attend, participate, and employ the targeted skills enhances outcome and generalization of skills (see Bernal, 1984).

Barkley (1987) developed a PMT program for parents of children between the ages of 2 and 11 years who display noncompliant behaviors, whether alone or in concert with other childhood disorders, including ADHD, ODD, and CD. Goals of the program include increasing parental knowledge of the causes of childhood misbehavior, improving parental behavior management skills and competence, and improving child compliance with parental rules and commands (Barkley, 1987). The program is organized into 10 sequential instructional units. Each unit comprises didactic presentations, opportunities to learn and rehearse specific behavior management skills (e.g., methods to increase compliance, decrease disruptive behavior, appropriate use of timeout), and homework assignments. Parents are taught to reduce or eliminate their ineffective attending behaviors and to begin to increase more effective forms of attending to children; to increase child compliance by contingently responding to compliance with positive social reinforcement; to shape positive, appropriate child behaviors; to develop comprehensive behavior management programs and punishment procedures (e.g., response cost, time out); and to manage child noncompliance in public settings.

Forehand and McMahon (1981) developed a PMT program intended for use by parents of children between the ages of 3 and 12 years who exhibit noncompliant behaviors, whether alone or in concert with other childhood disorders. Goals of the program include increasing parental knowledge about the causes of childhood misbehavior, particularly the coercive patterns of interaction maintained through negative reinforcement; improving proactive parenting skills that utilize positive reinforcement; improving the effectiveness of parental disciplinary behaviors; and improving child compliance with parental rules and commands. The program is organized into two phases, differential attention and compliance training, with several subcomponents in each phase. The program attempts to teach five skills: two types of reinforcement skills (appropriate attending behaviors and use of rewards), an extinction procedure (ignoring), use of appropriate commands, and a response-cost procedure (time out from reinforcement). Each subcomponent has objectives relating to the acquisition of skills, activities designed to reach the objective, and behavioral performance criteria to ensure that the parent has obtained competence in the particular skill. Several methods are used to teach parents these skills, including didactic presentations, modeling, role playing, and home practice exercises.

Webster-Stratton (1984, 1987, 1994) developed a PMT for use with children who exhibit noncompliant and conduct-disordered type behavior. It is generally implemented in group format, though it can be adapted for individual use. The program is built around commercially available videotapes and an accompanying manual. The videotapes contain 250 two-minute vignettes, each depicting parents interacting with children and attempting to manage child behaviors. The vignettes illustrate concepts such as nurturance, sensitivity, individual differences in children, and behavioral management skills. Some of the vignettes include both appropriate and inappropriate parental interventions or behaviors. After viewing each vignette, the therapist facilitates a discussion about the interactions. Parents are given homework assignments to practice parenting skills between sessions. Several outcome studies have demonstrated that parents report high levels of satisfaction with the program and that it produced positive changes in parent-child interactions, parental perceptions of child behaviors, and child compliance and reductions in deviant child behavior, which were maintained during a 1-year follow-up (Webster-Stratton, 1984, 1987). A modification (Webster-Stratton, 1994) included additional video vignettes that address a broader range of behaviors, including personal self-control, communication skills, and problem-solving skills, and attempt to strengthen social support; some further improvements have been noted.

The following issues relating to patient selection and enhancing effectiveness for PMT have been noted in the literature. First, not all families with disruptive, behavior-disordered children benefit from PMT. Among the factors that contraindicate the use of PMT are significant parental psychopathology (e.g., severe depression, psychosis, substance abuse, or severe marital discord). If these conditions exist, they need to be addressed before the parents undertake PMT. Second, the programs reviewed here have been designed for implementation in a relatively time-limited manner (e.g., 10 sessions). However, some parents require intermittent "booster" sessions or may even need to periodically repeat the entire program in order to enhance long-term effectiveness. Third, there has been discussion concerning whether the effects of clinic-based PMT generalizes to other settings or circumstances and what, if anything, might enhance generalizability. Evidence suggests that generalizability may be enhanced if the program provides parents with knowledge of social learning principles, in-session opportunities for modeling and behavioral practice, and feedback and reinforcement for the acquisition and appropriate use of the targeted skills.

The literature supports the following conclusions: (1) PMT is an effective method of increasing child compliance, increasing positive parental child-management behaviors, and improving the quality of parent-child interactions; (2) the effects of PMT generalize from the clinic to the home and the school settings; (3) in most cases, these effects are maintained over time (with follow-ups ranging from several months to 4.5 years); (4) effects generalize to nontargeted child behaviors; (5) effects generalize to untreated siblings of the referred child; and (6) parent training is associated with long-term decreases in aggression, destructiveness, and inappropriate verbal behaviors. Finally, some evidence suggests that maternal depression and marital discord may improve as a consequence of parent training. Evidence suggests, then, that PMT is a practical, effective method of dealing with noncompliance and a wide variety of externalizing behaviors and conduct problems (Feldman & Kazdin, 1995).

Family System Interventions

The PMT approaches just discussed have diminishing usefulness as the child reaches adolescence. During adolescence the child begins to deal with the developmental tasks of separating from the family of origin, developing an independent identity, and asserting independence. Utilizing a PMT program with families of adolescents may prove ineffective and may trigger a complementary escalation in parent-adolescent conflicts. Attempts have therefore been made to develop family system interventions for use with adolescents who exhibit disruptive behavior disorders (Alexander & Parsons, 1982; Barkley et al., 1992; Morris, Alexander, & Waldron, 1990; Robin & Foster, 1989). Barkley et al. (1992) developed a modification of the previously discussed PMT for use with adolescents. The program made changes in the session on developing parental positive attention, and the time-out procedure was altered to include brief periods of grounding (isolation to the home) for rule violations. Alexander and colleagues have developed functional family therapy (FFT), which combines systems, behavioral, and cognitive approaches to address problem behaviors in the adolescent. The primary goal of treatment is to change communication and interpersonal interaction patterns to create more positive, adaptive interactions in the family system. This includes increasing reciprocity, positive reinforcements, clear communication, and negotiation of conflictual issues. Robin and Foster (1989) developed an approach that focuses on communication training, cognitive restructuring, problem-solving skills training, and functional/structural interventions in a goal-oriented treatment sequence. Treatment involves four distinct phases: engagement, skill building, resolution of intense problems, and disengagement/termination. Robin and Foster (1989) provide an outline of a standardized treatment format.

To date, only a limited literature is available that has examined the efficacy of these approaches in families with disruptive behavior disordered adolescents. Barkley et al. (1992) compared the modified PMT, the approach developed by Robin and Foster (1989), and structural family therapy in a sample of comorbid ADHD/ODD adolescents. All three treatments produced statistically significant improvements in a number of areas, including communication, number of conflicts, anger intensity, and externalizing/aggressive and delinquent symptoms. However, less than a third of the sample produced clinically significant changes, with no differences noted between groups. Alexander & Parsons (1983) found that FTT produced improvements in family interaction and lower recidivism rates in a sample of delinquent adolescents referred to juvenile court.

SUMMARY AND COMMENTS

Children with oppositional defiant or conduct disorders typically exhibit chronic emotional, behavioral, and social maladjustment, which is often evident in early childhood and continues through childhood and adolescence and perhaps into adulthood. In addition, there is very often comorbidity (e.g., ADHD, mood disorders, alcohol or drug abuse). Finally, these children often find themselves in stressful familial and social contexts, with higher than normal rates of psychopathology among parents and siblings. The children frequently come to the attention of a mental health professional as the result of a specific act, or pattern of acts, which is troubling to parents, teachers, or others in the child's environment. Treatment of these children often yields minimal long-term benefits because it is limited to the specific presenting circumstances and does not adequately address the broader context in which the circumstances occur, including the developmental course of the child, possible comorbidity, possible psychopathology in parents or other family members, and possible chronic familial dysfunction.

On the basis of what is empirically known, and of our clinical experience, we offer some observations and recommendations about the assessment and treatment of these children. First, the recommended approach taken toward these children and their families is one that is comprehensive, multimodal, and longitudinal. Goals should include ameliorating the presenting concerns, identifying and ameliorating existing comorbidity, and attempting to move the long-term course toward more favorable outcomes. This often involves multiple treatment targets, multiple modes of intervention, long-term management, and intermittent booster sessions. Second, the assessment process must be more comprehensive than is often the case. In particular, issues of comorbidity in the child, existing psychopathology in the parents and family, and the child's functioning in extrafamilial settings (e.g., school) are often inadequately evaluated. Better long-term outcomes are likely to result from more complete identification of existing circumstances and needs. Third, it is highly recommended that treatment of these children begin earlier than often occurs. Problems are often evident in the preschool or early elementary years, but treatment is frequently not initiated; when parents express concerns to primary physicians, teachers, or other professionals, they are often told, "He's young, he'll outgrow it." Usually this advice is given because the professional is unaware of what can be done. We have found that multimodal interventions in the preschool years (e.g., a PMT program with the parent, perhaps in combination with psychotropic medication) are often potent and can have a significant impact on the long-term adjustment of the child and the family (e.g., Tremblay et al., 1995). Fourth, it is recommended that efforts be made to ensure that the treatment of these children is multidisciplinary and that professionals cross-refer these children and families more than is commonly done. This is necessary because, typically, no professional group has the training or expertise to provide all of the treatment modalities that may be indicated. For example, if the child first sees a psychologist or social worker, he may be less likely to receive psychotropic medication; similarly, if the child first sees a psychiatrist, the parents may be less likely to become involved in a PMT program. In most cases, outcome is enhanced through multiple treatment modalities, requiring that professionals of various disciplines work together cooperatively. Fifth, it is recommended that treatment professionals recognize the chronic nature of the difficulties which these children experience and follow the child and the family over the long run, similar to medical follow-up of an individual with a chronic illness. Too often, presenting concerns are addressed, perhaps successfully, and the child and the family are discharged from treatment. Often, however, problems recur, the parents become demoralized, and they do not return for further treatment. Better long-term outcomes are likely to occur if the child and family remain in treatment (with infrequent contacts during periods of relative stability). In this circumstance, parents are often more willing to address new problems that emerge, and the professional may be able to intervene successfully before the problem escalates. Finally, it is recommended that psychopathology in the parent be addressed. This is often a difficult issue to approach, requiring sensitivity and a sense of timing, as parents may become uncomfortable and discontinue treatment of the child. We have found, however, that the long-term course for the child often improves when the issue of possible parental psychopathology is successfully addressed and appropriate treatment initiated.

REFERENCES

Abikoff, H., Klein, R., Klass, E., & Ganeles, D. (1987, October). Methylphenidate in the treatment of conduct disordered children. In H. Abikoff (Chair), *Diagnosis and treatment issues in children with disruptive behavior disorders.* Symposium conducted at the annual meeting of the American Academy of Child and Adolescent Psychiatry, Washington, DC.

Achenbach, T. M. (1991a). *Manual for the Child Behavior Checklist/ 4–18 and 1991 Profile.* Burling-

ton: University of Vermont, Department of Psychiatry.

Achenbach, T. M. (1991b). *Manual for the Teacher's Report Form and 1991 Profile.* Burlington: University of Vermont, Department of Psychiatry.

Achenbach, T. M. (1991c). *Manual for the Youth Self-Report and 1991 Profile.* Burlington: University of Vermont, Department of Psychiatry.

*Alessi, N., Naylor, M. W., Ghaziuddin, M., & Zubieta, J. K. (1994). Update on lithium carbonate therapy in children and adolescents. *Journal of the American Academy of Child and Adolescent Psychiatry, 33,* 291–304.

Alexander, J. F., & Parsons, B. V. (1982). *Functional family therapy.* Monterey, CA: Brooks/Cole.

Alexander, J. F., & Parsons, B. V. (1983). Short-term behavioral intervention with delinquent families: Impact upon family process and recidivism. *Journal of Abnormal Psychology, 81,* 219–225.

Altepeter, T. S., & Walker, C. E. (1992). Prevention of physical abuse of children through parent training. In D. J. Willis, E. W. Holden, & M. Rosenburg (Eds.), *Child abuse prevention.* New York: Wiley.

American Psychiatric Association. (1987). *Diagnostic and statistical manual of mental disorders* (3rd ed., rev.). Washington, DC: Author.

American Psychiatric Association. (1991). *DSM-IV options book: Work in progress.* Washington, DC: Author.

*American Psychiatric Association. (1994). *Diagnostic and statistical manual of mental disorders* (4th ed.). Washington, DC: Author.

Baer, R. A., & Nietzel, M. T. (1991). Cognitive and behavioral treatment of impulsivity in children: A meta-analytic review of the outcome literature. *Journal of Clinical Child Psychology, 20,* 400–412.

*Barkley, R. A. (1987). *Defiant children: A clinician's manual for parent training.* New York: Guilford Press.

Barkley, R. A., Guevremont, D. C., Anastopoulos, A. D., & Fletcher, K. E. (1992). A comparison of three family therapy programs for treating family conflicts in adolescents with Attention-Deficit Hyperactive Disorder. *Journal of Consulting and Clinical Psychology, 60,* 450–462.

Barratt, E. S. (1993). The use of anticonvulsants in aggression and violence. *Psychopharmacology Bulletin, 29,* 75–81.

Barrickman, D. O., Perry, P. J., Allen, A. J., Kuperman, S., Arndt, S. V., Herrmann, K. J., & Schumacher, E. (1995). Bupropion versus methylphenidate in the treatment of Attention Deficit Hyperactive Disorder. *Journal of the American*

Academy of Child and Adolescent Psychiatry, 34, 649–657.

Beck, A. T. (1993). *The Beck Depression Inventory.* San Antonio, TX: Psychological Corporation.

Bernal, M. E. (1984). Consumer issues in parent training. In R. F. Dangel & R. A. Polster (Eds.), *Parent training: Foundations of research and practice.* New York: Guilford Press.

*Braswell, L., & Kendall, P. C. (1988). Cognitive-behavioral methods with children. In K. S. Dobson (Ed.), *Handbook of cognitive-behavioral therapies.* New York: Guilford Press.

*Breen, M. J., & Altepeter, T. S. (1990). *Disruptive behavior disorders in children: A treatment-focused assessment.* New York: Guilford Press.

Brown, R. T., Jaffe, S. L., Silverstein, J., & Magee, H. (1991). Methylphenidate and adolescents hospitalized with conduct disorder: Dose effects on classroom behavior, academic performance and impulsivity. *Journal of Clinical Child Psychology, 20,* 282–292.

Burns, G. L., & Patterson, D. R. (1991). Factor structure of the Eyberg Child Behavior Inventory: Unidimensional or multidimensional measure of disruptive behavior? *Journal of Clinical Child Psychology, 20,* 439–444.

Butcher, J. N., Dahlstrom, W. G., Graham, J. R., Tellegen, A., & Kaemmer, B. (1989). *Minnesota Multiphasic Personality Inventory (MMPI-2). Manual for administration and scoring.* Minneapolis: University of Minnesota Press.

Butcher, J. N., Williams, C. L., Graham, J. R., Archer, R. P., Tellegen, A., Ben-Porath, Y. S., & Kaemmer, B. (1992). *MMPI-A (Minnesota Multiphasic Personality Inventory-Adolescent): Manual for administration, scoring and interpretation.* Minneapolis: University of Minnesota Press.

Cadoret, R. J. (1978). Psychopathology in adopted-away offspring of biologic parents with antisocial behavior. *Archives of General Psychiatry, 35,* 176–184.

Camp, B. W., & Bash, M. A. S. (1985). *Think aloud: Increasing social and cognitive skills—A problem-solving approach.* Champaign, IL: Research Press.

Campbell, M., Adams, P. B., Small, A. M., Kafantaris, V., Silva, R. R., Shell, J., Perry, R., & Overall, J. E. (1995). Lithium in hospitalized aggressive children with conduct disorder: A double-blind and placebo-controlled study. *Journal of the American Academy of Child and Adolescent Psychiatry, 34,* 1262–1272.

*Campbell, M., & Cueva, J. E. (1995). Psychopharmacology in child and adolescent psychiatry: A review of the past seven years. Part II. *Journal of the American Academy of Child and Adolescent Psychiatry, 34,* 1262–1272.

Campbell, M., Gonzalez, N. M., & Silva, R. R. (1992). The pharmacologic treatment of conduct disorders and rage outbursts. In L. Kramer (Ed.), *Psychiatric Clinics of North America.* Philadelphia: W. B. Saunders.

Campbell, M., Green, W. H., & Deutsch, S. I. (1985). *Child and adolescent psychopharmacology.* Beverly Hills, CA: Sage Publications.

Campbell, M., Small, A. M., Green, W. H., Jennings, S. J., Perry, R., Bennett, W. G., & Anderson, L. (1984). Behavioral efficacy of haloperidol and lithium carbonate: A comparison in hospitalized aggressive children with conduct disorder. *Archives of General Psychiatry, 41,* 650–656.

Campbell, M., Small, A. M., Padron-Gayol, M., Locascio, J. J., Kafantaris, V., & Overall, J. E. (1990). Lithium in aggressive children with conduct disorder. *Clinical Neuropharmacology, 13,* (Suppl. 2), 615–616.

Campbell, M., & Spencer, E. K. (1988). Psychopharmacology in child and adolescent psychiatry: A review of the past five years. *Journal of the American Academy of Child and Adolescent Psychiatry, 27,* 269–279.

Caspi, A., Elder, G. H., & Herbener, E. S. (1990). Childhood personality and the prediction of life-course patterns. In L. Robins & M. Rutter (Eds.), *Straight and devious pathways from childhood to adulthood.* Cambridge: Cambridge University Press.

Chess, S., & Thomas, A. (1990). Continuities and discontinuities in temperament. In L. Robins & M. Rutter (Eds.), *Straight and devious pathways from childhood to adulthood.* Cambridge: Cambridge University Press.

Cloninger, C. R., Reich, T., & Guze, S. G. (1978). Genetic environmental interactions and antisocial behavior. In R. D. Hare & D. Schalling (Eds.), *Psychopathic behavior: Approaches to research.* New York: Wiley.

Conners, C. K. (1989). *Conners' Rating Scales Manual.* North Tonawanda, NY: Multi-Health Systems.

Conners, C. K. (1994). *Conners' Continuous Performance Test—computer program* (version 3.0). North Tonawanda, NY: Multi-Health Systems.

Costello, A. J., Edelbrock, C., Dulcan. M. K., Kalas, R., & Klaric, S. (1987). *Diagnostic Interview Schedule for Children.* Pittsburgh: Western

Psychiatric Institute and Clinic, School of Medicine, University of Pittsburgh.

Dangel, R. F., & Polster, R. A. (Eds.). (1984). *Parent training: Foundations of research and Practice*. New York: Guilford Press.

Derogatis, L. R. (1983). *SCL-90-R: Administration, Scoring and Procedures Manual-II*. Towson, MD: Clinical Psychometric Research.

*Dulcan, M. K. (1990). Using psychostimulants to treat behavioral disorders of children and adolescents. *Journal of child and adolescent psychopharmacology*, 1, 7–20.

Eichelman, B. (1987). Neurochemical and psychopharmacologic aspects of aggressive behavior. In H. Y. Meltzer (Ed.), *Psychopharmacology: The third generation of progress*. New York: Raven Press.

Eyberg, S. M. (1980). Eyberg Child Behavior Inventory. *Journal of Clinical Child Psychology*, 9, 22–28.

Eyberg, S. M., & Robinson, E. A. (1983). Conduct problem behavior: Standardization of a behavior rating scale with adolescents. *Journal of Clinical Child Psychology*, 12, 347–356.

*Farrington, D. P., Loeber R., & Van Kammen, W. B. (1990). Long-term criminal outcomes of hyperactive-impulsive-attention deficit and conduct problems in childhood. In L. Robins & M. Rutter (Eds.), *Straight and devious pathways from childhood to adulthood*. Cambridge: Cambridge University Press.

Feldman, J. M., & Kazdin, A. E. (1995). Parent management training for oppositional and conduct problem children. *The clinical psychologist*, 48, 3–5.

Forehand, R. L., & McMahon R. J. (1981). *Helping the noncompliant child: A clinician's guide to parent training*. New York: Guilford Press.

Frick, P. J., Lahey, B. B., Applegate, B., Kerdyck, L., Ollendick, T., Hynd, G. W., Garfinkel, B., Greenhill, L., Biederman, J., Barkley, R. A., McBurnett, K., Newcorn, J., & Waldman, I. (1994). DSM-IV field trials for the disruptive behavior disorders: Symptom utility estimates. *Journal of the American Academy of Child and Adolescent Psychiatry*, 32, 1262–1272.

Frick, P. J., Lahey, B. B., Loeber, R., Stouthamer-Loeber, M., Christ, M. A. G., & Hanson, K. (1992). Familial risk factors to oppositional defiant disorder and conduct disorder: Parental psychopathology and maternal parenting. *Journal of Consulting and Clinical Psychology*, 60, 49–55.

Gammon, G. D., & Brown, T. E. (1993). Fluoxetine

and methylphenidate in combination for treatment of attention deficit disorder and comorbid depressive disorder. *Journal of child and adolescent psychopharmacology*, 3, 1–10.

Gordon, M. (1982). *The Gordon Diagnostic System*. DeWitt, NY: Gordon Systems.

Haapasalo, J., & Tremblay, R. E. (1994). Physically aggressive boys from ages 6 to 12: Family background, parenting behavior, and prediction of delinquency. *Journal of Consulting and Clinical Psychology*, 62, 1044–1052.

Herbert, M. (1978). *Conduct disorders of childhood and adolescence: A behavioral approach to assessment and treatment*. New York: Wiley.

Herjanic, B., & Reich, W. (1982). Development of a structured psychiatric interview for children: Agreement between child and parent on individual symptoms. *Journal of Abnormal Child Psychology*, 10, 307–324.

Hinshaw, S. P. (1991). Stimulant medication and the treatment of aggression in children with attentional deficits. *Journal of Clinical Child Psychology*, 20, 301–312.

Hinshaw, S. P., Heller, T., & McHale, J. P. (1992). Covert antisocial behavior in boys with attention deficit hyperactivity disorder: External validation and effects of methylphenidate. *Journal of Consulting and Clinical Psychology*, 59, 785–798.

Hunt, R. D. (1987). Treatment effects of oral and transdermal clonidine in relation to methylphenidate—An open pilot study in ADDH. *Psychopharmacology Bulletin*, 23, 111–114.

*Hunt, R. D., Capper, L., & O'Connell, P. (1990). Clonidine in child and adolescent psychiatry. *Journal of child and adolescent psychopharmacology*, 1, 87–101.

Husain, S. A., & Cantwell, D. P. (1991). *Fundamentals of child and adolescent psychopathology*. Washington, DC: American Psychiatric Association.

Jary, M. L., & Stewart, M. A. (1985). Psychiatric disorder in the parents of adopted children with aggressive conduct disorder. *Neuropsychobiology*, 13, 7–11.

Kafantaris, V., Campbell, M., Locascio, J. J., Padron-Gayol, M., & Small, A. M. (1992). Carbamazepine in hospitalized aggressive conduct-disordered children: An open pilot study. *Psychopharmacology Bulletin*, 28, 193–199.

Kazdin, A. E. (1985). *Treatment of antisocial behavior in children and adolescence*. Homewood, IL: Dorsey Press.

*Kazdin, A. E. (1987). Treatment of antisocial

behavior in children: Current status and future directions. *Psychological Bulletin, 102,* 187–203.

Kemph, J. P., DeVane, C. L., Levin, G. M., Jarecke, R., & Miller, R. L. (1993). Treatment of aggressive children with clonidine: Results of an open pilot study. *Journal of the American Academy of Child and Adolescent Psychiatry, 32,* 1262–1272.

*Kendall, P. C. (1993). Cognitive-behavioral therapies with youth: Guiding theory, current status, and emerging developments. *Journal of Consulting and Clinical Psychology, 61,* 235–247.

*Kendall, P. C., & Braswell, L. (1985). *Cognitive-behavioral therapy for impulsive children.* New York: Guilford Press.

Kline, R. (1991). Preliminary results: Lithium effects in Conduct Disorders. In *CME Syllabus and Proceedings, 144th Annual Meeting of the American Psychiatric Association,* New Orleans, pp. 119–120.

Kolvin, I., Nicol, A. R., Garside, R. F., Day, K. A., & Tweedle, E. G. (1982). Temperamental patterns in aggressive boys. In R. Porter & G. M. Collins (Eds.), *Temperamental differences in infants and young children* (CIBA Foundation Symposium No. 89). London: Pitman.

Kovacs, M. (1992). *The Children's Depression Inventory Manual.* North Tonawanda, NY: Multi-Health Systems.

Kovacs, M., & Pollock, M. (1995). Bipolar disorder and comorbid conduct disorder in childhood and adolescence. *Journal of the American Academy of Child and Adolescent Psychiatry, 34,* 715–723.

La Greca, A. M. (1990). *Through the eyes of the child: Obtaining self-reports from children and adolescents.* Boston: Allyn and Bacon.

Lochman, J. E. (1990). Modifications in childhood aggression. In M. Hersen, R. Eisler, & P. M. Miller (Eds.), *Progress in behavior modification* (Vol. 25). Newbury Park, CA: Sage Publications.

Lochman, J. E. (1992). Cognitive-behavioral intervention with aggressive boys: Three-year follow-up and preventive effects. *Journal of Consulting and Clinical Psychology, 60,* 426–432.

Lochman, J. E., & Dodge, K. A. (1994). Social-cognitive processes of severely violent, moderately aggressive and nonaggressive boys. *Journal of Consulting and Clinical Psychology, 62,* 366–374.

Loeber, R. (1982). The stability of antisocial and delinquent child behavior: A review. *Child Development, 53,* 1431–1446.

Loeber, R. (1988). Natural histories of conduct problems, delinquency, and associated substance abuse: Evidence for developmental progressions. In B. B. Lahey & A. E. Kazdin (Eds.), *Advances in clinical child psychology* (Vol. 11). New York: Plenum Press.

Loeber, R., Green, S. M., Keenan, K., & Lahey, B. B. (1995). Which boys will fare worse? Early predictors of the onset of conduct disorder in a six-year longitudinal study. *Journal of the American Academy of Child and Adolescent Psychiatry, 34,* 1262–1272.

McLeer, S. V., Callaghan, M., Henry, D., & Wallen, J. (1994). Psychiatric disorders in sexually abused children. *Journal of the American Academy of Child and Adolescent Psychiatry, 33,* 313–319.

Merry, S. N., & Andrews, L. K. (1994). Psychiatric status of sexually abused children 12 months after disclosure of abuse. *Journal of the American Academy of Child and Adolescent Psychiatry, 33,* 939–944.

Miller, L. S., Klien, R. G., Piacenti, J., Abikoff, H., Shah, M. J., Samoilov, A., & Guardino, M. (1995). The New York Teacher Rating Scale for disruptive and antisocial behavior. *Journal of the American Academy of Child and Adolescent Psychiatry, 34,* 359–370.

Morris, S. B., Alexander, J. F., & Waldron, H. (1990). Functional family therapy: Issues in clinical practice. In I. R. H. Falloon (Ed.), *Handbook of behavior therapy.* New York: Guilford Press.

O'Dell, S. L. (1985). Progress in parent training. In M. Hersen, R. M. Eisler, & P. M. Miller (Eds.), *Progress in behavior modification* (Vol. 19). New York: Academic Press.

Offord, D. R., & Bennett, K. J. (1994). Conduct Disorder: Long-term outcomes and intervention effectiveness. *Journal of the American Academy of Child and Adolescent Psychiatry, 33,* 1069–1078.

Ollendick, T. H., & Hersen, M. (1989). *Handbook of child psychopathology* (2nd ed.). New York: Plenum Press.

Olweus, D. (1980). Familial and temperamental determinants of aggressive behavior in adolescent boys: A causal analysis. *Developmental Psychology, 16,* 644–660.

*Patterson, G. R. (1982). *Coercive family process.* Eugene, OR: Castalia.

*Patterson, G. R. (1986). Performance models for antisocial boys. *American Psychologist, 41,* 432–444.

Patterson, G. R., & Stouthamer-Loeber, M. (1984). The correlation of family management practices and delinquency. *Child Development, 55,* 1299–1307.

Pelcovitz, D., Kaplan, S., Goldenberg, B., Mandel, F., Lehane, J., & Guarrera, J. (1994). Post-traumatic stress disorder in physically abused adolescents. *Journal of the American Academy of Child and Adolescent Psychiatry, 33*, 305–312.

Pelham, W. E., Swanson, J. M., Furman, M. B., & Schwindt, H. (1995). Pemoline effects on children with ADHD: A time-response by dose-response analysis on classroom measures. *Journal of the American Academy of Child and Adolescent Psychiatry, 34*, 1504–1513.

Platt, J. E., Campbell, M., Green, W. H., & Grega, D. M. (1984). Cognitive effects of lithium carbonate and haloperidol in treatment-resistant aggressive children. *Archives of General Psychiatry, 41*, 657–662.

Pliszka, S. R. (1987). Tricyclic antidepressants in the treatment of children with attention deficit disorder. *Journal of the American Academy of Child and Adolescent Psychiatry, 2*, 127–132.

Pliszka, S. R. (1991a). Anticonvulsants in the treatment of child and adolescent psychopathology. *Journal of Clinical Child Psychology, 20*, 277–281.

Pliszka, S. R. (1991b). Antidepressants in the treatment of child and adolescent psychopathology. *Journal of Clinical Child Psychology, 20*, 313–320.

Quay, H. C., & Peterson, D. R. (1987). *Manual for the Revised Behavior Problem Checklist*. Coral Gables, FL: University of Miami, Department of Psychology.

Quiason, N., Ward, D., & Kitchen, T. (1991). Buspirone for aggression [letter]. *Journal of the American Academy of Child and Adolescent Psychiatry, 30*, 1026.

Quinton, D., Rutter, M., & Gulliver, L. (1990). Continuities in psychiatric disorders from childhood to adulthood in the children of psychiatric patients. In L. Robins & M. Rutter (Eds.), *Straight and devious pathways from childhood to adulthood*. Cambridge: Cambridge University Press.

Rapoport, J. L. (1983). The use of drugs: Trends in research. In M. Rutter (Ed.), *Developmental neuropsychiatry*. New York: Guilford Press.

Reich, W., Earls, F., Frankel, O., & Shayka, J. J. (1993). Psychopathology in children of alcoholics. *Journal of the American Academy of Child and Adolescent Psychiatry, 32*, 995–1002.

Reynolds, W. M. (1987). *Reynolds Adolescent Depression Scale: Professional Manual*. Odessa, FL: Psychological Assessment Resources.

Riddle, M. A., Hardin, M. T., Cho, S. C., Woolston, J. L., & Leckman, J. F. (1988). Desipramine treatment of boys with attention-deficit hyperactivity disorder and tics: Preliminary clinical experience. *Journal of the American Academy of Child and Adolescent Psychiatry, 6*, 811–814.

*Robin, A. L., & Foster, S. L. (1989). *Negotiating parent-adolescent conflict: A behavioral-family systems approach*. New York: Guilford Press.

Robins, L. N. (1981). Epidemiological approaches to natural history research: Antisocial disorders in children. *Journal of the American Academy of Child Psychiatry, 20*, 566–680.

Robins, L. N., & McEvoy, L. (1990). Conduct problems as predictors of substance abuse. In L. Robins & M. Rutter (Eds.), *Straight and devious pathways from childhood to adulthood*. Cambridge: Cambridge University Press.

Russo, M. F., Loeber, R., Lahey, B. B., & Keenan, K. (1994). Oppositional defiant and conduct disorders: Validation of the *DSM-III-R* and an alternative diagnostic option. *Journal of Clinical Child Psychology, 23*, 56–68.

Safer, D. J., & Allen, D. (1976). *Hyperactive children*. Baltimore: University Park Press.

Sanson, A., Smart, D., Prior, M., & Oberklaid, F. (1993). Precursors of hyperactivity and aggression. *Journal of the American Academy of Child and Adolescent Psychiatry, 32*, 1207–1216.

Satterfield, J., Swanson, J., Schell, A., & Lee, F. (1995). Prediction of antisocial behavior in attention-deficit hyperactivity disorder boys from aggression/defiance scores. *Journal of the American Academy of Child and Adolescent Psychiatry, 34*, 185–190.

Schachar, R., & Tannock, R. (1995). Test of four hypotheses for the comorbidity of attention-deficit hyperactivity disorder and conduct disorder. *Journal of the American Academy of Child and Adolescent Psychiatry, 34*, 639–648.

Schroeder, J. S., Mullin, A. V., Elliott, G. R., Steiner, H., Nichols, M., Gordon, A., & Paulos, M. (1989). Cardiovascular effects of desipramine in children. *Journal of the American Academy of Child and Adolescent Psychiatry, 28*, 376–379.

Sheard, M. H. (1978). The effects of lithium and other ions on aggressive behavior. In L. Valzelli (Ed.), *Modern problems in pharmacopsychiatry* (Vol. 13). New York: Karger.

Stewart, M. A., Cummings, C., Singer, S., & deBlois, C. S. (1981). The overlap between hyperactive and unsocialized aggressive children. *Journal of Child Psychology and Psychiatry, 22*, 23–45.

Sussman, N. (1994). The uses of buspirone in psychiatry. *Journal of Clinical Psychiatry Monograph, 12*, 3–19.

Tremblay, R. E., Pagani-Kurtz, L., Masse, L. C., Vitaro, F., & Pihl, R. O. (1995). A bimodal preventive intervention for disruptive kindergarten boys: Its impact through mid-adolescence. *Journal of Consulting and Clinical Psychology, 63,* 560–568.

*Trimble, M. R. (1990). Anticonvulsants in children and adolescents. *Journal of child and adolescent psychopharmacology, 1,* 107–124.

Turecki, S., & Tonner, L. (1985). *The difficult child.* New York: Bantam.

Ullmann, R. K., Sleator, E. K., & Sprague, R. L. (1988). *Manual for the ADD-H Comprehensive Teacher's Rating Scale.* Champaign, IL: MeriTech.

Walker, C. E., & Roberts, M. C. (Eds.). (1992). *Handbook of clinical child psychology* (2nd ed). New York: Wiley.

Webster-Stratton, C. (1984). Randomized trial of two parent training programs for families with conduct-disordered children. *Journal of Consulting and Clinical Psychology, 52,* 666–678.

Webster-Stratton, C. (1987). *The parents and children series.* Eugene, OR: Castalia.

Webster-Stratton, C. (1994). Advancing videotape parent training: A comparison study. *Journal of Consulting and Clinical Psychology, 62,* 583–593.

Weiner, J. M. (1991). *Textbook of child and adolescent psychiatry.* Washington, DC: American Psychiatric Association.

World Health Organization. (1992). *ICD-10 classification of mental and behavioral disorders: Clinical descriptions and diagnostic guidelines.* Geneva: Author.

World Health Organization. (1993). *ICD-10 classification of mental and behavioral disorders: Diagnostic criteria for research.* Geneva: Author.

Wozniak, J., Biederman. J., Kiely, K., Ablon, J. S., Faraone, S. V., Mundy, E., & Mennin, D. (1995). Mania-like symptoms suggestive of childhood-onset bipolar disorder in clinically referred children. *Journal of the American Academy of Child and Adolescent Psychiatry, 34,* 867–876.

Yoshikawa, H. (1994). Prevention as cumulative protection: Effects of early familial support and education on chronic delinquency and its risks. *Psychological Bulletin, 115,* 28–54.

*Indicates references that the authors recommend for further reading.

8

Feeding Disorders of Infancy and Early Childhood

Thomas R. Linscheid
Laura Bennett Murphy

INTRODUCTION

The newest revision of the *Diagnostic and Statistical Manual of Mental Disorders* (APA, 1994), or DSM-IV, reflects a change in structure and content with respect to feeding and eating disorders that first appear in childhood. The previous manual had included anorexia nervosa and bulimia nervosa within this category. The new manual, however, distinguishes these two diagnoses in a separate section called "eating disorders." An additional section titled "feeding and eating disorders of infancy and early childhood" was created to include pica, rumination disorder, and a new categorical diagnosis, feeding disorder of infancy and early childhood. This chapter (1) describes each of the feeding disorders and (2) offers a review of assessment and treatment strategies for intervention with children and families.

307.52 Pica

Pica is the persistent ingestion of nonnutritive substances. Ingestants can include paint, plaster, hair, cloth, toys, feces, sand, and bugs.

Reported cases of pica are rare, although the condition may not be uncommon among preschool aged children (APA, 1994). Nonetheless, estimates suggest that as many as 5% of institutionalized individuals with mental retardation may evidence pica (Danford & Huber, 1982). It has been suggested that pica typically spontaneously remits in early childhood (Miller, O'Neil, Malcolm, & Currey, 1985). However, because of potential serious health consequences such as lead poisoning, choking, intestinal blockage, parasites, and death, aggressive intervention may be indicated. To meet DSM-IV diagnostic criteria, the eating of nonnutritive substances must last for at least one month, be developmentally inappropriate, and not be culturally sanctioned. Consequently, geophagia, the deliberate eating of earth common among certain African American females with rural southern origins, is not considered pica. If pica occurs in individuals with mental retardation or pervasive developmental disorder, symptoms must be severe enough to warrant a separate diagnosis clinically.

Youngsters with pica typically do not display food aversions. Rather, the pica is in addition to, not in place of, appropriate eating behavior. While vitamin or mineral deficiencies have been implicated, there is little empirical support to suggest that these deficiencies are causal. Still, Lofts, Schroeder, and Maier (1990) found a supplement of chelated zinc to be effective in treating some cases of pica. More commonly, pica and vitamin deficiencies co-occur in the context of familial poverty, neglect, and poor parental supervision.

A number of causes for pica have been postulated, including oral fixation, inadequate stimulation, parental inattention, and modeling (Fultz & Rojahn, 1988; Halmi, 1985; Wicks-Nelson & Israel, 1997). The most parsimonious explanations, however, focus on the self-stimulating and self-injurious nature of the behavior (Fisher, Piazza, Bowman, Kurtz, Sherer, & Lachman, 1994). In fact, McLoughlin (1988) reports that the risk of death is higher from pica than from other types of self-injurious behaviors.

Assessment of pica must include a description of the ingesting behavior, including contextual factors, antecedents, and consequences of the behavior. Because of the risk of parasitic infection, lead poisoning, and other health complications, a complete medical examination also is indicated. Developmental assessment of the child with the Bayley Scales of Infant Development (Bayley, 1993) or other appropriate devices is necessary both to document potential negative sequelae of the disorder (e.g., developmental delays subsequent to lead poisoning) and to document whether the behavior occurs within the context of pervasive developmental delays. Finally, a comprehensive assessment should include an appraisal of the home environment, attending to environmental dangers (peeling lead-based paint), sources of appropriate stimulation, parental caregiving practices, and dietary suitability.

Interventions typically begin by maintaining an adequate and balanced diet for the child. Second, interventions with the parents are beneficial to encourage developmentally appropriate stimulation and supervision. Third, removal of all possible dangerous substances that the child could ingest is vital. Lead-based paint should be removed from the walls and

replaced with a nontoxic substitute. Finally, a number of behavioral intervention techniques have been suggested that typically involve some combination of differential reinforcement, discrimination training, extinction, and punishment. These have been inconsistently successful (Bucher, Reykdal, & Albin, 1976). Fisher et al. (1994) suggest that the variability in treatment efficacy likely is a function of the limits of functional analysis with pica and the lack of empirical selection of punishers when these are included in a treatment package. These authors suggest that ineffective punishers may underlie treatment difficulties. Certainly, for many youngsters with pica, punishment increases the probability of quickly suppressing behavior that is self-injurious and dangerous. Duker and Nielen (1993) and Fisher et al. (1994) have demonstrated significant decreases in pica behavior in controlled settings using a treatment package of response-contingent procedures that have included punishment for nonnutritive ingestion.

307.53 Rumination Disorder

Rumination is a rare but medically serious phenomenon most often found in infants and individuals with mental retardation. It is the practice of voluntarily bringing previously ingested food back into the oral cavity and then either ejecting it or rechewing and swallowing. In order to meet DSM-IV diagnostic criteria, the rumination must have lasted for at least 30 days following a period of normal eating, must not be caused by diagnosable organic conditions, and must not occur in conjunction with anorexia nervosa or bulimia nervosa. If rumination occurs in individuals with mental retardation or pervasive developmental disorder, symptoms must be severe enough to warrant a separate diagnosis clinically.

It is important to note that rumination itself is not associated with retching, gagging, or any apparent distress or displeasure. On the contrary, the individual appears to be enjoying the act, much like a self-stimulatory behavior (e.g., rocking). Indeed, a major feature to consider in the differential diagnosis is the lack of distress during the act of rumination, because nearly all of the medical conditions that lead to vomiting are associated with distress (e.g., gastrointestinal reflux, pyloric stenosis). However, to rule out an organic cause for the vomiting, a medical evaluation is necessary. While weight loss, leading to starvation, is the major cause for concern, social interactions with the infant or individual with mental retardation can be adversely affected by the unpleasant nature of this behavior.

Two main theories of etiology have been proposed. Psychodynamic postulations center on a disturbed mother-child interaction (Lourie, 1955; Richmond, Eddy, & Green, 1958). The infant attempts to derive pleasure, denied by the faulty interaction, by turning to its own body for satisfaction. Mothers of ruminating infants are described as unable to relate to their infants, fearful of the infant's death, and unable to want, accept, or give to their baby (Richmond, Eddy, & Green, 1958). One must exercise caution in accepting psychodynamically oriented interpretations as they are based on a very small number of cases and have never been empirically demonstrated. In addition, attempting to assess a mother-child interaction once rumination has developed is fraught with problems of establishing cause and effect.

More parsimonious are behavior-based explanations that suggest rumination is a habit maintained by its consequences, that is, pleasurable self-stimulation and/or the increased attention the individual receives from a caregiver (Cunningham & Linscheid, 1976). Nearly 40 years ago, Kanner (1957), describing 53 cases, recognized this etiologic explanation when he said, "Whatever the primary occasion may have been, the habit nature of this act can hardly be questioned" (p. 468). Situations in which there is less than optimal stimulation can lead to development of self-stimulatory behaviors. A mother (caregiver) who is unable to give time and attention to her infant or an institutional setting for individuals with mental retardation can set the stage for the development of self-stimulatory behaviors, which may include rumination.

Treatment begins with an assessment of (1) the environment in order to determine the amount of stimulation and (2) the seriousness of the medical status of the ruminator. Treatments have ranged from nonintrusive counseling interventions directed at caregivers when rumination is not severe or life threatening to very intense and intrusive measures made necessary by life-threatening weight loss and dehydration secondary to rumination.

The most straightforward treatment approach is to provide increased attention, interaction, and stimulation. Some infants decrease the rate of rumination when admitted to the hospital and provided with stimulating and interactive nursing care. When this occurs, treatment is often directed at improving the home environment and caregiver-infant interaction. Treatment may take the form of coaching the caregiver in more effective and mutually satisfying interactions. If maternal or caregiver psychopathology (e.g., maternal depression) prevents appropriate infant stimulation, psychotherapeutic or pharmacological interventions may be necessary.

In severe cases, behaviorally based aversive conditioning procedures have been applied with dramatic success. Several studies, conducted in the 1970s, used contingent mild electric shock to treat rumination in infants and individuals with mental retardation (Cunningham & Linscheid, 1976; Lang & Melamed, 1969; Linscheid & Cunningham, 1977; Toister, Colin, Worley, & Arthur, 1975). In these studies, life-threatening rumination was successfully treated within a matter of days. Rast and colleagues (Rast, Johnson, Drum, & Conrin, 1981) experimentally demonstrated a relationship between amount of food eaten and rumination. Working with mentally retarded individuals, they documented decreases in rumination when individuals were allowed to eat as much as they desired, compared to when they ate a standard nutritionally and calorically adequate diet.

307.59 Feeding Disorder of Infancy and Early Childhood

The diagnosis of feeding disorder of infancy or early childhood represents a significant addition to the current manual. Historically, the behaviors associated with this disorder have been considered a primary medical condition (failure to thrive) and have not been under the purview of mental health specialists in spite of effective interventions. Youngsters with feeding disorders sometimes carried a concurrent diagnosis of reactive attachment disorder, yet the feeding problems were not specifically viewed as psychological in nature. The current diagnostic formulation consists of four central features:

> 1) A feeding disturbance as manifested by persistent failure to eat adequately with significant failure to gain weight or significant loss of weight over at least 1 month;
> 2) The disturbance is not due to an associated gastrointestinal or other general medical condition (e.g., esophageal reflux);
> 3) The disturbance is not better accounted for by another mental disorder (e.g., Rumination Disorder) or by lack of available food; and
> 4) The onset is before age 6 years. (APA, 1994, p. 99)

These criteria characterize the disorder as a primary problem with the feeding interaction, which leads to growth impairment. The diagnosis also identifies several associated features of the disorder. Infants with a feeding disorder have been described as difficult and irritable, particularly during mealtime (APA, 1994). Apathy and developmental delays may coexist with this disorder. Comorbidity of neuroregulatory and/or preexisting developmental difficulties in the infant may contribute to feeding problems as the infant is less responsive to the feeding situation.

Difficulties in the parent-child relationship further contribute to the feeding problems. These parent-child interaction difficulties may revolve solely around the feeding exchange or may be reflective of more broad-based and generalized problems, including but not limited to child abuse and neglect. Parental psychopathology also has been indicated as a potential contributing factor. In fact, the diagnostic criteria note that if feeding behavior and weight improve upon the child's removal from the home, this diagnosis should be considered. Finally, the negative sequelae of malnutrition may exacerbate the associated symptoms (i.e., irritability, apathy, developmental delay) and contribute to the perpetuation of the feeding problems (APA, 1994).

Central to this diagnosis is the failure to eat adequately, which leads to concomitant poor growth or weight loss. Unlike the diagnosis of anorexia nervosa, the specific criteria for what constitutes insufficient oral intake or significant weight loss are not specified. This allows freedom for early intervention before (1) the feeding interaction patterns become entrenched, and (2) the caloric inadequacy and weight loss become extreme. However, the ambiguity may lead to problems with reliability and validity in the diagnostic process. As this is a new diagnostic category, data on reliability are not available.

Distinctions have been made in the literature between behavioral feeding disorders and nonorganic failure to thrive (FTT) (see Benoit, 1993, for a review). Nonorganic failure to thrive is not a diagnosis but rather a symptom defined as growth failure, often indicated when weight falls below the 5th percentile on growth charts (Drotar, 1988) and/or there is a deceleration in the rate of weight gain from birth (Drotar et al., 1985). Further, these growth decelerations typically are observed to improve upon hospitalization. Benoit (1992) notes that not all youngsters with FTT demonstrate a feeding disorder and not all children with a feeding disorder develop or exhibit failure to thrive. A feeding disorder may be both a cause and a consequence of FTT (Drotar, 1988). The association between feeding disorders and FTT has not been established and represents an area ripe for further investigation.

As the current classification scheme involves both problems with feeding and growth, it may include the severe pediatric condition FTT, while recognizing less extreme problems in the feeding dynamic. While this allows inclusion and eligibility for services at an earlier point, it also may lead to difficulties in clarity both clinically and conceptually.

Drotar (1989) suggests that increased specificity and the classification of psychosocial variables in FTT would enhance clarity and aid in assessment and treatment. Research clearly documents the complexity of the feeding dynamic, including the potential contribution of both proximal/individual variables and family/environmental variables on the interaction. The current diagnostic formulation does not assist the clinician in differentiating multiple pathways of etiology for feeding disorders, which may predict the utility of various intervention strategies. Further, while this diagnosis is not intended for those children for whom a medical condition clearly underlies the feeding problem, it offers little guidance in forming a differential diagnosis in cases of mild medical conditions that coexist and may or may not be contributing to the feeding problems. For example, children with a history of reflux, Down syndrome, or choking may demonstrate resistance to eating. As detailed later in this chapter, careful assessment of antecedents and biophysical associated factors is essential in diagnosis and treatment planning. Further, future research must address the issue of parsimony or need for greater differentiation within this categorical scheme.

EPIDEMIOLOGICAL DATA

Research suggests that children with FTT make up 1–5% of all pediatric hospital admissions for infants (Berwick, 1980; Bruenlin, Desai, Stone, & Swilley, 1983). The current DSM-IV uses these numbers to estimate the prevalence of the new diagnosis of feeding disorder of infancy and early childhood (APA, 1994). Epidemiological data further indicate that 3.5–20% of infants in rural and urban ambulatory care settings present with FTT (Altemeier, O'Connor, Sherrod, Yeager, & Vietze, 1985; Benoit, 1993; Mitchell, Gorrell, & Greenberg, 1980; Drotar, 1988).

However, the epidemiological data regarding feeding disorders indicate that prevalence rates range from 6–35%, suggesting that a substantial number of young children may be affected (Benoit, 1993; Jenkins, Bax, & Hart, 1980; Palmer & Horn, 1978; Richman, 1981). The highest rates of feeding disorders occur within the developmentally disabled population (Jenkins et al., 1980). Infants born prematurely make up another risk group for the development of food refusal or aversion at the introduction of oral feeding (Geertsma, Hyams, Pelletier, & Reiter, 1985).

Feeding disorders appear with equal frequency among both males and females (APA, 1994). Later onset (in the second or third year) is associated with lower morbidity, particularly with respect to developmental delays and growth retardation (APA, 1994).

Drotar (1988) observes that FTT affects a "soberingly" large number of children. Clearly, feeding disorders may affect an even more substantial number of children. Thus, one recognizes the potential threat posed for both the physical and the psychological well-being of children. These youngsters may be subjected to the negative consequences of malnutrition, dehydration, and, potentially, rumination (see Drotar, 1988, for a review). Further, evidence suggests that children with nonorganic FTT are at increased risk for behavioral and learning problems, as well as poor ego control and resiliency (Drotar & Strum, 1988, 1992; Singer & Fagan, 1984).

Consequently, feeding disorders in general and FTT in particular may represent a potentially significant cost to society (Drotar, 1988), cost that includes hospitalization and treatment of chronic physical, developmental, and behavioral disorders, as well as the expense of institutionalization and foster care placement that may be required.

REVIEW OF THEORETICAL MODELS

Infants and young children with feeding disorders constitute a heterogeneous group. Again, there appear to be multiple pathways by which disruptions in the feeding interaction occur. Consequently, the differing models presented

should be considered not necessarily competing models but rather attempts to describe
heterogeneity and within group differences.

Biomedical Models

Biomedical theories of etiology may be categorized as one of three types: risk, homeostatic, or
traumatic.

Biomedical Risk

As described earlier in this chapter, certain conditions appear to be associated with increased
risk for feeding problems and/or FTT. Typically, the mechanisms through which these risk
factors evolve into feeding problems are not
well defined. Children with FTT exhibit higher
rates of prematurity than is the norm (25–41%)
(see Drotar, 1988, for a review; Geertsma et al.,
1985). Further, undernutrition and low birth
weight have been implicated in contributing
to later feeding problems (Als, Tronick, Adamson, & Brazelton, 1976; Frank, 1985; Woolston,
1983).

In addition to medical risk conditions, the
biological makeup of the child may place him
or her at risk. Youngsters with a feeding disorder have been noted to be vulnerable to infection and have more difficulty recovering from
these infections (Mitchell et al., 1980; Frank,
1985). Sherrod, O'Connor, Vietze, and Altemeier (1985) report that children with FTT
were ill more often than controls during the
first months after birth. Finally, exposure to
teratogens such as lead may play a role in some
children's failure to gain weight and the development of FTT (see Drotar, 1988, for a review).

Homeostatic Factors

Chatoor, Dickson, Schaefer, and Egan (1985)
argue that, in some infants, feeding problems
may stem from primary problems in the tasks of
self-regulation. These children struggle to form
the basic cycles of sleep, feeding, and elimination. The task of progression from reflexive

sucking to motivated oral feedings does not
occur.

The authors report that difficulties at this
stage of development may arise from organic/
constitutional difficulties (e.g., being a "col-
icky" child) or medical problems (Chatoor
et al., 1985). Constitutional vulnerabilities may
include predisposition to overstimulation, difficulty being calmed, a low sensory threshold,
irritability, and passivity with brief periods of
wakefulness. Medical problems may include
poor coordination of the oral musculature, poor
integration of sucking and breathing, respiratory distress that prohibits or limits feedings,
and anatomic problems of the gastrointestinal
tract (e.g., necrotizing enterocolitis, esophageal
atresia).

These constitutional and medical vulnerabilities may lead a child to fall asleep, demonstrate poor sucking, gag, and cry during
feedings. Further, subsequent to the primary
problems with self-regulation, these infants
may not give clear signals to initiate and terminate feeding sessions. This conglomeration
of symptoms acts to interfere with appropriate
feeding interactions with the primary caregiver.

Trauma

The third classification of biomedical theories of feeding problems includes threatening
events that lead to anxiety around the feeding
interaction. Benoit (1993) describes posttraumatic eating disorder (PTED) as a syndrome of
food refusal secondary to traumatic oral experiences. Oral trauma may include experiences
of gagging or choking on food or be related
to medical procedures such as the insertion of
an endotracheal or nasogastric feeding tube.
She describes that with the increasing numbers of infants surviving with complex medical
problems, more children are experiencing these
traumas and the concomitant anxiety around
feeding. Further, early medical conditions may
require the delayed onset of age-appropriate
eating skills. Due to early surgeries or health
problems, bottle feeds and solid food may not
be introduced in a timely fashion. Research suggests that failure to introduce fluids and solids

during critical periods may preclude the development of normal feeding skills (Illingworth & Lister, 1964).

Thus, biomedical variables such as preexisting medical conditions, self-organizational deficits, and traumatic experiences may all serve to place a child at risk for the development of feeding disorders. These factors must be considered in the assessment process and provide appropriate targets for intervention efforts. The presence of these problems may indicate the involvement of occupational or physical therapists or anxiety reduction techniques, in addition to more traditional psychological and behavioral interventions described later in this chapter.

Interpersonal Models

Interpersonal models typically examine the dyad of mother and child, both in the feeding situation and with respect to their general relatedness and attachment. Some limited and preliminary attention has been paid to the role of the father in the development of feeding disorders, as well (Drotar & Sturm, 1987). This section reviews interpersonal correlates of feeding problems in the areas of interpersonal risk (including demographic factors), behavioral models, and attachment models.

Interpersonal Risk

Several factors associated with the family structure have been identified as placing a youngster at heightened risk for feeding problems and FTT, as well as differentiating groups of children with FTT from healthy controls.

Drotar and Eckerle (1989) documented that the family environment of children with FTT differed from that of healthy peers. In particular, families of children with FTT exhibited lower levels of cohesion and expressiveness. Further, these families scored lower on dimensions of intellectual and cultural orientations. In a follow-up study, the authors report that families of children with FTT demonstrated

less optimal familial relationships than did controls but that the quality of family relationships was not stable over time (Drotar, Pallotta, & Eckerle, 1994). In other words, the authors suggest that there are greater discontinuities in family functioning in families with a child who exhibits FTT than in families of healthy children.

Drotar and Sturm (1987) propose a model by which paternal influences lead to the development of feeding disorders and/or FTT in the infant. They suggest that the pathway of impact moves primarily through the mother, who could be viewed as the moderating "variable." These authors suggest that (1) conflictual relationships between the parents, (2) inconsistent paternal support for the mother, (3) paternal psychopathology (e.g., substance use, domestic violence), (4) poor paternal nutritional standards, and (5) the father's infantilization of the child may all act to interfere with the maternal-child feeding dyad.

Specifically, these paternal variables affect the mother's emotional state and anxiety so that she may underfeed the child, have difficulty setting limits, or be less attentive to the child's eating behavior. Further, they argue that a child who is exposed to violence and potentially limited money for food (in the case of paternal substance abuse) may exhibit apathy and underfeeding.

Clearly, this evidence suggests that global family functioning and parental interactions may have both direct and indirect effects on the presentation of food to the child and the child's receptivity to the feeding exchange and must be examined in the assessment process. These family variables may also be part of the intervention program.

Behavioral Models

Behavioral models maintain that all parent-child interactions provide opportunity for contingency experiences (Linscheid & Rasnake, 1985). These experiences, in turn, allow the child to develop a sense of mastery and efficacy in his or her ability to influence the environment. Thus, maternal responsiveness to child behavior has been linked to learning in general, and to feeding behavior in particular (see Linscheid & Rasnake, 1985, for a review). Ramey, Heiger, and Klisz (1972) report that infants with FTT receive less response-contingent stimulation in general than do healthy infants. Within the feeding interaction, Drotar et al. (1990) indicate that mothers of children with FTT were observed to terminate feedings arbitrarily or noncontingently more often than controls.

Consequently, in families where the parent-child interaction is dysfunctional and deficient with respect to these contingency experiences, the infant fails to elicit appropriate care-giving and the parent struggles to intervene effectively with the child's behavioral and feeding problems (Linscheid & Rasnake, 1985). A conceptualization scheme proposed by Linscheid and Rasnake (1985) differentiates two different behavioral pathways to disrupted feeding interactions. Type I FTT or Type I feeding disturbance includes early age of onset (i.e., infancy) and a generalized dysfunctional parent-child relationship. These relationship difficulties are observed in multiple areas of interaction, not just the feeding situation. In Type I feeding problems there exists pervasive parental deprivation that affects the child's receptivity to engagement and feeding.

In contrast, Type II typically emerges later in development (usually 8 months old or older) and occurs in the context of the child's assuming direct control over the feeding situation. Typically, this pattern of feeding problem occurs as the parent (1) introduces solid food into the diet and (2) negotiates the transition of control of the feeding situation to the child. The most common problems falling under this rubric include resistance to texture variety, mealtime behavior problems (tantrums, spitting), inappropriate food habits or selection, and delays in self-feeding skills. Food refusal likely develops from both classical and operant conditioning paradigms. Extrapolating from this model, a feeding disorder results from (1) the lack of contingency between the child's behavior and the parental response or (2) "accidentally" conditioned wrong or inappropriate behavior.

Attachment Models

The behavior of infants with a feeding disorder stemming from poor attachment or disengagement is comparable to that of the infant with a Type I feeding disorder. The explanation of cause, however, does not use the classical conditioning terminology. Rather, attachment models suggest that feeding represents the primary means through which the mother and infant interact, thus facilitating the development of the affectional bond necessary for survival and good psychological adjustment (Bowlby, 1989). Through this critical and proximal relationship, the child develops skills of reciprocal interaction. When these developmental tasks are thwarted, generalized apathy and resignation on the part of the infant are observed in multiple settings, including feeding.

Observations of infants with FTT and their mothers during the feeding interaction demonstrate a generalized "lack of pleasure" in the interaction (Chatoor et al., 1985). Little intimacy occurs (e.g., loose physical contact, no eye contact, few verbalizations). The infants appear listless, may show atypical muscle tone, and also may experience diarrhea and vomiting (Chatoor et al., 1985). Mothers demonstrate less positive affect and less adaptive social interactions (Drotar et al., 1990). The feeding problems are viewed as secondary to the more generalized problems of poor attachment.

Psychological Models

These models examine the contribution of the infant alone in the feeding dynamic. Both a behavioral and dynamic model are presented.

Behavioral

Thompson, Palmer, and Linscheid (1977) dramatically demonstrated the role of the child in the feeding exchange and the child's ability to directly affect the caregiver's behavior. This study was a single study design in which the authors treated a 30-month-old male whose diet was devoid of meat, fruit, and vegetables.

After a baseline observation of three meals with the mother, the authors instituted a behavioral treatment program (such as that described in the following sections) until the child was successfully eating all target foods.

Following the intervention, the authors observed the mother (who had been excluded from the treatment) feed the child. During the posttreatment feeding, the child ate previously nonpreferred foods. Further, the mother's behavior had changed. Critical statements dropped from 7% to 0%. Positive statements rose from 12% to 23%. The child evidenced more cooperative (from 18% to 53%) and fewer noncompliant responses (from 41% to 21%). Again, these interactional changes occurred solely from changing the behavior of the child. The mother's behavior was in a sense "controlled" by the behavior of the child.

Psychodynamic Model

In describing feeding disturbances that emerge in toddlerhood, Chatoor and Egan (1983) assert that in the second half of the second year the child is navigating the tasks of somatopsychological differentiation as part of the effort at separation and individuation. They suggest that, to the extent that the child's efforts at self-feeding are thwarted, the child becomes angry. This constitutes a direct threat to the child's psychological need to individuate. In this anger, the child assumes control by refusing food. The caregiver, typically the mother, may become anxious and perhaps more dogmatic. The child's refusal continues escalating the cycle into a "battle of spoons" (Chatoor et al., 1985). The ongoing food refusal then represents failed efforts at separation.

In conclusion, the models described represent the multiple pathways through which feeding disorders may develop. Rich in complexity, these models highlight the interaction of organic, emotional, and social dimensions that contribute to the development of maladaptive feeding interactions. While differing in the "worldview" of how disordered behavior emerges, they all clearly suggest that (1) a child with disruptions in the feeding exchange may have multiple needs, and (2) assessment and intervention can take several forms.

ASSESSMENT

The assessment of children with eating and feeding disorder of infancy and early childhood incorporates a number of areas. Consistent with previously reviewed theories of etiology, assessment of a child with a feeding disorder involves three primary domains: developmental status, environmental and social variables, and specific behaviors and behavioral interactions during feeding or mealtimes. The goals of assessment are to (1) assist in the differentiation between organic and psychological factors that may be active, (2) determine family, social, and environmental factors operative in the disorder, and (3) assess specific behaviors and behavioral interactions between child and caregiver. Assessment in these areas is necessary for effective treatment planning.

Developmental assessment of the infant involves the determination of the infant's developmental level in the social and cognitive areas. This assessment should involve at least a standardized infant assessment test such as the Bayley Scales of Infant Development (Bayley, 1993) or other infant development scales. The assessment of cognitive development can be useful in targeting specific infant stimulation remedial activities and as a measure of progress during and following intervention (Drotar, 1989).

As indicated earlier, Drotar and Eckerle (1989) have shown that children with failure-to-thrive have different family environments from children with healthy peers. The assessment of family functioning is generally accomplished through clinical interview and standardized psychological questionnaires such as the Family Environment Scale (Moos & Moos, 1981). Drotar and Eckerle (1989) found that the three subscales of the Family Environment Scale—Cohesion, Expressiveness, and Intellectual-Cultural Orientation—successfully differentiated between families who had infants with nonorganic FTT and a control group. It is also important to assess general levels of stress within families, mother-father interactions, and overall support mechanisms for the infant's mother. There are several commonly used measures of family stress and maternal support, including the Family Environment Scale (Moos & Moos, 1981), the parenting stress index (Abidin, 1990), and the Family Relationship Inventory (Holohan & Moos, 1983). Marital adjustment and mother-father stress can be assessed with a number of marital adjustment such as the Dyadic Adjustment Scale (Spanier & Thompson, 1982). Increased incidence of psychopathological conditions in the mothers of infants with FTT has been suggested (Polan et al., 1991). Especially prevalent are personality disorders and depression. An instrument such as the SCL-90 (Derogatis, 1983) can be used to assess psychological functioning in the mother or primary caregiver.

The role of the father has been increasingly recognized in the development of nonorganic FTT, as described earlier. For effective treatment planning, the relationship between the child's father and mother must be assessed and considered when designing interventions that involve the entire family.

The third area of assessment involves the documentation of actual behaviors in the feeding situation. This includes parent-child interactions during meal times. Highly structured behavioral observation techniques have been developed to measure these behaviors and interactions (Babbitt et al., 1994; Riordan, Iwata, Finney, Wohl & Stanley, 1984; Thompson, Palmer, & Linscheid, 1977). Specifically, amount eaten is often measured by bites accepted or by weighing food before and after feeding. Specific child behaviors such as crying, spitting food out once accepted, gagging, or turning head away from food presented are measured with frequency counts or duration-based techniques such as interval recording. Interactional measures that document a parent's response to a specific child behavior or vice versa often yield useful information about a parent's ability to attend to appropriate child behaviors (cf. Thompson, Palmer, & Linscheid, 1977). While these direct behavioral

observation methods are time consuming, they can also be very revealing as to the exact nature of feeding problems during meal times and their relationship to parent-child interaction difficulties. Structured interviews as described by Linscheid and Rasnake (1985) also are helpful.

Several studies have shown specific behavioral differences between infants with organic FTT and nonorganic FTT and infants who are physically healthy. Powell, Low, and Speers (1987) found that, compared with controls, infants with nonorganic FTT demonstrated significantly more deviant behaviors. These infants showed decreases in motor activity response to stimuli, amount of smiling, overall activity, eye contact and fine motor activities. However, Drotar (1989) questions whether specific, observed behaviors can be used to differentiate between organic and nonorganic FTT infants because of the great degree of overlap in many of the behaviors observed in the groups. Drotar further suggests that assessment of intellectual development and biological and environmental risk factors must be considered with the behavioral observations, since these factors can affect the infants overall activity level and responsiveness.

Observation of the mother-child interaction during feedings is especially important. Mothers who have not bonded well, have their own emotional disturbance, or simply lack ability to detect the infant's needs and cues feed their babies with a distinct disinterest or lack of awareness (Schmidt & Mauro, 1989). Observation of mother's touch during feeding is also important, as Polan and Ward (1994) showed that mothers of infants with nonorganic growth problems provided less touch than mothers of most normally growing infants.

The assessment of parent-child interaction is extremely important, but two things should be kept in mind during the assessment. First, for the child who is currently acutely or chronically malnourished, social responsiveness may be decreased as a function of the malnourished condition, rather than as an ongoing permanent trait of the child. Until the child is returned to a adequate nutritional state, it is impossible to determine if a child's unresponsiveness is a cause or an effect of the malnourished condition. Second, as discussed previously, parent-child interaction is a bidirectional process (cf. Linscheid & Rasnake, 1985) in which decreased or inappropriate parental interactions during the feeding situation may be in response to infant characteristics rather than the cause of infant feeding problems. When direct observations of the feeding situation or parent-child interaction occur, these factors must be kept in mind to prevent forming the wrong conclusion as to cause.

INTERVENTION

Intervention in feeding disorders of infancy and early childhood can be broad or very specific. Broad interventions include services ranging from social welfare to early intervention to supportive counseling with parents and family. More specific interventions most often relate to the effectiveness of behavioral interactions during the feeding situation itself (Linscheid & Rasnake, 1985; Linscheid, Budd, & Rasnake, 1995). The nature of these interventions is summarized in the remainder of this chapter. The reader is encouraged to obtain additional readings in this area, as the following is meant only to be a review.

While the literature on multielement interventions directed primarily at the families of infants with FTT is not extensive, the results are not inspiring. For example, Casey et al. (1994) found that the assignment of preterm infants, who are at increased risk for FTT, to either an intense multielement intervention program directed at supporting the family or a control follow-up group revealed no differences in the incidence of FTT at 3-year follow-up. The intense intervention included weekly home visits during the first year of life and biweekly visits thereafter until the child reached age three. The purpose of these visits was to provide family support and education. In addition, the child attended a child development center 5 days a week from age 12 months to 3 years. After controlling for a number of factors, group membership did significantly contribute to the prediction of IQ at 36 month of age for the

children who did develop FTT. The authors also found that high compliance within the group of parents with infants who developed FTT was significantly related to IQ score at 36 months of age.

Similarly, Drotar, Nowak, Malone, Eckerle, and Negray (1985) did not find a difference between intervention strategies that utilized home visits, attempts to modify ineffective family coping strategies and dysfunctional patterns related to nurturing of the child. The interventions differed in frequency of contact and focus. In a family-centered-approach group, intervention was primarily directed at family functioning. In a parent-centered group, support and educational interventions focused on improving the mother's parenting skills as they affect the parent-child interaction, nutritional management, and relationship building. The authors found no relationship between outcome and group membership. Generally, they found that a less severe nutritional status of the child at the time of diagnosis and a higher family income were related to enhanced cognitive developmental outcome. Another factor found to be related to improved outcome was the ratio of adults to children within the family. It is interesting to note that the factors related to the improved outcome in both of the studies just described were inherent in the family and were not changed as a result of intervention. While these results may be discouraging in terms of intervention outcome, research in this area is still quite crude. It simply goes against logic that assisting families to better understand the nutritional needs of infants, obtain appropriate and adequate food, and provide for infant stimulation and promoting compliance with medical appointments and other medical treatment regimens would not improve outcome for children with early feeding problems.

Interventions Specifically Directed at Feeding

Under the assumption that difficulties in feeding and poor weight gain in infants or children can be attributed to ineffective feeding practices, interventions have been directed towards several specific problems. These include improving infant and child compliance during mealtimes, increasing quantity, variety, and texture of foods accepted by the child, and training parents in effective feeding techniques.

As reviewed earlier, Linscheid and Rasnake (1985) suggested two working subtypes, Type I and Type II, to describe feeding problems in infants and children. Type I feeding problems involve infants generally 8 months of age or younger whose inadequate intake leads to actual weight loss or weight gain below the expected level. With Type I feeding problems, the nature of the mother-infant relationship is dysfunctional and is characterized by the lack of the development of affectional bonds, decreased developmentally appropriate signs of social responsivity in the infant, and various behavioral symptoms such as excessive sleep, weak cry, hypomotility, and poor muscle tone. Although Type I feeding disorders often occur because of multiple family and social difficulties that may be addressed by intervention strategies as described previously, the feeding situation can serve as an excellent setting in which to train mothers in more effective interactional behaviors. The feeding situation can be used to increase what many have called synchrony between infant and mother. Synchrony involves appropriate eye contact, sensitivity to the child's signals, and the ability to respond immediately and appropriately with a consistent approach (Ainsworth, 1979). Interventions in situations where it is clear that attachment is not established involve direct modeling of appropriate infant-child interaction and coaching of the mother or caregiver in ways to appropriately respond to infant cues. Providing these "contingency" experiences (Goldberg, 1977) for a parent who seems unable to detect infant needs by infant behaviors can be particularly effective.

While mother-infant attachment and contingency experience training are the central focus of this type of intervention, care must be taken not to assume or convey the impression that the feeding problem is the mother's fault. Mothers or caregivers can perceive this attitude very quickly, and resistance, as a defense

against blame, can develop, especially since most mother attribute their child's condition to organic factors (Sturm & Drotar, 1989). Indeed, it is important to remember that problems of interaction between mother and child can be the result of an undetected neurophysiologically based feeding disorder. Ramsey, Gisel, and Boutry (1993) found no differences in early clinical symptoms, infant feeding behavior, and mother-infant interactions between groups of infants with nonorganic FTT and those whose growth failure could be explained organically.

In Type II feeding problems as defined by Linscheid and Rasnake (1985), the etiology is generally traceable to ineffective behavioral management of the feeding situation. In many cases, medical conditions that may have resolved have interfered with the normal development of feeding skills, and ineffective behavioral strategies for handling these difficulties may have emerged (Ginsberg, 1988). Type II feeding problems generally develop near the end of the first year of life and before age two. Both the transition to solid foods and the parent's inability to adjust to changing appetites and food preferences can set the stage for Type II feeding disorders. It has been suggested that this transition needs to occur at this age for infants and children to develop the ability to handle the variety of textures that are found in normal diets (Illingworth & Lister, 1964). Failure to introduce solids during this time often results in texture-related feeding problems involving prolonged subsistence on liquid or pureed textures. This is a common problem in children who, because of a medical condition, have not been allowed to or were not able to eat by mouth until the critical period has passed.

Also placing children at risk for Type II feeding problems is the natural reduction in appetite that occurs after age one. While children have been growing rapidly during the first year of life (tripling their birth weight), growth rate slows dramatically during the second year of life. Consequently, children who may have been feeding regularly and enthusiastically at set intervals during the first year of life begin to show total disinterest in food during some meals or decreased appetite and increased selectivity at others (Linscheid, 1992). Behavior-based feeding problems can occur during this time for a number of reasons. Parental efforts to increase food intake beyond what a child naturally desires can lead to offers of less nutritious foods such as sweets and desserts. Ineffective parental efforts to intervene at mealtimes can lead to mealtime tantrums and parental frustration, casting a negative emotional tone on mealtimes. Decreased intake at mealtimes can also lead parents to supply additional between-meal snacks, thereby decreasing appetite at mealtime for a more normal mixture and variety of foods. Many authors have described useful behavioral techniques for addressing specific mealtime behavior problems (Babbit et al., 1994; Linscheid, 1992; Linscheid, Budd, & Rasnake, 1995; Riorden, Iwata, Wohl, & Finney, 1984). Behavioral feeding treatments can be conducted on an outpatient or inpatient basis. Inpatient treatment is usually undertaken when outpatient attempts have been unsuccessful, the child's weight or nutritional status suggests impending medical problems, or other medical conditions must be closely monitored during the feeding treatment.

Generally, behavioral interventions for feeding difficulties involve developing goals such as increasing variety, increasing quantity, or increasing food texture. Goals may also include self-feeding or the reduction of disruptive mealtime behaviors (e.g., throwing food, tantrums). Using individually determined reinforcers and punishers, individualized treatment plans are developed. In order to ensure that children are hungry at treatment mealtimes, some type of appetite manipulation is often used. This is generally accomplished by simply restricting the child's access to food or calorie-containing liquids between meals. During the meal itself, compliance with the therapist's request (e.g., accepting a bite of a nonpreferred food or texture) is reinforced with social praise and perhaps access to a small quantity of a preferred food. Noncompliance (e.g., refusing a bite of food, spitting food out) may be treated with extinction (simple ignoring) or a brief time-out in which the therapist physically turns away from the child and prevents access to preferred foods. It can be seen that access to preferred food and the manipulation of social praise and attention, coupled with manipulations to increase hunger, are the main components of behavioral feeding treatments. Progress is measured by a variety of methods depending on treatment goals. For example, if a treatment goal is to increase intake, data on calories eaten or bites accepted or the patient's daily weight may serve as outcome measures.

Parent training is an essential component of behavior-based feeding interventions. This is especially important when treatment is done on an outpatient basis, since parents are instructed by a therapist during clinic or home visits but actually conduct most of the treatment themselves at home (Werle, Murphy, & Budd, 1993). Home-based treatment will likely become more common as managed care continues to emphasize outpatient care. In a full capitation system, sending therapists to the home can be cost-effective, whereas under fee-for-service models, travel time and time lost between meals make this practice financially impossible. Advances in communication technology will also facilitate home-based treatment. For example, parents can be asked to videotape meals at home for review by therapists, and, in the near future, videophone capabilities may allow direct live observation of home-based feedings by office-based therapists who can coach and instruct patents during actual meals.

During inpatient treatment, parents may not participate in the initial feeding treatments, since children have developed certain habits in the presence of their parents and having the parents out of the room during feedings can produce faster results. Parents may observe the initial feedings via one-way mirrors or videotape. Once progress begins, parents are brought into the feedings and gradually assume more control of the feeding while being coached by the behavior therapist (Linscheid, Budd, & Rasnake, 1995).

RELATIONSHIP TO ICD-10 DIAGNOSTIC CODES

In the International Classification of Diseases (ICD-10) classification system, rumination disorder is included under F98.2, "feeding disorder of infancy and childhood" (World Health Organization, 1993). This category, with the exception of the inclusion of rumination, is very similar to the DSM-IV diagnosis of "feeding disorder of infancy and early childhood." It specifies a persistent failure to eat adequately, and onset is before age six. It specifies an absence of organic disease, as do the DSM-IV criteria, and stipulates the absence of other behavioral or mental ICD disorder, other than mental retardation.

ICD-10 provides a separate diagnostic category for pica (F98.3, pica of infancy and childhood), which very closely approximates the DSM-IV criteria. While ICD-10 specifies that the child must be above 2 years of age, DSM-IV indicates only that the behavior is inappropriate for the child's developmental level. Both specify that pica should not be diagnosed if the eating of nonnutritive substances is part of a cultural practice.

SUMMARY

DSM-IV provides the diagnosis of "feeding disorder of infancy and early childhood" and provides a new structure for diagnosis. Diagnostic criteria are based on actual weight and feeding behaviors and do not assume disturbances in attachment or psychological functioning deficits in either parent or child. This is a significant step forward as we have shown that there are multiple pathways and great heterogeneity in the presentation of and the therapeutic approaches to this disorder. Multielement assessment of several domains of function is necessary to fully understand the complexities and contributory factors in any one child's feeding disorder. On the basis of the assessment, clinicians may choose a more broad-based or a more specific intervention in response to the child's unique needs. The effectiveness of specific interventions has been documented, but more research is needed on multielement assessment and intervention strategies.

REFERENCES

Abidin, R. R. (1990). *Parenting Stress Index manual* (3rd. ed.). Charlottesville, VA: Pediatric Psychology Press.

Ainsworth, M. (1979). Infant-mother attachment. *American Psychologist, 34,* 932–937.

Als, H., Tronick, E., Adamson, L., & Brazelton, T. (1976). The behavior of the full-term but underweight newborn infant. *Developmental Medicine and Child Neurology, 18,* 590–602.

Altemeier, W., O'Connor, S., Sherrod, K., Yeager, T., & Vietze, P. (1985). A strategy for managing nonorganic failure to thrive based on a prospective study of antecedents. In D. Drotar (Ed.), *New directions in failure to thrive: Implications for research and practice.* New York: Plenum Press.

American Psychiatric Association (APA). (1994). *Diagnostic and statistical manual of mental disorders* (4th ed.). Washington, DC: Author.

*Babbitt, R. L., Hoch, T. A., Coe, D. A., Cataldo, M. F., Kelly, K. J., Stackhouse, C., & Perman, J. A. (1994). Behavioral assessment and treatment of pediatric feeding disorders. *Behavioral and Developmental Pediatrics, 15,* 278–291.

Bayley, N. (1993). *Bayley Scales of Development, Second Edition Manual.* San Antonio, TX: Psychological Corporation.

*Benoit, D. (1993). Failure to thrive and eating disorders. In C. Zeanah (Ed.), *Handbook of infant mental health.* New York: Guilford Press.

Berwick, D. M. (1980). Nonorganic failure to thrive. *Pediatrics in Review, 1,* 265–270.

Bithoney, W. G., & Rathbun, J. M. (1983). Failure to thrive. In M. D. Levine, A. C. Carey, A. D. Crocker, & R. J. Gross (Eds.), *Developmental behavioral pediatrics.* Philadelphia: W. B. Saunders.

Bowlby, J. (1989). The role of attachment in personality development and psychopathology. In S. Greenspan & G. Pollack (Eds.), *The course of life: Infancy.* Madison, CT: International Universities Press.

Bruenlin, D. C., Desai, V. J., Stone, M. E., & Swilley, J. (1983). Failure to thrive with no organic etiology: A critical review. *International Journal of Eating Disorders, 2,* 25–49.

Bucher, B., Reykdal, B., & Albin, J. (1976). Brief physical restraint to control pica in retarded children. *Journal of Behavior Therapy and Experimental Psychology, 7,* 141–144.

*Casey, P. H., Kelliher, K. J., Bradley, R. H., Kellogg, K. W., Kirby, R. S., & Whiteside, L. (1994). A multifaceted intervention for infants with failure-to-thrive. *Archives of Pediatric Adolescent Medicine*, 148, 1071–1077.

*Chatoor, I., Dickson, L., Schaefer, S., & Egan, J. (1985). A developmental classification of feeding disorders associated with failure to thrive: Diagnosis and treatment. In D. Drotar (Ed.), *New directions in failure to thrive: Implications for research and practice*. New York: Plenum Press.

Chatoor, I., & Egan, J. (1983). Nonorganic failure to thrive and dwarfism due to food refusal: A separation disorder. *Journal of the American Academy of Child Psychiatry*, 22, 294–301.

Cunningham, C. E., & Linscheid, T. R. (1976). Elimination of chronic infant ruminating by electric shock. *Behavior Therapy*, 7, 231–234.

Danford, D., & Huber, A. (1982). Pica among mentally retarded adults. *American Journal of Mental Deficiency*, 87, 141–146.

Derogatis, L. (1983). *SCL-90-R: Administration, scoring, and procedures manual-II for the revised version*. Towson, MD.: Clinical Psychometric Research.

Drotar, D. (1988). Failure to thrive. In D. Routh (Ed.), *Handbook of pediatric psychology*. New York: Guilford Press.

*Drotar, D. (1989). Behavioral diagnosis in nonorganic failure to thrive: A critique and suggested approach to psychological assessment. *Behavioral and Developmental Pediatrics*, 10, 48–55.

*Drotar, D., & Eckerle, D. (1989). The family environment in nonorganic failure to thrive: A controlled study. *Journal of Pediatric Psychology*, 14, 245–257.

*Drotar, D., Eckerle, D., Satola, J., Pallotta, J., & Wyatt, B. (1990). Maternal interactional behavior with nonorganic failure to thrive infants: A case comparison study. *Child Abuse and Neglect*, 14, 41–51.

*Drotar, D., Nowak, M., Malone, C., Eckerle, D., & Negray, J. (1985). Early psychological outcomes in failure to thrive: Predictions from an interactional model. *Journal of Clinical Child Psychology*, 14, 105–111.

*Drotar, D., Pallotta, J., & Eckerle, D. (1994). A prospective study of family environments of children hospitalized for nonorganic failure to thrive. *Developmental and Behavioral Pediatrics*, 15, 78–85.

Drotar, D., & Sturm, L. (1987). Paternal influences in nonorganic failure to thrive: Implications for psychosocial management. *Infant Mental Health Journal*, 8, 37–50.

*Drotar, D., & Sturm, L. (1988). Prediction of intel-lectual development in young children with early histories of nonorganic failure to thrive. *Journal of Pediatric Psychology*, 13, 281–296.

Drotar, D., & Sturm, L. (1992). Personality development, personality solving and behavioral problems among preschool children with early histories of nonorganic failure to thrive: A controlled study. *Journal of Developmental and Behavioral Pediatrics*, 13, 266–273.

*Duker, P., & Nielen, M. (1993). The use of negative practice for the control of pica behavior. *Journal of Behavior Therapy and Experimental Psychiatry*, 24, 249–253.

*Fisher, W., Piazza, C., Bowman, L., Kurtz, P., Sherer, M., & Lachman, S. (1994). A preliminary evaluation of empirically derived consequences for the treatment of pica. *Journal of Applied Behavior Analysis*, 27, 447–457.

Frank, D. (1985). Biologic risks in nonorganic failure to thrive. Diagnostic and therapeutic implications. In D. Drotar (Ed.), *New directions in failure to thrive: Implications for research and practice*. New York: Plenum Press.

*Fultz, S., & Rojahn, J. (1988). Pica. In M. Hersen & C. Last (Eds.), *Child behavior therapy casebook*. New York: Plenum Press.

*Geertsma, M., Hyams, J., Pelletier, J., & Reiter, S. (1985). Feeding resistance after parenteral hyperalimentation. *American Journal of Diseases of Children*, 139, 255-256.

*Ginsberg, A. J. (1988). Feeding disorders in the developmentally disabled population. In D. C. Russo & J. K. Kedesty (Eds.), *Behavioral medicine with the developmentally disabled* (pp. 21–41). New York: Plenum Press.

Goldberg, S. (1977). Social competence in infancy: A model of parent-infant interaction. *Merrill-Palmer Quarterly*, 23, 161–176.

Halmi, K. (1985). Eating disorders. In H. Kaplan & B. Sadock (Eds.), *Comprehensive textbook of psychiatry* (4th ed.) Baltimore: Williams and Wilkins.

Holohan, C. J., & Moos, R. H. (1983). The quality of social support: Measures of family and work relationships. *British Journal of Clinical Psychology*, 22, 157–162.

Illingworth, R., & Lister, J. (1964). The critical or sensitive period, with special reference to certain feeding problems in infants and children. *Journal of Pediatrics*, 65, 839–848.

Jenkins, S., Bax, M., & Hart, H. (1980). Behavioral problems in preschool children. *Journal of Child Psychology and Psychiatry*, 21, 5–17.

Kanner, L. (1957). *Child psychiatry* (3rd ed.). Springfield, IL: Charles C. Thomas.

Lang, P. J., & Melamed, B. G. (1969). Avoidance conditioning therapy of an infant with chronic ruminative vomiting. *Journal of Abnormal Psychology, 74,* 139–142.

*Linscheid, T. R. (1992). Eating problems in children. In C. E. Walker & M. C. Roberts (Eds.), *Handbook of clinical child psychology* (2nd ed., pp. 451–473). New York: Wiley.

*Linscheid, T. R., Budd, K. S., & Rasnake, L. K. (1995). Pediatric feeding disorders. In M. C. Roberts (Ed.), *Handbook of pediatric psychology* (2nd ed., pp. 501–515). New York: Guilford Press.

Linscheid, T. R., & Cunningham, C. E. (1977). A controlled demonstration of the effectiveness of electric shock in the elimination of chronic infant rumination. *Journal of Applied Behavior Analysis, 10,* 500.

Linscheid, T., & Rasnake, L. K. (1985). Behavioral approaches to the treatment of failure to thrive. In D. Drotar (Ed.), *New directions in failure to thrive: Implications for research and practice.* New York: Plenum Press.

Lofts, R., Schroeder, S., & Maier, R. (1990). Effects of serum zinc supplementation on pica behavior of persons with mental retardation. *American Journal on Mental Retardation, 95,* 103–109.

Lourie, R. S. (1955). Treatment of psychosomatic problems in infants. *Clinical Procedures in Children's Hospitals, 2,* 142–151.

McLoughlin, I. (1988). Pica as a cause of death in three mentally handicapped men. *British Journal of Psychiatry, 152,* 842–845.

Miller, P., O'Neil, P., Malcolm, R., & Currey, H. (1985). Eating disorders. In H. Adams & P. Sutker (Eds.), *Comprehensive handbook of psychopathology.* New York: Plenum Press.

*Mitchell, W. G., Gorrell, R. W., & Greenberg, R. (1980). Failure to thrive: A study in a primary care setting, epidemiology and follow-up. *Pediatrics, 65,* 971–977.

Moos, A. H., & Moos, B. S. (1981). *Family environment scale manual.* Palo Alto, CA: Consulting Psychologist Press.

Palmer, S., & Horn, S. (1978). Feeding problems in children. In S. Palmer & S. Ekvall (Eds.), *Pediatric nutrition in developmental disorders.* Springfield, IL: Charles C. Thomas.

Polan, J. H., Kaplan, M. D., Kessler, D. B., Shindledecker, R., Newmark, M., Stern, D. N., & Ward, M. J. (1991). Psychopathology in mothers of infants with failure-to-thrive. *Infant Mental Health Journal, 12,* 55–64.

*Polan, H. J., & Ward, M. J. (1994). Role of mother's touch in failure to thrive: A preliminary investigation. *Journal of the American Academy of Child and Adolescent Psychiatry, 33,* 1098–1105.

*Powell, G. F., Low, J. F., & Speers, M. A. (1987). Behavior as a diagnostic aid in failure-to-thrive. *Journal of Behavioral and Developmental Pediatrics, 8,* 18–24.

Ramsey, M., Gisel, E. G., & Boutry, M. (1993). Nonorganic failure to thrive: Growth failure secondary to feeding-skill disorder. *Developmental Medicine and Child Neurology, 35,* 285–297.

Ramey, C., Hieger, L., & Klisz, D. (1972). Synchronous reinforcement of focal responses in failure to thrive infants. *Child Development, 43,* 1449–1455.

Rast, J., Johnson, J. M., Drum, C., & Conrin, J. (1981). The relation of food quantity to rumination behavior. *Journal of Applied Behavior Analysis, 14,* 121–130.

Richman, N. (1981). A community survey of characteristics of one to two year olds with sleep disturbances. *Journal of the American Academy of Child Psychiatry, 20,* 281–291.

Richmond, J. B., Eddy, E., & Green, M. (1958). Rumination: A psychosomatic syndrome of infancy. *Pediatrics, 22,* 49–55.

Riordan, M. M., Iwata, B. A., Finney, J. W., Wohl, M. K., & Stanley, A. E. (1984). Behavioral assessment and treatment of food refusal by handicapped children. *Journal of Applied Behavior Analysis, 17,* 327–341.

*Schmidt, B. D., & Mauro, R. D. (1989). Nonorganic failure to thrive: An outpatient approach. *Child Abuse & Neglect, 13,* 235–248.

Sherrod, K., O'Connor, S., Vietze, P., & Altemeier, W. (1985). Child health and maltreatment. *Child Development, 55,* 1174–1183.

*Singer, L., & Fagan, J. (1984). Cognitive development in the failure to thrive infant: A three year longitudinal study. *Journal of Pediatric Psychology, 91,* 363–383.

Spanier, G. B., & Thompson, L. (1982). A confirmatory analysis of the Dyadic Adjustment Scale. *Journal of Marriage and Family, 44,* 731–738.

*Sturm, L., & Drotar, D. (1989). Maternal attribution of nonorganic failure to thrive. *Family Systems Medicine, 9,* 53–64.

Thompson, R. J., Palmer, S., & Linscheid, T. R. (1977). Single-subject research design and interaction analysis in the behavioral treatment of a child with a feeding problem. *Child Psychiatry and Human Development*, 8, 43–53.

Toister, R. P., Colin, J., Worley, L. M., & Arthur, D. (1975). Faradic therapy of chronic vomiting in infancy: A case study. *Journal of Behavior Therapy and Experimental Psychiatry*, 6, 55–59.

*Werle, M. A., Murphy, T. B., & Budd, K. S. (1993). Treating chronic food refusal in young children: Home-based parent training. *Journal of Applied Behavior Analysis*, 26, 421–433.

Wicks-Nelson, R., & Israel, A. (1997). Disorders of basic physical functions. In *Behavior disorders of childhood* (3rd ed.). Upper Saddle River, NJ: Prentice Hall.

*Woolston, J. (1983). Eating disorders in infancy and early childhood. *Journal of the American Academy of Child Psychiatry*, 22, 114–121.

World Health Organization. (1993). *ICD-10 classification of mental and behavioral disorders: Diagnostic criteria for research*. Geneva: Author.

*Indicates references that the authors recommend for further reading.

9

Tic Disorders and Stereotypic Movement Disorders

Lee H. Matthews
Michael D. Chafetz

Disorders covered within this chapter relate to the American Psychiatric Association *Diagnostic and Statistical Manual of Mental Disorders* (Fourth Edition) (1994) classifications of "tic disorders" and "stereotypic movement disorder," and each will be covered in separate sections. In 1992, the World Health Organization published *The ICD-10 Classification of Mental and Behavioural Disorders: Clinical Descriptions and Diagnostic Guidelines*, which uses many of the same basic categories of description for the tic disorders and movement disorders.

Beyond the diagnostic differences for the disorders covered in this chapter are larger issues concerning the structure of the DSM-IV and ICD-10 classification systems with regard to the major diagnostic classes. For the reader interested in this broader perspective for these systems, both were recently reviewed by Thangavelu and Martin (1995). These authors discuss the development of both systems and provide a comparison of the two systems, using the ICD-10 organization rather than the DSM-IV as the basis for their comparison. Diagnostic systems are also influenced by societal and historical pressures. Alarcon (1995) noted that culture has a strong influence on the information obtained and the interpretation of those data in reaching a diagnosis. He described some of the effects of culture on the DSM-IV and ICD-10 systems and urged consideration of multiple factors such as stress, comorbidity, and daily functioning in reaching a global rather than an ethnocentric categorization of disorders.

The format used throughout this chapter consists of reference to the DSM-IV (APA, 1994) definitions of the various categories of disorders, their historical perspective, epidemiology, theoretical models, methods of assessment, and treatment techniques, with relevant comments to ICD-10 (WHO, 1992) when appropriate. Each of these areas is covered from a variety of perspectives, including biomedical, psychological, and social/interpersonal.

A tic is defined by DSM-IV (APA, 1994) as a "sudden, rapid, recurrent, nonrhythmic, stereotyped motor movement or vocalization" (p. 100). Other features mentioned by ICD-10 (1992) as distinguishing tics from other motor disorders are the circumscribed nature of the movements; their repetitiveness; the ease with which voluntary suppression may be possible for a period of time; and, often, their disappearance during sleep. Tics usually include head movements, but other parts of the body are also involved in many cases.

The seemingly contradictory statement that "tics" (small t) are not always "Tics" (large T) points up the problems involved in defining, assessing, and diagnosing the various DSM-IV (1994) and ICD-10 classifications of tic disorder and stereotypic movement disorders. The lack of rhythmicity differentiates tics from the stereotyped repetitive movements seen in autism or mental retardation. In these disorders, manneristic motor activities tend to comprise more complex and variable movements than those usually seen with tics (ICD-10; WHO, 1992). However, both tics and stereotypies may be present in these populations.

In general, tics do involve involuntary recurrent motor movements or vocalizations (Leckman, Towbin, Ort, & Cohen, 1988). While it may be possible to distinguish easily between a simple motor tic such as a blinking eye (a tic disorder) and picking at the skin (a stereotypic movement disorder), it may be more difficult to differentially diagnose that same stereotypic behavior from a more complex motor tic disorder, such as grooming behaviors or facial gestures (Cohen, Leckman, & Towbin, 1989). In addition, conclusive evidence is lacking whether the classifications for the tic disorders represent distinct problems or a continuum of severity of the same problem (American Psychiatric Association, 1987). Stereotyped movements or habits, although rhythmic, are viewed as intentional behaviors, as are compulsions (Golden & Hood, 1982). Obsessive-compulsive activities sometimes resemble complex tics but differ in that their form tends to be defined by their purpose (such as touching some object or turning a number of times), rather than by the muscle groups involved (ICD-10; WHO, 1992). These stereotypic movement disorders are covered later in the chapter.

TIC DISORDERS

Historical Perspective

Meige and Feindel in 1907 published an extensive book on the types and treatment of tics (as cited in Wright, Schaefer, & Solomons, 1979, p. 626). The major defining characteristic of the classification of tic disorders is abnormality in the child's (or adult's) motor movement or vocalization. A tic is a rapid, sudden, nonrhythmic, recurrent stereotyped motor movement or vocalization (Shapiro & Shapiro, 1981b). While both motor and vocal tics may be classified as "simple" or complex," there is disagreement as to what constitutes such a division for either type. Simple vocal tics include barking, grunting, throat clearing, sniffing, and snorting. Complex vocal tics include coprolalia (use of obscene or socially unacceptable words); echolalia (repeating the last heard word, phrase, or sound of another person or a last-heard sound); palilalia (repeating one's own sounds or words); and repeating words or phrases out of context. Simple motor tics include eye blinking, eye squinting, facial grimacing, neck jerking, and shoulder shrugging. Keshavan (1988) reported 10 cases of simple tics of the ear. Complex motor tics are echokinesis (mimicking or imitation of the movements of someone who is being observed), facial gestures, grooming behaviors, jumping, self-biting or hitting, smelling objects, stamping, or touching.

The four major DSM-IV (APA, 1994) classifications of tic disorder are "Tourette's disorder," "chronic motor or vocal tic disorder," "transient tic disorder," and "tic disorder, not otherwise specified."

TOURETTE'S DISORDER

Historical Perspective

DSM-IV (APA, 1994) classifies Tourette's disorder under "tic disorders," as did DSM-III-R (1987) under the same diagnostic number (307.23). Perhaps the best known of the tic disorders, although one of the rarer of the movement disorders, its unusual and often bizarre presentations have resulted in considerable interest in its etiology and treatment (Kerbeshian & Burd, 1994; Robertson, 1994). Historically called Tourette's Syndrome, or Gilles de la Tourette syndrome, it has been recognized as a distinct diagnostic entity for well over 100 years, since Gilles de la Tourette, a pupil of Charcot, first described a chronic tic of the face and body accompanied by speech aberrations in one of his patients ("Miss X" or "Miss de M") in a two-part paper published in 1885 (Kolb & Whishaw, 1990). This disorder often includes echolalia and coprolalia. Gilles de la Tourette's patient had episodes of echolalia, including barking "like a dog." On one occasion, "a dog came and barked under the window of her room. She immediately began involuntarily to echo the dog's barking. . . ." The patient apparently continued this behavior for several hours, unable to sleep until early in the morning, due to "her body being wracked by muscular spasms that accompanied the noisy barking, exactly like the dog's. . . ." The patient, "Miss X," who was described as a 15-year-old female, "belonging to an upper-class family," also displayed coprolalia, to the obvious distress of the family, as "one had to wonder how and where she picked up the words she continually uttered . . ." (Kolb & Whishaw, 1990, pp. 300–301).

Tourette also recorded what may be the first attempt at treatment for the coprolalia, as the patient's mother ordered her governess to shout substitute words at the patient several times per day, "to substitute the vulgar words with indifferent and banal exclamations . . ." (Kolb & Whishaw, 1990, p. 300).

Until Gilles de la Tourette's paper was published, this syndrome was seen as either an undifferentiated chorea or a symptom of hysteria, going by a variety of names depending on the country of observation. Other early cases were reported before the turn of the century by Itard (1825) and Beard (1880), prior to the publication of Tourette's paper.

One of the earliest accounts of an apparent victim of this disorder was Prince de Condé, who was a member of the seventeenth-century French Court of King Louis XIV. Records indicate that he was seized by "barking attacks" at royal receptions and made it a practice to stand next to a window so that he could stuff curtains in his mouth. Retrospective studies suggest that Samuel Johnson, the noted English writer, also exhibited a number of the signs of this disorder, including tics of the mouth, torso, and feet, and he was also noted for making unusual vocalizations (Medical Mystery: Tourette's, 1981). Recently, it has been suggested that Leo Tolstoy's description of the character Nikolai in the novel *Anna Karenina* incorporates many of the features of Tourette's syndrome (Hurst & Hurst, 1994).

Mahmood Abdul-Rauf, an NBA starting professional basketball player, is considered quite competitive, despite continuing treatment for his Tourette's disorder. At various times in his career, his medication has had to be adjusted to control the symptomatology.

Tourette's disorder is characterized by the presence of shouted obscenities (coprolalia) or other vocal disturbances in about 60% of patients. Vocalizations include "sounds such as clicks, grunts, yelps, barks, sniffs, snorts, and coughs" (DSM-IV; APA, 1994, p. 102). Additional symptoms include mimicking the movements of others, compulsive touching of persons or objects, and periodic displays of jumping or aggressive behavior (Martin, 1977). Studies of sign language incorporated into tic behavior suggest that obscenities vocalized in Tourette's disorder are due to "a random generation of high-probability sequences of phonemes" (Lang, Consky, & Sandor, 1993). Compulsive thought patterns also occur in some patients. About 50% of children with Tourette's disorder suffer from diagnosable learning disabilities, which can be related to tic severity, use of medication, executive dysfunction (problems with higher mental reasoning), comorbidity with other problems affecting life in the classroom, or stigma associated with the disorder (Singer, Schuerholz, & Denckla, 1995).

Diagnostic Description

DSM-IV (APA, 1994, p. 103) specifies five diagnostic criteria for Tourette's disorder:

a. At least two motor and one or more vocal tics present some time during the illness, but these do not have to be seen concurrently.

b. The tics occur several times a day for more than one year without a tic-free period of more than 3 months.

c. The disturbance causes distress or impairment in life functioning.

d. Onset before 18 years of age.

e. Disturbance is not due to substance use effects or a general medical condition.

The "essential features" of Tourette's disorder are the tics listed in Criterion A. Tourette's disorder is distinguished from its closest competitor, chronic motor or vocal tic disorder, only by the requirement in Criterion A of multiple motor tics and at least one vocal tic. Thus, the underlying disease process in Tourette's may be seen as capturing a larger number of motor control circuits in the brain.

In ICD-10 (WHO, 1992) the disorder is called "combined vocal and multiple motor tic disorder (de la Tourette's syndrome)," but the features and description are essentially identical. Golden (1978) has suggested that Tourette's disorder and chronic multiple tics are probably representative of the same continuum and are not different and separable disorders.

In 50% of cases, Tourette's starts with a single tic of the eyes, head, or face and may include sniffling, hacking, throat clearing, tongue protrusion, snorting, barking, or other signs. Some patients present with two to eight of these signs initially, but all eventually have involuntary movements and some vocal tics (Shapiro & Shapiro, 1982). Symptoms appear between the ages of two and 15, typically around 7 or 8 years of age.

Many of the characteristics of the tics (e.g., anatomical location, severity, frequency) may change over time. This change may hamper a classification already rendered difficult because of its sole reliance on behavioral characteristics (Chafetz, 1986) without the insight provided by neurobiologically based taxa (systems of classification) for movement disorders (Golden, 1982; Yates, 1970). Instead of describing behavioral criteria, Ollendick (1989)

reviewed helpful functional criteria such as whether the tics are tonic (almost continuous and relatively long-lasting movement) or clonic (rapid movement with short duration), and the degree of complexity of the tic. DSM-IV (APA, 1994, p. 100) examples of complex tics include "touching, squatting, deep knee bends, retracing steps, and twirling when walking." With this greater complexity, the differential diagnosis between tics and stereotyped, rhythmic behaviors becomes more difficult. The criteria of voluntary control, occurrence during sleep, and the presence of muscle atrophy are helpful in distinguishing tics from other organic conditions such as spasms, choreas, and tremors of cerebellar origin (Yates, 1970).

Comings (1995) has asserted that the objective criteria found in DSM-III (APA, 1980) and DSM-III-R (APA, 1987) have been replaced by subjective criteria in DSM-IV (APA, 1994), particularly in the impairment/distress criterion, which, it is noted, may occur because of social stigma or anxiety about having tics in social situations. Freeman, Fast, and Kent (1995) also argue that the lack of definition of distress and impairment impeded research, and First, Frances, and Pincus (1995) suggest waiving this criterion in research settings.

The Tourette Syndrome Association has developed its own classification system (Tourette Syndrome Classification Study Group, 1993), based on the older DSM-III-R (APA, 1987) model but also including two categories, "definite" (tics observed by someone else) and "historical" (not reliably witnessed), for each of the diagnostic categories, as well as inclusive and exclusive features for both motor and vocal tics. This system has other categories of tic disorders not included in DSM-III-R. In an older psychiatric glossary (American Psychiatric Association, 1975), a tic is considered an expression of emotional conflict or the result of neurologic disease, but DSM-IV (APA, 1994) merely notes that emotional problems, along with obsessions and compulsions, are "commonly associated symptoms." Other complications that sometimes occur with Tourette's disorder include physical injury (e.g., retinal detachment from head banging), orthopedic problems, and skin problems. Several authors

(Golden, 1977a; Shapiro & Shapiro, 1982) have noted the difficulty with accurate diagnosis of this disorder and the frequent long delay between onset of the symptoms and effective diagnosis. Many patients suffer the affliction for 10 years or more before the illness is properly diagnosed (Medical Mystery: Tourette's, 1981); the throat-clearing grunts frequently seen with the disorder are often mistaken for allergic rhinitis. The presence of such noises in a child with facial tics increases diagnostic certainty.

Epidemiology

Using 1994 census estimates of 260 million individuals in the United States, current estimates of the number of people with Tourette's disorder range between 130,000 (0.05%) and 4.16 million individuals (1.6%) (Ollendick, 1989). Lucas and Rodin (1973) reported only seven cases in 1.5 million clinic visits, but Woodrow (1974) suggested prevalence rates from 4 per 1 million to a high of 1 per 1,000 in psychiatric patients. About 30% of children with either Tourette's disorder or transient tics had a family history of tics (Wilson, Garron, & Klawans, 1978). Golden (1978), as well as Messiha and Carlson (1983), have reported similar findings. Gender differences in this disorder usually favor males over females by about 3:1 to 3.6:1 (Corbett, Matthews, Connell, & Shapiro, 1969; Kelman, 1965). Some evidence favors a higher incidence rate in Jewish children (Shapiro & Shapiro, 1982).

Theoretical Models

Tourette's disorder is transmitted as an autosomal dominant gene (Eapen, Pauls, & Robertson, 1993), but linkage analyses suggest that abnormalities in dopamine receptors and catecholamine metabolizing enzymes, which are associated in successful symptom treatment, do not have a major effect on the etiology of the disease (Brett, Curtis, Robertson, & Gurling, 1995). In a recent twin study (Hyde, Fitzcharles, & Weinberger, 1993), 16 of 18 twin pairs with one tiqueur were concordant for Tourette's, and the earlier vocal tiqueur had a more severe course of the disease. The genes associated with expression of Tourette's disorder difficulties also result in a spectrum of neuropsychiatric problems that include obsessive-compulsive and schizoid behaviors (Comings, 1994).

Although the evidence for a genetic model in Tourette's disorder is clear, there continues to be evidence favoring environmental influence. The diathesis-stress model proposed by Ascher (1948) suggests that the hereditary disposition and an emotional stressor must be present to manifest the disorder. Stressors include removal of teeth, tonsillectomy, birth of siblings, start of school, automobile accidents, parental illness, parental quarreling, or separation from parents; diseases considered of etiological importance include mumps, measles, chicken pox, whooping cough, scarlet fever, encephalopathy, and cholera (Matthews, Leibowitz, & Matthews, 1992). Tic manifestation varies in response to different environmental conditions that include both augmenting and decreasing factors (Silva, Munoz, Barickman, & Friedhoff, 1995). Factors associated with decreased symptomatology include sleeping, talking to friends, and reading for pleasure, while augmenting factors include feeling anxious or upset, experiencing emotional trauma, watching TV, being alone, and attending social gatherings.

That tic behavior is responsive to environmental stimuli continues to fuel the many behavioral theories of tic behavior. Learning theories emphasize either the operant model, in which tics produce contingencies that are reinforcing, or the respondent model, in which tics are regarded as learned habits that have attained peak behavioral strength (Ollendick, 1989). With the former model, treatments focus on manipulating environmental stimuli that may serve as reinforcers or punishers, while treatments based on the second model focus on the behavior itself.

Older psychoanalytic theory suggests that the various tics and explosive verbalizations represent symbolic expressions of repressed emotional states (Ascher, 1948). Although these emotional states are presently conceptualized as being "augmenting" or "precipitating," there is the occasional misdiagnosis based upon circular analytic reasoning. For example, Comings and Comings (1993) reported on the case of a 7-year-old boy with Tourette's disorder who was diagnosed mistakenly as having been sexually abused by his father.

Assessment

Behavioral observation using objective time-sampling procedures by the examiner, an informant in the tiqueur's natural environment (home or school), or self-monitoring are becoming increasingly popular (Ollendick, 1989). The self-monitoring instruments may be especially valuable as they increase the tiqueur's awareness of the tics, making them vulnerable to therapeutic change.

The Motor Tic, Obsession and Compulsion, and Vocal Tic Evaluation Survey (MOVES) is a self-report scale for assessing Tourette symptoms that can be quickly and easily completed by adults or children (Gaffney, Sieg, & Hellings, 1994). MOVES has five subscales: Motor Tics, Vocal Tics, Obsessions, Compulsions, and Associated Symptoms, and these correlate significantly with independent examiner-rated scales that include the Yale Tourette's Syndrome Global Severity Scale, Shapiro Tourette Clinical Rating Scale, and other scales for obsessive and compulsive symptoms. Another self-report instrument is the Tourette's Syndrome Questionnaire. Clinician methods used to assist in differential diagnosis include flowcharts and a clinical rating scale, the Tourette's Syndrome Global Scale (Ollendick, 1989).

A variety of measures have been found to be reliable and valid in assessing the severity of Tourette's disorder. Walkup, Rosenberg, Brown, and Singer (1992) evaluated four scales, the Hopkins Motor and Vocal Tic Scale, the Tourette's Syndrome Severity Scale, the Tourette's Syndrome-Clinical Global Impression Scale, and the Yale Global Tic Severity Scale. Interjudge reliability and validity was obtained across three judges over 20 patients, and the results indicated that these measures were essentially equally effective in rating overall severity and in their interjudge reliability.

In addition to these assessment procedures, an examination should include EEG and other physiological studies, because Lucas and Rodin (1973) found that more than half of Tourette's patients show abnormal patterns that include bilateral sharp waves, diffused background disorganization, and, less frequently, unilateral temporal shifts and sharp waves. Iakupova, Smirnov, Kozlova, and Gobachevskaia (1993–1994) showed both EEG abnormalities and autonomic dysregulation in Tourette's patients. Neuropsychological examination also shows cerebral abnormalities, though these are not clearly localized (Thompson & Thelen, 1986). The corpus callosum of Tourette's patients may also be somewhat smaller than same-age-and-sex peers, as shown on MRI imaging (Peterson, Leckman, Duncan, & Wetzles, 1994). Children with Tourette's may also have learning difficulties related to executive dysfunction associated with the disease process, with coexisting attentional problems, or with the use of tic-suppressing medication (Singer et al., 1995).

Treatment

Biological

Because of the effectiveness of low doses of antipsychotic agents, especially haloperidol, in treating Tourette's and other tic disorders (Gelenberg, Bassuk, & Schoonover, 1991), interest in both causative factors and treatment has centered on dopaminergic agents. In a British kindred study, none of the markers for dopamine receptor gene loci, or for catecholamine synthetic enzymes, showed any relationship to the etiology of Tourette's disorder (Brett et al., 1995). In a related study, the serotonin1A receptor and tryptophan oxygenase genes were excluded from causing susceptibility to Tourette's and chronic multiple tics (Brett, Curtis, Robertson, & Gurling, 1995). Although many of these related receptors can be excluded as causative agents, they are clearly affected in dopamine-blocking studies with drugs effective in treating Tourette's, even when dopamine receptor availability is not shown to be abnormal (George, Robertson, Costa, & Ell, 1994). The use of clonidine has proven effective in some children with Tourette's, as have other drugs that include clonazepam, s-blockers, desipramine, and calcium-channel blockers (Gelenberg et al., 1991). Other treatments that have been reported as effective include marijuana (Hemming & Yellowlees, 1993) and the use of weak electromagnetic fields (Sandyk, 1995).

Although clearly a "last resort" method, neurosurgical intervention has been used in the treatment of Tourette's disorder. Rauch, Baer, Cosgrove, and Jenike (1995) reviewed 36 cases with a variety of operational sites and noted that there was no evidence that any procedure was superior to all others, with the exception that cingulotomy seemed to be ineffective in alleviating tics. These authors present the theoretical rationale for such operations. Recommendations for future experimental neurosurgery are also given.

Psychological

With only slight disagreement in the literature, "negative" or "massed practice" techniques have been used with success (Lahey, McNees, & McNees, 1973; Ollendick, 1989; Varni, Boyd, & Cataldo, 1978). These techniques involve training subjects to repeat the obscenities or behavioral tics until they could no longer do so. Systematic desensitization in combination with other behavioral treatments has also been helpful in reducing tic behavior (O'Brien & Brennan, 1979). Removing the opportunity to obtain reinforcement, such as in a timeout procedure, has produced striking results in the treatment of coprolalia (Lahey et al., 1973).

Psychoanalytic treatments, although of historical interest, have produced minimal success. These treatments usually attempt to provide insight into the instinctual impulses thought to be at the root of a tiqueur's problems. With this insight, ticquers are supposed to channel these impulses into more acceptable realms (Ollendick, 1989). Other psychotherapies that operate at a general level of insight and do not focus on specific behaviors, environmental stimuli, or other related environmental factors also have not met with much success (Ollendick, 1989). The idea that ticquers suffer from repressed emotions as the cause of their tic behaviors has led to allied treatments such as hypnotherapy (Culbertson, 1989), sleep therapy, insulin coma, carbon dioxide inhalation, and electroconvulsive therapy, which have met with variable success (Matthews et al., 1992).

Social/Interpersonal

The finding, by Silva et al. (1995), that environmental factors play a part in the severity of tic behavior supports the continued use of combined social/behavioral techniques in the treatment of Tourette's disorder. In particular, certain environmental factors may serve to reinforce tic behaviors, thus strengthening and helping to maintain them. Miller (1970) eliminated vocal and facial tics in a 5-year-old boy by utilizing the reinforcement of incompatible behaviors in the classroom and at home, with the boy's parents and school teachers as therapists. The removal of parental attention, a powerful reinforcer of many pathological behaviors, has been a helpful treatment in eliminating tics.

CHRONIC MOTOR OR VOCAL TIC DISORDER

Diagnostic Description

In the category "Chronic Motor or Vocal Tic Disorder," DSM-IV (1994, p. 104) diagnostic criteria include:

a. Both multiple motor tics and one or more vocal tics have been present at some time during the disorder (but not necessarily concurrently).

b. The tics occur many times per day (often in clusters), nearly every day, or they occur intermittently throughout a period of more than 1 year, in which there is never a tic-free period of more than 3 consecutive months.

c. There is significant impairment in social, occupational or other areas of functioning or marked personal distress.

d. Onset is prior to age 18 years.

e. The disorder is not due to a general medical condition or the direct physical effect of a substance.

f. Criteria have never been met for Tourette's disorder.

In ICD-10 (1992), this disorder has the same name, with motor or vocal tics (but not both). The tics may be either single or multiple (but usually multiple) and last for more than a year.

The critical feature in the differential diagnosis of this disorder is the presence at any one time of either motor tics or vocal tics, but not both. A diagnosis of Tourette's disorder, by contrast, requires the existence of both multiple motor tics and one or more vocal tics at the same time.

Tics must be differentiated from other movement disorders such as dyskinesia, spasms, and chorea. Tics are most frequently confused with chorea, although patients with tics usually have a longer asymptomatic period between movements and always perform the movements in the same stereotyped manner. Yates (1970) provided classic but still useful criteria for making differential diagnosis of tics from organic conditions in tabular form. Stereotyped movements or habits, although rhythmic, are viewed as intentional behaviors, as are compulsions (Golden & Hood, 1982). These stereotypic movement behaviors are covered later in the chapter.

Epidemiology

Although incidence rates vary, Head and her associates (Head & Sallee, 1994; Head, Sallee, & Shannon, 1993) indicate that tics are the most common movement disorder of childhood. Rates from 1% to 14% of children have been cited (Achenbach & Edelbrock, 1983; Azrin & Nunn, 1977; Zausmer & Dewey, 1987). Most cases of motor tics and Tourette's have their onset in children from 7 to 10 years of age, a time span originally described by Gilles de la Tourette (Corbett et al., 1969; Holvey & Talbott, 1972). Comings and Comings (1985) noted that 20% of their sample had an onset before kindergarten, in marked contrast to Werry, Carlielle, and Fitzpatrick (1983), who reported that tics do not seem to occur in children under age five. The male:female ratio is approximately 3:1 (Zahner, Clubb, Leckman, & Pauls, 1988). There may be a higher incidence among children of Jewish and other eastern European ancestry (Lucas & Rodin, 1973; Shapiro & Shapiro, 1982), although some research (Comings & Comings, 1985) has disputed the higher rate in Jewish children.

Retrospective studies (Corbett et al., 1969; Matthews & Barabas, 1985) suggest spontaneous recovery within 1 month to over a year, with a recovery rate of at least 50% after 2 to 15 years. However, some evidence exists that tics may recur in later adult life and that stress may precipitate a relapse (Klawans & Barr, 1985).

The child may have the ability to suppress the tic for a few minutes or even a few hours; thus, variability of symptoms can be expected over time. While the most common form of tic appears to be the eye blink or other facial tic, the entire head or the torso may be involved. Multiple tics may occur sequentially, simultaneously, or randomly. Tics increase during stress and markedly diminish in sleep. In some instances, the individual is aware of the mannerism, but in most cases it is automatic and unconscious (Golden, 1987; Golden & Hood, 1982; Jankovic & Fahn, 1986; Valente & Valente, 1983; Woody & Laney, 1986).

Tics do not usually occur by themselves in any one patient. In many cases, additional emotional or behavioral difficulties also exist. Frequently cited coexisting disorders include obsessive-compulsive disorders, reported in 10–40% of cases (Head, Sallee, & Shannon, 1993; Towbin, 1996); attention-deficit/hyperactivity disorder, with a suggested comorbidity rate of approximately 25% (Caine et al., 1988; Head, Salee, & Shannon, 1993; Jagger, Proshoff, Cohen, Kidd, Carbonari, & John, 1982); and mood, anxiety, conduct, and oppositional disorders (Hynd & Hooper, 1992).

Other causes and conditions have been less well associated with tics. Several authors have noted some relationship to learning disabilities (Clementz, Lee, & Barclay, 1988; Lerer, 1987) or other psychological factors (Keshavan, 1988; Tibbetts, 1981), including auditory hallucinatory experiences (Kerbeshian & Burd, 1985) or posttraumatic stress (Fahn, 1982; Kivalo, 1979; Zikis, 1983). Self-injurious behaviors (discussed in the Stereotypic Movement Disorder section of this chapter) have also been associated with the presence of tic disorders (Head & Sallee, 1994).

Theoretical Models

Genetic or other familial factors may play a role in the onset of tics, as a disproportionate number of children with tics have a close relative with one or more tics (Clementz et al., 1988; Golden, 1983; Zausmer & Dewey, 1987). Abe and Oda (1978, 1980) found that children of parents who had had themselves had tics in childhood had an increased prevalence rate of 20–25% compared to 10% in controls. A family history of tics was found in about 10–30% of all cases. Price, Leckman, Pauls, Cohen, and Kidd (1986), as well as Shapiro and Shapiro (1981b), have reported significant positive concordance rates in identical twins and negative concordance rates in fraternal twins.

Soft neurological signs have been reported in 87% of children studied, suggesting a single autosomal dominant genetic transmission (Elston, Granje, & Lees, 1989; Golden, 1977b). Abnormality of CNS dopamine metabolism as a factor in the development of tics has been reported (Golden, 1983). More specifically, tics are probably due to excessively high levels of dopamine activity. Evidence linking tic disorders to dopamine activity includes findings that drugs that increase dopamine activity exacerbate tics and drugs that reduce dopamine activity (neuroleptics such as haloperidol) can be effective in treating tic disorders (Gittelman & Kanner, 1986; Zamula, 1988). As further support for the dopamine hypothesis, numerous authors (Burns, 1980; Burd, Kerbeshian, Fisher,

& Gascon-Generoso, 1986; Chandler, Barnhill, Gualtieri, & Patterson, 1989; Golden, 1983; Shapiro & Shapiro, 1981a) have noted that tics may be caused or exacerbated by anticonvulsant or stimulant medications and may not remit with discontinuation of that treatment.

Psychodynamic and psychoanalytic theories stress that tics represent repressed feelings of conflicts expressed in a symbolic manner (Cavernar, Spaulding, & Sullivan, 1979; Zivkovic, 1977). As such, they are often viewed as hysterical reactions in which the tics may represent a symbolic attempt to ward off danger (e.g., blinking the eye or repeatedly turning the head) or as a manifestation of angry feelings, revealed by tics that resemble a hitting motion.

Mahler (1949) presents perhaps the classic formulation based on psychodynamic theory. She and other authors suggested that tics serve many different functions that fall within various categories. One type, systematic tics (such as transient tics), indicates tension phenomena; an example is the eye twitches that might be experienced under strong emotional stress. Second, tics may be a sign of primarily reactive behavior disorders on the verge of internalization. For example, the tic is an indicator of a reaction to what was originally a situational stressor (in the same way that anger might be a reaction to being sexually abused). However, such responses (anger or tic) begin to become internalized (incorporated) into the child's view of self. The end result is that the tic becomes part of the child's body-self image. A third category is the tic as a symptom or symptom substitute of neurosis or psychosis. That is, the tic either serves as an indicator of underlying psychopathology or is the manifestation of an internal psychic conflict that in other children would be expressed in a variety of psychological disorders such as depression, anxiety, or psychosis. Mahler (1949) also said that, in some cases, the unconscious fantasies that produce the tics concern movement or paralysis. Cavernar et al. (1979) cited unresolved oedipal conflicts as the etiology of such disorders. Silber (1981) discussed the case of a patient with a tic and a recurrent dream stimulated by observation of the primal scene. Missildine (1964), as well as Fisher, Kerbeshian, and Burd (1986), proposed birth order as a major factor. Gerard (1946) said that tics are an ego defense, with the tic serving as a partial substitute for the impulsive expression.

Behavioral models may be based on respondent or operant techniques. Early models emphasized a drive-reducing conditioned response. Interventions focused on building an incompatible habit of not performing the tic. Massed or negative practice is most often used to accomplish this goal (Kaliappan & Murphy, 1982; Teichman & Eliahu, 1986). The patient performs the unwanted behavior until fatigue occurs. It is assumed that the fatigue state is aversive and that responses incompatible with the tic are reinforced during the rest period by the avoidance of fatigue.

Habit reversal was originally described by Azrin and Nunn (1973) and is based on the assumption that tic-like disturbances begin as reactions to trauma or stress. The tics persist because of response chaining, lack of interpersonal awareness of each tic, and excessive practice and social tolerance for the tic. The intervention, to be described under treatment later in the chapter, aims at strengthening incompatible responses by having the patient practice a behavior pattern that is opposite the tic, as well as eliminating any social reinforcement from attention.

Behavioral and cognitive models, such as that presented by Bandura (1969), suggest that unwitting reinforcement by increased attention or stress by significant others may serve to maintain the ticing behavior. Other authors (Bachman, 1972; Skinner, 1953) suggest that tics begin as purposeful movements in response to specific stimuli, but, eventually, similar movements are carried out automatically in a purposeless fashion. For example, a neck tic may have its origin in a collar that was too tight or otherwise annoying.

Social/interpersonal or environmental models place emphasis on the role of social interaction, interpersonal stress, or social modeling as primary causative agents. For example, tics are sometimes acquired by imitating other tiqueurs. Other interpersonal factors include a background history of emotional tension (Bakwin & Bakwin, 1972); serious home conflicts or family disruption (Miller, 1970; Ollendick, 1981); and psychiatrically ill parents (Bruch & Thum, 1968). In a description of "pseudotics" in two patients with Tourette's syndrome, Dooley, Stokes, and Gordon (1994) noted that these tics were linked to sexual abuse in one case and to academic difficulties in the other. Resolution of these situations resulted in the elimination of the tics, although both patients still had their Tourette's symptoms.

Negishi (1983) noted a relationship between family dynamics and onset of tics. However, Abe and Oda (1980) found no more psychological symptoms in the mothers of 3-year-old tiquers (who themselves had tics in childhood) than in a control sample of 1,000 mothers.

Assessment

The assessment of tics and the differential diagnosis especially of more complex motor tics may be difficult. Family history should be examined. A current medical examination should be obtained. A clinical interview with attention to onset of symptoms and associated behavioral problems is critical. The use of parental rating scales can be used to measure both the range of symptoms and their severity. Behavioral observations, if possible in a variety of situations (classroom, at play, in social interaction) are also of assistance. Personality testing may help to determine if the tic disorder is the primary behavior problem or is secondary to other psychological disturbances, such as the frequently associated disorders of attention-deficit/hyperactivity disorder or obsessive-compulsive disorder mentioned earlier. Each of these areas of assessment is discussed in greater detail later in this section.

Clinical assessment should focus on the historical progression of the tic symptoms. Jagger et al., (1982) postulated a rostral-caudal progression in the manifestation of motor tics, with tics of the face, head, and shoulders occurring well before motor tics of the extremities and torso. In general, with Tourette's disorder, onset of phonic (vocal) tics typically occurs after the onset of motor tics, with fewer than 5% of patients showing only phonic tics (Hynd & Hooper, 1982). Thus, a parental report of a long history of only motor tics in the absence of any later development of phonic symptoms may facilitate making a diagnosis of chronic tic disorder (or, to a lesser degree, transient tic disorder or tic, NOS disorder), rather than Tourette's.

In making a differential diagnosis between chronic tics and Tourette's disorder, the pattern of onset of symptoms as well as the severity of symptoms needs to be assessed. Since Tourette's requires the presence of both motor and vocal tics, use of the Motor Tic, Obsession and Compulsion, and Vocal Tic Evaluation Survey (MOVE) which has scales for both motor and vocal tics, will help with diagnosis (the survey is described in the Tourette's section in this chapter).

In the clinical assessment of tics, the presence or absence of certain signs for the various tic disorders is necessary, but some assessment of the severity (frequency or variety) of symptoms will also facilitate understanding and designing treatment interventions. A number of different parental, self-report, and clinician/observer rating scales, such as the Hopkins Motor and Vocal Tic Scale, Tourette Syndrome Symptom List, Tourette Syndrome Questionnaire, Tourette Syndrome Global Scale, Tourette Syndrome Severity Scale, and Yale Global Tic Severity Scale (Leckman & Cohen, 1988; Leckman, Towbin, Ort, & Cohen, 1988; Walkup, Rosenberg, Brown, & Singer, 1992) will facilitate this component of the assessment.

As an example of such measures, the Tourette's Syndrome Global Scale (Harcherik, Leckman, Detlor, & Cohen, 1984) consists of two major domains: a motor and phonic tic domain and a social functioning domain. In the first domain, tics are subdivided into the categories of simple motor, complex motor, simple vocal, and complex vocal tasks. Time-sampling techniques are used to obtain measures of frequency, complexity, and disruption of activities. In the social-functioning domain, items related to motor restlessness, behavior problems, and level of daily functioning (school or occupation) are assessed. In a study comparing four of these measures, Walkup et al. (1992) reported that each one was equally effective in determining overall severity, and all four had good inter-rater reliability.

Personality assessment also can be helpful in detecting the presence of other psychological problems. One such widely used instrument is the Personality Inventory for Children (PIC), a parent-informant measure of the child's cognitive, emotional, and behavioral status. This instrument consists of 420 true-false questions, with 16 standard profile scales and four more generalized factor scales (Wirt, Lachar, Klinedinst, & Seat, 1984). Another widely used series of personality assessment instruments is the parent, teacher, and youth versions of the Child Behavior Checklist (CBCL). All versions of the CBCL are well validated and have been used extensively in assessing the social and behavioral functioning of children (Achenbach, 1991a, 1991b, 1991c).

Rosenberg, Brown, and Singer (1995) examined the incidence of behavioral symptoms in children with tic disorders using the Child Behavior Problem Checklist and a motor and verbal tic severity measure. They noted a complex range of factors that influenced the degree of behavioral disturbance exhibited by tic disorder patients. Behavior problems were not directly related to age. There was a significant difference in symptoms between those patients who were on medication and those who were not, suggesting that medication needs to be taken into account when doing research in this area. In patients not on medication, there was a significant positive correlation between behavioral problem frequency and tic severity that was not seen in a group of patients on medication. These authors also noted that the range of coping skills was highly variable. There were patients with severe tics who apparently were not susceptible to developing behavioral problems; the authors called these "resilient." Patients who had mild tics and who developed much more severe behavioral problems were referred to as "vulnerable."

The existence of other disorders, either as primary or secondary, may or may not be helpful with diagnosis. For example, Tourette's patients have frequently been reported to have significantly higher rates of simple phobia and obsessive-compulsive disorder than do tic disorder patients (Head, Sallee, & Shannon, 1993).

Some authors have indicated that tic disorders and Tourette's occur frequently in children with a primary diagnosis of obsessive-compulsive disorder (Hynd & Hooper, 1992; Swedo & Leonard, 1994). However, Shapiro and Shapiro (1992), in a methodological review of 21 articles, discussed problems with many of these studies, based on issues such as adequacy of the clinical and control samples, definitions, and diagnostic procedures. While noting the considerable clinical indications for such an association, these authors concluded that the evidence from the studies reviewed does not adequately support such an association.

Treatment

Although the various models for treatment are presented separately, all of the tic disorders require a careful review of associated problems. Treatment should always include education of the child, family, and school personnel with regard to the natural history and behavioral manifestation of these disorders, as well as the integration of treatment modalities (Scahill, Ort, & Hardin, 1993).

Biological

Several authors have recently reviewed psychotropic medications, especially neuroleptics (Shapiro & Shapiro, 1996; Towbin & Cohen, 1996) and reported a 50–90% reduction in the frequency of ticing with a variety of medications. Reductions of 70–85% in tiqueurs with haloperidol has been reported by several authors (Golden & Hood, 1982; Shapiro & Shapiro, 1996) although this medication is associated with a high incidence of side effects. Regardless, most if not all, of the symptoms

seen in chronic tics and Tourette's are suppressed with this drug, and, over time, smaller doses may be required to obtain the same clinical results (Cohen, Riddle, & Leckman, 1992).

Riddle, Hardin, Cho, Woolston, and Leckman (1988) used desipramine, while Goetz, Tanner, and Klavan (1984) successfully treated 21 patients who were intolerant of haloperidol with fluphenazine hydrochloride. Eggers, Rothenberger, and Berghause (1988) used tiapride and noted positive therapeutic action with few side effects. Polak, Molcan, and Dimova (1985), in a study of 30 children, found that penfluridol was somewhat superior to haloperidol, but both were more effective than thioridazine. Leung and Fagan (1989) say that drugs should not be used unless the tic is seriously disabling, due to drugs' possible risks and lack of curative value. Shapiro, Shapiro, and Fulop (1987) reviewed the use of pimozide in tics. Troung, Bressman, Shale, and Fahn (1988) suggest the use of clonazepam, to be combined later with clonidine, followed by the use of haloperidol only if these other medications and combinations fail. This recommendation was made because of the risk of tardive dyskinesia with haloperidol. Other drugs used to decrease tics have included chlorpromazine, clonazepam, and clonidine (Troung et al., 1988).

Psychological

A variety of behavioral techniques have been successfully employed in reducing or eliminating tics (Azrin & Peterson, 1989). A recent review by Peterson, Campise, and Azrin (1994) of approximately 350 articles on tics and habit disturbances indicated that these disorders could be effectively controlled by behavioral and pharmacological methods.

Carr (1995) presented a table defining the competing responses of various types of tics that have been reported in the literature from 1973 to 1990. He also included a brief history of the competing response practice treatment, as well as a basic explanation of the procedure. Other behavioral techniques that have been effective include operant conditioning (Schulman, 1974); negative or massed practice (Kaliappan & Murphy, 1982; Teichman & Eliahu, 1986); self-monitoring (Carr, 1995; Ollendick, 1981); reciprocal inhibition techniques by autogenic training (Uchiyama, 1976); and habit reversal (Azrin & Nunn, 1973).

Perhaps the most widely used of the behavioral techniques is habit reversal. In their original study, Azrin and Nunn (1973) presented data on 12 patients with various tic-like symptoms. Marked decreases in the targeted behaviors occurred within one day, with an average percentage reduction below the base rate of 95%, going to 99% after 3 weeks. Self-report follow-up at 5 months indicated continued absence or reduction in targeted behaviors. As an example of this technique, if a client had a shoulder tic, treatment would consist of having the client press the muscles to hold the shoulder down, followed by relaxation of the muscles. For any tic, the initial focus would be on practicing movements that provide muscular opposition to the tic. In addition to the motor component, Azrin and Nunn (1973) would increase awareness of each tic by having the client carry a counter to record each occurrence of the tic.

A recent article by Woods and Miltenberger (1995) reviews the research on habit reversal and notes that use of these methods results in rapid and long-lasting treatment. Further component analysis identified the use of awareness training to help the patient identify the occurrence of the tic and the use of a competing response as the two primary factors in treatment effectiveness. Several variations on this method have been used, including self-monitoring, awareness training, competing response practice, and social support procedures using family members (Finney, Rapoff, Hall, & Christophersen, 1983; Miltenberger, Fuqua, & McKinley, 1985; Pray, Kramer, & Lindskog, 1986; Zikis, 1983a).

Self-monitoring procedures have been observed to be tic-inhibiting, with rates of 50–100% reduction and the occurrence of long-lasting remission of symptoms (Ollendick, 1981). As an example of such a behavioral intervention, Ollendick (1981) used a multiple baseline design in working with an 11-year-old boy with a chronic motor tic of the eye. A baseline was obtained using 20-minute time samples over a period of 5 days, by both the patient's mother and his teacher. The patient was then instructed in the use of a self-monitoring procedure in which he used a wrist counter to record the frequency of tics during specified time periods for an additional 5 days. Finally, the patient was instructed in a competing response technique, in which he was taught to tense the muscle groups that would result in a competing response to the tic. The results indicated that the use of the self-monitoring technique reduced the frequency of tics by approximately 50% following the initial self-monitoring. With the introduction of the competing response technique, the frequency of the tic was reduced to a near-zero level, with that level maintained on a 1-year follow-up.

Kaliappan and Murphy (1982) used negative or massed practice techniques to rapidly reduce the rate of tics. Pinkerton, Hughes, and Wenrich (1982) reviewed studies on operant techniques in which combination methods were used. One such technique combined an aversive stimulus (exposure to smelling salts) with a negative or massed practice technique. The combination was successful in reducing the frequency of eye-blink tics that had occurred over 4 years in a patient after only one 80-minute treatment session.

Biofeedback, desensitization, and other relaxation and feedback methods have also been used successfully (Mishra, 1985; Poth & Barnett, 1983; Tansey, 1986). The eye-squinting tic of a 9-year-old girl was initially reduced 54% by the use of facial relaxation techniques. The child was then taught to engage in voluntary, low-frequency blinking at home contingent on the occurrence of the tic. Voluntary blinking was incompatible with eye squinting, and the treatment method also utilized the blinking as a response-cost method. Results indicated that the frequency of the tic decreased to zero during the first 6 weeks of treatment and was not present on a 2-year follow-up (Azrin & Peterson, 1989).

Aversive techniques have included the use of electric shock, avoidance of a loud noise, incompatible responses, and response cost (Singh, 1981). Although effective, such methods should be used only after all other positive procedures have been attempted.

Tension reduction techniques were used by Evers and Van de Wetering (1994). They consider the motor tics to be a tension-reducing response to a specific sensory stimulus. Once the sensory stimulus has been identified, the patient learns a competing alternative response to the motor tic that also reduces the sensory stimulus. Stress reduction techniques were also used in this intervention.

Social/Interpersonal

Schulman (1974) successfully removed multiple tics by reducing parental attention. Levine and Ramirez (1989) describe a home-based treatment program of contingent negative practice. This model, in use since 1973, focuses on the parents as primary change agents. It has been successful in children with motor movement disorders, tics, and stuttering.

Matesevac (1991, 1993) noted in her description of the treatment of impulse disorders, including tics, that these disorders and their treatment are impacted by developmental issues and associated interpersonal problems. She suggests that psychotherapy is not appropriate for the direct treatment of Tourette's or chronic tics but that it can be used to help with the interpersonal consequences of such disorders. She also points out some of the limitations in using only single focused interventions (medication only, behavioral only) from a more global biopsychosocial perspective.

TRANSIENT TIC DISORDER

Diagnostic Description

The primary feature of "transient tic disorder" is its temporary nature. DSM-IV (APA, 1994, p. 105) criteria are essentially:

a. Single or multiple motor and/or vocal tics.

b. The tics occur several times a day, most days for at least 4 weeks, but no longer than 12 consecutive months.

c. The tic causes marked distress or significant impairment in social, occupational or other functioning.

d. Onset is prior to 18 years of age.

e. The tic is not due to direct effects of a substance or medical condition.

f. Criteria have never been met for Tourette's or Chronic Motor or Vocal Tic.

Other features of this disorder are the same as Tourette's, but the severity of impairment and the magnitude of the symptoms are usually much less. The diagnostic criteria have changed slightly from DSM-III-R (APA, 1987) in that the length of time the tic must have been present has increased from 2 weeks to 4 weeks.

In ICD-10 (WHO, 1992), "transient tic disorder" has to meet the general diagnostic criteria for a tic disorder, but the tics do not persist for longer than 12 months.

Epidemiology

Few data are available just on the subclassification of transient tics. Corbett et al. (1969) noted a mean age of onset of all types of tics at about 7 years. Historically, there may be some changes in the presentation of this disorder, as ICD-10 (1992) indicates that this is the most common tic and is most frequent about the age of 4 or 5 years. These tics usually take the form of eye blinking, facial grimacing, or head jerking. In some cases, the tics occur as a single episode, but in other cases there are remissions and relapses over a period of months. The frequency and/or initial symptoms of tic disorders, especially with transient tics, appears to increase with stressful times, such as starting school or the onset of puberty. Eapen, Srinath, and Devi (1989) reported the results from India of 30 children, ages 3 to 16, seen in a child guidance center and diagnosed with tic disorders. They noted that 15 (half the children) had transient tic disorder, 10 had chronic tic disorder, and the remaining 5 had Tourette's syndrome. These authors also reported that 30% of children in this sample had other associated psychiatric problems. Genetics may play a role, as about 10% of all cases have a family history of tics (Corbett et al., 1969). Malatesta (1990) noted the presence of six behavioral and emotional problems in addition to the transient tic disorder for which her 9-year-old patient was referred.

Theoretical Models

All of the biological, psychological, and psychosocial models mentioned previously under the other sections on tic disorders apply to this subclassification.

As further support for a biological basis, Wilson et al. (1978) reported that 30% of children with either Tourette's or transient tics had a family history of tics. Unfortunately, those data are not broken out by the type of tic to determine if a family history is more critical in Tourette's or transient tic disorder.

Eapen et al. (1989), in their report on a child guidance center in India, found that psychosocial stressors were present in 36.6% of children with various types of tics. Malatesta (1990) cited psychosocial factors, especially hypersensitivity to evaluation, as critical in the formulation of a case study of a 9-year-old who had an increased frequency of tics in the presence of his father.

Assessment

The assessment of transient tics, with emphasis on the length of time symptoms have been present, is essentially the same as outlined above in the Tourette's and chronic tic sections. Background history, clinical interview, parental reports, behavioral observations, rating scales, and personality assessment are all elements that should be included. Ollendick and Ollendick (1990) discussed the criteria for transient tic disorder and advocated the use of the Tourette Syndrome Global Scale (TSGS) in the behavioral assessment of this disorder.

Malatesta (1990) describes a case of behavioral assessment of a 9-year-old with transient tics that emphasizes the interconnectedness of behavioral and social interactions in the etiology of tics. The patient had several other physical, emotional, and behavioral problems, in addition to his motor tic. In this case, the frequency of transient tics appeared to be etiologically related to his social interaction with his father. Monitoring of EMG and tic rates in play situations while the child was being watched by one of his parents or another observer was obtained. The results indicated that the highest rates of EMG and frequency of tics occurred when the child was observed by his father, with the lowest rates being obtained when the child knew he was being observed by his mother.

Treatment

The biological, psychological, and social/interpersonal intervention methods previously described in other sections of this chapter have similar applications to transient tics. Eapen et al. (1989) reported that the children with transient tic disorder had a better outcome using parental counseling and psychotherapy than those with other types of tics.

TIC DISORDER, NOT OTHERWISE SPECIFIED
Diagnostic Description

This category is for disorders that do not meet DSM-IV (APA, 1994, p. 105) criteria for a specific tic disorder, such as tics that lasting less than 4 weeks or tics with onset after age 18. In actual clinical use, this category in the DSM-IV (APA, 1994) appears to be used primarily for tics with onset in adulthood. In ICD-10 (WHO, 1992), the similar categories are "other tic disorders" and "tic disorder, unspecified." The latter is a nonrecommended residual category for a disorder that fulfills the general criteria for a tic disorder but in which the specific subcategory cannot specified or in which the features do not meet the criteria for any other tic disorders.

To return to the DSM-IV (APA, 1994) adult use of these criteria, for example, Alberca and Ochoa (1994) describe a cluster tic syndrome consisting of pain attacks and trigeminal neuralgia, primarily in individuals between the ages of 20 and 70. They report on 27 previous cases in the literature and 10 new cases. Tarlow (1989), in his handbook on behavioral treatment for adult medical disorders, presents chapters on both tic disorders and Tourette's. He describes assessment strategies and treatment methods.

Epidemiology

No systematic data appear to be available on incidence rates for this subclassification of tics.

Theoretical Models

The biological, psychological, and social/interpersonal models mentioned previously in the other sections of this chapter apply to this subclassification. In a study involving adults, Evers and Van de Wetering (1994) consider motor tics to be tension-reducing responses to a specific sensory stimulus. Thus, stress factors and learning principles are important to their formulation.

Assessment

The assessment process for this disorder is essentially the same as outlined in the Tourette's and chronic tic sections. Additional clinical interview and personality assessment might be used to obtain an especially detailed history of any possible toxic exposure, drug or medication usage, including over-the-counter medications, especially in those patients with onset of symptoms of less than 4 weeks' duration. Drug and other conditions that may producing tic-like symptoms with onset in adults are stimulants and excessive caffeine ingestion.

Treatment

The variety of biological, psychological, and interpersonal intervention methods previously described in this chapter have applications to these tics. Behavioral techniques appear to be especially effective with these disorders. Fuata and Griffiths (1992) treated a vocal tic in a 28-year-old, using a modification of the habit-reversal technique that included a cognitive component. The therapy reduced the tic and was still effective at a 6-month follow-up.

Evers and Van de Wetering (1994) used their tension-reduction model in treating two adults, ages 40 and 35. The patients learned socially acceptable alternative responses for their tics, focused on the specific sensory stimulus identified during behavioral assessment. Behavioral techniques were also used to reduce stress, which was secondarily associated with the tics.

Kaplan (1991) used muscle tension and relaxation exercises in combination with EMG biofeedback to markedly reduce the frequency of facial tics in a 47-year-old. The patient practiced tensing and relaxing while observing EMG feedback, as well as practicing the technique outside the therapy session. From a base rate of 122 tics in 5 minutes, the technique reduced tics to 29 in the same time.

COMMENTS

The changing criteria for the tic disorders over the various diagnostic revisions and different organization versions of diagnostic classifications have not seemed to reduce the debate over the defining characteristics of these disorders. Several authors have suggested that conclusive evidence is lacking as to whether the classifications for the tic disorders represent distinct problems, separate clinical entities, or a continuum of severity of the same problem (DSM-III-R; APA, 1987; Eapen, & Robertson, 1994; Golden, 1990).

Treatment for Tourette's and other tic disorders will also benefit from better behavioral classificatory schemes (Chafetz, 1986) in which the behaviors are regarded as part of an underlying regulatory process that is dysfunctional in some way. This approach may help to refine the behavioral foci of treatment, as well as define the ancillary behavioral and psychological problems that may respond to other therapies. As the development of these classificatory schemes proceeds, the relationship of Tourette's to other tic disorders may become clearer.

As receptor and other molecular technologies improve, investigations into the etiology of Tourette's disorder should yield more fruit. In particular, dopaminergic and other treatments that are now partially effective will become more focused on the molecular mechanisms and therefore more helpful in treating this disorder. Moreover, neuroimaging techniques may provide insight into the mechanisms by which behavioral treatments and certain dopaminergic agents are helpful, as they have done with drug and behavioral therapy for obsessive-compulsive disorder (Baxter et al., 1992). In this study, glucose metabolic rates were changed similarly with behavioral and drug treatments in the head of the right caudate nucleus. These kinds of studies may help refine the behavioral techniques as well as the pharmacology.

STEREOTYPIC MOVEMENT DISORDERS

Historical Perspective

Repetitive movements have been described for almost 300 years. Nehemia Grew in 1701 noted repeated actions without variation, usually viewed now as intentional (Golden & Hood, 1982). As Sprague and Newell (1996) point out, even today, the descriptor term "stereotypy" is not even used in the PsycINFO database. The primary features of these movement disorders is motor behavior that is seemingly driven, repetitive, and nonfunctional. In extreme cases of stereotypic movement disorder, severe mutilation and life-threatening injuries may occur. These "self-injurious behaviors" (SIB) (Tate & Baroff, 1966) are covered later in this section.

Although the movement disorders in this section have been well described in the professional literature for many decades, they have been classified in a variety of ways. In the earlier part of this century, they were often referred to as "habit" disturbances. Even within the American Psychiatric Association mental disorders system, these and related disorders have historically been labeled under several classifications. In DSM-II (APA, 1968), many of these disorders were listed under "special symptoms", and in DSM-III (APA, 1980) as either "stereotyped movement disorders" or under "other symptom disorders." With the advent of DSM-III-R (APA, 1987), the stereotyped movement disorders were separated from the tic disorders and placed in their own category of "stereotypy/habit disorder." Even then, it was noted that conclusive evidence was lacking as to whether the tic and movement disorders represented distinct classes of problems or represented a continuum of severity (if not symptoms) of the same problem (DSM-III-R; APA, 1987). At that time, "common wisdom" (and the diagnostic system) considered tic disorders to be involuntary in nature, while the movement disorders were thought to be at least partially under voluntary control. While this so-called "distinction" did not survive the most recent DSM-IV (APA, 1994) revision within the criteria listing, it remains, in slightly changed form, as a differential diagnostic feature. Several repetitive behaviors, such as breath holding, hyperventilation, teeth grinding (bruxism), and swallowing air (aerophagia), which were previously listed in DSM-III-R (APA, 1987), are no longer listed in DSM-IV (APA, 1994) by name but presumably could still be diagnosed under this category.

Diagnostic Description

For "stereotypic movement disorder," the DSM-IV (1994, p. 121) diagnostic criteria include:

a. Repetitive, seemingly driven, and nonfunctional (that is, no constructive purpose) motor behavior. These include behaviors such as: hand shaking or waving; body rocking; head banging; self-hitting or self-biting; skin-picking or scratching; and body manipulations such as poking at bodily orifices (anus poking, nose picking).

b. The behavior interferes with normal activities or results in self-inflicted bodily injury that requires medical attention (or would result in injury if not prevented or restrained).

c. If Mental Retardation is present, the stereotypic or self-injurious behavior is of sufficient severity to become a focus of treatment.

d. The behavior is not better accounted for by a compulsion, tic, or part of a Pervasive Developmental Disorder or hair pulling (Trichotillomania).

e. The behavior is not due to the direct physiological effects of a substance or a general medical condition.

f. The behavior persists for 4 weeks or longer.

These criteria also carry a specifier "with self-injurious behavior" (SIB) if the behavior results in or would result in bodily damage requiring specific medical treatment if protective measures were not taken. This subsection is discussed later.

In ICD-10 (WHO, 1992), these disorders are called "stereotyped movement disorders" and are further classified as being "non-self-injurious," "self-injurious," or "mixed." The ICD-10 system specifies that these disorders are stereotypic movements that do not form part of any recognized psychiatric or neurological condition. Other excluded conditions, such as abnormal involuntary movements, movement disorders of organic origin, nail biting, nose picking, thumb sucking, obsessive-compulsive disorder, and trichotillomania are covered under other diagnostic categories.

The ICD-10 movements that are noninjurious include body rocking, head rocking, hair plucking, hair twisting, finger-flicking mannerisms, and hand flapping. Nail biting, thumb sucking, and nose picking are not included as they were judged not to be good indicators of

psychopathology and were not seen as a health concern.

Stereotyped self-injurious behavior includes repetitive head banging, face slapping, eye poking, and biting of hands, lips, or other body parts in the ICD-10 system.

Differential diagnosis should consider self-stimulating behaviors, such as rocking and thumb sucking, which are common at certain ages in normal infants. Thus, these diagnoses are given only when the disturbance either causes physical injury to the child or markedly interferes with normal activities. As noted earlier, stereotyped movements "appear to be more driven and intentional, whereas tics have a more involuntary quality and are not rhythmic" (DSM-IV; APA, 1994, p. 120).

When the behaviors involve self-induced injuries, the possibility of a "factitious disorder with predominantly physical signs and symptoms," based on the patient's motivation to assume a "sick" role, should be investigated.

Epidemiology

Movement disorders of a rhythmic nature appear transitionally in infants, apparently as part of normal development. Thelen (1979) observed 20 children every other week from age 4 weeks to 1 year and noted that at around 6 months of age stereotypic behavior of all types, such as rocking, waving, banging, bouncing, and thumping movements, accounted for 10–20% of observed behavior. Body rocking, head rolling, head banging, hair twirling, and bed rocking, as well as other rhythmic movements, occur in a variety of forms (Werry, Carlielle, & Fitzpatrick, 1983). These motor habits are relatively common, occurring in 15–20% of normal pediatric clinic patients. Although usually transitory, about 5% of children have symptoms for months or even years, but these usually disappear at 2.5 to 3 years of age. Such habits are three and a half times more common in boys than in girls (Bakwin & Bakwin, 1972).

Head banging occurs in approximately 3.5% of infants of normal intellect and is about three and a half times as common in boys as in girls (Kravits, Rosenthal, Teplitz, Murphy, & Lesser, 1960), although higher rates have been reported. DeLissovoy (1961) found an incidence rate as high as 15.2% in the normal population between 19 and 32 months of age, with a 22.3% rate in boys, as opposed to 7.4% in girls. Onset is between 5 and 11 months and lasts about 17 months. About 67% of head bangers also rock. The usual duration is approximately 15 minutes but the activity may continue for an hour or more. In infants, the frontal-parietal region is most frequently struck, and such banging may lead to soft tissue swelling (Sormann, 1982). The most common position is for the child to be on his knees and hands in the crib. Abe, Oda, and Amatomi (1984) in a 5-year follow-up of 34 children who were head-bangers at age three, found that only three children still had the symptom.

Head rolling or head rocking may begin as early as 2 to 3 months of age. Incidence rates increase up to 6 or 7 months, and rocking of the body and head banging usually first appear after 8 months of age. Body rocking is often a repetitive movement in a seated position and frequently begins or becomes more intense when a child goes from the sitting to the standing stage, although the rocking may occur any time a child is passing from one developmental phase to another (Brody, 1960). Schwartz, Gallagher, and Berkson (1986) have shown there are topographical differences in body rocking between retarded and normal infants.

Bramble (1995) presents two case reports of severe and chronic head banging. These two boys (ages 12 and 11 years) reportedly had head-banging behavior initially while they were suffering from recurrent and severe otitis media as toddlers. They had been symptom-free for many years but then had another onset of symptoms. In adults, such behaviors may occur even during sleep, as reported by Kempenaers, Bouillon, and Mendlewicz (1994) in a case study of a 34-year-old female.

Stereotypic movements are more common in individuals with autism, mental retardation, or schizophrenia, with rates of 24% to more than 50% reported for these populations (Dura, Mulick, & Rasnake, 1987; Morrison, 1973).

In autism, the presence of stereotypic movements has been positively correlated with overall symptomatology and severity of illness, as well as negatively correlated with IQ. Baumeister and Forehand (1973) estimated that two-thirds of institutionalized mentally retarded individuals exhibited these behaviors. Matson (1989) noted, in a study of severe and profoundly retarded nonambulatory patients, that 34% had at least one class of stereotypy and 11% had multiple classes of these behaviors, with 7% having four types of stereotypy, including rhythmic movements, bizarre posturing, self-restraint, and object manipulation. Prior to the development of neuroleptics, stereotypic behavior was frequently reported in patients with catatonic schizophrenia, ranging from simple repetitive motor acts to complex or bizarre gestures. Morrison (1973) noted that 24% of 250 such schizophrenic patients had stereotypic behavior.

In a study on eye poking, Jan, Good, Freeman, and Espezel (1994) assessed 21 children (ages 18 months to 20 years) and reported in a prospective study that eye poking was a chronic, stereotyped, self-injurious act. They said that this behavior was seen primarily among severely mentally disabled individuals who might or might not be somewhat visually impaired. These authors noted that the etiology was unclear, although it is probably multifactorial.

Stereotypic behavior has been associated with obsessive-compulsive disorder (OCD), and both OCD and self-injurious behavior frequently are co-expressed in patients with Tourette's disorder (Primeau & Fontaine, 1987). Swedo and Leonard (1994) reviewed research suggesting a relationship between childhood-onset obsessive-compulsive disorder (OCD) and pediatric movement disorders such as tics and Tourette's syndrome. Obsessive-compulsive symptoms are also manifest in Sydenham's chorea, a neurologic variant of rheumatic fever that results in neuropsychiatric symptomatology.

In mentally retarded populations, the presence of obsessive-compulsive disorder is associated with an increase in stereotypic behavior of 32%, an increase in self-injurious behavior of

40% and a comorbid prevalence of both SIB and stereotypic behavior of 37% compared to control populations of retarded individuals without obsessive-compulsive disorder (Bodfish et al., 1995).

Theoretical Models

Stereotypic behaviors have been viewed as serving either an arousal function or its opposite, a tension-reduction function (Berkson & Gallagher, 1986). In the first model, recurrent sequences of motor movement provide the stimulation that is lacking from the environment. In the second, stereotypic behaviors arise in states of increased stress and thus enable the organism to dissipate frustration or anxiety.

Other theorists (Lewis, Baumeister, & Mailman, 1987; Thelen, 1981a) have suggested that these behaviors are simply disinhibited primitive motor programs and the spontaneous output of disregulated neural pathways that occurs when higher cortical functions are disrupted.

The theory that stereotypic behavior is dopamine mediated may best account for the occurrence of these behaviors in a variety of settings. Pharmacologic agents with the ability to increase dopaminergic activity, such as amphetamines, cocaine, levodopa, and methylphenidate, produce stereotypic behavior. Conversely, agents that inhibit dopamine synthesis or are dopamine-receptor antagonists, such as the neuroleptics, block the production of stereotypic behavior, even when an individual is given an amphetamine that would normally induce stereotypic behavior (Shulman, Sanchez-Ramos, & Weiner, 1996).

Swedo and Leonard (1994) noted the frequent comorbidity of OCD and Sydenham's chorea and similar postulates that suggest basal ganglia dysfunction for both disorders and proposed that Sydenham's chorea may serve as a medical model for OCD.

Any process that causes damage to the dopamine pathways of the basal ganglia or other components of the extrapyramidal system has the potential to produce stereotypic behavior. Thus, traumatic injury, infectious processes, toxic exposure or metabolic insults, genetic diseases, neurodegenerative diseases, tumors, and vascular events are all potential producers of stereotypic behavior (Shulman et al., 1996).

Swedo and Leonard (1994) describe recent advances in the pharmacotherapy of childhood-onset OCD and note that the medications (e.g., neuroleptics) that are effective in treating tics and other movement disorders are distinctly different from those that are efficacious for OCD (e.g., serotonin reuptake blockers).

Ridley and Baker (1982) suggest that stereotypy is associated with cognitive inflexibility and social and sensory isolation due to some deficit in CNS regulatory function. Other authors (Gedye, 1989; Hutt & Hutt, 1968) found associations between stereotyped movement and the presence of desynchronized EEG activity, often frontal lobe in location.

Thelen (1980) suggested that the amount of vestibular stimulation was a critical factor in the etiology of rocking (although such activities were also associated with being in close proximity to a caregiver). He found an inverse relationship between the amount of holding, moving, and touching of the child and the amount of stereotyped behavior. Rhythmical leg movements have been found to reduce heart rate in normal school-age children (Soussignan & Koch, 1985), suggesting a functional and adaptive purpose to such behaviors.

The most widely accepted behavioral view of these disorders is that behaviors such as hand flapping and body rocking are maintained by their sensory consequences such as vestibular or visual stimulation. Thus, the behaviors continue to be performed because their sensory feedback is reinforcing. As long ago as the 1940s, Lourie (Thelen, 1979) proposed that the sensory feedback from rhythmic movements in childhood, which facilitated normal development, is abnormally maintained by the reward associated with the control of that specific feedback. Unfortunately, the testing of this concept is difficult. For example, how do you describe the feedback in a child who displays body rocking, beyond saying that some kinesthetic and/or vestibular stimulation is important? It is easier to select examples of stereotypes related to objects, such as a child twirling a bottle cap or a piece of string, and then see if changing the stimulus properties of the object changes the reinforcing value of that object. For example, Lovaas and his associates (Lovaas, Newsom, & Hickman, 1987) found that if the physical characteristics of a piece of string being twirled by an autistic child were changed (e.g., by making it wider), these changes quickly reduced the level of that stereotypic behavior, at least temporarily. Additional support for this theory of feedback control as reinforcement is provided by Buyer, Berkson, Winnega, and Morton (1987), in a study of mentally retarded clients who engaged in body rocking. When given choices between being rocked in a rocking chair at the client's previously determined rate by another person or being able to control their own rate of rocking, they most often chose the latter. This tendency was most strongly noted in those clients with the highest tested developmental levels.

Changes in the environment, especially in the level of stimulation available, can increase or decrease the frequency of stereotypic behavior. Infants without social stimulation demonstrate increased levels of abnormal stereotypic behaviors, as do children raised in institutional environments (Guess & Carr, 1991).

Assessment

The individual to be assessed should have a complete medical examination. Clinical assessment should focus on the historical progression of symptoms. A detailed family history should be obtained. Neef (1994) edited a special issue of the *Journal of Applied Behavioral Analysis* on functional analysis approaches to behavioral assessment and treatment, which is an outstanding reference for both current theoretical thinking on analysis of stereotypic movements and SIB and on research into treatment methods. As this collection of articles points out, information should be obtained regarding onset, duration, the situations in

which the stereotypic behavior occurs, a precise behavioral description, parental responses, associated behaviors, and some measure of whether the child's functioning has been impaired or whether the behavior is an indication of another severe emotional disturbance or deprivation.

The use of parental rating scales, such as the Child Behavior Checklist (Achenbach, 1991a, 1991b, 1991c) or the Personality Inventory for Children (Wirt, Lachar, Klinedinst, & Seat, 1984), may be helpful. Sprague and Newell (1996), in a review of methods of assessing stereotypic movements based on standards for test construction, noted that "none of the current instruments meet these ideal standards, and most of the widely used instruments are quite inadequate when measured against these psychometric standards" (p. 107). Matson (1989) noted that "there are no instruments devoted specifically to the assessment of self-injury or stereotypies" (p. 267) and concluded that behavioral specification of the targeted movements was the best assessment method.

Personality assessment to measure levels of anxiety, attention deficit hyperactivity, or compulsive symptoms may be useful for ruling out such disorders as primary diagnoses in the presence of a movement disorder. The Symptom Checklist-90-Revised (Derogatis, 1983) and the Obsessive-Compulsive Checklist (Brown, 1978) for adolescents may also be helpful in providing information about the type of symptoms experienced.

Although there are diagnostic criteria for the stereotypic movement disorders, studies of the relationship between various stereotypic behaviors that relied on formal observations in the classroom and teacher reports of the existence have indicated very low agreement. Even when specific behaviors are combined into broader categories, the agreement rates rarely exceed 33% (Schultz & Berkson, 1995). Different types of movement disorders are often misdiagnosed, even by experts. For example, when two groups of psychiatrists with experience in either autism or in medication-related dyskinesias were asked to rate children blindly as having one disorder or the other, they tended to overdiagnose the disorder with which they were most familiar (Meiselas et al., 1989). Thus, careful behavioral analysis of the movement disorder is important.

Treatment

Biological

There is contradictory evidence as to the effects of antipsychotic drugs in the treatment of stereotypic behaviors, at least with mentally retarded populations. Baumeister and Sevin (1990) reviewed the evidence that supports the use of these drugs, while other studies have reported either a lack of efficacy or an exacerbation of stereotypic behavior (Heistad, Zimmermann, & Doebler, 1982). The other class of drugs that has been examined relatively systematically for its effects on stereotypic behavior is the opiate antagonists. While effective for self-injurious behaviors, drugs such as naltrexone have not been found to be effective for stereotypic behaviors in mentally retarded populations (Sandman, Barron, & Coleman, 1990).

Psychological

Several recent reviews have been published on behavioral treatments. Peterson, Campise, and Azrin (1994) reviewed approximately 350 articles about behavior therapy and pharmacological treatment for tic disorders, self-destructive oral habits, and other stereotypic or habit disturbances (hair pulling, nail biting, and thumb sucking). The research shows these tic and habit disorders can be effectively treated with behavioral or pharmacological approaches. Controlled treatment-outcome studies have shown that the most effective behavioral treatments reduce the frequency of these tic and habit disorders by more than 90% and eliminate the disorders in 40–70% of cases. The most widely used and successful form of intervention involves reinforcing incompatible behaviors through the use of differential reinforcement of other behaviors (DRO) and differential reinforcement of incompatible behaviors (DRI) techniques.

Turpin (1993) provided an annotated, selective bibliography on the management of tics and movement disorders that includes seven books, seven general research articles, eight reviews of psychological management, and 11 reports on the efficacy of psychological treatment, all published in the United States and the United Kingdom between 1982 and 1992.

Bramble (1995), in a study reported earlier, used a variety of treatment approaches, including behavior modification techniques and advice regarding sleep habits, that proved highly successful with two preadolescent boys with chronic head banging.

Aurand, Sisson, Aach, and Van Hasselt (1989) evaluated the efficacy of differential reinforcement of incompatible behavior (DRI) and the use of response-interruption behavioral interventions in reducing stereotypic behaviors, including tongue chewing (TC), hand flapping (HF), and head weaving (HW) exhibited by a moderately retarded 4-year-old child with visual impairment. The DRI involved verbal praise and soft physical touch. Efficiency of DRI alone was first evaluated with TC. This method had minimal impact on the target behavior, so a response interruption component of inhibiting the target behavior was added. The combination of techniques was effective in suppressing TC and, later, HF and HW. Followup showed that the behavior change occurred across settings and for up to 2 months after treatment. Following intervention, the child displayed less self-stimulatory and more on-task behavior during a group activity.

Treatment based on the sensory consequence theory, described earlier, has used "sensory extinction" by reducing or masking the sensory consequences of the stereotypic behavior. Rincover, Cook, Peoples, and Packard (1979) have used these techniques with a variety of behaviors. In one study, they reduced a child's plate-spinning behavior at a table by carpeting the surface of the table. The lack of auditory feedback resulted in an almost total elimination of plate spinning.

Matthews et al. (1992) reported removal of a positive reinforcing event (presentation of music) to reduce the rate of body rocking in a severely retarded adolescent. The client had a history of high-frequency body rocking whenever she sat down, regardless of location, including when riding in the car. A tape recorder was used, with a microswitch attached to the back of the sofa where this client usually sat in a developmental day care center. As long as she sat still, the music was on. Increased rocking resulted in termination of the music. Following control of the behavior in this environment, variable-interval schedules were used to maintain her nonrocking behavior. Stimulus generalization was obtained by the use of similar techniques in other locations. For example, her family was instructed to turn off the radio in the car if she began to rock.

Rosenberg (1995) used hypnosis in the elimination of a rhythmic movement disorder in an adult. The client, a 26-year-old woman with nighttime "rocking," was treated successfully, using a hypnotically induced image of her watching a TV set on which the program showed her sleeping beside her husband without rocking.

Social/Interpersonal

Thompson and Thelen (1986), in a review, noted that the use of alternative activities, in general, easily reduces the rate of stereotypic behavior and that normal social interaction reduces such behavior for short periods, even in severely retarded institutionalized infants.

Morrissey, Franzini, and Karen (1992) compared the effectiveness of light calisthenics to relaxation techniques in the control of self-stimulatory behavior in four developmentally disabled boys (ages 8 to 13 years) residing in a group home. Data showed that the light calisthenics treatment reduced self-stimulatory behavior in all four of the clients to varying degrees, while the relaxation treatment led to reductions in self-stimulatory behavior in three of them.

A more interactive and cognitive approach to the treatment of both stereotypic and self-injurious behaviors (SIB) is the use of functional communication training (FCT). This technique involves training the child to substitute appropriate verbal alternatives for problem behaviors (Durand, 1982). For example, hand flapping or rocking behaviors, which appear to be escape-motivated behaviors to avoid task demands in class, were reduced by teaching children to ask appropriately for assistance on these tasks.

SELF-INJURIOUS BEHAVIORS

Diagnostic Description

Self-injurious behaviors (SIB) have been described in association with a variety of diagnostic classifications. Under the DSM-IV (APA, 1994) classification of stereotypic movement disorder, the specifier "with self-injurious behavior" is listed. In extreme cases of stereotypic movement disorder, severe mutilation and life-threatening injuries may result (Benians & Goldacre, 1984). The occurrence of the more severe forms of these stereotypic movement behaviors, such as self-hitting, head banging, and self-biting, are the most common of the "self-injurious" (Tate & Baroff, 1966) or "self-mutilation" behaviors (Phillips & Muzaffer, 1961). In general, these disorders occur much more often in developmentally delayed populations (Baumeister & Rollings, 1976). Such disorders are also associated with sensory handicaps, obsessive-compulsive behavior, and schizophrenia. The general term "self-injurious behavior" (SIB) is used to cover all of these disorders in this section.

As mentioned earlier, in behaviors involving self-induced injuries, the possibility of a "factitious disorder with predominantly physical signs and symptoms," based on the patient's motivation to assume a "sick" role, should be investigated. Self-mutilation may also be associated with some psychotic or personality disorders, but in such cases it is usually done with premeditation, is more complex in nature, and may have a meaning for the individual within the context of the underlying type of severe symptomatology. For example, the self-mutilation might be in response to a delusion that aliens are growing under the skin. In such cases, the diagnosis might more appropriately be "self-mutilation associated with certain psychotic disorders and personality disorders."

Neef (1994), in the special issue of the *Journal of Applied Behavioral Analysis* on functional behavior analysis mentioned earlier, included articles on separate topographies of aberrant behavior, extinction procedures for SIB, hand mouthing, and future directions for the use of functional analysis in a variety of clinical settings. Wright et al. (1979) stated that SIB is more likely to be an indication of severe disturbance than is body rocking or other compulsive types of habits.

Epidemiology

Several investigators (DeLissovoy, 1961; Green, 1967) report that in normal children from the ages of 9 months to 6 years, SIB of various forms is frequently observed. It occurs in 11–17% of children at ages 9 to 18 months and in 9% at 2 years of age but by 5 years of age is virtually absent (Williams, 1974). Johnson and Day (1992) examined data from 34 epidemiological surveys and summarized the findings across several dimensions, including overall frequency and distribution of SIB depending on age, gender, and handicapping condition, response characteristics, settings (residential, hospital, home), and related drug administration.

Theoretical Models

Symons (1995) reviewed seven theories and current treatment methods for SIB and concluded that further development is needed, especially regarding the role of environmental factors in the formulation and application of treatment for these behaviors.

Hellings and Warnock (1994) point out that low serotonin levels have been associated with increased SIB and impulsive and aggressive behaviors in a variety of psychiatric disorders, such as obsessive-compulsive disorders (OCD), and that serotonin reuptake inhibitors are effective in treating OCD. The increased rates of body rocking and head banging in children with intellectual or sensory handicaps (Gresty & Halmagyi, 1981; Jones, 1988) suggest some central nervous system involvement in the etiology of these behaviors.

Carr and McDowell (1980) found that SIB was maintained by social attention. While Money, Wolff, and Annecillo (1972) cited higher rates of SIB in abused children than in neglected or normal children as support for a social hypothesis, an alternative explanation, based on increased knowledge of the effects of "mild" head injury in the intervening years since this article was originally published, might be that this behavior is due to mild organic dysfunction, which is often associated with physical abuse.

Functional analysis studies of SIB have indicated that an action, such as hand biting, while behaviorally similar in appearance across individuals, may serve different functions. For example, SIB might be more frequent in academic-task situations as an escape response, allowing the child to avoid a teacher demand. When seen at times when the child is alone, the SIB may be maintained by its self-stimulatory function. Other children may exhibit SIB during play or when subject to social disapproval for the behavior by others, suggesting that it serves as a demand for attention. Treatment that does not take into account these various functions might be only partially successful overall, although very effective for the particular function targeted (Shapiro & Kratochwill, 1988).

Iwata, Pace, Dorsey, et al. (1994) summarized data from 152 single-subject analyses of the reinforcing functions of SIB. The results indicated that social reinforcement (both positive and negative) was a determinant of SIB in more than two thirds of the sample, with automatic (sensory) consequences accounting for one-fourth of the cases.

Bachman (1972) and others (Bandura, 1969; Mace, Browder, & Lin, 1987; Skinner, 1953; Thelen, 1981b) suggested that self-injurious behavior may develop if the behavior leads to the avoidance of even more aversive consequences (avoidance hypothesis) by delaying external demands, or if an aversive event is paired with a positive reinforcer that maintains a given activity (discriminative stimulus-conditioned reinforcer hypothesis). Durand (1982) found that SIB was also maintained as a way to escape from task demands, such as requirements to engage in classroom activities (Iwata, Dorsey, Slifer, Bauman, & Richman, 1994; Shapiro & Kratochwill, 1988).

Buyer et al. (1987) postulate self-stimulation as a factor that is dependent on developmental age. Since SIB often seems to occur only in the presence or absence of specific stimuli and is maintained by social reinforcement that follows it (Lane & Dormath, 1970), SIB may be a learned operant under the control of environmental stimuli (Edelson, Taubman, & Lovaas, 1983; Mace et al., 1987).

Iwata, Pace, Cowdery, and Miltenberger (1994), while investigating the role of extinction methods in reduction or elimination of head banging (SIB) with three children with moderate or severe mental retardation, noted that the behavior was maintained by different reinforcement contingencies. In one client, the SIB was positively reinforced by attention from adults (attention). A second child was negatively reinforced by escape from educational tasks (escape), while the third child's SIB appeared to be automatically reinforced (sensory) or "self-stimulatory" in nature, since no specific external reinforcer could be identified. This study again points out the need for careful behavioral analysis of SIB to determine etiological factors.

A variety of explanations for these behaviors have been presented in the psychodynamic literature (Kennedy & Moran, 1984). SIB is seen as a response to maternal deprivation (Greenberg, 1964; Spitz, 1945), an anxiety-reducing response (Clerk, 1972), a repression of hostility (Saul, 1976), disturbed narcissism (Kohut, 1972), libidinal fixation or displaced genital damage (Friedman, Glasser, Laufer, Laufer, & Wohl, 1972), and self-aggression as a result of oral fixation (Clerk, 1972).

Green (1967) postulated that self-stimulatory patterns may be avoidance behaviors or adaptive responses to a reduction in social or environmental stimulation. As adaptive responses, they serve to increase sensory input. However, the child, in waving his or her hands, may accidentally hit the head and a random head banging pattern can develop.

Treatment

Biological

Sprague (1977), in a review of psychopharmacology in children, indicated that neuroleptics reduce bizarre or stereotypical behavior but also suppress learning performance. Other authors (Aman, White, & Field, 1984; Haskell & Joffe, 1984; Kravitz et al., 1960; Richardson & Zaleski, 1983) have successfully used tranquilizing or sedative drugs, such as naloxone and clonidine, for chronic SIB.

Chengappa, Baker, and Sirri (1995) obtained rapid reduction in chronic and severe SIB in an adult diagnosed with borderline personality disorder by the atypical use of clozapine, after the patient had failed to respond to other psychotropic medications and behavioral interventions.

Hellings and Warnock (1994) described the successful use of fluoxetine in three patients with Prader-Willi syndrome, a condition often associated with SIB as manifested by compulsive skin picking and skin gouging. Two of the patients showed a reduction in skin picking, while the third had a decrease in explosive outbursts. King (1995) described a case study of a 19-year-old with face slapping, head banging, and forearm banging who was also successfully treated with fluoxetine.

Linn, Rojahn, Helsel, and Dixon (1988) investigated the acute effects of transcutaneous electric nerve stimulation (TENS) on self-injurious behavior (head banging and self-biting) in two multiply handicapped adolescent clients with mental retardation. The TENS device has conventionally been utilized to reduce or eliminate intractable pain. Although the use of the TENS unit resulted in a clear suppression of the SIB, concurrently recorded behaviors in the patient with head banging (e.g., body rocking, vocalization) were unaffected by the treatment. The authors concluded that, while TENS had selective effects on SIB, its use did not achieve clinically significant results.

Haynes, Wilson, Jaffe, and Britton (1979) used biofeedback and relaxation training in nine patients with atopic eczema and severe scratching. A total of eight sessions in 4 weeks produced 50% reduction in the size of the affected skin areas, based on photographic analysis.

Psychological

A variety of behavioral techniques have been used for the elimination of self-stimulatory and SIB. Reviews of treatment methods (Bachman, 1972; Johnson & Baumeister, 1978; Jones, 1988; Jordon, Singh, & Repp, 1989; Linscheid, Copeland, Jacobstein, & Smith, 1981; Rincover, 1986; Singh, 1981) found many treatments to be highly effective. These methods include differential reinforcement (Carr & McDowell, 1980; Peterson & Peterson, 1968); behavioral contracting (Frazier & Williams, 1973); aversive techniques (Baroff & Tate, 1968; Browning & Stover, 1971); extinction (Lovaas & Simmons, 1969); overcorrection (Harris & Romanczyk, 1976; Linscheid, Copeland, Jacobstein, & Smith, 1981; Shapiro, Barrett, & Ollendick, 1980; Strauss, Rubinoff, & Atkeson, 1983); visual screening (Jordon, Singh, & Repp, 1989); water mist (Dorsey, Iwata, Ong, & McSween, 1980); and time out (Solnick, Rincover, & Peterson, 1977; Tate & Baroff, 1966). Although many of the studies involved children with severe behavioral disorders or mental retardation, these techniques can be successfully applied to normal children.

The method of differential reinforcement of other behaviors (DRO) to reduce or eliminate SIB has been reported, but it has frequently been noted not to be effective alone. Cowdery, Iwata, and Pace (1990) concluded that, of the hundreds of research articles published, only a handful reported positive results when DRO was the only form of treatment. These authors reported a case study of self-scratching using a DRO schedule mediated with token reinforcement. This 9-year-old patient had exhibited the problem for at least 6 years and had never attended school due to the severity of his SIB. He had spent most of the 2-year period prior to the study in various hospitals. The program offered reinforcement for longer and longer periods of not scratching, and allowed him to exchange pennies for activities on the unit. At the end of treatment, he was discharged to his home after his parents were taught to maintain the token system. The authors note that, although suppression of the SIB was rapid, side effects, such as negative emotional outbursts, did occur with this method. They did find that the use of the token reinforcement was superior to the DRO system. Although this procedure was successful in markedly reducing the frequency of SIB, so the client was no longer considered to be at significant risk, however, it did not eliminate the behavior, thus preventing complete healing of all his wounds.

In a later study (Vollmer, Iwata, Zarcone, Smith, & Mazaleskim, 1993), DRO was compared to an alternative procedure, noncontingent reinforcement (NCR), which is normally used as a control procedure. The authors noted that both procedures were highly effective in reducing SIB but concluded that NCR reduced several of the limitations seen with the DRO schedule.

Allen and Harris (1966) taught a parent to eliminate self-scratching in a 5-year-old child who had been scratching for more than 1 year. SIB was so severe that the child bled and had large sores and scabs on her face and on one arm and one leg. Analysis of the interactions between child and parent indicated that almost all of the mother's verbalizations to the child were critical. A token program was instituted in which the child was given points for nonscratching. In addition, use of tangible reinforcers in the form of new Barbie doll items were given, with items initially purchased in the afternoon of each scratch-free day, placed out of reach but in plain view, and given to the child the next morning if no scratching had occurred that night. At the end of 6 weeks, every sore was healed completely, with no further scratching on a 4-month follow-up.

Martin and Conway (1976) used bright light as an aversive stimulus to eliminate nocturnal rocking in a normal 25-month-old. Dougherty and Lane (1976) used a time-out procedure, with parents serving as therapists. The child's pacifier was removed or replaced contingent upon the occurrence or nonoccurrence of head banging. Prytula, Joyner, and Schnelle (1981) utilized a school program to control head-banging behavior in the home. A preschooler who engaged in frequent head banging at home (with rates from 13 to 50 episodes per evening) but infrequent head banging at school was placed on a contingency program to reduce the rate of this behavior. While the child's mother was obtaining baseline data on head banging at home, in the school the child was observed in order to determine his preferred activities. A criterion was set for number of head-banging episodes. Each morning, the mother sent a daily "report card" consisting of a smiling or frowning face to school, indicating if the child had met the criterion. Participation in the child's preferred activity was contingent upon his having a smiling face on the report card. A frowning face resulted in a loss of the activity and the teacher's voicing her disappointment for the child's loss because he had banged his head at home. As treatment progressed, the number of head-banging episodes was reduced to zero. From the initial base rate of approximately 14 episodes per day, within 2 days after initiation of the program the rate was fewer than two episodes per day.

Self-biting has higher incidence rates in patients with developmental disabilities or mental retardation. Hile and Vatterott (1991, 1992) summarized treatment results with these populations reported in 43 articles published over 2 decades (1970–1990). They ranked each article according to the level of physical restrictiveness of the treatment on a scale of 1 to 4. The ranking was designed to allow clinicians to make informed treatment decisions, given the concerns over the excessive use of physical restraint with such populations. They concluded that a differential reinforcement (DRO) procedure, coupled with social time-out or the use of brief informational restraint, can provide an effective intervention for eliminating self-biting.

SIB hand mouthing was reduced in two adults with profound retardation by a simple response-blocking procedure (Reid, Parsons, Phillis, & Green, 1993). The behavior was hypothesized to serve a self-stimulatory function. The intervention by the experimenters was to place their own palms in front of the patient's mouth to prevent entry of the patient's own hand. Results indicated marked reductions in the rates of mouthing throughout the course of the day, even when the intervention was not being used.

In the previously described Iwata, Pace, Cowdery, and Miltenberger (1994) study on the use of extinction methods in reduction or elimination of SIB, each client was exposed to at least two of three functional variations of extinction, using either reversal or multiple-baseline designs. The results of these interventions indicated that reductions in SIB were observed only when implementation of extinction involved discontinuation of the reinforcement (attention, escape, or sensory stimulation) previously shown to be responsible for maintaining the behavior.

Van Houten (1993) reported on the use of wrist weights to reduce self-injury from face slapping. Following a functional analysis that suggested that face slapping was maintained by sensory consequences, the 10-year-old patient wore soft wrist weights for progressively longer periods. Data on the frequency of face slapping were collected before the use of the weights, during their use, and after the weights were removed. When the weights were worn for 30 minutes each day, face slapping decreased during 5-minute observation periods before and after the wearing of the weights. Continued use of the weights led to an elimination of the behavior, and the use of protective headgear was eliminated by the end of the study. Follow-up for 5 months indicated that face slapping did not reoccur.

Bar and Kuypers (1973) used aversive and relaxation techniques to treat an adult with a 4-year history of severe lichen simplex disease that was complicated by the client's scratching. The patient was instructed to scratch, at which time he was shocked on the hand and told to say, "Don't scratch." Relaxation techniques were also taught. After 19 days of treatment, scratching had disappeared, and on 13-month follow-up there was no further scratching.

Social/Interpersonal

Nonbehavioral treatments have been described by several authors (Greenberg, 1964; Jorgenson, 1974; Lasich & Bassa, 1985). The suggested therapeutic strategies include use of distracting stimulation, such as reading; sensory stimulation by playing music; or vestibular stimulation to reduce rocking rates. Rosenberg (1995) described the successful use of hypnosis in treating a 26-year-old with nighttime rocking. Following trance induction, a visual image technique was used in which the patient was asked to visualize herself watching a TV program in which she was sleeping without rocking.

Harris (1968) used psychoanalytic play therapy to resolve the psychosexual conflict that was supposedly producing head banging. Kohut (1972) investigated the relationship between narcissism and aggression and suggested that psychoanalysis was of value in taming narcissistic rage manifested by self-mutilation.

COMMENTS

This chapter has covered tics disorders and stereotypic movement disorders. Debate continues regarding the appropriate diagnostic criteria for these disorders. Kendell (1988), writing not just about tics and movement disorders but about diagnoses for all mental disorders at the time of the first-draft editions of ICD-10 (WHO, 1992) and DSM-IV (APA, 1994), called for an international "lingua franca" nomenclature. He also discussed the perspective relations between the emerging ICD-10 and DSM-IV criteria and the need for these two standard references to use similar

terms and symptoms. Although the two publications have contributed to the progress in universalizing the criteria for diagnoses, much work remains to be done. Kendell (1991), discussing the American Psychiatric Association's controversial decision to publish a revision of the DSM-III in 1987 before setting up the task force to produce the DSM-IV, stated that this decision impaired the association's ability to influence the format of ICD-10, because by then major decisions had already been made by the World Health Organization. He noted that, for a combination of scientific, political, and financial reasons, the APA was unwilling to use the ICD-10 system. He pointed out that there may be some advantage to research workers in having two widely used but different systems but that both systems are likely to exist in an uneasy competition. He concluded his article by noting that other branches of medicine and learning progressed not by the development of new classifications but by the development of new technologies, new concepts, and clarifying basic mechanisms (p. 301).

With regard to treatment, Tourette's disorder appears very responsive to pharmacologic intervention. Although a variety of etiological factors are associated with the occurrence of all of the other tic and movement disorders (including some SIB, which appears to be the result of genetically determined diseases), the most effective methods of controlling these behaviors in normal children has been the use of operant-conditioning techniques. The special issue of the *Journal of Applied Behavioral Analysis* on the functional analysis model of assessment (Neef, 1994) is likely to have a significant impact on the evaluation of these disorders. The use of behavioral interventions, especially DRO schedules and habit-reversal techniques, appears to be the treatment of choice for most of the tic and movement disorders. These procedures produce rapid and complete cessation of the behaviors in the majority of cases. Although there is a variety of theories about the etiology of these disorders, there remain relatively few studies involving intervention procedures with "normal" children. The majority of the literature, especially with regard to behavioral intervention techniques, continues to place heavy emphasis on the more severely impaired populations. It is our hope that, with the effectiveness of these interventions and the relative ease with which they can be applied, even by parents, the use of such techniques will increase in the future.

REFERENCES

Abe, K., & Oda, N. (1978). Follow-up study of children of childhood tiqueurs. *Biological Psychiatry*, 13, 629–630.

Abe, K., & Oda, N. (1980). Incidence of tics in the offspring of childhood tiqueurs: A controlled follow-up study. *Developmental Medicine and Child Neurology*, 22 (55), 649–653.

Abe, K., Oda, N., & Amatomi, M. (1984). Natural history and predictive significance of head-banging, head-rolling, and breath-holding spells. *Developmental Medicine and Child Neurology*, 26 (5), 644–648.

Achenbach, T. M. (1991a). *Manual for the Child Behavior Checklist/4–18 and 1991 profile*. Burlington: University of Vermont, Department of Psychiatry.

Achenbach, T. M. (1991b). *Manual for the Teacher's Report Form and the 1991 profile*. Burlington: University of Vermont, Department of Psychiatry.

Achenbach, T. M. (1991c). *Manual for the Youth Self-Report and 1991 profile*. Burlington: University of Vermont, Department of Psychiatry.

Achenbach, T. M., & Edelbrock, C. (1983). *Manual for the Child Behavior Checklist and revised child behavior profile*. Burlington: University of Vermont.

Alarcon, R. D. (1995). Culture and psychiatric diagnosis: Impact on DSM-IV and ICD-10. *Psychiatric Clinics of North America*, 18 (3), 449–465.

Alberca, R., & Ochoa, J. J. (1994). Cluster tic syndrome. *Neurology*, 44 (6), 996–999.

Allen, K. E., & Harris, F. R. (1966). Elimination of a child's excessive scratching by training the mother in reinforcement procedures. *Behavioral Research and Therapy*, 4, 79–84.

Aman, M. G., White, A. J., & Field, C. (1984). Chlorpromazine effects on stereotypic and conditioned behaviour of severely retarded patients: A pilot study. *Journal of Mental Deficiency Research*, 28 (4), 253–260.

American Psychiatric Association. (1980). *Diagnostic and statistical manual of mental disorders* (3rd ed.). Washington, DC: Author.

American Psychiatric Association. (1987). *Diagnostic and statistical manual of mental disorders-revised* (3rd ed.). Washington, DC: Author.

American Psychiatric Association. (1994). *Diagnostic and statistical manual of mental disorders* (4th ed.). Washington, DC: Author.

Ascher, E. (1948). Psychodynamic considerations in Gilles de la Tourette's disease with a report of five cases and discussion of the literature. *American Journal of Psychiatry*, 105, 267–275.

Aurand, J. C., Sisson, L. A., Aach, S. R., & Van Hasselt, V. B. (1989). Use of reinforcement plus interruption to reduce self-stimulation in a child with multiple handicaps. *Journal of the Multi-handicapped Person*, 2 (1), 51–61.

Azrin, N. H., & Nunn, R. G. (1973). Habit reversal: A method of eliminating nervous habits and tics. *Behaviour Research and Therapy*, 11, 619–628.

Azrin, N. H., & Nunn, R. G. (1977). *Habit control in a day*. New York: Simon & Schuster.

Azrin, N. H., & Peterson, A. L. (1988). Habit reversal for the treatment of Tourette syndrome. *Behaviour Research and Therapy*, 26 (4), 347–351.

Azrin, N. H., & Peterson, A. L. (1989). Reduction of an eye tic by controlled blinking. *Behavior Therapy*, 20 (3), 467–473.

Bachara, G. H., & Phelan, W. J. (1980). Rhythmic movement in deaf children. *Perceptual and Motor Skills*, 50 (3), 933–934.

Bachman, J. A. (1972). Self-injurious behavior: A behavioral analysis. *Journal of Abnormal Psychology*, 80, 211–224.

Bakwin, H., & Bakwin, R. M. (1972). *Behavior disorders in children* (4th ed.). Philadelphia: W. B. Saunders.

Bandura, A. (1969). *Principles of behavior modification*. New York: Holt, Rinehart & Winston.

Bar, L. H., & Kuypers, R. M. (1973). Behavior therapy in dermatological practice. *British Journal of Dermatology*, 88, 591–598.

Barnard, J. D., Cristopherson, E. R., & Wolf, M. M. (1976). Parent-mediated treatment of children's self-injurious behavior using overcorrection. *Journal of Pediatric Psychology*, 1, 56–61.

Baroff, G. S., & Tate, B. G. (1968). The use of aversive stimulation in the treatment of chronic self-injurious behavior. *Journal of American Academy of Child Psychiatry*, 7, 454–470.

Baumeister, A. A., & Forehand, R. (1973). Stereotyped acts. In N. R. Ellis (Ed.), *International review of research in mental retardation* (pp. 55–69). New York: Academic Press.

Baumeister, A. A., & Rollings, J. P. (1976). Self-injurious behavior. In N. R. Ellis (Ed.), *International review of research in mental retardation* (pp. 1–34). New York: Academic Press.

Baumeister, A. A., & Sevin, J. A. (1990). Pharmacologic control of aberrant behavior in the mentally retarded: Toward a more rational approach. *Neuroscience and Biobehavioral Reviews, 14*, 253–262.

Baxter, L. R., Schwartz, J. M., Bergman, K. S., Szuba, M. P., Guze, B. H., Mazziotta, J. C., Alazraki, A., Selin, C. E., Ferng, H. K, Munford, P., & Phelps, M. E. (1992). Caudate glucose metabolic rate changes with both drug and behavior therapy for obsessive-compulsive disorder. *Archives of General Psychiatry, 49*, 681–689.

Beard, G. (1880). Experiments with the "jumpers" or "jumping Frenchmen" of Maine. *Journal of Nervous and Mental Diseases, 7*, 487.

Benians, R., & Goldacre, P. (1984). Non-accidental injury in children: Two cases of concealment of self injury. *British Medical Journal, 289* (6458), 1583–1584.

Berkson, G., & Gallagher, R. J. (1986). Control of feedback from abnormal stereotyped behaviors. In M. G. Wade (Ed.), *The development of coordination, control and skill in the mentally handicapped* (pp. 7–24). Amsterdam: North Holland.

Bodfish, J. W., Crawford, T. W., Powell, S. B., Parker, D. E., Golden, R. N., & Lewis, M. H. (1995). Compulsions in adults with mental retardation: Prevalence, phenomenology, and comorbidity with stereotypy and self-injury. *American Journal of Mental Retardation, 100*, 183–192.

Bramble, D. (1995). Two cases of severe head-banging parasomnias in peripubertal males resulting from otitis media in toddlerhood. *Child Care, Health and Development, 21* (4), 247–253.

Brett, P. M., Curtis, D., Robertson, M. M., & Gurling, H. (1995). Exclusion of the 5-HT1A serotonin neuroreceptor and tryptophan oxygenase genes in a large British kindred multiply affected with Tourette's syndrome, chronic motor tics, and obsessive-compulsive behavior. *American Journal of Psychiatry, 152*, 437–440.

Brett, P. M., Curtis, D., Robertson, M. M., & Gurling, H. (1995). The genetic susceptibility to Gilles de la Tourette syndrome in a large multiple affected British kindred: Linkage analysis excludes a role for the genes coding for dopamine D1, D2, D3, D4, D5 receptors, dopamine beta hydroxylase, tyrosinase, and tyrosine hydroxylase. *Biological Psychiatry, 37*, 533–540.

Brody, S. (1960). Self-rocking in infancy. *Journal of the American Psychoanalytic Association, 7*, 464–491.

Brown, S. (1978). Emotional disorders. In S. Gellis & B. Kagan (Eds.), *Current pediatric therapy* (8th ed.). Philadelphia: W. B. Saunders.

Browning, R. M., & Stover, D. O. (1971). *Behavior modification in child treatment*. Chicago: Aldine-Atherton.

Bruch, H., & Thum, L. C. (1968). Maladie des tics and maternal psychosis. *Journal of Nervous and Mental Disease, 146*, 446–456.

Burd, L., Kerbeshian, J., Fisher, W., & Gascon-Generoso, G. (1986). Anticonvulsant medications: An iatrogenic cause of tic disorders. *Canadian Journal of Psychiatry, 31* (5), 419–423.

Burns, M. E. (1980). Droperidol in the management of hyperactivity, self-multilation and aggression in mentally handicapped patients. *Journal of International Medical Research, 8* (1), 31–33.

Buyer, L. S., Berkson, G., Winnega, M., & Morton, L. (1987). Stimulation and control as components of stereotyped body-rocking. *American Journal of Mental Deficiency, 91* (5), 543–547.

Caine, E. D., McBride, M. C., Chiverton, P., Bainford, K. A., Rediess, S., & Shiao, J. (1988). Tourette syndrome in Monroe County school children. *Neurology, 38*, 472–475.

Campbell, M., Locascio, J. J., Choroco, M. C., Spencer, E. K., Malone, R. P., Kafanteris, V., & Overall, J. E. (1990). Stereotypies and tardive dyskinesia: Abnormal movements in autistic children. *Psychopharmacology Bulletin, 26*, 260–266.

Cantwell, D. P., & Baker, L. (1980). Psychiatric and behavioral characteristics of children with communication disorders. *Journal of Pediatric Psychology, 5*, 161–178.

Carr, E. G., & McDowell, J. J. (1980). Social control of self-injurious behavior of organic etiology. *Behavior Therapy, 11*, 402–409.

Carr, J. E. (1995). Competing responses for the treatment of Tourette syndrome and tic disorders. *Behaviour Research and Therapy, 33* (4), 455–466.

Cavernar, J. O., Spaulding, J. G., & Sullivan, J. L. (1979). Child's reaction to mother's abortion: Case report. *Military Medicine, 144*, 412–413.

Chafetz, M. D. (1986). Taxonomy in psychology: Looking for subatomic units. *The Journal of Psychology, 120* (2), 121–135.

Chandler, M. L., Barnhill, J. L., Gualtieri, C. T., & Patterson, D. R. (1989). Tryptophan antagonism of stimulant-induced tics. *Journal of Clinical Psychopharmacology, 9* (1), 69–70.

Chengappa, K. N. R., Baker, R. W., & Sirri, C. (1995). The successful use of clozapine in ameriorating severe self-mutilation in a patient with borderline personality disorder. *Journal of Personality Disorders, 9* (1), 76–82.

Clementz, G. L., Lee, R. L., & Barclay, A. M. (1988). Tic disorders of childhood. *American Family Physician, 38* (2), 163–170.

Clerk, G. (1972). An ego-psychological approach to the problem of oral aggression. *International Journal of Psychoanalysis, 53*, 77–82.

Cohen, D. J., Leckman, J. F., & Towbin, K. E. (1989). Tic disorders. In *Treatments of psychiatric disorders: A task force report of the American Psychiatric Association* (Vol. 1–3 & Index Vol., pp. 687–714). Washington, DC: American Psychiatric Association.

Cohen, D. J., Riddle, M. A., & Leckman, J. F. (1992). Pharmacotherapy of Tourette's syndrome and associated disorders. *Psychiatric Clinics of North America, 15*, 109–129.

Comings, D. E. (1994). Tourette syndrome: A hereditary neuropsychiatric spectrum disorder. *Annals of Clinical Psychiatry, 6*, 235–247.

Comings, D. E. (1995). "DSM-IV criteria for Tourette's": Response. *Journal of the American Academy of Child and Adolescent Psychiatry, 34*, 401–402.

Comings, D. E., & Comings, B. G. (1985). Tourette syndrome: Clinical and psychological aspects of 250 cases. *American Journal of Human Genetics, 37* (3), 435–350.

Comings, D. E., & Comings, B. G. (1993). Sexual abuse or Tourette's syndrome? *Social Work, 38*, 347–350.

Corbett, J. A., Matthews, A. M., Connell, P. H., & Shapiro, D. A. (1969). Tics and Gilles de la Tourette's syndrome: A follow-up study and critical reviews. *British Journal of Psychiatry, 115*, 1229–1241.

Cowdery, G. E., Iwata, B. A., & Pace, G. M. (1990). Effects and side effects of DRO as treatment for self-injurious behavior. *Journal of Applied Behavioral Analysis, 23*, 497–506.

Culbertson, F. M. (1989). A four-step hypnotherapy model for Gilles de la Tourette's syndrome. *American Journal of Clinical Hypnosis, 31* (4), 252–256.

DeLissovoy, V. (1961). Head-banging in early childhood: A study of incidence. *Journal of Pediatrics, 58*, 803–805.

Dooley, J. M., Stokes, A., & Gordon, K. E. (1994). Pseudo-tics in Tourette syndrome. *Journal of Child Neurology, 9* (1), 50–51.

Dorsey, M. F., Iwata, B. A., Ong, P., & McSween, T. E. (1980). Treatment of self-injurious behavior using a water mist: Initial response suppression and generalization. *Journal of Applied Behavioral Analysis, 13* (2), 343–353.

Dougherty, E. H., & Lane, J. R. (1976). Naturalistic alternatives to extinction: An application to self-injurious bedtime behavior. *Journal of Behavior Therapy and Experimental Psychiatry, 7*, 373–375.

Duchowny, M. S., Resnick, T. J., Deray, M. J., & Alvarez, L. A. (1988). Video EEG diagnosis of repetitive behavior in early childhood and its relationship to seizures. *Pediatric Neurology, 4* (3), 162–164.

Dura, J. R., Mulick, J. A., & Rasnake, L. K. (1987). Prevalence of stereotypy among institutionalized nonambulatory profoundly mentally retarded people. *American Journal of Mental Deficiency, 91*, 548–549.

Durand, V. M. (1982). A behavioral/pharmacological intervention for the treatment of severe self-injurious behavior. *Journal of Autism and Developmental Disorders, 12* (3), 243–251.

Eapen, V., Pauls, D. L., & Robertson, M. M. (1993). Evidence for autosomal dominant transmission in Tourette's syndrome: United Kingdom cohort study. *British Journal of Psychiatry, 162*, 593–596.

Eapen, V., & Robertson, M. M. (1994). All that tics may not be Tourette's. *British Journal of Psychiatry, 164* (5), 708.

Eapen, V., Srinath, S., & Devi, M. G. (1989). Descriptive study of tic disorder in children. *Indian Journal of Psychological Medicine, 12* (2), 17–22.

Edelson, S. M., Taubman, M. T., & Lovaas, D. I. (1983). Some social contexts of self-destructive behavior. *Journal of Abnormal Child Psychology, 11* (2), 299–311.

Eggers, C., Rothenberger, A., & Berghaus, U. (1988). Clinical and neurobiological findings in children suffering from tic disease following treatment with tiapride. *European Archives of Psychiatry and Neurological Sciences, 237* (4), 223–229.

Elston, J. S., Granje, F. C., & Lees, A. J. (1989). The relationship between eye-winking tics, frequent eye-blinking and blephar spasm. *Journal of Neurology, Neurosurgery and Psychiatry, 52* (4), 477–480.

Evers, R. A., & van de Wetering, B. J. M. (1994). A treatment model of motor tics based on a specific tension-reduction technique. *Journal of Behavior*

Therapy and Experimental Psychiatry, 25 (3), 255–260.

Fahn, S. (1982). A case of post-traumatic tic syndrome. *Advances in Neurology, 35,* 349–350.

Finney, J. W., Rapoff, M. A., Hall, C. L., & Christophersen, E. R. (1983). Replication and social validation of habit reversal treatment for tics. *Behavior Therapy, 14* (1), 116–126.

First, M. B., Frances, A., & Pincus, H. A. (1995). "DSM-IV criteria for Tourette's": Reply. *American Academy of Child and Adolescent Psychiatry, 34,* 402.

Fisher, W. W., Kerbeshian, J., & Burd, L. (1986). A treatable language disorder: Pharmacological treatment of pervasive developmental disorder. *Journal of Developmental & Behavioral Pediatrics, 7* (2), 73–76.

Foxx, R. M., & Azrin, N. H. (1973). The elimination of autistic self-stimulatory behavior by overcorrection. *Journal of Applied Behavior Analysis, 6,* 1–14.

Frazier, J. R., & Williams, B. R. (1973). The application of multiple contingencies to rocking behavior in a non-related child. *Journal of Behavior Therapy and Experimental Psychiatry, 4,* 289–291.

Freeman, R. D., Fast, D. K., & Kent, M. (1995). DSM-IV criteria for Tourette's. *Journal of the American Academy of Child and Adolescent Psychiatry, 34,* 400–401.

Friedman, M., Glasser, M., Laufer, E., Laufer, M., & Wohl, M. (1972). Attempted suicide and self-mutilation in adolescence: Some observations from a psychoanalytic research project. *International Journal of Psychoanalysis, 53,* 179–183.

Fuata, P., & Griffiths, R. A. (1992). Cognitive behavioural treatment of a vocal tic. *Behaviour Change, 9* (1), 14–18.

Gaffney, G. R., Sieg, K., & Hellings, J. (1994). The MOVES: A self-rating scale for Tourette's syndrome. *Journal of Child and Adolescent Psychopharmacology, 4,* 269–280.

Gedye, A. (1989). Extreme self-injury attributed to frontal lobe seizures. *American Journal of Mental Retardation, 94* (1), 20–26.

Gelenberg, A. J., Bassuk, E. L., & Schoonover, S. C. (1991). *The practitioner's guide to psychoactive drugs* (3rd ed.). New York: Plenum Press.

George, M. S., Robertson, M. M., Costa, D. C., & Ell, P. J. (1994). Dopamine receptor availability in Tourette's syndrome. *Psychiatry research: Neuroimaging, 55,* 193–203.

Gerard, M. W. (1946). The psychogenic tic in ego

development. *Psychoanalytic Study of the Child, 2,* 133–141.

Goetz, C. G., Tanner, C. M., & Klawans, H. L. (1984). Fluphenazine and multifocal tic disorders. *Neurology, 41* (3), 271–272.

Golden, G. S. (1977a). The effect of central nervous system stimulants on Tourette's syndrome. *Annals of Neurology, 2,* 69–70.

Golden, G. S. (1977b). Genetic aspects of Tourette syndrome. *Neurology, 27,* 400.

Golden, G. S. (1978). Tics and Tourette's: A continuum of symptoms. *Annals of Neurology, 4,* 145–148.

Golden, G. S. (1982). Movement disorders in children: Tourette syndrome. *Developmental and Behavioral Pediatrics, 3,* 209–216.

Golden, G. S. (1983). Tics in childhood. *Pediatric Annals, 12* (11), 821–824.

Golden, G. S. (1987). Tic disorders in childhood. *Pediatric Review, 8* (8), 229–234.

Golden, G. S. (1990). Tourette syndrome: Recent advances. *Neurologic Clinics, 8* (3), 705–714.

Golden, G. S., & Hood, O. J. (1982). Tics and tremors. *Pediatrics Clinic of North America, 29* (1), 95–103.

Green, A. H. (1967). Self-mutilation in schizophrenic children. *Archives of General Psychiatry, 17,* 234–244.

Greenberg, N. H. (1964). Origins of head-rolling (Spasmus Nutans) during early infancy. *Psychosomatic Medicine, 26,* 162–171.

Gresty, M., & Halmagyi, G. M. (1981). Head nodding associated with idiopathic childhood nystagmus. *Annals of the New York Academy of Science, 374,* 614–618.

Guess, D., & Carr, E. (1991). Emergence and maintenance of stereotypy and self-injury. *American Journal of Mental Retardation, 96,* 299–319.

Harcherik, D. F., Leckman, J. F., Detlor, J., & Cohen, D. J. (1984). A new instrument for clinical studies of Tourette's syndrome. *Journal of the American Academy of Child Psychiatry, 23,* 153–160.

Harris, M. (1968). The child psychotherapist and the patient's family. *Journal of Child Psychotherapy, 2,* 50–63.

Harris, S. L., & Romanczyk, R. G. (1976). Treating self-injurious behavior of a retarded child by overcorrection. *Behavior Therapy, 7,* 235–239.

Haskell, E. L., & Joffe, R. (1984). Clonidine in a case of atypical tic disorder. *Canadian Journal of Psychiatry, 29* (8), 704–706.

Haynes, S. N., Wilson, C. C., Jaffe, P. G., & Britton, B. V. (1979). Biofeedback treatment of atopic dermatitis: Controlled case studies of eight cases. *Biofeedback and Self-Regulation, 4,* 195–209.

Head, L. A., & Sallee, F. R. (1994). Tic disorders. In M. Hersen, R. T. Ammerman, & L. A. Sisson (Eds.), *Handbook of aggressive and destructive behavior in psychiatric patients* (pp. 429–444). New York: Plenum Press.

Head, L. A., Sallee, F. R., & Shannon, M. P. (1993). Tic disorders. In R. T. Ammerman, C. G. Last, & M. Hersen (Eds.), *Handbook of prescriptive treatments for children and adolescents* (pp. 300–314). Boston, MA: Allyn and Bacon.

Heistad, G. T., Zimmermann, R. L., & Doebler, M. I. (1982). Long-term usefulness of thioridazine for institutionalized mentally retarded patients. *American Journal of Mental Deficiency, 87,* 243–251.

Hellings, J. A., & Warnock, J. K. (1994). Self-injurious behavior and serotonin in Prader-Willi syndrome. *Psychopharmacology Bulletin, 30* (2), 245–250.

Hemming, M., & Yellowlees, P. M. (1993). Effective treatment of Tourette's syndrome with marijuana. *Journal of Psychopharmacology, 7,* 389–391.

Hile, M. G., & Vatterott, M. K. (1991). Two decades of treatment for self-injurious biting in individuals with mental retardation or developmental disabilities: A treatment-focused review of the literature. *Journal of Developmental and Physical Disabilities, 3* (1), 81–113.

Hile, M. G., & Vatterott, M. K. (1992). Two decades of treatment for self-injurious biting in individuals with mental retardation or developmental disabilities: A treatment-focused review of the literature: Erratum. *Journal of Developmental and Physical Disabilities, 4,* 97.

Holvey, D. N., & Talbott, J. H. (1972). *The Merck manual of diagnosis and therapy.* Rahway, NJ: Merck, Sharp, & Dohme Research Laboratories.

Hurst, M. J., & Hurst, D. L. (1994). Tolstoy's description of Tourette Syndrome in *Anna Karenina. Journal of Child Neurology, 9* (4), 366–367.

Hutt, S. J., & Hutt, C. (1968). Stereotype, arousal, and autism. *Human Development, 11,* 277–286.

Hyde, T. M., Fitzcharles, E. K., & Weinberger, D. R. (1993). Age-related prognostic factors in the severity of illness of Tourette's syndrome in monozygotic twins. *Journal of Neuropsychiatry and Clinical Neurosciences, 5,* 178–182.

Hynd, G. W., & Hooper, S. R. (1992). *Neurological basis of childhood psychopathology.* Newbury Park, CA: Sage Publications.

Iakupova, L. P. Smirnov, A. I., Kozlova, I. A., & Gorbachevskaia, N. L. (1993–1994). Neurophysiological aspects of the study of children with the Gilles de la Tourette syndrome. *Journal of Russian and East European Psychiatry, 26,* 39–44.

Itard, J. M. G. (1825). Memories of some involuntary functions of the appearance of movement, grasp, and voice. *Archives of General Medicine,* 8, 358.

Iwata, B. A., Dorsey, M. F., Slifer, K. J., Bauman, K. E., & Richman, G. S. (1994). Toward a functional analysis of self-injury. *Journal of Applied Behavior Analysis, 27,* 197–209.

Iwata, B. A., Pace, G. M., Cowdery, G. E., & Miltenberger, R. G. (1994). What makes extinction work: An analysis of procedural form and function. *Journal of Applied Behavior Analysis, 27* (1), 131–144.

Iwata, B. A., Pace, G. M., Dorsey, M. F., Zarcone, J. R., Vollmer, T. R., Smith, R. G., Rodgers, T. A., Lerman, D. C., Shore, B. A., Mazaleski, J. L., Goh, H., Cowdery, G. E., Kalsher, M. J., McCosh, K. C., & Willis, K. D. (1994). The functions of self-injurious behavior: An experimental-epidemiological analysis. *Journal of Applied Behavior Analysis, 27,* 215–240.

Jagger, J., Proshoff, B. A., Cohen, D. J., Kidd, K. K., Carbonari, C. M., & John, K. (1982). The epidemiology of Tourette syndrome: A pilot study. *Schizophrenia Bulletin, 8,* 267–279.

Jan, J. E., Good, W. V., Freeman, R. D., & Espezel, H. (1994). Eye-poking. *Developmental Medicine and Child Neurology, 36* (4), 321–325.

Jankovic, J., & Fahn, S. (1986). The phenomenology of tics. *Movement Disorders, 1* (1), 17–26.

Johnson, W. L., & Baumeister, A. A. (1978). Self-injurious behavior: A review and analysis of methodological details of published studies. *Behavior Modification, 2,* 465–487.

Johnson, W. L., & Day, R. M. (1992). The incidence and prevalence of self-injurious behavior. In J. K. Luiselli, J. L. Matson, & N. N. Singh (Eds.), *Self-injurious behavior: Analysis, assessment, and treatment* (pp. 21–56). New York: Springer.

Jones, R. S. (1988). Treating high-rate stereotyped behaviours in children. *Child Care and Health Development, 14* (3), 175–188.

Jordon, J., Singh, N. N., & Repp, A.C. (1989). An evaluation of gentle teaching and visual screening in the reduction of stereotypy. *Journal of Applied Behavioral Analysis, 22* (1), 9–22.

Jorgenson, H. (1974). The use of a contingent music

activity to modify behaviors which interfere with learning. *Journal of Music Therapy, 11,* 41–44.

Kaliappan, K. V., & Murphy, H. N. (1982). Negative practice and tics: A case analysis. *Journal of Psychological Research, 26* (2), 61–62.

Kaplan, G. M. (1991). The use of biofeedback in the treatment of chronic facial tics: A case study. *Medical Psychotherapy: An International Journal, 4,* 71–76.

Kelman, D. H. (1965). Gilles de la Tourette's disease: A review of the literature. *Journal of Child Psychology and Psychiatry, 6,* 219–226.

Kempenaers, C., Bouillon, E., & Mendlewicz, J. (1994). A rhythmic disorder in REM sleep: A case report. *Sleep, 17,* (3), 274–279.

Kendell, R. E. (1988). Priorities for the next decade. In J. E. Mezzich & M. von Cranach (Eds.), *International classification in psychiatry: Unity and diversity.* (pp. 332–340). New York: Cambridge University Press.

Kendell, R. E. (1991). Relationship between the DSM-IV and the ICD-10. *Journal of Abnormal Psychology, 100* (3), 297–301.

Kennedy, H., & Moran, G. S. (1984). The developmental roots of self-injury and response to pain in a 4-year-old boy. *Psychoanalytic Study of Children, 39,* 195–212.

Kerbeshian, J., & Burd, L. (1985). Auditory hallucinosis and atypical tic disorder: Case reports. *Journal of Clinical Psychiatry, 46* (9), 398–399.

Kerbeshian, J., & Burd, L. (1994). Tourette's syndrome: A developmental psychobiological view. *Journal of Developmental & Physical Disabilities, 6* (3), 203–218.

Keshavan, M. S. (1988). The ear wigglers: Tics of the ear in 10 patients. *American Journal of Psychiatry, 145* (11), 1462–1463.

King, B. H. (1995). Fluoxetine reduced self-injurious behavior in an adolescent with mental retardation. *Journal of Child and Adolescent Psychopharmacology, 1* (5), 321–329.

Kivalo, A. (1979). An evaluation and follow-up study of children with tics. *Psychiatria Fennica,* 59–63.

Klackenberg, G. (1949). Thumbsucking: Frequency and etiology. *Pediatrics, 4,* 418–424.

Klawans, H. L., & Barr, A. (1985). Recurrence of childhood multiple tic in late adult life. *Archives of Neurology, 42* (11), 1079–1080.

Kohut, H. (1972). Thoughts on narcissism and narcissistic rage. *Psychoanalytic Study of the Child, 27,* 360–400.

Kolb, B., & Whishaw, I.Q. (1990). *Fundamentals of human neuropsychology.* New York: W. H. Freeman.

Kravitz, H., Rosenthal, V., Teplitz, Z., Murphy, J., & Lesser, R. (1960). A study of head banging in infants and children. *Disease of the Nervous System, 21,* 203–208.

Lahey, B. B., McNees, M. P., & McNees, M. C. (1973). Control of an obscene "verbal tic" through time-out in an elementary school classroom. *Journal of Applied Behavior Analysis, 6,* 101–104.

Lane, R. G., & Dormath, R. P. (1970). Behavior therapy: A case history. *Hospital and Community Psychiatry, 21,* 150–153.

Lang, A. E., Consky, E., & Sandor, P. (1993). "Signing tics": Insight into the pathophysiology of symptoms in Tourette's syndrome. *Annals of Neurology, 33,* 212–215.

Lasich, A. J., & Bassa, F. (1985). Stereotyped movement disorder of rocking. *Journal of Nervous and Mental Disease Disorders, 173* (3), 187–190.

Leckman, J. F., & Cohen, D. J. (1988). Descriptive and diagnostic classifications of tic disorders. In D. J. Cohen, R. D. Bruun, & J. F. Leckman (Eds.), *Tourette's syndrome and tic disorders: Clinical understanding and treatment* (pp. 3–19). New York: Wiley.

Leckman, J. F., Towbin, K. E., Ort, S. I., & Cohen, D. J. (1988). Clinical assessment of tic disorder severity. In D. J. Cohen, R. D. Bruun, & J. F. Leckman (Eds.), *Tourette's syndrome and tic disorders: Clinical understanding and treatment* (pp. 55–78). New York: Wiley.

Lerer, R. J. (1987). Motor tics, Tourette syndrome, and disabilities. *Journal of Learning Disabilities, 20* (5), 266–270.

Leung, A. K., & Fagan, J. E. (1989). Tic disorders in childhood (and beyond). *Postgraduate Medicine, 86* (1), 251–252, 257–261.

Levine, F. M., & Ramirez, R. (1989). Contingent negative practice as a home-based treatment of tics and stuttering. In C. E. Schaefer, & J. M. Briesmeister (Eds.), *Handbook of parent training: Parents as co-therapists for children's behavior problems.* New York: Wiley.

Lewis, M. H., Baumeister, A. A., & Mailman, R. B. (1987). A neurobiological alterative to the perceptual reinforcement hypothesis of stereotyped behavior: A commentary on "self-stimulatory behavior and perceptual reinforcement." *Journal of Applied Behavior Analysis, 20,* 253–258.

Linn, D. M., Rojahn, J., Helsel, W. J., & Dixon, J. (1988). Acute effects of transcutaneous electric nerve stimulation on self-injurious behavior. *Journal of the Multihandicapped Person, 1* (2), 105–119.

Linscheid, T. R., Copeland, A. P., Jacobstein, D. M., & Smith, J. L. (1981). Overcorrection treatment for nighttime self-injurious behavior in two normal children. *Journal of Pediatric Psychology, 6,* 29–35.

Lloyd, J., Kauffman, J., & Weygant, A. (1982). Effects of response-cost contingencies on thumb-sucking and related behaviours in the classroom. *Educational Psychology, 2* (2), 167–173.

Lourie, R. S. (1949). The role of rhythmic patterns in childhood. *American Journal of Psychiatry, 105,* 653–660.

Lovaas, I., Newsom, C., & Hickman, C. (1987). Self-stimulatory behavior and perceptual reinforcement. *Journal of Applied Behavioral Analysis, 20,* 45–68.

Lovaas, O., & Simmons, J. Q. (1969). Manipulation of self-destruction in three retarded children. *Journal of Applied Behavior Analysis, 2,* 143–152.

Lucas, A. R., & Rodin, E. A. (1973). Electroencephalogram in Gilles de la Tourette's disease. *Diseases of the Nervous System, 34,* 85–89.

Mace, F. C., Browder, D. M., & Lin, Y. (1987). Analysis of demand conditions associated with stereotypy. *Journal of Behavioral Therapy and Experimental Psychiatry, 18* (1), 25–31.

Mahler, M. S. (1949). A psychoanalytic evaluation of tic in psychopathology of children: Symptomatic and the syndrome. *Psychoanalytic Study of the Child, 3,* 279–285.

Malatesta, V. J. (1990). Behavioral case formulation: An Experimental assessment study of transient tic disorder. *Journal of Psychopathology and Behavioral Assessment, 12* (3), 219–232.

Martin, A. (1977). Tourette's syndrome. *Children Today, 6,* 26–27.

Martin, R. D., & Conway, J. B. (1976). Aversive stimulation to eliminate infant nocturnal rocking. *Journal of Behavior Therapy and Experimental Psychiatry, 7,* 200–201.

Matesevac, H. (1991). Toward a psychological understanding of Tourette syndrome (TS). *Psychotherapy, 28* (4), 643–645.

Matesevac, H. (1993). Treatment of impulse disorders: Tic, OCD and ADHD. In L. F. Koziol, C. E. Stout, & D. H. Ruben (Eds.), *Handbook of childhood impulse disorders and ADHD: Theory and practice.* Springfield, IL: Charles C. Thomas.

Matson, J. L. (1989). Self-injury and stereotypies. In T. H. Ollendick & M. Hersen (Eds.), *Handbook of child psychopathology* (2nd ed., pp. 265–275). New York: Plenum Press.

Matthews, L. H., Leibowitz, J. M., & Matthews, J. R. (1992). Tics, habits, and mannerisms. In C. E. Walker & M. C. Roberts (Eds.), *Handbook of clinical child psychology* (2nd ed., pp. 283–302). New York: Wiley.

Matthews, W., & Barabas, G. (1985). Recent advances in developmental pediatrics related to achievement and social behavior. *School Psychology Review, 14* (2), 182–187.

Medical mystery: Tourette's. (1981, January). *M.D.,* 62–64.

Meiselas, K. D, Spencer, E.K., Oberfield, R., Peselow, E. D., Angrist, B., & Campbell, M. (1989). Differentiation of stereotypies from neuroleptic-related dyskinesias in autistic children. *Journal of Clinical Psychopharmacology, 9,* 207–209.

Messiha, F. S., & Carlson, J. C. (1983). Behavioral and clinical profiles of Tourette's disease: A comprehensive overview. *Brain Research Bulletin, 11,* 195–204.

Miller, A. L. (1970). Treatment of a child with Gilles de la Tourette's syndrome using behavior modification techniques. *Journal of Behavior Therapy and Experimental Psychiatry, 1,* 319–321.

Miltenberger, R. G., Fuqua, R. W., & McKinley, T. (1985). Habit reversal with muscle tics: Replication and component analysis. *Behavior Therapy, 16* (1), 39–50.

Mishra, M. N. (1985). Behaviour modification applied to some problems of children. *Dayalbagh Educational Institute Research Journal of Education, 3* (1), 34–36.

Missildine, W. H. (1964). Intrafamilial relationships of children with tics. *Feelings and Their Medical Significance, 6,* 1–4.

Money, J., Wolff, G., & Annecillo, C. (1972). Pain agnosia and self-injury in the syndrome of reversible somatotropin deficiency (psychosocial dwarfism). *Journal of Autism and Childhood Schizophrenia, 2,* 127–139.

Morrison, J. R. (1973). Catatonia. *Archives of General Psychiatry, 28,* 39–41.

Morrissey, P. A., Franzini, L. R., & Karen, R. L. (1992). The salutary effects of light calisthenics and relaxation training on self-stimulation in the developmentally disabled. *Behavioral Residential Treatment, 7* (5), 373–389.

Neef, N. A. (Ed.). (1994). Special issue on functional analysis approaches to behavioral assessment and treatment. *Journal of Applied Behavioral Analysis, 27* (2).

Negishi, Y. (1983). Psychotherapeutic study of tics in childhood: On relationship between family dynamics and onset. *Psychiatry and Neurology of Japan, 37* (1), 1–23.

Noel, L. P., & Clarke, W. N. (1982). Self-inflicted ocular injuries in children. *American Journal of Ophthalmology, 94* (5), 630–633.

Nunn, R. G., & Azrin, N. H. (1976). Eliminating nail-biting by the habit reversal procedure. *Behavior Research and Therapy, 14,* 65–67.

O'Brien, J. S., & Brennan, J. H. (1979). The elimination of a severe long-term facial tic and vocal distortion with multi-facet behavior therapy. *Behavior Therapy and Experimental Psychiatry, 10,* 257–261.

Ollendick, D. G. (1989). Tics and Tourette's disorder. In T. H. Ollendick & M. Hersen (Eds.), *Handbook of child psychopathology* (2nd ed., pp. 277–290). New York: Plenum Press.

Ollendick, T. H. (1981). Self-monitoring and self-administered overcorrection: The modification of nervous tics in children. *Behavior Modification, 5,* 75–84.

Ollendick, T. H., & Ollendick, D. G. (1990). Tics and Tourette syndrome. In A. M. Gross & R. S. Drabman (Eds.), *Handbook of clinical behavioral pediatrics: Applied clinical psychology* (pp. 243–252). New York: Plenum Press.

Peterson, A. A., Campise, R. L., & Azrin, N. H. (1994). Behavioral and pharmacological treatments for tic and habit disorders: A review. *Journal of Developmental and Behavioral Statistics, 15* (6), 430–441.

Peterson, B. S., Leckman, J. F., Duncan, J. S., & Wetzles, R. (1994). Corpus callosum morphology from magnetic resonance images in Tourette's syndrome. *Psychiatry Research: Neuroimaging, 55,* 85–99.

Peterson, R. F., & Peterson, L. R. (1968). The use of positive reinforcement in the control of self-destructive behavior in a retarded boy. *Journal of Experimental Child Psychology, 6,* 351–360.

Phillips, R. H., & Muzaffer, A. (1961). Some aspects of self-mutilation in the general population of a large psychiatric hospital. *Psychiatric Quarterly, 35,* 421–423.

Pinkerton, S. S., Hughes, H., & Wenrich, W. W. (1982). *Behavioral medicine: Clinical applications.* New York: Wiley.

Polak, L., Molcan, J., & Dimova, N. (1985). Butyrophenons are superior to thioridazine in the treatment of tic in children. *Activitas Nervosa Superior, 27* (1), 46–47.

Poth, R., & Barnett, D. W. (1983). Reduction of a behavioral tic with a preschooler using relaxation and self-control techniques across settings. *School Psychology Review. 12* (4), 472–476.

Pray, B., Kramer, J. J., & Lindskog, R. (1986). Assessment and treatment of tic behavior: A review and case study. *School Psychology Review. 15* (3), 418–429.

Price, R. A., Leckman, J. F., Pauls, D. L., Cohen, D. J., & Kidd, K. K. (1986). Gilles de la Tourette's syndrome: Tics and central nervous system stimulants in twins and nontwins. *Neurology, 36* (2), 232–237.

Primeau, F., & Fontaine, R. (1987). Obsessive disorder with self-mutilation: A subgroup responsive to pharmacotherapy. *Canadian Journal of Psychiatry, 32,* 699–701.

Prytula, R. E., Joyner, K. B., & Schnelle, J. F. (1981). Utilizing the school for control of head-banging behavior of a child at home. *Psychological Reports, 48* (3), 887–894.

Rauch, S. L., Baer, L., Cosgrove, G. R., & Jenike, M. A. (1995). Neurosurgical treatment of Tourette's syndrome: A critical review. *Comprehensive Psychiatry, 36* (2), 141–156.

Reid, D. H., Parsons, M. B., Phillips, J. F., & Green, C. W. (1993). Reduction of self-injurious hand mouthing using response blocking. *Journal of Applied Behavior Analysis, 26,* 139–140.

Richardson, J. S., & Zaleski, W. A. (1983). Naloxone and self-mutilation. *Biological Psychiatry, 18* (1), 99–101.

Riddle, M. A., Hardin, M. T., Cho, S. C., Woolston, J. L., & Leckman, J. F. (1988). Desipramine treatment of boys with attention-deficit hyperactivity disorder and tics: Preliminary clinical experience. *Journal of the American Academy of Child and Adolescent Psychiatry, 27* (6), 811–814.

Ridley, R. M., & Baker, H. F. (1982). Stereotypy in monkeys and humans. *Psychological Medicine, 12* (1), 61–72.

Rincover, A. (1986). Behavioral research in self-injury and self-stimulation. *Psychiatric Clinics of North America, 9* (4), 755–766.

Rincover, A., Cook, A. R., Peoples, A., & Packard, D. (1979). Sensory extinction and sensory reinforcement principles for programming multiple adaptive behavior change. *Journal of Applied Behavior Analysis, 12,* 221–233.

Robertson, M. M. (1994). Gilles de la Tourette syndrome: An update. *Journal of child Psychology & Psychiatry & Allied Disciplines, 35* (4), 597–611.

Rosenberg, C. (1995). Elimination of a rhythmic movement disorder with hypnosis: A case report. *Sleep, 18* (7), 608–609.

Rosenberg, L. A., Brown, J., & Singer, H. S. (1992). Behavioral problems and severity of tics. *Journal of Clinical Psychology, 51* (6), 760–767.

Sandman, C. A., Barron, J. L., & Coleman, H. (1990). An orally administered opiate blocker, naltrexone, attenuates self-injurious behavior. *American Journal of Mental Retardation, 95*, 93–102.

Sandyk, R. (1995). Improvement of right hemispheric functions in a child with Gilles de la Tourette's syndrome by weak electromagnetic fields. *International Journal of Neuroscience, 81*, 199–213.

Saul, L. J. (1976). A psychoanalytic view of hostility: Its genesis, treatment, and implications for society. *Humanitas, 12*, 171–182.

Scahill, L., Ort, S. I., & Hardin, M. T. (1993). Tourette's syndrome: II. Contemporary approaches to assessment and treatment. *Archives of Psychiatric Nursing, 7* (4), 209–216.

Schulman, M. (1974). Control of tics by maternal reinforcement. *Journal of Behavior Therapy and Experimental Psychiatry, 5*, 95–96.

Schultz, T., & Berkson, G. (1995). Definition of abnormal focused affections and exploration of their relation to abnormal stereotyped behaviors. *American Journal of Mental Retardation, 100*, 376–390.

Schwartz, S. S., Gallagher, R. J., & Berkson, G. (1986). Normal repetitive and abnormal stereotyped behavior of nonretarded infants and young mentally retarded children. *American Journal of Mental Deficiency, 90* (6), 625–630.

Shapiro, E., Barrett, R. P., & Ollendick, T. H. (1980). A comparison of physical restraint and positive practice overcorrection in treating stereotypic behavior. *Behavior Therapy, 11*, 227–233.

Shapiro, E. S., & Kratochwill, T. R. (1988). *Behavioral assessment in schools: Conceptual foundations and practical applications.* New York: Guilford Press

Shapiro, A. K., & Shapiro, E. (1981a). Do stimulants provoke, cause, or exacerbate tics and Tourette syndrome? *Comprehensive Psychiatry, 22* (3), 265–273.

Shapiro, A. K., & Shapiro, E. (1981b). The treatment and etiology of tics and Tourette syndrome. *Comprehensive Psychiatry, 22* (2), 197–205.

Shapiro, A. K., & Shapiro, E. (1982). An update on Tourette syndrome. *American Journal of Psychotherapy, 36* (3), 379–390.

Shapiro, A. K., & Shapiro, E. (1989). Tic disorders. In H. I. Kaplan & B. J. Sadock (Eds.), *Comprehensive textbook of psychiatry, Vols. 1 & 2* (5th ed., pp. 1865–1878). Baltimore: Williams & Wilkins.

Shapiro, A. K., & Shapiro, E. (1992). Evaluation of the reported association of obsessive-compulsive symptoms of disorder with Tourette's disorder. *Comprehensive Psychiatry, 33* (3), 152–165.

Shapiro, A. K., & Shapiro, E. (1996). Treatment of tic disorders with neuroleptic drugs. In M. A. Richardson & G. Haugland (Eds.), *Use of neuroleptics in children: Clinical practice, No. 37* (pp. 137–170). Washington, DC: American Psychiatric Press.

Shapiro, A. K., Shapiro, E., & Fulop, G. (1987). Pimozide treatment of tic and Tourette disorders. *Pediatrics, 79* (6), 1032–1039.

Shapiro, A. K., Shapiro, E., & Wayne, H. (1972). Birth, development, and family histories and demographic information in Tourette's syndrome. *Journal of Nervous and Mental Disease, 155*, 335–344.

Shulman, L. M., Sanchez-Ramos, J. R. & Weiner, W. J. (1996). In R. L. Sprague & K. M. Newell (Eds.), *Stereotyped movements* (pp. 17–34). Washington, DC: American Psychological Association.

Silber, A. (1981). A tic, a dream and the primal scene. *International Journal of Psychoanalysis, 62* (3), 259–269.

Silva, R. R., Munoz, D. M., Barickman, J., & Friedhoff, A. J. (1995). Environmental factors and related fluctuation of symptoms in children and adolescents with Tourette's disorder. *Journal of Child Psychology and Psychiatry and Allied Disciplines, 36*, 305–312.

Singer, H. S., Schuerholz, L. J., & Denckla, M. B. (1995). Learning difficulties in children with Tourette syndrome. *Journal of Child Neurology, 10*, S58-S61.

Singh, N. N. (1981). Current trends in the treatment of self-injurious behavior. *Advances in Pediatrics, 28*, 377–440.

Skinner, B. F. (1953). *Science and human behavior.* New York: Macmillan.

Solnick, J. V., Rincover, A., & Peterson, C. R. (1977). Some determinants of the reinforcing and punishing effects of timeout. *Journal of Applied Behavior Analysis, 10*, 415–424.

Sormann, G. W. (1982). The headbangers tumour. *British Journal of Plastic Surgery, 35* (1), 72–74.

Soussigan, R., & Koch, P. (1985). Rhythmical stereotypies (leg-swinging) associated with reductions in heart-rate in normal school children. *Biological Psychology, 21* (3), 161–167.

Spitz, R. A. (1945). Hospitalism: An inquiry into the genesis of psychiatric conditions in early childhood. *Psychoanalytic Study of the Child, 1,* 53–74.

Sprague, R. L. (1977). Psychopharmacotherapy in children. In M. McMillan (Ed.), *Child psychiatry: Treatment and research*. New York: Brunner/Mazel.

Sprague, R. L., & Newell, K. M. (Eds.). (1996). *Stereotyped movements*. Washington, DC: American Psychological Association.

Strauss, C. C., Rubinoff, A., & Atkeson, B. N. (1983). Elimination of nocturnal headbanging in a normal seven-year-old girl using overcorrection plus rewards. *Journal of Behavior Therapy and Experimental Psychiatry, 14* (3), 269–273.

Swedo, S. E., & Leonard, H. H. (1994). Childhood movement disorders and obsessive-compulsive disorder. *Journal of Clinical Psychiatry, 55* (3, Suppl.), 32–37.

Symons, F. J. (1995). Self-injurious behavior: A brief review of theories and current treatment perspectives. *Developmental Disabilities Bulletin, 23* (1), 90–104.

Tansey, M. A. (1986). A simple and a complex tic (Gilles de la Tourette's syndrome): Their response to EEG sensorimotor rhythm biofeedback training. *International Journal of Psychophysiology, 4* (2), 91–97.

Tarlow, G. (1989). *Clinical handbook of behavioral therapy: Adult medical disorders*. Cambridge, MA: Brookline Books.

Tate, B. G., & Baroff, G. S. (1966). Aversive control of self-injurious behavior in a psychotic boy. *Behaviour Research and Therapy, 4,* 281–287.

Teichman, Y. E., & Eliahu, D. (1986). A combination of structural family therapy and behavior techniques in treating a patient with two tics. *Journal of Clinical Child Psychology, 15* (4), 311–316.

Thangavelu, R., & Martin, R. L. (1995). ICD-10 and DSM-IV: Depiction of the diagnostic elephant. *Psychiatric Annals, 25* (1), 20–28.

Thelen, E. (1979). Rhythmical stereotypes in normal human infants. *Animal Behaviour, 27,* 699–715.

Thelen, E. (1980). Determinants of amounts of stereotyped behavior in normal human infants. *Ethology and Sociobiology, 1,* 141–150.

Thelen, E. (1981a). Kicking, rocking and waving: Contextual analysis of rhythmical stereotypies in normal human infants. *Animal Behavior, 29* (1), 3–11.

Thelen, E. (1981b). Rhythmical behavior in infancy: An ethological perspective. *Developmental Psychology, 17,* 237–257.

Thompson, D. F., & Thelen, E. (1986). The effects of supplemental vestibular stimulation on stereotyped behavior and development in normal infants. *Physical & Occupational Therapy in Pediatrics, 6,* 57–66.

Tibbets, R. W. (1981). Neuropsychiatric aspects of tics and spasms. *British Journal of Hospital Medicine, 25* (5), 454, 456–457.

Tourette Syndrome Classification Study Group (1993). Definitions and classification of tic disorders. *Archives of Neurology, 50* (10), 1013–1016.

Towbin, K. E. (1996). Obsessive-compulsive disorder. In J. M. Wiener (Ed.), *Diagnosis and psychopharmacology of childhood and adolescent disorder* (2nd ed., pp. 375–399). New York: Wiley.

Towbin, K. E., & Cohen, D. J. (1996). Tic disorders. In J. M. Wiener (Ed.), *Diagnosis and psychopharmacology of childhood and adolescent disorder* (2nd ed., pp. 349–374). New York: Wiley.

Troung, D. D., Bressman, S., Shale, H., & Fahn, S. (1988). Clonazepam, haloperidol, and clonidine in tic disorders. *Southern Medical Journal, 81* (9), 1103–1105.

Turpin, G. (1993). The management of tics and movement disorders. *British Journal of Clinical Psychology, 32* (2), 257–258.

Uchiyama, K. (1976). Effects of reciprocal inhibition through autogenic training relaxation on psychogenic tics. *Bulletin of Clinical and Consulting Psychology, 15,* 1–10.

Valente, M. B., & Valente, S. M. (1983). Tics in children and adolescents. *Pediatric Nursing, 9* (5), 323–326.

Van Houten, R. (1993). The use of wrist weights to reduce self-injury maintained by sensory reinforcement. *Journal of Applied Behavior Analysis, 26* (20), 197–203.

Varni, J. W., Boyd, E. F., & Cataldo, M. F. (1978). Self-monitoring, external reinforcement, and timeout procedures in the control of high rate tic behaviors in a hyperactive child. *Journal of Behavior Therapy and Experimental Psychiatry, 9,* 353–358.

Vollmer , T. R., Iwata, B. A., Zarcone, J. R., Smith, R. G., & Mazaleski, J. L. (1993). The role of attention in the treatment of attention-maintained self-injurious behavior: Noncontingent reinforcement and differential reinforcement of other behavior. *Journal of Applied Behavior Analysis, 26,* 9–21.

Walkup, J., Rosenberg, L. A., Brown, J., & Singer, H. S. (1992). The validity of instruments measuring tic severity in Tourette's syndrome. *Journal of the American Academy of Child and Adolescent Psychiatry, 31* (3), 472–477.

Werry, J. S., Carlielle, J., & Fitzpatrick, J. (1983). Rhythmic motor activities (stereotypies) in children under five: Etiology and prevalence. *Journal of American Academy of Child Psychiatry, 22* (4), 329–336.

Williams, C. (1974). Self-injury in children. *Developmental Medicine and Child Neurology, 16,* 88–90.

Wilson, R. S., Garron, D. C., & Klawans, H. L. (1978). Significance of genetic factors in Gilles de la Tourette's syndrome: A review. *Behavior Genetics, 8,* 503–510.

Wirt, R. D., Lachar, D., Klinedinst, J. K., & Seat, P. D. (1984). *Multidimensional description of child personality: A manual for the Personality Inventory for Children.* Los Angeles: Western Psychological Services.

Woodrow, K. M. (1974). Gilles de la Tourette's disease: A review. *American Journal of Psychiatry, 131,* 1000–1003.

Woods, D. W., & Miltenberger, R. G. (1995). Habit reversal: A review of applications. *Journal of Behavior Therapy and Experimental Psychiatry, 26* (2), 123–131.

Woody, R. C., & Laney, M. (1986). Tics and Tourette's syndrome: A review. *Journal of Arkansas Medical Society, 83* (1), 53–55.

World Health Organization. (1992). *ICD-10 classification of mental and behavioural disorders: Clinical descriptions and diagnostic guidelines.* Geneva: Author.

Wright, L., Schaefer, A. B., & Solomons, G. (1979). *Encyclopedia of pediatric psychology.* Baltimore: University Park Press.

Yates, A. J. (1970). *Behavior therapy.* New York: Wiley.

Zahner, G. E. P., Clubb, M. M., Leckman, J. F., & Pauls, D. L. (1988). The epidemiology of Tourette's syndrome. In D. J. Cohen, R. D. Bruun, & J. F. Leckman (Eds.), *Tourette's syndrome and tic disorders: Clinical understanding and treatment* (pp. 79–87). New York: Wiley.

Zamula, E. (1988). Taming Tourette's tics and twitches. *FDA Consumer Report, 22,* 104–110.

Zausmer, D. M., & Dewey, M. E. (1987). Tics and heredity: A study of the relatives of child tiqueurs. *British Journal of Psychiatry, 150,* 628–634.

Zikis, P. (1983). Treatment of an 11-year-old obsessive-compulsive ritualizer and tiqueur girl with in vivo exposure and response prevention. *Behavioural Psychotherapy, 11* (1), 75–81.

Zivkovic, M. (1977). Some beginning results of using the new projective personality test. *Perceptual and Motor Skills, 45* (3, PT1), 910.

10
Elimination Disorders

Michael C. Luxem
Edward R. Christophersen

Elimination disorders of childhood are typically presented as dysfunctions of bowel and/or bladder control. Some elimination disorders are organic in origin and are most often associated with anatomical lesions (e.g., anal stenosis), neurological impairments (e.g., myelomeningocele and Hirschprung disease), endocrine and metabolic disorders (e.g., diabetes insipidus), smooth-muscle disease, urinary-tract infection, or certain drug therapies (e.g., methylphenidate, codeine-containing medications). Disorders of bowel and bladder control that have no known cause are frequently presumed to be nonorganic in origin and are described as being idiopathic or "functional" in origin. Functional elimination disorders are often characterized by significant behavioral involvement with respect to disease etiology and/or maintenance. This chapter examines those elimination disorders of childhood in which behavior is thought to play an important role. Functional disorders of bowel control include chronic constipation, toileting refusal, and functional encopresis (soiling). Functional disorders of bladder control include diurnal enuresis (day wetting) and nocturnal enuresis (night wetting). For reviews of both of these disorders and their treatments, see Christophersen and Rapoff (1992), Schaefer (1979), Walker (1978), Walker, Kenning, and Faust-Campanile (1989), and Walker, Milling, and Bonner (1988); for reviews of nocturnal enuresis and its treatments, see Alon (1995), Cohen (1975), and Shortliffe et al. (1993).

DISORDERS OF BOWEL CONTROL

Introduction

Historical Perspective

The term "functional encopresis" refers to a class of elimination disorders in which bowel control is expected but not acquired, or, once established, is lost or not routinely practiced. According to Anthony (1957), Fowler (1882) reported observing cases of functional encopresis shortly before the turn of the century, and Weissenberg (1926) was among the first to describe its clinical features. Data-based studies of functional encopresis, however, did not appear until almost four decades later; their emergence may have been retarded, in part, by the Victorian-era belief that the development of bowel habits, personality, and social morality were closely related. This widespread perception may have been founded on the so-called Jesuitical hypothesis, which proposed that

> decisive experiences for the formation of the personality are all transacted during the first five years of life within the orbit of the nursery world. It is during this period that the workings of the bowel and bladder are said to be invested with strong ideas of goodness and badness constituting a system of "sphincter morality." (cf. Anthony, 1957, p. 146)

In the early 1900s, proponents of the Mental Hygiene Movement taught that "by learning that one uses the toilet quietly and privately the child first gets the idea that society requires certain arbitrary things" (Bender, 1938, p. 578), suggesting that children who failed to learn bowel control were at risk for social deviance. In 1929, readers of the popular magazine *Parents* were advised to begin bowel training their infants "as soon as the umbilicus has healed [because] praise and rewards given when the child has practiced self-control strengthens his desire to establish right habits" (Selbert, 1929, pp. 17–18). Given the Victorian view of bowel-control training, early studies that attempted to assess and treat functional encopresis of children were almost exclusively psychodynamic in orientation. Although seriously lacking in methodological rigor, many such investigations nonetheless "revealed" psychiatric neuroses underlying encopretic child behavior (e.g., Huschka, 1942; Richmond, Eddy, & Garrand, 1954). Psychoanalytic treatments of encopresis-related personality conflicts and character defects, however, were often prolonged, ineffective, and/or inconclusive (Huschka, 1942), and clinical interest in psychodynamic interventions for functional encopresis failed to develop. (For an empirically based critique of the psychoanalytic model in this regard, cf. Achenbach & Lewis, 1971). By mid-century, it was observed that

> clinicians on the whole, perhaps out of disgust, prefer neither to treat [encopretic children] nor to write about them. The literature as compared with [that concerning] enuresis is surprisingly scanty and what there is seems superficial, as if the children had been observed from a respectable distance. (Anthony, 1957, p. 157)

Fortunately, clinical perceptions of functional encopresis etiology changed. In 1958, the pediatric gastroenterologist Murray Davidson made the astute observation that

> often the real problem of the impaction [and resulting encopresis] is overlooked while the physician ponders the psychodynamics. . . . Emotional problems are frequently apparent in parents and children when constipation and failure in toilet training are associated. Whether the emotional difficulties represent the cart or the horse is not always clear. (Davidson, 1958, p. 752)

Since Davidson's (1958) landmark paper, trends in the assessment and treatment of functional encopresis have reflected a more symptomatic approach, one in which chronic constipation is seen as the "horse" and behavioral difficulties as the "cart."

Diagnostic Description and Critique of DSM-IV

According to the American Psychiatric Association's (1994) *Diagnostic and Statistical Manual* (DSM-IV), the essential diagnostic feature of encopresis is repeated passage of feces in inappropriate places, such as in the child's clothing or on the floor. By DSM-IV definition, (a) passage must occur at least once a month for three months, (b) the chronological age of the child (or its developmental equivalent) must be at least 4 years, and (c) the behavior must not be due exclusively to the direct physiological effects of a substance, (e.g., laxatives) or to a general medical condition except through a mechanism involving constipation. Inappropriate stooling is described in DSM-IV as being involuntary or intentional; when involuntary, it is said to be related often to constipation, fecal impaction, and retention of stool with subsequent "overflow incontinence," that is, passage of liquid stool around and/or through the fecal impaction. (See discussion of toileting refusal).

DSM-IV recognizes two essential subtypes of functional encopresis: (a) encopresis with constipation and overflow incontinence and (b) encopresis without constipation and overflow incontinence. This distinction represents an improvement over previous DSM editions (e.g., DSM-III-R; American Psychiatric Association, 1987), in which functional encopresis was subtyped as "primary" if the child had never acquired fecal continence (where the criterion for continence is at least one year's duration of bowel control) and "secondary" when continence was previously evident. Levine (1992) points out that a classification based on encopresis onset and history of fecal continence may be too general, as some encopretic children appear to be partially toilet trained. Previous DSM subtyping of functional encopresis as "primary" and "secondary" (if such a distinction is reliable and valid) may be of interest to the basic researcher, but as a method of differential diagnosis it does not suggest to the clinician a corresponding course of treatment. DSM-IV is an advancement with regard to treatment; when, on physical examination or by history, functional encopresis can be subtyped as encopresis with constipation and overflow incontinence, the indication for rectal disimpaction and constipation management follows logically. Unfortunately, the clinical distinction between full bowel movements and fecal soiling (as overflow incontinence) is sometimes difficult because the encopretic child may, at various times, streak and stain, pass little "rocks," soil, or pass incomplete movements (Levine, 1981).

When evidence of constipation and overflow incontinence is lacking, the encopretic behavior is, according to DSM-IV, "usually associated with the presence of Oppositional Defiant Disorder or Conduct Disorder [when soiling is deliberate] or may be the consequence of anal masturbation" (American Psychiatric Association, 1994, p. 106). Clinical assumption of the DSM-IV subtype encopresis without constipation and overflow incontinence, however, should be approached with caution. First, chronic constipation in children can be difficult to assess from parental reports and/or from non-radiologic physical examination. Second, some observers suspect that virtually all children with encopresis retain stools at least intermittently (e.g., Levine, 1981). Third, although DSM-IV suggests that "constipation may develop for psychological reasons (e.g., anxiety about

defecating in a particular place or a more general pattern of oppositional behavior) leading to avoidance of defecation" (p. 106), empirical evidence to support this view is lacking.

Without corroborating medical evidence and a reliable behavioral history to support it, the suggestion that functional encopresis is secondary to a child behavioral disorder or that it is symptomatic of child sexual deviance or abuse can lead to assessments and treatments that are unnecessary and possibly even harmful to the child. When suspicion of sexual involvement in the etiology of encopresis is aroused, it is best to weigh the evidence against the observation of Nolan and Oberklaid (1993) that "occasional [encopretic] patients will present with a history of sexual abuse, but this is most unlikely to be related causally to fecal incontinence" (p. 448).

Regarding the diagnostic significance of the clinical presentation of constipation in encopresis assessment, Benninga, Büller, Heyman, Tytgat, and Taminiau (1994) identified a distinct subgroup of encopretic children (N = 50) who presented without clinical evidence of constipation. Moreover, this subgroup exhibited normal colonic transit time and normal rectal manometric features that distinguished them from a sample of children (N = 111) showing encopresis with constipation. Given this evidence, a third subtype, encopresis without constipation but with overflow incontinence, may warrant consideration for inclusion in future DSM editions. Similarly, consideration of a fourth subtype, encopresis with constipation, but without overflow incontinence, may be justified. (See the discussion under Toileting Refusal.)

Diagnostic Description and Critique of ICD-10

The World Health Organization's *International Classification of Mental and Behavioral Disorders: Clinical Descriptions and Diagnostic Guidelines* (ICD-10) (World Health Organization, 1992) provides a brief but useful definition and diagnostic description of nonorganic encopresis. ICD-10 defines the condition as "repeated voluntary or involuntary passage of feces, usually of normal or near-normal consistency, in places not appropriate for that purpose in the individual's own sociocultural setting." Furthermore ICD-10 states that "the condition may represent an abnormal continuation of normal infantile incontinence, it may involve a loss of continence following the acquisition of bowel control, or it may involve the deliberate deposition of feces in inappropriate places in spite of normal physiological control" (World Health Organization, 1992, p. 286). Regarding diagnosis, ICD-10 differentiates among the causal factors of inadequate toilet training, psychological disorder, and physiological retention. The manual points out that encopresis may accompany or follow physiological conditions, such as anal fissure or gastrointestinal infection, and that encopresis and constipation may coexist.

Benefits of ICD-10's diagnostic description include its recognition of the potential roles of toilet training, bowel-movement retention, and/or predisposing and comorbid features in the etiology of functional encopresis. Unlike DSM-IV, however, ICD-10 provides no objective criteria for diagnosing functional encopresis, such as the number of soilings per given period. In addition, ICD-10 places little emphasis on the importance of overflow incontinence in assessing the severity of functional encopresis. Last, ICD-10 suggests that "there is usually some degree of associated emotional/behavioral disturbance" in cases of encopresis, though there is little empirical health-behavior research to support this view (see earlier section on diagnostic description and critique of DSM-IV).

Epidemiology

The prevalence of functional encopresis is estimated to be approximately 3% in the clinic-referred pediatric population (Levine, 1975), and roughly 1–2% in the child population at large (Bellman, 1966). Epidemiological reports of the prevalence of encopresis by child age are rare; in a study conducted in Sweden, Bellman (1966) found that, in a sample of more than 9,000 children, 8.1% of 3-year-olds, 2.8%

of 4-year olds, 2.2% of 5-year-olds, 1.9% of 6-year-olds, and 1.5% of 7-year-olds reportedly soiled their clothing. Because discussion of bowel movements tends to be socially embarrassing for many people, disclosure of child toileting problems—including confidential disclosure within the medical setting—is often difficult for parents; for this reason, childhood encopresis is sometimes called "the hidden disease." (cf. Brody, 1992). As a result, the true prevalence of functional encopresis in children may be significantly higher than current estimates suggest (cf. Mesibov, Schroeder, & Wesson, 1977). The disorder occurs approximately three to six times more frequently in boys than in girls (Levine 1975; Schaefer, 1979; Wright 1975). According to DSM-IV, functional encopresis can persist with intermittent exacerbation for years, but it is rarely chronic. Most untreated cases do not persist beyond adolescence (Lavietes, 1989). Although 15% of the fathers of encopretic children surveyed in the Bellman (1966) study were reportedly encopretic as children, there are few data to suggest encopresis is an inherited disorder.

Brief Review of Bowel Function and Theoretical Models of Pathogenesis

In contrast to the psychodynamic view of the etiology of functional encopresis that suggested primarily psychological causes, Davidson (1958) stressed the importance of physiological mechanisms that contribute to constipation, fecal impaction, bowel-movement withholding, and bowel distention. Data-based studies conducted since Davidson's (1958) seminal paper tend to support the physiological model (cf. Schaefer, 1979). An overview of bowel physiology and its apparent role in the etiology of functional encopresis is presented here.

The colon serves two major functions. One function is temporary storage of feces until they are eliminated from the body by routine defecation. In the normally functioning bowel, the rectum remains empty until feces, stored in the sigmoid colon, enter the rectal vault and initiate a series of coordinated autonomic reflexes. Distention of, and/or pressure against, the internal anal sphincter alerts the brain, via afferent neural pathways, that defecation is necessary and imminent. If defecation is inconvenient or socially inappropriate, the external anal sphincter is contracted voluntarily, and defecation is postponed for a short period. When defecation is convenient and socially appropriate, closure of the glottis, voluntary contraction of the abdominal wall and application of downward pressure against the abdominal organs exerted by the fixation of the diaphragm and inflation of the lungs, plus voluntary release of the external anal sphincter, initiate defecation (Loening-Baucke, 1996). Toilet training acquaints the child with the relevant proprioceptive feedback from the colon and rectum and helps the child coordinate abdominal pressure and relaxation of the external anal sphincter with timely positioning over the potty chair or toilet. The second function of the colon is the resorption of water and salts from stored feces (Wrenn, 1989). Any action that reduces colonic motility, including voluntary bowel-movement withholding, can extend this process, resulting in excessive fecal dehydration and hardening, which, among other things, can lead to constipation.

CHRONIC CONSTIPATION. The term "constipation" refers to significant changes in the frequency, size, consistency, and/or ease of passing stools (Loening-Baucke, 1992). These variables change with child development and diet. Normal infants tend to pass a stool after each feeding; breast-fed infants generally have lower stooling frequencies than formula-fed infants (cf. Hyams et al., 1995). A progressive decrease in stooling frequency, with a corresponding increase in stool size, typically begins at about 6 months of age and continues until about the fourth year, when the normal child tends to pass one stool daily (Weaver & Steiner, 1984). Deviation from this developmental pattern of stooling may be indicative of normal biological diversity, or it may suggest symptoms of constipation.

Numerous physiological and/or behavioral conditions may contribute to constipation (cf. Owens-Stively, 1995). Physiological conditions include hereditary factors (e.g., genetically acquired abnormally long gastrointestinal transit time and/or overly efficient gastrointestinal absorption of water), dietary habits (e.g., insufficient consumption of dietary fiber, excessive consumption of bland foods and/or dairy products), environmental effects (e.g., lead poisoning), various illnesses (e.g., irritable bowel syndrome), and negative side effects of some medications (e.g., opiates). Research by Stern et al. (1995) suggests that some encopretic children excrete certain gastrointestinal hormones that are different than those secreted by normal children, but cause-and-effect relationships with respect to constipation and/or encopresis remain unclear. Behavioral factors that contribute to constipation include insufficient exercise (which can occur during prolonged illness or hospitalization), insufficient fluid intake, changes in daily routine (which can occur during travel and stressful family events), excessive use of laxatives, incompetent toilet training, and/or voluntary bowel-movement withholding to avoid painful defecation or to obtain secondary social gain.

Complaints of chronic pediatric constipation are common (Klish, 1994), and the incidence of such complaints may be increasing. Data compiled from the National Disease and Therapeutic Index show that, for the period 1958 to 1986, there was a twofold rise in the number of physician visits for the treatment of constipation in children aged from birth to 9 years of age and that the prevalence of constipation in this age group was second only to that of persons over the age of 65 years. For the period from 1983 to 1986, physician visits per 100,000 population were approximately 1.8% in the pediatric population and approximately 3.5% in the geriatric population (Sonnenberg & Koch, 1989). Loening-Baucke (1993) reports that the prevalence of chronic pediatric constipation may range as high as 8%.

In infants and young children, chronic constipation is often accompanied by signs of abdominal discomfort, fits of screaming and crying before, during, and after defecation, and bowel-movement withholding (so-called retention) to avoid defecation (Loening-Baucke, 1992); other symptoms can include unusual stool size (e.g., very large or very narrow/stringy), day and night wetting (if the child is toilet trained), and/or loss of appetite (Owens-Stively, 1995). Many parents may recognize dry and hard-formed stools as evidence of constipation, but they may tend to disregard changes in stool consistency, including pebbly stools, as indicative of constipation. Constipation-related stooling abnormalities such as frequent, small stools or infrequent, large stools may not always be distressing to the child. The significance of such episodes may be overlooked or underestimated by parents, and only half of parents recognize constipation symptoms in their children (Loening-Baucke, 1996).

Acute episodes of child constipation are generally infrequent and of short duration (usually a few days), and they are generally easily treated with improvements in diet and exercise. Chronic constipation in children may be persistent or intermittent in duration, and its symptoms can vary from week to week, depending on such things as diet, exercise, family activities, and travel. Limited use of lubricants, bulk-forming laxatives, stimulants, and/or cathartics is sometimes curative, but many cases of chronic pediatric constipation are refractory, especially when treatment is overly conservative and/or inconsistent. When severe and protracted, chronic constipation is often described by the term "obstipation."

Relatively little is known today about the etiology, treatment, and long-term outcome of chronic pediatric constipation. Levine (1982), seeing constipation as the primary cause of functional encopresis, found it in 79% of 102 encopretic pediatric outpatients (Levine, 1975). Levine and Bakow (1976) reported that 33% of 127 encopretic children in their study had reported histories of constipation in infancy. In a study of 174 children age four and younger, Loening-Baucke (1993) found that initial symptoms of idiopathic chronic constipation in children were infrequent (fewer than three bowel moments per week) bowel movements (58%), palpable abdominal mass

(67%), painful bowel movements, often with screaming (77%), and severe stool withholding (97%). Treatment in the Loening-Baucke (1993) study consisted of parent education, fecal disimpaction, prevention of future impaction with daily administration of milk of magnesia taken by mouth, promotion of regular bowel habits with dietary fiber and milk of magnesia, and, for preschoolers, positive reinforcement for toilet sitting and toilet use for bowel movements. At follow-up (mean 2.7 years posttreatment), 52% of the children were traced; 63% had recovered (i.e., they had no soiling and experienced three or more bowel movements per week). The recovery rate for children younger than 2 years of age was significantly better than that of children older than 2 years.

In reviewing the medical charts of 227 children presenting at a gastroenterology clinic for the treatment of difficult defecation, Partin, Hamill, Fischel, and Partin (1992) found that, of 74 children younger than 3 years, 86% presented with pain, 71% had fecal impaction, and 97% had histories of severe bowel-movement withholding. Of the children older than 3 years, 85% presented with fecal soiling, 57% were experiencing painful defecations, 73% had fecal impaction, and 96% had histories of severe withholding. From these data, Partin and his colleagues concluded "painful defecation frequently precedes chronic fecal impaction and fecal soiling in American children. Early, effective treatment of painful defecation in infancy might reduce the incidence of chronic fecal impaction and fecal soiling in school-age children" (p. 1007).

Though the pathogenesis of functional encopresis is not clear, the role of painful defecation, chronic constipation, and toileting refusal appears prominent. Levine (1975) found that 60% of the 102 encopretic children in his descriptive study had histories of toilet-training resistance (i.e., toileting refusal); in their study of 127 encopretic children, Levine and Bakow (1976) found the rate to be 45%.

TOILETING REFUSAL. The term "toileting refusal" describes an adaptive behavior-deficit "disorder" of early childhood in which opposition to toilet training is deemed developmentally and socially inappropriate (Schmitt, 1987; cf. Berk & Friman, 1990; Brazelton, 1962). Schmitt (1987) suggests many children with toileting refusal have excellent bowel and bladder control" when they want to. They can postpone bowel movements until no one is watching. They can wet themselves deliberately when the parent is on the telephone or nursing a younger sibling. Many of these children refuse to sit on the toilet or sit there only if the parent brings up the subject and marches them into the bathroom" (p. 32). One recent study, however, suggests that some children who exhibit toileting refusal are not more oppositional than most children, that some have histories of chronic constipation, and that they sometimes exhibit overt symptoms of emotional and/or physical distress before, during, and/or after defecation (Luxem, Christophersen, Purvis, & Baer, 1996). Ten of 11 children in this study were under the age of four and, by DSM-IV standards, were too young to be diagnosed with functional encopresis. None of the 10 children had reported histories of overflow incontinence, but at least six had histories of chronic constipation. Had these six children been over the age of 4 years, accurate subtyping according to DSM-IV would have not been possible because DSM-IV makes no provision for the subtype, encopresis with constipation and without overflow incontinence.

Toileting refusal has been attributed to (a) psychosocial stresses during toilet training (Levine, 1981, 1982), (b) coercive or overpermissive toilet training (Huschka, 1942; Richmond et al., 1954), (c) fear of toilets (Ashkenazi, 1975; Doleys & Arnold, 1975; Walker & Werstlein, 1980), (d) differential maternal attention to refusal (Conger, 1970; Lal & Lindsey, 1968), (e) lack of adequate foot supports required for "bearing down" during defecation (Davidson et al., 1963); (f) mild constipation, episodic hard-stooling, painful defecation, and/or anal-fissure irritation (Christophersen & Rapoff, 1992; Levine, 1975; Rappaport & Levine, 1986), and (g) toileting-training specific oppositional behavior (Schmitt, 1987).

Toileting refusers may be at risk for developing encopresis (Christophersen & Rapoff, 1992). The mechanism by which toileting refusal may contribute to a loss of bowel control is as follows. When voluntary bowel-movement withholding prevents defecation, progressive impaction ensues as peristaltic movements of the colon compress bowel matter into a firm, hard mass. When normal bowel capacity is exceeded, a large-caliber stool is passed painfully. To avoid recurrence of this event, the constipated child may inadvertently initiate a vicious "pain-retention-pain" cycle (Rappaport & Levine, 1986) in which each stool-withholding episode decreases colonic motility, increases constipation and fecal desiccation, and leads to progressive fecal hardening and impaction. Occasional liquid fecal matter and fecal-stained mucous passing involuntarily around and/or through the hardened fecal mass produces what is termed overflow incontinence. Although the observable symptoms of overflow incontinence mimic those of diarrhea, the condition is in fact a "ballvalve" effect (Suckling, 1962) in which the stool concretion distends the rectum, obstructs the anal opening, and prevents defecation—hence the term "paradoxical diarrhea," in which liquid stool passes around and/or through the hardened fecal masses. Well-intentioned parents, observing what they perceive as diarrhea, sometimes administer over-the-counter antidiarrheal agents to the child. This treatment only exacerbates the problem because these preparations hasten the resorption of water and salts from the bowel contents and thus make the retained bolus of stool dryer, harder, more impacted, and more painful to pass. Over time, the impacted bowel distends to accommodate the large fecal mass. Chronic dilation of the rectum (megarectum) and colon (megacolon), secondary to impaction, is thought to contribute to reduced rectal and sigmoidal motility, diminished normal sensation of rectal fullness (the "call to stool"), reduced bowel-muscle tone, and impaired coordination of internal and external anal sphincters required for normal defecation (Fleisher, 1976; Meunier, Moillard, & Marechal, 1976).

Encopretic children who complain, "I didn't feel it coming," when soiling occurs may, in fact, be reliable reporters who are experiencing symptoms of anorectal hyposensitivity. The encopretic child with reduced bowel-muscle tone may be unable to evacuate the bowels completely during defecation, leading to involuntary retention of feces. Research by Loening-Baucke (1984, 1987), Loening-Baucke and Cruikshank (1986), and Loening-Baucke, Cruikshank, and Savage (1987), among others, suggests that some children with chronic constipation and encopresis exhibit abnormal contraction of the external anal sphincter during defecation (anismus), a condition that is thought to lead to delayed, impacted, painful, and infrequent bowel movements (Cox et al., 1994). Whether these colorectal dysfunctions are the cause or the effect of megacolon, however, is not clear (Tharper, Davies, Jones, & Rivet, 1992).

Assessment

Medical Assessment

Although parent-reported measures of child behavior are notoriously untrustworthy, toileting-refusal and fecal soiling (when not concealed by the child) are so salient to parents that their report is generally used as its measure. Because encopretic children commonly hide their soiled clothes from their parents (Bellman, 1966), the reliability of child self-report and/or the counting of soiled clothes to estimate soiling accidents, however, is decidedly low. Medical assessment of toileting refusal and functional encopresis symptoms should include an assessment of the child's development in general and toileting readiness in particular (Azrin & Foxx, 1974; see Table 10.1). After ruling out organicity (Davidson et al., 1963), the medical exam should typically include a rectal examination to assess for constipation and impaction (Levine, 1983; Schmitt, 1984) and, if indicated, radiography to detect occult stool retention (Barr, Levine, Wilkinson, & Mulvihill, 1979).

The child's stooling history is a critical component of the medical assessment, and it should include review of the child's stooling patterns (from infancy), stooling frequency (stools per week), stool size (small, normal, large, very large), stool consistency (loose, pebbly, stringy or mucous-striped, normal, hard/dry), and other possible indicators of stooling problems such as anal-skin irritation, anal fissures, and/or bright-red blood in the stool. In addition, the child's history of urination, wetting, and related disorders (especially urinary tract infections), needs to be assessed. Family medical histories of chronic constipation, abnormal stooling patterns, toileting refusal, encopresis, enuresis, and related conditions should not be overlooked.

Assessment of the child's toilet-training history is of paramount importance and should include investigation of the child's toilet-training onset(s) and training duration(s) for bowel and bladder training, the method(s) used, the child and parent responses, and training outcomes, both positive and negative. The child's soiling history should include information about (a) soiling frequency, place, and time of day, (b) "paradoxical" diarrhea, large, and/or foul-smelling stools, (c) appropriate toilet use, if any (frequency, place, time), (d) child and parent responses to accidents as well as responses of others (e.g., siblings, teachers, classmates), (e) previous treatments for soiling, including medical, behavioral, and counseling interventions. Assessment of previous treatments and their effects often reveals important clues concerning parent and/or child ability and/or willingness to comply with treatment recommendations. Data concerning the child's health habits can be telling and should include inquiry into the child's daily diet (intake of high-fiber foods, dairy-products, liquids, and snack foods), eating and sleeping habits, and exercise habits (Doleys, 1981; Levine, 1982, 1992; Wright, 1973).

Behavioral Assessment

Use of child-behavior rating scales, such as the Achenbach Child Behavior Checklist (CBCL)

TABLE 10.1 Toilet-Training Readiness Checklist

1. Does your child urinate a good deal at one time rather than dribbling through the day?
   Yes ___ No ___

2. Does your child stay dry for several hours at a time? Yes ___ No ___

3. Does your child have enough finger and hand coordination to pick up objects easily?
   Yes ___ No ___

4. Does your child walk from room to room easily without help? Yes ___ No ___

5. Can your child carry out the following instructions when asked?
   a. Point to his nose. Yes ___ No ___
   b. Point to her eyes. Yes ___ No ___
   c. Point to his mouth. Yes ___ No ___
   d. Point to her hair. Yes ___ No ___
   e. Sit down on a chair. Yes ___ No ___
   f. Stand up. Yes ___ No ___
   g. Walk to a specific place in another room. Yes ___ No ___
   h. Imitate you in a simple task like playing patty-cake. Yes ___ No ___
   i. Bring your a familiar toy. Yes ___ No ___
   j. Put one familiar object with another, like putting a doll in a wagon. Yes ___ No ___

SCORING

If your answers to questions 1 and 2 are yes, your child has the necessary bladder control to begin toilet training. If your answers to questions 3 and 4 are yes, your child has the physical skills to begin toilet training.

If your child can follow eight of the ten instructions in question 5, your child has the verbal and social skills to begin toilet training.

If your child does not meet all of these criteria, you should delay toilet training until he can meet them.

Source: Azrin, N. H., Foxx, R. M. 1974. *Toilet Training in Less Than a Day.* New York: Simon and Schuster, pp. 36–37.

(Achenbach & Edelbrock, 1983), have historically revealed no systematic differences between encopretic and normal children of the same age and gender; they also show that encopretic children tend to be better adjusted than same-age, same-sex samples of "behavior problem" children (Friman, Mathews, Finney, Christophersen, & Leibowitz, 1988; Gabel, Hegedus, Wald, Chandram, & Chiponis, 1986; Loening-Baucke, Cruikshank, & Savage, 1987). In a comprehensive study comparing 90 children with Attention-deficit disorder (with and without hyperactivity) (American Psychiatric Association, 1987) with learning-disabled and control children, Barkley, DuPaul, and McMurray (1990) found no group differences with respect to toilet training. However, in examining 167 encopretic children in an encopresis clinic at a tertiary-care facility, Johnston and Wright (1993) found the prevalence of T scores on the CBCL Hyperactivity Scale above 70 (i.e., more than two standard deviations above the mean) in that sample to be ten times greater than expected in the normal population (cf. also

Benninga et al., 1994; Young, Brennen, Baker, & Baker, 1994). Whether the sample in this study is representative of most encopretic children presenting for treatment is not known. Without more data to support its use, comprehensive psychological testing beyond initial diagnostic screening is not indicated (Boon & Singh, 1991; Wright, 1973).

The lack of conclusive data showing systematic behavioral differences between encopretic and nonencopretic children should not be interpreted to suggest that children experiencing functional encopresis present without significant behavioral and psychological features. According to DSM-IV,

> the child with Encopresis often feels ashamed and may wish to avoid situations (e.g., camp or school) that might lead to embarrassment. The amount of impairment is a function of the effect on the child's self-esteem, the degree of social ostracism by peers, and the anger, punishment, and rejection on the part of caregivers. (American Psychiatric Association, 1994, p. 106)

In some cases, routine use of the CBCL (Achenbach & Edelbrock, 1991) in evaluating common behavioral problems of children reveals symptoms of the "hidden disease" (cf. Brody, 1992)—specifically, questions numbers 6 and 49, pertaining to bowel movements outside of toilet and constipation, respectively—that parents may simply interpret as further evidence of child behavioral noncompliance and oppositional responding. Given this potentially widespread misconception, encopresis-related conflict at home is probably common. At the extreme, problems of toilet training are thought to provoke some child abuse, even fatal child abuse (Krugman, 1984). Thus, no treatment plan should overlook the importance of treating the child within the context of social contingencies (see discussion of social/interpersonal treatment).

Treatments

The physiological mechanisms described, and the implications for significant behavioral involvement, suggest multiple foci of functional encopresis intervention: constipation and impaction, bowel-movement withholding and toileting refusal, colorectal dysfunction, and family education and counseling. The pediatric and child psychology literatures reveal many medical, behavioral, and medical-behavioral functional encopresis treatments, a few drug interventions (Gavanski, 1971; Murray, Li, McClung, Heitlinger, & Rehm, 1990), some family-systems efforts (McColgan, Pugh, & Pruitt, 1985), and some play-therapy treatments (Carey, 1990). Although many studies that have evaluated these treatments exhibit serious methodological flaws in subject representativeness, measurement, and/or experimental design, "package-type" medical-behavioral interventions appear to offer the most effective treatment approach for managing pediatric functional encopresis (e.g., O'Brien, Ross, & Christophersen, 1986).

Medical Treatments

Medical procedures in these intervention packages generally involve variations of what has come to be known as the "pediatric approach." Originally described by Davidson, Kuglar, & Bauer (1963), this intervention is a three-phase treatment consisting of: (a) bowel clean-out using large doses of mineral oil (a lubricant taken by mouth), followed by (b) bowel reconditioning to normalize stool size and consistency and to normalize stooling frequency using (i) small, daily administrations of mineral oil to soften and lubricate stools, (ii) increased consumption of high-fiber foods and liquids to increase stool bulk and improve consistency (cf. Houts, Mellon, & Whelan, 1988), (iii) scheduled toilet-sits with foot supports to provide leverage for bearing down during defecation, and (c) continuous follow-up to monitor for symptom recurrence. In 12 weeks of clinical trials with 119 severely constipated children, Davidson et al. (1963) found parents reported a 90% success rate when using this regimen.

Other medical treatments include: (a) bulk-forming laxatives (e.g., Metamucil®, Fiberall®, Citrucel®) to increase stool size and stool water content, (b) stimulant laxatives (e.g.,

Senokot®, Dulcolax®, Ex-Lax®, Modane®, Nature's Remedy®) containing bisacodyl, senna extracts, castor oil, phenolphthalein, danthron, and/or cascara to promote bowel contractions, (c) stool softeners (e.g., Colace®, Surfak®, dark Karo® syrup, Maltsupex®) containing ducusate sodium or malt extract, and/or sorbitol-containing fruits and fruit juices (prunes, pears; cf. American Academy of Pediatrics, 1991) to soften stools for easier passage, (d) saline laxatives (e.g., Phillip's® Milk of Magnesia, Fleet® enema) containing magnesium hydroxide, magnesium citrate, or sodium phosphate to increase water in the gastrointestinal tract and stimulate colonic motility, (e) rectally administered glycerin suppositories (e.g., Fleet®, Dulcolax®) to simulate rectal fullness and trigger defecation, (f) various combinations of these agents (e.g., Agoral®, Senokot-S®, Haley's M-O®, Correctol®, Peri-Colace®, Doxodan®), and (f) prescription cathartics (e.g., Chronulac®, Duphalac®, Cephula®) containing laculose and hospital-administered polyethylene-glycol gastrointestinal lavage treatments (e.g., Colyte®, Go-Lytely®) (Christophersen & Rapoff, 1992; Davidson, 1958; Davidson, Kugler, & Bauer, 1963; Owens-Stively, 1995; Pettei and Davidson, 1993; Wright, 1975). Routinization of eating and sleeping are recommended to promote bowel regularity (Christophersen & Rapoff, 1992). (Cf. Owens-Stively, 1995, for an outstanding resource for helping families understand and implement many aspects of the pediatric approach.)

Psychological Treatments

As indicated in the section on historical perspectives, psychodynamic approaches to the treatment of functional encopresis have largely been supplanted by symptomatic approaches. As a result, psychological treatments reported in the contemporary research literature are typically found in combined medical-psychological treatments. Psychological treatments in these regimens include behavioral approaches, biofeedback training, and clinical hypnosis.

BEHAVIORAL TREATMENTS. Behavioral treatments include: (a) positive reinforcement of appropriate bowel movements and nonsoiling, using such reinforcers as snacks, toys, and candy (Ashkenazi, 1975; Doleys & Arnold 1975), praise and approval (Christophersen & Rainey, 1976; Peterson & London, 1965; Schmitt, 1987; Young, 1973), and so-called "child time," or exclusive, positive parental attention or involvement in an activity of the child's own choosing (O'Brien, Ross, & Christophersen., 1986; Wright, 1973), (b) toileting prompts (O'Brien, Ross, & Christophersen, 1986; Young, 1973), and (c) various behavior-reduction techniques for suppressing inappropriate bowel movements, such as contingent ignoring for soiling (Giles & Wolf, 1966), simple correction or overcorrection as a means of toileting-accident restitution and cleanliness training (Azrin & Foxx, 1974; Christophersen & Rainey, 1976; O'Brien, Ross, & Christophersen, 1986; Schmitt, 1987), routinized toilet-sits or so-called "positive practice" toileting rehearsal (Azrin & Foxx, 1971; Christophersen & Rainey, 1976; Foxx & Azrin 1973a; O'Brien, Ross, & Christophersen, 1986), and time-out for soiling (Edelman, 1971; O'Brien, Ross, & Christophersen, 1986; for information on the time-out technique, cf. Christophersen, 1990).

BIOFEEDBACK TRAINING. Biofeedback training is a developing area of research in the treatment of encopresis. First described by Engel, Nikoomanesh, and Schuster (1974) in treating fecally incontinent children with myelomeningocele, this technique involves inserting an inflatable balloon into the rectum to simulate the sensation of rectal fullness. The balloon is connected to a manometric transducer, and a display/recording device informs the encopretic child when, and to what degree, the rectum is distended. Using this information, some encopretic children can be trained to control voluntary contractions of the external anal sphincter and to time those contractions with simulated bowel sensations that mimic the natural "call to stool" (Whitehead, Parker, Masek, Cataldo, & Freeman, 1981). More recent research suggests that electromyographic feedback may be more effective than balloon feedback in treating constipation related to spastic pelvic-floor syndrome (Bleijenberg & Kuijpers, 1994).

Cox et al. (1994) conducted a study in which 26 constipated encopretic children with anismus were randomly assigned to one of two groups. A control group received only a standard medical intervention consisting of enemas, laxative therapy, and dietary modification. Children in the experimental group received the same standard intervention; they also underwent electromyographic biofeedback training to treat their paradoxical constriction. At a 16-month follow-up, parents of the biofeedback-group children reported significantly greater improvement in their children with respect to their constipation, encopresis, laxative use, and painful bowel movements, compared to the children who did not undergo biofeedback training.

Benninga, Büller, and Taminiau (1993) studied 29 patients, ages 5 to 16 years, to evaluate the effects of biofeedback training in treating children with chronic constipation and encopresis. Evidence of external anal contraction or decreased rectal sensation in 16 (55%) and 8 (27%) of the children, respectively, was identified on manometry. After an average of five biofeedback training sessions, 90% of the children learned to relax the external anal sphincter, and 63% normalized rectal sensation, with significant increases in defecation frequency and decreases in encopresis being reported. At six weeks, 55% of the children were clinically symptom-free, and results for these children were sustained at 12-month follow up. Three children relapsed within the following 6-month period; two were then successfully treated with one extra training session. A controlled study by Loening-Baucke (1995) suggests that long-term (approximately 4 years) outcome of biofeedback treatment for chronic constipation and encopresis in children is not superior to conventional treatment, but further research with representative sampling is needed to confirm this finding.

CLINICAL HYPNOSIS. Some so-called cyber-physiologic approaches (Culbert, Reaney, & Kohen, 1994) may hold promise for improving the effects of functional encopresis treatments. These individualized self-regulation techniques involve the integration of self-hypnosis and biofeedback methods to treat a variety of biobehavioral disorders in children. Cyberphysiologic approaches attempt to take therapeutic advantage of the child's innate imaginative abilities and natural drive for control and self-mastery. Some regimens involving this techniques have been shown to be beneficial in treating cases involving panic disorder, muscle/facial pain, and migraine headache (Culbert, Reaney, & Kohen, 1994). Olness (1976) has reported clinical evidence to suggest that, with the aid of self-hypnosis and positive reinforcement, some preschool-age children with histories of treatment failure for bowel-movement withholding and encopresis apparently are able to change their bowel habits when convinced that the change is of their own making. Integration of self-hypnosis with biofeedback for the treatment of disorders of bowel control awaits further study.

Suggested Medical-Behavioral Treatment for Toileting Refusal and Encopresis

Several clinician-researchers have reported or reviewed effective medical-behavioral protocols for treating encopresis (e.g., Christophersen & Rapoff, 1992; Schaefer, 1979; Walker, 1978; Walker, Milling, & Bonner, 1988). In the experience of the authors, an effective protocol for treating both toileting refusal and encopresis is as follows (refer to earlier sections for details and references): For *toileting refusal* treatment, a one-week regimen of bowel conditioning (Phase I) consisting of (a) child behavioral compliance training, (b) dietary modification to increase high-fiber foods intake (total grams per day equal to the child's age plus 5; (cf. Williams, Bollola, & Wydner, 1995), increase liquids intake (as much as the child will accept), and reduce (if not eliminate) dairy-products intake and to begin mineral-oil therapy (1–2 tablespoons/day, or until orange-colored oil is observed leaking into the child's pants), (c) routinization of eating, sleeping, and vigorous outdoor play, with sedentary activities (e.g., TV viewing) limited to 1–2 hours/day), and (d) shaping of toilet-sitting compliance and relaxation, if indicated. Following this regimen, the addition (not substitution) of the following procedures (Phase II) for remedial toilet training, usually for a period of 1–3 weeks: (a) one-time enema-induced bowel cleanout (one or two over-the-counter pediatric-size enemas, the commercial solution being replaced with a 50/50 mixture of milk and molasses (cf. Loening-Baucke, 1996), then, on the following day and for days thereafter, (b) daily administration of adult-size glycerine suppositories 15–20 minutes before mealtime (usually dinner) to control the child's time and place of defecation, (c) use of footstools if child is using an adult toilet, (d) prompting to secure toilet-sitting compliance when defecation appears imminent, along with pleasant games or activities to enhance distraction and relaxation once the child is seated and immediately after appropriate toilet use, and (e) exclusive time (15–20 minutes), with the parent engaged in a play activity of the child's own choosing. Once the child exhibits signs of interest in independent toileting, mineral-oil therapy is faded out over a two-week period, and the contingency is applied: "If you use the potty today, we won't need the medicine [i.e., the suppositories] tonight." For the *encopresis* treatment, Phases I and I are initiated simultaneously rather than sequentially. When implementing any toileting refusal and encopresis treatments, it is essential that parents obtain the approval of the child's physician.

Daily at-home record keeping by the parent is useful when monitoring treatment implementation and treatment effects. When evaluating treatment-resistant cases of toileting refusal or encopresis, review of the daily diary often reveals obvious treatment-effect (or non-effect) relationships. Recommendations tend to follow logically. In the experience of the authors, including increasing dietary fiber intake, increasing mineral oil and/or administering lactulose (e.g., Chronulac®, 1 teaspoon three times daily, by prescription) (or other suitable laxative in the appropriate dose) to soften stools, and/or decreasing dairy-products intake frequently produces a desirable therapeutic outcome.

Provision of special incentives for appropriate toileting is sometimes beneficial, but it is generally used to initiate, rather than maintain, appropriate toileting habits. Parents are encouraged to allow naturally occurring contingencies (e.g., pleasant bodily sensations, rapid return to play activities, sense of self-mastery) to be the child's "reward" for appropriate toileting. When independent, routine toileting is deemed possible, positive practice, overcorrection, (see Table 10.2), and time-out are implemented immediately following each toileting accident.

Social/Interpersonal Treatments

No treatment approach for managing functional encopresis is complete without sensitive and competent family education and counseling. Levine (1992) advocates a "demystification" process by which the child and the child's family learn that (a) encopresis is a common ailment in children, (b) simple drawings and diagrams can help explain how abnormal bowel, functioning can lead to encopresis, (c) the child is not to blame for his or her abnormal bowel functioning, and (d) effective treatment plans are available. Patients and families need to know, however, that functional encopresis treatment is a long-term project. In general, 4 to 6 weeks of consistent treatment is required before substantial improvement in encopretic symptoms is observed; long-term maintenance is needed to prevent constipation and impaction. Thus, provisions must be made for follow-up care that includes, at least during the first month of treatment, daily record keeping of treatments and treatment effects. Routine telephone contact between the family and clinician is vital for assessing progress, making modifications to the treatment plan, and encouraging treatment compliance.

Securing pediatric compliance (cf. Christophersen, 1994; Rapoff & Christophersen, 1982)

TABLE 10.2 Toileting Accidents

After they have been toilet trained, some children occasionally have periods of frequent wetting or soiling. The children should first be examined by a physician to rule out physical conditions, such as urinary tract infections, that may be causing the accidents.

When you find your child with wet or soiled pants, use the following guidelines:

1. *Show verbal disapproval for the wetting or soiling.*
   a. Tell the child why you are displeased, saying something like, "You wet your pants."
   b. Express your disapproval of the accident by saying something like, "You shouldn't wet your pants. You should go in the potty."

2. *Have the child do positive practice of self-toileting.*
   a. Tell your child what you are doing and why by saying something like, "Bobby wet his pants. Bobby has to practice going to the bathroom."
   b. The child walks quickly to the toilet or potty chair.
   c. The child quickly lowers her pants and sits on the potty.
   d. After sitting 1 or 2 seconds (do not allow urination), the child quickly raises his pants.
   e. The child goes to another part of the house and repeats steps b through d for 10 trials. Five of the trials should start where the child had the accident; the other five trials should start from several different places in the house.
   f. If the child refuses to do the positive practice trials or if he has a temper tantrum, put him in time-out. After time-out has ended, begin the positive practice from where you left off.

3. *Make the child responsible for cleaning up.*
   a. If there is wetness on the floor, have the child get a cloth and wipe up the wetness.
   b. With minimum assistance, require the child to remove her soiled pants.
   c. Have the child put her soiled clothes in an appropriate place, like a soiled-clothes hamper.
   d. If the child is dirty, require her to clean herself or take a quick bath.
   e. Have the child put on clean clothes.

4. *After the accident has been corrected, do not continue to talk about it.* Your child should start with a clean slate.

5. *Remember to praise and hug your child when he eliminates in the toilet.* "Catch 'em being good!"

Source: Adapted from Azrin, N. H., and Foxx, R. M. 1976. *Toilet Training in Less Than a Day.* New York: Pocket Books, 1976.

in the treatment of bowel disorders is sometimes difficult. Children who have received rectal enemas may be reluctant to repeat the experience, especially if previous enemas were administered forcefully. Because initial bowel clean-out is often required as a prerequisite for reestablishing bowel control, it is often important to convince the parent(s) and the child that this procedure is a "necessary evil" and certainly a lesser of two evils when compared to the embarrassment and inconvenience of fecal soiling (Levine, 1992). Acknowledging the encopretic child's predicament is often helpful, especially when the child denies being distressed by the his or her condition.

Alternative methods of bowel clean-out may be medically effective but socially objectionable because of (a) the extended duration (usually one or more days) and the unpredictability with which these methods evacuate the bowel contents (as with large doses of mineral oil) and/or (b) the aversive administration procedure. For example, Tolia, Lin, and Elitsur (1993) compared the effectiveness and acceptability of mineral-oil therapy with that of an orally consumed, pineapple-flavored isotonic intestinal lavage solution containing polyethylene glycol-3550 (Colyte®). In their randomized-assignment study of 36 children over the age of two, these researchers found that, while the children in the lavage group had more frequent bowel movements and showed more effective clearance of abdominal and rectal fecal lumps than the mineral-oil group, treatment compliance in the lavage group was poorer than in the mineral-oil group.

The use of rectal suppositories can be objectionable to children (and their parents) as well. Age-appropriate presentation of the rationale and contingencies for suppository use can help enhance suppository-use compliance. In the authors' experience, toileting-refusal children and encopretic children are generally very accepting of the explanation, "If you use the potty today, we [the parent and child] won't need the medicine [i.e., the suppositories] tonight." This approach seems to suggest to the child that (a) he or she has some control over the use of the suppositories, (b) the parent and child are working together, and (c) suppository use is medically therapeutic and not intended as punishment. In conducting a parent-satisfaction survey of families who participated in treatment for toileting refusal, Luxem (1994) found that, on average, parental administration of suppositories using this approach was rated 3.60 on a Likert-type scale where a score of 0 was "extremely easy," a score of 4 was "neither easy nor difficult," and a score 7 was "extremely difficult." Child acceptance of suppositories use was rated 4.80.

Once soiling has been brought under control, long-term maintenance of positive treatment effects is critical. Factors that contribute to cure include systematic fading of procedures (mineral-oil therapy in particular), prophylactic care (especially maintenance of dietary modifications), establishment of routine toilet use, and insistence on the child's acceptance of responsibility for personal hygiene.

Comments

It is unfortunate that contemporary pediatric medicine and clinical child psychology texts do not place more emphasis on what would obviously be the most effective form of treatment for chronic constipation, toileting refusal, and/or functional encopresis—prevention. Although this situation surely reflects the lack of empirical research regarding the etiology of these conditions, a common-sense approach suggests the use of anticipatory guidance (Christophersen, 1986), timely toilet-training readiness assessment, and patience in planning and executing child toilet training.

Because developmental immaturity, behavioral noncompliance, and/or attention-deficit/hyperactivity symptoms in the child may frustrate toilet-training attempts and contribute to bowel-movement withholding and toileting refusal, measures of child behavior (Achenbach, 1994) and toilet-training readiness (Azrin & Foxx, 1974), when administered by unbiased observers, should be applied. Parents should be reminded that, despite the trend toward early toilet training (Seim, 1989), most children do not actually acquire reliable bowel control until they are 3 or 4 years old (Berk & Friman, 1990). Thus, unnecessarily long toilet-training efforts may be avoided by postponing training until late in the child's second year. Last a "bowel-healthy" approach to meal planning and early regulation of the child's eating, sleeping, and exercise habits, may help avoid problems of irregular stooling, constipation, impaction, and painful defecation that may contribute to the development of functional disorders of bowel control (cf. Behrman & Vaughan, 1987; Carpenter, 1994; Levine, 1992).

DISORDERS OF BLADDER CONTROL

Introduction

Enuresis was first recognized as a medical problem in 1550 B.C., according to Glicklich (1951), who concluded that the disorder was born with civilization and will always be with us. It is certainly one of the most widespread problems to come to the attention of behavioral practitioners and pediatricians. In Glicklich's review, which covered more than 100 years of practice, a number of therapeutic procedures were reviewed, some of which, by today's standards, would be considered barbaric, such as the use of acid burns just inside the urinary meatus to awaken the enuretic child as soon as the bed wetting began to occur.

Diurnal enuresis or day wetting has received far less discussion in the literature than has nocturnal enuresis or night wetting. Therefore, mention of day wetting in this chapter is limited to those areas in which literature on the topic is available for review.

Historical Perspective

Mowrer and Mowrer (1938) described the first legitimate behavioral procedure for the treatment of nighttime enuresis long before any commercially available drugs were available for managing the condition. The bell-and-pad method, as it came to be called, involved placing two low-voltage-conducting foil pads on the child's bed, situated in such a way that, when the child started wetting, the two pads would complete a circuit, resulting in the bell ringing, which, by design, was supposed to awaken the enuretic child, interrupt the wetting process, and permit the child to finish voiding into a toilet. The bell-and-pad alarm has been popular over the years, with various brands of systems sold though large department and catalog stores. There are also a number of companies that market bed-wetting alarms through pharmacies and through direct-mail outlets. Typically, the prices are all about the same. Some large clinics and teaching hospitals now offer enuresis clinics, where professional staff members assist families in the implementation of the bell-and-pad alarms.

Diagnostic Description and Critique of DSM-IV

Enuresis is defined in DSM-IV (American Psychiatric Association, 1994) as the repeated voiding of urine into the bed or clothes, whether involuntary or intentional. The behavior is clinically significant when manifested by either a frequency of twice a week for at least 3 consecutive months or the presence of clinically significant distress or impairment in social, academic, or other important areas of functioning. The chronological age of the child must be at least 5 years (or equivalent developmental level), and the enuretic behavior must not be due, exclusively, to the direct physiological effect of a substance (e.g., a diuretic) or a general medical disorder (e.g., diabetes, spina bifida, or a seizure disorder).

Although DSM-IV presents diagnostic symptoms of enuresis, these apply only to night wetting, not to day wetting. To the authors' knowledge, there is no consensus in the published literature as to what constitutes day wetting. Hjalmas (1992) proposes that "leakage" be defined by at least 1 ml. of urine at least once a week in a child older than 5 years in the absence of disease, injury, or congenital malformation.

Diagnostic Description and Critique of ICD-10

The World Health Organization's *International Classification of Mental and Behavioral Disorders* clinical descriptions and diagnostic guidelines (ICD-10) (World Health Organization, 1992) states that nonorganic enuresis is characterized by involuntary voiding by day and/or by night; it may constitute a monosymptomatic condition, or it may be associated with a more widespread emotional or behavioral disorder. However, ICD-10 allows that there is uncertainty over the mechanisms involved in the association and that "there is no straightforward, unambiguous way of deciding between the alternatives in the individual case" (p. 285).

With respect to diagnostic guidelines, ICD-10 states that "there is no clear-cut demarcation between an enuresis disorder and the normal variations in the age of acquisition of bladder control" (p. 285). This said, ICD-10 suggests that enuresis is not ordinarily diagnosed in a child under the age of five (or with a mental age of 4 years). A diagnosis of primary nonorganic enuresis is made only if the involuntary voiding of urine occurs at least "several" times per week.

Given the lack of objectivity in the ICD-10 clinical description and diagnostic guidelines concerning functional enuresis, the manual does not offer any distinct advantage over use of the DSM-IV, except for its recognition of daytime enuresis.

Epidemiology

About 40% of children wet the bed at 3 years of age; the prevalence declines slowly thereafter: 22% at 5 years, 10% at 10 years, and 3% at 15 years (Binderglas, 1975). A positive family history of clinical enuresis has been frequently noted. When both parents were enuretic, 77% of children are enuretic; when one parent was enuretic, 42% of children are enuretic; and when neither parent had a history of enuresis, only 15% of children are enuretic (Cohen, 1975).

Enuresis is generally a self-limiting condition with a spontaneous cure rate of 12 to 15% per year (Binderglas, 1975). Shelov and participants (1981) reported on a survey in which parents and pediatricians were asked at what age children should be dry at night. On average, parents thought children should be dry at night at a much younger age than did the physicians (2.75 years versus 5.13 years, respectively).

Hjalmas (1992) quoted a study, conducted in Gothenburg among 35,567 school students, that reported that day wetting of any kind occurred in 6% of the students. Day wetting at least once a week was found in 3.1% of the girls and 2.1% of the boys. Most of the day-wetting children also had increased urgency; this condition was reported in 82% of the girls and 74% of the boys. Bed wetting at least once a week was reported by only 2.9% of the girls and 3.8% of the boys. Combined daytime and nighttime incontinence was reported by 17% of the children, while 22% wet only by day and 61% only by night. None of the 35,567 children had a previously indicated organic cause for their incontinence. The researchers did report a strong correlation between bacteria and day wetting in girls, but not in boys. Hjalmas stated that the researchers did not know whether the bacteria caused the disturbance of bladder function, or vice versa.

Brief Review of Psychopathology and Theoretical Models

A number of etiologic factors has been proposed for enuresis, including food allergies, deep sleep, small bladder capacity, developmental delays, and faulty training techniques (Cohen, 1975; McKendry & Stewart, 1974; Simonds, 1977). However, no definitive cause of enuresis has been identified. There is general agreement that enuresis is not primarily a psychopathological disorder (Olness, 1975; Perlmutter, 1976; Werry & Cohrssen, 1965). However, secondary emotional and behavioral problems may develop as a result of coping with enuresis.

Numerous treatments for enuresis have been suggested, including diet restrictions, psychotherapy, retention-control training, drugs, and behavioral methods. Assuming that enuretics have a smaller bladder capacity than non-enuretic children, it has been suggested that small bladder capacity may be due to spasms of the smooth muscle in the bladder wall. This spasm may have an allergic basis; therefore, removal of substances that irritate the bladder wall may arrest enuresis (Christophersen & Rapoff, 1992). Recent promotion of the drug DDAVP® has included speculation that enuresis is the result of a hormone deficiency.

Short-term psychotherapy has been recommended by some clinicians for the treatment of enuresis (Sperling, 1965). However, the few comparative studies that have been done have shown short-term psychotherapy is no more effective than no treatment and that more direct methods, such as using a urine alarm, are more effective. Psychotherapy may be indicated in those few cases where significant psychopathology is suspected in addition to the fact that the child is enuretic (Cohen, 1975; Lovibond, 1964).

Assessment

Typically, assessment of enuresis involves ruling out significant pathology, both medical and behavioral. Medical pathology, for example, a urinary tract infection, produces such physical symptoms as burning on urination, a discharge from the urinary meatus, and perhaps a low-grade fever, but only urinalysis and urine culture can accurately identify a urinary tract infection. Children can have an asymptomatic urinary tract infection, in which case they have no symptoms but a urine culture results in the growth of bacteria.

Psychopathology can often be ruled out with a detailed clinical history. The history focuses on prior family history of emotional problems, as well as the onset and the course of the present complaint. Table 10.3 provides the foundation for our discussions with the parents of children referred for evaluation and treatment of enuresis.

In addition to the clinical history, many clinicians use a rating scale like the Achenbach Child Behavior Checklist or the Conners Parent and/or Teacher Rating Scale (e.g., Friman, Mathews, Finney, Christophersen, & Leibowitz, 1988), without any need, initially, for any more extensive psychological evaluation.

Daytime wetting, which involves essentially the same medical and psychological evaluation, has received much less attention in the medical and psychological literature. Day wetting may be considered incomplete toilet training, rather than a separate clinical entity. The diagnostic criteria in DSM-IV do not differentiate between day wetting and night wetting, although the treatment of these two types of enuresis is usually quite different.

Van Gool, Vijverberg, and deJong (1992) caution that a standard medical history may fail to disclose the pathophysiology behind patterns of bladder/sphincter dysfunction. They identified four patterns of bladder/sphincter dysfunction associated with day wetting secondary to pathophysiology: urge syndrome, staccato voiding, fractionated and incomplete voiding, and lazy-bladder syndrome. They also reported a strong correlation between recurrent urinary tract infections and nonneuropathic bladder/sphincter dysfunction, implying that the detection and treatment of bladder/sphincter dysfunction is essential in

every child with recurrent urinary tract infections, especially in the presence of vesico-ureteral reflux. Hurley (1990) took the position that day wetting is mainly a behavioral problem, while night wetting is mainly a developmental problem. Although van Gool et al. (1992) and Hurley (1990) may appear to contradict each other, the four criteria recommended by van Gool et al. (1992) can be used to rule out pathophysiology prior to considering behavior management procedures.

TREATMENT
Medical Treatments

The drug most commonly used to treat enuresis has been imipramine (Tofranil®, a tricyclic antidepressant). In general, this drug stops enuresis completely in 40 to 50% of enuretic children; another 10–20% show considerable improvement. The relapse rate after the drug is discontinued is high, however, with about two thirds of enuretics resuming wetting frequently enough to warrant further treatment. The FDA has recommended that imipramine be used only as contemporary adjunctive therapy for enuretic children 6 years of age and older (Medical Economics Data Production Company, 1994) and, even then, only for short periods of time, e.g., 3 weeks. Like any other powerful pharmacological agent, imipramine has potentially serious side effects and should be reserved for those cases where more conventional therapies are not practical or effective and there is sufficient pressure from the family on the child to cease bed-wetting.

Recently, the efficacy and safety of the use of desmopressin (DDAVP, a hormone nasal spray used to treat diabetes insipidus) for nocturnal enuresis has been examined, with an improvement noted in from 10–60% of the patients, typically with an increase in enuresis after the medication is discontinued.

Moffatt, Harlos, Kirshen, & Burd (1993) reported on a total of 689 subjects from 18 studies of DDAVP, and calculated that an average of only 24% of the subjects achieved short-term dryness. In three studies that reported on

TABLE 10.3 Enuresis Intake Form

PARENTS

1. What word does your child use for urinating? _____

2. Has your child ever been potty trained? _____

	Age Started	Age Accomplished
Bladder trained? ___	___	___
Bowel trained? ___	___	___

3. What potty-training method did you use? _____

   _____

4. Was there ever a time when your child did not wet the bed? Yes ___ No ___

5. If so, when did bed-wetting begin? _____

6. When did you decide it as a problem? _____

   Your spouse? _____

   Your child? _____

7. What about bed-wetting makes it a problem for you? _____

   For your spouse? _____

   For your child? _____

8. Does your child wet the bed every night? _____

   If not, how often? _____

9. Has your child ever gone for any length of time not wetting the bed? _____

   How long? ___ How often? ___

10. What methods have you used in the past to stop the bed-wetting? _____

    _____

    _____

    For how long? _____

11. Are you still using any of these methods? _____

12. What is your child's responsibility when he wets the bed? _____

13. Does your child ever wet her pants during the day? _____ How often? _____

    How much? Small ___ Medium ___ Large ___

TABLE 10.3 (*continued*)

14. Does your child ever dribble in his pants during the day? _____

15. Does your child ever complain of burning when she urinates? _____

16. Does your child have to go more frequently than you think is normal? _____

17. Does your child complain that it doesn't feel like he has completely emptied his bladder when finished? _____

18. When your child has to urinate, can she wait a while, or does she have to go right then or have an accident? _____

19. Have you ever noticed any irritation around the end of his penis/her meatus? _____

20. Has your child ever had a work-up for a urinary tract infection or any other urinary problem? ____

    When? _____

    By whom? _____

    Where? _____

    Results? _____

21. Is your child a sound sleeper? _____

22. When your child stays overnight with relatives or a friend, does he wet the bed? _____

23. What do you believe causes bed-wetting? _____

    _____

24. Has your child ever had problems with constipation? Yes ___ No ___

25. Has your child ever soiled? Yes ___ No ___

26. To your knowledge, did anyone in either the biological mother's or father's family wet the bed? If so, who? _____

CHILD

1. Tell me why you're here. _____

   _____

2. Do you want to stop wetting the bed? _____

3. Does wetting the bed cause you any problem? _____

   _____

4. What do Mom and Dad do when you wet the bed? _____

   _____

5. Have you ever gone without wetting the bed? _____

6. When you wet the bed, what do you do about it? _____

_____

7. What do you like to do with your mom? _____

_____

   With your dad? _____

_____

long-term dryness, only 5.7% maintained dryness after stopping DDAVP. The authors concluded that, on the basis of current knowledge, DDAVP is inferior to conditioning alarms as a primary therapy (p. 420).

An article in a Danish journal (Ankjaer & Sejr, 1994) reported a cost-effectiveness analysis of the use of DDAVP for enuresis. While the authors estimated that the use of urine-alarm training would save the socialized Danish medical care system 19.2 million kroner annually ($3.3 million), the use of DDAVP would cost the system 44.8 million kroner ($7.8 million). This is the first such article that has actually addressed the issue of cost-benefit considerations regarding widespread usage of DDAVP.

There are some children for whom imipramine or DDAVP is effective but whose parents are either uncomfortable about long-term use of medication or concerned about the toxicology of the drugs used to treat enuresis. In these cases, we sometimes recommend that the medication only be used on nights when the child wants to have a friend for an overnight stay or when the enuretic child wants to stay overnight at a friend's house or attend a scout campout or some similar event. The medication is then, used only before bedtime on the evening of the overnight.

Psychological Treatments

For more than 4 decades, the standard behavioral treatment for enuresis has been the bell-and-pad procedure originally reported by Mowrer and Mowrer (1938). In general, studies have shown that the urine-alarm treatment initially eliminates enuresis in approximately 75% of enuretics, with treatment duration ranging from a mean of 5 weeks to 12 weeks (Doleys, Ciminero, Tollison, Williams, & Wells, 1977). Relapse rates are generally high, occurring, on average, in 46% of cases, although reinstatement of the procedures usually results in a complete cure (Taylor & Turner, 1975). The urine-alarm treatment has also been shown to be superior to no treatment, short-term psychotherapy, and imipramine (DeLeon & Mandell, 1966; McKendry et al., 1975; Werry & Cohrssen, 1965). Possible disadvantages of this treatment include the length of treatment necessary to effect a cure, the inconvenience of awakening during the night, and malfunctions of the urine alarm (Christophersen & Rapoff, 1992).

The major adaptation of the urine-alarm treatment that has produced the most promising results is dry-bed training (Azrin, Sneed, & Fox, 1974). Dry-bed training combines a number of behavioral procedures, including cleanliness training, positive practice, nighttime awakening, retention control training, and positive reinforcement. Success with dry-bed training averages approximately 85%, with relapse rates reported between 7% and 29%, with a mean of 18%. As with urine-alarm treatment, relapsed children were cured when the training procedures were reinstated. Table 10.4 provides a treatment summary, suitable for distribution to parents after the decision has been made to use dry-bed training and after the treatment procedures have been verbally described and discussed with the parents and the enuretic child.

Perhaps the major reason physicians do not recommend urine-alarm/dry-bed training is that they are not acquainted with it during their residency training. In fact, only 5% of physicians are trained in the use of urine-alarm/dry-bed training, compared with almost 100% of physicians who are trained in the pharmacological management of enuresis (Determining Reasonable Expectations, 1990).

Interestingly, dry-bed training has also been shown to be effective with adults, with higher cure rates and lower relapse rates than have been reported with children (van Son, Mulder, & van Londen, 1990). The researchers reported using dry-bed training successfully with nine adults, three men and six women, whose average age was 26 years, with a mean treatment duration of 15 weeks.

Arousal training, which combines the use of a urine alarm and rewards for the child for awakening, has recently been credited with a success rate of 98%, with no drop-outs from treatment. Data reported after a follow-up 2.5 years later indicated that the arousal training group was still dry 92% of mornings, compared with 77% for the urine alarm with specific instructions and 72% with the urine alarm only (van Londen, van Londen-Barentsen, van Son, & Mulder, 1993).

Over the years, various authors have reported on the use of hypnosis as a treatment for enuresis. The first such report, Olness (1975), showed a cure rate of almost 80% with hypnosis. Unfortunately, replication of these results has never appeared in a peer-reviewed journal. Recently, Banaerjee, Srivastav, and Palan (1993) compared hypnosis with imipramine drug treatment in enuretics ranging in age from 5 to 16 years. After treatment and at 9-month follow-up, the hypnosis group reported vastly superior results (68% of the hypnosis group were still dry, while only 24% of the imipramine group was still dry).

The toilet-training procedures described in Azrin and Foxx's *Toilet Training in Less Than a Day* (1974) were based on their published research that described almost 100% cure rates (Foxx & Azrin, 1993G). In their book, they describe a procedure for eliminating day wetting called "positive practice." Positive practice involves having the child practice going to the bathroom, on the potty, 10 times after each accident. The authors have recommended positive-practice procedures for toileting accidents since the Azrin and Foxx book was published (Christophersen, 1994). Table 10.2 (see section on disorders of bowel control) presents a treatment summary of the positive-practice procedures for the treatment of day wetting.

Social/Interpersonal Treatments

The negative psychosocial consequences of enuresis are common (Warzak, 1993), secondary to the impact of enuresis on family members and others. The enuretic child may be at increased risk for emotional—or even physical abuse—from family members and may experience stress related to fear of detection by peers. These factors may contribute to the loss of self-esteem that the enuretic child often experiences (Warzak, 1993).

Comments

The prevalence of nocturnal enuresis, combined with the availability of several treatment modalities (drugs, urine alarm, dry-bed training, and hypnosis) has produced a large body of literature on the topic. Parents and clinicians must choose between the ease and expense of medications that are marginally effective and the difficulty of urine-alarm procedures that are far more effective but require significantly more effort on the part of the caregiver. Both drugs and urine-alarm procedures can be implemented by the vast majority of health care providers. The use of hypnotherapy, however, requires rather extensive training, produces middle-of-the-road results, and

TABLE 10.4 Dry-Bed Training Procedures

I. Recording: Use calendar progress chart to record dry or wet from previous night.
    a. Parent praises child if dry.
    b. Parent encourages child to keep working if wet.

II. At bedtime
    a. Child feels sheets and comments on their dryness.
    b. Child describes what he will do if he has the urge to urinate.
    c. Child describes current need to urinate and does so.
    d. Parent expresses confidence in child and reviews progress.
    e. Alarm is placed on bed.
    f. Alarm is connected and tested.
    g. Child goes to sleep.

III. Nightly awakening
    a. Awaken child once during night.
        1. Use minimal prompt in awakening, but be sure the child is awake.
        2. Child feels sheets and comments on dryness.
        3. Parent praises child for dry sheets.
        4. Child goes to bathroom, urinates as much as possible, returns to bed.
        5. Child feels sheets again.
        6. Child states what he will do if he feels urge to urinate.
        7. Parent expresses confidence to child.
        8. Keep alarm on bed if it has not sounded before awakening.
        9. If alarm has sounded more than 30 minutes before scheduled awakening, awaken at scheduled time.
        10. If alarm has sounded less than 30 minutes before scheduled awakening, awaken at scheduled time.

    b. Adjust time of nightly awakening.
        1. On first night, awaken child 5 hours before his or her usual time of awakening.
        2. After child has six consecutive dry nights, awaken him or her 1 hour earlier the next night. Continue to move the awakening time 1 hour earlier after each six dry nights until the awakening time is 8 hours before the usual time of awakening.
        3. When dry for 14 nights at 8-hour awakening, discontinue awakening and discontinue alarm.

IV. When alarm sounds
    a. Awaken child and give mild reprimand for wetting.
    b. Child feels sheets and comments on wetness.
    c. Child walks to bathroom and finishes voiding.
    d. Child takes quick bath.
    e. Child changes into dry clothes.
    f. Child removes wet sheets and places them in laundry.
    g. Child remakes bed with dry sheets.
    h. Child feels bed sheets and comments on dryness.
    i. Do not reconnect alarm.
    j. Child returns to sleep.

V. During day
    a. Child and parents describe progress to relevant friend or family member.
    b. Parents repeatedly express confidence in child and praise him or her.
    c. Parent calls therapist at set times to report progress.

is moderately expensive. Obviously, the clinician who has all treatment modalities available can inform the client or family of the options, including the degree of difficulty, the cost, and the expected level of effectiveness, and let the family choose between the options.

There are varying recommendations regarding the age at which nocturnal enuresis becomes a clinical problem suitable for treatment. While Azrin, Sneed, and Foxx (1974) suggest that children over four years of age are ready for treatment, Christophersen (1994) recommends waiting until the child is over seven years and is concerned about his or her wetting. Day wetting has been successfully treated with positive practice (Azrin & Foxx, 1974; Christophersen, 1994), but little systematic research has been reported on this clinical entity.

CONCLUDING REMARKS

Great strides have been made during the past 20 years in the treatment of elimination disorders. The combination of results from basic research studies, epidemiological studies, and the findings from objective research studies comparing various treatment modalities have provided physicians and psychologists with information that can be used to make informed decisions regarding the diagnostic workup, as well as when and how to proceed in the management of soiling, toileting refusal, night wetting, and day wetting. While at one time these problem areas were not well understood and treatment was only marginally successful, we now have the technology to intervene effectively with the vast majority of patients who present with disorders of elimination.

REFERENCES

Achenbach, T. M. (1991). *Manual for the Child Behavior Checklist /4–18 and 1991 Profile*. Burlington: University of Vermont Department of Psychiatry.

Achenbach, T. M. (1994/1988). *Manual for the Child Behavior Checklist /2–3 and 1994 Profile*. Burlington: University of Vermont Department of Psychiatry.

Achenbach, T. M., & Edelbrock, C. (1983). *Manual for the Child Behavior Checklist and Revised Child Behavior Profile*. Burlington: University Associates in Psychiatry.

Achenbach, T. M., & Lewis, M. (1971). A proposed model for clinical research and its application to encopresis and enuresis. *Journal of the American Academy of Child and Adolescent Psychiatry, 10*, 845–852.

*Alon, U. S. (1995). Nocturnal enuresis. *Pediatric Nephrology, 9*, 94–103.

American Pediatric Association (1991). The use of fruit juices in the diets of young children. *AAP News, February*, 11–12.

American Psychiatric Association. (1987). *Diagnostic and statistics manual of mental disorders-revised* (3rd ed.). Washington, DC: Author.

*American Psychiatric Association. (1994). *Diagnostic and statistics manual of mental disorders* (4th ed.). Washington, DC: Author.

Ankjaer, J. A., & Sejr, T. E. (1994). Costs of the treatment of enuresis nocturna: Health economic consequences of alternative methods in the treatment of enuresis nocturna. *Ugeskr-Laeger, 156*, 4355–4360.

Anthony, E. J. (1957). An experimental approach to the psychopathology of childhood: Encopresis. *British Journal of Medical Psychology, 30*, 146–175.

Ashkenazi, Z. (1975). The treatment of encopresis using a discriminative stimulus and positive reinforcement. *Journal of Behavior Therapy and Experimental Psychiatry, 6*, 155–157.

Azrin, N. H., & Foxx, R. M. (1971). A rapid method of toilet training the institutionalized retarded. *Journal of Applied Behavior Analysis, 4*, 89–99.

*Azrin, N. H., & Foxx, R. M. (1974). *Toilet training in less than a day*. New York: Simon & Schuster.

*Azrin, N. H., Sneed, T. J., & Foxx, R. M (1974). Dry-bed training: Rapid elimination of childhood enuresis. *Behavior Research and Therapy, 12*, 147–156.

Banaerjee, S., Srivastav, A., & Palan, B. M. (1993). Hypnosis and self-hypnosis in the management of nocturnal enuresis: A comparative study with imipramine therapy. *American Journal of Clinical Hypnosis, 36*, 113–119.

Barkley, R. A., DuPaul, G. J., & McMurray, M. B. (1990). Comprehensive evaluation of Attention

Deficit Disorder with and without hyperactivity as defined by research criteria. *Journal of Consulting and Clinical Psychiatry, 58*, 775–798.

*Barr, R. G., Levine, M. D., Wilkinson, R. H., & Mulvihill, D. (1979). Chronic and occult stool retention: A clinical tool for its evaluation in school-aged children. *Clinical Pediatrics, 18*, 674–686.

Behrman, R. E., & Vaughan, V. C. (Eds.). (1987). *Nelson textbook of pediatrics* (13th ed.). Philadelphia: W. B. Saunders.

Bellman, M. (1966). Studies on encopresis. *Acta Paediatrica Scandanavica, 170*, (Supplement).

Bender, L. (1938). Mental hygiene and the child. *American Journal of Orthopsychiatry, 8*, 574–582.

Benninga, M. A., Büller, H. A., Heyman, H. S. A., Tytgat, G. N. J., & Taminiau, J. A. J. M. (1994). Is encopresis always the result of constipation? *Archives of Diseases in Children, 71*, 186–193.

Benninga, M. A., Buller, H. A., & Taminiau, J. A. J. M. (1993). Biofeedback training in chronic constipation. *Archives of Diseases of Children, 68*, 126–129.

*Berk, L. B., & Friman, P. C. (1990). Epidemiologic aspects of toilet training. *Clinical Pediatrics, 29*, 278–282.

Binderglas, P. M. (1975). The enuretic child. *Journal of Family Practice, 5*, 375–380.

Bleijenberg, G., & Kuijpers, H. C. (1994). Biofeedback treatment of constipation: A comparison of two methods. *American Journal of Gastroenterology, 89*, 1021–1026.

Boon, F. F. L., & Singh, N. (1991). A model for the treatment of encopresis. *Behavior Modification, 15*, 355–371.

*Brazelton, T. B. (1962). A child-oriented approach to toilet training. *Pediatrics, 29*, 121–128.

Brody, J. E. (1992, January 29). Personal health: Silence on fecal incontinence is harmful; From 1 to 2 percent of children over 4 have the problem. *New York Times.*

Carey, L. (1990). Sandplay therapy with a troubled child. *Arts in Psychotherapy; 17*, 197–209.

Carpenter, R. O. (1994). Disorders of elimination. In F. A. Oski, C. D. DeAngelis, R. D. Feigin, J. A. McMillan, & J. P. Warsaw (Eds.), *Principles and practice of pediatrics* (2nd ed., pp. 747–753). Philadelphia: Lippincott.

Christophersen, E. R. (1986). Anticipatory guidance in discipline. *Pediatric Clinics of North America, 33*, 789–798.

Christophersen, E. R. (1990). *Beyond discipline: Parenting that lasts a lifetime.* Kansas City, MO: Westport.

*Christophersen, E. R. (1994). *Pediatric compliance: A guide for the primary care provider.* New York: Plenum Press.

*Christophersen, E. R., & Rainey, S. K. (1976). Management of encopresis through a pediatric outpatient clinic. *Journal of Pediatric Psychology, 4*, 38–41.

*Christophersen, E. R., & Rapoff, M. A. (1992). Toileting problems in children. In C. E. Walker & M. Roberts (Eds.), *Handbook of clinical child psychology.* New York: Wiley.

*Cohen, M. W. (1975). Enuresis. *Pediatric Clinics of North America, 22*, 545–560.

Conger, J. C. (1970). The treatment of encopresis by the management of social consequences. *Behavior Therapy, 1*, 386–390.

*Cox, D. J., Sutphen, J., Borowitz, S., Dickens, M. N., Singles, J., & Whitehead, W. E. (1994). Simple electromyographic biofeedback treatment for chronic pediatric constipation/encopresis: Preliminary report. *Biofeedback Self-Regulation, 19*, 41–50.

Culbert, T. P., Reaney, J. B., & Kohen, D. P. (1994). "Cyberphysiologic" strategies for children; The clinical hypnosis/biofeedback interface. *International Journal of Clinical and Experimental Hypnosis, 42*, 97–117.

*Davidson, M. (1958). Constipation and fecal incontinence. *Pediatric Clinics of North America, 5*, 749–757.

*Davidson, M., Kugler, M. M., & Bauer, C. H. (1963). Diagnosis and management in children with severe and protracted constipation and obstipation. *Journal of Pediatrics, 62*, 261–275.

DeLeon, G., & Mandell, W. (1966). A comparison of conditioning and psychotherapy in the treatment of functional enuresis. *Journal of Clinical Psychology, 22*, 326–330.

Determining reasonable expectations: A multi-disciplinary roundtable discussion on special problems in toilet training. (1990). Durham: Duke University Medical Center, Office of Continuing Medical Education.

Dick, D. (1987). *Yesterday's babies: A history of babycare.* London: Bodley Head.

Doleys, D. M., & Arnold, S. (1975). Treatment of childhood encopresis: Full cleanliness training. *Mental Retardation, 13*, 14–16.

*Doleys, D. M., Ciminero, A. R., Tollison, J. W., Williams, D. L., & Wells, K. C. (1977). Dry-bed training and retention control training: A comparison. *Behavior Therapy, 8*, 541–548.

Edelman, R. T. (1971). Operant conditioning treatment of encopresis. *Journal of Behavior Therapy and Experimental Psychiatry, 2,* 71–73.

Ellett, M. L. (1990). Constipation/encopresis: A nursing perspective. *Journal of Pediatric Health Care, 4,* 141–146.

Engel, B. T., Nikoomanesh, P., & Schuster, M. M. (1974). Operant conditioning of retrosphincteric responses in the treatment of fecal incontinence. *New England Journal of Medicine, 290,* 636–649.

Fleisher, D. R. (1976). Diagnosis and treatment of disorders of defecation in children. *Pediatric Annals, 5,* 700–722.

Fowler, G. B. (1882). Incontinence of faeces in children. *American Journal of Obstetrics, 15,* 985.

Foxx, R. M., & Azrin, N. H. (1973a). *Toilet training the retarded.* Champaign, IL: Research Press.

*Foxx, R. M., & Azrin, N. H. (1973b). Dry pants: A rapid method of toilet training children. *Behavior Research and Therapy, 11,* 435–442.

*Friman, P. C., Mathews, J. R., Finney, J. W., Christophersen, E. R., & Leibowitz, J. M. (1988). Do encopretic children have clinically significant behavior problems? *Pediatrics, 82,* 407–409.

Gabel, S., Hegedus, A. M., Wald, A., Chandra, R., & Chiponis, D. (1986). Prevalence of behavior problems and mental health utilization among encopretic children: Implications for behavioral pediatrics. *Developmental and Behavioral Pediatrics, 7,* 293–297.

Gavanski, M. (1971). Treatment of non-retentive secondary encopresis with imipramine and psychotherapy. *Canadian Medical Association Journal, 104,* 46–48.

Giles, D. K., & Wolf, M. M. (1966). Toilet training institutionalized, severe retardates: An application of operant behavior modification techniques. *American Journal of Mental Deficiency, 70,* 766–780.

*Glicklich, L. B. (1951). An historical account of enuresis. *Pediatrics, 8,* 859–876.

Hjalmas, K. (1992). Functional daytime incontinence: Definitions and epidemiology. *Scandinavian Journal of Urology and Nephrology, 141,* 39–44.

*Houts, A. C., Mellon, M. W., & Whelan, J. P. (1988). Use of dietary fiber and stimulus control to treat retentive encopresis: A multiple-baseline investigation. *Journal of Pediatric Psychology, 13,* 435–445.

Hurley, R. M. (1990). Enuresis: The difference between night and day. *Pediatric Review, 12,* 167–170.

Huschka, M. (1942). The child's response to coercive bowel training. *Psychosomatic Medicine, 4,* 301–308.

Hyams, J. S., Treem, W. R., Etienne, N., Weinerman, H., MacGilpin, D., Hine, P., Choy, K., & Burke, G. (1995). Effect of infant formula on stool characteristics of young infants. *Pediatrics, 95,* 50–54.

Issenman, R. M., Hewson, S., Pirhonen, D., & Taylor, W. (1987). Are chronic digestive complaints the result of abnormal dietary patterns? *Annals of Diseases of Children, 141,* 679–672.

Johnston, B. D., & Wright, J. A. (1993). Attentional dysfunction in children with encopresis. *Journal of Developmental and Behavioral Pediatrics, 14,* 381–385.

Krugman, R. D. (1985). Fatal child abuse: Analysis of 24 cases. *Pediatrician, 12,* 68–72.

Klish, W. J. (1994). Functional constipation and encopresis. In F. A. Oski, C. D. DeAngelis, R. D. Feigin, J. A. McMillan, & J. B. Warshaw (Eds.), *Principles and practice of pediatrics* (2nd ed., pp. 1843–1845). Philadelphia: Lippincott.

Lal, H., & Lindsey, O. R. (1968). Therapy of chronic constipation in a young child by rearranging social consequences. *Behaviour Research and Therapy, 6,* 484–485.

Lavietes, R. L. (1989). Functional encopresis. In H. I. Kaplan & B. J. Sadock (Eds.), *Comprehensive textbook of psychiatry* (5th ed.), Baltimore: Williams and Wilkins.

*Levine, M. D. (1975). Children with encopresis: A descriptive analysis. *Pediatrics, 56,* 412–416.

*Levine, M. D. (1981). The schoolchild with encopresis. *Pediatrics in Review, 2,* 285–290.

*Levine, M. D. (1982). Encopresis: Its potentiation, evaluation, and alleviation. *Pediatric Clinics of North America, 29,* 315–330.

*Levine, M. D. (1983). Encopresis. In M. D. Levine, W. B. Carey, A. C. Crocker, & R. T. Gross (Eds.), *Developmental-behavioral pediatrics* (pp. 586–595). Philadelphia: W. B. Saunders.

*Levine, M. D. (1992). Encopresis. In M. D. Levine, W. B. Carey, & A. C. Crocker (Eds.), *Developmental-behavioral pediatrics* (pp. 389–397). Philadelphia: W. B. Saunders.

*Levine, M. D., & Bakow, H. (1976). Children with encopresis: A study of treatment outcome. *Pediatrics, 58,* 845–852.

Levine, M. D., Carey, W. B., & Crocker, A. C. (Eds.). (1992). *Developmental-behavioral pediatrics* (2nd ed.). Philadelphia: W. B. Saunders.

Loening-Baucke, V. (1984). Abnormal rectoanal function in children recovered from chronic constipaton and encopresis. *Gastroenterology* 87 1299–1304.

*Loening-Baucke, V. (1987). Factors responsible for persistence of childhood constipation. *Journal of Gastroenterology and Nutrition, 6,* 915–922.

*Loening-Baucke, V. (1993). Constipation in early childhood: Patient characteristics, treatment, and longterm follow up. *Gut, 33,* 1400–1403.

*Loening-Baucke, V. (1995). Biofeedback treatment for chronic constipation and encopresis in childhood: Long-term outcome. *Pediatrics, 96,* 105–110.

*Loening-Baucke, V. (1996). Encopresis and soiling. *Pediatric Clinics of North America, 43,* 279–298.

*Loening-Baucke, V., & Cruickshank, B. (1986). Abnormal defecation dynamics in chronically constipated children with encopresis. *Journal of Pediatrics, 108,* 562–566.

*Loening-Baucke, V., Cruickshank, B., & Savage, C. (1987). Defecation dynamics and behavior profiles in encopretic children. *Pediatrics, 80,* 672–679.

Lovibond, S. H. (1964). *Conditioning and enuresis.* Oxford: Pergamon.

Luxem, M. C., & Christophersen, E. R. (1994). Behavioral toilet training in early childhood: Research, practice, and implications. *Journal of Developmental and Behavioral Pediatrics, 15,* 370–378.

Luxem, M. C., Christophersen, E. R., Purvis, P., & Baer, D. M. (1996). Behavioral-medical treatment of pediatric toileting refusal. *Journal of Developmental and Behavioral Pediatrics, 18,* 34–41.

McColgan, E. B., Pugh, R. L., & Pruitt, D. B. (1985). Encopresis: A structural/strategic approach to family treatment. *American Journal of Family Therapy, 13,* 46–54.

McKendry, J. B., & Stewart, D. A. (1974). Enuresis. *Pediatric Clinics of North America, 21,* 1019–1029.

McKendry, J. B., Stewart, D. A., Khanna, F., & Netley, C. (1975). Primary enuresis: Relative success of three methods of treatment *Canadian Medical Association Journal, 113,* 953–955.

Medical Economics Data Production Company. (1994). *Physicians' desk reference* (48th ed.). Montvale, NJ: Author.

Mesibov, G. B., Schroeder C. S., & Wesson, L. (1977). Parental concerns about their children. *Journal of Pediatric Psychology, 2,* 13–17.

Meunier, P., Mollard, P., & Marechal, J. M. (1976). Physiopathology of megarectum: The association

of megarectum with encopresis. *Gut, 17,* 224–227.

*Moffatt, M. E., Harlos, S., Kirshen, A. J., & Burd, L. (1993). Desmopressin acetate and nocturnal enuresis: How much do we know? *Pediatrics, 92,* 420–425.

*Mowrer, O. H., & Mowrer, W. M. (1938). Enuresis—A method for its study and treatment. *American Journal of Orthopsychiatry, 8,* 436–459.

Murray, R. D., Li, B. U., McClung, H. J., Heitlinger, L., & Rehm, D. (1990). Cisapride for intractable constipation in children: Observations from an open trial. *Journal of Pediatric Gastroenterology and Nutrition, 11,* 503–508.

Nolan, T., & Oberklaid, F. (1993). New concepts in the management of encopresis. *Pediatrics in Review, 14,* 447–451.

*O'Brien, S., Ross, L. V., & Christophersen, E. R. (1986). Primary encopresis: Evaluation and treatment. *Journal of Applied Behavior Analysis, 19,* 137–145.

Olness, K. (1975). The use of self-hypnosis in the treatment of childhood enuresis. *Clinical Pediatrics, 14,* 273–279.

Olness, K. (1976). Autohypnosis in functional megacolon in children. *American Journal of Clinical Hypnosis, 19,* 28–32.

Olness, K., McParland, F. A., & Piper, J. (1980). Biofeedback: A new modality in the treatment of children with fecal soiling. *Journal of Pediatrics, 96,* 505–509.

Olness, K., & Tobin, J. (1982). Chronic constipation in children: Can it be managed by diet alone? *Postgraduate Medicine, 72,* 149–154.

*Owens-Stively, J. (1995). *Childhood constipation and soiling: A practical guide for parents and children* (2nd ed.). Minneapolis: Children's Health Care.

*Partin, J. C., Hamill, S. K., Fischel, J. E., & Partin, J. S. (1992). Painful defecation and fecal soiling in children. *Pediatrics, 89,* 1007–1009.

Perimutter, A. D. (1976). Enuresis. In T. P. Kelalis & L. R. King (Eds.), *Clinical pediatric urology* (pp. 166–181). Philadelphia: W. B. Saunders.

Peterson, D. R., & London, P. (1965). A role for cognition in the behavioral treatment of a child's elimination disturbance. In L. P. Ullmann & L. Krasner (Eds.), *Case studies in behavior modification* (pp. 289–295). New York: Holt, Rinehart, & Winston.

Pettei, M. J., & Davidson, M. (1993). Constipation and encopresis. In F. D. Burg, J. R. Ingelfinger, & E. R. Wald (Eds.), *Gellis and Kagan's current pediatric therapy* (pp. 198–200). Philadelphia: W. B. Saunders.

Rapoff, M. A., & Christophersen, E. R. (1982). Improving compliance in pediatric practice. *Pediatric Clinics of North America, 29,* 339–357.

*Rappaport, L. A., & Levine, M. D. (1986). The prevention of constipation and encopresis: A developmental model and approach. *Pediatric Clinics of North America, 33,* 859–869.

Richmond, J. B., Eddy, E. J., & Garrand, S. D. (1954). The syndrome of fecal soiling and megacolon. *American Journal of Orthopsychiatry, 24,* 391–401.

Robinson, E. A., Eyberg, S. M., & Ross, A. W. (1980). The standardization of an inventory of child conduct problem behaviors. *Journal of Clinical Child Psychology, 9,* 23–29.

*Schaefer, C. E. (1979). *Enuresis and encopresis: Cause and therapy.* New York: Van Reinhold.

Schmitt, B. D. (1987). Toilet training refusal: Avoid the battle and win the war. *Contemporary Pediatrics, 4,* (12), 32–50.

Schmitt, R. D. (1984). Encopresis. *Primary Care, 11,* 497–511.

Seim, H. C. (1989). Toilet training in first children. *Journal of Family Practice, 29,* 633–636.

Selbert, N. (1929, January). Train your baby to regularity. *Parents, 17.*

Shelov, S. P., & Participants. (1981). Enuresis: A contrast of attitudes of parents and physicians. *Pediatrics, 67,* 707–710.

*Shortliffe, L. M. D., et al. (July 1993). Primary nocturnal enuresis. *Clinical Pediatrics, Special Edition,* 1–40.

Simonds, J. D. (1977). Enuresis: A brief survey of current thinking with respect to pathogenesis and management. *Clinical Pediatrics, 16,* 79–82.

Sonnenberg, A., & Koch, T. R. (1989). Physician visits in the United States for constipation: 1958 to 1986. *Digestive Diseases and Sciences, 34,* 606–611.

Sperling, M. (1965). Dynamic considerations and treatment of enuresis. *Journal of American Academy of Child Psychiatry, 4,* 19–31.

Stern, H. P., Stroh, S. E., Fiedorek, S. C., Kelleher, K., Mellon, M. W., Pope, S. K., & Rayford, P. L. (1995). Increased plasma levels of pancreatic polypeptide and decreased plasma levels of motilin in encopretic children. *Pediatrics, 96,* 111–117.

Suckling, P. (1962). The ball-valve rectum due to impacted faeces. *Lancet, 2,* 1147.

Taylor, P. D., & Turner, R. K. (1975). A clinical trail of continuous intermittent and overlearning "bell and pad" treatments for nocturnal enuresis. *Behaviour Research and Therapy, 3,* 281–293.

Tharper, A., Davies, G., Jones, T., & Rivett, M. (1992). Treatment of childhood encopresis—a review. *Child Care, Health, and Development, 18,* 343–353.

Tolia, V., Lin, C. H., & Elitsur, Y. (1993). A prospective randomized study with mineral oil and oral lavage solution for treatment of faecal impaction in children. *Alimentary Pharmacology and Therapeutics, 7,* 523–529.

Van Gool, J. D., Vijverberg M. A., & de Jong, T. P. (1992). Functional daytime incontinence: Clinical and urodynamic assessment. *Scandinavian Journal of Urology and Nephrology, Supplement, 141,* 58–69.

Van Londen, A., van Londen-Barentsen, M. W., van Son, M. J., & Mulder, G. A. (1993). Arousal training for children suffering from nocturnal enuresis: A 2-½-year follow-up. *Behaviour Research and Therapy, 31,* 613–615.

Van Son, M. J., Mulder, G., & van Londen, A. (1990). The effectiveness of dry-bed training for nocturnal enuresis in adults. *Behaviour Research and Therapy, 28,* 347–349.

*Walker, C. E. (1978). Toilet training, enuresis, and encopresis. In P. Magrab (Ed.), *Psychological management of pediatric problems* (Vol. 1). Baltimore: University Park Press.

*Walker, C. E., Kenning, M., & Faust-Campanile, J. (1989). Enuresis and encopresis. In E. J. Mash & R. A. Barkley (Eds.), *Treatment of childhood disorders* (pp. 436–448). New York: Guilford Press.

*Walker, C. E., Milling, L. S., & Bonner, B. L. (1988). Incontinence disorders: Enuresis and encopresis. In D. K. Routh (Ed.), *Handbook of pediatric psychology* (pp. 363–397). New York: Guilford Press.

Walker, C. E., & Werstlein, R. (1980). Use of relaxation procedures in the treatment of toilet phobia in a 4-year-old child. *Behavior Therapist, 3,* 17–18.

Warzak, W. J. (1993). Psychosocial implications of nocturnal enuresis. *Clinical Pediatrics, Special Supplement,* 38–40.

Weaver, I. T., & Steiner, H. (1984). The bowel habits of young children. *Archives of Diseases of Children, 59,* 649–652.

Weissenberg, G. B. (1926). Uber enkopresis. Z. *Kinderpsychiatr., 1,* 69.

Werry, J. S., & Cohrssen, J. (1965). Enuresis—

An etiologic and therapeutic study. *Journal of Pediatrics, 67,* 423–431.

Whitehead, W. E., Parker, L. H., Masek, B. J., Cataldo, M. F., & Freeman, J. M. (1981). Biofeedback treatment of fecal incontinence in patients with myelomeningocele. *Developmental Medicine and Child Neurology, 23,* 313–322.

Williams, C. L., Bollolla, M., & Wydner, E. L. (1995). A new recommendation for dietary fiber in childhood. *Pediatrics (Supplement) 96,* 985–987.

World Health Organization. (1992). *ICD-10 classification of mental and behavioural disorders: Clinical descriptions and diagnostic guidelines* (pp. 286–288). Geneva: Author.

Wrenn, K. (1989). Fecal impaction. *New England Journal of Medicine, 321,* 658–662.

Wright, L. (1973). Handling the encopretic child. *Professional Psychology, 4,* 136–144.

Wright, L. (1975). Outcome of a standardized program for treating psychogenic encopresis. *Professional Psychology, 6,* 453–456.

Young, G. C. (1973). The treatment of childhood encopresis by conditioned gastro-ileal reflex training. *Behaviour Research and Therapy, 11,* 499–501.

Young, M. H., Brennen, L. C., Baker, R. D., & Baker, S. S. (1994). *Functional encopresis: Symptom reduction and behavioral improvement, 16,* 226–232.

*Indicates references that the author recommends for further reading.

11
Organic Symptoms

Kevin R. Krull
Rosario Castillo

This chapter begins by comparing and contrasting the classification of organic mental disorders. Major features of child and adolescent diagnoses are presented, along with a critique of diagnostic systems. Epidemiological information is highlighted, and guidelines for the assessment and diagnosis of organic syndromes are reviewed. The chapter concludes by posing pertinent questions as yet unanswered by the field and suggesting future directions for research to resolve the difficulties in the classification of organic mental disorders in childhood.

The diagnosis of organic mental conditions is based on a combination of medical and psychological data that indicate the presence of disturbance, either mental or behavioral, resulting from suspected or known brain injury. By the very fact that the disturbance is a resultant of a change in the state of the brain, the diagnosis of this disorder typically carries with it a long and persistent course of pathology. Given the existence of brain pathology or damage, the probability of a full recovery and return to premorbid levels of functioning is typically less than that associated with behavioral or nonorganic mental disorders.

The study of mental or behavioral disorders resultant to brain impairment has grown in popularity and given rise to a relatively new discipline of psychology called neuropsychology. This discipline, as it pertains to children and adolescents, has arisen from a variety of psychological and nonpsychological fields, including clinical child psychology, school psychology, cognitive psychology, experimental psychology, behavioral neurology, and special education. In its current state, neuropsychology is as distinct from clinical psychology as neurology is from internal medicine. In that light, a comprehensive review and discussion of organic syndromes as they pertain to children and adolescents is beyond the scope of a single book chapter. Therefore, a more focused discussion of common childhood disorders and diagnostic systems is presented.

CLASSIFICATION OF ORGANIC SYMPTOMS

Diagnostic and Statistical Manual of Mental Disorders, Third Edition, Revised

The classification of organic mental conditions under the *Diagnostic and Statistical*

Manual of Mental Disorder (Third Edition, Revised) (DSM-III-R) (American Psychiatric Assocation, 1987) involved differentiation of "syndromes" from "disorders." Organic mental syndromes were defined as psychological and/or behavioral symptoms that were believed to be associated with brain dysfunction, though direct identification or evidence of a brain injury was not available. Organic mental disorders, on the other hand, involved similar psychological and or behavioral symptoms suggesting organicity, with the addition of direct reference to a known or suspected brain injury. Since the lack of knowledge of the existence of a brain dysfunction or injury and its connection to a mental disorder does not suggest that the brain injury cannot or does not produce the specific mental disorder, this distinction between "syndrome" and "disorder" was meaningless and has subsequently been eliminated from the new classification system (i.e., *Diagnostic and Statistical Manual of Mental Disorders*, Fourth Edition; APA, 1994).

Diagnosis of organic mental conditions (OMC) in DSM-III-R was based on symptoms or syndromes that fall into six categories: (1) delirium and dementia; (2) amnestic syndromes; (3) organic delusional, mood, and anxiety disorders; (4) organic personality disorders; (5) organic conditions associated with intoxication and withdrawal; and (6) organic conditions not otherwise specified. Delirium is an altered level of arousal characterized by poor attention, disorientation, and memory impairment. The apparent memory impairment results from the fluctuations in attention and disorientation. Delirium is seen in individuals suffering from acute brain injuries, such as closed head injuries or exposure to toxic substances. In addition to overt brain trauma, the classification of the causes of delirium included those acute or withdrawal phases of drug or alcohol dependence. Dementia is an impairment in long- and short-term memory, associated with changes in reasoning, thinking, and or language processes. The key or primary symptom though is the memory impairment. Brain injury that results in disturbance of select cognitive abilities (i.e., language) but leaves memory functions intact was not classified as dementia. The classification of dementias under DSM-III-R differentiated between those that occurred in the "senium" (late onset) and those that occurred in the "Presenium" (early onset). Two of the common forms of dementia included Alzheimer's disease and multi-infarct dementia. Alzheimer's disease is a degenerative disorder that occurs in mid- to late adulthood, while multi-infarct dementia results from multiple strokes or altered blood flow in the brain. Both of these conditions are associated with primary memory deficits. Amnestic syndromes are characterized by memory impairment without loss of other cognitive functions. True amnestic syndromes are rare, since most brain injuries do not affect memory processes without some disruption of other cognitive abilities. Organic delusional, mood, anxiety, and personality disorders are alterations in emotional functioning or behavioral traits associated with brain injury. The brain injury is believed to be responsible for the alteration in affect or personality due to the temporal relationship between the injury and the behavioral change. The problem with this category arises from the fact that many injuries may result in a reactive change in affect due to the loss associated with the incident. The change in affect may not have an organic basis, and distinguishing between organic and reactive causes may not be possible.

The DSM-III-R classification system was not only inadequate for classification of organic mental conditions in adults; it was practically useless for classification of organic conditions in children. Obviously, children do not have senile dementias such as Alzheimer's or senile dementia NOS (i.e., not otherwise specified), two categories in the DSM-III-R classification. Dementias associated with childhood typically included the multi-infarct dementia and presenile dementia NOS. However, children rarely have cerebral infarcts or strokes, leaving presenile dementia NOS as the only possible diagnosis of a dementing process. Dementia itself implies a degenerative process, or a progressive decline from previous levels of functioning. The vast majority of organic mental syndromes in children are not degenerative and instead may be associated with a single traumatic event. Furthermore, the disorder resulting from the trauma may have a larger effect on altering the course of normal brain development than it does on producing a decline in current levels of brain functioning (Fletcher, Miner, & Ewing-Cobbs, 1987). Deficits in attention are common in children following brain impairment. In fact, most brain injuries that occur in childhood, whether due to a physical or to a chemical alteration in the brain, are associated with deficits in attention or arousal. Attention deficits, when accompanied by disorientation and memory disturbances, could be classified as a delirium. However, although children may be somewhat disoriented, frequent fluctuations in their level of arousal is not common, making the diagnosis of a delirium unusual. Since children are typically too young to be diagnosed with a personality disorder, diagnosis of an organic personality disorder is equally unlikely and inappropriate. Children do experience changes in mood following brain injury, though these changes rarely occur without some changes in cognitive processes, as well. Finally, the category of drug or alcohol intoxication and withdrawal is typically restricted to a small sample of children during mid- to late adolescence. Younger children and infants may be at risk for exposure to toxic substances, though they do not typically engage in regular alcohol or drug abuse. Thus, the vast majority of children with altered mental and/or behavioral functioning associated with a change in the state of the brain receive a general, typically useless diagnosis of organic mental syndrome NOS. Such a diagnosis may be useful in obtaining reimbursement from health insurance carriers or other third-party payers, but it does very little to describe the type or severity of the symptoms the child is experiencing following brain impairment.

Diagnostic and Statistical Manual of Mental Disorders, Fourth Edition

The classification of organic mental conditions described in the *Diagnostic and Statistical*

Manual of Mental Disorders, Fourth Edition (DSM-IV) (APA, 1994) has improved slightly, though it is still very problematic for use with children. Categories of disorders in DSM-IV have been reorganized to include: (1) delirium, dementia and amnesia, and other cognitive disorders; (2) mental disorders due to general medical conditions; and (3) substance related disorders. The focus of this discussion of DSM-IV diagnosis as it relates to organic mental conditions in children is on the first two categories in the new classification system.

DSM-IV has made substantial improvements in the categorization of organic mental conditions, though it is far from a comprehensive system of diagnosis of brain pathology as it relates to children. For the most part, classification is still based on a dementia process. That is, the mental condition associated with brain impairment is viewed as a decline from previous levels of functioning. However, instead of being restricted to a selection among an Alzheimer's dementia, vascular dementia, or an other unspecified dementia, clinicians may also select from specific causes of brain pathology. In addition to the classical dementia categories, a diagnosis of "dementia due to other general medical conditions" can be given. This later category includes dementia due to a human immunodeficiency virus (HIV), head trauma, Parkinson's disease, Huntington's disease, Pick's disease, Creutzfelt-Jakob disease, or "other general medical conditions." Outside of high-risk groups such as children with sickle-cell disease, children undergoing cranial irradiation, and children with diabetes, cerebral vascular insults are rare. Children do not experience strokes or cerebral vascular lesions as frequently as adults. Thus, the diagnosis of "dementia due to other general medical conditions" can be more useful. However, out of the predetermined categories, few are likely to be observed in childhood. For example, children do not typically experience Parkinson's disease, which is a progressive disturbance in memory and motor functions, and they rarely experience Huntington's disease, which is also characterized by a progressive disturbance in memory and motor functions. Creutzfelt-Jakob disease is extremely rare, occurring at a rate of less than 1:1,000,000, and typically results in death within months of the initial diagnosis (Swiam, 1991). Thus, there is no need for a diagnostic category to describe the mental conditions resulting from the disease.

Those disorders included in DSM-IV that are most likely to be seen during childhood or adolescence include dementia due to HIV, head trauma, and other general medical conditions. These other general medical conditions may include brain tumors, hydrocephalus, endocrine disorders, nutritional disorders, infections, and organ failure. Thus, the majority of causes for organic mental symptoms in childhood are appropriate for inclusion into two specific and one general category. The criteria for dementia in the DSM-IV classification is defined by cognitive deficits, including the primary symptom of memory impairment combined with one of the following: aphasia (a disturbance of higher-order language functions), apraxia (a disturbance in controlled movements), agnosia (a disturbance in the ability to recognize identify objects), or executive deficits (a group of deficits characterized by poor decision making, planning, reasoning, and mental control). As in DSM-III-R, the condition must represent a decline from previous levels of functioning and must include a disturbance of memory processes. Organic mental conditions that include an impairment in language abilities, controlled movement, or reasoning processes, though not a disturbance in memory, do not meet the criteria for a dementia, regardless of the extent of the other processes.

An amnestic disorder involves the onset of a memory impairment (decline from previous levels) that is not directly due to a delirium or dementia. Furthermore, the disorder is identified as being either transient or chronic in nature. Pure memory disorders (i.e., conditions that do not cause other disturbances in cognitive functions) are very rare in children, and in adults, for that matter. Most acquired brain deficits in children produce a disturbance in attention, language, psychomotor functions, or perceptual/spatial skills. Thus, diagnosis of an amnestic disorder is quite unlikely. Although memory impairment is common in childhood following a brain injury, it rarely occurs in isolation.

The final option in DSM-IV for diagnosis of an organic mental condition in childhood is that of "cognitive disorder NOS." This is the catch-all category for those conditions that do not fit into any of the previous categories. Unfortunately, it is probably the most appropriate one for the majority of organic mental conditions seen in children. Children who experience a brain injury and go on to display symptoms of cognitive dysfunction characterized by deficits in language, visual perception, attention, reasoning, or motor control should be diagnosed with cognitive disorder NOS. A case can be made for the diagnosis of children with co-occurring memory disturbances, as well. Typically, a memory impairment warrants a diagnosis of a dementia in childhood. However, as stated previously, a dementia implies a decline from previous levels of functioning. The diagnosis does not in any way consider the developmental aspect of brain functioning. Since the child is still developing cognitive skills, what qualifies as a "decline" in cognitive abilities? Is it more appropriate to define decline from previous levels of functioning or from levels the child would have achieved as an adult if the injury had not occurred? Obviously, no one can clearly determine the precise levels of functioning a child would have obtained under normal circumstances, though estimates of projected functioning can be obtained through knowledge of the child's demographics (such as parental occupation or education). The brain impairment may not be associated with a decline in functioning as much as it is with an altered developmental trajectory. That is, the child who experiences a brain injury may appear to "recover" quickly from the injury and display no immediate deficits, then go on to develop new cognitive skills or abilities, such as memory, at an impaired level. Thus, the memory deficits exhibited by the child 3 years after the injury may represent not a decline in cognitive abilities but instead a failure to develop age-appropriate cognitive abilities. Under these circumstances a diagnosis of dementia is inappropriate.

International Classification of Diseases, Tenth Revision

An alternative to diagnosis of organic mental conditions using DSM classification is to employ the World Health Organization's (WHO) *International Classification of Diseases* (ICD) criteria. ICD-10, which is the most recent revision of the international system, includes criteria for the classification of physical as well as mental diseases. The ICD-10 *Classification of Mental and Behavioural Disorders* (WHO, 1992) includes a section on "organic, including symptomatic, mental disorders." Classification using this system includes the use of codes for the diagnosis of the psychopathology as well as the underlying brain or physical disorder, which is similar to the use of Axis I and Axis III diagnoses in DSM. In general, diagnosis within this ICD-10 category involves an etiology based in cerebral disease, injury, or dysfunction. The two primary clusters of diagnoses include: (1) those that involve cognitive dysfunction, such as disorders of memory, learning, attention, or general intellect and (2) those that involve disturbance of perception, mood, emotion, behavior, or personality. Although the age of onset of these disorders can occur at any time, most are described as having an onset during middle to late adulthood.

Categories of organic mental conditions in ICD-10 include: (1) dementia, (2) amnestic disorders, (3) delirium, and (4) other mental disorders resulting from brain dysfunction. In general, dementia is defined as a chronic and progressive deterioration of higher cognitive functions, including memory and thinking, that is evident for at least a 6-month period. A disturbance of consciousness or arousal is not present for dementias in this category. Specific subtypes of dementia include Alzheimer's disease, vascular dementia, dementias resulting from other specified diseases, and unspecified dementia. Alzheimer's disease is further broken down into early onset, late onset, atypical/mixed onset, and unspecified onset. Vascular dementia includes an acute subtype, a multi-infarct subtype, a subcortical subtype, and other or unspecified subtypes. Other specified dementias include those arising from Pick's disease, Creutzfeldt-Jakob disease, Huntington's disease, Parkinson's disease, HIV disease, or another specified disease. Additional symptoms of delusions, hallucinations, depression, or mixed symptoms can be added to the dementia diagnosis though fifth-character coding.

Like DSM-IV, ICD-10 coding of an organic amnestic disorder includes primary symptoms of impaired recent and/or remote memory without a disturbance in attention or consciousness. Disorders characterized by memory impairment combined with impairment in language, motor control, visual perception, or higher-order reasoning are typically not given this classification.

Diagnosis of delirium in the ICD-10 system is restricted to primary symptoms of disturbed consciousness, including disorders of attention, perception, thinking, psychomotor functioning, behavior, and emotional regulation. These symptoms are viewed as transient and fluctuating during their course.

Diagnosis of other organic mental disorders not included in the categories already listed must meet several criteria listed in the ICD-10. These include evidence of cerebral disease, a temporal relationship between the onset of symptoms and the onset of the disease, the presence of recovery of the symptoms after improvement in the course of the disease, and the absence of evidence of other nonorganic causes for the symptoms. Once these criteria are met, a diagnosis of organic mental disorder can include primary symptoms of hallucinosis, catatonic behavior, delusional or schizophrenic-like behavior, disturbance of mood, anxiety, dissociative experiences, emotional lability, mild cognitive declines, or other specified symptoms. Specified changes in personality and behavior include diagnoses of a nonreversible organic personality disorder, a reversible postencephalitic condition, and a postconcussional condition that which may present as primary symptoms of irritability.

Like the DSM-IV classification, ICD-10 categories are slanted toward ease of diagnosis of organic mental conditions in adults. Diagnosis of disorders of children can be made, but they often involve using general, nondescriptive categories. For example, the most frequent cause of brain dysfunction in childhood is closed head injury (Goldstein & Levin, 1987). Diagnosis of this condition in ICD-10 results in the use of the code F02.8, which is the code for the "dementia in other specified diseases—other category." This same code would be used for a child who experiences a disturbance in memory and thinking as a reult of cranial irradiation for the treatment of leukemia. Thus, two very different diseases that require different treatments, have different accompanying cognitive or mental symptoms, and carry different prognoses can receive the same ICD-10 diagnosis.

In addition to grouping different etiologies in the same disease diagnosis, DSM-IV and ICD-10 do little to distinguish between among types of cognitive symptoms. Basic distinctions among memory, attention or consciousness, and thinking are made. Memory disorders without disorders of attention or thinking are classified as "amnestic"; disorders of memory and thinking with good attention and consciousness are classified as "dementia"; disorders of attention or consciousness, which produce poor performance on measures of memory and thinking, are classified as "delirium." This basic distinction is practically useless in working with organic conditions. In children, memory disorders rarely present without disturbances in "thinking" or other cognitive processes, making a diagnosis of organic amnesia extremely unlikely. In addition, when brain injury results in disorders of attention, which is a very common outcome of many diseases, the disturbance is often not transient or fluctuating. Instead, the deficit in the control of attention is seen across many environments and situations, making the diagnosis of delirium inappropriate outside of acute recovery. Thus, one is left with a diagnosis of dementia or other mental disorders due to a medical condition.

Dementia is often an inappropriate diagnosis for children for the following reasons: (1) A disturbance in attention is a common outcome of brain injury or disease in childhood; and (2) As previously stated, the primary deficit in the child may involve not a decline in levels of cognitive functioning but instead a failure to properly develop cognitive skills or to reach expected potentials. That is, the end result of the brain injury in the child may be an acquired delay or a premature plateau in the development of new cognitive processes. In addition, a diagnosis of a dementia in childhood does nothing to identify primary symptoms of importance. This classification says nothing about the child's expressive or receptive language abilities, visual-perceptual or perceptual motor skills, academic development, or abstract reasoning or planning abilities. Knowledge of these specific deficits conveys more information about the child's organic mental condition than does the term "dementia." Furthermore, knowledge of specific symptoms provides more useful information for the development and comparison of treatment programs aimed at servicing children with brain dysfunction.

As is evident from the discussion, diagnosis of organic mental conditions in childhood is not a straightforward process. Many of the diagnoses used for adults may not be appropriate for children. Table 11.1 presents the categories of diagnoses for organic symptoms in DSM-III-R, DSM-IV, and ICD-10, with those appropriate for use with children identified.

EPIDEMIOLOGY OF ORGANIC MENTAL CONDITIONS

Epidemiological data on the diagnosis of organic mental conditions in children are somewhat confusing and potentially misleading. Given the restricted categories that are applicable to children, as described earlier, and the large number of medical conditions that result in brain dysfunction in children, base rates for organic mental disorders are difficult to assess. In addition, not all brain injuries result in mental disorders, and some organic-like mental disorders may not be associated with a history of injury or insult or contain evidence of

TABLE 11.1. Comparison of the Diagnostic Classification Systems for Organic Symptoms.

DSM-III-R *Organic Mental Disorders* *(etiology known)*	DSM-IV *Delirium, Dementia, and Amnestic* *and Other Cognitive Disorders*	ICD-10 *Organic, Including Symptomatic,* *Mental Disorders*
Dementia	*Delirium*	*Dementia in Alzheimer's Disease*
Alzheimer's Disease	General Medical Condition*	*Vascular Dementia*
Multi-Infarct Dementia	Substance Intoxication*	Multi-Infarct*
Not Otherwise Specified*	Substance Withdrawal	Subcortical*
Psychoactive Substance-Induced	Not Otherwise Specified	Mixed Cortical and Subcortical*
Intoxication*	*Dementia*	Other*
Withdrawal	Alzheimer's	Unspecified*
Delirium	Vascular*	*Dementia in Other Diseases*
Dementia	Human Immunodeficiency Virus*	Pick's Disease
Amnestic Disorder	Head Trauma*	Creutzfeldt-Jakob Disease
Delusional Disorder	Parkinsons's Disease	Huntington's Disease
Mood Disorder	Huntington's Disease	Parkinson's Disease
Anxiety Disorder	Pick's Disease	Human Immunodeficiency Virus*
Personality Disorder	Creutzfeldt-Jakob Disease	Other Specified Diseases*
Organic Mental Syndromes (etiology unknown)	General Medical Condition*	Unspecified Dementia*
Delirium*	Substance-Induced*	*Organic Amensic Syndrome* *
Dementia	Multiple Etiologies*	*Delirium (not substance induced)* *
Amnestic Syndrome*	Not Otherwise Specified*	*Other Mental Disorders*
Delusional Syndrome*	*Amnestic Disorder*	Organic Hallucinosis
Mood Syndrome*	General Medical Condition*	Organic Catatonic Disorder
Anxiety Syndrome*	Substance-Induced*	Organic Delusional Disorder
Personality Syndrome	Not Otherwise Specified*	Organic Mood Disorder*
Intoxication and Withdrawal*	*Other Cognitive Disorders*	Organic Anxiety Disorder*
Not Otherwise Specified*	Not Otherwise Specified*	Organic Dissociative Disorder
		Organic Emotionally Labile*
		Mild Cognitive Disorder*
		Other Specified Mental Disorder*
		Unspecified Mental Disorder*
		Personality and Behavioral Disorders
		Organic Personality Disorder
		Postencephalitic Syndrome*
		Postconcussional Syndrome*
		Other Specified Disorder*
		Unspecified Disorder*
		Unspecified Organic/Symptomatic Disorder *

Note: DSM-III-R = Diagnostic and Statistical Manual of Mental Disorders—Third Edition—Revised
    DSM-IV = Diagnostic and Statistical Manual of Mental Disorders—Fourth Edition
    ICD-10 = International Classification of Diseases—Tenth Edition
    * = Diagnoses appropriate for use with children

brain dysfunction on neurological tests. Many children may thus be diagnosed with a developmental disorder due to the clinician's inability to identify the brain injury or dysfunction. Furthermore, recent advances in neuroimaging techniques provide evidence that supports the notion that developmental disorders such as specific learning disabilities and attention-deficit/hyperactivity disorders may result from structural or functional brain pathology (Hynd et al., 1993; Leonard et al., 1994; Zametkin et al., 1993).

Although data are sparse on the diagnosis of organic mental conditions in children, data do exist on the occurrence of brain injury and brain disease in childhood. For example, closed head injuries are the leading cause of death in childhood, accounting for more than 100,000 hospitalizations per year (Goldstein & Levin, 1987). Incidence rates of such injuries have been placed as high as 150 to 200 per 100,000 children (Kalsbeek, McLaurin, Harris, & Miller, 1980; Kraus, Fife, Cox, Ramstein, & Conroy, 1986). However, since minor head injuries may involve fewer symptoms of cognitive dysfunction, many children may go undiagnosed. As compared to head injuries, cerebral vascular lesions are relatively rare in childhood, occurring at a rate of 2.5 per 100,000 children (Schoenberg, Mellinger, & Schoenberg, 1978). Pediatric brain tumors occur with a similar frequency of about 2 to 3 per 100,000 children (Dennis et al., 1991). HIV, once a rare occurrence in childhood, has unfortunately moved up in its incidence and is now the ninth leading cause of death in children (Fletcher et al., 1991; Pizzo & Wilfert, 1992). Thus, a decline in cognitive functioning or a plateau in the development of cognitive abilities resulting from HIV disease appears to be a much more likely occurrence than previously.

DIAGNOSIS OF ORGANIC MENTAL CONDITION

Historical Data

The diagnosis of organic mental conditions rests on the combination of a thorough developmental history, brain imaging studies, and extensive neuropsychological testing. The history should include information on pre-, peri-, and postnatal development of the child, as well as information on the health of the mother during pregnancy. History of head trauma or lesion, exposure to toxic substances (e.g., lead, alcohol or drugs, viral or bacterial infections), and poor physical and mental health is of particular importance. Most of the historical information necessary for a diagnosis is obtained during a standard thorough interview with parents and the child, if the child is at an age appropriate to comprehend the questions. Readers are directed to Baron, Fennell, and Voeller (1995) for

an example of a good developmental history questionnaire.

When significant events are discovered, additional information about the circumstances surrounding that event is needed. For example, if a child is described as having an injury to the brain, detailed information about the injury should include: (1) The cause of the injury (e.g., a head injury versus an infection; open versus closed head injury); (2) The location of the injury in the brain; (3) The maturity of the child, chronological as well as the estimated developmental age; (4) The severity of the illness or injury, which can often be estimated by the duration of coma, if present, or the length of hospitalization or treatment; and (5) Deficits or changes observed in the child's behavior or mental state. Care must be taken to ensure that the mere presence of a head injury is not taken as definitive proof that the child has an organic mental condition. Children with a history of head trauma can also suffer from other mental disorders. For example, a child may have a history of a benign tumor near the posterior fossa, one of the three most common sites for pediatric brain tumors (Swiam, 1991), which is associated with very few residual cognitive deficits, and go on to develop a reactive depression due to the disruption in the familial, educational, and social routines the treatment of the tumor may involve. In addition, certain disorders may have tendency to co-occur with organic mental symptoms. Children with attention-deficit/hyperactivity disorder, predominantly of the hyperactive-impulsive type, are at risk for obtaining head injuries due to their impulsiveness (Segalowitz & Lawson, 1995). They are more likely to act impulsively (e.g., run into the street without looking for approaching cars), thus increasing the risk for traumatic brain injuries. These children then display an organic mental condition in addition to their premorbid attention deficit.

Medical Data

Organic mental conditions, by definition, imply an etiology of organic brain impairment.

Although historical reports can be used as data to suggest the likelihood of brain impairment, brain imaging is certainly more definitive. Substantial improvement in brain imaging has occurred over recent years. Imaging techniques allow for the examination of brain structure as well as brain function, both of which are important in the diagnosis of organic mental conditions. Structural imaging devices include computerized tomography (CT) and magnetic resonance imaging (MRI). Both CT and MRI provide images based on differences in the densities of matter, allowing for the discrimination of fluid, bone, and tissue substances (Kalat, 1995). These scans result in a picture of various brain structures, without the representation of the functional capacity of those structures. Functional imaging produces images of neuronal activity, as opposed to gross structure. Common functional imaging devices include electroencephalograpy (EEG), positron emission tomography (PET), and functional MRI (f MRI). Electroencephalography involves the recording of electrical fluctuations from the scalp and is sensitive to abnormal electrical discharges, which are frequently indicative of brain dysfunction (Kooi, 1971). Fluctuations can be recorded during baseline monitoring (i.e., when the individual is not actively involved in a task), or they can be evoked by a specific stimulus, as in event-related potential recording (ERP). When conducted in this fashion, fluctuations indicative of sensory, perceptual, attention, and memory processes can be identified. EEG recordings are useful in the identification of global brain deficits and seizure activity. However, in regard to seizure disorders, an EEG should never be used in isolation as evidence of absence. That is, a normal EEG does not preclude the presence of a seizure disorder. The EEG identifies a seizure only when it is actively occurring. If a brain area is not actively seizing, an EEG may appear normal. PET analysis involves the recording of glucose metabolism throughout the brain during participation in various cognitive tasks. Areas of the brain that are more active during the task use more glucose. This technique has been found to demonstrate differences in the brains of patients with dementia during performance of memory tasks (Meltzer & Frost, 1994), as well as individuals diagnosed with attention-deficit/hyperactivity disorder (Zametkin et al., 1993). However, due to the fact that the imaging process employs the use of radioactive tracers, PET has limited applicability with the prepubescent child. This imaging process requires radioactive tracers to enter the body's bloodstream and travel to the brain, where they are detected through the emission process. However, once in the bloodstream, the radioactive tracers can travel to other organs as well. In the prepubescent child, exposure of the gonadal organs to radioactivity may have long-term consequences to development and potential reproductivity. Functional magnetic resonance imaging (f MRI) utilizes changes in magnetic fields associated with blood oxygenation to create images of brain functioning. Areas of the brain that are more active use more oxygen and are therefore distinguishable from less active areas (Ogawa et al., 1992). The f MRI technique does not require radioactive tracers and thus holds more promise in the identification and understanding of organic mental symptoms in children.

Neuropsychological Data

Documentation of mental dysfunction is the second component of the diagnosis of an organic mental condition. Identification of an impairment in attention, memory, or other cognitive functions is necessary. Although family members or friends typically report disturbance in the patient, the use of a formal neuropsychological evaluation is much more sensitive and reliable. For example, apparent lapses of memory in a 14-year-old male can result from a variety of factors, including depression, drug abuse, epilepsy, or some other neurological deficit. All of these conditions can cause the adolescent to appear to "forget" material; however, only the neurological conditions meet criteria for an organic mental condition. Furthermore, the presence of a history of brain injury or illness does not necessarily mean that the "forgetting" is due to that injury. For example, an adolescent or child can experience an injury during a motor vehicle accident that may produce a paralysis and subsequent depression, though not a true dementia or amnesia. The depression resulting from the loss of movement can cause the child to be distractible and inattentive and thereby appear to "forget" information.

When a complete neuropsychological evaluation is not available or is not possible to obtain, brief assessment of the child's mental status can be conducted in a relatively short period of time. The Children's Orientation and Amnesia Test (Ewing-Cobbs, Levin, Fletcher, Miner, & Eisenberg, 1990) can be useful in the assessment of global functioning. This test is a children's version of the popular Galveston Orientation and Amnesia Test (Levin, O'Donnell, & Grossman, 1979), which has been used often to assess global functioning in adults following head trauma. However, the reader should be cautioned that these tests are useful for quick global assessment and tracking of moderate to severe injury and do not provide data for specific deficits or identify mild impairments.

A neuropsychological evaluation involves the administration and interpretation of tests of general cognitive functioning, attention, memory, language, spatial perception, motor control, reasoning and mental flexibility, and emotional or behavioral functioning. Table 11.2 presents common neuropsychological tests grouped according to typical cognitive processes assessed. This table is not intended to be an exhaustive coverage of neuropsychological measures but instead lists common tests employed for assessing neuropsychological functioning in children.

A properly trained neuropsychologist can provide interpretations of the test results in light of brain-behavior relationships. With a comprehensive battery of measures, decisions can be made as to whether the "forgetting" is associated with attentional deficits (as in delirium), memory deficits (as in dementia), or emotional disturbances (as in depression). In addition, documentation of functions such as language, spatial perception, and reasoning or mental flexibility form the basis of a decision

to diagnose an individual with amnesia or a dementia.

The data derived from a neuropsychological evaluation also allow for comparisons to norm-referenced samples of children of similar age or educational level. Knowledge of how the child is functioning as compared to his or her peers is not only a basis for the establishment of current dysfunction but provides for future comparisons of the expected development of cognitive abilities. Data indicating that a child's expressive language abilities are at the thirtieth percentile (low average range) 18 months after a traumatic brain injury takes on an entirely new meaning if additional data exist to indicate that the child's performance on the same tasks fell at the eightieth percentile three months after the injury. Without the evidence of a decline in the rate of development of skills, the child's expressive deficit may go untreated.

TREATMENT OF ORGANIC MENTAL CONDITIONS

Treatment of organic mental conditions depends to a large extent on the symptoms and cause(s) of the disorder. As outlined earlier, the symptoms and causes can vary widely and often are independent of one another. Since the identification and understanding of specific symptoms resulting from brain dysfunction in childhood is a rapidly and newly emerging field, treatment options have not received the systemic study they deserve. The dearth of treatment investigations has also been stymied by the falsely held notion that children recover more fully from brain injury than do adults; thus, if greater plasticity exists in the child's brain, why develop treatment programs for brain injury? This notion of greater plasticity in the brains of children has been a topic of hot debate. Although there is evidence for developmental plasticity, as in synaptic reorganization, evidence for regeneration of neuronal cells following injury does not exist (Spreen, Risser, & Edgell, 1995). Instead, the injury may interfere with the development of ongoing or future cognitive processes (Fletcher, Miner, &

TABLE 11.2. Cognitive Processing Assessed through a Pediatric Neuropsychological Evaluation and Common Tests Used for the Assessment

Cognitive Area	Process	Test
General Intellect	Comprehensive	Wechsler Intelligence Scale for Children—Third Edition (Wechsler, 1991)
		Differential Abilities Scale (Elliot, 1990)
		Stanford-Binet—Fourth Edition (Thorndike, Hagen, & Sattler, 1986)
	Simultan/ Successive	Kaufman Assessment Battery for Children (Kaufman & Kaufman, 1983)
Visual Perceptual and Motor	Comprehensive	Developmental Test of Visual Perception—Second Edition (Hammill, Pearson, & Voress, 1993)
	Graphomotor	Developmental Test of Visual-Motor Integration (Beery, 1989)
		Rey Osterrieth Complex Figure (Spreen & Strauss, 1991)
	Visual Perception	Motor-Free Visual Perception Test (Colarusso & Hammill, 1972)
		Test of Visual Perceptual Skills (Gardner, 1982)
	Fine Motor	Purdue Pegboard Test (Tiffin, 1968)
Language	Comprehensive	Clinical Evaluation of Language Fundamental—Third Edition (Semel, Wiig, & Secord, 1995)
		Test of Language Development—Second Edition (Newcomer & Hammill, 1991)
	Receptive	Peabody Picture Vocabulary Test—Revised (Dunn & Dunn, 1981)
		Receptive One-Word Picture Vocabulary Test—Revised (Gardner, 1990)
	Expressive	Boston Naming Test (Kaplan, Goodglass, & Weintraub, 1983)
		Expressive One-Word Picture Vocabulary Test—Revised (Gardner, 1985)
		Controlled Oral Word Association (Benton & Hamsher, 1983)
	Phonology	Auditory Analysis Test (Rosner, 1979)
		Lindamood Auditory Conceptualization Test (Lindamood & Lindamood, 1979)
		Word Attack Subtest (Woodcock & Johnson, 1989)
Attention	Sustained	Gordon Diagnostic System [Omissions] (Gordon, 1983)
		Continuous Performance Test [Omissions] (Conners, 1992)
	Focused/Selective	Coding (Wechsler, 1991)
		Symbol Search (Wechsler, 1991)
		Stroop Color Word Test (Golden, 1978)
	Inhibition	Gordon Diagnostic System [Commissions] (Gordon, 1983)
		Continuous Performance Test [Commissions] (Conners, 1992)
		Stroop Color Word Test [Interference] (Golden, 1978)
Memory	Comprehensive	Test of Memory and Learning (Reynolds & Bigler, 1994)
		Wide-Range Assessment of Memory and Learning (Sheslow & Adams, 1990)
	Storage vs. Retrieval	Selective Reminding Test (Hannay & Levin, 1985)
		Visual Selective Reminding Test (Fletcher, 1985)
	Chunking	Children's Auditory Verbal Learning Test—Second Edition (Talley, 1992)
		California Verbal Learning Test—Children's Version (Delis, Kramer, Kaplan, & Ober, 1994)
	Recognition	Continuous Visual Recognition Memory Test (Hannay, Levin, & Grossman, 1979)
Executive Functions	Abstraction	Wisconsin Card Sorting Test (Heaton, 1981)
		Children's Category Test (Boll, 1993)
		Ravens Progressive Matrices (Raven, 1938; 1947)
		Test of Nonvernal Intelligence—Second Edition (Brown, Sherbenou, & Johnsen, 1990)
	Planning	Tower of London (Krikorian, Bartok, & Gay, 1994)
		Tower of Hanoi (Leon-Carrion et al., 1991)
		Rey-Osterrieth Complex Figure (Spreen & Strauss, 1991)
		Porteus Mazes (Porteus, 1968)
	Flexibility	Wisconsin Card Sorting Test (Heaton, 1981)
		Trail-Making Test (Reitan & Wolfson, 1985)

Cognitive Area	Process	Test
Academic Achievement	Comprehensive	Wechsler Individual Achievement Test (Psychological Corporation, 1992)
		Woodcock-Johnson—Revised Tests of Achievement (Woodcock & Johnson, 1989)
		Kaufman Tests of Educational Achievement (Kaufman & Kaufman, 1985)
		Peabody Individual Achievement Test—Revised (Markwardt, 1989)
	Basic	Wide-Range Achievement Test—Third Edition (Wilkinson, 1993)
	Reading	Stanford Diagnostic Reading Test (Karlsen, Madden, & Gardner, 1984)
		Gray Oral Reading Test—Revised (Wiederholt & Bryant, 1986)
	Writing	Test of Written Language—Third Edition (Hammill & Larsen, 1996)
	Arithmetic	Key Math—Revised (Connolly, 1988)
Behavior	Adaptive	Vineland Adaptive Behavior Scales (Sparrow, Balla, & Cicchetti, 1984)
	Observational Ratings	Child Behavior Checklist (Achenbach & Edelbrock, 1983)
		Conners Rating Scales (Goyette, Conners, & Ulrich, 1978)
	Self Report	Reynold's Depression Scales (Reynolds, 1986, 1988)
		Children's Depression Inventory (Kovacs, 1992)
		Revised Children's Manifest Anxiety Scale (Reynolds & Richmond, 1985)
		Minnesota Multiphasic Personality Inventory—Adolescent Version (Butcher, Williams, Graham, Archer, Tellegen, Ben-Porath, & Kaemmer, 1992)

Ewing-Cobbs, 1987), where the emergence of additional deficits occurs as more sophisticated or complex skills are required of the child.

Treatment of the organic deficit has received more attention than has treatment of the mental condition in children with brain pathology. Common neurosurgical treatments in children or adolescents include removal of brain tumors, removal of brain areas that are believed to generate seizure activity, and the placement of shunts in children with hydrocephalus to reduce ventricular pressure resulting from the buildup of cerebral spinal fluid. Resection of seizure foci is conducted to reduce seizure activity and thus may improve mental functioning. If the seizure is severe enough that it spreads to other areas of the brain, thereby disrupting the function of these areas, improvement in overall functioning may result following the ablation. Similarly, the placement of a shunt into the lateral ventricles of a hydrocephalic patient will reduce the effects of the pressure the addition fluid places on surrounding brain areas, and improvement in overall functioning of the child may result. It should be noted, however, both of these treatments also result in the lesion of portions of the brain that may function normally and thus may lead to additional deficits in the child.

Pharmacotherapy is also a well-studied area in specific types of brain pathology. Various medications have been used for the treatment of seizure disorders, with both positive and negative outcomes. Overall, these medications have been found to decrease the frequency of seizures and thus the degree of disruption the seizure event places on the child's life. However, when certain drugs are used in early childhood, additional deficits may result. For example, several studies have found phenobarbitol to be effective in seizure management; however, when it is given regularly during early childhood, declines in cognitive functioning have been noted (Chen, Kang, & So, 1996; Riva & Devati, 1996).

Additional medications have been found to be effective in the treatment of certain cognitive deficits in children. Pharmacotherapy has been employed with children following acute brain injury. Children who experience attentional deficits following organic brain injury have been found to respond positively to stimulant medication (Hornstein, Lennihan, Seliger, Lichtman, & Schroeder, 1996; Kaelin, Cifu, & Matthies, 1996; Kraus, 1995). The same stimulants used to treat disorders such as attention-deficit/hyperactivity disorder have also been found to be effective in the treatment of attention deficits following traumatic brain injury, though the degree of improvement is typically not as high. However, to date, no systematic research into the pharmacotherapeutic treatment of organic mental disorders in children has been reported. Thus, most results are based on anecdotal or clinical case study reports.

The specific treatment of the cognitive or behavioral deficit produced by an organic brain injury depends largely on the nature of the specific deficit produced by the injury. Due to the complexity of the conditions, therapists who specialize in the treatment of certain disorders are often necessary. For example, deficits in the expression of language resulting from injury to the left hemisphere of the brain (i.e., aphasia) warrant referral to a speech and language therapist. Treatment of visual-motor integration deficits in a child following a traumatic brain injury is best performed by an occupational therapist who has experience working with such cases.

Systematic investigations into the applicability of psychosocial treatments in children with brain dysfunction are rare. When such treatment is employed, it often involves either the adaptation of the child to the environment or the modification of the environment to meet the needs of the child. For example, children with severe memory impairment following hydrocephalus can be taught to make use of a memory notebook and a wristwatch equipped with multiple alarms. Children with motor control deficits (i.e., apraxia) following brain injury can use computers to complete school assignments instead of writing them by hand. The environments of children with persistent attentional deficits that don't respond to medication can be modified to reduce distractions, and timed assignments can be altered to accommodate the decreased vigilance. Any number of treatments can be attempted as long as the clinician is keenly aware of the specific deficits the brain injury has produced.

CONCLUSIONS

A mental disorder implies abnormal behavior and/or thought processes. The term "organic" implies a physiological state of being. Thus, organic mental conditions by definition include abnormal behavior or thought processes associated with changes in the physical functioning or state of the brain. However, not all mental disorders that co-occur with the presence of brain abnormalities are classified as organic mental disorders. Instead, this classification is limited to mental disorders with onset following the occurrence of acquired brain pathology. Thus, the change in brain state is believed to be the cause of the mental disturbance. Developmental disorders, some of which have identifiable differences in brain physiology, are not classified as organic mental conditions. For example, brain imaging studies have identified functional differences in the brains of children with ADHD, differences that decline with the administration of psychostimulants. Does this evidence imply that the ADHD is an "organic" condition? No identified age or stage of development exists for the determination of an "acquired" deficit. Does a child who experiences a brain injury during the birth process or in infancy and goes on to develop an impulsive, inattentive, and hyperactive behavior style have an organic mental condition or ADHD? Although the current status of neuroimaging does not allow for the differential diagnosis of these two conditions, continued advances in the state of the art will undoubtedly permit such discrimination in the near future.

As stated previously, organic impairment to the brain may not necessarily cause a decline in cognitive functioning of the child. Mild to moderate impairment may be associated with a temporary decline, followed by a quick return to baseline. However, in the developing brain this pattern does not imply a lack of cognitive dysfunction. The mild to moderate injury may change the course of brain development, with a lack of or altered growth in cognitive functions. Thus, the cognitive level may not decline but instead may fail to mature properly because of the injury. The "deficit" may not be identifiable for many years after the injury occurs. For example, a 4-year-old child who experiences a mild traumatic brain injury to the frontal lobes may display no deficits in cognitive processes for years to come. As the child nears adolescence, however, impaired abstract thought processes and mental flexibility may become evident. These deficits may result from improper or incomplete development of the frontal lobe structures responsible for such processes. A failure to mature in cognitive functioning does not fit the criteria for a dementing process or an amnesia and thus cannot be diagnosed in DSM-IV unless the "cognitive disorder NOS" category is used. Cognitive disorder NOS is a heterogeneous group of disorders, which unfortunately is probably the most appropriate category for the majority of disorders resulting from brain injury in childhood.

Is differential diagnosis of organic mental conditions in children important? Are various medical conditions associated with similar patterns of dysfunction in childhood so that the diagnosis of "dementia due to a general medical condition" or "cognitive disorder NOS" suffices? As should be clear from the discussion, DSM-IV has done little to assist in the diagnosis of organic mental dysfunction in childhood. Most childhood conditions associated with organic impairment are diagnosed under an unspecified category, which does little to assist in classification. If the purpose of the entire diagnostic process is to ensure reimbursement for clinical services, then differential diagnosis is not necessary. On the other hand, if the purpose of the diagnostic process is to improve communication among professionals so that advances in the understanding and treatment of organic mental conditions occur, then differential diagnosis is essential.

REFERENCES

Achenbach, T., & Edelbrock, C. (1983). *Manual for the Child Behavior Checklist and Revised Child Behavior Profile*. Burlington: University of Vermont.

American Psychiatric Association. (1987). *Diagnostic and statistical manual of mental disorders* (3rd ed., rev.). Washington, DC: Author.

American Psychiatric Association. (1994). *Diagnostic and statistical manual of mental disorders* (4th ed.). Washington, DC: Author.

Annegers, J. (1983). The epidemiology of head trauma in children. In K. Shapiro (Ed.), *Pediatric head trauma*. New York: Futura Publishing Co.

Baron, I., Fennell, E., & Voeller, K. (1995). *Pediatric neuropsychology in medical settings*. New York: Oxford University Press.

Beery, K. (1989). *The Developmental Test of Visual-Motor Integration: Administration, scoring, and teaching manual* (3rd rev.). Cleveland, OH: Modern Curriculum Press.

Benton, A., & Hamsher, K. (1983). *Multilingual aphasia examination*. Iowa City, IA: AJA Associates.

Boll, T. (1993). *Children's Category Test*. San Antonio, TX: Psychological Corporation.

Brown, L., Sherbenou, R., & Johnsen, S. (1990). *Test of Nonverbal Intelligence—second edition*. Austin, TX: ProEd.

Butcher, J., Williams, C., Graham, J., Archer, R., Tellegen, A., Ben-Porath, Y., & Kaemmer, B. (1992). *MMPI-A: Manual for administration, scoring, and interpretation*. Minneapolis: University of Minnesota Press.

Chen, Y., Kang, W., & So, W. (1996). Comparison of antiepileptic drugs on cognitive function in newly diagnosed epileptic children: A psychometric and neurophysiological study. *Epilepsia*, 37 (1): 81–86.

Colarusso, R., & Hammill, D. (1972). *Motor-Free Visual Perceptual Test*. Novato, CA: Academic Therapy.

Conners, C. (1992). *Continuous Performance Test Computer Program*. North Tonawanda, NY: Multi-Health Systems.

Connolly, A. (1988). *Key Math—Revised: A diagnostic inventory of essential mathematics*. Circle Pines, MN: American Guidance Service.

Dalby, P., & Obrzut, J. (1991). Epidemiologic characteristics and sequelae of closed head-injured children and adolescents: A review. *Developmental Neuropsychology*, 7, 35–68.

Delis, D., Kramer, J., Kaplan, E., & Ober, B. (1994). *California Verbal Learning Test—Children's version*. San Antonio, TX: Psychological Corporation.

Dennis, M., Spiegler, B., Hoffman, H., Hendrick, E., Humphreys, R., & Becker, L. (1991). Brain tumors in children and adolescents: I. Effects on working, associative and serial-order memory of IQ, age at tumor onset and age of tumor. *Neuropsychologia*, 29, 813.

Dunn, L., & Dunn, L. (1981). *Peabody Picture Vocabulary Test—Revised manual*. Circle Pines, MN: American Guidance Service.

Elliott, C. (1990). *Differential Abilities Scale: Administration and scoring manual*. San Antonio, TX: Psychological Corporation.

Ewing-Cobbs, L., Levin, H., Fletcher, J., Miner, M., & Eisenberg, H. (1990). The Children's Orientation and Amnesia Test: Relationship to severity of acute head injury and to recovery of memory. *Neurosurgery*, 27 (5), 683–691.

Fletcher, J. (1985). Memory for verbal and nonverbal stimuli in learning disability subgroups: analysis by selective reminding. *Journal of Experimental Child Psychology*, 40 (2), 244–259.

Fletcher, J., Francis, D., Pequenat, W., Raudenbusch, S., Bornstein, M., Schmitt, F., Brouwers, P., & Stover, E. (1991). Neurobehavioral outcomes in diseases of childhood: Individual change model foe pediatric immunodeficiency virus. *American Psychologist*, 46, 1267.

Fletcher, J., Miner, M., & Ewing-Cobbs, L. (1987). Age and recovery from head injury in children: Developmental issues. In H. Levin, J. Grafman, & H. Eisenberg (Eds.), *Neurobehavioral recovery from head injury*. New York: Oxford University Press.

Gardner, M. (1982). *Test of Visual-Perceptual Skills (nonmotor): Manual*. Los Angeles, CA: Western Psychological Services.

Gardner, M. (1985). *Receptive One-Word Picture Vocabulary Test: Manual and form*. Novato, CA: Academic Therapy Publications.

Gardner, M. (1990). *Expressive One-Word Picture Vocabulary Test—Revised: Manual and form*. Novato, CA: Academic Therapy Publications.

Golden, J. (1978). *Stroop Color Word Test*. Chicago, IL: Stoelting.

Goldstein, F., & Levin, H. (1987). Epidemiology of pediatric closed head injuries: Incidence, clinical characteristics, and risk factors. *Journal of Learning Disabilities*, 20, 518–525.

Gordon, M. (1983). *The Gordon Diagnostic System*. Dewitt, NY: Gordon Systems.

Goyette, C., Conners, C., & Ulrich, R. (1978). Normative data on Revised Conners Parent and Teacher Rating Scales. *Journal of Abnormal Child Psychology*, 6, 221–236.

Hammill, D., & Larsen, S. (1996). *Test of Written Language—Third edition*. Austin, TX: ProEd.

Hammill, D., Pearson, N., & Voress, J. (1993). *Developmental Test of Visual Perception—Second edition*. Austin, TX: ProEd.

Hannay, H., & Levin, H. (1985). Selective Reminding Test: An examination of the equivalence of four forms. *Journal of Clinical and Experimental Neuropsychology*, 7, 251–263.

Hannay, H., Levin, H., & Grossman, R. (1979). Impaired recognition memory after head injury. *Cortex*, 15 (2), 269–283.

Heaton, R. (1981). *Wisconsin Card Sorting Test manual*. Odessa, FL: Psychological Assessment Resources.

Hornstein, A., Lennihan, L., Seliger, G., Lichtman, S., & Schroeder, K. (1996). Amphetamine in recovery from brain injury. *Brain Injury*, 10 (2), 145–148.

Hynd, G., Hern, K., Novey, E., Eliopulos, D., Marshall, R., Gonzalez, J., & Voeller, K. (1993). Attention deficit-hyperactivity disorder and asymmetry of the caudate nucleus. *Journal of Child Neurology*, 8 (4), 339–347.

Kalat, J. (1995). *Biological psychology* (5th ed.). Pacific Grove, CA: Brooks/Cole.

Kaelin, D., Cifu, D., & Matthies, B. (1996). Metylphenidate effect on attention deficit in the acutely brain-injured adult. *Archives of Physical Medicine and Rehabilitation*, 77 (1), 6–9.

Kalsbeek, W., McLaurin, R., Harris, B., & Miller, J. (1980). The national head injury and spinal cord injury survey: Major findings. *Journal of Neurosurgery*, 53, 19–31.

Kaplan, E., Goodglass, H., & Weintraub, S. (1983). *The Boston Naming Test* (2nd ed.). Philadelphia: Lea & Febiger.

Karlsen, B., Madden, R., & Gardner, E. (1984). *Stanford Diagnostic Reading Test—Third edition*. San Antonio, TX: Psychological Corporation.

Kaufman, A., & Kaufman, N. (1983). *Kaufman Assessment Battery for Children*. Circle Pines, MN: American Guidance Service.

Kaufman, A., & Kaufman, N. (1985). *Kaufman Test of Educational Achievement*. Circle Pines, MN: American Guidance Service.

Kooi, K. (1971). *Fundamentals of electroencephalography*. New York: Harper & Row.

Kovacs, M. (1992). *Children's depression inventory*. North Tonawanda, NY: Multi-Health Systems.

Kraus, J., Fife, D., Cox, P., Ramstein, K., & Conroy, C. (1986). Incidence, severity, and external causes of pediatric brain injury. *American Journal of Disabilities in Children, 140,* 687–693.

Kraus, M. (1995). Neuropsychiatric sequelae of stroke and traumatic brain injury: The role of psychostimulants. *International Journal of Psychiatry in Medicine, 25* (1), 39–51.

Krikorian, R., Bartok, J., & Gay, N. (1994). Tower of London procedure: a standard method and developmental data. *Journal of Clinical and Experimental Neuropsychology, 16* (6), 840–850.

Leon-Carrion, J., Morales, M., Forastero, P., Dominguez-Morales, M., Murillo, F., Jimenez-Baco, R., & Gordon, P. (1991). The computerized Tower of Hanoi: A new form of administration and suggestions for interpretation. *Perceptual and Motor Skills, 73* (1), 63–66.

Leonard, C., Voeller, K., Lombardino, L., Morris, M., Hynd, G., Alexander, A., Andersen, H., Garofalakis, M., Honeyman, J., Mao, J., et al. (1994). Anomalous cerebral structure in dyslexia revealed with magnetic resonance imaging. *Archives of Neurology, 50* (5), 461–469.

Levin, H., O'Donnell, V., & Grossman, R. (1979). The Galveston Orientation and Amnesia Test. A practical scale to assess cognition after head injury. *Journal of Nervous and Mental Disease, 167* (11), 675–684.

Lindamood, C., & Lindamood, P. (1979). *Lindamood Auditory Conceptualization—Revised.* Austin, TX: ProEd.

Markwardt, F. (1989). *Peabody Individual Achievement Test—Revised.* Circle Pines, MN: American Guidance Service.

Meltzer, C., & Frost, J. (1994). Partial volume correction in Emission-Computed Tomography: Focus on Alzheimer's Disease. In R. W. Thatcher, M. Hallettt, T. Zeffiro, E. R. John, & M. Huerta (Eds.), *Functional neuroimaging.* San Diego: Academic Press.

Newcomer, P., & Hammill, D. (1991). *Test of Language Development—Second edition.* Austin, TX: ProEd.

Ogawa, S., Tank, D., Menon, R., Ellerman, J., Kim, S., Merkle, H., & Ugurbil, K. (1992). Intrinsic signal changes accompanying sensory stimulation: Functional brain mapping with magnetic resonance imaging. *Proceeding of the National Academy of Sciences, 89,* 5951–5955.

Pizzo, P., & Wilfert, C. (1992). *Pediatric AIDS: The challenge of HIV infection in infants.* Baltimore: Williams and Wilkins.

Porteus, S. (1968). New applications of the Porteus Maze tests. *Perceptual and Motor Skills, 26* (3), 787–798.

Raven, J. (1938). *Progressive Matrices: A perceptual test of intelligence: Individual form.* London: H. K. Lewis.

Raven, J. (1947). *Colored Progressive Matrices Sets A, Ab, B.* London: H. K. Lewis.

Reitan, R., & Wolfson, D. (1985). *The Halstead-Reitan Neuropsychological Test Battery.* Tucson, AZ: Neuropsychological Press.

Reynolds, C., & Bigler, E. (1994). *The Test of Memory and Learning.* Austin, TX: ProEd.

Reynolds, C., & Richmond, B. (1985). *What I Think and Feel (RCMAS).* Los Angeles: Western Psychological Services.

Reynolds, W. (1986). *Reynolds Adolescent Depression Scale.* Odessa, FL: Psychological Assessment Resources.

Reynolds, W. (1988). *Reynolds Child Depression Scale.* Odessa, FL: Psychological Assessment Resources.

Riva, D., & Devoti, M. (1996). Discontinuation of phenobarbital in children: effects on neurocognitive behavior. *Pediatric Neurology, 14* (1), 36–40.

Rosner, J. (1979). Screening for perceptual skills dysfunction: An up-date. *Journal of the American Optometric Association, 50* (10), 1115–1119.

Sattler, J. (1992). *Assessment of Children: Revised and updated third edition.* San Diego, CA: Jerome M. Sattler.

Schoenberg, B., Mellinger, J., & Schoenberg, D. (1978). Cerebrovascular disease in infants and children: A study of incidence, clinical features, and survival. *Neurology, 28,* 763

Segalowitz, S., & Lawson, S. (1995). Subtle symptoms associated with self-reported mild head injury. *Journal of Learning Disabilities, 28* (5), 309–319.

Semel, E., Wiig, E., & Secord, W. (1995). *Clinical Evaluation of Language Fundamentals—Third edition: Examiner's manual.* San Antonio, TX: Psychological Corporation.

Sheslow, D., & Adams, W. (1990). *Wide-Range Assessment of Memory and Learning.* Wilmington, DE: Jastak Associates.

Sparrow, S., Balla, D., & Cicchetti, D. (1984). *Vineland Adaptive Behavior Scale.* Circle Pines, MN: American Guidance Service.

Spreen, O., Risser, A. H., & Edgell, D. (1995). *Developmental neuropsychology.* New York: Oxford University Press.

Spreen, O., & Strauss, E. (1991). *A compendium of*

neuropsychological tests: Administration, norms, and commentary. New York: Oxford University Press.

Swaiman, K. (1989). Pediatric neurology. St. Louis: Mosby.

Talley, J. (1992). Children's Auditory Verbal Learning Test. Odessa, FL: Psychological Assessment Resources.

Thorndike, R. L., Hagen, E. P., & Sattler, J. M. (1986). The Stanford-Binet Intelligence Scale: Fourth edition. Guide for administering and scoring (2nd ed.). Chicago: Riverside.

Tiffin, J. (1968). Purdue Pegboard Examiner's Manual. Rosemont, IL: London House.

Wechsler, D. (1991). Wechsler Intelligence Scale for Children—Third edition. San Antonio, TX: Psychological Corporation.

Wechsler, D. (1992). Wechsler Individual Achievement Test. San Antonio, TX: Psychological Corporation.

Wiederholt, J., & Bryant, B. (1986). Gray Oral Reading Tests—Revised. Austin, TX: ProEd.

Wilkinson, G. (1993). The Wide-Range Achievement Test: Administration Manual. Wilmington, DE: Wide-Range.

Woodcock, R., & Johnson, M. (1989). Woodcock-Johnson Revised Psychoeducational Battery. Allen, TX: DLM Teaching Resources.

World Health Organization. (1992). ICD-10 Classification of Mental and Behavioural Disorders. Geneva: Author.

Zametkin, A., Liebenauer, L., Fitzgerald, G., King, A., Minkunas, D., Herscovitch, P., Yamanda, E., & Cohen, R. (1993). Brain metabolism in teenagers with Attention-Deficit Hyperactivity Disorder. Archives of General Psychiatry, 50, 333–340.

12

Substance-Related Disorders

Mari Radzik
Brandi J. Freeman
Richard G. MacKenzie

The use of alcohol and other drugs among adolescents continues to be of serious concern among clinicians, researchers, public policy makers, and, most importantly, parents. As the rates of accidental deaths related to alcohol and drug use continue to rise among adolescents (MacKenzie & Kipke, 1992), it is critical for health care workers to fully understand the adolescent in order to intervene with carefully matched treatments that clearly address the adolescent's specific needs. This chapter reviews the historical perspective of substance use and abuse, the substance-related disorders as delineated by DSM-IV, the epidemiology of substance use among adolescents, and the major influences and consequences of adolescent substance use. Practical approaches to assessment and treatment of the adolescent are followed by appendices and references.

The language of substance abuse has changed over the years and can be confusing; therefore, it would be helpful to clarify some of the terminology found in the literature. For example, ATOD and AOD are abbreviations for "*a*lcohol, *t*obacco, and *o*ther *d*rugs" and "*a*lcohol and *o*ther *d*rugs." The term "illicit drug use" refers to the use of controlled substances (e.g., marijuana and lysergic acid diethyamide [LSD]) or those drugs that are abused (not under the direction of a physician) but are available by prescription (e.g., tranquilizers). The term "licit" refers to those drugs that are available to adults, but generally not available to adolescents, such as alcohol or tobacco (O'Malley, Johnston, & Bachman, 1995). The phrases "chemical dependency, addiction, and habit" are still in use but less so than "substance abuse, use, or misuse." The latter have become the favored vernacular among researchers and clinicians. Despite the confusion of the wording, the terminology crystallizes some of the changes in the thinking in the field of chemical dependency.

ADOLESCENCE AND SUBSTANCE ABUSE

The nature of adolescent substance use and abuse needs to be viewed within the context of the pubertal changes of physical and emotional development (Brooks-Gunn & Graber, 1994; Trad, 1994). Like any change confronting humankind, adapting to adolescence requires skill, self-efficacy, and the willingness to take risks. Despite the many changes and adjustments, most adolescents negotiate adolescence well and ease into adulthood without difficulty (Mishne, 1986; Trad, 1994). Yet there are times when the common pubertal changes become stressful for adolescents. Menarche, for example, can often be a developmental "crisis" for some girls. For a male, the deepening of his voice imports the beginning of adulthood (Kestenberg, 1967, Neinstein, 1991). For some adolescents, one way of managing the difficult stressors of moving into adulthood with the necessary abandonment of childhood is through the use of illicit or licit substances. Consequently, the initiation into substance use may be a result of many complex and inter-relating events, including normal developmental stressors, dysfunctional family relations, lack of economic or emotional support, intrafamilial substance use, or psychiatric conditions (Malinosky-Rummell & Hansen, 1993; Norton, 1994; Patton, 1995; Peters, Maltzman, & Villone, 1994). Only by understanding the relationship between developmental issues, cultural, societal, and familial influences, will the clinician begin to tease out the underlying dynamics that promote drug use and define its role in any individual adolescent's life.

Historical Perspective

Since the beginning of documented civilization, historians from different cultures and at different times have mentioned the use of alcohol and mood/mind-altering substances. For example, as Brust (1993) points out in his review, alcohol (ethanol), has been manufactured from fruits and vegetables since the Paleolithic period, marijuana has existed as far back as the third millennium in China, and opioids have been used for six thousand years. More recently, New World explorers found Native Americans smoking tobacco and then disseminated the product in Europe (Brust, 1993).

In the twentieth century, the illicit use of psychostimulants has gained in popularity. Amphetamine-like compounds have been available since the 1920s, when ephedrine was found in the ma huang plant (*Ephedra vulgaris*). Cocaine, derived from a South American plant, *Erythroxylon coca*, has enjoyed periods of popularity from the early 1900s, first as a popular elixir to the current popular crystalline form, "crack cocaine." Even more recently, in the 1950s, the disinhibiting anesthetic phencyclidine, or "PCP," was developed for veterinarian use. Due to the intense mind-body dissociation and associated illusionogenic properties, PCP became a drug of abuse during the 60s and the 70s (Brust 1993). Last, inhalants have been used in many forms for centuries. Religious ceremonies have included scents or vapors as a part of rituals and ceremonies. The discovery of diethyl ether in the thirteenth century introduced inhalant use to the nonreligious segments of the population (Brust, 1993). In sum, the use of substances to cope, alter moods, or reach another level of consciousness has been an acceptable form of communication and expression for most of humankind.

Adolescent Substance Use as a Problem

Not until the past few decades has substance use and misuse been described as a significant problem among adolescents. Reasons for this fairly recent concern about adolescent substance use is a result of the potentially greater access to illicit drugs youth have had in the past few decades. For example, due to drug trafficking, illicit substances have become more available around the United States and in local communities (Li & Feigelman, 1994). Moreover, it has become recognized that substance use has become less stigmatizing among adolescents and is viewed less as a problem among their peers (Johnston, O'Malley, & Bachman, 1994).

A prominent development in the adolescent substance abuse literature has been the awareness that substance misuse may have an inextricable dysfunctional relationship between family members (Norton, 1994; Patton, 1995). Through the work of family systems therapists and organizations such as Alcoholics Anonymous, it has become understood that family substance abuse affects all members of a family. With the creation of adjunct family groups and adolescent groups, substance use among adolescents has been addressed. Further research has linked parental substance use with their children's later substance use (Morrison, Rogers, & Thomas, 1995). The links are both environmental and genetic; for example, the relationship between alcoholics with alcoholic parents has been repeatedly substantiated (Morrison, Rogers, & Thomas, 1995).

Psychosocial Factors Influencing Substance Use

Along with familial influences, other psychosocial factors play an essential role in adolescent substance use. These factors include cultural, environmental, interpersonal, and intrapersonal situations (Leigh, 1985). Ethnicity, acculturation, or cultural background influences the adolescent's substance use. Since not all cultures view substance use similarly (Charles et al., 1994), it is vital to address cultural attitudes toward substance abuse with the adolescent. How a culture dictates the use of substances is important to determine, but it is generally the excessive use of a substance that brings the adolescent to the attention of an aware and involved caregiver and then onto the clinician.

Modern day adolescents are influenced by many aspects of their environment. They may be influenced to misuse substances through the media, family, social, and occupational influences, and through peers. All of these factors can condition the adolescent to accept substance use as an acceptable way to cope with environmental and life stressors (Malinosky-Rummell & Hansen, 1993; Peters et al., 1994). Often substance use is then related to minor infractions and involvement with delinquent behaviors, which may become an ongoing way to cope with environmental stressors (Leigh, 1985).

Interpersonally, the adolescent's initiation into substance use may include other factors, such as parental and peer influences. Just as the most recent "Monitoring the Future" surveys (Johnston, O'Malley, & Bachman, 1994, 1995) have determined, peer influences play a vital role in how adolescents become involved with substance use. Furthermore, the media has instrumentally influenced adolescents' attitudes that smoking or drinking excessively are acceptable social activities with little perceived risk (Johnston et al., 1994).

Last, the adolescent's personality structure and his or her own value and belief system can affect the decision to misuse drugs or alcohol. If an adolescent is depressed, anxious, or acting out, substance use may become a way to express and cope with painful emotions and internal processes. It is difficult to say how well personality determines drug use, but is important to bear in mind that a few mental disorders include diagnostic criteria that incorporates the inappropriate use of substances (e.g., conduct disorder, oppositional defiant disorder, and antisocial personality disorder).

DSM-IV DIAGNOSTIC DESCRIPTION OF SUBSTANCE-RELATED DISORDERS

The fourth edition of the *Diagnostic and Statistical Manual of Mental Disorders* (DSM-IV, American Psychiatric Association, 1994) has expanded the substance use section to one of the largest in the manual. By using DSM-IV, a clinician is able to make a multiaxial evaluation and diagnosis of a patient. This multiaxial system is meant to organize and facilitate dialogue between clinicians and health care professionals; especially those utilizing a biopsychosocial treatment and intervention model.

To review briefly, criticisms of DSM-IV do exist; for example, a DSM-IV diagnosis one may be perceived by the client as "labeling." DSM-IV addresses this issue by encouraging the clinician to use flexibility and a holistic view rather than a rigid categorical approach. With sensitivity and awareness of the potential of placing a diagnostic "label" of substance abuse on an adolescent, DSM-IV allows the clinician to accurately diagnose an adolescent with a substance-related disorder.

A further criticism of DSM is that cultural issues are not addressed by the diagnostic criteria system. In response, the latest version of DSM reviews many culturally specific symptoms and syndromes, which may be a consideration when placing the adolescent's cultural context within his or her dominant culture. To correct stereotyping and cultural insensitivity, it is the clinician's responsibility to prevent "labeling" the client and to become fully aware of culturally specific issues.

DSM-IV describes substance-related disorders as those "disorders related to the taking of a drug of abuse (including alcohol), to the side effects of a medication, and to toxin exposure" (APA, 1994, p. 175). To clarify, a substance is referred to as any drug of abuse—a medication or a toxin. DSM-IV surveys eleven classes of substances. A DSM-IV diagnosis can be made on any of these substances, with polysubstance dependence a possible diagnosis if there is evidence of multiple substance misuse.

In DSM-IV, the term substance-related disorders is divided into two groups. The first group, substance use disorders, is broken into two further categories, substance dependence and substance abuse. Substance dependence is defined as a triad of cognitive, behavioral, and physiological symptoms that continue despite the individual's substance-related problems. To receive a substance dependence diagnosis, the individual uses the substance such that tolerance, withdrawal, and/or compulsive substance use-taking behaviors are present. A DSM-IV diagnosis of substance dependence is given if three or more diagnostic criteria occur at any time in the same 12-month period. The criteria include tolerance; withdrawal; substance taken in larger amounts; desire or efforts to control the use; increased time, obtaining, using, or recovering from the use; important activities are reduced because of the substance use; and use continues despite knowledge of a persistent or recurrent problem exacerbated by the substance use. The diagnosis is further delineated whether the individual is physiologically dependent on the substance and what level of remission he or she is in currently (APA, 1994).

Substance abuse is defined in DSM-IV as a maladaptive pattern of substance use in which there are significant negative consequences. The diagnosis applies if, within the same 12-month period, the substance use leads to impairment or distress leading to societal failures, use in hazardous situations, legal problems, and continued use and the symptomatic criteria of substance dependence has not been met for the drug in question. Similar to the diagnosis of substance dependence, the substance abuse diagnosis is further delineated as to whether the individual is physiologically dependent on the substance and what level of remission he or she is in currently (APA, 1994).

The second category includes substance-induced disorders. Substance-induced disorders describe a wide spectrum of conditions that are induced by substances, medications, or toxins. The conditions include delirium, persistent dementia, amnestic disorders, psychotic disorders, mood and anxiety disorders, sexual dysfunction, and sleep disorders. If diagnosed, the prefix substance-induced is added to the condition to clearly identify the etiology of the disorder (APA, 1994).

Another diagnosis, substance intoxication, is defined as a reversible process due to exposure or ingestion of a substance. All behavioral or physiological changes are due to the substance and not to another general medical condition or mental disorder. Most behavioral changes then can be attributed to the substance and are dose dependent and related to the tolerance level of the person (APA, 1994).

Last, DSM-IV defines substance withdrawal as the syndrome of behavioral and physiological changes that occur when the substance is reduced or terminated. Further, the syndrome causes distress to the person on a social or occupational level and is not due to another general medical condition or is not related to a mental disorder.

DSM-IV, ICD-9, and ICD-10 Comparisons

Briefly reviewed here, DSM-IV contains only a portion of the codes provided by the *International Classification of Diseases*, 9th revision, Clinical Modification (ICD-9-CM, World Health Organization, 1992). Within the next several years, it is anticipated that ICD-9 will be replaced with ICD-10 (World Health Organization, 1993), which is primarily used outside of the United States. To assist this transition, DSM-IV codes and terms were prepared to coordinate with the rating system of the ICD-10. In Appendix G of DSM-IV, codes are provided to help the clinician find the corresponding codes necessary for ICD-9-CM diagnosis. For the equivalent DSM-IV codes and terms related to substance use in ICD-9 and ICD-10-CM, review the codes in the medication-induced disorders section of Appendix G. Moreover, to review the compatible codes between DSM-IV and ICD-10, Appendix H in DSM-IV presents the classification codes. For a more complete description see DSM-IV (APA, 1994), pages 813 to 841.

EPIDEMIOLOGY OF ADOLESCENT SUBSTANCE USE

Based on a trend that started in 1991 and 1992, the most recent "Monitoring the Future" survey found that American adolescent drug use continues to rise (Johnston et al., 1995). The study began documenting substance use patterns among American adolescents in 1975 and has provided data annually. The most recent survey analyzed the data of approximately 50,000 adolescents in the eighth, tenth, and twelfth grades (O'Malley et al., 1995). The past two surveys found American adolescents using a greater number of illicit drugs (Johnston et al., 1994, 1995). It appears that concurrent to increased drug use, the belief that drugs are dangerous has declined among adolescents. This is a concern for the clinician, since the study also found that peers increasingly influence each other's drug and alcohol using behaviors.

More specifically, the study found that adolescent substance misuse of hallucinogens, inhalants, stimulants, barbiturates, cocaine, and crack (alkaloidal or "rock" cocaine) has risen since 1992 (Johnston et al., 1994, 1995). The researchers found increased usage of marijuana, illicit drugs, and slight elevations in the use of alcohol. Marijuana use trends are of particular interest because marijuana is considered a "gateway" drug. The study found that

the most pronounced increase of marijuana use was among twelfth graders. Johnston and colleagues also found that inhalant use was most dramatic among eighth graders. This is of concern because many inhalants are common household substances and are usually considered primitive or unsophisticated and are not illegal to own (Johnston et al., 1995).

An important finding of the "Monitoring the Future" study was the fact that, among youth, attitude toward drug use was related to the perceived level of drug dangerousness. The study found a continued decline, which started in 1991, in perceived risk for drug use among peer groups (Johnston et al., 1995). This result is important to consider because the influence of peers on adolescent behaviors is an integral part of the developmental phase of adolescence. It appears that behavior among peers, such as drug using, is related to the adolescent's view that drug use is not dangerous. For example, Johnston and colleagues (1995) found that peer disapproval has declined concurrent with the increase of marijuana use.

For an overview of the rates of adolescent use of substances such as alcohol, tobacco, cigarettes, alcohol, marijuana, illicit drugs, stimulants, and inhalants, see Table 12.1.

BRIEF REVIEW OF ETIOLOGIC MODELS OF SUBSTANCE USE

The following section describes major causal models of substance abuse that can be applied toward adolescent substance use. Appropriate interventions with adolescents will be addressed in the intervention section. Many interrelated factors influence a person's decision to use substances. These include psychological (intrapersonal and interpersonal), biological, environmental, and cultural factors (Leigh, 1985). More specific to adolescent substance use, the four primary variables found to influence adolescents are parental influences, peer influences, adolescent beliefs and values, and participation in minor delinquent activities (Leigh, 1895). Despite the numerous theories that explain substance use, the astute clinician must consider the interplay between these

TABLE 12.1. Substance Use Trends*—High School Seniors.

Substance	1988	1989	1990	1991	1992	1993	1994	1995
Alcohol	64	60	57	54	51	51	51	51
Tobacco	29	28	29	28	28	30	31	34
Marijuana	18	17	14	14	12	15	17	21
Cocaine	3	3	2	1	1	1	1	2
Inhalants	3	2	3	2	2	3	3	3
Stimulants	5	4	4	3	3	4	4	4
Smokeless tobacco	10	8	na	na	11	11	11	12
LSD	na	2	2	2	2	2	3	4
Any illicit substance	21	20	17	16	14	18	22	24

*Trends in recent use (past 30 days), expressed in percent. From: Johnston, O'Malley, and Bachman (1995).

influences and a theory of substance use when working with the adolescent.

Developmental Model

The developmental model views substance use as a predictable progression of behaviors and attitudes from experimentation to psychological and physical dependence. During the initial experimental phase, substance use is generally not perceived as harmful since it is often used recreationally or in a social environment. In these contexts, substance use may be viewed as exciting and perceived to be under control. Following this phase, regular use is defined by the development of tolerance and an increased need to use a substance repeatedly. Daily use begins and eventually disrupts normal activities. The early pleasures found in using become replaced by negative feelings. The final stage of dependence is marked by use in spite of multiple negative consequences as categorized by DSM-IV.

Gateway Model

Often linked with the developmental model, since it too progresses from benign to dangerousness, the gateway model views substance use as progressing from no drug use to "less dangerous" substances, like alcohol or cigarettes, to marijuana, to "more dangerous" substances, such as other illicit drugs.

Problem Behavior Theory

As described by Jessor and Jessor (1977), the problem behavior theory focuses on the interaction of personal, physiologic (or genetic) factors and environmental factors that contribute to the adolescent's decision to use. They explain that among certain adolescents, substance use is viewed as a normative way of life. Among adolescents with poor coping and social skills, substance use is often a means to manage personal problems such as academic failure, boredom, social anxiety, or low self-esteem (Leigh, 1985).

Disease Model

The disease (or genetic) model grew out the more punitive "moral model" in which it was believed that the alcohol or substance abuser lacked the "moral fiber" to resist temptations, or lacked moral character or the strength of will to resist earthly temptations. The disease model emerged as a less judgmental form of the moral model's view that a person lacked the ability or skill to *not* use drugs or alcohol. The disease model views addictive behaviors as stemming from physical dependence and physiologic factors, including genetic influences.

One example of disease model theory is the current view that alcoholism is a disease. In this view, alcoholism is perceived as a predictable and progressive condition, similar to a chronic illness, and one that cannot be "cured." The disease model also implies that the alcoholism is a primary condition, not a secondary symptom stemming from another underlying physical cause or emotional disorder. In support of this view, the American Medical Association declared alcoholism a disease in 1956. With the official sanctions of other associations, such as the World Health Organization, the disease model allows persons to seek treatment, especially those who may have avoided treatment under the moral model view of substance use (Marlatt & Gordon, 1985; Petraitis, Flay, & Miller, 1995).

Cognitive Models

Briefly, the theory behind cognitive models is based on the rationale that feelings and behaviors are determined by thoughts and perceptions (Wright, Beck, Newman, & Liese, 1993). In this fashion, dysfunctional thoughts give rise to feelings or beliefs that ultimately lead to problematic behaviors and actions. Undoing this connection requires the individual to change the activating dysfunctional beliefs. The cognitive model suggests that substance abuse occurs when specific beliefs increase the opportunity for use or when the beliefs are activated, or triggered, by certain social situations (Wright et al., 1993). Because cognitive therapy is an active collaboration between the therapist and the individual, it is a practical intervention tool for the substance abusing adolescent.

Social Learning Model

The social learning model plays an important role in understanding substance use. Social learning models suggest that behaviors are learned through the observation of others' behaviors (Dusenbury, Khuri, & Millman, 1992). High-status individuals such as older and more popular peers, media and sports figures, or family members, have enormous power to influence the substance using behaviors among adolescents. Observed behaviors that are rewarded with positive outcomes (e.g., becoming more popular) are the most influential and tend to repeated or learned quickly. Since adolescents place great value on peer opinions and struggle to fit in, the social learning model integrates the oftentimes difficult social milieu of adolescence with the decision to use drugs or alcohol (Dusenbury et al., 1992).

One example of a social learning model intervention is relapse prevention. Marlatt based his relapse prevention approach on social-learning theory and described it as a "self-control program that combines behavioral skill training, cognitive interventions, and lifestyle change components" (Marlatt & Gordon, 1985, p. 3). The relapse prevention model also utilizes both the behavioral and cognitive components of the cognitive-behavioral techniques of cognitive behaviorists such as Beck, Mahoney, and Meichenbaum. The cognitive behavioral interventions rely on the interconnectedness between thoughts and behaviors. By understanding these connections, one can then make changes in behaviors in a proactive sense.

Addictive Behavior Model

Another model based on social learning theory is the addictive behavior model. This model views addictive behaviors as a series of bad habits that have been so overlearned, or overconditioned, as to become detrimental. As such, the addictive behaviors can then be *unlearned* through studying the determinants such as antecedent situations, thoughts, beliefs, and expectations. Consequences are evaluated to inhibit any further maladaptive behaviors. The concept of immediate gratification, compulsive behaviors, and expectations are evaluated in addictive behavior therapy as an attempt to undo past learned behaviors.

In summary, clinicians should view the substance abuse theory ascribed to as a confluence of three main factors; the adolescent's social world, attitude, and intrapersonal world with influences from the past, present, and future (Petraitis et al., 1995).

CONSEQUENCES OF ADOLESCENT SUBSTANCE ABUSE

The consequences of ongoing adolescent substance use may at the beginning appear inconsequential but as use progresses, the consequences may become profound. For example, the impact on the psychosocial development of the adolescent is less clear toward the beginning, but as he or she grows into adulthood and continues to use, the impact becomes more serious as financial gain, employment, education, and establishment of self and family may become impinged.

Long-term substance use is related to psychiatric conditions such as suicide and depression, affective disorders, eating disorders, and personality disorders (Bentler, 1992; MacKenzie & Kipke, 1992). When a situation such as this exists, the "dually-diagnosed" clients become more challenging for the clinician. The dual diagnosed individual suffers from a comorbidity of substance related disorders and a mental disorder, such as an affective disorder or a psychotic disorder. A client struggling with an affective disorder can often mask depressed feelings with substance use as tolerance of the depression wanes. The onset of major depression generally precedes alcohol or other drug use. With depression comes the associated problem of suicide. Often the associated problem of suicide risk is exacerbated by the use of substances. Since suicide is currently one of the five leading causes of adolescent death, it is important to treat the adolescent's depression concurrent to the substance use treatment. It has been shown that substance use is highly correlated with the increase of adolescent suicide attempts (MacKenzie & Kipke, 1992). Reasons for this behavior include the fact that substance use either releases the inhibition toward suicide or may inadvertently contribute to completed suicides by adolescents.

Among the eating disordered adolescents, especially those with bulimia nervosa, there is a trend toward concurrent substance use. Eating disorders are often classified as addictions since it is felt that the same lack of external control rules the young person (MacKenzie & Kipke, 1992). Therefore, the eating disordered adolescent is also at risk for suicide and self-injurious behaviors, and requires integrated management by both medical care and mental health care providers.

ASSESSMENT OF ADOLESCENT SPECIFIC SUBSTANCE ABUSE

Much of the focus of adolescent substance abuse research has been centered on epidemiology, health and social consequences, associated at-risk behaviors, and treatment approaches, with little focus on adolescent-specific assessment tools. A developmentally sensitive assessment is essential in the unfolding of an appropriate diagnostic plan for change. Rather than using an adolescent-specific measure, a clinician often will rely on the validity of specific measures designed for adult use as screening or treatment planning instruments (Argeriou, Mcarty, Mulvey, & Dailey, 1994; Parrish, 1994). For example, research addressing the differences in adolescent and adult substance issues has been primarily limited to alcohol (Leccese & Waldron, 1994). Compared to adults, it has been shown that adolescents consume less alcohol overall, consume more in one sitting, consume in different settings, and exhibit less physical dependence with fewer medical problems directly related to the use of alcohol (Leccese & Waldron, 1994). Adolescents are most commonly referred by parents concerned about poor school performance, in comparison to the adult being referred by his or her employer. Due to the different nature of complaints between adolescents and adults, the adolescent's primary reason for the visit leaves an opportunity for an underlying diagnosis of substance abuse to go unrecognized. Therefore, it is important to utilize adolescent-specific measures whenever possible (Blum, 1987; Hughes, Power, & Francis, 1992; Kaminer, 1994; Parrish, 1994).

Before a clinician can choose an assessment tool, it is beneficial to investigate the purpose of the assessment, the population served, and the available resources. For example, it would not be advantageous for the clinician who routinely provides treatment for substance abusing clients, and needs detailed information to guide treatment planning, to administer a screening instrument. The clinician would be better aided by a comprehensive assessment tool that would elicit specific information among various life domains. Screening instruments are generally inexpensive and time efficient to administer. A screening instrument often will be used to determine if further comprehensive evaluation is needed or to serve as a preliminary step in substance abuse assessment. On the other hand, comprehensive instruments may act as helpful tools in individualized treatment planning or in a DSM-IV diagnosis. Generally, comprehensive instruments elicit information about functioning in a variety of psychosocial areas; however, they often are inadequate in settings where large numbers of adolescents must be seen in a limited amount of time. For example, a screening instrument may be useful in school-based health clinics or adolescent medicine units. There are many instruments that can be used for the pretreatment assessment of alcohol and other drug abuse. The following section reviews conventional assessment tools, screening instruments, and comprehensive substance abuse assessment instruments, and discusses special assessment issues. See Appendix A for information on obtaining many of the measures reviewed.

It is beneficial to review the benefits and drawbacks of three most conventional rating scales. The clinician should be well versed in commonly used substance abuse screenings, regardless of the age of the target population. The following screening tools have documented benefit for use with older adolescents (Anderson, 1987). The CAGE (Mayfield, McLead, & Hall, 1974), the Michigan Alcoholism Screening Test (MAST) (Selzer, 1971), and the Drug Abuse Screening Test (DAST) (Skinner, 1982) are the most well-known alcohol and drug assessment tools.

The acronymic CAGE is a beneficial tool because it is composed of four short questions, which take approximately 15 minutes to self-administer or to conduct by the clinician:

C: Have you ever felt the need to **Cut down** on your drinking?
A: Have other people **Annoyed** you by criticizing your drinking?
G: Have you ever felt bad or **Guilty** about your drinking?
E: Have ever had a drink (**Eye-opener**) first thing in the morning?

Two or more "yes" answers indicate a diagnosis of alcoholism. Despite the simplicity of the CAGE, the screening tool was shown by Bush and colleagues to correctly identify 75% of alcoholics and 96% of nonalcoholics (Bush, Shaw, Cleary, Del Banco, & Aronson, 1987).

The original form of the MAST has 25 items that require a "yes" or "no" answer reflecting the respondent's self-perceptions of alcohol problems and negative consequences. The MAST has also been developed in shorter versions, the "b-MAST" and the "SMAST" (Selzer, Vinokur, & Van Rooijen, 1975). A sample question from the MAST is "Have you ever gotten into trouble at work because of your drinking?" Like the CAGE, the MAST indicates the diagnosis of alcoholism by the number of "yes" responses. The MAST can be administered in approximately 7 minutes.

To meet the need for a drug screening tool, the DAST was developed from items on the MAST (Skinner, 1982). The DAST is a 20-item questionnaire that produces a quantitative index of problems related to illicit drug use or abuse. Similar to the MAST for alcohol use or abuse, no information on frequency or length of use is obtained using the DAST. It may be self-administered or given in interview format in about 5 minutes.

Substance Abuse Screening Instruments

Drug and Alcohol Problem (DAP) Quick Screen

The DAP (Schwartz & Wirtz, 1990) is a 30-item questionnaire developed by pediatricians to meet the need for a quick drug and alcohol screening tool in primary health care settings.

The DAP requires a "yes," "no," or "uncertain" response on short items focusing on substance use, friends, parents, and peer group substance use and involvement in high-risk behaviors, conflict with parents, misbehavior in school, beliefs about alcohol and drug use, and symptoms of depression. A score of six or more "yes" responses indicates a high-risk adolescent. Some data on validity pertaining to the DAP are provided in Schwartz and Wirtz (1990), although further research is needed.

Drug Use Screening Inventory (DUSI)

The DUSI (Tarter, 1990; Tarter & Hegedus, 1991), is a 149-item instrument containing a personal history form, a drug use screening instrument, and a demographic, medical, and treatment/prevention summary plan. The main purpose of the DUSI is to identify problems with substance abuse, physical and mental health, and psychosocial adjustment. This instrument gauges ten domains: substance use behavior, behavior patterns, health status, psychiatric disorder, social skill, family system, school work, work performance, peer relationships, and leisure/recreation. The DUSI may be administered by self-report, with the use of paper and pencil, or by computer. The questionnaire is formatted with "yes" or "no" items and takes approximately 20 to 40 minutes to complete. The scoring is computed as follows: an Absolute Problem Density score indicates the percentage of problem behaviors for each of the ten domains; a Relative Problem Density score indicates the severity of problems in each domain compared to the overall number of problems indicated by a "yes" response for all ten domains; and an Overall Problem Index, which is the average of the number of "yes" responses over the ten domains. Tarter suggests the information acquired from the DUSI should be viewed as implicative and not definitive in that the findings should generate hypotheses regarding the areas requiring comprehensive diagnostic evaluation (Tarter, 1990). The DUSI is reported by Leccese and Waldron (1994) to display adequate content validity.

Perceived Benefit of Drinking Scale

This is a measure in which respondents are asked to register their support or disapproval to five statements regarding reasons for alcohol use. Petchers and Singer (1987) created the 1-minute screening tool to be used in primary health care settings. Petchers and colleagues expanded the instrument to include a Reason for Drug Use Scale that can be used to inquire about beliefs regarding both alcohol and other drug use (Petchers, Singer, Angelotta, & Chow, 1988). Leccese and Waldron suggest the Perceived Benefit of Drinking Scale to possess adequate internal consistency and divergent validity based on the authors' evidence supporting the measure (Leccese & Waldron, 1994).

Personal Experience Screening Questionnaire (PESQ)

This 38-item questionnaire is divided into three sections: problem severity, psychosocial risk, and drug use history. The PESQ screens for substance abuse problem severity, frequency and onset of use, defensiveness, and psychosocial functioning, with respondents answering "never," "once or twice," "sometimes," or "often." Taking 10 minutes to self-administer, this quick screening tool is often used to evaluate the need for a more comprehensive assessment tool, and to make appropriate referrals. Winters (1992) reported that the PESQ exhibited satisfactory discriminate validity and internal consistency.

Problem Oriented Screening Instrument for Teenagers (POSIT)

The POSIT (Rahdert, 1991) is a screening tool consisting of 139 yes/no items measuring functioning in ten sectors: substance use, physical health, mental health, family relationships, peer relationships, educational status, vocational status, social skills, leisure/recreation, and aggressive behavior. Points are given for responses in each area, with established cutoffs to mark the need for further assessment. The purpose of this tool is to indicate "red flags" that will necessitate further evaluation. This instrument is administered by self-report and takes 30–45 minutes. Currently, the psychometric properties of the POSIT have not been reported.

Substance Abuse Subtle Screening Inventory–Adolescent (SASSI–A)

This 81-item questionnaire is composed of 55 true/false items indirectly asking substance abuse-related questions and 26 items directly asking how often certain situations involving substance use have occurred (Miller, 1990). It is presumed that responses to the indirect items can be divided into categories or criterion groups (i.e., problem substance using). The SASSI–A includes scales designed to determine the validity of alcohol and drug use, attributes (obvious and subtle), and defensiveness. This self-report questionnaire may be completed in 20 minutes. Research findings report limited validity data, yet present no information on reliability.

Comprehensive Substance Abuse Assessment Instruments

Miller and Rollnick (1991) suggest that eight domains should be covered in a comprehensive evaluation: (1) alcohol/drug use, (2) life problems, (3) dependence syndrome, (4) functional analysis, (5) biomedical effects, (6) neuropsychological effects, (7) family history, and (8) other psychological problems. The following comprehensive substance abuse assessment instruments attempt to include these essential domains pertinent to an extensive assessment of the adolescent substance abuser.

Adolescent Diagnostic Interview (ADI)

The ADI (Winters & Henley, 1993) is a 45 to 60-minute structured or computerized interview designed to assess DSM-III-R criteria for psychoactive substance use disorders. The interview probes drug use history and signs of abuse versus dependence for various categories of substances. Psychosocial stressors and levels of functioning are also examined with attention to involvement with peers, opposite sex relationships, school behavior and performance, and home behavior. At the present time there is no information on the psychometric soundness of the ADI or whether the DSM criteria has been reevaluated.

Adolescent Drug Abuse Diagnosis (ADAD)

The ADAD (Friedman & Utada, 1989) is a 150-item measurement that focuses on nine items: medical, school/employment, social, family, psychological, legal, alcohol and drugs to aid in diagnosis, treatment planning, and research. Friedman and Utada modeled the ADAD after the adult assessment measure the Addiction Severity Index (ASI) (McLellan, Luborsky, Woody, & O'Brien, 1980). Each of nine items is measured on a 10-point scale to rate the degree of severity. This structured interview may be completed in approximately 45–60 minutes. High interrater agreement, test-retest reliability, and criterion-related validity were reported by Friedman and Utada (1989, as cited in Leccese & Waldron, 1994).

Adolescent Problem Severity Index (APSI)

The APSI (Metzger, Kushner, & McLellan, 1991) is a 45 to 60-minute semistructured interview that assesses seven domains: legal, family relationships, school and work, medical, psychosocial adjustment, personal relationships, and substance abuse. Risk factors in each area and severity ratings are compiled to assist the interviewer in determining the need for treatment. At present time there have been no published reports on the psychometric properties of the APSI.

Personal Experience Inventory (PEI)

The PEI is part of an assessment battery developed as part of the Minnesota Chemical Dependency Adolescent Assessment Project. The complete battery consists of the Personal Experience Inventory (PEI), the Adolescent

Diagnostic Interview (ADI), and the Personal Experience Screening Questionnaire (PESQ). The PEI (Winters & Henley, 1989) is a 276-item designed to document the severity of personal and peer risk factors, environmental risk factors, special problems (e.g., abuse), severity and frequency of drug use, and faking. The PEI may be completed in approximately 45–60 minutes by self-report or computer. The measure is composed of two parts. The first, the chemical involvement section, includes items on alcohol and other drugs. There are five "basic" scales measuring problems of alcohol and drug involvement, effects of use, personal consequences, and polydrug use. Problem severity scores are also provided for five "clinical" scales gauging transitional use, psychological benefits from use, social–recreational use, preoccupation, and loss of control. Three validity indices are included to detect defensiveness, "faking" bad, and neglectful responding. Second, the psychosocial scale, includes eight personal risk or personal adjustment scales, four family and peer environmental risk scales, six problem screens (including eating disorder, sexual abuse, physical abuse, and suicide risk), and psychiatric referral. Adequate reliability and predictive validity have been documented in Toneatto and Tucker (1992).

Teen-Addiction Severity Index (T-ASI)

The T-ASI (Kaminer, Bukstein, & Tarter, 1991) is a 32 to 62-item structured interview taking approximately 45–60 minutes to complete. The T-ASI is modeled after an adult focused measure (the ASI), and addresses seven subscales: chemical use, school status, employment-support status, family relationships, legal status, peer-social relationships, and psychiatric status. The interviewee and interviewer use a 5-point scale in each domain to assess the need for treatment. Kaminer and colleagues report good reliability, although they suggest the need for a larger scale psychometric study across different patient populations to ascertain validity (Kaminer et al., 1991).

General Assessment Tools

HEADSS Psychosocial Assessment Interview

The HEADSS was developed to be used with adolescents (Berman, 1987). HEADSS is an acronym for Home, Education/Employment, peer group Activities, Drug Use and Abuse, Sexual Behavior, and Suicidality/Depression (see Table 12.2). By asking carefully worded questions in those areas that are sensitive to adolescent development, the clinician builds rapport and potentially discovers red flags. Along with further modifications, Goldenring and Cohen (1988) suggest the interview be done in the absence of parents, family members, or other adults unless otherwise requested. This approach is taken to assure confidentiality, build trust, and to communicate that the adolescent is the primary interest.

Drug Screening

In addition to the above substance abuse measurements, drug screening is another tool that may contribute useful information. There are some circumstances when a drug screen would present valuable information: medical emergencies, a tool for measuring abstinence in rehabilitation, and other circumstances involving sports physicals, motor vehicle accidents, and high-risk adolescent pregnancies. It is important to discuss three concerns for the health care provider in regards to drug testing (Woolf & Shannon, 1995):

1. Is the test available and accurate?
2. Will the information learned be important and timely to medical management?
3. Are there issues of consent?

Although drug screens do not provide information in regards to patterns of use of drugs, abuse, or dependence, it may act as one part of an assessment tool, or to support abstinence in treatment. Drug testing may provide a way of documenting the presence or absence of recent drug use. It is beneficial for the adolescent to fully understand the purpose of the drug screen. Drug screening in a treatment setting must

TABLE 12.2. H.E.A.D.S.S Interview

H Describe your client's living situation. With whom does the client live? One or both parents? Relatives? Recent moves? Runaway?

E Which is the last grade the client completed? How does the client perform in school? Any recent changes? Does the client want more schooling? Does the client enjoy school? Any current or past employment?

A How and with whom does your client spend free time? Describe peer relationships. Has the client ever been arrested?

D Does your client use drugs or alcohol (now or in the past)? How about family members? How about peers? Has the client ever used a needle while getting high? Does the client or do others see the clients drug use as a problem? What are the amounts, frequency, and patterns of use/abuse, and car use while intoxicated? How does the client pay for drugs and or alcohol?

S Is your client sexually involved (present or past)? With men or women? Rate of condom use? What is the degree and types of sexual experience and acts? How old was the client when he or she first engaged in sex willingly? Has the client ever been physically, emotionally, or sexually abused?

S Is the client depressed? Is the client suicidal? If yes, further assess. Has the client ever attempted suicide? If so, describe situation, including method, outcome, and precipitating event. Does the client think about hurting someone else?

Adapted from Goldenring, J. M., and Cohen, E. (1988). Getting into adolescents' heads. *Contemporary Pediatrics*, 7, 75–90.

occur randomly and, if possible, be observed or monitored. It is necessary for the practitioner to have a plan in regards to the drug test result, including appropriate follow-up referrals and/or treatment plan adjustments. Specimen collection is of particular concern due to the possible implications and results of a positive result. There are several laboratory techniques for effective drug screening that are timely and inexpensive.

Although drug screens do not provide information in regards to patterns of use of drugs, abuse, or dependence, it may act as one part of an assessment tool, or to support abstinence in treatment. Drug testing may provide a way of documenting the presence or absence of recent drug use. It is beneficial for the adolescent to fully understand the purpose of the drug screen. Drug screening in a treatment setting must occur randomly and, if possible, be observed or monitored. It is necessary for the practitioner

to have a plan in regards to the drug test result, including appropriate follow-up referrals and/or treatment plan adjustments. Specimen collection is of particular concern due to the possible implications and results of a positive result. There are several laboratory techniques for effective drug screening that are timely and inexpensive.

The American Academy of Pediatrics has endorsed the philosophy that, unless emergent circumstances exist, involuntary drug screens should not be conducted. This includes the request for a drug screen by a parent who suspects his or her child is abusing drugs (Neinstein, 1991).

In summary, the types of instruments available for the assessment of alcohol and other drug use and abuse may be classified as either (1) for the measurement of the frequency, amount, and duration of use of the various types of substances, and assessment of the problems related to the use and or abuse, or (2) for the determination of the presence (in the past or in the present) of a condition that is formally diagnosed in a medical sense, based on DSM criteria, and diagnosed as either "drug abuse" or "drug dependency" or "alcohol abuse" or "alcohol dependency." Most drug treatment programs do not need to use the second type of instrument to establish a formal diagnosis for most of their clients, either as a criterion for admission to the program or for other purposes. In other situations it is helpful to use the second type of instrument to determine admission into an inpatient treatment for detoxification, and to determine whether a client is currently in a state of dependency. In such instances, both types of instruments should be used, or the second diagnostic instrument should be used in combination with one of the broad spectrum instruments.

TREATMENT

Many of the existing treatment approaches are designed for the substance using and abusing adult. The adolescent substance abuser has different needs than an adult and requires a more comprehensively integrated treatment approach that accesses multiple services. The wide range of developmental issues facing an adolescent may include physical maturation, peer-group membership issues, sex-role identity, sexual relationships, and autonomy and individuation. According to Morrison and colleagues, the treatment of young people must be described as habilitation, not as rehabilitation because, in contrast to the adult, the adolescent does not have a prior level of successful functioning from which to return (Morrison, Smith, Wilford, Ehrlich, & Seymour, 1993).

The principal treatment options for adolescents are as follows: pretreatment services, outpatient, inpatient/residential treatment, and services that support independent living. Each of these treatment options include various levels and types of care. Depending on the assessed need of the adolescent, the treatment options may be conceptualized along a continuum of services ranging from least intensive to most intensive.

Pretreatment Services

These programs do not include primary treatment, but focus on primary prevention and early intervention. Primary prevention programs are usually school or community based and are directed at adolescents who have not yet used alcohol and other drugs. Early intervention is a psychoeducational approach for adolescents who have not used substances, but who are considered to be at high risk for alcohol- and other drug-related problems.

Outpatient Treatment

These services span a wide range of intensity, including nonintensive outpatient treatment, intensive outpatient treatment, and day treatment or partial hospitalization. Nonintensive outpatient treatment typically consists of less than 9 hours per week of regularly scheduled sessions focused on substance use and abuse issues. Intensive outpatient treatment may be an after school or weekend program lasting approximately 9–20 hours per week. Day treatment or partial hospitalization is the most intensive outpatient category consisting of treatment 20 hours per week in a structured program. Although each program varies in philosophy and programming, some treatment components included in outpatient services are group therapy, family therapy, individual therapy, case management, peer socialization/recreational activities, 12-step referrals, drug testing, relapse prevention, and aftercare.

Inpatient Treatment/Residential Care

This level of care may include intensive medical, psychiatric, and psychosocial treatment on a 24-hour basis. Services defined as inpatient/residential care include medically "monitored" intensive inpatient treatment, medically "managed" intensive inpatient treatment, intensive residential treatment, psychosocial residential care, halfway house living, and group home living. Medically intensive inpatient settings provide care for individuals who need special attention due to a medical and/or psychiatric condition that requires around-the-clock attention. The usual length of stay is 7–45 days with the average stay of 21–28 days. Intensive residential treatment is modeled after the adult therapeutic community and is appropriate for dually diagnosed adolescents with many psychosocial problems. Psychosocial residential care is an adolescent, alcohol- and drug-focused model lasting 6–24 months. Unlike intensive residential treatment, psychosocial residential care services are specific to the dually diagnosed adolescent with a substance abuse diagnosis and a coexisting mental disorder that lacks the severity of requiring medical or psychiatric intervention. Halfway houses and group home living are service alternatives that offer minimal substance abuse treatment in a minimally controlled environment. An adolescent may focus on educational needs while learning independent living skills.

Just as outpatient services vary between programs yet carry common treatment components, inpatient treatment services vary, although they display essentially similar components. Some of the fundamental treatment services include structure, dual diagnosis capabilities, pharmacologic interventions, arrangements with medical care, role modeling, client participation in the therapeutic milieu, family groups, individual and group therapy, school/vocational training, recreational programs, relapse prevention, and 12-step support.

It is extremely important that treatment service match the need of the adolescent in both intensity and philosophy. Treatment programs of the same level of intensity may differ in individual philosophies of addiction, treatment components, and types of staff employed. Some important issues in treatment matching include education level, cognitive functioning, geographic proximity, cultural issues, and language barriers. In response to increasing demands of the alcohol and other drug treatment provider community, the American

Society Addiction Medicine (ASAM) and the National Association of Addiction Treatment Providers (NAATP) utilized previous criteria from NAATP and the Greater Cleveland Hospital Association/Northern Ohio Chemical Dependency Treatment Directors Association to develop national guidelines for the implementation of a patient placement system that aids in rational clinical decision making and quality of care. In the Center for Substance Abuse Treatment's (CSAT) "Guidelines for the Treatment of Alcohol-and Other Drug-Abusing Adolescents" enhanced adolescent-specific criteria are presented to assist the adolescent substance abuse provider in treatment matching (Schonberg, 1993). For an overview of CSAT guidelines on treatment matching strategy for adolescents, see Appendix B for the "Client Assessment Criteria" continuum.

Services That Support Independent Living

Finally, aftercare issues are crucial when addressing the recovering adolescent. A supportive environment that provides drug-free social activities is advantageous. Continued involvement in the recovering community, such as attendance at 12-step meetings, provides the adolescent with drug-free peers and sober role models. The role of the family is very important in aftercare. If possible, family involvement begins during the adolescent's treatment with continuation as the adolescent reintegrates into the family. It is critical for the family to become educated on addiction issues so that they are able to provide a supportive recovery environment and learn strategies to address prior dysfunctional family roles. The clinician should provide a referral for the family to a support group such as Al-Anon, so family members can learn how others have dealt with anger, disappointment, and possible frustration.

Specific Treatment Approaches and Interventions

Some basic components in the different levels of care were listed earlier without the description of specific interventions. The following section discusses specific treatment approaches and interventions. Just as there are many theories about substance abuse, there are many theoretical rationales about treatment. For example, there are some questions regarding the assignment of the disease model with adolescents. Lawson and Lawson (1992) express concern that the disease model is not as suitable for adolescents as it might be for adults. The proponents of this concept are concerned that factors of the disease model regarding loss of control, physical addiction, and health-related problems due to drugs and alcohol often do not exist in the adolescent. This perspective views adolescent substance abuse as a behavior rather than a disease. Even those who align with the disease concept for its use with adolescents agree that, at least in certain cases, adolescent behavior regarding alcohol or other drugs may not represent addictive disease (Morrison et al., 1993). Adolescent substance abuse may be difficult to diagnose due to unique developmental issues of the adolescent, such as risk taking, experimentation, and feelings of invulnerability. Many adolescents "age out" of specific behaviors that could classify them as alcohol and or drug abusive or dependent. However, regardless of the former issues, many believe that addictive disease exists in the adolescent population and that the basics of the addictive disease model are the same for preadolescents, adolescents, and adults. Morrison and colleagues state "addiction is a disease in and of itself, carrying its own psychopathology and characterized by compulsion, loss of control, and continued use in spite of adverse consequences" (1993, p. 325). The proponents of this theory believe abstinence from all psychoactive drugs is necessary to treat addiction, a disease that is chronic, progressive, incurable, and potentially fatal.

As described, there are different theoretical treatment approaches to treating the adolescent with substance use and abuse issues. Again, the importance of treatment matching is particularly valuable due to the fact that outpatient alcohol treatment dropout rates range between 52% and 75% by the fourth session; and inpatient recidivism rates average 55% to 65% (McLellan, O'Brian, & Kron et al., 1980). No

individual approach to alcohol and drug treatment is superior for all individuals. Different types of individuals respond best to different treatment approaches; therefore, the clinician must be aware of various treatment methods. The next section describes various relapse prevention techniques developed by Marlatt, discusses Gorski's Cenaps Model, describes the harm reduction approach, introduces pharmacotherapy, and concludes with an outline of motivational interviewing. The following models view relapse prevention from a cognitive-behavioral orientation defined by Marlatt and Gordon (1985) as a central theme. Characteristics of cognitive-behavioral approaches have been found to be particularly suited for the adolescent (Zarb, 1992).

Marlatt's Model of Relapse Prevention

Marlatt's model of relapse prevention, as described earlier in the chapter, conceptualizes addiction as a set of habit patterns that have been reinforced by pharmacological and social reinforcement contingencies. In this model, addictive behaviors represent a category of "bad habits" and are presumed to lie along a continuum of use rather than being defined in terms of fixed categories, such as excessive use (loss of control) or total abstinence. Marlatt asserts that behavior itself is not a disease. Marlatt's model is very extensive and we focus here on the essentials of the fundamental interventions. Rawson and colleagues suggest the following "key points" to conceptualizing the relapse prevention model by Marlatt and Gordon (Rawson, Obert, McCann, & Marinelli-Casey, 1993):

1. **Addiction treatment is the process of habit change**. It is thought that substance abusers have developed maladaptive coping skills. Therefore, it is necessary to learn alternative coping skills rather than using drugs or alcohol. Some of these options to maladaptive coping skills may include role playing, refusal skills, substitute methods of expressing affective states, and new

cognitive strategies (such as relaxation techniques).

2. **The nature of a relapse—bypassing the abstinence violation effect.** According to Marlatt and Gordon (1985), a relapse may be predicted by cognitive and behavioral events. Clients may be taught high-risk states (such as boredom, being around using friends, money, and certain times of the day), behavioral warning signs (including compulsive behavior, spending time with drug users, failure to attend to recovering activities, and returning to a secondary drug), cognitive warning signs (such as drug dreams, relapse justification, fantasizing about drug-using days, and rationalizations to discontinue new recovery behaviors), and affective warning signs (including periods of emotionality previously associated with drug use). Clients are made aware of these warning signs to anticipate a relapse. Marlatt also provides the clinician with specific behavioral strategies by describing a range of coping responses to high-risk situations. It is suggested that self-efficacy is promoted by educating the recovering substance abuser about alternate metaphors to explain addiction and recovery-related concepts. For example, drug use after a period of abstinence is framed as a "slip" or "lapse" rather than a relapse or re-addiction. The slip or lapse is used as information for "the bigger picture," hence minimizing shame that could facilitate a return to an extended relapse episode.

3. **Lifestyle modification changes.** When alcohol and other drug use is restrained, it is important that healthy, non-drug-using activities are reinforced. For example, exercise, community activities, self-help support, and family activities are encouraged.

Gorski's Cenaps Model

Similar to Marlatt's view of relapse prevention, Gorski's Cenaps model has contributed to the field of substance abuse treatment. The Cenaps model combines essential principles of AA and the Minnesota Model Treatment. Unlike Marlatt, Gorski views chemical dependency as a chronic disease, with total abstinence as well as personality and lifestyle changes mandatory for full recovery. Gorski may be appealing for the adolescent who has displayed loss of control with drugs and alcohol, whose behaviors are continually more risky than peers, and who displays some readiness for treatment. Gorski is most known for his acknowledgment of neurological factors in the recovery of alcoholics and his regard given to the Post-Acute Withdraw (PAW) Syndrome. The essential concepts from Gorski's Cenaps model are as follows (Gorski, 1990):

1. **Stabilization.** Detoxification and immediate abstinence are the primary goals.
2. **Self-Assessment History.** Drinking or drug use is reviewed with attention to the individual's personalized warning signs identification list.
3. **Relapse Education.** Films and lectures are used to introduce information about the "disease concept" of addiction and factors involved in high-risk situations, including relapse warning signs.
4. **Warning Signs Identification.** A list of relapse warning signs is composed by the client or patient to include irrational thoughts, unmanageable feelings, and self-defeating behaviors.
5. **Coping Skills.** Clients or patients are taught skills training (e.g., mental rehearsal, role-playing, and therapeutic assignments) to increase their ability to cope with warning signs.
6. **Recovery Planning.** Alternative activities (e.g., recreational activities) are identified that will address issues associated with warning signs.
7. **Inventory Planning.** A daily recovery

plan is made addressing positive goals with a review of potential warning signs.

8. **Involvement of Others.** Significant others, including spouses, parents, 12-Step sponsors, and employers, are educated on relapse warning signs.

9. **Relapse Plan Update.** Monthly plans are devised for the first 3 months, quarterly until the 12th month, semi-annually for 3 years. These sessions review and revise goals, review progress, develop skills for newly identified problem areas, and revise recovery program activity list.

Harm Reduction Approach

Harm reduction, harm minimization, and risk reduction are terms that describe methods based on the assumption that habits can be placed along a continuum ranging from lowest amount of risk to highest amount of risk (Marlatt, Somers, & Tapert, 1993). The goal of the harm reduction approach is to move the individual along the continuum to the behavior with the least amount of harm. Marlatt and colleagues cite several themes of the model (Marlatt et al., 1993, pp. 149–151):

1. "harm reduction is broad based and inclusive"
2. "harm reduction tends to normalize rather than marginalize substance abusers"
3. "harm reduction places substance use on a continuum, relating levels of use to the severity of the problems engender for each level"
4. "harm reduction de-emphasizes the use of absolute restrictions on drug use as the primary means of reducing substance use problems."

Harm reduction methods are applicable to AIDS prevention, treatment of ongoing active addictive behaviors (e.g., methadone maintenance), and secondary prevention of harmful addictive or excessive behaviors. Marlatt and colleagues suggest the harm reduction approach be considered when intervening with a particular adolescent subgroup—the "college drinker"—due to patterns of binge drinking and the likelihood that the "college drinker" will experience more acute alcohol-related problems at certain times and, in particular settings. Because college drinkers rarely identify themselves as alcoholics or problem drinkers, the harm reduction approach may help accelerate the process of maturing out of risky drinking behavior. Miller and colleagues (as cited in Marlatt et al., 1993) discuss the paradox of controlled drinking programs for problem drinkers, suggesting that many clients exposed to this approach eventually end up abstaining from alcohol. The harm reduction approach may be considered a valuable option for the substance-abusing adolescent population due to evidence that suggests controlled drinking is a more attainable goal for some problem drinkers, just as abstinence works best for others (Peele, 1991).

Medications in the Treatment of Addiction

Treating adolescent substance abuse should include psychosocial interventions in addition to pharmacotherapy (when medications are required) since the latter alone may not be sufficient. In other words, "it should be understood that medication treatment is almost always an adjunct to psychosocial treatment and rarely is pharmacotherapy alone adequate treatment for a patient who is drug dependent" (Wesson & Ling, 1991, p. 365). The therapeutic uses of medications can be categorized into two functions: (1) to help patients stop abusing drugs and (2) to help patients prevent relapse to drug use. For example, a pharmacologic intervention may reduce acute drug withdrawal symptoms, medically maintain a patient, or decrease drug craving. Although the use of medications for the treatment of adolescent addiction may be limited to special populations, substance abusers often ask questions about pharmacotherapy or request to be treated with medication. Thus, familiarity regarding medications and substance abuse treatment is necessary. Again it must be restated that pharmacological interventions typically are not appropriate for the adolescent population unless the patient has not responded to ongoing psychosocial interventions.

Motivational Interviewing

How can clinicians treat the adolescent who is ambivalent about taking action toward treatment? Here we present a brief explanation of motivational interviewing and discuss the stages of change to aid the clinician in facilitating an intervention with a resistant youth.

Motivational interviewing is a technique that promotes readiness and change. Miller and Rollnick (1991) view motivation as a state of readiness or eagerness to change, which may fluctuate or be influenced. They suggest that overtly direct and highly confrontational approaches tend to be less effective than empathetic styles of addressing substance abuse. To understand how change occurs, Prochaska and DiClemente (1992) have developed a model of change. The model of change may be viewed as a circle or wheel with a series of stages through which people pass in the course of changing a problem. In their research with smokers, Prochaska and DiClemente found that people ordinarily went around the wheel between three and seven times before quitting. The stages are pre-contemplation, contemplation, determination, action, maintenance, and, permanent exit. The clinician's task is to meet the client at his or her appropriate level and guide a client through the wheel with interventions appropriate to the client's level. For example, it would be nonproductive to promote interventions that suggest action when a client is in a state of contemplating the benefits and the risks of alcohol and other drug use. When the clinician provides strategies appropriate to the level of change, the client may be moved toward commitment and change.

Miller and Rollnick (1991) describe five general principles underlying the principal of motivational interviewing (DARES):

1. **D**evelop *discrepancy*. The client presents the argument for change. A motivating discrepancy is that between "where I see myself being, and where I want to be."

2. **A**void *argumentation*. Argumentation with the client is strongly discouraged. If the clinician is in this position the strategy should be changed. It is suggested that labeling is unnecessary.

3. **R**oll *with resistance*. Invite new perceptions in the client, reframe but do not push against resistance.

4. **E**xpress *empathy*. Create a supportive client-centered environment. Acceptance facilitates change, while pressure to change blocks it.

5. **S**upport *self-efficacy*. Provide optimism in the possibility of change.

The above techniques may be helpful for the use with adolescents because they provide a nonjudgmental approach designed to increase self-esteem and self-efficacy, decrease dissonance, and motivate change.

CONCLUSION

In summary, treatment of adolescent substance-related disorders requires interventions that are similar yet dissimilar to those used with adults. The most important areas to incorporate in an adolescent-focused substance use treatment program include the following: an awareness of adolescent developmental changes; an understanding of the etiological factors that influence substance use; issues of trust and confidentiality (which are crucial for the therapeutic alliance); well-matched treatments that meet the specific substance abusing needs for the adolescent; and, finally, multidisciplinary adjunct care, such as medical support, schooling, psychological counseling, and job training. Further, it is imperative that clinicians evaluate their own ability to work with oftentimes difficult adolescents. Self-awareness and understanding will enhance clinicians' ability to work well with the substance using adolescent.

REFERENCES

*American Psychiatric Association. (1994). *Diagnostic and statistical manual of mental disorders* (4th ed.). Washington, DC: Author.

Anderson, P. (1987). Early intervention in general practice. In *Helping the problem drinker: New initiatives in primary care*. London: Croon Helm.

Argeriou, M., Mcarty, D., Mulvey, K., & Dailey, M. (1994). Use of the Addiction Severity Index with homeless substance abusers. *Journal of Substance Abuse Treatment, 11*, 359–365.

Bentler, P. M. (1992). Etiologies and consequences of adolescent drug use: Implications for prevention. *Journal of Addictive Diseases, 11* (3), 47–61.

Berman, H. S. (1987). Talking HEADS, interviewing adolescents. *HMO Practice, 1*(1), 3–11.

Blum, R. W. (1987). Adolescent substance abuse diagnostic and treatment issues. *Pediatric Clinics of North America, 34*, 523–537.

Brooks-Gunn, J., & Graber, J. A. (1994). Puberty as a biological and social event: Implications for research on pharmacology. *Journal of Adolescent Health, 15*, 663–671.

*Brust, J. C. M. (1993). *Neurological aspects of substance abuse*. Boston: Butterworth-Heinemann.

Bush, B., Shaw, S., Cleary, P., DelBanco, T. L., & Aronson, M. D. (1987). Screening for alcohol abuse using CAGE questionnaire. *American Journal of Medicine, 82*, 231–235.

Charles, M., Masihi, E. J., Siddiqui, H. Y., Jogarao, S. V., D'Lima, H., Mehta, U., & Britto, G. (1994). Culture, drug abuse, and some reflections on the family. *Bulletin on Narcotics, 66* (1), 67–86.

Dusenbury, L., Khuri, E., & Millman, R. B. (1992). Adolescent substance abuse: A sociodevelopmental perspective. In L. Lowinson, P. Ruiz, R. Millman & J. Langrod (Eds.), *Substance abuse, a comprehensive textbook* (2nd ed., pp. 832–842). Baltimore: Williams and Wilkins.

Friedman, A. S., & Utada, A. (1989). A method for diagnosing and planning the treatment of adolescent drug abusers: The Adolescent Drug Abuse Diagnosis (ADAD) instrument. *Journal of Drug Education, 19*, 285–312.

*Goldenring, J. M., & Cohen, E. (1988). Getting into adolescents' heads. *Contemporary Pediatrics, 7*, 75–90.

*Gorski, T. T. (1990). The CENAPS model of relapse prevention: Basic principles and procedures. *Journal of Psychoactive Drugs, 22*, 125–133.

*Hughes, S. O., Power, T. G., & Francis, D. (1992). Defining patterns of drinking in adolescence: A cluster analytic approach. *Journal of Studies on Alcohol, 53*, 40–47.

Jessor, R., & Jessor, S. L. (1977). *Problem behavior and psychosocial development: A longitudinal study of youth*. New York: Academic Press.

*Johnston, L. D., O'Malley, P. M., & Bachman, J. G. (1994, December 12). Illicit drug use by American high school seniors. *News and Information Services of the University of Michigan*.

*Johnston, L. D., O'Malley, P. M., & Bachman, J. G. (1995, December 15). Drug use rises again in 1995 among American teens. *News and Information Services of the University of Michigan*.

*Kaminer, Y. (1994). *Adolescent substance abuse: A comprehensive guide to theory and practice*. New York: Plenum.

Kaminer, Y., Bukstein, O., & Tarter, R. E. (1991). The Teen-Addiction Severity Index: Rationale and reliability. *International Journal of the Addictions, 26*, 219–226.

Kestenberg, J. (1967). Phases of adolescence with suggestions for correlations of psychic and hormonal organizations, II: Prepuberty, diffusion, and reintegration. *Journal of the American Academy of Child Psychiatry, 6*, 577–614.

Lawson, G. W., & Lawson, A. W. (1992). *Adolescent substance abuse: Etiology, treatment and prevention*. Gathersburg, MD: Aspen.

Leccese, M., & Waldron, H. B. (1994). Assessing adolescent substance use: A critique of current measurement instruments. *Journal of Substance Abuse Treatment, 11*, 553–563.

Leigh, G. (1985). Psychosocial factors in the etiology of substance abuse. In T. E. Bratter & G. G. Forrest (Eds.), *Alcohol and substance use: Strategies for clinical intervention* (pp. 3–48). New York: Free Press.

Li, X., & Feigelman, S. (1994). Recent and intended drug trafficking among male and female urban African-American early adolescents. *Pediatrics, 93*, 1044–1049.

*MacKenzie, R. G., & Kipke, M. D. (1992). Substance use and abuse. *Comprehensive adolescent health care* (pp. 765–786). St. Louis: Quality Medical Publishing.

Malinosky-Rummell, R., & Hansen, D. J. (1993). Long-term consequences of childhood physical abuse. *Psychological Bulletin, 114* (1), 68–79.

*Marlatt, G. A., & Gordon, J. R. (1985). *Relapse prevention: Maintenance strategies in the treatment of addictive behaviors*. New York: Guilford Press.

*Marlatt, G. A., Somers, J. M., & Tapert, S. F. (1993). Harm reduction: Application to alcohol abuse problems. In *Behavioral treatments for drug abuse and dependence*. Rockville, MD: National Institute of Drug Abuse (NIH Pub. #93-3684).

Mayfield, D., McLead, G., & Hall, P. (1974). The CAGE questionnaire: Validation of a new alcoholism screening instrument. *American Journal of Psychiatry, 131,* 1121–1123.

McLellan, A. T., Luborsky, L., Woody, G. E., & O'Brien, C. P. (1980). An improved diagnostic evaluation instrument for substance abuse patients: The Addiction Severity Index. *Journal of Nervous and Mental Disease, 168,* 26–33.

McLellan, A. T., O'Brian, C. P., Kron, R., et al. (1980). Matching substance abuse patients to appropriate treatments: A conceptual and methodical approach. *Drug and Alcohol Dependency, 5,* 189–195.

Metzger, D. S., Kushner, H., & McLellan, A. T. (1991). *Adolescent Problem Severity Index administration manual.* Philadelphia: Biomedical Computer Research Institute.

Miller, G. (1990). *Substance Abuse Subtle Screening Inventory-Adolescent (SASSI-A).* Bloomington, IN: SASSI Institute.

Miller, W. R., & Rollnick, S. (1991). *Motivational interviewing: Preparing people to change addictive behavior.* New York: Guilford Press.

Mishne, J. M. (1986). *Clinical work with adolescents.* New York: Free Press.

Morrison, M. A., Smith, D. E., Wilford, B. B., Ehrlich, P., & Seymour, R. B. (1993). At war in the fields of play: Current perspective on the nature and treatment of adolescent chemical dependency. *Journal of Psychoactive Drugs, 25,* 321–330.

Neinstein, L. S. (1991). *Adolescent health care.* Baltimore: Urban & Schwarzenberg.

Norton, J. H. (1994). Addictions and family issues. *Alcohol, 11,* 457–460.

O'Malley, P. M., Johnston, L. D., & Bachman, J. G. (1995). Adolescent substance use: Epidemiology and implications for public policy. *Pediatric Clinics of North America, 42,* 241–260.

Parrish, S. R., Jr. (1994). Adolescent substance abuse: The challenge for clinicians. *Alcohol, 11,* 453–455.

Patton, L. H. (1995). Adolescent substance abuse. *Pediatric Clinics of North America, 42,* 283–293.

Peele, S. (1991). What works in addiction treatment and what doesn't: Is the best therapy no therapy? *International Journal of the Addictions, 24,* (12A), 409–417.

Petchers, M. K., & Singer, M. I. (1987). Perceived Benefit of Drinking Scale: Approach to screening for adolescent alcohol abuse. *Journal of Pediatrics, 110,* 977–981.

Petchers, M. K., Singer, M. I., Angelotta, J. W., & Chow, J. (1988). Revalidation and expansion of an adolescent substance abuse screening measure. *Developmental and Behavioral Pediatrics, 9* (1), 25–20.

Peters, K. R., Maltzman, I., & Villone, K. (1994). Childhood abuse of parents of alcohol and other drug misusing adolescents. *International Journal of the Addictions, 29,* 1259–1268.

Petraitis, J., Flay, B. R., & Miller, T. Q. (1995). Reviewing theories of adolescent substance use: Organizing pieces in the puzzle. *Psychological Bulletin, 117* (1), 67–86.

Rahdert, E. R. (Ed.). (1991). *The Adolescent Assessment/Referral System manual.* Rockville, MD: U. S. Department of Health and Human Services.

Rawson, R. A., Obert, J. L., McCann, M. J., & Marinelli-Casey, P. (1993). Relapse prevention strategies in outpatient substance abuse treatment. *Psychology of Addictive Behaviors, 7* (2), 85–95.

Selzer, M. L. (1971). The Michigan Alcoholism Screening Test: The quest for a new diagnostic instrument. *American Journal of Psychiatry, 127,* 1653–1658.

Selzer, M. L., Vinokur, A., & Van Rooijen, L. (1975). A self-administered Short Michigan Alcoholism Screening Test (SMAST). *Journal of Studies on Alcohol, 36,* 117–126.

*Schonberg, S. K. (1993). *Guidelines for the treatment of alcohol and other drug abusing adolescents.* Rockville, MD: U.S. Department of Health and Human Services.

Schwartz, R. H., & Wirtz, P. W. (1990). Potential substance abuse detection among adolescent patients using the drug and alcohol (DAP) quick screen, a 30-item questionnaire. *Clinical Pediatrics, 29* (1), 38–43.

Skinner, H. A. (1982). The Drug Abuse Screening Test. *Addictive Behavior, 7,* 363–371.

Tarter, R. E. (1990). Evaluation and treatment of adolescent substance abuse: A decision tree method. *American Journal of Drug and Alcohol Abuse, 16,* 1–46.

Tarter, R. E., & Hegedus, A. M. (1991). The Drug Use Screening Inventory: Its application in the evaluation and treatment of alcohol and other drug abuse. *Alcohol Health and Research World, 15* (1), 65–75.

Toneatto, T., & Tucker, J. A. (1992). Personal experience inventory. *Measurement and Evaluation in Counseling and Development, 25* (2) 91–94.

Trad, P. V. (1994). Developmental vicissitudes that promote drug abuse in adolescents. *American Journal of Drug and Alcohol Abuse, 20,* 459–481.

Wesson, D. R., & Ling, W. (1991). Medications in the treatment of addictive disease. *Journal of Psychoactive Drugs, 23,* 365–370.

Winters, K. C. (1992). Development of an adolescent alcohol and other drug abuse screening scale: Personal Experience Screening Questionnaire. *Addictive Behaviors, 17,* 479–490.

Winters, K. C., & Henley, G. A. (1989). *Personal Experience Screening Inventory Test and manual.* Los Angeles: Western Psychological Services.

Winters, K. C., & Henly, G. A. (1993). *Adolescent Diagnostic Interview Schedule and manual.* Los Angeles: Western Psychological Services.

Woolf, A. D., & Shannon, M. W. (1995). Clinical toxicology for the pediatrician. *Pediatrics Clinics of North America, 42* (2), 317–333.

World Health Organization. (1992). *International classification of diseases* (9th Rev., Clinical modification). Geneva: Author.

World Health Organization. (1993). *International classification of diseases* (10th Rev.). Geneva: Author.

Wright, F. D., Beck, A. T., Newman, C. F., & Liese, B. S. (1993). Cognitive therapy of substance abuse: theoretical rationale. In *Behavioral treatments for drug abuse and dependence.* Rockville, MD: National Institute of Drug Abuse (NIH Pub. #93-3684).

Zarb, J. (1992). *Cognitive-behavioral assessment and therapy with adolescents.* New York: Brunner Mazel.

*Indicates references that the authors recommend for additional reading.

APPENDIX 12.A.

The following names and addresses are presented as recommended drug and alcohol assessment measures often used with adolescents.

DAP: Schwartz and colleagues provide a sample questionnaire in Schwartz and Wirtz (1990). Copies of the instrument are available from the authors.

DUSI: The DUSI may be purchased through the Gordian Group, Hartsville, South Carolina, (803) 383-2200.

PESQ: A copy of the instrument may be obtained through Western Psychological Services, Los Angeles, CA, (213) 478-2061.

POSIT: To receive a copy of the POSIT, order the Adolescent Assessment-Referral System (AARS) through the National Clearinghouse for Alcohol and Drug Information, Rockville, MD; 1-800-729-6686 information on reliability.

SASSI: The SASSI Institute, 4403 Trailridge Road, Bloomington, IN, 47408, may be contacted for more information.

ADI: The ADI may be obtained through PAR Psychological Assessment Resources, Inc., Odessa, FL, 1-800-331-TEST.

ADAD: This measurement may be obtained by consulting the Belmont Research Center, 4081 Ford Road, Philadelphia, PA, 19131.

APSI: Inquiries regarding the APSI should be directed to David Metzger, Ph.D., Addiction Research Center, University of Pennsylvania, 3900 Chestnut Street, Philadelphia, PA, 19115.

PEI: Inquires concerning the PEI may be directed to Western Psychological Services, Los Angeles, CA, (213) 478-2061.

T-ASI: Inquiries about the T-ASI may be made to the Western Psychiatric Institute, 2811 O'Hara Street, Pittsburgh, Pennsylvania, or Yifrah Kaminer, M.D., Bradley Hospital, 1011 Veteran's Memorial Parkway, East Providence, Rhode Island, 02915.

APPENDIX 12.B. Client Assessment Criteria

Toxicity/Withdrawal	Medical	Intrapersonal	Interpersonal	Environmental	Type of Treatment
No history of use; no current use	Only those medical conditions that can be handled without patient medical management	Developmentally appropriate; effective coping skills; moderate to high emotional/cognitive functioning	Demonstrates developmentally appropriate, prosocial interpersonal behavior; maintains responsible relationships with significant others	May have no significant impact	**Primary prevention**
Positive history of use; no current use	Positive history of use; no current use	Less effective coping skills; but competent emotional/cognitive functioning	Demonstrates developmentally appropriate prosocial interpersonal behavior; maintains responsible relationships with significant others; and history of AOD and/or other risk-related behaviors that increase the potential for developing psychoactive substance use disorder (PSUD); able to function in a nonstructured setting	One or more environmental/contextual factors that increase personal vulnerability (family history of AOD problems) indicate need for intervention	**Early intervention**
Problem(s) resulting from use; no current use, or low to moderate use without anticipated withdrawal	Problem(s) resulting from use; no current use, or low to moderate use without anticipated withdrawal	Less effective coping skills; less competent emotional/cognitive functioning; still able to function in a nonstructured setting	Identified deficiencies in relationships with significant others and history of AOD and/or other risk-related behaviors that increase the potential for developing PSUD; able to function in a nonstructured setting	Environmental/contextual factors affect the individual, but do not warrant removal from current living situation; needs to be supported by minimal treatment	**Outpatient treatment**
Detoxification services not required	No special medical services required on site	Dysfunctional coping skills; emotional/cognitive/psychiatric impairment; requires supervision in structured setting, ADL and other psychosocial rehabilitation	Dysfunctional relationships and behaviors that do not pose an immediate threat to self and/or others but that require behavior management within a structured setting that provides supervision, ADL, and other psychosocial rehabilitation	Environmental/contextual factors dictate individual must be removed from adverse influences of current living situation	**Residential psychosocial care**
Detoxification services not required	No special medical services required on site	Adequate coping skills; has moderate to high level of emotional/cognitive functioning but requires some supervision	Ability to establish prosocial relationships that support recovery; able to self-regulate behavior with minimal structure/supervision	Environmental/contextual factors dictate individual must be removed from current living situation or other adverse circumstances	**Halfway house**
Detoxification services not required	No special medical services required on site	Adequate coping skills; has moderate to high level of emotional/cognitive functioning; able to live independently	Ability to establish prosocial relationships that support recovery; self-regulates behavior consistent with standards of responsible group living without supervision	Environmental/contextual factors dictate individual must be removed from current living situation or other adverse circumstances	**Group home/group living**

Source: Schonberg, S. K. (1993). *Guidelines for the treatment of alcohol- and other drug-abusing adolescents.* Rockville, MD: U.S. Department of Health and Human Services.

13

Depression and Bipolar Disorder in Children and Adolescents

Nadine J. Kaslow
Shannon S. Croft
Carrie A. Hatcher

This chapter first reviews the research on unipolar depressive disorders in youth and then turns to bipolar disorders. Given the relative dearth of data on bipolar disorders in youth, we focus on depression in youth.

CHILD AND ADOLESCENT DEPRESSION

Historical Perspective

Cases of depression in young people were reported in the seventeenth century. Historically, however, little attention was paid to this condition. Prior to the 1970s, the dominant psychoanalytic theory maintained that depression could not occur among children due to their level of psychological development. Other theories held that depressive symptoms were "masked" by other symptoms or were transitory phenomena. These views limited the examination of depression in youth. A transition occurred when childhood depression was acknowledged as a mental disorder at the Fourth Congress of the Union of European Pedopsychiatrists in 1970. Over the past 25 years, childhood depression has received increased attention, and our understanding of childhood mood disorders has been enhanced by the proliferation of diagnostic classification schemas, assessment devices for measuring symptoms and associated sequelae, findings from epidemiological studies, and intervention and prevention efforts.

Diagnostic Description

Mood Disorder Due to a General Medical Condition

This diagnosis is made when the child's medical history, physical examination, or laboratory findings reveal that the mood disturbance is due to the direct physiologic effects of a medical condition. In the fourth edition of the *Diagnostic and Statistical Manual of Mental Disorders* (DSM-IV) (American Psychiatric Association, 1994), one may receive a depression diagnosis on Axis I and an Axis III diagnosis if the depression is not the consequence of a medical condition.

Substance-Induced Mood Disorder

A DSM-IV substance-induced mood disorder is diagnosed when a youth develops a mood disturbance within a month of alcohol or drug intoxication or withdrawal, and the substance use caused the mood disturbance. In the tenth revision of the *International Classification of Diseases* and *Related Health Problems* (ICD-10) (World Health Organization, 1992), this is classified under "Mental and Behavioural Disorders due to Psychoactive Substance Use."

Major Depressive Disorder (MDD)

Also termed unipolar depression, MDD is characterized by a history of one or more major depressive episodes without manic, hypomanic, or mixed episodes of mood disturbance. For a DSM-IV major depressive episode, the youth's symptoms must cause impairment, must reflect a change from baseline, and may not be secondary to uncomplicated bereavement; the diagnosis also requires at least five of the following symptoms during the same 2-week period (according to ICD-10, less than a 2-week period if symptoms are severe and of rapid onset): (1) depressed or irritable mood; (2) anhedonia; (3) decreased weight or appetite or failure to make expected weight gains; (4) sleep disturbance; (5) psychomotor agitation or retardation; (6) fatigue or loss of energy; (7) feelings of worthlessness or inappropriate guilt; (8) concentration difficulties or indecisiveness; and (9) thoughts of death and/or suicide. One symptom must be depressed or irritable mood or anhedonia. Although ICD-10 does not specify the number of symptoms needed to meet criteria for a depressive episode, similar symptoms constitute this diagnostic category. While criteria for a major depressive episode are virtually identical for youth and adults, DSM-IV acknowledges that psychomotor retardation, hypersomnia, and delusions are rare in prepubertal children, whereas somatic complaints, irritability, and social withdrawal may be prominent.

In DSM-IV, descriptive specifiers for the most recent episode refer to severity of depression, presence of psychotic features, remission status, chronicity and course, and the presence of catatonic, melancholic, or atypical features. ICD-10 distinguishes between mild, moderate, and severe depressions and notes the presence of somatic features. Recurrent episodes have their own category in ICD-10 ("recurrent depressive disorder"), whereas DSM-IV describes this feature as a modifier.

Dysthymic Disorder (DD)

According to DSM-IV, DD is characterized by chronically depressed or irritable mood and two of the following: appetite change, sleep change, decreased energy, low self-esteem, difficulty concentrating, and feelings of helplessness. A similar symptom picture is described in ICD-10. For youth to receive a DSM-IV diagnosis of DD, symptom duration must be at least 1 year (as opposed to 2 years for adults), without a symptom free period of 2 months. If a MDD is superimposed on a DD, both diagnoses are made (double depression). DD before age 21 is specified as early onset.

Adjustment Disorder with Depressed Mood (ADDM)

This DSM-IV diagnosis is made when the child's symptoms reflect a maladaptive reaction to a stressor(s) and his or her depressive features do not meet the criteria for MDD or DD. Depressive symptoms may be mixed with anxiety (adjustment disorder with mixed anxiety and depressed mood) and/or conduct disturbance (adjustment disorder with mixed disturbance of emotions and conduct). In DSM-IV, adjustment disorders occur within 3 months of the stressor's onset and cannot persist longer than 6 months after the stressor terminates. Adjustment disorders can be acute or chronic according to DSM-IV (brief or prolonged in ICD-10).

Depressive Disorder Not Otherwise Specified (NOS)

When depressive features do not meet the criteria for MDD, DD, or ADDM (minor depression, depression superimposed on schizophrenia spectrum disorders, depressions without clear etiology), a DSM-IV depressive disorder NOS is diagnosed (the ICD-10 category is "other mood (affective) disorders" or "unspecified mood (affective) disorder").

Comorbid Conditions

Most depressed youth meet the criteria for at least one comorbid condition (McCracken, 1992). Comorbidity increases with the severity of the depression (Fleming & Offord, 1990). MDD often is comorbid with anxiety disorders, attention deficit and disruptive behavior disorders, DD, or eating and substance-related disorders (Angold & Costello, 1993; Fleming & Offord, 1990).

Critique of DSM-IV

Although developmental psychopathologists worked to include distinct diagnostic criteria for childhood mood disorders in DSM-IV, this proposal was rejected on the basis of the view that there were insufficient data to support such a stance. DSM-IV criteria for mood disorders lack a developmental perspective, failing to account for children's cognitive, affective, and interpersonal competencies and biological maturation (Cicchetti & Schneider-Rosen, 1986). Future diagnostic criteria should address the unique features of mood disorders in youth and delineate developmentally appropriate signs of depression.

Although DSM-IV attends more than its predecessors to cultural features, the criteria still reflect a dearth of attention to such factors. Given that specific patterns of depressive symptoms occur in different cultures (Canino & Spurlock, 1994), future diagnostic schema need to acknowledge culture-specific symptom patterns in mood disorders in childhood.

Epidemiology

The prevalence of depression varies depending on setting, disorder, age, sex, sociocultural background, informant, and measurement devices (Fleming & Offord, 1990). Prevalence rates for mood disorders range from 2–5% in community samples and 10–50% in psychiatric settings (Fleming & Offord, 1990; McCracken, 1992; Petersen et al., 1993). Rates of depressive disorders increase with age (Fleming & Offord, 1990). Measurement artefacts, puberty, and changes in risk and/or protective factors may explain this trend (Harrington, 1993).

There are no consistent sex differences in depression rates in prepubertal youth (Angold, 1988). However, by age 15, females are twice as likely as males to receive a depressive diagnosis (Nolen-Hoeksema & Girgus, 1994), a finding that may be attributable to differences in sex role socialization patterns, cognitive styles and coping patterns, variability in stresses encountered in early adolescence, maladaptive expressions of distress, and hormonal factors (Petersen et al., 1993).

Depressive episodes in children and adolescents tend to be of relatively long duration, with protracted time to recovery (e.g., Hanna, 1992; Kovacs, 1989). Depressive disorders tend to recur, and the number of prior episodes predicts the likelihood of reoccurrence throughout the life span (Hanna, 1992; Harrington, 1993; Kovacs, 1989). Factors influencing the course of depressive disorders include the nature of the depressive picture, comorbid psychiatric disorders, age and sex, parental mood disorders, and family environment (e.g., Harrington, 1993).

Brief Review of Psychopathology and Theoretical Models

Genetic and Neurobiological Factors

While research on the neurobiology of depression in youth has proliferated (e.g., Emslie, Weinberg, Kennard, & Kowatch, 1994), no specific model has been supported by research. Furthermore, genetic and environmental factors appear to act synergistically in causing depression.

GENETIC FACTORS. Children with a family history of depression are at increased risk for depression, particularly if a parent evidences depression (Hammen, 1991). Monozygotic twins, even when reared apart, have a higher rate of mood disorder than dizygotic twins. Adopted children of biologic parents with a positive history for depression have more depression than do adopted controls.

NEUROBIOLOGY. Abnormalities in neurotransmitter systems (e.g., acetylcholine, norepinephrine, serotonin, neuropeptides) have been observed and postulated to be of etiological significance in adult depression. Data on these neurotransmitter systems in depressed children are sparse.

Sleep and neuroendocrine abnormalities in depressed adults may indicate a dysfunction of the limbic system and the hindbrain, areas of the brain that may be involved with affective illness (Puig-Antich, 1987). Although early studies failed to demonstrate sleep abnormalities in depressed children, prepubertal children studied after recovery from depression have improved sleep continuity compared to when they were depressed and have decreased rapid eye movement (REM) latency and increased REM density compared to normal and nondepressed controls (Emslie et al., 1994; Puig-Antich, 1987). Shortened REM latency may reflect a depressive trait or indicate a past depressive episode.

Neuroendocrine markers in depressed youth yield a variety of abnormalities, including growth hormone abnormalities and elevated serum thyrotropin (Emslie et al., 1994). Cortisol hypersecretion, found in some depressed adults, is not observed consistently in children (Puig-Antich, 1987). The dexamethasone suppression test (DST) may have some utility in identifying an abnormality in the response of the hypothalamic-pituitary-adrenal axis in depressed youth (Casat, Arana, & Powell, 1989).

Taken together, these preliminary data make it premature to postulate a neurobiological etiological model of childhood depression. However, neurobiology is an exciting field for study that may advance our understanding of the pathophysiology of childhood depression.

Psychological Factors

PSYCHODYNAMIC PERSPECTIVE. Although psychoanalytic theorists implicate childhood events in the etiology of adult depression, there is a paucity of psychodynamic theories of child and adolescent depression, largely due to the classic psychoanalytic view that children could not experience depression because they lack a well-formed superego, stable self-representation, future time orientation, and capacity to tolerate dysphoric affects (Bemporad, 1994). In the 1950s and 1960s, ego-psychological perspectives on childhood depression emerged (Sandler & Joffee, 1965), theorizing that children became depressed when they lost or were unable to attain the emotional support needed to maintain their narcissistic integrity. The resultant helplessness in the face of deprivation leads vulnerable children to become depressed. Sandler and Joffee (1965) noted that children with a neurobiological predisposition, separation-individuation difficulties, and unrealistic expectations of self and others were at high risk for depression. Another ego-analytic view was that depressed children's cognitive distortions reflect problematic parent-child interactions that produce low self-esteem, a perceived lack of instrumentality, dependence on others for gratification, and a view of the environment that often renders them unhappy (Bemporad, 1994).

According to recent object relations models and attachment theory, early disruptions in attachment predispose individuals to depression and sensitize them to loss (Bowlby, 1981). Thus, depression emerges in youth who feel helpless and form negative self and object representations because they failed to form or maintain stable and secure attachments with their parents.

COGNITIVE AND BEHAVIORAL PROCESSES. Data on contingency reinforcement relates parent- and self-reported social skills deficits to youths' current levels of depression and predicts future depressive symptoms. For example, many depressed youth are reluctant to interact with their peers (i.e., social skills deficit), who in turn begin to avoid them (i.e., negative reinforcement), an interpersonal experience that only serves to further their social isolation. However, unlike depressed adults, there is insufficient evidence regarding differential participation by depressed and nondepressed youth in pleasurable and unpleasurable activities. With regard to the cognitive model, depressed children report more negatively distorted cognitions, particularly regarding loss and self-concept, than their nondepressed peers. While some research finds correlations between self-reported depression and subjective indices of cognitive functioning, other data indicate that depressed youth rate themselves more negatively than nondepressed youth despite comparable task performance. Further, depressed youth often feel hopeless and thus are at risk for suicidal behavior. Studies of learned helplessness reveal that children who endorse depressive symptoms evidence deficits in instrumental responding, an external locus of control, "personal helplessness" (perceived incompetence), and contingency uncertainty and "universal helplessness" (perceived noncontingency). The bulk of the work on attributional patterns reveals that, compared to nondepressives, depressed youngsters evidence a more internal, stable, and global attributional pattern for negative events and a more external, unstable, and specific attributional style for positive events. This way of construing the causes of negative events predicts later depressive symptoms, suggesting that this maladaptive attributional style may be a risk factor for depression. In examining the self-control model, researchers report that depressed children have impaired self-monitoring, evaluation, and reinforcement. For comprehensive reviews of this research, see Garber and Hilsman, 1992 and Kaslow, Brown, and Mee, 1994.

In sum, depressed youth report negative cognitive patterns similar to those of depressed adults. However, data are scant regarding whether or not these cognitions are specific to depression in children. Also, it is unclear if these cognitive and behavioral processes are of etiological significance. To understand the etiological role of cognitive patterns in depressive disorders, it is important to use a multimethod assessment of cognitions in children, conduct longitudinal follow-up studies of high-risk children, and ascertain empirically the origins of negative cognitive styles (Garber & Hilsman, 1992). Although the major cognitive models of depression appear applicable for understanding depression in children and adolescents, the validity of these models will be enhanced if they are integrated with developmental theory.

LIFE STRESS. A major psychosocial model suggests that stress, particularly high cumulative levels of negative life events, places a child or adolescent at risk for depression, and stressful experiences correlate with depression (for reviews, see Compas, Grant, & Ey, 1994; Garber & Hilsman, 1992). Although chronic stress is associated with depressive symptoms, this link is mediated or moderated by other variables. Further, there appears to be a reciprocal relation between depression and stress.

According to the diathesis-stress model, people who interpret life events as reflecting negatively on themselves and their futures are more vulnerable to depression when experiencing important stressful life events than are people without this cognitive proclivity (Garber & Hilsman, 1992). Not only can chronic stressors lead to the development of a tendency to interpret events negatively, but this negative cognitive style may place one at risk for more aversive experiences. The limited research provides tentative support for this model's validity (Garber & Hilsman, 1992; Turner & Cole, 1994).

DEVELOPMENTAL PSYCHOPATHOLOGY. A developmental psychopathology frame conceptualizes the genesis and symptom presentation of depression over the life span. This model holds that depression occurs when a lack of integration of interpersonal, cognitive, and affective competencies interferes with successful negotiation of developmental tasks (Cicchetti & Schneider-Rosen, 1986; Rutter, 1986).

One psychosocial pathway for the development and maintenance of depressive disorders in youth results from complex transactions among interpersonal variables, cognitive processes, and life stress (Hammen, 1992). Specifically, insecure parental attachment may be significant in the etiology of depressotypic cognitive processes, leading to a more depressive perspective on self, world, and future. This negative cognitive style may lead to a sense of helplessness and hopelessness, impeding the development of normal peer and sibling relations.

Similarly, it has been purported that depression results from a "loss" of intimate relatedness and is connected to the development of negative self-perceptions in the context of early mother-child experiences (Bowlby, 1981; Cicchetti & Schneider-Rosen, 1986). Maladaptive early relationships may make one vulnerable to problematic patterns of relating to others, and these interpersonal difficulties may constitute stressful life events and shape negative cognitions about self and others. This interpersonal vulnerability is evident in children of depressed mothers, and data suggest a reciprocal influence between the depressed child and depressed mother (e.g., Hammen, 1991).

Social/Interpersonal Factors

FAMILY FUNCTIONING. Despite documentation that "depression runs in families" (Hammen, 1991), only recently has significant attention been paid to the role of the family in the etiology and maintenance of childhood depression (for review, see Kaslow, Deering, & Racusin, 1994). Depressed youth come from families with high rates of psychopathology, particularly mood and substance use disorders. The risk of transmission of depression within a family is high (Hammen, 1991). Children of depressed parents are at risk for myriad emotional and behavioral disorders and evidence multiple impairments, notably in the interpersonal and the cognitive spheres.

Children of families characterized by divorce, single parenthood, and low SES are at high risk for depression. These children often reside in families with many negative life events, notably loss and child maltreatment.

Depressed youth describe their families as less cohesive, supportive, and adaptable and more controlling and conflictual than do their nondepressed peers (e.g., Cumsille & Epstein, 1994). They report less secure attachment to their parents than do nondepressed psychiatric patients and nonpsychiatric controls. Communication patterns in these families are portrayed as hostile, tense, and punitive.

Data indicating an association between family functioning and childhood depression have led to the development of family-oriented models of childhood depression. The mechanisms proposed to account for the transmission of depression from parents to children include genetic predisposition, maladaptive parent-child interactions, and marital discord (for review, see Hammen, 1991; Kaslow et al., 1994). Given that the primary social context in which children are embedded is the family, it is reasonable to hypothesize that family-related negative life events, attachment difficulties, and the transmission of depressive cognitions may be important in the genesis of depression in youth.

EXTRAFAMILIAL FUNCTIONING. Peer relationship and social status difficulties both contribute to the development of depressive symptoms and reflect the presence of depression (Hammen, 1992). Depressed youth often are rejected or viewed negatively by their peers and teachers (e.g., Bell-Dolan, Reaven, & Peterson, 1993; Dalley, Bolocofsky, & Karlin, 1994; Rudolph, Hammen, & Burge, 1994), and their peer problems persist after the resolution of the depressive episode (e.g., Puig-Antich et al., 1993). Individuals most likely to evidence peer problems have a history of problematic relations with their parents (Puig-Antich et al., 1993). Not surprisingly, depressed children have limited social self-confidence and perceive themselves more negatively in terms of social problem-solving ability (Marton, Connolly, Kutcher, & Korenblum, 1993). However, although some studies find that depressed children have impaired social problem-solving, social information processing, and conflict negotiation skills (Quiggle, Garber, Panak, & Dodge, 1992; Rudolph et al., 1994), these findings have not been replicated consistently (Marton et al., 1993). Until longitudinal studies examine the temporal association between depression and social functioning deficits, the complex interplay between nonfamilial interpersonal problems and child depression will remain unclear.

Assessment

Psychosocial Approach

A psychosocial assessment of mood disorders in youth uses a multitrait, multimethod, multi-informant approach to examine individual and contextual factors. This strategy enhances diagnostic reliability and validity, addresses interinformant discrepancies, and portrays the child's impairments and competencies across domains (e.g., cognitive, affective, and interpersonal functioning, adaptive behavior, negative life events) and settings. A psychosocial evaluation involves interviews with the child or adolescent and appropriate caretakers and other relevant family members, completion of behavior ratings scales by multiple informants (e.g., child, parents, teachers, peers, clinicians), and findings from psychological testing data.

SEMISTRUCTURED INTERVIEWS. Semistructured diagnostic clinical interviews, devised to evaluate depressive and comorbid disorders, include the Diagnostic Interview Schedule for Children, the Schedule for Affective Disorders and Schizophrenia in School-Age Children (K-SADS), the Child Assessment Scale, the Diagnostic Interview for Children and Adolescents, and the Interview Schedule for Children (for review, see Hodges, 1994). These interviews, which provide some standardization to the interview process and yield information that facilitates differential diagnosis, also may yield more valid information. Some argue that diagnostic interviews are optimal for assessing the syndrome of depression, asserting that symptom checklists and questionnaires yield information about individual symptoms and psychological distress, rather than clinical depression (Hodges, 1994).

SELF-REPORT QUESTIONNAIRES. Self-report questionnaires, the dominant assessment method, address the child's perceptions of his or her internal state. Most self-report measures, which are appropriate for children ages eight and older, provide a rapid tool for determining the severity of depressive symptoms. Common self-report measures that have adequate reliability and validity include: the Children's Depression Inventory, the Children's Depression Scale, the Depression Self-Rating Scale, the Reynolds Child Depression Scale, the Reynolds Adolescent Depression Scale, the Center for Epidemiological Studies Depression Scale, and the Beck Depression Inventory (for review, see Reynolds, 1994). While self-report measures offer important clinical information, they should be used in conjunction with clinical interviews that offer a more comprehensive diagnostic picture (Reynolds, 1994).

Assessment example. Samantha, a 12-year-old African American female, was referred by her teacher to the school psychologist for deterioration in school performance. At the first appointment, in addition to talking with the counselor, Samantha completed a Children's Depression Inventory (CDI) (Kovacs, 1992). She scored 23 (> 19 indicates potential clinical depression). Consistent with Stark's (1990) recommendation for a three-phase assessment, the CDI was readministered 1 week later; she scored 21. At neither time did she endorse the suicide item. Given her self-report of depressive symptoms, clinical interviews, including the Diagnostic Interview Schedule for Children (DISC), were administered to Samantha and to her mother. Both of her parents completed the Child Behavior Checklist, and her teacher completed the Teacher Rating Form. Although Samantha was consistent in her report of depressive symptoms during the semistructured clinical interview and her teacher's rating of her was high on the anxious-depressed subscale, neither of her parents reported that Samantha had depressive symptoms or other psychological problems. To integrate the discrepant data, a meeting was held with Samantha, her parents, her older brother, and her teacher. After receiving permission from Samantha, the evaluator shared with the family those CDI subscales and individual items from the CDI and the DISC that Samantha endorsed, as well as the teacher's ratings. The parents agreed to monitor more closely Samantha's self-esteem, involvement in positive activities, and affective state, the three clusters of depressive symptoms reported. A follow-up appointment was scheduled for 2 weeks later.

Medical Approach

When evaluating a youth for depression, a medical work-up should rule out underlying organic causes. Depression may be substance induced, and a drug screen for commonly abused substances may be indicated. Since many prescribed medications (e.g., corticosteroids, anticonvulsants, some antibiotics) are associated with depression, a thorough drug history should be obtained (Kashani & Breedlove, 1994).

In addition to a physical examination, the laboratory workup is designed to rule out medical conditions that cause depression. A hematologic profile with differential should be obtained to look for signs of infection or anemia. A thyroid stimulating hormone (TSH) level should be obtained to evaluate for thyroid disease. An electrolyte panel, including liver and kidney (BUN, creatinine) function tests, evaluate for potential metabolic abnormalities, parathyroid disease, adrenal dysfunction, and kidney disorders (Weller & Weller, 1991). Other tests may include an EEG to look for seizures and an ECG if a tricyclic antidepressant trial is likely.

Treatment

Psychosocial Interventions

PSYCHOSOCIAL TREATMENT STUDIES WITH CHILDREN. The first empirical treatment study with groups of depressed children compared the relative efficacy of 10-session role play, cognitive restructuring, attention placebo, and waiting list conditions for fifth and sixth graders with elevated self-reported depression scores and teacher referrals (Butler, Miezitis, Friedman, & Cole, 1980). The role-play intervention emphasized social problem-solving training and rehearsal of social skills. The cognitive restructuring condition focused on identifying depressive and maladaptive cognitive patterns and developing more adaptive cognitions. Although both experimental conditions were effective, children in the role-play group showed comparatively fewer self-reported depressive symptoms and more improved classroom functioning. No follow-up was conducted.

Stark, Reynolds, and Kaslow (1987) compared 12-session group interventions of self-control therapy, behavior problem-solving therapy, and a waiting list control for fourth through sixth graders with elevated self-reported depression scores. The self-control groups taught adaptive self-monitoring, self-evaluating, self-consequating, and appropriate causal attributions. The behavioral problem-solving group consisted of education, self-monitoring of pleasant events, and group problem solving directed toward improving social behavior. Postintervention and follow-up assessments found that participants in both active interventions reported an amelioration of depressive symptoms; waiting list subjects reported minimal change. Although findings comparing the two interventions were equivocal, the pattern suggested that the self-control intervention was more useful.

Stark and colleagues (Stark, Rouse, & Livingston, 1991) evaluated self-control therapy for fourth through seventh graders with high levels of depressive symptoms. This 24- to 26-session cognitive-behavioral treatment, consisting of self-control and social skills training, cognitive restructuring, and problem-solving, was compared to a traditional counseling condition designed to control for nonspecific elements of the intervention. For the cognitive-behavioral group, monthly family meetings encouraged parents to assist their children in applying their new skills and to increase the frequency of positive family activities. In the counseling condition, monthly family sessions addressed improving communication and increasing pleasant family events. At postintervention and 7-month follow-up, both groups revealed decreased self-reported depression; however, at postintervention, those in the cognitive-behavioral group were more improved on a semistructured interview and endorsed fewer depressive cognitions.

Liddle and Spence (1990) randomly assigned 7- to 11-year-olds with elevated depressive symptoms on self-report measures and a diagnostic interview to 8-week social competence training (e.g., social skills, interpersonal problem solving, and cognitive restructuring regarding social situations), attention-placebo control, and no-treatment control groups. Although all groups showed reduced self-reported depressive symptoms that continued during follow-up, no differential treatment effects were found, and no changes in social competence were revealed.

Kahn, Kehle, Jenson, and Clark (1990) compared three psychoeducational group interventions (cognitive-behavioral, relaxation training, self-modeling) and a wait-list control for 10- to 14-year-olds selected on self- and parent reports and clinical interview. Decreases in depressive symptoms and improved self-esteem were noted in children in the three experimental conditions relative to the wait-list control. Improvements were maintained at 1-month follow-up. There were no significant differences between the experimental conditions.

While these studies suggest that a variety of intervention approaches may be efficacious in ameliorating depressive symptoms and more effective than no intervention, no single treatment appears superior. Most studies were conducted in schools with nonreferred children with depressive symptoms; thus, the generalizability of the findings to children with depressive disorders is unclear (Asarnow, 1990; Harrington, 1993). Further, there are no data regarding which specific component(s) of these multifaceted interventions may be most beneficial (Asarnow, 1990). Finally, these outcome studies fail to accommodate developmental differences in children's competencies and do not assess the effectiveness of various interventions strategies for youth at different ages and developmental level. Future research needs to integrate developmental research findings on the cognitive, affective, and social functioning of youth in devising and implementing therapies for depressed children.

PSYCHOSOCIAL TREATMENT STUDIES WITH ADOLESCENTS. Treatment studies with depressed adolescents have used cognitive-behavioral interventions, a family psychoeducational program, and interpersonal psychotherapy. Reynolds and Coates (1986) conducted the first treatment outcome study of adolescent depression. Nonreferred high school students who self-reported high levels of depressive symptoms were assigned randomly to cognitive-behavioral self-control therapy (10 sessions), relaxation training (10 sessions), or a wait-list control. Posttreatment and 5-week follow-up results revealed that both therapies were more effective than the control condition in reducing depression and anxiety and enhancing academic self-concept. No differences were found between the active conditions.

Fine, Forth, Gilbert, and Haley (1991) compared a 12-week social-skills training group to a therapeutic support group for psychiatric outpatient adolescents who met diagnostic criteria for MDD or DD. The social-skills groups taught specific skills (recognizing feelings, assertiveness, communication skills, social problem solving); the therapeutic support groups facilitated discussions of common concerns and adaptive ways to address difficult situations. At posttreatment, youth in the support groups had less clinical depression and higher self-concepts than those in the social-skills groups. At 9-month follow-up, between-group differences were no longer evident; adolescents in the support groups maintained their gains and those who received social-skills training continued to improve.

The most sophisticated treatment research has been conducted by Lewinsohn, Clarke, Hops, and Andrews (1990), who assigned high school students ages 14–18 with DSM depressive disorders to cognitive-behavioral group treatment for the adolescent only, concurrent cognitive-behavioral treatment groups for the depressed adolescent and his or her parents, and a wait-list control. The cognitive-behavioral intervention, based on the Coping with Depression (CWD) course for adults, was adapted to address the concerns and competencies of adolescents. The CWD 14-session multiple-component intervention focused on experiential learning and skills training (increasing pleasant activities, relaxation, controlling depressive thoughts, improving social interaction and communication, and negotiation and conflict resolution skills). The seven-session complementary parent intervention aimed at enhancing parents' capacity to reinforce and promote their adolescent's adaptive changes to increase the likelihood that treatment effects would be maintained and generalized. Posttherapy assessment indicated that, compared to youth in the wait-list condition, fewer adolescents in the active treatment groups met criteria for depression, and the treated children showed greater reductions in self-reported depressive and anxious symptoms and maladaptive cognitions and more involvement in positive events. Gains were maintained at 2-year follow-up. Although a trend indicated that the adolescent-and-parent CWD condition was more effective than the adolescent-only CWD condition, only a few between-group differences reached statistical significance.

Brent, Poling, McKain, and Baugher (1993) examined a 2-hour psychoeducational program for parents of adolescents with mood disorders. This program was associated with improved parental understanding of mood disorders and modification of dysfunctional beliefs about the etiology, course, and treatment of adolescent depression.

After a 12-week open trial of individual interpersonal psychotherapy modified for clinically depressed adolescents (IPT-A) (Mufson, Moreau, Weissman, & Klerman, 1993), adolescents reported decreases in depressive symptoms, no longer met criteria for a depressive disorder, and evidenced improvements in other psychological symptoms and physical distress. IPT-A also appeared to improve overall social functioning.

In sum, these studies indicate that short-term therapies, regardless of their theoretical underpinnings, effectively decrease depressive symptoms in adolescents. However, it is premature to conclude that any given intervention is the most effective, and it is unclear which intervention is optimal for any given adolescent. Larger-scale and more rigorous studies will facilitate the development, implementation, and evaluation of psychosocial interventions for depressed adolescents.

Biological Interventions

MEDICATION TREATMENT. Pharmacological intervention targets those neurotransmitter systems most implicated in depression (see Schatzberg & Nemeroff, 1995). Both tricyclic antidepressants (TCAs) and specific serotonin reuptake inhibitors (SSRIs) inhibit the uptake of serotonin. TCAs also inhibit the reuptake of norepinephrine. The mechanism of action likely involves not only increasing intrasynaptic serotonin/norepinephrine but also the down-regulation of neuroreceptors and other effects on the neurons via second-messenger systems.

Initially, open trials of TCAs (e.g., imipramine, nortriptyline, amitriptyline) yielded encouraging results for prepubertal youth; findings were less clear for adolescents (for review, see Harrington, 1993; Ryan, 1992). More methodologically sophisticated double-blind studies of TCAs failed to demonstrate superiority of drug over placebo (e.g., Geller et al., 1992; Puig-Antich et al., 1987). Consistent with these data, open trials of two SSRIs, fluoxetine (prozac) and fluvoxamine (luvox), yielded positive results in adolescent depression (e.g., Apter et al., 1994; Boulous, Kutcher, Gardner, & Young, 1992), while a placebo-controlled double-blind study of fluoxetine failed to demonstrate superiority of medication over placebo (Simeon, DiNicola, Ferguson, &

Copping, 1990). Explanations of the disparity of results between child or adolescent and adult populations focus on pharmacokinetics and brain developmental neurochemical differences (Ryan, 1992). Until more large-scale, methodologically sound studies are conducted, it may be premature to conclude from research that medications are not useful.

Despite the equivocal empirical support for antidepressant medications, many child psychiatrists advocate their use. However, TCAs are associated with problematic side effects in children (e.g., cardiac changes) and may be lethal in overdose (Ryan, 1992). Data suggest that some adolescents treatment-refractory to TCAs may benefit from lithium augmentation (e.g., Strober, Freeman, Rigali, Schmidt, & Diamond, 1992). Monoamine oxidase inhibitors (MAOIs), useful for some adults, rarely are used with youth because of the dietary restrictions required when taking this class of medication (e.g., Ryan, 1992). Recently, there has been interest in using the SSRIs for treating depressed children and adolescents. SSRIs have few harmful side effects and tend not to be dangerous in overdose (Rosenberg, Holttum, & Gershon, 1994). However, the SSRIs are more expensive than the TCAs, and for some families this cost may be prohibitive. Fortunately, some pharmaceutical companies have offered indigent programs for low-income individuals.

ELECTROCONVULSIVE THERAPY (ECT). ECT, a medical procedure in which an electrical current is applied to elicit a generalized seizure in an anesthetized patient, has been hypothesized to result in changes in neurotransmitter function and may alter the metabolic activity of some regions of the brain. There is a reluctance to use ECT to treat depressed children and adolescents, due to the lack of documented efficacy of this treatment for youth and the potential negative sequelae of ECT (brief organic impairment and long-term cognitive deficits, alteration of seizure threshold, anxiety, disinhibition) (Bertagnoli & Borchardt, 1990). The American Psychiatric Association Task Force on ECT (1990) recommends that ECT be used only for youth for whom other treatments are not effective or safe. Despite concerns, some case reports document the efficacy of this approach in 80% of depressed youth (e.g., Bertagnoli & Borchardt, 1990).

Prevention

Prevention trials for depression are recent, although a number of programs designed for youth following stressful events (e.g., divorce, bereavement) have implications for preventing depression (Asarnow, 1992). Jaycox, Reivich, Gillham, and Seligman (1994) explored the efficacy of a group cognitive and social problem-solving program for 10- to 13-year-olds with elevated depressive symptoms and parental conflict. Results revealed greater diminution of symptoms for youth in the experimental than control condition at postintervention and 6-month follow-up.

Clarke and colleagues (1995) compared a 15-session group cognitive preventive intervention program and a treatment-as-usual control condition for adolescents with self-reported depressive symptoms who did not meet diagnostic criteria for a mood disorder. A survival analysis indicated that at a 12-month follow-up, adolescents in the experimental group were less likely than controls to meet the diagnostic criteria for a mood disorder. These findings support the utility of prevention programs in reducing the risk for mood disorders in at-risk youth.

Related prevention efforts focus on children at high risk for depression (e.g., children of affectively ill parents). Beardslee and colleagues (1993) compared clinician-based and lecture-based cognitive psychoeducational prevention programs for addressing family members' behaviors and attitudes regarding the illness. Families in the clinician-based group were more positive about the program and developed more adaptive attitudes and behaviors for coping with stress than did families in the lecture-based program. These changes may be associated with improved parental management of high-risk children and more adaptive child coping, both of which may decrease the child's risk for depression (Beardslee et al., 1993).

Given that depressive disorders recur and interfere with a child's development and functioning, clinical researchers need to design and implement prevention programs aimed at reducing the risk of childhood mood disorders and the impact of these conditions on the youth's functioning. Attention should be paid to developing preventive intervention programs for children and adolescents at risk for depression (e.g., those with low levels of persistent dysphoria; children of depressed parents). Additional efforts should be devoted to relapse prevention.

BIPOLAR DISORDERS

Historical Perspective

Although bipolar disorder in children and adolescents was noted by Kraepelin (1921), little attention was paid to this condition prior to Anthony and Scott's (1960) review that offered diagnostic criteria for childhood onset mania and enumerated the extant theories of childhood mania. The occurrence of mania remained controversial through the 1970s, and it was not until DSM-III (APA, 1987) that diagnostic criteria were established for diagnosing bipolar disorder in children and adolescents. However, current criteria for bipolar disorders lack attention to developmental differences in symptom presentation. For example, irritability is more common than euphoria in children, but the reverse is true for adolescents (Krasa & Tolbert, 1994). Since the publication of DSM-III-R, the need to differentiate mania from other forms of psychopathology (e.g., ADHD) has been noted. Despite the deleterious effects of bipolar disorder on children's development, this illness remains understudied.

Diagnostic Description

Variables that account for the well-documented difficulties in diagnosing childhood manic disorders include: (1) the low base rate of the phenomena; (2) fluctuations in symptom presentation; (3) similarities in symptom profiles of mania and other child disorders; and (4) differences in the behavioral manifestations of the symptoms across the life span (Bowring & Kovacs, 1992). In both DSM-IV and ICD-10, there are no differences in the criteria for manic and hypomanic episodes for youth and for adults.

To meet DSM-IV criteria for any form of bipolar disorder, the child or adolescent must have had at least one manic or hypomanic episode. To meet DSM-IV criteria for a manic episode (mania in ICD-10), the individual must have "a distinct period of abnormally and persistently elevated expansive or irritable mood lasting at least 1 week (or any duration if hospitalization is necessary)" (APA, 1994; p. 332), with three or more of the following symptoms: inflated self-esteem or grandiosity, decreased need for sleep, pressured speech or hyperverbosity, flight of ideas or racing thoughts, distractibility, increase in goal-directed activity or psychomotor agitation (increased energy in ICD-10), or impulsive overinvolvement in pleasurable and potentially harmful activities (includes ICD-10 symptoms of loss of social inhibition). Symptoms impair functioning and are not attributable to the effects of a substance or a medical problem.

DSM-IV criteria for a hypomanic episode differ only in terms of duration and level of impairment. When a child or adolescent meets criteria for both a major depressive and a manic episode nearly daily for 1 week, he or she is diagnosed as having had a mixed episode. Bipolar disorders may not be superimposed on a schizophrenia spectrum disorder, delusional disorder, or psychotic disorder NOS.

With a history of either a manic or a mixed episode (past or current), the patient is diagnosed with a bipolar I disorder (DSM-IV). If there has never been a manic or mixed episode, but there has been at least one hypomanic (past or present) and one major depressive episode, a DSM-IV bipolar II diagnosis is made ("other bipolar affective disorders" in ICD-10). There are enumerable sets of criteria for bipolar I disorder in DSM-IV and ICD-10 that address the nature of the current or most recent episode (manic, hypomanic, mixed, depressed), features and severity of the depressed or manic state, chronicity, onset, and course. ICD-10 presents mania with psychotic symptoms as a separate diagnostic entity. Youth who do not meet full criteria for a bipolar disorder but manifest significant bipolar features receive a DSM-IV diagnosis of "bipolar disorder not otherwise specified" or an ICD-10 diagnosis of "bipolar affective disorder unspecified."

Youth with cycles of hypomanic and depressive symptoms who never meet criteria for a major depressive episode are diagnosed with cyclothymic disorder in DSM-IV or ICD-10. According to DSM-IV, the symptom pattern for those under 19 must last at least 1 year, in contrast to adults, who must evidence this presentation for 2 or more years. ICD-10 specifies early or late onset.

Differential diagnosis of bipolar disorders in youth is complex, given the overlap between symptoms of bipolarity and other disorders (attention-deficit and disruptive behavior, psychotic, substance abuse, anxiety, other mood disorders) and the high incidence of the comorbidity of these disorders (e.g., Biederman et al., 1995; Krasa & Tolbert, 1994).

Epidemiology

Although the median age of onset for bipolar illness is 18 years (Burke, Burke, Reiger, & Rae, 1990), there is a paucity of prevalence and incidence data of bipolar disorders in youth (McCracken, 1992). A recent epidemiological study of teens found a lifetime prevalence of bipolar spectrum disorders (primarily bipolar II and cyclothymia) of 1% (Lewinsohn, Klein, & Seeley, 1995). These youth evidence significant impairments and a chronic and relapsing course (Lewinsohn et al., 1995; Strober et al., 1995). Juvenile-onset depressions are a common precursor of bipolar disorders (e.g., Geller, Fox, & Clark, 1994). Those prepubertal depressed youth most likely to develop bipolar I disorder in adolescence have a multigenerational family history of depressive and bipolar conditions (e.g., Geller et al., 1994) or evidence psychotic symptoms during their depressive

episode (Strober, Lampert, Schmidt, & Morrell, 1993).

Assessment

Comprehensive assessment of manic symptoms should include a complete medical evaluation to rule out medical conditions likely to present with manic-type symptoms (e.g., hyperthyroidism, drug intoxication) (Weller & Weller, 1991). In addition, a thorough psychiatric interview, with attention to psychiatric and family history, is essential. Since a bipolar disorder diagnosis depends on symptom course, this diagnostic impression should be reevaluated throughout the patient's development.

Standard structured and semistructured diagnostic interviews (e.g., Diagnostic Interview for Children and Adolescents, Revised; Diagnostic Interview Schedule for Children; Children's Schedule for Affective Disorders and Schizophrenia; Interview Schedule for Children) can aid in making a DSM-compatible diagnosis of bipolar disorder in youth (for review, see Fristad, Weller, & Weller, 1992). These interviews are useful in assessing comorbid psychiatric conditions, as well as in differentiating mania from ADHD, conduct disorder, and schizophrenia spectrum disorders. Some rating scales may aid in assessing manic symptoms in youth. The Mania Rating Scale is helpful in quantifying the severity of manic symptoms in youth and in distinguishing between mania and ADHD (Fristad et al., 1992). The Child Behavior Checklist (CBCL) is a useful screening tool for identifying clinically referred manic children (Biederman et al., 1995).

Treatment

There is a dearth of treatment studies for mania in children and adolescents (Kafantaris, 1995). No psychosocial treatment outcome studies have been published, and the literature on psychotherapy is limited. It has been recommended that psychosocial treatment include psychoeducation, school intervention, and family treatment (e.g., Weller, Weller, & Fristad, 1995). The psychoeducation should provide information to the patient and the family regarding the nature of the disorder, appropriate medication management, and ways to reduce stress that may precipitate a manic or depressive episode. Interventions with school personnel and possibly the child's peers may include providing information about the disorder itself, developing and implementing behavioral plans, and offering instruction regarding ways to enhance the child's self-esteem. Family intervention should include attaining a history, reviewing with the family the diagnosis and probable course of the disorder, and identifying and addressing family interactional and interpersonal problems.

The bulk of the literature focuses on medication use. Although in clinical practice lithium is the primary medication used in children and adolescents with acute mania, no well-controlled double-blind studies document its efficacy (Botteron & Geller, 1995; Kafantaris, 1995). However, two large open-trial studies support its utility (DeLong & Aldershof, 1987; Strober et al., 1988), and a naturalistic study supported the use of lithium to prevent future manic episodes in adolescents (Strober et al., 1995). One must be aware that lithium may have significant side effects for youth (e.g., weight gain, acne). Pharmacokinetic differences between children and adults suggest different dosing strategies (e.g., Rosenberg et al., 1994). Although adjunctive use of neuroleptics (antipsychotics) is common for treating manic episodes in adults, research reveals that lithium alone improves both manic and psychotic symptoms in youth (Varanka, Weller, Weller, & Fristand, 1988). These medications should be added to a lithium regimen only when necessary, given that the risk of tardive dyskinesia due to neuroleptic use is elevated in those with mood disorders (e.g., Botteron & Geller, 1995).

Although no well-controlled studies document the efficacy of anticonvulsant medications (e.g., carbamezapine, valproic acid) for manic symptoms in youth, these drugs are used clinically both alone and as adjuncts to lithium (e.g., Botteron & Geller, 1995; Kafantaris, 1995). A few studies support the use of anticonvulsants to augment lithium in treating manic symptoms in youth (e.g., Papatheodorou, Kutcher, Katic, & Szalai, 1995).

CONCLUSION

Childhood depression is a serious mental health problem that significantly impairs development and adaptive functioning within an ecological context. Research on the assessment, diagnosis, epidemiology, and course of depressive disorders has proliferated during the past two decades. Still, there is a paucity of research testing of etiological models, particularly those that integrate environmental and biological factors. Even more alarming is the dearth of treatment outcome and prevention research documenting the efficacy of various psychosocial and pharmacological therapies for depressed children and adolescents. Theory-driven intervention and prevention studies may shed light not only on which treatment is most effective for which child but also on the multifaceted etiology of depressive disorders in children. These treatment studies must take into account the comorbidity of disorders and the covariation of psychological problems in children and adolescents. Future research should be conducted within a developmental psychopathology framework and should be targeted toward enhancing our understanding of the complex interplay between the psychological and biological factors involved in the etiology and maintenance of depressive disorders in youth.

While bipolar disorders affect a relatively smaller number of youth, this serious condition is underdiagnosed in childhood and adolescence. There are virtually no data regarding effective interventions that integrate psychosocial and pharmacological treatment. The possibilities for further research in this area are vast, and empirical investigations are needed. Specifically, developmentally sensitive diagnostic assessment tools will improve the diagnosis of childhood mania, and systematic treatment

outcome studies will inform both psychotherapeutic and pharmacologic treatment.

REFERENCES

American Psychiatric Association. (1987). *Diagnostic and statistical manual of mental disorders* (3rd ed., rev.). Washington, DC: Author.

American Psychiatric Association. (1994). *Diagnostic and statistical manual of mental disorders* (4th ed.). Washington, DC: Author.

American Psychiatric Association Task Force on ECT. (1990). The practice of ECT: Recommendations for treatment, training, and privileging. *Convulsive Therapy, 6*, 85–120.

Angold, A. (1988). Childhood and adolescent depression: I. Epidemiological and aetiological aspects. *British Journal of Psychiatry, 152*, 601–617.

Angold, A., & Costello, E. J. (1993). Depressive comorbidity in children and adolescents: Empirical, theoretical, and methodological issues. *American Journal of Psychiatry, 150*, 1779–1791.

Anthony, E. J., & Scott, S. P. (1960). Manic depressive psychosis in childhood. *Journal of Child Psychology and Psychiatry, 1*, 53–72.

Apter, A., Ratzoni, G., King, R., Weizman, A., Iancu, I., Binder, M., & Riddle, M. (1994). Fluvoxamine open-label treatment of adolescent inpatients with obsessive compulsive disorder or depression. *Journal of the American Academy of Child and Adolescent Psychiatry, 33*, 342–348.

Asarnow, J. R. (1990). Psychosocial intervention strategies for the depressed child: Approaches to treatment and prevention. *Child and Adolescent Psychiatric Clinics of North America, 1*, 257–283.

Beardslee, W. R., Salt, P., Porterfield, K., Rothberg, P. S., van de Velde, P., Swatling, S., Hoke, L., Moilanen, D. L., & Wheelock, I. (1993). Comparison of preventive interventions for families with parental affective disorder. *Journal of the American Academy of Child and Adolescent Psychiatry, 32*, 254–263.

Bell-Dolan, D. J., Reaven, N. M., & Peterson, L. (1993). Depression and social functioning: A multidimensional study of the linkages. *Journal of Clinical Child Psychology, 22*, 306–315.

Bemporad, J. R. (1994). Dynamic and interpersonal theories of depression. In W. M. Reynolds & H. F. Johnston (Eds.), *Handbook of depression in children and adolescents* (pp. 81–95). New York: Plenum Press.

Bertagnoli, M. W., & Borchardt, C. M. (1990). A review of ECT for children and adolescents. *Journal of the American Academy of Child and Adolescent Psychiatry, 29*, 302–307.

Biederman, J., Faraone, S., Mick, E., & Lelon, E. (1995). Psychiatric comorbidity among referred juveniles with major depression: Fact or artifact? *Journal of the American Academy of Child and Adolescent Psychiatry, 34*, 579–590.

Biederman, J., Wozniak, J., Kieley, K., Ablon, S., Faraone, S., Mick, E., Mundy, E., & Kraus, I. (1995). CBCL clinical scales discriminate prepubertal children with structured interview-derived diagnosis of mania for those with ADHD. *Journal of the American Academy of Child and Adolescent Psychiatry, 34*, 464–471.

Botteron, K. N., & Geller, B. (1995). Pharmacologic treatment of childhood and adolescent mania. *Child and Adolescent Psychiatric Clinics of North America: Pediatric Psychopharmacology II, 4*, 283–302.

Boulous, C., Kutcher, S., Gardner, D., & Young, E. (1992). An open naturalistic trial of fluoxetine in adolescents and young adults with treatment-resistant major depression. *Journal of Child and Adolescent Psychopharmacology, 2*, 103–111.

Bowlby, J. (1981). *Attachment and loss, Vol. 3: Sadness and depression.* Harmondsworth, Middlesex: Penguin.

Bowring, M. A., & Kovacs, M. (1992). Difficulties in diagnosing manic disorders among children and adolescents. *Journal of the American Academy of Child and Adolescent Psychiatry, 31*, 611–614.

Brent, D. A., Poling, K., McKain, B., & Baugher, N. (1993). A psychoeducational program for families of affectively ill children and adolescents. *Journal of the American Academy of Child and Adolescent Psychiatry, 32*, 770–774.

Burke, C. K., Burke, J. D., Jr., Reiger, D. A., & Rae, D. (1990). Age at onset of selected mental disorders in five community populations. *Archives of General Psychiatry, 47*, 511–518.

Butler, L., Miezitis, S., Friedman, R., & Cole, E. (1980). The effect of two school-based intervention programs on depressive symptoms in preadolescents. *American Educational Research Journal, 17*, 111–119.

Canino, I. A., & Spurlock, J. (1994). *Culturally diverse children and adolescents: Assessment, diagnosis, and treatment.* New York: Guilford Press.

Casat, C. D., Arana, G. W., & Powell, K. (1989). The DST in children and adolescents with major depressive disorder. *American Journal of Psychiatry, 146,* 503–507.

Cicchetti, D., & Schneider-Rosen, K. (1986). An organization approach to childhood depression. In M. Rutter, C. E. Izard, & P. B. Read (Eds.), *Depression in young people: Developmental and clinical perspectives* (pp. 71–134). New York: Guilford Press.

Clarke, G. N., Hawkins, W., Murphy, M., Sheeber, L. B., Lewinsohn, P. M., & Seeley, J. R. (1995). Targeted prevention of unipolar depressive disorder in an at-risk sample of high school adolescents: A randomized trial of a group cognitive intervention. *Journal of the American Academy of Child and Adolescent Psychiatry, 34,* 312–321.

Compas, B. E., Grant, K. E., & Ey, S. (1994). Psychosocial stress and child and adolescent depression: Can we be more specific? In W. M. Reynolds & H. F. Johnston (Eds.), *Handbook of depression in children and adolescents* (pp. 509–523). New York: Plenum Press.

Cumsille, P. E., & Epstein, N. (1994). Family cohesion, family adaptability, social support, and adolescent depressive symptoms in outpatient clinic families. *Journal of Family Psychology, 8,* 202–214.

Dalley, M. B., Bolocofsky, D. N., & Karlin, N. J. (1994). Teacher-ratings and self-ratings of social competency in adolescents with low- and high-depressive symptoms. *Journal of Abnormal Child Psychology, 22,* 477–485.

DeLong, G. R., & Adershof, A. L. (1987). Long-term experience with lithium treatment in childhood: Correlation with clinical diagnosis. *Journal of the American Academy of Child and Adolescent Psychiatry, 26,* 389–394.

Emslie, G. J., Weinberg, W. A., Kennard, B. D. & Kowatch, R. A. (1994). Neurobiological aspects of depression in children and adolescents. In W. M. Reynolds & H. F. Johnston (Eds.), *Handbook of depression in children and adolescents* (pp. 1430–165). New York: Plenum Press.

Fine, S., Forth, A., Gilbert, M., & Haley, G. (1991). Group therapy for adolescent depressive disorder: A comparison of social skills and therapeutic support. *Journal of the American Academy of Child and Adolescent Psychiatry, 30,* 79–85.

Fleming, J. E., & Offord, D. R. (1990). Epidemiology of childhood depressive disorders: A critical review. *Journal of the American Academy of Child and Adolescent Psychiatry, 29,* 571–580.

Fristad, M., Weller, E., & Weller, R. (1992). Bipolar disorder in children and adolescents. *Child and Adolescent Psychiatric Clinics of North American, 1,* 13–29.

Garber, J., & Hilsman, R. (1992). Cognitions, stress, and depression in children and adolescents. *Child and Adolescent Psychiatric Clinics of North America, 1,* 129–167.

Geller, B., Cooper, T. B., Graham, D., Fetner, H., Marstellar, F., & Wells, J. (1992). Pharmacokinetically designed double-blind placebo-controlled study of nortriptyline in 6- to 12-year-olds with major depressive disorder. *Journal of the American Academy of Child and Adolescent Psychiatry, 31,* 34–44.

Geller, B., Fox, L. W., & Clark, K. A. (1994). Rate and predictors of prepubertal bipolarity during follow-up of 6- to 12-year-old depressed children. *Journal of the American Academy of Child and Adolescent Psychiatry, 33,* 461–468.

Hammen, C. (1991). *Depression runs in families: The social context of risk and resilience of children of depressed mothers.* New York: Springer-Verlag.

Hammen, C. (1992). Cognitive, life stress, and interpersonal approaches to a developmental psychopathology model of depression. *Development and Psychopathology, 4,* 189–206.

Hanna, G. L. (1992). Natural history of mood disorders. *Child and Adolescent Psychiatric Clinics of North America, 1,* 169–181.

Harrington, R. (1993). *Depressive disorder in childhood and adolescence.* West Sussex, England: Wiley.

Hodges, K. (1994). Evaluation of depression in children and adolescents using diagnostic clinical interviews. In W. M. Reynolds & H. F. Johnston (Eds.), *Handbook of depression in children and adolescents* (pp. 183–208). New York: Plenum Press.

Jaycox, L. H., Reivich, K. J., Gillham, J., & Seligman, M. E. P. (1994). Prevention of depressive symptoms in school children. *Behavioral Research and Therapy, 32,* 801–816.

Kafantaris, V. (1995). Treatment of bipolar disorder in children and adolescents. *Journal of American Academy of Child and Adolescent Psychiatry, 34,* 732–741.

Kahn, J. S., Kehle, T. J., Jenson, W. R., & Clark, E. (1990). Comparison of cognitive-behavioral, relaxation, and self-modeling interventions for depression among middle-school students. *School Psychology Review, 19,* 196–211.

Kashani, J. H., & Breedlove, L. (1994). Depression in medically ill youngsters. In W. M. Reynolds & H. F. Johnston (Eds.), *Handbook of depression in children and adolescents* (pp. 427–443). New York: Plenum Press.

Kaslow, N. J., Brown, R. T., & Mee, L. L. (1994). Cognitive and behavioral correlates of childhood depression: A developmental perspective. In W. M. Reynolds & H. F. Johnston (Eds.), *Handbook of depression in children and adolescents* (pp. 97–121). New York: Plenum Press.

Kaslow, N. J., Deering, C. G., & Racusin, G. R. (1994). Depressed children and their families. *Clinical Psychology Review, 14,* 39–59.

Kovacs, M. (1989). Affective disorder in children and adolescents. *American Psychologist, 44,* 209–215.

Kovacs, M. (1992). *Children's Depression Inventory Manual.* North Tonawanda: Multi-Health Systems.

Kraepelin, E. (1921). *Manic depressive insanity and paranoia.* Edinburgh: E. & S. Livingstone.

Krasa, N. R., & Tolbert, H. A. (1994). Adolescent bipolar disorder: A nine-year experience. *Journal of Affective Disorders, 30,* 175–184.

Lewinsohn, P. M., Clarke, G. N., Hops, H., & Andrews, J. (1990). Cognitive-behavioral treatment for depressed adolescents. *Behavior Therapy, 21,* 385–401.

Lewinsohn, P. M., Klein, D., & Seeley, J. (1995). Bipolar disorders in a community sample of older adolescents: Prevalence, phenomenology, comorbidity, and course. *Journal of the American Academy of Child and Adolescent Psychiatry, 34,* 454–463.

Liddle, B., & Spence, S. H. (1990). Cognitive-behaviour therapy with depressed primary school children: A cautionary note. *Behavioural Psychotherapy, 18,* 85–102.

Marton, P., Connolly, J., Kutcher, S., & Korenblum, M. (1993). Cognitive social skills and social self-appraisal in depressed adolescents. *Journal of the American Academy of Child and Adolescent Psychiatry, 32,* 739–744.

McCracken, J. T. (1992). The epidemiology of child and adolescent mood disorders. *Child and Adolescent Psychiatric Clinics of North America, 1,* 53–72.

Mufson, L., Moreau, D., Weissman, M. M., & Klerman, G. L. (1993). *Interpersonal psychotherapy for depressed adolescents.* New York: Guilford Press.

Nolen-Hoeksema, S., & Girgus, J. S. (1994). The emergence of gender differences in depression during adolescence. *Psychological Bulletin, 115,* 424–443.

Papatheodorou, G., Kutcher, S. P., Katic, M., & Szalai, J. P. (1995). The efficacy and safety of divalproex sodium in the treatment of acute mania in adolescents and young adults: An open clinical trial. *Journal of Clinical Psychopharmacology, 15,* 110–116.

Petersen, A. C., Compas, B. E., Brooks-Gunn, J., Stemmler, M., Ey, S., & Grant, K. E. (1993). Depression in adolescence. *American Psychologist, 48,* 155–168.

Puig-Antich, J. (1987). Sleep and neuroendocrine correlates of affective illness in childhood and adolescence. *Journal of Adolescent Health Care, 8,* 505–529.

Puig-Antich, J., Kaufman, J., Ryan, N. D., Williamson, D., Dahl, R. E., Lukens, E., Todak, G., Ambrosini, P., Rabinovich, H., & Nelson, B. (1993). The psychosocial functioning and family environment of depressed adolescents. *Journal of the American Academy of Child and Adolescent Psychiatry, 32,* 244–253.

Puig-Antich, J., Perel, J., Lupatkin, W., Chambers, W., Tabrizi, M., King, J., Goetz, R., Davies, M., & Stiller, R. (1987). Imipramine in prepubertal major depressive disorders. *Archives of General Psychiatry, 44,* 81–89.

Quiggle, N. L., Garber, J., Panak, W. F., & Dodge, K. A. (1992). Social information processing in aggressive and depressed children. *Child Development, 63,* 1305–1320.

Reynolds, W. M. (1994). Assessment of depression in children and adolescents by self-report questionnaires. In W. M. Reynolds & H. F. Johnston (Eds.), *Handbook of depression in children and adolescents* (pp. 209–234). New York: Plenum Press.

Reynolds, W. M., & Coates, K. I. (1986). A comparison of cognitive-behavioral therapy and relaxation training for the treatment of depression in adolescents. *Journal of Consulting and Clinical Psychology, 54,* 653–660.

Rosenberg, D. R., Holttum, J., & Gershon, S. (1994). *Textbook of pharmacotherapy for child and adolescent psychiatric disorders.* New York: Brunner/Mazel.

Rudolph, K. D., Hammen, C., & Burge, D. (1994). Interpersonal functioning and depressive symptoms in childhood: Addressing the issues of specificity and comorbidity. *Journal of Abnormal Child Psychology, 22,* 355–371.

Rutter, M. (1986). The developmental psychopathology of depression: Issues and perspectives. In M. Rutter, C. E. Izard, & P. B. Read (Eds.), *Depression in young people: Developmental and clinical perspectives* (pp. 3–30). New York: Guilford Press.

Ryan, N. D. (1992). The pharmacologic treatment

of child and adolescent depression. *Psychiatric Clinics of North America, 15*, 29–40.

Sandler, J., & Joffee, N. G. (1965). Notes on childhood depression. *International Journal of Psychoanalysis, 46*, 88–96.

Schatzberg, A. F., & Nemeroff, C. B. (Eds.). (1995). *Textbook of psychopharmacology*. Washington. DC.: American Psychiatric Press.

Simeon, J., DiNicola, V., Ferguson, H., & Copping, W. (1990). Adolescent depression: A placebo controlled fluoxetine treatment study and follow-up. *Progress in Neuro-psychopharmacology and Biological Psychiatry, 14*, 791–795.

Stark, K. D., Reynolds, W. R., & Kaslow, N. J. (1987). A comparison of the relative efficacy of self-control therapy and a behavioral problem-solving therapy for depression in children. *Journal of Abnormal Child Psychology, 15*, 91–113.

Stark, K. D., Rouse, L. W., & Livingston, R. (1991). Treatment of depression during childhood and adolescence: Cognitive-behavioral procedures for the individual and family. In P. Kendall (Ed.), *Child and adolescent therapy* (pp. 165–206). New York: Guilford Press.

Strober, M., Freeman, R., Rigali, J., Schmidt, S., & Diamond, R. (1992). The pharmacotherapy of depressive illness in adolescents: II. Effects of lithium augmentation in nonresponders to imipramine. *Journal of the American Academy of Child and Adolescent Psychiatry, 31*, 16–20.

Strober, M., Lampert, C., Schmidt, S., & Morrell, W. (1993). The course of major depressive disorder in adolescents: I. Recovery and risk of manic switching in a follow-up of psychotic and nonpsychotic subtypes. *Journal of the American Academy of Child and Adolescent Psychiatry, 32*, 34–42.

Strober, M., Morell, W., Burroughs, J., Lampert, C., Danforth, H., & Freeman, R. (1988). A family study of bipolar I disorder in adolescence: Early onset of symptoms linked to increased familial loading and lithium resistance. *Journal of Affective Disorders, 15*, 255–268.

Strober, M., Schmidt-Lackner, S., Freeman, R., Bower, S., Lampert, C., & DeAntonio, M. (1995). Recovery and relapse in adolescents with bipolar affective illness: A five-year naturalistic, prospective follow-up. *Journal of the American Academy of Child and Adolescent Psychiatry, 34*, 724–731.

Turner, J. E., & Cole, D. A. (1994). Developmental differences in cognitive diatheses for child depression. *Journal of Abnormal Child Psychology, 22*, 15–32.

Varanka, T. M., Weller, R. A., Weller, E. B., & Fristad, M. A. (1988). Lithium treatment of manic episodes with psychotic features in prepubertal children. *American Journal of Psychiatry, 145*, 1557–1559.

Weller, E. B., & Weller R. A. (1991). Mood disorders. In M. Lewis (Ed.), *Child and adolescent psychiatry: A comprehensive textbook* (pp. 646–664). Baltimore: Williams and Wilkins.

Weller, E., Weller, R., & Fristad, M. (1995). Bipolar disorder in children: Misdiagnosis, underdiagnosis, and future directions. *Journal of the American Academy of Child and Adolescent Psychiatry, 34*, 709–714.

World Health Organization. (1992). *ICD-10 classification of mental and behavioral disorders*. Geneva: Author.

14
Anxiety Disorders

Christopher A. Kearney
Diane Wadiak

INTRODUCTION
Historical Perspective

Ever since Hall's (1904) description of adolescence as a period of "storm and stress," clinical researchers have been fascinated by the phenomenon of fear and anxiety disorders in youngsters. Part of this fascination was the basis for some classic, early studies in clinical psychology, including Watson and Rayner's (1920) induction of rodent phobia into Little Albert and Jones's (1924) desensitization of phobia in Peter. Interest in anxious youngsters also helped form the basis for several principles of psychodynamicism. For example, Freud's case of horse phobia in little Hans helped contribute to ideas about projection and other defense mechanisms. Such principles were later extended to other anxiety-related problems, such as "school phobia" (e.g., Johnson, Falstein, Szurek, & Svendsen, 1941).

The reemergence of the behavioral perspective and ego psychology in the 1950s and 1960s was also intimately tied to the study of fear and anxiety in youngsters. For example, Bandura and colleagues' early studies (e.g., 1967) on modeling and phobia in children demonstrated the importance of social learning in this population. Several case studies utilizing desensitization to treat fearful youngsters were also introduced (e.g., Lazarus, Davison, & Polefka, 1965). In addition, Erickson's (1959) psychosocial stages of development were marked by "crises" that had to be resolved to facilitate future development. One important stage was "identity versus identity diffusion" in adolescence. Here, Erickson postulated that adolescents either successfully integrate various self-concepts (e.g., son, student, boyfriend) into a consolidated whole or experience anxiety over diffuse gender and occupational roles. Later theorists (e.g., Marcia, 1980) expanded upon this view, hypothesizing that anxiety in youngsters may result from failures in heterosexual relationships, acceptance of physical changes, development of self-reliance, formation of ethical and religious convictions, and decisions about career goals.

Since 1980, clinical research into childhood fear and anxiety disorders has concentrated on categories listed in the *International Classification of Diseases* (ICD; World Health Organization, 1992) and, especially, the *Diagnostic and Statistical Manual of Mental Disorders* (DSM;

American Psychiatric Association, 1994). Several changes in DSM childhood anxiety disorders categories have taken place since 1980 and are presented in more detail elsewhere (see Kearney & Sims, 1997). Specifically, provisions were made for separation anxiety, avoidant, and overanxious disorder in DSM-III and DSM-III-R. In DSM-IV, however, avoidant disorder was eliminated, and overanxious disorder was integrated into generalized anxiety disorder.

Diagnostic Description

ICD-10 lists several anxiety disorders specific to youngsters. Social anxiety disorder of childhood is characterized by a "wariness of strangers and social apprehension or anxiety when encountering new, strange or socially threatening situations" for at least 4 weeks (WHO, 1994, p. 306). Symptoms include self-consciousness, interference with peer relationships, and positive interactions with persons well known to the child. Phobic anxiety disorder of childhood is characterized by a "persistent or recurrent fear (phobia) that is developmentally phase-appropriate (or was so at the time of onset) but which is abnormal in degree and is associated with significant social impairment" for at least 4 weeks (WHO, 1994, p. 306). In addition, generalized anxiety disorder of childhood is characterized by "extensive anxiety and worry" (WHO, 1994, p. 309) for at least 6 months. Criteria parallel those listed in DSM-IV for generalized anxiety disorder. Other ICD-10 emotional disorders of childhood include sibling rivalry, identity, overanxious, and separation anxiety disorder.

Criteria for separation anxiety disorder in ICD-10 are almost identical to those listed in DSM-IV. In DSM-IV, separation anxiety disorder is defined as developmentally inappropriate and "excessive anxiety concerning separation from home or from those to whom the person is attached" (APA, 1994, p. 110) for at least 4 weeks. Symptoms include worry about potential harm to self or others, school and sleep refusal behavior, avoidance of being left alone, nightmares, somatic complaints, and interference in daily life functioning. Separation anxiety disorder is currently the only DSM anxiety disorder specific to children.

Also in DSM-IV, adult anxiety disorders may be applied to children if appropriate criteria are met. Those that parallel the older categories of avoidant and overanxious disorder are social phobia (social anxiety disorder) and generalized anxiety disorder, respectively. Social phobia is characterized by "marked and persistent fear of social or performance situations in which embarrassment may occur" for at least 6 months (APA, 1994, p. 411). Symptoms in children may include (1) discomfort evidenced by crying or withdrawal, (2) avoidance of social and performance situations, and (3) interference with daily functioning. Generalized anxiety disorder is characterized by "excessive anxiety and worry occurring more days than not . . . about a number of events" for at least 6 months (p. 432). Symptoms in children may include difficulty controlling worry, somatic complaints, and interference in daily functioning.

Other DSM anxiety diagnoses may also be applicable to youngsters. These include (1) panic disorder, or ongoing panic attacks or worry about having an attack; (2) specific phobia, or irrational fear of a specific stimulus; (3) obsessive-compulsive disorder (OCD), or recurrent, bizarre, and anxiety-provoking thoughts with repetitive behaviors performed to reduce their aversiveness; and (4) posttraumatic stress disorder (PTSD), or the reexperience or reenactment of a traumatic event accompanied by physiological arousal and avoidance. In addition, several new DSM anxiety disorders have been delineated, including acute stress disorder, anxiety disorder due to a general medical condition, and substance-induced anxiety disorder. Finally, other diagnoses relevant to anxious youngsters include adjustment disorder with anxiety, as well as several personality disorders (e.g., borderline) with anxiety-related criteria.

Epidemiology

The overall prevalence of anxiety disorders in youngsters is debatable but probably ranges from 9–21% (e.g., Kashani & Orvaschel, 1990). Specific prevalence rates for separation anxiety disorder vary from 3–5% in children and up to 2.4% in adolescents (e.g., Bird et al., 1988). The prevalence of the older DSM categories of avoidant and overanxious disorder has been reported to be about 1% and 4%, respectively (e.g., McGee et al., 1992). Prevalence rates for adult anxiety disorders in children are often disputed, but general figures have been reported for panic disorder (0.6–0.8%), specific phobia (1.3–3.1%), and obsessive-compulsive disorder (0.5–2.0%; Eisen & Kearney, 1995). With respect to posttraumatic stress disorder, occurrence in youngsters is rare except in cases of maltreatment (e.g., Kendall-Tackett, Williams, & Finkelhor, 1993).

Theoretical Etiological Models of Fear and Anxiety Disorders in Youngsters

The etiology of anxiety disorders in youngsters is debatable as well, but contemporary models tend to fall into one of three categories: behavioral, cognitive, and biological. Behavioral models have focused on the learning principles of classical and operant conditioning, as well as observation. With respect to the former, children are thought to develop fear or anxiety disorder by associating neutral with nonneutral stimuli. For example, a child may learn to pair fear with a dog after an aversive experience. Another scenario involves linkage of fear to internal physical sensations, a theory that has been used to explain the etiology of panic disorder (Wolpe & Rowan, 1988).

In addition, children may develop fear and anxiety via reward from others. Parents, for example, often reinforce fears of strangers in their children or inadvertently reward anxious responses with extra attention or privileges. Unfortunately, this operant conditioning model is highly limited in its utility for explaining most types of fear and anxiety. In response, several researchers (Mowrer, 1960) have proposed a two-factor theory for this population. Two-factor theory holds that an anxious reaction is developed through classical conditioning and maintained or reinforced through operant conditioning. However, this theory is based on an intimate association between fear and avoidance, which is not always the case, and it tends to de-emphasize the role of positive reinforcement in the creation of anxiety (Barrios & O'Dell, 1989). In response to this, Delprato and McGlynn (1984) developed their approach-withdrawal theory. Here, fear and avoidance are learned via classical conditioning but maintained by avoidance and a rewarding approach to a nonaversive situation. Unfortunately, these models do not explain how some children develop fear or anxiety without repeated presentations of an aversive stimulus. Instead, social learning and principles related to self-efficacy (Bandura, 1977) likely play a key role in these situations.

Cognitive models of fear and anxiety disorder have become increasingly popular in recent years and are based on the premise that youngsters compare information received from the general environment to existing cognitive structures. Examples include Beck and Emery's (1985) schema theory, Clark's (1986) catastrophic misinterpretation theory, and Reiss's (1991) expectancy-anxiety sensitivity theory. A key characteristic of these theories is that a person develops an anxiety disorder by perceiving anxiety symptoms to be extremely destructive. In essence, normal physiological changes are considered to be aversive or dangerous. A person may then expect negative consequences to follow such symptoms, and therefore avoid situations that cue them. Whether children have the cognitive developmental level (e.g., memory) necessary for these perceptions and expectancies is still debated, however (Nelles & Barlow, 1988).

Finally, several biological variables have been linked to fear and anxiety disorders, although much of this work has been done with adults. Several family and twin studies indicate that genetic factors may be operating in the development of anxiety disorders, especially panic, obsessions, and blood-injury phobia (Torgersen, 1993). Dysfunctions in neurochemical substances such as gamma aminobutyric acid (generalized anxiety), norepinephrine (panic,

PTSD), and serotonin (OCD) have also been implicated. Other potentially important biologically related factors include basal ganglia changes (OCD), hyperventilation syndrome and mitral valve prolapse (panic), preparedness, and behavioral inhibition (see Biederman et al., 1993; Eisen & Kearney, 1995).

ASSESSMENT

The assessment of fear and anxiety disorders in youngsters has received a substantial amount of attention in recent years, and several excellent instruments and techniques have been developed. In this section, we briefly cover those procedures most commonly employed, empirically supported, and clinically useful. These include structured interviews, child self-report measures, parent and teacher rating scales, behavioral observations, physiological assessment, and formal psychological testing.

Structured Interviews

The most common assessment technique in clinical child psychology is, of course, the interview. Problems with unstructured interviews are widely known, and several researchers have therefore developed semistructured or structured interviews for youngsters with fear and anxiety disorders. In almost all cases, these interviews are designed to reflect DSM criteria. The reader is referred elsewhere for a complete description of these interviews (e.g., Silverman, 1994), but major ones include the Schedule for Affective Disorders and Schizophrenia in School-Aged Children (Puig-Antich & Chambers, 1978), the Diagnostic Interview for Children and Adolescents (Herjanic & Reich, 1982), the Child Assessment Schedule (Hodges, McKnew, Cytryn, Stern, & Kline, 1982), the Diagnostic Interview Schedule for Children (Costello, Edelbrock, & Costello, 1985), the Interview Schedule for Children (Kovacs, 1985), and the Child and Adolescent Psychiatric Assessment (Angold et al., in press). These interviews may be generally used for

youngsters ages 6–18 years, and most have child and parent versions to derive composite diagnoses.

The structured interview most commonly used to assess youngsters with fear and anxiety disorders, however, is the Anxiety Disorders Interview Schedule for Children (ADIS-C; Silverman & Nelles, 1988). The ADIS-C was originally designed to solicit information about DSM-III/DSM-III-R anxiety disorders in children and has been subsequently revised to reflect DSM-IV criteria. In the most recent version of the interview, detailed information is also solicited about school refusal behavior, interference in daily functioning, interpersonal relationships, avoided situations, somatic complaints, and individual anxiety symptoms (i.e., type, frequency, intensity; Silverman & Albano, 1996). In the parent version, questions are also asked about externalizing problems (e.g., conduct disorder) and sleep and elimination problems, among others.

Structured interviews for children with anxiety disorders are popular because they supposedly improve assessment consistency across clients and, therefore, reliability estimates. Unfortunately, this is not often the case. Silverman's (1991, 1994) reviews in this area indicate that test-retest (0.10–1.0) and interrater (0.22–1.0) reliabilities for these clinical interviews are highly variable. In general, reliability for the overall presence of an anxiety disorder tends to be much better than for specific syndromes. With respect to individual syndromes, the one most reliably diagnosed tends to be separation anxiety disorder. Overall, reliability seems to improve with the use of inpatient samples, short interview intervals, similar sources of information, and clinicians or raters who are similarly trained. With respect to the validity of these interviews, no definitive conclusions can yet be drawn (Silverman, 1994).

Part of the problem for the variable psychometric strength of clinical interviews may be too rigid a reliance on DSM criteria. As noted elsewhere (e.g., Kearney & Sims, 1997), DSM criteria are often insensitive to developmental considerations. For example, no differentiation is made for childhood versus adolescent versus adult panic disorder, despite their many symptomatological differences. As a result, clinicians may be soliciting a variety of answers to the interview questions or be interpreting ambiguous answers differently. In a related manner, frequent DSM criteria changes for childhood anxiety disorders may also contribute to reliability problems. Finally, mixing different child and parent reports about anxiety symptoms is often poisonous to good reliability (Klein, 1991). To address these problems, it may be necessary to simplify the DSM taxonomy, consider more stable factors such as the function of behavior, or incorporate more dimensional measures into the interview process.

Child Self-Report Measures

Within the past few years, several child self-report measures have been developed that are specific to fear and anxiety symptoms. Some of the most prevalent measures are briefly described here. The most common measure of general fearfulness is the Fear Survey Schedule for Children—Revised (Ollendick, 1983), an 80-item instrument that contains items related to failure and criticism, the unknown, minor injury and small animals, danger and death, and medical fears (Ollendick, King, & Frary, 1989). The Louisville Fear Schedule for Children (Miller, Barrett, Hampe, & Noble, 1972) may also be used to measure fears of animals, physical danger, darkness, public places, and school. A common measure of general anxiety is the Revised Children's Manifest Anxiety Scale (Reynolds & Paget, 1981), a 37-item instrument that assesses four factors: lie, worry/oversensitivity, concentration, and physiological anxiety. In addition, the State-Trait Anxiety Inventory for Children, published by Spielberger (1973), contains two 20-item scales that measure acute and characterological anxiety. In general, the test-retest and inter-rater reliability and concurrent validity of these measures are good, although the discriminative validity of the latter two measures is debatable (James, Reynolds, & Dunbar, 1994).

Other self-report measures have been developed specifically to assess social anxiety. For example, La Greca and Stone (1993) created the Social Anxiety Scale for Children—Revised (SASC-R) to evaluate fear of negative evaluation, social avoidance, and distress. The SASC-R has demonstrated good internal consistency and concurrent validity. In addition, the Social Phobia and Anxiety Inventory (SPAI) has been found to be reliable and valid for use with adolescents (Clark et al., 1994). Factor analyses have confirmed the validity of the SPAI's two factors: social phobia and agoraphobia.

Another specific self-report measure is the Test Anxiety Scale for Children—Revised (TASC-R), a 30-item yes-no instrument that is related to school achievement (Clinkenbeard & Murphy, 1990). However, reliability is only moderate. In addition, the Generalized Anxiety Scale for Children is a 45-item measure of chronic, generalized anxiety (with lie scale) that has shown good test-retest reliability (Witt, Heffer, & Pfieffer, 1990). Finally, the Children's Anxiety Sensitivity Index (CASI) was produced by Silverman, Fleisig, Rabian, and Peterson (1991) to measure the belief that one's anxiety symptoms have negative consequences. The CASI has displayed moderate reliability and validity and appears related to fear, anxiety, and panic.

Other self-report measures may be particularly helpful in measuring the construct of negative affectivity, or the confluence of anxiety and depressive symptoms that is often seen in children. One example is the Negative Affect Self-Statement Questionnaire composed by Ronan, Kendall, and Rowe (1994). Separate versions are available for youngsters ages 7–10 (14 items) and 11–15 (39 items) years. Another example is the Daily Life Stressors Scale, a 30-item measure developed by Kearney, Drabman, and Beasley (1993) to assess regular stressful events as well as symptoms of negative affectivity in children and adolescents. Kearney and Silverman (1993) also designed the School Refusal Assessment Scale to measure the function of school refusal behavior, including the avoidance of stimuli that provoke negative affectivity and escape from aversive social or evaluative situations. Finally, many clinicians who work with children with anxiety problems employ the Children's Depression

Inventory (Kovacs, 1992). The CDI is a 27-item measure of depression experienced within the 2 preceding weeks. Each of these scales has displayed excellent reliability and validity.

More general child self-report measures are also available. For example, Achenbach (1991a) developed the Youth Self-Report (YSR) for persons aged 11–18 years. The YSR is a 118-item measure of internalizing and externalizing problems rated on a 0–2 scale by youngsters. The internalizing scales of somatic complaints and anxious/depressed are most relevant to anxious youngsters, but a gender-specific profile of many different problems can be plotted. The YSR has demonstrated good internal consistency, long-term stability, and content and criterion-related validity. In addition to the YSR, other general scales may be used for anxious children. For example, the Piers-Harris Self-Concept Scale (Piers, 1984) is an 80-item yes-no measure of general self-esteem that contains an anxiety subscale. Also, clinicians may administer any number of personality inventories that contain items relevant to fear and anxiety in different situations. Examples include the Minnesota Multiphasic Personality Inventory—Adolescent Version (Butcher et al., 1992) and the Behavior Assessment System for Children (Reynolds & Kamphaus, 1992), among others (Eisen & Kearney, 1995).

Parent and Teacher Rating Scales

Rating scales are also available for parents and teachers of anxious children. One of the most well-known parent scales is the Child Behavior Checklist (CBCL; Achenbach, 1991b), a 118-item measure of internalizing and externalizing behaviors. Items related to anxiety problems involve fearfulness, nervousness, self-consciousness, and worrying, among others. In addition, related problems may be assessed. For example, the anxious/depressed factor of the CBCL tends to be highly comorbid with attention problems and aggressive and delinquent behavior (McConaughy & Skiba, 1993). Related scales include the Conners Parent Rating Scale (Conners, 1990) and the Quay-Peterson Revised Behavior Problem Checklist (Quay &

Peterson, 1987). A synthesized version of these scales, the ACQ Behavior Checklist, has also been reported (Achenbach, Howell, Quay, & Conners, 1991). All display excellent reliability and validity.

Other parent rating scales that are useful for evaluating anxious children include the Louisville Behavior Check List (Miller, 1967) and the Personality Inventory for Children (Wirt, Lachar, Klinedinst, & Seat, 1984). Both assess anxiety symptoms as well as other dimensions, such as externalizing behavior, affect, and cognitive ability. In addition, family environment and marital functioning are commonly related to anxiety in children. Family environment is often measured via the Family Environment Scale (Moos & Moos, 1986), and the Parental Expectancies Scale has been recently developed to help clinicians identify unreasonable patterns of parental pressure that may be placed on anxious children (Spasaro et al., 1995). Finally, marital satisfaction is often assessed via the Marital Adjustment Scale (Locke & Wallace, 1959) or the Dyadic Adjustment Scale (Spanier, 1976). All display adequate reliability and validity. The reader should also note that parental psychopathology is sometimes related to childhood anxiety disorders and must be assessed carefully.

With respect to teachers, the most common measure is the Teacher Report Form (TRF; Achenbach, 1991c). The TRF is structured like the CBCL and is useful for obtaining a clinical picture of how an anxious child functions in school (e.g., academically, with peers, in performance situations). A related but shorter measure is the Conners Teacher Rating Scale (CTRS; Conners, 1990), in two versions of 28 and 39 items. The psychometric strength of both scales is very good. Teacher measures are sometimes evaluated in conjunction with sociometric measures or peer ratings of a child's behavior.

Behavior Observations

Intense behavioral observations are critical to the assessment of anxious children because of the covert nature of the problem. In addition, social desirability effects inherent in other methods may be more easily controlled in observations. In general, behavioral observations of this population take the form of behavioral approach tests, observational ratings, role-play tests, and self-monitoring. Behavioral approach tests, or BATs, require a child to gradually approach a feared stimulus under the direction and supervision of a therapist. This procedure is particularly useful for children with specific phobia or social or generalized anxiety. The reader is referred to Eisen and Silverman (1991), Evans and Harmon (1981), Kelley (1976), and Matson (1981) for specific examples.

A BAT usually consists of separate 5-minute phases, including adaptation, baseline, walking baseline, the approach itself, and postbaseline. In adaptation, the child is placed in a setting free of distractions and fearful stimuli and allowed to rest and habituate to the surroundings. The baseline period follows and is identical to adaptation except that measures of fear (e.g., heart rate) are taken. Walking baseline is similar to baseline except that the child is asked to walk around the setting. This is done to see if changes in fear measures are due to simple moving around or actual exposure to the fearful stimulus about to be introduced. The fourth phase is the core of the BAT and involves exposure of the fear- or anxiety-provoking stimulus to the child. Examples include taking a test, talking to an unknown person, and walking toward a dog. Preferably, this should continue until fear decreases or for 5 minutes, although some cases may be so severe that only a limited exposure is possible. Finally, postbaseline involves placing the child in the original setting to monitor the length of time needed for a return to the resting state.

These phases are often conducted in analog settings or under simulated conditions (e.g., tape recording of thunder). However, we suggest that naturalistic settings (e.g., school) be used if possible. In many cases, the three major response sets of anxiety (cognitive, behavioral, physiological) are concurrently assessed during this process, which may be conducted at pre- and posttreatment. Although the test is clinically useful and often reliable, its external validity is unclear.

Clinical researchers also employ observational rating systems to measure a broad spectrum of motor behaviors in anxious children. In this method, raters assess a variety of categories indicative of anxiety, including verbalizations, trembling, avoidance, absence of eye contact, and body rigidity (Kendall, 1994). Some well-known examples include the Observer Rating Scale of Anxiety (Melamed & Siegel, 1975), the Behavior Profile Rating Scale (Melamed et al., 1978), the Procedure Behavior Rating Scale (Jay & Elliot, 1984), and the Preschool Observation Scale of Anxiety (Glennon & Weisz, 1978). Behavioral observation scores often distinguish clinical from nonclinical youngsters, but reliability and validity have been established on a preliminary basis only.

Role-play tests require a youngster to respond to an anxiety-provoking event as if the event were actually occurring. This approach is most commonly used for socially anxious children. An example is the Behavioral Assertiveness Test for Children (Bornstein, Bellack, & Hersen, 1977), which involves the videotaping and analysis of children asked to respond to models in simulated social situations. Unfortunately, the psychometric strength of role-play tests for children has not been well supported.

Finally, self-monitoring procedures involve the recording of anxious behavior by the children themselves. Many clinical researchers who work with anxious children utilize diaries to obtain daily information about anxiety and depression intensity, somatic complaints, avoided situations, and the antecedents and consequences of anxious reactions. Beidel, Neal, and Lederer (1991) were among the first to empirically test the daily diary approach and found moderate reliability and validity. Compliance is often problematic, however. Thought-listing and think-aloud procedures may also be added to this category of assessment. Thought-listing involves the self-recording of cognitions surrounding an anxious reaction (Kendall & Chansky, 1991), whereas think-aloud procedures involve the verbalization and audiotaping of cognitions that are later coded into categories (Houston, Fox, & Forbes, 1984). These methods are often hampered, however, by reactivity and cognitive limitations.

Dadds and colleagues (1994) issued several recommendations for future work in this area. Specifically, they suggested that research into behavioral observations be extended to include familial interactions, sequences and duration of anxious behaviors, and threat stimuli. To initiate this process, the authors developed their Family Anxiety Coding Schedule to measure variables such as the positive or negative valence of behavior, reassurance, consequences to anxiety reactions, offered solutions, questions, and affect, among others. The preliminary reliability of this method is excellent, and the tool may allow clinicians to obtain a greater wealth of data than possible with previous methods.

Physiological Assessment

The assessment measures just described are useful for examining cognitive and behavioral components of anxious reactions but are less useful for evaluating physiological components. Because increased physiological arousal is a key characteristic of many anxiety disorders, it should be monitored closely. Unfortunately, the use of physiological indices for anxious children represents a relatively new area of study.

The easiest and most common physiological measures for anxious children are those that evaluate cardiovascular functioning. Heart rate and blood pressure, for example, are practical measures that distinguish anxious from nonanxious children and are sensitive to treatment effects. A good apparatus for measuring heart rate is the Vantage Night Vision ($400; Polar Electro, Port Washington, New York), which includes a rubber strap/transmitter fitted around the chest and a watch on the wrist. Heart rate is automatically recorded, and supporting computer interfacing equipment ($400) and software ($60) are available.

Measures of respiration may also be used in physiological assessment. In addition, blood volume (level of blood in tissue) and blood volume pulse changes (blood flow through tissue

with each heartbeat) can be monitored and seem particularly relevant to fears of blood, tests, and heights. Finally, skin temperature is used to measure the flow of blood to the extremities and can provide an indirect assessment of physiological arousal.

In addition to cardiovascular activity, other bodily systems are relevant to anxious children. For example, the electromyogram may be used to measure electrical activity in tense muscles. Measures of electrodermal skin conductance and resistance, determined by placing electrodes on specific body areas such as the hands, also help to define anxiety via sweat gland activity. Evoked responses following the presentation of an anxiety-provoking stimulus can also be closely watched. In related fashion, sweat indices are available to measure general physiological arousal. A full discussion of the recommended methodology of these measures may be found in reviews by Beidel (1989) and King (1994).

Computerized physiological recording and biofeedback apparati to measure these variables are available through Multi-Health Systems (North Tonawanda, New York) and Lafayette Instrument (Lafayette, Indiana). The former produces surface-mount equipment (i.e., for placement on the person's body), and the latter produces biofeedback software and needed accessories to interface with personal computers. Neither type of equipment requires extensive technical training for usage. However, the cost of these apparati range from $100 to $3600.

Although clinically useful, mixed results have been found regarding the reliability and validity of physiological measures for anxious children. A major threat to the psychometric strength of these measures is artifactual variables such as movement, electrical interference, and temperature (King, 1994). In addition, changes in physiological functioning from treatment are not always related to changes in behavior or thought. The lack of normative data for these measures is also problematic. Given the limited use of these indices as well as their questionable validity, we recommend that clinicians adhere to basic assessments of cardiovascular activity such as heart rate and blood pressure.

Formal Psychological Testing

Formal psychological testing has traditionally held a limited role in the assessment of anxiety disorders in youngsters, but several measures should be considered. Intelligence tests, for example, are useful for ruling out alternative explanations for poor school performance such as learning disabilities or mild mental retardation. In addition, an assessment of a child's cognitive functioning is often critical to making decisions about treatment. For example, knowing that an 11-year-old child possesses excellent memory and abstract thinking abilities may allow a clinician to consider the use of cognitive therapy.

Subtests of intelligence scales may also be useful during behavioral observations. These subtests may act as standardized stimuli that allow therapists to observe children's problem-solving strategies and reactions to psychosocial stressors. In particular, Wechsler performance subscales (see Wechsler, 1989, 1991) such as block and geometric design, animal pegs, and mazes are useful for these purposes. In addition, behavioral observations during intelligence test-taking may indicate whether deficits or differences among verbal and performance subscale scores are simply a function of test anxiety. For example, some children are less anxious and therefore score better on verbal, covert problem-solving tasks than on performance, overt problem-solving tasks.

In addition, projective testing may help youngsters project feelings of frustration, dependency, and abandonment that may otherwise be hidden. Specifically, projective tests such as the Rorschach Inkblot Test or the Thematic Apperception Test may be clinically useful when speaking to depressed clients or those overly concerned with social desirability. Perhaps the most useful aspect of these tests, however, is their rapport-building quality. The ambiguous and nonthreatening nature of projective tests is sometimes helpful with clients who are initially resistant or hostile (see Finch & Politano, 1994).

TREATMENT

The treatment of anxiety disorders in youngsters can involve a great many techniques and procedures. Therefore, only those most commonly used and empirically supported are presented here. We divide treatments into four basic categories: behavioral, cognitive, pharmacological, and parent- and family-oriented.

Behavioral Treatments

Behavioral approaches to treating anxiety disorders in youngsters concentrate on overt symptoms such as avoidance or inappropriate social behaviors. Behavioral approaches most pertinent to the treatment of anxiety disorders include systematic desensitization, implosion and flooding, interoceptive exposure, response prevention, and modeling.

Systematic desensitization (Wolpe, 1982) is often thought of as a three-step process and is most useful for reducing phobias of specific objects or situations. The technique is based on classical conditioning and involves gradual approach toward an aversive stimulus while simultaneously practicing some incompatible response. Common examples of incompatible responses include anger, laughter, and relaxation. Relaxation training is a common first step in systematic desensitization and usually requires a client to tense and release various muscle groups. Several protocols for this are available (see Ollendick & Cerny, 1981). In most cases, the person begins by tensing his or her hands and holding tight for a few seconds before releasing quickly. A concentration on the difference between tension and relaxation is emphasized. Tension and release are then spread to other areas of the body, including arms, neck, shoulders, face, stomach, legs, and feet. Particular attention should be paid to body areas that are problematic in stressful situations.

The second step in systematic desensitization involves the construction of an anxiety hierarchy. An anxiety hierarchy is a list of usually 5–10 items about an aversive stimulus that are ranked from least to most anxiety-provoking. For example, a child afraid of dogs might list "seeing films of dogs" as number six on his or her anxiety hierarchy, followed by increasingly difficult items such as "being in a pet store," "walking in a neighborhood where dogs might be," "peering over a fence at a dog," "seeing a leashed dog 10 feet away," and "petting a dog." Therapists must be careful not to form items that are too far apart in difficulty level, and intermediate steps may need to be added if a child is unable to progress easily from one item to the next.

The final step in systematic desensitization involves pairing relaxation with each successive step on the anxiety hierarchy. Such pairing may be done via imagination first and later in real-life or in vivo situations. In general, mildly to moderately anxiety-provoking items are desensitized first to give the child a sense of self-efficacy and to prepare him or her for more fearful stimuli. At each step, the child is informed about the upcoming procedure and allowed to terminate the exposure should it become too aversive. In many cases, desensitization is paired with modeling, cognitive procedures, or coping skills to enhance the therapeutic effect. Desensitization is effective for treating a variety of fears and is one of the most commonly used therapy techniques for anxious children.

Implosive therapy and flooding are related to systematic desensitization but rely more on the process of extinction (Marks, 1975; Stampfl & Levis, 1967). In essence, a fearful child is exposed to the most aversive object or situation first. Such exposure may be imaginal (implosion) or in vivo (flooding) and is often valuable if time constraints are an issue. The person engages in this exposure until habituation, or lessened fear and anxiety, occur. Several cautions must be voiced about this procedure, however. For example, we do not recommend the approach for children under age 7 years, in cases where the fear is extreme or diffuse,

if the risk of sensitization is at least moderate, and if prior implosion or flooding methods were unsuccessful. Little research has been done regarding these procedures with children, although some reports are available about their efficacy for youngsters with PTSD or school refusal behavior (Eisen & Kearney, 1995).

Interoceptive exposure is a relatively new behavioral approach to treating anxiety disorders in general and panic disorder in particular. This approach is best for persons who have paired fear and anxiety with internal sensations such as hyperventilation, dizziness, rapid heartbeat, and hot flushes, among others. In essence, a person afraid of a specific physical symptom is asked to engage in some procedure that will elicit the symptom. Relaxation training or some other agent (e.g., drug) can then be administered. For example, a person overconcerned about shortness of breath may be asked to breathe through a small straw for 60 seconds and then to practice relaxation. A full description of these procedures is available from Craske and Barlow (1990). The reader should note that this procedure has been utilized extensively with adults but not with youngsters, and caution should therefore be employed.

Response prevention is a behavioral technique most often associated with the treatment of obsessive-compulsive disorder. This procedure is generally introduced following some exposure to a "contaminant" or stimulus that provokes an anxious response. Following the exposure, the client is instructed not to engage in any activity (i.e., a compulsion) typically used to reduce anxiety. For example, a person who compulsively washes his or her hands may be required to dirty his or her hands and not wash. Clients may also be restrained from other behaviors such as checking. In many cases, the therapist will need to enlist the support and supervision of family members and friends. The use of response prevention is very effective in treating obsessive-compulsive disorder (e.g., Kearney & Silverman, 1990), and the reader is referred to Riggs and Foa (1993) for a detailed description of the procedure.

Finally, modeling is another common behavioral method of treating fear and anxiety disorders in youngsters. Modeling essentially refers to learning by observation or imitation, and various types of therapeutic modeling can be used. These types include (1) imaginal/covert, or imagining a peer or other who is positively interacting with an aversive stimulus, (2) symbolic, or viewing films that depict peers or others who are positively interacting with an aversive stimulus, and (3) live/participant, or direct observation of peers or others who are positively interacting with an aversive stimulus. These procedures are cost-effective and efficacious with children with phobias over a long period of time. Positive treatment outcome seems particularly related to the client's increased age, resemblance to the model, and low defensiveness (Barrios & O'Dell, 1989).

Modeling may also be used to build social skills that are often deficient in anxious children. Common targets for socially anxious youngsters include assertiveness, eye contact, facial expression, interruptions, appropriate verbalizations, and voice control, among others. Here, a child is usually asked to watch others engage in low-level tasks such as conversations or high-level tasks such as oral presentations. Following this procedure, the child is asked to attempt the task on his or her own. Afterward, the therapist provides detailed feedback as well as reinforcement for effort and appropriate responses. This cycle is repeated continuously until the child is proficient. Then, real-life practice exercises are assigned (Cartledge & Milburn, 1995). These may include situations such as public speaking, approaching others, dating, and nonverbal interaction, among others. Modeling appears best for specific phobias and social anxiety but may serve as a useful adjunct for treating OCD, PTSD, and panic disorder.

Cognitive Treatments

Cognitive treatments of fear and anxiety disorders in youngsters are often employed in addition to behavioral approaches. In many cases, cognitive treatment involves teaching a client coping strategies to identify and alter negative thinking patterns or to replace the patterns with more adaptive cognitions. Several methods have been developed to accomplish this process, including examination of evidence, decatastrophizing and decentering, looking at alternatives and cognitive rehearsal, and cognitive self-control programs. We discuss these briefly with cautions regarding their use with children and adolescents.

Children with anxiety disorders often have thoughts about events that are somewhat irrational in nature. The reader is referred elsewhere for a complete listing of different types of irrational thoughts (e.g., Haaga & Davison, 1986). A common cognitive distortion is arbitrary inference or "jumping to conclusions," in which youngsters form a negative conclusion about an event without supporting evidence. For example, an older child may be convinced that his parents will get into a severe car accident should they leave to go out for dinner. In the "What is the Evidence?" technique developed by Beck and his colleagues (1979, 1985), clients are required to list the evidence for and against the dire consequences they believe will occur. In the example presented here, the child would be asked to list all of the car accidents his parents have been in and what damage occurred, as well as evidence against the possibility and severity of the event. Assuming the evidence against highly outweighs the evidence for, the client should give a realistic probability of the event occurring (e.g., 5%) and test the probability against upcoming events. This technique is useful for youngsters with anxious apprehension about events like separation.

In related fashion, the therapist may also implement decatastrophization, or an illustration that even the most dire outcomes do not imply complete disaster. For example, many persons who experience panic attacks misinterpret the symptoms as overly dangerous. In decatastrophization (or the "What if" technique; Beck et al., 1979, 1985), the therapist challenges the client to design the "worst-case" scenario to a proposed situation and identify the "true" source of anxious apprehension, which is often not as harmful as the client originally thought.

For example, a therapist might ask about the worst consequences of experiencing dizziness and hyperventilation in a department store. The client may then state that having to suddenly escape the building might be embarrassing because everyone would stare and laugh. In addition to examining the evidence for and against this scenario (e.g., are the symptoms and escape actually noticeable to others?), the therapist can point out to the client that his or her focus of fear might be more the act of leaving the store than the actual physical symptoms.

The therapist may also employ decentering, which requires the client to assess whether he or she observes others with the same attention to detail that he or she assumes others apply to them. For example, clients who are afraid to eat in public places are sometimes convinced that others are closely watching their eating habits. However, these same clients often don't apply the same assumed practice in their own behavior; that is, they rarely watch others with such intensity. Such a contradiction should be pointed out in different situations. Decatastrophizing and decentering may best be used with persons who experience panic attacks and social anxiety.

Following a continually successful pattern of examining one's cognitions and identifying maladaptive patterns, a client may be asked to implement alternative and more positive ways of thinking. Specifically, the therapist should help the client develop coping thoughts or strategies to use in a given situation, positive self-statements that can be used in time of stress (e.g., "I can do this"), and solutions to common problems that arise in the client's life. Such procedures can be readily combined with behavioral treatments like exposure. With practice, the client should be able to develop coping, self-statement, and problem-solving strategies on his or her own in response to hypothetical scenarios posed by the therapist or real-life circumstances. This process is sometimes referred to as cognitive rehearsal.

Comprehensive cognitive therapies for youngsters have been recently refined by several prominent researchers (e.g., Kendall et al., 1992; Silverman, 1989). In a cognitive self-control procedure, youngsters are instructed to monitor their own thoughts and related affect, to use self-statements to control anxious apprehension, to assess their own performance in more positive terms, and to reinforce themselves for the successful use of these procedures. In Kendall et al.'s (1992) FEAR program, for example, youngsters are required to monitor symptoms of anxiety and fear (**F**), identify expectations (**E**) or worries that negative consequences will occur, employ appropriate actions and attitudes (**A**) in the anxiety-provoking situation, and evaluate the results and reward (**R**) themselves accordingly. This approach has been utilized as part of an integrated protocol to successfully treat clinically anxious youngsters (Kendall, 1994). Cognitive coping procedures and positive self-statements have also been successfully used as part of a multicomponent treatment program for adolescents with panic disorder and social phobia (Albano et al., 1995; Ollendick, 1995).

The use of cognitive procedures with this population will undoubtedly enjoy more substantial attention in the future, but clinicians should be aware of certain limitations. For example, the therapy components described in this section require a specific cognitive developmental level and accompanying ability to verbalize different thoughts and feelings. In addition, adequate memory, reasoning, attention, and comprehension are required. As a result, cognitive procedures may be more useful for adolescents than children, who may require more behaviorally or family-oriented treatment approaches.

Pharmacological Treatments

In addition to psychological therapies, various pharmacological treatments have emerged to address fear and anxiety disorders in youngsters. The reader should note, however, that pharmacotherapies are usually empirically tested against a drug placebo and not against psychosocial treatment. Indeed, the need is acute for studies that compare pharmacotherapy with psychotherapy. In this section, we summarize the evidence for leading pharmacological agents for childhood anxiety disorders.

Antidepressant medication has been an integral aspect of treatment in this area. These agents influence the reuptake and general metabolism of various neurotransmitters, in particular increasing levels of norepinephrine (e.g., desipramine) and serotonin (e.g., fluoxetine). Some of the earliest drug trials in this area were conducted with children with separation anxiety disorder and "school phobia" (e.g., Gittelman-Klein & Klein, 1971, 1973). In these studies, increased levels of imipramine were linked to significantly reduced somatic complaints, fear, and anxiety. However, later work with antidepressants produced more mixed results. For example, some investigators found that the antidepressants clomipramine and imipramine worked equally well as placebo in treating children with separation anxiety disorder (Berney et al., 1981; Klein, Koplewicz, & Kanner, 1992). Other researchers, however, found some improvement in clinician ratings using imipramine (Bernstein, Garfinkel, & Borchardt, 1990). At this point, definitive conclusions cannot yet be made regarding the efficacy of antidepressant medication for these childhood anxiety problems.

Antidepressant medications have also been used to treat obsessive-compulsive disorder in youngsters. For example, clomipramine has been found to be effective compared to placebo in several investigations (e.g., DeVeaugh-Geiss et al., 1992; Flament et al., 1985; Leonard et al., 1989). In addition, fluoxetine and fluvoxamine have been found to help reduce OCD symptoms in combination with psychosocial treatment or other drugs (e.g., Apter et al., 1994; Riddle et al., 1992; Simeon, Thatte, & Wiggins, 1990). Efficacy may be limited, however, by the presence of comorbid conditions such as eating or personality disorders. Fluoxetine has also been found to be effective for children with general anxiety, social phobia, and separation anxiety disorder (Birmaher et al., 1994).

The use of antidepressant medication to treat childhood anxiety disorders continues to draw attention, but some cautions should be noted. First, side effects may be present to a significant degree in some youngsters. These include tachycardia, hypertension, dry mouth, dizziness, drowsiness, blurred vision, seizures, and constipation, among others (Simeon & Wiggins, 1995). Second, dosage levels must be carefully monitored because of vastly different absorption and metabolic rates in youngsters. In general, recommended daily dosage levels for tricyclic antidepressants range from 10–25 milligrams (in 3–5 mg/kg divided doses), with a maximum medication regimen of six months. For fluoxetine, an initial dose range of 0.5–1.0 mg/kg has been suggested (Simeon & Wiggins, 1995). In cases where drug therapy is utilized, we recommend concurrent psychosocial treatment to boost therapeutic efficacy, address related conditions, and monitor compliance.

In addition to antidepressants, anxiolytic medications have become more commonly used to treat anxious youngsters. The most popular have been alprazolam, clonazepam, and buspirone, which affect gamma aminobutyric acid or dopamine receptors, but studies regarding their efficacy are either mixed or preliminary. For example, positive treatment effects for alprazolam have been found to be mild (Simeon & Ferguson, 1987) or no different from placebo (Simeon et al., 1992) in the treatment of youngsters with overanxious or avoidant disorder. The use of clonazepam has enjoyed more support, particularly in the treatment of panic (e.g., Kutcher & MacKenzie, 1988). In addition, Leonard and her colleagues (1994) suggested that the combined use of fluoxetine and clonazepam may be effective in treating childhood-onset obsessive-compulsive disorder. However, one controlled investigation has not supported the use of clonazepam for separation anxiety and other disorders (Graae, Milner, Rizzotto, & Klein, 1994). Finally, only preliminary evidence is available to suggest that buspirone is effective for treating generalized anxiety (e.g., Kutcher, Reiter, Gardner, & Klein, 1992).

Although the use of anxiolytics to treat childhood anxiety disorders is becoming more popular, the reader should note that several side effects may occur. These include aggravation of impulsivity and aggression, drowsiness, and ataxia, among others. Initial dosage levels for alprazolam (0.25–0.50 mg; Simeon et al., 1992), clonazepam (0.5–2.0 mg; Graae et al., 1994), and buspirone (10–40 mg; Simeon, 1991) have been reported in the literature. In general, should anxiolytic treatment be used, investigators in the area recommend a maximum regimen of four months and concurrent treatment with psychosocial therapies (Simeon & Wiggins, 1995).

Overall, pharmacological treatments for childhood anxiety disorders have produced only fair results except for obsessive-compulsive disorder. As a result, clinicians should use extreme caution when considering these agents, and researchers should devote more attention to the study of their efficacy on a larger scale. We recommend that drug therapy be considered as a primary treatment for childhood anxiety only under certain conditions. These conditions include extremely severe symptomatology, long-term chronicity of the disorder, history of resistance to psychological intervention, and lack of significant comorbidity (Reiter, Kutcher, & Gardner, 1992).

Parent- and Family-Oriented Treatments

In the preceding three sections, we described treatments for anxious children that concentrate on the youngsters themselves. However, there are many cases when the therapist must include family members and others to successfully resolve a fear or anxiety problem. In this section, we cover parent- and family-oriented techniques that are most pertinent to this population. Specifically, we discuss contingency management, contracting, paradoxical treatment, and communication skills and problem-solving training. The reader should note, however, that empirical data are only preliminary regarding many of these procedures for anxious children. As a result, great care should be taken when implementing them in treatment.

In some cases involving anxious youngsters, parents can be the main focus of treatment. Parent training for this population is pertinent when (1) externalizing problems such as noncompliance are comorbid with the child's anxiety, (2) children are modeling fearful or anxious reactions from their parents, (3) parents are intentionally or inadvertently reinforcing fear or anxiety in their children, and/or (4) support for the child and his or her motivation are at issue. The various components of parent training in general and contingency management in particular are fully described elsewhere (e.g., Barkley, 1989; Eisen & Kearney, 1995; Forehand & McMahon, 1981), but are briefly outlined here.

Therapists who engage in parent training to treat anxious youngsters should probably concentrate first on enhancing parental attention. Because parents are often not good monitors of their children's behavior, detailed and daily diaries should be kept about salient child behaviors and verbalized thoughts and feelings. Subsequently, parents should be taught to give clear and simple commands to their children. In particular, parents should refrain from commands (1) in the form of questions, criticism, or sarcasm, and (2) that increase childhood anxiety and dependence. Instead, commands should be short, concise, and at least partially oriented toward fulfilling the goals of treatment (e.g., identifying negative thoughts, reducing avoidance of feared situations).

In related fashion, parents should be instructed to reinforce behaviors incompatible with childhood fear and anxiety. Examples include approach toward social settings, adaptive verbal behaviors, and relaxation. Conversely, excessive behavior such as somatic complaints, reassurance-seeking, and tantrums should be ignored, especially if attention is a primary motivating variable. Following the successful practice of this approach, parents can help shape a child's behavior toward more difficult goals (e.g., petting a dog, going to school). Positive or negative contingencies for successful or failed goal attainment, respectively, should also be established. Positive contingencies can be set up in a daily or weekly token economy, whereas negative contingencies could include time-out or revocation of privileges among others.

Family-oriented treatment approaches are also useful for many anxious children, especially when broader issues such as conflict are relevant. In our clinical practice with youngsters with school refusal behavior, for example, contingency contracting is commonly used. Contracting involves the negotiation of some formal, written agreement among family members about a given issue, such as school attendance or excessive reassurance-seeking. The first step is to define one current problem as specifically as possible. During this initial process, the use of reframing may facilitate communication and help define problems in a positive manner. Then, family members (e.g., parents and child) may be separated so that the therapist can shuttle back and forth with proposed solutions. When the negotiation process is complete and all parties have agreed to a solution, the contract is drawn. All family members are asked to read and sign the contract daily for its duration, which should not be longer than a few days. At subsequent therapy sessions, contracts should be examined for adherence, contribution to treatment, and potential modification toward increased difficulty and detail. This therapeutic technique is particularly useful for conflictive and detached families.

Paradoxical treatments are sometimes useful if a child's anxious behavior is embedded in certain family processes that serve to maintain the behavior. For example, a child may show excessive separation anxiety to shift parental attention toward himself or herself and away from marital conflict. In this case, the therapist might ask the child to increase overt symptoms (e.g., tantrums) to make clear to the parents the purpose of the behavior. Paradoxical techniques include symptom prescription, paradoxical intention, and paradoxical letters (see Weeks & L'Abate, 1982), but these should be used only if the therapist has good rapport and is quite comfortable with the family.

Communication skills and problem-solving training may be employed when families experience considerable difficulty interacting or resolving ongoing disputes. These approaches can often be implemented in the context of the cognitive and behavioral treatments mentioned earlier. For example, modeling and role play of appropriate familial interactions can parallel a child's imitation of a model. In addition, cognitive restructuring to decrease "mindreading" for the entire family can parallel a child's identification and alteration of negative thinking patterns. Communication skills and problem-solving training can also be used to modify poor speaking and listening skills, clarify messages between parties, and develop realistic solutions without fear of retribution. Specific protocols for these approaches are available (e.g., Bornstein & Bornstein, 1986). Overall, therapists should consider the treatment of families of anxious children in many cases, particularly those involving comorbidity, enmeshment, detachment, and persistent conflict.

COMMENTS

The study of fear and anxiety disorders in children and adolescents continues to represent a fascinating and fruitful but fickle area. Our knowledge of what causes these problems, how to classify them, and which methods of assessment and treatment to use has grown tremendously in the past several years. However, the reader should be aware of several cautions when addressing this population. We briefly address some of these here, with a particular focus on the theme of future integration.

With respect to etiology, it is important to point out that traditional views, by themselves, are probably inadequate for explaining most cases of fear and anxiety. Past theorists have often clung tightly to one perspective (e.g., psychosocial, neuroscientific) without much regard to others. However, growing evidence indicates that changes in cognitions and behavior often create substantial effects on neurobiological processes and genetic expression (Barlow, 1994). Conversely, of course, changes in physical functioning influence thinking patterns and overt behavior. Because the field of clinical psychology is migrating toward an integration of perspectives to explain most mental disorders, we recommend that clinicians and researchers adopt a similar approach for children with fear and anxiety problems. Specifically, the interaction of biological predispositions, psychological vulnerabilities, environmental stressors, sociocultural demands, familial variables, and proximal functional influences must be considered (see Albano, Chorpita, & Barlow, 1996, for initial integrative models of childhood anxiety).

With respect to classification, a major roadblock to fully understanding youngsters with fear and anxiety disorders has been a strict dichotomy between categorical and dimensional approaches. Clinicians have typically adhered to the ICD and DSM classification systems despite ongoing changes and drawbacks (e.g., vague criteria, questionable reliability and validity, stigmatization). However, dimensional approaches can also be faulted for inconsistent usage among clinicians, significant comorbidity, and poor linkage to treatment. As a result, some clinical researchers have suggested an amalgamation of the best features of both taxonomic approaches. Indeed, the DSM and other nosological systems now incorporate some dimensional components. Prototypes of a categorical-dimensional approach have been presented elsewhere for anxious children (see Kearney & Sims, 1997), and these may help to improve the flexibility, psychometric strength, and clinical utility of taxonomies for this population.

With respect to assessment, a burgeoning literature has been developed regarding the evaluation of youngsters with fear and anxiety disorders. Still, some key issues remain. First, although reliability and validity have been well established for some assessment measures, a great deal of work remains for others. A related problem is the high correlation between measures of anxiety and depression in youngsters. Second, many assessment procedures for anxious children lack an emphasis on developmental differences that may be important for treatment. Third, clinicians have a tendency to adhere to one set of assessment techniques (e.g., behavioral) without employing others (e.g., physiological) that may be just as crucial. Fourth, informant variance, or discrepancies in information across sources (e.g., parents, child), is endemic to this population. As a result of these issues, we recommend that clinicians employ an integrative, multimethod, multisource assessment approach to fully examine behavioral, cognitive, and physiological aspects of anxiety in children.

Finally, with respect to treatment, clinical researchers must be sensitive to different factors that influence therapeutic effectiveness for anxious youngsters. For example, to address the many factors that cause and maintain childhood anxiety disorders, clinicians should be prepared to employ a variety of treatment procedures for a particular case. Specifically, practitioners and researchers should be more sensitive to a prescriptive approach, where one of several treatment options is tailored to an individual client (see Kearney, Eisen, & Schaefer, 1995). Second, the rift between clinicians and researchers must be mended so that effective psychotherapies are disseminated widely. This "communication gap" is also pertinent to managed care and the possibility that any national health care policy could favor pharmacological agents over equally effective psychosocial therapies (see American Academy of Child and Adolescent Psychiatry practice parameters, 1993; Barlow, 1994). Third, it is clear that not all youngsters have adequate access to psychological or pharmacological treatment. This is particularly true of minority populations who, for a variety of reasons, may not be referred to specialized anxiety disorder clinics. Finally, our knowledge is limited about many of our psychological therapies, including differential gender influences, improvements in positive functioning, and long-term outcome, among others. These areas must be studied further.

The study of anxiety disorders in children and adolescents is truly a rewarding but challenging endeavor. We have outlined some of the major perspectives, techniques, procedures, and issues relevant to anxious children, but the reader is encouraged to go beyond this chapter and delve into the many intricacies that mark this population. Because so much attention has focused on other areas of clinical child psychology (e.g., hyperactivity) for so long, a full understanding of childhood anxiety disorders remains elusive. We therefore encourage our readers to be sensitive about recognizing fear and anxiety in children and to be innovative when addressing this population.

REFERENCES

Achenbach, T. M. (1991a). *Manual for the Youth Self-Report and 1991 profile*. Burlington: University of Vermont, Department of Psychiatry.

Achenbach, T. M. (1991b). *Manual for the Child Behavior Checklist/4–18 and 1991 profile*. Burlington: University of Vermont, Department of Psychiatry.

Achenbach, T. M. (1991c). *Manual for the Teacher's Report Form and 1991 profile*. Burlington: University of Vermont, Department of Psychiatry.

*Achenbach, T. M., Howell, C. T., Quay, H. C., & Conners, C. K. (1991). National survey of problems and competencies among four- to sixteen-year-olds. *Monographs of the Society for Research in Child Development*, 56, Serial N. 255.

Albano, A. M., Chorpita, B. F., & Barlow, D. H. (1996). Childhood anxiety disorders. In E. J. Mash & R. A. Barkley (Eds.), *Child psychopathology* (pp. 196–241). New York: Guilford Press.

Albano, A. M., Marten, P. A., Holt, C. S., Heimberg, R. G., & Barlow, D. H. (1995). Cognitive-behavioral group treatment for social phobia in adolescents: A preliminary study. *Journal of Nervous and Mental Disease*, 183, 649–656.

American Academy of Child and Adolescent Psychiatry. (1993). Practice parameters for the assessment and treatment of anxiety disorders. *Journal of the American Academy of Child and Adolescent Psychiatry*, 32, 1089–1098.

*American Psychiatric Association. (1994). *Diagnostic and statistical manual of mental disorders* (4th ed.). Washington, DC: Author.

Angold, A., Prendergast, M., Cox, A., Harrington, R., Simonoff, E., & Rutter, M. (in press). The Child and Adolescent Psychiatric Assessment (CAPA). *Psychological Medicine*.

Apter, A., Ratzoni, G., King, R. A., Weizman, A., Iancu, I., Binder, M., & Riddle, M. A. (1994). Fluvoxamine open-label treatment of adolescent inpatients with obsessive-compulsive disorder or depression. *Journal of the American Academy of Child and Adolescent Psychiatry*, 33, 342–348.

Bandura, A. (1977). Self-efficacy: Toward a unifying theory of behavioral change. *Psychological Review*, 84, 191–215.

Bandura, A., Grusec, J. E., & Menlove, F. L. (1967). Vicarious extinction of avoidance behavior. *Journal of Personality and Social Psychology*, 5, 16–23.

Barkley, R. A. (1989). Attention-deficit hyperactivity disorder. In E. J. Mash & R. A. Barkley (Eds.), *Treatment of childhood disorders* (pp. 39–72). New York: Guilford Press.

Barlow, D. H. (1994). Psychological interventions in the era of managed competition. *Clinical Psychology: Science and Practice*, 1, 109–122.

*Barrios, B. A., & O'Dell, S. L. (1989). Fears and anxieties. In E. J. Mash & R. A. Barkley (Eds.), *Treatment of childhood disorders* (pp. 167–221). New York: Guilford Press.

*Beck, A. T., & Emery, G. (1985). *Anxiety disorders and phobias: A cognitive perspective*. New York: Basic Books.

Beck, A. T., Rush, A. J., Shaw, B. F., & Emery, G. (1979). *Cognitive therapy of depression*. New York: Guilford Press.

*Beidel, D. C. (1989). Assessing anxious emotions: A review of psychophysiological assessment in children. *Clinical Psychology Review*, 9, 717–736.

Beidel, D. C., Neal, A. M., & Lederer, A. S. (1991). The feasibility and validity of a daily diary for the assessment of anxiety in children. *Behavior Therapy*, 22, 505–517.

Berney, T., Kolvin, I., Bhate, S. R., Garside, R. F., Jeans, J., Kay, B., & Scarth, L. (1981). School phobia: A therapeutic trial with clomipramine and short-term outcome. *British Journal of Psychiatry*, 138, 110–118.

Bernstein, G. A., Garfinkel, B. D., & Borchardt, C. M. (1990). Comparative studies of pharmacotherapy for school refusal. *Journal of the American Academy of Child and Adolescent Psychiatry*, 29, 773–781.

Biederman, J., Rosenbaum, J. F., Bolduc-Murphy, E. A., Faraone, S., Chaloff, J., Hirshfeld, D. R., & Kagan, J. (1993). Behavioral inhibition as a temperamental risk factor for anxiety disorders. *Child and Adolescent Psychiatric Clinics of North America*, 2, 667–684.

Bird, H. R., Canino, G., Rubio-Stipec, M., Gould, M. S., Ribera, J., Sesman, M., Woodbury, M., Huertas-Goldman, S., Pagan, A., Sanchez-Lacay, A., & Moscoso, M. (1988). Estimates of the prevalence of childhood malajustment in a community survey in Puerto Rico: The use of combined measures. *Archives of General Psychiatry, 45*, 1120–1126.

Birmaher, B., Waterman, G. S., Ryan, N., Cully, M., Balach, L., Ingram, J., & Brodsky, M. (1994). Fluoxetine for childhood anxiety disorders. *Journal of the American Academy of Child and Adolescent Psychiatry, 33*, 993–999.

Bornstein, M. R., Bellack, A. S., & Hersen, M. (1977). Social skills training for unassertive children: A multiple-baseline analysis. *Journal of Applied Behavior Analysis, 10*, 183–195.

Bornstein, P. H., & Bornstein, M. T. (1986). *Marital therapy: A behavioral-communications approach.* New York: Pergamon.

Butcher, J. N., Williams, C. L., Graham, J. R., Archer, R. P., Tellegen, A., Ben-Porath, Y. S., & Kaemmer, B. (1992). *Minnesota Multiphasic Personality Inventory—Adolescent manual.* Minneapolis: University of Minnesota Press.

Cartledge, G., & Milburn, J. F. (1995). *Teaching social skills to children and youth: Innovative approaches* (3rd ed.). Boston: Allyn and Bacon.

Clark, D. B., Turner, S. M., Beidel, D. C., Donovan, J. E., Kirisci, L., & Jacob, R. G. (1994). Reliability and validity of the Social Phobia and Anxiety Inventory for adolescents. *Psychological Assessment, 6*, 135–140.

Clark, D. M. (1986). A cognitive approach to panic. *Behavior Research and Therapy, 24*, 461–470.

Clinkenbeard, P. R., & Murphy, S. C. (1990). Measuring student motivation. In C. R. Reynolds & R. W. Kamphaus (Eds.), *Handbook of psychological and educational assessment of children* (pp. 589–605). New York: Guilford Press.

Conners, C. K. (1990). *Conners' Rating Scales manual.* North Tonawanda, NY: Multi-Health Systems.

Costello, E. J., Edelbrock, C. S., & Costello, A. J. (1985). Validity of the NIMH diagnostic interview for children: A comparison between psychiatric and pediatric referrals. *Journal of Abnormal Child Psychology, 13*, 579–595.

*Craske, M. G., & Barlow, D. H. (1990). *Therapist's guide for the mastery of your anxiety and panic.* Albany: Graywind.

*Dadds, M. R., Rapee, R. M., & Barrett, P. M. (1994). Behavioral observation. In T. H. Ollendick, N. J. King, & W. Yule (Eds.), *International handbook of phobic and anxiety disorders in children and adolescents* (pp. 349–364). New York: Plenum Press.

Delprato, D. J., & McGlynn, F. D. (1984). Behavioral

theories of anxiety disorders. In S. M. Turner (Ed.), *Behavioral treatment of anxiety disorders* (pp. 63–122). New York: Plenum Press.

DeVeaugh-Geiss, J., Moroz, G., Biederman, J., Cantwell, D., Fontaine, R., Griest, J. H., Reichler, R., Katz, R., & Landau, P. (1992). Clomipramine hydrochloride in childhood and adolescent obsessive-compulsive disorder: A multicenter trial. *Journal of the American Academy of Child and Adolescent Psychiatry, 31*, 45–49.

*Eisen, A. R., & Kearney, C. A. (1995). *Practitioner's guide to treating fear and anxiety in children and adolescents: A cognitive-behavioral approach.* Northvale, NJ: Jason Aronson.

Eisen, A. R., & Silverman, W. K. (1991). Treatment of an adolescent with bowel movement phobia using self-control therapy. *Journal of Behavior Therapy and Experimental Psychiatry, 22*, 45–51.

Erickson, E. H. (1959). *Identity and the life cycle.* New York: International Universities Press.

Evans, P. D., & Harmon, G. (1981). Children's self-initiated approach to spiders. *Behaviour Research and Therapy, 19*, 543–546.

Finch, A. J., & Politano, P. M. (1994). Projective techniques. In T. H. Ollendick, N. J. King, & W. Yule (Eds.), *International handbook of phobic and anxiety disorders in children and adolescents* (pp. 381–393). New York: Plenum Press.

Flament, M., Rapoport, J. L., Berg, C. J., Sceery, W., Kilts, C., Mellstrom, B., & Linnoila, M. (1985). Clomipramine treatment of childhood obsessive-compulsive disorder: A double-blind controlled study. *Archives of General Psychiatry, 42*, 977–983.

Forehand, R. L., & McMahon, R. J. (1981). *Helping the noncompliant child: A clinician's guide to parent training.* New York: Guilford Press.

Gittelman-Klein, R., & Klein, D. F. (1971). Controlled imipramine treatment of school phobia. *Archives of General Psychiatry, 25*, 204–207.

Gittelman-Klein, R. G., & Klein, D. F. (1973). School phobia: Diagnostic considerations in light of imipramine effects. *Journal of Nervous and Mental Disease, 156*, 199–215.

Glennon, B., & Weisz, J. R. (1978). An observational approach to assessment of anxiety in young children. *Journal of Consulting and Clinical Psychology, 46*, 1246–1257.

Graae, F., Milner, J., Rizzotto, L., & Klein, R. G. (1994). Clonazapam in childhood anxiety disorders. *Journal of the American Academy of Child and Adolescent Psychiatry, 33*, 372–376.

*Haaga, D. A., & Davison, G. C. (1986). Cognitive change methods. In F. H. Kanfer & A. P. Goldstein

(Eds.), *Helping people change: A textbook of methods* (3rd ed., pp. 236–282). New York: Pergamon.

Hall, G. S. (1904). *Adolescence*. Englewood Cliffs, NJ: Prentice Hall.

Herjanic, B., & Reich, W. (1982). Development of a structured psychiatric interview for children: Agreement between child and parent on individual symptoms. *Journal of Abnormal Child Psychology, 10*, 307–324.

Hodges, K., McKnew, D., Cytryn, L., Stern, L., & Kline, J. (1982). The Child Assessment Schedule (CAS) diagnostic interview: A report on reliability and validity. *Journal of the American Academy of Child and Adolescent Psychiatry, 21*, 468–473.

Houston, B. K., Fox, J. E., & Forbes, L. (1984). Trait anxiety and children's state anxiety, cognitive behaviors, and performance under stress. *Cognitive Therapy and Research, 8*, 631–641.

*James, E. M., Reynolds, C. R., & Dunbar, J. (1994). Self-report instruments. In T. H. Ollendick, N. J. King, & W. Yule (Eds.), *International handbook of phobic and anxiety disorders in children and adolescents* (pp. 317–329). New York: Plenum Press.

Jay, S. M., & Elliot, C. (1984). Behavioral observation scales for measuring children's distress: The effects of increased methodological rigor. *Journal of Consulting and Clinical Psychology, 52*, 1106–1107.

Johnson, A. M., Falstein, E. I., Szurek, S. A., & Svendsen, M. (1941). School phobia. *American Journal of Orthopsychiatry, 11*, 702–711.

Jones, M. C. (1924). The elimination of children's fears. *Journal of Experimental Psychology, 7*, 382–390.

Kashani, J. H., & Orvaschel, H. (1990). A community study of anxiety in children and adolescents. *American Journal of Psychiatry, 147*, 313–318.

Kearney, C. A., Drabman, R. S., & Beasley, J. F. (1993). The trials of childhood: The development, reliability, and validity of the Daily Life Stressors Scale. *Journal of Child and Family Studies, 2*, 371–388.

*Kearney, C. A., Eisen, A. R., & Schaefer, C. E. (1995). General issues underlying the diagnosis and treatment of child and adolescent anxiety disorders. In A. R. Eisen, C. A. Kearney, & C. E. Schaefer (Eds.), *Clinical handbook of anxiety disorders in children and adolescents* (pp. 3–15). Northvale, NJ: Jason Aronson.

Kearney, C. A., & Silverman, W. K. (1990). A preliminary analysis of a functional model of assessment and treatment for school refusal behavior. *Behavior Modification, 14*, 340–366.

Kearney, C. A., & Silverman, W. K. (1993). Measuring the function of school refusal behavior: The School Refusal Assessment Scale. *Journal of Clinical Child Psychology, 22*, 85–96.

*Kearney, C. A., & Sims, K. E. (1997). Anxiety problems in childhood: Diagnostic and dimensional aspects. In J. A. den Boer (Ed.), *Clinical management of anxiety: Theory and practical applications* (pp. 371–397). New York: Marcel Dekker.

Kelley, C. K. (1976). Play desensitization of fear of darkness in preschool children. *Behaviour Research and Therapy, 14*, 79–81.

*Kendall, P. C. (1994). Treating anxiety disorders in children: Results of a randomized clinical trial. *Journal of Consulting and Clinical Psychology, 62*, 100–110.

Kendall, P. C., & Chansky, T. E. (1991). Considering cognition in anxiety-disordered children. *Journal of Anxiety Disorders, 5*, 167–185.

*Kendall, P. C., Chansky, T. E., Kane, M. T., Kim, R. S., Kortlander, E., Ronan, K. R., Sessa, F. M., & Siqueland, L. (1992). *Anxiety disorders in youth: Cognitive-behavioral interventions*. New York: Pergamon.

Kendall-Tackett, K. A., Williams, L. M., & Finkelhor, D. (1993). Impact of sexual abuse on children: A review and synthesis of recent empirical studies. *Psychological Bulletin, 113*, 164–180.

*King, N. J. (1994). Physiological assessment. In T. H. Ollendick, N. J. King, & W. Yule (Eds.), *International handbook of phobic and anxiety disorders in children and adolescents* (pp. 365–379). New York: Plenum Press.

Klein, R. G. (1991). Parent-child agreement in clinical assessment of anxiety and other psychopathology: A review. *Journal of Anxiety Disorders, 15*, 187–198.

Klein, R. G., Koplewicz, H. S., & Kanner, A. (1992). Imipramine treatment of children with separation anxiety disorder. *Journal of the American Academy of Child and Adolescent Psychiatry, 31*, 21–28.

Kovacs, M. (1985). The interview schedule for children (ISC). *Psychopharmacology Bulletin, 21*, 991–994.

Kovacs, M. (1992). *Children's Depression Inventory manual*. North Tonawanda, NY: Multi-Health Systems.

Kutcher, S. P., & Mackenzie, S. (1988). Successful clonazepam treatment of adolescents with panic disorder. *Journal of Clinical Psychopharmacology*, 8, 299–301.

Kutcher, S. P., Reiter, S., Gardner, D. M., & Klein, R. G. (1992). The pharmacotherapy of anxiety disorders in children and adolescents. *Psychiatric Clinics of North America*, 15, 41–67.

La Greca, A. M., & Stone, W. L. (1993). Social Anxiety Scale for Children—Revised: Factor structure and concurrent validity. *Journal of Clinical Child Psychology*, 22, 17–27.

Lazarus, A. A., Davison, G. C., & Polefka, D. A. (1965). Classical and operant factors in the treatment of a school phobia. *Journal of Abnormal Psychology*, 70, 225–229.

Leonard, H. L., Swedo, S. E., Rapoport, J. L., Koby, E. V., Lenane, M. C., Cheslow, D. L., & Hamburger, S. D. (1989). Treatment of childhood obsessive compulsive disorder with clomipramine and desipramine: A double-blind crossover comparison. *Archives of General Psychiatry*, 46, 1088–1092.

Leonard, H. L., Topol, D., Bukstein, O., Hindmarsh, D., Allen, A. J., & Swedo, S. E. (1994). Clonazepam as an augmenting agent in the treatment of childhood-onset obsessive-compulsive disorder. *Journal of the American Academy of Child and Adolescent Psychiatry*, 33, 792–794.

Locke, H. J., & Wallace, K. M. (1959). Short-term marital adjustment and prediction tests: Their reliability and validity. *Journal of Marriage and Family Living*, 21, 251–255.

Marcia, J. (1980). Identity in adolescence. In J. Adelson (Ed.), *Handbook of adolescent psychology*. New York: Wiley.

Marks, I. M. (1975). Behavioral treatments of phobic and obsessive-compulsive disorders: A critical appraisal. In M. Hersen, R. M. Eisler, & P. M. Miller (Eds.), *Progress in behavior modification* (Vol. 1, pp. 65–158). New York: Academic.

Matson, J. L. (1981). Assessment and treatment of clinical fears in mentally retarded children. *Journal of Applied Behavior Analysis*, 14, 287–294.

McConaughy, S. H., & Skiba, R. J. (1993). Comorbidity of externalizing and internalizing problems. *School Psychology Review*, 22, 421–436.

McGee, R., Feehan, M., Williams, S., & Anderson, J. (1992). DSM-III disorders from age 11 to age 15 years. *Journal of the American Academy of Child and Adolescent Psychiatry*, 31, 50–59.

Melamed, B. G., & Siegel, L. J. (1975). Reduction of anxiety in children facing hospitalization and surgery by use of filmed modeling. *Journal of Consulting and Clinical Psychology*, 43, 511–521.

Melamed, B., Yurcherson, R., Fleece, E. L., Hutcherson, S., & Hawes, R. (1978). Effects of filmed modeling on the reduction of anxiety-related behaviors in individuals varying in level of previous experience in the stress situation. *Journal of Consulting and Clinical Psychology*, 46, 1357–1367.

Miller, L. C. (1967). Louisville Behavior Check List for males, 6–12 years of age. *Psychological Reports*, 21, 885–896.

Miller, L. C., Barrett, C. L., Hampe, E., & Noble, H. (1972). Factor structure of childhood fears. *Journal of Consulting and Clinical Psychology*, 39, 264–268.

Moos, R. H., & Moos, B. S. (1986). *Family Environment Scale Manual* (2nd ed.). Palo Alto, CA: Consulting Psychologists Press.

Mowrer, O. H. (1960). *Learning theory and behavior*. New York: Wiley.

*Nelles, W. B., & Barlow, D. H. (1988). Do children panic? *Clinical Psychology Review*, 8, 359–372.

Ollendick, T. H. (1983). Reliability and validity of the revised Fear Survey Schedule for Children (FSSC-R). *Behavior Research and Therapy*, 21, 685–692.

Ollendick, T. H. (1995). Cognitive behavioral treatment of panic disorder with agoraphobia in adolescents: A multiple baseline design analysis. *Behavior Therapy*, 26, 517–531.

*Ollendick, T. H., & Cerny, J. A. (1981). *Clinical behavior therapy with children*. New York: Plenum Press.

Ollendick, T. H., King, N. J., & Frary, R. B. (1989). Fears in children and adolescents: Reliability and generalizability across gender, age and nationality. *Behavior Research and Therapy*, 27, 19–26.

Piers, E. V. (1984). *Piers-Harris Children's Self-Concept Scale: Revised manual 1984*. Los Angeles: Western Psychological Services.

Puig-Antich, J., & Chambers, W. (1978). *The Schedule for Affective Disorders and Schizophrenia for School-Aged Children*. New York: New York State Psychiatric Institute.

Quay, H. C., & Peterson, D. R. (1987). *Manual for the Revised Behavior Problem Checklist*. Coral Gables, FL: University of Miami.

Reiss, S. (1991). Expectancy model of fear, anxiety, and panic. *Clinical Psychology Review*, 11, 141–153.

*Reiter, S., Kutcher, S., & Gardner, D. (1992). Anxiety disorders in children and adolescents: Clinical and related issues in pharmacological treatment. *Canadian Journal of Psychiatry, 45,* 444–450.

Reynolds, C. R., & Kamphaus, R. W. (1992). *Behavior Assessment System for Children manual.* Circle Pines, MN: American Guidance.

Reynolds, C. R., & Paget, K. D. (1981). Factor analysis of the Revised Children's Manifest Anxiety Scale for blacks, whites, males, and females with a national normative sample. *Journal of Consulting and Clinical Psychology, 49,* 352–359.

Riddle, M. A., Scahill, L., King, R. A., Hardin, M. T., Anderson, G. M., Ort, S. I., Smith, J. C., Leckman, J. F., & Cohen, D. J. (1992). Double-blind, crossover trial of fluoxetine and placebo in children and adolescents with obsessive-compulsive disorder. *Journal of the American Academy of Child and Adolescent Psychiatry, 31,* 1062–1069.

*Riggs, D. S., & Foa, E. B. (1993). Obsessive-compulsive disorder. In D. H. Barlow (Ed.), *Clinical handbook of psychological disorders* (2nd ed., pp. 189–239). New York: Guilford Press.

Ronan, K. R., Kendall, P. C., & Rowe, M. (1994). Negative affectivity in children: Development and validation of a self-statement questionnaire. *Cognitive Therapy and Research, 18,* 509–528.

Silverman, W. K. (1989). *Self-control manual for phobic children.* Unpublished manuscript.

Silverman, W. K. (1991). Diagnostic reliability of anxiety disorders in children using structured interviews. *Journal of Anxiety Disorders, 5,* 101–124.

*Silverman, W. K. (1994). Structured diagnostic interviews. In T. H. Ollendick, N. J. King, & W. Yule (Eds.), *International handbook of phobic and anxiety disorders in children and adolescents* (pp. 293–315). New York: Plenum Press.

Silverman, W. K., & Albano, A. M. (1996). *Anxiety Disorders Interview Schedule for DSM-IV: Parent and child version.* San Antonio, TX: Psychological Corporation.

Silverman, W. K., Fleisig, W., Rabian, B., & Peterson, R. A. (1991). The Child Anxiety Sensitivity Index. *Journal of Clinical Child Psychology, 20,* 162–168.

*Silverman, W. K., & Nelles, W. B. (1988). The Anxiety Disorders Interview Schedule for Children. *Journal of the American Academy of Child and Adolescent Psychiatry, 27,* 772–778.

Simeon, J. G. (1991). Buspirone effects in adolescent psychiatric disorders. *European Neuropsychopharmacology, 1,* 421.

Simeon, J. G., & Ferguson, H. B. (1987). Alprazolam effects in children with anxiety disorders. *Canadian Journal of Psychiatry, 32,* 570–574.

Simeon, J. G., Ferguson, H. B., Knott, V., Roberts, N., Gauthier, B., Dubois, C., & Wiggins, D. (1992). Clinical, cognitive, and neurophysiological effects of alprazolam in children with overanxious and avoidant disorders. *Journal of the American Academy of Child and Adolescent Psychiatry, 31,* 29–33.

Simeon, J. G., Thatte, S., & Wiggins, D. (1990). Treatment of adolescent obsessive-compulsive disorder with a clomipramine-fluoxetine combination. *Psychopharmacology Bulletin, 25,* 285–290.

*Simeon, J. G., & Wiggins, D. M. (1995). Pharmacotherapy. In A. R. Eisen, C. A. Kearney, & C. E. Schaefer (Eds.), *Clinical handbook of anxiety disorders in children and adolescents* (pp. 550–570). Northvale, NJ: Jason Aronson.

Spanier, G. B. (1976). Measuring dyadic adjustment: New scales for assessing the quality of marriage and similar dyads. *Journal of Marriage and the Family, 38,* 15–28.

Spasaro, S., Eisen, A. R., Kearney, C. A., Albano, A. M., & Barlow, D. H. (1995, March). *Reliability and validity of the Parental Expectancies Scale in a child anxiety disorders sample.* Paper presented at the meeting of the Eastern Psychological Association, Boston, MA.

Spielberger, C. D. (1973). *Manual for the State-Trait Anxiety Inventory for Children.* Palo Alto, CA: Consulting Psychologists Press.

Stampfl, T. G., & Levis, D. J. (1967). Essentials of implosive therapy: A learning-based psychodynamic behavioral therapy. *Journal of Abnormal Psychology, 72,* 496–503.

*Torgersen, S. (1993). Relationship between adult and childhood anxiety disorders: Genetic hypothesis. In C. G. Last (Ed.), *Anxiety across the lifespan: A developmental perspective* (pp. 113–127). New York: Springer.

Watson, J. B., & Rayner, R. (1920). Conditioned emotional reactions. *Journal of Experimental Psychology, 3,* 1–14.

Wechsler, D. (1989). *Wechsler Preschool and Primary Scale of Intelligence-Revised.* New York: Psychological Corporation.

Wechsler, D. (1991). *Wechsler Intelligence Scale for Children-Third Edition* (WISC-III). New York: Psychological Corporation.

*Weeks, G. R., & L'Abate, L. (1982). *Paradoxical psychotherapy: Theory and practice with individuals, couples, and families*. New York: Brunner/Mazel.

Wirt, R. D., Lachar, D., Klinedinst, J. K., & Seat, P. D. (1984). *Multidimensional description of child personality: A manual for the Personality Inventory for Children*. Los Angeles: Western Psychological Services.

Witt, J. C., Heffer, R. W., & Pfieffer, J. (1990). Structured rating scales: A review of self-report and informant rating procedures and issues. In C. R. Reynolds & R. W. Kamphaus (Eds.), *Handbook of psychological and educational assessment of children* (pp. 364–394). New York: Guilford Press.

*Wolpe, J. (1982). *The practice of behavior therapy* (3rd ed.). New York: Pergamon.

Wolpe, J., & Rowan, V. C. (1988). Panic disorder: A product of classical conditioning. *Behavior Research and Therapy, 26*, 441–450.

*World Health Organization. (1992). *International classification of disease* (10th ed.). Geneva: Author.

World Health Organization. (1994). *Pocket guide to the ICD-10 classification of mental and behavioral disorders*. Washington, DC: American Psychiatric Press.

*Indicates references that the author recommends for further reading.

15
Factitious Disorders and Factitious Disorder by Proxy

Loren Pankratz

Factitious means arising from an unnatural or manufactured source. A factitious disorder, then, is a condition in which symptoms do not arise from the natural course of disease but are feigned or produced by the patient. The apparent goal is to satisfy a need to assume the role of patient. This chapter considers instances in which the diagnosis of factitious disorder might be appropriate for a child or adolescent. It should be kept in mind that a child may be the victim of a caregiver who wants the child in the role of patient, a phenomenon reviewed in the second part of this chapter.

FACTITIOUS DISORDERS

Historical Perspective

The history of childhood deception provides some insight into our current understanding of the pathology of factitious disorder. Young children lie beginning at an early age (DePaulo, et al., 1985; Triplett, 1900). Usually they are not very successful, but as they grow they become adept at fooling their peers and adults. The theory, here, is that young children lack the cognitive skills to appreciate how the situation

appears to the intended victim. To lie successfully, the child must mature sufficiently to appreciate the perspective of another while simultaneously creating information that causes the victim to accept the false story. Surprisingly, Chandler, Fritz, and Hala (1989) discovered that children as young as 2.5 years are already capable of engaging in a variety of well-crafted deceptive practices aimed at instilling false beliefs in others. However, this precocity may still not imply that the child fully recognizes how the victim construes the information.

A case can be made, of course, that deception is an important developmental task for all humans. At times it is necessary to speak falsely (the white lie) and avoid revealing personal preferences in order to cooperate in social interactions. Similarly, suppression of information is essential for a private life.

Delbruch, a German physician, was perhaps the first to study seriously problematic liars (Healy & Healy, 1915; Larson, 1932). For several years he studied five disturbed adolescents whose lies did not originate in childhood fantasy, delusion, or poor memory. Hence, he coined the phrase "pseudologica fantastica" to refer to their extraordinary tall tales. In one case he had trouble determining whether the child belonged in a reformatory or an insane asylum. In another, he concluded that constitutional psychosis, hysteria, moral insanity, and psychopathy were all interrelated.

In the early 1900s William Healy established the Juvenile Psychopathic Institute in Chicago, where he catalogued the "swindles, pathological accusations, and lies" of youth (Healy & Healy, 1915). In one instance he gathered the extensive history of a young female who simulated medical disorders like diabetes and tuberculosis to gain admission to 18 different hospitals. Although she claimed to be 16 or 17 years old, Healy discovered that she was 27. Patients who practice such deceit are now identified as having "pseudoadolescent Munchausen syndrome" (Shaner & Eth, 1988).

Although there were many fascinating early studies of deception, no "psychology of deception" ever emerged. Hyman (1989) suggested that deception is illuminated by subfields of psychology, but the understanding of deception itself is not supported by a body of psychological propositions. Nevertheless, clinicians should not be surprised to find children and adolescents engaged in a variety of medical and psychological deceptions.

Diagnostic Description

Factitious disorders imply the intentional production or feigning of physical or psychological symptoms for purposes more complex or convoluted than simple malingering. Indeed, the motivation is presumed to be a desire to assume the sick role. *The Diagnostic and Statistical Manual of Mental Disorders* (DSM-IV) includes three types of factitious disorders: those showing predominantly psychological signs and symptoms (300.16); those showing predominantly physical signs and symptoms (300.19); and those showing combined psychological and physical signs and symptoms (300.19). The *International Classification of Mental and Behavioral Disorders* (ICD-10) published by the World Health Organization, classifies factitious disorders under "other disorders of adult personality

and behavior." Presumably the diagnosis could be applied to children and adolescents when appropriate.

Epidemiology

No estimates of epidemiology are available for children. Factitious disorders are considered rare, but the consequences of missing the diagnosis can be serious. Factitious disorders with psychological symptoms in children are rarely described except in single case-study reports.

Brief Review of Psychopathology and Theoretical Models

Just as deception falls on a continuum from white lie to pseudologica fantastica, factitious disorders also occur across a spectrum. They range from the feigning of symptoms (mimicry) to serious, surreptitious, self-inflicted disorders. Sometimes clinicians mistakenly believe patients can be dismissed after the diagnosis of factitious disorder is made, perhaps because they have confused factitious with fictitious. However, the diagnosis refers not to the state of the physical findings but instead to the fact that information was manufactured, withheld, or distorted. Thus, a child may have heated a thermometer by friction, or he may have self-injected a noxious or infectious substance. Both cases create a factitious fever, but a patient with an infection needs specific medical attention. It is important to remember that symptoms might be only mimicry, or they might reflect serious pathology.

How might children develop a factitious disorder? We have some insight into this question from the study of adult Munchausen syndrome patients. The Munchausen syndrome refers to patients with factitious disorders who travel from hospital to hospital, usually spinning tall tales (pseudologica fantastica) about their diseases or their (usually fictitious) accomplishments (Pankratz, 1981; Pankratz & Jackson, 1994). As children, many of these patients experienced rejection, mistreatment, and parental loss (Griffith, 1988; O'Shea et al., 1982). For them, the hospital provides a haven or refuge. Hospital staff are accepting and sympathetic even when inflicting pain, and patients learn to create symptoms to remain in a sick role. On the other hand, the hospital can also be a source of excitement or sensation fulfillment (Justus, Kreutzinger, & Kitchens, 1980; Pankratz & McCarthy, 1986). Solomon's (1980) theory of acquired motivation suggests that activities that initially cause fear and distress (like skydiving or rock climbing) can eventually become pleasurable. Perhaps, in some similar way, patients may become addicted to the hospital (Barker, 1962).

All chronically ill children are at risk for developmental behavior problems, and it is important to consider ways of management to prevent the reinforcement of malingering (Creer, Weinberg, & Molk, 1974). In other instances, the sick role may elicit care from parents who might otherwise punish or neglect their children. Care-eliciting behaviors are prominent in several medical and psychiatric disorders (Henderson, 1974). Nurture is almost always available for those who are sick (Feldman & Escalona, 1991). Further, sickness can project an image of helplessness that provides the individual with an excuse for poor personal performance. Symptoms may be a self-handicapping strategy that excuses the child from failure (Smith, Snyder, & Perkins, 1983).

Assessment

Factitious disorders are best differentiated from malingering by an analysis of the goal. In malingering, the goal is easily understandable, simple, and usually of brief duration. Like their adult counterparts, however, children with factitious disorders may have apparent secondary gain (Rogers, Bagby, & Rector, 1989). Malingering children are either attempting to avoid some understandably unpleasant responsibility, activity, or expectation, or they expect to receive some benefit from being sick. However, a child who persists in a sick role to stay home from school might eventually earn the diagnosis of factitious disorder. At some point the goal is no

longer understandable, and the sick role eventually must be judged pathological.

Malingering should have an understandable cost-benefit balance for the child. Thus, a child who malingers typically mimics an illness with little cost. However, when self-infections or self-injuries become costly, dangerous, or bizarre beyond what can reasonably be considered an understandable tradeoff, some other diagnosis must be explored. Malingering is a game or trick that does not arise in the context of a mental disorder, nor does it deserve a psychiatric label. Only when the sick role becomes part of the child's life can the diagnosis of factitious disorder be considered.

Many adults with factitious disorder also abuse prescription medications; however, no information is available about this in children. Adults often claim that their problems with drugs are iatrogenic, although it is usually impossible to know whether the symptoms or the drug seeking came first. Drug seekers who submit to invasive medical procedures or who injure themselves seriously should be given the additional diagnosis of factitious disorder.

Childhood somatoform disorders point less to deception than to a lifestyle focused on illness and symptoms, and precursors of this disorder develop quite early. The symptoms in somatoform disorder, which can be quite wide in range, constitute the experience and communication of somatic distress (Lipowski, 1988). Bodily symptoms, whether real or imagined, take on meaning or significance that is not understandable from the physical findings. Such symptoms are not the result of schemes or self-inflicted activity, although the patient might lie to preserve self-esteem or to ensure additional examination. Patients with somatoform disorders might complain about symptoms, but they lack the duplicity of patients with factitious disorders.

Patients with factitious disorder lie to stay in the sick role; patients with somatoform disorder fear they are doomed to live in it. Thus, somatoform patients usually seem overly revealing and more naive than duplicitous. They complain bitterly about all the treatments that have not helped, whereas patients with factitious disorder hide their history of multiple procedures. The symptoms of patients with somatoform disorders are not intentional or voluntary. In factitious disorder the symptoms are intentional, in that the patient can decide where or how to produce them, however, the diagnostic manual properly refrains from describing them as voluntary, although sometimes patients' actions seem quite compulsive and sometimes quite deliberate. This difference can be seen clearly in surreptitious dermatologic self-injury. In some instances the behavior appears quite compulsive (as in cheilitis or some purpuras), while in others the injury appears more manipulative (as in cigarette burns or cupping).

The medical literature describes simulation of a wide range of symptoms in children. However, one should not place too much confidence in the diagnosis provided, especially in studies where children are described as subjects along with adults. Psychogenic stomach pain, for example, may not always be psychogenic according to the guidelines of the diagnostic manual (Raymer, Weininger, & Hamilton, 1984; Wasserman, 1988). Although feigned seizures are usually identified as psychogenic, other diagnoses might be more technically correct (Lancman et al., 1994; Morgan et al., 1984). It would be helpful to know if the seizures of these children were associated with an obvious payoff, as in malingering, or if they were psychologically convoluted, as in factitious disorder.

Similarly, literature that focuses on factitious symptoms may describe children who actually have a somatization disorder or are malingerers. It is important not to confuse factitious symptoms with the diagnosis of factitious disorder; for example, patients can have symptoms of depression without the diagnosis of depression. The distinction between symptom and diagnosis is not trivial. Children have been described with symptoms of factitious renal stones (Lachman & Morgan, 1983; Sneed & Bell, 1976), factitious skin lesions (Putnam & Stein, 1985; Sheppard, O'Loughlin, & Malone, 1986), and factitious fevers (Aduan et al., 1979; Herzberg & Wolff, 1972). However, not all of the children with these factitious symptoms should be diagnosed as having a factitious disorder.

Schade and colleagues (1985) were more explicit in differentiating malingering from factitious disorders in their study of brittle diabetics with manipulated symptoms. Malingering teenagers omitted their insulin injections or were noncompliant with diet in the context of an identifiable event such as an argument with a family member, peer pressure, or an impending exam at school. Patients with factitious disorder were more devious in their surreptitious manipulations, usually identified through the astute observations of specially trained nurses. Patients with factitious disorders were more familiar with their disease and the infusion devices, and the timing of their manipulations was not associated with identifiable events. In other words, children with factitious disorders were more complex in the manipulation of their disease and in terms of their goals. The symptoms created can be extremely serious; one 12-year-old boy manipulated his diabetic disease to such an extent that he was continually in a life-threatening condition (Sheehy, 1992).

Fras (1973) suggested that anorexia nervosa, which bears many similarities to a factitious disorder, should be treated as one. Prescribed treatments and diets are sabotaged, while food is surreptitiously consumed. Voluntary, self-induced complications are common, such as those secondary to vomiting and enema or laxative abuse (Brown, 1985; Shur, et al., 1988). Although the deceptions are important to remember, there seems little need to give a child with anorexia the additional diagnosis of factitious disorder.

In summary, malingerers *pretend* to be sick, especially when someone is watching, and patients with somatoform disorders often feel that they are doomed to be sick. Patients with factitious disorder seek the sick role, creating or pretending symptoms to ensure their status. The diagnosis is not dependent on the medical findings. Instead, the diagnosis is confirmed by deceptive interactions with health care professionals that are designed to maintain the sick role.

Treatment

Clinicians must remember that patient deceptions may have a wide band of underlying psychopathology. The deceptions of malingerers are usually narrow in focus; therefore, therapists can often devise alternative routes for patients to accomplish their goals. Similarly, simple dermatologic self-injury may be maintained more by habit than by psychological distress. Stewart and Kernohan (1972) noted that, whenever the wounds of young dental patients were openly discussed, they all cooperated in stopping their habit without resentment or protest. Reich and Gottfried (1983) noted that patients with factitious disorders sometimes give up their artifice when confronted, even if they deny their role in creating symptoms.

Careful assessment of developmental pathology will suggest how entrenched a factitious disorder might be. More comprehensive intervention in the social system of the child may be necessary for some cases of factitious disorder. Mims and Antonello (1994) described extensive assessment and intervention procedures necessary for modification of well-practiced deceptive behaviors. First, assessment is conducted across all the social systems of the child. Then, problems are identified according to categories such as situational, cognitive, emotional, educational, and so on. Intervention includes specific roles for both health care professionals and members of the patient's social system.

Deceptions in a medical setting, once discovered, may trigger a variety of responses. Some will feel betrayed, duped, or used and complain that the patient has wasted time and resources. However, patients have always brought their pathology to physicians, and we should not be surprised when their pathology includes deception. On the other hand, some professionals have excessive curiosity, keeping patients that should be discharged.

Consultants are often pressured to endorse a certain viewpoint when called for an opinion, and the hidden expectation might be to transfer or punish the patient. Careful gathering of information is essential because different members of the patient's team might have quite different opinions. The sensitive clinician will ensure that everyone contributes to the development of a treatment program that all can support.

Most authors who have written about the management of factitious disorders suggest that treatment must begin with confrontation. Confrontation usually implies conflict; however, patient confrontation is merely the process of presenting the information one has and its implications. As much as this approach is feared, Reich and Gottfried (1983) note that the relationship between patient and staff often improves after confrontation. It is helpful to enter the initial confrontation session with some face-saving strategies for the patient and the family (Eisendrath, 1989).

Inevitably, the patient's family will know the diagnosis. Their response is impossible to predict. Some families become enraged at the child, and some accuse the doctor of failing to find the real cause.

Patients with chronic factitious disorders, and their families, are notoriously resistant to psychological treatment. Therefore, the first task is to consider management: focusing not so much on cure as on containment. Management requires a clear problem list so that the patient can be provided those services, and only those services, that are necessary. The patient and family must be reassured that they will not be abandoned. During the early stages, there is no need for probing questions and searching for motives.

Management requires obtaining information about such things as service utilization from sources outside the patient's own report. Some mental health clinicians are uncomfortable in such a role because they believe it communicates doubt that can damage the relationship. Indeed, Loftus (1993) discovered that some therapists responded emotionally when questioned about whether their patients always provide authentic reports. Such therapists should consider whether they are suitable for treatment roles with patients who have factitious disorders.

In contrast, addiction models of therapy incorporate surveillance for compliance as part of the recovery process. The therapist must manage self-destructive acts with unambiguous actions while not rejecting the patient. Often there is an expectation that patients will stop producing symptoms that arise from their own hand once their tricks have been discovered. Families especially need a plan of action for when the simple solutions do not work.

Comments

Children have sometimes been associated with the Munchausen syndrome. Although this syndrome does not appear in the diagnostic manual, it is often used to describe severe forms of factitious disorder. Most commonly, the Munchausen label is reserved for those who travel from hospital to hospital telling outrageous stories about their lives or their symptoms (Pankratz, 1981; Pankratz & Jackson, 1994).

Some children have been inappropriately diagnosed as suffering from the Munchausen syndrome. For example, Tec (1975) described the antics of a 10-year-old boy who feigned symptoms in response to his father's pressure to play football and whose symptoms were explored extensively over several hospitalizations. In my judgment, this case fails to meet the criteria for Munchausen syndrome because the family did not use multiple providers. The child's goal was simply to avoid something he feared.

There are, however, descriptions of adolescents that do appear to fit the Munchausen diagnosis. All of the classic characteristics were evident in an adolescent girl who had 23 hospitalizations, 13 major surgeries, and innumerable physician office visits (Paperny, Hicks, & Hammar, 1980). This girl was very literate about medical terminology and procedures. She induced a wide variety of symptoms, including rectal and vaginal bleeding, vomiting attacks, and septic arthritis. Her joint aspirates revealed atypical organisms, but her constant changing of physicians hampered accurate diagnosis. Each physician thought the needle marks around her joints were from prior aspirations, when in fact she had been injecting feces.

One review of Munchausen cases suggested that the mean age of onset is about 21 years of age. In 186 cases where the information was available, 41% of the patients had developed the syndrome (presumably, *characteristics* of the syndrome) by 18 years of age. Parents were aware that their children were faking illness but did not have an understanding that they were seeking nurture unavailable at home (Raymond, 1987).

A 15-year-old girl with factitious Cushing's syndrome demonstrated a remarkable number of Munchausen characteristics through several hospitalizations (Witt & Ginsberg-Fellner, 1981). She was well versed in the symptoms, pathophysiology, and diagnostic procedures of her disorder, and she repeatedly asked for invasive tests and surgical adrenalectomy. Eventually, physicians discovered she was taking prednisone, probably supplied by a pharmacist who was her cousin. When the ruse was discovered, her family refused to return for follow-up care. This outcome suggests a collusion of the family with the patient. The participation of the family raises the question of Munchausen syndrome by proxy, which is the topic of the next section.

FACTITIOUS DISORDER BY PROXY

Historical Perspective

In 1964 Douglas Pickering described three hospitalized children who had high levels of salicylate. Even though two died, the parents of the children maintained it was impossible that their child could have ingested that much aspirin. Although Pickering believed that the parents could have been unaware or oblivious to the actions of their children, he cautiously raised the possibility that the children were purposely poisoned.

The following year Dine (1965) reported on a 19-month-old child with numerous hospitalizations for mysterious neurologic symptoms and seizures. He eventually discovered that the mother was poisoning her child with phenothiazines that she had been prescribed for a postpartum psychosis. Soon other clinicians recognized this same distressing variation of child abuse. The children involved were similar in many respects to physically battered children (Shnaps et al., 1981).

It was Roy Meadow, however, who captured the broader nature of this problem and named it Munchausen syndrome by proxy (Meadow, 1977). Meadow, a pediatrician in Leeds, England, identified mothers involved in bizarre games with doctors. These mothers brought their children to the hospital with fabricated illnesses and watched with feigned innocence as the physicians tried to make a diagnosis. The mothers' behavior was reminiscent of the Munchausen syndrome, but by proxy in these cases.

Although this phenomenon was originally called Munchausen syndrome by proxy, DMS-IV uses the label "factitious disorder by proxy." However, the Munchausen term, being more whimsical and thus more memorable (London, 1968), continues to dominate the medical literature. In addition, Munchausen syndrome by proxy is used in ICD-10.

Munchausen syndrome by proxy is a diagnosis not of the child but of the adult perpetrator. However, adults have also been identified as victims (Repper, 1995; Sigal, Altmark, & Carmel, 1986), usually in cases involving the more vulnerable elderly (Smith & Sinanan, 1972). When the pretense is psychiatric symptoms, the condition has been called the "gaslight" phenomenon, so named after a play in which a husband tries to get his wife into a lunatic asylum (Barton & Whitehead, 1969). However, the gaslight phenomenon has not been used to describe interactions with children, who are the focus of this chapter.

Diagnostic Description and Critique

Factitious disorder by proxy involves the intentional production of symptoms, or the feigning of symptoms, in another person who is under the individual's care. The motivation for the perpetrator is either to assume the sick role by proxy or to become involved in the drama of medical care. External incentives, such as economic gain, are absent (or at least not primary), and the behavior is not better accounted for

by another mental disorder. For example, one troublesome but disturbed mother wrapped her children in toilet paper and aluminum foil rather than blankets, making unusual claims about their health (Warner & Hathaway, 1984). Presumably her primary diagnosis of psychosis would exclude the diagnosis of factitious disorder by proxy.

The diagnosis is listed in Appendix B of DSM-IV, which contains "Criteria sets and axes provided for further study." These listings need more research to determine if they have sufficient consistency to be considered for a separate diagnosis. Boundaries for inclusion and exclusion need to be established. It may be that the use of "factitious" instead of "Munchausen" will encourage the inclusion of a broader range of problems. The ICD-10 code for Munchausen syndrome by proxy presents it as a subset of maltreatment syndromes. It is, therefore, a form of child abuse. If the "Munchausen syndrome by proxy" label is used, the perpetrator's behaviors should be sufficiently distinctive from ordinary child abuse to warrant the diagnostic code (T 74.8).

Epidemiology

Schreier and Libow (1993) surveyed 870 pediatric neurologists and 388 pediatric gastroenterologists who reported 273 confirmed cases of Munchausen syndrome by proxy and 192 cases in which the diagnosis was seriously implicated. The average length of time to diagnosis was more than a year in 19% of the cases and more than 6 months in 33%. Rosenberg (1987) suggested that the average time taken to uncover the proxy diagnosis was more than 14.9 months. More widespread general knowledge about the syndrome would presumably reduce the time needed for its proper identification.

Unfortunately, more widespread general knowledge about the syndrome has probably resulted in false identifications. Meadow (1994) suggested that the syndrome is now being overused, with improper methods employed to make the diagnosis. This problem is of particular concern within sudden infant death syndrome (SIDS), where mothers in grief may feel accused. Light and Sheridan (1990) suggested that 0.27% of the population of infants being monitored in infant apnea programs represented Munchausen syndrome by proxy, which is a very small percentage.

Attention has focused on families who report multiple episodes of illness that require resuscitation (Light & Sheridan, 1990), particularly when those episodes are not witnessed by a professional (Mitchell et al., 1993). Unfortunately, these cases are difficult to identify properly because of the broad range of customary presentations. Indeed, Morley (1992) pointed out that the majority of apnea cases are witnessed only by the mothers, and many mothers express their concern by spending lots of time at the baby's side. Many read and become knowledgeable about the medical conditions of the child. More recently, concern about these deaths has been limited to situations in which one sibling has already died of SIDS, again about 3% of all cases. Symptoms in a second child, then, are highly suspicious.

One percent of attendees at an asthma clinic received the diagnosis (Godding & Kruth, 1991), and as many as 5% of allergy patients were thought to represent some issues of proxy (Warner & Hathaway, 1984). Only three examples of Munchausen syndrome by proxy were found among 4,585 patients in a regional pediatric rheumatology population (Denardo et al., 1994).

Presentations of factitious disorder by proxy for psychiatric symptoms (Fisher, Mitchell, & Murdoch, 1993) and for developmental disabilities (Stevenson & Alexander, 1990) are rare. More commonly, mothers will doctor-shop for the purpose of obtaining financial benefits, such as Social Security, for pretended psychiatric or developmental disorders.

Brief Review of Psychopathology and Theoretical Models

The diagnostic manual implies that factitious disorder by proxy is a behavioral problem of a parent characterized by deceptive interactions

with a physician that result, or have the potential of resulting, in harm to the child. The area covered by this definition is surprisingly large and lacks clear landmarks to guide the uncertain clinician.

Does one include the hyperconcerned mother who may embellish or falsify the severity of her child's illness to entice the physician into a more careful examination? Does one include the parents who want biological explanations for behavioral problems? Deception in the medical setting may cause harm to the child, but the minor twisting of truth is probably common. When, then, does deceptive behavior on the part of the mother rise to a level that it should be considered factitious?

Harm is a complex dimension for consideration. Herman-Giddens and Berson (1989) described parents who engaged in unusual, often harmful genital care of their children. The mothers usually presented their children as having a long history of genital infections and recurrent discharge. Harmful genital care is probably on the borderland of factitious disorder by proxy. Although this problem should be of concern to clinicians, the focus of these mothers seems to be more an obsession with the child's genitalia than a wish to deceive the doctor or harm the child.

A parent might claim that he or she had no way of knowing the potential for harmful outcome. In such cases, the clinician must make a judgment about what the parent had reason to know or should have known. There are, in fact, many unintended ways of harming children that fall outside factitious disorder by proxy. For example, parents whose children have had close encounters with death frequently create psychological problems in these children whom they dearly love (Green & Solnit, 1964).

Bools, Neals, and Meadow (1992) considered that extreme cases of medical neglect might be a part of this syndrome. Their criteria imply, however, that the abuse must appear repeatedly in the health care context and that acute symptoms and signs of illness cease when the child is separated from the perpetrator. Similarly, Munchausen syndrome by proxy was considered by Godding and Kruth (1991) in

17 mothers of asthmatic children who failed to administer relief to their children during an attack. These mothers withheld preventative treatment or knowingly used ineffective treatments. However, it is important to differentiate a clinical problem from one of intentional abuse.

Unusual forms of child abuse, like intentional burns (Montrey & Barcia, 1985), should probably not be considered factitious disorder by proxy unless played out in the context of ongoing medical care. On the other hand, certain prenatal abuse syndromes (Porter, Heitsch, & Miller, 1993) and some fabricated psychiatric syndromes (Fisher, Mitchell, & Murdoch, 1993) might be appropriate for the proxy diagnosis. Similarly, collusion of parent and child in the feigning of symptoms might be a critical sign of distress and potential harm (MacDonald, 1989; Masterson, Dunworth, & Williams, 1988). Guandolo (1985) described a 5-year-old boy who feigned sleep, lethargy, and pain when his mother brought him to the physician's office.

Children can be easily harmed through invasive medical procedures. Meadow noted that shamefully doctors sometimes injured the children more than the mothers did. Warner and Hathaway (1984) suggested that pediatricians harmed children indirectly through their unwitting collusion with mothers who wrongly believed in a food allergy as the explanation of the child's problem. Finally, Meadow (1994) noted that physicians can cause harm by allowing factitious disorders to persist. He mentioned a child who learned from his mother that they could deceive physicians by insisting that he was urinating through his umbilicus (Mitchels, 1983) This child matured, and as a young man he appeared in numerous emergency departments of teaching hospitals with the same story—and the senior house officers referred him to the surgeons. Meadow decried the fact that physicians wasted service and reinforced the illness role because doctors could not say what a bartender in any local pub would have said: "You've got a screw loose."

Rosenberg (1987) suggested that Munchausen syndrome by proxy may be defined as a cluster of symptoms including: (1) illness in a child that is simulated or produced by a parent, (2) presentation of the child for medical assessment and care, usually persistently, (3) denial of knowledge by the perpetrator about the etiology of the illness, and (4) abatement of acute symptoms when the child is separated from the perpetrator. Factitious disorder by proxy, in my view, should retain a strict definition to avoid confusion with more general child abuse and be based on factual information, not speculation. Many categories of illness presentations can be mistaken for factitious disorder by proxy (Ostfeld & Feldman, 1996); the diagnosis should be made on the appearance of a syndrome, not isolated symptoms.

As this chapter goes to press, the dimensions of the diagnosis continue to be debated (Fisher & Mitchell, 1995; Meadow, 1995; Morley, 1995). Clinicians should acknowledge the current uncertainty and carefully assess behaviors of the mother that put the child at risk.

Assessment

Signs of Munchausen syndrome by proxy can be detected in characteristics of the child, the parent, and the historical records. In the child, warning signals include persistent or recurrent illnesses that cannot be explained. Signs are often at variance with the general health of the child. That is, the child may have fever and not look ill, or he may have blood loss and not look as if he has been bleeding. The diseases of these children often do not make clinical sense, and experienced specialists frequently remark that they have never seen a case like this.

Munchausen syndrome by proxy should be considered when treatments are not tolerated and traditional therapy is not successful. Intravenous lines come out unexpectedly, seizures do not respond to anticonvulsants, and prescribed drugs are vomited. One should also be suspicious when dramatic symptoms are reported but not observed.

Certain disorders are likely candidates for proxy. Meadow reported that epilepsy was the most commonly feigned complaint, followed by bleeding disorders, allergy complaints, and neurological symptoms (Meadow, 1982, 1984). Mothers with nursing education are apparently able to concoct more exotic disorders than mothers who have not had such training. Physical examination should involve a search for other signs of abuse.

Rogers et al. (1976) outlined a drug-screening program for children suspected of having been poisoned. A specific search is more likely to be successful than a blind search, because prescribed medications can obscure the presence of other drugs (Lorber, Reckless, & Watson, 1980). Remember that a parent can overdose a child with medications prescribed for the child (Mahesh, 1988).

In addition, signs will likely be evident in the perpetrator as well. A thorough social history should include inquiry into the health of all family members. Other factitious or unexplained symptoms, especially those similar to the child's, should warn the clinician. Reports of other infant death or abuse should be noted. Light and Sheridan (1990) rightly suggest that the history should be taken in a way that can establish a pattern of truth telling, exaggeration, or poor reality testing.

The clinician should also be alert for nursing or paramedical training, especially in the case of mothers. When fathers are the active caretakers, their role in perpetrating the syndrome may make detection more difficult, because their styles may be quite different from those of mothers (Jones et al., 1993; Makar & Squier, 1990; Single & Henry, 1991).

One would expect mothers with this syndrome to be quite disturbed. A wide spectrum of pathology has been noted (Atoynatan et al., 1988), but most parents appear surprisingly normal at first observation. Indeed, many seem to be loving parents who often spend inordinate amounts of time with their children and sometimes refuse to leave them alone in the hospital. They may spend time making friends with nurses, performing volunteer tasks for other mothers, and interacting with the junior medical staff. This involvement may serve to reduce suspicion and avoid confrontation. Sometimes the parents are unusually calm while the staff

is in distress, although exceptions are noted (Rogers et al., 1976). In a study of 97 mothers identified in the medical literature, an overwhelming number were described as having an affable and friendly demeanor. Nevertheless, the mothers' loneliness and isolation were also apparent when the women were interviewed. Ten percent of the perpetrators had a diagnosis of Munchausen syndrome, with Munchausen features evident in another 14%.

Children with mothers who have Munchausen syndrome have been described as having the Polle syndrome, a reference to Baron Münchhausen's child, who died at an early age (Burman & Stevens, 1977; Verity et al., 1979). Strassburg and Peuckert (1977) objected to the use of this term because the parents had no part in this child's death, and the usage does not correspond with other historical facts. Indeed, the use of the term "Polle syndrome" probably creates unnecessary diagnostic clutter. Further, Munchausen syndrome is named after the storybook character created by Rudolf Raspe, not the historical baron upon whom his stories were based (Pankratz, 1986). Nevertheless, it is important to remember that the medical history of the mother is an important part of the child's medical history.

Covert video surveillance is the most controversial method of assessment (Bartholomew, 1994; Editor, 1994; Foreman & Farsides, 1993; Wade, 1994). Alternatives with fewer ethical and legal implications should be considered first, although delay may endanger the child (Feldman, 1994a; Williams & Bevan, 1988). A camera focused on a child should be used solely for the child's protection and should not create entrapment or in any way increase the likelihood of an illegal act (Epstein et al., 1987; Frost, Glaze, & Rosen, 1988). The use of video surveillance resulted in confirmation of abuse in 30 of 34 cases at the North Staffordshire Hospital, as well as a confession of two murders (Samuels & Southall, 1994). Evans (1995) vigorously criticized this report, suggesting that the protocol should have been submitted to an independent committee for ethical assessment. Nevertheless, legal consideration of this approach has been generally favorable (Yorker, 1996).

Treatment

When Meadow encountered his first case of Munchausen syndrome by proxy, he confronted the mother in an indirect manner. Subsequently the child died. This had a profound effect on Meadow, and he began to recommend a much more direct approach. He subsequently told each mother that he knew exactly what she was doing. In these later cases, the mothers did not admit their roles, but the problems stopped. Not all cases end so easily.

In the United States, strict laws govern the reporting of child abuse. Therefore, treatment must be considered within this context. Evidence suggests that children are at risk even in mild cases because of subsequent developmental and emotional problems (Nading & Duval-Arnould, 1984; Roth, 1990). Furthermore, such children and their siblings are often objects of continued medical fabrications (Alexander, Smith, & Stevenson, 1990; McGuire & Feldman, 1989). In one large study, 43% of the siblings of victims of factitious disorder by proxy were also abused or neglected (Bools, Neals, & Meadow, 1993). Thirty-nine percent had been victims of fabricated illnesses, and 17% had suffered from failure to thrive, nonaccidental injury, or inappropriate medication. Eleven of the siblings had died without medically conclusive reasons. Thus, in confirmed cases of factitious disorder by proxy, management must involve the larger family.

It should be noted that reporting is not a solution, and unexpected complications are certain to follow. Attorneys and judges may have difficulty believing the bizarre allegations against parents, and they need to be carefully educated (Waller, 1983). But what about *suspected* factitious disorder by proxy?

Suspected abuse can have various meanings. One might consider (suspect) a diagnosis of factitious disorder by proxy during the assessment process. Precipitous reporting would be ill advised, however, if child protective service workers were unnecessarily thrust into the assessment process when a clinical resolution would be sufficient. Suddenly, clinicians are cast into adversarial roles with the parents, and

ancillary staff may split into factions (Blix & Brack, 1988). Caseworkers, who may have good experience with traditional abuse but not with this unusual variation, may not have the experience or expertise to make a diagnosis in an area where experts disagree.

On the other hand, engaging a family in extended therapy, with the hope that the problem will disappear, may delay needed intervention. Instead, the clinician should consider the evidence for abuse, the risks created by deception, and the factors that suggest a poor prognosis.

The primary goal of management is the safety of the child. Certain factors suggest the importance of removing a child from the home or denial of reunification: history of severe abuse (especially during infancy), unexplained deaths of siblings, lack of insight, history of factitious disorder in the mother, insistence that only medical problems are at issue, and lack of understanding by the broader social support system. Pervasive denial of responsibility is characteristic of this syndrome (Feldman, 1994b), which creates a poor prognosis and a strain on therapists, who feel responsible for producing results.

A pediatrician, knowledgeable about the child's history and about factitious disorder by proxy, should be assigned by the court as gatekeeper for all the child's health care needs (Ostfeld & Feldman, 1996). In most cases the treatment process will involve multiple social services to provide remedial skills to the parents.

Because no standards of care currently exist for factitious disorder by proxy, treatment should emerge from the assessment findings, not from the diagnostic label. The assessment of parenting skills, for example, will provide directions for necessary skill training. Similarly, assessment of the social support system and individual personality assessment will suggest strategies.

Libow and Schreier (1986) described the proxy syndrome along a spectrum running from Help Seekers to Doctor Addicts to Active Inducers. Confrontation with the Help Seeker often allows the mother to communicate her anxiety, exhaustion, or depression.

Doctor Addicts, on the other hand, may be more suspicious, antagonistic, and paranoid. They insist that their child is ill, resist psychiatric intervention, and are likely to flee to other treatment settings. The Active Inducers are most commonly associated with the sensational aspects of the syndrome.

Understanding this spectrum may help the clinician create an appropriate intervention. One mother came to trust her physicians sufficiently so that she was able to admit causing the factitious illness (Kravitz & Wilmott, 1990). As a result, clinicians were able to provide strong support without confrontation. Nicol and Eccles (1985) were able to address the simplistic religious beliefs of one mother as part of her therapy.

Comments

This writer has now written 14 reports on cases initially presented as factitious disorder by proxy. In only two of these cases did I conclude that the diagnosis was applied appropriately. I believe the false conclusions resulted mostly from attraction to a faddish, exotic diagnosis. Sometimes complex clinical issues were thrown into the legal arena, diverting attention from difficult management responsibilities.

In one case a mother repeatedly brought her two children to pediatricians for trivial problems. However, there was no evidence of injury, and physicians never engaged in invasive testing. The symptoms of the children were merely those typical of childhood, quite in contrast to symptoms described or created by most proxy mothers. To complicate matters, this mother had personal qualities that most people strongly disliked, and the state caseworkers decided they should remove her children from her care. This writer's assessment was that she had a somatization disorder, which had not been identified despite repeated evaluations by many clinicians, and she was merely bringing her children to the doctor in the same way she had sought medical attention for herself. She had no discernible intention to harm or deceive.

Another falsely accused mother was extremely bright, which perhaps resulted in her holding unreasonably high expectations for her oldest child. Mood disorders were evident on both sides of the family, and this mother sought repeated psychiatric hospitalizations for her son on the basis of what she considered a manic-depressive disorder. However, the severity of his symptoms, as described by her, was not evident while he was an inpatient. Eventually, the possibility of a Munchausen syndrome by proxy with psychological signs was raised. A child psychiatrist who reviewed the voluminous records made his case for the proxy diagnosis in each setting, and on this basis legal charges were brought against the mother and the father to remove the child from their custody.

This second mother was not trying to assume a sick role by proxy. If she sometimes appeared to be engaged in a "game" with the clinicians, it was not one she enjoyed. She was often in disagreement with the psychiatrists about management strategies, but she sincerely loved her child and cooperated fully when taught good behavioral management techniques. Ironically, legal charges were initiated after the child had successfully lived at home for several months. Although it was easy to understand their concern for the child, one wonders whether the child psychiatrist and district attorney were simply fascinated with this unusual diagnosis. Charges were dropped after these issues were delineated in a report.

In neither of these cases did the mother conspire against a physician to create the impression of illness she knew was false. Neither intentionally withheld, distorted, or manufactured information to deceive a physician. All had problems that should have been managed clinically. Instead, they became entangled in legal controversy.

In another case I found minor but sufficient signs to make the diagnosis of factitious disorder by proxy. However, these problems in the medical setting were overshadowed by a far more pervasive pattern of abuse and neglect. I carefully reviewed this mother's problems of bad judgment, alcohol and drug abuse, and household disarray that put her children at serious risk. Even in this case, it seemed to me that the fascination with her factitious disorder by proxy diverted everyone's attention from her massive, long-standing problems to the point that they were unable to act on the more immediate issues of the child's safety.

Munchausen syndrome by proxy is another set of pathologic parental behaviors that hospitals and clinics must learn to identify, carefully assess, and manage with sensitivity.

ACKNOWLEDGMENT

The author wishes to thank Scott Smoler, D.O., for comments on sections of this chapter.

REFERENCES

Aduan, R. P., Fauci, A. S., Dale, D. C., Herzberg, J. H., & Wolff, S. M. (1979). Factitious fever and self-induced infection. *Annals of Internal Medicine*, 90, 230–242.

*Alexander, R., Smith, W., & Stevenson, R. (1990). Serial Munchausen syndrome by proxy. *Pediatrics*, 86, 581–585.

*Atoynatan, T. H., O'Reilly, E., & Loin, L. (1988). Munchausen syndrome by proxy. *Child Psychiatry and Human Development*, 19, 3–13.

Barker, J. C. (1962). The syndrome of hospital addiction (Munchausen syndrome). *Journal of Mental Science*, 108, 167–182.

*Bartholomew, A. A. (1994). Video tape and patients' rights. *Australian and New Zealand Journal of Psychiatry*, 28, 524–525.

Barton, R., & Whitehead, J. A. (1969). The gaslight phenomenon. *Lancet*, 1, 1258.

*Blix, S., & Brack, G. (1988). The effects of a suspected case of Munchausen's syndrome by proxy on a pediatric nursing staff. *General Hospital Psychiatry*, 10, 402–409.

*Bools, C. N., Neals, B. A., & Meadow, S. R. (1992). Co-morbidity associated with fabricated illness (Munchausen syndrome by proxy). *Archives of Disease in Childhood*, 67, 77–79.

*Bools, C. N., Neals, B. A., & Meadow, S. R. (1993). Follow up of victims of fabricated illness (Munchausen syndrome by proxy). *Archives of Disease in Childhood*, 69, 625–630.

Brown, N. W. (1985). Medical consequences of eating disorders. *Southern Medical Journal*, 78, 403–405.

Burman, D., & Stevens, D. (1977). Munchausen family. *Lancet*, 2, 456.

*Ceci, S. J., & Bruck, M. (1993). Suggestibility of the child witness: A historical review and synthesis. *Psychological Bulletin*, 113, 403–439.

Chandler, M., Fritz, A. S., & Hala, S. (1989). Small-scale deceit: Deception as a marker of two-, three-, and four-year-olds' early theories of mind. *Child Development*, 60, 1263–1277.

Creer, T. L., Weinberg, E., & Molk, L. (1974). Managing a hospital behavior problem: Malingering. *Journal of Behavior Therapy and Experimental Psychiatry*, 5, 259–262.

Denardo, B. A., Tucker, L. B., Miller, L. C., Szer, I. S., & Schaller, J. G. (1994). Demography of a regional pediatric rheumatology patient population. *Journal of Rheumatology*, 21, 1553–1561.

DePaulo, B. M., Stone, J. I., & Lassiter, G. D. (1985). Deceiving and detecting deceit. In B. R. Schlenker (Ed.), *The self in social life* (pp. 323–370). New York: McGraw-Hill.

Dine, M. S. (1965). Tranquilizer poisoning: An example of child abuse. *Pediatrics*, 36, 782–785.

Editor. (1994). Spying on mothers. *Lancet*, 343, 1373–1374.

Eisendrath, S. J. (1989). Factitious physical disorders: Treatment without confrontation. *Psychosomatics*, 30, 383–387.

Epstein, M. A., Markowitz, R. L., Gallo, D. M., Holmes, J. W., & Gryboski, J. D. (1987). Munchausen syndrome by proxy: Considerations in diagnosis and confirmation by video surveillance. *Pediatrics*, 80, 220–224.

Evans, D. (1995). The investigaton of life-threatening child abuse and Munchausen syndrome by proxy. *Journal of Medical Ethics*, 21, 9–13.

Feldman, M. D. (1994a). Spying on mothers (letter). *Lancet*, 344, 132.

Feldman, M. D. (1994b). Denial in Munchausen syndrome by proxy: The consulting psychiatrist's dilemma. *International Journal of psychiatry in Medicine*, 24, 121–128.

Feldman, M. D., & Escalona, R. (1991). The longing for nurturance: A case of factitious cancer. *Psychosomatics*, 32, 226–227.

Fisher, G. C., & Mitchell, I. (1995). Is Munchausen syndrome by proxy really a syndrome? *Archives of Disease in Childhood*, 72, 530–534.

*Fisher, G. C., Mitchell, I., & Murdoch, D. (1993).

Munchausen's syndrome by proxy. *British Journal of Psychiatry, 162*, 701–703.

Foreman, D. M., & Farsides, C. (1993). Ethical use of covert videoing techniques in detecting Munchausen syndrome by proxy. *British Medical Journal, 307*, 611–613.

Fras, I., & Coughlin, B. E. (1971). The treatment of factitial disease. *Psychosomatics, 12*, 117–122.

Frost, J. D., Glaze, D. G., & Rosen, C. L. (1988). Munchausen's syndrome by proxy and video surveillance. *American Journal of Diseases of Children, 142*, 917–918.

Guandolo, V. L. (1985). Munchausen syndrome by proxy: An outpatient challenge. *Pediatrics, 75*, 526–530.

*Godding, V., & Kruth, M. (1991). Compliance with treatment in asthma and Munchausen syndrome by proxy. *Archives of Disease in Childhood, 66*, 956–960.

Green, M., & Solnit, A. J. (1964). Reactions to the threatened loss of a child: A vulnerable child syndrome. *Pediatrics, 1*, 58–66.

Griffith, J. L. (1988). The family systems of Munchausen syndrome by proxy. *Family Process, 27*, 423–437.

Healy, W., & Healy, M. T. (1915). *Pathological lying, accusation, and swindling*. Boston: Little, Brown and Company.

Henderson, S. (1974). Care-eliciting behavior in man. *Journal of Nervous and Mental Disease, 159*, 172–181.

Herman-Giddens, M. E., & Berson, N. L. (1989). Harmful genital care practices in children: A type of child abuse. *Journal of the American Medical Association, 261*, 577–579.

Herzberg, J. H., & Wolff, S. M. (1972). Chronic factitious fever in puberty and adolescence: A diagnostic challenge to the family physician. *Psychiatry in Medicine, 3*, 205–212.

Hyman, R. (1989). The psychology of deception. *Annual Review of Psychology, 40*, 133–154.

Jones, J. G., Butler, H. L., Hamilton, B., Perdue, J. D., Stern, H. P., & Woody, R. C. (1986). Munchausen syndrome by proxy. *Child Abuse and Neglect, 10*, 33–40.

Jones, V. F., Badgett, J. T., Minella, J. L., & Schuschke, L. A. (1993). The role of the male caretaker in Munchausen syndrome by proxy. *Clinical Pediatrics, 32*, 245–247.

Justus, P. G., Kreutziger, S. S., & Kitchens, C. S. (1980). Probing the dynamics of Munchausen's syndrome. *Annals of Internal Medicine, 93*, 120–127.

Kravitz, R. M., & Wilmott, R. W. (1990). Munchausen syndrome by proxy presenting as factitious apnea. *Clinical Pediatrics, 28*, 587–592.

*Krener, P., & Adelman, R. (1988). Parent salvage and parent sabotage in the care of chronically ill children. *American Journal of Diseases of Children, 142*, 945–951.

Lachman, B. S., & Morgan, J. S. (1983). Factitious renal stone as a sign of internal conflict about sexual intercourse in an adolescent. *Journal of Adolescent Health Care, 4*, 123–125.

Lancman, M. E., Asconape, J. J., Graves, S., & Gibson, P. A. (1994). Psychogenic seizures in children: Long-term analysis of 43 cases. *Journal of Child Neurology, 9*, 404–407.

Larson, J. A. (1932). *Lying and its detection*. Chicago: University of Chicago Press.

*Libow, J. A., & Schreier, H. A. (1986). Three forms of factitious illness in children: When is it Munchausen syndrome by proxy? *American Journal of Orthopsychiatry, 56*, 602–611.

Light, M. J., & Sheridan, M. S. (1990). Munchausen syndrome by proxy and apnea (MBPA). *Clinical Pediatrics, 29*, 162–168.

Lipowski, Z. J. (1988). Somatization: The concept and its clinical application. *American Journal of Psychiatry, 145*, 1358–1368.

Loftus, E. F. (1993). The reality of repressed memories. *American Psychologist, 48*, 518–537.

London, S. J. (1968). The whimsy syndromes. *Archives of Internal Medicine, 122*, 448–452.

Lorber, J., Reckless, J. P. D., & Watson, J. B. G. (1980). Nonaccidental poisoning: The elusive diagnosis. *Archives of Disease in Childhood, 55*, 643–646.

MacDonald, T. M. (1989). Myalgic encephalomyelitis by proxy (letter). *British Medical Journal, 299*, 1030.

Mahesh, V. K. (1988). Application of pharmacokinetics in the diagnosis of chemical abuse in Munchausen syndrome by proxy. *Clinical Pediatrics, 27*, 243–246.

Makar, A. F., & Squier, P. J. (1990). Munchausen syndrome by proxy: Father as a perpetrator. *Pediatrics, 85*, 370–373.

*Masterson, J., Dunworth, R., & Williams, N. (1988). Extreme illness exaggeration in pediatric patients: A variant of Munchausen's by proxy? *American Journal of Orthopsychiatry, 58*, 188–195.

*McGuire, T. L., & Feldman, K. W. (1989). Psychologic morbidity of children subjected to Munchausen syndrome by proxy. *Pediatrics, 83*, 289–292.

*Meadow, R. (1977). Munchausen syndrome by proxy. *Lancet, 2,* 343–345.

Meadow, R. (1984). Factitious illness: The hinterland of child abuse. *Recent Advances in Pediatrics, 7,* 217–232.

*Meadow, R. (1985). Management of Munchausen syndrome by proxy. *Archives of Disease in Childhood, 60,* 385–393.

Meadow, R. (1989). Munchausen syndrome by proxy. *British Medical Journal, 299,* 248–250.

*Meadow, R. (1995). What is, and what is not, "Munchausen syndrome by proxy"? *Archives of Disease in Childhood, 72,* 534–538.

Meadow, S. R. (1994). Who's to blame—mothers, Munchausen or medicine? *Journal of the Royal College of Physicians of London, 28,* 332–337.

*Mims, J., & Antonello, J. L. (1994). Treatment of nonepileptic psychogenic events in adolescent patients using the systems model for intervention. *Journal of Neuroscience Nursing, 26,* 298–305.

Mitchell, I., Brummitt, J., DeForest, J., & Fisher, G. (1993). Apnea and factitious illness (Munchausen syndrome) by Proxy. *Pediatrics, 92,* 810–814.

*Mitchels, B. (1983). Munchausen syndrome by proxy—protecting the child. *Journal Forensic Science Society, 23,* 105–111.

Montrey, J. S., & Barcia, P. J. (1985). Nonaccidental burns in child abuse. *Southern Medical Journal, 78,* 1324–1326.

Morgan, M. E. I., Manning, D. J., Williams, W. J., & Rosenbloom, L. (1984). Fictitious epilepsy (letter). *Lancet, 2,* 233.

Morley, C. J. (1992). Experts differ over diagnostic criteria for Munchausen syndrome by proxy (letter). *British Journal of Hospital Medicine, 48,* 197.

*Morley, C. J. (1995). Practical concerns about the diagnosis of Munchausen syndrome by proxy. *Archives of Disease in Childhood, 72,* 528–529.

Nading, J. H., & Duval-Arnould, B. (1984). Factitious diabetes mellitus confirmed by ascorbic acid. *Archives of Disease in Childhood, 59,* 166–179.

*Nicol, A. R., & Eccles, M. (1985). Psychotherapy for Munchausen syndrome by proxy. *Archives of Disease in Childhood, 60,* 344–348.

O'Shea, B. M., McGennis, A. J., Lowe, N. F., & O'Rourke, M. H. (1982). Psychiatric evaluation of a Munchausen's syndrome. *Irish Medical Journal, 75,* 200–202.

*Ostfeld, B. M., & Feldman, M. D. (1996). Factitious disorder by proxy: Clinical features, detection, and management. In M. Feldman & S. Eisendrath, (Eds.), *The spectrum of factitious disorders.* Washington, DC: American Psychiatric Press.

Pankratz, L. (1981). A review of the Munchausen syndrome. *Clinical Psychology Review, 1,* 65–78.

Pankratz, L. (1986). Münchhausen versus Munchausen. *Medical Journal of Australia, 145,* 301.

Pankratz, L., & Jackson, J. (1994). Habitually wandering patients. *New England Journal of Medicine, 331,* 1752–1755.

Pankratz, L., & McCarthy, G. (1986). The ten least wanted patients. *Southern Medical Journal, 79,* 613–620.

Paperny, D., Hicks, R., & Hammar, S. L. (1980). Munchausen's syndrome. *American Journal of Diseases of Children, 134,* 794–795.

Pickering, D. (1964). Salicylate poisoning: The diagnosis when its possibility is denied by the parents. *Acta Paediatrica Scandinavica, 53,* 501–504.

Porter, G. E., Heitsch, G. M., & Miller, M. M. (1993). Munchausen syndrome by proxy (letter). *Medical Journal of Australia, 158,* 720.

*Putnam, N., & Stein, M. (1985). Self-inflicted injuries in childhood. *Clinical Pediatrics, 24,* 514–518.

Raymer, D., Weininger, O., & Hamilton, J. R. (1984). Psychological problems in children with abdominal pain. *Lancet, 1,* 439–440.

Raymond, C. A. (1987). Munchausen's may occur in younger persons. *Journal of the American Medical Association, 257,* 3332.

*Reich, P., & Gottfried, L. A. (1983). Factitious disorders in a teaching hospital. *Annals of Internal Medicine, 99,* 240–247.

Repper, J. (1995). Munchausen syndrome by proxy in health care workers. *Journal of Advanced Nursing, 21,* 299–304.

Rogers, D., Tripp, J., Bentovim, A., Robinson, A., Berry, D., & Goulding, R. (1976). Non-accidental poisoning: An extended syndrome of child abuse. *British Medical Journal, 1,* 793–796.

Rogers, R., Bagby, M., & Rector, N. (1989). Diagnostic legitimacy of factitious disorder with psychological symptoms. *American Journal of Psychiatry, 146,* 1312–1314.

*Rosenberg, D. A. (1987). Web of deceit: A literature review of Munchausen syndrome by proxy. *Child Abuse and Neglect, 11,* 547–563.

Roth, D. (1990). How "mild" is mild Munchausen syndrome by proxy? *Israel Journal of Psychiatry and Related Sciences, 27,* 160–167.

Samuels, M. P., & Southall, D. (1994). Welfare of

the child must come first (letter). *British Medical Journal, 308*, 1101–1102.

Schade, D. S., Drumm, D. A., Duckworth, W. C., & Eaton, R. P. (1985). The etiology of incapacitating, brittle diabetes. *Diabetes Care, 8*, 12–20.

*Schreier, H. A., & Libow, J. A. (1993). Munchausen syndrome by proxy: Diagnosis and prevalence. *American Journal Orthopsychiatry, 63*, 318–321.

Shaner, A., & Eth, S. (1988). Pseudoadolescent Munchausen syndrome. *Comprehensive Psychiatry, 29*, 561–565.

Sheehy, T. W. (1992). Care report: Factitious hypoglycemia in diabetic patients. *American Journal of Medical Science, 304*, 298–302.

Sheppard, N. P., O'Loughlin, S., & Malone, J. P. (1986). Psychogenic skin disease: A review of 35 cases. *British Journal of Psychiatry, 149*, 636–643.

Shnaps, Y., Frand, M., Rotem, Y., & Tirosh, M. (1981). The chemically abused child. *Pediatrics, 68*, 119–121.

Sigal, M. D., Altmark, D., & Carmel, I. (1986). Munchausen syndrome by adult proxy: A perpetrator abusing two adults. *Journal of Nervous and Mental Disease, 174*, 696–698.

Single, T., & Henry, R. L. (1991). An unusual case of Munchausen syndrome by proxy. *Australian and New Zealand Journal of Psychiatry, 25*, 422–425.

Smith, C. G., & Sinanan, K. (1972). The "gaslight phenomenon" reappears—a modification of the ganser syndrome. *British Journal of Psychiatry, 120*, 685–686.

Smith, T. W., Snyder, C. R., & Perkins, S. C. (1983). The self-serving function of hypochondriacal complaints: Physical symptoms as self-handicapping strategies. *Journal of Personal and Social Psychology, 44*, 787–797.

Sneed, R. C., & Bell, R. F. (1976). The Dauphin of Munchausen: Factitious passage of renal stones in a child. *Pediatrics, 58*, 127–130.

Solomon, R. ,L. (1980). The opponent-process theory of acquired motivation: The costs of pleasure and the benefits of pain. *American Psychologist, 35*, 691–712.

Stevenson, R. D., & Alexander, R. (1990). Munchausen syndrome by proxy presenting as a developmental disability. *Developmental and Behavioral Pediatrics, 11*, 262–264.

Stewart, D. J., & Kernohan, D. C. (1972). Self-inflicted gingival injuries. *Dental Practitioner, 22*, 418–426.

Strassburg, H. M., & Peuckert, W. (1977). Not "Polle syndrome," please (letter). *Lancet, 1*, 166.

Tec, L. (1975). Precursors of Munchausen's syndrome in childhood. *American Journal of Psychiatry, 132*, 757.

Triplett, N. (1900). The psychology of conjuring deceptions. *American Journal of Psychology, 11*, 439–510.

Verity, C. M., Winckworth, C., Burman, D., Stevens, D., & White, R. J. (1979). Polle syndrome: Children of Munchausen. *British Journal of Medical Practice, 2*, 422–423.

*Wade, R. (1994). Video tape and patients' rights. *Australian and New Zealand Journal of Psychiatry, 28*, 525–526.

*Waller, D. A. (1983). Obstacles to the treatment of Munchausen by proxy syndrome. *Journal of the American Academy of Child Psychiatry, 22*, 80–85.

Warner, J. O., & Hathaway, M. J. (1984). Allergic form of Meadow's syndrome (Munchausen by proxy). *Archives of Disease in Childhood, 59*, 151–156.

Wasserman, A. L. (1988). Psychogenic basis for abdominal pain in children and adolescents. *Journal of the American Academy of Child Psychiatry, 27*, 179–184.

Williams, C., & Bevan, V. T. (1988). The secret observation of children in hospital. *Lancet, 2*, 780–781.

Witt, M. E., & Ginsberg-Fellner, F. (1981). Prednisone-induced Munchausen syndrome. *American Journal of Diseases of Children, 135*, 852–853.

Yorker, B. C. (1996). Legal issues in factitious disorder by proxy. In M. Feldman & S. Eisendrath (Eds.), *The spectrum of factitious disorders*. Washington, DC: American Psychiatric Press.

*Indicates references that the author recommends for further reading.

16
Somatoform Disorders

John V. Campo
Manuel D. Reich

INTRODUCTION

Historical Perspective

Somatoform disorders are diagnosed in "the presence of physical symptoms that suggest a general medical condition, and are not fully explained by a general medical condition, by the direct effects of a substance, or by another mental disorder" (American Psychiatric Association, 1994, p. 445). They are defined by the presence of physical symptoms that suggest a physical disorder in the absence of physical pathology or demonstrable pathophysiologic findings.

The term "somatization" is commonly used descriptively and has been defined as the experience of physical symptoms in situations where medical evaluation shows no apparent physical pathology or where the physical symptoms exceed what would be expected on the basis of the medical findings (Kellner, 1991; Lipowski, 1988). In this chapter, the term "somatization" is used descriptively unless otherwise specified, but it is important to note that it has also been used to refer to a presumed mechanism of symptom production or as the defining label for a categorical psychiatric disorder known as

somatization disorder, one of the somatoform disorders. The multiple meanings are reminiscent of past uses of the term "hysteria," which has referred to a mechanism of symptom production, a clinical presentation characterized by multiple unexplained somatic symptoms in a variety of organ systems, and a dramatic personality style associated with the amplification and exaggeration of distress (Slavney, 1990).

Somatoform disorders and the conceptualization of somatization are unique to modern Western medicine and its biomedical paradigm, which emphasizes the importance of physical disease as the cause of physical suffering (Fabrega, 1990). Physical disease is considered to be an objectively verifiable disturbance that is accountable to a pathophysiologic process, is reducible to biophysical or biochemical terms, and has a natural history and course. In contrast, illness simply refers to the patient's subjective distress and related behaviors. Western medicine appears to be somewhat unique in that the subjective complaints of the patient are investigated by physicians in an attempt to validate their presence by associating them with the physical signs of disease. The Western system of externally validating the physical suffering of patients did not develop in traditional Chinese or Indian medicine, where the patient's symptoms and symptom complexes formed the basic data of medicine (Fabrega, 1990).

The term "neurosis" was originally applied to patients who suffered from a variety of physical discomforts unassociated with any evidence of tissue pathology (Goldberg & Bridges, 1988), and a psychological model of illness developed alongside the biomedical model as a result of the conceptual problems posed by patients with physical symptoms in the absence of recognizable physical disease (Weiner & Fawzy, 1989). This split between the physical and the psychological has evolved to be exemplified in the disciplines that have developed to care for sick and suffering individuals in our culture. Traditional medicine and its related disciplines have maintained a primarily biomedical focus, while the mental health disciplines have been simplistically relegated to the realm of the psychological or the mind. Nevertheless, despite the advances of modern medicine and the utility of the biomedical model, physicians continue to be confronted by patients who report significant physical distress in the absence of physical disease.

Somatization has long been recognized as a problem in children and adolescents, and the topic has been recently reviewed (Campo, 1993; Campo & Fritsch, 1994; Campo & Garber, 1998; Garralda, 1992). During the nineteenth century, the French physician Briquet described a number of patients with both single and multiple medically unexplained physical symptoms, with the majority of patients developing their sufferings prior to age 20 and one-fifth prior to puberty; early onset was associated with an especially poor prognosis (Mai & Merskey, 1980). Freud (1962) emphasized the importance of childhood experiences in the development of so-called hysterical symptoms. Modern interest in childhood somatization, particularly recurrent pain, was stimulated largely by the work of Apley (1958, 1975).

Classification

The *Diagnostic and Statistical Manual of Mental Disorders*, Fourth Edition (DSM-IV) (American Psychiatric Association, 1994) includes physical symptoms among the criteria for a number of psychiatric disorders such as anxiety disorders and mood disorders. Physical symptoms assume a special role in the DSM-IV category of "somatoform disorders," which are defined by the presence of physical symptoms that suggest a physical disorder but that are not fully explained by the presence of a general medical condition, the direct effects of a substance, or another mental disorder, such as panic disorder, for example (APA, 1994). Further, the reported symptoms must cause distress and/or some degree of functional impairment, do not appear to be intentionally produced, and the patient does not appear to experience any sense of control over the symptoms. The reader is referred to DSM-IV (APA, 1994) and to the *Classification of Mental and Behavioral Disorders* (ICD-10) (World Health Organization, 1992) for details of the current diagnostic nomenclature. In ICD-10, the somatoform disorders are characterized by the repeated presentation of physical symptoms and persistent requests for medical investigations in spite of repeated negative findings and reassurances by doctors that the symptoms have no physical basis (WHO, 1992).

Somatoform disorders are distinguished from factitious disorders and malingering, where the physical symptoms are judged to be intentionally produced or feigned and appear to be under the voluntary control of the patient (APA, 1994). In factitious disorder, physical symptoms are deliberately feigned or self-inflicted by the patient, with the patient's goal appearing to be an internal one in the form of the psychological gain presumably associated with the sick role. In factitious disorder by proxy, a parent or caretaker feigns, simulates, or causes disease in a child with the motivation being an internal one for the caretaker. Malingering, in contrast, is the deliberate feigning, simulation, or production of physical symptoms in pursuit of an external incentive, such as the avoidance of a particular responsibility or punishment, or the pursuit of financial gain.

"Psychological factors affecting medical condition" is the diagnosis applied in DSM-IV when psychological factors adversely affect a known general medical condition, such as migraine associated with anxiety or depression (APA, 1994). When the symptom is limited to pain associated with a general medical condition, it is classified under pain disorder in DSM-IV (discussed later). Pains or symptoms due to known or inferred psychophysiologic mechanisms such as muscle tension or migraine but still believed to be produced or exacerbated by psychological factors are diagnosed as "psychological or behavioral factors associated with disorders or diseases classified elsewhere" in ICD-10 (WHO, 1992).

There are seven specific somatoform disorders in DSM-IV: somatization disorder, undifferentiated somatoform disorder, conversion disorder, pain disorder, hypochondriasis, body dysmorphic disorder, and somatoform disorder, not otherwise specified (APA, 1994).

The diagnosis of "somatization disorder" is historically based on the earlier diagnostic conceptualizations of hysteria and Briquet's syndrome and refers to a recurrent disorder beginning before age 30 and characterized by multiple and varied somatic complaints that result in medical help seeking and/or significant functional impairment. The diagnostic criteria are quite specific and require a history of pain in at least four different sites across the course of the disturbance and at least two gastrointestinal symptoms, one sexual or reproductive symptom, and one pseudoneurologic symptom other than pain (APA, 1994). The DSM-IV criteria have been based on an extensive body of work by psychiatric researchers in the Midwestern United States (see Cloninger, 1994). In the past, the diagnosis had been based on elaborate symptom counts from an extensive list of physical symptoms, with the DSM-IV diagnosis constituting a significant simplification of the diagnostic process and being based on what appear to be the core features of this empirically derived disorder.

The prevalence of somatization disorder in the pediatric population is unknown, but the diagnosis as previously defined in earlier editions of DSM appears to be rare in prepubertal children (Offord et al., 1987; Walker, Garber, & Greene, 1991). Even the current diagnostic criteria may prove difficult to apply to children, given the requirement for reports of a sexual or reproductive symptom, which appeared to limit the pediatric utility of earlier categorizations (Garber et al., 1991; Livingston & Martin-Cannici, 1985; Walker et al., 1991). Nevertheless, children who meet the criteria for earlier diagnostic formulations have been reported (Kriechman, 1987; Livingston & Martin-Cannici, 1985).

The diagnostic guidelines for "somatization disorder" are not as restrictive in ICD-10, where the diagnosis requires at least 2 years of multiple and variable physical symptoms for which no physical explanation can be found, persistent refusal by the patient to accept the advice or reassurance of several doctors, and some degree of functional impairment as a result of the symptoms and resulting behaviors (WHO, 1992).

A diagnosis more likely to be made in children and adolescents is that of "undifferentiated somatoform disorder," which is applied when there are one or more physical complaints present for at least 6 months (e.g., fatigue, gastrointestinal symptoms, urinary complaints) and the other criteria for the diagnosis of a somatoform disorder are met (APA, 1994). The ICD-10 diagnosis of undifferentiated somatoform disorder is made in cases of pediatric somatization where the typical clinical picture of somatization disorder is not fulfilled (WHO, 1992).

The diagnosis of "conversion disorder" is made when one or more deficits or symptoms that affect voluntary motor or sensory function and that suggest a neurological or other general medical condition are present, other criteria for a somatoform disorder are met, and emotional or psychological factors are judged to be associated with the symptoms or deficits as a result of observations that the symptoms or deficits are preceded by conflicts or other stressors (APA, 1994). This definition of conversion disorder is a return to the more traditional conceptualization of the diagnosis as limited to symptoms that suggest neurologic disease or pseudoneurologic symptoms, a retreat from earlier editions of DSM where conversion disorder was unique in that the diagnosis was based on a presumed mechanism of symptom production. There are four subtypes in DSM-IV, depending on whether the symptoms presented are primarily motor, sensory, nonepileptic seizures, or mixed.

What is classified in DSM-IV as "conversion disorder" is classified in ICD-10 as "dissociative [conversion] disorders" (WHO, 1992). The diagnoses are based on the type of symptoms or deficits presented, with categories dedicated to dissociative motor disorders, dissociative convulsions, dissociative anaesthesia and sensory loss, mixed dissociative disorders, and dissociative disorder, unspecified.

"Pain disorder" is diagnosed when pain in one or more anatomical sites is the predominant focus of clinical presentation, is of sufficient severity to warrant clinical attention, and causes significant distress or functional impairment (APA, 1994). Psychological factors are judged to play a significant role in the onset, intensity, worsening, or maintenance of the pain, and the pain is not intentionally produced or feigned. There are three subtypes: pain disorder associated with psychological factors, where psychological factors are judged as playing the major role in the genesis or maintenance of the pain; pain disorder associated with both psychological factors and a general medical condition, where psychological factors and a general medical condition are judged to play important roles in the development or maintenance of pain; and pain disorder associated with a general medical condition, which is not considered a mental disorder, is coded on Axis III, and in which psychological factors are judged to play no more than a minimal role. The mental disorder diagnoses are specified as acute if of less than 6 months' duration and chronic if the duration is 6 months or greater. The ICD-10 category "persistent somatoform pain disorder" is less specific than those in DSM-IV but includes complaints of persistent pain that cannot be fully explained by a physiological process or physical disorder (WHO, 1992).

In DSM-IV, the term "hypochondriasis" refers to at least 6 months of preoccupation or belief by a patient that a serious physical disease is present, and the preoccupation or belief persists despite appropriate medical evaluation and reassurance (APA, 1994). The patient's disease conviction is not exaggerated and out of contact with reality, as in delusional disorder, somatic type. Hypochondriasis is also not diagnosed when the belief or preoccupation is limited to an imagined defect in appearance. In such circumstances, "body dysmorphic disorder" is diagnosed instead, as it is in circumstances where a slight physical anomaly is present, but the patient's concern is excessive (APA, 1994). The ICD-10 diagnosis "hypochondriacal disorder" lacks duration criteria and includes presentations that would be classified as body dysmorphic disorder in DSM-IV but otherwise parallels the DSM-IV category (WHO, 1992).

Other disorders that appear in ICD-10 but not in DSM-IV include "somatoform autonomic dysfunction" and "neurasthenia," though categories comparable to those in ICD-10 were considered for inclusion in DSM-IV but ultimately eliminated from the final draft. Somatoform autonomic dysfunction addresses symptoms that are presented by the patient as appearing to be due to a physical disorder of a system or organ that is largely controlled and innervated by the autonomic nervous system and associated with symptoms of autonomic arousal (WHO, 1992). There are specific subcategories of the diagnosis depending on whether the symptoms appear to be based in a particular organ system, including the heart and cardiovascular system, the upper gastrointestinal tract, the lower gastrointestinal tract, the respiratory system, and the genitourinary system. Neurasthenia is a concept with a long history in Western medicine (Wessely, 1990). Diagnostic guidelines in ICD-10 include persistent and troubling complaints of fatigue after mental effort and/or minimal physical effort, as well as at least two symptoms from a list that includes muscular aches and pains, dizziness, headache, sleep disturbance, inability to relax, irritability, and dyspepsia (WHO, 1992).

"Somatoform disorder, not otherwise specified" is diagnosed when symptoms consistent with a somatoform disorder are present, but criteria for a specific disorder are not met (APA, 1994). Examples include unexplained physical symptoms such as fatigue or hypochondriacal concerns that are of less than 6 months' duration. ICD-10 includes a similar category, called "somatoform disorder, unspecified," to account for presentations not addressed by other ICD-10 categories (WHO, 1992).

Epidemiology

There is little information available regarding the incidence and prevalence of specific somatoform disorders in children and adolescents, but review of the literature indicates that medically unexplained physical symptoms are exceedingly common in children and adolescents (Campo & Fritsch, 1994; Garralda, 1992). Recurrent complaints of pain are especially common in school-age children and adolescents, with the most common symptoms being headache, reported in 10–30% (Aro, Paronen, & Aro, 1987; Belmaker, Espinoza, & Pogrund, 1985; Garber, Walker, & Zeman, 1991; Larson, 1991; Oster, 1972; Rutter, Tizard, & Whitmore, 1970), and recurrent abdominal pain, which has been reported in 10–25% (Apley, 1975; Belmaker et al., 1985; Garber et al., 1991; Oster, 1972). Approximately 4% of pediatric visits are for complaints of abdominal distress, and 2% focus on headache, suggesting that abdominal discomfort may generate special concern (Starfield et al., 1984). Other commonly reported symptoms include fatigue, dizziness, nausea and vomiting, limb pains, and chest pain (Garber et al., 1991).

It is important to note that pseudoneurological symptoms, or symptoms suggestive of a neurological disorder in the absence of demonstrable neurologic disease, are unusual in community samples of children and adolescents in most modern Western cultures (Garber et al., 1991; Rutter et al., 1970; Stefansson, Messina, & Meyerowitz, 1976). Such symptoms appear to become increasingly common

in specific settings, such as tertiary referral pediatric centers and pediatric neurology services, where nonepileptic seizures, faints, falls, and abnormalities of gait or sensation are the most commonly reported conversion symptoms (Goodyer, 1981; Goodyer & Mitchell, 1989; Grattan-Smith, Fairley, & Procopis, 1988; Lehmkuhl, Blanz, Lehmkuhl, & Braun-Scharm, 1989; Leslie, 1988; Maloney, 1980; Spierings, Poels, Sijben, Gabreels, & Renier, 1990; Steinhausen, Aster, Pfeiffer, & Gobel, 1989; Volkmar, Poll, & Lewis, 1984).

In a school-based sample of more than 500 children from grades 3 through 12, nearly half reported at least one physical symptoms in a 2-week period, with 15% reporting at least four symptoms and 1% endorsing 13 or more (Garber et al., 1991). There is additional evidence that polysymptomatic presentations are quite common, with a somatization syndrome being identified in 4.5% of boys and 10.7% of girls ages 12–16 years in the Ontario Child Health Study (Offord et al., 1987). Approximately a third of patients with recurrent pediatric pain experience additional physical symptoms (Apley, 1975; Oster, 1972). Further, a somatic complaints syndrome was identified by principal-components analysis in a study that employed the Child Behavior Checklist protocols of more than 8,000 children and adolescents referred for mental health services (Achenbach, Conners, Quay, Verhulst, & Howell, 1989). The Child Behavior Checklist is a well-accepted and empirically sound measure of emotional and behavioral problems in children and adolescents.

Age appears to be an important variable in the epidemiology of pediatric somatization, but there are few comprehensive longitudinal studies to provide much guidance regarding the development of somatization across the life span (Campo & Fritsch, 1994). Polysymptomatic presentations become more common with increasing age (Achenbach et al., 1989; Offord et al., 1987). Recurrent abdominal pain may be the most common symptom in early childhood (Apley, 1975), with headache becoming more prominent in late childhood (Oster, 1972). Pseudoneurologic symptoms are quite rare prior to age six (Grattan-Smith et al., 1988; Lehmkuhl et al., 1989; Leslie, 1988; Volkmar et al., 1984), and, though they remain unusual in community samples, they become increasingly common through adolescence (Stefansson et al., 1976).

Girls are more likely than boys to seek medical care for their physical complaints (Lewis & Lewis, 1989). Pseudoneurologic or conversion symptoms appear to be more prevalent in girls across all ages (Goodyer & Mitchell, 1989), but the more common complaints, such as those of recurrent pain, occur equally in boys and in girls prior to puberty, after which there is a predominance of somatic symptom reporting by females (Aro & Taipale, 1987; Garber et al., 1991; Oster, 1972; Rauste-von Wright & von Wright, 1981; Walker & Greene, 1991). Girls also appear to be more consistent in the reporting of somatic symptoms over time than are boys (Rauste-von Wright & von Wright, 1981; Walker & Greene, 1991).

Low socioeconomic status and low levels of parental education have been associated with somatic symptom reporting in childhood in some studies (Aro, Paronen, & Aro, 1987; Steinhausen et al., 1989), but not in others (Stevenson, Simpson, & Bailey, 1988; Walker & Greene, 1991). The role of social and cultural factors in pediatric somatization requires further study. Cultural factors may be important in the presentation of pseudoneurologic symptoms, as conversion symptoms are one of the most common psychiatric presentations in Turkey (Turgay, 1980) and India (Srinath, Bharat, Girimaji, & Seshadri, 1993).

Psychopathology and Theoretical Models

Somatization has been viewed in a variety of ways from a theoretical perspective (Simon, 1991). One conceptualization is that somatization may represent a learned set of interpersonal or social behaviors, with operant conditioning, classical or respondent conditioning, and social learning all potentially playing a role. The motivation may be the benefits and relief from usual obligations afforded by attainment of the sick role, including school avoidance (Goodyer

& Taylor, 1985; Slavney, 1990). There is some empirical support for the notion that physical complaints may influence parental attitudes towards the responsibilities and behaviors of children, especially when the physical symptoms are legitimized by the diagnosis of a physician (Walker, Garber, & Van Slyke, 1995). The so-called secondary gain of a symptom refers to its social and familial reinforcement (Wooley, Blackwell, & Winget, 1978). The interest and attention a parent gives to the symptom may influence the behavior and response of the child (Mechanic, 1964).

Somatization has also been understood from a psychodynamic perspective, with patients manifesting emotional or psychological distress physically and the symptoms arising as a consequence of a defensive process in which awareness of potentially troubling emotions, conflicts, or memories is subverted by the development of physical illness (Simon, 1991). From the perspective of attachment theory, the symptoms may allow the patient to maintain proximity to important attachment figures, thus serving a care-eliciting function (Henderson, 1974). Systemic thinkers have viewed somatization as serving a homeostatic or communicative function within families, perhaps allowing the family to avoid conflict (Mullins & Olson, 1990).

A more psychobiological perspective considers somatization in some of its forms to be a consequence of the physiology of emotional arousal (Kellner, 1991; Simon, 1991). Cognitive factors may also be important, with some individuals showing a heightened preoccupation and/or sensitivity to physical sensations combined with a tendency to react to physical symptoms with negative cognitions that frame the symptoms as alarming and worthy of serious concern (Barsky, 1992).

Finally, somatization may be considered a consequence of psychiatric disorder per se (Simon, 1991), and there is considerable evidence that medically unexplained physical symptoms are associated with psychiatric symptoms in children and adolescents (see Campo & Fritsch, 1994). Children with recurrent abdominal pain have been shown to present with symptoms of, predominantly, anxiety and, to a lesser extent, depression more commonly than controls (Garber, Zeman, & Walker, 1990; Hodges, Kline, Barbero, & Woodruff, 1985; Walker, Garber, & Greene, 1993; Wasserman, Whitington, & Rivera, 1988). Similarly, studies of children with anxiety disorders (Beidel, Christ, & Long, 1991; Last, 1991) and depressive disorders (McCauley, Carlson, & Calderon, 1991; Ryan et al., 1987) suggest that somatic complaints are quite common. Parents of children with recurrent abdominal pain also appear to be more vulnerable to symptoms of anxiety and depression (Garber et al., 1990; Walker & Greene, 1989). Further, having a parent with somatization disorder (Livingston, 1993) or alcoholism and antisocial behavior (Routh & Ernst, 1984) may increase the likelihood of pediatric somatization.

ASSESSMENT

The assessment of the pediatric patient with troubling and presumably medically unexplained physical symptoms should be comprehensive and broad-based. Ensuring that appropriate medical assessment has taken place is essential, and the clinician should be willing and ready to initiate further medical assessment if the clinical picture changes or if the initial assessment raises new concerns about undiagnosed physical disease. It is important to remember that all medically unexplained symptoms are not necessarily representative of a psychiatric disorder such as somatoform disorder and that physical symptoms may at times simply be unexplained. A broad view of the differential diagnosis for patients with medically unexplained physical symptoms includes undiagnosed physical disease, somatoform disorder or an associated psychiatric disorder such as an anxiety or mood disorder, factitious illness, malingering, and so-called psychophysiologic disorders, where a pathophysiologic process appears to be present that is exacerbated by psychological factors.

Too often, the absence of findings of clearcut physical disease on initial evaluation may engender the conviction that the symptoms must be "psychogenic" in origin. Patients and families may quickly feel dismissed and may become concerned that their complaints have not and will not be taken seriously, fearing that the professionals have prematurely closed the door on the possibility of discovering serious physical disease. There are certainly numerous reports in the literature of patients with presumed somatoform complaints who were subsequently discovered to suffer from a physical disease that explained the original symptoms, particularly in patients with conversion disorders (e.g., Caplan, 1970; Rivinus, Jamison, & Graham, 1975). It is important to remember, however, that this appears to be of low probability with common complaints such as RAP, where a physical disease is found in less than 10% of cases (Apley, 1975; Walker et al., 1994). Relatively recent studies of patients with conversion symptoms also suggest that the likelihood of later discovering undiagnosed physical disease that explained the original symptoms is less than 10% (Maisami & Freeman, 1987; Spierings, Poels, Sijben, Gabreels, & Renier, 1990; Volkmar et al., 1984).

Conversely, and perhaps more frequently, patients with unexplained physical symptoms may receive excessive and inappropriate medical investigations and evaluations by anxious professionals or, worse, by professionals who are convinced of the absence of serious physical disease but uncomfortable with exploring emotional and behavioral issues with the patient and family. It is not only fear of an undiagnosed physical disease that may motivate patients, families, and clinicians to pursue potentially dangerous and unnecessary medical treatments and procedures but also concerns related to the stigma of physical complaints without medical validation and the potential diagnosis of psychiatric disorder. Further, medical professionals receive more training and have a greater degree of comfort in pursuing the diagnosis of physical disease than in the evaluation and treatment of psychiatric disorder.

It is important to remember that there is no substitute for common sense in the assessment of patients with unexplained physical symptoms, and professionals often need to pay careful attention to their own emotions and reactions in the evaluatory process, as the anxiety of the patient and/or family can at times be contagious and a source of distraction from sound clinical practice. Not only are unnecessary medical tests and treatments potentially physically dangerous, but continued investigations may serve to communicate to the family and patient that the clinician expects to find physical disease, which can maintain somatization by giving the patient and family the impression that a serious physical disease has been missed and making any attempts to reassure them seem disingenuous (Goodyer & Taylor, 1985; Grattan-Smith et al., 1988).

Ideally, the diagnosis of a somatoform disorder should not simply be an exercise in excluding physical disease but should be based on positive findings as well (Dubowitz & Hersov, 1976; Friedman, 1973; Goodyer & Taylor, 1985; Maisami & Freeman, 1987). While it is seldom possible to definitively and convincingly demonstrate the absence of physical disease beyond any doubt, and it may not be possible or desirable to demonstrate that a particular symptom is "psychogenic" in nature, several "clues" to the identification of somatization and the diagnosis of a somatoform disorder exist (Campo & Garber, 1998; Friedman, 1973; Goodyer & Taylor, 1985). These include: contiguity of the symptom with psychosocial stressors or the presence of a particularly severe stressor; the presence of a diagnosable psychiatric disorder; association of the symptom with psychological or interpersonal gain for the child; existence of a model for the symptom within the child's immediate environment; the symptom's having an apparent communicative or symbolic meaning within the patient's social milieu; the symptom's violation of known anatomic or physiologic patterns judging from current scientific knowledge; and responsiveness of the symptom to placebo, suggestion, or psychological treatment. It should be evident that these clues to the diagnosis are not definitive by any means, and, though a constellation of clues taken together may be most

persuasive (Friedman, 1973), virtually all the clues to somatization mentioned may also be noted in patients with documented physical disease (e.g., Walker et al., 1993). Indifference of the patient to the physical symptoms ("la belle indifférence") has also been noted as a clue to the diagnosis of conversion disorder (Leslie, 1988; Maisami & Freeman, 1987; Volkmar et al., 1984), but the subjective nature of this finding has caused others to minimize its significance (Dubowitz & Hersov, 1976; Goodyer, 1981; Spierings et al., 1990).

Further complicating matters, somatization and demonstrable physical disease may be associated or coexist in a number of ways. The presence of a chronic medical illness may increase the risk of experiencing symptoms consistent with somatization (Kellner, 1986; Livingston, 1993; Pilowsky et al., 1982). Similarly, many children appear to develop what appears to be a somatoform disorder after experiencing an acute illness or accident, which may appear to act as a precipitant (Carek & Santos, 1984; Creak, 1938; Dubowitz & Hersov, 1976; Leslie, 1988). Children with medically unexplained physical symptoms may be more likely to have family members who suffer from a physical illness, disability, or somatization (Belmaker, 1984; Bergman & Stamm, 1967; Livingston, 1993; Walker et al., 1991; Walker et al., 1994; Zuckerman, Stevenson, & Bailey, 1987). It may be that a young person's observation or experience of the potential benefits associated with the sick role, including the avoidance of uncomfortable responsibilities or the availability of special benefits, may ultimately predispose to somatization in vulnerable individuals (Wooley, Blackwell, & Winget, 1978).

Somatization may be one of the most common presentations of psychiatric disorder in pediatric medical settings, with somatization often being associated with elevated rates of psychopathology in the identified patient and the family (Campo & Fritsch, 1994). Mental health professionals can help educate and provide the necessary back-up for colleagues who are not comfortable or proficient in psychiatric and psychological assessment. A careful assessment for the presence of psychopathology in the child or adolescent is essential, with careful attention being paid to the presence of anxiety and depressive symptoms. There are several instruments that can enhance the clinical interview to assess psychiatric symptoms in children. The Child Behavior Checklist (CBCL) is a 118-item questionnaire that rates problem behavior on a three-point scale (Achenbach & Edelbrock, 1983). Gadow and Sprafkin (1995) have also developed DSM-IV-based checklists for psychopathology in children and adolescents that are clinically useful.

Anxiety symptoms are especially common in children with recurrent complaints of pain, such as those with RAP (Garber et al., 1990; Hodges, Kline, Barbero, & Woodruff, 1985; Walker et al., 1993; Wasserman, Whitington, & Rivera, 1988). School refusal is not uncommon, particularly among children with prominent somatic complaints and associated anxiety (Last, 1991). Depressive symptoms are also common in somatizing children and adolescents (Garber et al., 1991; Kashani, Lababidi, & Jones, 1982; Kowal & Pritchard, 1990; Larson, 1991).

Obtaining supporting information from parents, health care providers, other relevant professionals, and the school is intrinsic to a sound evaluation in most cases, with school nurses often being a very useful source of information about the child's functioning at school. The presence of school difficulties, particularly learning problems, may be especially important clinically, as a skills deficit such as a learning disorder may provide motivation for school avoidance per se (Silver, 1982), and physical symptoms may also serve as "self-handicapping strategies," thus serving to provide a ready "explanation" for why a particular child may not be performing up to expectations (Walker, Garber, & Van Slyke, 1995).

Previous medical and psychiatric records should be reviewed, and the clinician should be alert to any inconsistencies or distortions in the history, as this can sometimes be a clue in the differential diagnostic process, suggesting the possibility of malingering, a factitious disorder, or factitious disorder by proxy. Medical or psychiatric records hand-carried by a parent should be handled with some degree of suspicion depending on the circumstance, as falsified records have been offered by offending caretakers in some cases of factitious disorder by proxy. In factitious disorder by proxy, the suspected parent may be medically knowledgeable, may have a history of work or intense interest in a health-related profession, and may have a history of multiple unexplained physical symptoms or even factitious illness themselves; the parent may deliver an implausible history, often relating a litany of traumatic events for the patient or family, and the child's symptoms may be surprisingly quiescent in the parent's absence (Schreier & Libow, 1993).

Careful family assessment may reveal the presence of psychiatric disorder, somatization, and/or physical illness and disability, as well as a possible model for the patient's symptoms (Apley, 1975; Garber et al., 1990; Livingston, 1993; Walker et al., 1991; Walker & Greene, 1989; Walker et al., 1993). Separation fears and a sense of parental "overprotection" may be evident (Bergman & Stamm, 1967; Grattan-Smith et al., 1988; Lehmkuhl et al., 1989; Robinson et al., 1990), and the affected child may be considered especially "vulnerable" (Green & Solnit, 1964). The clinician should also be alert to the possibility of marital conflict, communication difficulties within the family, and parent-child relational problems (Campo & Fritsch, 1994; Campo & Garber, 1998). Systemic thinkers have viewed the patient's physical symptoms at times as serving a specialized function within the family system, potentially appearing to allow the family to preserve its current level of function at the expense of allowing the family to avoid significant interpersonal conflicts, most often parental conflict (Mullins & Olson, 1990). Indeed, the family may represent one level at which biological, psychological, and social influences most evidently come together (Wood, 1993).

In addition to a family assessment, consideration of peer interactions and social function is important. The somatizing child may be the object of peer ridicule, isolative, and avoidant of interactions with peers such as intramurals or scouting. Inquiries about friends, after-school activities, hobbies, and free-time avocations may reveal social difficulties.

Somatization may be associated with negative life events such as the loss or death of a family member or other close relation (Aro, 1987; Aro et al., 1989; Greene, Walker, Hickson, & Thompson, 1985; Hodges, Kline, Barbero, & Flanery, 1984; Livingston, 1993; Maloney, 1980; Scaloubaca, Slade, & Creed, 1988). Maltreatment can be associated with somatization, with sexual maltreatment being especially important to consider in cases of conversion disorder, genitourinary complaints, or chronic, polysymptomatic somatization (Klevan & De-Jong, 1990; Livingston et al., 1988; Rimza, Berg, & Locke, 1988). Other stressors such as parental conflict, family illness, and school difficulties may also be associated with somatization (Poikolainen et al., 1995), highlighting the importance of careful history.

TREATMENT

Overview

An understanding of prognosis is often helpful in approaching treatment, but our current knowledge of the expected prognosis for children and adolescents with medically unexplained physical symptoms is sorely limited, with most available studies having significant methodologic limitations (Campo & Fritsch, 1994). There is a shortage of well-designed longitudinal studies, and most available studies have concentrated on the presence or absence of the original symptom as the sole outcome measure, despite the fact that other outcomes, such as functional status or psychiatric status, might be of relevance.

Follow-up studies of children and adolescents with RAP show that 25–50% continue to experience some degree of abdominal discomfort in adulthood (Apley & Hale, 1973; Christensen & Mortensen, 1975; Liebman 1978; Stickler & Murphy, 1979; Stone & Barbero, 1970). In a recent follow-up study that examined RAP patients 5 to 6 years after original

assessment, former RAP patients reported significantly higher levels of abdominal discomfort, other somatic symptoms, and functional disability than did formerly healthy controls (Walker, Garber, Van Slyke, & Greene, 1995). In addition, former RAP patients were reported by parents to have higher levels of internalizing emotional symptoms such as anxiety and depression than formerly well patients in the study. Correspondingly, the RAP patients had significantly higher levels of mental health service utilization. There was also a trend suggesting that former RAP patients had visited medical clinics more frequently in the year prior to the follow-up assessment.

With regard to patients who have pseudoneurologic or conversion symptoms, significant clinical improvement or complete recovery has been reported in 50–100% of such patients from the standpoint of the physical symptom alone (Bangash, Worley, Kandt, 1988; Goodyer, 1981; Goodyer & Mitchell, 1989; Grattan-Smith et al., 1988; Kotsopolous & Snow, 1986; Lehmkuhl et al., 1989; Leslie, 1988; Maisami & Freeman, 1987; Proctor, 1958; Schneider & Rice, 1979; Spierings et al., 1990; Turgay, 1990; Wyllie et al., 1991).

The variables that predict later outcome are currently unknown, and although multiple somatic symptoms and greater chronicity of somatization have been reported to predict poor outcomes (Ernst, Routh, & Harper, 1984; Grattan-Smith et al., 1988; Robins & O'Neal, 1953), other reports do not support this view (Goodyer & Mitchell, 1989; Lehmkuhl et al., 1989; Walker et al., 1991). Conversion symptoms or pseudoneurologic symptoms may be especially predictive of later functional impairment (Goodyer & Mitchell, 1989; Robins & O'Neal, 1953), but this has not been conclusively demonstrated in the pediatric age group.

A thorough and conscientious assessment is the foundation for successful treatment intervention. Throughout the treatment, objective data and corresponding clinical information are essential. The clinician must have a firm, unbiased conviction regarding the validity of the objective data, which form the basis of treatment. Treatment can take place in the primary-care or subspecialty medical setting, the pediatric hospital, the psychiatric outpatient setting, or, in certain circumstances, during an inpatient psychiatric hospitalization.

Since somatization is relatively common in the pediatric medical setting, mental health professionals should take an active role in working with health care professionals, particularly in the primary-care setting. Acquainting the primary-care professional with the importance of considering psychological issues early in the assessment of patients with common physical symptoms such as recurrent abdominal pain or headaches is particularly important, given the role of somatic symptoms as an initial presentation of psychiatric disorder in medical settings. Availability and a willingness to be contacted for telephone consultation are important, as physicians may be reluctant to refer directly to a mental health professional. Ideally, the physical presence of a mental health professional in the primary medical setting or subspecialty clinic allows for greater coordination of collaborative efforts. Such a presence in the medical setting undermines the institutionalized dichotomy between soma and psyche that can become stigmatizing and destructive in the treatment of somatization and allows the psychiatric, psychological and medical assessments and interventions to become part of a unified process.

Preparation of the patient and the family for referral is important. Involving a mental health professional early in the process allows the physician to explain that the common overlap between physical symptoms and emotional distress makes psychological/psychiatric assessment essential in the diagnostic process. Evidence for symptoms of anxiety, depression, or other related difficulties should be discussed frankly and without embarrassment, communicating that the professional approaches such difficulties with the same seriousness as clearcut physical disease and does not view psychiatric disorder as a sign of "weakness" or as something "shameful."

As in any clinical situation, an empathic approach to the patient's experience of somatic distress is often useful, and the patient's suffering should be acknowledged. The clinician should not take issue with the subjective reality of the physical symptom and should not insist on explanations or descriptions of the condition in psychological terms, at least early in the treatment. Correspondingly, efforts by the patient or family to focus on the discovery of a single, clear psychological etiology for the symptom should be gently discouraged. Early on, this approach is not helpful and may serve to fortify a sense of defensiveness and resistance to treatment. The mere conscious confession and realization of the psychological and emotional aspects of the disorder are generally insufficient to effect a cure. Instead, acknowledging the reality of the physical suffering of patients who have become angry, confused, and troubled as a consequence of dealing with physical symptoms in the absence of physical disease may help develop the sort of therapeutic alliance that can allow their condition to be understood and appropriately treated. Evaluating, explaining, or reinterpreting the patient's and the family's experience with prior physicians and other professionals may also help in establishing a therapeutic working relationship.

The presenting condition should be discussed with the patient and the family and the diagnosis stated in a positive manner, as with any other illness (Campo, 1995; Campo & Garber, 1998). A thoughtful discussion of the formulation and associated psychosocial stressors can be therapeutic, particularly when the clinician takes time to educate the patient and the family about the complexities of the mind-body relationship and the problems associated with the traditional false dichotomy between the physical and the emotional or psychological. Parents may gain insight into their child's emotional world and environmental stressors, and children may feel understood following an explanation that they had neither the vocabulary nor the sophistication to express in their own terms. Formal treatment follows an interactive discussion with the patient and the family in which the clinician's impression is communicated in a comfortable and confident manner, unless, of course, serious doubt regarding etiology remains. As with any condition, particularly those of a psychiatric nature, the clinician must avoid communicating any sense of reserve or shame regarding the diagnosis, as this may strengthen resistance to treatment by communicating a sense of stigma and generate feelings of embarrassment or self-reproach for patients and family members (Campo & Garber, 1998).

Once the diagnosis of a somatoform disorder has been made and explained to the patient and family, additional diagnostic evaluation should be strictly limited. Pressure for continued medical testing and diagnostic procedures may continue on the part of parents, patient, or other family members, and it is the job of the clinician to discourage further invasive or sophisticated testing unless the clinical picture changes or new information becomes available.

Reassurance, encouragement, and scientifically based optimism on the part of the clinician are useful tools in achieving a successful outcome. At first, reassurance that the patient's condition will not lead to death or increased physical morbidity may be helpful and has been recommended in the treatment of somatizing adults (Kellner, 1991) and children (Goodyer & Mitchell, 1989; Grattan-Smith et al., 1988; Maisami & Freeman, 1987; Schulman, 1988; Thompson & Sills, 1988). However, it has been pointed out (Warwick & Salkovskis, 1985) that excessive reassurance may serve to maintain somatization, particularly in cases where the patient or a parent struggles with obsessional and hypochondriacal fears. Therefore, the clinician may choose to minimize and diminish any reliance of the patient or family on reassurance alone as treatment progresses, with illness worry eventually becoming a problem to be solved together rather than one dependent solely on the perceived special knowledge and training of the clinician.

The clinician needs to continually assess the family's understanding of the condition and the treatment. Some families and patients assume that the professional will be entirely responsible for effecting "cure." Others have difficulty accepting that a serious physical disease is not present. Usually, successful treatment is a collaborative venture involving the patient, the family, and the professional. The responsibilities of the individual parties should be delineated clearly and early in treatment. The degree to which the symptom interferes with daily life, day-to-day functioning, and psychosocial development needs to be clarified. Defining realistic and shared functional goals for the patient becomes an important task, with a focus on functional improvement rather than an unequivocal "cure" being encouraged (Kellner, 1991).

Particularly in situations where diagnostic uncertainty persists, it is important to remember that a successful treatment response may provide supportive evidence that the patient's difficulties have a significant psychological component and reflect somatization. A positive treatment response can then be used to encourage continued treatment, thereby avoiding potentially dangerous and costly medical and surgical interventions. The use of placebo is generally discouraged, however, as this approach may inadvertently contribute to the belief that the symptom is caused by physical disease and, if unsuccessful, forces the clinician to once again attempt to convince the patient that serious physical disease is not present.

Psychosocial Treatments

The treatment of somatizing children has traditionally been viewed as a two-step process, with removal of the physical symptom being followed by psychological interventions (Shapiro & Rosenfeld, 1987). Symptom removal has been effected by suggestion (Proctor, 1958; Rock, 1971), encouragement (Gold, 1965), or the use of chemical abreaction with medications such as amobarbital (Laybourne & Churchill, 1972). Current clinical experience suggests, however, that intervention should proceed without waiting until symptom removal is accomplished. Indeed, it is counterproductive to allow the patient or the family to develop the expectation that a return to regular function and productivity can only follow the resolution of the symptom. An effort to help the family and the patient understand the presenting symptoms as less threatening is generally beneficial, allowing anxiety in the system to decrease and permitting other treatment interventions to be introduced (Kellner, 1986; Kotsopolous & Snow, 1986; Lehmkuhl et al., 1989; Maisami & Freeman 1987; Schulman, 1988).

The currently favored approach is one that is considered rehabilitative. This encourages the patient to return to usual activities, while discouraging behaviors associated with the sick role (Dubowitz & Hersov, 1976; Leslie, 1988; Maisami & Freeman, 1987; Schulman, 1988). A rehabilitative focus encourages a significant shift of responsibility to the patient for a successful return to healthy functioning. This, in turn, discourages the notion that the patient can return to normal developmental functioning only when the symptoms have disappeared. Thus, the patient's role is reframed from that of a passive recipient of care to an active collaborator with the professional and the family. This approach respects the power of the symptom and of the sick-role expectation, yet presents a model to overcome the symptom, an accomplishment of which the patient can be proud.

In keeping with a rehabilitative paradigm, the use of physical therapy has been recommended in the treatment of children with conversion symptoms (Dubowitz & Hersov, 1976; Leslie, 1988; Maisami & Freeman, 1987; Thompson & Sills, 1988). Physical therapy should be used cautiously so as to avoid needless identification of the patient with the sick role but can at times allow a gradual return of the patient to prior functioning in a manner that is potentially "face saving" (Bolton & Cohen, 1986).

There are few controlled trials of psychosocial treatment in pediatric somatization. A few studies demonstrate self-monitoring techniques and cognitive behavioral methods as being successful in the treatment of children with RAP (Finney, Lemanek, Cataldo, Katz, & Fuqua, 1989; Sanders et al., 1989; Sanders, Shepherd, Cleghorn, & Woolford, 1994). Most other available treatment reports focus on un-

controlled case examples or series (see Campo & Fritsch, 1994, for review).

A behavioral paradigm is often useful in approaching somatization in children and adolescents. This requires the cooperation of family members and the collaboration of others who have significant contact with the child. The crucial element in treatment is positive reinforcement for healthy, adaptive, developmentally normal behavior. This approach has been emphasized in a number of case studies and reports (Delameter, Rosenbloom, Conners, & Hertweck, 1983; Dubowitz & Hersov, 1976; Klonoff & Moore, 1986; Lehmkuhl et al., 1989; Maisami & Freeman, 1987; Mansdorf, 1981; Mizes, 1985; Sank & Biglan, 1974).

Along with positive reinforcement for adaptive behavior, rewards associated with the sick role need to be minimized. This is best conceptualized as extinction or withdrawal of reinforcement of the symptom (Delameter et al., 1983). This process, generally described as "minimizing secondary gain," often presents practical problems for parents, who may have difficulty implementing recommendations that involve confronting their own fears and concerns, as well as what have become accepted patterns of family behavior. Parents may feel that it is punitive to restrict access to friends on a day that the child has been absent from school, often driven by a tenderhearted but generally unhelpful belief that the child's illness has already imposed excessive restrictions on the child, who must then "deserve" any possible respite and enjoyment. A technique that helps parents implement a plan to decrease secondary gain is to return to a discussion of the goals of treatment. Parental fears, anger, and guilt should be explored, and the firmness that treatment demands of them should be reframed as thoughtful kindness over the long term. This discussion may need to be repeated throughout the treatment and used to provide empathy or support. It is a useful intervention to prevent unexpressed hostility and ambivalence from influencing the parents' behavior. In addition, the clinician must realize that enabling the parents to utilize a behavior plan is a process. The parents' relationship with the clinician, in a sense, mirrors the relationship with the child. The parents will respond to positive feedback from the clinician and also need to be reminded in a neutral and nonjudgmental manner that inability to set limits or indulgence of the child will, naturally, impede progress toward the desired goal. Similarly, the clinician's kind but firm approach to the patient provides a potentially useful model for parents in the treatment process.

In an example of a particularly tough-minded intervention, time-out was utilized in the treatment of a 10-year-old girl with RAP; use of a time-out procedure resulted in a reduction of pain complaints over the course of treatment (Miller & Kratochowill, 1979). The use of time-out is not generally worthy of consideration in most clinical situations involving somatization; neither is punishment per se. What is called for, however, is a firmness and a willingness to place expectations upon the child that may appear unfair but are necessary to return the patient to normal functioning. A related and powerful approach is negative reinforcement (Leslie, 1988), which involves lifting restrictions that have theoretically been imposed by the illness. For example, discharge from the hospital might be allowed only if the patient evidences sufficient physical improvement, or repeated somatic complaints and requests for special treatment may be addressed by strict bed rest, with confinement being lifted only when the patient is able to assume usual function and responsibilities. Another example is forbidding the use of a wheelchair to allow the child access to outside activity with peers. This approach also allows for more traditional positive reinforcement as the impairment is overcome. Such an approach discourages the child from becoming comfortable in the sick role.

A successful treatment program most often incorporates elements of some of the aproaches mentioned. While pursuing treatment, the clinician frequently needs to disabuse family members and perhaps other professionals of the belief that the treatment is unfair, unkind, and possibly harmful to the child. Particularly in the beginning phases of treatment, the child will be most resistant, complain loudly, and present obstacles to the interventions suggested. At this point, the treating clinician must be persistent until measurable improvement can be witnessed and used to encourage further interventions.

Cognitive-behavioral approaches have been demonstrated to be successful in the treatment of school-aged children with RAP (Finney et al., 1989; Sanders et al., 1989; Sanders et al., 1994). Sanders et al. (1989) employed a multimodal treatment method that included differential reinforcement of healthy behavior, cognitive coping-skills training, and self-monitoring techniques. Although the sample size was small, the positive results of the study are encouraging, with the treated group of patients doing significantly better than controls. Extending this research, a cognitive behavioral family intervention was compared to standard pediatric care for 7- to 14-year-old children with RAP, resulting in higher levels of parental satisfaction with treatment, greater improvements in functionality, higher rates of complete elimination of the pain, and lower levels of relapse at 6- and 12-month follow-up than standard pediatric care (Sanders et al., 1994). Finney et al. (1989) completed a small, controlled trial of treatment for children with RAP in a primary-care setting that was successful in demonstrating a reduction in complaints of pain, school absenteeism, and health care utilization in the experimental treatment group as compared to an untreated control group. Treatment was multimodal and included self-monitoring of the symptoms, limiting parental reinforcement of illness behavior, relaxation training, administration of a dietary fiber supplement, and strong encouragement of participation in routine activities such as school. The reduction in medical care utilization was not accounted for by an effect on RAP-related visits alone, suggesting that some of the reduction in visits may have resulted from a generalization of the treatment to other types of illnesses and complaints. It is unclear which components of the multimodal interventions described were responsible for the positive results, but such trials are important in that they are likely to approximate clinical practice and demonstrate that effective treatment is possible.

Encouraging results have been reported regarding the use of self-management techniques such as training in coping and relaxation (Linton, 1986; Masek, Russo, & Varni, 1984), hypnosis (Caldwell & Steward, 1981; Elkins & Carter, 1986; Williams & Singh, 1976), and the use of biofeedback (Klonoff & Moore, 1986; Mizes, 1985).

Although individual psychotherapy is widely used, there are no controlled studies of its efficacy (Campo & Fritsch, 1994; Campo & Garber, 1998). Psychotherapy incorporating psychodynamic understanding, interpretation, expressive interventions, and an interpersonal perspective may be integrated with cognitive behavioral and other treatments. Perceived intrapsychic gain associated with somatization has been referred to by psychodynamic writers as the "primary gain" of the symptom and may allow the patient to avoid painful memories, thoughts, or affects (Simon, 1991). Early in treatment, particularly when integrated with a cognitive-behavioral approach, psychodynamically informed interventions are best kept simple and closely related to a particular intervention. Lengthy or heavily interpretative speculations should be avoided, but comments based on a psychodynamic understanding of the patient may promote change, help the patient feel understood by the treating professionals, and provide fertile ground for cognitive and behavioral methods, which may be more concrete and overtly acceptable to patients and families. More intensive individual psychotherapy around issues related to somatization can take place once adequate function and adaptation have been achieved. Excessive attention to the psychological meaning of the symptoms may interfere with the primary goal of treatment, namely a return to relatively normal function. Since patients may be reluctant or unable to identify emotions or express feelings, techniques such as keeping a journal may be especially helpful, particularly if somatization follows a traumatic event (Pennebaker & Susman, 1988).

There are no reports regarding the use of group psychotherapy in the treatment of somatizing children and adolescents (Campo & Fritsch, 1994), but clinical experience suggests that the group setting may be useful. The group provides a setting for discussion of common issues, peer pressure and encouragement, in a context where emotions and feelings unable to be expressed individually or in other settings may be explored.

The use of family therapy in the treatment of children and adolescents with somatization has been advocated (Goodyer, 1981; Liebman, Hoenig, & Berger, 1976; Mullins & Olson, 1990). As with any successful treatment of children, work with parents and families is essential. Minuchin and colleagues (1975) worked with a variety of psychosomatic conditions that emphasized the patient's physical symptoms as serving a particular function within the family system and suggested that the family's focus on the child's physical symptom may distract the family from other areas of conflict and serve to preserve homeostasis in the system. In addition to conflict avoidance, this group describes specific patterns of family interaction, including enmeshment, parental overprotection, familial rigidity, and poor conflict resolution (Minuchin et al., 1975; Minuchin, Rosman, & Baker, 1978). Later writers such as Mullins and Olson (1990) have attempted to update the family-systems approach to somatization. Wood (1993) has critically examined and challenged early family-systems conceptualizations of the so-called psychosomatic family and made sophisticated attempts to integrate a family-systems view within a more comprehensive biopsychosocial understanding. Despite the great interest in family therapy, however, research regarding its efficacy in pediatric somatization is limited (Campo & Fritsch, 1994; Campo & Garber, 1998).

A close working relationship with the primary-care physician or referring specialist is essential. In many cases, somatizing children have been seen by many physicians, each with little information regarding the other's recommendations. It is preferred to consolidate the care of somatizing children with a single primary physician or team leader. This improves communication and also decreases the risk of treatment efforts being repeated, diluted, or misinterpreted. Work with adults with somatization disorder has shown that a simple consultation letter from a consulting psychiatrist to the primary-care physician outlining a suggested approach to the somatizing patient was effective in improving patient satisfaction with the care provided and in reducing health care expenditures (Smith, Monson, & Ray, 1986). An extension of the study to somatizing patients with medically unexplained physical symptoms who did not meet full criteria for somatization disorder also demonstrated an improvement in physical functioning and a significant cost offset for patients who received the treatment intervention (Smith, Rost, & Kashner, 1995).

For some patients, the physician can become an important attachment figure. A subset of these patients may be persistently somatizing in an effort to seek out the company of their doctor, who may be viewed as a source of comfort and care. For these patients, regularly scheduled office visits to the primary-care physician may paradoxically be of benefit. In this way, they can see the physician without the requirement that they be sick. Instructing primary-care providers about their potential role as an attachment figure is important, as patients and families may develop concerns that involvement in treatment with a mental health professional will result in their being dismissed by the primary physician.

Another area of extreme importance is close communication with the school. School absenteeism or school refusal is commonly associated with pediatric somatization. School officials may benefit from a better understanding of the patient's difficulties and may be a source of useful information and suggestions regarding practical interventions. The clinician may also serve as a bridge to help bring together the school and the patient's family, as tension has often developed regarding frequent absences and requests for special treatment of the child. It is often useful to help define what constitutes a legitimate, medically excused school absence for both the family and the school. This requires close collaboration between the treating mental health professional, the primary-care physician, the parents, and the school. The patient has to understand that absence from school without the approval of the collaborative treatment team and an appropriate medical excuse will be viewed as truancy and that the school will take the appropriate action. With such a treatment plan, the cooperation of the school can benefit the treatment effort. Once it is clear that any excuses for school absences need to come from the primary physician alone, the tendency to "doctor-shop," particularly for medical excuses, will be curtailed.

Most somatizing pediatric patients will be best managed on an outpatient basis. However, there are circumstances when inpatient treatment may be beneficial. These cases involve refractory school refusal, persistent and escalating somatization, and situations where outpatient treatment options have been exhausted, as well as in cases where there is significant diagnostic uncertainty (Campo & Garber, 1998). Potential benefits of inpatient pediatric treatment of somatization in children and adolescents have been suggested in several reports based on anecdotal observations (Goodyer, 1985; Kotsopolous & Snow, 1986; Lemkuhl et al., 1989; Leslie, 1988; Maisami & Freeman, 1987). One advantage of inpatient treatment is that it allows for close observation by skilled personnel and greater control over the behavioral treatment of the patient (Delameter et al., 1983). Since the child is removed from the environment in which the symptoms developed, the inpatient staff can utilize alternate ways of dealing with the patient, family members, and other important figures in the child's life. The improvement in functioning that can be demonstrated in the inpatient setting may help to reassure family members that physical disease is not driving the patient' symptoms, reduce their anxiety, and convince them that psychosocial treatment is important. A multidisciplinary approach to inpatient treatment is desirable and can often be best accomplished on a pediatric medical psychiatry inpatient unit (Campo & Raney, 1995). Rigorous discharge planning should incorporate the principles previously discussed, with a coordinated transition to outpatient or intermediate levels of care.

Pharmacologic Treatment

Review of the existing literature reveals no available studies that address the use of psychotropic medication in pediatric somatization (Campo & Fritsch, 1994; Campo & Garber, 1998). However, these patients frequently suffer from concomitant anxiety, depression, or other psychiatric difficulties that may respond to treatment with medication. Antidepressant medication has been shown to reduce somatic symptoms in depressed adults, and anxiolytic medications such as benzodiazepines and antidepressants may alleviate somatic symptoms in patients suffering from anxiety disorders (see Kellner, 1991). Remaining alert to the presence of a previously undiagnosed psychiatric disorder is especially important, given the possibility that the presence of a disorder such as panic disorder may provide a context for the use of psychotropic medication that may serve to treat the psychiatric disorder and any associated somatic symptoms.

Clinical experience indicates that many pediatric patients benefit from the use of psychotropic medication in the relief of medically unexplained physical symptoms, particularly recurrent complaints of pain or fatigue, but definitive statements and recommendations must await appropriate controlled studies. In patients who experience physical symptoms predominantly associated with emotional arousal and anxiety, a short course of anxiolytic medication might be beneficial in helping the patient and the family begin to understand the connection between the physical and the emotional life of the child. In the short term, the use of a benzodiazepine may demonstrate to the patient and the family that the physical symptoms are the result of anxiety and emotional arousal, rather than the product of serious physical disease (Campo & Garber, 1998). Low doses of lorazepam (Ativan) at 0.5 mg three times daily, or of clonazepam 0.25 mg once or twice per day, are often effective and blunt physical symptoms associated with emotional arousal. The principal side effect of these agents is sedation.

Tricyclic antidepressants, selective serotonin reuptake inhibitors (SSRIs), and other antidepressants may also be useful in pediatric somatization. The SSRIs are especially useful in anxious patients and in patients with comorbid anxiety and depression. These medications are generally well tolerated but should be begun at a low dose and gradually titrated upward due to the sensitivity of anxious and somatizing patients to side effects. Potential side effects include a transient increase in anxiety, including the precipitation of panic anxiety, gastrointestinal symptoms such as nausea and diarrhea, the development of mania or hypomania in vulnerable individuals, and sexual dysfunction, which may be especially confusing for adolescents. In terms of beginning doses for specific agents, sertraline (Zoloft) might be begun at 25 mg per day, fluvoxamine (Luvox) at 25 mg twice a day, and fluoxetine (Prozac) or paroxetine (Paxil) at 10 mg per day. Low doses are sometimes effective, but most patients require a gradual increase to more typical therapeutic doses. In addition, the SSRIs may benefit patients with obsessional illness worry, given their efficacy in the treatment of pediatric obsessive compulsive disorder (e.g., Riddle et al., 1992). Controlled trials of treatment in children and adolescents with specific disorders are needed. Reviews by Kutcher, Reiter, and Gardner (1995) and Allen, Leonard, and Swedo (1995) provide more detailed information regarding the treatment of pediatric anxiety disorders. Riddle (1995) provides a comprehensive review of recent developments in pediatric psychopharmacology. Please refer to the relevant manufacturer's literature and to standard pharmacologic texts for information regarding specific agents, potential side effects, drug-drug interactions, and contraindications.

COMMENTS

Clearly, there is much to be learned about the nature of somatoform disorders in children and adolescents, and their careful study may eventually reveal much about the relationship between emotional and physical health. Empirical studies of psychosocial and biological interventions are needed to help guide the work of clinicians in addressing these common but frequently difficult-to-manage problems. The category of somatoform disorders is somewhat unique in that it often serves as a way of codifying problems generated by the mind-body split characteristic of Western medicine, as well as the split between the so-called mental health disciplines and traditional medicine. Consequently, dealing with pediatric somatization requires a certain degree of flexibility, both intellectually and practically. It may well be that new ways of conceptualizing the problems posed by patients with physical symptoms that defy traditional medical explanations will be important in providing a framework for future empirical work, including work regarding practical treatment efforts. In a climate where cost and concerns about excessive health care utilization are becoming increasingly prominent, interest and attention to these disorders should also increase. Somatoform disorders offer an example of the impracticality of segregating the delivery of physical and behavioral health care, as well as an example of how solid behavioral health consultation and intervention might not only improve the well-being of patients and their families but might also reduce or serve to contain health care expenditures.

REFERENCES

Achenbach, T. M., Conners, C. K., Quay, H. C., Verhulst, F. C., & Howell, C. T. (1989). Replication of empirically derived syndromes as a basis for taxonomy of child/adolescent psychopathology. *Journal of Abnormal Child Psychology, 17,* 299–323.

Achenbach, T. M., & Edelbrock, C. (1983). *Manual for the Child Behavior Checklist and Revised Child Behavior Profile.* Burlington, VT: University of Vermont.

Allen, A. J., Leonard, H., & Swedo, S. E. (1995). Current knowledge of medications for the treatment of childhood anxiety disorders. *Journal of the American Academy of Child and Adolescent Psychiatry, 34,* 976–986.

American Psychiatric Association. (1987). *Diagnostic and statistical manual of mental disorders,* (3rd ed., rev.). Washington, DC: Author.

American Psychiatric Association. (1991). *DSM-IV options book: Work in progress.* Washington, DC: Author.

American Psychiatric Association. (1994). *Diagnostic and statistical manual of mental disorders,* (4th ed.), Washington, DC: Author.

Apley, J. (1958). A common denominator in the recurrent pains of childhood. *Proc. Royal Society of Medicine, 51,* 1023–1024.

Apley, J. (1975). *The child with abdominal pain.* Oxford: Blackwell.

Apley, J., & Hale, B. (1973). Children with recurrent abdominal pain: How do they grow up? *British Medical Journal, 3,* 7–9.

Aro, H. (1987). Life stress and psychosomatic symptoms among 14- to 16-year-old Finnish adolescents. *Psychological Medicine, 17,* 191–201.

Aro, H., Hanninen, V., & Paronen, O. (1989). Social support, life events and psychosomatic symptoms among 14–16-year-old adolescents. *Social Science and Medicine, 29,* 1051–1056.

Aro, H., Paronen, O., & Aro, S. (1987). Psychosomatic symptoms among 14–16-year-old Finnish adolescents. *Social Psychiatry, 22,* 171–176.

Aro, H., & Taipale, V. (1987). The impact of timing of puberty on psychosomatic symptoms among fourteen- to sixteen-year-old Finnish girls. *Child Development, 58,* 261–268.

Bangash, I. H., Worley, J. G., & Kandt, R. S. (1988). Hysterical conversion reactions mimicking neurological disease. *American Journal of Diseases in Children, 142,* 1203–1206.

Barsky, A. J. (1992). Amplification, somatization, and the somatoform disorders. *Psychosomatics, 13,* 28–33.

Barsky, A. J., Goodson, J. D., Lane, R. S., & Cleary, P. D. (1988). The amplification of somatic symptoms. *Psychosomatic Medicine, 50,* 510–519.

Bass, C. M., & Murphy, M. R. (1990). Somatization disorder: Critique of the concept and suggestions for future research. In C. M. Bass (Ed.), *Somatization: Physical symptoms and psychological illness.* New York: Blackwell Scientific Publications.

Beidel, D., Christ, M. A. G., & Long, P. J. (1991). Somatic complaints in anxious children. *Journal of Abnormal Child Psychology, 19,* 659–670.

Belmaker, E. (1984). Nonspecific somatic symptoms in early adolescent girls. *Journal of Adolescent Health Care, 5,* 30–33.

Belmaker, E., Espinoza, R., & Pogrund, R. (1985). Use of medical services by adolescents with nonspecific somatic symptoms. *International Journal of Adolescent Medicine and Health, 1,* 150–156.

Bergman, A. B., & Stamm, S. J. (1967). The morbidity of cardiac non-disease in school children. *New England Journal of Medicine, 276,* 1008–1013.

Bohman, M., Cloninger, C. R., von Knorring, A. L., & Sigvardsson, S. (1984). An adoption study of somatoform disorders: III. Cross-fostering analysis and genetic relationship to alcoholism and criminality. *Archives of General Psychiatry, 41,* 872–878.

Bolton, J., & Cohen, P. (1986). 'Escape with honour': The need for face-saving. *Bulletin of Anna Freud Centre, 9,* 19–33.

Bridges, K. W., & Goldberg, D. P. (1985). Somatic presentation of DSM-III psychiatric disorders in primary care. *Journal of Psychosomatic Research, 29,* 563–569.

Caldwell, T. A., & Stewart, R. S. (1981). Hysterical seizures and hypnotherapy. *American Journal of Clinical Hypnosis, 23,* 294–298.

Campo, J. V. (1993). Medical issues in the care of child and adolescent inpatients. In A. S. Bellack & M. Hersen (Eds.), *Handbook of behavior therapy in the psychiatric setting.* New York: Plenum Press.

Campo, J. V. (1995). Somatization disorder. In R. T. Ammerman & M. Hersen (Eds.), *Handbook of child behavior therapy in the psychiatric setting.* New York: Wiley.

Campo, J. V., & Fritsch, S. L. (1994). Somatization in children and adolescents. *Journal of the American Academy of Child and Adolescent Psychiatry, 33,* 1223–1235.

Campo, J. V., & Garber, J. (1998). Somatization. In R. T. Ammerman & J. V. Campo (Eds.), *Handbook of Pediatric Psychology and Psychiatry* (pp. 137–161). Boston: Allyn and Bacon.

Campo, J. V., & Raney, D. R. (1995). The pediatric medical-psychiatric unit in a psychiatric hospital. *Psychosomatics, 36,* 438–444.

Caplan, H. L. (1970). Hysterical 'conversion' symptoms in childhood. Unpublished M. Phil. Thesis. University of London.

Carek, D. J., & Santos, A. B. (1984). Atypical somatoform disorder following infection in children—a depressive equivalent? *Journal of Clinical Psychiatry, 45,* 108–111.

Carlson, G., & Kashani, J. H. (1988). Phenomenology of major depressive disorder from childhood through adulthood: An analysis of 3 studies. *American Journal of Psychiatry, 145,* 1222–1225.

Christensen, M. F., & Mortensen, O. (1975). Long-term prognosis in children with recurrent abdominal pain. *Archives of Diseases of Children, 50,* 110.

Cloninger, C. R. (1994). In G. Winokur and P. J. Clayton (Eds.), *The medical basis of psychiatry* (pp. 169–192). Philadelphia: W. B. Saunders.

Cloninger, C. R., Reich, T., & Guze, S. B. (1975). The multifactorial model of disease transmission: III. Familial relationship between sociopathy and hysteria (Briquet's Syndrome). *British Journal of Psychiatry, 127,* 23–32.

Cloninger, C. R., Sigvardsson, S., von Knorring, A. L., & Bohman, M. (1984). An adoption study of somatoform disorders: II. Identification of two discrete somatoform disorders. *Archives of General Psychiatry, 41,* 863–871.

Creak, M. (1938). Hysteria in childhood. *British Journal of Childhood Diseases, 35,* 85–95.

Delamater, A. M., Rosenbloom, N., Conners, K., & Hertweck, L. (1983). The behavioral treatment of hysterical paralysis in a ten-year-old boy: A case study. *Journal of the American Academy of Child Psychiatry, 1,* 73–79.

Derogatis, L., Lipman, R. S., Rickels, K., Ulenhuth, E. H., & Covi, L. (1974). The Hopkins Symptom Checklist (HSCL): A self-report inventory. *Behavioral Science, 19,* 1–15.

Dubowitz, V., & Hersov, L. (1976). Management of children with non-organic (hysterical) disorders of motor function. *Developmental Medicine and Child Neurology, 18,* 358–368.

Elkins, G. R., & Carter, B. D. (1986). Hypnotherapy in the treatment of childhood psychogenic coughing: A case report. *American Journal of Clinical Hypnosis, 29,* 59–63.

Ernst, A. R., Routh, D. K., & Harper, D. C. (1984). Abdominal pain in children and symptoms of somatization disorder. *Journal of Pediatric Psychology, 9,* 77–86.

Fabrega, H. (1990). The concept of somatization as a cultural and historical product of Western medicine. *Psychosomatic Medicine, 52,* 653–672.

Faull, C., & Nicol, A. R. (1986). Abdominal pain in six-year-olds: An epidemiological study in a new town. *Journal of Child Psychology and Psychiatry, 27,* 251–260.

Fenton, G. W. (1986). Epilepsy and hysteria. *British Journal of Psychiatry, 149,* 28–37.

Finney, J. W., Lemanek, K. L., Cataldo, M. F., Katz, H. P., & Fuqua, R. W. (1989). Pediatric psychology in primary healthcare: Brief targeted therapy for recurrent abdominal pain. *Behavior Therapy, 20,* 283–291.

Freud, S. (1962). The aetiology of hysteria. In J. Strachey (Ed.), *The standard edition of the complete psychological works of Sigmund Freud* (pp. 191–221). London: Hogarth Press.

Friedman, S. B. (1973). Conversion symptoms in adolescents. *Pediatric Clinics of North America*, 20, 873–882.

Gadow, K. D., & Sprafkin, J. (1995). *Adolescent Supplement to the Child Symptom Inventories Manual*. Stony Brook, NY:Checkmate Plus, Ltd.

Garber, J., Walker, L. S., & Zeman, J. (1991). Somatization symptoms in a community sample of children and adolescents: Further validation of the children's somatization inventory. *Psychological Assessment*, 3, 588–595.

Garber, J., Zeman, J., & Walker, L. S. (1990). Recurrent abdominal pain in children: Psychiatric diagnoses and parental psychopathology. *Journal of the American Academy of Child and Adolescent Psychiatry*, 29, 648–656.

Garrick, T., Ostrov, E., & Offer, D. (1988). Physical symptoms and self-image in a group of normal adolescents. *Psychosomatics*, 29, 73–80.

Garralda, M. E. (1992). A selective review of child psychiatric syndromes with a somatic presentation. *British Journal of Psychiatry*, 161, 759–773.

Gold, S. (1965). Diagnosis and management of hysterical contracture in children. *British Medical Journal*, 1, 21–23.

Goldberg, D. P., & Bridges, K. (1988). Somatic presentations of psychiatric illness in the primary care setting. *Psychosomatic Research*, 32, 137–144.

Goodwin, J., Simms, M., & Bergman, R. (1979). Hysterical seizures in 4 adolescent girls. *American Journal of Orthopsychiatry*, 49, 698–703.

Goodyer, I. M. (1981). Hysterical conversion reactions in childhood. *Journal of Child Psychology and Psychiatry*, 22, 179–188.

Goodyer, I. M. (1985). Epileptic and pseudoepileptic seizures in childhood and adolescence. *Journal of the American Academy of Child Psychiatry*, 1, 3–9.

Goodyer, I. M., & Mitchell, C. (1989). Somatic and emotional disorders in childhood and adolescence. *Journal of Psychosomatic Research*, 33, 681–688.

Goodyer, I. M., & Taylor, D. C. (1985). Hysteria. *Archives of Diseases of Children*, 60, 680–681.

Grattan-Smith, P., Fairley, M., & Procopis, P. (1988). Clinical features of conversion disorder. *Archives of Diseases of Children*, 63, 408–414.

Green, M., & Solnit, A. J. (1964). Reactions to the threatened loss of a child: A vulnerable child syndrome. *Pediatrics*, 34, 58–66.

Greene, J. W., Walker, L. S., Hickson, G., & Thompson, J. (1985). Stressful life events and somatic complaints in adolescents. *Pediatrics*, 75, 19–22.

Gross, M. (1979). Incestuous rape: A cause for hysterical seizures in 4 adolescent girls. *American Journal of Orthopsychiatry*, 49, 704–708.

Henderson, S. (1974). Care eliciting behavior in man. *Journal of Nervous and Mental Disorders*, 159, 172–181.

Hodges, K., Kline, J. J., Barbero, G., & Flanery, R. (1984). Life events occurring in families of children with recurrent abdominal pain. *Journal of Psychosomatic Research*, 28, 185–188.

Hodges, K., Kline, J. J., Barbero, G., & Flanery, R. (1985), Depressive symptoms in children with recurrent abdominal pain and in their families. *Journal of Pediatrics*, 107, 622–626.

Hodges, K., Kline, J. J., Barbero, G., & Woodruff, C. (1985). Anxiety in children with recurrent abdominal pain and their parents. *Psychosomatics*, 26, 859–866.

Kashani, J. H., Lababidi, Z., & Jones, R. S. (1982). Depression in children and adolescents with cardiovascular symptomatology: The significance of chest pain. *Journal of the American Academy of Child Psychiatry*, 21, 187–189.

Kellner, R. (1986). *Somatization and hypochondriasis*. New York: Praeger.

Kellner, R. (1991). *Psychosomatic syndromes and somatic symptoms*. Washington, DC.: American Psychiatric Press.

Klevan, J. L., & DeJong, A. R. (1990). Urinary tract symptoms and urinary tract infection following sexual abuse. *American Journal of Diseases of Children*, 144, 242–244.

Klonoff, E. A., & Moore, D. J. (1986). "Conversion reactions" in adolescents: A biofeedback-based operant approach. *Journal of Behavior Therapy & Experimental Psychiatry*, 17, 179–184.

Kotsopoulos, S., & Snow, B. (1986). Conversion disorders in children: A study of clinical outcome. *Psychiatric Journal of the University of Ottawa*, 11, 134–139.

Kowal, A., & Pritchard, D. (1990). Psychological characteristics of children who suffer from headache: A research note. *Journal of Child Psychology and Psychiatry*, 31, 637–649.

Kriechman, A. M. (1987). Siblings with somatoform disorders in childhood and adolescence. *Journal of the American Academy of Child and Adolescent Psychiatry*, 26, 226–231.

Kutcher, S., Reiter, S., & Gardner, D. (1995). Pharmacotherapy: Approaches and applications. In J. S. March (Ed.), *Anxiety disorders in children and adolescents* (pp. 341–385). New York: Guilford Press.

LaBarbera, J. D., & Dozier, J. E. (1980). Hysterical seizures: The role of sexual exploitation. *Psychosomatics, 21,* 897–903.

Larson, B. S. (1991). Somatic complaints and their relationship to depressive symptoms in Swedish adolescents. *Journal of Childhood Psychology and Psychiatry, 32,* 821–832.

Lask, B., & Fosson, A. (1989). *Childhood illness: The psychosomatic approach.* New York: Wiley.

Last, C. G. (1991). Somatic complaints in anxiety disordered children. *Journal of Anxiety Disorders, 5,* 125–138.

Laybourne, P. C., & Churchill, S. W. (1972). Symptom discouragement in treating hysterical reactions of childhood. *International Journal of Child Psychotherapy, 1,* 111–123.

Lehmkuhl, G., Blanz, B., Lehmkuhl, U., & Braun-Scharm, H. (1989). Conversion disorder: Symptomatology and course in childhood and adolescence. *European Archives of Psychiatry and Neurological Sciences, 238,* 155–160.

Leslie, S. A. (1988). Diagnosis and treatment of hysterical conversion reactions. *Archives of Diseases of Children, 63,* 506–511.

Lewis, C. E., & Lewis, M. A. (1989). Educational outcomes and illness behaviors in participants in a child-initiated care system: A 12-year follow-up study. *Pediatrics, 84,* 845–850.

Liebman, R., Honig, P., & Berger, H. (1976). An integrated treatment program for psychogenic pain. *Family Process, 15,* 397–405.

Liebman, W. H. (1978). Recurrent abdominal pain in children: A retrospective survey of 119 patients. *Clinical Pediatrics, 17,* 149–153.

Linton, S. J. (1986). A case study of the behavioural treatment of chronic stomach pain in a child. *Behaviour Change, 3,* 70–73.

Lipowski, Z. J. (1988). Somatization: The concept and its clinical application. *American Journal of Psychiatry, 145,* 1358–1368.

Livingston, R. (1993). Children of people with somatization disorder. *Journal of the American Academy of Child and Adolescent Psychiatry, 32,* 536–544.

Livingston, R., & Martin-Cannici, C. M. (1985). Multiple somatic complaints and possible somatization disorder in prepubertal children. *Journal of the American Academy of Child Psychiatry, 24,* 603–607.

Livingston, R., Taylor, J. L., & Crawford, S. L. (1988). A study of somatic complaints and psychiatric diagnosis in children. *Journal of the American*

Academy of Child and Adolescent Psychiatry, 27, 185–187.

Looff, D. H. (1970). Psychophysiologic and conversion reactions in children. *Journal of the American Academy of Child Psychiatry, 9,* 318–331.

Mai, F. M., & Merskey, H. (1980). Briquet's treatise on hysteria. *Archives of General Psychiatry, 37,* 1401–1405.

Maisami, M., & Freeman, J. M. (1987). Conversion reactions in children as body language: A combined child psychiatry/neurology team approach to the management of functional neurologic disorders in children. *Pediatrics, 80,* 46–52.

Maloney, M. J. (1980). Diagnosing hysterical conversion reactions in children. *Journal of Pediatrics, 97,* 1016–1020.

Mansdorf, I. J. (1981). Eliminating somatic complaints in separation anxiety through contingency management. *Journal of Behavior Therapy and Experimental Psychiatry, 12,* 73–75.

Masek, B., Russo, D. C., & Varni, J. W. (1984). Behavioral approaches to the management of chronic pain in children. *Pediatric Clinics of North America, 31,* 1113–1131.

McCauley, E., Carlson, G. A., & Calderon, R. (1991). The role of somatic complaints in the diagnosis of depression in children and adolescents. *Journal of the American Academy of Child and Adolescent Psychiatry, 30,* 631–635.

Mechanic, D. (1962). The concept of illness behavior. *Journal of Chronic Diseases, 15,* 189–194.

Mechanic, D. (1964). The influence of mothers on their children's health attitudes and behavior. *Pediatrics,* 444–453.

Mikail, S. F., & von Baeyer, C. L. (1990). Pain, somatic focus, and emotional adjustment in children of chronic headache sufferers and controls. *Social Sciences and Medicine, 31,* 51–59.

Miller, A. J., & Kratochwill, R. T. (1979). Reduction of frequent stomach ache complaints by time out. *Behavior Therapy, 10,* 211–218.

Minuchin, S., Baker, L., Rosman, B. L., Liebman, R., Milman, L., & Todd, T. C. (1975). A conceptual model of psychosomatic illness in children. *Archives of General Psychiatry, 32,* 1031–1038.

Minuchin, S., Rosman, B. L., & Baker, L. (1978). *Psychosomatic families: Anorexia nervosa in context.* Cambridge, MA: Harvard University Press.

Mizes, J. S. (1985). The use of contingent reinforcement in the treatment of a conversion disorder: A multiple baseline study. *Journal of Behavior Therapy and Experimental Psychiatry, 16,* 341–345.

Mullins, L. L., & Olson, R. A. (1990). Familial factors

in the etiology, maintenance, and treatment of somatoform disorders in children. *Family Systems and Medicine, 8,* 159–175.

Murphy, M. R. (1990). Classification of the somatoform disorders. In M. Bass (Ed.), *Somatization: Physical symptoms and psychological illness.* New York: Blackwell Scientific Publications.

Nemiah, J. C. (1977). Alexithymia. Theoretical considerations. *Psychotherapy and Psychosomatics, 28,* 199–206.

O'Brien, W. H., & Haynes, S. N. (1993). Behavioral assessment in the psychiatric setting. In A. S. Bellack & M. Hersen (Eds.), *Handbook of behavior therapy in the psychiatric setting.* New York: Plenum Press.

Offord, D. R., Boyle, M. H., Szatmari, P., Rae-Grant, N. I., Links, P. S., Cadman, D. T., Byles, J. A., Crawford, J. W., Blum, H. M., Byrne, C., Thomas, H., & Woodward, C. A. (1987). Ontario Child Health Study: II. Six-month prevalence of disorder and rates of service utilization. *Archives of General Psychiatry, 44,* 832–836.

Oster, J. (1972). Recurrent abdominal pain, headache and limb pains in children and adolescents. *Pediatrics, 50,* 429–436.

Parsons, T. (1964). *Social structure and personality.* New York: Free Press.

Pennebaker, J. W., & Susman, J. R. (1988). Disclosure of traumas and psychosomatic processes. *Social Sciences and Medicine, 26,* 327–332.

Pennebaker, J. W., & Watson, D. (1991). The psychology of physical symptoms. In L. J. Kirmayer & J. M. Robbins (Eds.), *Current concepts of somatization: Research and clinical perspectives.* Washington, DC: American Psychiatric Press.

Pilowsky, I. (1969). Abnormal illness behavior. *British Journal of Medicine and Psychiatry, 42,* 347–351.

Pilowsky, I., Bassett, D. L., Begg, M. W., & Thomas, P. G. (1982). Childhood hospitalization and chronic intractable pain in adults: A controlled retrospective study. *International Psychiatry in Medicine, 12,* 75–84.

Poikolainen, J., Kanerva, R., & Lonnquist, J. (1995) Life events and other risk factors for somatic symptoms in adolescence. *Pediatrics, 96,* 59–63.

Proctor, J. T. (1958). Hysteria in childhood. *American Journal of Orthopsychiatry, 28,* 394–407.

Rauste-von Wright, M., & von Wright, J. (1981). A longitudinal study of psychosomatic symptoms in healthy 11–18-year-old girls and boys. *Journal of Psychosomatic Research, 25,* 525–534.

Riddle, M. A. (Guest Ed.). (1995). *Child and adolescent clinics of North America, Pediatric*

Psychopharmacology II. Philadelphia: W. B. Saunders.

Riddle, M. A., Schaill, L., King, R. A., Hardin, M. T., Anderson, G. M., Ort, S. I., Smith, J. C., Leckman, J. F., & Cohen, D. J. (1992). Double-blind crossover trial of fluoxetine and placebo in children and adolescents with obsessive-compulsive disorder. *Journal of the American Academy of Child and Adolescent Psychiatry, 31,* 1062–1069.

Rimsza, M. E., Berg, R. A., & Locke, C. (1988). Sexual abuse: Somatic and emotional reactions. *Child Abuse and Neglect, 12,* 201–208.

Rivinus, T. M., Jamison, D. L., & Graham, P. J. (1975). Childhood organic neurological disease presenting as psychiatric disorder. *Archives of Diseases of Children, 40,* 115–119.

Robins, E., & O'Neal, P. (1953). Clinical features of hysteria in children—with a note on prognosis: A two- to seventeen-year follow-up study of 41 patients. *Nervous Child, 10,* 246–271.

Robinson, J. O., Alverez, J. H., & Dodge, J. A. (1990). Life events and family history in children with recurrent abdominal pain. *Journal of Psychosomatic Research, 34,* 171–181.

Rock, N. (1971). Conversion reactions in childhood: A clinical study on childhood neuroses. *Journal of the American Academy of Child Psychiatry, 10,* 65–93.

Routh, D. K., & Ernst, A. R. (1984). Somatization disorder in relatives of children and adolescents with functional abdominal pain. *Journal of Pediatric Psychology, 9,* 427–437.

Rutter, M., Tizard, J., & Whitmore, K. (1970). *Education, health and behavior.* London: Longman Group.

Ryan, N. D., Puig-Antich, J., Ambrosini, P., Nelson, B., & Krawiec, V. (1987). The clinical picture of major depression in children and adolescents. *Archives of General Psychiatry, 44,* 854–861.

Sanders, M. R., Rebgetz, M., Morrison, M., Bor, W., Gordon, A., Dadds, M., & Shepherd, R. (1989). Cognitive-behavioral treatment of recurrent nonspecific abdominal pain in children: An analysis of generalization, maintenance, and side effects. *Journal of Consulting and Clinical Psychology, 57,* 294–300.

Sanders, M. R., Shepherd, R. W., Cleghorn, G., & Woolford, H. (1994). The treatment of recurrent abdominal pain in children: A controlled comparison of cognitive-behavioral family intervention and standard pediatric. *Journal of Consulting and Clinical Psychology, 62,* 306–314.

Sank, L. I., & Biglan, A. (1974). Operant treatment

of a case of recurrent abdominal pain in a 10-year-old boy. *Behavior Therapy, 5*, 677–681.

Scaloubaca, D., Slade, P., & Creed, F. (1988). Life events and somatization among students. *Journal of Psychosomatic Research, 32*, 221–229.

Schneider, S., & Rice, D. R. (1979). Neurologic manifestations of childhood hysteria. *Journal of Pediatrics, 94*, 153–156.

Schreier, H. A., & Libow, J. A. (1993). *Hurting for Love: Munchausen by Proxy Syndrome.* New York: Guilford.

Schulman, J. L. (1988). Use of a coping approach in the management of children with conversion reactions. *Journal of the American Academy of Child and Adolescent Psychiatry,* 785–788.

Shapiro, E. G., & Rosenfeld, A. A. (1987). *The somatizing child.* New York: Springer-Verlag.

Shields, J. (1982). Genetical studies of hysterical disorders. In A. Roy (Ed.), *Hysteria.* New York: Wiley.

Shorter, E., Abbey, S. E., Gillies, L. A., Singh, M., & Lipowski, Z. J. (1992). Inpatient treatment of persistent somatization. *Psychosomatics, 33*, 295–301.

Siegel, M., & Barthel, R. P. (1986). Conversion disorders on a child psychiatry consultation service. *Psychosomatics, 27*, 201–204.

Silver, L. B. (1982). Conversion disorder with pseudoseizures in adolescence: A stress reaction to unrecognized and untreated learning disabilities. *Journal of the American Academy of Child Psychiatry, 5*, 508–512.

Simon, G. E. (1991). Somatization and psychiatric disorder. In L. J. Kirmayer & J. M. Robbins (Eds.), *Current concepts of somatization: Research and clinical perspectives.* Washington, DC: American Psychiatric Press.

Slavney, P. R. (1990). *Perspectives on "hysteria."* Baltimore: Johns Hopkins University Press.

Smith, G. R., Monson, R. A., & Ray, D. C. (1986). Psychiatric consultation in somatization disorder. *New England Journal of Medicine, 314*, 1407–1413.

Smith, G. R., Rost, K., & Kashner, T. M. (1995). A trial of the effect of a standardized psychiatric consultation on health outcomes and costs in somatizing patients. *Archives of General Psychiatry, 52*, 238–243.

Spierings, C., Poels, P. J. E., Sijben, N., Gabreels, F. J. M., & Renier, W. O. (1990). Conversion disorders in childhood: A retrospective follow-up study of 84 patients. *Developmental Medicine and Child Neurology, 32*, 865–871.

Srinath, S., Bharat, S., Girimaji, S., & Seshadri, S. (1993). Characteristics of a child inpatient population with hysteria in India. *Journal of the American Academy of Child and Adolescent Psychiatry, 32*, 822–825.

Starfield, B., Katz, H., Gabriel, A., Livingston, G., Benson, P., Hankin, J., Horn, S., & Steinwachs, D. (1984). Morbidity in childhood—a longitudinal view. *New England Journal of Medicine, 310*, 824–829.

Stefansson, J. G., Messina, J. S., & Meyerowitz, S. (1976). Hysterical neurosis, conversion type: Clinical and epidemiological considerations. *Acta-Psychiatra Scandinavian, 53*, 119–138.

Steinhausen, H. D., Aster, M. V., Pfeiffer, E., & Gobel, D. (1989). Comparative studies of conversion disorders in childhood and adolescence. *Journal of Child Psychology Psychiatry, 30*, 615–621.

Stevenson, J., Simpson, J., & Bailey, V. (1988). Research note: Recurrent headaches and stomachaches in preschool children. *Journal of Child Psychology and Psychiatry, 29*, 897–900.

Stickler, G. B., & Murphy, D. B. (1979). Recurrent abdominal pain. *American Journal of Diseases of Children, 133*, 486–489.

Stone, R., & Barbero, G. (1970). Recurrent abdominal pain in childhood. *Pediatrics, 45*, 732–738.

Thomson, A. P. J., & Sills, J. A. (1988). Diagnosis of functional illness presenting with gait disorder. *Archives of Diseases of Children, 63*, 148–153.

Turgay, A. (1980). Conversion reactions in children. *Psychiatric Journal of the University of Ottawa, 5*, 287–294.

Turgay, A. (1990). Treatment outcome for children and adolescents with conversion disorder. *Canadian Journal of Psychiatry, 35*, 585–589.

Volkmar, R. R., Poll, J., & Lewis, M. (1984). Conversion reactions in children and adolescents. *Journal of the American Academy of Child and Adolescent Psychiatry, 23*, 424–430.

Walker, L. S., Garber, J., & Greene, J. W. (1991). Somatization symptoms in pediatric abdominal pain patients: Relation to chronicity of abdominal pain and parent somatization. *Journal of Abnormal Child Psychology, 19*, 379–394.

Walker, L. S., Garber, J., & Greene, J. (1993). Psychosocial correlates of recurrent childhood pain: A comparison of pediatric patients with recurrent abdominal pain, organic illness, and psychiatric disorders. *Journal of Abnormal Psychology, 102*, 248–258.

Walker, L. S., Garber, J., & Greene, J. W. (1994).

Symptom maintenance in pediatric patients: The role of negative life events, child competence, and parent somatic complaints. *Journal of Consulting and Clinical Psychology, 62*, 1213–1221.

Walker, L. S., Garber, J., & Van Slyke, D. A. (1995). Do parents excuse the misbehavior of children with physical or emotional symptoms? An investigation of the pediatric sick role. *Journal of Pediatric Psychology, 20*, 329–345.

Walker, L. S., Garber, J., Van Slyke, D. A., & Greene, J. W. (1995). Long-term health outcomes in patients with recurrent abdominal pain. *Journal of Pediatric Psychology, 20*, 233–245.

Walker, L. S., & Greene, J. W. (1989). Children with recurrent abdominal pain and their parents: More somatic complaints, anxiety, and depression than other patient families? *Journal of Pediatric Psychology, 14*, 231–243.

Walker, L. S., & Greene, J. W. (1991). Negative life events and symptom resolution in pediatric abdominal pain patients. *Journal of Pediatric Psychology, 16*, 341–360.

Warwick, H. M., & Salkovskis, P. M. (1985). Reassurance. *British Medical Journal, 290*, 1028.

Warwick, H. M., & Salkovskis, P. M. (1988). Hypochondriasis. In J. Scott, J. M. Williams, & A. T. Beck (Eds.), *Cognitive therapy: A clinical casebook*. London: Helm.

Wasserman, A. L., Whitington, P. F., & Rivera, F. P. (1988). Psychogenic basis for abdominal pain in children and adolescents. *Journal of the American Academy Child and Adolescent Psychiatry, 27*, 179–184.

Watson, D., & Pennebaker, J. W. (1989). Health complaints, stress, and distress: Exploring the central role of negative affectivity. *Psychology Review, 96*, 234–254.

Weiner, H., & Fawzy, F. (1989). An integrative model of health, disease, and illness. In S. Cheren (Ed.), *Psychosomatic medicine: Theory, physiology, and practice*. Madison: International Universities Press.

Wessely, S. (1990). Old wine in new bottles: Neurasthenia and 'ME'. *Psychological Medicine, 20*, 35–53.

Williams, D. T., & Singh, M. (1976). Hypnosis as a facilitating therapeutic adjunct in child psychiatry. *Journal of the American Academy of Child Psychiatry, 15*, 326–342.

Williams, D. T., Spiegel, H., & Mostofsky, D. I. (1978). Neurogenic and hysterical seizures in children and adolescents: Differential diagnostic and therapeutic considerations. *American Journal of Psychiatry, 135*, 82–86.

Wood, B. (1993). Beyond the "psychosomatic family": A biobehavioral family model of pediatric illness. *Family Process, 32*, 261–278.

Wooley, S. C., Blackwell, B., & Winget, C. (1978). A learning theory model of chronic illness behavior: Theory, treatment, and research. *Psychosomatic Medicine, 40*, 379–401.

World Health Organization. (1988). *International classification of diseases (10th rev.)*. Geneva: Author.

World Health Organization. (1992). *ICD-10 classification of mental and behavioural disorders: Clinical descriptions and diagnostic guidelines*. Geneva: Author.

Wyllie, E., Friedman, D., Luders, H., Morris, H., Rothner, D., & Turnbull, J. (1991). Outcome of psychogenic seizures in children and adolescents compared with adults. *Neurology, 41*, 742–744.

Zuckerman, B., Stevenson, J., & Bailey, V. (1987). Stomachaches and headaches in a community sample of preschool children. *Pediatrics, 79*, 677–682.

17

Dissociative Disorders in Childhood and Adolescence

Heather R. Wallach
Stephen J. Dollinger

HISTORICAL PERSPECTIVE

Midway through the nineteenth century, the physician Antoine Despine reported on his treatment of an 11-year-old girl with numerous somatic complaints, including paralysis and extreme pain upon movement (Ellenberger, 1970; Fine, 1988; Greaves, 1993; Sanders, 1986). The child, Estelle, also experienced hallucinations and visions and was amnestic for events around her. Following a slight improvement from physiological treatments, Estelle was diagnosed by Despine with " 'ecstatis,' a condition that could be cured by animal magnetism" (Ellenberger, 1970, p. 129). Despine commenced "magnetic" treatment (analogous to hypnotherapy), at which time different personality states emerged. During hypnotic episodes, Estelle demonstrated marked changes in physical and psychological functioning. Using therapeutic principles similar to those applied during modern treatment of dissociative disorders, Despine worked with Estelle and her mother to reduce the frequency of dissociative episodes and to begin restoring Estelle to healthy physical and psychological functioning (Fine, 1988).

Although this early report of pathological dissociation has been described as the first "truly objective study of multiple personality" (Ellenberger, 1970, p. 129), writings on dissociative disorders have, until recent years, focused attention almost exclusively on adult cases of dissociation. A historical review of dissociative phenomena begins with Gmelin's description, in 1791, of identity changes in a German woman during the French Revolution (Greaves, 1993). Case studies of pathological dissociative reactions (generally, in adults) continued appearing during the eighteenth and nineteenth centuries (Carlson, 1981; Rosenzweig, 1988; Sanders, 1986). Theoretical work included de Tour's concept of dissociation or "psychological dissolution" (reviewed in van der Hart & Friedman, 1989), and Durand's writings on polypsychism (reviewed in Sanders, 1986), in which an individual's mind was believed to be physically divided into a number of distinct parts, each with unique ego development and functioning. Other investigations included observations of automatic writing, by Taine, and of hypnosis, by Jean Martin Charcot, Morton Prince, Freud, and others (reviewed in Putnam, 1989a, 1989b; Sanders, 1986; van der Hart & Horst, 1989). With its apparent capacity to gain access to different states of consciousness, hypnosis became a research tool for investigating dissociative barriers. And, in clinical work, hypnotherapy gained in popularity as a treatment for hysterical conditions or conversion disorders; it was hypothesized that hypnotism permitted the expression and release of thoughts and feelings that were held apart or "dissociated" from everyday awareness. Kluft (1985a, 1985b) and Greaves (1980, 1993) provide reviews of the history of dissociation, including theoretical developments, as well as case histories of individuals with dissociative disorders; Kluft's (1985a, 1985b) focus is on instances of childhood dissociation.

Although such clinical and theoretical work provided a foundation for dissociation theory, Pierre Janet has been credited as being the first person to have systematically investigated dissociative phenomena (Putnam, 1989a). On the basis of his observations of patients under his care, and drawing from earlier work, Janet described dissociation as a significant alteration in one's identity combined with amnesia for events that occurred during the period of identity disruption:

> Things happen as if an idea, a partial system of thought, emancipated itself, became independent and developed itself on its own account. The result is, on the one hand, that it develops far too much, and on the other hand, that consciousness appears no longer to control it. (Janet, quoted in Putnam, 1989a, p. 415)

This disturbance of identity, coupled with memory loss, was believed to occur when individuals who suffered from "psychological misery" were unable to maintain an integrated sense of self (Janet, reviewed in van der Hart & Friedman, 1989, p. 6). In considering Despine's young patient, it can be noted that, although Estelle's symptoms developed after a mild fall, her history included earlier and more traumatic life events, including a near-fatal illness at age five and, 2 years later, her father's own death from cholera (Ellenberger, 1970; Fine, 1988).

Although reports of dissociation continued to emerge during the beginning of the twentieth century (Greaves, 1993), those reviewing the history of dissociation note an apparent decrease in interest in dissociative phenomena beginning during the 1930s and 1940s. Greaves (1993) has termed the period from 1944 to 1957 a "blackout time" (p. 362) for publications on the most severe form of pathological dissociation, multiple personality disorder (MPD), now called dissociative identity disorder (DID) by the American Psychiatric Association (1994) in the *Diagnostic and Statistical Manual of Mental Disorders* (DSM-IV), and this appears to have been the case for writings on other dissociative phenomena as well (Putnam, 1989b).

A number of factors appear to have contributed to the waning interest in dissociation during this time period. Because most published reports of dissociation were clinical case studies or poorly designed, single-participant experiments, there was a growing skepticism regarding the validity of dissociative disorders (Putnam, 1989b). Putnam (1989b) noted that during the 1930s "dissociation . . . was demoted to the role of an obscure, minor phenomena" (pp. 4–5).

One dissociative disorder in particular, MPD, was challenged as being an iatrogenically created "artifact of personality" (Putnam, 1989b, p. 33), or easily created under conditions of high suggestibility, such as hypnosis (Spanos, Weekes, & Bertrand, 1985). During the same time period, psychoanalytic theory emerged as a dominant model of psychopathology, and theories of dissociation faded in prominence (Putnam, 1989b; van der Hart & Horst, 1989).

The growing identification and treatment of schizophrenia following Bleuler's work in this area (reviewed in Sanders, 1986) also began to overshadow reports of dissociative pathology (Greaves, 1993; Sanders, 1986). Behaviors presumed to be characteristic of dissociative reactions in adults (e.g., auditory hallucinations, loss of motor control, periods of stupor and trance-like states, and changes in personality functioning) could also be explained as symptoms of schizophrenia (Kluft, 1987; Sanders, 1986), and Bleuler's description of schizophrenia was inclusive of some aspects of multiple personality disorder (Greaves, 1993). Although at least one case of childhood dissociation is known to have been misdiagnosed as schizophrenia (McElroy, 1992), there is some indication that this diagnostic confusion is less likely to occur with children and adolescents. Gilbert and Dollinger (1992) note, for example, that hallucinations in children are not necessarily indicative of a psychotic process and may likely represent a hysterical or dissociative reaction to stress.

Other factors, however, may have contributed to the low rate in diagnosis of dissociative disorders in children prior to the 1980s. On the basis of retrospective accounts from adult MPD patients, Kluft (1985b) has offered a list of seven factors that may contribute to the low diagnosis rate of multiple personality disorder in childhood. Among these, we regard three as most notable: that fluctuating findings suggested a different diagnosis (e.g., psychosis, learning disability); that other explanations for specific symptoms are more readily available (e.g., lying, imaginary companionship, or primitive ego functions); and that children may be unaware of their condition. As noted, Kluft (1985b) offered further explanations, as well. A review of additional writings on other dissociative disorders in childhood shows that many factors in this list are applicable not only to childhood MPD/DID and what Fagan and McMahon (1984) have termed "incipient mpd," but to other dissociative disorders as well.

The 1960s and 1970s saw a resurgence in interest in incidences of pathological dissociation; observation of dissociative reactions in Vietnam War veterans suffering from post traumatic stress disorder highlighted a connection between trauma and dissociation (Garcia, 1990). Of special relevance to the apparent increase in dissociative disorders was a greater recognition of childhood sexual abuse and the observed relationship between childhood trauma and later dissociation (Garcia, 1990; Putnam, 1989b). Indeed, modern theories of dissociation emphasize the influence of exposure to traumatic events on subsequent dissociative reactions. In reviewing the history of multiple personality disorder in childhood, Kluft (1985b) presents a timeline of the number of cases reported for children and

adolescents. He observes a steady increase, beginning just prior to 1980, in the rate at which this dissociative disorder was diagnosed in children and adolescents. Although the majority of work to date with children and adolescents has focused on this most severe and chronic dissociative disorder, recent findings with various child dissociation assessment scales have begun to identify a continuum of dissociative experiences that more comprehensively portrays the range of both normative and pathological dissociations in young persons (Evers-Szostak & Sanders, 1992; Hornstein & Putnam, 1992; Malinosky-Rummell & Hoier, 1991; Putnam, Helmers, & Trickett, 1993; Tyson, 1992). Such empirical work also begins to address one of the factors considered by Kluft to contribute to the "non-recognition" (1985b, p. 173) of dissociative disorders in children and adolescents, specifically, limited information regarding characteristics of dissociative disorders in young persons.

Historical accounts of dissociative disorders in children and adolescents are thus found in a limited number of reports. In recent years, however, attention has shifted toward identifying and describing dissociative experiences both in adults and, most recently, in young persons. The remainder of this chapter defines the concept of dissociation, both as a normative and as a maladaptive event, examines major diagnostic classification systems for the dissociative disorders, discusses assessment and diagnosis of dissociative disorders in children, and reviews various treatment protocols that have been applied to help young persons with dissociative disorders and their families.

THE DISSOCIATIVE CONTINUUM

Pierre Janet's understanding of dissociative phenomena is in fact quite similar to contemporary theories, in particular, his description of the role of traumatic events on dissociative experiences (Putnam, 1989a; van der Hart & Horst, 1989). Research in several countries has provided much empirical data to support an association between traumatic events and the subsequent capacity to dissociate as a defensive response to such events (Sandberg & Lynn, 1992; Sanders & Giolas, 1991; Sanders, McRoberts, & Tollefson, 1989; Terr, 1991).

Current models of dissociation also recognize (more explicitly than did Janet) that dissociative phenomena are not pathological per se but rather occur along a continuum that ranges from normative to maladaptive experiences of dissociation. At present, dissociation is commonly defined as:

> a process whereby certain mental functions which are ordinarily integrated with other functions presumably operate in a more compartmentalized or automatic way usually outside the sphere of conscious awareness or memory recall. (Ludwig, 1983, p. 93)

Empirical findings support a continuum theory for dissociative experiences. Dissociation at low levels has been found to be present within nonclinical populations without any known psychiatric history (Bernstein & Putnam, 1986; Martin & Labott, 1986; Ross, Joshi, & Currie, 1990). More pathological instances of dissociation are likely to be associated with traumatic experiences (often beginning during childhood) such as physical and sexual abuse, maltreatment, and neglect (Bernstein & Putnam, 1986; Coons, 1994; Irwin, 1994; Ross, Ryan, Voigt, & Edie, 1991; Sandberg & Lynn, 1992; Sanders & Giolas, 1991; Sanders et al., 1989; Schultz, Braun & Kluft, 1989; Terr, 1991). Furthermore, subgroups of college students who reported physical and emotional abuse during childhood have obtained higher scores on objective scales of dissociation relative to the scores of nonabused peers (Ross, Ryan, Anderson, Ross, & Hardy, 1989; Ross et al., 1991; Sandberg & Lynn, 1992; Sanders et al., 1989).

Normative Dissociation

A number of common, "everyday" experiences of dissociation are similar in adults and young persons, including daydreaming, overabsorption in tasks (e.g., while reading books, watching television or movies), or failing to notice or remember what someone has said (Evers-Szostak & Sanders, 1992). However, children seem to experience a broader range of dissociative experiences (Putnam, 1991). Normative experiences of dissociation in young children include being amnestic for experiences in their early life and having a high involvement in fantasy activities with high absorption, including daydreaming and imaginary companions (Putnam, 1991; Putnam et al., 1993):

> The looser cohesion of young children is an important asset of childhood and not a sign of pathology. The very looseness and vulnerability to fragmentation that characterizes young children form an important avenue through which the child is able to turn to adults for self-object functions which will lay down profound supplies of self esteem, self-soothing, ambition, values, internal warmth, empathy, vigor, and organization which are the stuff of deeper and healthier adulthood functioning. (Albini & Pease, 1989, p. 149)

Initial data on patterns of child dissociation were based primarily on comparisons to age-related changes in hypnotic capacity and on records of and recollections by adults with dissociative disorders (Braun & Sachs, 1985; Carlson & Putnam, 1989; Kluft, 1985b). More recently, construction of objective assessment scales to quantify experiences in both adults and young persons has helped clarify the nature of normative and pathological dissociations (Bernstein & Putnam, 1986; Evers-Szostak & Sanders, 1992; Putnam et al., 1993). Numerous studies of dissociative experiences have found evidence for the existence of dissociative responses in normative groups of children, adolescents, and adults. For most individuals, dissociative capacity appears to follow a general developmental path, characterized by levels of dissociation that rise gradually and steadily throughout childhood, peak during late childhood or early adolescence, then level off and decline steadily throughout adulthood (Evers-Szostak & Sanders, 1992; Putnam, 1991).

Maladaptive Dissociation

Three general criteria have been proposed to help distinguish between maladaptive and normative dissociation—an alteration in identity, changes in memory functioning, and a history of exposure to traumatic events (Nemiah, 1981; Putnam, 1989b). Both case studies and empirical research on dissociation indicate that significant changes in identity do occur (Dell & Eisenhower, 1990; Hornstein & Putnam, 1992; Malenbaum & Russell, 1986; Riley & Mead, 1988; Tyson, 1992; Weiss, Sutton, & Utecht, 1985). Hornstein and Putnam (1992) found that children diagnosed with MPD or with dissociative disorder not otherwise specified (DDNOS) consistently demonstrated identity disturbances such as alter personality states, age regression, and marked changes in personality. Likewise, individual case histories on adolescents with problems of depersonalization and derealization have reported severe shifts in identity functioning, including feeling like a "stranger in a strange world" (McKellar, 1978, p. 1580) and the sensation of being detached from one's surroundings (Dollinger, 1983).

Memory disturbances are also evident in individuals with pathological dissociation; amnesia for personal information or general knowledge is commonly identified in both adults and young persons. Dell and Eisenhower (1990) reported that 9 of 11 adolescents (82%) diagnosed with MPD reported such symptoms. Hornstein and Putnam (1992) list a number of other problems of memory functioning in children and adolescents with dissociative disorders, such as wandering off, and a tendency to lose possessions.

Maladaptive dissociative reactions, in particular those characteristic of the more severe dissociative disorders (DID, DDNOS), have been etiologically linked to a history of repeated traumatic events during childhood, generally originating when the child is between 5 and 10 years of age (Albini & Pease, 1989; Coons, Bowman, & Milstein, 1988). Such traumatic experiences are generally severe physical, sexual, and/or emotional abuse, often initiated by family members (Stern, 1984). A number of clinical researchers believe that the most extreme dissociative pathology develops as the young child dissociates repeatedly to escape from the distress of severe abuse (Coons et al., 1988; Nash, Hulsey, Sexton, Harralson,

& Lambert, 1993; Putnam, 1989b; Stern, 1984; Wilbur, 1984). At first an adaptive method for managing overwhelming stress, dissociation becomes disruptive to the individual's overall functioning and can pose a threat to the individual's (and others') health and safety (Hornstein & Tyson, 1991; Putnam, 1985; Wilbur, 1984).

Braun and Sachs (1985) have proposed a diathesis-stress model composed of predisposing factors that contribute to the development of the most extreme dissociative disorder, MPD, or dissociative identity disorder, as well as precipitating and perpetuating factors that maintain DID pathology. Predisposing factors include an inborn dissociative ability, hypnotic susceptibility, high intelligence, and exposure to trauma during childhood. Symptoms of the illness are then evoked by precipitating events, most commonly "some form of abuse that triggers dissociative episodes" (Braun & Sachs, 1985, p. 48). Finally, MPD is maintained as the individual continues to use dissociation as a "preferred" (Braun & Sachs, 1985, p. 50) coping mechanism and experiences stressful life events (e.g., ongoing abuse, loss of significant others). Dell and Eisenhower (1990) reported that MPD adolescents least likely to benefit from treatment were those living in an environment in which physical, emotional, or sexual abuse continued. Similarly, Kluft's (1984a, 1984b) four-factor model for the development of MPD involves a child's predisposing tendency to dissociate, use of such ability during traumatic experiences, the development of a system of alter personality states, and the maintenance of such pathological functioning as the child is re-exposed to traumatic events.

DIAGNOSTIC CLASSIFICATION SYSTEMS

DSM—Previous and Current Diagnostic Categories

In the most current edition of the *Diagnostic and Statistical Manual of Mental Disorders*

(DSM-IV; APA, 1994), the American Psychiatric Association recognizes five dissociative disorders: dissociative amnesia, dissociative fugue, depersonalization disorder, DID, and DDNOS. The dissociative disorders are maintained in a separate category and are described in DSM-IV as involving "a disruption in the usually integrated functions of consciousness, memory, identity, or perception of the environment" (APA, 1994, p. 477).

There is limited information in DSM-IV regarding the occurrence of dissociative disorders in childhood and adolescence. In the third edition of DSM (APA, 1980), sleepwalking was considered a disorder of childhood with a dissociative component. However, with the revisions to DSM-III in 1987 (DSM-III-R), sleepwalking disorder was removed from the section on disorders first diagnosed in childhood and was reassigned to the category "sleep disorders."

The first two editions of the DSM clearly identified underlying stress as contributing to the development and expression of dissociative pathology:

> The chief characteristic of these disorders is 'anxiety' which may be directly felt and expressed or which may be unconsciously and automatically controlled by the utilization of various psychological defense mechanisms. . . . (APA, 1952, p. 31)

Diagnostic titles reflected this theoretical stance towards etiology: within the original *Diagnostic and Statistical Manual* (APA, 1952) dissociative pathology was described as a psychoneurotic disorders—specifically, "dissociative reaction," which included symptoms of dissociation, shifts in personality functioning, disturbances of memory, and fugue behaviors. Physical symptoms arising due to underlying anxiety were indicative of a "conversion reaction" and were not considered to involve dissociative processes. Revisions published in 1968, in DSM-II, maintained this explicit connection between underlying stress or anxiety and dissociation, yet combined conversion reaction and dissociative reaction diagnoses into one new diagnostic category, hysterical neurosis,

with two subcategories, entitled "conversion type" and "dissociative type." In addition, depersonalization, which was formerly considered simply a symptom of a dissociative reaction, now was considered as a separate diagnostic entity, depersonalization disorder.

The introduction of DSM-III, in 1980, represented a key paradigmatic shift in the classification of mental illness, with a general emphasis on description of symptoms as a stronger emphasis on an atheoretical stance toward possible etiologies (Wilson, 1993). This shift is perhaps reflected in the subtle change in the way the dissociative disorders were described. A discussion of the relationship between dissociation and stress had previously been found in the overarching introductory description of the dissociative disorders. However, in DSM-III (APA, 1980) such theoretical musings were now given only a brief mention under the "course and predisposing factors" section for each specific diagnosis. Interestingly, this change came at a time when a growing scientific interest in the dissociative disorders began to demonstrate a strong association between exposure to traumatic events and subsequent dissociative reactions (Putnam, 1989b).

DSM-III also made further distinctions among the types of dissociative pathology; with diagnostic categories consisting of psychogenic amnesia, psychogenic fugue, multiple personality, depersonalization disorder, and atypical dissociative disorder. Finally, the older hysterical neurosis, conversion type, was reclassified in a new section entitled "Somatoform Disorders" and divided into conversion disorder and psychogenic pain disorder. DSM-III-R (APA, 1987) retained these general diagnostic categories, although atypical dissociative disorder was renamed DDNOS and the conditions under which this diagnosis could be made were expanded. Likewise, DSM-IV (APA, 1994) has made limited changes from DSM-III-R in the classification of the dissociative disorders, with the exception of renaming several diagnoses— MPD has become DID, and psychogenic amnesia and psychogenic fugue have become dissociative amnesia and dissociative fugue, respectively.

ICD-10 Diagnostic Categories

In comparison with DSM-IV (APA, 1994), the World Health Organization's *International Classification of Mental and Behavioral Disorders* (ICD-10) (1992) classification system retains a more explicit theoretical connection between trauma and dissociation. The general description of the dissociative disorders within ICD-10 (WHO, 1992) is similar to that offered in DSM-IV (APA, 1994). In contrast to DSM-IV, however, ICD-10 makes a greater number of distinctions between different types of dissociative pathology that appear to have a higher potential for overlap (WHO, 1992). For example, trance and possessive disorder overlaps in description with MPD, whereas dissociative convulsions overlaps with dissociative stupor. Moreover, the "convulsions" and "trance" categories also overlap in symptom picture. Furthermore, although the majority of empirical work on the dissociative disorders has involved MPD/DID research, ICD-10 classifies MPD as a subcategory under "other dissociative disorders" (WHO, 1992, p. 160), given the controversy surrounding the validity of this disorder.

Diagnostic Challenges

Although the dissociative disorders appear etiologically linked to childhood traumas, a formal diagnosis is seldom made until late adolescence or early adulthood, at the earliest. For example, data on diagnosis of DID (MPD) reveals an average of nearly 7 years between initial psychiatric contact and a later diagnosis of DID/MPD (Coons et al., 1988). Common misdiagnoses during childhood and adolescence have included internalizing problems, such as mood, anxiety, and adjustment disorders, as well as externalizing problems, including conduct disorder and attention-deficit disorder (Dell & Eisenhower, 1990; Putnam et al., 1993). Putnam et al. (1993) note that a diagnosis of schizophrenia or psychosis is often applied to explain symptoms of hallucinations. In adolescents, borderline personality disorder

was also found to be a common prior diagnosis (Dell & Eisenhower, 1990). Furthermore, co-morbid problems related to abuse history (e.g., posttraumatic stress disorder [PTSD], mood disorder) may further complicate diagnostic judgment. In an examination of adolescents with MPD, all patients met the criteria for at least one other DSM-III-R diagnosis and were found to have at least some characteristics of other diagnoses (Dell & Eisenhower, 1990). The authors proposed a hierarchical model in which the presence of MPD, and posttraumatic stress disorder, an "abuse/trauma related-diagnosis" (Dell & Eisenhower, 1990, p. 365) be considered "diagnostically superordinate" (p. 364) to other, more common childhood diagnoses. This implies a treatment focus on abuse-related issues and dissociative pathology, rather than other problems, such as conduct disorder, attention-deficit disorder, or mood disorder. Kluft's (1985b) own observations in diagnosis and treatment of a group of adolescent females support this.

With the exception of sleepwalking disorder, briefly considered a mental disorder of childhood, DSM classification systems have been limited in their discussion of dissociative pathology in childhood. Similarly, ICD-10 gives only a cursory mention of childhood or adolescent instances of dissociation in the category of "transient dissociative [conversion] disorders occurring in childhood and adolescence" (WHO, 1992, p. 161). This diagnosis is listed, yet no definition or guidelines for diagnostic criteria are provided.

Empirical evidence for the clinical validity of these disorders in childhood is limited, but a growing canon of research in this area has begun to clarify this issue (Dell & Eisenhower, 1990; Malinosky-Rummell & Hoier, 1991; Putnam, 1991; Putnam et al., 1993; Sanders & Giolas, 1991; Tyson, 1992). Individual case reports point to the existence of MPD/DID and DDNOS in children as young as 3 to 5 years of age, and reports of depersonalization in adolescence exist as well (Dollinger, 1983; Fagan & McMahon, 1984; McKellar, 1978; Riley & Mead, 1988; Rinsley, 1971; Shimizu & Sakamoto, 1986). Objective scales to quantify dissociative experiences have been helpful as well in describing the range of normative and pathological dissociations that may occur in childhood and adolescence (Evers-Szostak & Sanders, 1992; Putnam et al., 1993). It has also been suggested that the dissociative disorders may take on a different form with regard to both the quality and the severity of childhood symptoms (Fagan & McMahon, 1984; Peterson, 1990; Tyson, 1992). Tyson (1992) found support for this hypothesis; examination of symptomology in a group of dissociating children aged 8 to 12 years revealed a number of differences relative to adults with MPD. Differences included fewer somatic complaints, a more equal sex ratio, and a clinical picture that was "less florid, less clearly delineated, and apparently less stable" (Tyson, 1992, p. 26). Likewise, McElroy (1992) reviews findings that suggest differences in the clinical presentation of dissociative disorders in children and in adults.

THEORIES OF DISSOCIATION

Supernatural/Possession Theories

Primarily during the nineteenth century and before, supernatural theories of dissociative phenomena were not uncommon, with treatment based in spiritually related activities. Although such explanations have declined in popularity since the emergence of modern medical and psychological models, DSM-IV recognizes "possession trance . . . attributed to the influence of a spirit, power, deity, or other person" (APA, 1994, p. 490) among the criteria for the DDNOS category and provides cross-cultural examples. In a similar manner, the World Health Organization's (1993) ICD-10 diagnostic system maintains a separate category under the dissociative disorders labeled "trance and possession disorders" (p. 156).

Biological Models

Research into brain structure and function in dissociating individuals has revealed some differences in electrophysiological functioning compared with nondissociating persons (Herbert, 1982; Larmore, Ludwig, & Cain, 1977; Mesulam, 1981; Thigpen & Cleckley, 1954). A study of adults identified temporal lobe abnormalities in electrophysiological functioning among patients with dissociative symptomatology (Mesulam, 1981). This finding supported the inference that some individuals with dissociative symptoms may in fact be experiencing epilepsy centered in the temporal lobe region (Mesulam, 1981). Further support for EEG differences related to dissociation comes from a review by Herbert (1982) of work by Frank Putnam. Putnam's work indicates that adult MPD patients showed significant variation in the amplitude and latency of EEG measures as a function of different personality states. Control subjects, instructed to simulate MPD-like personality states, in contrast, showed EEG patterns that appeared normal and were constant across time (Herbert, 1982).

However, other research has failed to reveal consistent differences in the EEG records of dissociative disordered patients, in particular, MPD individuals. Coons and coauthors (Coons, Milstein, & Marley, 1982) concluded that EEG differences found in two MPD patients and one control participant were likely indicative of "changes in emotional state" (p. 825) rather than underlying functional or structural differences related to alter personality functioning.

Neurochemical changes related to state-dependent learning theory have also been proposed to account for differences in knowledge and skill levels evident during different dissociative and nondissociative states among individuals with dissociative disorders (Braun, 1984). Findings on adult MPD patients suggest that a number of other physiological measures (e.g., muscle tension, galvanic skin response, and visual acuity), as well as somatic symptoms such as headaches can differ among alter personality states (Miller, 1989; Putnam, 1984, 1989b).

Finally, a heritable capacity to dissociate has been tentatively established via an association with findings on the genetic predisposition for hypnotic susceptibility. Morgan (1973) conducted a study of heritable hypnotic capacity and calculated a heritablity index (h^2) of 0.64 in monozygotic twins. Other researchers have worked to link hypnotic susceptibility with dissociative capacity (Frischholz, 1985; Frischholz, Lipman, Braun & Sachs, 1992). Studying college students, Frischholz and co-authors (1992) found low but statistically significant correlations between dissociation and hypnotizability.

There is some limited evidence to suggest that an association between hypnotizability and dissociation also exists in children (Putnam, 1989b; Spiegel, 1984). Age-related changes in hypnotic capacity appear to follow a developmental curve similar to that for dissociative ability (Putnam, 1991). At present, however, results are conflicting regarding this relationship and whether either of these phenomena has biological antecedents. Carlson and Putnam (1989) have integrated theories of hypnotic capacity with those for dissociation by arguing that they exist as "two overlapping phenomena," each with distinct characteristics, but sharing some features (p. 34). Further work is necessary to clarify biologically based explanations for dissociative phenomena.

Psychological Theories

The current primary psychological model describing the development of dissociative disorders etiologically links the dissociative disorders to a history of repeated traumatic event during childhood, generally originating between 5 and 10 years of age (Coons et al., 1988). Such traumatic experiences often involve severe physical, sexual, and/or emotional abuse, often initiated by family members (Stern, 1984). Dissociative disorders are believed to develop as the young child dissociates repeatedly to escape from the psychological distress associated with severe physical, emotional, and/or sexual abuse (Coons et al., 1988; Nash et al., 1993; Putnam, 1989b). At first an adaptive method for managing overwhelming stress, dissociation into alter personalities becomes disruptive to the individual's overall functioning and can pose a threat to the individual's (and others') health and safety (Putnam, 1989b; Wilbur, 1984).

Research in several countries has provided much data to support an association between traumatic events and the subsequent capacity to dissociate as a defensive response to such events (Sandberg & Lynn, 1992; Sanders & Giolas, 1991; Sanders et al., 1989). Research with adult MPD/DID patients has demonstrated a strong relationship between the disorder and conditions of extreme and repetitive sexual, physical, and emotional abuse during childhood. In one survey, therapists indicated that 98% of MPD patients with whom they had worked had reported being abused as children (Schultz et al., 1989).

Investigations of children and adolescents also demonstrate a strong relationship between abusive experiences and subsequent maladaptive dissociations (Dell & Eisenhower, 1990; Hornstein & Putnam, 1992; Sanders & Giolas, 1991). A study that compared sexually abused girls with a nonclinical, nonsexually abused group of girls reported significantly higher scores on three different dissociation measures for the sexually abused group (Malinosky-Rummell & Hoier, 1991). Atlas and Hiott (1994) found that adolescent inpatients with a history of physical and/or sexual abuse obtained moderate to severe levels of dissociation on an objective scale of dissociative experiences.

Intrapsychic theories point to issues of identity confusion and identity development, especially with regard to phenomena of depersonalization and derealization (Meares & Grose, 1978; Meyer, 1961): "The depersonalization syndrome can be understood as arising from the conflicts associated with the new and unstable relation of the ego to the outer world" (Meyer, 1961, p. 160). Additional intrapsychic theories for depersonalization based in the psychodynamic tradition have included double-bind theory and issues of boundary confusion (Rinsley, 1971). Greaves (1993) highlights the use of defense mechanisms such as regression, denial, and projection by MPD individuals. Such theories, however, appear based on case studies rather than empirical investigations.

ASSESSMENT

Classification systems such as DSM-IV (APA, 1994) and the World Health Organization's (1992) ICD-10 are the first step in diagnosis insofar as they offer diagnostic criteria for the dissociative disorders. Assessment approaches that are more specifically geared toward identification of dissociative disorders in children and adolescents can be instrumental in the diagnosis of pathological dissociations in young persons. Because dissociative disorders offer a varied and fluctuating clinical presentation across time and setting, a multimodal, multiobserver assessment is recommended, involving self-report and interview data, direct observation, general evaluation of psychological and cognitive functioning, and use of more specific dissociation scales that have been developed in recent years.

Self-Report and Interview Data

Even with adults who report dissociative symptomology, self-report data can be inaccurate due to periods of amnesia and other distortions in time perception and memory (Putnam et al., 1993). Because their understanding of temporal continuity is still developing, children may have difficulty in providing an accurate record of dissociative experiences. Young children are also expected to experience normative dissociative experiences at a higher rate than older children. Putnam et al. (1993) note that:

> In fact, discontinuity of experience is probably the norm for young children, who recurrently cycle through sleep and drowsy states and thus often find themselves in new or changed surroundings without any awareness of what has occurred. (p. 41)

Putnam (1989b) notes that use of the mental status exam with adult MPD patients has revealed a general pattern of marked changes in presentation both during individual interviews and across different times of assessment. This can include changes in speech patterns, physical appearance, motor abilities, and judgment.

Patients may show signs of thought disorder, have long-term memory problems, or report auditory hallucinations that originate from inside the head, rather than externally. During assessment of adolescents, it might also be helpful to examine for prior or ongoing substance use that may be exacerbating dissociative symptoms or perhaps be the primary cause of periods of dissociation.

Some symptoms that individuals experiencing dissociation might report include a sense of feeling "separated" from their environment (depersonalization and derealization), somatic complaints, imaginary friends, forgetfulness, and auditory hallucinations; they may also report being accused of lying (Albini & Pease, 1989; Hornstein & Putnam, 1992; Putnam, 1991; Putnam et al., 1993; Ross, Heber, Norton, & Anderson, 1989; Ross, Ryan, et al., 1989).

Observations and Archival Data

Direct interview of a child or adolescent on different occasions may also permit observation of dissociative phenomena; the young person may demonstrate marked changes in cognitive or affective functioning from one occasion to the next as different demands are placed upon him or her (Dell & Eisenhower, 1990; Fagan & McMahon, 1984; Tyson, 1992; Vincent & Pickering, 1988). Putnam et al. (1993) has noted that "frequent trance-like behavior" (p. 42) may be the best indication of the presence of pathological dissociation.

Behavioral data gathered from reliable observers such as parents and other family members, foster parents or guardians, and teachers can help supplement self-report data, as there may be discrepancies between information obtained from the child and that gathered from other sources. Children may be observed talking to themselves or to imaginary companions, show changes in skills or abilities across time or situation, have marked changes in mood, be sexually precocious, or be observed in "trance-like" states (Fagan & McMahon, 1984; Kluft, 1985b; Putnam et al.,

1993; Tyson, 1992). For example, school personnel might report high levels of inattentiveness during class, overabsorption in activities, and inconsistent academic performance. For children and adolescents who have been hospitalized to manage severe pathology, ongoing observations by members of the treatment team may help identify such behavior patterns as well (Hornstein & Tyson, 1991). Many of these behaviors are also common symptoms of other difficulties children can experience, so caution must be exercised in gathering and integrating information from multiple sources. Hornstein and Putnam (1992) list a number of clusters within which behaviors associated with dissociative disorders can occur; there is a considerable amount of overlap with behaviors characteristic of a number of internalizing disorders (e.g., anxiety, depression) and externalizing disorders of childhood such as attention-deficit/hyperactivity disorder, conduct disorder, and oppositional defiant disorder.

It should be noted that the symptoms discussed are not diagnostic of dissociation in and of themselves, nor are they indicative of maladaptive dissociative processes per se. Rather, they may become diagnostically relevant within the context of a broad-based assessment of a child's overall functioning and history. For example, imaginary friends are not unique to a dissociating child, but rather are a normal developmental process. However, Putnam et al. (1993) notes extreme examples of this in some dissociating children, including arguing with and threatening themselves or talking about themselves in the third person.

General Psychological Testing—Objective Measures

While attempts have been made to use traditional personality measures such as the Minnesota Multiphasic Personality Inventory (MMPI) to assess the presence of dissociative disorders in adults, evaluation of MMPI profiles have not identified any distinct profile patterns representative of dissociative disorders. In a review of research reporting the MMPI profiles

of adult DID patients, Putnam (1989b) stated that such individuals are "polysymptomatic on the MMPI" (p. 87). Although no formal interpretive standards exist for the MMPI with respect to dissociative identity disorder, common elevations have been reported by Coons et al. (1988) on scale 8 (Schizophrenia) in combination with scales 2 (Depression), 4 (Psychopathic Deviate), 6 (Paranoia), and 7 (Psychasthenia) (Bliss, 1984; Coons et al., 1988). Some common features associated with each of these scale score elevations are unpredictable and bizarre behavior, difficulty in forming intimate relationships, social isolation, suicidal ideation with high risk for actual suicide attempts, problems in logic, and poor judgment (Greene, 1991). Certainly this is consistent with what is known about DID and DDNOS from the observations by clinicians and researchers.

Limited data exist on general psychological testing with children and adolescents who are suspected of presenting with maladaptive dissociation. In a group of children referred for a variety of psychological problems, Evers-Szostak and Sanders (1992) reported moderate positive correlations between the Obsessive-Compulsive and the Aggressive scales of the Child Behavior Checklist (CBCL; Achenbach & Edelbrock, 1983) and the Children's Perceptual Alteration Scale (CPAS; Evers-Szostak & Sanders, 1992). The CPAS is a self-report measure developed to quantify children's subjective reports on dissociation, and the CBCL is a general symptom checklist used to identify a wide variety of symptoms associated with internalizing and externalizing problems of childhood and adolescence. The authors suggest that associations between the CPAS and portions of the CBCL may point to externalizing aspects of the dissociation in children. The authors do not report specific CBCL items that contributed to correlations between the CPAS and specific CBCL scales.

A dissociation subscale was derived intuitively from seven CBCL items; the final subscale contained six items that related to dissociation symptoms such as confusion, absorption, and labile mood (Malinosky-Rummell & Hoier, 1991). This dissociation scale was able to distinguish a group of sexually abused girls from a group of nonabused girls. However, elevations on the CBCL were not unique to this dissociative subscale and may have represented a general level of pathology among this group of abused girls. At present, normative data for this dissociation subscale are not available (Malinosky-Rummell & Hoier, 1991).

Tests of intellectual functioning, while not specifically able to identify dissociative phenomena in either adults or young persons, can nonetheless be helpful in supporting diagnoses of dissociative disorders. Marked differences in test scores or differences in apparent intellectual functioning at different times or in different settings might suggest that dissociation is occurring to an extent that it interferes with a child's or adolescent's ability to learn, retain, and process information in a consistent and integrative manner. In their initial evaluation of an 8-year-old who presented dissociative pathology, Fagan and McMahon (1984) reported a difference of more than 20 points favoring her WISC-R Verbal over her Performance IQ score. The authors note the potential for higher achievement with this child, as WRAT scores were above grade level. Follow-up testing after three months of treatment for a dissociative disorder showed a marked improvement in WISC-R Performance score, with a gain of 14 points in Performance scale score.

Projective Measures

Projective tests used during adult assessment of dissociative disorders have included the Rorschach Inkblot test and the Thematic Apperception Test (TAT), although use of the TAT has been limited (Armstrong & Loewenstein, 1990; Battle, 1985; Gilbertson, Torem, & Kemp, 1989; Labott, Leavitt, Braun, & Sachs, 1992; Wagner, Allison, & Wagner, 1983; Wagner & Heise, 1974). Armstrong and Loewenstein (1990) reported on use of the TAT as part of an assessment battery given to MPD subjects; however, no individual or group content analysis was reported with their results.

For tests such as the TAT and the Rorschach, the theoretical basis is that, in the absence of specific instruction or highly directive stimuli (e.g., such as items on the MMPI or CBCL), an individual will have only his or her own internal resources available for managing the demands of the test (Exner, 1993). Thus, projective techniques essentially require clients to use their own personality and experience to structure an ambiguous stimulus in order to respond to it; as such, it can reflect internal coping skills (cf. Ronan, Colavito, & Hammontree, 1993). The advantage of using such tests when assessing the dissociative disorders is that pathology related to these illnesses is most evident where little explicit support or guidance is forthcoming from the environment (Labott et al., 1992; Wagner & Heise, 1974). Because of the absence of clear task demands in the Rorschach test, the test is expected to reveal the general ability of a person to rely upon his or her unique internal coping mechanisms for managing a stressful or problem solving situation. Individuals with dissociative disorders are characterized by their tendency to engage in dissociative behaviors when placed under psychological duress, and it is expected that the quality and content of their Rorschach responses will reflect this coping style (Wagner & Heise, 1974).

Some research with the Rorschach test has sought to identify patterns evident among dissociative disorder patients, specifically, those with DID (Armstrong & Loewenstein, 1993; Barach, 1986; Lovitt & Lefkof, 1985; Wagner, Allison, & Wagner, 1983). Although results from these studies are conflicting, the studies have differed methodologically in a number of ways (Wallach, 1995). Differences have included the system of Rorschach test administration and interpretation used, the client/patient populations sampled, and qualitative differences in the criteria used to distinguish the presence or absence of dissociative phenomena in Rorschach test protocol (Labott et al., 1992; Young, Wagner, & Finn, 1994).

Information on projective testing in children and adolescents appears limited to several clinical case reports. As part of an overall assessment battery given to a 10-year-old male diagnosed with MPD, the Rorschach was administered upon hospitalization to the "primary" personality of the child (Weiss, Sutton, & Utect, 1985). According to the authors, this Rorschach protocol contained responses indicative of MPD, including "rapidly shifting percepts to the same stimulus" (p. 497) and "unsteady boundaries" (p. 498). Follow-up Rorschachs were given some months later to each of the two alter personality states identified. The authors noted that the Rorschach protocols from each "alter" appeared somewhat similar to the original protocol, yet contained differences in percept content, with more aggressive and fearful responses. Finally, several months prior to discharge, another Rorschach was administered to the initial, primary personality state, with responses indicating more stable boundaries, and "fewer shifts in perception" (Weiss et al., 1985, p. 498).

Hypnosis

Hypnotic techniques have been used in both diagnosis and treatment of dissociative disorders in children and adolescents as well as in adults. As an assessment tool, hypnotic induction has been used to obtain information about traumatic events that the child may have dissociated from conscious awareness. Hypnosis is also used during assessment to identify those aspects of personality functioning that have been separated from everyday awareness, in particular, with suspected cases of MPD/DDNOS. However, hypnosis may be best used as a treatment adjunct to enhance mastery and alleviate symptoms, rather than mainly to retrieve information (cf. Kluft, 1991). We discuss hypnosis in more detail later.

Dissociation Scales and Symptom Checklists

In recent years, objective measures have been developed to help quantify dissociative experiences. Beginning primarily with adult research, dissociation scales have identified a wide variety of dissociative experiences that occur in normative and clinical populations. Such assessment tools have provided empirical support for a dissociative continuum that had previously been understood on the basis of clinical observation analogies to theories of hypnotic capacity. The Dissociative Experiences Scale (DES; Bernstein & Putnam, 1986) has demonstrated good reliability and validity in measuring dissociative experiences in both normative and mentally ill samples of adolescents and adults (Atlas & Hiott, 1994; Ensink & van Otterloo, 1989; Malinosky-Rummell & Hoier, 1991; Riley & Mead, 1988; Ross, Ryan, et al., 1989; Sanders & Giolas, 1991). Furthermore, the DES reliably differentiates between individuals without any psychiatric history, individuals with nondissociative disorders (e.g., schizophrenia), and those with a dissociative disorder (Bernstein & Putnam, 1986; Ross, Norton, & Anderson, 1988).

In groups of college students with no reported psychiatric history, DES scores are consistently lower than those obtained by individuals with dissociative identity disorder and other psychiatric groups (Bernstein & Putnam, 1986; Frischholz et al., 1990; Ross et al., 1990). Mean DES scores typical of college students have been reported to range between 5.6 (medical students; Ross et al., 1988) and 23.8 (undergraduate students; Frishholz et al., 1990). Other groups of young adults have obtained mean DES scores of 14.6 (undergraduate students; Sanders et al., 1989), and 15.4 (community sample; Ross et al., 1990). Mean scores on the DES obtained by dissociative disorder patients (MPD, DDNOS) have ranged between 36.4 and 55.0 (Ross et al., 1988; Ensink & van Otterloo, 1989; Frischholz et al., 1990).

Within a normative college population, a subgroup of students who report traumatic childhood events, including abuse, have been found to score higher on the DES than their nonabused peers (Sanders et al., 1989). This supports theories that link dissociation with prior traumatic experiences (Janet, reviewed in van der Hart & Friedman, 1989; Putnam, 1989a, 1989b; Sanders, 1986). When students who reported a history of a variety of forms of childhood trauma were separated from their nonabused peers, abused students were found to have significantly higher DES scores ($M = 22.6$) than students who denied a history of abuse ($M = 11.9$). This may indicate that, within a general college sample, the average DES scores may be elevated by a subgroup of students who have been victims of childhood trauma.

To assess dissociative experiences in younger individuals, several assessment scales have recently been created, some which are revisions of earlier adult-based measures (Evers-Szostak & Sanders, 1992; Liner, 1989, as cited in Malinosky-Rummell & Hoier, 1991; Putnam et al., 1993). Dissociation scales for young children have been developed with consideration for developmental differences in the dissociative experiences of young persons and of adults. For example, this has resulted in the inclusion of items relevant to school functioning, sexual precocity, and peer relations (Evers-Szostak & Sanders, 1992; Putnam et al., 1993).

The Child Dissociative Checklist (CDC; Putnam et al., 1993) reliably distinguishes among normal control girls, sexually abused children, and children with diagnoses of dissociative disorders. With the CDC, low levels of dissociative experiences have been recorded in normal control participants, and dissociative experiences have been measured along a continuum extending to high levels of dissociation in children with MPD/DDNOS (Putnam et al., 1993). The CDC contains 20 items rated by an adult observer (e.g., parent or teacher) for the frequency with which they occur in a child. Sample items tap six areas related to dissociative pathology, including changes in identity, personality, and knowledge ("Child shows rapid changes in personality," "Child is unusually forgetful or confused about things that he or she should know"), acting-out behaviors ("Child has intense outbursts of anger"), and dissociation and trance ("Child goes into a daze or trance-like state at times or often appears 'spaced-out,'" "Child refers to him- or herself in the third person . . . or at times insists on being called by a different name") (Putnam et al., 1993, pp. 740–741). Higher scores are indicative of more extensive dissociation; control girls obtained a mean score of 2.3, sexually abused girls obtained a mean score of 6.0, and children with DDNOS and MPD obtained mean scores of 16.8 and 24.5, respectively. Also of note, the variance was greater for victims and patient groups (SDs ranging from 4.7 to 6.4) than for controls ($SD = 2.7$). This suggests that high scores are diagnostic, because controls rarely obtain high scores. However, low scores may not be diagnostic, because some patients occasionally obtain low scores.

A different assessment approach is used with the CPAS (Evers-Szostak & Sanders, 1992), an adaptation of an earlier adult scale entitled the Perceptual Alteration Scale (Sanders, 1986). The CPAS is a self-report measure designed to obtain information directly from children about their dissociative experiences. Sample items tap a number of dimensions related to dissociative pathology, including dissociation ("When someone calls me, I don't recognize my name"), amnesia ("I do not remember what people tell me"), and marked changes in behavioral and emotional functioning ("I steal things, but I don't want to" and "My feelings change, but I don't want them to") (Evers-Szostak & Sanders, 1992, p. 92). Children who were receiving psychological evaluation or treatment for a variety of problems obtained significantly higher CPAS scores than did a control group of children receiving routine pediatric examinations. Evers-Szostak and Sanders (1992) recommend further research with the CPAS to obtain data on specific groups of children, including those with abuse histories and those suspected of having dissociative disorders. Similar to results of Putnam et al. (1993) with the CDC, CPAS data supported a continuum of dissociative experiences, with low levels of dissociation observed in the control group (Evers-Szostak & Sanders, 1992).

A number of symptom checklists have recently been complied to help organize the wide array of information that may be gathered throughout the assessment period via the approaches discussed, and they are reviewed in Tyson (1992). Predating the DSM-IV (APA, 1994) use of the term, Peterson (1990) used the term "dissociative identity disorder" to describe children who shared the following characteristics: amnesia and/or trance-like behavior, marked behavior changes, and at least three of the following: "Refers to self in third person or uses another name to refer to self. . . . Has imaginary companion. . . . Is seen as infrequently lying. . . . Has antisocial behaviors. . . . Is sexually precocious. . . . Has intermittent depression. . . . Has frequent sleep problems. . . . Has auditory hallucinations from inside the head" (Peterson, 1990, p. 6). Tyson (1992) applied these criteria (Peterson, 1990) to six cases of childhood dissociation and noted that six of these criteria were present in all children: amnesia, trance, behavior changes, lying, conduct problems, and depression. The remaining symptoms were all present in some of these children. Furthermore, Tyson (1992) noted that these symptoms have occurred frequently in prior samples of children with pathological dissociation.

Tyson (1992) also found a number of additional features reported in earlier papers to be present in his sample, including a family history of dissociation, poor response to earlier treatment, and "passive influence experiences" (Kluft, 1984, in Tyson, 1992, p. 25), personal history of abuse and amnesia for abuse events (Putnam, 1981, in Tyson, 1992), and social skills deficits and pseudoseizures (Fagan & McMahon, 1984, in Tyson, 1992).

Medical History/Family Psychiatric History

A comprehensive social and medical family history can help identify risk factors relevant to children with dissociative disorders. Useful background information includes parental psychiatric history, in particular for the dissociative disorders (Hornstein & Tyson, 1991). Clinical observation and published case histories report an intrafamilial incidence of dissociative disorders, with children of parents with dissociative disorders often demonstrating dissociative pathology as well (Braun, 1985; Coons, 1994; Malenbaum & Russell, 1986; Mann & Sanders, 1994; Weiss et al., 1985). In a retrospective study examining case histories of 18 adult MPD patients, Braun (1985) reported that all had a family history of dissociation, with an average of more than four family members with dissociative experiences. In five of these 18 MPD patients, the mother or the stepmother also had a confirmed diagnosis of multiple personality disorder. A retrospective approach was taken by Coons (1994), who researched the incidence of psychiatric problems in children of adults with a diagnosis of MPD. Thirty-nine percent of children of MPD patients had received psychiatric diagnoses across a variety of problem areas, including conduct disorder (N=3), developmental disorder and mental retardation (N=2), personality disorders (N=2), and dissociative disorders (N=2). Further support for an association between parental and child dissociation comes from a study that showed significant correlations between the self-reports of dissociative experiences in young males (ages 8–11) with self-reported dissociation experienced by these boys's fathers (Mann & Sanders, 1994).

Information regarding family and individual medical background can help to rule out possible seizure disorders such as epilepsy (Mesulam, 1981). A thorough medical history is also important where there are concerns regarding physical and/or sexual abuse of the identified child or adolescent client. Confirmation of ongoing abuse may necessitate the young person's removal from the abusive environment into a safe care setting. Medical treatment has also been reported as a precursor to dissociation in the absence of any known abuse experiences. Dell & Eisenhower (1990) review the case of an adolescent male who developed and sustained dissociative pathology (specifically, alter personalities) following "medical/surgical trauma in very early childhood" (p. 365).

Putnam (1991) also notes a high prevalence of sleep problems (approximately 75%) in child cases of dissociative disorders, including problems of sleepwalking, nightmares and night terrors. In a sample of 64 children with dissociative disorders, nearly 70% of DDNOS and nearly 90% of MPD children reported experiences of traumatic nightmares.

TREATMENT OF DISSOCIATIVE DISORDERS IN CHILDHOOD AND ADOLESCENCE

Despite a growing number of clinical treatment reviews during the past decade, experimental outcome research for treatment of child and adolescent dissociative disorders is not yet available (Dell & Eisenhower, 1990; Fagan & McMahon, 1984; Hornstein & Tyson, 1991; McElroy, 1992; McMahon & Fagan, 1993). As with treatment of adults with dissociative disorders, the majority of work appears to be focused on psychotherapeutic approaches to treatment, with pharmacological agents used adjunctively to manage associated symptoms of depression, anxiety, and agitation.

To date, case studies of psychotherapeutic treatment for dissociative disorders in children have often involved a multimodal systems therapy approach, with attention to individual, intrapsychic elements of the child as well as external factors such as family, home environment, and school settings (Dell & Eisenhower, 1990; Fagan & McMahon, 1984; Hornstein & Tyson, 1991; McMahon & Fagan, 1993). Although not an explicitly sequential process, a general pattern has been reported for treatment, with the primary tasks of the therapist and/or treatment team being to ensure the health and safety of the young client, provide ongoing education to both child and family regarding the dissociative disorder, develop a therapeutic alliance, identify all aspects of maladaptive functioning that may be occurring, manage behavior problems, reduce episodes of dissociation as a coping mechanism, do abreactive work to resolve trauma-related issues, and perform follow-up work to sustain positive effects of treatment (Dell & Eisenhower, 1990; Hornstein & Tyson, 1991).

Health and Safety

Given that dissociative pathology is often related to high levels of family disruption, specifically, severe physical, sexual, and/or emotional abuse, information gathered during the assessment phase regarding the stability and safety of the child's family environment should be used to assess both the current and the future safety for the child (Dell & Eisenhower, 1990; McMahon & Fagan, 1993). In their treatment of 11 adolescent cases of MPD, Dell and Eisenhower (1990) noted that all adolescents with a severe history of family abuse were considered "treatment failures" (p. 356). Conversely, a supportive family environment has been associated with more positive treatment outcomes (Fagan & McMahon, 1984). When children or adolescents require extensive evaluation or stabilization or present with behaviors harmful to themselves or others, Hornstein and Tyson (1991) suggest inpatient hospital treatment to provide structure and safety.

Education

Like adults suffering from dissociative disorders, children may be confused and distressed about features of dissociation such as memory loss. An ongoing task during therapy is to educate the child or adolescent client and his or her family regarding the nature of the diagnosis, including information on identifying and managing symptoms (Dell & Eisenhower, 1990). Dell & Eisenhower (1990) refer to this approach as "Detoxification, Stabilization, and Alliance-Building" (p. 362) in the treatment of adolescents with multiple personality disorder. Information disseminated appropriately to the young person's school is also helpful, enabling teachers to provide a consistent environment and to offer supportive understanding for dissociative behaviors that may occur (Dell & Eisenhower, 1990; Fagan & McMahon, 1984). Riley & Mead (1988) report on a case of childhood multiple personality in which the primary caregiver (guardian mother) was taught and encouraged to use strategies that supported "reintegration" (p. 43) of the child's personality functioning.

Another aspect of education may be teaching caregivers how to provide a stable and nonabusive environment that does not sustain maladaptive dissociation. For such families, this may require adjunctive treatment such as family therapy or work with abusers (Dell & Eisenhower, 1990; Hornstein & Tyson, 1991; McMahon & Fagan, 1993).

Therapeutic Alliance

The development of a trusting relationship between therapist and client is considered an essential component in treatment of most problems, and with most therapeutic approaches. Children or adolescents who may likely have had repeated experiences of abuse or intrusion may be particularly wary of others (Dell & Eisenhower, 1990; Dollinger, 1983; Fagan & McMahon, 1984; Hornstein & Tyson, 1991; McMahon & Fagan, 1993). Play therapy has been used in treatment of childhood MPD, including trust-building activities:

> Gaining entry into the heart of the child with MPD is not an easy task. Play therapy, because it speaks the universal language of childhood and lets the therapist function in a role that avoids authority and judgment, provides an ideal route of access. Play therapy brings adult and child together where hopes as well as painful struggles can be explored. . . . (McMahon & Fagan, 1993, p. 254)

Reduced Use of Dissociation as Coping Mechanism

With an increased understanding of and ability to identify dissociative patterns, clients can begin to explore means to decrease the incidence of maladaptive dissociations. Abreactive work involves assisting the client in bringing to consciousness those traumatic experiences that were dissociated or split off from everyday awareness. The working through of traumatic experiences in a safe (nonabusive), nonjudgmental environment can help the individual to manage negative feelings without retreating into dissociative behaviors (Hornstein & Tyson, 1991; McMahon & Fagan, 1993). A variety of

nonspecific therapeutic approaches have been used in helping children develop more adaptive coping strategies. Play therapy and guided imagery activities can involve helping children develop mastery over feelings through construction of internal "safe havens" or "helpers" in a controlled manner. Such strategies are used with not only children but also with adults (Horevitz, 1995).

In addition to interpersonal therapeutic work, traditional behavior management programs that provide positive reinforcement for appropriate expression of feelings can support more adaptive functioning (Hornstein & Tyson, 1991). Hornstein and Tyson (1991) suggest that time-out techniques or redirection that remove positive reinforcement for inappropriate behaviors such as aggressiveness may be useful as well. Differential reinforcement of low rates (DRL) of "blacking out," combined with family therapy, was successful in treating an adolescent's depersonalization (Dollinger, 1983).

Abreaction involves the expression and release of memories for traumatic events that were previously unavailable to conscious awareness due to dissociation or amnestic barriers (Fagan & McMahon, 1984; Kluft, 1985b; McMahon & Fagan, 1993; Putnam, 1989b; Wilbur, 1984). This process, in addition to the retrieval and reliving/reconstructing of critical memories, may be important, although clinicians are urged to proceed when the client is ready for such work and then to proceed with caution (and supervision) toward these goals (Horevitz, 1995). As noted by Horevitz, such memories can "evoke profoundly disorganizing affective states, shame, and existential crises" (p. 405). The reframing and reviewing of such memories should be done in and out of hypnosis so as to integrate such experience with the patient's personal life history. In some cases, this goal can be accomplished only under the control of an inpatient setting.

A common aspect of adult therapies for MPD/DID is integrative work, following abreaction, to "unify" those aspects of the self that have been dissociated (Kluft, 1985b; Kluft, 1991; Putnam, 1989b; Wilbur, 1984). Integration involves the organization of material recalled during the abreactive process and is a process designed to result in "a synthesis of the previous separate elements of each alter into a more unified global personality structure" (Putnam, 1989b, p. 300). Therapeutic techniques that have been used to support integration of previously repressed or dissociated memories include constructing a timeline of traumatic events, providing feedback to clients via audio or video recording of sessions, validating and supporting emotional expression, and resolving any conflicting memories (e.g., by different alters) of traumatic events (Putnam, 1989b). The interested reader is directed to a discussion by Putnam (1989b) for further information on the specific components and stages of integrative work.

There is some debate whether or not such integration is necessary or recommended for children with dissociative disorders (Kluft, 1985b). Although some descriptions of therapy that have been reported do refer to integration as a task to be completed with child clients as well, a contrasting viewpoint has been offered. An examination of the normal developmental course of dissociation in normal children reveals that, for young children in particular, dissociation at low to moderate levels is expected. The "integration" of a young person receiving treatment for a dissociative disorder may erroneously place a child at a developmental level for dissociation that is *not* age-appropriate:

> In our opinion it seems to be preferable to allow the natural, more gradual establishment of cohesion to unfold rather than to bypass the normally looser self-cohesion of the preschool and young latency child in favor of a prematurely cohesive but emptier child. (Albini & Pease, 1989, p. 149)

Follow-up Work

When dissociative symptoms appear to have remitted and the child appears to be functioning in an age-appropriate manner, it has been recommended that therapists provide continued support for the child and family. At present there are no known standard guidelines for total treatment length or for the extent of follow-up work that should occur after termination of formal treatment. Decisions regarding issues of termination and follow-up work appear to be based on a combination of clinical judgment, relative improvements observed in a given child (including reduction or elimination of dissociative symptoms), and family variables. Some general markers for improvement include achievement of more adaptive functioning that is fairly consistent across settings, reduction in anxiety, reduction in use of dissociation as a coping mechanism, and improved ability to manage one's feelings (Hornstein & Tyson, 1991).

Such ongoing contact can help in management of later developmental issues that may have been delayed or distorted by dissociative pathology (Dell & Eisenhower, 1990; Fagan & McMahon, 1984). Additional follow-up work can include continued family therapy to support an ongoing and healthy environment in which the young person can develop (Dell & Eisenhower, 1990; Fagan & McMahon, 1984).

Biological/Pharmacological Treatment

Reports of biological treatments for dissociative disorders in young persons are limited. In adults, medications have been used to treat nondissociative symptoms, including depression and anxiety. Putnam (1989b) offers a concise review of the efficacy of various medications in treating such symptoms; in general, treatment outcomes have been mixed. Case reports of children and adolescents with dissociative disorders also have reported the use of medication to manage associated symptoms of anxiety and depression (Meyer, 1961; Weiss et al., 1982), although Putnam (1991) observes that pharmacologic treatments "appear to be even less effective as adjunctive treatments in children than they are in adults" (p. 528). It has also been suggested that medications may be contraindicated when treating dissociative disorders. For example, McKellar (1978) cautioned against the use of medication in treatment of depersonalization in an adolescent male, arguing that medications might serve to exacerbate feelings of "clouding of consciousness" (p. 1581) rather than attenuate symptoms of depersonalization.

Treatment Duration

One difference between adults and child or adolescent treatment that remains under debate relates to the required length of treatment. Initial reports of treatment of dissociative disorders indicated that treatment was short-term relative to treatment of dissociative disorders in adults (Bowman, Blix, & Coons, 1985; Kluft, 1985b; Riley & Mead, 1988). One reason for this may be that the dissociative symptomatology may be less deeply entrenched for younger persons. In addition, for very young children diagnosed with DID or incipient cases of DID, there may be fewer alter personality states, and those that exist may be less distinct and less well developed (Peterson, 1990). However, empirical data on treatment outcomes is limited at this time. A number of adolescent cases of MPD, for example, have shown a high resistance to treatment, including a high dropout rate (Dell & Eisenhower, 1990).

Dell and Eisenhower (1990) reported that, among a group of adolescents receiving treatment for dissociative disorders, the average length of therapy differed as a function of treatment outcome. Teens who were continuing in treatment but were not yet integrated participated in psychotherapy for an average of 14.7 months; clients who were integrated and were continuing in supportive therapy participated in treatment for nearly 2.5 years (29 months; Dell & Eisenhower, 1990). Adolescents considered to be treatment failures (treatment dropouts) received treatment for an average of 6.4 months; treatment failure was attributed to continuing exposure of these clients to abuse at home.

Reports of the duration of individual psychotherapy (from case reports) have varied across different case studies, with Weiss et al. (1985) reporting inpatient treatment of a 10-year-old girl lasting at least two years, with a follow-up study of the child's functioning 18 months following discharge from hospital. McMahon & Fagan (1993) also report an approximate treatment length of 2 years, with information on the client's functioning at 5 years after treatment onset. Finally, McElroy's (1992) review of two child dissociation cases reports a total of 66 therapy sessions for one child (age nine) and approximately 60 individual therapy sessions for the other girl (age six), although the time frame for these sessions is not reported for either case.

CONCLUDING COMMENTS

Within the past one or two decades, knowledge regarding child and adolescent dissociative disorders has increased as data from newly developed child dissociation scales (e.g., CPAS; Evers-Szostak & Sanders, 1992; CDC; Putnam et al., 1993) and symptom checklists (e.g., Tyson, 1992) have been integrated with information from clinical reports and case studies, as well as findings from the adult literature on dissociative disorders. Work in all of these areas has helped to better describe the nature of both normative and pathological instances of dissociation in children and adolescents.

Developments in the assessment and diagnosis of dissociative pathology go hand in hand with progress in intervention for such children. From this continued enhanced ability to identify dissociative pathology in young persons has emerged an interest in examining treatment options for this population. Clinical reports have thus far described general, broad-based protocols for treatment of dissociative disorders in children and adolescents, with attention on both short-term and longer-term outcomes (Dell & Eisenhower, 1990; Fagan & McMahon, 1984; Hornstein & Tyson, 1991; McMahon & Fagan, 1993). Future directions might involve expansion of such clinical work into more rigorous experimental designs to examine treatment efficacy.

At present, several goals for treatment have been identified with dissociative disorder children and adolescents, including management of behavioral acting-out, reduction of dissociative pathology, education of client and family regarding dissociative disorders, working through of traumatic events, and maintenance of treatment gains. An overarching theme for these goals appears to be assisting the child in gaining a sense of mastery over his or her environment. For a child who has likely experienced a world low in organization and security and high in unpredictable and fearful, even dangerous events, the ability to regain a sense of mastery in an adaptive manner may be the child's greatest accomplishment in treatment.

REFERENCES

Achenbach, T. M., & Edelbrock, C. (1983). *Manual for the Child Behavior Checklist and Revised Child Behavior Profile.* Burlington: University Associates in Psychiatry.

Albini, T. K., & Pease, T. E. (1989). Normal and pathological dissociations of early childhood. *Dissociation, 2* (3), 144–150.

American Psychiatric Association. (1952). *Diagnostic and statistical manual of mental disorders.* Washington, DC: Author.

American Psychiatric Association. (1968). *Diagnostic and statistical manual of mental disorders* (2nd ed.). Washington, DC: Author.

American Psychiatric Association. (1980). *Diagnostic and statistical manual of mental disorders* (3rd ed.). Washington, DC: Author.

American Psychiatric Association. (1987). *Diagnostic and statistical manual of mental disorders* (3rd ed., rev.). Washington, DC: Author.

American Psychiatric Association. (1994). *Diagnostic and statistical manual of mental disorders* (4th ed.). Washington, DC: Author.

Armstrong, J. G., & Loewenstein, R. J. (1990). Characteristics of patients with multiple personality and dissociative disorders on psychological testing. *Journal of Nervous and Mental Disease, 178,* 448–454.

Atlas, J. A., & Hiott, J. (1994). Dissociative experiences in a group of adolescents with history of abuse. *Perceptual and Motor Skills, 78,* 121–122.

Barach, P. (1986). *Rorschach signs of MPD in multiple personality disorder and non-multiple personality disorder in victims of sexual abuse.* Paper presented at 3rd International Conference on Multiple Personality/Dissociative States, Chicago, IL.

Battle, A. O. (1985). Rorschach evaluation of two personalities in a patient. *British Journal of Projective Psychology, 30,* 11–23.

Bernstein, E. M., & Putnam, F. W. (1986). Development, reliability, and validity of a dissociation scale. *Journal of Nervous and Mental Disease, 174,* 727–733.

Bliss, E. L. (1984). A symptom profile of patients with multiple personalities, including MMPI results. *Journal of Nervous and Mental Disease, 172,* 197–202.

Braun, B. G. (1984). Towards a theory of multiple personality and other dissociative phenomena. *Psychiatric Clinics of North America, 7* (1), 171–193.

Braun, B. G. (1985). The transgenerational incidence of dissociation and multiple personality disorder: A preliminary report. In R. P. Kluft (Ed.), *Childhood antecedents of multiple personality* (pp. 127–150). Washington, DC: American Psychiatric Press.

Braun, B. G., & Sachs, R. G. (1985). The development of multiple personality disorder: Predisposing, precipitating, and perpetuating factors. In R. P. Kluft (Ed.), *Childhood antecedents of multiple personality* (pp. 37–64). Washington, DC: American Psychiatric Press.

Carlson, E. T. (1981). The history of multiple personality in the United States: I. The beginnings. *American Journal of Psychiatry, 138* (5), 666–668.

Carlson, E. B., & Putnam, F. W. (1989). Integrating research on dissociation and hypnotizability: Are there two pathways to hypnotizability? *Dissociation, 2* (1), 32–38.

Coons, P. M. (1994). Confirmation of childhood abuse in child and adolescent cases of multiple personality disorder and dissociative disorder not otherwise specified. *Journal of Nervous and Mental Disease, 18* (8), 461–464.

Coons, P. M., Bowman, E. S., & Milstein, V. (1988). Multiple personality disorder: A clinical investigation of 50 cases. *Journal of Nervous and Mental Disease, 176,* 519–527.

Coons, P. M., Milstein, V., & Marley, C. (1982). EEG studies of two multiple personalities and a control. *Archives of General Psychiatry, 39,* 823–825.

Dell, P. F., & Eisenhower, J. W. (1990). Adolescent multiple personality disorder: A preliminary study of eleven cases. *Journal of American Academy of Child and Adolescent Psychiatry, 29*, 359–366.

Dollinger, S. J. (1983). A case report of dissociative neurosis (depersonalization disorder) in an adolescent treated with family therapy and behavior modification. *Journal of Consulting and Clinical Psychology, 51*, 479–484.

Ellenberger, H. F. (1970). *The discovery of the unconscious: The history and evolution of dynamic psychiatry.* New York: Basic Books.

Ensink, B. J., & van Otterloo, D. (1989). A validation of the Dissociative Experiences Scale in the Netherlands. *Dissociation, 2* (4), 221–224.

Exner, J. E., Jr. (1993). *The Rorschach: A comprehensive system: Vol. 1.* (3rd ed.). New York: Wiley.

Evers-Szostak, M., & Sanders, S. (1992). The Children's Perceptual Alteration Scale (CPAS): A measure of children's dissociation. *Dissociation, 5* (2), 91–97.

Fagan, J., & McMahon, P. P. (1984). Incipient multiple personality disorder in children: Four cases. *Journal of Nervous and Mental Disease, 172* (1), 26–36.

Fine, C. G. (1988). The work of Antoine Despine: The first scientific report on the diagnosis and treatment of a child with multiple personality disorder. *American Journal of Clinical Hypnosis, 31* (1), 33–39.

Frischholz, E. J. (1985). The relationship among dissociation, hypnosis, and child abuse in the development of multiple personality disorder. In R. P. Kluft (Ed.), *Childhood antecedents of multiple personality* (pp. 99–126). Washington, DC: American Psychiatric Press.

Frishholz, E. J., Braun, B. G., Sachs, R. G., Hopkins, L., Shaeffer, D. M., Lewis, J., Leavitt, F., Pasquotto, J. N., & Schwartz, D. R. (1990). The Dissociative Experiences Scale: Further replication and validation. *Dissociation, 3* (3), 151–153.

Frischholz, E. J., Lipman, L. S., Braun, B. G., & Sachs, R. G. (1992). Psychopathology, hypnotizability, and dissociation. *American Journal of Psychiatry, 149*, 1521–1525.

Garcia, F. O. (1990). The concept of dissociation and conversion in the new edition of the International Classification of Diseases (ICD-10). *Dissociation, 3* (4), 204–208.

Gilbert, B. O., & Dollinger, S. J. (1992). Neurotic disorders of children: Obsessive-compulsive, phobic, conversion, dissociative, and post-traumatic stress disorders. In C. E. Walker & M. C. Roberts (Eds.), *Handbook of clinical child psychology* (2nd ed., pp. 359–374). New York: Wiley.

Gilbertson, A., Torem, M., & Kemp, K. (1989). *The validity of proposed Rorschach signs in the diagnosis of multiple personality disorder.* Paper presented at 6th International Conference on Multiple Personality/Dissociative States, Chicago, IL.

Greaves, G. B. (1980). Multiple personality 165 years after Mary Reynolds. *Journal of Nervous and Mental Disease, 168*, 577–596.

Greaves, G. B. (1993). A history of multiple personality disorder. In R. P. Kluft & C. G. Fine (Eds.), *Clinical perspectives on multiple personality disorder* (pp. 355–380). Washington, DC: American Psychiatric Press.

Greene, R. L. (1991). *The MMPI-2/MMPI: An interpretive manual.* Boston: Allyn & Bacon.

Herbert, W. (1982). The three brains of Eve: EEG data. *Science News, 121*, 356.

*Horevitz, R. (1995). Hypnosis in the treatment of multiple personality disorder. In J. W. Rhue, S. J. Lynn, & I. Kirsch (Eds.), *Handbook of clinical hypnosis* (pp. 395–424). Washington, DC: American Psychiatric Association.

*Hornstein, N. L., & Putnam, F. W. (1992). Clinical phenomenology of child and adolescent dissociative disorder. *Journal of the American Academy of Child and Adolescent Psychiatry, 31* (6), 1077–1085.

Hornstein, N. L., & Tyson, S. (1991). Inpatient treatment of children with multiple personality/dissociative disorders and their families. *Psychiatric Clinics of North America, 14* (3), 631–648.

Irwin, H. J. (1994). Proneness to dissociation and traumatic childhood events. *Journal of Nervous and Mental Disease, 182* (8), 456–460.

Kluft, R. P. (1985a). The natural history of multiple personality disorder. In R. P. Kluft (Ed.), *Childhood antecedents of multiple personality* (pp. 197–238). Washington, DC: American Psychiatric Press.

Kluft, R. P. (1985b). Childhood multiple personality disorder: Predictors, clinical findings, and treatment results. In R. P. Kluft (Ed.), *Childhood antecedents of multiple personality* (pp. 167–196). Washington, DC: American Psychiatric Press.

*Kluft, R. P. (Ed.). (1985c). *Childhood antecedents of multiple personality.* Washington, DC: American Psychiatric Press.

Kluft, R. P. (1987). First-rank symptoms as a diagnostic clue to multiple personality disorder. *American Journal of Psychiatry, 144*, 293–298.

Kluft, R. P. (1991). Hypnosis in childhood trauma. In W. C. Wester & D. J. O'Grady (Eds.), *Clinical hypnosis with children* (pp. 53–68). New York: Brunner/Mazel.

Labott, S. M., Leavitt, F., Braun, B. G., & Sachs, R. G. (1992). Rorschach indicators of multiple personality disorder. *Perceptual and Motor Skills*, 75, 147–158.

Larmore, K., Ludwig, A. M., & Cain, R. L. (1977). Multiple personality: An objective case study. *Psychiatric Clinics of North America*, 7 (1), 149–159.

Lovitt R., & Lefkof, G. (1985). Understanding multiple personality with the Comprehensive Rorschach System. *Journal of Personality Assessment*, 49, 232–294.

Ludwig, A. M. (1983). The psychobiological functions of dissociation. *American Journal of Clinical Hypnosis*, 26 (2), 93–99.

Malenbaum, R., & Russell, A. T. (1986). Multiple Personality Disorder in an 11-year-old boy and his mother. *Journal of the American Academy of Child and Adolescent Psychiatry*, 26 (3), 436–439.

Malinosky-Rummell, R. R., & Hoier, T. S. (1991). Validating measures of dissociation in sexually abused and nonabused children. *Behavioral Assessment*, 13, 341–357.

Mann, B., & Sanders, S. (1994). Child dissociation and the family context. *Journal of Abnormal Child Psychology*, 22 (3), 373–387.

Martin, R. B., & Labott, S. M. (1986). *Dissociation, stress, and disturbance in a normal population.* Paper presented at the 3rd National Conference on Multiple Personality/Dissociative States, Chicago, IL.

McElroy, L. P. (1992). Early indicators of pathological dissociation in sexually abused children. *Child Abuse and Neglect*, 16, 833–846.

McKellar, A. (1978). Depersonalization in a 16-year-old boy. *Southern Medical Journal*, 71 (12), 1580–1581.

*McMahon, P. P., & Fagan, J. (1993). Play therapy with children with multiple personality disorder. In R. P. Kluft & C. G. Fine (Eds.), *Clinical perspectives on multiple personality disorder* (pp. 253–276). Washington, DC: American Psychiatric Association.

Meares, R., & Grose, D. (1978). On depersonalization in adolescence: A consideration from the viewpoints of habituation and "identity." *British Journal of Medical Psychology*, 51, 335–342.

Mesulam, M. (1981). Dissociative states with abnormal temporal lobe EEG: Multiple personality and the illusion of possession. *Archives of Neurology*, 38, 176–181.

Meyer, J. E. (1961) Depersonalization in adolescence. *Psychiatry*, 24, 357–360.

Miller, S. D. (1989). Optical differences in cases of multiple personality disorder. *Journal of Nervous and Mental Disease*, 177, 480–486.

Morgan, A. H. (1973). The heritability of hypnotic susceptibility in twins. *Journal of Abnormal Psychology*, 82, 55–61.

Nash, M. R., Hulsey, T. L., Sexton, M. C., Harralson, T. L., & Lambert, W. (1993). Long-term sequelae of childhood sexual abuse: Perceived family environment, psychopathology, and dissociation. *Journal of Consulting and Clinical Psychology*, 61 (2), 276–283.

Nemiah, J. C. (1981). Dissociative disorders. In A. M. Freedman & H. I. Kaplan (Eds.), *Comprehensive textbook of psychiatry* (3rd ed., pp. 1544–1561). Baltimore: Williams and Wilkins.

Peterson, G. (1990). Diagnosis of childhood MPD. *Dissociation*, 3 (1), 3–9.

Putnam, F. W. (1989a). Pierre Janet and modern views of dissociation. *Journal of Traumatic Stress*, 2 (4), 413–429.

Putnam, F. W. (1989b). *Diagnosis and treatment of multiple personality disorder.* New York: Guilford Press.

Putnam, F. W. (1991). Dissociative disorders in children and adolescents: A developmental perspective. *Psychiatric Clinics of North America*, 14 (3), 519–531.

*Putnam, F. W., Helmers, K., & Trickett, P. K. (1993). Development, reliability, and validity of a child dissociation scale. *Child Abuse and Neglect*, 17, 731–741.

Riley, R. L., & Mead, J. (1988). The development of symptoms of multiple personality disorder in a child of three. *Dissociation*, 1 (3), 41–46.

Rinsley, D. B. (1971). The adolescent inpatient: Patterns of depersonalization. *Psychiatric Quarterly*, 45 (3), 3–22.

Ronan, G. F., Colavito, V. A., & Hammontree, S. R. (1993). Personal problem-solving system for scoring TAT responses: Preliminary validity and reliability data. *Journal of Personality Assessment*, 61, 28–40.

Rosenzweig, S. (1988). The identity and idiodynamics of the multiple personality "Sally Beauchamp": A confirmatory supplement. *American Psychologist*, 43 (1), 45–48.

Ross, C. A., Heber, S., Norton, G. R., & Anderson, G. (1989). Differences between multiple personality disorder and other diagnostic groups on structured interview. *Journal of Nervous and Mental Disease*, 179, 487–491.

Ross, C. A., Joshi, S., & Currie, R. (1990). Dissociative experiences in the general population. *American Journal of Psychiatry*, 147, 1547–1552.

Ross, C. A., Norton, G. R., & Anderson, G. (1988). The Dissociative Experiences Scale: A replication study. *Dissociation, 1* (3), 21–22.

Ross, C. A., Ryan, L., Voigt, H., & Edie, L. (1991). High and low dissociators in a college student population. *Dissociation, 4* (3), 147–151.

Ross, C. A., Ryan, L., Anderson, G., Ross, D., & Hardy, L. (1989). Dissociative experiences in adolescents and college students. *Dissociation, 2* (4), 239–242.

Sandberg D. A., & Lynn, S. J. (1992). Dissociative experiences, psychopathology and adjustment, and child and adolescent maltreatment in female college students. *Journal of Abnormal Psychology, 101*, 717–723.

Sanders, S. (1986). A brief history of dissociation. *American Journal of Clinical Hypnosis, 29* (2), 83–85.

Sanders, B., & Giolas, M. H. (1991). Dissociation and childhood trauma in psychologically disturbed adolescents. *American Journal of Psychiatry, 148*, 50–54.

Sanders, B., McRoberts, G., & Tollefson, C. (1989). Childhood stress and dissociation in a college population. *Dissociation, 2* (1), 17–23.

Schultz, R., Braun, B. G., & Kluft, R. P. (1989). Multiple personality disorder: Phenomenology of selected variables in comparison to major depression. *Dissociation, 2*, 45–51.

Shimizu, M., & Sakamoto, S. (1986). Depersonalization in early adolescence. *Japanese Journal of Psychiatry and Neurology, 40*, 603–608.

Sirles, E. A., Smith, J. A., & Kusama, H. (1989). Psychiatric status of intrafamilial sexual abuse victims. *Journal of the American Academy of Child and Adolescent Psychiatry, 28* (2), 225–229.

Spanos, N. P., Weekes, J. R., & Bertrand, L. D. (1985). Multiple personality: A social psychological perspective. *Journal of Abnormal Psychology, 94*, 361–376.

Spiegel, D. (1984). Multiple personality as a post-traumatic stress disorder. *Psychiatric Clinics of North America, 7* (1), 101–110.

Stern, C. R. (1984). The etiology of multiple personalities. *Psychiatric Clinics of North America, 7* (1), 149–159.

Terr, L. (1991). Childhood traumas: An outline and overview. *American Journal of Psychiatry, 148* (1), 10–20.

Thigpen, C., & Cleckley, H. (1954). A case of multiple personality. *Journal of Abnormal and Social Psychology, 49*, 135–151.

*Tyson, G. M. (1992). Childhood MPD/dissociation identity disorder: Applying and extending current diagnostic checklists. *Dissociation, 5* (1), 20–27.

Van der Hart, O., & Friedman, B. (1989). A readers guide to Pierre Janet on dissociation: A neglected intellectual heritage. *Dissociation, 2* (1), 3–16.

Van der Hart, O., & Horst, R. (1989). The dissociation theory of Pierre Janet. *Journal of Traumatic Stress, 2*, 397–412.

Vincent, M., & Pickering, M. R. (1988). Multiple personality disorder in childhood. *Canadian Journal of Psychiatry, 33*, 524–529.

Wagner, E. E., Allison, R., & Wagner, C. (1993). Diagnosing multiple personalities with the Rorschach: A confirmation. *Journal of Personality Assessment, 47*, 143–149.

Wagner, E., E., & Heise, M. R. (1974). A comparison of Rorschach records of three multiple personalities. *Journal of Personality Assessment, 38*, 308–331.

Wallach, H. R. (1995). *Malingering of dissociative identity disorder on the Rorschach.* Unpublished M.A. thesis, Southern Illinois University at Carbondale.

Weiss, M., Sutton, P. J., & Utect, A. J. (1985). Multiple personality in a 10-year-old girl. *Journal of the American Academy of Child and Adolescent Psychiatry, 244*, 495–501.

Wilbur, C. B. (1984). Multiple personality and child abuse: An overview. *Psychiatric Clinics of North America, 7*, 3–7.

Wilson, M. (1993). DSM-III and the transformation of American psychiatry: A history. *American Journal of Psychiatry, 150* (3), 399–410.

World Health Organization. (1992). *ICD-10 classification of mental and behavioural disorders: Clinical descriptions and diagnostic guidelines.* Geneva: Author.

World Health Organization. (1993). *ICD-10 classification of mental and behavioral disorders: Diagnostic criteria for research.* Geneva: Author.

Young, G. R., Wagner, E. E., & Finn, R. F. (1994). A comparison of three Rorschach diagnostic systems and use of the hand test for detecting multiple personality in outpatients. *Journal of Personality Assessment, 62*, 485–497.

*Indicates references that the authors recommend for additional reading.

18

Gender Identity Disorder and Transvestic Fetishism

Kenneth J. Zucker
Susan J. Bradley

GENDER IDENTITY DISORDER

Historical Perspective

The term "gender identity" can be defined as a child's basic knowledge or understanding that he is a male ("a boy") or that she is a female ("a girl"). In this sense, the acquisition of gender identity is a type of cognitive milestone, typically achieved by the age of 3 years (Kohlberg, 1966). There is, however, also an emotional valence connected to such knowledge, which, in most children, has a positive connotation.

According to Money (1995), the term "gender identity" was apparently coined in the early 1960s by Evelyn Hooker, a psychologist well known for her studies of nonpatient homosexual men in the late 1950s (e.g., Hooker, 1957). Around the same time, Stoller (1964), a psychoanalyst, had coined a similar term, "core gender identity," which he defined along the same lines that have become mainstream in the normative cognitive-developmental literature (Kohlberg, 1966).

Despite the relative recency of the term "gender identity," prior generations of clinicians had become aware that there were adults who felt extremely uncomfortable with their gender identity, even to the point of wanting to transform their sex-related physical anatomy to correspond to their felt sense of having a cross-gender identity. By the 1950s, such individuals were referred to as "transsexuals" (e.g., Benjamin, 1954).

Because many adults with the syndrome of transsexualism claimed to have felt unhappy being a male or a female since early childhood, this prompted several investigators to study children who also appeared to be unhappy about being male or female (e.g., Green, 1974; Stoller, 1968a).

But it was only with the publication of the third edition of the *Diagnostic and Statistical Manual of Mental Disorders* (DSM) (American Psychiatric Association, 1980) that the official North American psychiatric nomenclature provided a formal diagnosis for children who were extremely unhappy with their gender identity.

As reviewed by Bradley et al. (1991), the placement of the gender identity disorder (GID) diagnosis for children within the DSM nomenclature has had somewhat of a vagabond career. In DSM-III, it was the only child psychiatric diagnosis not located in the section entitled "Disorders Usually First Evident in

Infancy, Childhood, or Adolescence." Instead, it was placed in the section entitled "Psychosexual Disorders." Following a recommendation by some members of the Subcommittee on Gender Identity Disorders, this was changed in the revised third edition of DSM (American Psychiatric Association, 1987), and the GID diagnosis was moved to the child section of the manual. Subsequently, there was criticism of this change because the largely adult diagnosis of transsexualism was also shifted to the child section (Pauly, 1992). After deliberation, the DSM-IV Subcommittee on Gender Identity Disorders (hereafter, the DSM-IV Subcommittee) recommended that both diagnoses be given a distinct section in the manual (Bradley et al., 1991); however, this did not occur; instead, a new section entitled "Sexual and Gender Identity Disorders" was created, which actually consisted of the same types of diagnoses that had constituted the "Psychosexual Disorders" section of DSM-III.

DSM-IV Diagnostic Description and Changes from DSM-III-R

Placement matters aside, there have been some rather significant developments in the conceptualization of GID in DSM-IV and in the diagnostic criteria. For example, there was a reduction in the number of diagnoses from three to one between DSM-III-R and DSM-IV. The DSM-IV Subcommittee took the position that the gender identity disorder of childhood, transsexualism, and gender identity disorder of adolescence or adulthood, nontranssexual type, were not qualitatively distinct disorders (as they were in DSM-III-R) but reflected differences in both developmental and severity parameters. As a result, the DSM-IV Subcommittee recommended one overarching diagnosis, gender identity disorder, that could be used, with appropriate variations in criteria, across the life cycle (Bradley et al., 1991).

Table 18.1 shows the DSM-IV criteria for GID. It can be seen that three criteria (Points A, B, and D) are required for the diagnosis, and Point C is an exclusion criterion.

Compared to DSM-III and DSM-III-R, there were five main changes in the criteria for use with children:

1. The A criterion reflects the child's cross-gender identification, indexed by a total of five behavioral characteristics, of which at least four must be manifested. Previously, these characteristics were listed in either the A or the B criterion in DSM-III-R. In addition, they are more descriptively distinct in DSM-IV.

2. The B criterion reflects the child's rejection of his or her own anatomic status and/or rejection of same-sex stereotypical activities and behaviors. In DSM-III-R, the B criterion also included some of the behavioral signs of cross-gender identification, which are now restricted to the A criterion.

3. The criteria for boys and girls are more similar than they were in DSM-III-R. For example, in DSM-III-R, girls had to have a "stated" desire to be a boy, whereas boys had to have an "intense" desire to be a girl. Zucker (1992) had noted that the basis for this distinction was unclear and was particularly confusing inasmuch as the phraseology had been identical for the two sexes in the DSM-III: "strongly and persistently *stated* desire to be a boy [girl]" (APA, 1980, p. 265, emphasis added). Moreover, the passage for girls in DSM-III-R contained no reference to intensity or chronicity. In DSM-IV, both boys and girls must manifest a "repeatedly" stated desire to be of the other sex. In addition, the other behavioral characteristics required for the diagnosis are more similar for boys and girls than they were in DSM-III-R.

4. In DSM-III-R, a girl's desire to be of the other sex could not be the result of a wish "merely . . . for any perceived cultural advantages from being a boy" whereas this proviso was not included for boys. In DSM-IV, the proviso applies to both boys and girls.

5. In DSM-III-R, the A criterion specified

that a child must show a "persistent and intense distress" about being a boy or a girl. This phrase did not appear in the DSM-III criteria, and in DSM-III-R it was not specified how one should assess such distress or in what ways it might be distinct from other operationalized components in the criteria. This phrase has been deleted in the DSM-IV A criterion, but the presence of distress must be inferred via impairment in "social, occupational, or other important areas of functioning" (Point D).

Appraisal of DSM-IV Criteria

Reliability and Validity

Can the DSM-IV diagnosis of GID be made reliably? Because the criteria have changed and because no field trials were conducted, this question cannot yet be answered. Zucker, Finegan, Doering, and Bradley (1984) conducted one study of the reliability of the earlier DSM-III criteria. The research involved 36 consecutive referrals to a specialized child and adolescent gender identity clinic. Kappas of .89 and .80 were obtained for the A and B criteria, respectively (both $ps < .001$).

TABLE 18.1 DSM-IV Diagnostic Criteria for Gender Identity Disorder

A. A strong and persistent cross-gender identification (not merely a desire for any perceived cultural advantages of being the other sex).
 In children, the disturbance is manifested by at least four (or more) of the following:
 1. repeatedly stated desire to be, or insistence that he or she is, the other sex
 2. in boys, preference for cross-dressing or simulating female attire; in girls, insistence on wearing only stereotypical masculine clothing
 3. strong and persistent preferences for cross-sex roles in make-believe play or persistent fantasies of being the other sex
 4. intense desire to participate in the stereotypical games and pastimes of the other sex
 5. strong preference for playmates of the other sex
 In adolescents and adults, the disturbance is manifested by symptoms such as a stated desire to be the other sex, frequent passing as the other sex, desire to live or be treated as the other sex, or the conviction that he or she has the typical feelings and reactions of the other sex.

B. Persistent discomfort with his or her sex or sense of inappropriateness in the gender role of that sex.
 In children, the disturbance is manifested by any of the following: in boys, assertion that his penis or testes are disgusting or will disappear or assertion that it would be better not to have a penis, or aversion toward rough-and-tumble play and rejection of male stereotypical toys, games, and activities; in girls, rejection of urinating in a sitting position, assertion that she has or will grow a penis, or assertion that she does not want to grow breasts or menstruate, or marked aversion toward normative feminine clothing.
 In adolescents and adults, the disturbance is manifested by symptoms such as preoccupation with getting rid of primary and secondary sex characteristics (e.g., request for hormones, surgery, or other procedures to physically alter sexual characteristics to simulate the other sex) or belief that he or she was born the wrong sex.

C. The disturbance is not concurrent with a physical intersex condition.

D. The disturbance causes clinically significant distress or impairment in social, occupational, or other important areas of functioning.

Source: Reprinted with permission of the American Psychiatric Association. In ICD-10 (World Health Organization, 1992), the comparable diagnosis is gender identity disorder of childhood, which utilizes the description that was in DSM-III-R.

In the Zucker et al. (1984) study, the validity of the DSM-III criteria was also assessed by comparing the children who met the complete criteria with those children who did not meet the complete criteria on a number of demographic variables and sex-typed behaviors. It should be noted that, by and large, the children who did not meet the complete DSM-III criteria showed at least some characteristics of cross-gender-identification and were not necessarily inappropriate, or false positive, referrals.

Zucker and Bradley (1995) provided an update of these initial analyses based on a considerably larger sample size. We found that the children who met the complete criteria for GID were significantly younger, of a higher social-class background, and more likely to come from an intact, two-parent family than the children who did not meet the complete criteria. The two subgroups did not differ significantly with regard to sex composition and IQ. Correlational analyses indicated that age, IQ, and social class and marital status of the parents were all significantly correlated with one another (absolute rs ranged from .32–.50).

To test which variables, if any, contributed to the correct classification of the subjects in the two diagnostic groups, a discriminant function analysis was performed. Age, sex, IQ, and marital status contributed to the discriminant function, with age showing the greatest power. In the DSM-III group, 82.6% were correctly classified, and in the non-DSM-III group, 68.8% were correctly classified.

The two diagnostic subgroups were then compared on several measures of sex-typed behavior. T-tests were performed, with age, social class, and marital status covaried. The DSM-III subgroup showed significantly more cross-gender behavior or less same-gender behavior than the non-DSM-III subgroup on 11 of 17 measures; thus, there seemed to be at least some behavioral differences between the two diagnostic subgroups in the degree of same-sex-typed or cross-sex-typed behavior, even after controlling for the demographic variables that also differed between the two subgroups (for details, see Zucker & Bradley, 1995).

Empirical Analyses

Initially, the DSM-IV Subcommittee had recommended that the DSM-III-R A and B criteria for children be collapsed into one criterion set. In part, they did so because the two sets of criteria appeared conceptually and empirically related (e.g., Bentler, Rekers, & Rosen, 1979; Rosen, Rekers, & Friar, 1977). As noted, research utilizing the DSM-III and DSM-III-R criteria found that younger children were significantly more likely to receive the diagnosis than were older children (Zucker & Bradley, 1995). This seemed to be due mainly to the fact that older children did not meet the A criterion; that is, despite marked clinical evidence of cross-gender identification, these children did not frequently verbalize the desire to be of the opposite sex. In part, this seemed a function of social desirability and fear of stigma.

If, in fact, the stated desire to be of the opposite sex is simply one of a series of behavioral markers suggestive of GID, then a factor analysis of these markers should yield one common factor. The DSM-IV Subcommittee tested this hypothesis in a reanalysis of parent-report and clinician ratings of cross-gender behavior in Green's (1987) sample of feminine and controls boys (Zucker et al., 1998). A principal-axis factor analysis with varimax rotation yielded one strong factor, accounting for 51.2% of the variance. The variable "son states wish to be a girl" was one of 15 cross-gender behaviors that loaded on this factor (all factor loadings > .40). Thus, there was some empirical support for the hypothesis.

As noted earlier, clinical experience and some research data suggested that the wish to change sex is negatively related to age, that is, older children may be less likely to verbalize this wish, perhaps because of social desirability factors. Green's (1987) data were reanalyzed to explore the relation between age and the verbalized wish to be of the opposite sex. Given the age effects suggested by other analyses (Zucker, 1992), Green's data were analyzed by comparing children between 3 and 9 and 9 and 12 years of age. It was found that the wish to be of the opposite sex was more common in the younger age group. Frequency of the wish to be of the opposite sex was not associated with several other demographic variables.

Given the changes in the Point A criterion (Table 18.1), Zucker et al. (1998) then reexamined the symptom ratings from parent interview data regarding a cohort of 54 children who did not meet the DSM-III criteria for GID (Zucker, 1992). In this analysis, we assessed whether children would meet the proposed DSM-IV A criterion for GID. Because these children did not repeatedly state the desire to be of the opposite sex, we coded as present or absent four remaining traits: cross-dressing, cross-sex roles in fantasy play, cross-sex activity/toy interests, and cross-sex peer preference. If all four traits were present, these children would meet the proposed cutoff for the A criterion. (We chose not to reanalyze the data on the 54 other children who met the DSM-III criteria for GID, since it was our impression that there would not be any substantive change, given that these children had already verbalized the wish to be of the opposite sex and had displayed marked cross-gender role behaviors.)

Of the 54 children, the mean number of symptoms rated as present was 2.36 ($SD =$ 1.33; range, 0–4). Only seven children did not have any symptoms rated as present. Of the 54 children, 16 (29.6%) had all four symptoms, thus meeting the criteria for Point A.

The subgroup that met the A criterion was also compared to the subgroup that did not with regard to the demographic variables of age, IQ, and parents' social class and marital status. There was a trend for the children who met the A criterion to be younger than the children who did not (8.0 vs. 9.4 years), $t(52) = 1.74$, $p = .087$ (two-tailed). Thus, age continued to be a correlate of diagnostic status, but the correlation appeared to be weaker than that found in earlier research (Zucker et al., 1984). None of the other demographic variables distinguished the two subgroups. These reanalyses suggest that the revisions to the diagnostic criteria may result in a modest increase in the number of cases that will meet the complete criteria.

Since these reanalyses were completed, the DSM-IV Subcommittee, with feedback from the DSM-IV main office, developed the B criterion (see Table 18.1), which should, if anything, make the diagnosis even harder to meet. Unfortunately, the reanalyses just described did not explicitly focus on this criterion, so this conjecture will require additional empirical analysis.

Cultural Influences

It was noted earlier that in DSM-IV the simple perception of a cultural advantage accruing to being the other sex is deemed inadequate for the A criterion. Unlike DSM-III or DSM-III-R, this exclusion requirement no longer applies only for girls.

Interestingly, the DSM-IV Subcommittee had initially recommended that this proviso be deleted, since it was argued that although the motivational basis for the desire to be the other sex may have relevance for such parameters as natural history and response to treatment, it was not clear why it should be used diagnostically (Bradley et al., 1991). For example, it could be argued that boys who wish to be girls perceive similar, albeit inverted, cultural advantages (e.g., "girls can wear dresses *and* pants," "girls don't have to play rough, boys do"). Empirical research will have to resolve the question of whether including this proviso has any clinical utility or validity.

Judgments of Persistence

Judgments of behavioral persistence are required in both the A and the B criteria. For example, the A criterion requires a clinical judgment in determining what qualifies as a "repeatedly stated desire to be . . . the other sex." What criteria should clinicians utilize in deciding whether the desire to change sex is persistent? To some extent, the answer to this question hinges on what is known about the prevalence and intensity of cross-sex wishes in the general population. Although it is likely that the persistent desire to change sex is relatively uncommon in the general population (for discussion, see Zucker & Bradley, 1995), there is really no "gold standard" for the clinician to use, and the DSM-IV does not provide explicit guidelines for addressing this matter. Of course, this is a problem not unique to diagnosing GID.

Clinical Impressions

Over the past couple of years, our group has been using the DSM-IV criteria for GID as part of routine clinical assessment. It is our impression that the Point A criteria are easy to diagnose, at least within a population of gender-referred children. In contrast, the Point B criteria appear to be more problematic, particularly with regard to preschoolers. For example, "aversion toward rough-and-tumble play" can be difficult to gauge when the boy has had little exposure to a peer group or activities in which rough-and-tumble play might be a part. "Rejection of male stereotypical toys, games, and activities" is easier to gauge, but, unless the rough-and-tumble criterion is met, the child does not meet the Point B criterion (assuming that there is no evidence of anatomic dysphoria). If this impression is accurate, then one runs the risk of making a false negative diagnosis.

Epidemiology

Prevalence

The prevalence of GID in children has not been formally studied by epidemiological methods. Nevertheless, Meyer-Bahlburg's (1985) characterization of GID as a "rare phenomenon" is not unreasonable.

On the basis of the number of persons receiving "cross-gender" hormonal treatment at the main adult gender identity clinic in the Netherlands, Bakker, van Kesteren, Gooren, and Bezemer (1993) inferred the prevalence of GID (transsexualism) to be 1 in 11,000 men and 1 in 30,400 women.

This approach suffers, however, from at least three limitations. First, it relies on the number of persons who attend specialty clinics that serve as gateways for surgical and hormonal sex reassignment, which may not see all adults with GID. Second, the assumption that GID in children will, in fact, persist into adulthood is not necessarily true. Last, unlike adult females

with GID, who are invariably attracted sexually to biological females, adult males with GID are about equally likely to be attracted sexually to biological males or females (Blanchard, 1985a). A childhood history of GID, or its subclinical manifestation, occurs largely among adults with GID who have a homosexual orientation. Estimates of the prevalence of childhood GID inferred from the prevalence of GID in adult males should take this into account.

Because GID in childhood is strongly associated with subsequent homosexuality (Green, 1987), the prevalence of GID might also be derived from the epidemiological literature on homosexuality. Determining the prevalence of homosexuality is, however, no simple task and has been beset by a host of methodological and interpretive problems.

On the basis of a reading of the original Kinsey data, Voeller (1990) concluded that "an average of 10% of the population [men and women combined] could be designated as Gay [homosexual]" (p. 33, italics omitted). Other scholars who have reworked the Kinsey terrain suggest much lower prevalence rates, typically between 2–6% for men and around 2% for women (e.g., Diamond, 1993; Fay, Turner, Klassen, & Gagnon, 1989; Rogers & Turner, 1991). Even lower estimates for men and women have emerged from studies pertaining to the AIDS epidemic (Laumann, Gagnon, Michael, & Michaels, 1994; Spira, Bajos, & the ACSF Group, 1994; Wellings, Field, Johnson, & Wadsworth, 1994).

The use of prevalence data on homosexuality to determine the prevalence of GID in children is based on retrospective studies that have shown that a substantial proportion of homosexual men and women recall greater rates of childhood cross-gender behavior than do their heterosexual counterparts (e.g., Bell, Weinberg, & Hammersmith, 1981).

To provide a more formal quantitative analysis of the retrospective literature pertaining to childhood sex-typed behavior and later sexual orientation, Bailey and Zucker (1995) conducted a meta-analysis based on 48 independent effect sizes from 41 different citations, 32 effect sizes for heterosexual and homosexual men and 16 effect sizes for heterosexual and homosexual women. In each of these studies, quantitative measures were available for various sex-typed behaviors (e.g., toy interests, roles in fantasy play, involvement in cross-dressing). In some studies, multi-items scales were employed, whereas others reported results separately for each item examined. The mean effect sizes (d) for recalled childhood sex-typed behavior for the within-sex sexual orientation comparisons were "large" by Cohen's (1988) criteria: 1.31 for men and 0.96 for women, respectively.

For 12 studies, frequency distributions for recalled sex-typed behavior were available, which were transformed into z scores. For these subsamples of homosexual and heterosexual men, 89% of homosexual men had scores for cross-sex-typed that exceeded the heterosexual median, in contrast to only 2% of heterosexual men whose scores exceeded the homosexual median. There was slightly more overlap for women—81% of homosexual women had scores that exceeded the heterosexual female median, and 12% of heterosexual women had scores that exceeded the homosexual female median.

From a prevalence perspective, however, these studies pose their own interpretive problems. For example, the specific behaviors assessed varied from one study to the next. How one should determine whether or not an individual was cross-gendered or not cross-gendered ("caseness") is rarely specified; moreover, as noted by Friedman (1988), among others, individuals classified as cross-gendered do not necessarily meet the complete diagnostic criteria for GID. A formal retrospective diagnostic study on the occurrence of GID during childhood among homosexual men and women (compared to heterosexual men and women) remains to be done.

Methodologically, these retrospective studies are most vulnerable to the criticism of memory distortions in recall; for example, it has been argued that homosexual adults might be more likely to recall cross-sex-typed behavior in childhood than heterosexual adults (for review and analysis of this criticism, see Bailey & Zucker,

1995). There are, however, at least two sources of data that argue against the distortion hypothesis. First, two studies have shown significant agreement in recalled cross-sex-typed behavior for ratings made by homosexual men and their mothers (Bailey, Miller, & Willerman, 1993; Bailey, Nothnagel, & Wolfe, 1995). Second, the retrospective data converge with prospective data on the relation between childhood cross-sex-typed behavior and a later homosexual sexual orientation (e.g., Green, 1987; Zucker & Bradley, 1995; Zuger, 1984).

More liberal estimates of prevalence of GID might be derived from studies of children in whom specific cross-gender behaviors were assessed (see, e.g., Zucker, 1985, pp. 87–95). For example, Fagot (1977) attempted to identify statistically preschool children with "moderate" levels of cross-gender behavior. Such children were defined as obtaining preference scores for opposite-sex activities that were at least 1 SD above the mean of the opposite sex and preference scores for same-sex activities that were at least 1 SD below the mean of their own sex. Based on this criterion, 7 (6.6%) of 106 boys and 5 (4.9%) of 101 girls displayed moderate cross-gender preferences.

Another source of information, based on a broader age range of children, comes from the widely used Child Behavior Checklist (CBCL) (Achenbach & Edelbrock, 1981), a parent-report behavior problem questionnaire with excellent psychometric properties. It includes two items (out of 118) that pertain to cross-gender identification: "behaves like opposite sex" and "wishes to be of opposite sex." In the standardization study, endorsement of both items was more common for girls than for boys, regardless of age and clinical status (referred vs. nonreferred). Among referred boys, the desire to be of the opposite sex was quite high for the 4- to 5-year-olds—15.5%—but dropped off sharply thereafter for older children. Among referred girls, the desire to be of the opposite sex was more stable (range, 4.2–8.3%) and was consistently higher than that of the nonreferred girls. Similar results were obtained from a newly developed parent-report questionnaire, the ACQ Behavior Checklist (Achenbach, Howell, Quay,

& Conners, 1991), which contained three items pertaining to cross-gender identification out of a total of 215 (two from the original CBCL and a third, "Dresses like or plays at being opposite sex"). If anything, endorsement of these items appeared to be less common on the new questionnaire than on the original CBCL, which supports the general point that extreme cross-gender behavior is relatively uncommon.

The main problem with such data is that they do not identify adequately patterns of cross-gender behavior that would be of use in determining "caseness." Thus, such data may be best viewed as screening devices for more intensive evaluation.

Incidence

On the basis of clinical experience, Lothstein (1983) speculated that parents who had been influenced by the cultural zeitgeist to use "nonsexist" socialization techniques might have inadvertently induced gender identity conflict in their children. There are, however, no systematic data regarding changes, or the lack thereof, in the incidence of GID over the past several decades.

Sex Differences in Referral Rates

Consistently, it has been observed that boys are referred more often than girls for concerns regarding gender identity. This has been reflected in both research studies and case reports of treatment. Since its inception in 1978, our clinic has had a referral ratio of 6.6:1 (N = 275) of boys to girls (Zucker, Bradley, & Sanikhani, 1997).

How might this disparity be best understood? Perhaps, due to a greater biological vulnerability, the true prevalence of psychosexual disorders is greater in males. For example, it has been noted that, among mammals, development along male lines is dependent on the production of androgen during early fetal development. If appropriate androgen secretion does not occur, or if cell receptors do not respond to circulating androgen, then fetal development proceeds along female

lines, despite the presence of XY sex chromosomes. The androgen-insensitivity (testicular feminization) syndrome (AIS) (see, e.g., Perez-Palacios, Chavez, Mendez, Imperato-McGinley, & Ulloa-Aguirre, 1987) in genetic males is the most poignant illustration of this possibility. In the AIS, cell receptors do not respond to male hormones secreted by the testes, but instead respond to the small amounts of estrogens that are also secreted by the testes. Although the internal physical components of masculine development commence, they do not get completed, and the external genitalia differentiate in the form of a blind vagina. At the time of puberty, there is no menstruation, but there is normal breast development. Accordingly, it has been suggested that male fetal development is more "complex" than female fetal development and thus more susceptible to errors that may affect postnatal psychosexual differentiation.

Whatever the contribution of biological events, social factors appear to play a role in accounting for the disparity in referral rates. For example, the peer group is less tolerant of cross-gender behavior in boys than in girls (reviewed by Zucker, 1985; see also Zucker, Wilson-Smith, Kurita, & Stern, 1995), which might influence the liklihood of clinical referral.

More direct clinical evidence for the differential reaction to cross-gender behavior in boys and girls comes from Green's studies of feminine boys and masculine girls. Green (1976) and Green, Williams, and Harper (1980) obtained parental assessments of the male peer group relations of 55 feminine and 45 control boys (all of whom proved conventionally masculine). The former had been referred by various professionals for participation in a research study. Green, Williams, and Goodman (1982) also obtained parental assessments of the female peer group relations of 50 masculine ("tomboy") girls and 49 feminine ("nontomboy") girls, who were solicited through newspaper advertisements.

Maternal ratings of same-sex peer group relations for these four groups of children showed that the masculine boys were more likely to have good same-sex peer group relations than were the feminine boys, especially as judged by the "good mixer" category. The masculine girls tended to do less well than the feminine girls with female peers, although this trend was not confirmed in the analysis of paternal ratings (Green et al., 1982). However, the masculine girls were less likely to be rejected by same-sex peers than were the feminine boys and were more likely to be regarded as leaders or good mixers. In interpreting these differences, it is important to note that the masculine girls, unlike the feminine boys, were not referred through clinical channels.

Adults (e.g., parents, teachers) are also less tolerant of cross-gender behavior in boys than in girls (e.g., Fagot, 1977, 1985; Langlois & Downs, 1980). Weisz and Weiss (1991) devised a "referability index" (RI) that reflected the frequency with which a child problem, adjusted for its prevalence in the general population, resulted in a clinic referral. All 118 items from the CBCL were analyzed in a comparison of clinic-referred and nonreferred children. Among parents in the United States, the 20 most referable problems (e.g., vandalism, poor schoolwork, attacks on people) appeared to be relatively serious. In contrast, the 20 least referable problems (e.g., bragging, teasing a lot, liking to be alone) appeared less so. Weiss (personal communication, March 4, 1992) indicated that, for boys, the CBCL item "wishes to be of opposite sex" had an RI of 91/118 (i.e., in the upper quartile) and "behaves like opposite sex" had an RI of 80/118. For girls, the RI was lower: 55/118 for "wishes to be of opposite sex" and 14/118 for "behaves like opposite sex." In addition to their immediate differential reactions to cross-gender behavior in boys and girls, adults are more likely to predict long-term atypical outcomes, such as homosexuality, in feminine boys than in masculine girls (Antill, 1987; Martin, 1990; McCreary, 1994).

These studies, particularly that of Weisz and Weiss (1991), led us to predict that girls would be required to display more extreme cross-gender behavior than boys before parents sought out a clinical assessment (Zucker & Bradley, 1995). We found that the mothers of gender-referred girls seen in our clinic were significantly more likely than the mothers of gender-referred boys to rate the two items pertaining to gender development on the CBCL as a 2 ("very true or often true" on a 0–2 point scale), 52% to 28%, respectively. This was not, however, the case for ratings by fathers. Although mother-father ratings for the two CBCL ratings were significantly correlated ($r[128] = .56$, $p < .001$), the mothers were more likely than the fathers to rate both items a 2 for both the boys and the girls, $\chi^2[1] = 5.11$ ($p < .05$) and 3.18 ($p < .10$), respectively.

A final possibility regarding the sex difference in referral rates is that the base rate of cross-gender behavior differs for boys and girls in the general population. The developmental literature is inconsistent on this point, but, if anything, girls are likely to display masculine behavior more than boys are likely to display feminine behavior (e.g., Sandberg et al., 1993). Thus, from a comparative standpoint, one would predict that girls need to show more cross-gender behavior than boys in order to be perceived as notably different from same-sex peers. To test this possibility, we analyzed CBCL normative data from the standardization sample (Achenbach & Edelbrock, 1981) by calculating the percentage of nonreferred boys and girls, ages 4 to 11 years, who received a rating of 2 on both CBCL items pertaining to gender development. Of 398 boys, none were given ratings of 2 on both items; of 398 girls, only two were rated in this way. Thus, it appears that the CBCL sex difference in our sample of gender-referred children does not seem to be accounted for by a sex difference in the way these items are rated for nonreferred children.

Age of Onset

Green (1976) reported that the age of onset of cross-gender behaviors in GID is typically during the preschool years. In his sample of boys, for example, 55% were cross-dressing by their third birthday, 80% were cross-dressing by their fourth birthday, and 90% were cross-dressing by their fifth birthday. Many experienced clinicians have observed repetitive, intense cross-gender behaviors even before a child's second birthday. Clinical data on girls reveal a similar age of onset (Zucker & Bradley, 1995). It is important to note that among more typical children a display of various gender role behaviors can also be observed during this period in the life cycle. This similarity suggests that the underlying mechanisms for both patterns may be the same, albeit mirror images.

Prognosis

Green (1987) has provided the most detailed information regarding long-term follow-up of boys with GID vis-à-vis gender identity and sexual orientation (for other follow-up reports, see Zucker & Bradley, 1995). Green originally assessed 66 extremely feminine boys and 56 control boys at a mean age of 7.1 years (range, 4 to 12 years). About two thirds of the boys in each of these groups were reevaluated at a follow-up mean age of 18.9 years (range, 14–24 years). Sexual orientation in fantasy and behavior was assessed by means of a semistructured interview schedule. Using Kinsey scale criteria, all 35 control boys were heterosexual in fantasy at follow-up. Of the 25 control boys who had experienced overt sexual relations, one was classified as bisexual, and the remainder were classified as heterosexual. In contrast, 33 of the 44 feminine boys (75%) were classified as either bisexual or homosexual; of the 30 feminine boys who had experienced overt sexual relations, 24 (80%) were classified as either bisexual or homosexual. Only one of the feminine boys, who was sexually attracted to males, was seriously entertaining the notion of sex reassignment surgery. Thus, homosexuality rather than GID persisting into late adolescence or young adulthood appears to be the most common long-term outcome associated with GID.

Why was GID in adolescence or young adulthood not a common outcome in Green's (1987) study? There are two main explanations. First, as noted by Weinrich (1985), the low base rate of GID in the adult population would require large sample sizes, even within the population of children with GID. Second, it is possible that the assessment process and, when it occurs, treatment alter the natural history of GID. Clinical experience and observation suggest that it is only those children who have not moved away from extreme cross-gender identification that remain at risk for continued GID in adolescence or adulthood (McCauley & Ehrhardt, 1984). Zucker and Bradley (1995) have found that the persistence of gender dysphoria (the felt distress about being a male or a female), including the wish for sex reassignment, was considerably higher among patients first assessed in adolescence and followed up later compared to patients who were first assessed in childhood and followed up in adolescence. Thus, it might be argued that there is more plasticity to GID in childhood than in adolescence if psychosocial efforts to alter it occur early in development.

Brief Review of Psychopathology and Theoretical Models

Associated Psychopathology

Apart from the GID itself, there is substantial evidence that, on average, children with GID manifest levels of general behavior problems at a level comparable to that of clinic-referred controls (Zucker & Bradley, 1995). On the CBCL, for example, boys with GID appear to show a predominance of internalizing difficulties (reviewed in Zucker & Bradley, 1995). In addition, two studies have shown that these boys manifest a high rate of separation anxious traits (Coates & Person, 1985; Zucker, Bradley, & Sullivan, 1996).

In boys with GID, CBCL psychopathology was shown to increase with age, which likely reflects the mediating impact of social ostracism, and with degree of maternal psychopathology (Zucker & Bradley, 1995); however, the nature of the relation between the associated psychopathology and the genesis of the GID itself remains unclear (for reviews of this issue, see Zucker & Bradley, 1995; Zucker & Green, 1992). Nevertheless, the presence of other forms of psychopathology in these youngsters needs to be considered in order to conduct a comprehensive diagnostic assessment.

Biological Factors

As noted earlier, children with GID do not show any gross biological anomaly. This does not, however, rule out the presence of other, more subtle biological factors that may be important in understanding the genesis of GID. In our view, such factors may, at present, be best understood as predisposing rather than fixed influences on the psychosexual differentiation of these children.

From this perspective, what biological factors might be of importance? To some extent, research that has guided conceptual thinking on this matter has considered biological factors that might be related to normative sex differences in the sex-typed behavior of boys and girls and to within-sex differences in sexual orientation, given that we now know that GID is associated with an increased liklihood of a later homosexual sexual orientation (Green, 1987).

Elsewhere, we have reviewed seven domains of biological research pertaining to both sex and within-sex sexual orientation differences: molecular genetics, behavior genetics, prenatal sex hormones, prenatal maternal stress, neuropsychological factors, neuroanatomy, and familial demographics (Zucker & Bradley, 1995). Here we provide a thumbnail sketch of the status of this research.

The molecular and behavior genetics of GID have not been studied. However, there is little evidence for familiality of GID based on the virtual absence of concordance among siblings. Prenatal sex hormones might play a role in affecting certain sex-dimorphic behaviors, such as activity level and proclivity for rough-and-tumble play; for example, boys with GID appear to be less active and to avoid rough-and-tumble play more than control boys, whereas girls with GID appear to be more active than control girls (Zucker & Bradley, 1995). Prenatal maternal stress, which may influence patterns of prenatal hormone levels, has not been studied. Neuropsychological variables, such as patterns of cognitive ability, might also be influenced by prenatal sex hormones. On one measure of visual-spatial ability, boys with GID performed significantly more poorly than both clinical and normal control boys; however, the link between depressed spatial ability and GID is unclear. Postmortem or in vivo studies of neuroanatomic structures have not been conducted for children with GID. Last, two familial demographic variables—sibling sex ratio and birth order—have been shown to differ between boys with GID and clinical control boys. Boys with GID have an excess of brothers (Blanchard, Zucker, Bradley, & Hume, 1995; Zucker et al., 1997) and are born later in the sibship than clinical control boys (Blanchard et al., 1995). The possible role of biological factors that are implicated by these altered familial demographic variables has been reviewed elsewhere (e.g., Blanchard et al., 1995; Zucker & Bradley, 1995); at present, such factors remain speculative and have not been verified empirically.

Psychosocial Factors

Elsewhere, we have reviewed several psychosocial variables thought to be of relevance in the genesis of GID (Zucker & Bradley, 1995). These include sex of assignment at birth, parent's prenatal sex preference, parental tolerance or reinforcement of cross-gender behavior, and psychological and psychiatric characteristics of the parents. We provide here a thumbnail sketch of the status of this research (for other recent reviews, see Coates, 1990; Green, 1987).

It is clear that sex of assignment at birth is irrelevant to the genesis of GID, since these children are invariably assigned to the correct biological sex (this contrasts with sex assignment in some infants with physical intersex conditions, in which decisions about the sex of rearing may be delayed or dealt with ambiguously). There is also no consistent evidence that parents preferred a child of the opposite sex, which may have induced ambivalent feelings about the child (Zucker et al., 1994). However, there does appear to be a subgroup of these youngsters, particularly the boys, whose mothers experience what we term "pathological gender mourning," in which the wish for a child of the opposite sex remains unresolved and affects gender-related aspects of parental socialization

(Zucker, 1996). Across most families, the most common socialization factor seems to be the tolerance or encouragement of cross-gender behavior during the toddler and preschool years, which, at the least, functions as a perpetuating factor (Green, 1987; Mitchell, 1991; Zucker & Bradley, 1995). Thus, in clinical assessment, it is important to focus on the extent to which parents have encouraged the cross-gender behavior or simply allowed it to emerge without any attempts to set limits. More important, one needs to understand the varying motivations related to such parenting, since this will help in devising a treatment plan. There is also some emerging evidence that the parents of children with GID manifest psychiatric and emotional difficulties that are at least commensurate with those of parents of clinical control children. However, the lack of specificity raises questions about the precise relevance such characteristics have for the genesis of GID, although plausible mechanisms have been proposed (Coates & Person, 1985; Coates & Wolfe, 1995; Marantz & Coates, 1991; Wolfe, 1990; Zucker & Bradley, 1995).

Assessment

Biomedical Tests

There are no known biological markers that identify children with GID. For such children, the parameters of biological sex, such as the sex chromosomes and the appearance of the external genitalia, are invariably normal (Green, 1976). It is not, however, uncommon for parents of children with GID to ask about the role of biological factors as an explanatory phenomenon, so it is necessary to review with them current theoretical ideas about their contribution (see earlier discussion).

Because there is some evidence that gender identity conflict or disorder is overrepresented among specific physical intersex conditions, particularly congenital adrenal hyperplasia in genetic females (Meyer-Bahlburg, 1994) and partial androgen-insensitivity syndrome in genetic males reared as girls, it is important to inquire about any physical signs of these conditions. However, it is rare that these conditions have not already been diagnosed prior to a clinical assessment for GID.

Psychological Tests and Structured Interviews

Table 18.2 provides information on several parent-report and behavioral measures that can be used to assess sex-typed behavior in children with GID. From a diagnostic standpoint, however, it should be recognized that no one test is a replacement for a diagnosis that is established by a good clinical interview that covers the behavioral signs for the diagnosis.

As one example, consider the Draw-a-Person (DAP) test, a relatively simple and probably crude marker of gender identification. On this test, children are asked to draw a person and then to identify the person's sex. Normative research has long shown that a large proportion of both boys and girls draw a person of their own sex first in response to this request (e.g., Jolles, 1952). In contrast, three studies with gender-problem children showed that children with GID were more likely than controls to draw an opposite-sex person first (Green, Fuller, & Rutley, 1972; Skilbeck, Bates, & Bentler, 1975; Zucker, Finegan, Doering, & Bradley, 1983). The percentage of gender-problem and control subjects in each of the three studies who drew an opposite-sex person first was 57% versus 24%, 32% versus 6%, and 61% versus 20%, respectively.

Although significant in each case, the false negative rate was considerably higher than the false positive rate. The high rate of false negatives may be interpreted in several ways. For example, given the nominal nature of the measure, the probability of an "incorrect" response is 50% by chance alone. It is also likely that gender-referred children vary in the degree to which they are cross-gender-identified, and this may contribute to greater variance on psychological testing. In an update of our original DAP study (Zucker & Bradley, 1995), we found that 72.4% of the gender-referred children who met the complete DSM-III criteria for GID

(N = 110) drew an opposite-sex person first, in contrast to only 30.3% of the gender-referred children who did not meet the complete criteria (N = 78); thus, the false negative rate was lower within the more extreme group.

The nominal nature of the DAP test precludes any type of continuous measurement; however, other potential indices of sex-typing on the DAP are amenable to more refined analyses. Zucker et al. (1983) found that gender-referred children drew taller opposite-sex persons than same-sex persons, whereas controls tended to draw taller same-sex persons than opposite-sex persons. Skilbeck et al. (1975) found that gender-referred boys provided more details in their drawings of females than in their drawings of males, which is a common observation noted in therapy with these boys (Coates, 1985). In general, drawings of males and females are of qualitative, clinical use in understanding the gender representations of children with GID.

We have developed a semistructured Gender Identity Interview schedule (Table 18.3) that can be used to obtain both quantitative and qualitative information from the child and that is useful as part of a clinical assessment (Zucker et al., 1993). Factor analysis identified two factors, which were labeled Cognitive Gender Confusion and Affective Gender Confusion. The following responses were obtained from a 5-year-old boy (IQ = 95) who met the DSM-IV diagnostic criteria for GID:

Interviewer (I): Are you a boy or a girl?
Child (C): A girl.
I: Are you a boy?
C: No.
I: When you grow up, will you be a mommy or a daddy?
C: A mom.
I: Could you ever grow up to be a daddy?
C: Sometimes.
I: Are there any good things about being a boy?
C: No.
I: Are there any things that you don't like about being a boy?
C: Yes.

I: Tell me some of the things that you don't like about being a boy.
C: I don't like being a boy Power Ranger and I don't like being a boy pig or something, like an animal. I like being a girl, girls are better.
I: Do you think it is better to be a boy or a girl?
C: Girl.
I: Why?
C: So I can do hair things and that's prettier [and] 'cause they wear beautiful bathing suits.
I: In your mind, do you ever think that you would like to be a girl?
C: Yes.
I: Can you tell me why?
C: 'cause it's funner and you can fling your hair around and do it in ponytails and pigtails.
I: In your mind, do you ever get mixed up and you're not really sure if you are a boy or a girl?
C: Sometimes.
I: Tell me more about that
C: I'm not really sure of that.
I: Do you ever feel more like a girl than like a boy?
C: Yes.
I: Tell me more about that.
C: I feel more like a girl than like a boy.
I: You know what dreams are, right? Well, when you dream at night, are you ever in he dream?
C: Yes . . . and I'm always a girl.
I: Tell me about those dreams.
C: I don't know.
I: Do you ever think that you really are a girl?
C: Yes. I really think that I'm a girl, I can't tell you because I can't tell you about it.

Treatment

Therapeutic interventions for GID are entirely psychosocial in nature, taking into account temperamental and psychological factors in the child and family dynamics. To our knowledge, there are no known pharmacological treatments.

TABLE 18.2. Description of Assessment Techniques

Reference	Measure	Content	Original/Additional References
Green (1976, 1987)	Parent report	Gender identity; gender role behaviors	Roberts, Green, Williams, & Goodman (1987)
Bates & Bentler (1973)	Parent report	Sex-typed games and activities	Meyer-Bahlburg, Feldman, & Ehrhardt (1985); Sandberg & Meyer-Bahlburg (1994); Zucker et al. (1985); modified by Meyer-Bahlburg, Sandberg, Dolezal, & Yager (1994)
Bates, Bentler, & Thompson (1973)	Parent report	Gender role behaviors	Bates, Bentler, & Thompson (1979); Meyer-Bahlburg et al. (1985)
Zucker & Bradley (1995)	Parent report	Gender identity; gender role behaviors	modified from Elizabeth & Green (1984)
Bates et al. (1973)	Parent report	Activity level/extraversion	modified version, Zucker & Bradley (1995)
Green, Fuller, Rutley, & Hendler (1972)	Free play	Masculine and feminine sex-typed play	
Rekers & Yates (1976)	Free play	Masculine and feminine sex-typed play	Zucker, Doering, Bradley, & Finegan (1982)
Green et al. (1972)	IT-Scale for Children	Projective measure of sex-typed preferences	Rekers, Rosen, & Morey (1990)
Green & Fuller (1973)	Fantasy play	Masculine and feminie fantasy play (stories)	
Green et al. (1972)	Draw-a-Person	Sex of first figure drawn; heights of same-sex and opposite-sex persons; content analysis	Rekers et al. (1990); Skilbeck et al. (1975) Zucker et al. (1983)
Zucker et al. (1996)	Gender constancy	"Stages" of gender constancy development	
Zucker et al. (1992)	Rorschach	Sex-typed responses; gender confusion	
Zucker et al. (1993)	Gender identity interview	Cognitive and affective gender identity confusion	

Source: Modified from Zucker, K. J., and Bradley, S. J. (1995, pp. 60–61). These assessment measures are the most readily accessible for clinical assessment. All have shown at least some discriminant validity, that is, they have distinguished gender-referred children from normal, sibling, and/or clinical controls. Some of the measures are appropriate for both boys and girls, whereas others (e.g., Bates et al., 1973) have been validated only for boys.

TABLE 18.3. Gender Identity Interview for Children (Boy Version)

1. Are you a boy or a girl? BOY ___ GIRL ___

2. Are you a (opposite of first response)? ___

3. When you grow up, will you be a Mommy or a Daddy? MOMMY ___ DADDY ___

4. Could you ever grow up to be a (opposite of first response)? Yes ___ No ___

5. Are there any good things about being a boy? Yes ___ No ___
   If YES, say: Tell me some of the good things about being a boy. (Probe for a maximum of three responses.)

   If YES or NO, ask: Are there any things that you don't like about being a boy? Yes ___ No ___

   If child answers YES, say: Tell me some of the things that you don't like about being a boy. (Probe for a maximum of three responses.)

6. Do you think it is better to be a boy or a girl? Yes ___ No ___
   Why? (Probe for a maximum of three responses.)

7. In your mind, do you ever think that you would like to be a girl? Yes ___ No ___
   If YES, ask: Can you tell me why? (Probe for a maximum of three responses.)

8. In your mind, do you ever get mixed up and you're not really sure if you are a boy or a girl?
   Yes ___ No ___
   If YES, say: Tell me more about that. (Probe until satisfied.)

9. Do you ever feel more like a girl than like a boy? Yes ___ No ___
   If YES, say: Tell me more about that. (Probe until satisfied.)

10. You know what dreams are, right? Well, when you dream at night, are you ever in the dream? If YES, ask: In your dreams, are you a boy, a girl, or sometimes a boy and sometimes a girl?
    BOY ___ GIRL ___ BOTH ___ NOT IN DREAMS ___
    (Probe regarding content of dreams.)

11. Do you ever think that you really are a girl? Yes ___ No ___
    If YES, say: Tell me more about that. (Probe until satisfied.)

Source: From Zucker, K. J., et al. (1993).

Several therapeutic approaches have been employed to treat children with GID, including behavior therapy, psychotherapy, family therapy, parental counseling, group therapy, and eclectic combinations of these strategies. As reviewed elsewhere (Green, 1974, 1987; Zucker, 1985, 1990; Zucker & Bradley, 1995; Zucker & Green, 1989), all of these strategies appear to have clinical utility; unfortunately, formal comparative studies have not been conducted, so the most efficacious types of treatment remain unclear (for specific references to the case report literature, see Zucker & Bradley, 1995).

Three general comments about treatment of GID will be made. First, clinical experience suggests that intervention can more readily reduce gender identity conflict during childhood than during adolescence. The prognosis for reducing severe gender dysphoria after puberty is rather poor. Accordingly, the earlier treatment begins, the better. Second, the importance of working with the parents of children with GID has been much discussed in the literature. When there is a great deal of marital discord and parental psychopathology, treatment of these problems will greatly facilitate more specific work on gender identity issues. Management of the child's gender behavior in his or her daily environment requires that the parents have clear goals and a forum in which to discuss difficulties. Because parental dynamics and parental ambivalence about treatment may contribute to the perpetuation of GID (Newman, 1976), it is important for the therapist to have an appropriate relationship with the parents in order to address and work through these issues. Last, the therapist needs to consider closely the goals of treatment (Zucker & Bradley, 1995). In part, this issue will be conceptualized within the therapist's theoretical framework, but it will also be a function of the parents' concern and, to some extent, of the child's concerns. Two short-term goals have been discussed in the clinical literature: the reduction or elimination of social ostracism and conflict and the alleviation of underlying or associated psychopathology. Longer-term goals have focused on the prevention of postpubertal gender dysphoria and homosexuality. Little disagreement about the advisability of preventing gender dysphoria in adolescence or adulthood has been expressed in the clinical literature. Contemporary and secular-minded clinicians are, however, sensitive to the importance of helping people integrate a homosexual sexual orientation into their sense of identity (Friedman, 1988; Green, 1987). Not surprisingly, however, the development of a heterosexual orientation is probably preferred by most parents of children with GID. It is therefore important that clinicians point out to such parents that, as of yet, there is no strong evidence that treatment affects later sexual orientation. Both authors, as well as other experienced clinicians in the field, have preferred to emphasize the merit of reducing childhood gender identity conflict per se and, when it is present, associated behavioral problems and to orient the parents of children with GID to the short-term goals of intervention.

Behavior Therapy

Rekers (1977, 1985) and colleagues used different types of behavioral techniques to treat GID, such as differential social attention or reinforcement, token economy, and self-regulation. There is evidence that specific sex-typed behaviors can be either reduced or increased in their frequency. The techniques have been subject to two main limitations—"stimulus specificity" and "response specificity." The first term refers to the phenomenon of a behavior reappearing (e.g., cross-dressing) in the absence of the stimulus condition under which it was modified (e.g., parental negative sanctions, new environment). The second term means that the treatment did not generalize or influence untreated behaviors, although they appear to be of the same type as the treated behavior; thus, a procedure might modify cross-dressing but not generalize to play with Barbie dolls, a behavior that was not specifically subject to formal treatment techniques (for a review, see Zucker, 1985).

Despite these limitations, an overall analysis of the behavior therapy case report literature suggests some impact on the presenting problem and apparently an impact on the child's overall sense of gender identity (Zucker, 1985). Rekers, Kilgus, and Rosen (1990) provided group analysis of 29 boys treated by behavior therapy techniques. At a mean follow-up of 51 months after treatment, it was found that "completion" of treatment accounted for 20% of the variance in change scores, as defined by a reduction in ratings of cross-gender identification. Unfortunately, no published longer-term follow-ups on this sample, in which their adolescent gender identity and sexual orientation were assessed, are available.

Psychotherapy

The English-language psychotherapy literature consists of a couple of dozen case reports (see Zucker & Bradley, 1995). Unlike in the behavior therapy case report literature, which use quantitative data, the psychotherapy literature is much more descriptive and qualitative in nature. Schultz's (1979) doctoral dissertation consisted of a detailed account of the psychotherapy of one boy with GID, which provides an unusual glimpse into the process of therapeutic intervention. Although difficult to quantify, the impression one gets from studying this literature is that many of the children had made gains by the end of their therapy. Because many of the parents of these children were in therapy and because in some instances the child received additional, concurrent treatments (e.g., as an inpatient), the precise mechanisms of change become even more difficult to identify. No systematic follow-up data on adolescent gender identity and sexual orientation are available from the psychotherapy case report literature.

Elsewhere, we have identified discernable themes in the psychotherapy case report literature (Zucker, 1985; Zucker & Bradley, 1995). These include an emphasis on the significance of the emergence of cross-gender behavior during the preoedipal years, with concomitant attention to early object relations and general ego functioning and evidence for developmental arrests. Attention is given to understanding the impact of the mother-child and the father-child relationships on the formation of the gender symptomatology and the parental psychodynamics that putatively underlie parental tolerance for the cross-gender behavior. In a sense, then, this literature takes a more contextual approach in understanding GID than does the behavior therapy literature.

Treatment of the Parents

Two rationales have been offered for the involvement of parents in treatment. The first emphasizes the hypothesized role of parental dynamics in the genesis or maintenance of the child's disorder. From this perspective, individual therapy with the child will probably proceed more smoothly and quickly if the parents are able to gain some insight into their own contribution to their child's difficulties. Many clinicians, including ourselves, who have worked extensively with gender-disturbed children subscribe to this rationale (e.g., Coates,

1985; Green, Newman, & Stoller, 1972; Newman, 1976; Stoller, 1978).

The second rationale is that parents need regular, formalized contact with the therapist to discuss day-to-day management issues that arise in carrying out the overall therapeutic plan. Our clinic, for example, suggests that parents disallow cross-dressing, discourage cross-gender role play and fantasy play, restrict playing with cross-sex toys, tell the child that they value him as a boy (or her as a girl), encourage same-sex peer relations, and help the child engage in more sex-appropriate or neutral activities. Some parents, especially the well functioning and intellectually sophisticated, are able to carry out these recommendations relatively easily and without ambivalence. Many parents, however, require ongoing support in implementing the recommendations, perhaps because of their own ambivalence and reservations about gender identity issues (see, e.g., Newman, 1976). Some of these parents find it difficult to believe that their child has a gender identity problem; others are reluctant to restrict their child's favorite fantasies or activities. Regular involvement with such parents then benefits the child's treatment. Although some case reports suggest that substantial therapeutic change can occur with minimal parental involvement, our experience is that parental involvement in therapy is required in the majority of cases. While we concur with other clinicians in the importance of addressing therapeutically familial and intrapersonal factors, we do not share the perspective of those clinicians whose therapeutic approach does not include limit-setting of the cross-gender behavior. Our view is that limit-setting helps the child to become less confused about his or her gender identity (from the "outside in," as we explain to some parents), whereas the traditionally more open-ended approach within individual psychotherapy sessions helps the child to work through the various conflicts that have contributed to the consolidation of a cross-gender identity (from the "inside out"). In general, contact with the parents is important in understanding the day-to-day problems experienced by children with GID.

Is there empirical evidence that working with the parents makes a difference? Again, systematic information on the question is scanty. The most relevant study found some evidence that parental involvement in therapy was significantly correlated with a greater degree of behavioral change in the child at a 1-year follow-up, but this study did not make random assignment to different treatment protocols (Zucker, Bradley, Doering, & Lozinski, 1985).

TRANSVESTIC FETISHISM

Historical Perspective

The literal meaning of the word "transvestism" is to wear the clothing of the opposite sex. In contemporary clinical sexology and in DSM-IV (APA, 1994), the term "transvestism" is delimited to describing biological males who cross-dress in women's clothing, accompanied, at least at times, by sexual arousal (e.g., Stoller, 1971), and that is how the term, or its variant, transvestic fetishism (TF), is used in this chapter.

At the outset, it needs to be emphasized that TF has been observed by generations of clinicians and researchers to occur virtually exclusively in biological males. Although Stoller (1982) reported on three cases of adult females who showed some features of sexual arousal associated with cross-dressing, the clinical and research literature remains silent on whether there is a truly analogous form of TF in biological females.

In the older clinical literature, the term "transvestism" was used in diverse ways, so without studying the actual case material, one could never be certain whether the patient was, by "modern" terminology, a transvestite (as defined here), a transsexual, or a homosexual cross-dresser or "drag queen" (Person & Ovesey, 1984). (Among homosexuals who cross-dress, sexual arousal never accompanies this activity.) Thus, any clinician or researcher who studies the extant literature must be very careful in recognizing that the term "transvestism" has been

used in diverse and, at times, confusing ways (for review, see Zucker & Blanchard, 1997).

Although TF (or, perhaps, its immature precursors) has been observed in prepubertal children, patients most commonly come to the attention of clinicians during their adolescence or adulthood.

DSM-IV Diagnostic Description and Changes from DSM-III-R

In the three recent editions of DSM, TF has been included in the section of the manual as one of the paraphilias. In DSM-IV, this placement is in the section entitled "Sexual and Gender Identity Disorders."

Table 18.4 shows the DSM-IV criteria for TF, which were developed on the basis of expert clinical consensus, that is, by the subcommittee responsible for the TF diagnosis, since there has been little in the way of formal empirical research, such as field trials, regarding the reliability and validity of the TF diagnostic criteria.

In our view, the wording of Criterion B raises substantial conceptual issues. Note that Criterion B is *not* met if there is an absence of distress or impairment in "social, occupational, or other important areas of functioning." In DSM-III-R, however, one could be given the diagnosis of TF *in the absence of distress* because Criterion B could be met if the person had simply "acted" on the urge to cross-dress.

Gert (1992) criticized Criterion B in DSM-III-R on the grounds that the diagnosis of TF could be made in the absence of distress and argued that it should be made only if there was associated distress. The changes in DSM-IV appear to reflect this criticism.

In our view, there are complex problems with the DSM-IV criteria for TF because of the wording of Criterion B. We have a population of males who engage in the behaviors and fantasies that define TF. But a diagnosis of TF can be made only for those males within this population who are distressed or impaired by such behaviors and/or fantasies. From a practical point of view, this is likely of little import, since individuals with TF who consult mental

---

TABLE 18.4. DSM-IV Diagnostic Criteria for Transvestic Fetishism

A. Over a period of at least 6 months, in a heterosexual male, recurrent, intense, sexually arousing fantasies, sexual urges, or behaviors involving cross-dressing.

B. The fantasies, sexual urges, or behaviors cause clinically significant distress or impairment in social, occupational, or other important areas of functioning.

Specify if
    With Gender Dysphoria: if the person has persistent discomfort with gender role or identity.

Source: Reprinted with permission of the American Psychiatric Association. In ICD-10 (World Health Organization, 1992), the comparable diagnosis is fetishistic transvestism.

---

health professionals are presumably, in some respect, distressed or impaired by their condition. But from a conceptual and philosophical standpoint, the matter seems confused and muddled. (It should be noted that Criterion B [distress or impairment] has been applied to all of the paraphilias in the DSM-IV. Thus, for example, one cannot give the diagnosis of pedophilia to an individual who is not distressed by the condition or if it does not cause impairment in social, occupational, or other important areas of functioning.)

Epidemiology

Prevalence

No formal epidemiological study has ever been conducted to assess the prevalence of TF. As noted earlier, however, TF is a disorder that appears to be unique to biological males. Without any formal documentation, Bullough and Bullough (1993) stated that the prevalence "figure of 1 percent of the adult male population is often mentioned, and it conforms with our own tentative conclusions; we will use it until better statistics are available" (p. 315). In our view, this claim is based on sheer conjecture and should in no way be taken as the result of any serious epidemiological effort.

Incidence

No formal epidemiological study has ever been conducted to assess the incidence of TF.

Chasseguet-Smirgel (1981), a psychoanalyst, speculated that "perversions" in general, which includes TF, were becoming more frequent but provided no systematic documentation. The increased visibility of men with TF appears to be, in part, the result of the development of what Bullough and Bullough (1993) characterized as "organized transvestism," that is, educational, social, and support groups that have emerged over the past few decades. As well, any casual observer of popular culture cannot escape notice of the amount of attention given to transvestism in the press, on television talk shows, and in films.

Age of Onset

Adolescents with TF are usually referred when they are discovered, typically by a parent or other adult authority figure (e.g., a group home worker), to be cross-dressing. In some instances, a parent might enter the youngster's room at night and inadvertently find him under the covers wearing his mother's underpants. In other instances, the mother becomes aware that her clothing is missing, often winding up intermingled with her son's laundry. At times, the mother or a sister might discover that her underclothing is stained with semen. In extreme cases, adolescents with TF engage in the behavior so compulsively that they wind up stealing underclothing from a store or break and enter neighbors' homes to obtain the clothing.

Unlike adolescents with GID, who usually self-refer or do so in agreement with an adult authority figure, adolescents with TF rarely self-refer. The initiative is invariably on the part of an adult.

Adolescents with TF vary in the degree to which they cross-dress. They also vary in the extent to which they acknowledge associated sexual arousal. Some adolescents report that they hold women's underclothing (e.g., underpants, nylons, stockings) only because they like its texture. The report of self-soothing with or without associated erotic arousal has long been part of the clinical picture associated with TF. (It should be noted that many adolescents with this disorder are extremely embarrassed and ashamed when they are discovered. The claim that they are not aroused sexually by the cross-dressing may be true, but they may also be lying. The clinician should recognize that talking about one's sexuality is difficult enough, let alone about a behavioral pattern that the adolescent is slowly recognizing is a cause of great concern on the part of his parents. It is very important to give the adolescent individual interview time to talk about his sexuality with an interviewer who is comfortable engaging in this topic.) Other adolescents report that they wear women's undergarments, are aroused by them, and subsequently masturbate. Some adolescents wear the clothing episodically; others compulsively wear the clothing under their own masculine apparel. In extreme cases, the adolescent engages in "full" cross-dressing, attempting to emulate the phenotype of a woman. Unlike adults with TF, who attempt to pass publicly as women, such attempts are very rare during adolescence. In addition to masturbation, some adolescents mutilate the female apparel (e.g., cutting it to pieces with a scissors) or defecate or urinate on it.

Like adults with TF, adolescents appear to be heterosexual in their sexual orientation. They report sexual fantasies involving females, and some have engaged in interpersonal sexual experiences with girls. They often report being sexually aroused without the use of female clothing, although some adolescents report being more aroused by clothing than by a female partner.

Because some individuals with TF can also experience severe gender dysphoria (Blanchard & Clemmensen, 1988), it is important to assess the youngster's feelings about being a boy. To some extent, the presence of gender dysphoria in a transvestitic youngster is disarming because their physical appearance is stereotypically masculine, as are their behavioral interests. This is in marked contrast to adolescents with GID, who often shape their physical appearance in a way that reflects their cross-gender identification.

The childhood gender development of adolescents with TF is typically masculine (e.g., in peer preference, toy and activity interests, involvement in sports) (Zucker & Bradley, 1995). The sole exception to this is that in a minority of youngsters there is a prepubertal onset of cross-dressing (e.g., use of mother's underpants, wearing or stroking of nylons); however, as suggested earlier, the use of these clothes is not to enhance a sense of feminine identification but rather seems to have some type of self-soothing function, which at times has been observed to be accompanied by penile erection. Cross-dressing of boys with GID usually involves outerwear (e.g., dresses, jewelry) to fuel the fantasy of being like a girl or a woman. In other words, the nature of cross-dressing in TF and in GID is qualitatively different.

Prognosis

By adulthood, the prognosis for any substantive change in TF is rather guarded; in fact, a subgroup of adult men with TF are at further risk for the development of gender dysphoria or full-blown GID (Zucker & Blanchard, 1997). Unfortunately, there is no formal information about the possibility of behavioral change in adolescents treated for TF.

Brief Review of Psychopathology and Theoretical Models

Associated Psychopathology

In our own experience (summarized in Zucker & Bradley, 1995), we have been impressed with the regularity of some other characteristics in our sample of adolescents with TF (N = 79). At the outset, we make no claim that these are representative features of TF in general, since our sample is a clinic-referred one. For example, many of our youngsters have been referred from group homes, indicating that they were no longer able to live with their families, often due to extreme psychopathology and dysfunction in their families of origins. This is obviously one type of sampling bias.

Comorbidity in psychiatric status has been common. Although some of these youngsters are overtly anxious, depressed, and withdrawn, the more common clinical presentation has been of a severely undercontrolled youngster, with diagnoses such as conduct disorder or attention-deficit/hyperactivity disorder. On the CBCL, these youngsters have shown, on average, extremely high levels of behavioral disturbance. Verbal IQ has been significantly lower than performance IQ. Language-related learning disabilities have been common, with attendant school failure. Because of their general behavioral difficulties, social relations have often been poor (e.g., conflicted or nonexistent peer relations). Although paternal absence has been high, so has maternal absence (e.g., by divorce, separation, placement in group homes). In fact, the rate of maternal absence has been significantly higher among our group of adolescent transvestites than it has in our other groups of adolescents with psychosexual problems, including those with GID. A minority of these youngsters have documented neurological dysfunction (e.g., epilepsy). We often request a neurological consult because of the clinical literature, albeit patchy and inconsistent, that has noted a relation between fetishistic behavior and neurological dysfunction (e.g., Epstein, 1973; Kolarsky, Freund, Machek, & Polak, 1967). For example, one 16-year-old youngster seen in our clinic developed epilepsy at age 10; shortly thereafter, his transvestitic behavior seemed to appear for the first time. At age 16, he was also found on occasion to wear diapers to school, which is a type of fetish that has been previously noted in the clinical literature on adults.

Biological Factors

If one takes as a starting point the assumption that TF is related more strongly to ordinary heterosexuality than to homosexuality, then one would expect men with TF to show biological traits (or corresponding behavioral markers) more similar to those of heterosexual men than to those of homosexual men (or, far that matter, of heterosexual women). For example, let us suppose that certain childhood sex-typed behaviors, such as toy preferences and involvement in rough-and-tumble play, are partly influenced by biological factors (see, e.g., Collaer & Hines, 1995). Given that these behaviors clearly distinguish preheterosexual boys from prehomosexual boys (Bailey & Zucker, 1995; Green, 1987), one would predict that pretransvestitic boys would be more similar to preheterosexual boys that to prehomosexual boys. As noted earlier, this is exactly what has been observed in retrospective studies of adolescent and adult males with TF. Unfortunately, in contrast to ordinary homosexuality and heterosexuality, very little work of this type has been conducted on men with TF. In this section, we summarize the material that is available.

Although case reports have documented the co-occurrence of TF between probands and fathers or male siblings or in monozygotic (identical) twin pairs, there is very little systematic research regarding familial patterns. Croughan, Saghir, Cohen, and Robins (1981) studied 70 men with TF and concluded that it was not familial; however, this judgment might be premature, given that evidence for familiality hinges on knowledge of base rates. Croughan et al. reported that 1% of fathers and 2% of brothers of their probands apparently cross-dressed. Given that we really know nothing about the prevalence of TF, it is difficult to know if these rates are, in fact, elevated.

Although brain mechanisms responsible for sexual arousal have not been definitively identified, there is a general consensus that limbic and temporal lobe structures are important for both sexual interest or arousal and for inhibition of sexual behaviors (Blumer & Walker, 1975). Generally, temporal lobe epilepsy (TLE) produces a state of hyposexuality. However, case reports of hypersexuality, and of fetishistic and transvestic behaviors associated with TLE, led Epstein (1973) to hypothesize that some forms of fetishism arise as a result of inhibition or release of limbic regions with seizure activity (see also Kolarsky et al., 1967). Other reports have linked TF and other types of fetishism with head injury (e.g., Miller, Cummings, McIntyre, Ebers, & Grode, 1986; Pandita-Gunawardena, 1990). This theory is supported by the fact that, in several cited cases, transvestic and fetishistic impulses were reduced or eliminated by either surgical removal of the irritating focus or medication to control the seizures (Walinder, 1965). The idea that abnormalities in limbic structures may facilitate transvestic behavior is illustrated by a case report in which such behavior, previously extinguished by behavioral treatment, returned with the development of a seizure-provoking mass and then diminished with treatment of the seizures (Ball, 1968; see also Hoenig, 1985).

In our clinic, referral for neurological assessment to rule out a temporal lobe focus revealed only one significant abnormality by history and EEG testing (total N = 79). However, three other adolescents had a documented history of epilepsy or EEG abnormality prior to the onset of TF, and a fourth had Tourette's syndrome. In one of the adolescents with an established seizure disorder, the frequency of transvestic behaviors escalated and a diaper fetish also began as seizure control diminished. Several other youngsters had had severe head injuries as toddlers, and several had been exposed to very severe environmental deprivation, both of which are suggestive of cerebral insult. Last, it is of interest that Bowler and Collacott (1993) have reported verbal learning disabilities in cross-dressing men, which dovetails nicely with our own finding that adolescent males with TF showed deficits in verbal IQ compared to performance IQ (Zucker & Bradley, 1995).

Psychosocial Research

There is very little methodologically adequate psychosocial research on the origin of TF. Much of the available work is primarily retrospective in nature and subject to many problems (e.g., demand characteristics, absence of validity checks). It appears that much of the research has been guided by general theoretical notions about the psychosocial determinants of ordinary heterosexuality and homosexuality. Unfortunately, these ideas are confusing, since TF has been more closely linked with homosexual development (or to the development of those transsexuals with a homosexual sexual orientation) than to heterosexual development, which we believe is inaccurate.

Some clinicians have suggested that the origin of TF results from forced cross-dressing during childhood, particularly by mothers or other female figures, as a form of punishment or humiliation—the so-called "petticoat punishment" (Stoller, 1968b). Stoller's explanation of why the transvestism persists is that "the passively endured experience of being a living puppet . . . was transformed into an active experience colored by sexual excitement. Now what had been traumatic was mastered, becoming his greatest pleasure. In this way the victim has his own sort of triumph" (p. 182).

Other clinicians have not shared this view, claiming that forced cross-dressing is rare. For example, Person and Ovesey (1978) stated that "Most often it is the child himself who initiates the cross-dressing. In the predominant pattern, the child spontaneously cross-dresses, the activity most often remains surreptitious, and it is not reinforced by the mother or a mother-surrogate" (p. 306). Person and Ovesey's view is similar to views advanced by various behaviorists, who often see the origin of TF as resulting from accidental exposure to women's clothing (e.g., Strzyzewsky & Zierhoffer, 1967). In our experience with TF in adolescents, we have never encountered a case where forced cross-dressing was reported, either by the patient himself or by the parents.

Even if the cross-dressing is not externally induced or reinforced, there are other ways to conceptualize the role of reinforcement processes. As noted earlier, cross-dressing is often reported to be soothing when it first occurs, and, when it is accompanied by sexual excitement, masturbation, and orgasm, there is an added reinforcing property (see, e.g., Crawford, Holloway, & Domjan, 1993; Laws

& Marshall, 1991). Thus, cross-dressing may be self-perpetuating because of the pleasure associated with it. Of course, the notion of some type of reinforcing property was the basis for the early efforts to treat TF by behavior therapy techniques, such as aversive conditioning (Bancroft, 1974).

In some of the formulations of TF by psychoanalytic theorists, cross-dressing has been viewed as a way of handling various forms of anxiety—separation anxiety, castration anxiety, and so on. In these accounts, cross-dressing can be viewed as a source of reinforcement because it reduces anxiety (Person & Ovesey, 1974a, 1974b, 1978). To date, this explanation has been based exclusively on inferences from clinical data, not on controlled empirical studies. Theorists such as Person and Ovesey (1974b, 1978) have argued that the personality organization of men with TF is largely preoedipal, which also explains why there is a concomitantly high rate of Axis II personality disorders. An aspect of their account that remains unexplained is why most men with preoedipal personality pathology do not manifest TF. In other words, there is a lack of specificity to the model—something else besides preoedipal pathology is needed to explain the development of TF in its own right.

The role of parents in the development of TF has been studied exclusively by retrospective self-report, never by a systematic study of the parents themselves. Various hypotheses have been proposed, and, at times, they have been contradictory. In one study, Newcomb (1985) found that men with TF were more likely than ordinary heterosexual men to characterize their parents as "less sex-typed or more sex-reversed in terms of dependence and affiliation" (p. 160), which was judged as support for a "pattern of parent sex-role reversal" (p. 160). In contrast, Newcomb found no differences in parental attributes when homosexual men were compared with heterosexual men. To some extent, these results are surprising, since it is homosexual men, not TF men, who are feminine during childhood. Thus, if parental sex-typed characteristics are in some way causally related to the child's sex-typed characteristics, one would expect to find atypical personality constellations in the parents of homosexual men, not in the parents of men with TF.

Another line of exploration has examined the quality of the parent-child relationship in TF, in which variables such as closeness and hedonic tone have been rated (Buhrich & McConaghy, 1978). Schott (1995), for example, found that men with TF recalled better relationships with their mothers than with their fathers, but so did a control sample (which, incidentally, was very poorly matched to the probands).

If one examines carefully the writings of certain psychoanalytic authors, who have been most interested in parental influences, it becomes apparent that the central maternal influence in TF has been judged to be hostility and anger toward males. This contrasts rather sharply with the observations made by psychoanalysts regarding maternal influences on homosexuality, such as smothering overcloseness and intrusiveness, which have also been implicated in an even more extreme manner with regard to transsexualism of the homosexual type (Stoller, 1968b).

In our clinical experience with TF in adolescents, the presence of severe mother-son conflict, characterized by anger, hostility, and rejection, has been common. These clinical observations were complemented by the objective finding that many of these youngsters had had, at some point prior to the onset of the TF, a long-term or permanent separation from their mothers (Zucker & Bradley, 1995). Of 79 adolescents, 36 were not living with their biological mothers at the time of assessment; another four adolescents had experienced a separation from their mothers but were living with them again at the time of the assessment. Thus, the rate of maternal separation was 50.6%, which was considerably higher than the rates of maternal separation among our comparison samples of gender-dysphoric and homosexual adolescents.

The clinical evidence of maternal-son distance and the co-occurring hostility have been used to explain the function of the transvestism, which is to maintain some kind of representational connection, in part analogous to other, more ordinary types of transitional objects, such as security blankets (Sullivan,

Bradley, & Zucker, 1995). However, other behaviors that at times accompany the cross-dressing, such as defecation in the mother's underwear or shredding it, point to the associated feelings of anger and unresolved conflict.

Assessment

Biomedical Tests

There are no known biological markers that identify children or adolescents with TF. As noted earlier, it may be important to conduct a pediatric neurological evaluation to rule out temporal lobe epilepsy or other abnormalities, especially in cases where there is evidence of cognitive impairment or a history of head injury.

Psychological Tests

In the literature on adults, self-report questionnaires on TF are available (Blanchard, 1985b), but it is unlikely that such information will add much beyond what can be gleaned from a detailed clinical interview that covers the core phenomenology. Phallometric assessment, which infers a subject's preference for various sexual stimuli (e.g., homosexual vs. heterosexual) on the basis of differential psychophysiological responsiveness (see, e.g., Freund, 1977; Quinsey & Lalumiere, 1996), can be used to assess TF (Blanchard, Racansky, & Steiner, 1986), but the use of this method may be quite stressful for some adolescents. The most problematic assessment issue with these adolescents is denial of the transvestitic behavior, despite overwhelming evidence to the contrary. This defensiveness will ultimately need to be considered in developing a therapeutic plan for intervention.

Treatment

There are virtually no therapeutic guidelines in the literature regarding the treatment of adolescents with TF. One can, however, peruse the adult literature that describes the treatment of transvestism with forms of behavior

therapy (e.g., Gelder & Marks, 1969; Langevin, 1983, pp. 211–232) and psychotherapy (e.g., Glasser, 1979; Greenacre, 1979). As with GID during adolescence, the prognosis for therapeutic change should be considered guarded. In our own clinic, it has been our impression so far that not only is the transvestism itself extremely complex to treat but that the associated psychopathology and family dysfunction are often so great that multiple forms of intervention targeted to multiple forms of impairment are required. Unfortunately, there is very little information on the long-term outcome of this disorder when it is diagnosed and treated during adolescence.

In our own clinic, several forms of therapeutic intervention have been considered. From a sheer informational point of view, we have found it useful to explain to parents and the adolescent what transvestism "is." Many parents, particularly the mothers, believe that the behavior signifies their son is homosexual or, less commonly, a "pervert" who is prone to sexual aggression. Many parents do not have a "label" for their child's behavior, so explaining the term "transvestism" can be helpful.

One therapeutic strategy that we recommend is to see whether the adolescent is able to develop alternative strategies of sexual arousal (e.g., masturbating to imagery without the wearing or thought of female clothing). To some extent, this approach is guided by fundamental assumptions about associative conditioning and operant behavior. A second therapeutic strategy is to identify the factors within the adolescent and the family that activate the need to self-soothe. Often times, it has been our impression that the stressor is related to mother-son conflict that has evolved over an extended period of time (Zucker & Bradley, 1995). This approach is based on the assumption that the cross-dressing serves some representational function pertaining to the adolescent's relationship with his mother, in which issues pertaining to closeness, hostility, and the need for comfort are fused.

Last, there has been some consideration of psychopharmacological treatment of TF. For example, if the patient shows a documented neurological condition (e.g., temporal-lobe epilepsy), then medications such as carbamezapine might be tried. The clinical observation of the anxiety-reducing function of cross-dressing has led to some preliminary study of the effects of buspirone (Federoff, 1988, 1992). Last, conceptualization of transvestism as a compulsive disorder has led to one controlled trial comparing clomipramine with desipramine, which yielded mixed evidence of the effectiveness of both medications (Kruesi, Fine, Valladares, Phillips, & Rapoport, 1992).

REFERENCES

Achenbach, T. M., & Edelbrock, C. S. (1981). Behavioral problems and competencies reported by parents of normal and disturbed children aged four through sixteen. *Monographs of the Society for Research in Child Development*, 46 (1, Serial No. 188).

Achenbach, T. M., Howell, C. T., Quay, H. C., & Conners, C. K. (1991). National survey of problems and competencies among four- to sixteen-year-olds. *Monographs of the Society for Research in Child Development*, 56 (3, Serial No. 225).

American Psychiatric Association. (1980). *Diagnostic and statistical manual of mental disorders* (3rd ed.). Washington, DC: Author.

American Psychiatric Association. (1987). *Diagnostic and statistical manual of mental disorders* (3rd ed., rev.). Washington, DC: Author.

American Psychiatric Association. (1994). *Diagnostic and statistical manual of mental disorders* (4th ed.). Washington, DC: Author.

Antill, J. K. (1987). Parents' beliefs and values about sex roles, sex differences, and sexuality: Their sources and implications. In P. Shaver & C. Hendrick (Eds.), *Sex and gender* (pp. 294–328). Newbury Park, CA: Sage Publications.

Bailey, J. M., Miller, J. S., & Willerman, L. (1993). Maternally rated childhood gender nonconformity in homosexuals and heterosexuals. *Archives of Sexual Behavior*, 22, 461–470.

Bailey, J. M., Nothnagel, J., & Wolfe, M. (1995). Retrospectively measured individual differences in childhood sex-typed behavior among gay men: Correspondence between self- and maternal reports. *Archives of Sexual Behavior*, 24, 613–622.

*Bailey, J. M., & Zucker, K. J. (1995). Childhood sex-typed behavior and sexual orientation: A con-

ceptual analysis and quantitative review. *Developmental Psychology*, 31, 43–55.

Bakker, A., van Kesteren, P. J. M., Gooren, L. J. G., & Bezemer, P. D. (1993). The prevalence of transsexualism in the Netherlands. *Acta Psychiatrica Scandinavica*, 87, 237–238.

Ball, J. R. B. (1968). A case of hair fetishism, transvestitism, and organic cerebral disorder. *Acta Psychiatrica Scandinavica*, 44, 249–254.

Bancroft, J. (1974). *Deviant sexual behavior: Modification and assessment*. Oxford: Oxford University Press.

Bates, J. E., & Bentler, P. M. (1973). Play activities of normal and effeminate boys. *Developmental Psychology*, 9, 20–27.

Bates, J. E., Bentler, P. M., & Thompson, S. K. (1973). Measurement of deviant gender development in boys. *Child Development*, 44, 591–598.

Bates, J. E., Bentler, P. M., & Thompson, S. K. (1979). Gender-deviant boys compared with normal and clinical control boys. *Journal of Abnormal Child Psychology*, 7, 243–259.

Bell, A. P., Weinberg, M. S., & Hammersmith, S. K. (1981). *Sexual preference: Its development in men and women*. Bloomington: Indiana University Press.

Benjamin, H. (1954). Transsexualism and transvestism as psychosomatic somato-psychic syndromes. *American Journal of Psychotherapy*, 8, 219–230.

Bentler, P. M., Rekers, G. A., & Rosen, A. C. (1979). Congruence of childhood sex-role identity and behaviour disturbances. *Child: Care, Health and Development*, 5, 267–283.

Blanchard, R. (1985a). Typology of male-to-female transsexualism. *Archives of Sexual Behavior*, 14, 247–261.

Blanchard, R. (1985b). Research methods for the typological study of gender disorders in males. In B. W. Steiner (Ed.), *Gender dysphoria: Development, research, management* (pp. 227–257). New York: Plenum Press.

Blanchard, R., & Clemmensen, L. H. (1988). A test of the DSM-III-R's implicit assumption that fetishistic arousal and gender dysphoria are mutually exclusive. *Journal of Sex Research*, 25, 426–432.

Blanchard, R., Racansky, I. G., & Steiner, B. W. (1986). Phallometric detection of fetishistic arousal in heterosexual male cross-dressers. *Journal of Sex Research*, 22, 452–462.

Blanchard, R., Zucker, K. J., Bradley, S. J., & Hume, C. S. (1995). Birth order and sibling sex ratio in homosexual male adolescents and probably pre-homosexual feminine boys. *Developmental Psychology*, 31, 22–30.

Blumer, D., & Walker, A. E. (1975). The neural basis of sexual behavior. In D. F. Benson & D. Blumer (Eds.), *Psychiatric aspects of neurologic disease* (pp. 199–217). New York: Grune & Stratton.

Bowler, C., & Collacott, R. A. (1993). Cross-dressing in men with learning disabilities. *British Journal of Psychiatry*, 162, 556–558.

*Bradley, S. J., Blanchard, R., Coates, S., Green, R., Levine, S. B., Meyer-Bahlburg, H. F. L., Pauly, I. B., & Zucker, K. J. (1991). Interim report of the DSM-IV subcommittee for gender identity disorders. *Archives of Sexual Behavior*, 20, 333–343.

Buhrich, N., & McConaghy, N. (1978). Parental relationships during childhood in homosexuality, transvestism and transsexualism. *Australian and New Zealand Journal of Psychiatry*, 12, 103–108.

Bullough, V. L., & Bullough, B. (1993). *Cross-dressing, sex, and gender*. Philadelphia: University of Pennsylvania Press.

Chasseguet-Smirgel, J. (1981). Loss of reality in the perversions—with special reference to fetishism. *Journal of the American Psychoanalytic Association*, 29, 511–534.

Coates, S. (1985). Extreme boyhood femininity: Overview and new research findings. In Z. De-Fries, R. C. Friedman, & R. Corn (Eds.), *Sexuality: New perspectives* (pp. 101–124). Westport, CT: Greenwood Publishing.

*Coates, S. (1990). Ontogenesis of boyhood gender identity disorder. *Journal of the American Academy of Psychoanalysis*, 18, 414–438.

Coates, S., & Person, E. S. (1985). Extreme boyhood femininity: Isolated behavior or pervasive disorder? *Journal of the American Academy of Child Psychiatry*, 24, 702–709.

*Coates, S., & Wolfe, S. (1995). Gender identity disorder in boys: The interface of constitution and early experience. *Psychoanalytic Inquiry*, 15, 6–38.

Cohen, J. (1988). *Statistical power analysis for the social sciences* (2nd ed.). Hillsdale, NJ: Lawrence Erlbaum.

*Collaer, M. L., & Hines, M. (1995). Human behavioral sex differences: A role for gonadal hormones during early development? *Psychological Bulletin*, 118, 55–107.

Crawford, L. L., Holloway, K. S., & Domjan, M. (1993). The nature of sexual reinforcement. *Journal of the Experimental Analysis of Behavior*, 60, 55–66.

Croughan, J. L., Saghir, M., Cohen, R., & Robins, E. (1981). A comparison of treated and untreated male cross-dressers. *Archives of Sexual Behavior*, 10, 515–528.

Diamond, M. (1993). Homosexuality and bisexuality in different populations. *Archives of Sexual Behavior*, 22, 291–310.

Elizabeth, P. H., & Green, R. (1984). Childhood sex-role behaviors: Similarities and differences in twins. *Acta Geneticae Medicae et Gemellologiae*, 33, 173–179.

Epstein, A. W. (1973). The relationship of altered brain states to sexual psychopathology. In J. Zubin & J. Money (Eds.), *Contemporary sexual behavior: Critical issues in the 1970s* (pp. 297–310). Baltimore: Johns Hopkins University Press.

Fagot, B. I. (1977). Consequences of moderate cross-gender behavior in preschool children. *Child Development*, 48, 902–907.

Fagot, B. I. (1985). Beyond the reinforcement principle: Another step toward understanding sex role development. *Developmental Psychology*, 21, 1097–1104.

Fay, R. E., Turner, C. F., Klassen, A. D., & Gagnon, J. H. (1989). Prevalence and patterns of same-gender sexual contact among men. *Science*, 243, 338–348.

Fedoroff, J. P. (1988). Buspirone hydrochloride in the treatment of transvestic fetishism. *Journal of Clinical Psychiatry*, 49, 408–409.

Fedoroff, J. P. (1992). Buspirone hydrochloride in the treatment of an atypical paraphilia. *Archives of Sexual Behavior*, 21, 401–406.

Freund, K. (1977). Psychophysiological assessment of change in erotic preference. *Behavior Research and Therapy*, 15, 297–301.

Friedman, R. C. (1988). *Male homosexuality: A contemporary psychoanalytic perspective*. New Haven: Yale University Press.

Gelder, M. G., & Marks, I. M. (1969). Aversion treatment in transvestism and transsexualism. In R. Green & J. Money (Eds.), *Transsexualism and sex reassignment* (pp. 383–413). Baltimore: Johns Hopkins University Press.

Gert, B. (1992). A sex-caused inconsistency in DSM-III-R: The definition of mental disorder and the definition of paraphilias. *Journal of Medicine and Philosophy*, 17, 155–171.

Glasser, M. (1979). Some aspects of the role of aggression in the perversions. In I. Rosen (Ed.),

Sexual deviation (2nd ed., pp. 278–305). New York: Oxford University Press.

*Green, R. (1974). *Sexual identity conflict in children and adults*. New York: Basic Books.

Green, R. (1976). One-hundred ten feminine and masculine boys: Behavioral contrasts and demographic similarities. *Archives of Sexual Behavior, 5*, 425–446.

*Green, R. (1987). *The "sissy boy syndrome" and the development of homosexuality*. New Haven: Yale University Press.

Green, R., & Fuller, M. (1973). Family doll play and female identity in preadolescent males. *American Journal of Orthopsychiatry, 43*, 123–127.

Green, R., Fuller, M., & Rutley, B. (1972). It-Scale for Children and Draw-a-Person test: 30 feminine vs. 25 masculine boys. *Journal of Personality Assessment, 36*, 349–352.

Green, R., Fuller, M., Rutley, B., & Hendler, J. (1972). Playroom toy preferences of fifteen masculine and fifteen feminine boys. *Behavior Research and Therapy, 3*, 425–429.

Green, R., Newman, L. E., & Stoller, R. J. (1972). Treatment of boyhood "transsexualism." An interim report of four years' experience. *Archives of General Psychiatry, 26*, 213–217.

Green, R., Williams, K., & Goodman, M. (1982). Ninety-nine "tomboys" and "non-tomboys": Behavioral contrasts and demographic similarities. *Archives of Sexual Behavior, 11*, 247–266.

Green, R., Williams, K., & Harper, J. (1980). Cross-sex identity: Peer group integration and the double standard of childhood sex-typing. In J. Samson (Ed.), *Childhood and sexuality* (pp. 542–548). Montreal: Editions Etudes Vivantes.

Greenacre, P. (1979). Fetishism. In I. Rosen (Ed.), *Sexual deviation* (2nd ed., pp. 79–108). New York: Oxford University Press.

Hoenig, J. (1985). Etiology of transsexualism. In B. W. Steiner (Ed.), *Gender dysphoria: Development, research, management* (pp. 33–73). New York: Plenum Press.

Hooker, E. (1957). The adjustment of the male overt homosexual. *Journal of Projective Techniques, 21*, 17–31.

Jolles, I. (1952). A study of validity of some hypotheses for the qualitative interpretation of the H-T-P for children of elementary school age; I. Sexual identification. *Journal of Clinical Psychology, 8*, 113–118.

Kohlberg, L. (1966). A cognitive-developmental analysis of children's sex-role concepts and attitudes. In E. E. Maccoby (Ed.), *The development*

of sex differences (pp. 82–173). Stanford, CA: Stanford University Press.

Kolarsky, A., Freund, K., Machek, J., & Polak, O. (1967). Male sexual deviation: Association with early temporal lobe damage. *Archives of General Psychiatry, 17*, 735–743.

Kruesi, M. J. P., Fine, S., Valladares, L., Phillips, R. A., & Rapoport, J. L. (1992). Paraphilias: A double-blind crossover comparison of clomiprimine versus desipramine. *Archives of Sexual Behavior, 21*, 587–593.

Langevin, R. (1983). *Sexual strands: Understanding and treating sexual anomalies in men*. Hillsdale, NJ: Lawrence Erlbaum.

Langlois, J. H., & Downs, A. C. (1980). Mothers, fathers, and peers as socialization agents of sex-typed play behaviors in young children. *Child Development, 51*, 1237–1247.

Laumann, E. O., Gagnon, J. H., Michael, R. T., & Michaels, S. (1994). *The social organization of sexuality: Sexual practices in the United States*. Chicago: University of Chicago Press.

Laws, D. R., & Marshall, W. L. (1991). Masturbatory reconditioning with sexual deviates: An evaluative review. *Advances in Behavior Research and Therapy, 13*, 13–25.

Lothstein, L. M. (1983). *Female-to-male transsexualism: Historical, clinical, and theoretical issues*. Boston: Routledge & Kegan Paul.

Marantz, S., & Coates, S. (1991). Mothers of boys with gender identity disorder: A comparison of matched controls. *Journal of the American Academy of Child and Adolescent Psychiatry, 30*, 310–315.

Martin, C. L. (1990). Attitudes and expectations about children with nontraditional and traditional gender roles. *Sex Roles, 22*, 151–165.

McCauley, E., & Ehrhardt, A. A. (1984). Follow-up of females with gender identity disorders. *Journal of Nervous and Mental Disease, 172*, 353–358.

McCreary, D. R. (1994). The male role and avoiding femininity. *Sex Roles, 31*, 517–531.

Meyer-Bahlburg, H. F. L. (1985). Gender identity disorder of childhood: Introduction. *Journal of the American Academy of Child Psychiatry, 24*, 681–683.

Meyer-Bahlburg, H. F. L. (1994). Intersexuality and the diagnosis of gender identity disorder. *Archives of Sexual Behavior, 23*, 21–40.

Meyer-Bahlburg, H. F. L., Feldman, J. F., & Ehrhardt, A. A. (1985). Questionnaires for the assessment of atypical gender role behavior: A methodological study. *Journal of the American Academy of Child Psychiatry, 24,* 695–701.

Meyer-Bahlburg, H. F. L., Sandberg, D. E., Yager, T. J., Dolezal, C. L., & Ehrhardt, A. A. (1994). Questionnaire scales for the assessment of atypical gender development in girls and boys. *Journal of Psychology & Human Sexuality, 6*(4), 19–39.

Miller, B. L., Cummings, J. L., McIntyre, H., Ebers, G., & Grode, M. (1986). Hypersexuality or altered sexual preference following brain injury. *Journal of Neurology, Neurosurgery, and Psychiatry, 49,* 867–873.

Mitchell, J. N. (1991). *Maternal influences on gender identity disorder in boys: Searching for specificity.* Unpublished doctoral dissertation, York University, Downsview, Ontario.

Money, J. (1995). *Gendermaps: Social constructionism, feminism, and sexosophical history.* New York: Continuum.

Newcomb, M. D. (1985). The role of perceived relative parental personality in the development of heterosexuals, homosexuals, and transvestites. *Archives of Sexual Behavior, 14,* 147–164.

*Newman, L. E. (1976). Treatment for the parents of feminine boys. *American Journal of Psychiatry, 133,* 683–687.

Pandita-Gunawardena, R. (1990). Paraphilic infantilism: A rare case of fetishistic behaviour. *British Journal of Psychiatry, 157,* 767–770.

Pauly, I. B. (1992). Terminology and classification of gender identity disorders. *Journal of Psychology & Human Sexuality, 5,* 1–14.

Perez-Palacios, G., Chavez, B., Mendez, J. P., Imperato-McGinley, J., & Ulloa-Aguirre, A. (1987). The syndromes of androgen resistance revisited. *Journal of Steroid Biochemistry, 27,* 1101–1108.

Person, E., & Ovesey, L. (1974a). The transsexual syndrome in males. I: Primary transsexualism. *American Journal of Psychotherapy, 28,* 4–20.

Person, E., & Ovesey, L. (1974b). The transsexual syndrome in males. II. Secondary transsexualism. *American Journal of Psychotherapy, 28,* 174–193.

Person, E., & Ovesey, L. (1978). Transvestism: New perspectives. *Journal of the American Academy of Psychoanalysis, 6,* 301–323.

Person, E. S., & Ovesey, L. (1984). Homosexual cross-dressers. *Journal of the American Academy of Psychoanalysis, 12,* 167–186.

Quinsey, V. L., & Lalumiere, M. L. (1996). *Assessment of sexual offenders against children.* Thousand Oaks, CA: Sage Publications.

Rekers, G. A. (1977). Assessment and treatment of childhood gender problems. In B. B. Lahey &

A. E. Kazdin (Eds.), *Advances in clinical child psychology* (Vol. 1, pp. 267–306). New York: Plenum Press.

*Rekers, G. A. (1985). Gender identity problems. In P. A. Bornstein & A. E. Kazdin (Eds.), *Handbook of clinical behavior therapy with children* (pp. 658–699). Homewood, IL: Dorsey.

Rekers, G. A., Kilgus, M., & Rosen, A. C. (1990). Long-term effects of treatment for gender identity disorder of childhood. *Journal of Psychology & Human Sexuality, 3,* 121–153.

Rekers, G. A., Rosen, A. C., & Morey, S. M. (1990). Projective test findings for boys with gender disturbance: Draw-a-Person test, IT scale, and Make-a-Picture Story test. *Perceptual and Motor Skills, 71,* 771–779.

Rekers, G. A., & Yates, C. E. (1976). Sex-typed play in feminoid boys vs. normal boys and girls. *Journal of Abnormal Child Psychology, 4,* 1–8.

Roberts, C. W., Green, R., Williams, K., & Goodman, M. (1987). Boyhood gender identity development: A statistical contrast of two family groups. *Developmental Psychology, 23,* 544–557.

Rogers, S. M., & Turner, C. F. (1991). Male-male sexual contact in the U.S.A.: Findings from five sample surveys, 1970–1990. *Journal of Sex Research, 28,* 491–519.

Rosen, A. C., Rekers, G. A., & Friar, L. R. (1977). Theoretical and diagnostic issues in child gender disturbances. *Journal of Sex Research, 13,* 89–103.

Sandberg, D. E., & Meyer-Bahlburg, H. F. L. (1994). Variability in middle childhood play behavior: Effects of gender, age, and family background. *Archives of Sexual Behavior, 23,* 645–663.

Sandberg, D. E., Meyer-Bahlburg, H. F. L., Ehrhardt, A. A., & Yager, T. J. (1993). The prevalence of gender-atypical behavior in elementary school children. *Journal of the American Academy of Child and Adolescent Psychiatry, 32,* 306–314.

Schott, R. L. (1995). The childhood and family dynamics of transvestites. *Archives of Sexual Behavior, 24,* 309–327.

Schultz, N. M. (1979). *Severe gender identity confusion in an eight-year-old boy.* Unpublished doctoral dissertation, Yeshiva University, New York, NY.

Skilbeck, W. M., Bates, J. E., & Bentler, P. M. (1975). Human figure drawings of gender-problem and school-problem boys. *Journal of Abnormal Child Psychology, 3,* 191–199.

Spira, A., Bajos, N., and the ACSF Group. (1994). *Sexual behaviour and AIDS.* Ashgate, England: Aldershot.

Stoller, R. J. (1964). The hermaphroditic identity of hermaphrodites. *Journal of Nervous and Mental Disease, 139*, 453–457.

Stoller, R. J. (1968a). Male childhood transsexualism. *Journal of the American Academy of Child Psychiatry, 7*, 193–209.

Stoller, R. J. (1968b). *Sex and gender (Vol. I). The development of masculinity and femininity.* New York: Jason Aronson.

Stoller, R. J. (1971). The term "transvestism." *Archives of General Psychiatry, 24*, 230–237.

Stoller, R. J. (1978). Boyhood gender aberrations: Treatment issues. *Journal of the American Psychoanalytic Association, 26*, 541–558.

Stoller, R. J. (1982). Transvestism in women. *Archives of Sexual Behavior, 11*, 99–115.

Strzyzewsky, J., & Zierhoffer, M. (1967). Aversion therapy in a case of fetishism with transvestistic component. *Journal of Sex Research, 3*, 163–167.

Sullivan, C. B. L., Bradley, S. J., & Zucker, K. J. (1995). Gender identity disorder (transsexualism) and transvestic fetishism. In V. B. Van Hasselt & M. Hersen (Eds.), *Handbook of adolescent psychopathology: A guide to diagnosis and treatment* (pp. 525–558). New York: Lexington Books.

Voeller, B. (1990). Some uses and abuses of the Kinsey scale. In D. P. McWhirter, S. A. Sanders, & J. M. Reinisch (Eds.), *Homosexuality/heterosexuality: Concepts of sexual orientation* (pp. 32–38). New York: Oxford University Press.

Walinder, J. (1965). Transvestism: Definition and evidence in favor of occasional derivation from cerebral dysfunction. *International Journal of Neuropsychiatry, 1*, 567–573.

Weinrich, J. D. (1985). Transsexuals, homosexuals, and sissy boys: On the mathematics of follow-up studies. *Journal of Sex Research, 21*, 322–328.

Weisz, J. R., & Weiss, B. (1991). Studying the "referability" of child clinical problems. *Journal of Consulting and Clinical Psychology, 59*, 266–273.

Wellings, K., Field, J., Johnson, A. M., & Wadsworth, J. (1994). *Sexual behaviour in Britain: The National Survey of Sexual Attitudes and Lifestyles.* London: Penguin Books.

Wolfe, S. M. (1990). *Psychopathology and psychodynamics of parents of boys with a gender identity disorder of childhood.* Unpublished doctoral dissertation, The City University of New York, New York.

World Health Organization. (1992). *International statistical classification of diseases and related health problems* (10th rev.). Geneva: Author.

Zucker, K. J. (1985). Cross-gender-identified children. In B. W. Steiner (Ed.), *Gender dysphoria: Development, research, management* (pp. 75–174). New York: Plenum Press.

Zucker, K. J. (1990). Treatment of gender identity disorders in children. In R. Blanchard & B. W. Steiner (Eds.), *Clinical management of gender identity disorders in children and adults* (pp. 25–47). Washington, DC: American Psychiatric Press.

Zucker, K. J. (1992). Gender identity disorder. In S. R. Hooper, G. W. Hynd, & R. E. Mattison (Eds.), *Child psychopathology: Diagnostic criteria and clinical assessment* (pp. 305–342). Hillsdale, NJ: Lawrence Erlbaum.

Zucker, K. J. (1996, March). *Pathological mourning in mothers of boys with gender identity disorder: Clinical evidence and some psychocultural hypotheses.* Paper presented at the meeting of the Society for Sex Therapy and Research, Miami Beach, FL.

Zucker, K. J., & Blanchard, R. (1997). Transvestic fetishism: Psychopathology and theory. In D. R. Laws and W. O'Donohue (Eds.), *Sexual deviance: Theory, assessment, and treatment* (pp. 253–279). New York: Guilford Press.

*Zucker, K. J., & Bradley, S. J. (1995). *Gender identity disorder and psychosexual problems in children and adolescents.* New York: Guilford Press.

Zucker, K. J., Bradley, S. J., Doering, R. W., & Lozinski, J. A. (1985). Sex-typed behavior in cross-gender-identified children: Stability and change at a one-year follow-up. *Journal of the American Academy of Child Psychiatry, 24*, 710–719.

Zucker, K. J., Bradley, S. J., Kuksis, M., Pecore, K., Birkenfeld-Adams, A., Doering, R. W., Mitchell, J. N., & Wild, J. (1996). *Gender constancy judgments in children with gender identity disorder: Evidence for a developmental lag.* Manuscript submitted for publication.

Zucker, K. J., Bradley, S. J., Lowry Sullivan, C. B., Kuksis, M., Birkenfeld-Adams, A., & Mitchell, J. N. (1993). A gender identity interview for children. *Journal of Personality Assessment, 61*, 443–456.

Zucker, K. J., Bradley, S. J., & Sanikhani, M. (1997). Sex differences in referral rates of children with gender identity disorder: Some hypotheses. *Journal of Abnormal Child Psychology, 25*, 217–227.

Zucker, K. J., Bradley, S. J., & Sullivan, C. B. L. (1996). Traits of separation anxiety in boys with gender identity disorder. *Journal of the American Academy of Child and Adolescent Psychiatry, 35*, 791–798.

Zucker, K. J., Doering, R. W., Bradley, S. J., & Finegan, J. K. (1982). Sex-typed play in gender-disturbed children: A comparison to sibling and psychiatric controls. *Archives of Sexual Behavior, 11*, 309–321.

Zucker, K. J., Finegan, J. K., Doering, R. W., & Bradley, S. J. (1983). Human figure drawings of gender-problem children: A comparison to sibling, psychiatric, and normal controls. *Journal of Abnormal Child Psychology, 11*, 287–298.

Zucker, K. J., Finegan, J. K., Doering, R. W., & Bradley, S. J. (1984). Two subgroups of gender-problem children. *Archives of Sexual Behavior, 13*, 27–39.

Zucker, K. J., & Green, R. (1989). Gender identity disorder of childhood. In T. B. Karasu (Ed.), *Treatments of psychiatric disorders* (Vol. 1, pp. 661–670). Washington, DC: American Psychiatric Association.

Zucker, K. J., & Green, R. (1992). Psychosexual disorders in children and adolescents. *Journal of Child Psychology and Psychiatry, 33*, 107–151.

Zucker, K. J., Green, R., Bradley, S. J., Williams, K., Rebach, H. M., & Hood, J. E. (1998). Gender identity disorder of childhood: Diagnostic issues. In T. A. Widiger, A. J. Frances, H. A. Pincus, R. Ross, M. B. First, W. Davis, & M. Kline, (Eds.), *DSM-IV sourcebook* (Vol. 4, pp. 503–512). Washington, DC: American Psychiatric Association.

Zucker, K. J., Green, R., Coates, S., Zuger, B., Cohen-Kettenis, P. T., Zecca, G. M., Lertora, V., Money, J., Hahn-Burke, S., Bradley, S. J., & Blanchard, R. (1997). Sibling sex ratio of boys with gender identity disorder. *Journal of Child Psychology and Psychiatry, 38*, 543–551.

Zucker, K. J., Green, R., Garofano, C., Bradley, S. J., Williams, K., Rebach, H. M., & Lowry Sullivan, C. B. (1994). Prenatal gender preference of mothers of feminine and masculine boys: Relation to sibling sex composition and birth order. *Journal of Abnormal Child Psychology, 22*, 1–13.

Zucker, K. J., Lozinski, J. A., Bradley, S. J., & Doering, R. W. (1992). Sex-typed responses in the Rorschach protocols of children with gender identity disorder. *Journal of Personality Assessment, 58*, 295–310.

Zucker, K. J., Wilson-Smith, D. N., Kurita, J. A., & Stern, A. (1995). Children's appraisals of sex-typed behavior in their peers. *Sex Roles, 33*, 703–725.

Zuger, B. (1984). Early effeminate behavior in boys: Outcome and significance for homosexuality. *Journal of Nervous and Mental Disease, 172*, 90–97.

*Indicates readings that the authors recommend for further reading.

19
Eating Disorders

Stacey Steinberg Nye
Craig L. Johnson

The past 20 years of evolving study and treatment of eating disorders have opened up many important pathways for sufferers. Most major medical schools and hospitals now have eating disorder clinics, and more practitioners are devoting their careers to the study and treatment of the problem. More recently, the threat of managed care has placed greater burdens on clinicians to treat more disturbed patients in less time. Clearly, further understanding of eating disorders is necessary to accomplish this daunting task.

HISTORY

Anorexia Nervosa

Anorexia nervosa emerged as a distinctive syndrom during the nineteenth century when Sir William Gull (1874) coined the term and provided case descriptions with a significant psychological component. Following these early reports, the most influential and lasting contribution to the modern conceptualization of anorexia nervosa emerged in the writing of Hilde Bruch (1973). She postulated that the falsification of early developmental learning experiences resulted in inaccurate perception and cognitive labeling of visceral and affective states, faulty perception of body boundaires and a deeply rooted sense of ineffectiveness and lack of autonomy, all of which are primary to the development of the syndrome.

Bulimia Nervosa

Although clinical descriptions of bulimia date back to the late 1800s, it was not until the 1940s that more detailed accounts of bulimic behavior began to emerge in the literature. In these early reports, however, the symptomatic behavior was always referred to as a symptom of anorexia nervosa. Bulimia among individuals who did not have histories of anorexia nervosa or obesity was first observed in 1976 by Boskind-Lodahl, who coined the term "bulimarexia" to describe the disorder. Shortly thereafter descriptive labels such as bulimia nervosa (Russell, 1979), dietary chaos syndrome (Palmer, 1979), and abnormal weight control syndrome (Crisp, 1981) emerged in the literature. Bulimia emerged as a distinct diagnostic entity with publication of the third edition of the *Diagnostic and Statistical Manual of Mental Disorders*

(DSM-III; American Psychiatric Association, 1980). The suggestion in DSM-III was that episodic binge eating was not only an isolated symptom but an essential component of a specific syndrome of disordered eating.

DIAGNOSTIC DESCRIPTION

Anorexia Nervosa

Anorexia nervosa is characterized by a refusal to maintain a minimally normal body weight, intense fear of gaining weight, disturbance in the perception of the shape or size of one's body, and amenorrhea in postmenarchal females. DSM-IV (APA, 1994) now specifies two types: "restricting type" describes those who don't engage in binge eating or purging behavior, and "binge eating/purging type" describes those who regularly engage in binge eating or purging behavior. The diagnostic criteria appear as follows:

Diagnostic criteria for 307.1 Anorexia Nervosa

A. Refusal to maintain body weight at or above a minimally normal weight for age and height (e.g., weight loss leading to maintenance of body weight less than 85% of that expected; or failure to make expected weight gain during period of growth, leading to body weight less than 85% of that expected).

B. Intense fear of gaining weight or becoming fat, even though underweight.

C. Disturbance in the way in which one's body weight or shape is experienced, undue influence of body weight or shape on self-evaluation, or denial of the seriousness of the current low body weight.

D. In postmenarchal females, amenorrhea, i.e., the absence of at least three consecutive menstrual cycles. (A woman is considered to have amenorrhea if her periods occur only following hormone, e.g., estrogen, administration.)

Specify type:
Restricting Type: during the current episode of Anorexia Nervosa, the person has not regularly engaged on binge-eating or purging behavior (i.e.,

self-induced vomiting or the misuse of laxatives, diuretics, or enemas.)

Binge Eating/Purging Type: during the current episode of Anorexia Nervosa, the person has regularly engaged in binge-eating or purging behavior (i.e., self-induced vomiting or the misuse of laxatives, diuretics, or enemas) (APA, 1994, pp. 535–536).

Bulimia Nervosa

Bulimia nervosa is characterized by binge eating and inappropriate compensatory methods to prevent weight gain. These episodes occur at least twice a week for a period of 3 months. In addition, self-evaluation is predominantly influenced by body shape and weight. DSM-IV now specifies two types: "purging type" describes those who regularly engage in purging behaviors such as self-induced vomiting or laxatives, and "nonpurging type" describes those who use other inappropriate compensatory behaviors, such as fasting or excessive exercise. The diagnostic criteria appear as follows:

Diagnostic Criteria for 307.51 Bulimia Nervosa

A. Recurrent episodes of binge eating. An episode of binge eating is characterized by both of the following:
1. eating, in a discrete period of time (e.g., within any 2-hour period), an amount of food that is definitely larger than most people would eat during a similar period of time and under similar circumstances.
2. a sense of lack of control over eating during the episode (e.g., a feeling that one cannot stop eating or control what or how much one is eating)

B. Recurrent inappropriate compensatory behavior in order to prevent weight gain, such as self-induced vomiting; misuse of laxatives, diuretics, enemas, or other medications; fasting; or excessive exercise.

C. The binge eating and inappropriate compensatory behaviors both occur, on average, at least twice a week for 3 months.

D. Self-evaluation is unduly influenced by body shape and weight.

E. The disturbance does not occur exclusively during episodes of Anorexia Nervosa.

Specify type:

Purging Type: during the current episode of Bulimia Nervosa, the person has regularly engaged in self-induced vomiting or the misuse of laxatives, diuretic, or enemas

Nonpurging Type: during the current episode of Bulimia Nervosa, the person has used other inappropriate compensatory behaviors, such as fasting or excessive exercise, but has not regularly engaged in self-induced vomiting or the misuse of laxatives, diuretics, or enemas. (APA, 1994, pp. 540–541)

Eating Disorder Not Otherwise Specified

"Eating disorder NOS" is the diagnostic category used for eating disorders that do not meet criteria for any specific eating disorder, such as bingeing and vomiting less than twice a week, having symptoms of anorexia nervosa without amenorrhea, or exhibiting a binge-eating disorder (recurrent episodes of binge eating in the absence of purging behaviors).

The diagnostic criteria for eating disorders from the ICD-9 are almost identical. They appear as follows:

307.1 Anorexia Nervosa
    Excludes: eating disturbance NOS (307.50)
      feeding problem (783.3)
        of nonorganic origin (307.59)
      loss of appetite (783.0)
        of nonorganic origin (307.59)

307.5 Other and unspecified disorders of eating
    Excludes: anorexia:
      nervosa (307.1)
      of unspecified cause (783.0)

      overeating, of unspecified cause (783.6)
      vomiting:
      NOS (787.0)
      cyclical (536.2)
        psychogenic (306.4)
    307.50 Eating disorder, unspecified
    306.51 Bulimia
      overeating of nonorganic origin
      (St. Anthony Publishing, 1995, pg. 88)

EPIDEMIOLOGY

Anorexia Nervosa

Anorexia appears to be more prevalent in industrialized societies, such as the United States, Canada, and the countries of Europe, where there is an abundance of food and attractiveness is linked to being thin. Anorexia nervosa rarely begins before puberty, yet the severity of associated mental illness may be greater among prepubertal individuals, and there is a better prognosis associated with the onset in early adolescence (APA, 1994). The mean age of onset is 17 years. The onset is often associated with a stressful life event, such as leaving home for college. The course and outcome are variable. Some individuals recover fully after a single episode, some exhibit a fluctuating pattern of weight gain and relapse, and others experience a chronically deteriorating course of illness with frequent hospitalizations. The long-term mortality is over 10%, resulting from starvation, suicide, or electrolyte imbalance.

Friends or family members who notice dramatic weight loss typically urge individuals with anorexia nervosa into treatment. Those with the illness usually have severe denial about the seriousness of their illness and are extremely resistant to treatment.

Prevalence rates are estimated at 0.5–2.1% (Barbosa-Saldivar & Van Itallie, 1979). There are limited data concerning prevalence among males.

Bulimia Nervosa

Bulimia nervosa also appears to be more prevalent in industrialized societies. Bulimia nervosa usually begins in late adolescence or early adult life. Binge eating frequently begins during or after an episode of dieting. Purging behaviors typically follow as a way to regain a sense of control and rid the body of excess calories. This cycle of disturbed eating may continue for several years before the individual seeks help. There is tremendous secrecy and shame associated with the illness, and the request for help comes when the individual no longer feels in control.

The prevalence of bulimia nervosa among adolescent and young adult females is approximately 1–3%; the rate of occurrence in males is approximately one-tenth of that in females. At least 90% of individuals with bulimia nervosa are female, while males have a higher prevalence of premorbid obesity than do females.

ETIOLOGY

It is difficult to outline what causes anorexia nervosa and bulimia nervosa since both are multidetermined, meaning that there is a combination of factors (biological, familial, sociocultural, and personality-related) that play a role in their development and perpetuation.

Biological Factors

Although there are clear medical side effects associated with anorexia nervosa and bulimia nervosa, such as electrolyte abnormalities, dehydration, edema, menstrual difficulties, cardiovascular problems, and dental decay (Gallo & Randel, 1981; Mitchell & Bantle, 1983), to date there is no consistent endocrine finding of etiological significance. Over the past several years, however, there has been an increasing body of literature suggesting that bulimia may be a variant of a biologically mediated affective disorder. The evidence includes reported symptoms of unipolar and bipolar depression (Glassman & Walsh, 1983; Russell, 1979), family studies (Hudson, Laffer, & Pope, 1982; Hudson, Pope, Jonas, & Yurgelund, 1983), and the effectiveness of antidepressant pharmacotherapy (Pope, Hudson, Jonas, & Yurgelund-Todd, 1983; Walsh, Haidgan, Devlin, Gladis, & Roose, 1991). Although further research is necessary to substantiate the prevalence of affective disorders among eating disorders, it is clear that overall the group experiences significant affective instability that may have predated the onset of eating disorder symptoms.

Family Characteristics

Studies that have investigated the nature of the family environment among eating disordered individuals have found the following: bulimic families tend to be characterized as disengaged, chaotic, and highly conflictual and as having a high degree of life stress (Johnson & Flach, 1985). Anorexic families tend to be characterized as enmeshed, overprotective, and conflict avoidant (Minuchin, Rosman, & Baker, 1978).

Sociocultural Factors

When one turns to the broader sociocultural context during the period of increased incidence, one can see how the group was selectively biased, as well as the specific symptom expression. It appears that two cultural events occurred simultaneously: (1) the onset of the feminist movement, and (2) the emphasis on thinness for women. Garner, Garfinkel, and O'Shaughnessy (1983) reviewed evidence suggesting that shifting cultural norms force contemporary women to face multiple, ambiguous, and often contradictory role expectations. These role expectations include accommodating more traditional feminine expectations such as physical attractiveness and domesticity, incorporating more modern standards for vocational and personal achievement, and taking advantage of increased opportunity for self-definition and autonomy. According to the authors, for those women who are psychologically robust, this provides personal freedom. For those who are more prone to relying on external stimuli to define their sense of self, this may put them at increased risk for affective instability.

Amid this milieu of increasing emphasis on achievement and confusion about how to express the drive to achieve, it appears that the pursuit of thinness has emerged as one way in which young women can compete among themselves and demonstrate self-control. In fact, the absence of weight control, leading to even moderate obesity, leads culturally to social discrimination, isolation, and low self-esteem (Wooley & Wooley, 1979).

Therefore, against the backdrop of confusing cultural expectations and high achievement expectations, it appears that the pursuit of thinness and the avoidance of obesity has emerged as one very concrete activity through which young women can compete and obtain consistently favorable social responses, thus enhancing self-esteem. It is extremely important to note, however, that not all young women exposed to this cultural milieu have developed eating disorders. Therefore, one must attempt to look more closely at the personality characteristics thought to be associated with eating disorders.

Personality Factors

Anorexics consistently have been found to be complaint, approval seeking, self-doubting, conflict avoidant, excessively dependent, perfectionistic, and socially anxious. Bulimics experience significant affective instability, which is manifested in depressed and highly variable mood states, impulsive behavior, low frustration tolerance, and high anxiety. Both have also been described as having difficulty identifying and articulating internal states (Bruch, 1973). Furthermore, in addition to the sociocultural factors that might contribute to women feeling dissatisfied with their bodies, women who experience difficulty modulating their internal states may feel more dissatisfaction, perhaps even rage, at bodies they experience as being defective containers of their affective states.

One can now see that when you take a child who may be at risk for affective instability, put him or her in a family that is volatile and disorganized, with parents who themselves may have difficulty with affect regulation, and add the sociocultural demands for thinness, you have a person at risk for feeling fundamentally out of control in her internal life. Given these circumstances, it is likely that the person will begin to seek some external adaptation in an attempt to gain control of her internal experience. Given the issues related to bodily experience, it seems

obvious that the adaptation will need to be focused in that arena. The pursuit of thinness thus emerges as a viable adaptation to the self-regulatory deficits that have been reviewed.

ASSESSMENT

The assessment process and the initial consultation are essential in getting an understanding of each individual's history and in identifying the unique meaning of the disturbed eating behavior to the individual. Once the specific adaptation has been identified, treatment needs to be tailored to each patient's special requirements.

Questionnaires may be utilized to assess specific eating behaviors and attitudes. Standardized intake forms, such as the Diagnostic survey for Eating Disorders—Revised (DSED-R; Johnson, 1984) and the Eating Disorders Inventory 1 & 2 (EDI 1 & 2; Garner, 1991; Garner, Olmsted, & Polivy, 1983) and the Eating Disorders Inventory—SC (ED-SC; Garner, 1991), provide useful information on symptoms and behavior such as weight history, dieting behavior, binge eating, purging and exercise behavior, and medical and psychiatric history. Both can be used as self-report instruments or guides for a semistructured interview. The EDI 1 & 2, which are scaled instruments, measure eating attitudes and behavior common in anorexia nervosa and bulimia, such as drive for thinness, body dissatisfaction, and perfectionism. Both instruments are useful not only for assessment but at treatment termination and follow-up.

After specifics about the eating disorder and its history are derived, it is important to ascertain associated features and comorbid disorders, such as depression, anxiety disorders, dissociative disorders, substance abuse, and personality disorders. Treatment history and medication trials, as well as suicide attempts and self-mutilative behaviors, are especially important.

Depression is common among patients with eating disorders (Glassman & Walsh, 1983). It is particularly important to ascertain whether depressive symptoms are manifestations of an

Axis I diagnosis of major depressive disorder or dysthymia or are related to the emotional and physiological effects of the eating disorder. Many times depressive symptoms subside after a period of adequate nutrition. If they do not, some patients may benefit from a trial of antidepressant medication (see treatment section). Useful measures for assessing depression include structured interviews such as the Schedule for Affective Disorders and Schizophrenia (SADS; Endicott & Spitzer, 1978) and the Hamilton Rating Scale for Depression (HRSD; Hamilton, 1960, 1967) and self-report scales such as the Beck Depression Inventory (BDI; Beck & Beamesderfer, 1974).

Patients with anorexia nervosa may also show obsessive-compulsive traits (Smart, Beumont, & George, 1976; Solym, Miles, & O'Kane, 1982). Typically the obsessional symptomatology is magnified by the severe starvation state. The Maudsley Obsessional-Compulsive Inventory (MOCI; Hodgson & Rachman, 1977) can be a useful self-report inventory for measuring obsessive-compulsive symptoms.

Susan Sands (1991) suggests that most bulimic patients subjectively experience some form of dissociation, from the trance state the bulimic feels after vomiting to frank multiple-personality disorder. She implies that the extent of the organization of early dissociated needs into a distinct self-state varies, with those who have suffered the most traumatic breaches of empathy having the most distinct self-states. The Dissociative Experiences Scale (DES; Burnstein & Putnam, 1986) can be utilized to understand the frequency and severity of the dissociative episodes.

Substance abuse and other addictive disorders are common among eating disorders (Bulik, 1987). People who lack the internal resources to soothe themselves can remedy their inadequacy by using mood-altering substances such as drugs, alcohol, or food. In addition, the drug or food itself may be used to fill up the individual or to act as a replacement for other people or relationships. Two commonly used self-report instruments for substance abuse are the Michigan Alcoholism Screening Test

(MAST; Selzer, 1971) and the Drug Abuse Screening Test (DAST; Skinner, 1982).

There is also a high frequency of Axis II disorders among eating disorder patients. At least a third to half of all patients seeking treatment for eating disorders also carry a personality disorder diagnosis, most commonly borderline personality disorder (Johnson, Tobin, & Enright, 1989). Borderline patients with eating disorders report more emotional distress, more sexual abuse, more self-mutilation or suicidal gestures, and greater perceived family disturbance than do other eating-disordered groups. The Millon Clinical Multiaxial Inventory (MCMI; Millon, 1982) can serve as a useful screening instrument for personality disorders.

Finally, it is essential to get a sense of the individual's willingness to change. For example, is the person being forced into treatment by family members, or is he or she voluntarily seeking help? How willing or able is the person to stick to a treatment contract, gain weight, or take responsibility for his or her behavior? These questions are crucial not only in determining the level of care but also in understanding the dynamics of the therapeutic relationship and the potential success of the treatment. It is nearly impossible to successfully treat individuals who don't want to get better, need to control their treatment, or need to sabotage achievement.

TREATMENT

Often individuals with anorexia nervosa are starved to such a degree that they are cognitively unavailable for psychotherapy. In such cases, refeeding is an essential first step. Once the individual begins to think more clearly, the therapy can begin to take place. Likewise, those with bulimia nervosa may need to stabilize medically, and behavioral interventions based on interrupting the binge purge cycle are needed. Before starting any kind of outpatient therapy, it is recommended that the patient be seen by a medical doctor to evaluate his or her medical status. Of particular importance are chest x-rays, EKGs, and labwork to measure electrolytes.

It is helpful to frame the illnesses as symptoms of other underlying disorders. Whereas they may have begun as related to a striving for thinness, the symptoms themselves began to take on other adaptive functions, such as affect regulation. Therefore, therapy should be aimed at (1) intervening behaviorally with the disturbed eating patterns; (2) exploring the underlying issues, such as traumas; (3) helping the patient learn more adaptive coping mechanisms.

Inpatient vs. Partial Hospital vs. Outpatient

Whereas hospitalization or residential treatment facilities used to be the frontline treatment for anorexia and bulimia, inpatient stays are currently reserved primarily for those who are medically unstable, have an accompanying depression that results in active suicidal ideation or an inability to take care of themselves, or have been actively engaged in outpatient or partial hospital treatment with no success. These stays tend to be quite brief and geared toward acute stabilization. Unfortunately, many patients quickly relapse when discharged to their regular living environment. Consequently, discharge planning focused on follow-up care is essential. While some residential facilities continue to treat chronic-eating-disorder patients, they are rarely funded by insurance and rely heavily on research grants and out-of-pocket payments.

Partial hospitalization currently treats those who were formerly hospitalized. It is utilized most typically as a step down from inpatient treatment or when outpatient treatment is no longer sufficient. Typically including intensive group therapy, structured menu-planning, and one or two meals and snacks per day, this approach is fairly effective in intervening in the symptom cycles, beginning to understand underlying issues for the disorder, and teaching more adaptive coping mechanisms. Weekend and evening programs are becoming more prevalent in order to help support patients during what are typically their most difficult times. One of the goals of partial hospitalization is to help the patient gradually learn to take greater responsibility for herself. Part-time schedules are usually employed once the patient has begun to stabilize. For example, patients may phase down to 2 or 3 days per week of treatment and return to work or school on other days. This is useful to ease the transition to outside life and outpatient treatment.

Outpatient and structured outpatient programs continue to be relied on heavily. These include individual, group, family, nutritional, and medication therapies. Free support groups as well as family education and support groups are helpful if not essential in managing patients between therapy sessions.

Treatment Components

Nutritional Counseling

It is useful in the treatment of eating disorders to enlist a nutritionist or registered dieticians to assume many of the responsibilities of management of the eating disorder sysmptoms. In the event that a nutritionist is not available or would impose a financial hardship, the individual therapist can take on these responsibilities within the course of the therapy. This management includes: (1) self-monitoring and meal planning, which requires the patient keep a journal of what was eaten, if the patient purged, and the accompany feelings; (2) supervise weight gain or weight stabilization with daily or weekly weights; (3) use of nutritional supplements; (4) reintroduction of "scary" foods; and (5) supervision of meals, snacks, and bathroom (done in the inpatient or partial hospital program).

Johnson and Connors (1987) suggest a "strategy for recovery" for bulimics, a four-stage cognitive-behavioral model that helps to interfere with the subsequent link or behaviors that occur during a binge-purge sequence. Many of these components can be utilized in the treatment of the anorexic patient, as well, particularly the education invovled in the prevention stage and the conceptualization of the starvation as serving a function similar to that of the bingeing and purging behaviors of the bulimic. Figure 19.1 illustrates those components.

The nutritionist is typically feared and despised by the eating disordered patient, for the nutritionist is the one "responsible" for weight gain or the reintroduction of scary foods. Those nutritionists who remain nonjudgmental and empathic with their patient's struggles, however, may best understand the tremendous struggle their patients face in giving up their symptoms.

FIGURE 19.1 Strategy for Recovery

Prevention

Normalizing food intake
    Physiological deprivation: semistarvation studies
    Psychological deprivation: restraint theory

    Changing eating habits
        Timing of eating
        Eating rituals
        Demystification of food groups

    Side effects of meal normalization
    Weight expectations
    Challenging the overvaluation of thinness

Self-monitoring: self-mastery through anticipating difficult situations
    Macro-level: major life repetitions
    Micro-level: daily behaviors

Self-enhancing activities: positive self-investment

↓

Prebinge State

Perspective: avoid immediate cognitive lapse
Identify mood state
Common precipitants to a binge episode
Alternative behaviors: "lists" used for delay

↓

Postbinge State

Commitment to nonpurging: purging reinforces binge/purge cycle
Alternative behaviors: lists used for delay; use of significant others

↓

Postbinge / Purge Sequence

Episodic disorder: need to recover
Relapse training: beliefs that mediate further episodes
Normal food intake: the best defense against binge eating is to eat

Individual Therapy

The individual therapist is essential in entering and understanding the world of the eating-disordered patient. The task of the therapist is to gain an understanding of the functions that the eating disorder serves, beyond weight regulation and coping with body image disturbances. Once these functions have been determined, the therapist, in the context of a safe and trusting relationship, can challenge the efficacy of the symptoms and begin to encourage the patient to take risks with more adaptive coping mechanisms. The individual psychotherapist should be able to use directive, symptom-focused interventions when indicated and should also be able to analyze the resistances to recovery. It is this duality of perspective within a safe therapeutic alliance that allows "working through" to occur.

Group Therapy

Group therapy includes brief psychoeducational groups, long-term process groups, patient-run support groups, and movement groups. Given the degree of shame that most individuals with eating disorders feel, group therapy is often essential in helping them see that they are not alone in their symptoms as well as experience their problems in relating to others. Psychoeducational groups are primarily didactic and focus on normalizing eating habits, correcting cognitive distortions, developing adaptive coping mechanisms, increasing assertiveness, and building self-esteem (Johnson & Connors, 1987).

Long-term, process-oriented groups can be both difficult and rewarding at the same time. Some individuals have difficulty committing, which may result in sporadic attendance, adversely affecting group cohesiveness. Often, also, a core membership develops of individuals who do not get better and do not leave the group (Johnson & Connors, 1987). In addition, those with severe character pathology may not be able to tolerate the affect that is stimulated in typical group conflicts, such as sharing time and competitiveness. Therefore, group selection based on a desire to have an adequate mix of patients with different degrees of severity of character pathology, as well as regular evaluation periods of the effectiveness of the group, is essential for its success.

Support groups are typically run by nonprofessionals and are available to individuals at no cost. Although the groups are typically open to anyone in the community with an eating disorder, it is important to monitor periodically the safety and appropriateness of the patient mix. For example, individuals should be encouraged to participate in additional treatment modalities besides the support group. Although this is not required for all patients, it should be a prerequisite for those with significant symptomatology. Those individuals who exhibit particularly poor boundaries or become suicidal during group time need firm limits to maintain the safety of the group. Active recruitment of new members who are functioning at a higher level is useful to maintain the hopefulness and adaptiveness of the group. The leader of the group should have regular supervision to help facilitate these goals.

Movement groups are focused primarily on getting in touch with one's body, as well as utilizing and developing nonverbal means of communication and affect expression. Nonverbal movement activities involve both structured activities, such as yoga, and expressive activities, such as mirroring. These groups are best used in inpatient or partial hospital settings, since they tend to be somewhat threatening and overstimulating to most patients. Careful screening of patients in order to select those without severe character pathology is needed to effectively run these groups on an outpatient basis.

Family Therapy/Multifamily Group

It has been found that many women with eating disorders have some degree of developmental conflict between their need to individuate and their need to conform to the perceived expectation of their families. Family therapy (or at least focus on family dynamics) can be extremely useful in helping such patients to function more separately and adaptively without the feared loss of all connection to their family. Although some families may be resistant to family therapy, it is important to predict that they will be affected as the patient changes in therapy.

According to object relations theory, there have been clear failures in the "holding environment" (Winnicott, 1965), or the total empathic care that the infant needs to receive during the first years of life, in anorexic and bulimic families. These failures are family-wide and multigenerational (Humphrey & Stern, 1988). Therefore, family therapy should attempt to provide a "good enough" holding environment to promote empathy, nurturance, containment of affect, reasonable limits, appropriate boundaires, and support for separation-individuation (Humphrey, 1991). Different techniques may be combined for optimal success and effectiveness, all within an empathic holding environment. Process-oriented techniques include observing and interpreting for the family members how their interactions reflect developmental deficits and adaptations through the generations (e.g., comparing the child's difficulties to the difficulties the parents might have with their own parents). Structural techniques are usually more confrontive and directive (Minuchin, Rosman, & Baker, 1978), such as suggesting family lunch sessions or asking a child to move her seat in order to dislodge herself from the parents' marital conflicts.

Multifamily groups are another way to accomplish the same goals of family therapy within a group setting. As in traditional group therapy, sometimes members are able to hear and tolerate advice and confrontation better from peers (other parents) than from professionals. In addition, what family members cannot identify or tolerate in their own children they may be able to recognize in and gain insight from peer families.

It is improtant to recognize with patients that in many cases families may remain unwilling or unable to change. It is useful for the therapist to assist the patient in exploring this possibility in order to prepare her for the need to change regardless of whether or not her family does. This is the essential task of separation that often takes place not only in the family therapy but in the individual therapy, as well.

Pharmacotherapy

There have been numerous double-blind placebo-controlled studies on the use of antidepressants in the treatment of bulimia nervosa. Seven studies examine the use of tricyclic antidepressants. Six of these studies compared the use of a tricyclic antidepressant to placebo (Agras, Dorian, Kirkley, Arnow, & Bachman, 1987; Barlow, Blouin, Blouin, & Perez, 1988; Hughes, Wells, Cunningham, & Isstrup, 1986; Mitchell & Groat, 1984; Pope, Hudson, Jonas, & Yurgelun-Todd, 1983; Walsh, Haidgan, Devlin, Gladis, & Roose, 1991), while one compared the use of desipramine to fenfluramine and to placebo (Blouin, Blouin, Perez, Bushnik, Zuro, & Mudler, 1988). In all of these studies, the use of tricyclic antidepressant led to a significant reduction in binge eating and/or vomiting frequency when compared to placebo. Although the tricyclics used to be the starting point for drug treatment, the sedative and anticholinergic side effects (particularly constipation) make it less desirable than other antidepressants.

Two controlled trials have examined the use of monoamine oxidase inhibitors (Kennedy, Piran, Warsh, Prendergrast, Mainprize, Whynot, & Garfinkel, 1988; Walsh, Gladis, Roose, Stewart, Stetner, & Glassman, 1988) and demonstrated reductions in binge frequency comparable to those found in the studies of tricyclics when compared to controls. However, numerous side effects make their use inadvisable as a first-line treatment for bulimia nervosa.

Three studies have used fluoxetine in the treatment of bulimia nervosa (Enas, Pope, & Velvine, 1989; Fluoxetine Bulimia Nervosa Collaborative Study Group, 1992; Freeman & Hampson, 1987). They report significant improvement with 60–80 mg dosages compared to placebo.

Although the results of drug trials are encouraging and significant improvement in bulimic symptoms has been found in most studies, abstinence rates achieved during treatment are poor and long-term outcome questionable.

Behavioral Contracts

Behavioral contracts can be a useful therapeutic tool in all treatment settings to assist patients in symptom control. The contents and specificity of the contract depends on the setting (inpatient, partial hospital, or outpatient), the severity of illness, and what specific terms the patient and treatment team feel are important to include for the recovery of the patient. In all cases, however, the contract serves a number of purposes.

Most important, the contract provides structure and predictability. Expectations, rewards, and consequences are delineated so tht all people involved (patient, treaters, families) know what is expected at all stages of treatment.

Patients know what consequences to expect if they are not doing well or what rewards they may put in place for abstinence from self-destructive symptoms. This structure guards against ambiguity and splitting among treaters.

The contract also provides a sense of autonomy. Patients are encouraged to coauthor their contracts in order to include components that they know are important to them, as well as to give them an increased sense of control of their treatment. They sign the contract as a symbol that they are signing onto treatment and are reminded that they have a choice as to whether they participate

or not. This structure identifies the expectations not only of the treaters but also of the patient.

Finally, contacts can be helpful in delineating how families and significant others can be involved, how they can be helpful and when they should back off. The contract is an agreement between patient and treaters, and it is the patient's responsibility to follow the contract, not the family's, unless stated specifically in the contract. This can be a tremendous relief to the patient, as well as the family. Figures 19.2–19.5 provide examples of treatment plans (contracts), activity levels, and recommended diet guidelines. The treatment guidelines may have many open spaces in order to include ways to tailor it to each individual patient.

There may be periodic resistance to developing or maintaining the contract by patients or staff. For example, patients may be reluctant to agree to certain limits to their behavior. They may try to "test" the therapist to see how much they can bend the contract before the therapist enforces consequences. Even staff may disagree on components of the contract or ways to enforce consequences of behavior. It is particularly important in cases of patients who utilize splitting as a defense to keep staff working together at all times. Education about the benefits of the contract and opportunities for staff to vent their feelings (e.g., fears that they might seem cruel) are essential for the contract's effectiveness. Behavioral contracts are most effective when utilized in an empathic and consistent manner.

Integrating the 12-Step Approach in Traditional Settings

There has been a recent movement to integrate a 12-step component with traditional psychotherapy for the treatment of eating disorders (Johnson & Sansone, 1993). Preliminary results show that long-term treatment that

FIGURE 19.2 Treatment Plan 1: Recommended for Weight Gain

Supervised Meals: You are expected to "eat all" at meals supervised by staff.

Bathrooms: You are required to use supervised bathroom times unless otherwise directed in treatment plan.

Weights: Done daily per below protocol:
1. You must not eat prior to being weighed except for a sip of water with medication.
2. You must void prior to being weighed and you may be asked for a random urine sample to test for hydration.
3. Weights are done in a hospital gown with no other clothing. No jewelry or hair items are to be worn. Hair must be dry.

Weight Gain: You are expected to gain ¼ lb. per day or 1¾ lbs. per week.

Activity: Your activity level is _____

_____

_____

Other: _____

_____

_____

Date:_____   Patient Signature:_____

FIGURE 19.3 Treatment Plan 2: Recommended for Weight Maintenance

Supervised Meals: You are expected to eat 2/3 of your portion at meals supervised by staff.

Bathrooms: You are required to use supervised bathroom times unless otherwise directed in treatment plan.

Weights: Done in clothing. _____

Activity: Your activity level is _____

_____

_____

Other: _____

_____

_____

Date:_____   Patient Signature:_____

FIGURE 19.4 Activity Guidelines

LEVEL I	LEVEL II	LEVEL III
Bedrest/chairrest (nonmoving activities).	Same except that patient may apply for a specified limited activity, i.e., attending movie, school/work hours.	Patients on this level may engage in normal daily activity.
Wheelchair may be required for some patients.	May walk, but only to *approved* activities.	Patients may apply to treatment team to engage in regular exercise program, including walking, sports, weightlifting.
Walking allowed to BR, but not more than once per hour.	Same	No participating in sports/weightlifting on this level.
Extra clothing layers to conserve body heat.	Same	Patients may apply to treatment team for approved amount of walking.
Time outside when temp less than 60 degrees limited to transportation to and from program.	Time outside limited to amount approved by treatment team when temp is below 60 degrees.	
Sponge bath, showering only when approved.	May shower but not more than 15 minutes per day.	

integrates psychodynamically oriented psychotherapy with a 12-step component can be useful in treating the more difficult-to-treat subpopulation of eating disordered patients with significant Axis I and Axis II comorbidity (Johnson, Tobin, & Enright, 1989; Mitchell & Groat, 1984). We provide here a brief description of one such program, as well as a description of the advantages and disadvantages (Laureate Psychiatric Clinic and Hospital, Johnson & Sansone, 1993) of the way it has integrated the 12-step model into its treatment.

The integrated approach developed when several eating-disordered patients became involved with Alcoholics Anonymous or Overeaters Anonymous and made remarkable recoveries. Table 19.1 presents the original 12 steps, published in 1939 (Alcoholics Anonymous World Services, 1939), elaborated in 1952 (Alcoholics Anonymous World Services, 1952), and modified in 1990 to include the area of eating disorders (Overeaters Anonymous, 1990).

The 12 steps have been interpreted from a psychotherapeutic perspective (partially adapted from Bean, 1975) to include formulations of (1) confronting denial, (2) establishing hope and faith, (3) confronting grandiosity/omnipotence, (4) establishing dependency into the relational sphere and away from substance, (5) introspection, (6) confession and catharsis, (7) penance and undoing, (8) confirmation of a new image of oneself, and (9) giving back through helping others.

Johnson and Sansone make some modifications in the 12-step philosophy to tailor it to their treatment of eating disorders. For example, the traditional goal in step one is abstinence from alcohol. However, given that food is essential to survival, unlike alcohol, it cannot be a target for abstinence. Other target symptoms are substituted, including dieting, purging, binge eating, or other self-destructive behaviors such as self-mutilation. In addition, some sects of Overeaters Anonymous encourage abstinence from specific substances such as white flour or sugar. This can be particularly problematic and can provoke some patients who are restrained eaters into counterregulatory binge eating, that is, bingeing on foods that have been deprived.

The original 12-step writings make frequent references to God, and many individuals may be turned off by the "religious" orientation of the program. Therefore, the 12-step organization has moved toward using the term "Higher

---

FIGURE 19.5 Diet Guidelines

1. No diet foods of any kind, including diet soda (caffeine or decaf), sugar substitute, diet jelly, diet dressings, diet syrup, diet candy, Dzerta, rice cakes.
2. No caffeine-containing noncaloric items, including coffee, tea, cola.
3. No decaf coffee, herbal tea, or soda.
4. No nonfat yogurt, skim milk, nonfat cottage cheese, or nonfat cheeses.
5. No gum.
6. No food from home.
7. No alcohol or alcohol-containing beverages.
8. Limits may be placed on the following if necessary: salt, water, condiments such as mustard, pepper, ketchup.
9. Food lists are to be handed in daily. Include all foods and beverages consumed (including water).
10. Food lists are also to be used to record any purging or exercise activity.
11. Patients are allowed to use the first few minutes of a meal or snack to use microwave and/or toaster and to get any needed utensils.
12. Patient use of the microwave is prohibited unless OK'd by staff supervising.
13. Patients are to refrain from eating disorder behaviors at the table, and, if you are unaware of what those behaviors may be, staff or patients will confront you.
14. No sharing of food or condiments.
15. No additional spices/condiments other than what is ordered on the menu.
16. Modifications to the above must be approved by the team and be written as part of the patients's treatment plan.

Date:_____ Patient Signature _____

TABLE 19.1 The Original 12 Steps

1. We admitted we were powerless over alcohol—that our lives had become unmanageable.
2. Came to believe that a power greater than ourselves could restore us to sanity.
3. Made a decision to turn our will and our lives over to the care of God as we understand him.
4. Made a searching and fearless moral inventory of ourselves.
5. Admitted to God, to ourselves, and to another human being the exact nature of our wrongs.
6. We're entirely ready to have God remove all these defects of character.
7. Humbly asked him to remove our shortcomings.
8. Made a list of all persons we had harmed, and became willing to make amends to them all.
9. Made direct amends to such people wherever possible, except when to do so would injure them or others.
10. Continued to take personal inventory and when we were wrong promptly admitted it.
11. Sought through prayer and meditation to improve our conscious contact with God as we understand Him, praying only for knowledge of His will for us and the power to carry that out.
12. Having had a spiritual awakening as the result of these steps, we tried to carry this message to alcoholics and to practice these principles in all our affairs.

Power" rather than God, and individuals are encouraged to identify their own personal higher power, such as one's 12-step group, sponsor, or therapist.

Finally, the 12-step philosophy stresses the concept of powerlessness. This notion is provocative, especially in working with women with eating disorders who already feel powerless and may be striving for empowerment. It can be useful to target the powerlessness, however, to areas with which the individual is obsessively concerned, such as weight, body size, and shape. If our patients can begin to understand and identify the things that cannot be controlled (such as their natural body size) and to distinguish them from the things they can control (such as their feelings about themselves), they can begin to make peace with those things that cannot be controlled and feel empowered to change the things that they can.

There are several advantages and disadvantages to the 12-step philosophy in the treatment of eating disorders. Alcoholics Anonymous does an excellent job of engendering hope and faith in individuals who are ready to give up. It can be very powerful to have successfully recovering people advise those who feel desperate and alone. The 12-step model also provides a common language that incorporates complicated psychological points and revises them into very simple and catchy phrases; this language can be learned quickly and accepted in any 12-step community. The 12-step model also provides a very concrete structure. There are distinct rituals, step-by-step assignments, inspirational literature and paraphernalia, and transitional objects such as abstinence chips or coins. Especially for those individuals who are intrapsychically chaotic and who have relied on their eating disorders for structure and identity, these things offer an adaptive substitution. Finally, by offering our patients the language and meaning of the 12-step philosophy, we create an opportunity for them to network anywhere. Especially for those patients who are transitioning from inpatient or partial hospital to less structured forms of treatment, it can be helpful to know that they can find free meetings

virtually from dawn until midnight, 7 days a week. This can be an invaluable support that most treatment programs cannot provide.

It is important to acknowledge some of the disadvantages of the 12-step philosophy. Often there are patients invovled in the programs who could be greatly helped by other therapeutic interventions in addition to the 12-step approach, for example, those who may have a biologically induced mood disorder that could be successfully treated with psychopharmacological interventions and those who could benefit from psychoeducational material (on topics such as dieting and sociocultural pressures on women) or from family interventions to assist with dysfunctional families. As noted, many of the difficult-to-treat patients have significant personality disorders (Johnson, Tobin, & Enright, 1989) that may be difficult to manage within the structure of the 12-step program. It can be useful for therapists to have ongoing communication with the sponsors of these patients to help them avoid destructive relationships.

In summary, it has been very beneficial to add a 12-step component to a traditional multidimensional treatment program. Especially in a world of shrinking health care dollars, innovative ways of adding support for this extremely needy and difficult-to-treat population are always welcome.

COMMENTS

There are numerous etiological theories, assessment techniques, and treatment modalities available to those in the field of eating disorders. Although the field continues to expand, certainly one of the most recent and daunting challenges is to find shorter and more cost-effective ways to treat very disturbed patients in order to accommodate the demands of managed care.

Prevention is critically important as one tries to accommodate to these demands. Most well-regarded therapists in the field are organizing community programs designed to confront the daunting task of size acceptance—in other words, challenging the media, fashion design-ers, manufacturers of diet products, and de-velopers of diet programs. This may also in-clude educating our physicians who mistreat their obese patients or revealing the names of clinics that give out prescription diet pills as if it were candy. Certainly this includes edu-cating our children of the positive components of self-esteem, those that have nothing to do with weight or body size. This is a large and frustrating task. Weight discrimination and the resulting obsession with thinness are rampant and recalcitrant. I believe that, in order to make any kind of a dent in this field, we all need to combat these pernicious influences.

REFERENCES

Agras, W. S., Dorian, B., Kirkley, B. G., Arnow, B., & Bachman, J. (1987). Imipramine in the treatment of bulimia: A double-blind controlled study. *International Journal of Eating Disorders*, 6, 29–38.

Alcoholics Anonymous World Services. (1939). *Alcoholics anonymous*. New York: Author.

Alcoholics Anonymous World Services. (1952). *Twelve Steps and Twelve Traditions*. New York: Author.

American Psychiatric Association. (1980). *Task force on nomenclature and statistics. Diagnostic and statistical manual of mental disorders* (3rd ed.). Washington, DC: Author.

American Psychiatric Association. (1994). *Diagnostic and Statistical Manual of Mental Disorders* (4th ed.). Washington, DC: Author.

Barbosa-Saldivar, J. L., & Van Itallie, T. B. (1979). Semistarvation: An overview of an old problem. *Bulletin of the New York Academy of Medicine*, 55, 744–797.

Barlow, J., Blouin, J., Blouin, A., & Perez, E. (1988). Treatment of bulimia with desipramine: A double-blind crossover study. *Canadian Journal of Psychiatry*, 33, 129–133.

Bean, M. (1975). Alcoholics anonymous. *Psychaitric Annals*, 1 (A), 7–61.

Beck, A. T., & Beamesderfer, A. (1974). Assessment of depression: The depression inventory. In P. Pichot (Ed.), *Psychological measurements in psychopharmacology: Modern problems in pharmapsychiatry*. Paris: Karger, Basil.

Blouin, A. G., Blouin, J. H., Perez, E. L., Bushnik, T., Zuro, C., & Mudler, E. (1988). Treatment of bulimia with fenfluramine and desipramine. *Journal of Clinical Psychopharmacology*, 8, 261–269.

Boskind-Lodahl, M. (1976). Cinderella's stepsisters: A feminist perspective on anorexia nervosa and bulimia. *Journal of Women in Culture and Society*, 2, 342–356.

Bruch, H. (1973). *Eating disorders: Obesity, anorexia nervosa, and the person within*. New York: Basic Books.

Bulik, C. M. (1987). Drug and alcohol abuse by bulimic women and their families. *American Journal of Psychiatry*, 144, 1604–1606.

Burnstein, E. M., & Putnam, F. W. (1986). Development, reliability, and validity of a dissociation scale. *Journal of Nervous and Mental Disease*, 174, 727–735.

Crisp, A. H. (1981). Anorexia nervosa at a normal weight! The abnormal weight control syndrome. *International Journal of Psychiatry in Medicine*, 11, 203–234.

Enas, C. G., Pope, H. G., & Velvine, L. R. (1989). *Fluoxetine in bulimia nervosa. Double-blind study*. Poster presented at the annual meeting of the American Psychiatric Association, San Francisco, CA.

Endicott, J., & Spitzer, R. L. (1978). A diagnostic interview: The Schedule for Affective Disorders and Schizoprehenia. *Archives of General Psychiatry*, 35, 831–837.

Fairburn, C. G., Kirk. J., O'Connor, M., & Cooper, P. J. (1986). A comparison of two psychological treatments for bulimia nervosa. *Behavior Research and Therapy*, 24, 629–643.

Freeman, C. P. L., & Hampson, M. (1987). Fluoxetine as a treatment for bulimia nervosa. *International Journal of Obesity*, 11 (Suppl. 3), 171–177.

Fluoxetine Bulimia Nervosa Collaborative (FBNC) Study Group. (1992). Fluoxetine in the treatment of bulimia nervosa. *Archives of General Psychiatry*, 49, 139–147.

Gallo, L., & Randel, A. (1981). Chronic vomiting and its effect on the primary dentition: Report of a case. *Journal of Dentition Child*, 48, 383–384.

Garner, D. M., Olmsted, M. P., & Polivy, J. (1983). Development and validation of a multidimensional eating disorder inventory for anorexia nervosa and bulimia. *International Journal of Eating Disorders*, 2, 15–34.

Garner, D. M. (1991). *Eating Disorders Inventory-2*. Odessa: Psychological Assessment Resources.

Garner, D. M., Garfinkel, P. E., & O'Shaughnessy. (1983). Clinical and psychometric comparison between bulimia in anorexia nervosa and bulimia in normal-weight women. *Report of the Fourth Ross Conference on Medical Research* (pp. 6–13). Columbus, OH: Ross Laboratories.

Glassman, A. H., & Walsh, B. T. (1983). Link between bulimia and depression unclear. *Journal of Clinical Psychopharmacology, 3,* 203.

Gull, W. W. (1874). Anorexia nervosa (apepsia hysterica, anorexia hysterica). *Transactions of the Clinical Society of London, 7,* 22–28.

Hamilton, M. (1960). A rating scale for depression. *Journal of Neurology, Neurosurgery, and Psychiatry, 23,* 56–61.

Hamilton, M. (1967). Development of a rating scale for primary depressive illness. *British Journal of School and Clinical Psychology, 6,* 278–296.

Hodgson, R. J., & Rachman, S. (1977). Obsessional-compulsive complaints. *Behavior Research and Therapy, 15,* 389–395.

Hudson, J. I., Laffer, P. S., & Pope, H. G., Jr. (1982). Bulimia related to affective disorder by family and response to the dexamethazone suppression test. *American Journal of Psychiatry, 137,* 695–698.

Hudson, J. I., Pope, H. G., Jonas, J. M., & Yurgelund, T. D. (1983). Family history study of anorexia nervosa and bulimia. *British Journal of Psychiatry, 142,* 133–138.

Hughes, P. L., Wells, L. A., Cunningham, C. J., & Isstrup, D. M. (1986). Treating bulimia with desipramine. *Archives of General Psychiatry, 43,* 182–186.

Humphrey, L. L. (1991). Object relations and the family system: An integrative approach to understanding and treating eating disorders. In C. Johnson (Ed.), *Psychodynamic treatment of anorexia nervosa and bulimia* (pp. 321–353). New York: Guilford Press.

Humphrey, L. L., & Stern, S. (1988). Object relations and the family system in bulimia. *Journal of Marital and Family Therapy, 14,* 337–350.

Johnson, C. (1984). The initial consultation for patients with bulimia and anorexia nervosa. In D. M. Garner & P. E. Garfinkel (Eds.), *Handbook of psychotherapy for anorexia nervosa and bulimia* (pp. 19–51). New York: Guilford Press.

Johnson, C., & Connors, M. E. (1987). *The etiology and treatment of bulimia nervosa.* New York: Basic Books.

Johnson, C. L., & Flach, R. A. (1985). Family characteristics of 105 patients with bulimia. *American Journal of Psychiatry, 142,* 1321–1324.

Johnson, C. L., & Sansone, R. A. (1993). Integrating the twelve-step approach with traditional psychotherapy for the treatment of eating disorders. *International Journal of Eating Disorders, 14,* 121–134.

Johnson, C., Tobin, D. L., & Enright, A. B. (1989). Prevalence and clinical characteristics of borderline patients in an eating disordered population. *Journal of Clinical Psychiatry, 50,* 9–15.

Kennedy, S. H., Piran, N., Warsh, J. J., Prendergrast, P., Mainprize, W., Whynot, C., & Garfinkel, P. E. (1988). A trial of isocarboxazid in the treatment of bulimia nervosa. *Journal of Clinical Psychopharmacology, 8,* 391–396.

Kirkley, G. B., Scheneider, J. A., Agras, W. S., & Bachman, J. (1985). Comparison of two group treatments for bulimia. *Journal of Consulting and Clinical Psychology, 5,* 43–48.

Millon, T. (1982). *Millon Clinical Multiaxial Inventory* (2nd ed.). Minneapolis: National Computer Systems.

Minuchin, S., Rosman, B. L., & Baker, L. (1978). *Psychosomatic families: Anorexia nervosa in context.* Cambridge, MA: Harvard University Press.

Mitchell, J., & Bantle, J. (1983). Metabolic and endocrine investigations in women of normal weight with the bulimia syndrome. *Biological Psychiatry, 18* (3), 355–365.

Mitchell, J. E., & Groat, R. (1984). A placebo-controlled, double-blind trial of amitriptyline in bulimia. *Journal of Clinical Psychopharmacology, 4,* 186–193.

Overeaters Anonymous. (1990). *The Twelve Steps of Overeaters Anonymous.* Los Angeles: Author.

Palmer, R. L. (1979). The dietary chaos syndrome: A useful new term? *British Journal of Medical Psychology, 52,* 187–190.

Pope, H. G., Hudson, J. I., Jonas, J. M., & Yurgelun-Todd, D. (1983). Bulimia treated with imipramine: A placebo-controlled, double-blind study. *American Journal of Psychiatry, 140,* 554–558.

Russell, G. (1979). Bulimia nervosa: An ominous variant of anorexia nervosa. *Psychological Medicine, 9,* 429–448.

Sands, S. (1991). Bulimia, dissociation, and empathy: A self-psychological view. In C. Johnson (Ed.), *Psychodynamic treatment of anorexia nervosa and bulimia* (pp. 34–50). New York: Guilford Press.

Selzer, M. L. (1971). Michigan Alcoholism Screening Test. The quest for a new diagnostic instrument. *American Journal of Psychiatry, 127,* 1653–1658.

Selvini-Palazzoli, M. (1978). *Self-starvation: From individual to family therapy in the treatment of anorexia nervosa*. Noahvale, NJ: Jason Aronson.

Skinner, H. A. (1982). The drug abuse screening test. *Addicitive Behaviors, 71*, 363–371.

Smart, D. E., Beumont, P. J. V., & George, G. C. W. (1976). Some personality characteristics of patients with anorexia nervosa. *British Journal of Psychiatry, 128*, 57–60.

Solyom, L., Miles, J. E., & O'Kane, J. (1982). A comparative psychometric study of anorexia nervosa and obsessional neurosis. *Canadian Journal of Psychiatry, 27*, 282–286.

St. Anthony's ICD-9-CM Code Book. (1995). Reston: St. Anthony Publishing.

Walsh, B. T., Haidgan, C. M., Devlin, M. J., Gladis, M., & Roose, S. P. (1991). Long-term outcome of anti-depressant treatment for bulimia nervosa. *American Journal of Psychiatry, 148*, 1206–1212.

Walsh, B. T., Gladis, M., Roose, S. P., Stewart, J. W., Stetner, F., & Glassman, A. H. (1988). Phenelzine vs. placebo—50 patients with bulimia. *Archives of General Psychiatry, 45*, 471–475.

Winnicott, D. W. (1965). *The maturation processes and the facilitating environment*. New York: International Universities Press.

Wooley, S., & Wooley, O. (1979). Obesity and women—I: A closer look at the facts. *Women's Studies International Quarterly, 2*, 69–79.

20
Sleep Disorders in Childhood and Adolescence

Charles R. Carlson
Matthew J. Cordova

INTRODUCTION
Historical Perspective

Informed discussion of sleep disorders in children and adolescents begins with an overview of current perspectives regarding the purpose and nature of normal sleep. There are numerous theories concerning the purpose of sleep. One group of theories posits that sleep provides a period of restoration in which deficits in somatic and central nervous system tissues are repaired (Adam & Oswald,1983; Hartmann, Orzack, & Branconnier, 1974). Another theory proposes that sleep is a necessary part of the learning process whereby information processing and memory consolidation occur (Block, Hennevin, & Leconte, 1981). It has also been suggested that sleep provides an opportunity for the elimination of unneeded neuronal connections to increase the efficiency of information processing (Crick & Mitchison, 1983). Others have characterized sleep as an energy conservation behavior with adaptive roots dating back over many generations (Snyder, 1966). Current theories have also been influenced by recent evidence suggesting that changes in immune function, hormone release, and tissue growth are linked with sleep patterns (Moldofsky, Lue, Davidson, & Gorczynski, 1988; Roffwarg, Muzio, & Dement, 1966; Sassin et al., 1969). Despite the various possible functions of sleep, most theorists agree that it is a necessary, though not sufficient, behavior for unimpaired daily living.

While the exact role of sleep has not been determined, it is well established that sleep deprivation can have significant negative physical and psychological consequences (Carskadon, Harvey, & Dement, 1981; Kales et al., 1979). Fatigue, excessive sleepiness, decreased attentiveness, decline in perceptual, cognitive, and psychomotor capabilities and performance, regressive behavior, and disoriented thought may result from prolonged sleep disruption (Kales et al., 1979). Sleep disorders in children are often associated with learning difficulties and disruptive behavior (Mindell, 1993). Furthermore, it appears that children require more time to recuperate from sleep deprivation than adults, so accumulation of daytime sleepiness can have detrimental effects, especially on school performance and social interactions with other children. Given this range of effects, and given the fact that approximately 30% of adults and 25% of children are estimated to suffer from some sort of sleep disturbance, further understanding of the characteristics of sleep, as well as knowledge of assessment and treatment strategies for sleep disorders, is important (Bixler et al., 1979; Lozoff, Wolf, & Davis, 1985; Mindell, 1993).

The architecture of the normal sleep pattern has been well described elsewhere (Aserinksy & Kleitman, 1955a, 1955b; Dement & Kleitman, 1957; Loomis, Harvey, & Hobart, 1935; Roffwarg et al., 1966), so only a brief overview is presented to remind the reader of essential principles important for understanding sleep dysfunctions. Five distinct stages of sleep have been identified using electroencephalography (EEG), electromyography (EMG), and electrooculography (EOG) and other polysomnographic measurements. Nonrapid eye movement (NREM) Stage 1 sleep, which accounts for approximately 4–5% of total sleep time, occurs during the transition from wakefulness to sleep and is characterized by low-voltage, high-frequency (diffuse alpha/theta) EEG waves, tonic muscle tone, and slow, rolling eye movements. Nonrapid eye movement Stage 2 sleep, which accounts for 45–50% of total sleep time, is identified by the emergence of specific EEG forms known as sleep spindles and K-complexes, tonic muscle tone, absence of eye movements, and low-voltage, mixed-frequency EEG waves. Together, NREM Stages 3 and 4 sleep account for 15–25% of total sleep time and are known as slow-wave (delta) or deep sleep. The presence of high-voltage, low-frequency delta EEG waves for more than 50% of the time marks the change from NREM Stage 3 to NREM Stage 4 sleep; both stages are characterized by tonic muscle tone and absence of eye movements. Rapid eye movement (REM) sleep is known for being that period of sleep where dreaming occurs. The REM periods appear cyclically and alternate with NREM stages every 80–120 minutes throughout the night in adults; infants have a REM/NREM cycle of 45–55 minutes. REM sleep accounts for 20–25% of total sleep time and is characterized by rapid saccadic eye movements, hypotonic muscle tone, and relatively low-voltage, mixed-frequency EEG waves (Aserin-

sky & Kleitman, 1955a, 1955b; Dement & Kleitman, 1957; Loomis et al., 1935; Roffwarg et al., 1966).

Over the course of the night, four to six cycles of NREM and REM stages may occur. Once sleep is initiated, stages progress sequentially from NREM Stage 1 to NREM Stage 4 sleep. The first NREM Stage 4 period of the night is often reached within 15 minutes after falling asleep. Sleep then cycles from NREM Stage 4 to NREM Stage 2 and back again (i.e., 4-3-2-3-4-3-2) for 1 to 2 hours. Following this initial cycling, the first REM stage may occur and becomes part of this sequence (i.e., 4-3-2-REM-2-3-4, etc.). The first REM period may be as brief as 5 minutes before NREM cycling begins again. As the night progresses, REM periods get longer and more intense, sometimes as long as 20 minutes, while NREM periods, especially Stages 3 and 4, get shorter (Carskadon, Keenan, & Dement, 1987; Coble, Kupfer, Reynolds, & Houck, 1987; Sheldon, Spire, & Levy, 1992c).

As children mature, total sleep time decreases and becomes more stable (see Table 20.1). During infancy, total sleep time averages 16–17 hours per day. Most of this time is spent in REM sleep and occurs in 2- to 4-hour sleep periods scattered throughout the day and night. The first 6 months of life are marked by consolidation of sleep periods, NREM/REM stage differentiation, and entrainment of sleep to primarily a diurnal pattern. By 6 months of age, total sleep time falls to approximately 13–14 hours per day, and REM sleep significantly decreases to from a third to a fourth of total sleep time. During childhood, total sleep time continues to decrease, falling to between 9.5 and 11 hours per day, and the sleep-wake cycle becomes more stable. During adolescence, the structure of bedtimes is typically reduced, and there are increased time demands (e.g., academic, social) on the child, often resulting in a significant sleep debt in many adolescents. Combined with an increased physiological need for sleep (e.g., 8–9 hours per night), this reduction in time available for sleep often contributes to sleep deprivation and the characteristic daytime sleepiness frequently seen in teenagers (Carskadon & Dement, 1987). Age

TABLE 20.1. Total Sleep Time (per 24 hours clock time) Across Age Groups

Age	Hours
1 week	16.5
1 month	15.5
3 months	15
6 months	14.25
12 months	13.75
2 years	13
5 years	11
10 years	9.75
16 years	8.5

Source: Modified from Ferber, R., *Solve your child's sleep problems.* New York: Simon & Schuster, 1985, p. 19. Copyright 1985 by Richard Ferber, M.D., with permission of Simon and Schuster.

of onset, course, and severity of sleep disorders are affected by the natural progression of sleep development in children and adolescents. Consequently, these factors must be considered carefully when performing an evaluation of sleep patterns (Carskadon et al., 1987; Coble et al., 1987; Sheldon et al., 1992c).

Diagnostic Description and Critique of DSM-IV

The *Diagnostic and Statistical Manual of Mental Disorders, Fourth Edition* (DSM-IV) divides sleep disorders into four main categories: primary sleep disorders, sleep disorders related to another mental disorder, sleep disorder due to a general medical condition, and substance-induced sleep disorder (American Psychiatric Assocation, 1994). Due to the scope and purpose of this chapter, we focus discussion on primary sleep disorders and, in particular, those disorders most prevalent in children. Primary sleep disorders, diagnosed only when the disturbance is not caused by a mental disorder, medical condition, or substance use or abuse, are divided into two subcategories: dyssomnias and parasomnias. The diagnoses that follow can also be listed as subtypes in cases where sleep disturbance is caused by a mental disorder, medical condition, or substance use or abuse.

Dyssomnias are abnormalities in the amount, quality, or timing of sleep. Several disorders exist within this subcategory. Primary Insomnia is characterized by difficulty initiating and/or maintaining sleep. These difficulties must be present for at least one month. Daytime fatigue, sleepiness, irritability, poor concentration, and nighttime fears, anxiety, and self-focused attention are also common features. Primary hypersomnia is manifested by excessive daytime sleepiness for at least 1 month, and sufferers exhibit excessive total sleep time, impaired alertness, poor concentration and school performance, sleep drunkenness, and an inability to experience refreshing sleep. Narcolepsy is characterized by excessive daytime somnolence, repeated sleep attacks, cataplexy (sudden loss of muscle tone often triggered after extreme emotion), sleep paralysis, and hypnagogic hallucinations (REM periods occurring between states of wakefulness and sleep) (APA, 1994).

Breathing-related sleep disorders are indicated by sleep disruption due to abnormalities in ventilation. These disorders are often associated with excessive sleepiness or insomnia. Three subtypes of breathing-related sleep disorders exist in DSM-IV: (1) obstructive sleep apnea, characterized by upper airway obstruction; (2) central sleep apnea syndrome, in which there is an episodic cessation of ventilation without airway obstruction; and (3) central alveolar hyperventilation syndrome, an impairment in ventilation control resulting in abnormally low arterial oxygen levels.

Circadian rhythm sleep disorder is identified by a persistent, recurrent pattern of sleep disruption resulting from a mismatch between the individual's internal sleep-wake regulatory system and his or her environmental demands. This disorder manifests as problems initiating and maintaining sleep and often alternates between insomnia and excessive sleepiness, though total sleep time is within normal limits. Subtypes of circadian rhythm sleep disorder include delayed sleep phase type, jet lag type, shift work type, and unspecified type.

Other dyssomnias can be subtyped under the category "dyssomnia not otherwise specified (NOS)." These include "restless legs syndrome" (somatosensory sensations that lead to an urge to move the legs) and idiopathic periodic limb movements (called "nocturnal myoclonus," limb jerks leading to brief arousals and subsequent restless sleep). As can be seen from these descriptions, dyssomnias encompass a wide variety of specific sleep disturbances involving the amount, quality, or timing of sleep.

Parasomnias are abnormal behavioral or physiological events that occur in association with sleep, specific sleep stages, or sleep-wake transitions. These disorders are often characterized by physiological activation at inappropriate times during the sleep-wake cycle. Nightmare disorder involves repeated frightening dreams that lead to awakening from REM-stage sleep. Nightmares usually occur during the last third of the night, when REM stages are longer and more intense and the individual usually retains recall of the sequence and content of the dreams. Sleep terror disorder is a disorder of arousal from NREM Stage 3 or 4 sleep in which the individual awakens abruptly with a panicky scream or cry and exhibits intense fear, confusion, and disorientation. Sleep terrors, also known as "pavor nocturnus" in children and "pavor incubus" in adults, occur during the first third of the night, when deep sleep is more concentrated, and are characterized by extreme autonomic arousal (tachycardia, tachypnea, perspiration) and amnesia for the event. Also related to NREM Stage 3 or 4 arousals during the first third of the night is sleepwalking disorder, which involves complex motor behaviors initiated during sleep that may range from sitting up in bed to walking or running about the home. Injuries are common during sleepwalking and the individual usually has little or no recall of the event (APA, 1994). Other diagnoses of sleep dysfunctions may be subtyped under the category "parasomnia not otherwise specified."

The *International Statistical Classification of Diseases and Related Health Problems* (ICD-10) differentiates between "nonorganic" sleep disorders and those suspected of having an organic basis (World Health Organization, 1992). According to ICD-10, emotional causes are considered to be the primary cause of nonorganic sleep disorders, whereas all other sleep disorders are classified under the heading "Diseases of the Nervous System." Similar to the DSM-IV sleep disorders classification, ICD-10 nonorganic sleep disorders are divided into dyssomnias and parasomnias. Together, these disorders include nonorganic insomnia, nonorganic hypersomnia, nonorganic disorder of the sleep-wake schedule, sleepwalking, sleep terrors, nightmares, and "other/NOS" categories (WHO, 1992). Sleep disorders falling under the ICD-10 category "Diseases of the Nervous System" include disorders of initiating and maintaining sleep, disorders of excessive somnolence, disorders of the sleep-wake schedule, sleep apnea, and narcolepsy and cataplexy. This alternative classification system reflects the fact that ICD-10 includes both physical and behavioral or mental disorders. Overall, the ICD-10 and the DSM-IV diagnostic classifications of sleep disorders are quite similar.

Other classification systems of sleep disorders have been developed. In 1979, the Association of Sleep Disorders Centers (ASDC) and the Association for the Psychophysiological Study of Sleep developed the *Diagnostic Classification of Sleep and Arousal Disorders* (1979). This system was further enhanced in 1990 with the *International Classification of Sleep Disorders (ICSD): Diagnostic and Coding Manual* (American Sleep Disorders Association, 1990). Both of these systems offer a more detailed classification of sleep disorders, with greater differentiation of subtypes, than do the DSM-IV and the ICD-10 systems. For example, the ICSD system divides "insomnias" (called "disorders of initiating or maintaining sleep") into several categories, including adjustment sleep disorder, inadequate sleep hygiene, limit-setting sleep disorder, sleep onset association disorder, excessive nocturnal fluids, psychophysiological insomnia, and others (American Sleep Disorders Association, 1990). There is, however, considerable overlap between DSM-IV/ICD-10 sleep disorders and the ICSD categories. In addition, the DSM-IV "not otherwise specified" categories and the sleep dysfunction categories other than the primary sleep disorders make for further consistency between these systems. Moreover, the text for each DSM-IV diagnostic category contains a section relating the diagnosis to the corresponding ICSD diagnosis. The DSM-IV categories, however, are more difficult to apply to children than the ICSD categories because of the clearer descriptive categories found in the ICSD's nosological framework. Epidemiological information in DSM-IV is offered primarily for adult populations. In addition, DSM-IV sleep disorder criteria are mostly descriptive, whereas the ICSD classification system takes etiology into account in several diagnostic subtypes. Although DSM-IV's classification system is not as detailed as the ICSD system, it does prove comprehensive and useful in the diagnosis, assessment, and treatment of sleep disorders.

Epidemiology

It is estimated that approximately 25% of children suffer from some sort of sleep disturbance during the course of childhood (Lozoff et al., 1985; Mindell, 1993). Dyssomnias are less prevalent in children than in adults, but many children suffer from these disorders (Mindell, 1993). Primary insomnia is rare in childhood and adolescence. When difficulty initiating or maintaining sleep during childhood does occur, it is usually associated with environmental and conditioning factors such as acute anxiety due to school or related issues, a change in family residence, poorly set limits by parents, absence of familiar routine or object (e.g., bottle, blanket, being rocked to sleep), or eating and drinking too close to bedtime. Onset is usually before age five, and insomnias of childhood usually resolve naturally over time (American Sleep Disorders Association, 1990; Ferber, 1985a).

Primary hypersomnia and narcolepsy are rare in children, with estimated prevalence rates of narcolepsy ranging from 0.03–0.16% of the population (Guilleminault, 1987b). Onset is rarely before puberty, although signs of excessive childhood sleepiness have retrospectively been reported by adult narcoleptics. Familial patterns have been reported in primary insomnia, primary hypersomnia, and narcolepsy, so there is some evidence for a genetic basis to these disorders.

Obstructive sleep apnea is the most common breathing-related sleep disorder in children, with onset usually before age 10. The frequency of obstructive sleep apnea in children is unknown, primarily because it often goes undetected by parents (Guilleminault, 1987c). It occurs more often in boys than in girls and is often associated with morbid obesity and soft-tissue abnormalities of the upper airway (Guilleminault, 1987c).

Circadian rhythm sleep disorders are also common in children and adolescents. The actual prevalence is unknown because the symptoms of this disorder are often confused with insomnia and/or hypersomnia. In children, they are usually associated with parental limit-setting difficulties, while adolescent sleep-wake schedule difficulties develop when social and school activities push bedtime later and later (Ferber, 1987a).

Parasomnias are also common in children. It is estimated that between 10–50% of children between the ages 3 to 5 years have nightmares, although the actual prevalence of nightmare disorder is unknown. Nightmare disorder usually begins between the ages of 3 and 6 years and is eventually outgrown in most cases (Kales et al., 1980b). Sleep terror episodes occur in 1–6% of children and are more common in males than in females. Onset occurs between the ages of 4 and 12, and sleep terrors usually resolve spontaneously by adolescence. A strong familial connection appears to exist both in sleep terrors and in sleepwalking. It is estimated that 10–30% of children have sleepwalked at least once, and 1–5% meet the criteria for sleepwalking disorder. Onset is usually between 4 and 8 years, with the peak prevalence at 12 years of age. Sleepwalking also usually disappears spontaneously by adolescence (Kales et al., 1980a, 1980c).

Factors That Influence Onset and Maintenance of Childhood and Adolescent Sleep Disorders

Several factors can be identified that may precipitate and/or maintain sleep disorders in children and adolescents. These include, but are not limited to, life stressors, parental reactions and attachment issues, cultural norms, physiological/medical conditions, and various psychopathological conditions. Stressful life events may create anxiety levels that disrupt sleep onset or quality. Moving, school transitions (e.g., reaching school age, changes in grade or school), parental marital discord or divorce, physical or sexual abuse, death of a family member, and birth of a sibling are all examples of life stressors that can influence sleep in children. While this list is clearly not exhaustive, it is representative of events that may lead to sleep difficulty in children and adolescents (Ferber, 1987a).

Sometimes children may have difficulty sleeping separately from their parents. It has been suggested that this may reflect insecure attachment and/or failure of the child to individuate and separate from his or her mother (Benoit, Zeanah, Boucher, & Minde, 1992). If parents do not set clear and consistent limits regarding cosleeping, this may foster disrupted sleep and increased parental distress (Benoit et al., 1992; Ellis, 1991). Other cultural factors that can influence sleep include parents who place differential emphasis on independence as a function of the gender and age of their child. Thus, certain norms of different cultures may lead to sleep disruption when superimposed on the demands of life in mainstream American culture. Conditions such as asthma, attention-deficit/hyperactivity disorder, epilepsy, mental retardation, chronic pain, fever, gastrointestinal problems, a recent medical procedure, and use of prescription and nonprescription drugs may also lead to sleep problems that may subsequently be maintained by conditioning effects (Ferber, 1987b). Finally, while psychopathology is often comorbid with sleep disorders in adults, it is rarely so in children. However, depression, anxiety, phobias, and obsessive-compulsive tendencies have been associated with increased sleep disturbance in children and adolescents (Kales et al., 1980a, 1980c).

ASSESSMENT

General Considerations

The following section should be read with the understanding that the mental health clinician works in conjunction with the patient's primary-care physician, and possibly other health care specialists, in treating a sleep disorder. A thorough medical evaluation will most likely precede a physician's referral of a patient to mental health services for assistance with sleep disturbances. However, if the mental health clinician is the first caregiver to see the patient, the clinician should refer the child or adolescent to a physician for a diagnostic work-up to rule out any physical basis for the sleep disruption. Similarly, the mental health clinician may want to consider referral to a sleep disorders clinic or consultation with a sleep disorders specialist as part of the initial assessment. Mental health professionals working collaboratively with primary-care physicians and sleep disorders specialists provide an effective treatment team for childhood and adolescent sleep disorder patients.

Treatment of sleep disorders is designed to address both the symptoms and the causal factors of the disturbance; therefore, it is essential to cast a broad net in assessment to identify the likely etiology of a sleep disruption. Assessment should begin with a clinical interview that includes a thorough description of the sleep problem (see Appendix A). The first occurrence, the frequency of disturbance, the time of night for each occurrence, the duration of each episode, and a detailed description of the behavior involved must first be established (Ware & Orr, 1983). If parasomnias are suspected, the clinician should assess carefully the presence of stereotypical or rhythmical movements, displacement from bed, the child's degree of arousal and agitation during an event, and the ability of the child to recall the event the next day (Clore & Hibel, 1993). Life events occurring around the time that the sleep disturbance began, as well as those that have occurred since, should be assessed. A common symptom of children who have been physically and/or sexually abused is sleep disruption (Sadeh et al., 1994). Posttraumatic stress disorder symptoms, such as nightmares, intrusive thoughts, and hyperarousal, may be sources of nighttime worries and difficulty sleeping through the night. Clearly, these statements should not be interpreted to mean that all or even most cases of childhood sleep disorders are related to abuse. However, the clinician should be alert to the possibility of such factors when assessing sleep disorders in children.

In addition, the interaction of parental behavior and the child's current sleep problem must be understood. What reinforcers and/or contingencies are maintaining the child's behavior? If the child wakes at night, what are the parents' responses? Is the child allowed to sleep in rooms or places other than his or her bedroom? What interventions by parents or health care professionals have been attempted, for how long, and how consistently? What is the degree of distress exhibited by the parents over the child's sleep problem? Parental distress is often a significant factor motivating them to seek assistance for a child's sleep problem (Ferber, 1985a).

Sleep disturbances must also be considered in the context of sleep hygiene, or the conditions that promote continuous and effective sleep. Evaluation of sleep hygiene should include information such as intake of food and liquids close to bedtime (with special attention to caffeine and alcohol), any current medications, and use of nicotine or illicit substances. In addition, a thorough description of the bedtime routine should include evening exercise (its intensity and proximity to bedtime), TV watching, reading (does child read on his or her own, or do parents read bedtime stories?), bathing (baths can sometimes wake a child up), and associations the child needs to fall asleep (e.g., blanket, stuffed animal, TV, music, toy, night light, parent rocking, reading, singing) (Thorpy,

1988). Furthermore, sleep hygiene assessment includes examining factors related to the sleep environment, such as room temperature, noise level, amount of light, and presence of other siblings (does the child share a room?) and/or pets (Sheldon, Spire, & Levy, 1992b).

Next, the clinical interview should assess the child's and family's psychiatric history, including sleep disturbances. Depression and anxiety are often related, though not always causally, with sleep disturbance. The potential familial pattern of certain sleep disorders makes it important to assess whether parents have had or currently have sleep disturbances independent of the child's problem. If a sleep disorder is or was present in a parent or family member, what treatment did the person receive? Has the child's disturbance followed a similar course? What were the parents' reactions to their own sleep problems? These are all questions that should be considered carefully by the clinician during the initial evaluation.

In addition, the child's medical history and developmental milestones should be evaluated. Sleep disorders are rarely caused by unitary psychological or physical factors but are usually the result of multiple interacting factors. As noted, if a thorough medical evaluation is not done prior to referral to the mental health clinician, it should soon follow (Thorpy, 1988).

Sleep diaries are an effective way to document the course of events in the child's sleep-wake cycle and, when filled out consistently over a two-week period, can provide a stable baseline against which to assess the effectiveness of interventions. Such a diary often provides information regarding the child's sleep-wake cycle that includes bedtime, sleep onset latency, sleep duration, wake episodes and specific behaviors, and time out of bed in the morning (see Figure 20.1). In addition, a 24-hour sleep diary can record daytime sleep behaviors and occurrences such as naps, homework, food or drink intake, medications, emotional states, sleepiness, exercise, fatigue, level of alertness, and stressful events that might influence sleep activity. It is also important to obtain sleep diary information on weekends and, if the opportunity presents itself, on holidays

FIGURE 20.1 Sample Sleep Log

Day	6	7	8	9	10	11	M	1	2	3	4	5	6	7	8	9	10	11	N	1	2	3	4	5

Child's Name: _____

Parents' Name: _____

Child's Age: _____ Birthdate: _____ Phone: _____

DIRECTIONS: 1. Draw an arrow down (v) when your child gets into bed. 2. Shade in the boxes when your child is sleeping. 3. Leave the boxes blank when your child is awake, even if in bed. 4. Draw an arrow up (ˆ) when your child gets out of bed. 5. NOTE: Each line of boxes represents parts of TWO Days.

Note: Sleep Log. M=midnight; N=noon.

Source: Modified from Ferber, R., *Solve your child's sleep problems. New York: Simon and Schuster, 1985, p. 105, with permission.*

in order to further understand how the sleep-wake cycle changes as a function of daytime activity structure. Such documentation can be especially helpful in the diagnosis of circadian rhythm sleep disorders, but it should be part of any standard sleep disturbance assessment (Thorpy, 1988).

Various sleep questionnaires can provide helpful data on which to base further inquiry into particular trouble areas. The Children's Sleep Behavior Scale, a 22-item Likert-type scale designed for evaluating sleep-related behaviors in the middle childhood years, can be used to identify major areas of concern and to compare current clinical presentation to normative data (Fisher, Pauley, & McGuire, 1989) (see Table 20.2). Circadian rhythm difficulties may be assessed in part with the Morningness/Eveningness Scale for Children (Carskadon, Vieira, & Acebo, 1993) (see Table 20.3). This brief self-report measure can provide information concerning possible phase shifts and the direction of such shifts. The Stanford Sleepiness Scale, a measure of subjective sleepiness levels, consists of a single seven-point scale ranging from very alert to excessively sleepy (Hoddes et al., 1973). This scale is sensitive to the effects of sleep deprivation and may be filled out at different times of the day to provide quantitative information regarding the severity of disturbance the child is experiencing (Herscovitch & Broughton, 1981).

Children's and adolescents' psychological distress and environmental stressor levels can be evaluated using various objective assessment measures to augment data obtained in the clinical interview. These include the Children's Depression Inventory (Kovacs, 1978), the Spielberger Child State-Trait Anxiety Inventory/State-Trait Anxiety Inventory, Form Y (Spielberger, Edwards, Montuon, & Lushene, 1970; Spielberger et al., 1968), the Coddington Life Events Scale (Coddington, 1972b), and the Minnesota Multiphasic Personality Inventory—Adolescent Form (Butcher et al., 1992). Since depression and anxiety can result from, as well as cause, sleep problems, it is important not to make causal conclusions pre-maturely. Similarly, children's sleep difficulties can cause family tension and parental marital discord, as well as develop from such stressors. Therefore, the clinician needs to take the time to carefully evaluate such issues. Other areas of concern, such as conduct problems, hyperactivity, inattentiveness, passivity, learning difficulty, psychosomatic complaints, impulsivity, anxiety, withdrawal, depression, problems in social relations, and aggressive behavior, can also be assessed using parent and teacher report on instruments such as the Revised Connors Rating Scale (Goyette, Connors, & Ulrich, 1978) and the Achenbach Child Behavior Checklist (Achenbach & Edelbrock, 1979). Caution and care in assessment are necessary because behavior problems can stem from or cause sleep disturbances.

While it is not necessary to seek consultation with a sleep disorders center in every case, overnight sleep evaluations can provide information that is important for the correct assessment, diagnosis, and treatment of a sleep disturbance. Referral to a sleep disorders center is essential in cases when narcolepsy or obstructive sleep apnea are suspected (American Sleep Disorders Association, 1992). Nocturnal polysomnography is usually performed for at least two nights in order to allow the child to get used to sleeping in a new environment. Measurements may include EEG, EOG, EMG, breath and arterial oxygen and carbon dioxide levels, nasal and oral airflow, abdominal/thoracic movements, and limb muscle activity. The documentation of the progression of sleep stages, duration of stages and their percentage of total sleep time, arousals, and characteristic behaviors provides empirical data on which to base diagnostic and treatment decisions. In addition, daytime polysomnographic tests, such as the Multiple Sleep Latency Test (MSLT) and the Maintenance of Wakefulness Test (MWT), can provide information on the severity of daytime sleepiness. These tests can be helpful in differential diagnosis, especially when narcolepsy or breathing-related sleep disorders are suspected, and can aid in the evaluation of treatment effectiveness.

TABLE 20.2. Children's Sleep Behavior Scale

Item	1	2	3	4	5
1. Does your child go to bed willingly?					
2. Is he/she a restless sleeper?					
3. Have you seen your child smiling while asleep?					
4. Does he/she wake up during the night?					
5. Have you heard your child talking in his/her sleep?					
6. Have you observed him/her sleep-walking?					
7. While asleep, does he/she ever sit up in bed?					
8. Does he/she grind his/her teeth while asleep?					
9. Have you heard your child laughing in his/her sleep?					
10. Has your child told you about having a frightening dream?					
11. Have you observed repetitive actions such as rocking or head banging while your child is asleep?					
12. Does he/she have problems with bed-wetting?					
13. Does your child fall asleep easily?					
14. Have you seen or heard your child having nightmares which he/she didn't remember the next day?					
15. Has he/she expressed a fear of sleeping in the dark?					
16. Is your child easy to wake in the morning?					
17. Have you observed your child having a nightmare during which he/she appeared extremely afraid or terrified?					
18. Have you looked in on your child and discovered that he/she was crying while asleep?					
19. Has he/she told you about having a pleasant dream?					
20. On the average, how many hours per night does he/she sleep?					
21. Does your child complain about difficulties going to sleep?					
22. Does he/she get up to go to the bathroom during the night?					

Note (1) Never = never in the past 6 months; (2) Rarely = once in the past 6 months; (3) Occasionally = two or three times in the past six months; (4) Quite often = four or five times in the past six months; (5) Often = six or more times in the past six months. For item #20, (1) 4–5 hours; (2) 6–7 hours; (3) 8–9 hours; (4) 10–11 hours; (5) 11+ hours.

Source: Reproduced from Fisher, B. E., Pauley, C., & McGuire, K. (1989). Children's sleep behavior scale: Normative data on 870 children in grades 1 to 6. Perceptual and Motor Skills, 68, 227–236, with permission.

The MSLT incorporates five nap opportunities at two hour intervals beginning at 9:30–10:00 A.M. For example, assessments may be scheduled for 10:00 A.M., 12:00 P.M., 2:00 P.M., 4:00 P.M., and 6:00 P.M., during a single day. For each nap opportunity, sleep latency is measured after the child assumes a relaxed state in bed and is instructed to fall asleep. Once asleep, the patient is allowed to sleep for 10 minutes. Over the five nap periods, an average sleep latency of less than 5 minutes or two or more sleep onset REM periods (SOREMPS) indicate the likelihood of narcolepsy (American Sleep Disorders Association, 1992). The MWT, an alternate measure of daytime sleepiness, involves five 10-minute nap opportunities and measures sleep latency from when the child is instructed to try to remain awake while in a semireclining position in a darkened room (Mitler, Gujavarty, & Browman, 1982). While it provides useful information concerning daytime sleepiness, this test has less diagnostic value than the MSLT as it lacks norms that reliably identify pathological sleepiness. When using the MSLT or the MWT, it is important to have a record of the child's sleep prior to the sleep laboratory sessions in

TABLE 20.3 Morningness/Eveningness Scale for Children

1. Imagine: School is canceled! You can get up whenever you want to. When would you get out of bed? Between . . .
   a. 5:00 and 6:30 A.M.
   b. 6:30 and 7:45 A.M.
   c. 7:45 and 9:45 A.M.
   d. 9:45 and 11:00 A.M.
   e. 11:00 A.M. and noon
2. Is it easy for you to get up in the morning?
   a. No way!
   b. Sort of
   c. Pretty easy
   d. It's a cinch
3. Gym class is set for 7:00 in the morning. How do you think you'll do?
   a. My best!
   b. Okay
   c. Worse than usual
   d. Awful
4. The bad news: You have to take a two-hour test.
   The good news: You can take it when you think you'll do your best. What time is that?
   a. 8:00 to 10:00 A.M.
   b. 11:00 A.M. to 1:00 P.M.
   c. 3:00 to 5:00 P.M.
   d. 7:00 to 9:00 P.M.
5. When do you have the most energy to do your favorite things?
   a. Morning! I'm tired in the evening
   b. Morning more than evening
   c. Evening more than morning
   d. Evening! I'm tired in the morning
6. Guess what? Your parents have decided to let you set your own bedtime. What time would you pick? Between . . .
   a. 8:00 and 9:00 P.M.
   b. 9:00 and 10:15 P.M.
   c. 10:15 P.M. and 12:30 A.M.
   d. 12:30 A.M. and 1:45 A.M.
   e. 1:45 and 3:00 A.M.
7. How alert are you in the first half hour you're up?
   a. Out of it
   b. A little dazed
   c. Okay
   d. Ready to take on the world
8. When does your body start to tell you it's time for bed (even if you ignore it)? Between . . .
   a. 8:00 and 9:00 P.M.
   b. 9:00 and 10:15 P.M.
   c. 10:15 P.M. and 12:30 A.M.
   d. 12:30 A.M. and 1:45 A.M.
   e. 1:45 and 3:00 A.M.
9. Say you had to get up at 6:00 A.M. every morning. What would it be like?
   a. Awful!
   b. Not so great
   c. Okay (if I have to)
   d. Fine, no problem
10. When you wake up in the morning how long does it take for you to be totally "with it?"
    a. 0 to 10 minutes
    b. 11 to 20 minutes
    c. 21 to 40 minutes
    d. more than 40 minutes

Note A score is derived by adding points for each answer: a = 1, b = 2, c = 3, d = 4, e = 5, except for items 1, 3, 4, 5, 6, 8, and 10, where point totals are reversed. The maximum score is 42 (maximal morning preference), and the minimum is 10 (minimal morning preference).

Source: Reproduced from Carskadon, M. A., Vieira, C., & Acebo, C. (1993). Association between puberty and delayed phase preference. Sleep, 16, 258–262, with permission.

order to evaluate the effects of the nighttime sleep disruption on daytime sleepiness.

Specific Considerations

Primary Insomnia

Parental distress over a child's difficulty initiating or maintaining sleep usually motivates the parents to seek clinical consultation (Ferber, 1987a). Careful evaluation of the degree of impairment experienced by the child and the coping strategies employed by the parents is necessary. Symptoms of insomnia in children include excessive daytime sleepiness, poor concentration, and declining school performance. The causes of insomnia in children are often different from those in adults. Poor sleep hygiene, nighttime fears, and parent/child interactions at bedtime, including poor limit setting, are often at the root of childhood insomnia (Ferber, 1987b). In addition, conditioning effects may maintain sleeplessness; for example, parental attention in response to a child's nighttime fears is reinforcing and may contribute to future episodes of difficulty initiating sleep. Medications, such as methylphenidate, and substances such as caffeine may also be involved. A 2-week sleep diary is an effective way to evaluate these factors, provided parents are consistent, comprehensive, and accurate in their records. As a wide variety of physiological conditions may result in insomnia, a thorough medical history and evaluation is generally indicated as a first step in the evaluation process (Kales, Soldatos, & Kales, 1982).

Primary Hypersomnia

Hypersomnia is often difficult to assess because it may be interpreted as occurring as a result of other sleep disturbances, such as parasomnias or insomnia. Also, differentiating between hypersomnia and narcolepsy may be difficult in cases when symptoms are not severe. For example, early-stage narcolepsy, in which the presence of auxiliary symptoms are not yet present, resembles hypersomnia. Hypersomnia symptoms include excessive daytime sleepiness, low alertness, attention problems, poor school performance, sleep drunkenness, and frequent unrefreshing daytime naps (Sheldon, Spire, & Levy, 1992a). Total sleep time that is more than 2 hours longer than the average for a child's age is considered clinically significant (see Table 20.1 for average sleep times across age groups). This excessive sleepiness occurs without the symptoms of narcolepsy (cataplexy, sleep paralysis, hypnagogic hallucinations, sleep attacks), though episodes of "microsleeps," that is, periods of sleep lasting up to 30 seconds during which external stimuli are not perceived and polysomnography indicates sleep, may occur. Polysomnography reveals MSLT of less than 7 minutes and no sleep-onset REM periods (SOREMPS). Medical evaluation of central nervous system functioning is essential and should include assessment of infections, seizures, head injury, other neurologic impairment, and use of medications, because these conditions are sometimes associated with excessive daytime sleepiness (Sheldon et al., 1992a).

Narcolepsy

The classic tetrad of narcoleptic symptoms includes excessive daytime sleepiness and sleep attacks, cataplexy, hypnagogic hallucinations (distortions in visual or auditory perception that occur at the onset or ending of the sleep period, e.g., the child is still "awake" but sees "monsters" or hears "footsteps" or "breaking glass"), and sleep paralysis (Guilleminault, 1987b). Daytime naps are refreshing and are usually followed by 2 to 4 hours of alertness before sleepiness ensues again. Average sleep latency on the MSLT of less than 5 minutes and the presence of two or more SOREMPS are pathognomic indicators of narcolepsy. In persons with narcolepsy, polysomnography reveals larger amounts of REM sleep than are typically seen in normal subjects. Narcolepsy is rarely seen before adolescence and is often difficult to assess in children because naps aren't considered bothersome at this age. Also, parents may not be familiar with the age-appropriate frequency and duration of naps. There can be severe social and academic ramifications related to narcolepsy, including stigmatization, impaired learning, and behavior problems. Familial history should be assessed, as narcolepsy has been found to be related to the human leukocyte antigen (HLA) DR2 (Honda, Asaka, Tanaka, & Juji, 1983).

Breathing-Related Sleep Disorders

In the assessment of breathing-related sleep problems, nocturnal polysomnography is always indicated. During these sessions, special attention is given to cardiovascular functioning and breathing parameters such as nasal/oral airflow, arterial blood oxygen saturation, and respiratory pauses (Guilleminault, 1987c). During apneic episodes, heart rate varies between bradycardia and tachycardia. Central sleep apnea is usually asymptomatic except for awakenings in which the child is scared because of feelings of choking and inability to catch his or her breath. Common symptoms of obstructive sleep apnea include nocturnal restless sleep, unusual sleep postures, snorts and snoring, morning headaches, daytime difficulty breathing, mouth breathing and subsequent dry mouth, and excessive daytime sleepiness (Guilleminault, 1987c). Children with obstructive sleep apnea often exhibit confusion, impaired memory, and poor judgment, especially in the morning. Other associated behaviors include speech articulation difficulties, nocturnal enuresis, excessive activity, attention problems, fidgeting, and pathological shyness. Obstructive sleep apnea is often associated with morbid obesity, craniofacial syndromes, respiratory allergies, and adenotonsillar enlargement or other soft-tissue deformities. Symptoms may be aggravated by alcohol intake, extended periods of time spent at high altitude, and allergies. If left untreated, risks include hypertension, cardiac arrhythmia, and Sudden Infant Death Syndrome (Guilleminault, 1987c).

Circadian Rhythm Sleep Disorder

Parents of children with circadian rhythm disturbances, especially sleep phase delay syndromes, usually seek clinical consultation because their children appear to have insomnia if they go to bed too early and exhibit excessive daytime sleepiness if they wake up too early (Ferber, 1987a). Such disturbances are usually socioenvironmentally produced and may be linked to parental work schedule, increased time demands, or poor sleep hygiene. The increased need for sleep in adolescence, combined with the shorter total sleep time that usually comes with increased academic and social demands, may lead to phase shifts and excessive daytime sleepiness (Carskadon & Dement, 1987). Assessment may include the "Owl and Lark" questionnaire and a 2-week sleep diary to document phase-shift direction. In addition, the patient may be asked to record body temperature every 3 hours during the day in order to determine whether a phase shift in peak body temperature has occurred; such a shift would indicate that a circadian rhythm disorder is likely to be present (Czeisler et al., 1981).

Nightmare Disorder

The primary assessment issue with nightmare disorder is differential diagnosis with sleep terror disorder. Nightmares occur during the last third of the night and involve frightening dreams that lead to an abrupt awakening from REM sleep, after which the child may be distressed but alert and consolable. Bodily movements and vocalizations are rare, and autonomic nervous system (ANS) activation is present but mild. In addition, the child stays in bed and usually has good recall of both the dream content upon awakening and the event the next day (Kales et al., 1980b). Nightmares often occur following traumatic experiences and stressful life events and may reflect underlying insecurity, depression, anxiety, and guilt (Association of Sleep Disorders, 1979). However, nightmares are common in children and adolescents and usually reflect acute anxiety. Clinical concerns are raised if nightmares occur nightly or persist after adolescence.

Sleep Terror Disorder and Sleepwalking Disorder

Disorders of arousal, both sleep terrors and sleepwalking occur during the first third of the night and involve a sudden awakening out of NREM Stage 3 or 4 sleep. Though the child's eyes may be open, the patient is unresponsive to parental attempts to awaken him or her. Sleep terrors involve intense vocalizations, frantic movement, confusion, extreme autonomic nervous system activation, and amnesia for the event upon awakening (Broughton, 1968). Sleepwalking is manifested by rhythmic movements that may involve rising from bed and walking or running about. Characteristics include reduced alertness and responsiveness, a blank stare, confusion and disorientation upon being awakened, and limited recall or amnesia for the event the next day. Both disorders can be precipitated by fever, bladder distention, or external stimuli, such as a loud noise. While both disorders can be influenced by traumatic events and related anxiety, concomitant psychopathology may be occasionally seen in adolescents (Carlson, White, & Turkat, 1982). In addition, there is some evidence that a genetic factor contributes to these disorders. Sleep terrors may be associated with high levels of inhibited aggression and anxiety suppression, as well as depression, phobias, and obsessive-compulsive tendencies. Sleepwalking may be associated with more outwardly directed behavioral patterns, such as aggression, acting out, and hyperactivity. Further, sleep terrors and sleepwalking may be exacerbated or maintained by conditions that increase NREM Stage 3 and 4 sleep, such as sleep deprivation and alcohol use (Kales et al., 1980a).

TREATMENT

General Considerations

While the literature on treatment of sleep disorders in adults is extensive, there are comparatively fewer studies of sleep disorder interventions for adolescents and children. Though many well-structured child and adolescent treatment studies do exist, several are limited by low subject numbers and lack of control groups. The proceeding treatment sections should be viewed in this light; clinicians need to be cautious in delivery of services in areas where there is not a strong experimental data base upon which to rely.

Psychological Approaches

Behavioral management is often the first step in treatment of sleep disorders in children and adolescents. Initial interventions should focus on sleep hygiene (Ferber, 1985a). Parents should be encouraged to help their child create both a bedtime routine and an environment that is conducive to sleep. Clear, simple, and consistent limits should be set and maintained concerning bedtime. A time by which the child will be in bed should be set and consistently enforced. Eating and drinking (especially of liquids that contain caffeine, such as colas, tea, and hot chocolate) close to bedtime should be discouraged, though steps should be taken to avoid having the child go to bed hungry. In addition, vigorous exercise in the hours immediately before bedtime should be avoided so as not to overstimulate the child and wake her or him up. Careful consideration of any medications the child is taking is necessary to avoid agents that may disrupt sleep (e.g., caffeine, alcohol in cough syrup, methylphenidate, certain antihistamine; parents should carefully check labels for additives and other stimulants). A bedtime ritual should be established if one is not already in place. This should include a pattern for grooming and personal hygiene, flossing and brushing teeth, and using the bathroom. Full bathing is often a "stimulant" before bedtime and is usually less disruptive if it is done earlier in the evening (Ferber, 1985a). Bedtime stories, lullabies, and the use of stuffed animals or a special blanket may help smooth the transition to bed. Once bedtime rituals are completed, the child should be left to fall asleep without parental action.

The child's room should be dark (night-lights or closet lights may be left on), quiet and maintained at a comfortable temperature (<75 degrees). Nighttime awakenings should be handled matter-of-factly, and, in the event that the child gets out of bed, she or he should be escorted back to bed, comforted, and left alone to fall asleep. As in the case of "tucking in," only if absolutely necessary should parents stay in the room while the child falls asleep. The process of withdrawing the parent's presence is described in a later section. Morning wake time should also be consistent. Parents may be compelled to let their child sleep late into the morning on weekends and holidays, but inconsistent sleep times may lead to phase shifts and difficulty setting limits when normal weekday schedules resume (Ferber, 1987a). Daytime sleep hygiene factors include limiting the duration of naps and the time of day they occur (late afternoon or evening naps may lead to excessive wakefulness at bedtime). Daytime ingestion of certain medications (e.g., methylphenidate) and caffeine may also disrupt nighttime sleep.

Behavior modification programs can be effective for children with a wide variety of sleep disturbances (Durand & Mindell, 1990; Piazza & Fisher, 1991a). Target behaviors should be set, and the contingencies maintaining those behaviors should be identified. In particular, it is often the case that parental reactions and attention become reinforcing to such disorders as insomnia and nightmares. With this in mind, parental responses to sleep disruption should be evaluated and modified so that parents provide comfort to the child without perpetuating the disturbance. For example, graduated extinction requires the parents to delay coming to the room of a child who has awakened (Durand & Mindell, 1990). Each time the child cries out or awakens, the parent waits a few minutes longer before coming to comfort the child; this occurs until the child learns to return to sleep on his or her own. Similarly, parents of a child with insomnia related to nighttime fears may have a habit of sitting in the child's room until she or he is asleep. The presence of a parent can be reinforcing and may perpetuate this behavior (Richman et al., 1985). Parents can "phase themselves out" by moving their chair closer to the door each night until the child can fall

asleep on his or her own without the presence of the parent.

Reinforcement programs are also successful (Ferber, 1985a). Such programs can range from getting to choose the book a parent will read if bedtime is abided by to earning points toward special privileges for "good sleep nights." Material reinforcers may be necessary at first but should be gradually withdrawn over time and replaced with more subtle social rewards, such as praise and affection. At the same time, it is important to identify the contingencies these new reinforcers will be competing with. In order for material or social reinforcers to be effective in changing sleep behavior, parents may need to alter their own behavior already in place. For example, a warm, cozy bed with "two big people" provides a very comforting and safe environment for a child who has had a nightmare; reinforcers equally comforting to the child should be sought as an alternative. Behavioral modification interventions, however, take time and must be adhered to consistently. At the beginning of such interventions, many parents report that their child's problems get worse rather than better. However, after this initial upsurge in symptoms, such programs are usually quite effective (Ferber, 1985a).

Relaxation training can be successful in reducing sleep-related anxiety in children and adolescents. Once these procedures have been learned, they can be self-employed by patients to alleviate sleep disturbances (Anderson, 1979). Several options for relaxation training exist. Breathing entrainment involves teaching slow, abdominal breathing to ensure optimal arterial carbon dioxide levels and adequate oxygen distribution throughout the body. Proper ventilation often reduces anxiety and promotes relaxation. Another alternative, progressive relaxation, is a process of tensing and releasing different muscle groups while attending to the sensations of tension and relaxation that occur (Bernstein & Borkovec, 1973). Finally, a more recent approach, stretch-based relaxation, alternates a series of muscle stretches with rest periods when the individual focuses on feelings of relaxation in the muscles following gentle stretching exercises (Carlson et al., 1990). These techniques help the patient learn to identify the physical sensations associated with anxiety and muscle tension and to take self-regulatory steps to counteract them.

There has been limited support for the use of hypnosis in the treatment of childhood sleep disorders, sleep terrors, and sleepwalking in particular (Kohen, Mahowald, & Rosen, 1992; Kramer, 1989). Typically, this intervention involves imagery tasks during which the child pictures him- or herself sleeping comfortably through the night. These peaceful images are then associated with self-assuring statements about the safety and peacefulness of sleep. However, studies on hypnosis as a treatment for childhood sleep disorders are typically case reports and do not use standardized methodology; therefore, the mental health clinician should be very cautious in pursuing this intervention (Kohen et al., 1992; Kramer, 1989).

While sleep disorders of childhood are seldom associated with severe psychopathology, psychological interventions focused on alleviating anxiety, depression, phobias, and low self-esteem related to impairment caused by a sleep disorder (e.g., narcolepsy) are often indicated (Guilleminault, 1987c). In addition, family therapy may be helpful to address animosity, frustration, marital discord, and other distress of family members in reaction to the patient's sleep disorder. At the same time, it is possible that stress levels in the home are contributing to the child's sleep disorder, and family therapy may focus on such factors as well.

Education and reassurance are often the most important methods of treatment (Guilleminault, 1987a, 1987b). Explanations of the possible etiology and underlying physiology of sleep disorders, especially those that involve more dramatic behaviors (e.g., sleep terrors and sleepwalking), can help parents and children understand why and how the disturbances occur. In addition, reassuring both parents and children that sleep difficulties are common and often spontaneously resolve may alleviate some of the distress involved with the disorder.

Another essential component of treatment is management of the sleep disorder (Guilleminault, 1987b). Steps such as making the child's room and surrounding areas safe in case of displacement from bed (i.e., sleep terrors or sleepwalking) and scheduling daytime naps to alleviate excessive sleepiness (i.e., narcolepsy, hypersomnia) are necessary for certain disorders. In most cases, several of the psychological interventions mentioned will be combined in order to treat childhood and adolescent sleep disorders successfully (Piazza & Fisher, 1991a; Richman et al., 1985).

Biological Approaches

Most clinicians would agree that pharmacological treatment of childhood and adolescent sleep disorders should be a last resort, to be considered only after behavioral approaches have been tried with limited success (Dahl, 1992). The potential for side effects, tolerance, and withdrawal, especially in children and adolescents, makes it essential to exhaust other treatment options before turning to medications. Exceptions include cases in which the disorder is causing extremely severe impairment or posing a lethal threat to the child (e.g., severe cataplexy in narcolepsy may lead to accidents). If pharmacologic treatment is employed, it is best used in conjunction with behavioral interventions, and several guidelines may prove useful. First, parents should be reminded that all medications should be dispensed with close supervision of the child's primary-care physician. Further, the lowest dosage possible should be given for the shortest amount of time possible. "Drug holidays" should be scheduled regularly to avoid tolerance, subsequent dosage increases, and/or side effects. If possible, the physician should introduce new drugs and increases in dosage on Friday nights so as to avoid unexpected side effects from these changes that might impair school performance (Dahl, 1992). Finally, it is generally agreed that the purpose of medications in treating childhood sleep disorders is to bring severe symptoms under control. In such severe cases, behavioral and pharmacologic treatment may be used together. Once behavioral and pharmacologic interventions are in place and have been shown to successfully manage the sleep disorder, upon the consent of the physician use of pharmacologic treatment should be decreased and ultimately eliminated.

Several medications have been used with success in treating sleep disorders, although most have been used primarily with adult patient populations. Therefore, physicians who dispense prescriptions to improve sleep in children and adolescents need to be prudent and cautious. Benzodiazapines, such as diazepam, have been used in treatment of arousal disorders because of their NREM Stage 3 and Stage 4 suppressive effects (Dahl, 1992). Tricyclic antidepressants, such as imipramine and protriptyline, have been shown to suppress REM Stage sleep and are often used in the treatment of cataplexy in narcoleptics. At the same time, central nervous system (CNS) stimulants, such as methylphenidate and pemoline, are used to manage daytime sleepiness (Dahl, 1992). Dosage is dependent on the patient's body weight and should be strictly monitored. It should be reiterated that the use of medications by a physician often represents a last resort in the treatment of childhood sleep disorders, unless there is severe impairment or impending danger to the child.

Specific Considerations for Behavioral Management

Primary Insomnia

Several behavioral treatments are suggested for childhood insomnia. First, evaluation and reform of sleep hygiene, including the establishment of a consistent routine, is necessary. This should involve deconditioning nonsleep behaviors associated with the child's bed (Ferber, 1985a). In order to associate the bed with relaxation and sleep, activities such as playing, studying, and sometimes even reading in bed should be avoided at all times. In addition, curtailment of time in bed can be effective. While it may initially result in sleep deprivation, delaying bedtime for an hour may help the child settle down and assume normal sleep. If this is successful, bedtime can be advanced 15 minutes each night until the original bedtime is

reached (Ollendick, Hagopian, & Huntzinger, 1991; Piazza & Fisher, 1991a). An alternative approach involves getting the child out of bed if he or she has trouble settling for more than 10 minutes. Allowing hours of sleeplessness to occur unattended can foster "nonsleep" associations with being in bed. After a few minutes out of bed, the child should be returned to bed for another try at going to sleep. Because parental attention can reinforce and perpetuate sleeplessness, steps should be taken to eliminate secondary gains for the child. These may include the "phase-out" (in which parents sit in the room and move progressively toward the door night by night) and graduated extinction (waiting longer and longer before coming to comfort the child) approaches described earlier (Durand & Mindell, 1990).

If insomnia is due to nighttime fears or anxiety, therapeutic interventions such as cognitive-behavioral techniques and relaxation training may be appropriate in selected cases (Ferber, 1985; Piazza & Fisher, 1991b). For example, use of one of the relaxation approaches described earlier in conjunction with repeating a calming self-statement (e.g., "Relax and go to sleep") can be quite effective in alleviating nighttime worries that impede sleep onset. Intrusive thoughts rarely can be "turned off," but they can be replaced by focusing attention on thoughts that are calming and relaxing. Pharmacologic treatment has not generally been recommended, although diazepam and imipramine have been used with limited success in children (Ollendick et al., 1991).

Primary Hypersomnia

The primary mode of treatment is management of daytime sleepiness. Strategic scheduling of naps during times of day when sleepiness is most severe can provide temporary relief, although this strategy may result in sleep drunkenness and lethargy (Sheldon et al., 1992a). For example, if a child typically experiences extreme sleepiness after lunch, brief (e.g., 20 minutes) naps should be scheduled at that time. Engaging the child in activities upon awakening may be one approach to minimizing postnap grogginess. Hypersomnia has been shown to have a poor response to medicine, and, though stimulants have shown some success, their use has not been recommended due to their side effects and to nighttime sleep disruption (Sheldon et al., 1992a). Thus, the best current treatment recommendations focus on managing sleepiness and avoiding or minimizing treatment side effects. The sparse literature on empirically established treatments for hypersomnia suggests that continued clinical research is needed to improve therapeutic approaches to excessive sleepiness in children and adolescents.

Narcolepsy

As with hypersomnia, the major focus of the treatment of narcolepsy is behavioral management. Daytime naps, 20–30 minutes in length, scheduled around noon and in late afternoon can be effective in controlling sleepiness. Unlike hypersomnia, narcoleptics usually wake from these naps refreshed and can function well for 2–4 hours before sleepiness returns. In addition, education of the patient, parents, and teachers is essential to help them create an understanding and supportive environment for the child. The symptoms and physiological underpinnings of narcolepsy should be explained. This can help eliminate resentment, frustration, and guilt experienced by family members, classmates, and friends. Parents and teachers should be sensitive to the fact that narcolepsy is a very frightening experience for the child. In particular, sleep paralysis and hypnagogic hallucinations can be alarming; it should be explained to the child that episodes of these sensations are temporary and will pass quickly. Parents may let the child fall asleep in a room other than the bedroom so that she or he can be near others to reduce the fear involved with these symptoms (Guilleminault, 1987a). In addition to managing daytime sleepiness, another goal of treatment is to eliminate cataplexy because of the accidents and impairment it can cause. Under the careful supervision of the primary-care physician, methylphenidate has

been given to relieve daytime sleepiness, and imipramine has been successful in eliminating cataplexy. When these medications are used, it is recommended that both be prescribed with the lowest dosage possible to avoid side effects, and care should be taken to schedule "vacations" from these medications (Karacan & Howell, 1988).

Breathing-Related Sleep Disorder

Close collaboration with the child's primary-care physician and referral to a respiratory specialist is indicated in most cases of breathing-related sleep disorder. Standard behavioral treatment includes weight loss through dieting, behavior modification of eating patterns, and exercise. Obstructive sleep apnea is often treated by surgical means such as tonsillectomy and/or adenoidectomy or other soft-tissue reconstruction (Potsic & Wetmore, 1990). Assessment and treatment of medical conditions or syndromes associated with sleep apneas should be made via referral to a physician (Guilleminault, 1987c).

Circadian Rhythm Sleep Disorder

Circadian rhythm disorders occur because the child's internal sleep-wake regulating cycle is mismatched with environmental demands. Behavioral shaping that involves advancing or delaying the child's bedtime is the most effective treatment (Czeisler et al., 1981; Sheldon, Spire, & Levy, 1992f). The most common childhood circadian disorder, sleep phase delay, can be treated in this way. If the child's time of sleep onset is delayed by a few hours and is later than the desired bedtime, bedtime can be *advanced* by 15 minutes each night (i.e., from 11:30 P.M. to 11:15 P.M. to 11:00 P.M., and so on) until the desired bedtime has been reached. At the same time, morning wake time should be advanced in 15-minute increments to maintain the same total sleep time. Special attention to sleep hygiene is essential, and each new bedtime or waketime should be strictly enforced (Czeisler et al., 1981). If sleep onset is delayed by *more than 4 hours*, the same incremental shift principles are applied. However, because it is easier to delay sleep schedules than to advance them, the desired bedtime is reached "the long way around." Preferably during a period of time when daytime demands and responsibilities are minimal (e.g., vacation), bedtime (and, one hopes, sleep onset) is *delayed* by 2 or 3 hours each day until the desired bedtime has been reached. For example, a child whose bedtime is 9:00 P.M. but who has experienced a sleep-phase delay and is unable to sleep until 3:00 A.M. should have bedtime (and in effect, sleep onset) delayed by a few hours each day (e.g., 3:00 A.M. to 5:00 A.M. to 7:00 A.M., and so on) until the desired bedtime is reached. As in the first scenario, it is important to delay waking time by 2 or 3 hours each day as well in order to maintain the same total sleep time (Sheldon et al., 1992f). These bedtime advances and shifts can be augmented by reinforcement programs to motivate the child to adhere to the new schedule (Sheldon et al., 1992f).

Nightmare Disorder

Primary treatment for nightmares includes reassurance and support of the child and parents, special attention to sleep hygiene, and management of sleep-related anxiety and fears. Reassurance that nightmares are a normal part of childhood sleep and that they usually spontaneously resolve should be given (Ferber, 1985a). In addition, steps should be taken to assure the child that he or she is safe and protected during sleep. Parents should be encouraged to be matter-of-fact and reassuring with their child following a nightmare. Parents who show excessive concern or anxiety may reinforce the frightening nature of the nightmare. There is a delicate balance the parent must strike in reassuring the child without unwittingly setting up reinforcers that increase the likelihood the child will seek nurturance from the parent through an increased incidence of nightmare reports. Attention to possible environmental and behavioral factors that can contribute to nightmares should be given, and anxiety-provoking stimuli (e.g., scary stories, violent television shows or movies) and traumatic experiences should be avoided.

In addition, several therapeutic techniques have been effective in the treatment of recurrent nightmares. Systematic desensitization combines relaxation training with exposure to anxiety provoking stimuli. A hierarchy of fearful situations or nightmare-related images is constructed and arranged from "least" to "most" anxiety provoking. The therapist then works with the child to approach each "higher" step in sequence while using relaxation techniques to alleviate anxiety (Ollendick et al., 1991). Another approach is to have the child tell and retell the nightmare, while practicing relaxation techniques. This combines the process of "working through" with desensitization (Ollendick et al., 1991). Another alternative, "dream reorganization," combines systematic desensitization and coping self-statements (e.g., "it's just a dream, it isn't real") to countercondition anxiety-provoking nightmare content (Palace & Johnston, 1989). After relaxation training and cognitive behavioral training aimed at developing reassuring self-statements, the child undergoes guided rehearsal of mastery endings to dream content hierarchy items. For instance, the child may develop a happy ending to a recurrent frightening dream; rehearsal of such alternative dreams may then lead to nightmare resolution (Palace & Johnston, 1989).

Sleep Terror Disorder and Sleepwalking Disorder

Because both sleep terrors and sleepwalking are disorders of arousal, similar treatment is indicated. A first goal of treatment involves management and prevention of injury, especially with sleepwalking. The potential risk of an accident while moving about during sleep should be addressed by ensuring that the child's room and surrounding areas are made safe. If the child does not have a ground-floor room, stairs should be gated or blocked, doors should be closed, windows should be locked, and objects that the child could step on should be cleared. Parents may consider using an alarm attached to the child's door to alert them that an episode is occurring. During a sleepwalking episode, the child should not be awakened but should be carefully guided back to bed. Though sleep terrors can involve moving about the home, in most cases the child sits bolt upright in bed and appears to be in great distress; again, the child should not be awakened but should be comforted and allowed to settle and resume sleeping. Another management technique involves identifying the time that sleep terrors or sleepwalking happen (usually during the first few hours of the night) and waking the child 15 minutes prior to their occurrence (Rickert & Johnson, 1988). These scheduled awakenings are then phased out over time. It has been suggested that this approach may reset the child's circadian rhythm and shape longer and longer periods of continuous sleep as it is phased out (Ricken & Johnson, 1988).

While the child seldom recalls sleep terrors or sleepwalking the next day, these dramatic behaviors can be extremely distressing to parents and other family members. Reassurance and education about the underlying physiology of arousal disorders can be comforting. As in all sleep disorders, reform of sleep hygiene is important and may contribute to a decrease in the frequency of sleep terror or sleepwalking episodes. Steps should be taken to avoid liquids close to bedtime and to minimize noise (both bladder pressure and noise can precipitate an episode). In addition, any situations leading to increases in NREM Stage 3 and Stage 4 sleep (e.g., sleep deprivation, drug and alcohol use) should be avoided. Therapeutic interventions for arousal disorders involve relieving anxiety associated with sleep and dreams. Hypnosis, as described earlier, has been shown in case studies to be successful in the treatment of sleep terrors, and relaxation training can further decrease anxiety (Kramer, 1989; Kohen et al., 1992).

Only if sleep terrors and sleepwalking are severe (occurring every night) and debilitating (leading to injury) should pharmacological treatment be considered. In addition, drug therapy should be employed in conjunction with the management and therapeutic interventions described earlier, and should be aban-doned as soon as behavioral means are deemed sufficient to manage the disorder. The benzodiazepine diazepam acts to suppress NREM Stage 3 and Stage 4 sleep and has been effective in treatment of children with sleepwalking and/or sleep terror disorder. However, side effects such as daytime sedation and alteration of normal sleep patterns are serious concerns (Dahl, 1992). Also, the long-term effects of suppression of NREM Stage 3 and Stage 4 sleep on growth hormone release, immune functioning, and other physiological processes have not been explored. It should be emphasized that sleep terrors and sleepwalking in childhood often resolve spontaneously as the child grows and matures, although occasionally they persist into adolescence and adulthood (Sheldon, Spire, & Levy, 1992d).

SUMMARY

Sleep disorders in children and adolescents can be successfully treated by a clinician working in close cooperation with a primary-care physician and a sleep disorders specialist. A combination of behavioral, psychotherapeutic, educational, and, on occasions, pharmacologic treatment will likely lead to management, if not resolution, of the disturbance. The etiology of sleep disorders is often multifactorial. In this light, several considerations should be noted. First, clinicians often must rely on parental report of their children's sleep difficulties. This information must be evaluated with care because parents may have biases related to past interactions with the child and to their own past and/or present sleep difficulties. Second, in some cases, sleep problems occur secondary to current or past sexual abuse. The clinician should be alert to this possibility and pursue it if indicated. In cases where abuse is suspected, parents may not know about or may be reluctant to report these traumatic events, thus failing to provide information that may have a bearing on the child's sleep difficulty. Third, parents do not usually witness an entire night of their child's sleep and may not have accurate or complete information. For example, if a child's nighttime arousals are not disruptive, neither parents nor children may be privy to them. That is one reason that referral to a sleep disorders specialist for overnight polysomnography may be helpful. Such an evaluation, however, can be costly and may be unwarranted if accurate information from parents can be gathered. While protocols of polysomnographic evaluations vary, costs may range from $800–1500 depending on the procedures administered, the length of the study, and the geographic region. It is more cost-efficient in the long run, however, to assess, diagnose, and treat a disorder with the help of polysomnography than to misdiagnose and unsuccessfully treat the disturbance over a period of time. Finally, when treating childhood and adolescent sleep disorders, the mental health clinician should collaborate closely the primary physician, especially when medications are involved. Taken together, these principles can set the stage for successful management of sleep disorders in children and adolescents.

REFERENCES

Achenbach, T. M., & Edelbrock, C. S. (1979). *Manual for the child behavior checklist and revised child behavior profile*. Burlington: Department of Psychiatry, University of Vermont.

Adam, K., & Oswald, I. (1983). Protein synthesis, bodily renewal and the sleep-wake cycle. *Clinical Science, 65*, 561–567.

American Psychiatric Association (1994). *The diagnostic and statistical manual of mental disorders* (4th ed.). Washington, DC: Author.

American Sleep Disorders Association (1992). The clinical use of the Multiple Sleep Latency Test. *Sleep, 15* (3), 268–276.

Anderson, D. R. (1979). Treatment of insomnia in a 13-year-old boy by relaxation training and reduction of parental attention. *Journal of Behavior Therapy and Experimental Psychiatry, 10* (1), 263–265.

Aserinsky, E., & Kleitman, N. (1955). A motility cycle in sleeping infants as manifested by ocular and gross bodily activity. *Journal of Applied Physiology, 8*, 11–18.

Aserinsky, E., & Kleitman, N. (1955). Two types of ocular motility occurring in sleep. *Journal of Applied Physiology, 8*, 1–10.

Association of Sleep Disorders Centers and Association for the Psychophysiological Study of Sleep (1979). Diagnostic classification of sleep and arousal disorders (1st ed.). *Sleep, 2*, 1–154.

Benoit, D., Zeanah, C. H., Boucher, C., & Minde, K. K. (1992). Sleep disorders in early childhood: Association with insecure maternal attachment. *Journal of the American Academy of Child and Adolescent Psychiatry, 31* (1), 86–93.

Bernstein, D. A., & Borkovec, T. D. (1973). *Progressive relaxation training: A manual for the helping professions*. Champaign, IL: Research Press.

Bixler, E. O., Kales, A., Soldatos, C. R., Kales, J. D., & Healey, S. (1979). Prevalence of sleep disorders in the Los Angeles metropolitan area. *American Journal of Psychiatry, 136*, 1257–1262.

Block, V. Hennevin, E., & Leconte, P. (1981). The phenomenon of paradoxical sleep augmentation after learning: Experimental studies of its characteristics and significance. In W. Fishbein (Ed.), *Sleep, dreams and memory* (pp. 1–18). Jamaica, NY: Spectrum.

Broughton, R. J. (1968). Sleep disorders: Disorders of arousal? *Science, 158*, 1070–1078.

Butcher, J. N., Williams, C. L., Graham, J. R., Archer, R. P., Tellegen, A., Ben-Porath, Y. S., & Kaemmer, B. (1992). *Minnesota Multiphasic Personality Inventory-Adolescent (MMPI-A): Manual for administration, scoring, and interpretation*. Minneapolis: University of Minnesota Press.

Carlson, C. R., Collins, F. L., Nitz, A. J., Sturgis, E. T., & Rogers, J. L. (1990). Muscle stretching as an alternative relaxation training procedure. *Journal of Behavior Therapy and Experimental Psychiatry, 21*, 29–38.

Carlson, C. R., White, D. K., & Turkat, I. D. (1982). Night terrors: A clinical and empirical review. *Clinical Psychology Review, 2*, 455–468.

Carskadon, M. A., & Dement, W. C. (1987). Sleepiness in the normal adolescent. In C. Guilleminault (Ed.), *Sleep and its disorders in children* (pp. 53–66). New York: Ravens Press.

Carskadon, M. A., Harvey, K., & Dement, W. C. (1981). Acute restriction of nocturnal sleep in children. *Perceptual and Motor Skills, 53*, 103.

Carskadon, M. A., Keenan, S., & Dement, W. C. (1987). Nighttime sleep and daytime sleep tendency in preadolescents. In C. Guilleminault (Ed.), *Sleep and it's disorders in children* (pp. 43–52). New York: Ravens Press.

Carskadon, M. A., Vieira, C., & Acebo, C. (1993). Association between puberty and delayed phase preference. *Sleep, 16*, 258–262.

Clore, E. R., & Hibel, J. (1993). The parasomnias of childhood. *Journal of Pediatric Health Care, 7*, 12–16.

Coble, P. A., Kupfer, D. J., Reynolds, C. F., III, & Houck, P. (1987). EEG sleep of healthy children 6 to 12 years of age. In C. Guilleminault (Ed.), *Sleep and its disorders in children* (pp. 29–41). New York: Ravens Press.

Coddington, R. D. (1972b). The significance of life events as etiologic factors in the disease of children. II. A study of a normal population. *Journal of Psychosomatic Research, 16*, 205–213.

Crick, F., & Mitchison, G. (1983). The function of dream sleep. *Nature, 304*, 111–114.

Czeisler, C. A., Richardson, G. S., Coleman, R. M., Zimmerman, J. C., Moore-Ede, M. C., Dement, W. C., & Weitzman, E. D. (1981). Chronotherapy: Resetting the circadian clocks of patients with delayed sleep phase insomnia. *Sleep, 4*, 1–21.

Dahl, R. E. (1992). The pharmacologic treatment of sleep disorders. *Psychiatric Clinics of North America, 15* (1), 161–178.

Dement, W., & Kleitman, N. (1957). Cyclic variations in EEG during sleep and their relation to eye movements, body motility, and dreaming. *Electroencephalography and Clinical Neurophysiology, 9*, 673–690.

Diagnostic Classification Steering Committee, Thorpy, M. J. (Chairman) (1990). *International classification of sleep disorders: Diagnostic and coding manual.* Rochester: American Sleep Disorders Association.

Durand, M. V., & Mindell, J. A. (1990). Behavioral treatment of multiple childhood sleep disorders: Effects on child and family. *Behavior Modification, 14* (1), 37–49.

Ellis, E. M. (1991). Watchers in the night: An anthropological look at sleep disorders. *American Journal of Psychotherapy, 45* (2), 211–220.

Ferber, R. (1985a). Sleep disorders in infants and children. In T. L. Riley (Ed.), *Clinical aspects of sleep and sleep disturbance* (pp. 113–157). Boston: Butterworth.

Ferber, R. (1985b). Solve your child's sleep problems. New York: Simon and Schuster.

Ferber, R. (1987a). Circadian and schedule disturbances. In C. Guilleminault (Ed.), *Sleep and its disorders in children* (pp. 165–175). New York: Ravens Press.

Ferber, R. (1987b). The sleepless child. In C. Guilleminault (Ed.), *Sleep and its disorders in children* (pp. 141–161). New York: Ravens Press.

Ferber, R., & Kryger, M. (1995). Principles and practices of sleep medicine in the child. Philadelphia: W. B. Saunders.

Fisher, B. E., Pauley, C., & McGuire, K. (1989). Children's sleep behavior scale: Normative data on 870 children in grades 1–6. *Perceptual and Motor Skills, 68*, 227–236.

Goyette, C. H., Connors, C. K., & Ulrich, R. F. (1978). Normative data on Revised Connors Parent and Teacher Rating Scales. *Journal of Abnormal Child Psychology, 46*, 221–236.

Guilleminault, C. (1987a). Disorders of arousal in children: Somnambulism and night terrors. In C. Guilleminault (Ed.), *Sleep and its disorders in children* (pp. 243–252). New York: Ravens Press.

Guilleminault, C. (1987b). Narcolepsy and its differential diagnosis. In C. Guilleminault (Ed.), *Sleep and its disorders in children* (pp. 181–194). New York: Ravens Press.

Guilleminault, C. (1987c). Obstructive sleep apnea syndrome in children. In C. Guilleminault (Ed.), *Sleep and its disorders in children* (pp. 213–224). New York: Ravens Press.

Hartmann, E., Orzack, M. H., & Branconnier, R. (1974). Deficits produced by sleep deprivation: Reversal by D- and L-amphetamine. *Sleep Research, 3*, 151.

Herscovitch, J., & Broughton, R. (1981). Sensitivity of the Stanford Sleepiness Scale to the effects of cumulative partial sleep deprivation and recovery oversleeping. *Sleep, 4* (1), 83–92.

Hoddes, E., Zarcone, V., Smythe, H., Phillips, R., & Dement, W. C. (1973). Quantification of sleepiness: A new approach. *Psychophysiology, 10*, 431–436.

Honda, Y., Asaka, A., Tanaka, Y., & Juji, T. (1983). Discrimination of narcoleptic patients by using genetic markers and HLA. *Sleep Research, 12*, 254 (abstract).

Kales, J. D., Kales, A., Soldatos, C. R., Caldwell, A. B., Charney, D. S., & Martin, E. D. (1980a). Night terrors: Clinical characteristics and personality factors. *Archives of General Psychiatry, 37*, 1413–1417.

Kales, J. D., Soldatos, C. R., & Caldwell, A. B. (1980b). Nightmares: Clinical characteristics and personality patterns. *American Journal of Psychiatry, 137*, 1197–2001.

Kales, J. D., Soldatos, C. R., & Kales, A. (1982). Treatment of sleep disorders. I: Insomnia. *Rational Drug Therapy, 17* (2), 1–7.

Kales, A., Soldatos, C. R., Caldwell, A. B., Kales, J. D., Humphreys, F. J., Charney, D. S., & Schweitzer,

P. K. (1980c). Somnambulism: Clinical characteristics and personality patterns. *Archives of General Psychiatry*, 37, 1406–1410.

Kales, A., Tan, T. L., Kollar, E. J., Naitoh, P., Preston, T. A., & Malmstrom, E. G. (1979). Sleep patterns following 205 hours of sleep deprivation. *Psychosomatic Medicine*, 32, 189–200.

Karacan, I., & Howell, J. W. (1988). Narcolepsy. In R. L. Williams, I. Karacan, & C. A. Moore (Eds.), *Sleep disorders: Diagnosis and treatment* (pp. 87–105). New York: Wiley.

Kohen, D. P., Mahowald, M. W., & Rosen, G. M. (1992). Sleep-terror disorder in children: The role of self-hypnosis in management. *American Journal of Clinical Hypnosis*, 34 (4), 233–244.

Kovacs, M. (1978). Children's Depression Inventory (CDI). Unpublished manuscript, University of Pittsburgh.

Kramer, R. L. (1989). The treatment of childhood night terrors through the use of hypnosis: A case study. *International Journal of Clinical and Experimental Hypnosis*, 37 (4), 283–284.

Loomis, A. L., Harvey, E. N., & Hobart, G. (1935). Further observations on the potential rhythms of the cerebral cortex during sleep. *Science*, 82, 198–200.

Lozoff, B., Wolf, A. W., & Davis, N. S. (1985). Sleep problems seen in pediatric practice. *Pediatrics*, 75, 477–483.

Mindell, J. A. (1993). Sleep disorders in children. *Health Psychology*, 12 (2), 151–162.

Mitler, M. M., Gujavarty, K. S., & Browman, C. P. (1982). Maintenance of wakefulness test: A polysomnographic technique for evaluating treatment in patients with excessive somnolence. *Electroencephalograhy and Clinical Neurophysiology*, 53, 658–661.

Moldofsky, H., Lue, F. A., Davidson, J. R., & Gorczynski, R. (1988). The effect of 40 hours of wakefulness on immune functions in humans. II. Interleukins-1- and -2- like activities. *Sleep Research*, 17, 34.

Ollendick, T. H., Hagopian, L. P., & Huntzinger, R. M. (1991). Cognitive-behavior therapy with nighttime fearful children. *Journal of Behavior Therapy and Experimental Psychiatry*, 22 (2), 113–121.

Palace, E. M., & Johnston, C. (1989). Treatment of recurrent nightmares by the dream reorganization approach. *Journal of Behavior Therapy and Experimental Psychiatry*, 20 (3), 219–226.

Piazza, C. C., & Fisher, W. W. (1991a). A faded bedtime with response-cost protocol for treatment of multiple sleep problems in children. *Journal of Applied Behavior Analysis*, 24, 129–140.

Piazza, C. C., & Fisher, W. W. (1991b). Bedtime fading in the treatment of pediatric insomnia. *Journal of Behavior Therapy and Experimental Psychiatry*, 22 (1), 53–56.

Potsic, W. P., & Wetmore, R. F. (1990). Sleep disorders and airway obstructions in children. *Otolaryngologic Clinics of North America*, 23 (4), 651–663.

Richman, N., Douglas, J., Hunt, H., Lansdown, R., & Levere, R. (1985). Behavioural methods in the treatment of sleep disorders: A pilot study. *Journal of Child Psychology and Psychiatry*, 26 (4), 581–590.

Rickert, V., & Johnson, M. (1988). Reducing nocturnal awakening and crying episodes in infants and young children: A comparison between scheduled awakenings and systematic ignoring. *Pediatrics*, 81, 203–212.

Roffwarg, W. P., Muzio, J. N., & Dement, W. C. (1966). Ontogenetic development of the human sleep-dream cycle. *Science*, 152, 604–619.

Sadeh, A., Hayden, R. M., McGuire, J. P., Sachs, H., & Civita, R. (1994). Somatic, cognitive, and emotional characteristics of abused children in a psychiatric hospital. *Child Psychiatry and Human Development*, 24, 191–200.

Sassin, J. F., Parker, D. C., Mace, J. W., Gotlin, R. W., Johnson, L. C., & Rossman, L. G. (1969). Human growth hormone release relation to slow-wave sleep and sleep-waking cycles. *Science*, 165, 513–515.

Sheldon, S. H., Spire, J. P., & Levy, H. B. (1992a). Disorders of excessive somnolence. In J. Fletcher (Ed.), *Pediatric sleep medicine* (pp. 91–105). Philadelphia: W. B. Saunders.

Sheldon, S. H., Spire, J. P., & Levy, H. B. (1992b). Disorders of initiating and maintaining sleep. In J. Fletcher (Ed.), *Pediatric sleep medicine* (pp. 69–90). Philadelphia: W. B. Saunders.

Sheldon, S. H., Spire, J. P., & Levy, H. B. (1992c). Normal sleep in children and young adults. In J. Fletcher (Ed.), *Pediatric Sleep Medicine* (pp. 14–27). Philadelphia: W. B. Saunders.

Sheldon, S. H., Spire, J. P., & Levy, H. B. (1992d). Parasomnias. In J. Fletcher (Ed.), *Pediatric sleep medicine* (pp. 119–135). Philadelphia: W. B. Saunders.

Sheldon, S. H., Spire, J. P., & Levy, H. B. (1992e). Pediatric sleep medicine. Philadelphia: W. B. Saunders.

Sheldon, S. H., Spire, J. P., & Levy, H. B. (1992f).

Sleep-wake schedule disorders. In J. Fletcher (Ed.), *Pediatric sleep medicine* (pp. 106–118). Philadelphia: W. B. Saunders.

Snyder, F. (1966). Toward an evolutionary theory of dreaming. *American Journal Psychiatry, 123,* 121.

Spielberger, C. D., Edwards, C. D., Montuori, J., & Lushene, R. (1970). *Children's State-Trait Anxiety Inventory.* Palo Alto, CA: Consulting Psychologists Press.

Spielberger, C. D., Gorsuch, R. L., Lushene, R., Vagg, P. R., & Jacobs, G. A. (1968, 1977). *State-Trait Anxiety Inventory, Form* Y. Palo Alto, CA: Consulting Psychologists Press.

Thorpy, M. J. (1988). Diagnosis, evaluation, and classification of sleep disorders. In R. L. Williams, I. Karacan, & C. A. Moore (Eds.), *Sleep disorders: Diagnosis and treatment* (pp. 9–25). New York: Wiley.

Ware, J. C., & Orr, W. C. (1983). Sleep disorders in children. In C. E. Walker & M. C. Roberts (Eds.), *Handbook of clinical child psychology* (pp. 381–405). New York: Wiley.

World Health Organization (1992). *International statistical classification of diseases and related health problems* (10th revision). Geneva: Author.

APPENDIX A. Sleep Disorders Cinical Interview Checklist

_____ *Parameters* (e.g., first occurrence, frequency, time of night, description of behavior, degree of distress, child's recall of event, etc.)

_____ *Life events* (e.g., birth of sibling, losses, school changes, moving, illness/injury to child/family member/friend, abuse, etc.)

_____ *Parental Reactions* (e.g., possible reinforcers, past interventions, degree of parental distress, etc.)

_____ *Sleep Hygiene* (e.g., food/liquid intake, medications, bedtime routine, sleep environment, etc.)

_____ *Child/Family Psychiatric History* (e.g., sleep disturbances, anxiety, depression, abuse, treatments received, etc.)

_____ *Child's Medical History* (e.g., pregnancy, complications at birth, developmental milestones, breathing difficulties, etc.)

Note. This is a summary of the minimal information to be collected and should be expanded upon as necessary. The clinical interview should be used in combination with the appropriate medical/physical examinations, questionnaires, sleep logs, polysomnographic evaluations, etc.

21

Impulse Control Disorders Not Elsewhere Classified

Steven D. Thurber
Robert A. Dahmes

The five dysfunctions classed under the rubric "impulse control disorders" constitute a residual diagnostic category in the fourth edition of the *Diagnostic and Statistical Manual* (DSM-IV) (American Psychiatric Association, 1994a), meaning that they refer to impulsivity and other specified symptoms ostensibly detached from other DSM classifications (e.g., substance abuse, antisocial personality disorder). Hence the phrase "not classified elsewhere." They apparently share a common "spring" to harmful action. This is the controversial irresistible impulse that may involve an overpowering urge to aggress, steal, set fires, gamble, or pull out one's own hair. These potentially injurious actions are the behavioral components of the syndromes included in this DSM-IV section: intermittent explosive disorder, kleptomania, pyromania, pathological gambling, and trichotillomania. The *International Classification of Disease* (ICD), Ninth Edition (World Health Organization, 1978), nomenclature for disorders of impulse control is similar in content to that in DSM-IV. However, an isolated explosive disorder, involving a single discrete episode of violence, is recognized in the ICD, whereas trichotillomania is conspicuously absent. The

tenth edition of ICD (WHO, 1992), returns trichotillomania to this diagnostic category and excludes any reference to isolated explosive disorder. Moreover, ICD-10 classifies trichotillomania, pathological gambling, pathological firesetting (pyromania), pathological stealing (kleptomania), and intermittent explosive disorder as habit and impulse disorders. The term "habit" may indicate that behaviors consistent with certain of the listed disorders may take place in an inveterate fashion and without necessarily having an antedating motivational impulse.

The origins of these impulse control disorders can be found in Pinel's and Esquirol's nineteenth-century concepts of "instinctive impulses" and "instinctive monomanias" (Browne, 1871). The impulse control syndromes were not included in the first two editions of the American Psychiatric Association's *Diagnostic and Statistical Manual*. Intermittent explosive disorder, pathological gambling, pyromania, and kleptomania were officially recognized in DSM-III (APA, 1980), while trichotillomania was added in the revised third edition (DSM-III-R; APA, 1987). The same categories were retained in DSM-IV (APA,

1994). These disorders may have their genesis in childhood or adolescence, perhaps coinciding with challenges related to acquiring internal control mechanisms and the development of self-regulation. Impulsive actions and failures to moderate deportment vis-à-vis appropriate social norms may be concomitants of developmental arrests or lags in cognitive growth such that behavior is not adequately guided by anticipated consequences (e.g., adverse effects on self or other people) or behavior-outcome relationships (see Kohlberg, 1975; Meichenbaum, 1977; Piaget, 1970). The propensity to act rather than engage in premeditated thought has also been discussed by psychodynamic theoreticians. Freud mentioned "acting out" as an expression of tension due to internal conflict that simultaneously precludes recollections of earlier traumatic and painful experiences (Freud, 1905). Developmentally, inconsistent deprivations and overindulgences early in life may impede the capacity to delay gratification and prevent impulses from becoming actuated. Although testable developmental models of the specific DSM impulse control disorders have yet to be constructed, perhaps the cognitive, cognitive-behavioral, and psychodynamic perspectives will provide certain foundation constructs for future theorizing.

The notion of the irresistible impulse appears central conceptually in the impulse control disorders (we have more to say about the irresistible impulse later in the chapter). It is therefore a curious fact that the irresistible impulse is explicitly listed in DSM-IV diagnostic criteria for only intermittent explosive disorder and kleptomania. Interestingly, and inexplicably, the irresistible impulse criterion was deleted from trichotillomania in DSM-IV and added to intermittent explosive disorder. In its general definition of impulse control disorders, ICD-9 cites a failure to resist an impulse as central but expands the notion to include "drives" and "temptations." In addition, a failure to resist impulses is listed as symptomatic in the ICD-9 definitions for pyromania, isolated explosive disorder, and kleptomania. In ICD-10, failure to resist impulses is specifically included

as symptomatic for kleptomania and trichotillomania only.

Another presumed common element among these disorders is a sense of tension or arousal prior to committing the harmful act. Again, curiously, tension and arousal are specifically mentioned as symptoms in the DSM-IV and ICD-10 criteria only for pyromania, trichotillomania, and kleptomania. A final presumed core characteristic of the impulse control disorders is a sense of pleasure, gratification, or release following act commission. Inexplicably, only three of the five DSM disorders (trichotillomania, pyromania, and kleptomania) designate the postevent emotionality as a diagnostic criterion. ICD-9 includes "an intense experience of gratification," with reference to committing theft in the kleptomania disorder. Moreover, the pyromaniac in the ICD criteria is presumed to experience "satisfaction" with the destruction caused by firesetting. ICD-10 retains "gratification" with reference to kleptomania; it deletes "satisfaction" and adds "intense excitement" as the aftermath of setting a fire. The emotional result of an episode of intermittent explosive disorder is "genuine regret or self-reproach." This ICD-9 notion of a sense of compunction following a violent outburst is highly disparate in relation to presumed consequences of other DSM-IV and ICD-10 impulse control dysfunctions. Perhaps for this reason it was expunged in ICD-10.

Similar diagnostic inconsistencies were discussed by McElroy, Hudson, Pope, Keck, and Aisley (1992) for the impulse control disorders of DSM-III-R (APA, 1987). In DSM-IV, only kleptomania diagnostically requires all three "essential features" of the impulse control disorders (see McElroy et al., 1992; Wise & Tierney, 1994): (a) the irresistible impulse, (b) tension or arousal, and (c) positive postevent emotionality. None of the ICD classifications includes the three "essential" criteria. Furthermore, ICD-10 includes the possibility of "habit" detached from "impulse." If kleptomania alone contains the core diagnostic elements, and if none of the ICD categories conforms to the essential elements, it can be asked reasonably if mistakes were made regarding symptom specification for most of the DSM-IV impulse control disorders and virtually all of the relevant dysfunctions listed in ICD. A related question concerns the legitimacy of classifying together disorders that do not share in common the posited essential characteristics. As a point of emphasis, the authors of ICD-10 state that these disorders are grouped together because of their broad descriptive similarities, not because they are known to share any other important features.

Nevertheless, all five disorders conflate around the matter of harm inflicted on self or others (hardly distinctive among DSM-IV and ICD syndromes). They may also be concatenated with respect to abnormalities in the serotonin neurotransmitter system and may hence have kinship with the so-called affective spectrum disorders that evince similar neurobiologic underpinnings (Stein, Hollander, & Liebowitz, 1993). If this finding has credence, it suggests that, based on serotonogenic considerations, the extant impulse control disorders might appropriately be classed with depression, certain eating disorders, chemical dependency, and self-mutilation in the diagnostic nomenclature.

Given the DSM and ICD symptom descriptions, together with convergent research information, the following generalizations appear warranted: the impulse control disorders (or "habit and impulse disorders") as a group involve: (a) the infliction of harm, (b) shared neurotransmitter anomalies, and (c) some combination of irresistible urges, preevent tension and arousal, and pleasure and release following the harmful act. In addition, it is possible for all to be subsumed as affective spectrum dysfunctions. If there is another area of consensus, it is, unfortunately, that this group of disorders has been poorly researched. Although DSM-IV represents a significant advancement in regard to empirical support for included syndromes, our computer-assisted literature review of the impulse control disorders indicated a paucity of published studies that used participants rigorously defined in terms of DSM or ICD diagnostic criteria. The state of affairs is even worse regarding research conducted solely with developing persons. However, let us be clear on this point. There is a fairly abundant literature on participants who evince the behavioral components of each impulse control syndrome, but the degree of congruence with all of the diagnostic criteria for a given disorder remains ambiguous or is simply not explicated. Thus, for example, there appears to be an extensive database on children who set fires but relatively little information on children who both set fires and display antedating tension or affective arousal combined with elevated curiosity about and fascination with fire, along with postevent gratification or relief (i.e., the DSM-IV diagnostic criteria for pyromania). That is to say, the database focuses on children who show the harmful behavior, but investigators have either neglected or been unable to ascertain the more subjective pre- and postbehavior criteria that in the aggregate define the more abstract diagnostic term "pyromania."

Another challenge faced by the diagnostician is to determine whether the symptoms of a given impulse control disorder occur in isolation from other, more pervasive DSM-IV and ICD dysfunctions. As discussed earlier, this is a residual section of DSM-IV. It is also a residual category of ICD-10. The listed symptoms may occur as concomitants of other syndromes and should be diagnosed only when found to be detached and distinctive from other DSM-IV and ICD-10 classifications. The result is that several of the disorders in this section have exclusionary criteria. For example, both DSM-IV and ICD-10 criteria state that pathological gambling should be excluded from consideration if the symptoms occur in conjunction with a manic episode. Similarly, kleptomania should not be diagnosed in the presence of antisocial personality disorder (DSM-IV) or depressive disorder (ICD-10). Such exclusionary criteria, by the way, represent a major difference between DSM-III-R and DSM-IV. ICD-9 states only that aggressive behavior must be distinguished from other mental disorders for the clinician to consider the diagnosis of intermittent and isolated explosive disorders. Again, a major change in ICD-10 involves the provision of several exclusionary criteria for most listed disorders. Pyromania, for example, is excluded as a diagnostic classification if fire setting occurs as part of a conduct disorder; trichotillomania is excluded if hair pulling takes place in conjunction with a stereotyped movement disorder.

More basic than whether there are common features that bind these disorders together or the extent to which they are distinct from other classifications is the question regarding their very existence as reliable and diagnostically efficient entities. In candor, the research evidence, to date, is insufficient to allow statements supporting the diagnostic validity of the impulse control disorders. We cannot state with any degree of empirical certainty that the dysfunctions actually exist as separate, homogeneous clusters of diagnostic features. We could find no information on the interjudge reliability of DSM-IV or ICD-10 classifications, for instance. We were unable to locate any published studies dealing with the relative importance of each delineated symptom of a given disorder in contributing to a particular diagnosis. For example, no studies on the "specificity" of inclusion criteria (i.e., the conditional probability of the presence of a symptom given the presence of a disorder) were discovered.

In sum, there are axiomatic weaknesses in these DSM-IV and ICD-10 sections, beginning with incomprehensible omissions with respect to the listing of apparently essential diagnostic features. In addition, unanswered questions remain concerning the homogeneity, diagnostic validity, and distinctiveness of inclusion criteria. Finally, we must wonder about the very existence of the disorders in relation to DSM-IV and ICD descriptions.

Nevertheless, and more optimistically, there is a fairly substantial assessment and treatment literature on developing persons who at least engage in what we have referred to as the more concrete, behavioral aspect of each disorder. The remainder of this chapter reviews and integrates research information germane to clinical application.

TRICHOTILLOMANIA

The term is a neologism coined by the nineteenth-century French dermatologist Francois H. Hallopeau (Hallopeau, 1889). It is derived from the Greek word for hair ("trichos") and means literally "hair-pulling madness". Trichotillomania involves the repetitive, chronic, self-directed plucking of one's own hair, usually from the scalp (most often from the crown and sides) but sometimes from the eyelashes, eyebrows, and auxiliary areas of the body. The DSM-IV inclusion criteria require increasing tension before the hair pulling or when attempting to resist the urge and a sense of pleasure, gratification, or relief attendant to the behavioral act; the result must be noticeable hair loss. The ICD-10 criteria are practically identical. ICD-10 excludes this diagnosis if hair pulling is part of a stereotyped movement disorder, mentioned earlier, or if the plucking represents a response to a delusion or a hallucination. The diagnosis is also excluded if there is a preexisting inflammation of the skin. Trichotillomania must be distinguished from other dermatological conditions characterized by localized or diffuse alopecia, including alopecia araeta (an apparent autoimmune disturbance) and tinea capitis(a fungal infection); the condition must be associated with significant distress and social or other impairments. The disorder can have serious medical ramifications, including a reduced capacity of the hair follicles to regenerate healthy hair. In addition, there is often attendant trichophaga (i.e., chewing and/or swallowing the hair). This can lead to trichobezoars, or hair casts in the stomach or intestines, resulting in complications such as intestinal bleeding, acute pancreatitis, and obstructive jaundice (Adam & Kashani, 1990).

The areas of hair loss are located primarily in the scalp region on the opposite side of the body from the individual's dominant hand (Wise & Tierney, 1994). The repetitive avulsion is often accomplished by twisting the hair around the fingers while simultaneously pulling (Stewart, Danton,& Maddin, 1978). Few patients report pain associated with hair plucking.

The incidence and prevalence of trichotillomania are difficult to establish; a variety of estimates have been reported. Krishnan et al. (1985) indicated a rate of three in every 500 patients seen by child psychiatrists; a report by Tynes and Winstead (1992) indicated that one of every 200 persons would experience this disorder by college age. Tynes and Winstead also reported a prototypical onset during childhood, with a more chronic developmental course associated with a later onset.

Perhaps the most comprehensive investigation of the epidemiology of trichotillomania was conducted by Christenson, Pyle, and Mitchell (1991). The retrospective reports of 2,534 first-year college students indicated a mean onset age of 13 years. As noted by Rothbaum and Ninan (1994), hair pulling rates reported by Christenson et al. (1991), resulting in visible alopecia but without preceding tension or postevent relief, occurred in 1.5% of men and 3.4% of women. This finding suggests that the tension/relief notion presented in the DSM-III-R, DSM-IV, and ICD-10 diagnostic criteria might well be extraneous to a reliable trichotillomania designation. There may be a higher female-to-male ratio but the data are not conclusive (Popkin, 1989).

Stroud (1983) suggests that most cases of trichotillomania in young children may be reactions to stressful events and are likely to attenuate spontaneously. However, we did not find corroborative evidence for this statement in more recent literature. Researchers also suggest that when the disorder is found in adolescents, a more chronic developmental course may obtain. The comorbidity of trichotillomania may be substantial: In children, nail biting, thumb sucking, and other forms of self-mutilation are fairly common. There is also comorbidity with mood disturbances, anxiety, and borderline personality disorder. In particular, trichotillomania has been posited by researchers and clinicians as a variant of obsessive-compulsive disorder (OCD). Stanley, Swann, Bowers, Davis, and Taylor (1992) however, found that in comparison to OCD patients, trichotillomania patients experienced more pleasure in performance, exhibited lower

levels of anxiety, and evinced reduced urges and severity of associated thoughts. Trichotillomania, in general, also appears to have an earlier onset than OCD.

A comprehensive listing and appraisal of assessment procedures for trichotillomania has been provided by Rothbaum and Ninan (1994):

a. Self-monitoring. To the extent of the patient's capabilities, he or she is asked to record each instance (frequency; duration) of hair pulling, including number of hairs, date, time, environmental setting, and associated thoughts. Rothbaum and Ninan note that self-monitoring is reactive in nature. As a baseline measure, it may not be accurate, since it is a mildly aversive procedure and may tend to reduce the behaviors in question. However, it can also be reframed as a quasi-therapeutic intervention.

b. Saving hairs. This is a subcomponent of self-monitoring and requires the patient to place every extracted hair in a container (usually an envelope) to be inspected by the therapist.

c. Clinical interviews. Direct questioning of the patient or caregivers aimed at extracting information on the when, where, how, and what (i.e., the aftermath of hair pulling, such as mouthing or chewing the hair) of the hair avulsion. The interview should also be directed toward information on the degree to which the patient is aware of the pulling, possible warning events that antedate the avulsion, history of the hair pulling (including possible family history), previous treatments, and so on. Rothbaum and Ninan (1994, p. 659) have also developed a standardized set of interview questions based on DSM-III-R criteria for trichotillomania. This approach could readily be adapted to reflect the minor changes in DSM-IV (i.e., the deletion of the irresistible impulse notion).

d. Observational ratings. The most frequently used and perhaps the best instrument from a technical standpoint is the Yale-Brown Obsessive-Compulsive Scale modified by Stanley, Prather, Wagner, Davis, and Swann (1993) for the assessment of trichotillomania. There are both adult and child forms. It is a 10-item clinician-rated ($0 =$ no symptoms; $4 =$ extreme symptoms) instrument with items dealing with time spent on thought ruminations, interference, distress, resistance, sense of control over thoughts, time spent on actual hairpulling, and associated interference, distress, resistance, and sense of control over the actual hair-pulling behavior. Analyzes by Stanley et al. (1993) indicate acceptable interrater, test-retest, and internal consistency reliabilities.

e. Photographs. This typically involves pictures of the primary area or areas of alopecia, with the use of a Polaroid camera for immediate feedback to the patient. In addition, the photographs are taken pre- and posttreatment by the clinician or even the patient. Ideally, a digital camera that provides the best resolution should be used, along with a measuring device in the photograph itself. According to Rothman and Ninan (1994), this is probably the single best assessment approach for trichotillomania.

The review of assessment procedures by Rothman and Ninan appears to cover the most frequently used methods in the measurement of this disorder and of the extent of its often disfiguring effects. In addition, therapeutic work with children, in which reliable self-monitoring is precluded because of age or noncompliance considerations, often requires the use of innovative evaluative techniques. For example, Dahlquist and Kalfus (1984) devised and implemented a creative approach with a 9-year-old girl. They operationally defined alopecia as an area of the scalp with a diameter of 0.3 cm that contains three or fewer hairs. At the time of treatment, the child showed baldness on the entire top of her head. A paper pattern was constructed corresponding to the size of the bald area. Next, three holes of the appropriate diameter were randomly cut in the pattern for sampling from the front, middle, and back areas of the bald spot. The pattern was placed on the bald area 5 cm above the bridge of the nose. Two judges then independently counted the hairs in the three sampling areas. The child was unaware of the placement of the sampling holes. Subsequently, the number of increased hairs in the main bald spot and in the sampling areas

served as the treatment outcome assessment measure.

The symbolic nature of hair pulling has been noted by psychodynamic practitioners. It may, for example, signify the penis, so that pulling becomes symbolic castration. Hair plucking may also be a manifestation of fixations or regressions in a psychosexual stage of development (Sorosky & Sticher, 1980). From the psychodynamic perspective, trichotillomania could relate motivationally to the development of control over one's body. In particular, this disorder may act as a psychodynamic defense against fears of separation and emotional deprivation. Indeed, the onset of trichotillomania has been documented by Oguchi and Miura (1977) as occurring following a loss within the mother-child relationship. Insight into this phenomenon on the part of adult caregivers ostensibly resulted in increased attention shown to the child, followed by an amelioration of the symptoms.

Although viewed somewhat disdainfully by psychodynamic theorists, the evidence is accumulating to suggest that hair extirpation may begin innocuously and progress to a series of habits that occur automatically, without awareness. This does not necessarily abrogate the possibility of psychodynamic etiology; it is possible for trichotillomania to become detached from its original causal source and become habitual by the time the patient presents for treatment (see de L Horne, 1977). Nevertheless, behavioral and cognitive-behavioral approaches, essentially devoid of etiological considerations, have seemingly become ascendant in the treatment of this disorder. The literature is replete with such treatment modalities as overcorrection (e.g., having the child brush her or his hair to excess following instances of hair pulling; Barrett & Shapiro, 1980); aversion therapy (e.g., administering mild electric shock while the patient views videotapes of hair avulsion; de L Horne, 1977); negative practice (e.g., repeating the motions of hair pulling without actually pulling the hair; Azrin, Nunn, & Frantz, 1980); punishment (e.g., hand slaps as a consequence of hair extirpation; Gray, 1979); or use of a rubber band around the wrist that is snapped after each hair-pulling episodes; Stevens, 1984); use of reinforcement techniques (e.g., small monetary rewards contingent on hair regrowth; Gardner, 1978; or praise of attractive hair; Dahlquist & Kalfus, 1984); behavioral contracting (use of a written document signed by the child acceding to terminating the hair plucking in order to earn points redeemable for a variety of possible reinforcers; Stabler & Warren, 1974); response prevention (e.g., closely trimming the hair of a three-year-old boy so that he was unable to grasp and pull; Massong, Edwards, Sitton, & Hailey, 1980); modifications of internal dialogues (e.g., use of calming self-statements; Ottens, 1982); and hypnosis (e.g., age regression; Rowen, 1981). In addition, various multicomponent approaches using a combination of modalities have been implemented (e.g., reinforcement combined with punishment; Blount & Finch, 1987).

Perhaps the most successful treatment approach is habit-reversal training, patterned after the work of Azrin and Nunn (1973). This is a multicomponent intervention, using cognitive-behavioral and behavioral modalities. Initially, the therapeutic goal is to enhance awareness of the frequency of hair pulling through self-monitoring and saving of hairs. This is followed by the introduction of procedures for increasing awareness of the very first movement of the hand in performing the habit. Next, situation awareness training is employed to engender cognizance of each environmental setting in which this first movement of the hand takes place. This may be accomplished by self-monitoring and by having the patient list and describe for the therapist each setting in which hair pulling occurs.

The next step in habit-reversal practice consists of teaching the child an incompatible motoric response that literally competes with hair pulling. This can be as simple as performing any movement that precludes the touching of the scalp or other area of the body involved in the trichotillomania. Clasping the hands together, squeezing the arms of a chair, and clenching the fists are commonly used competing habits. Rosenbaum and Ayllon (1981)

suggest maintaining the incompatible response for at least 2 minutes in reaction to urges to pull the hair, any antecedent warning conditions, or actual hair pulling. They also require adult caregivers to praise the child who practices the competing response appropriately and to prompt the child if she or he fails to perform the incompatible action. Rosenbaum and Ayllon (1981) also ask patients with trichotillomania to choose situations where hair extirpation occurs frequently, imagine that situation, and engage in symbolic rehearsal, that is, actually to practice the incompatible act while imagining the high-probability situation.

PATHOLOGICAL GAMBLING

Individuals rigorously classified as pathological gamblers must adhere to DSM-IV diagnostic criteria that define an addiction. The person must exhibit a progressive preoccupation with gambling; require progressively higher bets to maintain excitement (i.e., build up tolerance), experience withdrawal symptoms with the abrupt termination of gambling, gamble to avoid adverse mood states, deceive others in order to sustain gambling, request money from family and friends or commit illegal acts to pay gambling debts (e.g., forgery, fraud, embezzlement), and be unable to control the gambling as judged by unsuccessful attempts to modify or stop the behavior (see Wise & Tierney, 1994). ICD-10 more succinctly indicates that pathological gambling consists of frequent, repeated episodes that dominate the individual's life, with detrimental effects in social, occupational, and material areas and on family values and commitments. Ginsberg (1985) discusses what he deems the essence of pathological gambling. In an interview conducted at the World Series of Poker, the winner was asked what he would do with his monetary prize: "Lose it," he replied. Ginsberg thus focuses on the self-ruination involved in this disorder. Both the DSM-IV and ICD-10 exclusionary criteria cite gambling during manic episodes.

With the advent of legalized gambling in most states (48 out of 50) and throughout nearly the entire world (more than 90 countries), the incidence rate of so-called pathological gamblers has also increased; recent estimates put the rate at 2% to 3% of the adult population (APA, 1994). Surveys of problem gambling in developing persons have been accomplished mainly in the United Kingdom, where children and adolescents have access to "fruit machines," a type of slot machine. In a survey of 460 students (ages 11–16), 5.7% were categorized as meeting the criteria for pathological gamblers on fruit machines (Fisher, 1993). In fact, the sparse literature on gambling among children and adolescents is centered on this type of gambling in the United Kingdom. In the United States, Winters, Stinchfield, and Fulkerson (1993) found that 8.7% of 70 surveyed adolescents 15–18 years of age demonstrated what they termed "problem gambling." Returning to the United Kingdom, Griffiths (1990a) intensively studied 50 adolescents (mean age = 16.2 years) who habitually played the fruit machines. Among nine males classed as pathological gamblers, severe consequences, similar to those found in adults, were reported, including gambling debts, truancy, and stealing. In a related study (Griffiths, 1990b), male adolescents with an "addiction" to playing the fruit machines reported a mean onset age of 11 years; the excitement of gambling was the reported motivational source; peer pressure was involved only after the individual became established in a group of adolescents who also played the machines. An article by Moody (1989) indicated that the number of fruit machine gamblers involved in Gamblers Anonymous has increased rapidly over a 9-year period, representing about half of all new members. Of this number, 50% were listed as children; the remainder were in their late teens or early twenties.

A plethora of etiological speculations have been offered for pathological gambling, including unconscious needs for punishment (Bergler, 1957), latent homosexual propensities (Greenberg, 1980), and intermittent reinforcement with a "big win" early in the reinforcement schedule (Popkin, 1989). However, we must accede to a statement by Popkin to the effect that the cause of pathological gambling is currently unknown.

Individuals with gambling problems usually are seen by members of the mental health community for other difficulties. Therefore, it is not surprising that there is high comorbidity with other disorders. Among children and adolescents, excessive gambling has been found to be associated with attention-deficit disorder (Carlton & Manowitz, 1994), alcohol and cigarette use (Fisher, 1993), and solvent abuse (Griffiths, 1994). Interestingly, researchers and government officials in the United Kingdom found no relationship between fruit machine gambling and delinquency.

There appears to be a higher percentage of males who engage in problem gambling, but overall the quality and range of research in this domain are disappointing, with data stemming mainly from studies conducted with white males over the age of 30 (Murray, 1993a). Assessment procedures that may be germane to developing persons include a pathological gambling signs index patterned after the DSM diagnostic criteria (Lesieur, Blume, & Zoppa, 1986) and, in particular, an adaptation of this scale for use with adolescents, referred to as an adolescent gambling-problem severity scale.

Psychometric properties for the scale presented by Winters, Stinchfield, and Fulkerson (1993) are in the acceptable range. Griffiths (1992) likewise adapted DSM criteria in attempting to assess "addictions" to playing pinball machines.

Adult gamblers as a group appear heterogeneous, with no particular personality profile found to be characteristic (Murray, 1993a). There is no reason to suspect the existence of greater homogeneity among developing persons. The diversity among children and adolescents with gambling problems may require therapists to consider many possible interventions in devising treatment plans for them. Group therapy and Gamblers Anonymous may be beneficial (Gamblers Anonymous is based on a 12-step program like that of Alcoholics Anonymous, but without reference to a higher power), but we could find no evaluative studies of their effectiveness with children or adolescents. Covert sensitization also appears to hold promise as a treatment modality (Popkin, 1989). But virtually all general categories of treatment, from individual therapy to psychopharmacological interventions, have been used with adults. To our knowledge, no controlled treatment research has been reported for adults or children in this domain. Therefore, a multicomponent approach using several modalities appears warranted at this time (see Wise & Tierney, 1994).

KLEPTOMANIA

Kleptomania was listed among the instinctive monomanias of the nineteenth century (Popkin, 1989). The name is from the Greek for "stealing madness" (Goldman, 1991). As previously mentioned, it is the sole member of the group of impulse control disorders to have all the elements required by DSM-IV. DSM-IV requires recurrent failure to resist impulses to steal objects that have no immediate use or monetary value to the individual. It also requires preceding tension and postevent pleasure, gratitude, or relief. Moreover, the stealing cannot be related to anger , vengeance, delusions, hallucinations, conduct disorders, antisocial personality disorder, or a manic episode (the manic episode exclusionary criterion is the one change from DSM-III-R). The ICD-10 inclusion criteria for kleptomania or pathological stealing are practically identical to those of DSM-IV. The latter excludes this diagnosis if the stealing behavior can better be accounted for by conduct disorder, a manic episode, or antisocial personality disorder. The ICD-10 exclusionary criteria include stealing related to a depressive disorder or an organic mental disorder. It is important to note that, according to the source book that reports the corroborating empirical support for disorders listed in DSM-IV (APA, 1994), there is simply insufficient research on kleptomania to establish or refute the validity of the DSM criteria.

There is some evidence from the early research literature that kleptomania can appear initially in childhood (Chadwick, 1925). In the text *Treatment of Psychiatric Disorders*, Meeks (1989) describes a developmental course in which early stealing is viewed as a normal occurrence deriving from the egocentric inability of the young child to understand the rights of others and the concept of ownership. Deprivation of parental affection and sibling rivalries may lead to stealing designed to redress a perceived inequity. Later in development, stolen objects may acquire symbolic value similar to or perhaps antedating their meaning for the kleptomaniac.

The literature contains few studies of participants who have met acceptable DSM or ICD criteria (Murray, 1993b). We found virtually no studies in the past 20 years dealing with children and adolescents classified as kleptomaniacs. Although the adult database is largely retrospective and uncontrolled, it is estimated that six people per 1,000 population may evince this disorder, with perhaps the majority being female. The prototypical age of onset may be about 20 years of age (Goldman, 1991).

Historically, conforming to sex-role stereotypes of the nineteenth and early twentieth centuries, kleptomania was viewed as a form of mental illness occurring in women and related to diseases of the uterine organs (Mitchell, 1897). Psychoanalysts referred to such topics as direct sexual significance, hidden sexuality, and the female's symbolic acquisition of a penis as theoretical explanations for kleptomania (see Fenichel, 1945).

McElroy, Pope, Hudson, Keck, and White (1991) conducted structured interviews with adult patients who reportedly met the DSM criteria for kleptomania. Among other findings, these patients reported lifetime diagnoses of mood disorders, together with the existence of similar types of affective problems in first-degree relatives (however, this finding is confounded by the fact that the patients were recruited via psychiatric referral). The patients used terms such as "rush," "thrill," "high," and "euphoria" in describing their emotional states during acts of theft. Contrary to DSM-IV and ICD-10 criteria, however, they also described poststealing guilt and remorse. They also expressed a desire to atone for the thefts. Some even went so far as to return to a victimized store to purchase unneeded items as a type of atonement. Goldman (1991) also reports a sense of compunction commonly expressed by persons with kleptomania.

Approximately half of the participants in the McElroy et al. (1991) study indicated stressful or traumatic experiences, such as childhood physical and sexual abuse, that had occurred several years prior to their engaging in the stealing behavior. Convergent information is provided by Goldman (1991), who reported tumultuous and highly stressful childhood experiences among persons classified as having kleptomania, including concentration camp survival experiences and child abuse. Furthermore, according to Goldman, future kleptomaniacs may exist in chronic adverse affective states and may show a history of sexual dysfunctions and related mental preoccupations. In a recent review of the literature, Murray (1993b) indicates that kleptomania or shoplifting may be traceable to child neglect, child-parental separations, or a desire for vengeance against the father.

No research reports were located that describe procedures for assessing kleptomania. It may be that the act of theft speaks for itself eloquently. Beyond that, interviews have been used (as in McElroy et al. 1991), to ascertain the degree of correspondence with DSM and ICD criteria.

Within a sparse, inadequate adult literature, behavior therapy appears to be the treatment of choice. One investigator had a patient hold his breath while thinking of stealing (a type of aversive conditioning) (Keutzer, 1972). Another (Glover, 1985) attempted to associate mental images of nausea and vomiting with stealing behavior (a form of covert sensitization). Given what appear to be generally positive reactions of juveniles to behavioral therapies (Weisz, Weiss, Han, & Granger, 1995), these approaches might be considered initially in clinical interventions with children and adolescents who evince kleptomania-type problems. An effective multicomponent behavioral intervention for "uncontrollable stealing" of money and small objects by a 12-year-old girl involved a combination of self-monitoring of stealing behavior,

self-reinforcement for abstaining from stealing (e.g., "I did very well; I did not steal"), and a qualitative self-evaluation of overall progress. A family contingency contract specifying praise and monetary reinforcement for periods of non-stealing was also implemented.

PYROMANIA

The term "pyromania" first appeared in the scientific literature in the early part of the nineteenth century, in an 1833 article by Marc (cited in Bumpass, 1989). Like the other historical "manias," it is derived from the Greek; "pyro" refers to fire or heat. Unlike most DSM-IV and ICD-10 disorders of this type, this category is particularly germane to children, with a consensus in the literature that pyromania has its genesis in childhood. Indeed, there is abundant recent literature on children who set fires. However, as mentioned, this is a literature on fire setting and does not really deal with juveniles who conform to DSM or ICD criteria for pyromania. These criteria entail deliberate and purposeful fire setting (more than once), pre-event tension or emotional arousal, fascination with and curiosity about fire or associated characteristics (e.g., handling matches), and postevent pleasure, gratification, or relief. The fire setting cannot be related to financial gain or to a wish to conceal criminal activity; it cannot occur in response to a delusion or hallucination. Changes in DSM-IV involve exclusionary criteria for mania, conduct disorder, and antisocial personality disorder. ICD-10 substitutes "preoccupation" for "fascination" and "curiosity" and cites postevent "intense excitement." The diagnosis is precluded if fire setting is a concomitant of chemical intoxication, conduct disorder, organic disorders, or schizophrenia. Diagnostic difficulties in clinical work with children include the importance of distinguishing childhood intrigue and experimentation with fire and related paraphernalia (considered developmentally normal curiosities) from a more ingrained fire-setting disorder, together with the importance of differentiating fire-setting problems from a more pervasive conduct disorder. But to emphasize the point concerning extant literature, no cases of pyromania have been reported in the United States since the year 1970 (APA, 1994b). The diagnosis "pyromania" or "pathological fire setting" simply is not being made. Our inference from perusing the developmental literature in this domain is that (a) few juveniles conform to DSM criteria for pyromania; (b) the pre- and postfire setting subjective states are difficult, if not impossible, to assess reliably; and (c) fire setting is most often a manifestation of a conduct disorder (see Kolko, 1985).

Fire setting among juveniles occurs at prevalence rates of 2.3–17% of patients and 38–40% of nonpatients. It may be a predominantly male activity. The effects of fires set by children and young people may account for a large proportion of the more than $1 billion annual property damage in the United States. Besides property loss, fire setting is associated with physical injuries and death (see Kolko & Kazdin, 1991a; Wooden & Berkey, 1984).

It was Esquirol in 1837 who initially posited a connection between sexuality and fire setting (see Popkin, 1989). Psychoanalytic writings complemented Esquirol in equating fire setting, libidinal excitation, and urethroerotic fixations (see Freud, 1932). This sexual aspect of pyromania, or what is termed pyrolagnia, does not appear to be in the mainstream currently in relation to the understanding of this disorder in juveniles. The more recent scientific literature has focused on personality concomitants of fire setting, especially conduct disorders and antisocial dysfunctions. Familial disturbances noted as precursors of childhood fire setting have included depression, psychoses, and antisocial behavioral patterns among parents of fire setters (Bumpass, Fagelman, & Brix, 1983), together with elevated personal and marital distress, general family dysfunctions, and frequent parental absences and distancing from children (Gruber, Heck, & Mintzer, 1981; Kazdin & Kolko, 1986; Kolko & Kazdin, 1990).

The systematic contributions of David Kolko and Alan Kazdin stand out both theoretically and empirically in furthering our understanding of the dynamics of juvenile fire setting. Their conceptual model (Kolko & Kazdin, 1986) emphasizes the role of early developmental experiences with adult models (e.g., fathers who are firemen or furnace stokers; caregivers who smoke), fire, and fire-related objects (e.g., fire-starting materials such as matches). They report that fire interest may be almost universal among boys, starting as early as 2 years of age. Associated fire play may become a part of a child's behavior early in life. The Kolko-Kazdin model suggests that the child may lack the cognitive ability to comprehend fire-related hazards or to anticipate the many adverse consequences of fire play. The model also posits social skills deficiencies in fire-setting children, leading to unpleasant interpersonal transactions with peers, inadequate problem-solving capacities, and, ultimately, exclusion and social isolation. Moreover, this interpersonal ineffectiveness extends to the expression of anger; the fire setter may either be overcontrolled (i.e., the hostility is regulated by anxiety) or undercontrolled and destructive.

These model components occur in the context of limited supervision and poor parental monitoring of the child's activities. The child is allowed freedom beyond his or her capacity to behave responsibly. The result, in addition to fire setting, is a series of covert, concealed antisocial acts such as stealing, running away, and truancy. The uninvolved parents may also be poorly adjusted, with personality disorders, depression, and alcohol abuse being noteworthy. The aggregate impact of these factors is to produce a child who is unable to adapt to stressful events (e.g., a new sibling in the family or a divorce) that are found to antedate the fire setting behavior. Assessment instruments based on this model have been constructed. Research using these measures has yielded support for the theorizing of Kolko and Kazdin (discussed later).

One assessment instrument generated from the model is the Child Firesetting Interview (CFI). It consists of 46 items and is child administered, with a Likert-type 5-point response format. It is appropriate for use with children and adolescents age 6 years and above. There are six a priori dimensions that correspond to the components of the model: curiosity about fire; involvement in fire-related activities; knowledge about things that burn;

fire competence (knowledge, understanding about fire); exposure to models/materials; and a supervision/discipline dimension. Technical characteristics (Cronbach alphas; test-retest reliability; item-remainder correlations for the separate dimension scales) are in adequate ranges. Mean comparison of known fire setters and nonfire setters on the scale dimensions, a related discriminant function analysis, and correlations with other extant tests on fire setting supported the construct and concurrent validity of the instrument (Kolko & Kazdin, 1989a).

A measuring device that corresponds to the CFI (i.e., that is based on the same model) but that is constructed for parent responding is the Firesetting Risk Interview (FRI; Kolko & Kazdin, 1989b). It comprises 99 items, 15 a priori content areas or subscales, and again uses a 5-point Likert-type response format. The subscales are similar to those of the CFI (i.e., items purportedly assess the parent's perspective on the child's curiosity, involvement, exposure, knowledge, and competence in relation to fire and fire-related activities). Additional scales are intended to evaluate more explicitly than the CFI child-rearing practices and disciplinary techniques, parental supervision, and positive and negative behaviors of the child. Again, psychometric properties are within acceptable limits. Parents of actual fire setters described their children in the FRI items as showing the theorized curiosity, involvement, model exposure, and so on. The children were also perceived by parents as exhibiting elevated levels of negative social behaviors and as being exposed to both harsh discipline and ineffective mild punishment. Interestingly, and contrary to the Kolko and Kazdin model, fire setters were not found from the assessment of parental perceptions to be less skilled or less knowledgeable about fire and its dangers than nonfire setters. It is possible that fire-setting children possess adequate knowledge about the dangers of fire but willingly take risks in this regard.

The technical properties of the CFI and FRI lend credence to the model of fire setting on which the instruments are based. Further, ancillary research has corroborated other components of the model, especially those regarding covert antisocial actions, social skills deficiencies, parental distancing, and antedating stressful events (Jacobson, 1985; Kolko & Kazdin, 1990; Kolko & Kazdin, 1991a). We think the Kolko-Kazdin model continues to be germane; it accurately reflects the literature and can guide clinicians in gaining an understanding of juvenile fire setting behavior.

An additional measuring instrument developed by Kolko and Kazdin (1990) assesses the motivation for fire setting. Called the Firesetting Incident Analysis—Parent Version (FIAP), it consists of 50 Likert-type items designed to examine the most serious fire setting incident. The choices of motive are accidental firesetting, peer pressure, curiosity and experimentation, fun seeking, desire for a boost in self-confidence or a feeling of power, noncompliance with a request not to play with matches or fire, attention seeking, and a response to anger, family conflict, a school problem, or a problem with peers. Clinicians who work with fire setting juveniles should consider motivational states in treatment planning. For example, according to the authors, fire setting evoked by curiosity is more likely to occur among younger individuals from intact families; the fire setting will probably be a single, isolated incident. Remorse and guilt are probable emotional concomitants. Interventions with children showing this motivational source are more likely to be brief and involve didactic components centered on fire dangers and fire safety skills. Children who set fires in a more deliberate fashion are often motivated by anger or revenge and are likely to be repeating, emotionally disturbed offenders from dysfunctional families. Successful interventions will be more intensive and multimodal in nature.

An exemplary instance of the application of a multicomponent set of modalities is found in the work of McGrath, Marshall, and Prior (1979). The 11-year-old male fire setter was the second youngest of seven children (children who set fires often come from families with a large number of children; the fire setting may be related to the parental distancing and inadequate monitoring mentioned earlier). The family was also described as having multiple problems. The boy had serious deficiencies in social skills and was court referred after setting four dangerous fires, the last of which completely destroyed a group home in which he had been placed. The treatment of interpersonal deficiencies involved modeling, role playing, behavioral rehearsal, and videotaped feedback. An overcorrection procedure required the boy to light a piece of paper in a metal container and then extinguish the fire with water. He then had to clean and scrub thoroughly the container while repeating out loud such statements as "Fires can kill people." A covert sensitization technique consisted of having the child listen to audiotaped stories describing fire setting episodes similar to those in which the child had participated but with fictitious aversive consequences such as being personally trapped by the flames and being unable to breathe. This was followed by a relief scene. The final component consisted of fire safety instructions that included a discussion of fire dangers during a visit to the gutted group home burned down by the boy. Across a 2-year period, the treatment program was ostensibly effective; there was essentially no further fire setting.

An important principle emphasized in the McGrath et al. (1979) study is the difficulty inherent in the evaluation of a treatment program for a problem such as fire setting in which the behavior in question has a low frequency base rate to begin with and requires close supervision during treatment to ensure nonrecurrence. They suggest that evaluation of treatment assess collateral behaviors related to the targeted fire setting, such as the child's involvement in social activities and ability to cope with stressful events.

As might be surmised, the treatment literature on juvenile fire setters over the past 30 years has been dominated by behavioral approaches. Electro version therapy has perhaps been the most frequently used modality (Penny, Marcella, & Charlton, 1974). Holland (1969) chronicled a successful treatment using a contingency management program (e.g., removal of rewards for noncompliance; praise and tangible reinforcement for not lighting matches) implemented by the father of the fire setter.

Welsh (1971) employed a negative practice approach, requiring fire setters to light matches repeatedly in an ashtray.

An innovative behavioral approach with a more cognitive flavor was conducted by Stawar (1976). The participant was a 7-year-old boy with frequent fire-setting episodes (four in a 3-month period prior to treatment). On each occasion, the boy had found matches and immediately began to strike them. Treatment involved reading a fictitious story about a boy who found matches while playing (initially in the yard; subsequently, the location was shifted to rooms in the house and school and to other places the patient actually visited). The fictional character immediately took the matches to his mother, who then praised him for not striking them and gave the boy some of his favorite candy. After hearing the story twice in the first treatment session, the child was required to retell the story in his own words, aided by prompts and questions from the therapist. During the session the child was given penny candies simultaneously with the boy in the story. In later sessions, the boy could recall the story completely. Subsequently, the mother became involved in the home environment. She would place a nonfunctional book of matches in a place where it was likely to be found. The boy was rewarded for rapidly taking the matches to his mother; noncompliance was ignored. These "operantly structured fantasies" may generate preventive cognitive mediation processes and facilitate actual contingency management procedures in other settings. In any event, no fire setting by the 7-year-old boy was reported during the 2-week treatment period or on 3- and 7-month follow-up investigations.

As discussed as part of the multicomponent treatment approach of McGrath et al. (1979), didactic approaches dealing with fire safety and prevention may supplement other modalities. For the "curious" fire setter this may be the central treatment approach. In their fire safety prevention skills training (FSST; Kolko, Watson, & Faust, 1991), a group of juvenile fire setters is instructed using pictures and actual concrete objects. Sessions incorporate information about fires (positive and adverse), data concerning actual numbers of fires in the particular locality and the related damage, and discrimination training on incendiary objects that should be used only under adult supervision (lighters, matches). Sessions also focus on the functions of matches, taught through the use of a hand puppet. A role-playing procedure involves presenting matches to a supervising adult. The children are also required to complete a workbook on differentiating safe objects (e.g., a baseball) from objects that pose a fire danger (e.g., fireworks).

An innovative approach that encompasses cognitive and didactic features was reported by Bumpass, Fagelman, and Brix (1983). The child is first made aware that harmful actions such as fire setting stem from feeling states; in order to control fire setting the child must become aware of particular feelings that precede the fire setting behavior. The therapist then introduces what Bumpass et al. term the "graphing technique." Both the parents and the child are present and are asked to contribute. They generate detailed information about the events that preceded and followed the most recent fire setting episode. As the child observes, the triggering events that presage fire setting behavior and the postfire consequences are recorded in sequence on the bottom of a large sheet of graph paper. The child is then asked to describe feelings and their intensity for each of the listed events. The stronger the intensity, the greater its height on the graph. Parents may also discuss their own feelings in relation to the graphic portrayal. The intent of this approach is to engender awareness in the fire setter about instigating events and associated feelings that, according to Bumpass et al., constitute the causal mechanism in fire setting. The child is taught that the feelings can signal fire setting risk; therapy then focuses on constructive alternative actions to take in response to the feeling states. The authors used this technique with 29 patients, including children as young as 6.5 years old; subsequently, only two individuals set fires during an average follow-up period of 2.5 years.

As noted earlier, family discord may be a precursor of fire setting in children and adoles-

cents; indeed, this is part of the Kolko-Kazdin model. Somewhat inconsistent with the model, however, is the notion that fire setting in a child is a manifestation of disturbed family relationships; what is targeted for treatment are the disordered relationships, not the deviant behavior of a single family member. Eisler (1972), for example, assumed that the symptom of fire setting in a designated "patient" actually reflects a more general set of disturbances in the fire setter's family as a social system. The "designated" patient in Eisler's study was a 14-year-old boy who was referred for treatment following his confession to law enforcement officials that he had set several grass fires in the rural area in which he and his family resided. Prototypical of fire setters, the boy was described as a quiet loner with few friends. The boy had been adopted at birth by parents described as responsible and hard working. About 5 years prior to the boy's fire setting, the father had lost his business and had been working out of state in a series of jobs, with only occasional visits to home and family. About 1 year prior to Eisler's intervention, the father found employment that allowed him to return to live with the family. Family therapy centered on the apparent alliance between the patient and his mother and the ostensible distancing of the father, who felt like a pariah in his own family and tried to escape by engaging in many activities outside the home. The mother expressed dissatisfaction that her husband was not more active and responsible in his familial role.

A key factor in the fire setting, according to Eisler, was the unwritten, implicit family rule that prohibited the expression of anger and other negative feelings. Therapy incorporated having family members independently list their grievances. This apparently resulted in the boy's later open expressions of anger toward his father for his absences and his desire for a closer relationship with dad. The boy was also resentful toward his mother, who seemingly expected him to adhere to an adult role as a substitute father to younger siblings but in other ways treated him as a young child. The father, in turn, discussed his fears of being dominated by his wife. Although a rigorous evaluation was not implemented in this study, Eisler reported that the father eventually took on a more assertive role in the family and developed a more confident relationship with his wife. The family communication patterns evidenced greater openness, with a wider range of affect being expressed. There were no more instances of fire setting during in the year following family therapy.

In sum, there are a variety of fairly well-researched assessment techniques and treatment modalities for juvenile fire setting. The model presented by Kolko and Kazdin can serve as a conceptual guide for assessing fire setters and for planning interventions. There also seems to be a consensus among researchers and clinicians regarding the link between fire setting and social skills deficiencies, family discord, poor parental monitoring, curiosity about fire, and difficulties in anger expression. Again, whether the clinician focuses on the fire-setting juvenile directly or on the family unit, we believe that the multifaceted nature of fire setting requires a consideration of multicomponent treatment modalities.

INTERMITTENT EXPLOSIVE DISORDER

This may be the single most controversial classification among the impulse control disorders. Many psychiatrists and psychologists doubt the existence of such a clinical syndrome (Popkin, 1989). Our computer-assisted search of the medical and psychological literature indicated not a single rigorously controlled study on this ostensive disorder over the past 20 years. This classification has undergone some dramatic changes since the inception of the *Diagnostic and Statistical Manual* in 1952 (see Wise & Tierney, 1994). At that time the closest category to intermittent explosive disorder was "passive-aggressive personality, aggressive type." The term "episodic dyscontrol" was introduced by Menninger and Mayman in 1956. This was followed by the "explosive personality," introduced in DSM-II (APA, 1968). The diagnostic category "intermittent explosive disorder" was officially listed in ICD-9 in 1978

and became part of the diagnostic nomenclature of DSM-III-R (APA, 1987). Wise and Tierney (1994) note that intermittent explosive disorder was retained in DSM-IV "with some reservations."

The current criteria for this disorder involve: (a) several discrete failures to resist aggressive impulses resulting in assaultive acts or destruction of property, (b) inordinate aggressiveness in relation to the severity of the provocation, and (c) symptomatology exclusive of certain other mental disorder. Especially germane to developing persons are the exclusionary criteria for conduct disorder, attention-deficit/hyperactivity disorder, a manic episode, medications or substance abuse, and a general medical condition such as head trauma. ICD-10 simply lists intermittent explosive disorder as the single entry under the rubric "other habit and impulse disorders." No other inclusion or exclusion criteria are cited.

Although a great deal is known about aggression, including episodic violence, little is known (we would go so far as to say nothing is known) about intermittent explosive disorder in terms of actually studying persons who rigorously conform to diagnostic criteria. The central issue here, as in certain other presumed impulse control dysfunctions, is the matter of the irresistible impulse. There is little doubt that human beings evince episodic aggression that is extreme. But how does one assess and evaluate the DSM-IV-mandated irresistible aggressive impulse in order rigorously to diagnose and validate this classification? If a mental health professional happens adventitiously (however unlikely this is) to observe an uncharacteristic aggressive outburst in an individual and is able mystically and on the spot to rule out all DSM exclusionary criteria for intermittent explosive disorder, how, then, is the irresistible impulse measured scientifically? Does one simply ask the individual whether she or he acceded to an overwhelming urge that could not be resisted? If this is the approach, then one has to worry about all the potential contaminants of self-report information (see Nunnally, 1978). Scientific rigor requires an accounting of the extent to which self-report data are influenced by response sets such as acquiescence and social desirability. Since, to our knowledge, the irresistible impulse cannot be directly observed, the alternative is to infer the presence of the impulse from the violent behavior. This requires the mental health professional to take an illogical position: the inner determinant of the episodic aggression must be inferred from the very behavior it is supposed to cause. This is termed by Bandura (1986) as an interpretive circularity in which the description becomes the causal explanation. Furthermore, a syndrome that does not separate a presumed causal mechanism from the disordered behavior itself is outside the realm of scientific verification. This may explain why no well-controlled scientific studies were found on intermittent explosive disorder in our literature search. Whereas Monopolis and Lion (1983) chide practitioners who place patients in this category without reference to explicit diagnostic criteria, we suggest that a much larger group of mental health professionals should be scolded for supporting a presumed diagnostic classification that not only has no research substantiation but may be outside the realm of science.

It is not surprising to find that virtually no information exists on the treatment, course, or prognosis of rigorously defined intermittent explosive disorder (Wise & Tierney, 1994). It is therefore axiomatic that there are no data concerning this presumed disorder in juveniles. Nevertheless, there is an abundant research base on aggression in children and young people. Since aggression is discussed in other parts of this volume, (see chapter 7), we will be brief.

What can be said about the assessment of pronounced aggression and violence is that it requires a multidisciplinary evaluation that includes social and cognitive factors, stress tolerance, neurochemistry, habitual aversive interchanges within the family, and neuroanatomy (see Eichelman, 1992). It is also important to note in the assessment of developing persons information obtained from different assessment methods (e.g., rating scales, interviews) and sources (e.g., self and adult informants). This allows the clinician to ascertain the degree of convergence across methods and sources,

which in turn provides data on the degree to which the aggression occurs across situations and people (see Verhuist & Van der Ende, 1991).

A recent paper by Kruesi, Hibbs, Hamburger, Rapoport, Keysor, and Elia (1994) may be germane to our discussion because the authors dealt with the assessment of juveniles (ages 6.3 to 17.4 years) who engaged in severe forms of aggression such as cruelty to animals and acts that led to physical injuries. They used most of the important measuring instruments discussed in the literature on the assessment of aggression in children and adolescents. These include the aggression scale derived from the Conners Teacher Questionnaire (Loney & Milich, 1985) and the aggression scale from the parent-rated Child Behavior Checklist (CBCL; Achenbach & Edelbrock, 1983), together with direct observations and structured interviews such as the Diagnostic Interview for Children and Adolescents (DICA; Herjanic & Campbell, 1977). (It should also be mentioned that there is now a revised version of DICA [see Boyle, Offord, Racine, & Sanford, 1993].) The authors' discussion of the results emphasized the divergent but complementary data obtained across methods and sources and the importance of using multiple informants over a prolonged time period. The authors also addressed certain technical issues, such as error related to assessment method. It should also be mentioned that a relatively new assessment battery, the Adjustment Scales for Children and Adolescents (ASCA; McDermott, 1993) has recently been standardized nationally. The battery attempts to measure psychopathology across multiple situations. Included in the ASCA is a scale that purports to measure impulsive aggressiveness.

Although there is currently little, if any, validation of this diagnostic category, there are some formulations in clinical and social psychology that may relate to aperiodic expressions of aggression and that those involved in the next DSM or ICD revisions might consider. These formulations do not have the circularity problem mentioned earlier and have been scientifically investigated. Overcontrolled hostility entails tight, anxiety-related constraints exercised over anger and aggressiveness that are paradoxically associated with explosive, intermittent displays of violent behavior (Megargee, 1965). It is as if the angry feelings accumulate as excessive controls are exercised until a violent outburst occurs. Items from the Minnesota Multiphasic Personality Inventory (MMPI) are used to measure such overcontrol propensities; recently, theory and research in this area have been extended to adolescents (Truscott, 1990). This conceptualization has the advantage of a measured causal element (the overcontrol mechanisms) that can be investigated apart from aggressive acts themselves.

In Zillman's (1971) view, certain experiences, such as engaging in physical exercise or watching a motion picture, can activate biochemical factors that are maintained and applied to subsequent frustrating or irritating situations, producing more severe aggressiveness than would have been evoked by the situation alone. His "excitation transfer" formulation might account for aggression that appears to be disproportionate to the provocation.

The cognitive-behavioral treatment approaches for juvenile aggression consider developmental levels, extent of social skills acquisition, and cognitive distortions in the selection of treatment modalities and are recommended as the procedures of choice. They are designed to produce changes in thinking, feeling, and behavior. Aggressive children may have distortions involving, for instance, the misattribution of hostile intent to others; they also tend to employ quick, action-oriented solutions to problems that require more protracted ruminations. As reviewed by Kendall and Panichelli-Mindel (1995), cognitive behavioral interventions with aggressive children involve a variety of techniques tailored to remedy specific cognitive and social deficits and to engender more adaptive behavioral functioning. Self-talk is often used to dissipate anger; self-monitoring can be employed to engender greater awareness of cues that evoke aggression and associated thoughts and feelings. Modeling can be used to demonstrate effective problem solving, such as, for example, generating alternative solutions. Role playing is designed

to enable the child better to empathize with and take the perspective of others. Therapy often involves guided practice in perspective taking and can also employ contingency-based reinforcement.

EXAMPLES OF ASSESSMENT PROCEDURES

Throughout the chapter we have mentioned assessment techniques used by researchers and clinicians for the diagnosis of the impulse control disorders. In this section we present concrete exemplars.

The growth in the technical adequacy and popularity of standardized checklists and rating scales for use with developing persons has been well documented (see McDermott, 1993). Important topics that have emerged from research in this domain include the degree of correspondence between children and adult informants who complete the instruments independently and the extent to which psychopathology occurs specific to a given situation or more pervasively across environmental settings and people (see Thurber & Osborn, 1993). Checklists of this type often have specific items at least tangential (if not germane) to the impulse control disorders. The Child Behavior Checklist (CBCL; Achenbach & Edelbrock, 1983) contains single items related to fire setting, stealing, and aggression, for instance. The Adjustment Scales for Children and Adolescents (ASCA; McDermott, 1993) has a complete scale dealing with what is termed "impulsive aggressive" behaviors. However, no standardized assessment instrument, to our knowledge, attempts explicitly to measure DSM or ICD classifications, adhering to the delineated criteria.

With specific reference to the diagnostic classifications of this chapter, most investigators have simply taken the DSM criteria as the basis for a structured interview. Structured interviews have the advantage of being time-efficient and reliable (in comparison to more indirect methods of gathering information from children and adolescents), and they can be used by both professionals and lay persons (Herjanic & Reich, 1982).

The Trichotillomania Diagnostic Interview (Rothbaum & Ninan, 1994), was previously discussed. It is based on the DSM criteria for this disorder. These include: Failure to resist hair-pulling impulses; tension before plucking; subsequent relief, and so on. The items are scored by the interviewer according to this scale: ? = inadequate information; 1 = false; 2 = subthreshold; 3 = true. Representative questions include:

Do you pull out hair anywhere on your body? [related to DSM recurrent failure to resist impulses]

Are you unable to resist impulses to pull out your hair? [related, obviously, to the irresistible impulse]

Do you experience an increasing sense of tension before pulling out your hair?

Do you experience a sense of gratification or relief when alliance out the hair?

Griffiths (1992) constructed items from the DSM and used a "yes-no" format in evaluating gambling or "addictions" to playing machines (e.g., pinball machines). This is a typical question:

Have you done any of the following?

1. Frequently play (gamble) and obtain money to play
2. Frequently play with larger amounts of money
3. Need to play more to get more excited
4. Restless if you can't play
5. Return to win back your losses
6. Make repeated efforts to stop playing
7. Play instead of going to school/job
8. Sacrifice other activities to play
9. Continue to play even when you owe money

Another approach to assessment involves the modification of an existing instrument to reflect more directly a certain component of an impulse control disorder. As previously mentioned, Stanley et al. (1993) modified the Yale-Brown Obsessive Compulsive Scale for use with individuals suspected of having trichotillomania. This is also an example of a rating-scale assessment rather than a verbal interview. The Yale-Brown items are rated as follows: 0 = no symptoms; 1 = mild symptoms; 2 = moderate symptoms; 3 = severe symptoms; 4 = extreme symptoms. The modification involves substituting "thoughts about hair pulling" for the word "obsession" and "hair pulling" for "compulsion." For example, the Yale-Brown item #10 (degree of control over compulsive behavior) asks, "How strong is the drive to perform the compulsive behavior; how much control do you have over the compulsions?" This is altered to "How strong is the drive to perform the hair pulling? How much control do you have over the hair pulling?"

A more difficult approach, and one we advocate, requires the generation of an item pool that corresponds to a particular model or theory about the nature of the disorder. The developmental model of Kolko and Kazdin (1989a) was previously discussed. Their "Firesetting Risk Interview" is a parent-administered instrument, with a Likert-type response format (1 = not at all; 5 = almost always). Representative items, corresponding to their conceptual model of firesetting, are presented here:

How much does he/she want to play with fire?

How many times did your child hide matches, lighters, or other fire-starting materials?

How many family member have an interest in fire or a fascination with fire?

How often did you receive complaints from others about his/her play with fire?

To what extent has he/she been taught to use matches or lighters correctly?

PHARMACOTHERAPY

Despite the significant advances in pharmacotherapy of psychiatric disorders over the past decade, well-designed and controlled studies of medication effects on impulse control disorders are rare. Further, we must view with some reservation those studies that do appear, as the DSM or ICD diagnostic criteria for these disorders are not adhered to or are in a state of development and flux. An extensive computer-assisted review of the literature revealed only one placebo-controlled, double-blind study. Christenson, Mackenzie, Mitchell, and Callies (1991) reported that 15 participants who received fluoxetine for trichotillomania showed no improvement following an 18-week trial. In addition to the single technically adequate study, two investigations followed double-blind procedures. Mattes (1990) studied 80 patients with a variety of diagnoses, including attention-deficit disorder and intermittent explosive disorder. His findings suggested that the reduction of rage attacks in attention-deficit disorder was more effective with propranolol and that patients classified with an intermittent explosive disorder responded best to carbamazepine. Swedo, Leonard, Rapoport, and Lelane (1989) treated 13 female patients with the diagnosis of trichotillomania and found clomipramine to be more effective than desipramine.

The literature search indicated five open trials of psychopharmacologic agents with two of the impulse control disorders. Trichotillomania symptoms were reduced by SSRI medications alone in studies by Winchel, Jones, Stanley, and Molcho (1992) and by Koran, Ringold, and Hewlett (1992). Stein and Hollander (1992) added pimozide to the SSRIs and noted reductions in hair pulling. Christenson, Popkin, and Mackenzie (1991) report significant symptom relief in patients administered lithium. Patients diagnosed with intermittent explosive disorder were markedly improved when given propranolol in an open trial conducted by Jenkins and Maruta (1987).

In contrast to the few controlled studies and open trials of medication, there are a number of case reports and series that document the efficacy of pharmacologic agents in all of the impulse control disorders except pyromania. Trichotillomania has reportedly been effectively treated with SSRI medications (Bradford & Gratzer, 1995; Mahr, 1993; Sheikha, Wagner, & Wagner 1993). Tricyclic antidepressants and monoamine oxidase inhibitors have also demonstrated efficacy (Krishman, Davidson, & Guajardo, 1985; Tynes & Winstead,

1992). Patients with intermittent explosive disorder have responded to carbamazopine (Mattes, 1985), psychostimulants (Allen, Safer, & Covi, 1975), dilantin and pimozide (Monroe, 1974), lithium (Sheard, Marini, Bridges, & Wagner, 1976), and beta blockers (Yudofsky, Williams, & Gorman, 1981). Symptoms of kleptomania improved in a patient treated with lithium (Rocha & Rocha, 1992). McElroy, Keck, Pope, and Hudson (1989) also noted improvements in patients with kleptomania who received fluoxetine, trazodone, or tranylcypromine. Pathological gambling was reduced by lithium (Moskowitz, 1980) and by clomipramine (Hollander, Frenkel, DeCaria, & Trungold, 1992).

Several investigations suggest an underlying biochemical mechanism that is not yet clearly defined in certain of the impulse control disorders. The possibility of serotogenic etiology has previously been discussed. Virkkunen, Rawlings, Tokola, and Poland (1994) suggest a central serotonergic deficit in intermittent explosive disorder, whereas Eichelman (1988) considers the noradrenergic system to be implicated. Drake, Hietter, and Pakalnis (1992) reported that 7 of 23 patients with intermittent explosive disorder had abnormal EEG patterns compared to controls. Carrasco, Saiz-Ruiz, Hollander, & Cesar (1994) noted low platelet MAO activity in his participants with pathological gambling, whereas mood disorders were clearly associated in reports by Cusack, Malaney, and DePry (1993) and Linden, Pope, and Jonas (1986). Roy, Adinoff, Roehrich, and Lamparski (1988) questioned the likelihood of a functional disturbance in the noradrenergic system in patients with pathological gambling. Although a distinct biochemical substrate was not discussed in Rechlin and Joraschky's (1992) study, they noted a strong relationship between pyromania and suicidal and autoaggressive behaviors. McElroy, Hudson, Pope, Keck, and Aizley (1992) reported an association between pyromania and mood disorders, with a possibility of underlying serotonergic dysfunction.

As these studies suggest, there is no single theoretical explanation for the neurobiology of these heterogeneous disorders. We may speculate that, given the role of the frontal lobes in deliberation and judgment and of the basal ganglia in execution and movement, these areas of the brain are of critical importance in producing the symptoms associated with impulse control disorders. Serotonergic neurons arise in the raphe nucleus and send projections both to the frontal lobes and to the basal ganglia. The SSRIs may affect neural transmission between these two sites, resulting in symptom reduction. Other cortical areas that might be involved include the orbitofrontal cortex and the anterior cingulate cortex, which lie in close proximity to the frontal lobes, as well as the caudate nuclei within the basal ganglia. Considering the complexity of neural pathways between these various regions, their different neurotransmitters and their susceptibility to pharmacologic agents that affect nerve conduction, a likely explanation of the ostensible success of certain psychoactive agents is that they modify transmission between these cortical and subcortical structures. However, the exact nature of the possible dysfunctions is not clear at this time.

In recommending psychopharmacologic treatment for the impulse control disorders, research and experience clearly indicate that the clinician should assess the patient for comorbid psychiatric and neurological conditions. If any such conditions exist, they should be vigorously treated within established guidelines. For those patients who do not present with other psychiatric dysfunctions, the clinician may use the information presented here regarding responsiveness to medications. Of course, the use of medication in the impulse control disorders must be considered part of an overall treatment plan that includes the nonpharmacologic interventions described elsewhere in this chapter.

A cautionary note is in order at this point. Of all the studies, case reports, and case series reviewed, very few specifically dealt with developing persons. The physician should be well aware that pharmacologic treatment of these disorders remains investigational and experimental. However, this should not deter the practitioner from pursuing possible symptom reduction with medication after carefully pondering potential adverse reactions.

EPILOGUE

The "irresistible impulse," a carryover from nineteenth-century speculation, is the major historical antecedent of the current impulse control disorders. The term is devoid of empirical import and is perhaps logically indefensible (due to its interpretive circularity). Yet it continues to be sanctioned by prestigious national and (to a lesser extent) international organizations. We submit that these continuing sanctions defy logic and are scientifically unjustified; furthermore, they may be a disservice to the mental health professional. A practitioner, for example, who accedes to the mystical notion of "irresistible impulse" as a causal element in episodic aggression by an adolescent patient may not be inclined to investigate more established formulations, such as overcontrolled hostility, that are more scientifically defensible antedating conditions. The change in ICD-10 nosology that places greater emphasis on "habit" may signal a shift away from the antiquated "irresistible impulse" formulation. We further suggest that a construct that (a) cannot be measured, and (b) cannot be detached from the behaviors it purports to explain should not be granted anything beyond historical recognition.

The reliance in the DSM-IV and ICD-10 nomenclature on subjective postevent reactions as inclusion criteria is also an area of concern. Such assumed reactions can be evaluated only by retrospective self-reports and generally remain uncorroborated in the literature. It seems to us that a more parsimonious explanation for maintenance of behaviors involved in the impulse control disorders is simply reinforcement; engaging in the behaviors per se has implicit or explicit reinforcement value.

We also believe that, by default, researchers appear to have essentially eliminated the pre- and postevent subjective criteria as diagnostic necessities. Is it not sufficient for diagnosis and treatment to note that regardless of pre-event impulsivity, tension, and arousal, developing persons engage in hair pulling, shoplifting, types of gambling, fire setting, and aggressive acts and that a certain percentage will display a frequency and intensity of these actions to the extent of bringing harm to self and others? Psychiatric researchers and professionals can certainly measure reliably these acts and document that they and their deleterious consequences occur. Perhaps pre- and postevent subjective conditions are superfluous to reliable classification, research, and effective interventions.

REFERENCES

Achenbach, T. M. & Edelbrock, C. (1983). *Manual for the Child Behavior Checklist and Revised Child Behavior Profile*. Burlington: University of Vermont.

*Adam, B. S., & Kashani, J. H. (1990). Trichotillomania in children and adolescents: Review of the literature and case report. *Child Psychiatry and Human Development*, 20, 159–168.

Allen, R. P., Safer. D., & Covi, L. (1975). Effects of psychostimulants on aggression. *Journal of Nervous and Mental Diseases*. 160, 138–145.

American Psychiatric Association. (1952). *Diagnostic and statistical manual of mental disorders*. Washington, DC: Author.

American Psychiatric Association. (1968). *Diagnostic and statistical manual of mental disorders* (2nd ed.). Washington, DC: Author.

American Psychiatric Association. (1980). *Diagnostic and statistical manual of mental disorders* (3rd ed.). Washington, DC: Author.

American Psychiatric Association. (1987). *Diagnostic and statistical manual of mental disorders* (3rd ed., rev.). Washington, DC: Author.

American Psychiatric Association. (1994a). *Diagnostic and statistical manual of mental disorders* (4th ed.). Washington, DC: Author.

*American Psychiatric Association. (1994b). *DSM-IV source book*. Washington, DC: Author.

*Azrin, N. H., & Nunn, R. G. (1973). Habit-reversal: A method of eliminating nervous habits and tics. *Behavior Research and Therapy*, 11, 619–628.

Azrin, N. H., Nunn, R. G., & Frantz, S. E. (1980). Treatment of hairpulling (trichotillomania): A comparative study of habit reversal and negative practice training. *Journal of Behavior Therapy and Experimental Psychiatry*, 11, 13–20.

Bandura, A. (1986). *Social foundations of thought: A social cognitive theory*. Englewood Cliffs, NJ: Prentice-Hall.

Barrett, R. P., & Shapiro, E. S. (1980). Treatment of stereotyped hair-pulling with overcorrection: A case study with long-term follow-up. *Journal of Behavior Therapy and Experimental Psychiatry*, 11, 317–320.

Bergler, E. (1957). *The psychology of gambling*. New York: Universities Press.

Blount, R. L., & Finch, A. J. (1987). Reducing trichotillomania in a three-year-old girl. *Child and Family Behavior Therapy*, 9, 65–72.

Bradford, J. M. W., & Gratzer, T. G. (1995). A treatment for impulse control disorders and paraphilia: A case report. *Canadian Journal of Psychiatry* 40, 4–5.

Boyle, M. H., Offord, D. R., Racine, Y., & Sanford, M. (1993). Evaluation of the Diagnostic Interview for children and adolescents for use in general population samples. *Journal of Abnormal Child Psychology* 21, 663–681.

Browne, H. H. B. (1871). Moral mania. *American Journal of Insanity*, 27, 445–463.

Bumpass, E. R. (1989). Pyromania. *Treatments of psychiatric disorders* (pp. 2468–2472). Washington, DC: American Psychiatric Association.

Bumpass, E. R. Fagelman, F. D., & Brix, R. J. (1983). Interventions with children who set fires. *American Journal of Psychotherapy*, 37, 328–345.

Carlton, P. L. & Manowitz, P. (1994). Factors determining the severity of pathological gambling in males. *Journal of Gambling Studies*, 10, 147–157.

Carrasco, J. L., Saiz-Ruiz, R. J., Hollander, E., & Cesar, J. (1994). Low platelet monamine oxidase activity in pathological gambling. *Acta Psychiatrica Scandinavica*, 90, 427–431.

Chadwick, M. (1925). A case of kleptomania in a girl of ten years. *International Journal of Psycho-Analysis*, 6, 300–312.

Christenson, G. A., Mackenzie, T. B., Mitchell, J. E., & Callies, A. L. (1991). A placebo-controlled, double-blind crossover study of fluoxetine in trichotillomania. *American Journal of Psychiatry*, 148, 1566–1571.

Christenson, G. A., Popkin, M. K., & Mackenzie, T. B. (1991). Lithium treatment of chronic hair pulling. *Journal of Clinical Psychiatry*, 52, 162–170.

*Christenson, G. A., Pyle, R. L., & Mitchell, J. E. (1991). Estimated lifetime prevalence of trichotillomania in college students. *Journal of Clinical Psychiatry, 52*, 415–417.

Cusack, J. R., Malaney, K. R., & DePry, D. L. (1993). Insights about pathological gamblers. *Postgraduate Medicine, 93*, 169–176.

Dahlquist, L. M., & Kalfus, G. R. (1984). A novel approach to assessment in the treatment of childhood trichotillomania. *Journal of Behavior Therapy and Experimental Psychiatry, 15*, 47–50.

de L Horne, D. (1977). Behavior therapy for trichotillomania. *Behavior Research and Therapy, 15*, 192–196.

Drake, M. E., Hietter, S. A., & Pakalnis, A. (1992). EEG and evoked potentials in episodic-dyscontrol syndrome. *Neuropsychobiology, 26*, 125–128.

Eichelman, B. (1988). Toward a rational pharmacotherapy for aggressive and violent behavior. *Hospital and Community Psychiatry, 39*, 31–39.

Eichelman, B. (1992). Aggressive behavior from laboratory to clinic: Quo Vadit? *Archives of General Psychiatry, 49*, 488–492.

Eisler, R. M. (1972). Crisis intervention in the family of a firesetter. *Psychotherapy: Theory, research, and practice, 9*, 76–79.

Esquirol, J. E. D. (1845). *Mental maladies. A treatise on insanity*. Philadelphia.

Fenichel, O. (1945). *The psychoanalytic theory of neurosis*. New York: Norton.

Fisher, S. E. (1993). Gambling and pathological gambling in adolescents. *Journal of Gambling Studies, 9*, 277–288.

Freud, S. (1905). *Standard edition of the complete psychological works of Sigmund Freud. (v. 5)*. London: Hogarth Press.

Freud, S. (1932). In S. J. London (Ed.), *Complete psychological works of Sigmund Freud* (vol. 22, pp.181–193).

Gardner, G. G. (1978). Hypnotherapy in the management of childhood habit disorders. *Journal of Pediatrics, 92*, 838–840.

Ginsberg, G. L. (1985). Adjustment disorders and impulse control disorders. In H. I. Kaplan & B. J. Sadock (Eds.). *Comprehensive textbook of psychiatry* (5th ed., pp. 1098–1105). Baltimore: Williams and Wilkins.

Glover, J. H. (1985). A case of kleptomania treated by covert sensitization. *British Journal of Clinical Psychology, 24*, 213–214.

*Goldman, M. J. (1991). Kleptomania: Making sense of the nonsensical. *American Journal of Psychiatry, 148*, 986–996.

Gray, J. J. (1979). Positive reinforcement and punishment in the treatment of childhood trichotil-lomania. *Journal of Behavior Therapy and Experimental Psychiatry, 10*, 125–129.

Greenberg, H. R. (1980). Psychology of gambling. In H. I. Kaplan, A. M. Freedman, & B. J. Sadock (Eds.), *Comprehensive Textbook of Psychiatry* (3rd ed.). Baltimore: Williams and Wilkins.

Griffiths, M. D. (1989). Gambling in children and adolescents. *Journal of Gambling Behavior, 5*, 68–83.

Griffiths, M. D. (1990a). The acquisition, development, and maintenance of fruit machine gambling in adolescents. *Journal of Gambling Studies, 6*, 193–204.

Griffiths, M. D. (1990b). Addiction to fruit machines: A preliminary study among males. *Journal of Gambling Studies, 6*, 113–126.

Griffiths, M. D. (1992). Pinball wizard: The case of a pinball machine addict. *Psychological Reports, 71*, 160–162.

Griffiths, M. D. (1994). An exploratory study of gambling cross addictions. *Journal of Gambling Studies, 10*, 371–384.

Gruber, A. R., Heck, E. T., & Mintzer, E. (1981). Children who set fires: Some background and behavioral characteristics. *American Journal of Orthopsychiatry, 51*, 484–488.

Hallopeau, F. H. (1889). Alopecia par grottage. *Annals of Dermatology and Syphilology, 10*, 440.

Herjanic, B., & Campbell, W. (1977). Differentiating psychiatrically disturbed children on the basis of a structured interview. *Journal of Abnormal Child Psychology, 5*, 127–134.

Herjanic, B., & Reich, W. (1982). Development of a structured psychiatric interview for children: Agreement between child and parent on individual symptoms. *Journal of Abnormal Child Psychology, 10*, 307–324.

Holland, C. J. (1969). Elimination by the parents of firesetting behaviors in a seven-year-old boy. *Behavior Research and Therapy, 7*, 135–137.

Hollander, E., Frenkel, M., DeCaria, C. & Trungold, S. (1992). Treatment of pathological gambling with clomipramine. *American Journal of Psychiatry, 149*, 710- 711.

Jacobson, R. R. (1985). The subclassification of child firesetters. *Journal of Child Psychology and Psychiatry and Allied Disciplines, 26*, 769–775.

Jenkins, S., & Maruta, T. (1987). Therapeutic use of propranolol for intermittent explosive disorder. *Mayo Clinics Proceedings, 62*, 204–214.

*Kendall, P. C., & Panichelli-Mindel, S. (1995). Cognitive-behavioral treatments. *Journal of Abnormal Child Psychology, 4*, 107–123.

Keutzer, C. S. (1972). Kleptomania: A direct approach to treatment. *British Journal of Medical Psychology, 45*, 159–163.

Kohlberg, L. (1975). Counseling and counselor education: A developmental approach. *Counselor Education and Supervision, 14*, 250–256.

Kohlberg, L. (1978). The cognitive developmental approach in behavior disorders: A study of the development of moral reasoning. In B. Servan (Ed.), *Cognitive defects in the development of mental illness*. New York: Brunner/Mazel.

*Kolko, D. J. (1985). Juvenile firesetting: A review and methodological critique. *Clinical Psychology Review, 5*, 345–376.

Kolko, D. J., & Kazdin, A. E. (1986a). A conceptualization of firesetting in children and adolescents. *Journal of Abnormal Child Psychology, 14*, 49–61.

Kolko, D. J., & Kazdin, A. E. (1986b). Parent psychopathology and family functioning among childhood firesetters. *Journal of Abnormal Child Psychology, 14*, 315–329.

Kolko, D. J., & Kazdin, A. E. (1989a). The children's firesetting interview and psychiatrically referred and nonreferred children. *Journal of Abnormal Child Psychology, 17*, 609–624.

Kolko, D. J., & Kazdin, A. E. (1989b). Assessment of dimensions of childhood firesetting among patients and nonpatients: The Firesetting Risk Interview. *Journal of Abnormal Child Psychology, 17*, 157–176.

Kolko, D. J., & Kazdin, A. E. (1990). Matchplay and firesetting in children: Relationship to parent, marital, and family dysfunction. *Journal of Clinical Child Psychology, 19*, 229–238.

Kolko, D. J., & Kazdin, A. E. (1991a). Aggression and psychopathology in matchplaying and firesetting children: A replication and extension. *Journal of Clinical Child Psychology, 20*, 191–201.

Kolko, D. J., & Kazdin, A. E. (1991b). Motives of childhood firesetters: Firesetting characteristics and psychological correlates. *Journal of Child Psychology and Psychiatry and Allied Disciplines, 32*, 535–550.

Kolko, D. J., Watson, S., & Faust, J. (1991). Fire safety/prevention skills training to reduce involvement with fire in young psychiatric inpatients: Preliminary findings. *Behavior Therapy, 22*, 269–284.

Koran, L. M., Ringold, A., & Hewlett, W. (1992). Fluoxetine for trichotillomania: An open clinical trial. *Psychopharmacology Bulletin, 28*, 145–149.

Krishman, K. R., Davidson, J. F. & Guajardo, C.

(1985). Trichotillomania: A review. *Comprehensive Psychiatry, 26*, 123–128.

Kruesi, M. J. P., Hibbs, E. D., Hamburger, S. D., Rapoport, J. L., Keysor, C. S., & Elia, J. (1994). Measurement of aggression in children with disruptive behavior disorders. *Journal of Offender Rehabilitation, 21*, 159–172.

Lesieur, H. R., Blume, S. B., & Zoppa, R. M. (1986). Alcoholism, drug abuse, and gambling. *Alcoholism Clinical and Experimental Research, 10*, 33–38.

Linden, R. D., Pope, H. G., & Jonas, J. M. (1986). Pathological gambling and major affective disorders: Preliminary findings. *Journal of Clinical Psychiatry, 47*, 201–203.

Loney, J., & Milich, R. (1985). Hyperactivity, aggression, and inattention in clinical practice. In M. Wolraich & D. Routh (Eds.), *Advances in Developmental and Behavioral Pediatrics* (pp. 113–147). New York: JAI Press.

MaGrath, P., Marshall, P. G., & Prior, K. (1979). A comprehensive treatment program for a firesetting child. *Journal of Behavior Therapy and Experimental Psychiatry, 10*, 69–72.

Mahr, G. (1993). Feniluramine and trichotillomania. *Psychosomatics, 34*, 284.

Massong, S. R., Edwards, R. P., Sutton, L. R., & Hailey, B. J. (1980). A case of trichotillomania in a three-year-old treated b: response prevention. *Journal of Behavior Therapy and Experimental Psychiatry, 11*, 223–225.

Mattes, J. A. (1990). Metoprolol for intermittent explosive disorder. *American Journal of Psychiatry, 142*, 1108–1109.

McDermott, P. A. (1993). National standardization of uniform multisituational measures of child and adolescent behavior pathology. *Psychological Assessment, 5*, 413–424

*McElroy, S. L., Hudson, J. L., Pope, H. G., Jr., Keck, P. E., & Aizley, H. G. (1992). The DSM-III-R impulse control disorders not elsewhere classified: Clinical characteristics and relationship to other psychiatric disorders. *American Journal of Psychiatry, 149*, 318–327.

McElroy, S. L., Keck, P. E., Pope, H. G., & Hudson, J. I. (1989). Pharmacological treatment of kleptomania and bulimia nervosa. *Journal of Clinical Psychopharmacology, 9*, 358–360.

McElroy, S. L., Pope, H. G., Jr., Hudson, J. I., Keck, P. E., Jr., & White, K. L. (1991). Kleptomania: A report of 20 cases. *American Journal of Psychiatry, 148*, 652–657.

Meeks, J. (1989). Kleptomania. *Treatment of psychi-*

atric disorders (vol. 3, pp. 2457–2494). Washington, DC: American Psychiatric Association.

Megargee, E. I. (1965). Assault with intent to kill. *Trans-Action, 2*, 27–31.

Meichenbaum, D. H. (1977). *Cognitive behavior modification*. New York: Plenum Press.

Menninger, K. A., & Mayman, M. (1956). Episodic dyscontrol: A third order of stress adaptation. *Bulletin of the Menninger Clinic, 20*, 153–165.

Mitchell, S. W. (1897). The relation of nervous disorders in women to pelvic disease. *University of Medical Magazine 9*, 389–393.

Monopolis, S., & Lion, J. R. (1983). Problems in the diagnosis of intermittent explosive disorder. *American Journal of Psychiatry, 140*, 1200–1202.

Monroe, R. (1975). Anticonvulsants in the treatment of aggression. *Journal of Nervous and Mental Disease, 160*, 119–126.

Moody, G. (1989). Parents of young gamblers. *Journal of Gambling Behavior, 5*, 313–320.

Moskowitz, J. A. (1980). Lithium and lady luck: Use of lithium carbonate in compulsive gambling. *New York State Journal of Medicine, 80*, 785–788.

Murray, J. B. (1993a). Review of research on pathological gambling. *Psychological Reports, 72*, 791–810.

Murray, J. B. (1993b). Kleptomania: A review of the research. *Journal of Psychology, 126*, 131–138.

Mussen, P. E. (1979). *Carmicheal's manual of child psychology* (vol. 1, 3rd ed.). New York: Wiley.

Nunnally, J. C. (1978). *Psychometric theory*. New York: McGraw-Hill.

Oguchi, T., & Miura, S. (1977). Trichotillomania: Its psychopathological aspect. *Comprehensive Psychiatry, 8*, 437–454.

Ottens, A. J. (1982). A cognitive-behavioral modification treatment of trichotillomania. *Journal of American College Health, 31*, 78–81.

Penny, R. K., Marcella, P., & Charlton, D. (1974). Classical and operant conditioning program for a firesetting child. *Journal of the Ontario Association Children's Aid Society,1*, 4.

*Popkin, M. K. (1989). Impulse control disorders not elsewhere classified. In H. I. Kaplan & B. J. Sadock (Eds.), *Comprehensive Textbook of Psychiatry* (5th ed., pp. 1145–1154). Baltimore: Williams and Wilkins.

Rechlin, T., & Joraschky, P. (1992). Fin klinisch eindrucksvoller Fall von "pyromanem" Verhalten. *Praxis der Psychotherapie und Psychosomatik, 37*, 127–137.

Rocha, F. L., & Rocha, M. G. (1992). Kleptomania, mood disorder and lithium. *Arquivos de Neuro Psiquiatria, 50*, 543–546.

Rosenbaum, M. S., & Ayllon, T. (1981). The habit-reversal technique in treating trichotillomania. *Behavior Therapy, 12*, 473–481.

*Rothbaum, B. O., & Ninan, P. T. (1994). The assessment of trichotillomania. *Behavior Research and Therapy, 32*, 651–662.

Rowen, R. (1981). Hypnnotic age regression in the treatment of a self-destructive habit: Trichotillomania. *American Journal of Clinical Hypnosis, 23*, 195–197.

Roy, A., Adinoff, B., Roehrich, L., & Lamparski, D. (1988). Pathological gambling: A psychobiological study. *Archives of General Psychiatry, 45*, 369–373.

Sheard, M. H., Marini, J. L., Bridges, C. I., & Wagner, E. (1976). The effect of lithium on impulsive aggressive behavior in man. *American Journal of Psychiatry 133*, 1409–1413.

Sheikha, S. H., Wagner, K. D., & Wagner, R. F., Jr. (1993). Fluoxetine treatment of trichotillomania and depression in a prepubertal child. *Cutis, 51*, 50–52.

Sorosky, A. D., & Sticher, M. B. (1980). Trichotillomania in adolescence. *Adolescent Psychiatry, 8*, 437–454.

Stabler, B., & Warren, A. B. (1974). Behavior contracting in treating trichotillomania: Case note. *Psychological Reports, 34*, 401–402.

Stanley, M. A., Prather, R. C., Wagner, A. L., Davis, M. L., & Swann, A. C. (1993). Can the Yale-Brown Obsessive-Compulsive scale be used to assess trichotillomania? A preliminary report. *Behavior Research and Therapy, 31*, 171–177.

*Stanley, M. A., Swann, A. C., Bowers, T. C., Davis, M. L., & Taylor, D. J. (1992). A comparison of clinical features in trichotillomania and obsessive-compulsive disorder. *Behavior Research and Therapy, 30*, 651–652.

Stawar, T. L. (1976). Fable mod: Operantly structured fantasies as an adjunct in the modification of firesetting behavior. *Journal of Behavior Therapy and Experimental Psychiatry, 7*, 285–387.

Stein, D. J., & Hollander, E. (1992). Low-dose pimozide augmentation of serotonin reuptake blockers in the treatment of trichotillomania. *Journal of Clinical Psychiatry, 53*, 123–126.

Stein, D. J., Hollander, E., & Liebowitz, M. R. (1993). Neurobiology of impulsivity and the impulse control disorders. *Journal of Neuropsychiatry and Clinical Neurosciences, 5*, 9–17.

Stevens, M. J. (1984). Behavioral treatment of trichotillomania. *Psychological Reports, 55,* 987–990.

Stewart, W. D., Danton, J. C., & Maddin, S. (1978). *Dermatology—Diagnosis and treatment of cutaneous disorders* (4th ed.). Saint Louis: Mosby.

Stroud, J. D. (1983). Hair loss in children. *Pediatric Clinics of North America, 30,* 641–657.

Swedo, S. E., & Leonard, H. L. (1992). Trichotillomania: An obsessive-compulsive spectrum disorder? *Psychiatric Clinics of North America, 15,* 777–790.

Swedo, S. E., Leonard, H. L., Rapoport, J. L., & Lenane, M. C. (1989). A double-blind comparison of clomipramine and desipramine in the treatment of trichotillomania (hair pulling). *New England Journal of Medicine, 321,* 497–501.

Thurber, S., & Osborn, R. A. (1993). Comparisons of parent and adolescent perspectives on deviance. *Journal of Genetic Psychology, 154,* 25–32.

Truscott, D. (1990). Assessment of overcontrolled hostility in adolescence. *Psychological Assessment: A Journal of Consulting and Clinical Psychology, 2,* 145–148.

Tynes, L. L., & Winstead, D. K. (1992). Behavioral aspects of trichotillomania. *Journal of the Louisiana State Medical Society, 44,* 459–463.

*Verhuist, F. C., & Van der Ende, J. (1991). Assessment of child psychopathology: Relationships between different methods, different informants, and clinical judgment of severity. *Acta Psychiatrica Scandinavica, 84,* 155–159.

Virkkunen, M., Rawlings, R., Tokola, R., & Poland, R. E. (1994). CSF biochemistry, glucose metabolism, and diurnal activity rhythms in alcoholic, violent offenders, fire setters, and healthy volunteers. *Archives of General Psychiatry, 51,* 20–27.

Weisz, J. R., Weiss, B., Han, S. S., & Granger, D. A. (1995). Effects of psychotherapy with children and adolescents revisited: A meta-analysis of treatment outcome studies. *Psychological Bulletin, 117,* 450–468.

Weller, E. B., Weller, R. A., & Carr, S. (1989). Imipramine treatment of trichotillomania and coexisting depression in a seven-year-old. *Journal of the American Academy of Child and Adolescent Psychiatry, 28,* 952–953.

Welsh, R. S. (1971). The use of stimulus satiation in the elimination of juvenile fire-setting behavior. In A. M. Graziano (Ed.), *Behavior therapy with children* (pp. 283–289). Chicago: Aldine-Atherton.

Winchel, R. M., Jones, J. S., Stanley, B., & Molcho, A. (1992). Clinical characteristics of trichotillomania and its response to fluoxetine. *Journal of Clinical Psychiatry, 53,* 304–308.

Winters, K. C., Stinchfield, R., & Fulkerson, J. (1993). Patterns and characteristics of adolescent gambling. *Journal of Gambling Studies, 9,* 371–386.

*Wise, M. G., & Tierney, J. G. (1994). Impulse control disorders not elsewhere classified. In R. E. Hales, S. C. Yudofsky, & J. A. Talbot (Eds.), *Textbook of Psychiatry* (2nd ed., pp. 681–699). Washington, DC: American Psychiatric Press.

Wooden, W. S., & Berkey, M. L. (1984). *Children and arson: America's middle-class nightmare.* New York: Plenum Press.

World Health Organization. (1978). *Manual of the international statistical classification of disease* (9th rev.). Geneva: Author.

World Health Organization. (1992). *ICD-10 classification of mental and behavioral disorders: Clinical descriptions and diagnostic guidelines.* Geneva: Author.

Yudofsky, S., Williams, D., & Gorman, J. (1981). Propranolol in the treatment of rage and violent behavior in patients with chronic brain syndromes. *American Journal of Psychiatry, 138,* 218–220.

Zillman, D. (1971). Excitation transfer in communication-mediated aggressive behavior. *Journal of Experimental Social Psychology, 7,* 419–434.

*Indicates references that the authors recommend for additional reading.

22
Adjustment Disorders in Children and Adolescents

Stacy Overstreet
Chad C. Nelson
E. Wayne Holden

INTRODUCTION

The substantial attention given to the investigation of stress and coping paradigms in determining adjustment to both acute and chronic stressors attests to the central role that individual adaptation to stressful life events plays in determining developmental outcomes. It has long been recognized that even minor levels of stress can result in maladaptive behavioral, emotional, and physiological reactions in children and adults (Humphrey, 1984). The relationship of these responses to the development of more sustained psychopathology has been an area of significant concern for quite some time. Adjustment disorder (AD) is the psychiatric diagnostic category that addresses maladaptive reactions to life stress as one potential gateway to developing more sustained psychopathology in the future.

Historical Perspective

Despite limited research attention, AD has been considered an important diagnostic category for children since the 1960s. The Group for the Advancement of Psychiatry in 1966 suggested the use of a diagnostic category termed "reactive disorder," which involved a maladaptive and supposedly transient individual reaction to a psychosocial stressor (Tomb, 1991). This recommendation led to the inclusion of transient situational disturbances as a diagnostic category in the *Diagnostic and Statistical Manual of Mental Disorders*, Second Edition (DSM-II) (American Psychiatric Assocation, 1968). Diagnoses in this category were considered to represent acute reactions to life stressors in the absence of other diagnosable pathology. A time course was not included in the diagnostic criteria, but if symptoms did not subside when the stress was eliminated, then another diagnosis could be considered. The disorder was coded by developmental stage, with infancy, childhood, adolescence, adult life, and late life included. Stressor levels varied from quite mild to overwhelming.

DSM-III (APA, 1980) was the first diagnostic manual to include a specific section for AD. Operationalized and objective diagnostic criteria, including onset of symptoms within three months from the onset of the stressor(s), accompanying impairment in social and occupational functioning, maladaptive behavioral or emotional reactions, duration less than six months, and exclusionary criteria for other diagnoses and bereavement, were included. Eight different subtypes based on symptom patterns were also included, and coding of the diagnosis for individual developmental stages was discontinued. Diagnostic criteria were essentially the same for DSM-III-R (APA, 1987).

Current Diagnostic Description

The diagnostic criteria for AD in DSM-IV (APA, 1994) are included in a separate AD disorders section. The central feature of an AD in DSM-IV is the emergence of emotional or behavioral symptoms in response to an identifiable stressor that occurs within 3 months of the onset of the stressor. The symptoms must be clinically significant, with either significantly higher levels of distress than expected from exposure to the stressor or substantial impairment in social or occupational/academic functioning. Exclusionary diagnostic criteria to clarify the diagnosis of an AD include:

1. The symptoms cannot meet criteria for another Axis I disorder.
2. The symptoms cannot represent an exacerbation of a preexisting Axis I or Axis II disorder.
3. The symptoms cannot represent bereavement.
4. The symptoms cannot persist for more than 6 months beyond the termination of the stressor.

Furthermore, an AD diagnosis can be considered acute if the disturbance lasts less than 6 months or chronic if the disturbance lasts longer than 6 months.

Although the criteria for AD are generally written for and applicable to both children and adults, no specific recommendations are made for applying these criteria to children and adolescents at varying ages. It is assumed that the generic nature of the criteria lend themselves well to modification and subsequent application at varying developmental levels and for

males and females. It should be noted, however, that the lack of specificity for the application of AD criteria at varying developmental levels may result in an overdiagnosis bias that artificially inflates diagnostic rates. It is not known at this time where in the developmental continuum this is most likely to occur, although one might speculate that behaviorally and emotionally vulnerable developmental periods such as infancy/preschool and early adolescence are likely targets.

The absence of a firm grounding of AD criteria in developmental psychopathology models is compounded by the fact that interrater reliability is extremely low in studies that have evaluated AD diagnoses (Newcorn & Strain, 1992). Poor diagnostic reliability is related to the multiple interpretations that can be made of the nonspecific symptoms that go into the diagnosis. Reliability can be improved by strategies such as requiring the presence of at least three clinically significant symptoms for the diagnosis (Kovacs, Gatsonis, Pollock, & Parrone, 1994).

The diagnostic criteria in DSM-IV also provide for the subtyping of AD diagnoses by specifying the predominant symptoms that are displayed. Separate subtypes are included for AD with depressed mood, AD with anxiety, AD with mixed anxiety and depressed mood, AD with disturbance of conduct, AD with mixed disturbance of emotions and conduct, and an unspecified category. However, the level of symptom presentation is not clarified, nor are specific recommendations made for subtype differentiation depending on developmental level. Difficulties in accurately subtyping AD can result from the fact that interrater reliability of AD subtyping is even lower than for overall diagnoses, and significant concerns have been raised about limited predictive validity and poor corresponding diagnostic utility of AD subtypes (Newcorn & Strain, 1992). Placing another decision point in a diagnostic framework characterized by nonspecific criteria only compounds the problems with reliability encountered with the general diagnosis of AD. The general difficulty in differentiating anxiety from depression in children (March, 1995) and the frequent presence of behavioral symptoms that are emotionally based (Reed, Carter, & Miller, 1992; Weiner, 1992) are other developmentally specific factors that likely lower the ability of clinicians to subtype AD diagnoses in a reliable and valid fashion.

The International Statistical Classification of Diseases and Related Mental Health Problems, Tenth Revision (ICD-10) (World Health Organization, 1992) contains a brief description of AD within the section on reactions to severe stress and adjustment disorders. Similar to DSM-IV, diagnostic criteria in ICD-10 are generally described and not developmentally specific. The criteria include the occurrence of an identifiable stressor or significant life change that produces emotional or behavioral symptoms, with interference in social or occupational functioning. Individual vulnerability to stress is emphasized in determining the symptom pattern. As opposed to DSM-IV, ICD-10 does not specify a time interval from the occurrence of the stress to the onset of symptoms, symptom duration is not addressed, bereavement and phase of life problems are not excluded as stressors, and criteria for subtyping the disorder are not provided. Research addressing the comparability of ICD-10 and DSM-IV criteria for AD is not currently available.

Epidemiology

DSM-IV (1994) reports that AD is a common disorder in the general population of adults and children. Prevalence rate ranges from 5–20% are reported for individuals participating in outpatient mental health treatment. Once again, however, developmentally specific prevalence rates are not addressed within the context of the DSM-IV, making it impossible to place children and adolescents within this wide range.

Only one study to date has given attention to prevalence rates of AD in children within the general population. In a large, two-stage epidemiological study conducted in Puerto Rico, Bird and associates (1988) employed both structured and unstructured clinical assessment measures in diagnosing AD. Diagnosis of AD was based on the presence of the behavioral criteria in DSM-III and on a significant impairment in social and academic functioning, as measured by the Children's Global Assessment Scale (CGAS; Shaffer et al., 1983). Results of the study revealed that prevalence rates of AD varied as a function of the degree of impairment in academic and social functioning. When a cutoff score of 70 or below (mild to moderate impairment) on the CGAS was employed, the overall prevalence rate for AD was 7.6%. However, when the cutoff rate was lowered to reflect only severe impairments, the prevalence rate dropped to 4.6%. These results suggest that in about 40% of this sample, behavioral criteria for AD were present in the absence of significant impairment in academic and social functioning. This is an important finding, since the level of impairment in social or academic functioning is one of the qualifiers used to establish the diagnosis of AD.

In clinical populations, prevalence rates of AD have been higher but quite variable due to methodological and setting variations. In one of the largest and most systematic studies conducted, Fabrega, Mezzich, and Mezzich (1987), on the basis of semistructured interviews, reported a prevalence rate of 16% in subjects under 18 attending a university-based hospital clinic. No significant differences were found as a function of gender. In other studies, rates have varied from a low of 7% in an adolescent partial hospitalization program (Doan & Petti, 1988) to a high of 42% for adolescents presenting to an emergency room (Hillard et al., 1987). It is interesting to note that Jacobson et al. (1980) reported an AD prevalence rate range from 25–65% for children in pediatric settings who presented with psychiatric symptoms. In clinical settings, it is quite likely that AD may be the most frequently diagnosed disorder for children and adolescents.

Data are not currently available on age-specific prevalence rates or the incidence of AD in childhood or adolescent populations. This reflects the general absence of incidence data and more refined prevalence data on childhood psychiatric disorders (Holden & Schuman, 1995), rather than an omission specifically linked to

AD. The absence of such data, however, leaves the practicing clinician without any guiding information regarding peak ages of onset for AD.

The severity of symptoms of AD is constrained by the diagnostic criteria. More severe symptoms will likely cross the threshold for the diagnosis of another Axis I disorder. However, the available data on outcome and accompanying features indicates that AD may increase risk for other psychiatric problems and may be related to higher rates of mortality. The presence of AD has been associated with an increased frequency of comorbid psychiatric diagnoses, emergency room visits, psychiatric hospitalizations, and suicide attempts (Newcorn & Strain, 1992). A recent study that statistically controlled for the effects of comorbidity (Kovacs et al., 1994), however, reported that AD has value as a diagnostic entity and a relatively good short-term prognosis.

REVIEW OF PSYCHOPATHOLOGY AND THEORETICAL MODELS

Woolston's Model, Causality and Subtypes of AD

Conceptual models of AD provide an important foundation for guiding assessment and treatment. The most well-elaborated conceptual model of AD has been presented by Woolston (1988) (see Table 22.1). This model assumes that the causality involved in adjustment disorder is an important part of treatment. The author discusses the concept of causality as a

TABLE 22.1. Woodston's Subtypes of AD in Relation to Type of Causality

Type of Causality	Subtype of Adjustment Disorder
Point	Unspecified
Linear	Self-extinguishing
Circular	Self-sustaining, Self-generating
Helical	Interlocking chain, Kindling

foundation for the disorder from a hierarchical perspective and identifies several subtypes of AD in relation to the type of causality. He describes four types of causation:

1. *Point causality*. The most primitive form of causality is point causality, where magical thinking is heavily relied on and cause and effect are not separated in a rational way. Point causality may occur when stressors are faced by children who have a limited understanding of cause and effect or by those who encounter a sudden and extreme stressor, such as the sudden death of a parent. For stressors in which causality is perceived from a point perspective, therapy may focus on understanding the child's or adolescent's reasoning regarding the cause of the stressor and assisting with clarification of cause. In addition, assisting with coping can be incorporated into treatment.

2. *Linear causality*. The next level of causality is linear causality, in which there is one cause and one effect. With linear causality, past history, future development, and other possible factors are ignored. Although linear causality is more sophisticated than point causality, the fact that there is only one cause producing one effect makes this model applicable only to rather simple stressors. Adjustment disorders resulting from linear causality are considered self-extinguishing, in that the person returns to a previous level of functioning once the stressor has ceased. Examples of these types of stressors contributing to AD include temporary financial difficulties, failure to thrive secondary to malnutrition, and parental job loss. If possible, treatment should incorporate the removal of the stressor. If the stressor cannot be removed, as in cases of parental divorce, treatment should focus on effectively coping with the stressor.

3. *Circular causality*. An increasingly advanced concept of causality is what Woolston refers to as circular causality. This concept involves the use of "feedback" and "feedforward." Through feedforward, a cause produces an effect, which in turn produces another similar cause through feedback. The result of stressors in which circular causality is involved may be self-sustaining AD. Maladjustment persists

after the initial trauma has ended or the stressor has been removed. Although removed, the trauma or stressful situation triggers a maladaptive response that uses feedback to perpetuate the AD. An example of these types of stressors is found in children with failure to thrive secondary to emotional deprivation (Woolston, 1983). Treatment for self-sustaining AD should focus on short-term problem solving to assist the parent, child, or adolescent to cope with the stressor and preventive work to prevent further similar stressors and responses.

Similar to self-sustaining AD, self-generating AD continues after the ending of the stressor. In these types of disorders, a trauma or stressor initiates a response from the individual, which interacts with the intrinsic dysfunction of the individual. While treatment must focus on the stressor and removal or adaptation to the stressor, the internal dysfunction must also be addressed.

4. *Helical causality.* The most complex form of causality Woolston refers to is helical causality. Helical causality expands on the concept of circular causality in recognizing that the feedback that influences the cause in turn then changes the effect in some way. For example, adjustment to school failure may result in future anxiety when encountering difficult tasks in school, which may result in increased school failure, resulting in increased anxiety and low self-esteem.

Woolston describes two complex subtypes of AD related to helical causality. In an interlocking chain AD there are several intermediate links between the initial trauma or stressor and the final disturbance. These links may be separate, but they interlock to produce the final response. As an example of an interlocking AD, consider an individual who attempts to adapt to a stressor but, because he or she possesses inadequate self-esteem and judgement, produces a maladaptive response.

The last type of AD is what Woolston refers to as a kindling disorder. This type of disorder has a spreading, contagious action that is self-propagating and ensures perpetuation. The kindling disorders can occur intrinsically, when a stressor produces a threshold change in the individual, or extrinsically, when the recipient of a trauma or stressful event becomes the initiator of similar trauma. Sexual abuse, physical abuse, substance abuse, and suicide are all disturbances that have the tendency to spread from one person to another. With these types of disorders, treatment must focus on processing the current trauma and preventing the spread of similar traumas.

ASSESSMENT OF ADJUSTMENT DISORDER

Clinical Presentation of AD

Although AD is one of the most frequently diagnosed psychiatric conditions in children and adolescents (Chess & Thomas, 1984; Newcorn & Strain, 1992), it is also one of the most problematic diagnostic categories. The subsyndromal nature of the diagnostic category of AD has resulted in great variability in the presentation and diagnosis of AD in children and adolescents. The stressors in AD are often stressors incurred in everyday life, and their clinical implications are uncertain. The impact of life stressors, the capacity of a child to adapt, and the potential reactions vary enormously, depending on the child's developmental level, cognitive abilities, coping strategies, and available support systems.

Another factor that has led to confusion regarding the diagnosis of AD is that, unlike other diagnostic categories in DSM-IV, the diagnosis of AD is not guided by specific behavioral criteria, and this lack of specificity has called into question the utility of the diagnostic category. However, several studies have demonstrated the validity of the diagnosis in both children and adults (Bronisch & Hecht, 1989; Fabrega, Mezzich, & Mezzich, 1987; Kovacs, Gatsonis, Pollock, & Parrone, 1994; Snyder, Strain, & Wolf, 1990). Fabrega et al. (1987) found that adults diagnosed with AD displayed significantly higher levels of psychopathology than non-ill adults but significantly lower levels of psychopathology than adults who met the criteria for other DSM diagnoses. Other researchers have demonstrated that patients diagnosed with adjustment disorder with depressed mood are less severely impaired than those suffering from a major depression (Bronisch & Hecht, 1989; Snyder et al., 1990).

Although the clinical characteristics of AD vary from child to child, several studies have described common symptomatic presentations of AD in children and adolescents (Andreasen & Wasek, 1980; Kovacs et al., 1994), and the results indicate that the symptomatology is somewhat different from that observed in the adult population. Although depressive symptoms seem to be common in both adult and child populations (Andreasen & Wasek, 1980; Kovacs et al., 1994), behavioral symptoms are more common in adolescents than in adults (Andreasen & Wasek, 1980). In a sample of 8- to 13-year-old clinically referred patients with a research diagnosis of AD with depressed mood, Kovacs et al. (1994) found the most common symptoms were sadness (95%), suicidal ideation (58%), reduced ability to experience pleasure (42%), self-deprecation (42%), and irritability (32%). For the other types of AD, the most common symptoms were disobedience (55%), irritability (45%), sadness (45%), anger, physical fighting, and anxiety (36% each). In addition, 60% of the full sample had comorbid psychiatric disorders, of which conduct and/or attention-deficit disorders were the most frequent.

In summary, although the presentations of AD are diverse and based on many individual factors, this diagnostic category has been shown to be valid and clinically useful (Bronisch & Hecht, 1989; Fabrega, Mezzich, & Mezzich, 1987; Kovacs et al., 1994; Snyder et al., 1990). However, the lack of specificity of the diagnostic criteria for AD and the ease with which it may be assigned offer considerable potential for overuse of this diagnostic category (Newcorn & Strain, 1992). It has been argued that clinicians overuse and misapply the diagnosis of AD in an effort to protect individuals from more severe and stigmatizing psychiatric diagnoses (Kranzler, 1988). However, such efforts are not always in the best interests of the patient and may contribute to delays in appropriate treatment planning (Weiner & Del Gaudio, 1976). In addition, such overuse threatens the

reliability and validity of the diagnosis. It is highly recommended that the diagnosis of AD be approached cautiously in child and adolescent populations.

Differential Diagnosis of AD

According to DSM-IV, AD is a residual category, used when a maladaptive reaction to a stressor does not meet the criteria for another specific disorder, when the reaction is not merely an exacerbation of a preexisting condition, and when the reaction does not represent uncomplicated bereavement. Conditions to be considered when making the differential diagnosis include posttraumatic stress disorder, major depression, generalized anxiety disorder, separation anxiety disorder, disruptive behavior disorders, and psychological factors affecting physical condition. The following is a discussion of factors that should be considered when making the differential diagnosis.

AD versus Posttraumatic Stress Disorder (PTSD)

Although both AD and PTSD require the presence of a psychosocial stressor, PTSD is characterized by the presence of an extreme psychological stressor and a well-defined constellation of emotional and autonomic symptoms. AD, in contrast, is a reaction to a stressor of any severity and presents with a wide range of emotional and behavioral symptoms. In contrast to PTSD, AD and its subtypes are a series of symptom complexes representing nonspecific, individual reactions that are shaped by constitutional, developmental, and environmental factors; there is not a specific set of symptoms associated with given stressors. However, there are certain stressors that are more likely than others to result in an adjustment disorder.

Kovacs et al. (1994) and Andreasen and Wasek (1980) reported that school problems were the most common precipitant stressors in children and adolescents with AD, observed in 30% and 60% of the respective samples. In addition, family disruption through parental separation or divorce was also a common stressor and was identified in 23–25% of these samples. Other stressors noted by Kovacs et al. (1994) include peer rejection (identified in 13% of the sample) and parental illness (identified in 10% of the sample). Kovacs et al. (1985) also found that approximately 30% of a sample of children with newly diagnosed insulin-dependent diabetes met the criteria for AD.

On the basis of these findings, it is clear that the nature of the stressor precipitating a diagnosis of AD is quite different from that required for diagnosis of PTSD. In addition, there are differences in the psychological and behavioral sequelae of the disorders. In AD, reactions to stressors are diverse and no close stressor-response relationship has been demonstrated. In contrast, diagnosis of PTSD requires that the reactions to the stressor be characterized by very specific features, such as reexperiencing the traumatic event, emotional numbing, and physiological arousal.

AD versus Depression

In some cases, it may be difficult to differentiate between AD and situational (as opposed to endogenous) depression. The differential diagnosis between AD with depressed mood (ADDM) and major depression must be considered when a child presents with recent onset of depressive symptomatology that is associated with an identifiable stressor. If the symptoms are varied and severe enough to meet the criteria for a major depressive episode, that diagnosis, and not ADDM, must be made. However, such a qualitative distinction is sometimes difficult to make. For example, Hall and Benedek (1993) found that, in a sample of adults with the diagnosis of either ADDM or major depressive episode, severity of depression did not vary between the two but the more subtle, day-to-day mood variability did. Adults with ADDM displayed greater mood variability than did adults experiencing a major depressive episode.

Other research has also documented the difference in clinical presentation of major depression and ADDM. Snyder et al. (1990) found that, in a group of adults within a medical setting, ADDM was characterized by better recent functioning, greater severity of stressors, and decreased severity of psychiatric impairment than major depression. Bronisch and Hecht (1989) found similar differences between medical inpatients diagnosed with either ADDM or major depression. Individuals with ADDM reported less severe depressive symptomatology, and their social functioning was less impaired than that of individuals with major depression.

The results of these studies indicate that ADDM is a clinical entity distinct from major depression, with its own unique presentation, course, and prognosis. When symptoms are extreme and the criteria for major depression are clearly met, the differential diagnosis is clear. However, the differential diagnosis becomes more challenging in the case of children and adolescents, because presentation of depressive symptomatology is more diverse in this group than in adults.

AD versus Disruptive Behavior Disorders

The clinical subtype of AD with disturbance of conduct is used when the symptoms include the violation of the rights of others or of major age-appropriate norms and rules. In applying this diagnosis, it is important to rule out the presence of conduct disorder (CD) and oppositional defiant disorder (ODD). There are several ways to distinguish AD from CD and ODD. First, the typical course of CD and ODD is distinct from that of AD. In the case of CD and ODD, onset is typically gradual, occurring over the course of months or years, and there is a repetitive and persistent pattern of the inappropriate behaviors. This is not the typical pattern of conduct problems associated with AD, which develop rather suddenly in clear association with the onset of a psychosocial stressor and which cease with the termination of the stressor or its consequences. Second, both CD and ODD usually occur in late childhood or early adolescence and rarely after the age of 16 years. However, the emergence of conduct problems associated with AD varies not with age but with exposure to a stressor or stressors. Finally, the severity and persistence of conduct problems associated with AD do not meet the criteria for either CD or ODD.

AD versus Anxiety Disorders

The clinical subtype of AD with anxiety may often be difficult to distinguish from generalized anxiety disorder (GAD) and separation anxiety disorder (SAD). The subtype of AD with anxiety is used when the predominant manifestations are symptoms such as nervousness, worry, and jitteriness, which are similar to the symptoms observed in GAD. The other predominant manifestation of AD with anxiety includes fears of separation from major attachment figures, which is also the essential feature of SAD. Differential diagnosis is made based on the intensity of the symptoms, and the diagnosis of AD should be used only when the criteria are not met for GAD or SAD. Although the diagnosis of AD requires that the anxiety occur in response to a life stressor or stressors, if an individual has symptoms in response to a stressor that meet criteria for either GAD or SAD, the diagnosis of AD with anxiety is not applicable. There are several possible stressors that may evoke symptoms of anxiety and/or fears of separation in children and adolescents, including the death of a parent or divorce. After experiencing such an event, the young child may develop anxiety concerning separation from the attachment figure and may resist separation and display distress upon separation. In such a situation, when no other symptoms are present, the diagnosis of AD with anxiety may be made. However, if the anxiety becomes excessive and the child begins to display pervasive manifestations of the anxiety and fears (e.g., refusal to go to school or elsewhere, worry about possible harm befalling attachment figures, refusal to be alone or to go to sleep without being near attachment figure), the severity of the symptoms warrants the diagnosis of SAD.

AD versus Psychological Factors Affecting Medical Condition

The relationship between psychological and medical factors in these two conditions is re-versed. In AD, psychological symptoms can develop in response to the stress of having or being diagnosed with a medical condition. The diagnosis "psychological factors affecting medical condition" is applied when a medical condition is exacerbated by psychological symptoms. In some individuals, it is possible for both conditions to be present.

Assessment of AD

The assessment of AD should begin with a clinical interview in which the child's symptoms are carefully evaluated to determine whether the presenting symptoms are in fact maladaptive and not an "expected reaction" to an identifiable stressor. A thorough psychosocial history will allow the clinician to determine whether the presenting symptoms reflect a change from previous levels of functioning and when they occurred in relation to the stressor.

Although the clinical interview is a valuable assessment tool, it is often not sufficient to lead the clinician to a clear diagnosis of AD. For example, it may become clear during the interview that the presenting symptoms reflect a change in functioning, but the family and/or child may not be able to identify a clear stressor that preceded the symptoms. One objective measure that may be useful in such situations is the Life Event Scale (Coddington, 1981a, 1981b), which comes in two forms, one for children ages 6 to 11 and another for adolescents ages 12–18. Such a scale not only is useful in identifying the stressor or stressors that preceded presenting symptoms, but it may also reveal information that might be overlooked in the clinical interview. In addition, the scale provides a way of initiating discussions about sensitive or painful topics that may be difficult for the child to initially discuss face to face with an authority figure.

The clinician may also have difficulty determining the clinical significance of symptoms when making the diagnosis of AD. First, the clinician needs to know whether the degree of symptoms is significant given a child's age. In such situations, behavior checklists and self-report instruments such as the Child Behavior Checklist (CBCL; Achenbach, 1991a), the Youth Self-Report (YSR; Achenbach, 1991b), the Adjustment Scales for Children and Adolescents (ASCA; McDermott, Marston, & Stott, 1993), the Children's Depression Inventory (Kovacs, 1992), and the Revised Children's Manifest Anxiety Scale (Reynolds & Richmond, 1978) can be used to assess a variety of behavioral and emotional symptoms across a wide age range. In general, these scales are useful in identifying areas of functioning in which the child is experiencing significant disturbances. Although the clinical significance of more subtle variations in behavioral and emotional symptoms that do not reach the cutoff scores for abnormal behavior has not been empirically established for many of these measures (Drotar, Stein, & Perrin, 1995), a recent study using the ASCA developed a normative typology of behavior styles that define distinct variations of healthy, marginal, at-risk, and clinical behavior (McDermott & Weiss, 1995). Such distinctions could be helpful in distinguishing the subclinical behavioral and emotional problems associated with AD from those of normal and specific clinical populations.

Second, the clinician must determine whether the symptoms reflect a partial syndrome of a specific disorder or are of sufficient frequency and intensity to make the diagnosis of a specific disorder other than AD. Multiple measures of emotional functioning, including the clinical interview and standardized scales, are necessary to make the diagnosis of AD and to determine the clinical subtype. The utility of the standardized measures lies in their ability to distinguish between clinically significant levels of symptomatology that may indicate a specific anxiety or depressive disorder and subclinical levels of symptomatology that may indicate problems with adjustment but that do not meet the criteria for diagnosis of a specific anxiety or depressive disorder. Some common measures of anxiety and depression include the Revised Children's Manifest Anxiety Scale (RCMAS; Reynolds & Richmond, 1978), the State-Trait Anxiety

Inventory for Children (STAIC; Spielberger, Edwards, Lushene, Monturi, & Plazek, 1973), and the Children's Depression Inventory (CDI; Kovacs, 1992).

In summary, the assessment of AD requires a comprehensive evaluation of the child's functioning in a wide range of areas. The optimal evaluation will include a clinical interview with a detailed psychosocial history and standardized measures that identify stressors and quantify the intensity of behavioral and emotional symptomatology. After such a thorough evaluation, the clinician can feel confident regarding the differential diagnosis of AD.

TREATMENT OF ADJUSTMENT DISORDER

Although AD is a frequent diagnosis in children and adolescents (Andreasen & Wasek, 1980; Newcorn & Strain, 1992), little empirical research regarding the treatment of AD exists. Recent reviews on AD (Enzer & Cunningham, 1991; Tomb, 1991) in children and adolescents reveal that treatment often involves a multilevel approach. The treatment of AD has two general goals. These include addressing the acute symptoms related to the trauma or stressor and returning the child or adolescent to a healthy premorbid state by helping the child effectively cope with the ongoing stressor and gain a sense of mastery in coping (Enzer & Cunningham, 1991; Reid, 1989).

After a thorough evaluation of the individual, the family, the environment, the causal properties of the stressor, and the maladaptive response, the removal of the stressor should be considered (Enzer & Cunningham, 1991; Tomb, 1991). While removal of the identifiable stressor may greatly facilitate treatment and possibly return the child to previous functioning, this can not always be accomplished. Family death, loss from natural disasters, divorce, physical disfiguration, and diagnosis of a physical illness are all stressors that must be addressed and dealt with (see Table 22.2).

TABLE 22.2. Treatment Approaches for Various Adjustment Disorder Stressors

Treatment Approach	Stressors
Supportive Psychotherapy	Temporary stressors such as temporary financial difficulties, temporary parental unemployment
Individual Psychotherapy	Peer rejection, adjustment to new school, stressors involving underlying dynamic issues
Family Psychotherapy	Divorce, death of a family member
Group Psychotherapy	Chronic illness, disfigurement, death of friend or family member, disaster or trauma
Pharmacotherapy	Stressors resulting in inability to cope using own emotional resources or to learn personal ways of coping

Enzer and Cunningham (1991) address another type of stressor that may be possible to eliminate, although eliminating the stressor may not be in the best interest of the child. For example, it may be more profitable for the child or adolescent to learn to cope with and adapt to certain stressors, such as rejection from peers at a new school. With these stressors, therapy may include support and cognitive behavioral interventions to assist in problem solving.

Family Intervention

Because many of the stressors that face children and adolescents also impact the family, the consideration of family therapy as a mode of addressing the stressor and maladaptive adjustment has been suggested (Enzer & Cunningham, 1991; Reid, 1989; Tomb, 1991). With younger children, interventions that focus on work with the parents may be all that is needed to relieve the maladaptive adjustment to stressors. Assisting parents in understanding the child's view of the stressor and their response to their child may also serve a preventive purpose by bolstering parent's skills for coping with behavioral disturbance at a later time.

From a systemic viewpoint, family therapy may be crucial in adaptive adjustment to stressors. Well-functioning families can serve as protectors to children from stressors that the family and child encounter (Patterson, 1983). Therefore, stressors must significantly affect the family system before they can affect the individual child significantly. With family therapy, the impact of the stressor can be addressed with the hope of restoring the family system to its previous level of functioning. For example, parental hierarchies may break down as a result of family adjustment to a stressor, resulting in lack of consistency in child care and limit setting. Family therapy can address the meaning of the stressor for each family member and reestablish consistency in parenting and structure. These positive changes not only provide the child with a sense of stability but also allow the parents to resume their role in assisting the child in coping.

Individual Intervention

Individual therapy is also recommended for children and adolescents suffering from AD. Enzer and Cunningham (1991) and Tomb (1991) suggest that individual therapy can focus on the stressor and its meaning to the child or adolescent. Therapy can be brief, focused, and time limited, similar to the format described by Dulcan (1984). Several interventions have been suggested as components of individual therapy for patients with AD. These interventions have included relaxation training to reduce anxiety (Schatzberg, 1990) and cognitive problem solving to assist in coping with the trauma or stressor as well as symptoms of anxiety and depression that may be associated with the adjustment to the stressor (Enzer & Cunningham, 1991; Reid, 1989). For example, cognitive problem solving can teach children to (1) identify problems, (2) identify possible solutions to the problem, (3) choose an appropriate solution, and (4) evaluate the solution choice for future reference. Tomb (1991) recommends insight-oriented therapy for AD when underlying dynamic issues may be present.

Group/Classroom Intervention

Group interventions, whether taking place in a school or mental health setting, have also been suggested as a means of treating AD. Group psychotherapy allows individuals to increase their personal resources while gaining support from other group members (Reid, 1989). Such interventions allow a sense of shared experience and the opportunity to gain additional coping strategies. Despite the suggestion that group interventions may be useful for children with AD, there are virtually no studies that have outlined the components that would be necessary for the successful treatment of the disorder. From a cognitive-behavioral viewpoint, one could argue that coping strategies and problem-solving skills would be primary targets for treatment. Other targets for treatment may depend on the subtype of AD present. For example, when treating AD with depressed mood and/or anxiety, additional treatment components should include cognitive restructuring and relaxation training. On the other hand, when treating AD with disturbance of conduct, additional treatment components may include self-monitoring and self-control strategies. Much more research is needed to determine the efficacy of group treatment for children and adolescents with AD.

Pharmacological Intervention

Terr (1989) reported that psychopharmacological interventions are used with some children and adolescents who have experienced trauma. The use of pharmacological interventions for the treatment of AD has received mixed reviews. Enzer and Cunningham (1991) suggest that brief pharmacological interventions may be necessary for providing symptom relief so that other issues involved in adjustment can be addressed. Reid (1989), on the other hand, suggests that pharmacological interventions may rob the individual of the opportunity to use his or her own emotional resources and to learn personal ways of coping with current and future stressors. Vernberg and Vogel (1993) suggest that examination of the destructiveness of the person's response to the stressor or trauma, combined with clinical judgment, should be the basis for decisions regarding pharmacological assistance for symptom relief. When pharmacotherapy is chosen as an adjunctive treatment to psychotherapy for AD, choice of appropriate medications depends upon the predominant symptoms. For example, AD with depressed mood may be treated with tricyclic antidepressants or MAO inhibitors, AD with anxiety may be treated with benzodiazepines, and AD with disturbance of conduct may be treated with other mood stabilizers such as carbamazepine or clonidine (Enzer & Cunningham, 1991).

In summary, several approaches to intervention have been suggested in the treatment of AD in children and adolescents, but little research has been conducted on the efficacy of such interventions. After a thorough evaluation, clinical judgment is heavily relied upon to devise a comprehensive treatment plan. This treatment plan may encompass one or several intervention modalities, depending on the child's and family's adjustment, as well as the type of stressor or trauma experienced.

CONCLUSIONS

Adjustment disorder is the most frequently diagnosed condition in children and adolescents and appears to have at least moderate clinical utility. However, many questions regarding AD still remain to be answered. Although diagnostic criteria have become more specific over time, developmental variations in symptom presentation have not been adequately addressed. Documentation of symptoms specific to children and adolescents is necessary to further clarify developmental variations in AD. Moreover, the reliability of overall AD diagnoses is less than optimal, and the even lower reliability of AD subtype diagnoses suggests that subtyping should be pursued with caution. Further investigation of the effects of diagnostic criteria changes on reliability is recommended. Predictive validity and treatment response appear to be promising but have only recently been addressed in the literature and warrant continued investigation.

It is likely that clinicians will continue to find the AD diagnosis useful in their work with children and adolescents. This may be particularly true in settings where children are exposed to high rates of stressors without adequate environmental supports. The impact of cultural variations on the diagnosis of AD should be actively considered in both assessment and treatment. Interventions designed to promote self-extinguishing forms of AD are needed. Preventive interventions that bolster children's and family's coping skills in the face of life stressors will ultimately lead to decreases in the incidence and resulting high prevalence of AD.

REFERENCES

Achenbach, T. M. (1991a). *Manual for the Child Behavior Checklist and 1991 Profile*. Burlington: University of Vermont, Department of Psychiatry.

Achenbach, T. M. (1991b). *Manual for the Youth Self-Report and 1991 Profile*. Burlington: University of Vermont, Department of Psychiatry.

American Psychiatric Association. (1980). *Diagnostic and statistical manual of mental disorders* (3rd ed.). Washington, DC: Author.

American Psychiatric Association. (1987). *Diagnostic and statistical manual of mental disorders* (3rd ed., rev). Washington, DC: Author.

American Psychiatric Association. (1994). *Diagnostic and statistical manual of mental disorders* (4th ed.). Washington, DC: Author.

Andreasen, N. C., & Wasek, P. (1980). Adjustment disorders in adolescents and adults. *Archives of General Psychiatry, 37*, 1166–1170.

Bird, H. R., Canino, G., Rubio-Stipec, M., et al. (1988). Estimates of the prevalence of childhood maladjustment in a community survey in Puerto Rico: The use of combined measures. *Archives of General Psychiatry, 45*, 1120–1126.

Bronisch, T., & Hecht, H. (1989). Validity of adjustment disorder, comparison with major depression. *Journal of Affective Disorders, 17*, 229–236.

Chess, S., & Thomas, A. (1984). *Origins and evolution of behavior disorders from infancy to early adult life*. New York: Brunner-Mazel.

Coddington, R. D. (1981a). *Life Event Scale-Adolescents*. St. Clairsville, OH: Stress Research Company.

Coddington, R. D. (1981b). *Life Event Scale-Children*. St. Clairsville, OH: Stress Research Company.

Doan, R. J., & Petti, T. A. (1988). Clinical and demographic characteristics of child and adolescent partial hospital patients. *Journal of the American Academy of Child and Adolescent Psychiatry, 28*, 66–69.

Drotar, D., Stein, R. E., & Perrin, E. C. (1995). Methodological issues in using the child behavior checklist and its related instruments in clinical child psychology research. *Journal of Clinical Child Psychology, 24*, 184–192.

Dulcan, M. H. (1984). Brief psychotherapy with children and their families: The state of the art. *Journal of the American Academy of Child and Adolescent Psychiatry, 23*, 544–551.

Enzer, N. B., & Cunningham, S. D. (1991). Adjustment and reactive disorders. In J. M. Wiener (Ed.), *Textbook of child and adolescent psychiatry* (pp. 468–476). Washington, DC: American Psychiatric Press.

Fabrega, H., Mezzich, J. E., & Mezzich, A. C. (1987). Adjustment disorder as a marginal or transitional illness category in DSM-III. *Archives of General Psychiatry, 44*, 567–572.

Hall, D. P., & Benedek, D. M. (1993). Adjustment disorder criteria. *Hospital and Community Psychiatry, 44*, 592.

Hillard, J. R., Slomowitz, M., & Levi, L. S. (1987). A retrospective study of adolescents visits to a general hospital psychiatric emergency service. *American Journal of Psychiatry, 144*, 432–436.

Holden, E. W., & Schuman, W. B. (1995). Detection and management of mental health disorders in pediatric primary care. *Journal of Clinical Psychology in Medical Settings, 2*, 71–87.

Humphrey, J. H. (1984). Some general causes of stress in children. In J. H. Humphrey (Ed.), *Stress in childhood* (pp. 3–18). New York: AMS Press.

Jacobson, A. M., Goldberg, I. D., Burns, B. J., et al. (1980). Diagnosed mental disorder in children and use of health services in four organized health care settings. *American Journal of Psychiatry, 137*, 559–565.

Kovacs, M. (1992). *The Children's Depression Inventory*. New York: Multi-Health Systems.

Kovacs, M., Feinberg, T. L., Paulauskas, S., Finkelstein, R., Pollock, M., & Crouse-Novak, M. (1985). Initial coping responses and psychosocial characteristics of children with insulin-dependent diabetes mellitus. *Journal of Pediatrics, 106*, 827–834.

Kovacs, M., Gatsonis, C., Pollock, M., & Parrone, P. L. (1994). A controlled prospective study of DSM-III adjustment disorder in childhood: Short-term prognosis and long-term predictive validity. *Archives of General Psychiatry, 51*, 535–541.

Kranzler, E. M. (1988). Adjustment disorders. In C. J. Kestenbaum and D. T. Williams (Eds.), *Handbook of Clinical Assessment of Children and Adolescents* (pp. 812–828). New York: University Press.

March, J. S. (1995). *Anxiety disorders in children and adolescents*. New York: Guilford Press.

McDermott, P. A., Marston, N. C., & Stott, D. H. (1993). *Adjustment Scales for Children and Adolescents*. Philadelphia: Edumetric and Clinical Science.

McDermott, P. A., & Weiss, R. V. (1995). A normative typology of healthy, subclinical, and clinical behavior styles among American children and adolescents. *Psychological Assessment, 7* (2), 162–170.

Newcorn, J. H., & Strain, J. (1992). Adjustment disorder in children and adolescents. *Journal of the American Academy of Child and Adolescent Psychiatry, 31* (2), 318–326.

Patterson, G. R. (1983). Stress: A change agent for family process. In N. Garmezy & M. Rutter (Eds.), *Stress, coping and development in children* (pp. 235–264). New York: McGraw-Hill.

Reed, L. J., Carter, B. D., & Miller, L. C. (1992). Fear and anxiety in children. In C. E. Walker and M. C. Roberts (Eds.), *Handbook of clinical child psychology* (2nd ed., pp. 237–260). New York: Wiley.

Reid, W. H. (1989). Adjustment disorders. In W. H. Reid (Ed.), *The treatment of psychiatric disorders* (pp. 321–327). New York: Brunner/Mazel.

Reiff, M. I., Banez, G. A., & Culbert, T. P. (1993). Children who have attentional disorders: Diagnosis and evaluation. *Pediatrics in Review, 14*, 455–465.

Reynolds, C. R., & Richmond, B. O. (1978). "What I Think and Feel": A revised measure of children's manifest anxiety. *Journal of Abnormal Child Psychology, 6*, 271–280.

Schatzberg, A. F. (1990). Anxiety and adjustment disorder: A treatment approach. *Journal of Clinical Psychiatry, 51*, 20–24.

Shaffer, D., Gould, M. S., Brasic, J., Ambrosini, P., Bird, H. R., & Alvwahlia, S. (1983). A children's global assessment scale (CGAS). *Archives of General Psychiatry, 40*, 1228–1231.

Snyder, S., Strain, J. J., & Wolf, D. (1990). Differentiating major depression from adjustment disorder with depressed mood in the medical setting. *General Hospital Psychiatry, 12*, 159–165.

Spielberger, C. D., Edwards, C., Lushene, R., Monturi, J., & Plazek, S. (1973). *The State-Trait Anxiety Inventory for Children*. Palo Alto, CA: Consulting Psychologist Press.

Terr, L. C. (1989). Family anxiety after traumatic events. *Journal of Clinical Psychiatry, 50*, 15–19.

Tomb, D. A. (1991). Adjustment disorder. In M. Lewis (Ed.), *Child and adolescent psychiatry: A comprehensive textbook* (pp. 725–731). Baltimore: Williams and Wilkins.

Vernberg, E. M., & Vogel, J. M. (1993). Interventions with children after disasters. *Journal of Clinical Child Psychology, 22*, 485–498.

Weiner, A. S. (1992). Emotion problems of adolescence: Review of mood disorders. In C. E. Walker and M. C. Roberts (Eds.), *Handbook of clinical child psychology* (2nd ed., pp. 565–586). New York: Wiley.

Weiner, I. B., & Del Gaudio, A. C. (1976). Psychopathology in adolescence. *Archives of General Psychiatry, 33*, 187–193.

Woolston, J. L. (1983). Eating disorders in infancy and early childhood. *Journal of the American Academy of Child and Adolescent Psychiatry, 22*, 114–121.

Woolston, J. L. (1988). Theoretical considerations of the adjustment disorders. *Journal of the American Academy of Child and Adolescent Psychiatry, 27*, 280–287.

World Health Organization. (1992). *International statistical classification of diseases and related health problems* (10th rev.). Geneva: Author.

23
Personality Disorders

Sula Wolff

INTRODUCTION

This chapter differs from others in this book in that, with the exception of schizoid/schizotypal disorders, it deals not with childhood conditions themselves but with the childhood antecedents of important disorders in adult life. All child psychologists and psychiatrists need to be aware of the developmental psychopathology of these adult conditions so that they can take an informed long-term view of the relevant childhood disorders, be knowledgeable about the preventive aspects of their own work, and advise policymakers in the fields of health, education, and child care about effective community interventions. The hope is that such interventions in the lives of children and adolescents can, at least to some extent, prevent the later development of the more serious personality disorders of adult life, especially the antisocial disorders.

Personality disorders are defined by the *Diagnostic and Statistical Manual of Mental Disorders* (DSM-IV) (APA, 1994) and by the *International Classification of Mental and Behavioural Disorders* (ICD-10) (WHO, 1992) as enduring patterns of behavior (in DSM-

IV, experience too) that are deeply engrained, pervasive, and inflexible, and that manifest in a wide range of social and personal contexts, deviate markedly from the expectations of the culture, and are associated with subjective distress and impairment of social functioning. According to ICD-10, these disorders tend to appear in late childhood or adolescence and continue into adult life, but the diagnosis is not likely to be appropriate below the age of 16 or 17. DSM-IV states that personality disorders usually begin in early adult life or adolescence, sometimes even earlier, but that they should be diagnosed in those under 18 only if their features have been present for at least one year. In this scheme, the label "antisocial personality disorder" should never be applied to anyone under the age of 18, when "conduct disorder" is the preferred diagnosis.

Personality disorders are not often diagnosed by child psychiatrists (Hill and Rutter, 1994), and for good reasons. Many children with symptoms retrospectively associated with personality disorders never develop them. This is so especially for antisocial personality. Of affected adults, 60% have been seriously and another 30% moderately antisocial in childhood, but more than 50% of highly antisocial children do not become sociopathic in later life (Robins, 1978). The association for this disorder is very strong looking backward, but not looking forward (Rutter, 1989).

Personality disorder is by definition enduring, so to make such a diagnosis in childhood may suggest a gloomy prognosis. This applies particularly to the diagnosis of antisocial personality, which can act as a self-fulfilling prophesy and reinforce counterproductive negative responses on the part of parents, teachers, and the criminal justice system to antisocial and delinquent children. Hope, that essential ingredient of all treatment, must be preserved when the outcome for an individual child cannot be predicted (Wolff, 1993). Yet we shall see that for some types of personality disorder that manifest clearly in childhood, especially schizoid and schizotypal disorders, an early diagnosis improves the chances of appropriate treatment and education and results in a prognosis that is less gloomy than it might appear.

The discontinuity in diagnostic labeling between childhood and adult life can also have disadvantages. Spurious differences may be suggested between some of the pervasive developmental disorders of childhood, such as Asperger's disorder or schizoid disorder of childhood, and those personality disorders that make up cluster A of DSM-IV. This can impede explorations of the psychological functioning of affected people and of the etiology of the conditions.

A further disadvantage of different diagnostic conventions for children and adults is that it reinforces differences in attitude and practice for clinicians dealing with different age groups. Psychologists and psychiatrists for children and adolescents maintain their clinical concern even for youngsters likely to develop personality disorders in later life, and much child development research aims to disentangle the constitutional and environmental causes for such disorders. Psychiatrists for adults, especially in the United Kingdom, are sometimes less than tolerant of the therapeutic difficulties posed by seriously personality disordered patients. Psychiatrists will be helped towards greater understanding of affected people by a developmental perspective on these disorders derived from a knowledge of their childhood antecedents.

This chapter begins by considering constitutional factors that contribute to enduring childhood behaviors. The concept of temperament, its stability over time, and its genetic basis are discussed, followed by a description of two extremes of temperament: constitutional shyness and inhibition in the face of novelty and constitutional hyperactivity and disinhibition. Adult personality disorders likely to be related to such dispositions are mentioned: avoidant (DSM-IV) or anxious (avoidant) (ICD-10) personality disorder and the antisocial or borderline personality disorders of DSM-IV and the dissocial and emotionally unstable, impulsive type, personality disorders of ICD-10.

The next focus is the childhood antecedents, constitutional and environmental, of DSM-IV antisocial (ICD-10 dissocial) personality disorder. This disorder is not diagnosed in children, but its roots lie in childhood and adolescence. Antisocial behavior at any age contributes to the most common and the most serious psychiatric conditions, taking an enormous toll on individual and public health. Theoretically at least, these disorders are preventable, and it is in childhood and young adult life that prophylactic action is most urgent and most likely to pay off.

Finally, I address those conditions whose manifestations are both stable over time and and so similar in childhood and adult life that a personality disorder diagnosis is appropriate and helpful even in childhood. These make up cluster A personality disorders of DSM-IV, or, in ICD-10, schizoid and paranoid personality disorders and schizotypal disorder, at present here classified with the schizophrenias. The chapter ends with a discussion of what is a much more problematical diagnosis in childhood: borderline personality.

Two issues, however, need clarification to start with.

How Do We Decide That A Childhood Condition Is The Same As Its Counterpart In Later Life?

Although the manifestations of some clinical conditions change in the course of child development, equivalence between disorders of childhood and those of adult life must rely on a similarity of essential symptoms and signs. This is clearly so for schizophrenia beginning in childhood, for anorexia nervosa, for depressive illnesses, and for obsessive-compulsive disorders. It should apply equally to the diagnoses of the personality disorders. Confusion arises when "masked" diagnoses are inferred in childhood in the absence of the relevant symptomatology (Zeitlin, 1986), when, for example, depression is inferred in a child without evidence of a depressed mood state being elicited. In a study of people who had been psychiatrically referred both in childhood and in adult life, Zeitlin found symptoms to have greater continuity over time than diagnoses of syndromes.

What Are the Determinants of Continuity of Behavior and Experience in Childhood?

Constitutional, largely genetic factors certainly play a part, most obviously in determining the stability of intelligence and, as we shall see, aspects of temperament, too. But environmental continuities greatly contribute to the stability of behavior, including intelligence and temperament. These are continuities of the socioeconomic and cultural environment, of family circumstances and schooling, which often exert their influences throughout a person's childhood. A third potent source of continuity derives from mutually reinforcing interactions between the individual child and his or her caregivers, teachers, and peers. Often the effects of such interactions are to confirm and magnify the child's characteristic behavior. Finally, there are inner continuities based on remembered events and circumstances as they were experienced and perceived by the child at his or her particular developmental level. These determine children's cognitive set, their expectations of others, and their interpretations and responses to subsequent similar experiences.

CHILDHOOD TEMPERAMENT

Temperament is regarded as a constitutionally based source of individual variation in personality functioning, emerging early in life (Lamb et al., 1991). Experience determines the stability and transformation of temperamental qualities over time. Chess and Thomas's New York Longitudinal Study (1984) initiated the quest for enduring qualities of temperament that contribute to clinical disorders when parents and other important people in a child's life are unable to accommodate to his or her individual nature. Starting with the observation that, from birth onward, children differ from each other in their patterns of reactivity, these researchers explored the behavioral characteristics of a series of New York children by means of detailed parental interviews and observations of the children themselves at regular intervals as they grew up. Nine dimensions of temperament were defined: activity level, approach/withdrawal to novelty, positive or negative mood, threshold of sensitivity to stimuli, intensity of reactions, rhythmicity of biological functions, adaptability to novel situations and people, distractability, and persistence. The stability of ratings on these dimensions were low in very early childhood but increased with age. A cluster of traits that make up the "difficult child syndrome" (negative mood, intensity of reactions, poor adaptability, and low rhythmicity) correlated both with subsequent behavior disorders in early childhood and with maladjustment in later life. Approach/withdrawal, later included by other workers in a shyness/inhibition dimension (discussed later), accounted for more variance between children than any other trait and increased in stability during the preschool years. Activity level, intensity of response, threshold, and especially adaptability were also relatively stable over time (Plomin et al., 1988; Thomas & Chess, 1986).

On the basis of twin and adoption studies, and using questionnaires to measure the categories of temperament defined in the New York Study, Plomin and his colleagues suggested that three temperamental factors have a genetic basis: *activity*, most universally accepted as having high heritability; *sociability*, which loads on approach/withdrawal, adaptability, and threshold; and *emotionality*, with loadings on approach/withdrawal, mood, intensity, and threshold. From a clinical viewpoint, it was unfortunate that a fourth factor, *impulsivity*, was subsequently excluded because of difficulties of measurement. A twin study of very young children confirmed the heritabilities of all the temperamental traits that make up these three factors, and also of persistence, but not of rhythmicity (Cyphers et al., 1990), and a longitudinal twin study found activity level and approach/withdrawal to be heritable at all ages up to adolescence (Torgersen, 1989).

In an excellent review, Prior (1992) stresses the low levels of stability with age of the original nine catgories, compared with broad band factors, such as sociability and reactivity. The most stable traits are irritability, negative emotionality, and extreme inhibition, as well as the "difficult child" cluster, again only at the extreme. Prior, too, regrets that the clinically important traits related to impulsivity, attention regulation, distractability, soothability, and self-control, have not so far been fully addressed. She is among the few workers in the field to emphasise the considerable gender and social class differences of temperament, which have also not yet been fully explored. Boys are more hyperactive and negative in mood; parents respond to aspects of temperament, for example, shyness, differently in boys and girls, being more tolerant of shyness in their daughters than in their sons; and there is a consistent excess of children with a difficult temperament among lower socioeconomic groups.

Conduct-disordered children (most of whom are boys, often from socioeconomically deprived backgrounds), compared with children with emotional or no disorders, had the most deviant temperamental profiles, especially high activity, high intensity, and persistently negative mood. A deviant temperament, Prior holds, is a risk factor for antisocial behavior, but only in combination with other biological, relationship, and environmental variables.

Socioeconomic differences in childhood temperament reflect differences in parental assessments and expectations. Parents in lower socioeconomic groups have more negative perceptions of their children. In her Australian Temperament Project, Prior found relationships, biological factors, and temperament to operate additively in predicting later antisocial behavior.

CONSTITUTIONAL SHYNESS AND INHIBITION—A LINK WITH AVOIDANT PERSONALITY DISORDER?

Children's responsiveness to novel situations and people is one of the most stable aspects of childhood behavior. Between 10 and 15% of 2- and 3-year old children regularly become quiet, vigilant, and subdued when meeting unfamiliar people in unfamiliar settings (Kagan, 1994; Kagan et al., 1988). Kagan and his colleagues followed up cohorts of children who in their second year were observed to be either consistently shy or consistently sociable in such a context. By the age of 7.5, three-quarters of extremely inhibited children had remained so, and these had higher rates of anxiety disorders, as well as higher heart rates and larger pupils in unfamiliar settings than either children who had not been shy in their second year or that minority of shy children who had outgrown their shyness. Children at the extremes of sociability and disinhibition preserved these traits over time even more consistently. Moreover, children with extreme and stable shyness were found to have parents who themselves had an excess of current anxiety disorders (Hirschfeld et al., 1992).

Yet environmental factors also contributed to these developments: two-thirds of sociable children had been the first-born, without competing siblings in their earliest years, while two-thirds of shy children were later born.

In their adoption studies, Daniels and Plomin (1985) related infant shyness to parent ratings on an adult social temperament scale. They found infant shyness and maternal self-reports of shyness, introversion, and low sociability to be more highly correlated in natural, nonadoptive families than in adoptive families. They also observed that the self-assessments of biological mothers correlated with their adopted-away children's shyness even less. The authors suggest that shy, socially anxious mothers expose both themselves and their children less often to novel situations and that this then reinforces the constitutional predisposition of their children to social shyness and inhibition.

A great variety of descriptive terms and definitions is used in temperament research so that one can never be sure how comparable different research findings are. When Thapar and McGuffin (1996) in their Cardiff twin study found high neurotic symptom scores in children 8 to 16 years old to be highly heritable, we do not know how enduring these symptoms were or whether they were at all related to constitutional shyness. Nevertheless, a long-term outcome study of shy children is of great clinical relevance (Capsi & Elder, 1988). In this study, parent and teacher ratings of childhood shyness correlated with adult shyness at 30 years. Boys assessed as shy and reserved at 8 and 10 years were found at 40 to have married, embarked on fatherhood, and established careers later and to have inferior work achievements and more instability both at work and in marriage than men who had not been shy in middle childhood. Shy girls, by contrast, more often followed a conventional career of marriage and homemaking than nonshy girls; fewer of them were working, but the occupational status of their husbands was higher. The notion of "cumulative continuity" of personality traits emerges from this study: a person's disposition induces him or her to choose or construct particular environments, which in turn reinforce and sustain such dispositions; personal development is a sequence of reciprocal transactions between the individual and his or her environment, mediated both by behavioral and cognitive processes.

Clinical Diagnostic Issues

Children with extreme constitutional shyness, oversensitivity, and poor adaptability, labeled social sensitivity disorder in ICD-10 and social phobia in DSM-IV, are seen in clinical practice when their social withdrawal seriously impairs their social life outside the family and/or their functioning at school. Other family members are often similarly affected. We must await the more long-term follow-up of constitutionally shy children to know how many of them will in later life fulfill the criteria for avoidant personality disorder (DSM-IV and ICD-10), that is, pervasive patterns of social inhibition, feelings of inadequacy, and hypersensitivity to negative evaluations, with impairments in occupational and social activities and in intimate relationships. Only if this is found to be a common outcome can such children be said to suffer from a personality disorder.

Differential Diagnosis

Constitutional shyness in childhood, an enduring condition, needs to be differentiated from depressive illness (Hall & Hill, 1991), which has a definite time of onset and a characteristic mood disturbance and is best identified during a clinical interview with the child herself but which may be missed when only parents are interviewed (Angold et al., 1987). Several self-rating scales and standardized interviews for childhood depression are now available. The problems in their application in clinical practice and research are well summarized by Harrington (1994).

Constitutional shyness also needs to be distinguished from schizoid personality, where affected children lack the capacity for, and actively avoid, social relationships with peers. Constitutionally shy children, in contrast, long to mix and make friends and find their social inhibition painful. DSM-IV specifies that the term "social phobia" should be applied to constitutionally shy children only when they have an age-appropriate capacity for social relationships with familiar people, a capacity strikingly lacking in schizoid children. Again, the clinical interview with the child is the best way of establishing the diagnosis.

Treatment Approaches

As with other constitutionally based disorders, the most important intervention is to help the children, parents, and teachers understand the difficulties in terms of the child's temperamental disposition, rather than to search for hidden stressful life experiences or parental shortcomings, unless these are obviously also present. Rapid change should not be expected. Cognitive behavioral approaches and social skills training in small groups offer the best chance for improving an affected child's social integration.

CONSTITUTIONAL HYPERACTIVITY AND THE HYPERKINETIC SYNDROME (ADHD) AS CONTRIBUTORS TO LATER PERSONALITY DISORDERS

More common in clinical practice are children with hyperkinetic disorders (see also chapters 6 and 21). Activity level is one of the most heritable and enduring traits of childhood temperament. Kagan and Snidman (1991) found disinhibition with lack of fear, high levels of approach and sociability, and low physiological arousal to be stable over time in early childhood; Thapar et al. (1995) found childhood hyperactivity scores to be highly heritable. The temperamental traits of impulsivity, inattention, and low persistence have not yet been fully explored (Prior, 1992). Motor activity, disinhibition, and impulsivity are all possible contributors to the development of childhood attention-deficit/hyperkinetic disorder (DSM-IV) (hyperkinetic disorders of childhood in ICD-10) and to the antisocial and borderline personality disorders of later life. Developmental immaturity (hyperkinesis is highly associated with developmental delays of various types) and perinatal difficulties (commoner in

the more severe cases of the hyperkinetic syndrome) are possible, less well-established contributing factors (Taylor, 1994).

In a comparative study of pure hyperkinetic, mixed hyperkinetic/conduct-disordered, pure conduct-disordered, and normal boys, Taylor et al. (1991) found those with a mixed pathology to be the most disturbed, with greater educational impairments and higher rates of low IQ and neurodevelopmental disorders, than purely hyperkinetic children, and with earlier onset of conduct disorders than purely conduct-disordered children. Marital disharmony, parental hostility toward the child, poor parenting skills in coping with the child's difficulties, parental inconsistency, and maternal depression were high in all disturbed groups of children, but highest in the mixed hyperkinetic/conduct-disordered group. By contrast, marital disharmony and delinquency were commoner among parents of purely conduct-disordered children. Although inadequate parenting may in part be a response to the child's difficult behavior, its effect is to reinforce this. In most children of the mixed group, hyperkinesis had preceded the conduct disorder.

The Risk of Later Personality Disorder

The majority of children with pure hyperkinesis, and even some with transient conduct and school difficulties at adolescence, do well in later life (Taylor, 1994), especially if of good intelligence. Hyperkinesis tends to improve with age, but impulsivity may persist. How much childhood hyperkinesis and residual impulsivity contribute to the development of those adult personality disorders characterized by abnormal impulsivity: borderline personality disorder (DSM-IV), or (in ICD-10) the emotionally unstable personality disorders, impulsive and borderline types, is not known. Children with deficits in attention, motor control, and perception (DAMP) but *without conduct disorder* have been found at 16 years to fulfill the criteria for a variety of often overlapping personality disorders: DSM cluster A, borderline, and avoidant, but very rarely antisocial (Hellgren et al., 1994).

What is clear from a number of studies (Mannuzza et al., 1989; Weiss et al., 1979, 1985) is that children with mixed hyperkinetic and conduct disorders, especially boys and especially if also aggressive and exposed to socioeconomic disadvantage and family strife, have high risks for adult antisocial personality disorder and criminality. The separate childhood diagnostic category of hyperkinetic conduct disorder in ICD-10 reflects this.

Treatment and Prevention

This is not the place to detail the treatment of hyperkinetic children. But their increased risks of language and motor delays and of future antisocial and other personality disorders must be faced. Satterfield et al. (1987) showed that for *predelinquent* hyperactive boys, multimodal treatment, involving stimulant medication as well as intensive and long-term psychotherapy with behavioral, cognitive, and interpretative methods, was more effective in preventing later criminality than medication alone, and also cost-effective. The importance of clinical recognition of a hyperkinetic disorder on the basis of careful history taking and observation, and the benefits of accurate diagnosis and long-term, individually tailored multimodal treatment, including educational interventions, are well summarized by Taylor and Hemsley (1995).

Hyperkinetic children at greatest risk of later antisocial personality are those with accompanying antisocial, especially aggressive, behavior disorders, who are failing educationally, who come from disadvantaged families living in domestic strife, and whose parents are unable to modify their child-rearing practices to meet their children's needs. In my experience, such children often benefit from partial distancing from their adverse family environment in residential schools where their special educational needs are met and where they are helped to modify their behavior and their parents, too, are supported, without breaking family ties and

without the risks of multiple family and school placements that are almost inevitably associated with fostering.

CHILDHOOD ANTECEDENTS OF ANTISOCIAL PERSONALITY DISORDER

The strong relationship between childhood conduct disorder and antisocial personality in adult life was established by Robins (Robins & O'Neal, 1966). She sees childhood conduct disorder as the middle phase of a chronic psychiatric condition, beginning typically in early life and continuing into adulthood but one that can abort at any time (Robins, 1991). The number of conduct disorder symptoms is the best predictor of later antisocial personality, followed by early age of onset. Aggressive behavior, which tends to start very early, predicts antisocial conduct at adolescence more strongly than any other personal or environmental variable. Antisocial conduct beginning in adolescence has a better prognosis, especially when, as commonly, it occurs in girls and when it is not accompanied by low IQ, educational difficulties, and attention-deficit disorders, so common in antisocial boys.

Childhood Aggression as a Predictor of Later Antisocial Disorder

An early study (Olweus, 1979) found aggression to be one of the most stable personality characteristics, as predictable as IQ, especially in boys. It is determined by temperamental traits of high activity level and intensity; by mothers' expectations of aggressive/assertive behavior in their sons and their tolerance of aggression; and by parental "power-assertive" methods of child rearing (Olweus, 1980). In his longitudinal study in Sweden, Magnusson (1988, 1992) found that a subgroup of conduct-disordered boys who were also hyperactive with concentration difficulties and low physiological arousal wholly accounted for the continuity between childhood conduct disorder and adult criminality.

The persistence of aggressive conduct from middle childhood to adult life, especially in men, was confirmed by two comparative long-term longitudinal studies (Huesman et al., 1984 and Capsi et al., 1987; Capsi & Elder, 1988). These also documented the transmission of aggressiveness across the generations. Aggressive boys tend to become punitive fathers who in turn promote aggressiveness in their children. Low IQ, poor educational achievements, low socioeconomic status, and a punitive upbringing contribute to these developments. Aggressive boys in later life are also more likely to divorce and to have unstable work records. Aggressive girls, too, divorced more frequently in later life than other women and tended to marry men of lower occupational status and to become ill-tempered mothers. Aggression is thus very stable across the life span of individuals and across generations and is highly predictive of delinquency and antisocial personality disorder.

Constitutional Determinants of Aggression and Antisocial Conduct

Sex

Aggressive behavior is more common and more stable in boys than in girls. This may reflect social expectations, but constitutional factors—high levels of motor activity and greater muscularity—are likely to play a part. Boys are also more vulnerable to many adversities, reacting to parental discord, hostility, and family disruption with conduct disorders, which in turn evoke disapproval and rejection. Girls more often react with emotional disorders, and even conduct-disordered girls are in later life more likely to develop depressive and anxiety disorders than an antisocial personality (Maughan & Garratt, 1994; Wolff, 1993).

Early Puberty in Girls

Magnusson (1988) found that some girls who reached puberty early associated with older friends. They had higher rates of smoking, alcohol use, dating, and staying out late than their normally maturing age mates and early maturers with same-aged friends, behaviors that were socially disapproved of at their age. They tended to leave school earlier and with fewer qualifications than other girls. By the age of 26, although their sexual relationships were stable, they had had more children and slightly more recorded crime. Clearly, constitutionally determined early puberty, when it leads to mixing with older peers, carries a slight risk of later educational disadvantage and antisocial behavior.

Temperament

We have seen that traits of high activity, intensity, sociability, and impulsiveness, as well as low arousal and fearlessness, perhaps also persistently negative mood, promote aggressive and delinquent conduct in childhood. This process may in part be mediated, as we shall see, by an inadequate early development of conscience. In early adult life, a lack of "planfulness" has been identified as a risk factor for the adverse life events and circumstances (including a poor marital choice) that characterize people who had conduct disorders as children and that in turn contribute to their continuing antisocial difficulties (Champion et al., 1995; Quinton et al., 1993). Whether and how such lack of planfulness is related to temperamental impulsivity remains to be determined.

A Constitutional Obstacle to the Development of Conscience?

Once children are mature enough to be aware of how things ought to be and of their own competence and self-efficacy, in the second year of life (Kagan, 1981), child-rearing practices become powerful determinants of pro- or antisocial behavior and of conscience. But a third ingredient is necessary for the development of inner standards of what is right and inner mechanisms for self-control: empathy. The rudiments for this appear at birth, and in most children empathy develops rapidly in the second year, forming the basis for sympathetic and altruistic behavior (Wolff, 1996).

Empathy can be deficient for experiential reasons in seriously traumatized children (Hoffman, 1975) who miss out on normal early attachments, who repeatedly experience hostile and disrupted parenting, and who may themselves then become self-preoccupied, hostile, and even violent and retributive towards all others. But some children, those with schizoid/schizotypal disorders and Asperger's syndrome, are, as we shall see, constitutionally impaired in their capacity for empathic understanding of other people's thoughts and feelings. They suffer from a deficit of mentalizing abilities, or "theory of mind," an impairment of the capacity to imagine what goes on in the minds of others (Happe, 1994). Some affected people are callous from childhood onward, and a few develop antisocial, even criminal, behavior whose motivation often remains obscure.

These constitutional determinants may, at least in part, account for the genetic contribution to antisocial conduct, especially in adult life, revealed by the study of twins (Eaves et al., 1997).

Experiential Determinants of Aggression and Antisocial Conduct

Abnormal Early Attachments

Early parent loss and institutional care are common in the histories of antisocial people. Disrupted parent-child attachments foster aggression in children, especially when there is also parental discord. But disrupted and distorted early attachments are often so embedded in a network of other adversities—maternal depression, parental personality disorder, continued exposure to family disharmony, abusive experiences, repeated changes of substitute caregivers and of schooling, quite apart from poverty and exposure to delinquent peers—that the specific contributions of abnormal early bonding to later antisocial personality are not easily traced. An exception is the comparative follow-up of institutionalized children by Rutter et al. (1990), where the risk for adult criminality and personality disorder was significantly increased for boys but not girls when the disruption of family life had taken place in the first two years.

Coercive Child Rearing and the Early Development of Conscience

Chronic marital discord and hostility between parent and child foster antisocial development, especially in boys. Patterson (1986; Patterson & Dishion, 1988) has clarified the family processes involved. Many parents, especially in poor socioeconomic circumstances, depressed, exposed to external stresses, or using drugs or alcohol, have poor family management skills. They fail to monitor their child's behavior, threaten but do not follow through when their child misbehaves, and use coercive, punitive methods of control even for trivial noncompliance. The effect is that the child's irritating behavior stops temporarily, reinforcing the parents' punitiveness, only to recur and provoke ever more punitive responses from the parents. A mutually reinforcing sequence of increasingly violent interactions is set in train, parents and children "teaching" each other to become more and more aggressive. Children with a difficult temperament are most at risk of provoking such interactions, which interfere with expressions of mutual affection between children and parents and with mutual enjoyment of their relationship. Aggressive children from such families arrive at school with inadequate social skills, are rejected by other children, and, especially if also of low intelligence or with educational delays, fail academically. Not surprisingly, their self-esteem is poor.

Patterson was concerned with children in middle childhood. But we now have evidence that how parents socialize children in their early years profoundly affects their moral behavior and moral reasoning in later childhood. The effects of differences in mothers' early socializing styles on children's later development of guilt and conscience were investigated by Koshanska (1991) in a longitudinal study. Coercive and noncoercive rearing styles when children were

18–42 months old were compared with the children's contemporaneous compliance to their mothers' demands and with their affective/moral responses at 8–10 years to semiprojective stories. The main finding was that noncoercive child rearing and early compliance were associated with evidence for an internalized conscience in later years.

Temperament, however, also plays a part. Koshanska (1993) holds that children are best socialized when parents use inductive, that is, reasoning methods but do so with an emotional charge. Children who themselves have high levels of emotional tension then learn readily to make internal attributions about transgression and to feel appropriate guilt. But children with low levels of emotional tension learn poorly, evoke ever more coercion from parents, and have their external attributions reinforced every time they transgress and "get away with it" without feeling bad. Koshanska (1993) suggests that two components of conscience contribute to moral conduct: affective discomfort brought about by actual or potential wrong doing and the capacity for behavioral self-control. Both have temperamental underpinnings that may account for the differential effects of parental socialization methods. Fearfulness and social inhibition interact with high levels of moral motivation to reduce immoral behavior in situations of temptation. Less is as yet known about the interaction between parental socializing efforts and the childhood temperament dimension of impulsivity/behavioral control. Reasoning may be less effective in encouraging the internalization of standards for impulsive children. Inadequate early socialization is likely to be very important in the development of antisocial personality because children whose antisocial conduct starts early in life are most at risk. Magnusson (1996) has recently reviewed most clearly the evidence for an interactionist explanation of persistent antisocial behavior.

Shaw and Bell (1993) have clearly summarized how parents can contribute to their children's antisocial behavior: from neglectful parenting in the first year, fostering avoidant attachment in the infant and, later, noncompliance and hostile, acting-out on the part of the child, to a lack of maternal warmth and of the authoritative control needed to scaffold the child's efforts at prosocial behavior in the early years, and the coercive transactions in later childhood that Patterson identified. The Cardiff twin study suggests that antisocial behavior, at least in those between 8 and 16 years old, is indeed largely due to the shared environment to which social class factors make a small contribution. In this study, genetic effects were negligible, a finding not easily reconciled with the evidence, reviewed earlier, for the heritability of the temperamental factors contributing to antisocial conduct.

Parental Discord

Persistent parental discord is highly associated with conduct disorders in boys and with persistence of psychopathology from childhood into adult life. Rutter (1994) summarized the possible sequence of causal links and processes involved, including the role of an antisocial peer group and, later, of marriage to an unsupportive, deviant partner.

The Wider Environment

Child-rearing processes that engender childhood conduct disorders are commoner in family environments where parents are psychiatrically disturbed, drug or alcohol dependent, or themselves delinquent. Absence of intimate social supports and exposure to recurrent adverse life events and circumstances contribute to these difficulties. There is also evidence that children with conduct or emotional disorders themselves grow up into the sort of people who repeatedly encounter severely adverse events and circumstances of the kind known to precipitate psychiatric disorders (Champion et al., 1995). But we should not underestimate the effects of the wider social and economic environment on these processes. Socioeconomic disadvantage, universally associated with childhood antisocial conduct, is also associated with the occurrence of teenage pregnancy, with maternal depression, and with parental delinquency. And poor housing, unemployment, and ill health interfere with parental competence.

Educational Failure

A strong link between school failure and conduct disorders in childhood and adolescence has repeatedly been found. This is now thought to be accounted for by social class effects and by associated hyperactivity and attentional deficits (Maughan, 1995). Only when reading retardation and conduct disorder occur together in childhood is there a real risk of antisocial conduct beyond adolescence. The mediating factor here is truancy, which is associated with school failure and also predicts later delinquency (Maughan et al., 1996). Poor readers without childhood conduct disorders are at risk of persistent educational and occupational constraints, but not of an antisocial development in later life.

Peer Relationships and Stigma

Aggressive boys and boys who witness actual or verbal aggression between parents develop negative attributional styles; they infer hostile intent in other children when none is intended and react with defensive aggression. This increases their reputation for aggressiveness and evokes counteraggression from others (Dodge, 1980; Dodge et al., 1990). Such boys tend to be extruded from their peer group and to associate with other deviant youngsters, with the result that their antisocial behavior persists.

Labeling youngsters as delinquent can also be stigmatizing and cause a potentially transient disorder to persist. Adolescents with convictions, especially if these do not incur a definite sentence, are more likely to reoffend than young people with equally serious self-reported offenses who have not been convicted (West & Farrington, 1973).

FACTORS THAT PROTECT AGAINST AN ANTISOCIAL DEVELOPMENT

Constitutional Factors

Farrington and his colleagues (1988), in a longitudinal study of delinquent development, examined boys from a highly criminogenic background who, contrary to expectation, did not become delinquent. They differed from later delinquents in having been more "neurotic" in middle childhood, better behaved, less daring, and less sociable. Their parents were less delinquent, their mothers had thought well of them in childhood, and their siblings were better adjusted. Although persisting into adult life, constitutional shyness and inhibition as well as nervousness were thus protective against delinquency. High intelligence, physical attractiveness, and an easy temperament are other constitutional factors promoting resilience in the face of adversity and protecting children at risk from an antisocial development (Kolvin et al., 1988; Wolff, 1996).

Family Life

A harmonious family life protects vulnerable children, such as hyperkinetic children and children with developmental learning difficulties, from a delinquent development. And good parental supervision protects even children living in high-delinquency neighborhoods from becoming antisocial themselves (Kolvin et al., 1988).

Life Transitions

Perhaps the most important insights into the circumstances in which the progression from childhood antisocial conduct to adult antisocial personality (a criminal career, unstable marriage, poor child care, poor work adjustment, and/or substance abuse) can be halted have come from studies of important life transitions, especially from school into working life and marriage.

Sampson and Laub (1993), in a comprehensive reanalysis of the longitudinal data collected by Sheldon and Eleanor Glueck on 500 delinquent boys and their matched controls, developed the thesis that childhood pathways to adult crime or conformity are modified over the life course by social bonds: interdependence and attachments to people and commitments to educational and occupational goals. While juvenile delinquency is determined by the child's characteristics of IQ and temperament, by lack of family control, and by deficient bonding with family and school, delinquency after 17 is related only to the child's actual antisocial behavior (see also Robins, 1991) and to the quality of adult social ties. In both delinquent and control groups, it was job stability at 17–25 years, and marital attachment at 25–32, that correlated most highly with reduced later crime rates. Social bonds formed between 17 and 25 years were the strongest predictors for decreased crime and deviance between 25 and 32 years. Juvenile incarceration interfered with the development of work and marital bonds, and incarceration in adult life adversely affected their stability, with increased subsequent delinquency.

Quinton and Rutter's work (1988) is congruent with these ideas. Some girls who had been in institutional care and at risk of teenage pregnancy and marriage, marital discord, and poor mothering capacities for their own children, all indicative of an antisocial development, were protected from this fate by marriage to a nondeviant partner. And Farrington (1990) found lowered rates of offending in men at high risk of delinquency after marriage to a nondeviant wife.

PREVENTION OF CHILDHOOD CONDUCT DISORDER AND ANTISOCIAL PERSONALITY

The treatment of children with conduct disorders, which involves much effort (Bank et al., 1991; Kazdin, 1997) and is often not strikingly successful (Earls, 1994), is dealt with in chapter 7. Here the focus is on preventive measures that are potentially more likely to be effective (Farrington, 1995; Offord & Bennett, 1994). Conduct disorders and later antisocial personality are multiply determined, so, if only one of the interacting adversities can be made good, the chances of a more positive development are enhanced. Fergusson argues cogently for macrosociological changes and social reconstruction in order to minimize the number of seriously dysfunctional families in a community (Fergusson et al., 1994). And Offord advocates programs targeted on high-risk communities (Jones & Offord, 1989; Offord & Bennett, 1994). Such programs are more cost-effective than nationwide programs, while avoiding the stigma attached to interventions with individual families or children at risk.

Home Visiting Programs for Vulnerable Mothers

Numerous experimental programs have shown that specially trained and supported home visitors can help poor, unmarried, young mothers to achieve better health for their babies, better educational and work status for themselves, and more sensitive and less punitive care for their children, with the result that the children have better early language skills, make better school progress, and have fewer later behavior problems, including antisocial conduct (Graham, 1994; Larson, 1980; Seitz et al., 1985; Seitz & Provence, 1990; Shepherd & Farrington, 1995).

School-based Interventions

Good preschool education for socioeconomically disadvantaged children, initiated at first to boost intelligence and school progress, is now known to have long-term positive effects, not on intelligence but on school attainments and behavior, and to promote socioeconomic independence, low rates of teen-age pregnancy, and low delinquency rates in later life. It is also cost effective (Barnett & Escobar, 1990; Berrueta-Clement et al., 1984; Lazar & Darlington, 1982).

The quality of schools, their ethos, and their teaching methods have profound effects not only on educational progress but on the rates of behavior disorders and delinquency in childhood and adolescence. Although attempts to modify the school environment in the light of these findings have so far not been of proven value (Maughan, 1988), interventions in specific areas of school life have been successful in reducing childhood disorders, including conduct disorders (see Sylva, 1994), and are likely to have beneficial effects on adult personality.

Bullying, a common school occurrence known to be related to an antisocial development in later life, has been a recent focus of attention, and several school-based intervention programs have proved to be effective (Olweus, 1993; Smith & Sharp, 1994). The transition from primary to secondary school can be hazardous for socially and educationally disadvantaged children, leading to disaffection, truancy, drop-out, and delinquency. At least one low-cost special program to smooth the path of children on entry to secondary school is of known efficacy (Felner & Adan, 1988).

Less well evaluated has been the large-scale Newhaven Primary Prevention Project (Cauce et al., 1987; Comer, 1980). It ran for 20 years, used a "human systems management" approach, and improved children's academic achievements and behavior.

A Community Intervention

The Ontario Child Health Study (Boyle & Offord, 1990; Graham, 1994; Jones & Offord, 1989) incorporated a community-based, nonacademic skills program of sports, scouting, cross-country hiking, and so forth for children ages 5 to 15 years in a deprived public housing complex, to prevent conduct disorders. Outcome comparisons were with children in a similar setting but not in the program. The intervention was cost-effective, operational costs being more than offset by savings on law enforcement and property damage, but positive effects did not generalize and decreased when the program ended. Clearly, such programs should be ongoing and possibly school based.

SCHIZOID/SCHIZOTYPAL PERSONALITY DISORDER: AN APPROPRIATE DIAGNOSIS EVEN IN CHILDHOOD

In 1944 Asperger, unfamiliar with Kanner's first account of early infantile autism (1943),

reported on a series of children with what he called autistic psychopathy of childhood. He believed this to be a personality disorder with the following lifelong features: solitariness; abnormalities of gaze, expression, and gesture; insensitivity to social cues; lack of feeling for other people, at times amounting to callousness; over- and insensitivity; "autistic" intelligence, inventive rather than imitative; and specific interests in restricted fields such as mathematics, art, chemistry, and poisons, which could lead to creative achievements. Educational delays of all kinds were often present. Insistence on conformity could lead to outbursts of rage or tears. Social adaptation tended to improve with age, and the work adjustment of autistic psychopaths with high intelligence was good. But the basic personality features persisted, and intimate, including sexual, relationships were often limited. Asperger observed the full syndrome only in boys, although girls sometimes had a partial syndrome, often associated with brain damage. In every case, one or more biological relatives, male and female, were affected with the full or partial syndrome. Once familiar with Kanner's autism, Asperger (1979) drew a distinction between this and autistic psychopathy, believing that children affected by the latter were more awkwardly behaved, while in later life some had very exceptional achievements despite their eccentricities.

In 1980 we described a group of children seen in clinical practice with what we called schizoid personality disorder (Wolff & Chick, 1980) because they had the features of this condition as reported in the psychiatric literature before the advent of DSM. In DSM the schizoid category was subsequently split into schizotypal, schizoid and paranoid disorders, together constituting the type A personality disorders. Schizotypal disorder, the commonest, is found to greatest excess among biological relatives of schizophrenic patients. We realized at the time that our children also had the features of Asperger's autistic psychopathy, except that a third were girls.

Two controlled follow-up studies by "blind" interviewers, using standard semistructucred interviews, found the following core personality features of the children to be very stable over time: solitariness, children describing themselves or being described by others as "loners"; impaired empathy and emotional detachment; rigidity of mental set, especially the single-minded pursuit of special interests; increased sensitivity, at times with paranoid ideation; unusual or odd styles of communication, including overcommunicativeness and metaphorical use of language; and an unusual fantasy life, affected people appearing to blur the distinction between reality and fantasy, and occasionally engaging in pathological lying (Wolff, 1995). Our schizoid boys were of slightly above-average intelligence and had an upwardly skewed social class background. This was not so for the girls. An important finding was that multiple or serious developmental delays of all kinds, including language delays, occurred in half the affected boys and a third of the girls.

In 1981 Lorna Wing reported on a group of children with "Asperger's syndrome," which she held to be equivalent to high-functioning autism. Her account was seminal in initiating much research into what is now called the autistic spectrum, especially into the clinical features and psychological functioning of affected people (Frith, 1991; Happe, 1994) and into the genetic relationship with childhood autism. Asperger's syndrome now entered the ICD diagnostic classifications (ICD-9, including here schizoid disorder of childhood).

The prominence given to this syndrome had the beneficial effect of drawing attention to the educational and other needs of affected people, but it must be said that Wing's initial series of cases and those of others described as having Asperger's syndrome were very much more handicapped than our children with schizoid personality disorder, and probably also Asperger's own cases (Wolff, 1995). In contrast to our own series, most people with Asperger's syndrome were unemployed and unmarried in adult life, and many lived either with their families of origin or in sheltered care (Tantam, 1991).

Links with Autism

There is no question that the individual features of schizoid personality in childhood resemble those of childhood autism. Yet they are not the same. The deficits in social interaction did not markedly affect our children's attachments to their parents and usually manifested only on school entry. Peer relationships were the most impaired. Our children's special interest patterns were often sophisticated, quite unlike the repetitive, stereotyped behaviors of autistic children; and the unusual modes of communication of schizoid children were not, as in autism, immediately apparent but had to be carefully looked for. Moreover, our children were not deficient in imaginative play capacities. On the contrary, a number engaged in unusual imagination, much fantasy, and even pathological lying (Wolff, 1995). Only a minority had had earlier autistic symptoms and never the complete syndrome.

Yet clear genetic links have been established between Asperger's syndrome, schizoid personality, and childhood autism. Asperger's syndrome and autism sometimes aggregate in families (Gillberg, 1991); Asperger's syndrome has been found to excesss among biological relatives of autistic people (de Long et al., 1988; Gillberg et al., 1992), and schizoid personality traits in the parents of autistic children (Wolff et al., 1988).

Twin studies of autistic children have shown that nonaffected identical twins more often than expected have cognitive and social deficits, milder but similar to those of autism itself (Folstein & Rutter, 1988; LeCouteur et al., 1996); Bolton and his colleagues (1994) found a considerable excess among siblings of autistic people of "a lesser variant of autism" whose reported characteristics seem to resemble the features of schizoid personality as we described it.

Links with Schizophrenia

Our schizoid children closely resembled a group of schizotypal children reported by Nagy and

Szatmari (1986), one in 10 of whom later developed schizophrenia. In our second follow-up, we therefore incorporated the Baron schedule for schizotypal personality disorder (Baron et al., 1981) and found that, at a mean age of 27 years, three-quarters of our former patients fulfilled the criteria for this personality disoder. Moreover, in a search of the psychiatric records of the total cohort of 109 schizoid men and 32 schizoid women, all psychiatrically referred in childhood, a schizophrenic illness was found in seven of our schizoid subjects at a mean age of 27 years, an overall rate of 5%, compared with just one case among the matched controls of other referred children grown up (0.7%), and an estimated population prevalence at this age of 0.31–0.49% (Wolff, 1995). These findings support a schizophrenia spectrum diagnosis in our children.

In summary, a genetic association between autism and Asperger's syndrome and schizoid disorder has been established. Our work suggests there is also a link between schizoid disorder and schizophrenia. This appears at first sight to go in the face of the evidence that there is no excess of schizophrenia among biological relatives of autistic people and that autism is not among the psychiatric disorders that characterize relatives of schizophrenic patients. The findings can be reconciled by assuming that autism and schizophrenia, both recognized as having a multigenic causation, share a genetic predisposition to schizoid/schizotypal disorder, each condition in addition requiring other different genetic (and possibly organic) causes to be present, also.

Prognosis

The rate of later schizophrenia in our schizoid children, although greater than expected, was low and does not preclude a good prognosis. Indeed, our follow-up studies showed that, in later life, most schizoid children lived independent lives, and their work adjustment was only slightly worse than that of other referred children grown-up. Moreover, while they had

significantly fewer intimate sexual relationships than their matched controls, the actual marriage rates in the two groups were not significantly different. Our schizoid children were thus much less impaired in psychosocial functioning in adult life than were children currently diagnosed as having Asperger's syndrome according to ICD-10.

A search of the criminal records for our total group of 141 schizoid children as adults showed the boys in adult life to be no more delinquent than their matched controls but the girls to be more deviant. In both groups of referred children grown up, delinquency rates were, of course, somewhat higher than in the general population. Yet only one of our schizoid young men committed an incomprehensible, violent crime. It is important to note, however, that Asperger's syndrome has been diagnosed in a number of serious offenders (Wolff, 1995).

Diagnostic Issues

It is important to recognize schizoid/schizotypal disorders in childhood because the treatment needs of affected children differ from those of children whose difficulties are primarily due to adverse life experiences. Comorbidity may obscure the diagnosis, referred girls, in particular, often having associated conduct or emotional disorders. In both boys and girls, specific developmental delays are common, and schizoid children occasionally present with selective mutism. While Asperger's syndrome, as currently defined in ICD-10, is unlikely to be missed, the more subtle impairments of schizoid children need to be carefully looked for, especially when a child's symptoms cannot be accounted for by his or her life experiences.

Treatment Approaches

There are as yet no treatment outcome studies for this group of children. What follows is based on clinical experience. The clinical and educational needs of seriously impaired children with Asperger's syndrome are similar to those of children with high-functioning autism (see chapter 5). Clinicians, educationalists, and National Societies for Autistic people are beginning to develop appropriate services.

The needs of more mildly affected, often gifted, schizoid children are, however, different. They are not handicapped in the usual sense, but their behavior can be extremely difficult. The first step is to help parents, teachers, and the children themselves to recognize their difficulties as stemming from their constitutional personality makeup, their "nature"; that the parents, who may share some of their children's characteristics, are in no way to blame; and that the children are not wilfully awkward. The second step is to recognize that major changes in personality are not to be expected and that pressure for increased sociability and conformity is counterproductive. Family and the school have to accommodate to the child's needs. Small group teaching, even special schooling, may have to be arranged, and some affected children will need to be excused from team games or noisy playground activities. Teaching may have to build initially on the child's special interests, and children with reading, spelling or other educational delays require remedial education.

Secondary behavioral symptoms such as aggressive outbursts respond to behavioral treatment methods, and medication may be indicated for depressive symptoms or transient delusional states. Interpretative psychotherapy and intrusive family approaches are likely to make matters worse. What is helpful, above all, is for the clinician to accept long-term responsibility for care, to act as the child's advocate, and to help negotiate his or her path through the educational system and into a working life.

BORDERLINE PERSONALITY IN CHILDHOOD: A VALID DIAGNOSIS?

The meaning of this diagnostic term, much used by psychoanalytic writers, has fundamentally changed in recent classifications. It used to be applied to children and adults with conditions thought to be intermediate between psychosis and neurosis, and the psychoanalytic literature contains many descriptions of "borderline" children with ego deficits and abnormal psychological defenses who would now be labeled schizoid or schizotypal. In DSM-III the borderline category was split into schizotypal disorder, allied to schizophrenia, and borderline disorder, characterized by instability in behavior, relationships, identity, and emotional experiences, with impulsivity, suicidal behavior, oversensitivity to possible rejection, and vulnerability to psychotic episodes. Petti and Vela (1990) emphasize this distinction in their literature review of these conditions in childhood.

Etiologically, the newly defined borderline diagnosis in adult life has been linked to childhood experiences of abnormal attachments, family breakdown, and physical and especially sexual abuse (see Berelowitz & Tarnopolsky, 1993). Recently a group of adult patients with borderline personality disorder were, in comparison with dysthymic patients, found to have more enmeshed and unresolved patterns of responding to an Adult Attachment Interview, as well as scores of low maternal care and high maternal overprotection on the Parental Bonding Instrument (PBI) (Patrick et al., 1994). So far, there has been no exploration of the possible contribution to borderline personality of temperamental impulsivity, which is also likely to contribute to the other emotionally unstable personality type of ICD-10, impulsive personality.

The usefulness of the borderline diagnosis in childhood remains in doubt, although seriously disturbed children often fulfill its criteria. Greenman et al. (1986) applied Gunderson's Diagnostic Interview for Borderlines (DIB) retrospectively to the case notes of psychiatrically hospitalized children ages 6–12 years. Almost a third met the diagnostic criteria. But many borderline symptoms were found in other children, too, and there were high rates of comorbidity in those diagnosed as having BPD: conduct disorder, overanxious disorder, ADHD, and other personality disorders. The borderline children had been more delinquent, more aggressive, more assaultative, hostile, irritable, and demanding. Their most discriminating feature was episodes of psychotic thinking.

I find myself, with Robson (1991), in doubt about the validity of this elusive condition in childhood, especially since we do not know whether children given this diagnosis will continue to fulfil its criteria in adult life. Hill and Rutter (1994) consider the diagnosis to be helpful at least in adolescence, and Aarkrog (1994) found it to have considerable stability from adolescence into adult life. James et al. (1996) in a chart review found the DIB to identify 10% of adolescent in-patients as having BPD. Over half also had a major depressive disorder and of these one half had a family history of affective illness. Early separation from parents was no more common than in a group of psychiatric controls, but the rates of sexual abuse and maternal helplessness were higher. Recommended treatments include inpatient and family centered approaches (Robson, 1991), although James et al. (1996) caution against conjoint family therapy, suggesting that parents and adolescent should be seen separately, at least to start with.

SUMMARY

The childhood antecedents of many adult personality disorders have not been established. The only group of personality disorders that can be diagnosed with confidence in childhood are schizoid/schizotypal disorders because we know their characteristics endure into adult life. The diagnosis is important, affected children having specific treatment needs.

Avoidant personality is another candidate for early diagnosis, but its validity in childhood has yet to be confirmed. The same is true for borderline personality disorder, although in adolescence this diagnosis is more firmly based.

A great deal is known about the childhood causes of the most worrying condition, one that should never be diagnosed before adult life: antisocial personality disorder. Childhood conduct disorder is an almost universal antecedent. Among constitutional causes, hyper-

kinesis contributes to this development, and very rarely schizoid/schizotypal disorders do so also. The role of impulsivity has yet to be clarified. Dysfunctional family processes from early childhood onward are among the most powerful causes, and deficits in the macroenvironment contribute to these adversities. The prevention and amelioration of childhood conduct disorders should be a priority, not only for child psychologists and psychiatrists but for educationalists, health care workers, the criminal justice system, and, especially, government. Although the treatment of children with established conduct disorders is difficult and costly, much is known about effective, even cost-effective, preventive interventions. The problem is how to translate that knowledge into public policy and services for those at risk.

REFERENCES

Aarkrog, T. (1994). *Borderline adolescents 20 years later*. Vojens, Denmark: P. J. Schmidt A/S.

American Psychiatric Association. (1994). *Diagnostic and statistical manual of mental disorders* (4th ed.). Washington, DC: Author.

Angold, A., Weissmann, M. M., Merikangas, K. R., Prusoff, P., Wickramaratna, G., Gammon, G. D., & Warner, V. (1987). Parent and child reports of depressive symptoms in children at low and high risk of depression. *Journal of Child Psychology and Psychiatry, 28*, 901–915.

Asperger, H. (1944). Die autistischen Psychopathen im Kindesalter. *Archiv fuer Psychiatrie und Nervenkrankheiten, 177*, 76–137.

Asperger, H. (1979). Problems of infantile autism. *Communication, 13*, 45–52.

Bank, L., Marlowe, J. H., Reid, J. B., Patterson, G. R., & Weinrott, M. R. (1991). A comparative evaluation of parent-training interventions for families of chronic delinquents. *Journal of Abnormal Child Development, 19*, 15–33.

Barnett, W. S., & Escobar, C. M. (1990). Economic costs and benefits of early intervention. In S. J. Meisels and J. P. Shonkoff (Eds.), *Handbook of early childhood intervention* (pp. 560–582). Cambridge: Cambridge University Press.

Baron, M., Asnis, L., & Gruen, R. (1981). The schedule for schizotypal personalities (SSP): A diagnostic interview for schizotypal features. *Psychiatry Research, 4*, 213–228.

Berelowitz, M., & Tarnopolsky, A. (1993). The validity of borderline personality disorder: An updated review of research. In P. Tyrer and G. Stein (Eds.), *Personality disorder reviewed* (pp. 90–112). London: Gaskell, Royal College of Psychiatrists.

Berrueta-Clement, J. R., Schweinhart, L. J., Barnett, W. S., Epstein, A. S., & Weikhart, D. P. (1984). *Changed lives: The effects of the Perry Preschool Program on Youths through 19.* Monographs of the High/Scope Educational Research Foundation No. 8, Ypsilanti, Michigan.

Bolton, P., Macdonald, H., Pickles, A., Rios, P., Goode, S., Crowson, M., Bailey, A., & Rutter, M. (1994). A case-control family history study of autism. *Journal of Child Psychology and Psychiatry,* 35, 877–900.

Boyle, M. H., & Offord, D. R. (1990). Primary prevention of conduct disorder: Issues and prospects. *Journal of the American Academy for Child and Adolescent Psychiatry,* 29, 227–233.

Buss, A. H., & Plomin, R. (1984). *Temperament: Early developing personality traits* (pp. 84–85). Hillsdale, NJ: Lawrence Erlbaum.

Capsi, A., & Elder, G. H. (1988). Emergent family patterns: the intergenerational construction of problem behaviour and relationships. In R. H. Hinde and J. Stevenson-Hinde (Eds.), *Relationships within families: Mutual influences* (pp. 218–240), Oxford: Clarendon Press.

Capsi, A., Elder, G. H., & Bern, D. J. (1987). Moving against the world: Life course patterns of explosive children. *Developmental Psychology,* 23, 306–313.

Capsi, A., Elder, G. H., & Bern, D. J. (1988). Moving away from the world: Life course patterns of shy children. *Developmental Psychology,* 24, 824–831.

Cardoret, R. J., & Cain, C. (1980). Sex differences in predictors of antisocial behavior in adoptees. *Archives of General Psychiatry,* 37, 1171–1175.

Cauce, A. M., Comer, J. P., & Schwartz, D. (1987). Long-term effects of a systems-oriented school prevention program. *American Journal of Orthopsychiatry,* 57, 127–131.

Champion, L. A., Goodall, G., & Rutter, M. (1995). Behavioural problems in childhood and stressors in early adult life: A 20-year follow-up of London school children. *Psychological Medicine,* 25, 231–246.

Chess, S., & Thomas, A. (1984). *Origins and evolution of behavior disorders.* New York: Raven Press.

Comer, J. P. (1980). *School power: Implications of an intervention project.* New York: Free Press.

Cyphers, L. H., Phillips, K., Fulker, D. W., & Mrazek, D. A. (1990). Twin temperament during transition from infancy to early childhood. *Journal of the American Academy for Child and Adolescent Psychiatry,* 29, 392–397.

Daniels, D., & Plomin, R. (1985). Origins of individual differences in infant shyness. *Developmental Psychology,* 21, 118–121.

De Long, G. R., & Dwyer, J. T. (1988). Correlation of family history with specific autistic subgroups: Asperger's syndrome and bipolar affective disease. *Journal of Autism and Developmental Disorders,* 18, 593–600.

Dodge, K. A. (1980). Social cognition and children's aggressive behavior. *Child Development,* 51, 162–170.

*Dodge, K. A., Bates, J. E., & Pettit, G. S. (1990). Mechanisms in the cycle of violence. *Science,* 250, 1678–1683.

Earls, F. (1994). Oppositional-defiant and conduct disorders. In M. Rutter, E. Taylor, and L. Hersov (Eds.), *Child and adolescent psychiatry: Modern approaches* (3rd ed., pp. 308–329). Oxford: Blackwell.

Eaves, L. J., Silberg, J. L., Meyer, J. M., Maes, H. H., Simonoft, E., Pickles, A., Rutter, M., et al. (1997). Genetics and developmental psychopathology: 2. The main effects of genes and environment on behavioral problems in the Virginia twin study of adolescent behavioral development. *Journal of Child Psychology and Psychiatry,* 38, 965–980.

Farrington, D. (1990) Age, period, cohort and offending. In D. M. Gottfredson and R. V. Clarke (Eds.), *Policy and theory in criminal justice: Contributions in honour of Leslie Wilkins* (pp. 51–75). Aldershot: Avebury.

Farrington, D. P. (1995). The development of offending and antisocial behaviour from childhood: Key findings from the Cambridge study in delinquent development. *Journal of Child Psychology and Psychiatry,* 36, 929–964.

Farrington, D. P., Gallagher, B., Morley, L., St Ledger, R. J., & West, D. J. (1988). Are there any successful men from criminogenic backgrounds? *Psychiatry,* 51, 116–130.

Felner, R. D., & Adan, A. M. (1988). The school transitional environment project: An ecological intervention and evaluation. In R. H. Price, E. L. Cowen, R. P. Lorion, and J. Ramos-McKay (Eds.), *14 ounces of prevention: A casebook for practitioners* (pp. 111–122). Washington, DC: American Psychological Association.

Folstein, S., & Rutter, M. (1988). Autism: Familial aggregation and genetic implications. *Journal of Autism and Developmental Disorders,* 18, 297–331.

Frith, U. (Ed.). (1991). *Autism and Asperger syndrome* (pp. 37–92). Cambridge: Cambridge University Press.

Gillberg, C. (1991). Clinical and neurobiological aspects of Asperger syndrome in six family studies. In U. Frith (Ed.), *Autism and Asperger syndrome* (pp. 122–146). Cambridge: Cambridge University Press.

Graham, P. (1994). Prevention. In M. Rutter, E. Taylor, & L. Hersov (Eds.), *Child and adolescent psychiatry: Modern approaches*, (3rd ed., pp. 815–828). Oxford: Blackwell.

Greenman, D. A., Gunderson, J. G., Cane, M., & Saltzman, P. R. (1986). An examination of the borderline diagnosis in children. *American Journal of Psychiatry, 143,* 998–1003.

Hall, D. M. B., & Hill, P. (1991). Shy, withdrawn or autistic? *British Medical Journal, 302,* 125–126.

Happe, F. (1994). *Autism: An introduction to psychological theory.* London: UCL Press.

Harrington, R. (1994). Affective disorders. In M. Rutter, E. Taylor, & L. Hersov (Eds.), *Child and adolescent psychiatry: Modern approaches,* (3rd ed., pp. 330–350). Oxford: Blackwell.

Hellgren, L., Gillberg, I. C., Bagenholm, A., & Gillberg, C. (1994). Children with deficits in attention, motor control and perception (DAMP) almost grown up: Psychiatric and personality disorders at age 16 years. *Journal of Child Psychology and Psychiatry, 35,* 1255–1271.

*Hill, J., & Rutter, M. (1994). Personality disorders. In M. Rutter, E. Taylor, & L. Hersov (Eds.), *Child and adolescent psychiatry: Modern approaches* (3rd ed., pp. 688–696). Oxford: Blackwell.

Hirschfeld, D. R., Rosenbaum, J. F., Biederman, J., Bolduc, E. A., Faraone, S. V., Snidman, N., Reznick, J. S., & Kagan, J. (1992). Stable behavioral inhibition and its association with anxiety disorder. *Journal of the American Academy of Child and Adolescent Psychiatry, 31,* 103–111.

Hoffman, M. L. (1975). Developmental synthesis of affect and cognition and its implications for altruistic motivation. *Developmental Psychology, 11,* 607–622.

Huesmann, L. R., Eron, L. D., Lefkowitz, M. M., & Walder, L. O. (1984). Stability of aggression over time and generations. *Developmental Psychology, 20,* 1120–1134.

James, A., Berelowitz, M., & Vereker, M. (1996). Borderline personality disorder: A study in adolescence. *European Child and Adolescent Psychiatry, 5,* 11–17.

Jones, M. B., & Offord, D. (1989). Reduction of antisocial behavior in poor children by non-school skills development. *Journal of Child Psychology and Psychiatry, 30,* 737–750.

Kagan, J. (1981). *The second year: The emergence of self-awareness.* Cambridge, MA: Harvard University Press.

Kagan, J. (1994). *Galen's prophesy: Temperament in human nature.* New York: Basic Books.

Kagan, J., Reznick, J. S., & Snidman, N. (1988). Biological bases of childhood shyness. *Science, 240,* 167–171.

Kagan, J., & Snidman, N. (1991). Temperamental factors in human development. *American Psychologist, 46,* 856–862.

Kanner, L. (1943). Autistic disturbances of affective contact. *Nervous Child, 2,* 217–250.

Kazdin, A. E. (1997). Psychological treatment for conduct disorder in children. *Journal of Child Psychology and Psychiatry, 38,* 161–178.

Kolvin, I., Miller, F. J. W., Fleeting, M., & Kolvin, P. A. (1988). Risk/protective factors for offending with particular reference to deprivation. In M. Rutter (Ed.), *Studies of psychosocial risk: The power of longitudinal data* (pp. 77–95). Cambridge, Cambridge University Press.

Koshanska, G. (1991). Socialization and temperament in the development of guilt and conscience. *Child Development, 62,* 1379–1392.

*Koshanska, G. (1993). Towards a synthesis of parental socialization and child temperament in early development of conscience. *Child Development, 64,* 325–347.

Lamb, M. E., Nash, A., Teti, D. M., & Bornstein, M. H. (1991). Infancy. In M. Lewis (Ed.), *Child and adolescent psychiatry: A comprehensive textbook* (pp. 222–256). Baltimore: Williams and Wilkins.

Larson, C. (1980). Efficacy of prenatal and postpartum home visits on child health and development. *Pediatrics, 66,* 191–197.

Lazar, I., & Darlington, R. (1982). Lasting effects of early education: A Report for the Consortium for Longitudinal Studies. *Monographs of the Society for Research in Child Development.* (Serial No. 195) 47, 1–151.

Le Conteur, A., Bailey, A., Goode, S., Pickles, A., Robertson, S., Adhesman, I., & Rutter, M. (1996). A broader phenotype of autism: The clinical spectrum in twins. *Journal of Child Psychology and Psychiatry, 37,* 785–801.

Magnusson, D. (1988). *Individual development from an interactional perspective: A longitudinal study.* Hillsdale, NJ: Lawrence Erlbaum.

Magnusson, D. (1992). Individual development: A

longitudinal perspective. *European Journal of Personality*, 6, 119–138.

Magnusson, D. (1996). Interactionism and the person approach in developmental psychology. *European Child and Adolescent Psychiatry*, 5, Supplement 1, 18–22.

Mannuzza, S., Gittelman Klein, R., Horowitz Konig, P., & Giampino, T. L. (1989). Hyperactive boys almost grown up: IV. Criminality and its relationship to psychiatric status. *Archives of General Psychiatry*, 46, 1073–1079.

Maughan, B. (1988). School experiences as risk/protective factors. In M. Rutter (Ed.), *Studies of psychosocial risk: The power of longitudinal data* (pp. 200–220). Cambridge: Cambridge University Press.

Maughan, B. (1995). Annotation: Long-term outcomes of developmental reading problems. *Journal for Child Psychology and Psychiatry*, 36, 357–371.

Maughan, B., & Garratt, K. (1994). Conduct disorder: The gender gap. *Association for Child Psychology and Psychiatry Review and Newsletter*, 16, 277–282.

Maughan, B., Pickles, A., Hagell, A., Rutter, M., & Yule, W. (1996). Reading problems and antisocial behaviour: Developmental trends in comorbidity. *Journal for Child Psychology and Psychiatry*, 37, 405–418.

Nagy, J., & Szatmari, P. (1986). A chart review of schizotypal personality disorders in children. *Journal of Autism and Developmental Disorders*, 16, 351–367.

Offord, D. R., & Bennett, K. J. (1994). Conduct disorder: Long-term outcomes and intervention effectiveness. *Journal of the American Association for Child and Adolescent Psychiatry*, 33, 1069–1078.

Olweus, D. (1979). Stability of aggressive reaction patterns in males: A review. *Psychological Bulletin*, 86, 852–875.

Olweus, D. (1980). Familial and temperamental determinants of aggressive behaviour in adolescent boys: A causal analysis. *Developmental Psychology*, 16, 644–660.

*Olweus, D. (1993). *Bullying at school: What we know and what we can do*. Oxford: Blackwell.

Patrick, M., Hobson, R. P., Castle, D., Howard, R., & Maughan, B. (1994). Personality disorder and the mental representation of early social experience. *Development and Psychopathology*, 6, 375–388.

Patterson, G. R. (1986). Performance models for antisocial boys. *American Psychologist*, 41, 432–444.

Patterson, G. R., & Dishion, T. J. (1988). Multilevel family process models: Traits, interactions and relationships. In R. A. Hinde & J. Stevenson-Hinde (Eds.), *Relationships within families: Mutual influences* (pp. 283–310). Oxford: Clarendon Press.

Petti, T. A., & Vela, R. M. (1990). Borderline disorders of childhood: An overview. *Journal of the American Academy of Child and Adolescent Psychiatry*, 29, 327–337.

Plomin, R., De Fries, J. C., & Fulker, D. W. (1988). *Nature and nurture during infancy and early childhood*. Cambridge: Cambridge University Press.

*Prior, M. (1992). Childhood temperament. *Journal of Child Psychology and Psychiatry*, 33, 249–279.

Quinton, D., Pickles, A., Maughan, B., & Rutter, M. (1993). Partners, peers and pathways: Assortative pairing and continuities in conduct disorder. *Development and Psychopathology*, 5, 763–783.

Quinton, D., & Rutter, M. (1988). *Parenting breakdown: The making and breaking of intergenerational links*. Aldershot: Avebury.

Robins, L. N. (1978). Sturdy childhood predictors of adult anti-social behaviour: Replications from longitudinal studies. *Psychological Medicine*, 8, 611–622.

Robins, L. N. (1991). Conduct disorder. *Journal of Child Psychology and Psychiatry: Annual Research Review*, 32, 193–212.

Robins, L. N., & O'Neal, P. (1966). *Deviant children grown up*. Baltimore: Williams and Wilkins.

Robson, K. S. (1991). Borderline disorders. In M. Lewis (Ed.), *Child and adolescent psychiatry: A comprehensive text-book* (pp. 731–735). Baltimore: Williams and Wilkins.

Rutter, M. (1989). Pathways from childhood to adult life. *Journal of Child Psychology and Psychiatry*, 30, 23–51.

Rutter, M. (1994). Family discord and conduct disorder: Cause, consequence or correlate? *Journal of Family Psychology*, 8, 170–186.

Rutter, M., Quinton, D., & Hill, J. (1990). Adult outcome of institution-reared children: Males and females compared. In L. N. Robins and M. Rutter (Eds.), *Straight and devious pathways from childhood to adulthood* (pp. 135–157). Cambridge: Cambridge University Press.

Sampson, R. J., & Laub, J. H. (1993). *Crime in the making*. Cambridge, MA: Harvard University Press.

Satterfield, J. H., Satterfield, B. T., & Schell, A. M. (1987). Therapeutic interventions to prevent delinquency in hyperactive boys. *Journal of the American Academy of Child and Adolescent Psychiatry, 26,* 56–64.

Seitz, V., Rosenbaum, L. K., & Apfel, N. H. (1985). Effects of family support intervention: A ten-year follow-up. *Child Development, 56,* 376–391.

Seitz, V., & Provence, S. (1990). Care-giver-focused models of early intervention. In S. J. Meisels & J. P. Shonkoff (Eds.), *Handbook of early childhood intervention* (pp. 400–427). Cambridge: Cambridge University Press.

*Shaw, D. S., & Bell, R. Q. (1993). Developmental theories of parental contributors to antisocial behavior. *Journal of Abnormal Child Psychology, 21,* 493–518.

*Shepherd, J. P., & Farrington, D. P. (1995). Preventing crime and violence: Preschool education, early family support, and situational prevention can be effective. *British Medical Journal, 310,* 271–272.

Smith, P. K., & Sharp, S. (1994). *School bullying: Insights and perspectives.* London: Routledge.

Sylva, K. (1994). School influences on children's development. *Annual Review, Journal of Child Psychology and Psychiatry, 35,* 135–170.

Tantam, D. (1991). Asperger's syndrome in adulthood. In U. Frith (Ed.), *Autism and Asperger syndrome* (pp. 147–183). Cambridge: Cambridge University Press.

Taylor, E. (1994). Syndromes of attention deficit and overactivity. In M. Rutter, E. Taylor, & L. Hersov (Eds.), *Child and adolescent psychiatry: Modern approaches* (3rd ed., pp. 285–307). Oxford: Blackwell.

*Taylor, E., & Hemsley, R. (1995). Treating hyperkinetic disorders: Treatment needs care but is worth while. *British Medical Journal, 310,* 1617–1618.

Taylor, E., Sandberg, S., Thorley, G., & Giles, S. (1991). *The epidemiology of childhood hyperactivity.* Maudsley monographs no. 33. Oxford: Oxford University Press.

Thapar, A., Hervas, A., & McGuffin, P. (1995). Childhood hyperactivity scores are highly heritable and show sibling competitive effects: Twin study evidence. *Behavior Genetics, 25,* 537–544.

Thapar, A., & McGuffin, P. (1996). A twin study of antisocial and neurotic symptoms in childhood. *Psychological Medicine, 26,* 1111–1118.

Thomas, A., & Chess, S. (1986). The New York Longitudinal Study: From infancy to early adult life. In R. Plomin & J. F. Dunn (Eds.), *The study of temperament: Changes, continuities and challenges* (pp. 39–52). Hillsdale, NJ: Lawrence Erlbaum.

Torgersen, A. M. (1989). Genetic and environmental influences on temperamental development: Longitudinal study of twins from infancy to adolescence. In S. Doxiadis (Ed.), *Early influences shaping the individual* (pp. 269–281). London: Plenum.

*Tyrer, P., & Stein, G. (1993). *Personality disorder reviewed.* London: Gaskell.

Weiss, G., Hechtman, L., Perlman, T., Hopkins, J., & Wender, A. (1979). Hyperactives as young adults. A controlled prospective 10-year follow-up of 75 children. *Archives of General Psychiatry, 36,* 675–681.

Weiss, G., Hechtman, L., Milroy, T., & Perlman, T. (1985). Psychiatric status of hyperactives as adults: A controlled prospective 15-year follow-up of 63 hyperactive children. *Journal of the American Academy of Child and Adolescent Psychiatry, 24,* 211–220.

West, D. J., & Farrington, D. P. (1973). *Who becomes delinquent?* London: Heinemann.

Wing, L. (1981). Asperger's syndrome: A clinical account. *Psychological Medicine, 11,* 115–129.

Wolff, S. (1993). Personality disorder in childhood. In P. Tyrer & G. Stein (Eds.), *Personality disorder reviewed* (pp. 64–89). London: Gaskell.

Wolff, S. (1995). *Loners: The life path of unusual children.* London: Routledge.

Wolff, S. (1995). The concept of resilience. *Australian and New Zealand Journal of Psychiatry, 29,* 565–574.

Wolff, S. (1996). Morality. In M. Lewis (Ed.), *Child and adolescent psychiatry: A comprehensive textbook* (2nd ed., pp. 212–221). Baltimore: Williams and Wilkins.

Wolff, S., & Chick, J. (1980). Schizoid personality in childhood: A controlled follow-up study. *Psychological Medicine, 10,* 85–100.

Wolff, S., Narayan, S., & Moyes, B. (1988). Personality characteristics of parents of autistic children: A controlled study. *Journal of Child Psychology and Psychiatry, 29,* 143–153.

World Health Organization. (1992). *ICD-10 Classification of Mental and Behavioural Disorders: Clinical Descriptions and Diagnostic Guidelines.* Geneva: Author.

Zeitlin, H. (1986). *The natural history of psychiatric disorder in children.* Maudsley Monographs 29. Oxford: Oxford University Press.

*Indicates references that the author recommends for further reading.

24
Relational Problems: The Social Context of Child and Adolescent Disorders

Charles M. Borduin
Cindy M. Schaeffer
Naamith Heiblum

The progress of science is strewn, like an ancient desert trail, with the bleached skeletons of discarded theories that once seemed to possess eternal life.

— Arthur Koestler

During the past 3 decades, the mental health community has witnessed a major paradigmatic shift in the conceptualization and treatment of child and adolescent disorders. Traditional theories of child psychopathology, which postulate intrapersonal determinants of behavior, have been discarded by many mental health professionals in favor of approaches that emphasize the social ecology of child disorders. Indeed, there is now substantial evidence to suggest that children's emotional and behavioral disorders are often linked with relational problems in their family, peer, and school systems (Cicchetti, 1987; Lytton, 1990; Parker & Asher, 1987; Rubin & Mills, 1991; Wahler, 1990). Furthermore, there is growing empirical support for the effectiveness of family therapy and other systemic interventions in ameliorating the disorders of childhood and adolescence (Hazelrigg, Cooper, & Borduin, 1987; Henggeler, Borduin, & Mann, 1993; Kohler & Strain, 1990; Shadish et al., 1993). Despite this fundamental shift in the conceptualization and treatment of childhood disorders, the field's major diagnostic systems (i.e., the fourth edition of the *Diagnostic and Statistical Manual of Mental Disorders* [DSM-IV; American Psychiatric Association, 1994] and the 10th revision of the *International Classification of Diseases* [ICD-10; World Health Organization, 1992]) have been slow to incorporate these conceptual changes and still adhere to a fossilized, medical model of disorder (Denton, 1990; Kaslow, 1996; Rapoport & Ismond, 1990).

The purpose of this chapter is to help therapists provide competent evaluation and treatment services for relational problems of children and adolescents. Toward this end, we discuss the relational causes and correlates of children's behavioral and emotional problems, and we recommend that therapists adopt a broader, more ecologically oriented framework than the one that guides DSM-IV and ICD-10. We contend that the provision of competent services is based on an appreciation of interpersonal (i.e., relational) as well as intrapersonal factors in the etiology and maintenance of childhood disorders.

The chapter begins with a description of

how relational problems are considered within current psychiatric classification systems, followed by a brief discussion of epidemiological issues. Next, an overview of relational theories of childhood disorders is provided. Strategies for assessing different types of relational problems in children and adolescents are then presented. The final section provides treatment guidelines derived from our clinical work using an ecologically oriented treatment model.

HISTORY AND CRITIQUE OF THE DSM-IV AND ICD-10 CLASSIFICATION SYSTEMS

In the United States, DSM-IV represents the most widely used classification system among mental health professionals. Indeed, DSM-IV and its predecessors have strongly influenced treatment planning and clinical record keeping in both inpatient and outpatient mental health settings. Moreover, widespread use of this classification system has defined insurance reimbursement standards for mental health services and has profoundly influenced the scope and direction of psychopathology research (Denton, 1989; Patterson & Lusterman, 1996). Unfortunately, despite its avowed goal of ensuring that "DSM-IV reflects the best available clinical and research literature" (1994, p. xix), the American Psychiatric Association has been slow to recognize the important role of relational problems in childhood behavior disorders. The original DSM (American Psychiatric Association, 1952) consisted entirely of individually based diagnoses. The second edition of DSM (DSM-II; American Psychiatric Association, 1968) included a single relational category (i.e., "Marital Maladjustment"), while other relational problems were subsumed under the heading of "Non-Specific Conditions." The third edition of DSM (DSM-III; American Psychiatric Association, 1980) and its revision (DSM-III-R; American Psychiatric Association, 1987) improved on this cursory classification by including four categories of relational problems: "Marital Problems," "Parent-Child

Problems," "Other Specified Family Circumstances," and "Other Interpersonal Problems." Nevertheless, these relational problems were not given the same status as mental disorders and were listed as "V codes," conditions that were to be diagnosed only when no mental disorder could be diagnosed. DSM-IV continues to list relational problems as V codes and includes five such categories: "Parent-Child Relational Problem," "Partner Relational Problem," "Sibling Relational Problem," "Relational Problem Related to a Mental Disorder or General Medical Condition," and "Relational Problem Not Otherwise Specified."

Like DSM-IV, the ICD-10 classifications for mental health problems include diagnoses pertaining primarily to individuals and not to social relationships. ICD-10 offers three diagnoses that parallel the relational diagnoses of DSM-IV. First, similar to the "Partner Relational Problem" category in DSM-IV, ICD-10 includes the category "Relationship Disorder Not Otherwise Specified," which is used to classify problems within adult intimate relationships. Second, ICD-10 includes a category entitled "Sibling Rivalry Disorder," which is similar to the "Sibling Relational Problem" category of DSM-IV. Third, the ICD-10 provides the category "Other Childhood Disorders of Social Functioning," which is similar to "Relational Problem Not Otherwise Specified" in DSM-IV and can be used to classify other types of family or peer difficulties. Unlike DSM-IV, ICD-10 does not include a "Parent-Child Relational Problem" category but does include a category entitled "Reactive Attachment Disorder of Childhood"; the criteria for this latter disorder require that the child's attachment problems result from "severe parental neglect, abuse, or serious mishandling" and have their onset before age five (WHO, 1992, p. 383).

Clearly, the inclusion of several relational diagnoses in ICD-10 and DSM-IV reflects increased recognition that relational problems deserve attention from mental health professionals. Nevertheless, these relational diagnoses have been criticized because they lack clear operational criteria (e.g., for defining severity of impairment) and are too broad to provide meaningful or valid classifications of relational disorders (Cottone, 1989; Denton, 1990; Kaslow, 1993, 1996; Wynne, 1987). Moreover, the assignment of V code status to relational diagnoses in DSM-IV often precludes third-party reimbursement for such problems (Patterson & Lusterman, 1996). Because of these difficulties, relational problems are seldom used as primary diagnoses and are often used as secondary diagnoses for a wide range of child and adolescent disorders (e.g., disruptive behavior disorders, mood disorders).

EPIDEMIOLOGY

Recent large-scale epidemiological surveys of child (Anderson, Williams, McGee, & Silva, 1989) and adult (Kessler et al., 1994) disorders have not included an assessment of relational problems. In fact, to the authors' knowledge, there are no reliable data on the prevalence or incidence of relational diagnoses. This lack of data is likely due to the absence of an agreed upon system for classifying relationship disorders and to the "second-class" status that V code diagnoses (including relational problems) receive relative to other diagnostic categories in DSM-IV (Kaslow, 1996).

Although no prevalence rates are available, there is good reason to believe that childhood relational difficulties represent a significant clinical problem. Indeed, research has demonstrated that relational problems account, directly or indirectly, for a significant portion of variance in major childhood psychopathologies. For example, childhood disorders such as depression (see Burbach & Borduin, 1986; Kaslow, Deering, & Ash, 1996; Petersen et al., 1993, for reviews), anxiety problems (see Barrett, Rapee, Dadds, & Ryan, 1996; Dadds, 1995; Krohne & Hock, 1991), and conduct disorder (see Alexander & Pugh, 1996; Borduin, Henggeler, & Manley, 1995; Kazdin, 1995) have been linked with difficulties in both family and peer relations. Other problem behaviors such as adolescent substance abuse (see Hawkins, Catalano, & Miller, 1992; Newcomb & Bentler,

1989; Rhodes & Jason, 1990) and antisocial behavior (see Farrington, 1989; Henggeler, 1989) have also been linked with peer and family influences, as well as with school variables. Similarly, the psychological problems experienced by maltreated children are often accompanied by difficulties in family relations, given that parents are most often the perpetrators in the more than 3 million cases of child physical abuse, sexual abuse, or neglect reported annually in the United States (see Finkelhor & Dzuiba-Leatherman, 1994; Willis, 1995). Thus, even in the absence of epidemiological studies, there is considerable evidence that relational problems are common among children from various types of clinical populations.

THEORETICAL MODELS

Theoretical conceptualizations of relational problems have a long and rich history, beginning with the application of communication theory to family processes (Bateson, Jackson, Haley, & Weakland, 1956). Although an extensive review of such theories is beyond the scope of this chapter, this section provides a brief discussion of social learning and systems theories, which have been most influential in the conceptualization and treatment of child and adolescent relational problems.

Social Learning Theories

Social learning theorists contend that childhood disorders are a result of learning that occurs during children's repeated interactions with family members. For example, Patterson (1982; Patterson, Reid, & Dishion, 1992) has developed a coercion hypothesis to explain how families contribute to the development and maintenance of conduct-disordered behaviors in children. Patterson emphasizes the role of negative reinforcement in promoting coercive interchanges between parents and children: coercive (i.e., aversive) behavior on the part of one family member (parent or child) is reinforced when it leads to the termination of aversive behavior from another family member. Consider the example of a mother who yells and curses at her 8-year-old son to turn down the volume on his radio; the son hits the mother several times, and the mother terminates the exchange by glaring at the child and then walking out of his room. In this example, the hitting "worked" for the child in that it stopped the mother's cursing and yelling, and her leaving the room strengthened the son's tendency to use hitting again in similar situations. As this "training" continues over longer periods, there is often an acceleration of coercive interchanges, because family members learn that the continuation and escalation of their own aversive behavior leads to the removal of the other's aversive behavior.

Consistent with social learning theory, traditional behavioral parent training (e.g., Patterson, 1974) and some contemporary variations (e.g., Webster-Stratton, Hollinsworth, & Kolpacoff, 1989) provide parents with operant strategies for decreasing children's behavior problems and increasing their prosocial behaviors. Similarly, skills training (e.g., problem-solving skills, communication skills) has been used to address family problems such as parent-adolescent conflict (e.g., Noble, Adams, & Openshaw, 1989).

Social learning approaches have been criticized for reducing complex family processes to simple linear patterns and for focusing on a limited segment of family functioning rather than on the whole family system (see Mash, 1989). Perhaps in response to such criticisms, some behavioral approaches to child disorders have recently integrated key aspects of systems theory (see Miller & Prinz, 1990).

Family Systems Theories

Family systems theorists assert that a particular behavior problem or symptom must always be understood in terms of the social context in which it occurs. The family is viewed not simply as a collection of individuals but as a rule-governed system and an organized group that transcends the sum of its separate elements. Although a number of different approaches to intervening in the family system have been described, these approaches can be broadly classified as either aesthetic or pragmatic.

Aesthetic systems approaches (e.g., Bowen, 1978; Whitaker, 1976) originated from phenomenological, psychodynamic, and existential perspectives and maintain that problem behaviors or symptoms develop when a family is unable to foster the individual growth of its members. Bowen (1978) has suggested that child behavioral problems stem from emotional overinvolvement between family members and the intergenerational transmission of unresolved emotional issues. On the other hand, Whitaker (1976) has argued that children's symptoms are the result of restrictive family meaning systems or "narratives" that are shared and communicated in interactions between family members. In general, therapists who embody the aesthetic perspective view the presenting symptom or complaint as a "motor for growth" and argue that the immediate alleviation of symptoms can preclude the opportunity for a long-term, holistic healing of self (Keeney & Sprenkle, 1982). Thus, in spite of the presence of more than one family member during treatment sessions, these aesthetic family therapy approaches often emphasize change in intrapsychic structures over change in ongoing transactions.

In contrast to aesthetic approaches to family intervention, pragmatic systems approaches (e.g., Haley, 1987; Minuchin, 1974) are primarily concerned with the family interaction patterns that give rise to symptomatic behavior. Haley's (1987) strategic approach asserts that the symptoms exhibited by family members function to control the behavior of other family members, as in the case of a child who urinates in his clothing whenever his or her parents argue with each other. In this example, the child's enuresis serves the functions of distracting the parents from their conflict and uniting them in their concern for the child, thereby granting power to an otherwise helpless child. Similarly, Minuchin's (1974) structural approach posits that family relations are governed by implicit rules that serve to meet the individual needs of family members and to accomplish family tasks. Symptoms occur when the family structure is unable to adapt to changing family needs and circumstances. Both strategic and structural approaches focus directly on changing sequences of interaction between family members in order to alleviate symptoms. As such, these pragmatic approaches are designed to solve the presenting problem as quickly and efficiently as possible.

Multisystemic Therapy Model

Multisystemic Therapy (MST; Henggeler & Borduin, 1990; Henggeler et al., 1998) is an intensive, time-limited, home- and family-based treatment approach predicated on social-ecological (Bronfenbrenner, 1979) and family systems models of behavior. MST views individuals as being nested within a complex of interconnected systems that encompass individual (e.g., biological, cognitive), family, and extrafamilial (e.g., peer, school, neighborhood) factors. Behavior problems can be maintained by problematic transactions within and/or between the multiple systems in which family members are embedded. Moreover, to optimize the ecological validity of interventions, MST is conducted directly in the natural ecologies (home, school, community) of the youth and family. As such, MST aims to set the stage for lasting therapeutic change. Importantly, this ecological model of child behavior is strongly supported by the causal modeling literatures in the areas of child and adolescent psychopathology, where virtually all types of serious problems have been shown to be multiply determined (see Schoenwald, Borduin, & Henggeler, 1998).

Because MST is able to address the multiple relational contexts of children with serious emotional and behavioral disorders, our discussion of assessment and treatment strategies for children's relational problems will be based on MST principles and interventions. The following sections on relational assessment and relational treatment are organized using four of the most relevant diagnostic categories

from DSM-IV (i.e., "Parent-Child Relational Problem," "Partner Relational Problem," "Sibling Relational Problem," and "Relational Problem Not Otherwise Specified"). Unfortunately, DSM-IV does not include specific diagnostic categories for children's relational problems in extrafamilial systems (e.g., peers, school). Given this limitation in DSM-IV, the assessment and treatment of extrafamilial relations is discussed under the subsection heading of "Relational Problem Not Otherwise Specified," since the therapist will likely need to code extrafamilial relationship problems under this diagnostic category as well. It should also be noted that the use of a single relational diagnosis (e.g., "Sibling Relational Problem") seldom captures the broad range of relational problems found in children and adolescents with serious behavior disorders. Accordingly, the strategies that are described for each relational diagnosis should be considered as part of a more comprehensive approach to assessment and treatment.

ASSESSMENT

Traditionally, assessment of psychopathological disorders in children has focused on a relatively narrow range of behaviors and personality traits (e.g., impulsiveness, aggressiveness, withdrawal, sensation seeking) and has been conducted in settings outside the child's natural environment. However, in light of recent evidence (see Epidemiology section) pertaining to the relational correlates and causes of psychopathology in children and adolescents, it has become apparent that the scope of assessment needs to be broadened beyond the individual. Moreover, in the interest of ecological validity, the therapist should conduct his or her assessment in the same settings in which the child's problems occur, such as the home, the school, or the community.

Traditional assessment of individual mental health problems has also taken the form of paper-and-pencil instruments or projective measures. However, to the authors' knowledge, no single measure of social relations has sufficient validity for identifying clinically significant levels of relational problems in children or adolescents. Similarly, there are no diagnostic interviews that can be used to identify relational problems, given the absence of an explicit system for classifying relationship disorders. Rating scales can be used to assess various dimensions of family relations (e.g., Family Adaptability and Cohesion Evaluation Scales-II, Olson, Portner, & Bell, 1982; Family Environment Scale, Moos & Moos, 1986), marital relations (e.g., Marital Adjustment Test; Locke & Wallace, 1959), and peer relations (e.g., Inventory of Parent and Peer Attachment, Armsden & Greenberg, 1987; Missouri Peer Relations Inventory, Borduin, Blaske, Cone, Mann, & Hazelrigg, 1989), but such scales rely on global judgment and usually show little or no agreement between raters. These ambiguities make it difficult to recommend a circumscribed set of measures for relational assessment purposes. Moreover, in working with behavior-disordered children and adolescents over the past 15 years, the authors have found that the majority of assessment instruments rarely provide information that is not already discernable from the multimethod, multiperspective assessment outlined here. An exception pertains to the evaluation of academic difficulties in school. Here, it is often necessary to learn about the youth's intellectual strengths and weaknesses as well as his or her actual level of achievement. Intellectual tests and achievement tests are useful toward this end.

This section begins with some general guidelines pertaining to the assessment of behavior-disordered youths and the systems in which they are embedded. Next, strategies for assessing different types of relational problems in such youths are presented.

General Guidelines

It is essential to understand child and adolescent disorders within a framework that considers the youth's broader systemic context. More specifically, the therapist should attempt to determine how the child's problem behaviors "fit" with the individual characteristics of the child (e.g., intellectual functioning, moral reasoning,

attributional processes), the nature of family relations (e.g., affective qualities of parent-child and marital relations), and the many extrafamilial variables (e.g., peer relations, school performance) that can be linked with the presenting problems. The delineation of this fit has direct implications for the interventions that will be selected for implementation. Of course, the therapist should remember that assessment is an ongoing process and that new information should be continually integrated into his or her conceptualization of the particular case.

The therapist should evaluate key systems using multiple methods and multiple perspectives. For example, family relations can be evaluated through interviews with the entire family or through discussions with various family subsystems and individual family members. Interviews with the entire family can provide the therapist with an opportunity to observe parent-child interaction patterns and to obtain important information about areas of agreement and conflict in the family. Similarly, discussions with the parental dyad can often provide the therapist with an opportunity to assess marital relations as well as interparental cooperation.

Finally, the therapist should also consider the interactions between different relational systems, as well as within them. For example, if parents have a contentious relationship with their child's teachers and do not support the teachers' efforts to resolve child behavior problems in the classroom, it is likely that the child's behavior problems will continue. Similarly, parents who do not monitor their youth's peer relations may later find that the youth's involvement with deviant peers undermines parent-child relations. As such, problems that occur at the interface of systems can most easily be identified when the therapist obtains information directly from each of the social contexts (family, peer, school) in which the youth is embedded.

Parent-Child Problems

Two central dimensions of parental behavior, affect and control, have a significant influence on psychosocial development in children and should be assessed by the therapist. *Affect* reflects parental behaviors that are emotional in tone and that may range from warmth to rejection (Henggeler & Borduin, 1990). Warm parents convey acceptance to the child and are responsive to the child's needs, whereas rejecting parents are relatively hostile and tend to use criticism and even aggression when interacting with their child (Rothbaum & Weisz, 1994). The *control* strategies used by parents can range from permissiveness to restrictiveness; practically, this translates into the amount of structure and discipline that parents provide for the child (Henggeler & Borduin, 1990; Rothbaum & Weisz, 1994).

Parental Affect

Parental warmth provides a sense of emotional security for the child and sets the stage for the development of empathy and emotional responsiveness. This helps to explain why children who experience low parental warmth are at risk for the development of depressive disorders (see Burbach & Borduin, 1986; Reinherz et al., 1989; Rubin et al., 1992). Parents who provide their children with little warmth (i.e., emotional neglect) may or may not also be rejecting and hostile. Parental rejection and hostility have been associated with behavioral difficulties such as conduct problems and antisocial behavior (see Henggeler, 1989; Loeber & Schmaling, 1985; Patterson & Stouthamer-Loeber, 1984). On the other hand, parents who become too involved in their children's emotional lives (i.e., parental overprotection) may also contribute to the development of psychosocial problems in their children, including anxiety-withdrawal disorders and psychosomatic difficulties (see Hetherington & Martin, 1986).

Several key factors pertaining to individual family members can contribute to difficulties in parental-child affective relations. Child characteristics such as a difficult temperament or a physical handicap may lead to parental rejection of the child (Henggeler & Borduin, 1990). In such cases, the parent may reject the child in response to the cumulative stress of attempting

to meet the child's special needs. Parental factors such as deficits in child-rearing knowledge or skill and serious psychiatric disturbance can also interfere with emotional bonds between family members and should always be assessed.

Problems in the parent-child affective bond are best assessed through direct questioning of family members and through observation of their interactions. The therapist should ask how often the parent and child engage in mutually enjoyable activities that provide opportunities for emotional closeness. The therapist should also observe parent-child affective relations during family interviews or during a structured task (e.g., a play activity for younger children and their parents, a discussion between older children and their parents).

Parental Control

It is essential for parents to provide adequate limits and supervision so that children learn how to tolerate frustration and how to behave in socially acceptable ways. Parents who employ a permissive style of discipline (i.e., are indifferent toward child misbehaviors and fail to make maturity demands on the child) often do so at a high cost for both themselves and their children. Indeed, research has indicated that low parental monitoring of child behavior and inconsistent parental discipline are often linked with child behavior problems, particularly aggression and delinquency (Henggeler, 1989; Snyder & Patterson, 1987). On the other hand, parents who use an authoritarian style of discipline (i.e., require an unquestioning obedience to their authority and ignore the child's feelings and opinions) fail to promote the development of the child's social perspective-taking skills, often resulting in psychosocial difficulties such as depression, low self-esteem, and conduct problems (Henggeler & Borduin, 1990; Kazdin, 1995).

The therapist should assess the parents' rules and consequences for child misbehavior. If the parents are unable to identify what types of behavior they expect from their children, it is unlikely that the children will know how to behave appropriately. If parental rules are clear, problems with child compliance are more likely to be associated with inappropriate or inconsistent consequences for misbehavior. The therapist should assess whether there is consistency in the discipline strategies used by the individual parent (i.e., intraparental consistency), as well as between different parents (i.e., interparental consistency).

Several factors can contribute singly or in combination to ineffective parental control. One such factor is parental modeling of inappropriate behaviors. For example, parents who engage in criminal activity or are aggressive toward their spouse may have difficulty controlling delinquent or aggressive behaviors in their children. Another factor pertains to the amount and quality of social support that parents receive from spouses, extended family, or friends. The absence of a supportive social network attenuates parents' responsiveness to their children's needs and should routinely be assessed. Parental control can also be undermined by a lack of commitment to parenting, because of either career pursuits or unwanted parenthood. In these cases, it is important to assess the parents' priorities and willingness to make changes in the way they interact with their children.

Partner Problems

Marital difficulties are often at the root of child behavior problems (see Reid & Crisafulli, 1990, for an excellent review). For example, studies have found a strong link between marital discord and child conduct problems, especially for boys (e.g., Emery & O'Leary, 1982; Jouriles, Bourg, & Farris, 1991; Mann, Borduin, Henggeler, & Blaske, 1990). Given such findings, the quality of the parents' relationship should always be considered when assessing children's behavioral problems.

The assessment of parent-child relations can often provide the therapist with information that is relevant to marital relations. The marital relationship is the foundation of the family unit. As such, parental apathy or disagreements about discipline strategies should alert the therapist that marital difficulties probably exist. When meeting with the family, the therapist should observe the parents' behavior toward each other and should look for signs of cooperation and mutual respect. The therapist can also meet with parents without the children present to discuss child rearing and other important family responsibilities, such as division of labor in the household. In doing so, the therapist should be alert for signs of spousal dissatisfaction in these areas.

In families broken by divorce, continued discord between the former spouses can have an adverse effect on the entire family system. Such discord often indicates boundary problems where, years after the divorce, the children are still caught in the middle of the parents' conflicts. In such instances, the therapist can meet with the divorced parents, either singly or together, in an effort to assess issues that directly affect the children.

Sibling Problems

Behavior-disordered children often experience difficulties in their relations with siblings as well as with parents. For example, there is evidence that conduct-disordered children and adolescents are often aggressive toward their siblings (e.g., Loeber & Tengs, 1986; Loeber, Weissman, & Reid, 1983) and are frequently the targets of sibling aggression (e.g., Patterson, 1982, 1986). Moreover, older siblings often serve as models for a younger sibling and may reinforce the very behaviors (e.g., aggression, stealing, drug and alcohol abuse) that are identified as problems in the younger sibling. Thus, the development of an effective intervention plan for childhood behavior problems requires a careful assessment of the child's relations with his or her siblings. When meeting with the family, the therapist should ask about (and observe) the siblings' behavior toward each other and should look for signs of caring and cooperation.

Parents can have a significant influence on the quality of children's sibling relations. This influence often occurs through the parents' direct involvement in sibling interactions (e.g., by offering praise when siblings are sharing or cooperating, by providing punishment when siblings are arguing or fighting). However, parents also influence their children's sibling relations in ways that are less direct, such as through parental modeling of interpersonal problem-solving behaviors (e.g., cooperation, aggression) or through the parent's individual relationship with each of the siblings. Indeed, siblings who receive different amounts of attention from their parents often have relations characterized by high conflict and low warmth (Brody & Stoneman, 1987; Brody, Stoneman, & McCoy, 1994). In addition, differential treatment of siblings by parents contributes to mental health difficulties in the less-favored child, who is at risk for the development of low self-esteem, conduct problems, and delinquent behavior (Conger & Conger, 1994; Daniels, Dunn, Furstenburg, & Plomin, 1985).

The therapist should evaluate the extent of parental involvement (or interference) in children's sibling relations and should assess whether there are any inequities in the treatment that siblings receive from parents. In most cases, inequitable treatment of siblings by the parents is readily determined through interviews with the entire family or through discussions with various subsystems and individual family members. The therapist can also identify coalitions between parents and children by observing how each of the parents respond to positive and negative interactions between various siblings.

Relational Problems Not Otherwise Specified

As children mature, they are influenced by a growing number of persons outside their family. In particular, peers and teachers have an increasing influence on children's psychosocial development. The quality of a child's relations with peers and school personnel is determined, in part, by the quality of the parent's involvement with these extrafamilial systems. In this section, some guidelines are provided for assessing children's relations with peers and teachers, as well as family-peer and family-school linkages.

Peer Relations

The nature of children's peer relations and the context for those relations change with age (see Furman, 1982; Hartup, 1983). During the preschool years, children generally experience peer relations through shared play activities, where they learn about cooperation, social roles, and conflict resolution. In middle childhood, children's friendships or "chumships" with same-sex peers become a source of emotional support, trust, and external validation. During adolescence, same-sex friendships become even more intimate in nature and provide an important context for identity development; gradually, there is a shift away from strong same-sex friendships to the development of intimate relationships with members of the opposite sex. Thus, peer relations provide a wide range of essential experiences for the developing child and should always be assessed during the therapist's evaluation of the presenting problems.

The child's individual characteristics play an important role in his or her peer relations. Cognitive factors such as social perspective-taking skills, interpersonal problem-solving skills, and attributional processes all mediate children's behaviors toward peers. For example, aggressive children tend to attribute hostile intentions to peers and often fail to recognize the prosocial and benign intentions of peers (Crick & Dodge, 1994). Behavioral skills such as those involved in approaching and joining a group of peers, sustaining a conversation, and cooperating and sharing with peers are also related to the child's success in peer relations. When the therapist would like to directly assess the child's (or adolescent's) processing of social information or the child's behavioral skills, role-play procedures can often be used; the enactment of various social situations can provide opportunities to discuss problematic interchanges with the child and to probe the child's thinking behind his or her behavior.

The way that children interact with their peers is also affected by their family relations (see Parke & Ladd, 1992). Parents teach their infants and toddlers a great deal about regulating emotions and reading emotional cues through physical play with the child. As children mature, parents increasingly provide opportunities for social engagements with others, particularly peers, outside the immediate family. Security in family relations enhances feelings of self-competence, which, in turn, continue to facilitate peer relations. In late childhood and early adolescence, parent-child relations that are mutually positive and allow the child an increasing role in family decision making often lead to success in social relations outside the home.

Problems in the child's family relations can lead to difficulties in peer relations. For example, youths who do not feel supported and who lack opportunities for competent behavior within the family are more likely to turn to a deviant peer group for emotional security and self-esteem (e.g., Dishion, Patterson, Stoolmiller, & Skinner, 1991). In turn, involvement with deviant peers may place a strain on family relations by bolstering the youth's challenges to parental authority and further weakening parent-youth emotional bonds. Hence, the therapist should consider the linkage between family and peer relations in his or her evaluation of the child's ecology.

Information about the child's peer relations should be obtained from teachers, parents, siblings, and the child. The therapist should ask the teacher about the general reputations of the child's friends. The parents and siblings should also be asked about their impressions of these friends. (It is a negative sign if the child has kept the parents from having much contact with his or her peers.) Often, the child will be quite open about his or her friends: The child will describe the nature of their social activities, how they are performing in school, what their outside interests are, and what their families are like. When reports about the child's peer relations are contradictory or difficult to obtain, the therapist should conduct a more direct assessment of the child's interactions with peers. For younger children, the therapist can usually arrange to observe the child's peer interactions in the classroom or on the playground. For older children and adolescents, the therapist can often arrange to meet the youth's peers (e.g., at the family's home, at a local fast-food restaurant where peers congregate) to obtain firsthand impressions and information. Such assessment strategies rely heavily on the ability of the therapist to synthesize information, which is sometimes conflicting, and to "read" people.

School Relations

School is an extremely important system because children's academic performance sets the stage for future vocational and economic opportunities (Henggeler & Borduin, 1990). The school environment also provides children and adolescents with a milieu in which they have the opportunity to experience a variety of social roles. Although parents often emphasize problem behavior that the child presents within the family, the therapist should always evaluate the child's academic and social functioning in school. Academic and social difficulties frequently reflect the same underlying systemic dysfunctions. Thus, an understanding of one area can facilitate an understanding of the other. Moreover, information from teachers regarding the child's family (e.g., regarding parental involvement in the classroom or school) and peers can be used by the therapist to confirm or disconfirm impressions of these other systems.

The therapist should always ask the teachers whether the child displays behavior problems in school and whether these problems present any special difficulties to the teachers. The therapist should also ask the teachers about the youth's peer group, including their level of engagement in prosocial or antisocial activities, what leadership dynamics exist, the emotional quality of their relations, and their social status within the school. The therapist should also evaluate the child's relationships with the teachers. In some cases, the therapist will find that the child's difficulties are associated with a school environment that does not fully promote the child's motivation and efforts to learn. Hence, the process and direction of treatment can vary considerably based on information that is provided by the teachers.

TREATMENT

For both ethical and pragmatic reasons, the authors believe that the efficacy of any treatment for children's mental health problems should be demonstrated before it is widely disseminated to therapists. Accordingly, the interventions used in MST are usually adapted and integrated from pragmatic, problem-focused treatments that have empirical support for their effectiveness (see Hazelrigg et al., 1987; Shadish et al., 1993); these include strategic family therapy (Haley, 1987), structural family therapy (Minuchin, 1974), behavioral parent training (Schaefer & Briesmeister, 1989), and cognitive-behavioral therapies (Braswell & Bloomquist, 1991). Moreover, rigorous evaluation of outcome has been a cornerstone in the development of MST. Evaluations of MST have been completed at three sites (Memphis, Tennessee; Columbia, Missouri; and Simpsonville, South Carolina) with clinical samples that were composed mainly of multiproblem families. Specifically, clinical trials have demonstrated the efficacy of MST with inner-city juvenile offenders (Henggeler et al., 1986), abusive and neglectful families (Brunk, Henggeler, & Whelan, 1987), adolescent sexual offenders (Borduin, Henggeler, Blaske, & Stein, 1990), adolescents with substance abuse problems (Henggeler et al., 1991), serious juvenile offenders living in rural areas (Henggeler, Melton, & Smith, 1992; Scherer, Brondino, Henggeler, Melton, & Hanley, 1994), and violent and chronic juvenile offenders (Borduin et al., 1995). In general, these studies demonstrated the relative effectiveness of MST regarding numerous instrumental outcomes (e.g., decreased behavior problems, decreased association with deviant peers, improved family relations) and ultimate outcomes (e.g., fewer rearrests, less time incarcerated) in the treatment of serious behavior problems in youths.

Before discussing specific interventions used in MST for the treatment of relational problems, this section begins with some general guidelines for designing MST interventions. For a more extensive discussion of these guidelines and of specific interventions, see Borduin (1994), Borduin and Henggeler (1990), Henggeler and Borduin (1990), or Henggeler et al. (1998).

General Guidelines

Because the child is embedded in many systems in addition to the family (e.g., school, peer group, neighborhood) that influence and are influenced by the child, interventions should target sequences of behavior within and between these systems. The therapist should intervene directly in each of the social contexts in which problems occur.

Interventions should be developmentally appropriate and fit the developmental needs of the child and family. For example, interventions with younger adolescents usually place greater emphasis on the development of effective parental control strategies, whereas interventions with older adolescents focus on issues of emancipation and independence (for a detailed description of developmental processes in family systems, see Carter & McGoldrick, 1988; Minuchin, 1974).

Consistent with strategic family therapy models (see e.g., Haley, 1987), interventions should be present focused and action oriented, targeting specific and well-defined problems. The use of well-specified treatment goals, reached by consensus, provides necessary direction and purpose for therapy. Such goals also help to motivate the family's efforts toward change.

Once goals are established, interventions should be designed to promote daily or weekly effort by family members. This conveys the message that treatment involves commitment and effort on the part of family members. In addition, problems will be alleviated more rapidly if family members work actively on them.

Interventions should emphasize the positive and should use systemic strengths as levers for change (see Fisch, Weakland, & Segal, 1982). Reframing and positive connotation are used to decrease resistance to treatment. In addition, strengths of the systems are identified and used to attain the identified goals. For example, parental concern for the child might be used in motivating the parent to adopt more effective control strategies, or an adolescent's athletic or artistic talent might be used to promote involvement with prosocial peers.

Finally, interventions should be designed to promote responsible behavior and decrease irresponsible behavior among family members. Consequences for responsible and irresponsible behavior are clearly delineated, and parents learn to implement these consequences consistently and fairly.

Parent-Child Problems

Based on the results of the assessment of parental affect and parental control strategies, the therapist should design interventions that enable parents and children to change their problematic interaction styles in ways that promote positive development.

Parental Affect

When parental emotional neglect or rejection is due to knowledge/skill deficits, interventions should focus on opening lines of communication, helping parents see beyond their angry feelings, and helping parents and their children identify and engage in mutually enjoyed activities. To improve communication, the therapist can encourage the parent to comment on the child's positive behaviors; the child can also be encouraged to report his or her feelings about receiving positive parental feedback. In addition, the therapist can help the parent and child to plan pleasurable activities and can assign homework tasks involving these activities (see Haley, 1987, for a discussion of how to design homework tasks). Parents should be encouraged to not underestimate their own importance in their children's lives and to take responsibility for spending time with their children.

In addition to sharing positive experiences with their children, parents must demonstrate their affection to children in developmentally appropriate ways. Parents typically have a better idea of how to show affection to younger children than older children. Many adolescents, for example, are embarrassed by open displays of parental affection and may even discourage their parents from expressing affection toward them. The therapist can help the parent to appreciate the adolescent's need for parental love and to develop appropriate ways to express affection.

When parental emotional neglect or rejection is related to the stresses of trying to meet a child's special needs (e.g., a physical or intellectual handicap), interventions are often needed at several levels. The individual parent may need help to defuse anger or to alleviate guilt about personal and familial hardships incurred as a result of the child's special needs. The individual child may need help overcoming feelings of rejection and identifying personal strengths. Parent-child relations may be improved by helping parents clarify their feelings (love) for the child and explain why they sometimes do not show this love. Parent-community linkages may also need to be developed by helping the parent build a social support network or obtain child care assistance.

Some parents fail to develop a meaningful emotional attachment to the child because of a serious psychiatric disturbance (e.g., parental depression). Alternatively, severe stress such as marital discord or a recent divorce may have a negative impact on the parent's relationship with the child. Often, the alleviation of the parent's emotional or interpersonal problems (e.g., using cognitive-behavioral therapy with the individual parent or marital interventions with the couple) may be all that is needed to enhance parent-child affective relations. In extreme cases involving an incapacitated parent (e.g., a parent who is involved in extensive substance abuse or criminal activity and is unwilling to change), the therapist may need to identify a responsible adult from the child's ecology (e.g., an older sibling, an aunt or uncle, a grandparent, a teacher, a friend's parent) who is willing to serve as a surrogate parent for the child.

Parental Control

When it becomes apparent that a child's behavior problems are being maintained by a parent's style of discipline, several steps should be taken by the therapist. First, the therapist may need to explain the disadvantages associated with the parent's disciplinary style without blaming the parent for the behavior problem. Permissive parents may need to hear that impulse control problems and antisocial behavior can be a consequence of their giving in to a child's demands. Authoritarian parents can be told how extreme punitiveness can evoke anger and resentment in children. Once the therapist has presented a rationale to the parent for changing his or her disciplinary style, the therapist can help the parent to develop an effective method for handling the child's behavior problems.

The development of an effective approach to discipline usually begins with teaching the parent(s) to establish clear rules and expectations for the child's behavior. Rules should be stated in terms of positive behaviors (e.g., "Tim will be home by 9 P.M." as opposed to "Tim will not be late"). The expected behavior should be stated so clearly that anyone else (e.g., a babysitter, a grandparent) can tell whether or not it has occurred. The privilege that will be given or withheld when the rule is kept or broken should be listed with the rule, and rules should be posted in a public place (e.g., the refrigerator).

Next, parents should be taught that consequences must be inextricably linked to rules. Parents should be coached to respond to positive behaviors with consistent praise, affection, and increases in child privileges (e.g., four nights of meeting curfew results in an extra 10 minutes on a subsequent night). Likewise, parents must respond to negative behaviors with consequences that are immediate, developmentally appropriate, and aversive to the child. The therapist should encourage parents to develop punishments that are easily implemented, constructive, and helpful to parents, such as assigning the child extra chores or household tasks. If parents see a benefit to themselves for implementing punishments, they are much more likely to consistently do so.

Finally, parents should be taught how to effectively monitor a child's compliance or noncompliance with rules. The therapist should emphasize that the parent enforce rules in an unemotional way and that it is not the parent's responsibility to badger the child to follow rules. In this way, the parent can focus his or her efforts on monitoring the child's behavior and implementing the contingencies and can avoid becoming involved in negative emotional interchanges with the child. The therapist should also prepare parents for the likelihood that their child will react negatively to changes in their behavior and should provide parents with extra support, as needed, to "stick with" the program.

The therapist should also be prepared to deal with several potential impediments to effective parental discipline. When parental modeling of inappropriate behaviors (e.g., dishonesty, aggression) impedes effective discipline, the therapist can avoid blaming the parent by emphasizing the child's extreme susceptibility to influence from others and can help to arrange contexts that promote behavior change in the parent. When ineffective parental discipline is due to an absence of social support (e.g., a recently divorced, single parent), the therapist can temporarily provide support to the parent while helping the parent to develop a social network of understanding adults (e.g., other single parents). When a lack of commitment to parenting contributes to child behavior management problems, the therapist can promote attitudinal and behavioral change in the parent by helping the parent to understand the child's need for guidance, focusing on what the parent has to offer the child and emphasizing the long-term costs of lax parental control (for an extended discussion of behavioral parent training, see Hersen, Eisler, & Miller, 1994; Munger, 1993; Schaefer & Briesmeister, 1989).

Partner Problems

Marital difficulties may be linked to behavior problems because they interfere with parents' abilities to deliver consistent discipline, because parents in discord may model poor conflict resolution skills, or because the emotionally charged environment may be stressful to children. In cases where marital difficulties represent a likely cause of the child's behavior problems, the therapist should exercise caution before shifting the focus of treatment to the marital relationship. Indeed, when the presenting problem is the child's behavior, parents may see their marriage as irrelevant to the child's problem and are often reluctant to disclose details about their relationship to the therapist. It is important that the therapist acknowledge the child's problem and, together with the parents, set realistic goals for its resolution. The therapist can assign tasks to the parents that require their cooperation in addressing the child's problem. In most cases, marital problems will prevent the interparental consistency that is needed for effective child discipline. At this point the therapist can address likely reasons, including marital difficulties, for continued child behavior problems.

When marital difficulties are identified overtly, the therapist can design interventions to increase marital satisfaction and decrease marital conflicts (for an extended discussion of marital interventions, see Baucom & Epstein, 1990; Henggeler & Borduin, 1990; Jacobson & Gurman, 1995). Although some of these interventions may focus specifically on parenting, marital therapy alone may lead to improved parenting and child behavior. With the small minority of parents who are not willing to engage in marital therapy, the therapist should always clarify the effect of continued marital discord on the child. The parents should be told that it is absolutely essential to provide disciplinary consistency and to not undermine each other's authority. With this directive, some parents are able to maintain a "united front" to their children, whereas other parents may subsequently return for marital therapy or may decide to divorce.

In instances where conflict between divorced parents is adversely affecting the children, the therapist should explain to the parents that their behavior may have very serious long-term consequences for the children. The therapist should strongly recommend to the parents that each stop using the children to undermine the other. When meeting with divorced parents, the therapist should usually avoid any discussion of previous marital issues and focus exclusively on issues that are relevant for the children.

Sibling Problems

To the authors' knowledge, there are no empirically validated treatments that have been designed expressly to ameliorate problems in sibling relations. However, because sibling problems often occur in the presence of broader family difficulties, the therapist can rely on effective interventions that target these broader family problems. Nevertheless, the therapist should consider several issues when sibling problems are a family's presenting concern.

The therapist should always determine the severity of sibling conflicts before recommending any interventions to the parents. It is usually better for siblings to work out their own conflicts if these conflicts are relatively mild and do not involve acts or threats of physical harm. However, in cases of sibling violence, parents must send a clear message regarding the inappropriateness of aggression between family members. It is often the case that violence between siblings occurs in conjunction with parental physical abuse or spousal violence. In such cases, marital and family interventions are necessary to change the abusive interactions of all family members. Even so, the therapist may need to target sibling violence directly when working with violent families. Parents should never ignore violence between siblings and should provide firm consequences when it occurs.

Differential parental treatment of siblings usually occurs within the context of more extensive marital and family problems. For example, marital discord between the parents may lead to a father-mother-child "triangle" in which one parent forms a stable coalition (or peerlike relationship) with the child against the other parent (see, e.g., Mann et al., 1990). In such a family, the parent involved in the cross-generational coalition with the child almost always treats the child preferentially over his or her sibling(s). The therapist can use marital interventions to help resolve any difficulties that are impeding the couple's ability to function effectively as spouses and parents. In addition, the therapist should explain to the parent how preferential treatment of a child over his or her sibling can be detrimental to both children: the less favored child is likely to suffer from low self-esteem and to feel anger and resentment toward the favored sibling, and the favored sibling is likely to suffer from investing his or her emotional energy in the parent rather than in meeting important developmental tasks (e.g., development of peer relations). The therapist should encourage the parent to emphasize each child's strengths and to treat his or her children more equitably.

Relational Problems Not Otherwise Specified

Children's relations with peers and teachers often represent important targets for therapeutic interventions. When designing interventions for these extrafamilial systems, the therapist should always consider the linkages between each of these systems and the family system.

Peer Relations

When social skills deficits or cognitive processes are contributing to a child's difficulties with peers, interventions will often be needed with the individual child. Children with social skills deficits can be effectively coached in their behavioral skills for friendship making. Therapists can rely on a range of interventions to teach the child the requisite social skills (e.g., participating, cooperating, helping). For example, didactic instruction can be used to teach children conversational skills such as self-disclosure (e.g., offering information about oneself), questioning (e.g., asking others about themselves), and leadership bids (e.g., giving advice). The therapist can model appropriate

social skills and have the child practice new skills through role plays. The therapist can also coach the child regarding several aspects of peer interactions, including gaining entry into a peer group activity, cooperating with peers, asking questions and seeking information, helping and encouraging, communicating effectively, and engaging in appropriate nonverbal behaviors. Throughout this process, it is important that the therapist provide the child with appropriate feedback and reinforcement. Moreover, for these training procedures to be effective, the therapist must combine the training with structured opportunities to develop positive peer interactions.

Similarly, for children with deficits or biases in cognitive mediational processes, therapists can use cognitive-behavioral interventions such as self-instruction/self-control training (see, e.g., Braswell & Bloomquist, 1991; Kendall & Braswell, 1985) to improve the child's social perspective-taking skills and his or her ability to inhibit impulsive and aggressive behaviors toward peers. The goal of self-instructional training is to provide impulsive children with an internal cognitive framework that promotes a more reflective response style. When conducting self-instruction training, the therapist first rehearses the self-instruction protocol aloud for the child, and then the child repeats the self-instructions aloud for the therapist. After the instructions have been learned, the therapist whispers them while performing the task and has the child do the same. Finally, the therapist models the covert use of the instructions and has the child do the same. Training is complete when the child has internalized the use of on-task self-talk. Whenever possible, the therapist should demonstrate and explain this training procedure to parents and teachers so that they can also coach the child as necessary.

Because peer relations during early childhood are usually influenced by family relations, the therapist should consider the linkages between these relational systems when designing interventions for peer difficulties in younger children. Parents of toddlers and preschoolers can be taught how to engage in physical play with the child to enhance the child's ability to read emotional cues and to regulate his or her own emotions. Parents of young children must also provide the child with opportunities (e.g., informal play groups, preschool) for same-age peer interaction to promote the development of social skills. Parents can also be taught how to monitor their child's peer interactions when supervising peer activities; the parent should reinforce prosocial behaviors such as sharing and cooperation but should avoid frequent intrusions that prevent the development of other important social skills (e.g., conflict resolution, behaving assertively, expressing opinions).

The therapist should also consider family-peer linkages when developing interventions for adolescents' peer difficulties. In cases involving adolescents with serious clinical problems, the therapist will often need to help the parents decrease the adolescent's involvement with deviant peers and increase his or her association with prosocial peers. This course of action is generally recommended when (a) the adolescent has participated in illegal activities with his or her peers (especially violence or drug use), (b) the peers have no prosocial interests of any sort, or (c) the peers have parents who provide insufficient structure or monitoring of their children's activities. Of course, removing an adolescent from his or her peer group is an extremely difficult task and requires a great deal of energy and commitment from parents. Parents should be told to expect that the adolescent will respond angrily to their efforts to change the youth's peer affiliations and should be reminded of the likely long-term negative consequences (e.g., drug addiction, incarceration) of the youth's continued involvement with deviant peers.

Once the parents are committed to the process of changing their adolescent's peer affiliations, the therapist should help them to develop extremely unpleasant consequences for continued association with problem peers. These consequences should include those that the adolescent is likely to find especially aversive and that, under more normal circumstances, would seem quite unreasonable. For example, after establishing a set of procedures and guidelines for monitoring the who, what,

when, and where surrounding the adolescent's activities, the parents might respond to any violations of their guidelines by restricting the adolescent to the house and having him or her perform a 4-hour work detail that includes the most unpleasant household tasks (e.g., cleaning the toilet, bathtub, sinks, and kitchen floor). The parents must ensure the adolescent's compliance by inspecting his or her work and by having the adolescent redo any work that does not meet the parents' standards. Other relatively aversive activities, such as washing and waxing the car or vacuuming and dusting the entire house, can also be added to the adolescent's list of tasks should the adolescent continue to violate the parents' rules.

Equally important is the therapeutic task of helping the parents to actively support and encourage associations with nonproblem peers. Identification of the adolescent's talents and interests can provide an important vehicle for promoting his or her involvement with a new, more socially appropriate network of peers. For example, adolescents with musical talents can be encouraged to participate in organized musical groups (e.g., the school jazz band); adolescents with literary talents can be encouraged to join the staff of the school newspaper; mechanically talented adolescents can be enrolled in special vocational programs and can work as apprentices in certain employment settings; and athletically gifted youths can be encouraged to participate in organized sports. Whatever prosocial activity the adolescent selects, it is crucial that the parents provide the adolescent with practical support (e.g., a musical instrument, athletic equipment, transportation to and from an activity) and show interest in those activities at which their attendance is encouraged.

School Relations

There are several procedural and process level guidelines that therapists should use when interacting with educational professionals such as teachers and principals (see Henggeler & Borduin, 1990, for a more detailed discussion). First, to arrange a meeting with the child's teachers, it is important for therapists to go through normal administrative channels (e.g., by calling the principal or guidance counselor) after obtaining a signed release of information from the parents. Second, the therapist should behave in a nonthreatening manner during these initial phone conversations and should stress that the teachers can assist the therapist greatly in designing interventions for the child. Third, the therapist should meet with the teachers at the school at a time that is convenient for them and should treat them as equal-status colleagues. Finally, during the therapist-teacher conference, the therapist should convey respect for the teachers' expertise, emphasize common goals for the child, and avoid giving unsolicited advice. When these guidelines are followed, teachers are usually very cooperative with recommendations for school-based interventions. Conversely, if these guidelines are ignored, the therapist's recommendations may be resisted.

When a teacher's behavior-management practices inadvertently contribute to a child's misbehavior, the therapist must be especially skillful in the presentation of recommendations to the teacher. It is essential that the therapist couch his or her recommendations in the most positive terms possible and request feedback from the teacher regarding the probability of success of the proposed interventions. The therapist's recommendations should require as little of the teacher's time as possible and should place most of the responsibility for school-based interventions on the parents (e.g., by implementing rewards and punishments at home that are contingent on the child's behavior in school). Such an arrangement fosters parent-teacher cooperation and increases the likelihood that the child's behavior will improve.

Active parental involvement in the child's education should be an important goal of treatment. Parents may not value educational achievement because of their own difficulties in school. Parents should be told that, in many ways, they can have a greater impact on their child's education than teachers. The most influential way is to express strong interest in the child's performance and to support the child's efforts. Parents can be encouraged to structure the home environment in ways that promote child achievement, such as ensuring that there is a quiet time and place each day for their children to complete homework assignments. In addition, parents can be taught how to monitor the child's progress in school by insisting that their child inform them of test results and impending exams. Of course, parents should be encouraged to express satisfaction in their child's achievement.

It is essential that parents cooperate and communicate frequently with teachers. Children's academic performance usually deteriorates when parents and teachers are in conflict with each other. Family-school conflict is sometimes caused by a child who has learned to play parents and teachers against each other. In other cases, family-school conflict may be due to communication problems related to differences in parents' and teachers' sociocultural backgrounds. In most cases, the therapist can help to resolve problems in family-school relations by meeting jointly with parents and teachers to emphasize common goals for the child and to open channels of family-teacher communication.

SUMMARY

Although there is now substantial evidence to suggest that children's emotional and behavioral disorders are often linked with relational problems and that treatments of these disorders using relational interventions are quite effective, the field's major diagnostic systems (i.e., DSM-IV and ICD-10) still adhere to an individually oriented, medical model of child and adolescent disorders. Moreover, even though DSM-IV includes a number of diagnostic categories for relational problems, these categories are not sufficiently broad to capture the wide range of relational difficulties in children and adolescents.

In this chapter, we have suggested that therapists should adopt a broader, more ecologically oriented framework than the one that guides DSM-IV and ICD-10 and that treatments should target causes and correlates known to be linked with child and adolescent disorders. MST was developed to address the multiple relational contexts of children with serious emotional and behavioral disorders. From the social-ecological perspective of MST, child behavior problems can be maintained by problematic transactions within and/or between the multiple systems in which children and families are embedded. Importantly, this ecological approach to treatment is consistent with causal modeling literatures in the areas of child and adolescent psychopathology and has received empirical support in controlled clinical trials evaluating both short- and long-term outcomes. Thus, there are ethical and practical reasons for recommending MST for the treatment of children's mental health problems.

This chapter has offered some guidelines pertaining to the assessment and treatment of behavior-disordered youths and their systems. These guidelines do not provide a comprehensive set of instructions and should not be regarded as a blueprint for therapy. Instead, these guidelines are intended to offer the reader some direction for planning and implementing interventions for children's relational problems. We believe that it is essential to determine how the child's or adolescent's problem behaviors "fit" within his or her naturally occurring systems. The delineation of this fit has direct implications for the types of interventions that will be used and for the efficacy of those interventions in ameliorating the child's problems.

REFERENCES

Alexander, J. F., & Pugh, C. A. (1996). Oppositional behavior and conduct disorders of children and youth. In F. W. Kaslow (Ed.), *Handbook of relational diagnosis and dysfunctional family patterns* (pp. 210–224). New York: Wiley.

American Psychiatric Association. (1952). *Diagnostic and statistical manual of mental disorders*. Washington, DC: Author.

American Psychiatric Association. (1968). *Diagnostic and statistical manual of mental disorders* (2nd ed.). Washington, DC: Author.

American Psychiatric Association. (1980). *Diagnostic and statistical manual of mental disorders* (3rd ed.). Washington, DC: Author.

American Psychiatric Association. (1987). *Diagnostic and statistical manual of mental disorders* (3rd ed., rev.). Washington, DC: Author.

American Psychiatric Association. (1994). *Diagnostic and statistical manual of mental disorders* (4th ed.). Washington, DC: Author.

Anderson, J., Williams, S., McGee, R., & Silva, P. (1989). Cognitive and social correlates of DSM-III disorders in preadolescent children. *Journal of the American Academy of Child and Adolescent Psychiatry, 28,* 842–846.

Armsden, G. C., & Greenberg, M. T. (1987). The Inventory of Parent and Peer Attachment: Individual differences and the relationship to psychological well-being in adolescence. *Journal of Youth and Adolescence, 16,* 427–454.

Barrett, P. M., Rapee, R. M., Dadds, M. R., & Ryan, S. M. (1996). Family enhancement of cognitive style in anxious and aggressive children. *Journal of Abnormal Child Psychology, 24,* 187–203.

Bateson, G., Jackson, D., Haley, J., & Weakland, J. (1956). Toward a theory of schizophrenia. *Behavioral Science, 1,* 251–264.

Baucom, D. H., & Epstein, N. (1990). *Cognitive-behavioral marital therapy*. New York: Brunner/Mazel.

Borduin, C. M. (1994). Innovative models of treatment and service delivery in the juvenile justice system. *Journal of Clinical Child Psychology, 23* (Suppl.), 19–25.

Borduin, C. M., Blaske, D. M., Cone, L. T., Mann, B. J., & Hazelrigg, M. D. (1989). *Development and validation of a measure of adolescent peer relations: The Missouri Peer Relations Inventory*. Unpublished manuscript, University of Missouri, Department of Psychology, Columbia.

Borduin, C. M., & Henggeler, S. W. (1990). A multisystemic approach to the treatment of serious delinquent behavior. In R. J. McMahon & R. DeV. Peters (Eds.), *Behavior disorders of adolescence: Research, intervention, and policy in clinical and school settings* (pp. 62–80). New York: Plenum Press.

Borduin, C. M., Henggeler, S. W., Blaske, D. M., & Stein, R. (1990). Multisystemic treatment of adolescent sexual offenders. *International Journal of Offender Therapy and Comparative Criminology, 34,* 105–113.

Borduin, C. M., Henggeler, S. W., & Manley, C. M. (1995). Conduct and oppositional disorders. In

V. B. Van Hasselt & M. Hersen (Eds.), *Handbook of adolescent psychopathology: A guide to diagnosis and treatment* (pp. 349–383). Lexington, MA: Lexington Books.

Borduin, C. M., Mann, B. J., Cone, L. T., Henggeler, S. W., Fucci, B. R., Blaske, D. M., & Williams, R. A. (1995). Multisystemic treatment of serious juvenile offenders: Long-term prevention of criminality and violence. *Journal of Consulting and Clinical Psychology, 63*, 569–578.

Bowen, M. (1978). *Family therapy in clinical practice.* New York: Aronson.

*Braswell, L., & Bloomquist, M. L. (1991). *Cognitive-behavioral therapy with ADHD children: Child, family, and school interventions.* New York: Guilford Press.

Brody, G. H., & Stoneman, Z. (1987). Sibling conflict: Contributions of the siblings themselves, the parent-sibling relationship, and the broader family system. *Family Process, 29*, 39–53.

Brody, G. H., Stoneman, Z., & McCoy, J. K. (1994). Contributions of family relationships and child temperaments to longitudinal variations in sibling quality and sibling relationship styles. *Journal of Family Psychology, 8*, 274–286.

*Bronfenbrenner, U. (1979). *The ecology of human development: Experiments by nature and design.* Cambridge, MA: Harvard University Press.

Brunk, M., Henggeler, S. W., & Whelan, J. P. (1987). A comparison of multisystemic therapy and parent training in the brief treatment of child abuse and neglect. *Journal of Consulting and Clinical Psychology, 55*, 311–318.

Burbach, D. J., & Borduin, C. M. (1986). Parent-child relations and the etiology of depression: A review of methods and findings. *Clinical Psychology Review, 6*, 133–153.

Carter, B., & McGoldrick, M. (Eds.). (1988). *The changing family life cycle: A framework for family therapy* (2nd ed.). NY: Gardner.

Cicchetti, D. (1987). Developmental psychopathology in infancy: Illustration from the study of maltreated youngsters. *Journal of Consulting and Clinical Psychology, 55*, 837–845.

Conger, K. J., & Conger, R. D. (1994). Differential parenting and change in sibling differences in delinquency. *Journal of Family Psychology, 8*, 303–320.

Cottone, R. R. (1989). Defining the psychomedical and systemic paradigms in marital and family therapy. *Journal of Marital and Family Therapy, 15*, 225–235.

Crick, N. R., & Dodge, K. A. (1994). A review and reformulation of social information-processing mechanisms in children's social adjustment. *Psychological Bulletin, 115*, 74–101.

*Dadds, M. R. (1995). *Families, children, and the development of dysfunction.* Thousand Oaks, CA: Sage Publications.

Daniels, D., Dunn, J., Furstenberg, F. F., & Plomin, R. (1985). Environmental differences within the family and adjustment differences within pairs of adolescent siblings. *Child Development, 56*, 764–774.

Denton, W. (1989). DSM-III-R and the family therapist: Ethical considerations. *Journal of Marital and Family Therapy, 15*, 367–377.

Denton, W. (1990). A family systems analysis of DSM-III-R. *Journal of Marital and Family Therapy, 16*, 113–125.

Dishion, T. J., Patterson, G. R., Stoolmiller, M., & Skinner, M. L. (1991). Family, school, and behavioral antecedents to early adolescent involvement with antisocial peers. *Developmental Psychology, 27*, 172–180.

Emery, R. E., & O'Leary, K. D. (1982). Children's perceptions of marital discord and behavior problems of boys and girls. *Journal of Abnormal Child Psychology, 10*, 11–24.

Farrington, D. P. (1989). Early predictors of adolescent aggression and adult violence. *Violence and Victims, 4*, 79–100.

Finkelhor, D., & Dziuba-Leatherman, J. (1994). Victimization of children. *American Psychologist, 49*, 173–183.

*Fisch, R., Weakland, J. H., & Segal, L. (1982). *The tactics of change: Doing therapy briefly.* San Francisco, CA: Jossey-Bass.

Furman, W. (1982). Children's friendships. In T. M. Field, A. Huston, H. C. Quay, L. Troll, & G. E. Finley (Eds.), *Review of human development* (pp. 327–339). New York: Wiley.

*Haley, J. (1987). *Problem-solving therapy* (2nd ed.). San Francisco: Jossey-Bass.

*Hartup, W. W. (1983). Peer relations. In E. M. Hetherington (Ed.), *Handbook of child psychology: Socialization, personality, and social development* (pp. 103–196). New York: Wiley.

Hawkins, J. D., Catalano, R. F., & Miller, J. Y. (1992). Risk and protective factors for alcohol and other drug problems in adolescence and early adulthood: Implications for substance abuse prevention. *Psychological Bulletin, 112*, 64–105.

Hazelrigg, M. D., Cooper, H. M., & Borduin, C. M. (1987). Evaluating the effectiveness of family therapies: An integrative review and analysis. *Psychological Bulletin, 101,* 428–442.

Henggeler, S. W. (1989). *Delinquency in adolescence.* Newbury Park, CA: Sage Publications.

*Henggeler, S. W., & Borduin, C. M. (1990). *Family therapy and beyond: A multisystemic approach to treating the behavior problems of children and adolescents.* Pacific Grove, CA: Brooks/Cole.

Henggeler, S. W., Borduin, C. M., & Mann, B. J. (1993). Advances in family therapy: Empirical foundations. In T. H. Ollendick & R. J. Prinz (Eds.), *Advances in clinical child psychology* (vol. 15, pp. 207–241). New York: Plenum Press.

Henggeler, S. W., Borduin, C. M., Melton, G. B., Mann, B. J., Smith, L. A., Hall, J. A., Cone, L., & Fucci, B. R. (1991). Effects of multisystemic therapy on drug use and abuse in serious juvenile offenders: A progress report from two outcome studies. *Family Dynamics of Addiction Quarterly, 1,* 40–51.

*Henggeler, S. W., Borduin, C. M., Schoenwald, S. K., Pickrel, S. G., Roland, M. D., & Cunningham, P. B. (1998). *Multisystemic treatment for antisocial behavior in youth.* New York: Guilford Press.

Henggeler, S. W., Melton, G. B., & Smith, L. A. (1992). Family preservation using multisystemic therapy: An effective alternative to incarceration. *Journal of Consulting and Clinical Psychology, 60,* 953–961.

Henggeler, S. W., Rodick, J. D., Borduin, C. M., Hanson, C. L., Watson, S. M., & Urey, J. R. (1986). Multisystemic treatment of juvenile offenders: Effects on adolescent behavior and family interaction. *Developmental Psychology, 22,* 132–141.

Hersen, M., Eisler, R. M., & Miller, P. M. (Eds.). (1994). *Progress in behavior modification* (vol. 29). Pacific Grove, CA: Brooks/Cole.

Hetherington, E. M., & Martin, B. (1986). Family factors and psychopathology in children. In H. C. Quay & J. S. Werry (Eds.), *Psychopathological disorders of childhood* (3rd ed., pp. 332–390). New York: Wiley.

*Jacobson, N. S., & Gurman, A. S. (Eds.). (1995). *Clinical handbook of couple therapy.* New York: Guilford Press.

Jouriles, E. N., Bourg, W. J., & Farris, A. M. (1991). Marital adjustment and child conduct problems: A comparison of the correlation across subsamples. *Journal of Consulting and Clinical Psychology, 59,* 354–357.

Kaslow, F. W. (1993). Relational diagnosis: Past, present and future. *American Journal of Family Therapy, 21,* 195–204.

*Kaslow, F. W. (Ed.). (1996). *Handbook of relational diagnosis and dysfunctional family patterns.* New York: Wiley.

Kaslow, N. J., Deering, C. G., & Ash, P. (1996). Relational diagnosis of child and adolescent depression. In F. W. Kaslow (Ed.), *Handbook of relational diagnosis and dysfunctional family patterns* (pp. 171–185). New York: Wiley.

Kazdin, A. E. (1995). *Conduct disorders in childhood and adolescence* (2nd ed.). Thousand Oaks, CA: Sage Publications.

Keeney, B. P., & Sprenkle, D. H. (1982). Ecosystemic epistemology: Critical implications for the aesthetics and pragmatics of family therapy. *Family Process, 21,* 1–19.

Kendall, P. C., & Braswell, L. (1985). *Cognitive-behavioral therapy for impulsive children.* NY: Guilford Press.

Kessler, R. C., McGonagle, K. A., Zhao, S., Nelson, C. B., Hughes, M., Eshleman, S., Wittchen, H., & Kendler, K. S. (1994). Lifetime and 12-month prevalence of DSM-III-R psychiatric disorders in the United States. *Archives of General Psychiatry, 51,* 8–18.

Kohler, F. W., & Strain, P. S. (1990). Peer-assisted interventions: Early promises, notable achievements, and future aspirations. *Clinical Psychology Review, 10,* 441–452.

Krohne, H., & Hock, M. (1991). Relationships between restrictive mother-child interactions and anxiety of the child. *Anxiety Research, 4,* 109–124.

Locke, H. J., & Wallace, K. M. (1959). Short marital adjustment and prediction tests: Their reliability and validity. *Marriage and Family Living, 21,* 251–255.

Loeber, R., & Tengs, T. (1986). The analysis of coercive chains between children, mothers, and siblings. *Journal of Family Violence, 1,* 51–70.

Loeber, R., & Schmaling, K. B. (1985). Empirical evidence for overt and covert patterns of antisocial conduct problems: A meta-analysis. *Journal of Abnormal Child Psychology, 13,* 337–352.

Loeber, R., Weissman, W., & Reid, J. B. (1983). Family interactions of assaultive adolescents, stealers, and nondelinquents. *Journal of Abnormal Child Psychology, 11,* 1–14.

Lytton, H. (1990). Child and parent effects in boys' conduct disorder: A reinterpretation. *Developmental Psychology, 26,* 683–697.

Mann, B. J., Borduin, C. M., Henggeler, S. W., &

Blaske, D. M. (1990). An investigation of systemic conceptualizations of parent-child coalitions and symptom change. *Journal of Consulting and Clinical Psychology, 58,* 336–344.

*Mash, E. J. (1989). Treatment of child and family disturbance: A behavioral-systems perspective. In E. J. Mash & R. A. Barkley (Eds.), *Treatment of childhood disorders* (pp. 3–36). New York: Guilford Press.

Miller, G. E., & Prinz, R. J. (1990). Enhancement of social learning family interventions for child conduct disorder. *Psychological Bulletin, 108,* 291–307.

*Minuchin, S. (1974). *Families and family therapy.* Cambridge, MA: Harvard University Press.

Moos, R. H., & Moos, B. S. (1986). *Family Environment Scale manual* (2nd ed.). Palo Alto, CA: Consulting Psychologists Press.

Munger, R. L. (1993). *Changing children's behavior quickly.* Lanham, MD: Madison Books.

Newcomb, M. D., & Bentler, P. M. (1989). Substance use and abuse among children and teenagers. *American Psychologist, 44,* 242–248.

Noble, P. S., Adams, G. R., & Openshaw, D. K. (1989). Interpersonal communication in parent-adolescent dyads: A brief report on the effects of a social skills training program. *Journal of Family Psychology, 2,* 483–494.

Olson, D. H., Portner, J., & Bell, R. (1982). Family adaptability and cohesion evaluation scales. In D. H. Olson, H. I. McCubbin, H. L. Barnes, A. Larson, M. Muxen, & M. Wilson (Eds.), *Family inventories* (pp. 5–24). St. Paul, MN: University of Minnesota, Department of Family Social Science.

*Parke, R. D., & Ladd, G. W. (Eds.). (1992). *Family-peer relationships: Modes of linkage.* Hillsdale, NJ: Lawrence Erlbaum.

Parker, J. G., & Asher, S. R. (1987). Peer relations and later personal adjustment: Are low-accepted children at risk? *Psychological Bulletin, 102,* 357–389.

Patterson, G. R. (1974). Interventions for boys with conduct problems: Multiple settings, treatments, and criteria. *Journal of Consulting and Clinical Psychology, 42,* 471–481.

Patterson, G. R. (1982). *Coercive family process.* Eugene, OR: Castalia.

Patterson, G. R. (1986). The contribution of siblings to training for fighting: A microsocial analysis. In D. Olweus, J. Block, & M. Radke-Yarrow (Eds.), *Development of antisocial and prosocial behavior:*

Research, theories, and issues (pp. 235–261). New York: Harcourt, Brace, Jovanovich.

Patterson, G. R., Reid, J. B., & Dishion, T. J. (1992). *Antisocial boys.* Eugene, OR: Castalia.

Patterson, G. R., & Stouthamer-Loeber, M. (1984). The correlation of family management practices and delinquency. *Child Development, 55,* 1299–1307.

Patterson, T. E., & Lusterman, D. D. (1996). The relational reimbursement dilemma. In F. W. Kaslow (Ed.), *Handbook of relational diagnosis and dysfunctional family patterns* (pp. 46–58). New York: Wiley.

Peterson, A. C., Compas, B. E., Brooks-Gunn, J., Stemmler, M., Ey, S., & Grant, K. E. (1993). Depression in adolescence. *American Psychologist, 48,* 155–168.

Rapoport, J. L., & Ismond, D. R. (1990). *DSM-III-R training guide for diagnosis of childhood disorders.* New York: Brunner/Mazel.

*Reid, W. J., & Crisafulli, A. (1990). Marital discord and child behavior problems: A meta-analysis. *Journal of Abnormal Child Psychology, 18,* 105–117.

Reinherz, H. Z., Stewart-Berghauer, G., Pakiz, B., Frost, A. K., Moeykens, B. A., & Holmes, W. M. (1989). The relationship of early risk and current mediators to depressive symptomatology in adolescence. *Journal of the American Academy of Child and Adolescent Psychiatry, 28,* 942–947.

Rhodes, J. E., & Jason, L. A. (1990). A social stress model of substance abuse. *Journal of Consulting and Clinical Psychology, 58,* 395–401.

Rothbaum, F., & Weisz, J. R. (1994). Parental caregiving and child externalizing behavior in nonclinical samples: A meta-analysis. *Psychological Bulletin, 116,* 55–74.

Rubin, K. H., & Mills, R. S. L. (1991). Conceptualizing developmental pathways to internalizing disorders in childhood. *Canadian Journal of Behavioural Science, 23,* 300–317.

Rubin, C., Rubenstein, J. L., Stechler, G., Heeren, T., Halton, A., Housman, D., & Kasten, L. (1992). Depressive affect in "normal" adolescents: Relationship to life stress, family, and friends. *American Journal of Orthopsychiatry, 62,* 430–441.

*Schaefer, C. E., & Briesmeister, J. M. (Eds.). (1989). *Handbook of parent training: Parents as cotherapists for children's behavior problems.* NY: Wiley.

Scherer, D. G., Brondino, M. J., Henggeler, S. W., Melton, G. B., & Hanley, J. H. (1994). Multisystemic family preservation therapy: Preliminary findings from a study of rural and minority serious adolescent offenders. *Journal of Emotional and Behavioral Disorders, 2*, 198–206.

Schoenwald, S. K., Borduin, C. M., & Henggeler, S. W. (1998). Multisystemic therapy: Changing the natural and service ecologies of adolescents and families. In M. H. Epstein, K. Kutash, & A. J. Duchinowski (Eds.), *Community-based programming for children with serious emotional disturbance and their families: Research and evaluations.* New York: ProEd.

*Shadish, W. R., Montgomery, L. M., Wilson, P., Wilson, M. R., Bright, I., & Okwumabua, T. (1993). Effects of family and marital psychotherapies: A meta-analysis. *Journal of Consulting and Clinical Psychology, 61*, 992–1002.

Snyder, J., & Patterson, G. R. (1987). Family interaction and delinquent behavior. In H. C. Quay (Ed.), *Handbook of juvenile delinquency* (pp. 216–243). New York: Wiley.

Wahler, R. G. (1990). Who is driving the interactions? A commentary on "Child and parent effects in boys' conduct disorder." *Developmental Psychology, 26*, 702–704.

Webster-Stratton, C., Hollinsworth, T., & Kolpacoff, M. (1989). The long-term effectiveness and clinical significance of three cost-effective training programs for families with conduct-disordered children. *Journal of Consulting and Clinical Psychology, 55*, 542–549.

Whitaker, C. (1976). The hindrance of theory in clincial work. In P. J. Guerin (Ed.), *Family therapy: Theory and practice* (pp. 154–164). New York: Gardner Press.

Willis, D. J. (1995). Psychological impact of child abuse and neglect. *Journal of Clinical Child Psychology, 24* (Suppl.), 2–4.

World Health Organization. (1992). *Manual of the international classification of diseases, injuries, and causes of death, revision 10, with clinical modifications.* Geneva: Author.

Wynne, L. C. (1987). A preliminary proposal for strengthening the multiaxial approach of DSM-III: Possible family-oriented revisions. In G. L. Tischler (Ed.), *Diagnosis and classification in psychiatry: A critical appraisal of DSM-III* (pp. 477–488). New York: Cambridge University Press.

*Indicates references that the authors recommend for further reading.

25

Problems Related to Child Abuse and Neglect

John R. Lutzker, Kathryn M. Bigelow,
Cynthia Cupit Swenson, Ronald M. Doctor,
Maria Lynn Kessler

HISTORICAL PERSPECTIVE

Although child abuse and neglect (CAN) is a serious problem for society, it was formally recognized as such by the medical and professional community only in 1962 when Kempe, Silverman, Steele, Drogemueller, and Silver published their seminal article, "The Battered Child Syndrome." CAN's first appearance in the *Diagnostic and Statistical Manual of Mental Disorders* (DSM) was in DSM-IV, in which it was categorized as a V code. Previous editions of DSM had listed child abuse within parent-child problems.

Early professional attention to child abuse and neglect in the literature was restricted to research on the demographics of the disorder and to theoretical speculation as to the etiology of parents who perpetrate child abuse or neglect. Explanations of this disorder were first offered from a psychodynamic perspective, suggesting that parents who abuse their children do so because of unresolved intrapsychic reasons. Later theories suggested that the problem was more complex and that the parent, the child, and the social environment all play roles in CAN (Belsky, 1980, 1993; Garbarino, 1977; Lutzker &

Rice, 1984; Wolfe, 1991). In general, this latter orientation has prevailed, with some attention also given to possible biological determinants for parents. There are no data directly that link biological factors to child abuse; however, there are data that point to a biological role in aggressive behavior (National Research Council [NRC], 1993).

Attempts to treat child abuse and neglect began to appear in the literature in the late 1970s. Most reports were case studies or single-case experiments (Kazdin, 1982); most of these reports lacked sound methodology. After the first issue of *Child Abuse and Neglect: The International Journal* was published in 1978, reports of larger-scale programs also began to appear. With the introduction of socioecological theories, treatment was primarily focused on trying to remedy some of the socioecological problems associated with child abuse and neglect and included efforts to provide parent training, reduce stress to parents, and reduce community isolation of the family. This latter issue is what Wahler (1980) called "insularity." Additional attention was paid to poverty, poor housing conditions, single parenthood, substance abuse, poor interpersonal relationships, impulsivity, and lack of child care.

Among the earliest reports of treatment was parent training in child behavior management (Crimmins, Bradlyn, St. Lawrence, & Kelly, 1984; Crozier & Katz, 1979; Wolfe & Sandler, 1981). Other case studies described adding stress reduction (Egan, 1983; Gabinet, 1979; Wolfe, Sandler, & Kaufman, 1981) to parent training. Subsequently, a host of broad-based in-home programs have described services that include parent training and various forms of social support and parent education (Feldman, Case, & Sparks, 1992). In 1982, Lutzker, Frame, and Rice described an "ecobehavioral" approach to the treatment and prevention of CAN in which families received a host of services aimed at the factors that appear to be related to CAN. These services included parent training, stress reduction, basic skill training for children, home safety, nutrition, child health care, money management, problem solving, social support, self-control training, and comprehensive pre- and postnatal training for young, single parents. By "ecobehavioral," it was meant that the services were provided in-home and in situ, that assessment and treatment were multifaceted, and that there were active attempts to program for generalization of the skills that were taught.

From the work to date in the field, there are clearly two elements in the treatment and prevention of CAN: teaching new skills to parents and trying to alter their social ecologies to help alleviate the apparent stressors that contribute to CAN and providing ameliorative treatment to the victims of CAN. There has been a growing empirical literature in the former domain and very little empirical work in the latter. This chapter attempts to focus on what sound empirical work exists in both of these areas.

DIAGNOSTIC DESCRIPTION AND CRITIQUE OF DSM-IV

DSM-IV gives short shrift to CAN. Perhaps the reason for this is that CAN is, in fact, such a multifaceted problem and not a disorder of an individual. At minimum, it is an interaction between two people, a child and an adult. The behavioral and emotional sequelae of CAN run deep and long for children. The mitigating intrapersonal and sociological factors that may cause an adult to abuse or neglect a child may be too numerous and unspecific for the classification schemes usually associated with the DSM. Similarly, the *International Classification of Diseases* (ICD-10) has no code for acute stress reaction and posttraumatic stress disorder (PTSD), which are now known to be prevalent in child victims of abuse; like DSM-IV, ICD-10 does not fully recognize CAN as a specific disorder that affects parents or children.

One page of DSM-IV is devoted to "Problems Related to Abuse or Neglect." One paragraph notes that the section includes categories to be used when the clinical focus relates to one of these five categories: physical abuse of the child, sexual abuse of the child, neglect of the child, physical abuse of adult, and sexual abuse of adult. No defining characteristics are provided.

At minimum, DSM might provide definition and some known sequelae associated with CAN. For example, a common definition of physical abuse is that it involves physical harm perpetrated intentionally by an adult that involves observable marks on the child. Thus, physical abuse is an act of commission. Neglect is known to be a problem of omission in that it involves placing the child at risk of health and medical harm because of the failure to provides physically nurturing stimuli such as shelter, medical care, or sanitary living conditions. Sexual abuse can be defined as unwanted or forced sexual penetration, manipulation, or intimacy with a child or adolescent under the age of 16 by an adult.

The known sequelae of physical and sexual abuse and neglect are avoidance of adults or overdependence on adults, anxiety (symptoms that resemble PTSD), sexual acting out, precocious sexual verbal behavior, conduct disorder-like behavior, and withdrawal. It is also apparent that these sequelae can be very long lasting.

The diagnosis of CAN is also untraditional. For example, in most disorders covered in the

DSM, an individual has sought treatment because of discomfort from the disorder, such as any of the anxiety disorders, or the individual has failed in society and has come to the attention of professionals, such as in schizophrenia or any of the pervasive developmental disorders. With CAN, in most cases, a parent or parents has come to the attention of the legal system through the state or county's child protective service. Thus, rather than receiving a traditional diagnosis from a mental health professional, the parent has been labeled an abuser or as neglectful by a public agency. Although this is not always the case in that there are occasional self-referrals, by far the majority of CAN cases come through child protective service agencies.

Children who are abused or neglected may display a number of disorders specified in DSM, such as anxiety disorders, avoidant behaviors, and noncompliance, yet there are no diagnostic criteria that are specified for victims of CAN. In addition, it is virtually impossible to separate the role of the parent from any pathology shown by the child. Thus, CAN as a disorder for children can seldom be separated from the additional role of the parent in the disorder. As is evident in the review of the treatment literature, there is a relative dearth of applied research articles on the treatment of the child as victim, as there is on the treatment of parents. Nonetheless, we review here the applied treatment research that exists, most of which focuses on parents.

EPIDEMIOLOGY

Demographic prevalence indicates that the rate of substantiated or indicated child abuse and neglect in the United States is more than 1 million per year (U.S. Department of Health and Human Services, 1995). Children are abused from birth throughout adolescence. Abuse can range from a single incident to chronic incidence. It may involve all children in a family, or an individual child may be singled out as the victim of abuse. Abuse can range from a severe beating that produces serious welts, bruises, or fractures to torture such as tying children up or pouring scalding water on them or intentionally placing them in scalding bath water. Nearly half of the victims of maltreatment suffer from neglect. Twenty-four percent are physically abused, and 14% are sexually abused. Medical neglect and emotional maltreatment are reported for about 7% of the victims. The remaining 15% are reported for other types of maltreatment (U.S. Department of Health and Human Services, 1995).

It is believed that as many as a third of possible child physical abuse cases go unreported or unidentified (Warner & Hansen, 1994). Moderate injuries make up about 60% of child physical abuse (Warner & Hansen, 1994). Pathognomonic abuse is a specific kind of abuse that involves shaking a child violently, thus causing injury, loop, and bruise marks on the skin and spiral fractures (Altieri, 1990; Johnson, 1990).

The National Center on Child Abuse and Neglect (NCCAN) has noted that the incidence of abuse is positively correlated with age and gender (NCCAN, 1988). The prevalence of CAN is greater in younger children. As age increases, however, the risk of abuse or neglect decreases. Fifty-one percent of victims of child abuse or neglect are 7 years of age or younger (U.S. Department of Health and Human Services, 1995). For each type of maltreatment, age and gender are important variables. For neglect, it appears that age is the important factor. Neglect decreases as age increases for both males and females. This does not appear to be so for other types of maltreatment. For victims of physical abuse younger than age 12, males are more likely than females to be abused, while for victims 12 and older, females are more likely than males to be abused. Gender is a significant factor in prevalence of sexual abuse, with females twice as likely to be sexually abused as males (U.S. Department of Health and Human Services, 1995).

African American and Hispanic families have higher probabilities of being reported for abuse than other ethnic/racial groups, and low-income families have the highest rates of being reported among socioeconomic status groups.

Short- and long-term consequences of abuse may include perceptual-motor deficits, poor academic performance and lower scores on standardized intelligence and achievement tests, and negative social behaviors (Malinosky-Rummell & Hansen, 1993). The long-term effects are less clear, but clinicians report many DSM disorders of adult patients that may be the result of previous abuse or neglect. Malinosky-Rummell and Hansen (1993) reported that violent inmates and outpatients report higher rates of childhood physical abuse than do less violent comparison subjects. There is also evidence suggesting that childhood physical abuse relates to spouse abuse in adult men (Malinosky-Rummell & Hansen, 1993). Overall, individuals who have been abused demonstrate more violence than individuals who have not been abused. The estimates of intergenerational abuse range from 7%–70% (Malinosky-Rummell & Hansen, 1993). Thus, caution must prevail in considering this diagnosis.

More evidence exists showing that children who were the victims of CAN demonstrate more noncompliance and higher rates of conduct disorders than do comparison group children who are not the victims of CAN (Ammerman, Cassisi, Hersen, & Van Hasselt, 1986). There also appears to be a correlation between child abuse and subsequent adult substance abuse (Cavaiola & Schiff, 1988). Other long-term sequelae of CAN may include suicidal behavior, emotional problems, interpersonal problems, and academic difficulties. The occurrence of drug- and alcohol-related problems, suicidal behavior, and emotional problems is greater in individuals who report more than one form of childhood maltreatment than for individuals who report only one form of maltreatment (Malinosky-Rummell & Hansen, 1993).

There are multiple correlates and potential long-term sequelae of child sexual abuse. In a review of the literature, Beitchman, Zucker, Hood, daCosta, Akman, and Cassavia (1992) found that the effects of child sexual abuse are still to be clarified. Without control of variables such as the use of force or penetration by the perpetrator, age of onset of abuse, or the duration of abuse, it has been difficult to establish conclusions regarding the extent to which the sequelae are due to individual variables. When compared with women who do not report a history of child sexual abuse, women who do report a history of child sexual abuse show evidence of sexual disturbance, anxiety and fear related to force or threat of force during abuse, depression, and revictimization (Beitchman et al., 1992). Evidence supporting the relationship between child sexual abuse and multiple-personality and borderline personality disorders is lacking (Beitchman et al., 1992).

The data are equivocal at this point as to chronicity and prognosis in CAN. It is unclear what percentage of parents who were abused as children themselves become abusive parents. Similarly, the overall effectiveness of treatment programs has not been evaluated in most cases. Exceptions to this are cited in this chapter. What is known is that the reports of CAN have risen and there are few empirically driven programs aimed at assessing and treating it (whether the incidence has risen is unclear).

PSYCHOPATHOLOGY AND THEORETICAL MODELS

The issue of psychopathology among abusing parents calls attention to itself with the question "How could parents cause or allow to occur the serious physical harm of their child?" There is concern about the short-term and long-term psychological damage that CAN produces in children and as they become adults. In addition to suicidal behavior, emotional problems, and so on, there are other reported sequelae of being the victim of CAN. For example, it has been reported that victims of CAN display exaggerations in their behavior with nonfamilial adults. That is, they often display either isolate behavior, seldom interacting with adults, or, more commonly, display unusual attachment to even casual adult acquaintances. In addition, many victims of CAN display symptoms of posttraumatic stress disorder (PTSD). This includes nightmares, flashbacks, and generally elevated levels of anxiety.

Perpetrators of CAN have been described as having numerous disorders, often involving substance abuse, emotional lability, impulse control problems, antisocial personality, and difficulty with adult-adult relationships. As children, they often displayed many of the problems outlined earlier, such as poor academic performance, aggression, and noncompliance. It is important to remember, however, that data on these kinds of variables are correlational, often retrospective, and that there are perpetrators of CAN who have not displayed these characteristics and individuals who display these characteristics and do not engage in abuse.

In trying to explain the etiology of adults who abuse children, the earliest attempts focused on the psychopathology of the adult or the child (National Research Council, 1993). However, in the 1970s the focus shifted to a sociological model (Garbarino, 1977; Gil, 1970). More recently, ecological factors have been suggested as a major determinant (Belsky, 1980; Lutzker, 1984; Wolfe, 1991). This model suggests that family, community, society, and interpersonal factors may all contribute to CAN. Cicchetti and Carlson (1989) have noted that it is unlikely that there is a single risk factor in CAN. Rather, potentiating and contributing factors are likely different in each perpetrator, with some common factors being found among most perpetrators. The National Research Council (1993) has concluded that the etiology of CAN can best be described as a "developmental/ecological/transactional model" (p. 109).

Psychiatric Disorders

Although it seems likely that psychiatric disorders play a role in CAN, a consistent psychiatric profile has not evolved. There does, however, appear to be a set of consistent attributes among many parents involved in CAN. These are low self-esteem and an external locus of control, poor impulse control, negative affect, and antisocial behavior. Also, negative maternal attitudes and poor knowledge of child development appear to correlate with CAN (National Research Council, 1993).

Biological Variables

Biology as a contributing factor to CAN has been considered; however, these considerations have been based by analogy primarily from animal work. Even among animals the role of biological factors is unclear (Suomi, 1978). Clearly, children who have biological impairments are more at risk for CAN than are children who lack such impairments.

Parenting style seems to be a predictor of CAN. It is generally agreed that living with a parent with an authoritarian style or with a history of neglect and little involvement with the child places children at higher risk than that faced by children in homes wherein neither of these characteristics are present (Maccoby & Martin, 1983). The direct observational data suggest that the parent is more negative than the child in CAN families (Trickett & Susman, 1988). Dumas and Wahler (1985) noted a relationship between stressful life events and higher rates of abuse, but this research has not been replicated. Finally, poverty, unemployment, and dangerous neighborhoods all are correlated with higher rates of CAN.

ASSESSMENT

As with the treatment of a variety of other disorders, assessment of CAN is a necessary component for providing and evaluating treatment. This process involves the assessment of the potential risk to the child and provides for the development of individualized treatment plans and for the evaluation of the effects of treatment. While the research that thoroughly evaluates methods of assessing child abuse and neglect has been somewhat limited, the development of measurement devices has included measures that evaluate factors ranging from child management skills to home cleanliness. These assessment devices can be categorized into four domains: risk assessment, parent factors, child factors, and environmental factors.

Risk Assessment

Risk assessment involves the identification of the variables that may indicate that the risk for maltreatment is present and the degree to which it is present. The evaluation of parent factors, which has received the most attention, involves the assessment of parental psychopathology, the presence of child management skills, the quality of parent-child interactions, parent perception of child behavior problems, parental stress, anger and physiological arousal, knowledge of child development and behavior, problem-solving skills, and social support. Child factors include child development and child behavior problems. Environmental factors include variables such as cleanliness and safety.

Assessment of CAN should involve the use of several measures. Self-report ratings are used in assessing each of the domains listed, but a disadvantage of self-report is that parents may misrepresent their responses, either purposefully or not (Hansen & MacMillan, 1990). The use of direct observation, either in simulated or actual situations, can compensate in part for misrepresentation. Direct observation strategies also have limitations such as reactivity, that is, parents "staging" their behavior because they know that they are being observed. Measurement of physiological responses can also provide information regarding parental responses to highly arousing or stressful situations.

Many risk measures have been developed and are employed despite inadequate demonstrations of their psychometric properties (Doueck, Bronson, & Levine, 1992). Two devices that are widely used and have adequate psychometric properties include the Child Abuse Potential Inventory (CAPI; Milner, 1986) and the Childhood Level of Living Scale (CLLS; Hally, Polansky, & Polansky, 1980).

The CAPI is a widely used and researched measure of potential risk for physical abuse. In addition to an abuse potential score, there are six other scales: Rigidity, Unhappiness, Distress, Problems with Child and Self, Problems with Family, and Problems with Others. There are also three distortion indices, which include faking good, faking bad, and random responding. These scores are derived from combinations of scores on three validity scales: lie, random responding, and inconsistency. Procedures to test the reading level of the current version have indicated that the CAPI has a readability level of grade three. Evaluation of the CAPI has been extensive and has demonstrated support for its psychometric properties (Kaufman & Walker, 1986; Milner, 1986). A Spanish version of the CAPI is available, although little research is available regarding its use. Although estimates of internal consistency and predictive validity of the Spanish version have been reported, these studies were conducted in Argentina and Spain. Additional data are necessary to establish support for use of the CAPI with the various Spanish-speaking populations in the United States.

The Childhood Levels of Living Scale (Hally, Polansky, & Polansky, 1980) is used to measure the essential elements of child care and neglect. This is appropriate for parents of children ages four through seven and assesses nine factors; four are descriptive of emotional/cognitive care and five are descriptive of physical care.

In evaluating maltreatment within families, assessment of the parental factors that contribute to the risk for or incidence of abuse or neglect should be comprehensive and provide direction to the development and implementation of treatment plans. In many families, an assessment of parental psychopathology may be necessary. The Symptom-Checklist-90-Revised (Derogatis, 1983) is a 90-item self-report questionnaire that assesses several potential problems. Primary symptom scales include Somatization, Obsessive-Compulsive, Interpersonal Sensitivity, Depression, Anxiety, Hostility, Phobic Anxiety, Paranoid Ideation, and Psychoticism. Three global stress indices are Global Severity, Positive Symptom Distress, and Positive Symptom Total.

The use of the Minnesota Multiphasic Personality Inventory-2 (MMPI-2; Butcher, Dahlstrom, Graham, Tellegen, & Kaemmer, 1989) has been demonstrated with maltreating parents, as well as with parents at risk for maltreatment. A scale designed to assess substance abuse is also included.

An important component of assessment is the evaluation of parent's child behavior management skills. The Home Simulation Assessment (HSA; MacMillan, Olson, & Hansen, 1991) can be used to assess parent behavior in simulated child management situations and to measure the effects of training. An adult actor whose behavior is controlled by a clinician who is observing behind a one-way mirror portrays deviant child behavior in an attempt to assess parents' abilities to apply child management skills. Parents are provided with 10 tasks and asked to do their best to prompt the actor to complete the tasks. Parent performance is evaluated by calculating the percentage of correct instructions and responses to the various types of behavior demonstrated by the actor. Adequate interrater reliability has been demonstrated. The HSA is especially appropriate for parents with children placed outside the home and as an alternative to the observation of parents in situ (Macmillan, Olson, & Hansen, 1988).

High-Deviance Home Simulation Assessment (MacMillan, Olson, Hansen, 1991) which is an adaptation of and a supplement to the Home Simulation Assessment, introduces more demanding child management situations by presenting an additional actor in the simulated situation or by increasing the frequency of deviant behaviors displayed by the actor. In addition to coding parental response to child deviance in the 10 tasks, parent ratings of stress, anger, and anxiousness are collected. Interrater reliability, social validity, and effectiveness of measuring treatment outcome have been demonstrated. Differences between parent scores on the low-demand and the high-demand assessments may indicate a need for stress reduction or anger-control training (MacMillan, Olson, & Hansen, 1991). The types of deviant child behavior demonstrated by actors include verbal arguments, failure to attend to instructions, excuses for noncompliant behavior, compliance, noncompliance, rule violations, and escape from timeout (MacMillan, Olson, & Hansen, 1991). Although direct observation is the most desirable method of assessing parent performance, it can often be difficult or unethical to assess child management skills in the home setting with children present. Analogue assessment protects children from exposure to aggression and is efficient in assessing specific parent responses to child behavior that may not be demonstrated in actual child management situations with observers present (MacMillan, Olson, & Hansen, 1991).

Knowledge of Behavioral Principles as Applied to Children (KBPAC; O'Dell, Tarler-Benlolo, & Flynn, 1979) is a 50-item measure that can be used to evaluate parents' knowledge of child management principles. This may also be appropriate for assessing the effects of parent training. However, the measure requires an eighth-grade reading level. Furthermore, while parental knowledge of child management may be adequate, this knowledge may not be reflected in actual parent behavior.

The Parent Behavior Checklist (Fox, 1994) can be used to identify parenting strengths and needs. The PBC is appropriate for parents of children ages 1 to 4 years and measures three aspects of parenting: expectations, discipline, and nurturing.

There are several tools to evaluate the qualitative and stimulating aspects of the interactions between parents and children by utilizing direct observation procedures. Parent-child dyads are observed in semistructured situations, and specifically defined behaviors are observed and coded by a trained observer. Lutzker, Lutzker, Braunling-McMorrow, and Eddleman (1987) measured the quality of affective behaviors demonstrated by parents toward their young children; this included smiling, affectionate words, guided play, assuming the physical level of the child, affectionate touch, and eye contact. Similarly, the Dyadic Parent-Child Interaction Coding System (Eyberg, Bessmer, Newcomb, Edwards, & Robinson, 1994; Eyberg & Robinson, 1981) assesses several positive and negative parent and child behaviors. Some of the parent behaviors include commands, descriptive or reflective statements or questions, labeled praise, and critical statements. Child behaviors observed include whining, crying, yelling, compliance, noncompliance, and destructive behavior. The Behavioral Coding System (Forehand & McMahon, 1981) assesses the appropriateness of parental antecedents (commands, warnings, questions, and attends), child behaviors (compliance, noncompliance), and parental consequences (rewards and attends).

Parental stress, anger, and accompanying physiological arousal are often targeted for assessment. The Parenting Stress Index (PSI; Abidin, 1990; Loyd & Abidin, 1985) was designed to screen and diagnose the magnitude of family stress, which may increase the risk of dysfunctional parenting behaviors or behavior problems in the child. Three domains are assessed: parent characteristics, child characteristics, and other situations that are directly related to the role of being a parent (Abidin, 1990). The reliability of this measure has been demonstrated, supporting its use for both preliminary screening and for evaluating the effectiveness of intervention. The validity of the long form has been demonstrated, and since the short form was derived directly from the long form, it is likely that the short form is valid (Abidin, 1990). High scores on the child characteristics domain are often associated with children who display qualities that are contributing to the overall stress in the parent-child system. For parents of children with disabilities (hyperactivity, mental retardation, cerebral palsy, emotional disturbance, learning disabilities), the child characteristics domain score is usually elevated above the parent characteristics domain (Loyd & Abidin, 1985). Additional research has supported the cross-cultural utility of a Spanish version of the PSI with Latina mothers (Solis & Abidin, 1991).

Parental anger related to child behavior is also an area that can be assessed. The Novaco Anger Control Scale (NACS; Novaco, 1975) is a self-report measure designed to evaluate anger and arousal control problems. Brief descriptions of situations involving provocation are presented to the parent, who then rates on a 5-point scale the level of anger each situation would arouse.

The Parental Anger Inventory (PAI; DeRoma & Hansen, 1994) was designed to assess anger experienced by abusing parents in response to challenging child behaviors. Parents are asked to rate 50 child-related situations as problematic or nonproblematic and then to indicate the magnitude of anger elicited in each scenario, using a 5-point scale. This measure has been recommended for identifying anger-control problems and for evaluating treatment effects for anger-reduction intervention. Internal consistency and content validity of these instruments have been demonstrated.

Bauer and Twentyman (1985) presented parents with audiotaped descriptions of child-related and nonchild-related stressors and asked subjects to rate their level of annoyance. Measures obtained include amount of annoyance, peak annoyance, latency to annoyance, and latency to peak annoyance. Parents were also asked to rate the degree to which they thought the child engaged in purposefully annoying behavior. Abusive mothers showed more annoyance across both child-related and nonchild-related types of stressors. Furthermore, they attributed negative intentions to the child more frequently than did control parents. The measurement of physical arousal experienced in response to exposure to recorded or in vivo exposure to child deviance can function as a supplement to parent report of arousal. Differences between parent report and physiological data may be utilized in teaching parents to attend to the physiological signals that accompany arousal (Hansen & MacMillan, 1990).

Parent Expectations

Assessment of parents' expectations of child behavior and their knowledge of typical child development can be conducted. Unrealistic expectations about children are often displayed by maltreating parents. The Parent Opinion Questionnaire (Azar, Robinson, Hekimian, & Twentyman, 1984) is an 80-item questionnaire that assesses the level of parents' unrealistic expectations of appropriate child behavior. Parents are asked to rate whether they agree or disagree with the appropriateness of expecting a variety of child behaviors. Six subscales are scored: self-care, family responsibility and care of siblings, help and affection to parents, leaving children alone, proper behavior and feelings, and punishment. The Parent Opinion Questionnaire has been demonstrated to discriminate abusive and neglectful mothers from control mothers (Azar et al., 1984), as well as abusive mothers from control mothers whose partners were abusive (Azar & Rohrbeck, 1986).

The Family Beliefs Inventory (Roehling & Robin, 1986) measures unreasonable beliefs of parents about adolescents. It includes beliefs about ruination, perfectionism, approval, obedience, self-blame, and malicious intent. For the adolescents, the beliefs studied involve ruination, unfairness, autonomy, and approval.

Problem-Solving Skills

Problem-solving and coping skills represent yet another area for assessment. The Parent Problem-Solving Instrument contains 10 typical child-rearing problems presented in the form of a story (Wasik, Bryant, & Fishbein, 1980, cited in Azar et al., 1984). After the beginning and the end of each story are read, parents are asked to provide the middle, which is the solution to the problem. The PPSI differentiates between maltreating and nonmaltreating mothers. Maltreating mothers elaborate less on solutions, use fewer content categories in their solutions, and generate fewer solutions overall (Azar et al., 1984).

The Parental Problem Solving Measure (Hansen, Palotta, Tishelman, Conaway, & MacMillan, 1989) evaluates problem-solving abilities in child- and nonchild-related situations. It is administered by reading problematic situations to the parent and then asking the parent to imagine being in that situation and to "tell me all of the things you could do to solve the problem, and what you would do." Responses are rated on a 7-point scale for the number of solutions generated and the effectiveness of the best solutions. Two versions have been evaluated: a 25-item version (Hansen et al., 1989) and a 15-item version (Palotta, Conaway, Christopher, & Hansen, 1989).

Coping styles may be assessed using the Ways of Coping Checklist—Revised (Lazarus & Folkman, 1984), which comprises eight scales, including problem-focused coping, wishful thinking, detachment, seeking social support, focusing on the positive, self-blame, tension reduction, and keeping to self.

Wahler (1980) described the lack of social and emotional support and the high frequency of negative interactions and contacts as insularity. The extent to which a parent experiences insularity and the function of the contacts they do experience can be assessed by several measures. The Interpersonal Support Evaluation List (Cohen, Mermelstein, Kamarck, & Hoberman, 1985) assesses the extent to which social support fulfills the functions of tangible, appraisal, self-esteem, and belonging support. The Community Interaction Checklist (Wahler, Leske, & Rogers, 1979) evaluates the nature and the frequency of social contacts. A 20-item Network Orientation Scale, used in evaluating the effects of a social skills training package, assesses the willingness to utilize available social support resources. Finally, the Perceived Social Support Questionnaire (Procidano & Heller, 1983) evaluates the extent to which the needs for support and interaction are met by friends and family.

Child Behavior

In addition to the assessment of the parental factors that contribute to or maintain maltreatment toward children, an assessment of the needs of the child who has been abused is often necessary. Several child characteristics are associated with increased risk for maltreatment, particularly physical abuse (Ammerman, 1990). Factors such as prolonged crying, oppositional and defiant behavior, conduct problems, prematurity, and physical and developmental disability are all believed to contribute to stress within the family, which may exacerbate the risk for maltreatment (Ammerman, 1990).

Several parent-report measures for assessing child behavior problems are available. Two of the most common measures include the Child Behavior Checklist (CBCL; Achenbach & Edelbrock, 1983) and the Eyberg Child Behavior Inventory (ECBI; Eyberg & Ross, 1978). The CBCL (Achenbach & Edelbrock, 1983) consists of ratings of 118 items that describe specific behavior problems in children ages 2 to 16. The domains assessed include Schizoid or Anxious, Depressed, Uncommunicative, Obsessive-Compulsive, Somatic Complaints, Social Withdrawal, Ineffective, Aggressive, and Delinquent. The ECBI (Eyberg & Ross, 1978; Eyberg & Colvin, 1994) is a widely used rating scale that measures disruptive behaviors in children ages 2 to 16 and can be utilized repeatedly to assess change in behavior over time. Thirty-six common child behavior problems are rated on a 7-point scale for intensity. Parents are then asked to rate whether each behavior is a problem, providing a frequency score.

The Conners Rating Scales (Conners, 1990) are used to characterize patterns of problem behavior of children from 3–17 years of age. It includes scales for Conduct Disorder; Anxious-Shy; Restless-Disorganized; Learning Problem; Psychosomatic; Obsessive-Compulsive; Antisocial; and Hyperactive-Immature. Norms are available for the 93-item version for children ages 6 to 14 years. For the 48-item version, norms are available for children ages 3 to 17. Each version includes a 10-item Hyperactivity Index, which measures the extent to which the child displays behaviors indicative of ADHD.

In addition to measures of problem child behavior, assessment of the child's current level of development may be conducted through the use of well-validated and clinically useful scales such as the Bayley Scales of Development (Bayley, 1969) or the Vineland Adaptive Behavior Scales (Doll, 1964).

Other Risk Factors

The assessment of abuse or neglect within families can include an evaluation of the living conditions of the home. Two instruments have been utilized to assess the cleanliness and the safety of home environments. The Home Accident Prevention Inventory (HAPI; Tertinger, Greene, & Lutzker, 1984) assesses hazards that are accessible to children. Five categories of hazards are included: fire and electrical, suffocation by ingested objects, suffocation by mechanical objects, firearms, and solid and liquid poisons. The HAPI has been demonstrated to have adequate interrater reliability and content validity in identifying hazards and evaluating the effects of training to reduce accessible hazards in the home.

The Checklist for Living Environments to Assess Neglect (CLEAN; Watson-Perczel, Lutzker, Greene, & McGimpsey, 1988) evaluates the cleanliness of item areas within the home on three dimensions: presence of nonorganic or organic decaying matter, clothes and linens not belonging, and other objects not belonging. The CLEAN has also shown adequate interrater reliability and is effective in evaluating the effects of cleanliness training.

In evaluating immediate risks, parent factors, child factors, and environmental factors that contribute and/or maintain child maltreatment, several factors must be taken into account. As treatment of CAN should be comprehensive, so should assessment. Thorough evaluations should not be limited to parent factors alone but should involve all of the factors that are known to correlate with risk for maltreatment within families. Furthermore, a variety of methods for assessing these factors should be utilized. A combination of direct observational measures, self-report questionnaires, and interviews, when used together, is more likely to provide a thorough evaluation than one that relies on only one of these methods. It is also essential that the possibility of limited motivation, cooperation, and reading and writing abilities on the part of the parents be taken into account when assessing maltreating parents (Hansen & MacMillan, 1990).

One area that has been neglected in the evaluation of measures to assess families at risk for abuse or neglect has been the cultural factors that may influence parent behavior or even the assessment process itself. Language barriers limit the use of these instruments with many individuals who come to the attention of agencies that provide assessment and treatment of child abuse and neglect.

Assessment of Child Sexual Abuse

Following a sexual abuse report, the first step in managing the case is assessment of the child. Typically, two types of assessments are conducted, the forensic assessment and the clinical assessment. The purpose of the forensic assessment is to determine whether the child experienced sexual abuse and if so, to determine specific characteristics of the incident(s) and the current safety of the child. Forensic assessments are conducted by law enforcement officers, child protection workers, therapists, or a combination of professionals from these disciplines. The purpose of the clinical assessment is to determine child symptoms as a result of the trauma, to determine the treatment needs of the child, to assess the impact on the abuse on the family, and to assess family resources that will aid the child in recovery. In some communities, the forensic assessment and clinical assessment are conducted jointly, generally depending on the availability of a multidisciplinary team.

An essential prerequisite to beginning treatment with sexual abuse victims is a thorough clinical assessment composed of clinical interviews and standardized measures. Clinical interviews are conducted with the child and with the parent or guardian.

CLINICAL CHILD INTERVIEW. The child interview may consist of a basic clinical interview, including a mental status examination (Hughes & Baker, 1990). In addition, characteristics of the trauma should be assessed. The interviewer must be sensitive to the child's readiness to talk about the abuse and to the child's developmental level. If the child avoids talking about the trauma, use of activities such as puppet play or drawing may enable him or her to do so (Pynoos & Eth, 1986). Otherwise, trauma-related information can be obtained from the parent or guardian or from the forensic assessment report.

For school-age children and adolescents, a basic clinical child interview will include questions related to school, family, and self. To enable the child to talk openly about the experiences, the parent may be asked to give the child permission to talk about the trauma.

In the school section of the interview, children may be asked questions relating to where they attend school, their favorite subjects, attendance in any special classes, whether they like school, whether they get in trouble at school and why, their grades, changes in school performance, supportive relationships with teachers, peer relations, and whether the child has experienced a change in enjoyment of peer activities. It is also important to determine if the child has told any peers or school personnel about the abuse and whether those personnel have responded in a supportive manner.

In the family section of the interview, children may describe who lives in their household and their relationships with each individual, their relationships with extended family and parents residing outside the household, the child's understanding of how the family members view the alleged offender and how they feel about the child having disclosed the abuse. If the alleged offender is a family member, it is important to determine whether that individual is still living in the home with the child or how often that individual visits the home. If the child has been removed from the home via *ex parte* order or placed with another family member, how the child has experienced this separation from family should be assessed.

In the assessment-of-self section of the interview, a mental status examination is usually conducted to rule out psychosis, suicidal ideation, and homicidal ideation. Children may also be asked how they feel most of the time and whether they are experiencing depressed mood, sleep difficulties, nightmares, changes in appetite, fears, somatic complaints, or anger. An assessment of coping skills should also be conducted.

It is essential to the assessment of self that the clinician present specific questions in order to obtain a clear history of the sexual abuse. If age-appropriate, and if the child is able to do so, the child may be asked to tell what the alleged offender did, when the event(s) occurred, his or her age at the time of the abuse, and who may have known about the abuse. Specifics of the sexual abuse that may be associated with posttraumatic stress disorder should be explored. These specifics include: whether the child believed he or she or a loved one would die or be seriously injured, the frequency and duration of the abuse, whether penetration occurred, and responses of significant others to the abuse (Lipovsky, 1991). Furthermore, the child may be asked about reexperiencing the trauma; changes in concentration or memory; smells, sounds, and tastes that are reminiscent of the abuse; what the alleged offender said about the abuse; whether the child was told not to tell; what the child was told would happen if he or she told about the abuse; and what the child believes will happen now that the abuse has been disclosed. Furthermore, attributions such as self-blame and the basis for that blame should be assessed.

Finally, inquiries regarding other traumatic experiences should be made. These experiences may include physical abuse; presence at a natural disaster, fire, or car accident; life-threatening illnesses; or being witness to community, school, parental, or sibling violence. Few structured interviews for assessing multiple traumas have been developed and empirically tested. However, several structured interviews have demonstrated clinical utility. The Brief Assessment of Traumatic Events (BATE; Lipovsky & Hanson, 1992a; Lipovsky & Hanson, 1992b; Lipovsky, Hanson, & Hand, 1993) was designed as a clinical tool to assess the occurrence of various traumatic events. These include enduring physical or sexual abuse and witnessing family violence. Although this interview has not been empirically validated, it has been used clinically with outpatient and inpatient populations. The National Survey of Adolescents (Saunders & Kilpatrick, 1993) was developed as part of a national project to assess the prevalence of various types of trauma that adolescents ages 12–17 experience. Structured interviews have been developed for specifically assessing PTSD in children. These have added to the field

because they have enabled systematic collection of diagnostic data, which can be collected by individuals with limited professional training (Finch & Daugherty, 1993). However, at this juncture, the reliability and the validity of these measures are unknown. A child version (Reich, 1991a) and an adult version (Reich, 1991b) of the Diagnostic Interview for Children and Adolescents (DICA-R) include supplemental questions or "modules" for diagnosing PTSD in children. Similarly, the Diagnostic Interview Schedule for Children (DISC) contains a module for diagnosing PTSD in children. Once the psychometric properties of these scales are known, they may assist clinical and research efforts by reducing informant variability.

CLINICAL PARENT OR GUARDIAN CLINICAL INTERVIEW. The parent or guardian interview consists of a basic parent interview modified to obtain information relating to the sexual abuse. First, the parent or guardian may provide information regarding the presenting problem, duration of the problem, antecedents to the abuse and the consequences the parent applies following the described behavior. Second, information can be obtained about the child's educational history, medical and mental health history, developmental history, and learning, visual, or hearing impairments that may influence the standardized assessment. Third, the parent may provide information regarding the family history, names of friends and extended family members whom the child may discuss in treatment, family mental health and substance abuse history, and perception of the child's relationships with family members.

Fourth, parents or guardians may disclose specific characteristics of the abuse, the current legal status of the case, and their perception of the impact of the abuse on the child, themselves, and the family. If the alleged offender is a family member, the parent should be asked about the family's perception of the offense and his or her feelings toward the child and the offender. If children are placed in foster care or other programs outside the home, interviews should be conducted with the foster parent, birth parent, child protection worker, and other adults who are familiar with the child.

Standardized Measures

Although there is no current agreement on a standard battery for evaluation of children in child abuse research or clinical practice, several measures have consistently emerged for assessing trauma-related symptoms. In general, sexually abused children report some distress. However, parents and teachers tend to rate sexually abused children as experiencing more distress than the children acknowledge on self-reports (Waterman & Lusk, 1993). Currently, no extant empirical evidence indicates that standardized measures can provide definitive answers on whether or not abuse occurred. There is no "set of symptoms" that differentiates sexually abused children from nonsexually abused children (Kendall-Tackett, Williams, & Finkelhor, 1993). The goal of using standardized measures in assessment of children who have experienced sexual abuse is to determine symptoms they are experiencing to guide the treatment.

Child Measures

REVISED CHILDREN'S MANIFEST ANXIETY SCALE (RCMAS). The RCMAS (Reynolds & Richmond, 1978) consists of 37 statements that reflect symptoms of anxiety (e.g., "I worry a lot of the time") to which the respondent answers "Yes" or "No." In addition to an overall anxiety score, three factors can be assessed: Physiological Anxiety, Worry and Oversensitivity, and Concentration Anxiety. A Lie scale is designed to assess a social desirability response bias. Raw scores can be converted to T-scores based on age and sex norms for the purpose of normative comparisons (Reynolds & Paget, 1981). Internal consistency and test-retest reliability coefficients greater than .80 have been reported in several studies (Finch & Rogers, 1984). Although individual children may elevate on the RCMAS, in comparing children

who were sexually abused by their fathers to nonabused siblings, Lipovsky, Saunders, and Murphy (1989) found no significant differences on the RCMAS.

THE STATE/TRAIT ANXIETY SCALE FOR CHILDREN. The STAIC (Spielberger, 1973) consists of two 20-item scales, one assessing situationally specific anxiety (A-State) and the other assessing anxiety as a relatively stable characteristic of the individual (A-Trait). This scale has been widely used and has demonstrated strong internal consistency and validity (Finch, Montgomery, & Deardorff, 1974). Studies assessing sexually abused girls on the STAIC have yielded mixed results. Cohen and Mannarino (1988) found that sexually abused girls did not differ significantly from a nonclinical sample on the STAIC. In a subsequent study, Mannarino, Cohen, and Gregor (1989) found that sexually abused girls scored significantly higher on state anxiety than a clinical and nonclinical sample. At 6- and 12-month follow-up there were no significant differences between the groups (Mannarino, Cohen, Smith, & Moore-Motily, 1991).

CHILDREN'S DEPRESSION INVENTORY (CDI). This widely used 27-item measure assesses affective, cognitive, and behavioral symptoms of depression in children ages 7 to 17 (Kovacs, 1983). Raw scores can be converted to T-scores based on age and grade level norms (Finch, Saylor, & Edwards, 1985), and good reliability has been demonstrated (Smucker, Craighead, Craighead, & Green, 1986). Studies assessing sexual abuse victims have found higher ratings of depression among incest victims compared to their nonabused siblings (Lipovsky, Saunders, and Murphy, 1989) and no significant differences between sexually abused girls and a nonclinical sample (Cohen & Mannarino, 1988; Mannarino, Cohen, & Gregor, 1989).

TRAUMA SYMPTOM CHECKLIST—CHILDREN'S FORM (TSCC). The TSCC (Briere, 1989) is a 54-item scale designed to assess the sequelae of a variety of childhood traumas, including child abuse. The TSCC consists of six subscales, each of which measures a different hypothesized aspect of trauma-related psychopathology: Posttraumatic Stress, Anxiety, Depression,

Dissociation, Anger, and Sexual Concerns. The six subscales have been demonstrated to show good internal consistency (all α's > .83 except Sexual Concerns, α = .63; Lanktree, Briere, & Hernandez, 1991). Also, among a sample of sexually abused children, moderate correlations between the TSCC and both parent and child-report measures of known reliability and validity, the Child Behavior Checklist and the Children's Depression Inventory, support the concurrent validity of the scale (Lanktree et al., 1991).

To date, two published studies have been conducted using the TSCC to examine symptomatology of sexually abused children. In the initial study, Elliott and Briere (1994) found that children who recanted abuse allegations reported more anger and depression than children who had never disclosed, even though external evidence of abuse existed. Further, children who disclosed sexual abuse reported high levels of symptoms. Children who had not disclosed, despite external evidence of abuse, acknowledged low levels of distress, and nonabused children showed intermediate levels of symptoms. In the second study, Singer, Anglin, Song, and Lunghofer (1995) examined the relationship between exposure to violence or other trauma and symptoms in children. Having been a victim of sexual abuse was found to relate to the total TSCC score, as well as to scores on the Anxiety, Dissociation, Stress, and Depression subscales.

THE REACTION INDEX. The RI (Frederick, 1985) is a 20-item scale based on DSM-III-R (APA, 1987) criteria for PTSD. The scale can be administered in an interview or self-report format. Responses range from 0 to 4 ("None of the time," Little of the time," "Some of the time," "Much of the time"). A total score is obtained by summing the responses. The RI has good internal consistency (.85; Lonigan, Shannon, Finch, Daugherty, & Taylor, 1991), interrater reliability (.95; Applebaum & Burns, 1991), and concurrent validity with known cases of PTSD (.91; Frederick, 1985).

THE CHILDREN'S IMPACT OF TRAUMATIC EVENTS SCALE. The CITES (Wolfe, Gentile, & Wolfe, 1989) relates specifically to sexual abuse and includes a scale that assesses symptoms related to PTSD (i.e., intrusive thoughts). A high score on this scale has not been shown to confirm a PTSD diagnosis (Lipovsky, 1991).

Parent Measures

THE CHILD BEHAVIOR CHECKLIST—PARENT FORM (CBCL). The CBCL consists of 20 social competence and 113 behavior problem items applicable to children ages 4 to 16. Activity Involvement, Social Interaction, School Success, and broad-band Social Competence scores are derived from the social competence items. The behavior problem items form eight or nine factor-analyzed narrow-band problem scales, depending on gender and age. Three broad-band behavior problem scales, Internalizing, Externalizing, and Total Behavior Problems, are derived from the narrow-band scales. All three summary behavior problem scales, as well as the broad-band Social Competence score, can be compared across sexes and ages (Kazdin, Siegel, & Bass, 1992). The CBCL is one of the most widely used measures of child behavioral problems, and extensive normative and validity information is available (Achenbach & Edelbrock, 1983). The CBCL has been widely used in studies of sexually abused children. In general, parents tended to rate their sexually abused children as more symptomatic than nonabused children, but less than clinical comparison groups. These findings have been shown to maintain across 6- and 12-month follows-up (Mannarino, Cohen, Smith, & Moore-Motily, 1991).

THE PEDIATRIC EMOTIONAL DISTRESS SCALE (PEDS). The PEDS (Saylor, Swensen, Stokes, Wertlieb, & Casto, 1994; Swenson, Saylor, Stokes, Ralston, Smith, Hansen, & Saunders, 1994) is a parent rating scale consisting of 25 items that address theoretically derived, general behavior problems and trauma-related symptoms of young children. Good overall internal consistency has been obtained (α = .85), and three reliable factors have been identified: Anxious/Withdrawn, Acting Out, and Fearful

(Saylor et al., 1994). The PEDS shows good concurrent validity with the Eyberg Child Behavior Inventory (Eyberg & Ross, 1978) and the Reaction Index (Frederick, 1985). The ability of PEDS scores to distinguish traumatized from nontraumatized children supports its construct validity (Swenson et al., 1994). Stokes (1994) found that sexually abused children were rated as more symptomatic than were children who had experienced a hurricane and a nontrauma sample.

Although empirical studies comparing groups of sexually abused children to nonabused children on individual standardized measures have yielded mixed results regarding symptomatology, ample literature indicates that many of these children are likely to experience an emotional impact from the trauma (for a review see Kendall-Tackett, Williams, & Finkelhor, 1993). Standardized assessment is warranted on an individual level to determine the treatment needs of the child.

Developing an Assessment-Based Treatment Plan

Upon completion of the assessment, the results should be reported to the child and the parent. Then, an individual treatment plan should be written and agreed upon by the child, parent, and therapist. The goals of the treatment plan are written in behavioral and measurable terms and include the expected frequency of sessions to meet these goals. After developing the treatment plan, the therapist should explain what the child and the parent or guardian can expect to occur in treatment. The therapist may predict feelings of wishing to avoid attending future therapy appointments, normalize these feelings, and encourage the parent or guardian and child to attend the session despite these feelings.

TREATMENT
Biological Models

The search for new sources of predictors of child abuse has begun to focus on physiological states and reactivity in abused and abusive populations. Although this is relatively new area of study, it is fraught with subject selection and methodological inadequacies that often make interpretation of results difficult and cross-study comparisons almost impossible. A review of biological and genetic contributions to abuse has been published by Widom (1989). Similarly, McCanne and Milner (1991) tried to compare six published studies on physiological reactivity, and DeAngelis (1995), McNally (1991), and van de Kolk, Bessel, and Fisler (1994) provide insights into hyperarousal and its effects on the developmental process.

Physiological studies can be categorized roughly into four categories: (1) physiological responses to infant stimuli (usually crying) or (2) to stressful child behavior; (3) physiological arousal and self-regulation problems in abused children; and, (4) physiological arousal disorders such as PTSD and mental and physiological diseases in adults abused as children.

Physiological reactions to infant crying has received the most empirical attention of these four areas of investigation. Generally, this line of research finds that abusive parents are in a heightened state of arousal and tend to experience greater physiological (e.g., HR, GSR) reactivity than matched nonabusive parents (Boukydis & Burgess, 1982; Casanova, Domanic, McCanne, & Milner, 1994; Fodi & Lamb, 1980; Fodi & Senchak, 1990; Lester & Zeskind, 1982; Zeskind, 1987, 1983; and Zeskind & Lester, 1981). The use of stress management techniques seems to mediate this reactivity (Tyson & Sobschak, 1994). The hyperarousal hypothesis (Knutson, 1978) also is used as a predictor of poor responsiveness to stressful child behavior, usually in the form of noncompliance or tantrumming. The interested reader might consult Bauer and Twentyman (1985), Casanova, Domanic, McCanne, & Milner (1992), Friedrich, Tyler, & Clark (1985), and Wolfe, Fairbanks, Kelly, and Bradlyn (1983). Generally, the results support this hypothesis but are difficult to combine into metaanalyses and to interpret. In many cases, analog populations are used that are younger and less experienced than real abused adult populations, creating considerable variability in results.

The third and fourth areas are the newest and seem to offer great promise in the prevention and early identification areas. Abused children often develop self-regulation problems (area 3), as well as mental and physical diseases (area 4). McNally (1991), van de Kolk, Bessel, and Fisler (1994), and Beeghley and Cicchetti (1994) have empirically identified self-regulation problems in developing infants, toddlers, and children that lead to faulty coping behaviors, impulse control problems, and interpersonal stress and distress. Milner, Robertson, and Rogers (1990) suggest the use of their Childhood History Questionnaire (CHQ) to identify abused adults for study. And there is clearly emerging information that such abused adults suffer a range of personal travail, including PTSD and homelessness (Browne, 1993), health and pregnancy problems (Jacobs, 1992), and respondent bodily reactions such as asthma-like symptoms (When the Body Remembers, 1994), just to mention a few of what will undoubtedly be many personal struggles.

Psychological Models

Empirically driven treatment in CAN has largely come from behavioral and cognitive/behavioral perspectives. The earliest treatment literature focused on either behavior management training or stress reduction and anger management for parents. These strategies were derived from the logical assumption that CAN either was a function of poor parenting strategies (thus the need for parent training) or occurred because of the parent's inability to handle stress or anger.

One of the first case reports to describe parent training involved teaching parents involved in CAN to praise their children contingent upon appropriate behavior (Gilbert, 1976). This kind of parent training, with an exclusive focus on consequences for behavior, was the mode during the 1970s.

A more comprehensive parent training program was described by Wolfe and Sandler (1981). They gave parents reading assignments, modeled behavior management skills to the parents, required the parents to role play the skills, and provided feedback based on direct observation data; they also used contingency contracts with parents to help ensure parental compliance with the treatment regimens.

Using stress reduction and a number of other strategies, Wolfe, Edwards, Manion, and Koverola (1988) produced improvements in parenting skills along with improved ratings of their children's behavior by caseworkers. Wolfe et al. (1988) utilized modeling, instructions, therapist and video feedback, and in vivo desensitization to accomplish these improvements with young mothers.

Using a combination of stress reduction, communication training, and cognitive restructuring, Azar (1984) compared the results achieved by these strategies to those of insight-oriented treatment and to a control group. Families who participated in the combination of stress reduction and cognitive/behavioral techniques showed the most improvements. Azar and Wolfe (1989) have suggested that CAN parents must also be taught realistic expectations about child development.

An ecobehavioral model of treatment has been espoused by Lutzker (1992). He has suggested that the multifaceted nature of CAN requires multifaceted assessment and treatment. Project 12-Ways (Lutzker, 1984) and Project SafeCare (Lutzker, 1994) represent this model. Project 12-Ways has demonstrated the success of teaching a number of skills to families involved in CAN. These skills have included parent training (Dachman, Halasz, Bickett, & Lutzker, 1984), stress reduction (Campbell, O'Brien, Bickett, & Lutzker, 1983), self-control training for parents (Lutzker, 1984), assertiveness training (Lutzker, 1984), reciprocity counseling (Campbell et al., 1983), job finding, money management, nutrition training (Sarber, Halasz, Messmer, Bickett, & Lutzker, 1983), home safety (Barone, Greene, & Lutzker, 1986), home cleanliness (Watson-Perczel, Lutzker, Greene, & McGimpsey, 1988), and behavioral pediatrics (Kiesel, Lutzker, & Campbell, 1989). Other models tested include prevention programs through infant stimulation (Lutzker, Lutzker, Braunling-McMorrow, & Eddleman, 1987) and teaching infant health care skills to young mothers (Delgado & Lutzker, 1988).

Wolfe and Wekerle (1993) have categorized treatment in three ways: child focused, parent focused, and comprehensive. As has been suggested here, child-focused treatment has been minimal, but not nonexistent. For example, Culp, Heide, and Richardson (1987) showed that children who participated in a therapeutic day treatment program and who received individual and group treatment showed improvements in a number of domains as compared to a group of children who did not participate in therapeutic day care. Similarly, Culp, Little, Letts, and Lawrence (1991) found that another therapeutic day program had benefits on a number of developmental variables for children who had been abused.

Fantuzzo and his colleagues have repeatedly shown that a number of important social variables can be positively affected when abused or neglected children are exposed to a day program that included adult-mediated play sessions (Davis & Fantuzzo, 1989; Fantuzzo, Stovall, Schachtel, Goins, & Hall, 1987). Although this kind of research shows promising results, the relationship between therapeutic day programs for children who have been abused and abuse itself has not been shown.

As has been suggested here, parent-focused programs represent the mode treatment in CAN. Cognitive-behavioral interventions have attempted to improve parenting skills, change parental awareness, and change parent coping skills. For example, a number of studies have used relaxation, self-management, cognitive restructuring, and problem-solving skills to try to prevent CAN (Denicola & Sandler, 1980; Egan, 1983; Nomellini & Katz, 1983; Whiteman, Fanshel, & Grundy, 1987).

Comprehensive or multifaceted services such as the ecobehavioral model make up the third category of state-of-the-art intervention in CAN. Other examples are family-centered, home-based intervention services (Amundson, 1989) that provide a number of services. While these programs appear to be effective, they most often lack direct-observation data that reflect actual parent or child behavior change, and they lack the integrity of the independent variable. That is, there are few or no descriptions of performance criteria of those who implement the services.

It seems clear from the treatment literature that there are a number of procedures that seem to produce reliable behavior change in CAN families. Behavioral approaches involve the direct observation and treatment of behaviors that are related to CAN. Child behaviors that are observed usually involve positive behaviors such as instruction following, positive affect, and positive verbalizations. Negative behaviors involve aggression, negative verbalalizations, and failure to follow instructions. Parent behaviors usually involve the use and kinds of instructions (commands), affect, reinforcement, and planning activities.

Parent training involves teaching parents how to give instructions, how to set the occasion for appropriate child behavior, how to arrange activities, how to demonstrate affect, how to state rules, and how to provide consequences.

Cognitive strategies have utilized teaching problem-solving skills, changing expectations about child behavior, and changing the way that parents thinks about their children.

To summarize treatment in CAN, the focus has primarily been on the parent, but there have been a number of attempts to address the child and to examine the social or ecological variables associated with CAN and to offer direct services to try to alleviate some of the precipitating problems. The lack of involvement of male perpetrators in these programs causes necessary limitations in interpreting their overall efficacy. Further, lifestyle issues have not been clearly addressed, even with the ecobehavioral and ecological approaches. Finally, very little is known about cultural or ethnic differences and how treatment may have to be adjusted because of these variables.

Treatment of Child Sexual Abuse

When a child has been sexually abused, the incident(s) have likely had an impact on the entire family, in particular when the offender is a parent. Therefore, the siblings, nonoffending parent, offender, and close extended family members should also participate in treatment. Programs for treating nonoffending parents (Mara & Winton, 1990) and reunification of families (Meinig & Bonner, 1990) are described in the sexual abuse literature. The focus here is on direct, trauma-focused treatment of the child, recognizing the importance of ecological factors.

PRECONDITIONS TO TRAUMA-FOCUSED TREATMENT. Several preconditions should be met before initiating trauma-focused treatment. These include: (1) safety; (2) support; (3) crisis stabilization; and, (4) disclosure. Prior to beginning trauma-focused treatment, the therapist should determine if the child is in a safe environment. If the child is living with the alleged perpetrator, having unsupervised visits with the alleged perpetrator, or having phone contact that is harassing or otherwise inappropriate, then these issues should be resolved before proceeding with trauma-focused treatment (Lipovsky & Elliott, 1993). The therapist may work closely with Child Protective Services and Family Court to stop the child's contacts with the alleged perpetrator until it is safe, physically and psychologically, for the child to have these contacts.

Second, parental support has been shown to mediate the impact of sexual abuse on children (Everson, Hunter, Runyon, Edelsohn, & Coulter, 1989). The therapist should determine if there is a supportive adult in the child's life before beginning trauma-focused treatment. If the child's parent or guardian is not supportive and/or does not believe the child's report about the abuse, then the nonsupport should be addressed and clarified before proceeding with trauma-focused treatment with the child.

Third, during the course of the mental status examination, if the child indicates suicidal or homicidal intent or displays psychosis, then crisis stabilization is the immediate goal of treatment. Once the child is stabilized, then trauma focused treatment can proceed.

Fourth, trauma-focused treatment can be conducted only when the therapist has a clear understanding of whether the child experienced sexual abuse, the specific traumatic events, and the context in which those events occurred. If the child's experience is unclear, then the goal of treatment is to clarify what happened to the child before proceeding.

Treatment issues include:

a. *Confidentiality versus secrecy.* In the initial session the therapist reviews the purpose of treatment in developmentally appropriate language, reviews the treatment plan, and discusses confidentiality issues. It is often helpful to sexually abused children to make the distinction between confidentiality and secrecy so that they understand that the content of therapy is not secret, as the sexual abuse may have been. Specifically, confidentiality can be described as "nothing you say in this room will be told to anyone by me except if you are feeling like hurting yourself, hurting someone else or if you tell me about an older person hurting or touching you on your private parts." It should be explained that the child is free to tell whomever about the content of the therapy session. If therapy were a secret, then neither the child nor therapist could tell anyone what happened in the sessions (Hanson & Swenson, 1995). When describing the limits of confidentiality, children should be told that if the abuse has already been reported, it will not be reported again. Therefore, the child will not go through the interviews or medical exam again.

b. *Developmental issues.* Essential to maintaining the child's interest in the therapy session and to helping children communicate is the use of developmentally appropriate techniques.

c. *Loyalty conflicts.* Children who have been sexually abused by a family member may experience confusion regarding their feelings about the perpetrator. The therapist may assist the child by avoiding negative statements about the perpetrator and referring instead to the perpetrator as someone who broke the law or the rules about touching.

d. *Respecting/understanding cultural issues.* To aid in forming a working relationship with children and their families, developing cultural competence or the ability to share the worldview of the family and adapting clinical practice to respect that view is essential (Abney & Gunn, 1993). By becoming knowledgeable about the beliefs of the family and their culture, the therapist may come to understand the important distinction between characteristics of the family that are culturally congruent and those that are dysfunctional (Heras, 1992).

e. *The treatment environment.* To maximize the child's participation in treatment, the therapy environment should be safe, have some predictability, and have limits and rules. Providing family or conjoint treatment that includes the victim and a nonacknowledging, nontreated offender is contraindicated (Association for the Treatment of Sexual Abusers, 1993).

To increase predictability, therapy sessions may be conducted on the same day and at the same time of day each week. Also, children can be given the opportunity to make choices in treatment such as the amount of time to spend on recapitulation of the abuse, the method used to discuss the abuse (i.e., puppets, drawings, discussion), and whether to be accompanied to the session by a supportive adult.

Setting limits for the child during treatment is thought to be helpful in management of disruptive behavior and management of the child's anxiety. To aid in teaching the child appropriate touching rules and boundaries, the therapist should be cautious in touching or hugging the child without the child's permission. Also, children who display sexually reactive behavior may make attempts to touch the therapist inappropriately. This behavior can be dealt with by calmly stopping the child and making the rules for touching known.

A Theoretical Model for Treatment of Child Sexual Abuse

A classical conditioning model has been proposed for explaining fear and anxiety responses among adult sexual assault victims. Specifically, when previously neutral stimuli are paired with fear and anxiety, these stimuli become signals for danger and begin to elicit fear and anxiety, even in safe situations (Kilpatrick, Veronen, & Best, 1985). This model has been extended to explain children's fear and anxiety responses (Berliner & Wheeler, 1987). For example, if a neutral stimulus such as the smell of a certain cologne or perfume is paired with a sexual assault, later that smell may elicit fear and anxiety. The fear and anxiety response is manifested in three ways: physically, cognitively, and behaviorally (Lang, 1979). Treatment should include an explanation of this model and discovery of previously neutral cues that signal danger. If the model is explained in concrete, developmentally appropriate terms, including examples, school-age children (age eight and above) can generally exhibit comprehension (Hanson & Swenson, 1995). Treatment goals address the three channels through which anxiety and fear are manifested (Ribbe, Lipovsky, & Freedy, 1995).

Trauma-Focused Treatment in Sexual Abuse Cases

The literature on treatment of sexually abused children consists mainly of case studies (Kiser, Pugh, McColgan, Pruitt, & Edwards, 1991; Lindahl, 1988) and clinical descriptions of treatment approaches (Berliner & Wheeler, 1987; Pescosolido, 1993; Sirles, Walsma, Lytle-Barnaby, & Lander, 1988).

The first empirical evaluation of a cognitive-behavioral approach for treating PTSD in sexually abused children was conducted by Deblinger, McLeer, and Henry (1990). Nineteen 3–16-year-olds participated in 12 individual structured treatment sessions consisting of gradual exposure, modeling, education, coping, and prevention skills training. Nonoffending parents participated in sessions in which they were taught skills for dealing with their children's behavioral difficulties. Significant reductions were shown in the children's self-reported depression and state anxiety and trait anxiety scores and in parent reports of internalizing and externalizing behaviors. Children who had experienced oral sexual assault or penile penetration of the vagina or anus showed greater improvements on parent reports of internalizing and externalizing behaviors than did children who experienced touching, fondling with clothes on, or sexualized kissing.

Several studies that address the efficacy of group treatment have been conducted (De Luca, Boyes, Furer, Grayston, & Hiebert-Murphy, 1992; De Luca, Hazen, & Cutler, 1993). There were increases in self-esteem and decreases in self-report of anxiety and parent report of internalizing and externalizing behaviors. A similar group administered to preadolescent males resulted in decreases in depression and anxiety (Hack, Osachuk, & Deluca, 1994). In an evaluation of parallel groups for young children and their caregivers, Hall-Marley and Damon (1993) reported reductions in parent ratings of aggression and hyperactive behavior.

Components of Treatment

The limited empirical evidence of treatment efficacy and the broad clinical descriptions of treatment programs for sexually abused children indicate that several components of treatment are important to reducing trauma-related symptoms. These components include psychoeducation, anxiety management, graduated exposure, cognitive work, and sexual abuse education/prevention. A direct focus on the trauma the child experienced is the cornerstone of treatment (Berliner, 1991). However, directly addressing the sexual abuse may be difficult for the child, requiring the therapist to be sensitive to this difficulty and together with the child to creatively develop a means for dealing with the trauma.

PSYCHOEDUCATION. Psychoeducation involves providing a definition for all types of sexual abuse (e.g., touching, penetration, oral, exposure to pornography), discussing the child's affect and cognitions related to the abuse experiences, normalizing feelings, and providing an explanation of trauma-related symptoms as described in the theoretical model section. The major function of psychoeducation is to normalize feelings, rather than to normalize the experience. Children may learn that they are exhibiting "normal responses to an abnormal situation."

ANXIETY MANAGEMENT. A number of techniques may be taught to assist children in managing anxiety. This has included controlled breathing, relaxation, and guided imagery (Berliner & Wheeler, 1987). In fact, these cognitive-behavioral techniques have been empirically validated with sexually abused children (Deblinger et al., 1990) and with children who have anxiety disorders (Kendall, 1994). Several resources are available for teaching deep muscle relaxation to children (Ollendick & Cerny, 1981). In addition, simplified forms of deep muscle relaxation have been described for use with young children. For example, Deblinger (1995) asks children to act as if they are a tin soldier and then a wet noodle.

GRADUATED EXPOSURE. The purpose of graduated exposure is to break the link between anxiety and reminders of the abuse that did not previously elicit anxiety. First, a rationale for exposure should be presented to the child. The child's response is followed by a therapist's statement that the child will find out that nothing bad happens and will feel better. Children are then encouraged to do the same in therapy. That is, they are encouraged to "face their fears" so that they will start to feel less upset (Deblinger, 1992). Following a rationale, directed-exposure sessions involving recapitulation of the abuse are conducted. Stimuli that elicit lower levels of anxiety, such as questions like, "Where were you when the abuse occurred?" are presented first. The child is then instructed to recapitulate the abuse, noting any sights, sounds, or smells that occurred during the event. Children are encouraged to use anxiety management techniques when needed during exposures sessions. To help the child feel some control, choices of the exposure method can be offered (e.g., puppets, direct report). The child should not be forced to talk about difficult experiences but should be encouraged and presented with developmentally appropriate techniques that may assist. Finally, relaxation techniques that elicit calmness should be used to end the session.

COGNITIVE APPROACHES. Cognitive approaches focus on dealing with the child's subjective experience of the abuse and changing faulty attributions that may have been developed as a result of the abuse. For example, children often view something that they said, did, or wore as responsible for the abuse, rather than the perpetrator's behavior. Cognitive restructuring, guided self-dialogue, and thought stopping are used to correct thinking errors and reduce anxiety (Deblinger, McLeer, & Henry, 1990).

SEXUAL ABUSE EDUCATION/PREVENTION. The role of sexual abuse education and prevention in treatment is to correct inappropriate sexual information the child may have received from the perpetrator, to correct the child's own misperceptions regarding his or her body functioning, and to help ensure the child's safety from future abuse. Issues addressed include: (1) the right to say no; (2) facts on AIDS and sexually transmitted diseases; (3) facts on functions of sexual body organs and pregnancy; (4) how to recognize danger cues that may indicate the potential for re-abuse; (5) development of a safety plan; and (6) how to deal with sexualized feelings and behaviors (Deblinger, McLeer, & Henry, 1990). Each of these issues should be confronted using developmentally appropriate materials and with approval from the nonoffending parent.

CONSIDERING MULTIPLE SYSTEMS IN TREATMENT. In addition to trauma-focused treatment of the child, efforts should be made to assist the child with adjustment in school and activities outside school, with preparation for involvement in court, and with strengthening immediate family, extended family, and community relations. An ecological focus involves strong case management, contacts with teachers, contacts with all family members, and close work with attorneys, child protective services, and judges to work collaboratively in the best interest of the child.

SOCIAL/INTERPERSONAL. Family systems approaches have been common in the treatment of CAN. Although popular in the treatment of CAN, these approaches have had little to no empirical evaluation (NRC, 1993). The same is true for group therapy and paraprofessional approaches such as Parents Anonymous. Enriching the environment through home-based services and family preservation have shown considerable promise (Daro, 1988; NRC, 1993). The consensus among researchers is that evaluations of these programs, in general, have had too few outcome measures.

COMMENTARY

CAN is a serious societal problem. While affecting a child's physical and emotional well-being, it cannot be treated in a manner similar to singular disorders of children such as a phobia or anxiety disorder. The treatment of CAN necessarily involves the family and often involves other aspects of the child's social ecology.

While there have been individual treatment programs reported in the literature, the majority of reports come from research projects, usually affiliated with major university programs. These approaches in recent years have typically been multifaceted and have involved directive treatments such as parent training, stress reduction, the use of cognitive/behavioral techniques, and the active rearrangement of the families' social ecologies. These programs often involve treatment of the child only indirectly through the parent.

There have been a few reports of the direct treatment of children for the sequelae associated with CAN. Clearly, a truly multifaceted approach will include more of these treatments and will include better evaluations of them. Similarly, more research can be expected on the long-term effects of CAN on children and on the physiological effects on children and the biological bases of the behavior of CAN parents. As with all psychotherapeutic approaches at the end of the twentieth century and the beginning of the next, short-term, cost-effective programs that are demonstrably effective will survive funding cuts. Also, we can expect to see research on treatment programs that incorporate other media for training such as video, CD-ROM, and other media-interactive techniques. Finally, technological and statistical innovations may allow assessment to more closely match families to the "best-fit" services.

When it is considered that the professional history of CAN dates back only to 1962, it might be suggested that there has been rather remarkable progress in theory, treatment, and research. More progress, however, is clearly necessary with this overwhelming, serious problem.

ACKNOWLEDGMENT

Preparation of this manuscript was supported in part by a grant from the California Wellness Foundation. We are grateful for the help of Randi Sherman and Erica Kane in preparing this manuscript.

REFERENCES

Abidin, R. R. (1990). *Parenting Stress Index* (2nd ed.) Charlottesville: Pediatric Psychology Press.

Abney, V. D., & Gunn, K. (1993). A rationale for cultural competency. *APSAC Advisor*, 6 (3), 19–22.

Achenbach, T. M., & Edelbrock, C. S. (1983). *Manual for the Child Behavior Checklist and Revised Child Behavior Profile*. Burlington, VT: Thomas M. Achenbach.

Altieri, M. F. (1990). Child abuse: When to be suspicious and what to do then. *Postgraduate Medicine*, 87, 161–162.

American Psychiatric Association. (1987). *Diagnostic and statistical manual of mental disorders* (3rd ed., rev.). Washington, DC: Author.

*Ammerman, R. T. (1990). Etiological models of child maltreatment: A behavioral perspective. *Behavior Modification*, 14, 230–252.

*Ammerman, R. T., Cassisi, J. E., Hersen, M., & Van Hasselt, V. B. (1986). Consequences of physical abuse and neglect in children. *Clinical Psychology Review*, 6, 291–310.

Amundson, M. J. (1989). Family crisis care: A home-based intervention program for child abuse. *Issues in Mental Health Nursing*, 10, 285–296.

Applebaum, D. R., & Burns, G. L. (1991). Unexpected childhood death: Posttraumatic stress disorder in surviving siblings and parents. *Journal of Clinical Child Psychology*, 20, 114–120.

Association for the Treatment of Sexual Abusers (ATSA). (1993). *The ATSA practitioner's handbook*. Lake Oswego, OR: Author.

Azar, S. T. (1984). An evaluation of the effectiveness of cognitive-behavioral versus insight-oriented mothers groups with child maltreaters. Unpublished doctoral dissertation, University of Rochester.

Azar, S. T., Robinson, D. R., Hekimian, E., & Twentyman, C. T. (1984). Unrealistic expectations and problem-solving ability in maltreating and comparison mothers. *Journal of Consulting and Clinical Psychology*, 52, 687–691.

Azar, S. T., & Rohrbeck, C. A. (1986). Child abuse and unrealistic expectations: Further validation of the Parent Opinion Questionnaire. *Journal of Consulting and Clinical Psychology*, 54, 867–868.

*Azar, S. T., & Wolfe, D. A. (1989). Child abuse and neglect. In E. J. Mash & R. A. Barkeley (Eds.), *Treatment of childhood disorders* (pp. 451–493). New York: Guilford Press.

Barone, V. J., Greene, B. F., & Lutzker, J. R. (1986). Home safety with families being treated for child abuse and neglect. *Behavior Modification*, 10, 94–114.

Bauer, W. D., & Twentyman, C. T. (1985). Abusing, neglectful and comparison mothers' responses to child-related and non-child-related stressors. *Journal of Consulting and Clinical Psychology*, 53, 335–343.

Bayley, N. (1969). *Manual for the Bayley Scales of Infant Development*. New York: Psychological Corp.

Beeghly, M., & Cicchetti, D. (1994). Child maltreatment, attachment, and the self system: Emergence of an internal state lexicon in toddlers at high social risk. *Development and Psychopathology*, 6, 5–30.

Beitchman, J. H., Zucker, K. J., Hood, J. E., daCosta, G. A., Akman, D., & Cassavia, E. (1992). A review of the long-term effects of child sexual abuse. *Child Abuse & Neglect*, 16, 101–118.

*Belsky, J. (1980). Child maltreatment: An ecological integration. *American Psychologist*, 35, 320–335.

*Belsky, J. (1993). Etiology of child maltreatment: An ecological integration. *Psychological Bulletin*, 114, 413–431.

*Berliner, L. (1991). Clinical work with sexually abused children. In C. R. Hollin & K. Howells (Eds.), *Clinical approaches to sex offenders and their victims*. New York: Wiley.

Berliner, L., & Wheeler, J. R. (1987). Treating the

effects of sexual abuse on children. *Journal of Interpersonal Violence, 2* (4), 415–434.

Boukydis, C. F. Z., & Burgess, R. L. (1982). Adult physiological response to infant cries: Effects of temperament of infant, parent staus and gender. *Child Development, 53,* 1291–1298.

Briere, J. (1989). *Trauma Symptom Checklist for Children.* Odessa, FL: Psychological Assessment Resources.

Browne, A. (1993). Family violence and homelessness: The relevance of trauma histories in the lives of homeless women. *American Journal of Orthopsychiatry, 63,* 370–384.

Butcher, J. N., Dahlstrom, W. G., Graham, J. R., Tellegen, A., & Kaemmer, B. (1989). *Minnesota Multiphasic Personality Inventory-2 (MMPI-2): Manual for administration and scoring.* Minneapolis: University of Minnesota Press.

Campbell, R. V., O'Brien, S., Bickett, A., & Lutzker, J. R. (1983). In-home parent-training, treatment of migraine headaches, and marital counseling as an ecobehavioral approach to prevent child abuse. *Journal of Behavior Therapy and Experimental Psychiatry, 14,* 147–154. Indexed in the *Inventory of marriage and family literature,* Vol. X, Family Resource Center, 1984.

Casanova, G. M., Domanic, J., McCanne, T. R., & Milner, J. S. (1992). Physiological responses to non-child-related stressors in mothers at risk for child abuse. *Child Abuse and Neglect, 16,* 31–44.

Casanova, G. M., Domanic, J., McCanne, T. R., & Milner, J. S. (1994). Physiological responses to child stimuli in mothers with and without a childhood history of physical abuse. *Child Abuse and Neglect, 18,* 995–1004.

Cavaiola, A. A., & Schiff, M. (1988). Behavioral sequelae of physical and/or sexual abuse in adolescents. *Child Abuse and Neglect, 12,* 181–188.

Cicchetti, D., & Carlson, V. (Eds.). (1989). *Child maltreatment: Theory and research on the causes and consequences of child abuse and neglect.* New York: Cambridge University Press.

Cohen, J. A., & Mannarino, A. P. (1988). Psychological symptoms in sexually abused girls. *Child Abuse and Neglect, 12,* 571–577.

Cohen, S., Mermelstein, R., Kamarck, T., & Hoberman, H. M. (1985). Measuring the functional components of social support. In I. G. Sarason & B. R. Sarason (Eds.), *Social support: Theory, research, and applications* (pp. 73–94). The Hague: Martinus Nijhoff.

Conners, K. C. (1990). *Conners Rating Scales Manual.* North Tonawanda, NY: Multi-Health Systems.

Crimmins, D. B., Bradlyn, J. S., St. Lawrence, J. S., & Kelly, J. A. (1984). A training technique for improving the parent-child skills of an abusive-neglectful mother. *Child Abuse and Neglect, 8,* 533–539.

Crozier, J., & Katz, R. C. (1979). Social learning treatment of child abuse. *Journal of Behavior Therapy and Experimental Psychiatry, 10,* 213–220.

Culp, R. E., Heide, J., & Richardson, M. T. (1987). Maltreated children's developmental scores: Treatment versus nontreatment. *Child Abuse and Neglect, 11,* 29–34.

Culp, R. E., Little, V., Letts, D., & Lawrence, H. (1991). Maltreated children's self-concept: Effects of a comprehensive treatment program. *American Journal of Orthopsychiatry, 61,* 114–121.

Dachman, R. S., Halasz, M. M., Bickett, A. D., & Lutzker, J. R. (1984). A home-based ecobehavioral parent-training and generalization package with a neglectful mother. *Education and Treatment of Children, 7,* 183–202.

*Daro, D. (1988). *Confronting child abuse: Research for effective program design.* New York: Free Press.

Davis, S., & Fantuzzo, J. W. (1989). The effects of peer social initiations on the social behavior of withdrawn and aggressive maltreated preschool children. *Journal of Family Violence, 3,* 227–247.

DeAngelis, T. (1995). New threat associated with child abuse. *Monitor: The American Psychological Association, 26* (4), 1–2.

Deblinger, E. (1992). Child sexual abuse. In A. Freeman & F. M. Dattilio (Eds.), *Comprehensive casebook of cognitive therapy* (pp. 159–167). New York: Plenum.

*Deblinger, E. (1995, January). *Cognitive behavioral interventions for treating school-age sexually abused children.* Paper presented at the San Diego Conference for Responding to Child Maltreatment, San Diego, CA.

Deblinger, E., McLeer, S. V., & Henry, D. (1990). Cognitive behavioral treatment for sexually abused children suffering posttraumatic stress: Preliminary findings. *Journal of the American Academy of Child and Adolescent Psychiatry, 29* (5), 747–752.

Delgado, L. E., & Lutzker, J. R. (1988). Training young parents to identify and report their children's illnesses. *Journal of Applied Behavior Analysis, 21,* 311–319.

Deluca, R. V., Boyes, D. A., Furer, P., Grayston, A. D., & Hiebert-Murphy, D. (1992). Group treatment for child sexual abuse. *Canadian Psychology, 33* (2), 168–176.

DeLuca, R. V., Hazen, A., & Cutler, J. (1993). Evaluation of a group counseling program for preadolescent female victims of incest. *Elementary School Guidance and Counseling, 28* (2), 104–114.

Denicola, J., & Sandler, J. (1980). Training abusive parents in child management and self-control skills. *Behavior Therapy, 11,* 263–270.

Derogatis, L. R. (1983). *SCL-90-R: Administration, scoring, and procedures manual-II.* Towson, MD: Clinical Psychometric Research.

DeRoma, V. M., & Hansen, D. J. (1994, November). *Development of the Parental Anger Inventory.* Poster presented at the Association for the Advancement of Behavior Therapy Convention, San Diego, CA.

Doll, E. A. (1964). *Vineland Social Maturity Scale.* Circle Pines, MN: American Guidance Service.

Doueck, H. J., Bronson, D. E., & Levine, M. (1992). Evaluating risk assessment implementation in child protection: Issues for consideration. *Child Abuse and Neglect, 16,* 637–646.

*Dumas, J., & Wahler, R. G. (1985). Indiscriminate mothering as a contextual factor in aggressive-oppositional child behavior. *Journal of Abnormal Child Psychology, 13,* 1–17.

Egan, K. (1983). Stress management and child management with abusive parents. *Journal of Clinical Child Psychology, 12,* 292–299.

Elliott, D. M., & Briere, J. (1994). Forensic sexual abuse evaluations of older children: Disclosures and symptomatology. *Behavioral Sciences and the Law, 12,* 261–277.

Eyberg, S., Bessmer, J., Newcomb, K., Edwards, D., & Robinson, E. (1994). *Dyadic Parent-Child Interaction Coding System-II: A manual.* Unpublished manual, University of Florida, Gainesville.

Eyberg, S., & Colvin, A. (1994, August). *Restandardization of the Eyberg Child Behavior Inventory.* Poster presented at the annual meeting of the American Psychological Association, Los Angeles, CA.

Eyberg, S. M., & Robinson, E. A. (1981). *Dyadic Parent-Child Interaction Coding System: A manual.* Unpublished manuscript, Oregon Health Sciences University.

Eyberg, S. M., & Ross, A. W. (1978). Assessment of child behavior problems: The validation of a new inventory. *Journal of Clinical Child Psychology, 7,* 113–116.

Everson, M. D., Hunter, W. M., Runyon, D. K., Edelsohn, G. A., & Coulter, M. L. (1989). Maternal support following disclosure of incest. *American Journal of Orthopsychiatry, 59,* 197–207.

Fantuzzo, J. W., Stovall, A., Schactel, D., Goins, C., & Hall, R. (1987). Effects of peer initiations on the social behavior of socially withdrawn preschool children with a history of child maltreatment. *Journal of Behavior Therapy and Experimental Psychiatry, 18,* 357–363.

Feldman, M. A., Case, L., & Sparks, B. (1992). Effectiveness of a child-care training program for parents at risk for child neglect. *Canadian Journal of Behavioural Science, 24,* 14–28.

Finch, A. J., & Daugherty, T. K. (1993). Issues in the assessment of posttraumatic stress disorder in children. In C. F. Saylor (Ed.), *Children and disasters* (pp. 45–66). New York: Plenum.

Finch, A. J., Montgomery, L., & Deardorff, P. (1974). Reliability of state-trait anxiety with emotionally disturbed children. *Journal of Abnormal Child Psychology, 2,* 67–69.

Finch, A. J., & Rogers, T. R. (1984). Self-report instruments. In T. H. Ollendick & M. Hersen (Eds.), *Child behavior assessment: Principles and procedures.* New York: Pergamon Press.

Finch, A. J., Saylor, C. F., & Edwards G. E. (1985). Children's Depression Inventory: Sex and grade norms for normal children. *Journal of Consulting and Clinical Psychology, 53,* 424–425.

Fodi, A. M., & Lamb, M. E. (1980). Child abusers' responses to infant smiles and cries. *Child Development, 51,* 238–241.

Fodi, A. M., & Senchak, M. (1990). Verbal and behavioral responsiveness to the cries of atypical infants. *Child Development, 61,* 76–84.

*Forehand, R., & McMahon, R. (1981). *Helping the noncompliant child: A clinician's guide to parent training.* New York: Guilford Press.

Fox, R. A. (1994). *Parent Behavior Checklist.* Brandon, VT: Clinical Psychology Publishing.

Frederick, C. J. (1985). Children traumatized by catastrophic situations. In S. Eth & R. S. Pynoos (Eds.), *Post-traumatic stress disorders in children* (pp. 73–99). Washington, DC: American Psychiatric Press.

Friedrich, W. N., Tyler, J. D., & Clark, J. A. (1985). Personality and psychophysiological variables in abusive, neglectful and low-income control mothers. *Journal of Nervous and Mental Disorders, 173,* 449–460.

Gabinet, L. (1979). Prevention of child abuse and neglect in an inner city population: II. The program and the results. *Child Abuse and Neglect*, 3, 809–817.

*Garbarino, J. (1977). The human ecology of child maltreatment: A conceptual model for research. *Journal of Marriage and the Family*, 39, 721–735.

Gil, D. G. (1970). *Violence against children: Physical child abuse in the United States:* Cambridge, MA: Harvard University Press.

Gilbert, M. T. (1976). Behavioural approach to the treatment of child abuse. *Nursing Times*, 72, 140–143.

Hack, T. F., Osachuk, T. A. G., & Deluca, R. V. (1994). Group treatment for sexually abused preadolescent boys. *Families in Society, April*, 217–228.

Hall-Marley, S. E., & Damon, L. (1993). Impact of structured group therapy on young victims of sexual abuse. *Journal of Child and Adolescent Group Therapy*, 3 (1), 41–48.

Hally, C., Polansky, N. F., & Polansky, N. A. (1980). *Child neglect: Mobilizing services* (DHHS Publication No. OHDS 80–30257). Washington, DC: U.S. Government Printing Office.

Hansen, D. J., & MacMillan, V. M. (1990). Behavioral assessment of child abusive and neglectful families: Recent developments and current issues. *Behavior Modification*, 14, 255–278.

Hansen, D. J., Palotta, G. M., Tishelman, A. C., Conaway, L. P., & MacMillan, V. M. (1989). Parental problem-solving skills and child behavior problems: A comparison for physically abusive, neglectful, clinic, and community families. *Journal of Family Violence*, 4, 353–368.

Hanson, R. F., & Swenson, C. C. (1995, February). *Treatment of PTSD in child sexual abuse victims.* Paper presented at the First Annual South Carolina Professional Colloquium on Child Abuse, Charleston, SC.

Heras, P. (1992). Cultural considerations in the assessment and treatment of child sexual abuse. *Journal of Child Sexual Abuse*, 1 (3), 119–124.

Hughes, J. N., & Baker, D. B. (1990). *The Clinical Child Interview.* New York: Guilford Press.

Jacobs, J. L. (1992). Child sexual abuse victimization and later sequelae during pregnancy and childbirth. *Journal of Child Sexual Abuse*, 1 (1), 103–112.

Johnson, C. F. (1990). Inflicted injury versus accidental injury. *Pediatric Clinics of North America*, 37, 791–814.

Kaufman, K. S., & Walker, C. E. (1986). Review of the Child Abuse Potential Inventory. In J. D.

Keyser & R. C. Sweetland (Eds.), *Test critiques* (pp. 55–64). Kansas City, MO: Westport.

Kazdin, A. E., Siegel, T. C., & Bass, D. (1992). Cognitive problem-solving skills training and parent management training in the treatment of antisocial behavior in children. *Journal of Consulting and Clinical Psychology*, 60, 733–747.

Kazdin, A. E. (1982). *Single-case research designs.* New York: Oxford University Press.

Kempe, C. H., Silverman, F. N., Steele, B. F., Drogemueller, W., & Silver, H. K. (1962). The battered child syndrome. *Journal of Medical Association*, 181, 105–112.

Kendall, P. C. (1994). Treating anxiety disorders in children: Results of a randomized clinical trial. *Journal of Consulting and Clinical Psychology*, 62 (1), 100–110.

*Kendall-Tackett, K. A., Williams, L. M., & Finkelhor, D. (1993). Impact of sexual abuse on children: A review and synthesis of recent empirical studies. *Psychological Bulletin*, 113 (1), 164–180.

Kiesel, K. B., Lutzker, J. R., & Campbell, R. V. (1989). Behavioral relaxation training to reduce hyperventilation and seizures in a profoundly retarded epileptic child. *Journal of the Multihandicapped Person*, 2, 179–190.

Kilpatrick, D. G., Veronen, L. J., & Best, C. L. (1985). Factors predicting psychological distress among rape victims. In C. R. Figley (Ed.), *Trauma and its wake* (pp. 113–141). New York: Brunner/Mazel.

Kiser, L. J., Pugh, R. L., McColgan, E. B., Pruitt, D. B., & Edwards, N. B. (1991). Treatment strategies for victims of extrafamilial child sexual abuse. *Journal of Family Psychotherapy*, 2 (1), 27–39.

Knutson, J. G. (1978). Child abuse as an area of aggression research. *Journal of Pediatric Psychology*, 3, 20–27.

Kovacs, M. (1983). *The Children's Depression Inventory: A self-rated depression scale for school-age youngsters.* Unpublished manuscript, University of Pittsburgh.

Lang, P. J. (1979). A bio-informational theory of emotional imagery. *Psychophysiology*, 16, 495–511.

Lanktree, C. B., Briere, J., & Hernandez, P. (1991, August). *Further data on the Trauma Symptom Checklist for Children (TSC-C): Reliability, validity and sensitivity to treatment.* Paper presented at the annual meeting of the American Psychological Meeting, San Francisco, CA.

Lazarus, R. S., & Folkman, S. (1984). *Stress, appraisal, and coping.* New York: Springer.

Lester, B. M., & Zeskind, P. S. (1982). A biobehavioral perspective on crying in early infancy. In

H. Fitzgerald, B. M. Lester, & M. W. Yogman (Eds.), *Theory and research in behavioral pediatrics*, Vol. 1. New York: Plenum Press.

Lindahl, M. W. (1988). Letters to Tammy: A technique useful in the treatment of a sexually abused child. *Child Abuse and Neglect, 12,* 417–420.

Lipovsky, J. A. (1991). Posttraumatic stress disorder in children. *Family and Community Health, 14* (3), 42–51.

Lipovsky, J. A., & Elliott, A. N. (1993). Individual treatment of the sexually abused child. *The APSAC Advisor, 6* (3), 15–18.

Lipovsky, J. A., & Hanson, R. F. (1992a, October). *Multiple traumas in the histories of child/adolescent psychiatric inpatients.* Paper presented at the annual meeting of the International Society for Traumatic Stress Studies, Los Angeles, CA.

Lipovsky, J. A., & Hanson, R. F. (1992b, November). *Traumatic event histories of child/adolescent psychiatric inpatients: What is being done to our children?* Paper presented at the annual meeting of the Association for the Advancement of Behavior Therapy, Boston, MA.

Lipovsky, J. A., Hanson, R. F., & Hand, L. (1993, January). *Sexual abuse, physical abuse, and witnessing violence in child/adolescent inpatients: Relationship to psychopathology.* Paper presented at the San Diego Conference on Responding to Child Maltreatment, San Diego, CA.

Lipovsky, J. A., Saunders, B. E., & Murphy, S. M. (1989). Depression, anxiety, and behavior problems among victims of father-child sexual assault and nonabused siblings. *Journal of Interpersonal Violence, 4,* 452–468.

Lonigan, C. J., Shannon, M. P., Finch, A. J., Daugherty, T. K., & Taylor, C. M. (1991). Children's reactions to a natural disaster: Symptom severity and degree of exposure. *Advances in Behavior Research and Therapy, 13,* 135–154.

Loyd, B. H., & Abidin, R. R. (1985). Revision of the Parenting Stress Index. *Journal of Pediatric Psychology, 10,* 169–177.

*Lutzker, J. R. (1984). Project 12-Ways: Treating child abuse and neglect from an ecobehavioral perspective. In R. F. Dangel & R. A. Polster (Eds.), *Parent training: Foundations of research and practice* (pp. 260–291). New York: Guilford Press.

*Lutzker, J. R. (1992). Developmental disabilities and child abuse and neglect: The ecobehavioral imperative. *Behaviour Change, 9,* 149–156.

Lutzker, J. R. (Chair) (1994, November). *Child abuse*

intervention: Can we collect good data and provide real treatment? Symposium presented at the annual convention of the Association for the Advancement of Behavior Therapy, San Diego, CA.

Lutzker, J. R., Frame, J. R., & Rice, J. M. (1982). Project 12-Ways: An ecobehavioral approach to the treatment and prevention of child abuse and neglect. *Education and Treatment of Children, 5,* 141–155.

Lutzker, S. Z., Lutzker, J. R., Braunling-McMorrow, D., & Eddleman, J. (1987). Prompting to increase mother-baby stimulation with single mothers. *Journal of Child and Adolescent Psychotherapy, 4,* 3–12.

Lutzker, J. R., & Rice, J. M. (1984). Project 12-Ways: Measuring outcome of a large in-home service for treatment and prevention of child abuse and neglect. *Child Abuse and Neglect, 8,* 519–524.

Maccoby, E. E., & Martin, J. A. (1983). Socialization in the context of the family: Parent-child interaction. In P. H. Mussen & E. M. Heatherington (Eds.), *Handbook of child psychology: Socialization, personality, and social development* (pp. 1–102). New York: Wiley.

MacMillan, V. M., Olson, R. L., & Hansen, D. J. (1988, November). *The development of an anger inventory for use with maltreating parents.* Paper presented at the Association for the Advancement of Behavior Therapy Convention, New York, NY.

MacMillan, V. M., Olson, R. L., & Hansen, D. J. (1991). Low- and high-deviance analogue assessment of parent-training with physically abusive parents. *Journal of Family Violence, 6,* 279–301.

Malinosky-Rummell, R., & Hansen, D. J. (1993). Long-term consequences of childhood physical abuse. *Psychological Bulletin, 114,* 68–79.

Mannarino, A. P., Cohen, J. A., & Gregor, M. (1989). Emotional and behavioral difficulties in sexually abused girls. *Journal of Interpersonal Violence, 4,* 437–451.

Mannarino, A. P., Cohen, J. A., Smith J. A., & Moore-Motily, S. (1991). Six- and twelve-month follow-up of sexually abused girls. *Journal of Interpersonal Violence, 6,* 494–511.

Mara, B. A., & Winton, M. A. (1990). Sexual abuse intervention: A support group for parents who have a sexually abused child. *International Journal of Group Psychotherapy, 40* (1), 63–76.

McCanne, T. R., & Milner, J. S. (1991). Psychophysiological reactivity of physically abusive and at-risk subjects to child-related stimuli. In J. S. Milner

(Ed.), *Neuropsychology of Aggression* (pp. 147–166). Norwell, MA: Academic Publishers.

McNally, R. J. (1991). Assessment of post traumatic stress disorder in children. *Psychological Assessment: A Journal of Consulting and Clinical, 3,* 531–537.

Meinig, M. B., & Bonner, B. L. (1990). Returning the treated sex offender to the family. *Violence Update, 1* (2), 1–11.

*Milner, J. S. (1986). *The Child Abuse Potential Inventory: Manual* (2nd ed.). Webster, NC: Psytec.

Milner, J. S., Robertson, K. R., & Rogers, D. L. (1990). Childhood history of abuse and adult child abuse. *Journal of Family Violence, 5,* 15–34.

National Center on Child Abuse and Neglect (NCCAN). (1988). *Study of national incidence and prevalence of child abuse and neglect: 1988.* Washington, DC: U.S. Department of Health and Human Services.

*National Research Council. (1993). *Understanding child abuse and neglect.* Washington, DC: National Academy Press.

Nomellini, S., & Katz, R. C. (1983). Effects of anger control training on abusive parents. *Cognitive Therapy and Research, 7,* 57–68.

Novaco, R. W. (1975). *Anger control: The development and evaluation of an experimental treatment.* Lexington, MA: Lexington Books.

O'Dell, S. L., Tarler-Benlolo, L., & Flynn, J. M. (1979). An instrument to measure knowledge of behavioral principles as applied to children. *Journal of Behavior Therapy and Experimental Psychiatry, 10,* 29–34.

Ollendick, T. H., & Cerny, J. A. (1981). *Clinical behavior therapy with children.* New York: Plenum Press.

Palotta, G. M., Conaway, R. L., Christopher, J. S., & Hansen, D. J. (1989). *The Parental Problem-Solving Measure: Evaluation with maltreating clinical and community parents.* Paper presented at the Association for the Advancement of Behavior Therapy Convention, Washington, DC.

Pescosolido, F. J. (1993). Clinical considerations related to victimization dynamics and post-traumatic stress in the group treatment of sexually abused boys. *Journal of Child and Adolescent Group Therapy, 3* (1), 49–73.

Procidano, M., & Heller, K. (1983). Measures of perceived social support from friends and from family: Three validation studies. *American Journal of Community Psychology, 11,* 1–24.

Pynoos, R. S., & Eth, S. E. (1986). Developmental perspective on psychic trauma in childhood. In

C. R. Figley (Ed.), *Trauma and its wake* (pp. 36–52). New York: Brunner/Mazel.

Reich, W. (1991a). *Diagnostic Interview for Children and Adolescents-Child Version.* Unpublished manuscript, Washington University School of Medicine.

Reich, W. (1991b). *Diagnostic Interview for Children and Adolescents-Parent Version.* Unpublished manuscript, Washington University School of Medicine.

Reynolds, C. R., & Paget, K. D. (1981). Factor analysis of the Revised Children's Manifest Anxiety Scale for blacks, whites, males, and females. *Journal of Consulting and Clinical Psychology, 49,* 352–359.

Reynolds, C. R., & Richmond, B. O. (1978). "What I Think and Feel": A revised measure of children's manifest anxiety. *Journal of Abnormal Child Psychology, 6,* 271–280.

Ribbe, D. P., Lipovsky, J. A., & Freedy, J. R. (1995). Posttraumatic stress disorder. In A. R. Eisen, C. A. Kaemey, & C. E. Schaeffer (Eds.), *Clinical handbook of anxiety disorders in children and adolescents* (pp. 317–356). Northvale, NJ: Jason Aronson.

Roehling, P. V., & Robin, A. L. (1986). Development and validation of the Family Beliefs Inventory: A measure of unrealistic beliefs among parents and adolescents. *Journal of Consulting and Clinical Psychology, 54,* 693–697.

Sarber, R. E., Halasz, M. M., Messmer, M. C., Bickett, A. D., & Lutzker, J. R. (1983). Teaching menu planning and grocery shopping skills to a mentally retarded mother. *Mental Retardation, 21,* 101–106.

Saunders, B. E., & Kilpatrick, D. G. (1993). *Prevalence and consequences of child victimization: A longitudinal study.* National Institute of Justice Grant #93-IJ-CX-0023.

Saylor, C. F., Swenson, C. C., Stokes, S. J., Wertlieb, D., & Casto, Y. (1994, August). *The Pediatric Emotional Distress Scale: A brief new screening measure.* Paper presented at the American Psychological Association annual meeting, Los Angeles, CA.

Singer, M. I., Anglin, T. M., Song, L. Y., & Lunghofer, L. (1995). Adolescents' exposure to violence and associated symptoms of psychological trauma. *Journal of the American Medical Association, 273,* 477–482.

Sirles, E. A., Walsma, J., Lytle-Barnaby, R., & Lander, L. C. (1988). Group therapy techniques for work with child sexual abuse victims. *Social Work with Groups,* 11 (3), 67–78.

Smucker, M. R., Craighead, E., Craighead, L., & Green, B. J. (1986). Normative and reliability data for the Children's Depression Inventory. *Journal of Abnormal Child Psychology,* 14, 25–39.

Solis, M. L., & Abidin, R. R. (1991). The Spanish version Parenting Stress Index: A psychometric study. *Journal of Clinical Child Psychology,* 20, 372–378.

Spielberger, C. D. (1973). *Preliminary manual for the State-Trait Anxiety Inventory for Children.* Palo Alto, CA: Consulting Psychologists Press.

Stokes, S. J. (1994, April). *A comparison of children's reactions following three types of stressors.* Paper presented at the South Carolina Psychological Association Meeting, Myrtle Beach, SC.

Suomi, S. J. (1978). Maternal behavior by socially incompetent monkeys: Neglect and abuse of offspring. *Journal of Pediatric Psychology,* 3, 28–34.

Swenson, C. C., Saylor, C. F., Stokes, C. J., Ralston, M. E., Smith, D. E., Hanson, R. F., & Saunders, B. E. (1994, January). *Anxiety and fear in traumatized children: The validity of a new brief screening instrument.* Paper presented at the San Diego Conference for Responding to Child Maltreatment, San Diego, CA.

Tertinger, D. S., Greene, B. F., & Lutzker, J. R. (1984). Home safety: Development and validation of one component of an ecobehavioral treatment program for abused and neglected children. *Journal of Applied Behavior Analysis,* 17, 159–174.

Trickett, P. K., & Susman, E. J. (1988). Parental perceptions of child rearing practices in physically abusive and nonabusive families. *Developmental psychology,* 24, 270–276.

Tyson, P. D., & Sobschak, K. B. (1994). Perceptual responses to infant crying after EEG biofeedback assisted stress management training: Implications for physical child abuse. *Child Abuse and Neglect* 18, 933–943.

*U.S. Department of Health and Human Services, National Center on Child Abuse and Neglect. (1995). *Child Maltreatment 1993: Reports from the States to the National Center on Child Abuse and Neglect.* Washington, DC: U.S. Government Printing Office.

Van de Kolk, B. A., & Fisler, R. E. (1994). Childhood abuse and neglect and loss of self-regulation. *Bulletin of the Menninger Clinic,* 58 (2), 145–168.

Wahler, R. G. (1980). The insular mother: Her problem in parent-child treatment. *Journal of Applied Behavior Analysis,* 13, 207–219.

Wahler, R. G., Leske, G., & Rogers, E. S. (1979). The insular family: A deviance support system of oppositional children. In L. A. Hamerlynck (Ed.), *Behavioral systems for the developmentally disabled: I. School and family environments.* New York: Brunner/Mazel.

Warner, J. E., & Hansen, D. J. (1994). The identification and reporting of physical abuse by physicians: A review and implications for research. *Child Abuse and Neglect,* 18, 11–25.

Waterman, J., & Lusk, R. (1993). Psychological testing in evaluation of child sexual abuse. *Child Abuse and Neglect,* 17, 145–159.

Watson-Perczel, M., Lutzker, J. R., Greene, B. F., & McGimpsey, B. J. (1988). Assessment and modification of home cleanliness among families adjudicated for child neglect. *Behavior Modification,* 12, 57–81.

When the body remembers. (1994, March/April). *Psychology Today,* 27 (2), p. 9.

Whiteman, M., Fanshel, D., & Grundy, J. F. (1987). Cognitive-behavioral interventions aimed at anger of parents at risk of child abuse. *Social Work,* 32, 469–474.

Widom, C. S. (1989). Does violence beget violence? A critical examination of the literature. *Psychological Bulletin,* 106, 3–28.

Wolfe, D. A. (1991). *Preventing physical and emotional abuse of children.* New York: Guilford Press.

Wolfe, D. A., Edwards, B., Manion, I., & Koverola, C. (1988). Early intervention for parents at risk of child abuse and neglect: A preliminary investigation. *Journal of Consulting and Clinical Psychology,* 56, 40–47.

Wolfe, D. A., Fairbanks, J. A., Kelly, J. A., & Bradlyn, A. S. (1983). Child abusive parents' physiological responses to stressful and nonstressful behavior in children. *Behavioral Assessment,* 5, 363–371.

Wolfe, D. A., & Sandler, J. (1981). Training abusive parents in effective child management. *Behavior Modification,* 5, 320–335.

*Wolfe, D. A., & Wekerle, C. (1993). Treatment strategies for child physical abuse and neglect: A critical progress report. *Clinical Psychology Review,* 13, 474–500.

Wolfe, D., Sandler, J., & Kaufman, K. (1981). A competency-based parent training program for child abusers. *Journal of Consulting and Clinical Psychology, 49,* 633–640.

Wolfe, V. V., Gentile, C., & Wolfe, D. A. (1989). The impact of sexual abuse on children: A PTSD formulation. *Behavior Therapy, 20,* 215–228.

Zeskind, P. S. (1983). Production and spectral analysis of neonatal crying and its relation to other biobehavioral systems in the infant at risk. In T. Field & A. Sostek (Eds.), *Infants born at risk: Physiological, perceptual and cognitive processes* (pp. 23–43). New York: Grune & Stratton.

Zeskind, P. S. (1987). Adult heart-rate responses to infant cry sounds. *British Journal of Developmental Psychology, 5,* 73–79.

Zeskind, P. S., & Lester, B. M. (1981). Acoustic features and auditory perceptions of the cries of newborns with prenatal and perinatal complications. *Child Development, 49,* 580–589.

*Indicates references that the authors recommend for further reading.

26
Psychological Factors Affecting Medical Conditions

Gary R. Geffken
Linda Monaco
James R. Rodrigue

INTRODUCTION: HISTORICAL PERSPECTIVE

The interplay between psychological factors and the course of physical illness has been observed since the beginnings of recorded medicine. The writings of Hippocrates (460–377 B.C.) and his successors demonstrate that Greek medical practice accepted the relationship between personality attributes and humoral balance and disease (Hippocrates, Fourth Century B.C./1923). Furthermore, followers of Hippocrates believed that strong emotional experiences, such as anger, produced disturbed bodily functions. Similarly, Navajo tradition has attributed well-being and illness to mind-body interactions. However, despite the historical recognition of the interaction between mind and body, the classical Western medical model of illness has favored the clear demarcation between "physical" and "mental" illnesses. The dualistic approach to the mind and body reflects the Cartesian philosophy that the mind exists in a realm wholly separate from the physical world (Descartes, 1662/1955).

Recent research efforts have focused on studying the existence of the interrelationships between psychological and physical factors in examination of total well-being. Interest in such interactions led to the development of a discipline recognized as "psychosomatic medicine." The field of psychosomatic medicine may be regarded as both a scientific approach and an approach to clinical practice. As a body of scientific inquiry, psychosomatic medicine studied the interactions between psychological and physical functions. As a clinical application, psychosomatic medicine was concerned with diagnosing, treating, and ameliorating the psychological factors involved with illness. Psychosomatic disorders were considered disorders in organic functions caused by mental and emotional conditions. They were defined as diseases of adaptation, rooted in an organism's attempt to adapt physiologically to situational stressors. According to Wolman (1988), these disorders were either physiochemical, anatomical, or physiological in origin. Psychosomatic researchers, including representatives from physiological psychology, attributed influence over physical conditions to a number of psychological elements, including prolonged exposure to stress (Selye, 1956, 1976) and interactions between the environment and constitutional factors (Meyer, 1957; Dunbar, 1935, 1955).

According to Lipowski (1986), findings from psychosomatic research, specifically from the studies of Meyer and Dunbar, established the basis for future clinical studies on the relationship among environment, personality, and disease. In 1935, Flanders Dunbar wrote the first comprehensive review of the psychosomatic literature, which created a more complete frame of reference for practitioners to access and therefore heightened research capability. Four years later, the American Psychosomatic Society was founded, with Dunbar as the first editor of the organization's journal, *Psychosomatic Medicine*. The journal aimed to study the relationship between the psychological and the physical aspects of body function and to integrate psychosomatic theory into clinical practice.

In 1953, the Academy of Psychosomatic Medicine was founded, and researchers from a broad range of professions began conducting psychosomatic research. Alexander's specificity model best characterizes the writings from the psychoanalytic tradition (Alexander, 1950): specific emotional conflicts were associated with particular physical conditions; whether these conflicts resulted in dysfunction depended on individual characteristics. While Alexander's model of psychosomatic illness represents the most comprehensive model in psychoanalytic writings, Freud's work (1905/1963) incorporates elements of psychosomatic theory as well. According to Freud's theory of hysteria, both mental and physical factors contribute to the manifestation of the disorder. Thus, psychosomatic medicine as a study of illness represents a logical extension of research in psychoanalysis and in psychophysiology. Research in these areas formed the premise for contemporary research into the psychological factors that affect illness. In addition, this research contributed to psychoneuroimmunology, a field that investigates the effects of stress on the physiological and biological functions of the body.

The heightened awareness of the role of psychosocial factors in health has been accompanied by an increased involvement of clinical psychologists in medical settings. The increased involvement of clinical child psychologists in medical settings has given rise to the specialty field of pediatric psychology, a field that grew out of the recognition of the importance of assessing all factors that contribute to childhood illness, rather than giving primacy to biological factors alone. Many regard Jerome Kagan's (1965) article as the pioneering influence in pediatric psychology. According to Kagan, a liaison between pediatricians and psychologists was beneficial to both because it allowed the psychologist to confront practical issues and the pediatrician to understand the dynamics of psychology and physiology in symptom growth and health maintenance. Kagan suggested that the pediatrician and psychologist collaborate to understand whom the patient identifies with and which values and behaviors are rewarded at home before rendering a more complete diagnosis. Wright's (1967) expanded version of Kagan's model described a pediatric psychologist as someone trained in behavioral and cognitive assessment as well as development. For more than 30 years, pediatric psychologists have continued to apply these skills to clinical settings. At the present time, the pediatric psychologist has adopted a number of roles, including therapist and diagnostician.

As research and clinical interest in the psychological influences on physical symptoms has increased, so too has the response of the American Psychiatric Association. The development and expansion of the American Psychiatric Association's *Diagnostic and Statistical Manual of Mental Disorders* 316 category paralleled the growing interest in psychological influences on health. The category represents the formal means of recognizing the complex relationship between psychological factors and well-being and represents a departure from the historical diagnostic split between the two.

Psychological factors affecting illness were first diagnostically recognized in DSM-II (American Psychiatric Association, 1968) under the rubric "Psychophysiological Disorders." The manual characterized these disorders as "physical symptoms that are caused by emotional factors and involve a single organ system. The physiological changes involved usually accompany certain emotional states but in these disorders the changes are more intense and sustaining." Thus, DSM-II framed only general parameters of the disorder. Ten psychophysiological disorders were included under the DSM-II label: psychophysiologic skin disorders, musculoskeletal disorders, respiratory disorders, cardiovascular disorders, hemic and lymphatic disorders, gastrointestinal disorders, genitourinary disorders, endocrine disorders, disorders affecting organs of special sense, and an additional category titled "other psychophysiological disorders." The 316 category was revised in subsequent editions of the manual as research failed to confirm the hypothesis that intense emotional states were necessary causes of these disorders, the premise on which the DSM-II categorization was based.

The first operationalized criteria for the 316 diagnosis were provided in DSM-III (APA, 1980). The category enlarged the scope of psychological and behavioral factors believed to contribute to medical illness and thereby acknowledged the complex relationship between psychological factors and medical illness more appropriately than its predecessor (Linn & Spitzer, 1982). The diagnosis was applicable in cases where psychological factors exacerbated or maintained a medical condition as well as in situations where psychological symptoms resulted from physical disorders. Within the multiaxial format of this diagnostic framework, an Axis I diagnosis of "Psychological Factors Affecting Physical Conditions" (PFAPC) could be rendered concomitantly with another Axis I diagnosis if criteria for the second disorder were met; the appropriate physical disorder was rendered on Axis III.

According to Looney, Lipp, and Spitzer (1978), DSM-III's PFAPC was regarded a diagnostic modifier rather than a separate diagnostic entity. This observation suggests that the category's purpose was to focus attention on clinical information and not to foster assumptions about the organic nature of the condition.

The DSM-III-R (APA, 1987) 316 category remained unchanged from the DSM-III version.

According to Stoudemire (1995), the DSM-III and DSM-III-R diagnostic category of PFAPC lacked sufficient application in clinical settings. Furthermore, there was little evidence to suggest that PFAPC generated research in the medical or the psychiatric literature (Popkin, 1987). The DSM-IV Work Group for PFAPC revisions developed a number of possibilities for the 316 category, including the removal of the category from the mental disorders section of the manual in favor of its inclusion as a V code (Stoudemire, 1995). An exhaustive empirical literature review conducted by the work group revealed that, indeed, research supported the influence of psychological factors on physical well-being. Consequently, the category was retained and retitled "Psychological Factors Affecting Medical Conditions" (PFAMC); the category was placed in the DSM-IV section "Other conditions that may be the focus of clinical attention." The work group identified the major types of behavioral and psychological factors that affect medical conditions to make the category more clinically useful. However, these authors have found that pediatric psychologist clinicians working in the field certainly find the diagnosis of significant heuristic value; that is, the clinicians note issues of compliance and situational factors that regularly affect the medical conditions of children and adolescents.

A subcategorization format was developed to allow the clinician to specify the type of behavioral or psychological factors that is affecting the medical condition. Accordingly, the DSM-IV version of the 316 category allows clinicians to subtype psychological as well as behavioral factors believed to adversely affect medical conditions. Such factors include those that interfere with the course or treatment of a medical condition, those that exacerbate the symptoms of a medical condition, and those that may constitute additional health risks for the patient. Personality traits or coping styles that adversely affect a medical condition and stress-related physiological responses that exacerbate symptoms of a general medical condition are other subcategories. Of note, this category is considerably broader in scope compared to its DSM-II predecessor and encompasses a variety of psychological, social, and behavioral problems that may influence physical health.

These authors consider noncompliance with regimen as one subset of problems that should be included under the diagnosis of psychological factors affecting medical condition. Other problems commonly encountered are situational factors, which can involve the school or home setting and family members. Common differential diagnoses involve distinguishing adjustment reaction from psychological factors affecting medical condition. These authors would opt for the 316 diagnosis when the adjustment reaction is involved in the medical condition, in contrast to a situation where a child with a medical condition is having an adjustment reaction that does not basically affect the medical condition. Another common diagnostic differential is oppositional defiant disorder. When a child has oppositional characteristics, there may affect compliance with the regimen. If noncompliance is affecting the medical condition, these authors might opt for the 316 as the primary diagnosis, with the oppositional defiant disorder as the secondary diagnosis. Another common diagnostic differential covers parent-child problems. Again, when the parent and child conflict is directly involved in the medical condition, the 316 diagnosis may be primary.

"Psychological and behavioral factors associated with disorders or diseases classified elsewhere" is a diagnosis that appears in the *International Classification of Diseases* (ICD-10) (World Health Organization, 1992). ICD-10 is a broader classification system for all medical systems, of which the psychiatric system is a subset. The ICD-10 diagnosis indicates that it includes "psychological factors affecting physical condition." Like the DSM-IV 316 diagnosis, the ICD-10 diagnosis should be used to indicate those factors that play a significant role in the etiology of physical disorders, those that interfere with the course of a medical condition, or those that have influenced the manifestation of a medical condition. The ICD-10 diagnosis,

unlike the DSM-IV diagnosis, does not articulate those factors that constitute additional health risks, personality or coping styles, and stress related to physiological responses that exacerbate symptoms as subcategories as well. However, it should be noted that the factors not articulated in ICD-10 are not inconsistent with those factors that are described in both ICD-10 and DSM-IV.

Due to the fact that psychological factors play a role in the presentation of many medical conditions, the category is used only when psychological factors have a clinically significant effect on the course or outcome of the medical condition or when such factors place the individual at a higher risk for an adverse outcome. Whether or not a clinically significant effect exists is, of course, a clinical judgment. Psychological factors that affect a general medical condition include Axis I and Axis II disorders, as well as psychological symptoms that do not meet the full diagnostic criteria.

ASSESSMENT OF 316

The study of the interaction between physical and psychological factors is no longer confined within the "psychosomatic medicine" discipline or in any other individual field of scientific inquiry. Rather, the recognition of psychological factors related to illness continues to gain momentum among mental health and medical practitioners who recognize the importance of assessing psychological factors related to illness. Lipowski (1976) suggested that most medical disorders result from a combination of biological and psychosocial factors, rather than from one factor acting in isolation. The most current position among clinicians appears to be that the impact of psychological factors on health is not limited to illnesses in one particular category but may pervade a wide range of disorders.

Engel's (1977) biopsychosocial model embodies perhaps the most contemporary view of health. According to this model, behavior results from an interaction among psychological, physical, and social elements. The patient can be regarded as a system with interacting biological, psychological, and social subsystems. The model's systems approach permits the integration of biological, psychological, and social aspects of a patient's medical condition. Under this model, the clinician must understand and appreciate the contributions of each of these aspects to the patient's condition in order to provide the most effective treatment. This emphasis on context harkens back to Bronfenbrenner's (1979) ecological model. Bronfenbrenner's theories of how the past, family, peers, and social institutions all play a definitive role in forming the individual coalesced throughout the 1970s into this comprehensive developmental theory. According to Bronfenbrenner's model, when studying the developing child, the clinician is studying myriad elements, including the parents, the parent-child dyad, and the parent-spouse relationship. Ultimately, the study of children becomes the study of the family, friends, colleagues, and cultural practices that surround them. Bronfenbrenner's ecological perspective stressed the examination of the interaction of a changing organism within a changing environment that comprises the child's immediate settings as well as the social and cultural contexts of the relations between different settings such as home, school, and the workplace. Thus, a thorough assessment of the child's total environment is necessary to understand his or her condition.

In a medical setting, a comprehensive assessment to rule out a 316 diagnosis involves attention to a multitude of elements, including the physical, psychological, developmental, and social aspects of the patient. Each component of the patient's life merits simultaneous consideration in a psychological evaluation. When the patient is a child, there must also be an assessment of family functioning, communication, and decision-making processes. In addition, the child's social functioning in terms of peer relationships and school performance warrant careful assessment because these represent important aspects of the child's functioning.

Minuchin's writings (1978) suggest that assessment of familial transaction patterns is essential in the treatment of an ill child. His model of the "psychosomatic family" outlined four characteristics of overall family functioning that encouraged somatization in children. These four transactional patterns were identified as enmeshment, overprotectiveness, rigidity, and lack of conflict resolution. Enmeshment referred to an overinvolved family marked by intense family interactions. Overprotectiveness in the psychosomatic family was demonstrated by a high degree of concern that impeded the child's development of autonomy, competence, and interests outside the family. Rigidity referred to a heavy commitment to maintaining the status quo and avoiding conflict. Lack of conflict resolution in the family resulted from denial of the existence of any conflict. Minuchin also identified characteristic patterns of conflict-related behaviors (i.e., transactions) such as triangulation, parent-child coalition, and detouring. In triangulation and in the parent-child coalition, the spouse dyad is split in opposition while the child is an ally to one parent. In detouring, parents submerge their conflicts by protecting or blaming the ill child. These transactional sequences are frequently enacted within the psychosomatic family, and the pediatric psychologist must observe family patterns during assessment in an effort to detect them.

Minuchin (1978) credits the beginning of the study of the relationship between psychological factors and health to interventions with children with diabetes who had undergone numerous hospitalizations for ketoacidosis. Minuchin and his colleagues studied children with IDDM who had recurrent bouts of ketoacidosis. After ruling out organic bases for ketoacidosis, the researchers (Minuchin, Baker, Rosman, Liebman, Milman, & Todd, 1985) concluded that emotional arousal related to family issues was a direct influence on metabolic control. Other researchers, however, suggest that empirical data for the findings of Minuchin and his colleagues is lacking (Coyne & Anderson, 1988; Johnson, 1989).

EPIDEMIOLOGY

DSM-IV does not include categories for the incidence and prevalence of the 316 diagnosis. There is a lack of empirical data in this area.

MODELS FOR ASSESSMENT AND TREATMENT

A recent meta-analysis by Lavigne and Faier-Routman (1992) reviewed 87 studies of children's adjustment to physical disorders. The review indicated that children with chronic disorders show an increased risk for overall adjustment problems, with elevated levels of both internalizing and externalizing symptoms. The average change in effect size in overall psychological adjustment was approximately half a standard deviation. Of note, Wallander, Varni, Babani, Banis, and Wilcox (1988) indicated that although children with chronic illnessess experience higher levels of psychological adjustment problems when compared to healthy controls, their adjustment is typically better than that of a sample referred to mental health clinics. Collectively, these findings suggest that children with chronic illnesses are at risk for developing more psychosocial problems than well children. Thus, the 316 diagnosis may be particularly relevant for the clinician who comes into contact with patients who are chronically ill and who must comply with complex medical regimens. Cystic fibrosis, skin disorders, cancer, and juvenile rheumatoid arthritis are discussed briefly in this chapter. Insulin dependent diabetes mellitus (IDDM) serves as the primary model for the discussion.

Cystic Fibrosis

Cystic fibrosis (CF) is a disease that affects the respiratory, gastrointestinal, and reproductive systems. Proper management of CF is dependent, in part, on regular use of medication and maintenance of a high-calorie diet. The primary cause of death for patients with CF is pulmonary disease, which is highly correlated with malnutrition (Gurwitz, Corey, Francis, Crozier, & Levison, 1979). The 316 diagnosis may be applicable in a situation in which the patient does not comply with the medication regimen or does not adhere to an appropriate diet. Since the CF treatment recommendations suggest that children with CF consume 120% to 150% of the recommended daily allowance of calories for healthy children (MacDonald, Holden, & Harris, 1991), nutrition has often been targeted in CF treatment programs (Gurwitz et al., 1979). The increased caloric intake is necessary because of the demands of inadequate digestion, chronic lung infection, and malabsorption of nutrients. The need to maintain proper nutrition has been hypothesized to contribute to psychosocial problems such as increased parental anxiety and child behavior problems at mealtimes (MacDonald et al., 1991). Crist, McDonnell, Beck, Gillespie, and Mathews (1992) report that eating delays, spitting out food, and a variety of behavior problems at meals may be inadvertently rewarded by parents who use ineffective strategies (e.g., giving the child a second meal if the first one is refused). A diagnosis of 316 is appropriate for a patient who develops a behavior problem that interferes with the intake of necessary calories.

The literature regarding internalizing disorders in CF patients has failed to demonstrate that children with CF or their parents experience significant psychopathology when compared to normals. When assessed with self-report, children with CF do not appear to experience significant levels of depression and anxiety compared to healthy controls (Mullins, Youll, Olson, Reyes, & Volk, 1990). Furthermore, Thompson, Hodges, and Hamlett (1990) report that children with CF manifest fewer depressive symptoms and receive fewer depression, and dysthymic diagnoses than children referred to psychiatric settings. Given the standard CF nutritional and medication regimen, clinicians should monitor the child's internalizing symptoms through the course of the illness and render a 316 diagnosis when necessary.

Research on CF has focused on coping and adaptation to illness. Cowen, Corey, Keenan, Simmons, Arnt, and Levinson (1985) found that parents of children with CF cope relatively well with the child's illness and do not evidence higher levels of major psychopathology than controls. However, Quittner, DiGirolamo, Michel, and Eigen (1992) found that parents of recently diagnosed children evidenced significant levels of depression, parenting stress, and marital distress. Given this finding, the clinician should monitor parental adjustment during the course of the child's illness; the clinician should also monitor the impact of parental adjustment on the child.

Cancer

Medical treatment of acute lymphoblastic leukemia (ALL) usually includes an intensive 2- to 3-year regimen involving central nervous system prophylaxis and chemotherapy. Children and adolescents with cancer may experience physical side effects that may place them at risk for psychosocial difficulties (e.g., hair loss, weight loss or gain from medication, heightened fatigue). In a study of children with cancer, Noll, Bukowski, Rogosch, LeRoy, and Kulkarni (1990) reported that adolescents with cancer were considered more socially isolated than their peers. Furthermore, teachers reported that these children were less sociable than their peers. A 316 diagnosis may be appropriate for a child presenting with cancer who expresses feelings of depression and anxiety related to reduced social interactions.

Children with cancer may also experience a clinically significant amount of distress over medical procedures. This distress may be related to invasive medical procedures involved in ALL treatment, including venipunctures, lumbar punctures, and surgery. Studies suggest that certain parent behaviors (e.g., agitation, criticism) were associated with increased childhood distress (Blount, Sturges, & Powers, 1990). Adaptive coping behaviors were associated with the caregiver's distracting the child and attending to the child and the use of specific coping strategies such as humor and deep breathing during episodes of pain. A 316

diagnosis may be appropriate when distress levels become clinically significant.

Skin Disorders

There are few systematic studies on the psychological factors that affect dermatologic disorders (Van Moffaert, 1982). The DSM-IV Work Group for the 316 diagnostic category conducted an extensive review that identified a number of significant findings about many dermatologic conditions, including psoriasis and acne.

Psoriasis is a chronic skin disease characterized by dry patches covered with grayish scales. In 60% of the cases, disease onset occurs before age 30 (Gupta, Gupta, & Haberman, 1987). Psychological aspects of this disorder have been largely associated with the visibility of the disorder, as well as the need for care from others (Gupta et al., 1987). Ramsey and O'Reagan (1988) found that 55% of 104 psoriasis patients never experienced a complete remission from the condition, a fact that contributed to their eventual avoidance of social interactions. A diagnosis of 316 may be appropriate in instances where the patient avoids social interactions to a clinically significant degree. The association between psoriasis and depression has also been documented in the literature (Gupta, Schork, & Gupta, 1993).

Acne patients report a high frequency of diminished self-esteem and negative self-image (Rubinow, Peck, Squillace et al., 1988). Furthermore, anxiety and depression are two known clinical concomitants of severe acne (Van der Meeren et al., 1985). Severe acne may appear in children as well as young adults, suggesting that the clinician must screen patients for a possible 316 diagnosis.

Juvenile Rheumatoid Arthritis

Juvenile rheumatoid arthritis (JRA) is the most common connective tissue disease in children (Cassidy & Nelson, 1988). JRA can range in severity from mild to severe, and the disease is marked by periodic remissions and exacerbations. The regimen of JRA requires medication use and exercise. As a group, children with JRA have been found to be at risk for psychological and social adjustment problems (Wallander, Varni, Babani, Banis, & Wilcox, 1988). Research has suggested that the child's social environment is a significant predictor of the child's adaptation to the physical limitations of the disease. Social support, acceptance from peers, and family functioning have been identified as significant predictor variables of adjustment to illness (Varni, Wilcox, & Hanson, 1988). However, given the complex regimen of JRA, as well as the pain associated with the disorder, the clinician must consider the applicability of a 316 diagnosis with this population; for example, if adherence issues become problematic or if pain management becomes an issue, than a 316 diagnosis may be necessary.

Ross, Lavigne, Hayford, Berry, Sinacore, and Pachman (1994) examined the extent to which psychological variables are correlated with pain reported by children with JRA. Results indicated that higher levels of child self-reported anxiety, and maternal distress, were correlated with higher self-reported pain. Psychological variables had a significant impact on reported pain even after disease characteristics were taken into account. Therefore, psychological issues should be carefully monitored during the course of JRA.

Insulin-Dependent Diabetes Mellitus

Successful management of IDDM requires adherence to one of the most challenging regimens among the pediatric disorders. Maintaining health status requires monitoring of diet, insulin, and blood glucose and special attention to diet and exercise. A diagnosis of 316 is suitable for a child who does not adhere to the prescribed exercise, dietary, or insulin regimen or who is experiencing significant mood difficulties that affect compliance or health status.

The relevance of the 316 diagnosis becomes clear if IDDM management is conceptualized within the behavior-consequence framework

suggested by Gross (1987). From this standpoint, the youngster with IDDM experiences aversive consequences in return for a delayed reward. The immediate consequence of following the regimen involves inconvenience and physical discomfort, while the long-term reward is the avoidance of health complications. It is important to recognize that for the youngster, the immediate consequences of adherence are more salient than the potential delayed rewards. Given that choosing behavior in favor of long-term rewards is a difficult task for the child or young adult, the likelihood is that behavior will be controlled by its immediate consequences (Brigham, 1978; Gross & Wojnilower, 1984); thus, it is not surprising that a significant number of children with IDDM do not adhere to their medical regimens. Indeed, as many as 75% of patients with IDDM fail to follow their prescribed diets (Surwit, Scovern, & Feinglos, 1982), and it is estimated that 40–80% make errors in glucose testing and insulin administration (Johnson, Pollack, Silverstein, Rosenbloom, Spillar, McCallum, & Harkavay, 1982; Most, Gross, Davidson, & Richardson, 1986). This high rate of noncompliance and inaccuracy suggests that many clinicians treating children with IDDM may render 316 diagnoses and intervene with psychological treatment. Among children and adolescents with IDDM where nonadherence with the IDDM regimen is an issue, we consider the diagnosis of psychological factors affecting the medical condition, though the noncompliance is really a subset of that diagnosis.

Since health care behavior can be viewed from a behavior-consequence position, a pediatric psychologist may select patient education as a form of intervention in order to strengthen the relationship between behavior and consequence. Through patient education, the psychologist clarifies the relationship between medical adherence and long-term health. The pediatric psychologist may teach the child about health maintenance skills and provide an explanation of the impact of health behaviors on diabetes control. For example, the pediatrician and the pediatric psychologist might collaborate in instructing the youngster about proper insulin administration, healthy diet, blood glucose testing, and ketone testing and then teach the value of monitoring these elements. The goal in this type of education program is to increase adherence by establishing a clear relationship between current compliance and future health status.

Geffken and Johnson's (1994) review of the literature describes a close association between psychological adjustment and metabolic control in this period. However, the direction of this association is not always clear. Rather, Geffken and Johnson state that, in some cases, maladjustment may lead to poor compliance and diabetes control, while, in other cases, poor control may result in the child's becoming anxious or depressed. Nevertheless, a 316 diagnosis is relevant in both situations. Thus, the relationship between psychological adjustment and metabolic control is evident, but the exact nature of the relationship is bilateral. Given the complex relationship between health status and psychological variables, a thorough psychological assessment as well as a behavioral assessment of the child's medical regimen is crucial before a 316 diagnosis is rendered. This point is strengthened by Johnson's (1991) argument that assuming that a health status indicator is synonymous with adherence is inappropriate.

The distinction between a patient's health status and diabetes-related adherence is vital. Adherence or compliance refers to the patient's behavior in following a set of behavioral prescriptions given by the youngster's physician. Health status in diabetes, or what is referred to as metabolic control, refers to a set of biological variables reflected in part by the patient's blood glucose levels; when diabetes control is good, blood glucose levels are maintained within a desirable range.

Problems arise when health care providers use the terms "control" and "compliance" interchangeably. Sometimes patients are described globally as compliant or noncompliant as if compliance were a trait of the patient. Research on diabetes-related compliance behaviors has not supported the existence of such a trait (Glasgow, McCaul, & Schafer, 1987; Johnson,

Silverstein, Rosenbloom, Carter, & Cunningham, 1986). Patients may adhere to one aspect of a diabetes regimen (e.g., insulin injections) but not another (e.g., dietary recommendations). This example clarifies the importance of assessing each dimension of diabetes health care behavior.

Clarke, Snyder, and Nowacek (1985) found, in a survey of pediatric diabetologists, that 89% reported using the glycosylated hemoglobin, a measure of health status, to assess patient compliance. Johnson's (1990) review describes a literature that shows there is not a one-to-one relationship between compliance/adherence and health status/control. Another unreliable method of assessing adherence is use of health care provider ratings. Johnson (1991) further suggests that health care providers' knowledge of the health status of patients may merge with their ratings of adherence.

Assessment of 316 in Youths with IDDM

The 24-hour recall interview permits an assessment of each individual diabetes-related behavior (Johnson, Silverstein, Rosenbloom, Carter, & Cunningham, 1986). It focuses on actual behavior reported by the patient or the patient's parent. A number of studies in this area have yielded data suggesting that self-report may be useful, provided the reports are highly specific and time-limited (Freund, Johnson, Silverstein, & Thomas 1991; Johnson et al., 1986; Johnson, Freund, Silverstein, Hansen, & Malone, 1990; Spevack, Johnson, & Riley, 1991).

Skills tests based on observation of insulin injections, blood glucose monitoring, and urine ketone testing provide an important basis for assessing patient knowledge (Johnson, Lewis-Meert, & Alexander, 1981; Pollack & Johnson 1979). When these skills are deficient, inadvertent noncompliance may result. The patient may attempt to follow the doctor's behavioral prescriptions or advice regarding the best diabetes regimen, but because of lack of skill, may unintentionally not comply. It should be clear that this type of assessment can be critical in the assessment of psychological factors affecting medical condition.

Tests are also available to assess a broader range of diabetes-related knowledge tests. One such test is the Test of Diabetes Knowledge—Revised, Second Edition (Johnson, 1984). This is a multiple-choice test that assesses both factual knowledge about diabetes and how well these facts are applied in different situations or how problem solving is accomplished. Norms are available to allow comparison with same-age peers.

Developmental considerations are important in an assessment of diabetes. Research has shown that prior to age nine, youngsters are not capable of reliably giving themselves insulin injections in an accurate and appropriate way (Gilbert, Johnson, Spillar, McCallum, Silverstein, & Rosenbloom, 1982; Johnson, Pollack, Silverstein, Rosenbloom, Spillar, McCallum, & Harkavy, 1982). Similarly, research has shown that prior to 12 years of age, youngsters with diabetes may make critical errors in blood glucose testing (Harkavy, Johnson, Silverstein, Spillar, McCallum, & Rosenbloom, 1983; Johnson, Pollack, Silverstein, Rosenbloom, Spillar, McCallum, & Harkavy, 1982). The 316 diagnosis may be appropriate, on the basis of developmental considerations; for example, a child may be cognitively limited, rather than noncompliant in some other sense. Developmental considerations in the diagnosis of psychological factors affecting medical condition are an important issue, as are their treatment implications. For young children with insulin-dependent diabetes, problems with insulin injections definitely require parent training. However, if the patient is 19 years old, there would be a much stronger emphasis on working with the patient him- or herself. Likewise, with a 2-year-old with oppositional eating, the approach to treatment would focus almost exclusively on parent training, whereas with an adolescent there would be much greater involvement of the patient.

The data have shown there are developmental differences in diabetes-related knowledge (Johnson, 1984) and that adolescents may be more knowledgeable and may possess more of these diabetes-related skills; however, at times adolescents may be less adherent than younger patients (Johnson, Freund, Silverstein, Hansen,

& Mallone, 1990; Johnson, Silverstein, Rosenbloom, Carter, & Cunningham, 1986). Hence, when an individual assessment reveals that an adolescent is not mature enough for independent diabetes care, lack of parental supervision of diabetes-related skills may lead to failure to follow the prescription of the physician as well as a decline in the adolescent's health status.

An assessment of family factors is important in the assessment of 316 in the area of diabetes, as evidenced by considerable research. A study by Kovacs and colleagues (Kovacs et al., 1985) found that mild parental anxiety and depression were associated with the diagnosis of diabetes in the first six months after diagnosis. Mothers were also found to be more vulnerable that fathers. Numerous studies have described increased stress for mothers (Abidin, 1986; Borner & Steinhausen, 1987; Hauenstein, Marvin, Snyder, & Clarke, 1989). This research is understood as reflecting the fact that mothers are usually the primary caretaker for a child with diabetes. The same researchers (Hauenstein, Marvin, Snyder, & Clarke, 1989) found that mothers of youngsters with IDDM report receiving less support from their husbands than do mothers of a control group of healthy children. Other research on family factors has been more mixed. Some researchers (Anderson & Auslander, 1980; Anderson, Miller, Auslander, & Santiago, 1981; Gath, Smith, & Baum, 1980) found that limited family resources and/or family dysfunction were related to decreased health status in this population. Other researchers (Kovacs, Cass, Schnell, Goldston, & Marsh, 1989) found no relationship between the metabolic status of youngsters with diabetes and family functioning. Other research (Hanson, Henggler, Harris, Burghen, & Moore, 1989) found that only in youngsters with relatively newly diagnosed diabetes were family factors related to patient health. One of the more popular reports in the literature (Minuchin, Rosman, & Baker, 1978) suggested that unresolved family conflict was importantly related to recurrent episodes of diabetic ketoacidosis; however, other researchers (Coyne & Anderson, 1988) report that empirical data were lacking for this hypothesis. On the basis of this literature, it seems reasonable to posit that the clinician treating youngsters with IDDM should conduct a careful assessment of familial factors in addressing the issue of psychological factors that affect medical condition.

Another important issue where PFAMC may be involved with youngsters with diabetes concerns school-related problems. School problems may include poor attendance, the expression of excessive of physical complaints, and inadequate grades. In a report by Geffken et al. (1991), children admitted for specialized diabetes-related residential treatment missed an average of 22.5 days of school in the year preceding their admission. Similarly with a more representative sample of adolescents with IDDM, Ryan, Longstreet, & Morrow (1985) reported thirteen days missed on average from school, which was double the absences reported by a control group without diabetes. Clinicians working with children with difficult-to-manage diabetes may find that psychosocial issues become confused with medical issues, and school performance may suffer.

We are not aware of instruments for assessment that are available to tease out the different contributions of psychosocial and medical issues to problems with school performance. However, assessing any medical variables in the school situation may make a contribution to one's understanding of the school performance problem. Some conditions, such as diabetes, may have numerous medical markers, such as blood glucose levels or presence of ketones, available to assess. However, the constellation of variables in the situation over time is the critical issue. Problems of a repeated nature that are not experienced by most youngsters with the condition should alert the clinician to consider PFAMC.

Another important area where PFAMC may be identified in youngsters with diabetes is where the child has recurrent episodes of hypoglycemia; the issue may be surreptitious insulin administration (Orr, Eccles, Lawlor, & Golden, 1986). Some youngsters may attempt to cover dietary indiscretions by taking extra insulin, which results in hypoglycemia. An even more serious problem occurs with youngsters

who may be depressed or suicidal and who use unique diabetes-regimen behaviors as the means of self-destruction. Clearly, a careful assessment is very important with this problem.

PFAMC is evident in the incidence of eating disorders in youngsters with diabetes, which has been described in numerous case reports (Hillard & Hillard, 1984; Peveler & Fairburn, 1989; Powers, Malone, & Duncan, 1983; Rodrigue, Dandes, Geffken, Spevack, & Silverstein, 1990). There may be an increased prevalence of eating disorders with patients with diabetes, according to a review by Marcus and Wing (1990), though more controlled and rigorous studies are needed in this area. The emphasis on diet in diabetes may exacerbate atypical eating patterns in some youngsters with diabetes. It is also important to note that omission of insulin provides adolescents with diabetes a unique means for weight control, since skipping required insulin results in weight loss; however, this behavior can result in unintentional episodes of ketosis or, more serious, ketoacidosis. Assessment for indicators of eating-disordered behaviors is important in youngsters with diabetes.

General Issues in the Assessment of 316 with Youths

In recent years measures have been developed for the psychological assessment of issues related to specific medical conditions. While these vary across conditions, some of the issues, as indicated previously, involve an assessment of compliance with the regimen, which may be accomplished by obtaining a description of the patient's behavior as it relates to compliance over the day or two preceding the meeting with the doctor. For some conditions, these measures may exist in a very formalized way; for other conditions, they may be less formalized.

Another issue related to compliance is assessment of quality of life. Again, these may be quite disease-specific, given the issue, though the extent to which the regimen and symptoms of the conditions interfere with the life of the youngster and his or her family are an important issue. One would want to assess the patient's knowledge of the condition and the level of knowledge of the parents of the child with the condition. Again, this requires familiarity with the condition if a disease specific measure is not available. The clinician may want to assess attitudes of the child and of the parents, including their attitudes toward the medical staff who are treating the child. What are the child's and family's attitudes toward the stigmatization facing the child with the condition? Do the child and the parents feel that the child's condition is disruptive to the family or that the child uses the condition in a manipulative way to be excused from problems?

TREATMENT OF 316 IN YOUTHS WITH IDDM

In the pediatric setting, the 316 diagnosis is appropriate in a number of situations. The diagnosis may be suitable for an adolescent who experiences a major depressive episode that interferes with adequate recovery from a head injury. Similarly, the diagnosis is appropriate for a child with insulin-dependent diabetes mellitus whose refusal to administer insulin or to monitor diet interferes with diabetes control. The pediatric psychologist is faced with the challenge of measuring the interactive effects of environmental and biological factors on the child. In essence, the pediatric psychologist recognizes the special stresses that a chronic illness places on the child patient and on the family system and is available to the child as well as to the parents. Once the clinician has conducted a psychological assessment of the child and has determined that a 316 diagnosis is appropriate, the relationship among the child's attitudes, health care behavior, family interactions, and the child's developmental stage must be considered before a treatment plan is developed. Like other DSM-IV diagnoses, a 316 diagnosis does not dictate the treatment protocol. Rather, the treatment plan must be individualized to address the child's specific needs. Identification of psychological issues that need to be addressed and assessment of environmental

conditions and the family's willingness to help are all relevant for treatment planning.

The clinician's intervention does not end at the level of patient education and health promotion. Researchers have reported that newly diagnosed children with diabetes may experience anxiety, depression, and social withdrawal problems, which may remit within six to nine months (Kovacs, Feinberg, Paulauskas, Finklestein, Pollock, & Crouse-Novak, 1985). If these symptoms persist or become severe or if they interfere with medical adherence, a pediatric psychologist may provide emotional support for the child and encourage the child to continue peer relationships and to become involved in physical activities. The pediatric psychologist may identify and treat maladaptive coping strategies in ill children or help these children master the anxiety associated with their physical condition and new environment and to enhance their compliance with medical regimens (Peterson & Harbeck, 1988).

Treatment may also be directed at the family unit. In such cases, the unit of intervention is not the ill child but the transactional pattern. Interventions from the pediatric psychologist at the family level involve identifying and addressing pathological patterns in the family and include teaching family members to cope with medical procedures or the demands of the child's regimen and providing broad-based therapy. Family members may be taught to adapt to the child's medical procedures in order to limit both parental and child distress (Meng & Zastowsky, 1982). Behavioral techniques may be used to assist parents in acquiring specific skills needed for carrying out regimen requirements. In the case of IDDM, a family-based behavioral intervention program may be implemented. In this instance, parents may work together with a pediatric psychologist to form a reward system to increase the child's appropriate dietary intake, glucose testing, and regular exercise. While these interventions have a problem-based focus, the pediatric psychologist's interventions may encompass an even broader range with children with a 316 diagnoses. For example, a pediatric psychologist may focus on enhancing communication within the family, facilitating acceptance of the diagnosis, and increasing emotional support within the family.

Studies suggest that educational programs about diabetes and its management assist patients in acquiring information (Etzwiler & Robb, 1972; Heston & Lazar, 1980). However, research also suggests that cognitive developmental level is related to the degree of learning; some researchers (Gilbert, Johnson, Spillar, McCallum, Silverstein, & Rosenbloom, 1982) observed this in studying the effects of a peer modeling film of children learning to inject insulin, as did other researchers (Monaco, Geffken, & Silverstein, 1996) in training youngsters with diabetes to rotate insulin injection sites. It has, however, been evident that the positive results of educational programs are not always associated with improved health status (Etzwiler & Robb, 1972; Marrero, Kronz, Golden, Wright, Orr, & Fineberg, 1989). In fact, extending beyond the area of diabetes, Mazzuza's (1982) review of 320 articles found that there was limited evidence of improved health status after educational programming with chronically ill populations. Programs that target both knowledge and behavior are more likely to result in a meaningful change (Geffken & Johnson, 1994). The level of cognitive development may need to be addressed in many programs for children with diabetes (Moore, Geffken, & Royal, 1995), as well as those aimed at parents of children with diabetes.

An interesting line of educational research has been reviewed by Gonder-Frederick and Cox (1990), who studied individual differences in the symptoms experienced by patients with diabetes during periods of hyper- and hypoglycemia. While there are "classic" symptoms of hyper- and hypoglycemia, the literature in this area does not suggest that the classic symptoms of hypoglycemia are sufficiently widespread across the population of diabetes to warrant teaching these symptoms. Idiosyncratic patterns of symptoms associated with hypo- and, sometimes, hyperglycemia have been demonstrated and integrated into educational programs associated with significant improvement in patients' ability to accurately identify or estimate their own blood glucose levels in both adults and adolescents with IDDM (Cox, Gonder-Frederick, Lee, Julian, Carter, & Clarke, 1989; Nurick & Johnson, 1991). Family intervention studies have shown improved health status in both children and adolescents with diabetes (Anderson, Wolfe, Burkhart, Cornell, & Bacon, 1989; Satin, LaGreca, Zigo, & Skyler, 1989). However, other research has shown that family-based behavior therapy approaches have not resulted in improved metabolic control (Delamater, Smith, Bubb, Davis, Gamble, White, & Santiago, 1991; Wysocki, Green, & Huxtable, 1991). A judicious approach suggests that the clinician conceptualize each case individually before deciding whether to address familial factors affecting medical conditions in psychological treatment.

Residential treatment for chronically ill youngsters is very rare in the United States, though it occurs with greater frequency in Europe (Rosenbloom, 1983). A follow-up of the first 52 youngsters admitted to one of the few residential programs designed for youngsters with diabetes (at the University of Florida Health Science Center) indicated that psychological factors were affecting medical conditions, often to a life-threatening degree. Results showed numerous significant clinical improvements in this specialized treatment program with this exceptional population, which had problems with recurrent ketoacidosis, poor metabolic control, school attendance, and familial disruption. Residential treatment was associated with reduced hospitalizations for diabetes-related problems, improved blood glucose results, reduced school absenteeism, improved diabetes-related knowledge, and more normal attitudes toward their condition (Geffken, Lewis, Buithieu, Johnson, Silverstein, & Rosenbloom, 1991). Residential treatment has also been shown to be effective with diabetic youngsters with eating problems (Rodrigue et al., 1990) and in reducing needle phobia in youngsters with diabetes (Moore, Geffken, & Royal, 1995). Residential treatment remains a limited but important option for youngsters with diabetes where psychological factors affecting physical condition are life threatening in nature.

COMMENTS

There is a need for mental health professionals and health care professionals in general to identify areas of intervention where psychological factors are affecting medical conditions and to be able to recognize behaviors that are interfering with health maintenance or recovery. The current chapter cannot cover every possible diagnosis, given the multitude of possible diseases and illnesses and conditions for which the diagnosis of psychological factors affecting medical condition might be involved. However, it may be of value to provide the reader with a template that can serve as guide for the assessment and treatment of these problems. This template might focus on how to approach patients who might warrant a diagnosis of "psychological factors affecting medical conditions." The first recommendation is that the psychologist become familiar with the medical condition and its regimen; consultation with the referring physician and having access basic medical texts or a medical library will prove invaluable in this. Knowledge of the medical condition will allow the clinician to be sensitive to the need for the evaluation of potential risk factors with that condition. Given a behavioral framework for assessing risk, the clinician may then establish temporal relationships between external events and physical reactions. Involvement of family and peers and coordination with the school are important in this assessment. The reader may find it helpful to peruse such journals as the *Journal of Pediatric Psychology* and *Children's Health Care*, as well as numerous other journals, in providing a database for evaluation. There are numerous specialized journals, for example, if the clinician is interested in diabetes, such as *Diabetes Care* or *Diabetes Educator*. In addition, there are numerous texts, such as the *Source Book of Pediatric Psychology* and *The Handbook of Pediatric Psychology*, that are available for this purpose.

REFERENCES

Abidin, R. R., (1986). *Parenting Stress Index (PSI)—Manual.* Charolottesville, VA: Pediatric Psychology Press.

Alexander, F. (1950). *Psychosomatic medicine.* New York: W. W. Norton.

American Psychiatric Association. (1968). *Diagnostic and statistical manual of mental disorders* (2nd ed.). Washington, DC: Author.

American Psychiatric Association. (1980). *Diagnostic and statistical manual of mental disorders* (3rd ed.). Washington, DC: Author.

American Psychiatric Association. (1987). *Diagnostic and statistical manual of mental disorders* (3rd ed., rev.). Washington, DC: Author.

American Psychiatric Association. (1994). *Diagnostic and statistical manual of mental disorders* (4th ed.). Washington, DC: Author.

Anderson, B. J., & Auslander, W. (1980). Research on diabetes management and the family: A critique. *Diabetes Care, 3,* 671–696.

Anderson, B., Miller, J., Auslander, W., & Santiago, J. (1981). Family characteristics of diabetic adolescents: Relationships to metabolic control. *Diabetes Care, 4,* 586–594.

Anderson, B., Wolf, F. M., Burkhart, M. T., Cornell, R. G., & Bacon, G. E. (1989). Effects of peer group interventions on metabolic control of adolescents with IDDM: Randomized outpatient study. *Diabetes Care, 12* (3), 179–183.

Blount, R. L., Sturges, J. W., & Powers, S. W. (1990). Analysis of child and adult behavioral variations by phase of medical procedure. *Behavior Therapy, 20,* 585–601.

Borner, A., & Steinhauser, H. C. (1977). A psychological study of family characteristics in juvenile diabetes. *Pediatric and Adolescent Endocrinology, 3,* 46–51.

Brigham, T. A. (1978). Self-control. In A. C. Catania & T. A. Brigham (Eds.), *The handbook of applied behavior analysis.* New York: Irvington Press.

Bronfenbrenner, U. (1977). Toward an experimental ecology of human development. *American Psychologist, 32,* 513–531.

Cassidy, J. T., & Nelson, A. M. (1988). The frequency of juvenile arthritis. *Journal of Rheumatology, 15,* 535–536.

Clarke, W. L., Snyder, A. L., & Nowacek, G. (1985). Outpatient pediatric diabetes. I: Current practices. *Journal of Chronic Diseases, 38,* 85–90.

Cowen, L., Corey, M., Keenan, N., Simmons, R., Arnt, E., & Levison, H. (1985). Family adaptation and psychosocial adjustment to cystic fibrosis in the preschool child. *Social Science and Medicine, 20,* 553–560.

Cox, D. J., Gonder-Frederick, L. A., Lee, J. H., Julian, D. M., Carter, W. R., & Clarke, W. L. (1989). Blood glucose awareness training among patients with IDDM: Effects and correlates. *Diabetes Care, 12,* 313–318.

Coyne, J. C., & Anderson, B. J. (1988). The "psychosomatic family" reconsidered: Diabetes in context. *Journal of Marital and Family Therapy, 14,* 113–123.

Delamater, A. M., Smith, J. A., Bubb, J., Davis, S. G., Gamble, T., White, N. H., & Santiago, J. V. (1991). Family-based behavior therapy for diabetic adolescents. In J. H. Johnson & S. B. Johnson (Eds.), *Advances in child health psychology,* (pp. 293–306). Gainesville: University of Florida Press.

Descartes, R. (1662/1955). In R. Eaton (Ed.), *Selections.* New York: Scribner's.

Dunbar F. H. (1935). *Emotions and bodily changes: A survey of literature on psychosomatic relationships.* New York: Columbia University Press.

Dunbar F. H. (1955). *Mind and body: Psychosomatic medicine.* New York: Random House.

Engel, G. (1977). The need for a new medical model: A challenge for biomedicine. *Science, 196,* 129–135.

Etzwiler, D. D., & Robb, J. R. (1972). Evaluation of programmed education among juvenile diabetics and their familites. *Diabetes, 21,* 967–971.

Freud, S. (1905/1963). *Dora: A analysis of hysteria* (P. Rieff, Ed. and Trans.). New York: Macmillan.

Freund, A., Johnson, S. B., Silverstein, J., & Thomas, J. (1991). Assessing daily management of childhood diabetes using 24-hr. recall interviews: Reliability and stability, *Health Psychology, 10,* 200–208.

Gath, A., Smith, M., & Baum, J. (1980). Emotional, behavioral, and educational disorders in diabetic children. *Archives of Diseases in Childhood, 55,* 371–375.

Geffken, G. R., & Johnson, S. B. (1994). Diabetes: Psychological issues. In R. A. Olsen, L. L. Mullins, J. B. Gillman, & I. M. Chaney (Eds.), *A sourcebook of pediatric psychology,* Boston: Allyn and Bacon.

Geffken, G. R., Lewis, C., Buithieu, M., Johnson, S. B., Silverstein, J., & Rosenbloom, A. L. (1991). Follow-up of youngsters with IDDM after residential treatment. In S. R. Boggs (Ed.), *Advances in child health psychology: Supplemental abstracts.* Gainesville: University of Florida.

Gilbert, B. O., Johnson, S. B., Spillar, R., McCallum, M., Silverstein, J. H., & Rosenbloom, A. (1982). The effects of a peer-modeling film on children learning to self-inject insulin. *Behavior Therapy, 13,* 186–194.

Glasgow, R., & Anderson, B. (1995). Future directions for research on pediatric chronic disease management: Lessons from diabetes. *Journal of Pediatric Psychology, 20* (4), 389–402.

Glasgow, R. E., McCaul, K. D., & Schafer, L. C. (1987). Self-behaviors and glycemic control in type I diabetes. *Journal of Chronic Disease, 40,* 399–417.

Gonder-Frederick, L. A., & Cox, D. J. (1990). Symptom perception and blood glucose feedback in the self-treatment of IDDM. In C. S. Holmes (Ed.), *Neuropsychological and behavioral aspects of diabetes* (pp. 155–174). New York: Springer-Verlag.

Gonder-Frederick, L. A., & Cox, D. J. (1990). Symptom perception and blood glucose feedback in the self-treatment of IDDM. In C. Holmes (Ed.), *Neuropsychological and behavioral aspects of diabetes* (pp. 12–29). New York: Springer-Verlag.

Gross, A. M., & Wojnilower, D. A., (1984). Self-directed behavior in children: Is it self-directed? *Behavior Therapy, 15,* 501–514.

Gross, A. M. (1987). Noncompliance in young diabetics. *Journal of Compliance in Health Care, 2* (1), 7–21.

Gupta, M. A., Gupta, A. K., & Haberman, H. F. (1987). Psoriasis and psychiatry: An update. *General Hospital Psychiatry, 9,* 157–166.

Gupta, M. A., Schork, N. J., Gupta, A. K., et al. (1993). Suicidal ideation in psoriasis. *International Journal of Dermatology, 32,* 188–190.

Gurwitz, D., Corey, M., Francis, P. S., Crozier, D., & Levison, H. (1979). Perspectives in cystic fibrosis. *Pediatric Clinics of North America, 26,* 603–615.

Hanson, C. L., Henggeler, S. W., Harris, M. A., Burghen, G. A., & Moore, M. (1989). Family system variables and the health status of adolescents with insulin-dependent diabetes mellitus. *Health Psychology, 8* (2), 239–253.

Harkavy, J., Johnson, S. B., Silverstein, J., Spillar, R., McCallum, M., & Rosenbloom, A. (1983). Who learns what at diabetes summer camp. *Journal of Pediatric Psychology, 8,* 143–153.

Hauenstein, E. J., Marvin, R. S., Snyder, A. L., & Clarke, W. L. (1989). Stress in parents of children with diabetes mellitus. *Diabetes Care, 12* (1), 18–23.

Heston, J. V., & Lazar, S. J. (1980). Evaluating a

learning device for juvenile diabetic children. *Diabetes Care, 3* (6), 668–671.

Hillard, J. R., & Hillard, P. J. (1984). Bulimia, anorexia nervosa and diabetes: Deadly combinations. *Psychiatric Clinics of North America, 7,* 367–379.

Hippocrates. (4th Century B.C./1923). *On decorum and the physician*, Vol. II (W. H. S. Jones, Trans.). London: William Heinemann.

Johnson, S. B. (1984). *Test of diabetes knowledge—R2.* Gainesville: University of Florida, Department of Psychiatry.

Johnson, S. B. (1989). Juvenile diabetes. In T. H. Ollendick & M. Hersen (Eds.), *Handbook of child psychopathogy*, (2nd ed.). New York: Plenum Press.

Johnson, S. B. (1991). Compliance with complex medical regimens: Assessing daily management of childhood diabetes. In R. Prinz (Ed.), *Advances in behavioral assessment of children and families* (Vol. 5, pp. 113–139). Greenwich, CT: JAI Press.

Johnson, S. B., Freund, A., Silverstein, J., Hansen, C. A., & Malone, J. (1990). Adherence-health status relationships in childhood diabetes. *Health Psychology, 9,* 606–631.

Johnson, S. B., Lewis-Meert, C., & Alexander, B. (1981). *Administration and scoring manual for Chemstrip skill demonstration test.* Gainesville: University of Florida, Department of Psychiatry.

Johnson, S. B., Pollack, R. T., Silverstein, J. H., Rosenbloom, A. L., Spillar, R., McCallum, M., & Harkavy, J. (1982). Cognitive and behavioral knowledge about IDDM among children and parents. *Pediatrics, 69,* 708–713.

Johnson, S. B., Silverstein, J., Rosenbloom, A., Carter, R., & Cunningham, W. (1986). Assessing daily management in childhood diabetes. *Health Psychology, 5,* 545–564.

Kagan, J. (1965). The new marriage: Pediatrics and psychology. *American Journal of Diseases in Childhood, 110,* 272–278.

Kovacs, M., Feinberg, T. L., Paulausksa, S., Finkelstein, R., Pollock, M., & Crouse-Novak, M. (1985). Initial coping responses and psychosocial characteristics of children with insulin dependent diabetes mellitus. *Journal of Pediatrics, 106,* 827–834.

Kovacs, M., Kass, R. E., Schnell, T. M., Goldston, D., & Marsh, J. (1989). Family functioning and metabolic control of school-aged children with IDDM. *Diabetes Care, 12,* 409–414.

LaGreca, A., Auslander, W., Greco, W., Spetter, D., Fisher, & Santiago, J. (1994). *Journal of Pediatric Psychology, 20,* 449–476.

Lavigne, J. V., & Faier-Routman, J. (1992). Psychological adjustment to pediatric physical disorders: A meta-analytic review. *Journal of Pediatric Psychology, 17,* 133–158.

Linn, L., & Spitzer R. L. (1982). DSM-III: Implications for liaison psychiatry and psychosomatic medicine. *Journal of the American Medical Association, 247,* 3207–3209.

Lipowski, Z. J. (1986). Psychosomatic medicine: Past and present. I: Historical background. *Canadian Journal of Psychiatry, 31,* 2–7.

Looney, J. G., Lipp M. R., & Spitzer, R. L. (1978). A new method of classification for psychophysiological disorders. *American Journal of Psychiatry, 135,* 304–308.

MacDonald, A., Holden, C., & Harris, G. (1991). Nutritional strategies in cystic fibrosis: Current issues. *Journal of the Royal Society of Medicine, 84* (Suppl. 18), 28–35.

Marcus, M. D., & Wing, R. R. (1990). Eating disorders and diabetes. In C. S. Holmes (Ed.), *Neuropsychological and behavioral aspects of diabetes* (pp. 102–121). New York: Springer-Verlag.

Marrero, D. G., Kronz, K. K., Golden, M. P., Wright, J. C., Orr, D. P., & Fineberg, N. S. (1989). Clinical evaluation of computer-assisted self-monitoring of blood glucose system. *Diabetes Care, 12,* 345–350.

Mazzuca, S. A. (1982). Does patient education in chronic disease have therapeutic value? *Journal of Chronic Diseases, 35,* 521–529.

Meng, A., & Zastowny, T. (1982). Preparation for hospitalization: A stress inoculation training program for parents and children. *Maternal-Child Nursing Journal, 11,* 87–94.

Meyer, A. (1957). *The psychobiology of man.* Springfield, IL: Charles C. Thomas.

Minuchin, S. (1978). *Psychosomatic families: Anorexia nervosa in context.* Cambridge, MA: Harvard University Press.

Minuchin, S., Baker, L., Rosman, B. L., Liebman, R., Milman, L., & Todd, T. C. (1975). A conceptual model of psychosomatic illness in children. *Archives of General Psychology, 32,* 1031–1038.

Minuchin, S., Rosman, B. L., & Baker, L. (1978). *Psychosomatic families.* Cambridge, MA: Harvard University Press.

Monaco, L., Geffken, G. R., & Silverstein, J. (1996). Accuracy of injection site identification among children with insulin-dependent diabetes mellitus: A comparison of traditional and new visual aids. *Clinical Pediatrics, 25* (4), 191–199.

Moore, K., Geffken, G. R., & Royal, G. P. (1995).

Behavioral intervention to reduce child distress during self-injection, *Clinical Pediatrics, 34* (10), 530–534.

Most, R. S., Gross, A. M., Davidson, P. C., & Richardson, P. (1986). The accuracy of glucose monitoring by diabetic individuals in the home setting. *Diabetes Educator, 12,* 24–27.

Mullins, L. L., Youll, L. K., Olsen, R. A., Reyes, S., & Volk, R. J. (1990, August). *Children's coping with cystic fibrosis: Family factors and influences.* Paper presented at the meeting of the American Psychological Association, Boston, MA.

Noll, R. B., Bukowski, W. M., Rogosch, F. A., LeRoy, S., & Kulkarni, R. (1990). Social interaction between children with cancer and their peers: Teacher rating. *Journal of Pediatric Psychology, 15,* 43–56.

Nurick, M. A., & Johnson, S. B. (1991). Enhancing blood glucose awareness in adolescents and young adults with IDDM. *Diabetes Care, 15* (8), 493–509.

Olsen, R. A., Mullen, J. B., & Chaney, I. M. (Eds.). (1994). *A sourcebook of pediatric psychology.* Boston: Allyn and Bacon.

Orr, D. P., Eccles, T., Lawlor, R., & Golden, M. (1986). Surreptitious insulin administration in adolscents with insulin-dependent diabetes mellitus. *Journal of the American Medical Association, 256,* 3227–3230.

Peterson, L., & Harbeck, C. (1988). *The pediatric psychologist: Issues in professional development and practice.* Champaign, IL: Research Press.

Pevelar, R. C., & Fairburn, C. C. (1989). Anorexia nervosa in association with diabetes mellitus. *Journal of Clinical Psychiatry, 44,* 133–135.

Pollack, R. T., & Johnson, S. B. (1979). *Administration of scoring manual for the Test of Diabetes Knowledge skills demonstration.* Gainesville: University of Florida, Department of Psychiatry.

Popkin, M. K. (1987). Disorders with physical symptoms. In A. E. Skodol & R. L. Spitzer (Eds.), *Annotated bibliography of DSM-III.* Washington, DC: American Psychiatric Association Press.

Powers, P. S., Malone, J. T., & Duncan, J. A. (1983). Anorexia nervosa and diabetes mellitus. *Journal of Clinical Psychiatry, 44,* 133–135.

Quittner, A. L., DiGirolamo, A. M., Michel, M., & Eigen, H. (1992). Parental response to cystic fibrosis: A contextual analysis of the diagnosis phase. *Journal of Pediatric Psychology, 17,* 687–704.

Ramsey, B., & O'Reagan, M. (1988). A survey of the social and psychological effects of psoriasis. *British Journal of Dermatology, 118,* 195–201.

Rodrigue, J. R., Dandes, S. K., Geffken, G. R., Spevack, M., & Silverstein, J. (1990). Multimodal treatment of an adolescent with anorexia and insulin-dependent diabetes mellitus: A case report. *Family Systems Medicine, 8,* 349–358.

Rosenbloom, A. L. (1983). Need for residential treatment for children with diabetes mellitus. *Diabetes Care, 5,* 545–546.

Ross, C. K., Lavigne, J., Hayford, J., Berry, S., Sinacore, J., & Pachman, L. (1993). Psychological factors affecting reported pain in juvenile rheumatoid arthritis. *Journal of Pediatric Psychology, 8,* 561–573.

Routh, D. K. (Ed.). (1988). *Handbook of pediatric psychology.* New York: Guilford Press.

Rubinow, D. R., Peck, G. L., Squillace, K. M., et al. (1987). Reduced anxiety and depression in cystic acne patients after successful treatment with oral isotretinoin. *Journal of the American Academy of Dermatology, 17,* 25–32.

Ryan, C., Longstreet, C., & Morrow, L. (1985). The effects of diabetes mellitus on the school attendance and school achievement of adolecents. *Child: Care, Health, and Development, 11,* 229–240.

Satin, W., LaGreca, A. M., Zigo, M. A., & Skyler, J. S. (1989). Diabetes in adolescence: Effects of multifamily group intervention and parent simulation of diabetes. *Journal of Pediatric Psychology, 14,* 259–279.

Selye, H. (1956). *The stress of life.* New York: McGraw-Hill.

Selye, H. (1976). *Stress in health and disease.* Reading, MA: Butterworth.

Spevack, M., Johnson, S. B., & Riley, W. (1991). The effect of diabetes summer camp on adherence behaviors, glycemic control, and physician behavior. In J. Johnson & S. B. Johnson (Eds.), *Advances in child health psychology* (pp. 285–292). Gainesville: University of Florida Press.

Stoudemire, A. (1995). *Psychological factors affecting medical conditions.* Washington, DC: American Psychiatric Association Press.

Surwit, R. S., Scovern, A. W., & Feinglos, D. C. (1982). The role of behavior in diabetes care. *Diabetes Care, 5,* 337–342.

Van der Meeren, H. L. M., Van der Schaar, W. W., & Van den Hurk, C. M. A. M. (1985). The psychological impact of severe acne. *Cutis, 36,* 84–86.

Van Moffaert, M. (1982). Psychosomatics for the

practicing dermatologist. *Dermatologica, 165,* 73–87.

Varni, J. W., Wilcox, K. T., & Hanson, V. (1988). Mediating effects of family social support on child psychological adjustment in juvenile rheumatoid arthritis. *Health Psychology, 7,* 421–431.

Wallander, J. L., Varni, J. W., Babani, L. V., Banis, H. T., & Wilcox, K. T. (1988). Children with chronic physical disorders: Maternal reports of their psychological adjustment. *Journal of Pediatric Psychology, 13,* 197–212.

Wolman, B. (1988). *Psychosomatic disorders.* NY: Plenum Press.

World Health Organization. (1992). *ICD-10 Classification of Mental and Behavioural Disorders: Clinical descriptions of diagnostic guidelines.* Geneva: Author.

Wright, L. (1967). The pediatric psychologist: A role model. *American Psychologist, 22,* 323–325.

Wysocki, T., Green, L., & Huxtable, K. (1991). Reflectance meters with memory: Applications in behavioral assessment and intervention in juvenile diabetes. In J. H. Johnson & S. B. Johnson (Eds.), *Advances in child health psychology* (pp. 307–319). Gainesville: University of Florida Press.

27
Noncompliance

Heather Huszti
Roberta Olson

HISTORICAL PERSPECTIVE

Noncompliance has traditionally been considered a general impediment to the psychological treatment of children and adolescents. Noncompliance with treatment is not considered a distinct psychiatric disorder. The *Diagnostic and Statistical Manual of Mental Disorders*, Fourth Edition (American Psychiatric Association, 1994) provides a brief description of noncompliance with treatment (V15.81; ICD10 Z91.1):

> This category can be used when the focus of clinical attention is noncompliance with an important aspect of the treatment for a mental disorder or a general medical condition. The reasons for noncompliance may include discomfort resulting from treatment (e.g., medication side effects), expense of treatment, decisions based on personal value judgments or religious or cultural beliefs about the advantages and disadvantages of the proposed treatment, maladaptive personality traits or coping (e.g., denial of illness), or the presence of a mental disorder (e.g., Schizophrenia, Avoidant Personality Disorder). This category should be used only when the problem is sufficiently severe to warrant independent clinical attention.

(DSM-IV, 1994. Reprinted with permission from the Diagnostic and Statistical Manual of Mental Disorders, Fourth Edition. Copyright 1994 American Psychiatric Association.)

A comparison of this description of noncompliance with treatment and previous definitions in earlier editions of the *Diagnostic and Statistical Manual of Mental Disorders* reveals an expansion of the definition and the inclusion of additional behaviors considered to be reasons for noncompliance. In the most recent definition, both medical and mental health noncompliance are included, whereas the earlier definitions referred only to noncompliance with medical treatments and specifically excluded noncompliance with treatment that was due to a mental disorder (DSM III, DSM III-R). The most recent edition indicates that the diagnosis of noncompliance with treatment can be used even when there is the presence of a mental disorder. However, *International Classification of Diseases* (ICD-10) continues to define noncompliance as applying only to medical treatment and does not include a stipulation for noncompliance with mental health treatment.

Over time, the term "noncompliance" has taken on a negative connotation. Patients labeled as "noncompliant" are often viewed as being disobedient. Thus, the literature on compliance has begun to use the terms "adherence" and "nonadherence" to describe the performance or nonperformance of recommended treatment behaviors. The term "treatment cooperation" has also been used. In this chapter, "adherence" and "nonadherence" are used to avoid potentially negative connotations.

A frequently used definition of compliance or adherence is "the extent to which a person's behavior coincides with medical or health advice" (Haynes, 1979, pp. 2–3). The assumption of this definition is that there is one correct or most advantageous recommendation that should be followed. In reality, very different treatment regimes may be prescribed for the same diagnostic category or behavioral problem. In addition, even perfect adherence to a recommended regime may fail to ameliorate the symptoms or the problem. These issues require the clinician to examine the definition, assessment, and treatment of nonadherence.

Nonadherence can include a wide range of behaviors, including failure to take prescribed medications or refusal to wear medical appliances, follow medical regimes, attend scheduled appointments, or comply with agreed-upon clinician recommendations regarding behavior changes outside the sessions. It may be a result of errors of omission or errors of commission. For example, misunderstanding a medication schedule can result in medication errors in which too much or too little of the medication is taken. In mental health–related treatments, behavioral changes may require that new behaviors be instituted (i.e., practicing relaxation strategies) or that the patient learn to avoid old behaviors (i.e., spanking a child). Different aspects of nonadherence may negatively impact both short- and long-term outcomes in medical management and psychotherapeutic interventions with patients and families.

The preponderance of the literature on adherence has focused on medical nonadherence in adults and adolescents. A subset of these studies has examined adult psychiatric nonadherence with medications and appointment keeping. There have been fewer studies of nonadherence with psychotropic medications or psychotherapy interventions that have targeted the child or adolescent. Typically, when there is nonadherence with medication or psychotherapy treatment recommendations regarding a child, the parents are the target of the intervention to increase compliance. Most behavioral interventions with children have relied on teaching parents new and more appropriate skills for parent management. Nonadherence with medications or behaviors outside the therapy sessions usually focus on issues of parent education, parent-child interactions, behavioral interventions, or family systems issues.

An increasing number of children and adolescents are being treated with medications for ADHD, anxiety, depression, and behavior disorders. Approximately 1–2% of children in the United States have been diagnosed as having attention problems and are being treated with psychostimulant medications (Safer & Krager, 1988). There is little information on the number of children being treated with other psychotropic drugs or the level of adherence with these drugs. Most psychotropic medication used with children have been derived from research with adults.

An examination of the medical literature suggests that issues of nonadherence identified in medical studies are similar to those issues present in nonadherence to treatment for psychological or psychiatric disorders of children, adolescents, and families. Thus, it appears that both literatures are appropriate to examine when considering the assessment and treatment of nonadherence for either medical or psychological treatment.

PREVALENCE AND INCIDENCE

Noncompliance is not a unitary diagnosis. The incidence and prevalence of nonadherence vary with the behavior or diagnosis being studied, the treatment regime, the chronicity of the illness, the developmental level of the patient, the family system, and the method of measuring compliance. Each of these factors is examined in terms of the impact on nonadherence.

Illness—Chronicity and Severity

In general, nonadherence rates are greater when treatment regiments are chronic and more complex (Litt & Cuskey, 1980; Sackett & Snow, 1979). Studies of adults with chronic medical illnesses have suggested an overall compliance rate of approximately 50% (Haynes, 1976, 1979). Adults with schizophrenia have nonadherence rates with medications ranging from 16 to 75% (Hogarty, Schooler, Ulrich, Mussare, Farro, & Herron, 1979). An analysis of adolescents who stopped taking lithium after a manic episode found a high rate of recurrence of the illness. A meta-analysis of nonadherence rates for adolescents and adults taking lithium for the treatment of bipolar disorder reported the likelihood of a patient's being compliant with medications to be 60% (Basco & Rush, 1995). Studies show that children with chronic illnesses have a 55% greater risk of developing behavior problems, including nonadherence with medical treatment, than do controls (Gortmaker, Walker, Weitzman, & Sobol, 1990). Studies of parental compliance with regimes for chronic pediatric illness have found compliance rates ranging from 20 to 80%.

Issues of compliance do not necessarily follow logical assumptions. The severity of the illness and the consequences of nonadherence have not been significantly correlated with compliance rates. In fact, high rates of nonadherence are found in situations where lack of compliance can result in life-threatening consequences (Phipps & DeCuir-Whalley, 1990). Severe symptoms and rapid amelioration with the recommended medical treatment are more highly correlated with compliance with medication than the severity of the illness or the morbidity/mortality risks associated with nonadherence (La Greca, 1988). The majority of studies have suggested that greater treatment length and complexity are correlated with nonadherence. A consistent finding for psychotherapy and medication compliance is that compliance is lower when there is a comorbid diagnosis of substance abuse.

Outcome Factors

Patients may adhere to all of the clinician's recommendations regarding medications, medical testing, behavioral interventions, or skill practicing, yet find that the problems are not ameliorated. Compliance with the recommendations of the clinician does not guarantee success. In fact, treatment failures, even with complete compliance, occur in both acute and chronic problems.

Medication Factors

When pharmacological treatments with psychotropic medications are used, the prescribing doctor's goal is to find an optimal dose that has minimal side effects. Adherence to the recommended treatment almost certainly can be enhanced by the appropriate use of psychotropic medications that optimize benefits and are safe. Pharmacological factors that tend to reduce psychotropic medication compliance include complex medication regimes, dosages that are too high and create unacceptable side effects, or dosages that are too low and provides inadequate benefits and withdrawal reactions. Medications that create unacceptable side effects are frequently not taken as prescribed (Baldessarini, 1994). For example, children diagnosed with ADHD and given amphetamines can experience difficulty sleeping, headaches, stomachaches, or nightmares. If these side effects are severe, the parents and the child will be less compliant regarding the medication (Mason, 1996).

Patient Factors

Age is a contributing factor in nonadherence. The majority of studies have noted that adolescents tend to be more noncompliant than younger children (Johnson, Silverstein,

Rosenbloom, Carter, & Cunningham, 1986). Adolescence is a developmental period that is characterized by turmoil as young people struggle to establish their own identities separate from their families'. As a part of establishing their own identities, adolescents often reject the rules of their families and adopt the norms and rules of their peer group. This type of movement may be accompanied by increased family conflict and rebelliousness on the part of the adolescent. In addition, as peer groups assume greater importance, adolescents strive to be the same as their friends. For adolescents with a chronic illness, the difference between them and their peers may loom quite large, tempting them to ignore medical treatment in order to be the same as everyone else. Given these typical developmental patterns, it has been hypothesized that adolescents with chronic illnesses may be particularly at risk for nonadherence (Johnson et al., 1986; La Greca, 1988). In a recent study of adolescents with cancer, blood level compliance rates were measured for prophylactic oral trimethoprim/sulfamethaxazole. The nonadherence rate was 35% for this study group (Kennard, Stewart, Waller, Ruberu, Winick, Bawdon, & Buchanan, 1994). Several studies of children with diabetes found that, even when length of time since diagnosis was controlled, the older the child, the more problems there were with adherence and metabolic control (Allen, Tennen, McGrade, Affleck, & Ratzan, 1983; Anderson, Auslander, Jung, Miller & Santiago, 1990; La Greca, 1988).

Self-efficacy, or the confidence in one's ability to perform the required health behavior, may also be a factor in treatment adherence. A study of children and adolescents with cystic fibrosis (CF) and their caregivers looked at the relationship among educational, behavioral, and health status variables (Parcel et al., 1994). Controlling for the effects of all other variables, self-efficacy was found to be the most important self-management behavior for predicting adherence to recommended monitoring and treatment behaviors. The authors suggest that educational programs should include components designed to increase self-efficacy for the recommended treatment behaviors.

Family Variables

Children's and adolescents' behaviors occur within a social system. One of the most important influencing social systems is the family. A number of studies have examined the effects of family variables on adherence to treatment recommendations.

A 4-year longitudinal study of adolescents with diabetes (IDDM) and their parents found that the strongest predictor of long-term adherence was family conflict as experienced by the adolescent (Hauser, Jacobson, Lavori, Wolfsdorf, Herskowitz, Milley, Bliss, Wertlieb, & Stein, 1990). Compliance was improved when there was a greater perception of cohesion within the family by both the parents and the adolescents. Conversely, there was greater nonadherence when there was greater family conflict. In a companion study, child psychological variables were also examined. The child's coping and adjustment level were significantly related to compliance even when the effects of age were controlled (Jacobson et al., 1990). A study of children with juvenile rheumatoid arthritis identified family factors that affected compliance (Chaney & Peterson, 1989). Greater nonadherence with nonsteroidal anti-inflammatory drugs was associated with families that were more enmeshed or rigid.

Families with a child with a chronic illness may be at particularly high risk for conflicts regarding disease management during adolescence. Adolescence is a time of increasing independence and movement away from the family. For children with chronic illnesses, this desire to be independent may include taking increased responsibility for the illness. In addition, parents may be quite willing to turn responsibility over to adolescents, only to find that the adolescents do not complete the tasks effectively (Ingersoll, Orr, Herrold, & Golden, 1986). In cases where the adolescents do not perform the health-related tasks to the parents' satisfaction, family conflict may be increased.

One study that found that disagreements among children and adolescents with diabetes and their mother regarding who is responsible for diabetes-related tasks was associated with poorer adherence and overall poorer metabolic control (Anderson, Auslander, Jung, Miller, & Santiago, 1990). Increased conflict in families with children with insulin-dependent diabetes mellitus was also associated with poorer adherence (Hauser, Jacobson, Lavori, Wolfsdorf, Herskowitz, Milley, Bliss, Wertlieb, & Stein, 1990).

ASSESSMENT

Assessment of nonadherence is a difficult task. First, one must be clear on the definition being used. Generally, nonadherence is viewed as a failure to carry out a prescribed regimen. When nonadherence is seen from this perspective, assessment often takes on a punitive flavor. The patient and his or her family are questioned about why they failed to follow the prescribed routine (be it medication, exercise, or therapeutic homework), with an implied emphasis on their failure. However, a lack of treatment cooperation can also be viewed as adherence to a regimen other than that suggested by the health or mental health care provider. Patients and/or their families usually have some rationale for choosing which aspects of their treatment are carried out. Donovan and Blake (1992) have suggested that nonadherence may, in fact, represent a reasoned decision-making strategy. When recommended treatment regimes are extremely complex, time-consuming, or costly, the family may choose a balance between complying with recommendations and attempting to maintain a more normal and realistic goal for the child, adolescent, or family. By trying to understand the patient's perspective and rationale, the clinician can make the assessment process less threatening to all involved. This can result in increased information and a better understanding of the patient's view of his or her medical treatments. Ultimately, this increase in information can help mental health

care providers develop more effective forms of treatment.

It is also important to understand that treatment cooperation is not a unitary construct. Patient and family adherence or nonadherence to one aspect of treatment is not necessarily predictive of cooperation with another aspect of treatment (Glasgow & Anderson, 1995). In some studies of children with diabetes, there was little or no relationship between adherence to one aspect of treatment and the extent of adherence to another area (Glasgow, 1991; Johnson, 1992).

Medical treatments of many illnesses have grown increasingly complex, requiring a large number of different behaviors. Therefore, it is important to know what specific behaviors are required for the management of the illness or presenting problem. For example, perfect adherence to the administration of factor concentrate in the home for patients with hemophilia has 76 different steps (Sergis-Deavenport & Varni, 1983). Nonadherence can be defined as difficulties in any one of these steps. Behaviors can also be grouped. For instance, in the administration of factor concentrate, there are three basic classifications—reconstitution behaviors, syringe preparation behaviors, and infusion behaviors. Nonadherence is the failure to complete one of the behavioral groups. Alternatively, adherence can be viewed as the performance of those behaviors that must be performed in order to obtain a positive therapeutic outcome. For some illnesses, that might require less than 100% adherence; for others it may require perfect adherence. Thus, a patient may be seen as nonadherent if he or she misses one dose of a medication in a 10-day period or may not be considered nonadherent unless he or she takes less than 80% of the total pill count.

Thus, percentages of "nonadherence" reported in articles can differ widely, depending on the criterion used. Different criterion (e.g., one missed, 10% missed) for even simple measures of adherence, such as counting the number of missed and kept appointments or pills left in a bottle, can lead to different results. In reviewing studies of adherence, it is essential to be aware of the measurement strategies that have been used to assess medication and behavioral adherence. Different approaches to measurement are described below in more detail.

Patient/Family Self-Report

Patient verbal self-reports may be the least accurate method of assessment. Park and Lipman (1964) compared patient reports to actual pill counts and found that, in 40% of the cases, the reports did not match the count. It is often clear what the desired response is; patients generally know that they are supposed to take the prescribed medication. In fact, social desirability often creates instances of overestimation of adherence (Mathews & Christophersen, 1988). However, in many cases, patient and family verbal reports are the only measures of compliance available for a variety of reasons (sometimes the behavior cannot be observed; drug assays are too variable; treatment adherence does not have a physically measurable component). Several methods have been employed to enhance the accuracy of self-reports.

Patient and family estimates of adherence can be enhanced by asking direct informational questions about each specific behavior required by the protocol. In addition, requesting parents to recall health care behaviors in the past 24 hours is more accurate than getting estimates of longer-term behavior. Intermittent phone interviews with chronically ill children and parents in which they are asked to recall the past 24 hours of health care behaviors have been found to be a reliable and valid source of information on long-term treatment cooperation (Freund, Johnson, Silverstein, & Thomas, 1991).

Medical Staff Estimates

Medical staff judgments have often been used in clinical settings to estimate nonadherence. These estimates are often inaccurate. For example, in one study, medical staff (physicians, nurse practitioners, and medical residents) were asked to predict the adherence of parents with antibiotic treatment for otitis media (Finney, Hook, Friman, Rapoff, & Christophersen, 1993). The medical staff estimated an 86% compliance rate, while the actual rate was just 51%. Thus, almost half of the parents were noncompliant with the recommended 10-day course of antibiotics for their child's acute illness. Health care providers frequently base their estimates of compliance on the child's health status. This strategy ignores the possibility of individual response variability to medications (Johnson, 1994). Negative outcomes of treatment may indicate nonadherence or an incorrect and/or inadequate treatment regime.

Written Self-Report

Written diaries of behaviors or medications can help to assess problems with compliance and provide feedback on the effectiveness of the intervention. Tracking behaviors, such as temper tantrums or positive time with a parent, helps the child, adolescent, or parent identify progress or problems in the implementation of a behavior program. Written self-reports can be falsified, completed just before the session, or "forgotten." Unfortunately, parents who are not following the prescribed treatments are also the least likely to turn in accurate medication or behavioral records (Chaney & Peterson, 1989). Thus, it becomes difficult to obtain a true picture of what children and families actually do for treatment, as the most nonadherent families may be the most likely to avoid returning accurate reports of their behavior.

Pill Counts

Pill counts offer a simple assessment of adherence. When patients know they will be subject to this type of assessment, the reliability of the pill count decreases. Even when the pill count suggests cooperation, the clinician cannot tell whether the pills were taken on time. Pills containers that have a light-sensitive membrane can indicate when the pills were taken. Such measures are most frequently used with short-term medication assessments. A more expensive device to assess medication amount and timing is the Medication Event Monitor System, which contains a microprocessor in the cap of the medication container. The date and time are recorded each time the pill container is opened (Averbuch, Weintraub, & Pollock, 1988).

Drug Assays

Assessment of treatment cooperation using medication blood levels is more accurate than self-report or pill counts. But these assays must take into account the peaks and troughs that are associated with the time the medication is taken. In addition, medication effects and blood levels may vary within and between patients. For some types of medications, patient metabolism may vary by age, with changes often occurring in adolescence. Blood assays are expensive and usually reveal only short-term adherence. For children on a long-term medication, occasional blood assays may not reveal long-term compliance. Typically, children and adolescents are more likely to remember to take medications just before visiting the doctor and thus may show the drug in the blood on that day.

Treatment

Theoretical models and treatment modalities have ranged from micro- to macro-interventions. At one end of the spectrum are the strategies that have focused on specific educational and behavioral interventions to address individual factors associated with nonadherence. At the other end of the spectrum are theoretical models that attempt to explain the process an individual goes through in changing a complex behavior and maintaining that change over time.

Reminders

Various studies have found that the number of missed intake appointments can be reduced through the use of telephone reminders, mailed reminder cards, shorter waiting lists for a first appointment, or provision of expanded information about what will happen during the initial contact. Visual cues are helpful in obtaining compliance with acute problems or in teaching children complex health behaviors. Reminders on the refrigerator or calendars on the bathroom mirror can help children and adolescents become more responsible for their health care behaviors without the appearance of "parental nagging."

Practical issues such as transportation and financial barriers also lead to missed appointments. An assessment of these issues and solutions to these very real problems should be addressed during the first contact with the family. Often parents are not aware of special services or financial support that will help the child or family receive appropriate services.

Education

Medical disorders and their treatments are becoming increasingly complex. In many cases, it can be difficult for families to fully understand all of the nuances of the etiology of the disease and its treatment. This is particularly true initially, when parents and children may be overwhelmed by the diagnosis and unable to take in much additional information. This is also true of mental health disorders. Many families do not understand the causes and appropriate treatments for mood disorders, thought disorders, or oppositional defiant behaviors or the emotional impact of a medical illness.

Several studies have examined the impact of education regarding the cause and treatment of either acute or chronic health problems. Education typically has been found to have an initial positive impact on compliance (Colcher & Bass, 1972), and it is a necessary first step in preventing nonadherence, although alone it may not be effective with children or adolescents expected to follow a complex or aversive treatment regime (La Greca & Skyler, 1991). Modeling and coaching parents during psychotherapy sessions helps to teach parents new ways to cope with negative child behaviors. In-session modeling and parental practice has also been found to increase compliance with parental follow-through in the management of their child's behavior at home (Hembree-Kigin & McNeil, 1995).

Self-Monitoring

Self-monitoring of complex regimes for chronic illnesses has not brought about significant increases in compliance (Wysocki et al., 1989). Adherence to short-term interventions that use homework assignments such as diaries or checklists can enhance compliance with medication and psychotherapy recommendations. Compliance is increased when the child or parent is asked to keep a record of the assignment that is simple, easy to understand, and meaningful. Self-monitoring contains both assessment and treatment aspects and has been found to be an effective component in the treatment of depression, phobias, and child management strategies.

Changing Contingencies

One of the most consistent findings in the literature on compliance is the impact of positive reinforcement. Teaching parents to reinforce appropriate behavior has been found to be a successful motivator that has increased children's compliance with a wide range of behaviors. Incentives have been successful in improving compliance with medications regimes, medical procedures, self-care, toilet training, and behaviors such as practicing relaxation strategies, completing homework assignments, engaging in cooperative behavior between siblings, and obeying parental requests. Barkley's (1994) behavioral treatment for ADHD has found positive reinforcement of the child at home and school to be successful in increasing the number of appropriate behaviors. Complex behaviors can be monitored and shaped over time. A study of children with asthma found positive reinforcement of health behaviors

(e.g., taking medication, practicing relaxation, and monitoring pulmonary functioning) was effective in increasing their frequency and reducing emergency room and hospital stays (Olson & Chaney, 1983). The use of positive reinforcement to increase compliance can employ traditional learning strategies to teach behaviors and maintain behaviors over time. Typically, interventions using positive reinforcement are one component of a multidimensional treatment strategy.

Multimodal Interventions

Some of the most successful interventions have used multiple intervention strategies. A classical example is the treatment of ADHD, which may include education regarding the disorder, family and peer support of the child, consistent medication management, positive reinforcement for compliance with school and home rules, self-monitoring, and the teaching of problem-solving skills to the child (Barkley, 1994). Studies on teaching new behaviors such as techniques for coping with anxiety and fear have found that modeling, positive reinforcement, and imagery increase children's compliant behaviors with pain control strategies and medical treatment (Elliott & Olson, 1984).

A pilot study of a group intervention to increase adoption of diabetes management skills by patients between eight and 12 years of age yielded positive results (McNabb, Quinn, Murphy, Thorp, & Cook, 1994). In this study, children and their parents participated in six 1-hour group sessions (both separately and alone). Each session focused on a specific self-care behavior. Children learned and practiced the behavior, while parents were taught specific skills to promote their child's behavior. At the end of the session, children and parents met and developed specific goals for the coming week. Results indicated that children who participated in the group had significantly higher responsibility scores than the control group. Self-care behavior frequency was not significantly different between the two groups, suggesting that children assumed greater responsibility for their care without a decrease in the self-care behaviors. Finally, overall metabolic control was not significantly different between the two groups. This preliminary study suggests that a multimodal group intervention can be effective in increasing self-care behaviors in children.

Tailoring Interventions to the Cognitive, Social, and Emotional Level of the Patient

An increasing number of researchers have begun to study the impact of cognitive development on the level of adherence. Children at the concrete-operational level of cognitive development tend to have a linear and absolute view of health care. Young children believe that following adult recommendations will result in improved health or emotional well-being. Adolescents enter the stage of formal operations and can better understand the complexities and the less than perfect relationship between medical or psychological interventions and a positive outcome. Cognitive development during adolescence allows this group to have a better understanding of the complex issues involved in health maintenance.

Social and emotional issues become increasingly important with adolescents. This age group focuses on peer group expectations and appearances. Medical interventions that lead to weight gain, acne, or hair loss are particularly difficult for adolescents. As a result, adolescents may be noncompliant with medications that make them appear different from their peers (Friedman & Litt, 1987). Interventions that help the adolescent identify the range of issues and potential ways to solve these problems can be effective. Positive coping strategies have been associated with higher rates of compliance. Coping strategies include learning problem-solving skills, cognitive restructuring, and seeking peer support. Children and adolescents with higher self-esteem and more flexible coping styles have been found to be more compliant (Friedman et al., 1986; Jacobson et al, 1990). We have found that enhancing children's and adolescents' effective problem-solving, emotional coping and assertiveness skills has been effective in an overall, comprehensive, personalized treatment package.

Physician/Patient Communication

The literature does suggest that there is a link between the communication of a health care provider and the patient's compliance. One study found that compliance increases with information giving, positive communication, and requests for patient input (Roter & Hall, 1989). Another study found an association between compliance and relationship-enhancing techniques, education, behavior modification, and self-regulatory skills training (Meichenbaum & Turk, 1987). Other studies reviewed in this chapter suggest that these techniques are all useful in increasing patient compliance across a wide range of health-related behaviors. However, health care providers often do not use these techniques routinely. One interesting study performed a chart review of 108 children with juvenile rheumatoid arthritis (Thompson, Dahlquist, Koenning, & Bartholomew, 1995). Charts were reviewed for evidence of 17 specific health care provider behaviors known to increase patient adherence (Meichenbaum & Turk, 1987). Interestingly, the health care providers used relatively few of the compliance-enhancing behaviors. The most common behavior was recommending how often to perform the recommended activity (such as exercise, taking medication), which accounted for 61% of the compliance behaviors noted. More behavioral skills, such as using incentives, providing prompts or reminders, recommending self-monitoring, or checking past self-monitoring, occurred with less than 1% of the patients. Thus, mental health professionals working with children and adolescents who are noncompliant with medical recommendations should also consult with the child's health care providers. By increasing the health care provider's use of compliance-enhancing behaviors, the clinican may improve the patient's compliance.

Therapist-Patient Communication

The therapist-patient relationship impacts psychotherapy and medication compliance. A three-step model for use when working with families or adolescents has been found to improve compliance. First, it is essential to help the patient and family members to understand the diagnosis. Second, if medications are used, the potential side effects as well as the benefits should be thoroughly discussed. Finally, problems surrounding potential nonadherence with medications or homework assignments outside the session should be predicted. If nonadherence is viewed as a predictable behavior, problem-solving strategies can be applied to help the family or individual foresee and plan ways to reduce factors that lead to nonadherence.

The style and content of the therapist-patient communication regarding behaviors outside the sessions (e.g., homework, diet, exercise, relaxation practice, visual imagery) has been found to affect compliance. Three variables have been found to be associated with increased adherence (Conoley, Padula, Payton, & Daniels, 1994). First, it is important for the client to perceive a match between the problem and the recommendation. For example, parents are more likely to institute time-out procedures for temper tantrums than to spend "special time" with a disobedient child. Unless the parents can understand the relationship between increasing the level of positive reinforcement and the reduction of the child's aggression they are unlikely to comply with the therapist's recommendation. Clients' beliefs about their ability to carry out the recommendation also affect compliance. If the parents do not believe they can implement the recommendation because of their lack of knowledge, skill, or other resources, they will not comply. The third aspect involves making recommendations that focus on using the clients' strengths. Using these strategies can bring about an increase in compliance with counselor recommendations. A consistent finding across many studies is that a positive client-counselor relationship increases compliance and positive outcome for therapy.

Theoretical Models of Health-Related Behavioral Change

In developing treatment programs for individuals who are nonadherent, it is helpful to use a theoretical model to guide the interventions. The majority of behavioral intervention research has utilized a randomized experimental design. Although this design allows for the assessment of the overall effects of the intervention on the behavior of interest, it does not specifically evaluate the interaction of various elements within the intervention or how behavior change is affected by this interaction (Chen & Rossi, 1983). The use of theory-based models allows for an explicit, a priori prediction of the relationship between intervention components. Without this prediction, it is very difficult to fully understand which specific components, and in what specific combination, are most efficacious. When the relative contributions of individual components, as well as their interaction, are not well understood, it becomes quite difficult to modify interventions piloted in one type of population for use in a different one. By developing a sound theory-based intervention and basing the evaluation of behaviors on these theoretical principles, data can be gathered about the efficacy of individual components of the intervention and their interrelationships (Chen & Rossi, 1983). Once the effective components and their relationship to other elements of the intervention have been identified, it becomes easier to successfully transfer interventions to different populations and settings.

When intervening with children, adolescents, or families who are nonadherent, the goal is the adoption of a new, healthier behavior. There are a number of theoretical models that attempt to explain the adoption of health-related behaviors. Theories such as the Health Belief Model (HBM) (Becker, 1974) and the Theory of Reasoned Action (Ajzen & Fishbein,

1980) have been utilized in a number of studies. Another such model is the Transtheoretical Model of Change (also known as the Stages of Change) (TM), which was developed by Prochaska and DiClemente (1986). This model and possible therapeutic interventions that derive from it are discussed in further detail here.

Previous studies of the TM have shown the constructs of the model to be effective in encouraging behavioral change across a wide variety of health-related behaviors, including the acquisition of positive health behaviors as well as the cessation of unhealthy ones (Prochaska, 1994; Prochaska, Redding, Harlow, Rossi, & Velicer, 1994). The model posits that individuals do not change health-related behaviors in a dichotomous act but rather go through a series of predictable stages that can result in the long-term maintenance of the newly acquired behavior.

The TM categorizes five stages of change (SOC). In the first stage, *precontemplation*, individuals do not intend to change their behavior. These are the individuals who suggest that there is no reason for them to perform the recommended health-related behavior. In the second stage, *contemplation*, individuals are seriously considering making the change in their behaviors within the next 6 months. These are the individuals who might have thought about consistently using the recommended health-related behaviors within the next 6 months but not right now. In the third stage, *preparation*, individuals have made a commitment to make the behavioral change within the coming month and may have used the new behaviors sporadically. In the fourth stage, *action*, individuals have initiated the consistent use of the new behavior. Individuals in the action stage are performing the recommended health-related behaviors consistently. In the final stage, *maintenance*, individuals have consistently engaged in the new behavior for at least 6 months and thus are in the habit of consistently using the recommended regimen. Individuals can relapse from any of the four stages of change beyond precontemplation to any of the preceding stages. The model hypothesizes that individuals move through a series of relapses and subsequent progressions through the intervening stages before permanently acquiring the new health behavior (Prochaska & DiClemente, 1986).

The utility of the TM for intervention purposes lies in the matching of specific strategies and techniques to the individual's own particular stage of change to assist in movement to the next stage (Prochaska, DiClemente, & Norcross, 1992). These specific strategies are called processes of change (POC). The POC are techniques commonly used by counselors and health professionals to encourage behavioral change. However, in traditional counseling and other interventions, techniques to encourage change are not usually specifically matched to the individual's readiness to change. The TM has developed a template to match specific POCs to each SOC, thus accommodating the intervention to the individual's own readiness to acquire the new behaviors.

The TM has been used with an adolescent population as well as with adults (Prochaska et al., 1994). In one recent study, adolescents with hemophilia and HIV infection participated in an intervention based on the TM (Brown, Schultz, Forsberg, Butler, & Parsons, 1997). Adolescents received both individual and group interventions over the period of a year. At each session, participants completed forms that identified their current stages of change and received individual feedback about their current behaviors and their intentions to change those behaviors. The feedback contained specific information about types of activities (based on the processes of change) that could be used to encourage further change or to help maintain consistent use of safer sexual practices. Group sessions contained exercises that identified specific barriers to the use of safer sexual behaviors and allowed interveners to utilize activities that addressed the different stages of change for each individual. For instance, in a discussion of the barriers to using condoms, a variety of specific exercises used different processes of change that are effective for each of the stages of change. Although each individual's stage of change was kept private in the group sessions, it was clear in discussions that people had different ideas about safer sex. The interaction between individuals at earlier and later stages of change was extremely helpful. It was helpful for those individuals who felt change wasn't necessary to hear from peers about why it might be necessary, and talking about the importance of safer sex helped adolescents in maintenance to reinforce their own commitment to using safe-sex behavior consistently (Brown, Schultz, Forsberg, Butler, & Parsons, 1997). Therefore, group interventions using the TM approach might be quite useful with adolescents.

In working with adolescents, the TM could also be utilized within a family systems framework. As noted, increased family conflict is often associated with nonadherence. Family conflicts can be viewed within the context of the TM. The conflict may reflect the fact that different family members are in different stages of change. For example, adolescents with chronic diseases are often not in total control of the treatment for their disorder, and adolescents with diabetes are frequently reminded by their parents and medical providers to take their insulin, watch their diet, or check their blood levels. It is quite likely that parents and their children may be at different stages of change regarding the performance of these health-related behaviors. Clearly, individuals in different stages of change have different views of how to manage the adolescent's medical illness, which can lead to an increased risk of conflict within the family. For instance, an adolescent may be in precontemplation for checking his blood glucose levels (i.e., he or she sees no need for checking blood levels consistently), while his or her parent is in the action stage (and wants the blood level checked consistently). The TM offers a way to operationalize each family member's behavior and intentions around the recommended health-related behavior. Family members can be compared to determine if there are conflicts between them that result from being in different stages of change. Interventions can then be tailored to the stages of each family member, using a group model with specific activities tailored to each individuals' stage of change. In addition, separate group interventions for parents and adolescents with diabetes can also be performed, similar to those described for the acquisition and maintenance of safer sexual behaviors. A similar model can be developed for use with other types of chronic illnesses.

CONCLUSION

Nonadherence to recommended treatment regimens is a complex behavior. Nonadherence can contribute to myriad complications for both medical illness and mental disorders. Yet it is not a unilateral behavior that can be easily assessed and treated. Each recommended behavior may or may not be followed. The lack of treatment cooperation may have differing rates of complications, ranging from none to death, and patients may therefore be variably reinforced for nonadherence. Different factors may also maintain each treatment-related behavior. Therefore, careful assessment of the behavioral problems is critical, both to carefully define how the patient is being nonadherent and to fully understand the maintaining factors. The assessment methodology used should be chosen carefully, since different methods may lead to differing results. Self-report inventories must be viewed cautiously, but even blood assays can yield confusing results.

There is a broad range of interventions that can be utilized. Changes in health care provider behaviors can help to increase adherence, as can behavioral management programs. Finally, the use of theoretically based interventions is recommended. By using theoretically based interventions, the clinician can better understand the relationships between treatment components, which can allow for greater ease of use across different types of nonadherent behavior.

REFERENCES

Allen, D. A., Tennen, H., McGrade, B. J., Affleck, G., & Ratzan, S. (1983). Parent and child perceptions of the management of juvenile diabetes. *Journal of Pediatric Psychology, 8,* 129–141.

American Psychiatric Association. (1994). *Diagnostic and statistical manual of mental disorders* (4th ed.). Washington, DC: Author.

Anderson, B. J., Auslander, W. F., Jung, K. C., Miller, J. P., & Santiago, J. V. (1990). Assessing family sharing of diabetes responsibilities. *Journal of Pediatric Psychology,15*, 477–492.

Averbuch, M., Weintraub, M., & Pollock, D. J. (1988). Compliance monitoring clinical trials: The MEMS device. *Clinical Pharmacology Therapy, 43*, 185.

Ajzen, I., & Fishbein, M. (1980). *Understanding attitudes and predicting social behavior.* Englewood Cliffs, NJ: Prentice Hall.

Baldessarini, R. J. (1994). Enhancing treatment with psychotropic medicines. *Bulletin of the Menninger Clinic, 58* (2), 224–239.

Barkley, R. (1994). Attention deficit hyperactivity disorder: A handbook for diagnosis and treatment. New York: Guilford Press.

Basco, M. R., & Rush, A. J. (1995). Compliance with pharmacotherapy in mood disorders. *Psychiatric Annals, 25* (5), 269–279.

Becker, M. H. (1974). The health belief model and personal health behavior. *Health Education Monographs, 2.*

Brown, L., Schultz, J., Forsberg, A., Butler, R., & Parsons, J. T. (1997). A stage-based intervention for HIV positive adolescents with hemophilia: Results of the HBIEP. Manuscript in preparation.

Chaney, J., & Peterson, L. (1989). Family variables and disease management in juvenile rheumatoid arthritis. *Journal of Pediatric Psychology, 14,* 389–403.

Chang, P. (1994). Effects of interviewer questions and response type on compliance: An analogue study. *Journal of Counseling Psychology, 41,* 74–82.

Chen, H. T., & Rossi, P. H. (1983). Evaluating with sense: The theory-driven approach. *Evaluation Review, 7,* 283–302.

Colcher, I. S., & Bass, J. W. (1972). Penicillin treatment of streptococcal pharyngitis: A comparison of schedules and the role of specific counseling. *Journal of American Medial Association, 222,* 657–659.

*Conoley, C. W., Padula, M. A., Payton, D. S., & Daniels, J. A. (1994). Predictors of client implementation of counselor recommendations: Match with problem, difficulty level and building on clients strengths. *Journal of Counseling Psychology, 41,* 3–7.

*Donovan, J. L., & Blake, D. R. (1992). Patient non-compliance: Deviance or reasoned decision making? *Social Science and Medicine, 34,* 507–513.

Elliott, C., & Olson, R. A. (1984). The management of children's behavioral distress in response to painful medical treatments for burn injuries. *Journal of Behavior Therapy, 21,* 675–683.

Finney, J. W., Hook, R. J., Friman, P. C., Rappoff, M., & Christopherson, E. R. (1993). The overestimation of adherence to pediatric medical regiments. *Children's Health Care, 22,* 297–304.

Freund, A., Johnson, S. B., Silverstein J., & Thomas, J. (1991). Assessing daily management of childhood diabetes using 24-hour recall interviews: Reliability and stability. *Health Psychology, 10,* 200–208.

Friedman, I. M., & Litt, I. F. (1987). Adolescents' compliance with therapeutic regimens: Psychological and social aspects and intervention. *Journal of Adolescent Health Care, 8,* 52–65.

Friedman, I. M., Litt, I. F., King, D. R., Henson, R., Holtzman, D., Halverson, D., & Kraemer, H. C. (1986). Compliance with anticonvulsant therapy by epileptic youth. *Journal of Adolescent Health Care, 7,* 12–17.

*Glasgow, R. E. (1991). Compliance in diabetes regimens: Conceptualization, complexity, and determinants. In J. A. Cramer & B. Spilker (Eds.), *Patient compliance in medical practice and clinical trials.* New York: Raven.

Glasgow, R. E., & Anderson, B. J. (1995). Future directions for research on pediatric chronic disease management: Lessons from diabetes. *Journal of Pediatric Psychology, 20,* 389–402.

Gortmaker, S. L., Walker, D. K., Weitzman, M., & Sobol, A. M. (1990). Chronic conditions, socioeconomic risks and behavioral problems in children and adolescents. *Pediatrics, 85,* 267–276.

Hanson, C. L., De Guire, M. J., Schnikel, A. M., & Kolterman, O. G. (1995). Empirical validation for a family-centered model of care. *Diabetes Care, 18,* 1347–1356.

Hauser, S. T., Jacobson, A. M., Lavori, P., Wolfsdorf, J. I., Herskowitz, R. D., Milley, J. E., Bliss, R., Wertlieb, D., & Stein, J. (1990). Adherence among children and adolescents with insulin-dependent diabetes mellitus over a four-year longitudinal follow-up: II. Immediate and long-term linkages with the family milieu. *Journal of Pediatric Psychology, 15,* 527–542.

Haynes, R. B. (1976). A critical review of the "determinants" of patient compliance with therapeutic regimens. In D. L. Sackett & R. B. Haynes (Eds.),

Compliance with therapeutic regimens. Baltimore: Johns Hopkins University Press.

Haynes, R. B. (1979). Introduction. In R. B. Haynes, D. W. Taylor, & D. L. Sackett (Eds.), *Compliance in health care* (pp. 1–7). Baltimore: Johns Hopkins University Press.

*Hembree-Kigin, T. L., & McNeil, C. B. (1995). *Parent-child interaction therapy*. New York: Plenum Press.

Hogarty, G. E., Schooler, N. R., Ulrich, R. R., Mussare, F., Farro, O., & Herron, E. (1979). Fluphenazine and social therapy in the aftercare of schizophrenic patients: Relapse analysis of a two-year controlled study of fluphenazine decanoate and fluphenazine hydrochloride. *Archives of General Psychiatry*, 36, 1283–1294.

Huszti, H. (1995). Intrafamilial factors in compliance. Grant application to March of Dimes.

Ingersoll, G., Orr, D., Herrold, A., & Golden, M. (1986). Cognitive maturity and self-management among adolescents with insulin-dependent diabetes mellitus. *Journal of Pediatrics*, 108, 620–623.

Jacobson, A. M., Hauser, S. T., Lavori, P., Wolfsdorf, J. H. I., Herskowitz, R. D., Milley, J. E., Bliss, R., Gelfand, E., Wertlieb, D., & Stein, J. (1990). Adherence among children and adolescents with insulin-dependent diabetes mellitus over a four-year follow-up. *Journal of Pediatric Psychology*, 15, 511–526.

*Johnson, S. B. (1992). Methodological issues in diabetes research: Measuring adherence. *Diabetes Care*, 15, 1658–1667.

Johnson, S. B. (1994). Health behavior and health status: Concepts, methods and applications. *Journal of Pediatric Psychology*, 19, 129–141.

Johnson, S. B., Silverstein, J., Rosenbloom, A. L., Carter, R., & Cunningham, W. (1986). Assessing daily management in childhood diabetes. *Health Psychology*, 5, 545–564.

Kennard, B. D., Stewart, S. M., Waller, D. A., Ruberu, M. R., Winick, N. J., Bawdon, R. E., & Buchanan, G. (1994, August). *Psychological and family factors in noncompliant adolescent oncology patients*. Paper presented at the annual meeting of the American Psychological Association, Los Angeles, CA.

*La Greca, A. M. (1988). Adherence to prescribed medical regimens. In D. K. Routh (Ed.), *Handbook of pediatric psychology*. New York: Guilford Press.

La Greca, A. M., & Skyler, J. S. (1991). Psychosocial issues in IDDM: A multivariate framework. In

P. McCabe, N. Schneiderman, T. Field, & J. S. Skyler (Eds.), *Stress, coping and disease* (pp. 169–190). Hillsdale, NJ: Lawrence Erlbaum.

Litt, I. F., & Cuskey, W. R. (1980). Compliance with medial regimens during adolescence. *Pediatric Clinics of North America*, 27, 1–15.

Mason, P. J. (1996, September). *Helping teachers and parents cope with ADHD*. Presentation to Oklahoma Teachers Association, Tulsa, OK.

Mathews, J. R., & Christophersen, E. R. (1988). Measuring and preventing noncompliance in pediatric health care. In P. Karoly (Ed.), *Handbook of child health assessment*. (pp. 519–557). New York: Wiley.

McNabb, W. L., Quinn, M. T., Murphy, D. M., Thorp, F. K., & Cook, S. (1994). Increasing children's responsibility for diabetes self-care: The in control study. *Diabetes Educator*, 20, 121–124.

*Meichenbaum, D., & Turk, D. C. (1987). *Facilitating treatment adherence: A practitioner's guidebook*. New York: Plenum Press.

Olson, R. A., & Chaney, J. (1983 August). *Parent training with asthmatic children*. Paper presented at the American Psychological Association annual convention, Anaheim, CA.

*Parcel, G. S., Swank, P. R., Mariotto, M. J., Bartholomew, L. K., Czyzewski, D. J., Sockrider, M. M., & Seilheimer, D. K. (1994). Self-management of cystic fibrosis: A structural model for educational and behavioral variables. *Social Science and Medicine*, 38, 1307–1315

Park, L. C., & Lipman, R. S. (1964). A comparison of patient dosage deviation reports with pill counts. *Psychopharmacologia*, 6, 299–302.

Phipps, S., & DeCuir-Whalley, S. (1990). Adherence issues in pediatric bone marrow trasplantation. *Journal of Pediatric Psychology*, 15, 459–475.

Prochaska, J. O. & DiClemente, C. C. (1986). Toward a comprehensive model of change. In N. Miller & N. Heather (Eds.), *Treating addictive behaviors*. New York: Plenum Press.

*Prochaska, J. O., DiClemente, C. C., & Norcross, J. (1992). In search of how people change: Applications to addictive behaviors. *American Psychologist*, 47, 1102–1114.

Prochaska, J. O., Redding, C. A., Harlow, L. L., Rossi, J. S., & Velicer, W. F. (1994). The transtheoretical model of change and HIV prevention: A review. *Health Education Quarterly*, 21, 471–486.

*Prochaska, J. O., Velicer, W. F., Rossi, J. S., Goldstein, M. G., Marcus, B. H., Rakowski, W., Fiore, C., Harlow, L. L., Redding, C. A., Rosenbloom, D., & Rossi, S. R. (1994). Stages of change and decisional balance for twelve problem behaviors. *Health Psychology, 13*, 39–46.

Roter, D., & Hall, J. (1989). Studies of doctor-patient interaction. *Annual Review of Public Health, 10*, 163–180.

Sackett, D., & Snow, J. (1979). The magnitude of compliance and noncompliance. In R. Haynes, D. Taylor, & D. Sackett (Eds.), *Compliance in health care*. Baltimore: Johns Hopkins University Press.

Safer, D. J., & Krager, J. M. (1988). A survey of medication treatment for hyperactive/inattentive students. *Journal of American Medical Association, 260*, 2256–2258.

Sergis-Deavenport, E., & Varni, J. W. (1983). Behavioral assessment and management of adherence to factor replacement therapy in hemophilia. *Journal of Pediatric Psychology, 8*, 367–377.

*Thompson, S. M., Dahlquist, L. M., Koenning, G. M., & Bartholomew, L. K. (1995). Brief report: Adherence-facilitating behaviors of a multidisciplinary pediatric rheumatology staff. *Journal of Pediatric Psychology, 20*, 291–297.

Werry, J. S. (1993). Introduction: A guide for practitioners, professionals and the public. In J. S. Werry & M. G. Aman (Eds.), *Practitioner's guide to psychoactive drugs for children and adolescents* (pp. 3–21). New York: Plenum Press.

Wysocki, T., Green, L., & Huxtable, K. (1989). Blood glucose monitoring by diabetic adolescents: Compliance and metabolic control. *Health Psychology, 8*, 267–284.

*Indicates references that the authors recommend for further reading.

Index